The Legacy of Jihad

The Legacy of Jihad

Islamic Holy War and the Fate of Non-Muslims

Edited by Andrew G. Bostom, MD

Foreword by Ibn Warraq

 Prometheus Books

59 John Glenn Drive
Amherst, New York 14228-2197

Published 2005 by Prometheus Books

Inquiries should be addressed to
Prometheus Books
59 John Glenn Drive
Amherst, New York 14228–2197
VOICE: 716–691–0133, ext. 207
FAX: 716–564–2711
WWW.PROMETHEUSBOOKS.COM

09 08 07 06 05   5 4 3 2 1

Library of Congress Cataloging-in-Publication Data

The legacy of Jihad : Islamic holy war and the fate of non-Muslims / edited by Andrew G. Bostom with a foreword by Ibn Warraq.
    p. cm.
  Includes bibliographical references and index.
  ISBN 1-59102-307-6 (hardcover : alk. paper)
  1. Jihad. 2. War—Religious aspects—Islam. 3. Dhimmis. 4. Minorities (Islamic law) I. Bostom, Andrew G.

BP182.L45 2005
297.7'2—dc22

                                                          2005012250

Printed in the United States of America on acid-free paper

CONTENTS

PART 4: JIHAD—OVERVIEWS FROM IMPORTANT TWENTIETH-CENTURY SCHOLARS

PART 5: JIHAD, SEVENTH THROUGH ELEVENTH CENTURIES: SUMMARY TEXT

*Color Insert—Color-Coded Maps: Jihad, Seventh through Eleventh
Centuries; Illustrations of the Devshirme Levy, Conquest of Rhodes,
and Siege of Budapest, with Descriptions*

PART 6: JIHAD IN THE NEAR EAST, EUROPE, AND ASIA MINOR AND ON THE INDIAN SUBCONTINENT

PART 7: JIHAD SLAVERY

PART 8: MUSLIM AND NON-MUSLIM CHRONICLES AND EYEWITNESS ACCOUNTS OF JIHAD CAMPAIGNS

ACKNOWLEDGMENTS

This book would have been impossible to complete without the support and considerable sacrifice of my beloved wife, and best friend, Leah. Wise mentoring also brought this work to fruition. Special thanks are due to my mentors Bat Ye'or, Ibn Warraq, Hugh Fitzgerald, Ruth King, and David Littman. Their insights and boundless patience helped me avoid many pitfalls. A gifted trio of translators, Michael J. Miller, Dr. Michael Schub, and Fatemeh Masjedi, made invaluable contributions to this compendium. Mr. Miller deserves special credit for imposing discipline on my schedule. Timely and thorough technical assistance with the manuscript was provided by Wendy Mullen, Alyssa Lappen, Allie Marshall, and Tarrant Smith.

The book is dedicated to my mother, Rifka, and my beautiful children, Esther and Yonah. May Esther and Yonah and their children thrive in a world where the devastating institution of *jihad* has been acknowledged, renounced, dismantled, and relegated forever to the dustbin of history by Muslims themselves.

"The *Chachnama* is Arab or Muslim genre writing, a 'pleasant story of conquest,' the conquest of Sindh. But it is a bloody story, and the parts that get into the school books are fairy tales. . . . History as selective as this leads quickly to unreality. Before Mohammed, there is blackness, slavery, exploitation. After Mohammed, there is light: slavery and exploitation vanish. But did it? How can that be said or taught? What about all those slaves sent back from Sindh to the Caliph? What about the descendants of the African slaves who walk about Karachi? There is no adequate answer: so the faith begins to nullify or overlay the real world."

—V. S. Naipaul, *Among the Believers—An Islamic Journey*, 1981

"The deep knowledge—and pray God we have not lost it—that there is a profound moral difference between the use of force for liberation and the use of force for conquest."

—Ronald Reagan, Pointe de Hoc, Normandy, June 6, 1984,
the fortieth anniversary of D-Day

"Is the call for *jihad* against a particular people a religious right by those calling for it, or is it a human rights violation against the people on which *jihad* is declared and waged?"

—Dr. John Garang, United Nations, Geneva, March 22, 1999

A NOTE ON THE COVER ART

The cover illustration is titled "The Prophet, Ali, and the Companions at the massacre of the prisoners of the Jewish tribe of Beni Kuraizah [Banu Qurayzah]"; Author: Bazil (Muhammad Rafi); Published: nineteenth century; Kashmiri, 17 folio 108b. Reproduced by permission of The British Library.[1]

A consensus Muslim account of the massacre of the Qurayzah has emerged as conveyed by classical Muslim scholars of hadith (putative utterances and acts of Muhammad, recorded by pious Muslim transmitters), biographers of Muhammad's life (especially Ibn Ishaq), jurists, and historians.[2] This narrative is summarized as follows: Alleged to have aided the forces of Muhammad's enemies in violation of a prior pact, the Qurayzah were subsequently isolated and besieged. Twice the Qurayzah made offers to surrender and depart from their stronghold, leaving behind their land and property. Initially they asked to take one camel load of possessions per person, but when Muhammad refused this request, the Qurayzah asked to be allowed to depart without any property, taking with them only their families. However, Muhammad insisted that the Qurayzah surrender unconditionally and subject themselves to his judgment. Compelled to surrender, the Qurayzah were led to Medina. The men, with their hands pinioned behind their backs, were put in a court, while the women and children were said to have been put into a separate court. A third (and final) appeal for leniency for the Qurayzah was made to Muhammad by their tribal allies the Aus. Muhammad again declined, and instead he appointed as arbiter Sa'd Mu'adh from the Aus, who soon rendered his concise verdict: The men were to be put to death, the women and children sold into slavery, the spoils to be divided among the Muslims.

Muhammad ratified the judgment stating that Sa'd's decree was a decree of God pronounced from above the Seven Heavens. Thus some six hundred to nine hundred men from the Qurayzah were led on Muhammad's order to the Market of Medina. Trenches were dug, and the men were beheaded; their decapitated corpses were buried in the trenches while Muhammad watched. Male youths who had not reached puberty were spared. Women and children were sold into slavery, a number of them being distributed as gifts among Muhammad's companions. According to Muhammad's biographer Ibn Ishaq, Muhammad chose one of the Qurayzah women (Rayhana) for himself. The Qurayzah's property and other possessions (including weapons) were also divided up as additional "booty" among the Muslims. The following details have been chronicled consistently by Muslim sources: The arbiter (Sa'd Mu'adh) was appointed by Muhammad himself; Muhammad observed in person the horrific executions; Muhammad claimed as a wife a woman (Rayhana) previously married to one of the slaughtered Qurayzah tribesmen; the substantial material benefits (i.e., property, receipts from the sale of the enslaved) that accrued to the Muslims as a result of the massacre; the extinction of the Qurayzah.

Abu Yusuf (d. 798), the prominent Hanafi jurist who advised the Abbasid caliph Harun al-Rashid (d. 809), made the following observations about the Qurayzah massacre in his writings on jihad:

> Whenever the Muslims besiege an enemy stronghold, establish a treaty with the besieged who agree to surrender on certain conditions that will be decided by a delegate, and this man decides that their soldiers are to be executed and their women and children taken prisoner, this decision is lawful. This was the decision of *Sa'ad b. Mu'adh in connection with the Banu Qurayzahh* . . . it is up to the imam to decide what treatment is to be meted out to them and he will choose that which is preferable for religion and for Islam. If he esteems that the execution of the fighting men and the enslavement of their women and children is better for Islam and its followers, then he will act thus, *emulating the example of Sa'ad b. Mu'adh.*[3]

As reported by M. J. Kister, al-Mawardi (d. 1072), another eminent Muslim jurist from Baghdad, characterized the slaughter of the Qurayzah as a religious duty incumbent on Muhammad. Kister quotes al-Mawardi as follows: "[I]t was not permitted (for Muhammad) to forgive (in a case of) God's injunction incumbent upon them; he could only forgive (transgressions) in matters concerning his own person."[4] The notion that this slaughter was sanctioned by God as revealed to Muhammad was, according to Kister, reflective of "the current (as of 1986) Sunni view about the slaughter of the Banu Qurayzah."[5]

W. H. T. Gairdner, also relying exclusively upon Muslim sources characterizing the slaughter of the Qurayza, highlights the pivotal role that Muhammad himself played in orchestrating the overall events:

> The umpire who gave the fatal decision (Sa'ad) was extravagantly praised by Muhammad. Yet his action was wholly and admittedly due to his lust for personal vengeance on a tribe which had occasioned him a painful wound. In the agony of its treatment he cried out—"O God, let not my soul go forth ere thou has cooled my eye from the Bani Quraiza." *This* was the arbiter to whose word the fate of that tribe was given over. His sentiments were well-known to Muhammad, who appointed him. It is perfectly clear from that that their slaughter had been decreed. What makes it clearer still is the assertion of another biographer that Muhammad had refused to treat with the Bani Quraiza at all until they had "come down to receive the judgment of the Apostle of God." Accordingly "they came down"; in other words put themselves in his power. And only then was the arbitration of Sa'ad proposed and accepted—but not accepted until

it had been forced on him by Muhammad; for Sa'ad first declined and tried to make Muhammad take the responsibility, but was told "*qad amarak Allahu takhuma fihim*" "Allah has commanded you to give sentence in their case." From every point of view therefore the evidence is simply crushing that Muhammad was the ultimate author of this massacre.[6]

In the immediate aftermath of the massacre, the Muslims benefited substantially from the Qurayzah's assets, which they seized as booty. The land and property acquired helped the Muslims gain their economic independence. The military strength of the Muslim community of Medina grew because of the weapons obtained, and the fact that captured women and children taken as slaves were sold for horses and more weapons, facilitating enlargement of the Muslim armed forces for further conquests. Conversely, the Jewish tribe of the Qurayzah ceased to exist.

Finally, the Farsi text that borders the original illustration (above and below, but not reproduced on the cover art due to space constraints), apropos of its Persian Shiite context, focuses on the exploits of Ali:

Ali, who is the successor of God on the earth, and known to fight with a double-edged sword, ordered the warriors to cut off the heads of the nonbelievers. Zobair assisted him in finishing this job. Ali also ordered the distribution of the captives and their property [i.e., the "booty"] among the Muslims, in accord with Sa'ad (b. Mu'adh)'s [*see above*] decision regarding the fate of the defeated the Jews [i.e., the Qurayzah]. After the battle [and executions], Ali ordered everyone [of the Muslims] to return home. Sa'ad (b. Mu'adh) who had been very anxious during the battle, was now happy and praised God upon completion of his task. Then [later] they [i.e., the Muslims] celebrated and enjoyed beautiful women.[7]

NOTES

1. Charles Rieu, *Catalogue of the Persian Manuscripts in the British Museum, London, British Museum, 1966.* Supplement to the *Catalogue of the Persian Manuscripts in the British Museum* (London: British Museum Publications for the British Library, 1977), p. 211.

2. Summarized, here: M. J. Kister, "The Massacre of the Banū Qurayza: A Re-examination of a Tradition" *Jerusalem Studies in Arabic and Islam* 8 (1986): 61–96.

3. Abu Yusuf Ya'qub, *Le Livre de l'impot foncier,* trans. Edmond Fagnan (Paris: Paul Geuthner, 1921); English trans. in Bat Ye'or, *The Dhimmi—Jews and Christians under Islam* (Cranbury, NJ: Fairleigh Dickinson University Press, 1985), pp. 172–73.

4. Kister, "The Massacre of the Banū Qurayẓa," p. 69.

5. Ibid., p. 70.

6. W. H. T. Gairdner, "Muhammad without Camouflage," *Muslim World* 9 (1919): 36.

7. Translated by Fatemeh Masjedi.

FOREWORD

Ibn Warraq

Dr. Bostom has gathered together an impressive range of primary and secondary source documents relating to the theory and practice of jihad, and to a certain extent the conditions of *dhimmis*, non-Muslims living as oppressed tributaries in Islamic countries. The theory of the treatment of non-Muslims was in part derived and developed by theologians and Qur'anic commentators from Sura IX.29:

> Fight against such of those who have been given the Scripture as believe not in Allah nor the Last Day, and forbid not that which Allah hath forbidden by His messenger, and follow not the religion of truth, until they pay the tribute readily, being brought low.

Dr. Bostom is the first scholar to have had translated from the Arabic the works of such commentators on Sura IX.29 as al-Baydawi, al-Suyuti, al-Zamakhshari, and al-Tabari. Other primary sources translated for the first time into English include documents on jihad such as the one written by al-Ghazali, the celebrated Islamic mystic or Sufi, laying to rest the myth that Sufis always interpreted jihad as an inner moral struggle against one's lower instincts. Muslim jurists and philosophers include Shiites al-Hilli and al-Amili (the latter translated from Persian), and representatives of all four schools of Sunni jurisprudence, Averroes (Maliki), Ibn Taymiyya (Hanbali), Shaybani (Hanafi), al-Mawardi (Shafi'i), Ibn Qudama (Hanbali), and Ibn Khaldun (Maliki).

Similarly, Dr. Bostom is the first scholar to have overseen the translations of important, and, in some cases, neglected or forgotten, secondary sources from French works on jihad by Edmond Fagnan, Roger Arnaldez, Charles Emmanuel Dufourcq, Clement Huart, Dimitar Angelov, and Maria Mathilde Alexandrescu-Dersca Bulgaru.

Thus Dr. Bostom's collection is truly wide ranging, combining Shiite and Sunni, classical and modern, Qur'anic commentators and Islamic jurists and philosophers. There are regional examples of jihad campaigns as well as analyses of jihad slavery by some of the most learned modern scholars of the holy war. Dr. Bostom has even taken care to find and reproduce beautifully color-coded maps, with an accompanying chronology, depicting the initial five centuries of jihad conquests, and further primary documents detailing the havoc wrought by Muslims in the name of jihad across three continents, over the period of a millennium.

Scholars and nonspecialists alike should be grateful to Dr. Bostom for making these documents available for further research. I wrote "should be grateful"—but will everyone be pleased to have this comprehensive anthology that gainsays the myth of Islamic tolerance in an irrefutable way? And why did it take a nonspecialist such as Dr. Bostom, a scholar from another discipline—clinical epidemiology and randomized clinical trials in medicine—to discover, and have translated and published for the first time in English, this primary and secondary source material? Where were the Orientalists,[1] Islamologists, and professors of Near Eastern studies?

There are a number of scholars writing and living in the West whose works are widely read, respected, and influential but who, for various reasons, wish to play down the history of the *dhimmis*, including the Armenian genocide, and the periodic but persistent massacres of not only Jews and Christians, but the oft-neglected Hindus, Zoroastrians, and Buddhists, living under Islam. Some are concerned for the security of Israel and are grateful to Turkey for their treaties with Israel; hence these scholars do their best to deny or at least minimize the Armenian massacres. Since any discussion of *dhimmis* often ends in a discussion of the Armenian genocide, the negationist scholars are hostile to any works highlighting the plight of Jews and Christians under Islam in general. Others are simply Turkophiles, having made Turkey their field of speciality, and have friends and colleagues and even girlfriends or wives from Turkey. Others again are grateful to Turkey for its support during the cold war.

In an important essay, "The Pro-Islamic Jews," Bernard Lewis recounts how the romantic cult of Spain reaching its peak in Victor Hugo's *Hernani* influenced Jews who now nourished the illusion that they "had flourished in Muslim Spain, had been driven from Christian Spain, and had found refuge in Muslim Turkey."[2] But as Lewis points out, "The golden age of equal rights [in Spain] was a myth, and belief in it was a result, more than a cause, of Jewish sympathy for Islam. The myth was invented by Jews in nineteenth-century Europe as a reproach to Christians."[3] Something of the myth of the Golden Age of Spain persists to this day, and is perpetuated by politicians desperate to maintain social stability. Political leaders and the media in general in Europe are worried about the increasing number of Muslims in their respective countries, and are aware of the difficulties of assimilation. Under such circumstances the media will invite only those scholars who believe in the myth of Islamic tolerance. But European politicians, in their collective hatred and fear of the United States, have formed a strategic alliance with Arab states as a buffer to perceived threats from the only superpower, the Great Satan itself. In such a climate, an objective look at jihad and *dhimmis* is discouraged, and even scholars who should know better are swept along on the tide of anti-Americanism.

But long before the transformatiom of Europe into Eurabia,[4] many intellectuals had continued to treat Islam as a taboo subject for many reasons, including:

- Political correctness leading to Islamic correctness;
- The fear of playing into the hands of racists or reactionaries to the detriment of the West's Muslim minorities;
- Commercial or economic motives;
- Feelings of postcolonial guilt (wherein the entire planet's problems are attributed to the West's wicked ways and intentions);
- Plain physical fear; and
- The intellectual terrorism of writers such as Edward Said.

There are also tactical, political, and social reasons for playing down the role of jihad and *dhimmitude* in India, where communalism is a real danger, where religious passions run very high and can lead to riots leaving hundreds dead in their wake. For the sake of social harmony, it makes sense not to keep on harping on the past crimes of Islam.

As Lewis wrote,

> [We] may, indeed, we must study the history of Atlantic slavery and expose this great shame in the history of the Western world and the Americas north and south, in all its horror. This is a task which falls upon us as Westerners and in which others may and should and do join us. In contrast, however, even to mention—let alone discuss or explore—the existence of slavery in non-Western societies is denounced as evidence of racism and of imperialistic designs. The same applies to other delicate topics as polygamy, autocracy, and the like. The range of taboos is very wide.[5]

I should like to remind Bernard Lewis, his students, and his admirers of his own words,

> There was a time when scholars and other writers in communist eastern Europe relied on writers and publishers in the free West to speak the truth about their history, their culture, and their predicament. Today it is those who told the truth, not those who concealed or denied it, who are respected and welcomed in these countries. Historians in free countries have a moral and professional obligation not to shirk the difficult issues and subjects that some people would place under a sort of taboo; not to submit to voluntary censorship, but to deal with these matters fairly, honestly, without apologetics, without polemic, and, of course, competently. Those who enjoy freedom have a moral obligation to use that freedom for those who do not possess it. We live in a time when great efforts have been made, and continue to be made, to falsify the record of the past and to make history a tool of propaganda; when governments, religious movements, political parties, and sectional groups of every kind are busy rewriting history as they would wish it to have been, as they would like their followers to believe that it was. All this is very dangerous indeed, to ourselves and to others, however we may define otherness—dangerous to our common humanity. Because, make no

mistake, those who are unwilling to confront the past will be unable to understand the present and unfit to face the future.[6]

Finally, there are those who tell me that even though Dr. Bostom and many others may be right in exposing history hitherto repressed or simply denied, this was not the right historical moment to express it, in this hour of a conservative US administration whose members do not hide their Christian allegiances, at this time of a war on terror when we are trying to convince Muslims around the world that we are not at war with *them*, but with those who have a perverted interpretation of the great religion of Islam.

Sir Isaiah Berlin once described an ideologue as somebody who is prepared to suppress what he suspects to be true. Berlin then concluded that from that disposition to suppress the truth has flowed much of the evil of this and other centuries. The first duty of the intellectual is to tell the truth. By suppressing the truth, however honorable the motive, we are only engendering an even greater evil.

We are all beholden to Dr. Bostom for helping us to see more clearly and more honestly past events that have such an important bearing on present travails. In the words of Albert Schweitzer, "Truth has no special time of its own. Its hour is now, always, and indeed then most truly when it seems most unsuitable to actual circumstances."[7]

NOTES

1. I take Orientalist to mean "one versed in oriental languages and literature," as the *New Oxford Dictionary* defines it. It only became a term of abuse after the publication of Edward Said's distressingly inaccurate but influential work, *Orientalism*.

2. Bernard Lewis, "The Pro-Islamic Jews," in *Islam in History* (Chicago: Open Court, 1993), p. 148.

3. Ibid., p. 148

4. Bat Ye'or, *Eurabia—The Euro-Arab Axis* (Cranbury, NJ: Fairleigh Dickinson University Press, 2005), p. 384.

5. B. Lewis, "Other People's History," in *Islam and the West* (New York: Oxford University Press, 1993), p. 123.

6. Ibid., p. 130.

7. Norman Cousins, ed., *The Words of Albert Schweitzer* (New York: Newmarket Press, 1996), p. 19.

PART 1

1

JIHAD CONQUESTS AND THE IMPOSITION OF *DHIMMITUDE*—A SURVEY

Andrew G. Bostom

The late philosopher and theologian Jacques Ellul emphasized in his foreword to *Les Chretientes d'Orient entre Jihad et Dhimmitude. VIIᵉ–XXᵉ siecle* (1991), how contemporary historiography whitewashed the basic realities of jihad war:

> In a major encyclopedia, one reads phrases such as: "Islam expanded in the eighth or ninth centuries . . ."; "This or that country passed into Muslim hands. . . ." But care is taken not to say *how* Islam expanded, *how* countries "passed into [Muslim] hands." . . . Indeed, it would seem as if events happened by themselves, through a miraculous or amicable operation. . . . Regarding this expansion, little is said about *jihad*. And yet it all happened through war!
>
> . . . the *jihad* is an institution, and not an event, that is to say it is a part of the normal functioning of the Muslim world. . . . The conquered populations change status (they become *dhimmis*), and the *shari'a* tends to be put into effect integrally, overthrowing the former law of the country. The conquered territories do not simply change "owners."[1]

Writing more than six decades ago, Arthur Jeffery described the continuum from jihad to what has become known as *dhimmitude*—the sociopolitical status of those indigenous non-Muslim peoples vanquished by jihad campaigns:

> [Muhammad] did at least propose that all Arabia should be the land of Allah and planned vigorous measures to insure that within its borders the religion of Allah should be supreme. Communities of the People of the Book [Book = Bible; thus referring primarily to Jews and Christians] might remain within the land, but they

must be in subjection . . . deriving their rights from the supreme Muslim community, *not* from any recognized rights of their own. As the Arabs did not accept this without struggle, it had to be forced on them, and that meant war. But war in the cause of Allah is Holy War, and so even in the Prophet's lifetime we have the question of Jihad.[2]

Richard Bell, in his authoritative 1937 translation and exegesis of the Qur'an, demonstrates that Sura 9 *"is a chapter of war proclamations,"*[3] and verses 9.29 to 9.35, specifically, "form in effect a proclamation of war against Jews and Christians, and probably belong to the year IX [9 years after the Hijra] when an expedition was designed for the North which would involve war with Christians and possibly also with Jews."[4]

Jeffery belittled as "the sheerest sophistry" attempts

made in some circles in modern days to explain away all the Prophet's warlike expeditions as defensive wars or to interpret the doctrine of Jihad as merely a bloodless striving in missionary zeal for the spread of Islam. . . . The early Arabic sources quite plainly and frankly describe the expeditions as military expeditions, and it would never have occurred to anyone at that day to interpret them as anything else. . . . To the folk of his day there would thus be nothing strange in Muhammad, as the head of the community of those who served Allah, taking the sword to extend the kingdom of Allah, and taking measures to insure the subjection of all who lived within the borders of what he made the kingdom of Allah.[5]

The writings of Chiragh Ali Syed illustrate this apologetic modern sophistry, according to Jeffery, wherein "an . . . elaborate defense of Holy War . . . by a series of extraordinary interpretations and combinations of texts, he (Ali Syed) resolves Jihad into little more than a summons to vigorous missionary activity."[6]

Thirty years later, Maxime Rodinson warned more broadly that "[t]he anticolonial left, whether Christian or not, often goes so far as to sanctify Islam and the contemporary ideologies of the Muslim world. . . . Understanding has given away to apologetics pure and simple.[7]

The prescient critiques of Jeffery and Rodinson anticipated the state of contemporary scholarship on jihad. Two salient examples of this current apologetic trend will suffice.

Writing in 2002, Khaled Abou El Fadl, a professor of law at UCLA, maintained categorically that "Islamic tradition does not have a notion of holy war. Jihad simply means to strive hard or struggle in pursuit of a just cause. . . . Holy war (al-harb al-muqaddasah) is not an expression used by the Qur'anic text or Muslim theologians. In Islamic theology war is never holy; it is either justified or not."[8]

El Fadl's recent contention cannot be supported on either theological-juridical or historical grounds, and in fact contradicts the conclusion of an earlier essay he wrote.[9] Specifically, El Fadl wrote the following in 1999: "There is no doubt that Muslim jurists do equate just war with religious war (jihad)."[9]

His footnote for this quote cites the classical Hanbali jurist Ibn Taymiyya as well as two authoritative modern scholars of jihad, Majid Khadduri,[10] and Rudolph Peters.[11]

John Esposito's apologetic writings regarding expansionist military jihad simply ignore voluminous but inconvenient historical data. For example, he provides this ahistorical characterization of the entire period between the initial Islamic jihad conquests, in the fourth decade of the seventh century CE, and the first Crusade in 1099 CE: "Five centuries of peaceful coexistence elapsed before political events and an imperial-papal power play led to centuries-long series of so-called holy wars that pitted Christendom against Islam and left an enduring legacy of misunderstanding and distrust."[12]

Recently, Bat Ye'or analyzed Esposito's summary assessment of the first millennium of jihad conquests. Bat Ye'or notes how Esposito completely "ignores the concepts of jihad and dar al-harb,"[13] and she highlights the "thematic structure" of Esposito's selective overview, typical of the prevailing modern apologetic genre:[14]

> {H]istorical negationism, consisting of suppressing or sketching in a page or a paragraph, one thousand years of jihad which is presented as a peaceful conquest, generally welcomed by the vanquished populations; the omission of Christian and, in particular, Muslim sources describing the actual methods of these conquests: pillage, enslavement, deportation, massacres, and so on; the mythical historical conversion of "centuries" of "peaceful coexistence," masking the processes which transformed majorities into minorities, constantly at risk of extinction; an obligatory self-incrimination for the Crusades."[14]

The remainder of this essay, as well as the juridical texts, historical accounts, scholarly analyses, and excerpts from eyewitness accounts that follow, will provide the rationale for jihad as formulated by Muslim theologians and jurists, and highlight the global consequences of more than thirteen centuries of jihad campaigns during ancient, premodern, and modern times.

The essential pattern of the jihad war is captured in the great Muslim historian al-Tabari's recording of the recommendation given by Umar b. al-Khattab to the commander of the troops he sent to al-Basrah (636 CE), during the conquest of Iraq. Umar (the second "Rightly Guided Caliph") reportedly said: "Summon the people to God; those who respond to your call, accept it from them, (This is to say, accept their conversion as genuine and refrain from fighting them) but those who refuse must pay the poll tax out of humiliation and lowliness. (Qur'an 9:29) If they refuse this, it is the sword without leniency. Fear God with regard to what you have been entrusted."[15]

Jihad was pursued century after century, because jihad, which means "to strive in the path of Allah," embodied an ideology and a jurisdiction. Both were formally conceived by Muslim jurisconsults and theologians from the eighth and ninth centuries onward, based on their interpretation of Qur'anic verses (e.g., 9.5, 6; 9.29; 4.76–79; 2.214–15; 8.39–42),[16] and long chapters in the Traditions (i.e., hadith, acts and sayings of the Prophet Muhammad, especially those recorded by al-Bukhari [d. 869][17] and Muslim [d. 874][18]). The consensus on the nature of jihad from all four schools of Sunni Islamic jurisprudence (i.e., Maliki, Hanbali, Hanafi, and Shafi'i) is clear.

Ibn Abi Zayd al-Qayrawani (d. 996), Maliki jurist:

> Jihad is a precept of Divine institution. Its performance by certain individuals may dispense others from it. We Malikis [one of the four schools of Muslim jurisprudence] maintain that it is preferable not to begin hostilities with the enemy before having invited the latter to embrace the religion of Allah except where the enemy attacks first. They have the alternative of either converting to Islam or paying the poll tax (jizya), short of which war will be declared against them.[19]

Ibn Taymiyyah (d. 1328), Hanbali jurist

> Since lawful warfare is essentially jihad and since its aim is that the religion is God's entirely and God's word is uppermost, therefore according to all Muslims, those who stand in the way of this aim must be fought. As for those who cannot offer resistance or cannot fight, such as women, children, monks, old people, the blind, handicapped and their likes, they shall not be killed unless they actually fight with words (e.g., by propaganda) and acts (e.g., by spying or otherwise assisting in the warfare).[20]

From (primarily) the Hanafi school, as given in the *Hidayah* of Shaikh Burhanuddin Ali of Marghinan (d. 1196):

> It is not lawful to make war upon any people who have never before been called to the faith, without previously requiring them to embrace it, because the Prophet so instructed his commanders, directing them to call the infidels to the faith, and also because the people will hence perceive that they are attacked for the sake of religion, and not for the sake of taking their property, or making slaves of their children, and on this consideration it is possible that they may be induced to agree to the call, in order to save themselves from the troubles of war. . . . If the infidels, upon receiving the call, neither consent to it nor agree to pay capitation tax, it is then incumbent on the Muslims to call upon God for assistance, and to make war upon them, because God is the assistant of those who serve Him, and the destroyer of His enemies, the infidels, and it is necessary to implore His aid upon every occasion; the Prophet, moreover, commands us so to do.[21]

Al-Mawardi (d. 1058), Shafi'i jurist:

The mushrikun [infidels] of Dar al-Harb (the arena of battle) are of two types: First, those whom the call of Islam has reached, but they have refused it and have taken up arms. The amir of the army has the option of fighting them . . . in accordance with what he judges to be in the best interest of the Muslims and most harmful to the mushrikun. . . . Second, those whom the invitation to Islam has not reached, although such persons are few nowadays since Allah has made manifest the call of his Messenger . . . it is forbidden to . . . begin an attack before explaining the invitation to Islam to them, informing them of the miracles of the Prophet and making plain the proofs so as to encourage acceptance on their part; if they still refuse to accept after this, war is waged against them and they are treated as those whom the call has reached.[22]

Ibn Khaldun (d. 1406), Maliki jurist, renowned philosopher, historian, and sociologist, summarized these consensus opinions from five centuries of prior Sunni Muslim jurisprudence with regard to the uniquely Islamic institution of jihad: "In the Muslim community, the holy war is a religious duty, because of the universalism of the [Muslim] mission and [the obligation to] convert everybody to Islam either by persuasion or by force. . . . The other religious groups did not have a universal mission, and the holy war was not a religious duty for them, save only for purposes of defense. . . . Islam is under obligation to gain power over other nations."[23]

Finally, Shiite jurisprudence was in agreement with the Sunni consensus on the basic nature of jihad war, as reflected in this excerpt from the *Jami-i-Abbasi* (the popular Persian manual of Shia law) written by al-Amili (d. 1622), a distinguished theologian under Shah Abbas I: "Islamic Holy war [jihad] against followers of other religions, such as Jews, is required unless they convert to Islam or pay the poll tax."[24]

By the time of the classical Muslim historian al-Tabari's death in 923, jihad wars had expanded the Muslim empire from Portugal to the Indian subcontinent. Subsequent Muslim conquests continued in Asia, as well as on Christian lands in eastern Europe. The Christian kingdoms of Armenia, Byzantium, Bulgaria, Serbia, Bosnia, Herzegovina, Croatia, and Albania, as well as parts of Poland and Hungary, were also conquered and Islamized. When the Muslim armies were stopped at the gates of Vienna in 1683, more than a millennium of jihad had transpired.[25] These tremendous military successes spawned a triumphalist jihad literature. Muslim historians recorded in detail the number of infidels slain or enslaved, the cities and villages that were pillaged, and the lands, treasure, and movable goods seized. Christian (Coptic, Armenian, Jacobite, Greek, Slav, etc.), as well as Hebrew sources and even the scant Hindu and Buddhist writings that survived the ravages of the Muslim conquests independently validate this narrative, and complement the Muslim perspective by providing testimonies of the suffering of the non-Muslim victims of jihad wars.[26]

FROM JIHAD TO *DHIMMITUDE*

In *The Laws of Islamic Governance*[27] al-Mawardi (d. 1058), also examines the regulations pertaining to the lands and infidel (i.e., non-Muslim) populations subjugated by jihad. This is the origin of the system of *dhimmitude*. The native infidel population had to recognize Islamic ownership of their land, submit to Islamic law, and accept payment of the poll tax (*jizya*). Al-Mawardi highlights the most significant aspect of this consensus view of the *jizya* in classical Islamic jurisprudence: the critical connection between jihad and payment of the *jizya*. He notes that *"[t]he enemy makes a payment in return for peace and reconciliation."* Al-Mawardi then distinguishes two cases: (1) Payment is made immediately and is treated like booty, however *"it does, however, not prevent a jihad being carried out against them in the future"* (2) Payment is made yearly and will *"constitute an ongoing tribute by which their security is established."* Reconciliation and security last as long as the payment is made. *If the payment ceases, then the jihad resumes.* A treaty of reconciliation may be renewable, but must not exceed ten years. In the chapter "The Division of the Fay and the Ghaneemah [booty]," al-Mawardi examines the regulations pertaining to the land taken from the infidels. With regard to land taken through treaty, specifically, he indicates two possibilities: either the infidels convert or they pay the *jizya* and their life and belongings are protected. The nature of such "protection" is clarified in this definition of *jizya* by the respected Arabic lexicographer E. W. Lane, based on a careful analysis of the etymology of the term: "The tax that is taken from the free non-Muslim subjects of a Muslim government whereby they ratify the compact that assures them protection, *as though it were compensation for not being slain.*"[28]

Another important aspect of the *jizya* is the widely upheld view of the classical schools of Islamic jurisprudence about the deliberately humiliating imposition and procurement of this tax.[29] Here is a discussion of the ceremonial for collection of the *jizya* by the thirteenth-century Shafi'ite jurist an-Nawawi: "The infidel who wishes to pay his poll tax must be treated with disdain by the collector: the collector remains seated and the infidel remains standing in front of him, his head bowed and his back bent. The infidel personally must place the money on the scales, while the collector holds him by the beard, and strikes him on both cheeks."[30]

S. D. Goitein, in a seminal 1963 essay, highlighted the limitation of studying the potential economic and other adverse social consequences of the *jizya* without any reference to non-Muslim sources:

> There is no subject of Islamic social history on which the present writer had to modify his views so radically while passing from literary to documentary sources, i.e., from the study of Muslim books to that of the records of the Cairo Geniza as the jizya . . . or the poll tax to be paid by non-Muslims. It was of course, evident that the tax represented a discrimination and was intended,

according to the Koran's own words, to emphasize the inferior status of the non-believers. It seemed, however, that from the economic point of view, it did not constitute a heavy imposition, since it was on a sliding scale, approximately one, two, and four dinars, and thus adjusted to the financial capacity of the taxpayer. This impression proved to be entirely fallacious, for it did not take into consideration the immense extent of poverty and privation experienced by the masses, and in particular, their persistent lack of cash, which turned the "season of the tax" into one of horror, dread, and misery.[31]

Jewish, Coptic, Syriac, Armenian, and Serbian sources provide copious evidence that the *jizya-kharaj* was demanded from children, widows, orphans, and even the dead.[32] Indeed, these testimonies simply confirm what was prescribed at any rate by the Shafi'ite jurists, as expounded by an-Nawawi: "Our religion compels the poll tax to be paid by dying people, the old, even in a state of incapacity, the blind, monks, workers, and the poor, incapable of practicing a trade. As for people who seem to be insolvent at the end of the year, the sum of the poll tax remains a debt to their account until they should become solvent.[33]

Tax collectors were accompanied by soldiers, inspectors, surveyors, and money changers paid, fed, and lodged for several days at the taxpayers' expense.[34] Although theoretically prohibited, punishment and torture were used by tax collectors to complete their task.[35] The Armenian chronicler Ghevond describes this bleak situation in Armenia under Abbasid rule during the eighth century:

> One saw . . . horrible scenes of every sort of torture; nor did [they] forget to tax the dead; the multitude of orphans and widows suffered the same cruelty; priests and ministers at the holy sanctuary were forced by the vile punishments of flogging and whipping to disclose the names of the dead and their parents; in short the whole population of the country, smitten with enormous taxes, after having paid large sums of zuze [silver coins], also had to wear a lead seal around their necks . . . as for the lower classes of the population, it had been exposed to different sorts of torture: some suffered flagellation for being unable to pay exorbitant taxes; others were hanged on gibbets, or crushed under presses; and others were stripped of their clothing and thrown into lakes in the depths of an extremely cold winter: and soldiers spaced out on the banks prevented them clambering ashore and forced them to perish wretchedly.[36]

Endemic to Muslim-controlled Palestine, Syria, and Mesopotamia, as well as Armenia, such brutal practices led to an indelible process of expropriation of the *dhimmi* peasantry in particular. Onerous taxation, combined with indebtedness to Muslim creditors, forced Christian and Jewish peasants to abandon their mortgaged lands to their Muslim overlords, and go into exile or become slaves.[37] The later Turkish Muslim conquests and Islamization of Anatolia and the Balkans continued these processes between the eleventh and sixteenth centuries.[38]

Finally, two remarkable accounts demonstrate the humiliating conditions under which the *jizya* was still being collected within the modern era. An Italian Jew traveling in Morocco in 1894 reported the following:

> The kaid Uwida and the kadi Mawlay Mustafa had mounted their tent today near the Mellah [Jewish ghetto] gate and had summoned the Jews in order to collect from them the poll tax [*jizya*] which they are obliged to pay the sultan. They had me summoned also. I first inquired whether those who were European-protected subjects had to pay this tax. Having learned that a great many of them had already paid it, I wished to do likewise. After having remitted the amount of the tax to the two officials, I received from the kadi's guard two blows in the back of the neck. Addressing the kadi and the kaid, I said "Know that I am an Italian protected subject." Whereupon the kadi said to his guard: "Remove the kerchief covering his head and strike him strongly; he can then go and complain wherever he wants." The guards hastily obeyed and struck me once again more violently. This public mistreatment of a European-protected subject demonstrates to all the Arabs that they can, with impunity, mistreat the Jews.[39]

And in a letter from January 30, 1911, by Avram Elmaleh, head of the Fez boys' school, to the president of the Alliance Israelite Universelle in Paris, we learn the degrading conditions imposed upon the rabbinical leaders of the Moroccan Jewish community in connection with "community business" (i.e., such as payment of the *jizya*), even into the second decade of the twentieth century:

> I have the honor to acknowledge receipt of your letter No. 1283 of 30 January, enclosing a letter from Rabbi Vidal Sarfaty. The rabbi asks you to intervene with Si Mohamed el Mokri, the Moroccan Minister of Foreign Affairs, at present in Paris, for the abolition of the degrading custom imposed on Jews, not to enter Dar el Maghzen except barefoot. Unfortunately, the facts given in Rabbi Vidal's letter are correct. Jews must take off their shoes at the gate of Dar-Maghzen. Quite apart from the humiliation involved in this measure, it is an intolerable suffering for our co-religionists to be obliged to stand many hours barefoot on the earth of the Palace courtyard, which is either cold and damp or white-hot from the summer sun. Rabbi Vidal, a regular visitor to the Dar-Maghzen in connection with community business or on behalf of individuals, has often returned ill from a rather too long sojourn in front of the offices. It is my opinion that it would be impossible to obtain an order from the Sultan to allow Jews to enter the Palace with their shoes on. It is a concession which his pride would not permit, and one quite contrary to the Muslim conception of the relative positions of the Jews and themselves.[40]

The contract of the *jizya* or *dhimma* encompassed other obligatory and recommended obligations for the conquered non-Muslim *dhimmi* peoples.[41] Collectively, these "obligations" formed the discriminatory system of *dhimmitude* imposed upon non-Muslims—Jews, Christians, Zoroastrians, Hindus, and Buddhists—subjugated by jihad. Some of the more salient features of *dhimmitude* include: the prohibition of arms for the vanquished non-Muslims (*dhimmis*) and of church bells; restrictions concerning the building and restoration of churches, synagogues, and temples; inequality between Muslims and non-Muslims with regard to taxes and penal law; the refusal of *dhimmi* testimony by Muslim courts;[42] a requirement that Jews, Christians, and other non-Muslims, including Zoroastrians and Hindus, wear special clothes; and the overall humiliation and abasement of non-Muslims. It is important to note that these regulations and attitudes were institutionalized as permanent features of the sacred Islamic law, or sharia. The writings of the much lionized Sufi theologian and jurist al-Ghazali (d. 1111)—the famous theologian, philosopher, and paragon of mystical Sufism, who, as noted by the renowned scholar W. M. Watt, has been "acclaimed in both the East and West as the greatest Muslim after Muhammad"[43]—highlight how the institution of *dhimmitude* was simply a normative and prominent feature of the sharia:

> [T]he *dhimmi* is obliged not to mention Allah or His Apostle . . . Jews, Christians, and Majians must pay the *jizya* [poll tax on non-Muslims] . . . *on offering up the* jizya, *the* dhimmi *must hang his head while the official takes hold of his beard and hits* [*the* dhimmi] *on the protruberant bone beneath his ear* [*i.e., the mandible*]. . . . They are not permitted to ostentatiously display their wine or church bells . . . their houses may not be higher than the Muslim's, no matter how low that is. The *dhimmi* may not ride an elegant horse or mule; he may ride a donkey only if the saddle[-work] is of wood. He may not walk on the good part of the road. They [the *dhimmis*] have to wear [an identifying] patch [on their clothing], even women, and even in the [public] baths . . . [*dhimmis*] must hold their tongue.[44]

Ignaz Goldziher believed that Shi'ism manifested greater doctrinal intolerance toward non-Muslims, relative to Sunni Islam:

> On examining the legal documents, we find that the Shi'i legal position toward other faiths is much harsher and stiffer than that taken by Sunni Muslims. Their law reveals a heightened intolerance to people of other beliefs. . . . Of the severe rule in the Qur'an (9:28) that "unbelievers are unclean," Sunni Islam has accepted an interpretation that is as good as a repeal. Shi'i law, on the other hand, has maintained the literal sense of the rule; it declares the bodily substance of the unbeliever to be ritually unclean, and lists the touching of an unbeliever among the ten things that produce *najasa*, ritual impurity.[45]

Mohammad Baqer Majlesi (d. 1699), the highest institutionalized clerical officer under both Shah Sulayman (1666–1694) and Shah Husayn (1694–1722), was perhaps the most influential cleric of the Safavid Shi'ite theocracy in Persia. By design, he wrote many works in Persian to disseminate key aspects of the Shia ethos among ordinary persons. His Persian treatise *Risala-yi Sawa'iq Al-Yahud* (*Lightning Bolts against the Jews*), despite its title, was actually an overall guideline to anti-*dhimmi* regulations for all non-Muslims within the Shiite theocracy. In this treatise, Al-Majlisi describes the standard humiliating requisites for non-Muslims living under the sharia, first and foremost, the blood ransom *jizya*.[46] He then enumerates six other restrictions relating to worship, housing, dress, transportation, and weapons (specifically, i.e., to render the *dhimmis* defenseless), before outlining the unique Shiite impurity or *najas* regulations. It is these latter *najas* prohibitions that lead anthropology professor Laurence Loeb (who studied and lived within the Jewish community of southern Iran in the early 1970s) to observe, "Fear of pollution by Jews led to great excesses and peculiar behavior by Muslims."[47] According to Al-Majlisi,

> And, that they should not enter the pool while a Muslim is bathing at the public baths. . . . It is also incumbent upon Muslims that they should not accept from them victuals with which they had come into contact, such as distillates, which cannot be purified. If something can be purified, such as clothes, if they are dry, they can be accepted, they are clean. But if they [the *dhimmis*] had come into contact with those cloths in moisture they should be rinsed with water after being obtained. As for hide, or that which has been made of hide such as shoes and boots, and meat, whose religious cleanliness and lawfulness are conditional on the animal's being slaughtered [according to the sharia], these may not be taken from them. Similarly, liquids that have been preserved in skins, such as oils, grape syrup, [fruit] juices, myrobalan, and the like, if they have been put in skin containers or water skins, these should [also] not be accepted from them. . . . *It would also be better if the ruler of the Muslims would establish that all infidels could not move out of their homes on days when it rains or snows because they would make Muslims impure.* (Emphasis mine.)[48]

Bat Ye'or is an accomplished contemporary scholar[49] of those unique Islamic institutions that regulate the relations between Muslims and non-Muslims: jihad and its corollary institution, *dhimmitude*, the repressive and humiliating system of governance imposed upon those non-Muslims (i.e., *dhimmis*) subjugated by jihad. Although she coined the term *dhimmitude*, Bat Ye'or's characterization of the salient features of this institution is entirely consistent with the views of seminal scholars from the early and mid-twentieth century. Sir Jadunath Sarkar, for example, a preeminent historian of Mughal India, wrote the following in 1920 regarding the impact of centuries of jihad and *dhimmitude* on the indigenous Hindus of the Indian subcontinent:

> Islamic theology, therefore tells the true believer that his highest duty is to make "exertion (jihad) in the path of God," by waging war against infidel lands (dar-ul-harb) till they become part of the realm of Islam (dar-ul-Islam) and their populations are converted into true believers. After conquest the entire infidel popu-

lation becomes theoretically reduced to the status of slaves of the conquering army. The men taken with arms are to be slain or sold into slavery and their wives and children reduced to servitude. As for the non-combatants among the vanquished, if they are not massacred outright,—as the canon lawyer Shaf'i declares to be the Qur'anic injunction,—it is only to give them a respite till they are so wisely guided as to accept the true faith.

The conversion of the entire population to Islam and the extinction of every form of dissent is the ideal of the Muslim State. If any infidel is suffered to exist in the community, it is as a necessary evil, and for a transitional period only. Political and social disabilities must be imposed on him, and bribes offered to him from the public funds, to hasten the day of his spiritual enlightenment and the addition of his name to the roll of true believers. . . .

A non-Muslim therefore cannot be a citizen of the State; he is a member of a depressed class; his status is a modified form of slavery. He lives under a contract (zimma, or "dhimma") with the State: for the life and property grudgingly spared to him by the commander of the faithful he must undergo political and social disabilities, and pay a commutation money. In short, his continued existence in the State after the conquest of his country by the Muslims is conditional upon his person and property made subservient to the cause of Islam.

He must pay a tax for his land (kharaj), from which the early Muslims were exempt; he must pay other exactions for the maintenance of the army, in which he cannot enlist even if he offers to render personal service instead of paying the poll-tax; and he must show by humility of dress and behavior that he belongs to a subject class. No non-Muslim can wear fine dresses, ride on horseback or carry arms; he must behave respectfully and submissively to every member of the dominant sect.

As the learned Qazi Mughis-ud-din declared, in accordance with the teachings of the books on Canon Law: "The Hindus are designated in the Law as 'payers of tribute' (kharaj-guzar); and when the revenue officer demands silver from them, they should, without question and with all humility and respect, tender gold. If the officer throws dirt into their mouths, they must without reluctance open their mouths wide to receive it." By these acts of degradation are shown the extreme obedience of the zimmi [dhimmi], the glorification of the true faith of Islam, and the abasement of false faiths. God himself orders them to be humiliated, (as He says, "till they pay jaziya") with the hand and are humbled. . . . The Prophet has commanded us to slay them, plunder them, and make them captive. . . . No other religious authority except the great Imam (Hanifa) whose faith we follow, has sanctioned the imposition of jaziya on Hindus. According to all other theologians, the rule for Hindus is "Either death or Islam."

The zimmi is under certain legal disabilities with regard to testimony in law courts, protection under criminal law, and in marriage . . . he cannot erect new temples, and has to avoid any offensive publicity in the exercise of his worship. . . . Every device short of massacre in cold blood was resorted to in order to convert heathen subjects. In addition to the poll-tax and public degradation in dress and demeanor imposed on them, the non-Muslims were subjected to various hopes and fears. Rewards in the form of money and public employment were offered to apostates from Hinduism. The leaders of Hindu religion and society were systematically repressed, to deprive the sect of spiritual instruction, and their religious gatherings and processions were forbidden in order to prevent the growth of solidarity and sense of communal strength among them. No new temple was allowed to be built nor any old one to be repaired, so that the total disappearance of Hindu worship was to be merely a question of time. But even this delay, this slow operation of Time, was intolerable to many of the more fiery spirits of Islam, who tried to hasten the abolition of "infidelity" by anticipating the destructive hand of Time and forcibly pulling down temples.

When a class are publicly depressed and harassed by law and executive caprice alike, they merely content themselves with dragging on an animal existence. With every generous instinct of the soul crushed out of them, the intellectual culture merely adding a keen edge to their sense of humiliation, the Hindus could not be expected to produce the utmost of which they were capable; their lot was to be hewers of wood and drawers of water to their masters, to bring grist to the fiscal mill, to develop a low cunning and flattery as the only means of saving what they could of their own labor. Amidst such social conditions, the human hand and the human spirit cannot achieve their best; the human soul cannot soar to its highest pitch. The barrenness of intellect and meanness of spirit of the Hindu upper classes are the greatest condemnation of Muhammadan rule in India. The Muhammadan political tree judged by its fruit was an utter failure.[50]

Nearly four decades later, Antoine Fattal, whose 1958 *Le Statut Legal de Musulmans en Pays' d'Islam* remains the benchmark analysis of non-Muslims (especially Christians and Jews) living under the sharia (i.e., Muslim law), observed:

Even today, the study of the *jihad* is part of the curriculum of all the Islamic institutes. In the universities of Al-Azhar, Nagaf, and Zaitoune, students are still taught that the holy war [*jihad*] is a binding prescriptive decree, pronounced against the Infidels, which will only be revoked with the end of the world. . . . If he [the *dhimmi*] is tolerated, it is for reasons of a spiritual nature, since there is always the hope that he might be converted; or of a material nature, since he bears almost the whole tax burden. He has his place in society, but *he is constantly reminded of his inferiority*. . . . *In no way is the* dhimmi *the equal of the Muslim. He is marked out for social inequality and belongs to a despised caste; unequal in regard to individual rights; unequal in the Law Courts as his evidence is not admitted by any Muslim tribunal and for the same crime his punishment is greater than that imposed on Muslims*. . . . No social relationship, no fellowship is possible between Muslims and *dhimmis*.[51]

Bat Ye'or's seminal contribution to the study of jihad and *dhimmitude* has been her unique ability to accomplish two related tasks: (1) methodically pooling a vast, rich array of primary source data; (2) providing a brilliant synthetic analysis of these data to demonstrate convincingly the transformative power of jihad and *dhimmitude*, operating as designed, within formerly Christian societies of the Near East and Asia Minor. Mary Boyce, emeritus professor of Iranian studies at the University of London, has confirmed the external validity of Bat Ye'or's analytical approach in her description of how jihad and *dhimmitude* (without the latter being specifically identified as such) transformed Zoroastrian society in an analogous manner. Boyce has written comprehensive assessments of those Zoroastrian communities that survived the devastating jihad conquests of the mid-seventh through early eighth centuries.[52] The Zoroastrians experienced an ongoing, inexorable decline over the next millennium due to constant sociopolitical and economic pressures exerted by their Muslim rulers and neighbors. This gradual but continuous process was interspersed with periods of accelerated decline resulting from paroxysms of Muslim fanaticism—pogroms, forced conversions, and expropriations—through the latter half of the nineteenth century. Boyce describes these complementary phenomena based on a historical analysis, and her personal observations living in the central Iranian Yezd area during the 1960s:

> [I]n the mid nineteenth century disaster overtook Turkabad, in the shape of what was perhaps the last massed forcible conversion in Iran. It no longer seems possible to learn anything about the background of this event; but it happened, so it is said, one autumn day when dye-madder—then one of the chief local crops—was being lifted. All the able-bodied men were at work in teams in the fields when a body of Moslems swooped on the village and seized them. They were threatened, not only with death for themselves, but also with the horrors that would befall their women and children, who were being terrorized at the same time in their homes; and by the end of the day of violence most of the village had accepted Islam. To recant after a verbal acknowledgement of Allah and his prophet meant death in those days, and so Turkabad was lost to the old religion. Its fire-temple was razed to the ground, and only a rough, empty enclosure remained where once it had stood.
>
> A similar fate must have overtaken many Iranian villages in the past, among those which did not willingly embrace Islam; and the question seems less why it happened to Turkabad than why it did not overwhelm all other Zoroastrian settlements. The evidence, scanty though it is, shows, however, that the harassment of the Zoroastrians of Yazd tended to be erratic and capricious, being at times less harsh, or bridled by strong governors; and in general the advance of Islam across the plain, through relentless, seems to have been more by slow erosion than by furious force. The process was till going on in the 1960s, and one could see, therefore, how it took effect. Either a few Moslems settled on the outskirts of a Zoroastrian village, or one or two Zoroastrian families adopted Islam. Once the dominant faith had made a breach, it pressed in remorselessly, like a rising tide. More Moslems came, and soon a small mosque was built, which attracted yet others. As long as Zoroastrians remained in the majority, their lives were tolerable; but once the Moslems became the more numerous, a petty but pervasive harassment was apt to develop. This was partly verbal, with taunts about fire-

worship, and comments on how few Zoroastrians there were in the world, and how many Moslems, who must therefore posses the truth; and also on how many material advantages lay with Islam. The harassment was often also physical; boys fought, and gangs of youth waylaid and bullied individual Zoroastrians. They also diverted themselves by climbing into the local tower of silence and desecrating it, and they might even break into the fire-temple and seek to pollute or extinguish the sacred flame. Those with criminal leanings found too that a religious minority provided tempting opportunities for theft, pilfering from the open fields, and sometimes rape and arson. Those Zoroastrians who resisted all these pressures often preferred therefore in the end to sell out and move to some other place where their co-religionists were still relatively numerous, and they could live at peace; and so another village was lost to the old faith. Several of the leading families in Sharifabad and forebears who were driven away by intense Moslem pressure from Abshahi, once a very devout and orthodox village on the southern outskirts of Yazd; and a shorter migration had been made by the family of the centenarian "Hajji" Khodabakhsh, who had himself been born in the 1850s and was still alert and vigorous in 1964. His family, who were very pious, had left their home in Ahmedabad (just to the north of Turkabad) when he was a small boy, and had come to settle in Sharifabad to escape persecution and the threats to their orthodox way of life. Other Zoroastrians held out there for a few decades longer, but by the end of the century Ahmedabad was wholly Moslem, as Abshahi become in 1961. [Boyce's footnote: The last Zoroastrian family left Abshahi in 1961, after the rape and subsequent suicide of one of their daughters.] It was noticeable that the villages which were left to the Zoroastrians were in the main those with poor supplies of water, where farming conditions were hard.[53]

THE JIHAD CAMPAIGNS: A HISTORICAL OVERVIEW

Muhammad and the Inception of the Great Jihad

September 622 marks a defining event in Islam—the *hijra*. Muhammad and a coterie of followers (the Muhajirun), persecuted by fellow Banu Quraysh tribesmen who rejected Muhammad's authenticity as a divine messenger, fled from Mecca to Yathrib, later known as Al-Medina (Medina). Moshe Gil notes that Muslim sources described Yathrib as having been a Jewish city founded by a Palestinian diaspora population that had survived the revolt against the Romans.[54] Distinct from the nomadic Arab tribes, the Jews of the north Arabian peninsula were highly productive oasis farmers. These Jews were eventually joined by itinerant Arab tribes from southern Arabia who settled adjacent to them and transitioned to a sedentary existence.

Following Muhammad's arrival, he created a "new order," as described by Gil:

[E]stablishing a covenant between the tribes which imposed its authority on every clan and its members, [which] soon enabled him to attack the Jews and eventually wipe out the Jewish population of the town. Some were banned from the towns, others were executed, and their property—plantations, fields, and houses—was distributed by Muhammad among his followers, who were destitute refugees from Mecca. He also used the former property of the Jews to establish a war fund, setting up a well-equipped army corps of cavalry troops the likes of which had never before been seen on the Arabian peninsula. Muhammad evidently believed in the capacity of this army, imbued with fiery religious belief, to perform great and sensational feats of valor.[55]

W. M. Watt has emphasized Muslim religious zeal, not socioeconomic factors, as the predominant, sustaining motivation for the jihad conquests of early Islam:

As one reflects on the origin of Islam, it becomes clear that there was nothing inevitable about the development of a world religion from the economic and social circumstances of early seventh century Mecca. The malaise of the times might easily have found some alleviation without achieving anything more than transient and local importance. There were several moments in the early history of Islam when, if the scales had been tilted slightly in the other direction, there would never have been an Arab empire, and there would not now [i.e., as of this 1953 lecture] be 300 million Muslims. There were several battles where it was "touch and go" for Muhammad and his followers. That things happened as they did for the Arabs was perhaps sometimes just luck and good fortune—or perhaps not. What can hardly be doubted is that without the system of ideas we call Islam, the whole historical development would have been impossible. Islamic ideology alone gave the Arabs that outward-looking attitude which enabled them to become sufficiently united to defeat the Byzantine and Persian empires. Many of them may have been concerned chiefly with booty for themselves. But men who were merely raiders out for booty could not have held together as the Arabs did. The ideology was no mere epiphenomenon but an essential factor in the historical process.[56]

Richard Bell summarized Muhammad's final interactions with the Jews and Christians of Medina and northern Arabia. His analyses, based upon the sacred Muslim texts (i.e, Qur'an, hadith, and sira), authoritative Qur'anic commentaries, and the narratives of Muslim chroniclers of early Islam, also underscored the theological basis for the "Great Jihad":

His relations with the Jews form a part of all biographies of Muhammad, for they worked out to a bitter and savage conclusion in the course of his first few years residence in Medina. . . . Shortly after the Battle of Badr a Jewish tribe, the Bani Qainuqa, were deprived of their goods, and expelled from Medina. The Bani Nadir were similarly expelled some two years later, and finally the Bani Quraiza were besieged, and, after capitulation at discretion, were slaughtered, their goods confiscated, their women and children enslaved. This bitter hostility was no doubt due to the annoyance which the opposition of the Jews caused him . . . in Muhammad's mind there also rankled the old feeling that the Jews had misled him in regard to what the Revelation contained, and having discovered that Jesus had been a prophet to the Bani Isra'il whom the Jews had rejected, he may have in his own mind justified his harsh dealing with them by the reflection that they were renegades who had already more than once rejected the Divine message. . . . But when Muhammad's power began to spread in Arabia his attitude towards the Christians soon began to cool. Any real alliance or even peaceful accommodation was indeed impossible from the first. Muhammad complains (Q.2:113/114) that neither Jews nor Christians will be satisfied with him until he follows their milla or type of religion. It was just as impossible for him to make concessions. . . . Thus the relationship with the Christians ended as that with the Jews ended—in war. . . . We know that before the end of his life Muhammad was in conflict with Christian populations in the north of Arabia, and even within the confines of the Roman [Byzantine] Empire. What would have happened if he had lived we do not know. But probably the policy which Abu Bakr carried on was the policy of Muhammad himself. There could have been no real compromise. He regarded himself as vicegerent of God upon earth. The true religion could only be Islam as he laid it down, and acceptance of it meant acceptance of his divinely inspired authority. . . . The Hijra and the execution of the Divine vengeance upon the unbelievers of Mecca had given the immediate occasion for the organization of such a warlike community. The victory of Badr confirmed it. This is what it had grown to, a menace to whatever came in its way. Muhammad could bide his time, but he was not the man to depart from a project which had once taken hold of his mind as involved in his prophetic mission and authority. He might look with favor upon much in Christianity, but unless Christians were prepared to accept his dictation as to what the true religion was, conflict was inevitable, and there could have been no real peace while he lived.[57]

Only limited forays—*razzias* (raids)—against Byzantine civilization in Palestine occurred during Muhammad's lifetime.[58] Within two years of Muhammad's death, however, Abu Bakr, the first caliph, launched the Great Jihad.[59] The ensuing three decades witnessed Islamdom's most spectacular expansion, as Muslim armies subdued the entire Arabian Peninsula, and conquered territories that had been in Greco-Roman possession since the reign of Alexander the Great.[60] Despite Greek domination and Hellenization of these lands for over nine centuries (largely unaltered by the intervening Roman conquest), in less than two centuries, as Constantelos has observed, "[B]oth Hellenism and Christianity were eliminated as major ethnic, religious, and cultural forces in the Near East, save in Asia Minor and Cyprus."[61]

Walter Kaegi underscores the Byzantines' lack of adequate understanding, and hence strategic intelligence, about their Muslim adversary's organizational prowess and religious zeal: "Part of Byzantium's difficulties was generally poor intelligence on the Muslims and failure to act rapidly, properly, and decisively on what intelligence they did acquire about the Muslims. Although some Byzantines were immediately aware of the Islamic component in the motivation of Arabs, Byzantines generally underestimated the religious motivation of Arabs as Muslims, and understood very little about this new religion."[62]

Whether one subscribes to the theory of "lightning *jihad* conquests," or a more gradual process facilitated by continuous Arab Muslim migration and *razzias* under the banner of Islam, the result was a weakening and then a disintegration of both the Persian (and much of) the Byzantine empires and the Islamization of the Near East. Ibn Hudayl, a fourteenth-century Granadan author of an important treatise on jihad, outlined (and endorsed) those methods that in fact facilitated the jihad conquests of Byzantine and Persian territories, and, subsequently, the Iberian Peninsula and other parts of Christian Europe:

> It is permissible to set fire to the lands of the enemy, his stores of grain, his beasts of burden—if it is not possible for the Muslims to take possession of them—as well as to cut down his trees, to raze his cities, in a word, to do everything that might ruin and discourage him, provided that the imam (i.e., the religious "guide" of the community of believers) deems these measures appropriate, suited to hastening the Islamization of that enemy or to weakening him. Indeed, all this contributes to a military triumph over him or to forcing him to capitulate.[63]

The twentieth-century historian Charles Emmanuel Dufourcq characterized the impact of such repeated attacks:

> It is not difficult to understand that such expeditions sowed terror. The historian al-Maqqari, who wrote in seventeenth-century Tlemcen in Algeria, explains that the panic created by the Arab horsemen and sailors, at the time of the Muslim expansion in the zones that saw those raids and landings, facilitated the later conquest, if that was decided on: "Allah," he says, "thus instilled such fear among the infidels that they did not dare to go and fight the conquerors; they only approached them as suppliants, to beg for peace."[64]

Bat Ye'or makes a distinction between the plight of the inhabitants of rural versus city communities when subjected to these *razzias* and full-fledged jihad campaigns:

> [Rural] areas, particularly the plains and valleys populated with hamlets and villages, were ravaged by the Bedouins who set fire to crops, massacred and carried off the peasantry and their cattle, and left nothing but ruins. Townspeople were in a different position. Protected by their walls, they could defend themselves or negotiate the conditions of their surrender on payment of tribute to the Bedouin chiefs. This distinction mentioned in contemporary Christian accounts, is confirmed by later Muslim historians. In fact, the record of the precise progress of

the Arab conquests constituted a basic principle in the earliest stages of Muslim law, since it fixed not only the nature and taxation of the land, but also the legislation applicable to its indigenous inhabitants . . . the majority of the villages fell into the category of conquest without treaty. According to the strategy of jihad, the absence of a treaty allowed the massacre or enslavement of the conquered population, and the division of their property. Whatever the land, country, or people vanquished, this pattern invariably recurred in the . . . cycles of Islamization. . . . It reconciled the predatory habits of the Bedouins vis-à-vis the settled populations with the rules of jihad and, naturally, with the customary practices of the time.[65]

However, as Bat Ye'or also observes, actual practice, all too frequently for certain vanquished cities, mimicked the harsh jihad-mandated tenets for rural areas overrun in the absence of a treaty:

[T]own populations were not always spared. They often suffered massacre or slavery, always accompanied by deportations. This was the fate of the Christians and Jews of Aleppo, Antioch, Ctesiphon, Euchaita, Constantia, Pathos (Cyprus), Pergamum, Sardes, Germanicea (Marash), and Samosata—to cite but a few examples. In the course of the Umayyads' last attempt to take Constantinople (717), the Arab army commanded by Maslama carried out a pincer movement by land and sea and laid waste the whole region around the capital.[66]

By 750 CE—under the first four caliphs and the rulers of the Umayyad-Damascene Dynasty—Muslim invaders had defeated Persian armies capturing Babylonia, Susiana, Mesopotamia, and Armenia, and extending east to Sind on the Indian subcontinent. During their westward expansion, before they were repulsed at Narbonne and Poitiers, Muslim armies conquered all the Christian provinces of the eastern Mediterranean from Syro-Palestine to Egypt, continuing through the Maghreb (North Africa), and across the Mediterranean into the Iberian Peninsula.[67]

Dynastic and religious schisms following the Abbasid revolt (750 CE) stiffened Byzantine military resistance and limited the Abbasid caliphs' ambitions in the east, primarily, to raids along the frontiers with Anatolia and Armenia designed to pillage, sack, and acquire booty. Although the Abbasid state "orientalized" the caliphate, and lacked naval power of any importance, in the west, Muslim forces (i.e., decentralized, "organic formations") continued the Islamic expansion by maritime warfare.[68] Throughout the ninth and tenth centuries, Berbers and Arabs from Spain and North Africa launched raids along the coastal regions of France, Italy, and Sicily, and in the Greek archipelago.[69] Gabrieli provides important commentary regarding these naval *razzias*:

According to present-day concepts of international relations, such activities amounted to piracy, but they correspond perfectly to jihad, an Islamic religious duty. The conquest of Crete, in the east, and a good portion of the corsair warfare along the Provencal and Italian coasts, in the West, are among the most conspicuous instances of such "private initiative" which contributed to Arab domination in the Mediterranean.

. . . In the second half of the ninth century, a large number of Saracen (Muslim) raids occurred throughout Southern and Central Italy, but we do not get the impression of their ever having been part of a plan or organized conquest, as Musa's, Tariq's, and Asad's campaigns had been in Spain and Sicily. Their only object seems to have been destruction and looting which was also the object of the armed groups faced by Charles on the Balat ash-Shuhada near Poitiers.

. . . The no less classical themes of Arabic war poetry, the hamasah sanctified by jihad, ring out in the recollections and boasts of Ibn Hamdis, the Sicilian Abu Firas, who exalts the military successes of Islam on Calabrian soil, the landing of Muslim troops at Reggio and their exploits against the patricians whom they cut to pieces or put to flight.[70]

Halil Inalcik has placed the fourteenth-century Aegean Sea naval *razzias* of the Turkish maritime emirates in the context of jihad, citing, for example, the chapter of the Dusturname of Enveri concerning the actions of the emirate of Aydin.[71] Elizabeth Zachariadou describes the consternation of contemporary fourteenth-century Latin and Byzantine chroniclers observing the "spectacle" of Turkish emirs, "who were proud only because they were able to lead their ferocious soldiers" in such predatory attacks.[72] These raids—designed to pillage property and abduct captives for sale in slave markets—although merely ignoble piracy or brigandage from the perspective of the Christian chroniclers, nevertheless, as Zachariadou notes, were "for the Muslim Turks, a Holy War (Jihad), a praiseworthy and legitimate occupation, leading directly to Paradise."[73]

Gregory Palamus, a metropolitan of Thessalonica during the fourteenth century, wrote this commentary while living as a captive amongst the Turks in 1354, confirming (albeit with astonishment) that indeed the Turks attributed their victories over the Byzantines to their (the Muslims') love of God: "For these impious people, hated by God and infamous, boast of having got the better of the Romans by their love of God . . . they live by the bow, the sword and debauchery, finding pleasure in taking slaves, devoting themselves to murder, pillage, spoil . . . and not only do they commit these crimes, but even—what an aberration—they believe that God approves of them. This is what I think of them, now that I know precisely about their way of life."[74]

More than 550 years later, and a continent (and oceans) away, C. Snouck Hurgronje reported (in 1906) that similar acts of jihad piracy were still being performed against non-Muslims (both indigenous populations and Western traders) by the Muslim Acehnese of the Indonesian archipelago:

From Mohammedanism (which for centuries she [i.e., Aceh] is reputed to have accepted) she really only learnt a large number of dogmas relating to hatred of the infidel without any of their mitigating concomitants; so the Acehnese made a regular business of piracy and man-hunting at the expense of the neighboring non-Mohammedan countries and islands, and considered that they were justified in any act of treachery or violence to European (and latterly to American) traders who came in search of pepper, the staple product of the country. Complaints of robbery and murder on board ships trading in Acehnese parts thus grew to be chronic.[75]

JIHAD ON LAND

Jihad Conquests and Early Muslim Rule in Syro-Palestine

Moshe Gil, in his comprehensive analysis *A History of Palestine, 634–1099,* emphasizes the singular centrality that Palestine occupied in the mind of its pre-Islamic Jewish inhabitants, who referred to the land as "al-Sham." Indeed, as Gil observes, the sizable Jewish population in Palestine (who formed a majority of its inhabitants, when grouped with the Samaritans) at the dawn of the Arab Muslim conquest were "the direct descendants of the generations of Jews who had lived there since the days of Joshua bin Nun, in other words for some 2000 years."[76] He also explodes the ahistorical thesis of scholars who

> perceive an ethnic motivation behind the [jihad] conquests. They see Arabs everywhere: even the Canaanites and the Philistines were Arabs, according to their theories. This applies to an even greater degree to the population of Palestine and Syria in the seventh century, who were certainly Semites. Thus, according to their claims, the conquering Arab forces in the course of their battles, actually encountered their own people or at least members of their own race who spoke the same language. . . . This is of course a very distorted view: Semitism is not a race and only relates to a sphere of language. The populations met along the route of battle, living in cities or the country side, were not Arabs and did not speak Arabic. We do know of Bedouin tribes at that time who inhabited the borderlands and the southern desert of Palestine, west of the Euphrates (Hira) in the Syrian desert, Palmyra, and elsewhere. But the cultivated inner regions and the cities were inhabited by Jews and Christians who spoke Aramaic. They did not sense any special ties to the Bedouin; if anything it was the contrary. Their proximity and the danger of an invasion from that quarter disturbed their peace of mind and this is amply reflected both in the writings of the Church Fathers and in Talmudic sources.[77]

Gil concludes that views of the jihad conquest of Palestine expressed in the sources from the vanquished, indigenous non-Muslim populations

> reflect the attitude of the towns and villages in Palestine quite accurately; the attitude of a sedentary population, of farmers and craftsmen, toward nomads whose source of income is the camel and who frequently attack the towns, pillage and

slaughter the inhabitants, and endanger the lives of the wayfarer. These sources completely contradict the argument . . . to the effect that the villagers and townsmen in Palestine accepted the invasion of those tribes bearing the banner of Islam with open arms of their so-called racial affinity.[78]

Bat Ye'or summarizes the Arab Muslim conquest of Palestine as follows:

Abu Bakr organized the invasion of Syria [Syro-Palestine] which Muhammad had already envisaged. He gathered tribes from the Hijaz, Najd, and Yemen and advised Abu Ubayda, in charge of operations in the Golan, to plunder the countryside, but due to a lack of adequate weaponry, to refrain from attacking towns. Consequently, the whole Gaza region up to Cesarea was sacked and devastated in the campaign of 634. Four thousand Jewish, Christian, and Samaritan peasants who defended their land were massacred. The villages of the Negev were pillaged by Amr b. al-As, while the Arabs overran the countryside, cut communications, and made roads perilous. Towns such as Jerusalem, Gaza, Jaffa, Cesarea, Nablus, and Beth Shean were isolated and closed their gates. In his sermon on Christmas day 634, the patriarch of Jerusalem, Sophronius, lamented over the impossibility of going on pilgrimage to Bethlehem, as was the custom because the Christians were being forcibly kept in Jerusalem: "not detained by tangible bonds, but chained and nailed by fear of the Saracens," whose "savage, barbarous and bloody sword" kept them locked up in the town. . . . Sophronius, in his sermon on the Day of the Epiphany 636, bewailed the destruction of the churches and monasteries, the sacked towns, the fields laid waste, the villages burned down by the nomads who were overrunning the country. In a letter the same year to Sergius, the patriarch of Constantinople, he mentions the ravages wrought by the Arabs. Thousands of people perished in 639, victims of the famine and plague that resulted from these destructions.

The countryside [in Syro-Palestine, Iraq, Persia, and Armenia] suffered constant razzias, while those who escaped the sword swelled the contingents of enslaved women and children, shared out among the soldiers after the deduction of the fifth [share of the "booty"] reserved for the caliph.

According to [the Muslim chronicler] Baladhuri (d. 892 C.E.), 40,000 Jews lived in Caesarea alone at the Arab conquest, after which all trace of them is lost.[79]

The tenth-century Jacobite chronicler Michael the Syrian wrote that the ongoing Arab *razzias* and expeditions in Syro-Palestine (as well as Iraq, Persia, and Armenia) were characterized by repeated and systematic pillage: "The Taiyaye [Arabs] grew rich, increased and overran [the lands] which they took from the Romans [Byzantines] and which were given over to pillage.[80]

And following the surrender of the city of Damascus, he notes: "Umar [b. al-Khattab] sent Khalid [b. Walid] with an army to the Aleppo and Antioch region. There, they murdered a large number of people. No one escaped them. Whatever may be said of the evils that Syria suffered, they cannot be recounted because of their great number; for the Yaiyaye [Arabs] were the great rod of God's wrath."[81]

Gil further elaborates on the initial wave of jihad conquests, and details the lasting destruction they wrought:[82]

[A]t the time of the conquest, Palestine was inhabited by Jews and Christians. . . . The Arab tribes were to be found in the border areas, in keeping with arrangements made with the Byzantine rulers. . . . one can assume that the local population suffered immensely during the course of the war [i.e., jihad conquests] and it is very likely that many villages were destroyed and uprooted in the frontier regions, and that the lot of these local populations was very bitter indeed. It appears that the period of the conquest was also that of the destruction of the synagogues and churches of the Byzantine era, remnants of which have been unearthed in our own time and are still being discovered. The assumption is based both on what is said in a few Christian sources . . . and on Muslim sources describing 'Umar's [Umar b. al-Khattab] visits to al-Sham. There is no doubt that one of the main purposes of these visits was to establish order and put an end to the devastation and slaughter of the local population. . . . Towns in the western strip and the central strip (the region of the red sand hills and the swamps) in the Sharon, decreased from fifty-eight to seventeen! It is estimated that the erosion of the soil from the western slopes of the Judaean mountains reached—as a result of the agricultural uprooting during the Muslim period—the gigantic extent of 2,000 to 4,000 cubic meters. . . . We find direct evidence of the destruction of agriculture and the desertion of the villages in the fact that the papyri of Nessana are completely discontinued after the year 700. One can assume that at the time the inhabitants abandoned the place, evidently because of the inter-tribal warfare among the Arabs which completely undermined the internal security of the area.[82]

An archaeological analysis by Naphtali Lewis emphasizes that the distress of the inhabitants was exacerbated after the year 700. Conditions became unbearable, due to the general political situation and worsening attitudes toward the dhimmis, rendering the Negev a wasteland.

It was precisely at this period in the Caliphate of Abd-al-Malik and his sons (685–743 C.E.) that the Arab state embarked on a new, nationalistic policy. The official records of Islam began to be kept in Arabic . . . and non-Arabs began to be eliminated from government service. With this Arabization of rule came increasing fiscal burdens for the Christians-burdens which they could now no longer escape by conversion to Islam. . . . [This] may well have rendered life impossible for the villagers of the Negev, who had already before . . . had occasion to complain of fiscal oppression. In the period of their prosperity . . . the production of the Negev villages was supplemented by financial assistance from the Byzantine Emperors, in the form of stipends and emoluments paid the military settlers; in the first half-century of Arab rule, which terminated this positive support but otherwise changed conditions little, life could apparently still be sustained—and where life is even barely bearable people are generally reluctant to leave their homes; but when the government changed its policy and began to make conditions as a result become increasingly difficult, life in the southern desert became impossible and the Negev villages disappeared . . . growing Arab strength . . . drove out the Negev inhabitants; the weakness of central authority in the area would result from the growing depopulation and relapse into nomadism.[83]

Finally, Gil has translated these observations by the tenth-century Karaite commentator Yefet b. 'Ali expressing awareness of the fact that there was great destruction in Palestine and that there were places that remained uninhabited, while there were other places to which people returned and settled: "[T]he places which were completely destroyed so that no memory of them remains, like Samaria . . . and the second . . . are the places which have been destroyed and ruined, but despite this there are guards and people living there, such as Hebron and others."[84]

Gil also captures the stark, unromantic reality of Muslim-ruled Palestine during this era, which included the initial jihad conquest and establishment of Arab Muslim rule, from 634 to 661; Umayyad-Damascene rule, from 661 until 750; Abbasid-Baghdadian rule, from 750 through 878; Turco-Egyptian rule (Tulunids and Ikshidids) from 878 until 970—"interrupted" by Abbasid-Baghdadian rule again, between 905 and 930; nearly two generations of war including numerous participants, the dominant party being the Fatimids, from 970 through 1030; just over forty years of Fatimid-Egyptian rule, between 1030 and 1071; and a generation of (Seljuq) Turkish (or "Turcoman") rule encompassing most of Palestine, from 1071 until 1099.[85]

Dramatic persecution, directed specifically at Christians,[86] included executions for refusing to apostasize to Islam during the first two decades of the eighth century, under the reigns of Abd al-Malik, his son Sulayman, and Umar b. Abd al-Aziz. Georgian, Greek, Syriac, and Armenian sources report both prominent individual and group executions (for example, sixty-three out of seventy Christian pilgrims from Iconium in Asia Minor were executed by the Arab governor of Caesarea, barring seven who apostasized to Islam, and sixty Christian pilgrims from Amorion were crucified in Jerusalem).[87]

The Abbasids moved the capital city from Damascus (seat of the Umayyad Empire) to Baghdad, absorbed much of the Syrian and Persian culture, as well as Persian methods of governance, and ushered in a putative Golden Age. Gil and Bat Ye'or offer revealing assessments of this Golden Age *dhimmitude* and its adverse impact on the conquered, indigenous Jews and Christians of Palestine. Under early Abbasid rule (approximately 750–755 CE, perhaps during the reign Abul Abbas Abdullah al-Saffah), Greek sources report orders demanding the removal of crosses over churches, bans on church services and teaching of the scriptures, the eviction of monks from their monasteries, and excessive taxation.[88] Gil notes that in 772 CE, when Caliph al-Mansur visited Jerusalem,[89] "he ordered a special mark should be stamped on the hands of the Christians and the Jews. Many Christians fled to Byzantium."[89]

The following decade witnessed persistent acts of persecution as well. These details are provided by Gil:

> One source tells of a Muslim who converted to Christianity and became a monk, and was renamed Christophorous. He was beheaded on 14 April 789. At around the same time, evidently, there was an Arab attack on the monastery of St. Theodosius, near Bethlehem. The monastery was pillaged, many of the monks were slaughtered and some escaped. The attackers also destroyed two churches near that monastery. A Church source tells about the suffering endured by the monasteries in the Judean mountains during the inter-tribal warfare which broke out in 796. . . . While Bet Guvrin was being abandoned by its inhabitants, who were falling captive to the Arabs, assaults were being made in Ascalon, Gaza, and other localities. Everywhere there was pillage and destruction.[90]

Bat Ye'or elucidates the fiscal oppression inherent in eighth-century Palestine, which devastated the *dhimmi* Jewish and Christian peasantry: "Over-taxed and tortured by the tax collectors, the villagers fled into hiding or emigrated into towns."[91] She quotes from a detailed chronicle of an eighth-century monk, completed in 774: "The men scattered, they became wanderers everywhere; the fields were laid waste, the countryside pillaged; the people went from one land to another."[92]

The Greek chronicler Theophanes (as summarized by Gil) provides a contemporary description of the chaotic events that transpired after the death of the caliph Harun al-Rashid in 809 CE, and the ensuing fratricidal war that erupted between the brothers al-Amin and al-Ma'mun.

> According to him [Theophanes] these events caused the Christians an enormous amount of suffering. Many churches and monasteries in Jerusalem and its environs were abandoned, such as those of Sts Cyriac, Theodosius, Chariton, Euthymius, and Mar Saba. Four years later, in 813, the disturbances broke out anew and many Christians, both monks and laity, fled from Palestine to Cyprus and Constantinople, where they found refuge from the Arabs' terrible persecution in those days of anarchy and civil war. Palestine was the scene of violence, rape, and murder.[93]

Perhaps the clearest outward manifestations of the inferiority and humiliation of the *dhimmis* were the prohibitions regarding their dress "codes" and the demands that distinguishing signs be placed on the entrances of dhimmi houses. During the Abbasid caliphates of Harun al-Rashid (786–809) and al-Mutawwakil (847–861), Jews and Christians were required to wear yellow (as patches attached to their garments or hats).[94] Later, to differentiate further between Christians and Jews, the Christians were required to wear blue. In 850, consistent with Qur'anic verses associating them with Satan and hell,[95] al-Mutawwakil decreed that Jews and Christians attach wooden images of devils to the doors of their homes to distinguish them from the homes of Muslims. Bat Ye'or summarizes the oppression of the *dhimmis* throughout the Abbasid Empire under al-Mutawwakil as "a wave of religious persecution, forced conversions, and the elimination of churches and synagogues."[96]

Paroxysms of violent persecution erupted yet again in October and November 923 according to the patriarch of Alexandria, Sa'id b. Bitriq, as well as two Muslim chroniclers [summarized by Gil]:

> [T]he Muslims attacked . . . in Jerusalem on Palm Sunday (26 March 937) and set fire to the southern gates of Constantine's church and to half of the exedra, whereupon the Church of the Calvary and the Church of the Resurrection collapsed. . . . According to al-Makin and al-Maqrizi, the Church of the Resurrection and the Church of the Calvary were also robbed of their treasures. . . . It seems at the same time the Muslims attacked in Ascalon again. According to Yahya b. Sa'id, the assault was made on "the great church there, known by the name of Mary the Green. They destroyed it and robbed it of all its contents and then set fire to it.' . . . The bishop of Ascalon then left for Baghdad to get permission to rebuild the church, but he did not succeed. The church was left in ruins, for the Muslims who lived in Ascalon agreed amongst themselves that they would not allow it to be built again. As to the bishop, he never returned to Ascalon and remained in Ramla until his death.[97]

During the early eleventh-century period of al-Hakim's reign, religious assaults and hostility intensified. As Gil notes, "[T]the destruction of the churches at the Holy Sepulchre [1009 CE] marked the beginning of a whole series of acts of oppression against the Christian population, which according to reliable sources, extended to coercion to convert to Islam."[98]

Yahya b. Sa'id's description of the events surrounding the destruction of the churches of the Holy Sepulchre is summarized by Gil:

> They dismantled the Church of the Resurrection to its very foundations, apart from what could not be destroyed or pulled up, and they also destroyed the Golgotha and the Church of St Constantine and all that they contained, as well as the sacred grave stones. They even tried to dig up the graves and wipe out all traces of their existence. Indeed they broke and uprooted most of them. They also laid waste to a convent in the neighborhood. . . . The authorities took all the other property belonging to the Church of the Holy Sepulchre and its pious foundations and all its furnishings and treasures.[99]

Citing both Muslim (al-Quda'i, Ibn Khallikan, and Ibn Al-Athir) and non-Muslim (Bar Hebraeus) sources, Gil also describes the edicts al-Hakim imposed upon the Christians and Jews beginning in August 1011:

> They were ordered to wear black turbans. The Christians had to wear a cross the

length of a cubit and weighing five ratls around their necks; the Jews were obliged to wear a block of wood of similar weight . . . they had to wear some distinguishing mark in the bath-houses, and finally al-Hakim decided that there were to be separate bath-houses for their use. . . . Ibn Al-Athir conveys . . . that al-Hakim ordered (after the destruction of the Church of the Resurrection in Jerusalem . . .) that all the churches in the realm be destroyed, and this was done, and that the Jews and Christians were then to accept Islam, or emigrate to Byzantine lands. They were also obliged to wear special distinguishing signs. Many converted. . . . Bar Hebraeus speaks of thousands of churches which were destroyed in the Fatimid kingdom at that time; the decree regarding the wearing of the cross around the neck was also, he says, a means of pressuring the Christians to convert. The wooden block the Jews were obliged to wear, had to be in the shape of a calf, as a reminder of the golden calf.[100]

In a separate, focused analysis of the conditions of the dhimmis of Jerusalem, Gil concludes that during the early through the mid-eleventh century, the Jews suffered both economically and physically:

Economic conditions in Jerusalem were rather harsh, and the yeshiva often issued urgent appeals for aid. Besides, there were frequent acts of oppression on the part of the Muslim authorities. Very often special heavy taxes were imposed, which aggravated the already precarious situation of both the yeshiva and the Jewish population of Jerusalem. It must be remembered that taxation in Jerusalem was probably different from that found in other parts of the Muslim world. It seems that Jews there had to pay a comprehensive lump sum for the whole Jewish population of the city, regardless of its numbers. When the population decreased as a result of wars and Bedouin upheavals, the burden on each individual became heavier. In such situations the yeshiva was forced to borrow money, against heavy interest, from wealthy Muslims. When the time of repayment arrived, Jewish notables were in danger of being imprisoned, as the yeshiva was not in a position to accumulate the funds it had to return. In some cases people were actually incarcerated and it took a great deal of effort to collect the funds necessary for their release. An example is the letter written by Abraham, the son and main assistant of Solomon b. Yehuda, head of the yeshiva, to the sons of Mevasser, a family of parnasim of Fustat, asking them to keep their promise to send the aid in time to pay the *kharaj*.[101]

Muslim Turcoman rule of Palestine for the nearly three decades just prior to the Crusades (1071–1099) was characterized by such unrelenting warfare and devastation, that an imminent "End of Days" atmosphere was engendered.[102] For example, Gil describes one of Atsiz b. Awaq's jihad campaigns in Syro-Palestine around 1077:

Then Atsiz advanced on Jerusalem from Damascus, placed the city under siege, and promised its inhabitants the *aman*; on this basis, the inhabitants opened the gates of the city to him. Atsiz prevailed over Jerusalem, completely ignoring his promise of *aman*, and went on a rampage. He slaughtered 3,000 people there. . . . He also conducted campaigns of annihilation against Ramla, until all its people had fled, and against Gaza, where he murdered the entire population. He likewise massacred people in al-'Arish and elsewhere and wrought endless havoc in Damascus, where only 3,000 of the original 500,000 inhabitants had remained, due to starvation and scarcity. Jaffa, too, was attacked, and its governor . . . fled from the town to Tyre, together with all the city's inhabitants, while the walls of Jaffa were destroyed on Atsiz' orders.[103]

A contemporary Russian chronicle cited by Gil indicates that the Turcomans "destroyed and desolated the cities and the villages from Antioch to Jerusalem. They murdered, took captive, pillaged, set on fire; they destroyed churches and monasteries."[104]

Gil notes that these observations are confirmed by Geniza documents describing how "the Turcoman occupation denoted terrible calamities, such as the taking captive of the people of Ramla, the cutting off of roads, the obduracy of the commanders, the aura of anxiety and panic, and so on."[105] He continues, "We do not know what Atsiz' attitude was to the Jewish population in 1078, during the cruel suppression of the uprisings and the destruction of towns, but the fact that from this date onwards, we barely find letters from Palestine (apart from Ascalon and Caesarea) in the Geniza documents, speaks for itself."[106]

A contemporary poem by Solomon ha-Kohen b. Joseph, believed to be a descendant of the Geonim, an illustrious family of Palestinian Jewish religious leaders, speaks of destruction and ruin, the burning of harvests, the razing of plantations, the desecration of cemeteries, and acts of violence, slaughter, and plunder:

> They were a strange and cruel people, girt with garments of many colors,
> Armed and officered-chiefs among 'the terrible ones'
> And capped with helmets, black and red,
> With bow and spear and full quivers;
> And they trumpet like elephants, and roar as the roaring ocean,
> To terrify, to frighten those who oppose them,
> And they are wicked men and sinners, madmen, not sane,
> And they laid waste the cities, and they were made desolate
> And they rejoiced in their hearts, hoping to inherit.
> He [God] also remembered what they had done to the people of Jerusalem,
> That they had besieged them twice in two years,
> And burned the heaped corn and destroyed the places,
> And cut down the trees and trampled upon the vineyards,
> And surrounded the city upon the high mountains,
> And despoiled the graves and threw out the bones,
> And built palaces, to protect themselves against the heat,
> And erected an altar to slay upon it the abominations;

And the men and the women ride upon the walls,
Crying unto the God of gods, to quiet the great anger,
Standing the whole night, banishing sleep,
While the enemy destroy, evening and morning,
And break down the whole earth, and lay bare the ground,
And stand on the highways, intending to slay like Cain,
And cut off the ears, and also the nose,
And rob the garments, leaving them stand naked,
And also roar like lions, and roar like young lions;
They do not resemble men, they are like beasts,
And also harlots and adulterers, and they inflame themselves with males,
They are bad and wicked and spiteful as Sodomites.
And they impoverished the sons of nobles, and starved the delicately bred.
And all the people of the city went out and cried in the field,
And covered their lips, silent in their pains,
And they had no mercy on widows, and pitied not the orphans.[107]

Gil concludes that as a result of the Turcoman jihad,

Palestine was drawn into a whirlpool of anarchy and insecurity, of internal wars
among the Turks themselves and between them (generally in collaboration with
the Arab tribes) and the Fatimids. Here and there, in one or another area, a deli-
cate state of balance was arrived at for a few years. By and large, however, the
Turcoman period, which lasted less than thirty years, was one of slaughter and
vandalism, of economic hardship and the uprooting of populations. Terrible suffering, eviction and wandering, was the particular lot of the Jewish population,
and chiefly its leadership, the Palestinian yeshiva.[108]

Gil offers this sobering overall assessment from his extensive, copiously documented analysis of the initial period of Muslim rule of Palestine, from 634 to
1099: "These facts do not call for much interpretation; together they simply form
a picture of almost unceasing insecurity, of endless rebellions and wars, of
upheavals and instability.[109]

Jihad Conquests in Iraq

The conquest of the region corresponding (largely) to modern Iraq transpired
between 635 and 642 CE. Assisted by local Arabs (i.e., in areas with dense Arab
settlements, such as the Ubulla and Hira regions) and formal troop reinforcements
dispatched from Arabia, the Muslims expanded their *razzias* to include rural areas
and hamlets in southern and central Iraq, into the vicinity of Ctesiphon.[110] After the
important victory at al-Qadissiya in 636, a full-scale invasion of the villages bordering the Tigris and Euphrates rivers ensued, supported by reinforcements Caliph
Umar sent from the Hijaz (Medina).[111] Professor Morony, in his authoritative

analysis of the Islamization of Iraq, describes the initial impact of the jihad campaigns in Iraq on the Persian strongholds and populations, prior to al-Qadissiya:

> According to Arabic tradition, the first sweep made Khalid b. al-Walid coming up along the border of lower Iraq from the Yamama, took the lives of 70,000 people at Ullays, most of whom were from Aghishiyya. Afterwards, Aghishiyya itself was razed and its remaining population scattered in the countryside. . . . Abu Yusuf says that Khalid massacred the Persian garrisons at 'Udhayb and Najaf and took their women and children captive. . . . At Ayu Tamr the main Persian force . . . fled . . . when the citadel fell, all of their remaining defenders were killed. Along the Syrian border, the three strongholds of Husayd, Khanafis, and Musayyakh were reduced. At Husayd, large numbers of Persians were killed, along with the two commanders . . . while at Musayyakh the entire garrison . . . was killed in a dawn attack.[112]

The subsequent decisive Muslim victory at al-Qadissiya was a true military disaster for the Persians—their army was routed and the Persian general Rustam killed, followed by the inexorable destruction of the demoralized remnants of the Persian forces. These crushing military losses resulted in a massive displacement of refugees, which included the ruling Persian elites, and large-scale enslavement and deportation of those noncombatants who were captured as Muslim "booty." Morony highlights some of the dislocation wrought by the jihad enslavement of the sundry vanquished Persian populations:

> The initial result of captivity was the physical removal of a large number of Persian women and children from Iraq, most of whom were sent off to Medina with the other booty. According to [the Muslim historian] Ya'qubi, Khalid had taken captives at Kaskar and Baniqya. At Ullays captives are said to have been taken as never before. . . . At Ayn Tamr, after the garrison was slaughtered, all of the non-combatants in the fortress were taken captive. After Khalid left for Syria, in the campaign that lead up to the battle of the Bridge, more captives were taken at Zandaward and at Bitiq in Nahr Jawbar, Captives were also taken at Ubulla when it fell to 'Utba b. Ghazwan. . . . The redistribution of the Persian population of Iraq by carrying captive women and children off to the Hijaz or by relocating them in the new Islamic garrison towns of Basra and Kufa contributed to the depopulation of the districts east of the Tigris . . . most of the prisoners brought back by the Muslim armies that [later] conquered the Iranian plateau were taken to the slave markets in Basra or Kufa and redistributed from there. This caused the initial ethnic dislocation by the killing or flight of large numbers of Persians in the course of the conquest to be offset by a new, forced Persian immigration to the cities of lower Iraq.[113]

Morony characterizes the jihad raids that targeted the Nestorian and Monophysite Christian populations of towns along the Tigris and Euphrates, as follows:

Both Monophysite and Nestorian monasteries were raided. Monks were killed, taken prisoner, or driven to take refuge elsewhere. Large numbers of Monophysite [Christians] were killed, enslaved, or converted to Islam. The surrender of the citadel of Takrit to the Muslims in 637 was only an ad hoc arrangement by [grand Jacobite metropolitan of the East] Marutha preserved only the people and churches of Takrit, and did not include the rest of the Monophysite community in Iraq. On the Nestorian side, [bishop of Nineveh] Mar Ammeh's collaboration with the Muslims at Nineveh at the time of the conquest was similar. Since he was not even catholicos at the time, whatever advantage he gained for himself by collaboration did not extend to the rest of the Nestorian community.[114]

Bat Ye'or notes further, regarding the vanquished Christian communities, that "in Elam, the population was also decimated, and in Susa the notables were put to the sword."[115]

Jihad Conquests in Egypt

Philip Hitti, citing the Arab chronicler Abd-al-Hakam (d. 871), maintains that due to their oppression by the Orthodox Church in Egypt, and the imperial government in Constantinople, "The native Copts of Egypt . . . were instructed from the very beginning by their bishop of Alexandria to offer no resistance to the invaders . . . in view of the religious persecution to which they as Monophysites had been subjected.[116]

But Jacques Jarry[117] has pointed out that this narrative, as stated by Abd-al-Hakam, and similar Muslim sources, is simplistic and inaccurate. Jarry asserts that both the Greek-speaking collaborators of the Byzantines and the Melkites, followers of the Byzantine Church, were, within each party, divided in their attitudes toward the Muslims. The aristocrats or "blues," influential at court, requested a policy of at least temporary withdrawal, to attempt to organize their forces appropriately, as Heraclius had done in his campaigns against the Persians. The blues, in addition, were more Western oriented, and wanted to come to terms with Rome, in particular, being less interested in the Eastern domains. In contrast, the populist "greens" advocated a militant opposition to the Muslim invaders, which led, according to Jarry, to the wholesale annihilation of their towns during the Arab Muslim jihad conquests.

Moreover, the testimony of John, the Monophysite bishop of Nikiu, who wrote his chronicle around the year 700, some 150 years earlier than Hitti's source, characterizes the early Arab Muslim invasions in Egypt as brutal and without mercy. For example, when the Muslims captured the city of Bahnasa, the invaders slayed not only the commander of the Byzantine troops and all his companions, they also "put to the sword all that surrendered, and they spared none, whether old men, babes, or women."[118] Indeed, they perpetrated innumerable acts of violence, causing widespread panic.[119]

John of Nikiu, in fact, remonstrated against those "Egyptians who had apostasized from the Christian faith [Monophysites] and embraced the faith of the beast." Many Christian Copts, he adds, fled the Arabic invasions.[120] He acknowledges that due to their hostility to the emperor Heraclius (610–641) and Patriarch Kyros of Alexandria, the Copts of certain cities, such as Antinoe, cooperated with the invaders and submitted, becoming tributaries to the Muslims.[121] But John of Nikiu also indicates that the collapse of Alexandria, and of Egypt, resulted primarily from the impotence of Patriarch Kyros (who served as the prefect of Alexandria), and the tenuous position of the Byzantine government following Heraclius's death. Other Copts, moreover, in sizable numbers, refused to submit, and suffered intermittently "a panic [which] fell on all the cities of Egypt, and all their inhabitants took flight."[122] A multitude of Copts, not only the Greeks, were horrified and prepared for battle against the Arabs, having witnessed the devastation and slaughter they wrought in Alexandria after its surrender.[123] John of Nikiu records that Copts prayed to God to deliver them from "the enemies of the cross who plundered the country and took captives in abundance." They viewed the Islamic conquest as a yoke "heavier than the yoke which had been laid on Israel by Pharaoh"[124] and entreated the Almighty to do "unto them as He did aforetime unto Pharaoh."[125] Constantelos observes, "It is certain that because of fear or expediency many Christians, Orthodox and Copt, adopted Islam. How many of them abjured or remained crypto-Christians is unknown.[126]

He concludes that following the Arab Muslim jihad conquest of Egypt, the Arabs displayed essentially the same pattern of behavior toward the vanquished Christian populations they had exhibited in Syro-Palestine:

> Their attitude toward the Orthodox Church was determined by the relations between the caliphate and Constantinople. Their tolerance in peace-time changed during hostilities into violent outbursts which resulted in persecutions, the death of many Christians and the destruction of churches and other ecclesiastical institutions. For example, when the Arabic armies suffered repeated defeats during the reign of Emperor Tiberios II (698–705), Abd-al-Aziz, governor of Egypt and brother of Caliph Abd-al-Malik (685–705), unleashed a persecution against the Orthodox in Alexandria in 704. The mobs attacked the Christians, and Abd-al-Aziz ordered that all crosses be removed from Christian churches and that "Mohammed is the Great Apostle of God" and "God is neither born nor does He give birth" be written on their doors. The persecution was especially severe against monks and lasted for several years. The ecclesiastical administration of the Orthodox (Chalcedonian) patriarchate in Egypt was abolished for ninety-one years. Only two patriarchs (Kyros and Kosmas) governed in the early years of the Arabic occupation. From 651 to 742 there were only a few *locum tenenes* in the Orthodox patriarchate, while vacancies existed for several years even in the Coptic patriarchate.[127]

Early Jihad Conquests in Armenia

Initial Arab *razzias* into Armenia during 640 and 642 CE were followed a decade later by major campaigns of jihad conquest.[128] The Muslim historian al-Baladhuri (d. 892) recounts that Habib b. Maslama was dispatched by Mu'awaiya to gather "a body of men from Syria and Mesopotamia interested in the 'holy war' [jihad] and booty,"[129] for an expedition against Armenia.

According to Michael the Syrian, the population of Euchaita (on the River Halys) was massacred and enslaved by Habib's forces.[130] Armenian chroniclers describe how the Arabs, after decimating the non-Muslim populations of neighboring regions (Syria, Iraq) and forcing large numbers to apostasize to Islam, "entered the district of Daron [southwest of Lake Van] which they sacked, shedding rivers of blood. They exacted tribute and forced the women and children to be handed over to them.[131]

Dvin was captured in 642, and its population slaughtered. Afterward, according to Sebeos, "the Ishmaelites [Arabs] returned by the route whence they had come, carrying off in their wake a multitude of captives to the number of 35,000."[132] Sebeos maintains that the Arabs returned the following year to invade Armenia again, "wreaking ruin, and slavery."[133]

These devastating *razzias* were followed by what Arab historiography considers the more definitive conquest of Armenia, during the invasion of 654 CE.[134] Walter Kaegi summarizes this initial period of Muslim conquests in Armenia as follows: "The Muslim conquest was violent and destructive. A few Armenians did collaborate with Muslims from the beginning, for various motives. But chroniclers such as Sebeos describe the conquest as a calamity, not a liberation."[135]

Ter-Ghevondian contends that despite these devastating campaigns, Armenia managed to enjoy a considerable degree of independence until the onerous reign of the Umayyad caliph Abd al-Malik (685–705 CE).[136] Al-Baladhuri has provided this characterization of the events leading to Armenia's complete subjugation under 'Abd al-Malik:

> During the insurrection of ibn-az-Zubair [who had declared himself Caliph of Hijaz], Armenia rose and its nobles with their followers threw off their allegiance. When Muhammad ibn-Marwan held under his brother [the Umayyad caliph] Abd al-Malik the governorship of Armenia, he led the fight against them [the Armenians] and won the victory, slaughtering and taking captives. Thus he subdued the land [of Armenia].[137]

Ter-Ghevondian concludes: "Under the leadership of the Caliph's brother Muhammad b. Marwan, the Arab armies devastated Armenia and totally subjected it."[138]

Jihad Conquests and Early Muslim Rule on the Iberian Peninsula

The Iberian Peninsula was conquered in 710–716 CE by Arab tribes originating from northern, central, and southern Arabia. Massive Berber and Arab immigration and the colonization of the Iberian Peninsula followed the conquest. Most churches were converted into mosques. Although the conquest had been planned and conducted jointly with a faction of Iberian Christian dissidents, including a bishop, it proceeded as a classical jihad with massive pillages, enslavements, deportations, and killings. Toledo, which had first submitted to the Arabs in 711 or 712, revolted in 713. The town was punished by pillage and all the notables' throats were cut. In 730 the Cerdagne (in Septimania, near Barcelona) was ravaged and a bishop burned alive. In the regions under stable Islamic control, subjugated non-Muslim *dhimmis*—Jews and Christians—like elsewhere in other Islamic lands, were prohibited from building new churches or synagogues, or restoring the old ones. Segregated in special quarters, they had to wear discriminatory clothing. Subjected to heavy taxes, the Christian peasantry formed a servile class exploited by the dominant Arab ruling elites; many abandoned their land and fled to the towns. Harsh reprisals with mutilations and crucifixions sanctioned the Mozarab (Christian *dhimmis*) calls for help from the Christian kings. Moreover, if one *dhimmi* harmed a Muslim, the whole community lost its status of protection, leaving it open to pillage, enslavement, and arbitrary killing.[139]

By the end of the eighth century, the rulers of North Africa and Andalusia had introduced rigorous Maliki jurisprudence as the predominant school of Muslim law. Thus, as Evariste Lévi-Provençal observed three quarters of a century ago, "The Muslim Andalusian state thus appears from its earliest origins as the defender and champion of a jealous orthodoxy, more and more ossified in a blind respect for a rigid doctrine, suspecting and condemning in advance the least effort of rational speculation."[140]

Charles Emmanuel Dufourcq provides these illustrations of the resulting religious and legal discriminations *dhimmis* suffered, and the accompanying incentives for them to convert to Islam:

> A learned Moslem jurist of Hispanic Christian descent who lived around the year 1000, Ahmed ibn Said ibn Hazm (father of the famous mid-eleventh-century author Ibn Hazm) gives glimpses, in several of his juridical consultations, of how the freedom of the "infidels" was constantly at risk. Non-payment of the head-tax by a dhimmi made him liable to all the Islamic penalties for debtors who did not repay their creditors; the offender could be sold into slavery or even put to death. In addition, non-payment of the head-tax by one or several dhimmis—especially if it was fraudulent—allowed the Moslem authority, at its discretion, to put an end to the autonomy of the community to which the guilty party or parties belonged. Thus, from one day to the next, all the Christians in a city could lose their status as a protected people through the fault of just one of them.

Everything could be called into question, including their personal liberty. . . . Furthermore, non-payment of the legal tribute was not the only reason for abrogating the status of the "People of the Book"; another was "public outrage against the Islamic faith," for example, leaving exposed, for Moslems to see, a cross or wine or even pigs.

[B]y converting [to Islam], one would no longer have to be confined to a given district, or be the victim of discriminatory measures or suffer humiliations. . . . Furthermore, the entire Islamic law tended to favor conversions. When an "infidel" became a Moslem, he immediately benefited from a complete amnesty for all of his earlier crimes, even if he had been sentenced to the death penalty, even if it was for having insulted the Prophet or blasphemed against the Word of God: his conversion acquitted him of all his faults, of all his previous sins. A legal opinion given by a *mufti* from al-Andalus in the ninth century is very instructive: a Christian *dhimmi* kidnapped and violated a Moslem woman; when he was arrested and condemned to death, he immediately converted to Islam; he was automatically pardoned, while being constrained to marry the woman and to provide for her a dowry in keeping with her status. The *mufti* who was consulted about the affair, perhaps by a brother of the woman, found that the court decision was perfectly legal, but specified that if that convert did not become a Moslem in good faith and secretly remained a Christian, he should be flogged, slaughtered and crucified.[141]

Al-Andalus represented the land of jihad par excellence. Every year (or multiple times within a year as "seasonal" *razzias* [*ghazwa*]) raiding expeditions were sent to ravage the Christian Spanish kingdoms to the north, the Basque regions, or France and the Rhone valley, bringing back booty and slaves. Andalusian corsairs attacked and invaded along the Sicilian and Italian coasts, even as far as the Aegean Islands, looting and burning as they went. Many thousands of non-Muslim captives were deported to slavery in Andalusia, where the caliph kept a militia of tens of thousands of Christian slaves, brought from all parts of Christian Europe (the *Saqaliba*), and a harem filled with captured Christian women. Bat Ye'or summarizes these events as follows:

Breaking out of Arabia and from the conquered regions—Mesopotamia, Syria, Palestine—these successive waves of immigrants settled in Spain and terrorized southern France. Reaching as far as Avignon, they plundered the Rhone valley by repeated razzias. In 793 C.E., the suburbs of Narbonne were burned down and its outskirts raided. Calls to *jihad* attracted the fanaticized hordes in the ribats (monastery-fortresses) spanning the Islamo-Spanish frontiers. Towns were pillaged and rural areas devastated. In 981, Zamora and the surrounding countryside in the kingdom of Leon suffered destruction and the deportation of four thousand prisoners. Four years later, Barcelona was destroyed by fire and nearly all its inhabitants massacred or taken prisoner; several years after its conquest in 987, Coimbra remained desolate; Leon was demolished and its countryside ruined. In 997, Santaigo de Compostela was pillaged and razed to the ground. Three years later, Castille was put to fire and sword by Muslim troops and the population, captured in the course of these campaigns, enslaved and deported. The invasions by the Almoravides and the Almohades (eleventh to thirteenth centuries), Berber dynasties from the Maghreb, reactivated the *jihad*.[142]

Society was sharply divided along ethnic and religious lines, with the Arab tribes at the top of the hierarchy, followed by the Berbers who were never recognized as equals, despite their Islamization; lower in the scale came the *mullawadun* converts and, at the very bottom, the *dhimmi* Christians and Jews. The Andalusian Maliki jurist Ibn Abdun (d. 1134) offered these telling legal opinions regarding Jews and Christians in Seville around 1100 CE:

> No . . . Jew or Christian may be allowed to wear the dress of an aristocrat, nor of a jurist, nor of a wealthy individual; on the contrary they must be detested and avoided. It is forbidden to [greet] them with the [expression], "Peace be upon you." In effect, "Satan has gained possession of them, and caused them to forget God's warning. They are the confederates of Satan's party; Satan's confederates will surely be the losers!" (Qur'an 58:19 [modern Dawood translation]). A distinctive sign must be imposed upon them in order that they may be recognized and this will be for them a form of disgrace.[143]

Ibn Abdun also forbade the selling of scientific books to *dhimmis* under the pretext that they translated them and attributed them to their coreligionists and bishops. (In fact, plagiarism is difficult to prove since whole Jewish and Christian libraries were looted and destroyed.) Another prominent Andalusian jurist, Ibn Hazm of Cordoba (d. 1064), wrote that Allah has established the infidels' ownership of their property merely to provide booty for Muslims.[144]

In Granada, the Jewish viziers Samuel Ibn Naghrela and his son, Joseph, who protected the Jewish community, were both assassinated between 1056 to 1066, followed by the annihilation of the Jewish population by the local Muslims. It is estimated that up to five thousand Jews perished in the pogrom by Muslims that accompanied the 1066 assassination. This figure equals or exceeds the number of Jews reportedly killed by the Crusaders during their pillage of the Rhineland, some thirty years later, at the outset of the First Crusade. The Granada pogrom was likely to have been incited, in part, by the bitter anti-Jewish ode of Abu Ishaq, a well-known Muslim jurist and poet of the times, who wrote:

> Bring them down to their place and
> Return them to the most abject station.
> They used to roam around us in tatters
> Covered with contempt, humiliation, and scorn.
> They used to rummage amongst the dungheaps for a bit of a filthy rag
> To serve as a shroud for a man to be buried in. . . .
> Do not consider that killing them is treachery.
> Nay, it would be treachery to leave them scoffing.

[The translator then summarizes: "The Jews have broken their covenant (i.e., overstepped their station, with reference to the Covenant of Umar) and compunction would be out of place."][145]

The discriminatory policies of the Berber Muslim Almoravids, who arrived in Spain in 1086, and subsequently those of the even more fanaticized and violent Almohad Berber Muslims (who arrived in Spain in 1146–47) caused a rapid attrition of the pre-Islamic Iberian Christian (Mozarab) communities, nearly extinguishing them. The Almoravid attitude toward the Mozarabs is well reflected by three successive expulsions of the latter to Morocco in 1106, 1126, and 1138. The oppressed Mozarabs sent emissaries to the king of Aragon, Alphonso 1st le Batailleur (1104–1134), asking him to come to their rescue and deliver them from the Almoravids. Following the raid the king of Aragon launched in Andalusia in 1125–26 in responding to the pleas of Grenada's Mozarabs, the latter were deported en masse to Morocco in the fall of 1126.[146] Reinhart Dozy summarizes the events leading up, and surrounding the mass deportations, as follows:

[T]he Fakihs and the [Muslim] populace fostered against them [the Mozarabs] [an] envenomed hatred. In most towns they formed but a small community, but in the province of Granada they were still numerous, and near the capital they possessed a beautiful church, which had been built about 600 C.E. by Gudila, a [Visi]Gothic noble. This church was an offense to the Fakihs . . . they issued a fetwa decreeing its demolition. Yusuf [b. Tashifin, the Almoravid ruler] having given his approval, the sacred edifice was leveled with the ground (1099 C.E.). Other churches seem to have met with a similar fate, and the Fakihs treated the Mozarabs so oppressively that the latter at length appealed to Alfonso the Battler, King of Aragon, to deliver them from their intolerable burdens. Alfonso acceded to their request. In September, 1125, he set out with four thousand knights and their men-at-arms. . . . Alfonso, did not however, achieve the results he aimed at . . . the ultimate object of the expedition had been the capture of Granada, and this was not effected. Upon the withdrawal of the Aragonese army, the Moslems cruelly avenged themselves on the Mozarabs. Ten thousand of the Christians were already out of their reach, for knowing the fate in store for them they had obtained permission from Alfonso to settle in his territories, but many who remained were deprived of their property, maltreated in endless ways, thrown into prision, or put to death. The majority, however, were transported to Africa, and endured terrible sufferings, ultimately settling in the vicinity of Saleh and Mequinez (1126 C.E.). This deportation was carried out by virtue of a decree which the Kady Ibn Rushd—grandfather of the famous Averroes—had procured. . . . Eleven years later a second expulsion took place, and very few were left in Andalusia.[147]

The Almohads (1130–1232) wreaked enormous destruction on both the Jewish and Christian populations in Spain and North Africa. This devastation— massacre, captivity, and forced conversion—was described by the Jewish chronicler Abraham Ibn Daud and the poet Abraham Ibn Ezra. Suspicious of the sincerity of the Jewish converts to Islam, Muslim "inquisitors" (i.e., antedating their Christian Spanish counterparts by three centuries) removed the children from such families, placing them in the care of Muslim educators.[148] Maimonides, the renowned philosopher and physician, experienced the Almohad persecutions and had to flee Cordoba with his entire family in 1148, temporarily residing in Fez—disguised as a Muslim—before finding asylum in Fatimid Egypt. Indeed, although Maimonides is frequently referred to as a paragon of Jewish achievement facilitated by the enlightened rule of Andalusia, his own words debunk this utopian view of the Islamic treatment of Jews: "[T]he Arabs have persecuted us severely, and passed baneful and discriminatory legislation against us. . . . Never did a nation molest, degrade, debase, and hate us as much as they."[149]

Jihad Conquests of the Seljuk and Ottoman Turks and an Overview of the Rayah (Dhimmi) Condition under Ottoman Rule

The historian Michael the Syrian (Jacobite Patriarch of Antioch from 1166 to 1199 CE) in his chronicle reproducing earlier contemporary sources, made important observations regarding events that occurred beginning in the third decade of the eleventh century. He noted, "[T]he commencement of the exodus of the Turks to . . . Syria and the coast of Palestine . . . [where] [t]hey subdued all the countries by cruel devastation and plunder."[150] Subsequently, "Turks and Arabs were mixing together like a single people. . . . Such was the rule of the Turks amidst the Arabs."[151] Expanding upon this contemporary account, and the vast array of other primary sources—Arabic, Turkish, Greek, Latin, Serbian, Bulgarian, and Hungarian[152]—Bat Ye'or concludes,

> [T]he two waves of Muslim expansion, the Arab from the seventh century, and the Turkish four centuries later—are remarkably similar. . . . The great Arab and Turkish conquerors used the same military tactics and the same policies of consolidating Islamic power. This continuity resulted from the fact that the conquests took place within the framework of the common ideology of *jihad* and the administrative and juridical apparatus of the *shari'a*—a uniformity that defies time, since it adapts itself to diverse lands and peoples, being integrated into the internal coherence of a political theology. In the course of their military operations, the Turks applied to the conquered populations the rules of *jihad*, which had been structured four centuries earlier by the Arabs and enshrined in Islamic religious law.[153]

The Seljuk and Ottoman jihad campaigns were spearheaded by "Ghazi" (from the word *ghazwa* or *razzia*) movements, "Warriors of the Faith," brought together under the banner of Islam to fight infidels, and obtain booty. Wittek[154] and Vryonis[155] have stressed the significance of this movement, in its Seljuk incarnation, at the most critical frontier of Islam during the eleventh and twelfth centuries, that is, eastern Anatolia. Vryonis notes,

> When the Arab traveler al-Harawi passed through these border regions in the second half of the 12th century, he noted the existence of a shrine on the Byzantine-Turkish borders (near Afyon-Karahisar) which was reported to be the tomb of the Muslim martyr Abu Muhammd al-Battal, and at Amorium the tombs of those who fell in the celebrated siege of the city in 838. These constitute fascinating testimony to the fact that the ghazi-jihad tradition was closely intertwined into the nomadic society of Phrygia. Not only was there evidence of a nomadic invasion but also of an epic society in its heroic age, and it is from this milieu that the Turkish epics were shaped: the Battalname, the Danishmendname, and the Dusturname.[156]

Paul Wittek, citing the oldest known Ottoman source, the versified chronicle of Ahmedi, maintains that the fourteenth-century Ottomans believed they, too, "were a community of Ghazis, of champions of the Mohammedan religion; a community of the Moslem march—warriors, devoted to the struggle with the infidels in their neighborhood."[157] The contemporary Turkish scholar of Ottoman history, Halil Inalcik, has also emphasized the importance of Muslim religious zeal—expressed through jihad—as a primary motivation for the conquests of the Ottoman Turks: "The ideal of gaza, Holy War, was an important factor in the foundation and development of the Ottoman state. Society in the frontier principalities conformed to a particular cultural pattern imbued with the ideal of continuous Holy War and continuous expansion of the Dar ul Islam—the realms of Islam—until they covered the whole world."[158]

Incited by pious Muslim theologians, these Ghazis were at the vanguard of both the Seljuk and Ottoman jihad conquests. A. E. Vacalopoulos highlights the role of the dervishes during the Ottoman campaigns:

> [F]anatical dervishes and other devout Muslim leaders . . . constantly toiled for the dissemination of Islam. They had done so from the very beginning of the Ottoman state and had played an important part in the consolidation and extension of Islam. These dervishes were particularly active in the uninhabited frontier regions of the east. Here they settled down with their families, attracted other settlers, and thus became the virtual founders of whole new villages, whose inhabitants invariably exhibited the same qualities of deep religious fervor. From places such as these, the dervishes or their agents would emerge to take part in new military enterprises for the extension of the Islamic state. In return, the state granted them land and privileges under a generous prescription which required only that the land be cultivated and communications secured.[159]

Brief overviews of the Seljuk and Ottoman jihad campaigns, which ultimately Islamized Asia Minor, have been provided by Vryonis and Vacalopoulos. First, the schematic, clinical assessment of Vryonis:

The conquest, or should I say the conquests of Asia Minor were in operation over a period of four centuries. Thus the Christian societies of Asia Minor were submitted to extensive periods of intense warfare, incursions, and destructions which undermined the existence of the Christian church. In the first century of Turkish conquests and invasions from the mid-eleventh to the late twelfth century, the sources reveal that some 63 towns and villages were destroyed. The inhabitants of other towns and villages were enslaved and taken off to the Muslim slave markets.[160]

Vacalopoulos describes the conquests in more animated detail:

At the beginning of the eleventh century, the Seljuk Turks forced their way into Armenia and there crushed the armies of several petty Armenian states. No fewer than forty thousand souls fled before the organized pillage of the Seljuk host to the western part of Asia Minor. . . . From the middle of the eleventh century, and especially after the battle of Malazgirt [Manzikurt] (1071), the Seljuks spread throughout the whole Asia Minor peninsula, leaving terror, panic and destruction in their wake. Byzantine, Turkish and other contemporary sources are unanimous in their agreement on the extent of havoc wrought and the protracted anguish of the local population . . . evidence as we have proves that the Hellenic population of Asia Minor, whose very vigor had so long sustained the Empire and might indeed be said to have constituted its greatest strength, succumbed so rapidly to Turkish pressure that by the fourteenth century, it was confined to a few limited areas. By that time, Asia Minor was already being called Turkey . . . one after another, bishoprics and metropolitan sees which once throbbed with Christian vitality became vacant and ecclesiastical buildings fell into ruins. The metropolitan see of Chalcedon, for example, disappeared in the fourteenth century, and the sees of Laodicea, Kotyaeon (now Kutahya) and Synada in the fifteenth. . . . With the extermination of local populations or their precipitate flight, entire villages, cities, and sometimes whole provinces fell into decay. There were some fertile districts like the valley of the Maeander River, once stocked with thousands of sheep and cattle, which were laid waste and thereafter ceased to be in any way productive. Other districts were literally transformed into wildernesses. Impenetrable thickets sprang up in places where once there had been luxuriant fields and pastures. This is what happened to the district of Sangarius, for example, which Michael VIII Palaeologus had known formerly as a prosperous, cultivated land, but whose utter desolation he afterwards surveyed in utmost despair. . . . The mountainous region between Nicaea and Nicomedia, opposite Constantinople, once clustered with castles, cities, and villages, was depopulated. A few towns escaped total destruction—Laodicea, Iconium, Bursa (then Prusa), and Sinope, for example—but the extent of devastation elsewhere was such as to make a profound impression on visitors for may years to come. The fate of Antioch provides a graphic illustration of the kind of havoc wrought by the Turkish invaders: in 1432, only three hundred dwellings could be counted inside its walls, and its predominantly Turkish or Arab inhabitants subsisted by raising camels, goats, cattle, and sheep. Other cities in the southeastern part of Asia Minor fell into similar decay.[161]

The Islamization of Asia Minor was complemented by parallel and subsequent Ottoman jihad campaigns in the Balkans.[162] As of 1326, yearly *razzias* by the emirs of Asia Minor targeted southern Thrace, southern Macedonia, and the coastal areas of southern Greece. Around 1360 the Ottomans, under Suleiman (son of Sultan Orchan), and later Sultan Murad I (1359–1389), launched bona fide campaigns of jihad conquest, capturing and occupying a series of cities and towns in Byzantine and Bulgarian Thrace. Following the battle of Cernomen (September 26, 1371), the Ottomans penetrated westward, occupying within fifteen years a large number of towns in western Bulgaria and in Macedonia. Ottoman invasions during this period also occurred in the Peloponnesus, central Greece, Epirus, Thessaly, Albania, and Montenegro. By 1388 most of northeast Bulgaria was conquered, and following the battle of Kosovo (1389), Serbia came under Ottoman suzerainty. Vacalopoulos argues that internecine warring, as well as social and political upheaval, prevented the Balkan populations—Greeks, Bulgarians, Albanians, and Serbians—from uniting against the common Ottoman enemy, thus sealing their doom. Indeed, he observes that "[a]fter the defeat of the Serbs at Cirmen (or Cernomen) near the Hebrus River in 1371, Serbia, Bulgaria, and the Byzantine Empire became tributaries of the Ottoman Empire and were obliged to render assistance in Ottoman campaigns."[163]

Bayezid I (1389–1402) undertook devastating campaigns in Bosnia, Hungary, and Wallachia in addition to turning south and again attacking central Greece and the Peloponnesus. After a hiatus during their struggle against the Mongol invaders, the Ottomans renewed their Balkan offensive in 1421. Successful Ottoman campaigns were waged in the Peloponnesus, Serbia, and Hungary, culminating with the victory at the second battle of Kosovo (1448). With the accession to power of Mehmed II (1451–1481), the Ottomans commenced their definitive conquest of the Balkan Peninsula. Constantinople was captured on May 29, 1453, marking the end of the Byzantine Empire. By 1460 the Ottomans had completely vanquished both Serbia and the Peloponnesus. Bosnia and Trebizond fell in 1463, followed by Albania in 1468. With the conquest of Herzegovina in 1483, the Ottomans became rulers of the entire Balkan Peninsula.

Vacalopoulos, commenting on the initial Ottoman forays into Thrace during the mid-fourteenth century, and Dimitar Angelov, who provides an overall assessment highlighting the later campaigns of Murad II (1421–1451) and Mehmed II, elucidate the impact of the Ottoman jihad on the vanquished Balkan populations:

> From the very beginning of the Turkish onslaught [in Thrace] under Suleiman [son of Sultan Orchan], the Turks tried to consolidate their position by the forcible imposition of Islam. If [the Ottoman historian] Sukrullah is to be believed, those who refused to accept the Moslem faith were slaughtered and their families enslaved. "Where there were bells," writes the same author [i.e., Sukrullah], "Suleiman broke them up and cast them into fires. Where there were churches he destroyed them or converted them into mosques. Thus, in place of

bells there were now muezzins. Wherever Christian infidels were still found, vassalage was imposed on their rulers. At least in public they could no longer say '*kyrie eleison*' but rather 'There is no God but Allah'; and where once their prayers had been addressed to Christ, they were now to "Muhammad, the prophet of Allah."[164]

[T]he conquest of the Balkan Peninsula accomplished by the Turks over the course of about two centuries caused the incalculable ruin of material goods, countless massacres, the enslavement and exile of a great part of the population—in a word, a general and protracted decline of productivity, as was the case with Asia Minor after it was occupied by the same invaders. This decline in productivity is all the more striking when one recalls that in the mid-fourteenth century, as the Ottomans were gaining a foothold on the peninsula, the States that existed there—Byzantium, Bulgaria and Serbia—had already reached a rather high level of economic and cultural development. . . . The campaigns of Mourad II (1421–1451) and especially those of his successor, Mahomet II (1451–1481) in Serbia, Bosnia, Albania and in the Byzantine princedom of the Peloponnesus, were of a particularly devastating character. During the campaign that the Turks launched in Serbia in 1455–1456, Belgrade, Novo-Bardo and other towns were to a great extent destroyed. The invasion of the Turks in Albania during the summer of 1459 caused enormous havoc. According to the account of it written by Kritobulos, the invaders destroyed the entire harvest and leveled the fortified towns that they had captured. The country was afflicted with further devastation in 1466 when the Albanians, after putting up heroic resistance, had to withdraw into the most inaccessible regions, from which they continued the struggle. Many cities were likewise ruined during the course of the campaign led by Mahomet II in 1463 against Bosnia—among them Yaytzé, the capital of the Kingdom of Bosnia. . . . But it was the Peloponnesus that suffered most from the Turkish invasions. It was invaded in 1446 by the armies of Murad II, which destroyed a great number of places and took thousands of prisoners. Twelve years later, during the summer of 1458, the Balkan Peninsula was invaded by an enormous Turkish army under the command of Mahomet II and his first lieutenant Mahmoud Pasha. After a siege that lasted four months, Corinth fell into enemy hands. Its walls were razed, and many places that the sultan considered useless were destroyed. The work by Kritobulos contains an account of the Ottoman campaigns, which clearly shows us the vast destruction caused by the invaders in these regions. Two years later another Turkish army burst into the Peloponnesus. This time Gardiki and several other places were ruined. Finally, in 1464, for the third time, the destructive rage of the invaders was aimed at the Peloponnesus. That was when the Ottomans battled the Venetians and leveled the city of Argos to its foundations.[165]

In examining how the non-Muslim populations vanquished by the Ottoman jihad campaigns fared, it is useful to begin with the Jews, the least numerous population, who are also generally believed to have had quite a positive experience. Joseph Hacker studied the fate of Jews during their initial absorption into the Ottoman Empire in the fifteenth and sixteenth centuries. His research questions the uncritical view that from its outset the, "Jewish experience" in the Ottoman Empire "was a calm, peaceful, and fruitful one." Hacker notes: "It would seem to me that this accepted view of consistently good relations between the Ottomans and the Jews during the 15th century should be modified in light of new research and manuscript resources."[166]

The Jews, like other inhabitants of the Byzantine Empire, suffered heavily from the Ottoman jihad conquests and policies of colonization and population transfer (i.e., the surgun system). This explains the disappearance of several Jewish communities, including Salonica, and their founding anew by Spanish Jewish immigrants. Hacker observes, specifically:

> We possess letters written about the fate of Jews who underwent one or another of the Ottoman conquests. In one of the letters which was written before 1470, there is a description of the fate of such a Jew and his community, according to which description, written in Rhodes and sent to Crete, the fate of the Jews was not different from that of Christians. Many were killed; others were taken captive, and children were [enslaved, forcibly converted to Islam, and] brought to devshirme. . . . Some letters describe the carrying of the captive Jews to Istanbul and are filled with anti-Ottoman sentiments. Moreover, we have a description of the fate of a Jewish doctor and homilist from Veroia (Kara-Ferya) who fled to Negroponte when his community was driven into exile in 1455. He furnished us with a description of the exiles and their forced passage to Istanbul. Later on we find him at Istanbul itself, and in a homily delivered there in 1468 he expressed his anti-Ottoman feelings openly. We also have some evidence that the Jews of Constantinople suffered from the conquest of the city and that several were sold into slavery.[167]

Three summary conclusions are drawn by Hacker: (1) Strong anti-Ottoman feelings prevailed in some Byzantine Jewish circles in the first decades after the fall of Constantinople. These feelings were openly expressed by people living under Latin rule and to some extent even in Istanbul. (2) Mehmed II's policies toward non-Muslims made possible the substantial economic and social development of the Jewish communities in the empire, and especially in the capital, Istanbul. These communities were protected by him against popular hatred, and especially from blood libels. However, this policy was not continued by Bayezid II and there is evidence that under his rule the Jews suffered severe restrictions in their religious life. (3) The friendly policies of Mehmed, on the one hand, and the good reception by Bayezid II of Spanish Jewry, on the other, caused the Jewish writers of the sixteenth century to overlook both the destruction that Byzantine Jewry suffered during the Ottoman conquests and the later outbursts of oppression under both Bayezid II and Selim I.

Ivo Andric analyzed the *rayah* (meaning "herd" and "to graze a herd") or *dhimmi* condition imposed upon the indigenous Christian population of Bosnia for four centuries.[168] Those native Christian inhabitants who refused to apostasize to Islam lived under the Ottoman *Kanun-i-Rayah*, which merely reiterated the essential regulations of *dhimmitude* originally formulated by Muslim jurists and theologians in the seventh and eighth centuries CE.[169] Andric's presentation musters "a wealth of irrefutable evidence that the main points of the Kanun, just those that cut the deepest into the moral and economic life of Christians, remained in full force right up to the end of Turkish rule and as long as the Turks had the power to apply them . . . [thus] it was inevitable that the rayah decline to a status that was economically inferior and dependent."[170]

Andric cites a Bosnian Muslim proverb and a song honoring Sultan Bayezid II, whose shared perspectives reflect Muslim attitudes toward the Christian *rayahs*:

> "The rayah is like the grass,
> Mow it as much as you will, still it springs up anew."
> "Once you'd broken Bosnia's horns
> You mowed down what would not be pruned
> Leaving only the riffraff behind
> So there'd be someone left to serve us and grieve before the cross."[171]

These prevailing discriminatory conditions were exacerbated by Bosnia's serving as either a battlefield or staging ground during two centuries of Ottoman *razzias* and formal jihad campaigns against Hungary. Overcome by excessive taxation and conscript labor, "Christians therefore began to abandon their houses and plots of land situated in level country and along the roads and to retreat back into the mountains. And as they did so, moving ever higher into inaccessible regions, Muslims took over their former sites."[172]

Moreover, those Christians living in towns suffered from the *rayah* system's mandated impediments to commercial advancement by non-Muslims:

Islam from the very outset, excluded such activities as making wine, breeding pigs, and selling pork products from commercial production and trade. But additionally Bosnian Christians were forbidden to be saddlers, tanners, or candle-makers or to trade in honey, butter, and certain other items. Countrywide, the only legal market day was Sunday. Christians were thus deliberately faced with the choice between ignoring the precepts of their religion, keeping their shops open and working on Sundays, or alternatively, forgoing participation in the market and suffering material loss thereby. Even in 1850, in Jukic's "Wishes and Entreaties" we find him beseeching "his Imperial grace" to put an end to the regulation that Sunday be market day.[173]

Christians were also forced to pay disproportionately higher taxes than Muslims, including the intentionally degrading non-Muslim poll-tax.

This tax was paid by every non-Muslim male who had passed his fourteenth year, at the rate of a ducat per annum. But since Turkey had never known birth registers, the functionary whose job it was to exact the tax measured the head and neck of each boy with a piece of string and judged from that whether a person had arrived at a taxable age or not. Starting as an abuse that soon turned into an ingrained habit, then finally established custom, by the last century of Turkish rule every boy without distinction found himself summoned to pay the head tax. And it would seem this was not the only abuse. . . . Of Ali-Pasa Stocevic, who during the first half of the nineteenth century was vizier and all but unlimited ruler of Herzegovina, his contemporary, the monk Prokopije Cokorilo, wrote that he "taxed the dead for six years after their demise" and that his tax collectors "ran their fingers over the bellies of pregnant women, saying 'you will probably have a boy, so you have to pay the poll tax right away.' . . . The following folk saying from Bosnia reveals how taxes were exacted: "He's as fat as if he'd been tax collecting in Bosnia."[174]

The specific *Kanun-i-Rayah* stipulations that prohibited the *rayahs* from riding a saddled horse, carrying a saber or any other weapon in or out of doors, selling wine, letting their hair grow, or wearing wide sashes, were strictly enforced until the mid-nineteenth century. Hussamudin-Pasa in 1794 issued an ordinance that prescribed the exact color and type of clothing the Bosnian *rayah* had to wear. Barbers were prohibited from shaving Muslims with the same razors used for Christians. Even in bathhouses, Christians were required to have specifically marked towels and aprons to avoid confusing their laundry with laundry designated for Muslims. Until at least 1850, and in some parts of Bosnia well into the 1860s, a Christian upon encountering a Muslim was required to jump down from his (unsaddled) horse, move to the side of the road, and wait for the latter to pass.[175]

Christianity's loud and most arresting symbol, church bells, Andric notes, always drew close, disapproving Turkish scrutiny, and "[w]herever there invasions would go, down came the bells, to be destroyed or melted into cannon."[176] Predictably,

Until the second half of the nineteenth century, "nobody in Bosnia could even think of bells or bell towers." Only in 1860 did the Sarajevo priest Fra Grgo Martic manage to get permission from Topal Osman-Pasa to hang a bell at the church in Kresevo. Permission was granted, though, only on condition that "at first the bell be rung softly to let the Turks get accustomed to it little by little." And still the Muslim of Kresevo were complaining, even in 1875, to Sarajevo that "the Turkish ear and ringing bells cannot coexist in the same place at the same time"; and Muslim women would beat on their copper pots to drown out the noise. . . . [O]n 30 April 1872, the new Serbian Orthodox church also got a bell. But since the . . . Muslims had threatened to riot, the military had to be called in to ensure that the ceremony might proceed undisturbed.[177]

The imposition of such disabilities, Andric observes, extended beyond church ceremonies, as reflected by a 1794 proclamation of the Serbian Orthodox church in Sarajevo warning Christians not to "sing during . . . outings, nor in their houses, nor in other places. The saying 'Don't sing too loud, this village is Turk' testifies eloquently to the fact that this item of the *Kanun[-i-Rayah]* was applied outside church life as well as within."[178]

Andric concludes, "[F]or their Christian subjects, their [Ottoman Turkish] hegemony brutalized custom and meant a step to the rear in every respect."[179]

Paul Ricaut, the British consul in Smyrna, journeyed extensively within the Ottoman Empire during the mid-seventeenth century, becoming a keen observer of its sociopolitical milieu. In 1679 (i.e., *prior* to the Ottomans being repulsed at Vienna in September 1683; see later discussion of Ottoman "tolerance"), Ricaut published these important findings: (1) Many Christians were expelled from their churches, which the Ottoman Turks converted into mosques. (2) The "Mysteries of the Altar" were hidden in subterranean vaults and sepulchres whose roofs were barely above the surface of the ground. (3) Fearing Turkish hostility and oppression, Christian priests, particularly in eastern Asia Minor, were compelled to live with great caution and officiate in private obscurity. (4) Not surprisingly, to escape these prevailing conditions, many Christians apostacized to Islam.[180] Moreover, as Vryonis demonstrated convincingly for the earlier period between the eleventh and fifteenth centuries, the existence of cryto-Christianity and neomartyrs was not uncommon in the Christian territories of Asia Minor conquered by the waves of Seljuk and Ottoman jihad.[181] He cites, for example, a pastoral letter from 1338 addressed to the residents of Nicaea indicating widespread, forcible conversion by the Turks: "And they [Turks] having captured and enslaved many of our own and violently forced them and dragging them along alas! So that they took up their evil and godlessness."[182]

The phenomenon of forcible conversion, including coercive mass conversions, persisted throughout the sixteenth century, as discussed by Constantelos in his analysis of neomartyrdom in the Ottoman Empire: "[M]ass forced conversions were recorded during the caliphates of Selim I (1512–1520), . . . Selim II (1566–1574), and Murat III (1574–1595). On the occasion of some anniversary, such as the capture of a city, or a national holiday, many rayahs were forced to apostacize. On the day of the circumcision of Mohammed III great numbers of Christians (Albanians, Greeks, Slavs) were forced to convert to Islam."[183]

Reviewing the martyrology of Christians victimized by the Ottomans from the conquest of Constantinople (1453) through the final phases of the Greek War of Independence (1828), Constantelos notes: "[T]he Ottoman Turks condemned to death eleven Ecumenical Patriarchs of Constantinople, nearly one hundred bishops, and several thousand priests, deacons, and monks. It is impossible to say with certainty how many men of the cloth were forced to apostasize."[184]

However, the more mundane cases illustrated by Constantelos are of equal significance in revealing the plight of Christians under Ottoman rule, through at least 1867: "Some were accused of insulting the Muslim faith or of throwing something against the wall of a mosque. Others were accused of sexual advances toward a Turk; still others of making a public confession such as 'I will become a Turk' without meaning it."[185]

Constantelos concludes:

> The story of the neomartyrs indicates that there was no liberty of conscience in the Ottoman Empire and that religious persecution was never absent from the state. Justice was subject to the passions of judges as well as of the crowds, and it was applied with a double standard, lenient for Muslims and harsh for Christians and others. The view that the Ottoman Turks pursued a policy of religious toleration in order to promote a fusion of the Turks with the conquered populations is not sustained by the facts.[186]

Even the Turcophilic nineteenth-century travel writer Ubicini acknowledged the oppressive burden of Ottoman *dhimmitude* in this moving depiction:

> The history of enslaved peoples is the same everywhere, or rather, they have no history. The years, the centuries pass without bringing any change to their situation. Generations come and go in silence. One might think they are afraid to awaken their masters, asleep alongside them. However, if you examine them closely you discover that this immobility is only superficial. A silent and constant agitation grips them. Life has entirely withdrawn into the heart. They resemble those rivers which have disappeared underground; if you put your ear to the earth, you can hear the muffled sound of their waters; then they re-emerge intact a few leagues away. Such is the state of the Christian populations of Turkey under Ottoman rule.[187]

Vacalopoulos describes how jihad-imposed *dhimmitude* under Ottoman rule provided critical motivation for the Greek Revolution:

> The Revolution of 1821 is no more than the last great phase of the resistance of the Greeks to Ottoman domination; it was a relentless, undeclared war, which had begun already in the first years of servitude. The brutality of an autocratic regime, which was characterized by economic spoliation, intellectual decay and cultural retrogression, was sure to provoke opposition. Restrictions of all kinds, unlawful taxation, forced labor, persecutions, violence, imprisonment, death, abductions of girls and boys and their confinement to Turkish harems, and various deeds of wantonness and lust, along with numerous less offensive excesses—all these were a constant challenge to the instinct of survival and they defied every sense of human decency. The Greeks bitterly resented all insults and humiliations, and their anguish and frustration pushed them into the arms of rebellion. There was no exaggeration in the statement made by one of the beys if Arta, when he sought to explain the ferocity of the struggle. He said: "We have wronged the rayas [*dhimmis*] (i.e. our Christian subjects) and destroyed both

their wealth and honor; they became desperate and took up arms. This is just the beginning and will finally lead to the destruction of our empire." The sufferings of the Greeks under Ottoman rule were therefore the basic cause of the insurrection; a psychological incentive was provided by the very nature of the circumstances.[188]

Those scholars who continue to adhere to the roseate narrative of Ottoman "tolerance,"[189] the notion that an "easy-going tolerance, resting on an assumption not only of superior religion, but also of superior power,"[190] which it is claimed, persisted in the Ottoman Empire until the end of the seventeenth century, must address certain basic questions. Why has the quite brutal Ottoman devshirme-janissary system, which, from the mid-fourteenth through early eighteenth centuries, enslaved and forcibly converted to Islam an estimated five hundred thousand to 1 million non-Muslim (primarily Balkan Christian) adolescent males,[191] been characterized, reductio ad absurdum, as a benign form of social advancement, jealously pined for by "ineligible" Ottoman Muslim families? For example,

> The role played by the Balkan Christian boys recruited into the Ottoman service through the devshirme is well known. Great numbers of them entered the Ottoman military and bureaucratic apparatus, which for a while came to be dominated by these new recruits to the Ottoman state and the Muslim faith. This ascendancy of Balkan Europeans into the Ottoman power structure did not pass unnoticed, and there are many complaints from other elements, sometimes from the Caucasian slaves who were their main competitors, and more vocally from the old and free Muslims, who felt slighted by the preference given to the newly converted slaves.[192]

Scholars who have conducted serious, detailed studies of the devshirme-janissary system do not share such hagiographic views of this Ottoman institution. Vryonis, for example, makes these deliberately understated, but cogent observations:

> [I]n discussing the devshirme we are dealing with the large numbers of Christians who, in spite of the material advantages offered by conversion to Islam, chose to remain members of a religious society which was denied first class citizenship. Therefore the proposition advanced by some historians, that the Christians welcomed the devshirme as it opened up wonderful opportunities for their children, is inconsistent with the fact that these Christians had not chosen to become Muslims in the first instance but had remained Christians. . . . [T]here is abundant testimony to the very active dislike with which they viewed the taking of their children. One would expect such sentiments given the strong nature of the family bond and given also the strong attachment to Christianity of those who had not apostacized to Islam. . . . First of all the Ottomans capitalized on the general Christian fear of losing their children and used offers of devshirme exemption in negotiations for surrender of Christian lands. Such exemptions were

included in the surrender terms granted to Jannina, Galata, the Morea, Chios, etc.
. . . Christians who engaged in specialized activities which were important to the
Ottoman state were likewise exempt from the tax on their children by way of
recognition of the importance of their labors for the empire. . . . Exemption from
this tribute was considered a privilege and not a penalty.

. . . [T]here are other documents wherein their [i.e., the Christians] dislike
is much more explicitly apparent. These include a series of Ottoman documents
dealing with the specific situations wherein the devshirmes themselves have
escaped from the officials responsible for collecting them. . . . A firman . . . in
1601 [regarding the devshirme] provided the [Ottoman] officials with stern
measures of enforcement, a fact which would seem to suggest that parents were
not always disposed to part with their sons.

> " . . . to enforce the command of the known and holy fetva [fatwa] of
> Seyhul [Shaikh]-Islam. In accordance with this whenever some one of
> the infidel parents or some other should oppose the giving up of his son
> for the Janissaries, he is immediately hanged from his door-sill, his
> blood being deemed unworthy."[193]

Vasiliki Papoulia highlights the continuous desperate, often violent struggle
of the Christian populations against this forcefully imposed Ottoman levy:

> It is obvious that the population strongly resented . . . this measure [and the levy]
> could be carried out only by force. Those who refused to surrender their sons—
> the healthiest, the handsomest and the most intelligent—were on the spot put to
> death by hanging. Nevertheless we have examples of armed resistance. In 1565
> a revolt took place in Epirus and Albania. The inhabitants killed the recruiting
> officers and the revolt was put down only after the sultan sent five hundred janis-
> saries in support of the local sanjak-bey. We are better informed, thanks to the
> historic archives of Yerroia, about the uprising in Naousa in 1705 where the
> inhabitants killed the Silahdar Ahmed Celebi and his assistants and fled to the
> mountains as rebels. Some of them were later arrested and put to death . . .
> Since there was no possibility of escaping [the levy] the population resorted to
> several subterfuges. Some left their villages and fled to certain cities which enjoyed
> exemption from the child levy or migrated to Venetian-held territories. The result was
> a depopulation of the countryside. Others had their children marry at an early age. . . .
> Nicephorus Angelus . . . states that at times the children ran away on their own initia-
> tive, but when they heard that the authorities had arrested their parents and were tor-
> turing them to death, returned and gave themselves up. La Giulletiere cites the case
> of a young Athenian who returned from hiding in order to save his father's life and
> then chose to die himself rather than abjure his faith. According to the evidence in
> Turkish sources, some parents even succeeded in abducting their children after they
> had been recruited. The most successful way of escaping recruitment was through
> bribery. That the latter was very widespread is evident from the large amounts of
> money confiscated by the sultan from corrupt . . . officials. Finally, in their despera-
> tion the parents even appealed to the Pope and the Western powers for help.[194]

Papoulia concludes, "[T]here is no doubt that this heavy burden was one of the hardest tribulations of the Christian population.[195]

Why did the Tanzimat reforms, designed to abrogate the Ottoman version of the system of *dhimmitude*, need to be imposed by European powers through treaties, as so-called capitulations following Ottoman military defeats, and why, even then, were these reforms never implemented in any meaningful way from 1839 until the collapse of the Ottoman Empire after World War I?

Edouard Engelhardt made these observations from his detailed analysis of the Tanzimat period, noting that a quarter century after the Crimean War (1853–1856), and the second iteration of Tanzimat reforms, the same problems persisted: "Muslim society has not yet broken with the prejudices which make the conquered peoples subordinate . . . the raya [*dhimmis*] remain inferior to the Osmanlis; in fact he is not rehabilitated; the fanaticism of the early days has not relented. . . . [Even liberal Muslims rejected] . . . civil and political equality, that is to say, the assimilation of the conquered with the conquerors."[196]

A systematic examination of the condition of the Christian *rayas* was conducted in the 1860s by British consuls stationed throughout the Ottoman Empire, yielding extensive primary source documentary evidence.[197] Britain was then Turkey's most powerful ally, and it was in its strategic interest to see that oppression of the Christians was eliminated to prevent direct, aggressive Russian or Austrian intervention. On July 22, 1860, Consul James Zohrab sent a lengthy report from Sarajevo to his ambassador in Constantinople, Sir Henry Bulwer, analyzing the administration of the provinces of Bosnia and Herzegovina, again, following the 1856 Tanzimat reforms. Referring to the reform efforts, Zohrab states:

> The Hatti-humayoun, I can safely say, practically remains a dead letter . . . while [this] does not extend to permitting the Christians to be treated as they formerly were treated, is so far unbearable and unjust in that it permits the Mussulmans to despoil them with heavy exactions. False imprisonments (imprisonment under false accusation) are of daily occurence. A Christian has but a small chance of exculpating himself when his opponent is a Mussulman (. . .) Christian evidence, as a rule, is still refused (. . .) Christians are now permitted to possess real property, but the obstacles which they meet with when they attempt to acquire it are so many and vexatious that very few have as yet dared to brave them. . . . Such being, generally speaking, the course pursued by the Government towards the Christians in the capital (Sarajevo) of the province where the Consular Agents of the different Powers reside and can exercise some degree of control, it may easily be guessed to what extend the Christians, in the remoter districts, suffer who are governed by Mudirs (governors) generally fanatical and unacquainted with the (new reforms of the) law.[198]

In his comprehensive study of nineteenth-century Palestinian Jewry under Ottoman rule, Tudor Parfitt made these germane observations:

Inside the towns, Jews and other *dhimmis* were frequently attacked, wounded, and even killed by local Muslims and Turkish soldiers. Such attacks were frequently for trivial reasons: Wilson [in British Foreign Office correspondence] recalled having met a Jew who had been badly wounded by a Turkish soldier for not having instantly dismounted when ordered to give up his donkey to a soldier of the Sultan. Many Jews were killed for less. On occasion the authorities attempted to get some form of redress but this was by no means always the case: the Turkish authorities themselves were sometimes responsible for beating Jews to death for some unproven charge. After one such occasion [British Consul] Young remarked: "I must say I am sorry and surprised that the Governor could have acted so savage a part—for certainly what I have seen of him I should have thought him superior to such wanton inhumanity—but it was a Jew—without friends or protection—it serves to show well that it is not without reason that the poor Jew, even in the nineteenth century, lives from day to day in terror of his life."

. . . In fact, it took some time [i.e., at least a decade after the 1839 reforms] before these courts did accept *dhimmi* testimony in Palestine. The fact that Jews were represented on the meclis [provincial legal council] did not contribute a great deal to the amelioration of the legal position of the Jews: the Jewish representatives were tolerated grudgingly and were humiliated and intimidated to the point that they were afraid to offer any opposition to the Muslim representatives. In addition the constitution of the meclis was in no sense fairly representative of the population. In Jerusalem in the 1870s the meclis consisted of four Muslims, three Christians and only one Jew—at a time when Jews constituted over half the population of the city. . . . Some years after the promulgation of the hatt-i-serif [Tanzimat reform edicts] Binyamin [in an eyewitness account from *Eight Years in Asia and Africa from 1846 to 1855*, p. 44] was still able to write of the Jews— "they are entirely destitute of every legal protection." . . . Perhaps even more to the point, the courts were biased against the Jews and even when a case was heard in a properly assembled court where dhimmi testimony was admissible the court would still almost invariably rule against the Jews. It should be noted that a non-dhimmi [e.g., foreign] Jew was still not permitted to appear and witness in either the mahkama [specific Muslim council] or the meclis.[199]

The modern Ottomanist Roderick Davison acknowledges that the reforms failed, and offers an explanation based on Islamic beliefs intrinsic to the system of *dhimmitude*:

No genuine equality was ever attained . . . there remained among the Turks an intense Muslim feeling which could sometimes burst into an open fanaticism . . . More important than the possibility of fanatic outbursts, however, was the innate attitude of superiority which the Muslim Turk possessed. Islam was for him the true religion. Christianity was only a partial revelation of the truth, which Muhammad finally revealed in full; therefore Christians were not equal to Muslims in possession of truth. Islam was not only a way of worship, it was a way of life as well. It prescribed man's relations to man, as well as to God, and was the basis for society, for law, and for government. Christians were therefore inevitably considered second-class citizens in the light of religious revelation— as well as by reason of the plain fact that they had been conquered by the Ottomans. This whole Muslim outlook was often summed up in the common term *gavur* (or *kafir*), which means "unbeliever" or "infidel," with emotional and quite uncomplimentary overtones. To associate closely or on terms of equality with the *gavur* was dubious at best. "Familiar association with heathens and infidels is forbidden to the people of Islam," said Asim, an early nineteenth-century historian, "and friendly and intimate intercourse between two parties that are one to another as darkness and light is far from desirable." . . . The mere idea of equality, especially the anti-defamation clause of 1856, offended the Turks' inherent sense of the rightness of things. "Now we can't call a gavur a gavur," it was said, sometimes bitterly, sometimes in matter-of-fact explanation that under the new dispensation the plain truth could no longer be spoken openly. Could reforms be acceptable which forbade calling a spade a spade? . . . The Turkish mind, conditioned by centuries of Muslim and Ottoman dominance, was not yet ready to accept any absolute equality. . . . Ottoman equality was not attained in the Tanzimat period [i.e., mid- to late nineteenth century, 1839–1876], nor yet after the Young Turk revolution of 1908.[200]

Indeed, an influential member of the Ottoman Committee of Union and Progress, Sheik Abd-ul-Haq, a "progressive" Young Turk, made this revealing declaration writing in a Parisian Muslim review (*Le Mecherouttiete*, edited by Sherif Pasha, Paris) in August 1912:

Yes! The Musulman religion is in open hostility to all your world of progress. Understand, you European observers, that a Christian, whatever his position may be, by the mere fact of his being a Christian is regarded by us as a blind man lost to all sense of human dignity. Our reasoning with regard to him is as simple as it is definitive. We say: the man whose judgment is so perverted as to deny the existence of a one and only God, and to make up gods of different sorts, can only be the meanest expression of human degradation; to speak to him would be a humiliation for our intelligence and an insult to the grandeur of the Master of the Universe. The presence of such miscreants among us is the bane of our existence; their doctrine is a direct insult to the purity of our faith; contact with them is a defilement of our bodies; any relation with them a torture to our souls. Though detesting you, we have condescended to study your political institutions and your military organization. Over and above the new weapons that Providence procures for us through your agency, you have yourselves rekindled, the inextinguishable faith of our heroic martyrs. Our Young Turks, our Babis, our new Brotherhoods, all our sects, under various forms, are inspired by the same idea; the same necessity of moving forward. Towards what end? Christian civilization? Never! Islam is the one great international family. All true believers are brothers. A community of feeling and of faith binds them in mutual affection. It is for the Caliph to facilitate these relations and to rally the Faithful under the sacerdotal standard.[201]

Throughout the Ottoman Empire, particularly within the Balkans and, later, Anatolia itself, attempted emancipation of the *dhimmi* peoples provoked violent, bloody responses against those "infidels" daring to claim equality with local Muslims. The massacres of the Bulgarians (in 1876),[202] and more extensive massacres of the Armenians (1894–1896),[203] culminating in a frank jihad genocide against the Armenians during World War I,[204] epitomize these trends. Enforced abrogation of the laws of *dhimmitude* required the dismantling of the Ottoman Empire. This finally occurred after the Balkan Wars of independence and during the European Mandate period following World War I.

Lastly, why was there never a significant sharia-inspired slavery abolition movement within the Ottoman states, comparable to the courageous and successful campaigns lead by Western Christian statesmen (such as the evangelical parliamentarian William Wilberforce)[205] in Europe and America throughout the nineteenth century? Deliberately limited and ineffectual firmans issued by the Ottoman Porte failed to discourage East African slave trading,[206] and even British naval power, so successful in the Atlantic and Indian oceans,[207] was unable to suppress the Red Sea slave trade to the Ottoman Empire at the end of the nineteenth century.[208] Regardless, as Reuben Levy notes: "At Constantinople, the sale of women slaves, both negresses and Circassians [likely for harem slavery and/or concubinage], continued to be openly practiced until . . . 1908."[209]

The Timurid Jihad Conquests—An Overview

Amir Timur (whose name signifies "Iron" in Turkish) was born at Kash (Shahr-i-Sebz, the "Green City") in Transoxiana (some fifty miles south of Samarkand in modern Uzbekistan), on April 8 (or 11), 1336 CE. Amir Turghay, his father, was chief of the Gurgan or Chagtai branch of the Barlas Turks. By age thirty-four (1369/70), Timur had killed his major rival (Mir Husain), becoming the preeminent ruler of Transoxiana. He spent the next six to seven years consolidating his power in Transoxiana before launching the aggressive conquests of Persia, Afghanistan, and Iraq, and then attacking Hindustan (India) under the tottering Delhi Sultanate.[210]

Rene Grousset contrasts Jenghiz Khan's "straightforward planning" and "clean sweeps" with the "higgledy-piggledy" order of Timur's expeditions, and the often incomplete nature of the latter's conquests:

> Tamerlane's [Timur's] conquering activities were carried on from the Volga to Damascus, from Smyrna to the Ganges and the Yulduz, and his expeditions into these regions followed no geographical order. He sped from Tashkent to Shiraz, from Tabriz to Khodzhent, as enemy aggression dictated; a campaign in Russia occurred between two in Persia, an expedition into Central Asia between two raids into the Caucasus. . . . [Timur] at the end of every successful campaign left the country without making any dispositions for its control except Khwarizm and

Persia, and even there not until the very end. It is true that he slaughtered all his enemies as thoroughly and conscientiously as the great Mongol, and the pyramids of human heads left behind him as a warning example tell their own tale. Yet the survivors forgot the lesson given them and soon resumed secret or overt attempts at rebellion, so that it was all to do again. It appears too, that these bloodsoaked pyramids diverted [Timur] from the essential objective. Baghdad, Brussa (Bursa), Sarai, Kara Shahr, and Delhi were all sacked by him, but he did not overcome the Ottoman Empire, the Golden Horde, the khanate of Mogholistan, or the Indian Sultanate; and even the Jelairs of Iraq 'Arabi rose up again as soon as he had passed. Thus he had to conquer Khwarizm three times, the Ili six or seven times (without ever managing to hold it for longer than the duration of the campaign), eastern Persia twice, western Persia at least three times, in addition to waging two campaigns in Russia . . . [Timur's] campaigns "always had to be fought again," and fight them again he did.[211]

Timur's campaigns are infamous for their extensive massacres and emblematic "pyramids of heads." E. G. Brown cites "only a few" prominent examples:

As specimens of those acts mention may be made of his massacre of the people of Sistan 1383–4, when he caused some two thousand prisoners to be built up into a wall; his cold-blooded slaughter of a hundred thousand captive Indians near Dihli [Delhi] (December, 1398); his burying alive of four thousand Armenians in 1400–1, and the twenty towers of skulls erected by him at Aleppo and Damascus in the same year; and his massacre of 70,000 of the inhabitants of Isfahan in (November, 1387).[212]

Grousset emphasizes the important Islamic motivation for Timur's campaigns: "It is the Qur'an to which he continually appeals, the imams and dervishes who prophesy his success. His wars were to influence the character of the *jihad*, the Holy War, even when—as was almost always the case—he was fighting Muslims. He had only to accuse these Muslims of lukewarmness, whether the Jagataites of the Ili and Uiguria, whose conversion was so recent, or the Sultans of Delhi who . . . refrained from massacring their millions of Hindu subjects."[213]

The Turkish chronicle *Malfuzat-i-Timuri*, a putative autobiographical memoir of Timur,[214] translated into Persian by Abu Talib Husaini, illustrates these driving sentiments, complete with a Qur'anic quotation:

About this time there arose in my heart the desire to lead an expedition against the infidels, and to become a ghazi; for it had reached my ears that the slayer of infidels is a ghazi, and if he is slain he becomes a martyr. It was on this account that I formed this resolution, but I was undetermined in my mind whether I should direct my expedition against the infidels of China or against the infidels and polytheists of India. In this matter I sought an omen from the Qur'an, and the verse I opened upon [Q66:9] was this, "O Prophet, make war upon infidels and unbelievers, and treat them with severity." My great officers told me that the inhabitants of Hindustan were infidels and unbelievers. In obedience to the order of Almighty Allah I ordered an expedition against them.[215]

Timur's jihad campaigns against non-Muslims—whether Christians in Asia Minor and Georgia or Hindus in India—seemed to intensify in brutality. Brown highlights one particular episode that supports this contention, wherein Timur clearly distinguished between his vanquished Muslim and non-Muslim foes. After rampaging through (Christian) Georgia, where he "devastated the country, destroyed the churches, and slew great numbers of inhabitants," in the winter of 1399–1400, Timur, in August 1400, "began his march into Asia Minor by way of Avnik, Erzeroum, Erzinjan, and Sivas. The latter place offered a stubborn resistance, and when it finally capitulated Timur caused all the Armenian and Christian soldiers to be buried alive; but the Muhammadans he spared."[216]

The unparalleled devastation Timur wrought upon predominantly Hindu India further bolsters the notion that Timur viewed his non-Muslim prey with particular animosity. Moreover, there are specific examples of selective brutality directed against Hindus, cited in the *Malfuzat-i-Timuri*, from which Muslims are deliberately spared:

My great object in invading Hindustan had been to wage a religious war against the infidel Hindus, and it now appeared to me that it was necessary for me to put down these Jats [Hindus]. On the 9th of the month I dispatched the baggage from Tohana, and on the same day I marched into the jungles and wilds, and slew 2,000 demon-like Jats. I made their wives and children captives, and plundered their cattle and property. . . . On the same day a party of saiyids, who dwelt in the vicinity, came with courtesy and humility to wait upon me and were very graciously received. In my reverence for the race of the prophet, I treated their chiefs with great honour.[217]

On the 29th I again marched and reached the river Jumna. On the other side of the river I [viewed] a fort, and upon making inquiry about it, I was informed that it consisted of a town and fort, called Loni. . . . I determined to take that fort at once. . . . Many of the Rajputs placed their wives and children in their houses and burned them, then they rushed to the battle and were killed. Other men of the garrison fought and were slain, and a great many were taken prisoners. Next day I gave orders that the Musalman prisoners should be separated and saved, but that the infidels should all be despatched to hell with the proselyting sword. I also ordered that the houses of the saiyids, shaikhs and learned Musulmans should be preserved but that all the other houses should be plundered and the fort destroyed. It was done as I directed and a great booty was obtained.[218]

On the 16th of the month some incidents occurred which led to the sack of the city of Delhi, and to the slaughter of many of the infidel inhabitants. . . . On that day, Thursday, and all the night of Friday, nearly 15,000 Turks were engaged in slaying, plundering, and destroying. . . . The following day, Saturday, the 17th, all passed in the same way, and the spoil was so great that each man secured from fifty to a hundred prisoners—men, women, and children. There was no man who took less than twenty. The other booty was immense in rubies, diamonds, pearls and other gems; jewels of gold and silver, ashrafis, tankas of gold and silver of the celebrated 'Alai coinage; vessels of gold and silver; and brocades and silks of great value. Gold and silver ornaments of the Hindu women were obtained in such quantities as to exceed all account. Excepting the quarter of the saiyids, the 'ulama and the other Musulmans, the whole city was sacked.[219]

Timur left Samarkand with a large, powerful expeditionary force destined for India in April 1398. By October he had besieged Talamba, seventy-five miles northeast of Multan, subsequently plundering the town and massacring its inhabitants. He reached the vicinity of Delhi during the first week of December having forged a path of destruction—pillaging, razing, and massacring—en route through Pak Patan, Dipalpur, Bhatnar, Sirsa, and Kaithal. Prior to fighting and defeating an army under Sultan Nasir-ud-din Mahmud Tughluq on December 17, 1398, Timur had his forces butcher in cold blood one hundred thousand Hindu prisoners accumulated while advancing toward Delhi.[220] A. L. Srivastava describes what transpired after Timur's forces occupied Delhi on December 18, 1398:

> The citizens of the capital, headed by the *ulema*, waited on the conqueror and begged quarter. Timur agreed to spare the citizens; but, owing to the oppressive conduct of the soldiers of the invading force, the people of the city were obliged to offer resistance. Timur now ordered a general plunder and massacre which lasted for several days. Thousands of the citizens of Delhi were murdered and thousands were made prisoners. A historian writes: "High towers were built with the head of the Hindus, and their bodies became the food of ravenous beasts and birds . . . such of the inhabitants who escaped alive were made prisoners."[221]

Timur acquired immense booty, as well as Delhi's best (surviving) artisans, who were conscripted and sent to Samarkand to construct for him the famous Friday mosque. Leaving Delhi on January 1, 1399, for their return march to Samarkand, Timur's forces stormed Meerut on January 19, before encountering and defeating two Hindu armies near Hardwar.[222] The *Malfuzat-i-Timuri* indicates that at Hardwar, Timur's army

> displayed great courage and daring; they made their swords their banners, and exerted themselves in slaying the foe (during a bathing festival on the bank of the Ganges). They slaughtered many of the infidels, and pursued those who fled to the mountains. So many of them were killed that their blood ran down the mountains and plain, and thus (nearly) all were sent to hell. The few who escaped, wounded, weary, and half dead, sought refuge in the defiles of the hills. Their property and goods, which exceeded all computation, and their countless cows and buffaloes, fell as spoil into the hands of my victorious soldiers.[223]

Timur then traversed the Sivalik Hills to Kanra, which was pillaged and sacked, along with Jammu, "everywhere the inhabitants being slaughtered like cattle."[224]

Srivastava summarizes India's devastated condition following Timur's departure:

> Timur left [India] prostrate and bleeding. There was utter confusion and misery throughout northern India. [India's] northwestern provinces, including northern tracts of Rajasthan and Delhi, were so thoroughly ravaged, plundered and even burnt that it took these parts many years, indeed, to recover their prosperity. Lakhs [hundreds of thousands] of men, and in some cases, many women and children, too, were butchered in cold blood. The rabi crops [grown in October/November, harvested around March, including barley, mustard, and wheat] standing in the field were completely destroyed for many miles on both sides of the invader's long and double route from the Indus to Delhi and back. Stores of grain were looted or destroyed. Trade, coonerce and other signs of material prosperity disappeared. The city of Delhi was depopulated and ruined. It was without a master or a caretaker. There was scarcity and virulent famine in the capital and its suburbs. This was followed by a pestilence caused by the pollution of the air and water by thousands of uncared-for dead bodies. In the words of the historian Badauni, "those of the inhabitants who were left died (of famines and pestilence), while for two months not a bird moved wing in Delhi."[225]

The thirteenth-century chronicler Bar Hebraeus (d. 1286) provided this contemporary assessment of how the adoption of Islam radically altered Mongol attitudes toward their Christian subjects: "And having seen very much modesty and other habits of this kind among Christian people, certainly the Mongols loved them greatly at the beginning of their kingdom, a time ago somewhat short. But their love hath turned to such intense hatred that they cannot even see them with their eyes approvingly, because they have all alike become Muslims, myriads of people and peoples."[226]

Bar Hebraeus's observations should be borne in mind when evaluating Grousset's uncompromising overall assessment of Timur's deeds and motivations. After recounting Timur's 1403 ravages in Georgia, slaughtering the inhabitants, and destroying all the Christian churches of Tiflis, Grousset states:

> It has been noted that the Jenghiz-Khanite Mongol invasion of the thirteenth century was less cruel, for the Mongols were mere barbarians who killed simply because for centuries this had been the instinctive behavior of nomad herdsmen toward sedentary farmers. To this ferocity Tamerlane [Timur] added a taste for religious murder. He killed from Qur'anic piety. He represents a synthesis, probably unprecedented in history, of Mongol barbarity and Muslim fanaticism, and symbolizes that advanced form of primitive slaughter which is murder committed for the sake of an abstract ideology, as a duty and a sacred mission.[227]

Jihad Conquests on the Indian Subcontinent

The 570-year period between the initial Arab Muslim *razzias* (ordered by Caliph Umar) to pillage Thana (on the West Indian coast near Maharashtra) in 636–637 CE, and the establishment of the Delhi Sultanate (under Qutub-ud-din Aibak, a Turkish slave soldier), can be divided into four major epochs: (1) the conflict between the Arab invaders and the (primarily) Hindu resisters on the western coast of India from 636 to 713; (2) the Arab and Turkish Muslim onslaughts against the kingdom of Hindu Afghanistan from 636 to 870; (3) repeated Turkish efforts to subdue the Punjab from 870 to 1030, highlighted by the devastating campaigns of Mahmud of Ghazni (from 1000 to 1030); and, finally, (4) Muhammad Ghauri's conquest of northwestern India and the Gangetic valley between 1175 and 1206.[228]

This summary chronology necessarily overlooks the very determined and successful resistance that was offered by the Hindus to both the Arab (in particular) and Turkish invaders, for almost four centuries. For example, despite the rapidity of Mahmud of Ghazni's conquests—spurred by shock tactics and the religious zealotry of Islamic jihad—for almost 150 years, his successors could not extend their domain beyond the Punjab frontiers. Even after the establishment of the Delhi Sultanate (1206–1526), and the later Mughal Empire (1526–1707), Muslim rulers failed to Islamize large swaths of Indian territory and most of the populace.[229] The first Mughal emperor, Babur (1483–1530), made these relevant observations upon establishing his rule in India: "[Hindustan] is a different world . . . once the water of Sindh is crossed, everything is in the Hindustan way—land, water, tree, rock, people, and horde, opinion and custom. . . . Most of the inhabitants of Hindustan are pagans; they call a pagan a Hindu."[230]

Buddhist civilization within India, in stark contrast, proved far less resilient. Vincent Smith has described the devastating impact of the late-twelfth-century jihad *razzias* against the Buddhist communities of northern India, centered around Bihar, based exclusively on Muslim sources:

> The Muhammadan historian, indifferent to distinctions among idolators, states that the majority of the inhabitants were "clean shaven Brahmans," who were all put to the sword. He evidently means Buddhist monks, as he was informed that the whole city and fortress were considered to be a college, which the name Bihar signifies. A great library was scattered. When the victors desired to know what the books might be no man capable of explaining their contents had been left alive. No doubt everything was burnt. The multitude of images used in Medieval Buddhist worship always inflamed the fanaticism of Muslim warriors to such fury that no quarter was given to the idolators. The ashes of the Buddhist sanctuaries at Sarnath near Benares still bear witness to the rage of the image breakers. Many noble monuments of the ancient civilization of India were irre-

trievably wrecked in the course of the early Muhammadan invasions. Those invasions were fatal to the existence of Buddhism as an organized religion in northern India, where its strength resided chiefly in Bihar and certain adjoining territories. The monks who escaped massacre fled, and were scattered over Nepal, Tibet, and the south. After A.D. 1200 the traces of Buddhism in upper India are faint and obscure.[231]

Three major waves of jihad campaigns (exclusive of the jihad conquest of Afghanistan) that succeeded, ultimately, in establishing a permanent Muslim dominion within India, that is, the Delhi Sultanate, are summarized in the following discussion. The imposition of *dhimmitude* upon the vanquished Hindu populations is also characterized, in brief.

The Muslim chroniclers al-Baladhuri (in *Kitab Futuh al-Buldan*) and al-Kufi (in the *Chachnama*) include enough isolated details to establish the overall nature of the conquest of Sindh by Muhammad b. Qasim in 712 CE.[232] These narratives, and the processes they describe, make clear that the Arab invaders intended from the outset to Islamize Sindh by conquest, colonization, and local conversion. Al-Baladhuri, for example, records that following the capture of Debal, Muhammad b. Qasim earmarked a section of the city exclusively for Muslims, constructed a mosque, and established four thousand colonists there.[233] The conquest of Debal had been a brutal affair, as summarized from the Muslim sources by Majumdar.[234] Despite appeals for mercy from the besieged Indians (who opened their gates after the Muslims scaled the fort walls), Muhammad b. Qasim declared that he had no orders (i.e., from his superior al-Hajjaj, the Governor of Iraq) to spare the inhabitants, and thus for three days a ruthless and indiscriminate slaughter ensued. In the aftermath, the local temple was defiled, and "700 beautiful females who had sought for shelter there, were all captured." The capture of Raor was accompanied by a similar tragic outcome.

> Muhammad massacred 6000 fighting men who were found in the fort, and their followers and dependents, as well as their women and children were taken prisoners. Sixty thousand slaves, including 30 young ladies of royal blood, were sent to Hajjaj, along with the head of Dahar [the Hindu ruler]. We can now well understand why the capture of a fort by the Muslim forces was followed by the terrible *jauhar* ceremony (in which females threw themselves in fire kindled by themselves), the earliest recorded instance of which is found in the *Chachnama*.[235]

Practical, expedient considerations lead Muhammad to desist from carrying out the strict injunctions of Islamic law[236] and the wishes of al-Hajjaj[237] by massacring the (pagan) infidel Hindus of Sindh. Instead, he imposed the *jizya* and associated restrictive regulations of *dhimmitude* upon the vanquished Hindus. As a result, the *Chachnama* records, "some [Hindus] resolved to live in their native land, but others took flight in order to maintain the faith of their ancestors, and their horses, domestics, and other property."[238] Thus, a lasting pattern was set that would persist, as noted by Majumdar, until the Mughal Empire collapsed at the end of Aurangzeb's reign (in 1707),

> of Muslim policy towards the subject Hindus in subsequent ages. Something no doubt depended upon individual rulers; some of them adopted a more liberal, others a more cruel and intolerant attitude. But on the whole the framework remained intact, for it was based on the fundamental principle of Islamic theocracy. It recognized only one faith, one people, and one supreme authority, acting as the head of a religious trust. The Hindus, being infidels or non-believers, could not claim the full rights of citizens. At the very best, they could be tolerated as *dhimmis*, an insulting title which connoted political inferiority. . . . The Islamic State regarded all non-Muslims as enemies, to curb whose growth in power was conceived to be its main interest. The ideal preached by even high officials was to exterminate them totally, but in actual practice they seem to have followed an alternative laid down in the Qur'an [i.e., 9:29] which calls upon Muslims to fight the unbelievers till they pay the *jizya* with due humility. This was the tax the Hindus had to pay for permission to live in their ancestral homes under a Muslim ruler.[239]

Mahmud of Ghazni, according to the British historian Sir Henry Elliot, launched some seventeen jihad campaigns into India between 1000 and his death in 1030.[240] Utbi, Mahmud's court historian, viewed these expeditions to India as a jihad to propagate Islam and extirpate idolatry.[241] K. S. Lal illustrates this religious zeal to Islamize by force, as manifested during a twenty-three-year period between 1000 and 1023:

> In his first attack of frontier towns in C.E. 1000 Mahmud appointed his own governors and converted some inhabitants. In his attack on Waihind (Peshawar) in 1001–3, Mahmud is reported to have captured the Hindu Shahiya King Jayapal and fifteen of his principal chiefs and relations some of whom like Sukhpal, were made Musalmans. At Bhera all the inhabitants, except those who embraced Islam, were put to the sword. At Multan too conversions took place in large numbers, for writing about the campaign against Nawasa Shah (converted Sukhpal), Utbi says that this and the previous victory (at Multan) were "witnesses to his exalted state of proselytism." In his campaign in the Kashmir Valley (1015) Mahmud "converted many infidels to Muhammadanism, and having spread Islam in that country, returned to Ghazni." In the later campaign in Mathura, Baran and Kanauj, again, many conversions took place. While describing "the conquest of Kanauj," Utbi sums up the situation thus: "The Sultan levelled to the ground every fort . . . and the inhabitants of them either accepted Islam, or took up arms against him." In short, those who submitted were also converted to Islam. In Baran (Bulandshahr) alone 10,000 persons were converted including the Raja. During his fourteenth invasion in 1023 C.E. Kirat, Nur, Lohkot and Lahore were attacked. The chief of Kirat accepted Islam, and many people followed his example.[242]

These continuous jihad campaigns were accompanied by great destruction and acts of wanton cruelty. Utbi describes the slaughter that transpired during the attacks on Thanesar and Sirsawa:

> The chief of Thanesar was . . . obstinate in his infidelity and denial of Allah, so the Sultan marched against him with his valiant warriors for the purpose of planting the standards of Islam and extirpating idolatry. . . . The blood of the infidels flowed so copiously that the stream was discoloured, and people were unable to drink it. . . . Praise be to Allah . . . for the honour he bestows upon Islam and Musalmans.[243]
>
> [At Sirsawa, t]he Sultan summoned the most religiously disposed of his followers, and ordered them to attack the enemy immediately. Many infidels were consequently slain or taken prisoners in this sudden attack, and the Musalmans paid no regard to the booty till they had satiated themselves with the slaughter of the infidels. . . . The friends of Allah searched the bodies of the slain for three whole days, in order to obtain booty.[244]

Mahmud's final well-known expedition in Hindustan, to Somanath in 1025 CE, was similarly brutal, and destructive: "Mahmud captured the place [Somanath] without much difficulty and ordered a general slaughter in which more than 50,000 persons are said to have perished. The idol of Somanath was broken to pieces which were sent to Ghazni, Mecca, and Medina and cast in streets and the staircases of chief mosques to be trodden by the Muslims going there for their prayers."[245]

More than nine hundred years apart, remarkably concordant assessments of Mahmud's devastating exploits have been written by the eleventh-century Muslim scholar Alberuni (a counselor to Mahmud) and the contemporary Indian historian A. L. Srivastava. First Alberuni, from about 1030:

"Mahmud utterly ruined the prosperity of the country . . . by which the Hindus became like atoms of dust scattered in all directions, and like a tale of old in the mouth of the people. Their scattered remains cherish of course the most inveterate aversion towards all Muslims. This is the reason too why Hindu sciences have retired far away from those parts of the country conquered by us, and have fled to places which our hand cannot yet reach, to Kashmir, Benares, and other places."[246]

In 1950 Srivastava wrote:

> To the Indian world of his day Mahmud was a veritable devil incarnate—a daring bandit, an avaricious plunderer, and wanton destroyer of Art. He plundered many dozens of . . . flourishing cities; he razed to the ground great temples which were wonderful works of art; he carried thousands of innocent women and children into slavery; he indulged in wanton massacre practically everywhere he went; and . . . he forcibly converted hundred of . . . unwilling people to Islam. A conqueror who leaves behind desolate towns and villages and dead bodies of innocent human beings cannot be remembered by posterity by any other title.[247]

Lal believes that by the late twelfth century, Muhammad Ghauri was consummately prepared for the conquest and rule of India. Well-elaborated theological justifications for jihad, and comprehensive writings on India's geography and sociopolitical culture were readily available to him, complementing his powerful army of Turks, Persians, and Afghans.

> He now possessed Alberuni's *India* and Burhanuddin's *Hidayah*, works which were not available to his predecessor invader. Alberuni's encyclopedic work provided to the Islamic world in the eleventh century all that was militarily advantageous to know about India. Equally important was the Hidayah, the most authentic work on the laws of Islam compiled by Shaikh Burhanuddin Ali in the twelfth century. These and similar works, and the military manuals like the Siyasat Nama and Adab-ul-Harb, made the Ghauris and their successors better equipped for the conquest and governance of non-Muslim India. There need be no doubt that such works were made available, meticulously studied and constantly referred to by scholars attached to the courts of Muslim conquerors and kings.[248]

Muhammad Ghauri launched his first expeditions against Multan and Gujarat (in 1175 and 1178 CE, respectively). By 1191–92, following Ghauri's defeat of a Rajput confederation under Prithviraj Chauhan (and Prithviraj Chauhan's death), "Sirsuti, Samana, Kuhram, and Hansi were captured in quick succession with ruthless slaughter and a general destruction of temples, and their replacement by mosques. The Sultan then proceeded to Ajmer which too witnessed similar scenes. In Delhi an army of occupation was stationed at Indraprastha under the command of Qutub-ud-din Aibak who was to act as Ghauri's lieutenant in Hindustan. Later on Aibak became the first Sultan of Delhi."[249]

Qutub-ud-din Aibak's accession in 1206 (consistent with Muhammad Ghauri's desires and plans), marks the founding of the Delhi Sultanate.

Finally, the imposition of Islamic law upon the Hindu populations of India, that is, their relegation to *dhimmi* status, beginning with the advent of Muslim rule in eighth-century Sindh, had predictable consequences during both the Delhi Sultanate period (1206–1526), and the Mughal Empire (1526–1707). Srivastava highlights these germane features of Hindu status during the Delhi Sultanate:

> Throughout the period of the Sultanate of Delhi, Islam was the religion of the State. It was considered to be the duty of the Sultan and his government to defend and uphold the principles of this religion and to propagate them among the masses . . . even the most enlightened among them [the Sultans], like Muhammad bin Tughlaq, upheld the principles of their faith and refused permission to repair Hindu (or Buddhist) temples. . . . Thus even during the reign of the so-called liberal-minded Sultans, the Hindus had no permission to build new temples or to repair old ones. Throughout the period, they were known as *dhimmis*, that is, people living under guarantee, and the guarantee was that they

would enjoy restricted freedom in following their religion if they paid the *jizya*. The *dhimmis* were not to celebrate their religious rites openly . . . and never to do any propaganda on behalf of their religion. A number of disabilities were imposed upon them in matters of State employment and enjoyment of civic rights. . . . It was a practice with the Sultans to destroy the Hindu temples and images therein. Firoz Tghlaq and Sikander Lodi prohibited Hindus from bathing at the ghats [river bank steps for ritual bathers] in the sacred rivers, and encouraged them in every possible way to embrace the Muslim religion. The converts were exempted from the jizya and given posts in the State service and even granted rewards in cash, or by grant of land. In short, there was not only no real freedom for the Hindus to follow their religion, but the state followed a policy of intolerance and persecution. The contemporary Muslim chronicles abound in detailed descriptions of desecration of images and destruction of temples and of the conversion of hundreds and thousands of the Hindus. [Hindu] religious buildings and places bear witness to the iconoclastic zeal of the Sultans and their followers. One has only to visit Ajmer, Mathura, Ayodhya, Banaras and other holy cities to see the half broken temples and images of those times with their heads, faces, hands and feet defaced and demolished.[250]

R. C. Majumdar sees a continuum between the Delhi Sultanate and the subsequent Mughal Empire regarding the status of the Hindus:

So far as the Hindus were concerned, there was no improvement either in their material and moral conditions or in their relations with the Muslims. With the sole exception of Akbar, who sought to conciliate the Hindus by removing some of the glaring evils to which they were subjected, almost all other Mughal Emperors were notorious for their religious bigotry. The Muslim law which imposed many disabilities and indignities upon the Hindus . . . and thereby definitely gave them an inferior social and political status, as compared to the Muslims, was followed by these Mughal Emperors (and other Muslim rulers) with as much zeal as was displayed by their predecessors, the Sultans of Delhi. The climax was reached during the reign of Aurangzeb, who deliberately pursued the policy of destroying and desecrating Hindu temples and idols with a thoroughness unknown before or since.[251]

Majumdar also makes an interesting juxtaposition of Hindu cultural advancement under the lengthy period of Muslim colonial rule compared to the much shorter interval of British colonial rule: "Judged by a similar standard, the patronage and cultivation of Hindu learning by the Muslims, or their contribution to the development of Hindu culture during their rule . . . pales into insignificance when compared with the achievements of the British rule. . . . It is only by instituting such comparison that we can make an objective study of the condition of the Hindus under Muslim rule, and view it in its true perspective."[252]

JIHAD SLAVERY

The fixed linkage between jihad—a permanent, uniquely Islamic institution—and enslavement, provides a very tenable explanation for the unparalleled scale and persistence of slavery in Muslim dominions and societies. This general observation applies as well to "specialized" forms of slavery, including the (procurement and) employment of eunuchs, slave soldiering (especially of adolescents), other forms of child slavery, and harem slavery. Jihad slavery, in its myriad manifestations, became a powerful tool for both expansive Islamization and the maintenance of Muslim societies.

Juridical Rationale and Role in "Islamization"

Patricia Crone, in her recent analysis of the origins and development of Islamic political thought, makes an important nexus between the mass captivity and enslavement of non-Muslims during jihad campaigns and the prominent role of coercion in these major modalities of Islamization. Following a successful jihad, she notes:

> Male captives might be killed or enslaved, whatever their religious affiliation. (People of the Book were not protected by Islamic law until they had accepted *dhimma*.) Captives might also be given the choice between Islam and death, or they might pronounce the confession of faith of their own accord to avoid execution: jurists ruled that their change of status was to be accepted even though they had only converted out of fear. Women and children captured in the course of the campaigns were usually enslaved, again regardless of their faith. . . . Nor should the importance of captives be underestimated. Muslim warriors routinely took large numbers of them. Leaving aside those who converted to avoid execution, some were ransomed and the rest enslaved, usually for domestic use. Dispersed in Muslim households, slaves almost always converted, encouraged or pressurized by their masters, driven by a need to bond with others, or slowly, becoming accustomed to seeing things through Muslim eyes even if they tried to resist. Though neither the *dhimmi* nor the slave had been faced with a choice between Islam and death, it would be absurd to deny that force played a major role in their conversion.[253]

For the idolatrous Hindus enslaved in vast numbers during the waves of jihad conquests that ravaged the Indian subcontinent for well over a half millennium (beginning at the outset of the eighth century CE), the guiding principles of Islamic law regarding their fate were unequivocally coercive. Jihad slavery also contributed substantively to the growth of the Muslim population in India. Lal elucidates both of these points:

The Hindus who naturally resisted Muslim occupation were considered to be rebels. Besides they were idolaters (mushrik) and could not be accorded the status of Kafirs, of the People of the Book—Christians and Jews. . . . Muslim scriptures and treatises advocated jihad against idolaters for whom the law advocated only Islam or death. . . . The fact was that the Muslim regime was giving [them] a choice between Islam and death only. Those who were killed in battle were dead and gone; but their dependents were made slaves. They ceased to be Hindus; they were made Musalmans in course of time if not immediately after captivity . . . slave taking in India was the most flourishing and successful [Muslim] missionary activity. . . . Every Sultan, as [a] champion of Islam, considered it a political necessity to plant or raise [the] Muslim population all over India for the Islamization of the country and countering native resistance.[254]

Vryonis describes how jihad slavery, as practiced by the Seljuks and early Ottomans, was an important modality of Islamization in Asia Minor between the eleventh and fourteenth centuries:

A further contributing factor to the decline in the numbers of Christian inhabitants was slavery. . . . Since the beginning of the Arab razzias into the land of Rum, human booty had come to constitute a very important portion of the spoils. There is ample testimony in the contemporary accounts that this situation did not change when the Turks took over the direction of the djihad in Anatolia. They enslaved men, women, and children from all major urban centers and from the countryside where the populations were defenseless. In the earlier years before the Turkish settlements were permanently affected in Anatolia, the captives were sent off to Persia and elsewhere, but after the establishment of the Anatolian Turkish principalities, a portion of the enslaved were retained in Anatolia for the service of the conquerors.[255]

After characterizing the coercive, often brutal methods used to impose the devshirme child levy, and the resulting attrition of the native Christian populations (i.e., from both expropriation and flight), Papoulia concludes that this Ottoman institution, a method of Islamization par excellence, also constituted a de facto state of war:

[T]hat the sources speak of piasimo (seizure) aichmalotos paidon (capture) and arpage paidon (grabbing of children) indicates that the children lost through the devishirme were understood as casualties of war. Of course, the question arises whether, according to Islamic law, it is possible to regard the devishirme as a form of the state of war, although the Ottoman historians during the empire's golden age attempted to interpret this measure as a consequence of conquest by force be'anwa. It is true that the Greeks and the other peoples of the Balkan peninsula did not as a rule surrender without resistance, and therefore the fate of the conquered had to be determined according to the principles of the Koran regarding the Ahl-al-Qitâb: i.e. either to be exterminated or be compelled to convert to Islam or to enter the status of protection, of aman, by paying the taxes and particularly the cizye (poll-tax). The fact that the Ottomans, in the case of voluntary surrender, conceded certain privileges one of which was exemption from this heavy burden, indicates that its measure was understood as a penalization for the resistance of the population and the devshirme was an expression of the perpetuation of the state of war between the conqueror and the conquered . . . the sole existence of the institution of devshirme is sufficient to postulate the perpetuation of a state of war.[256]

Under Shah Abbas I (1588–1626 CE), the Safavid Shiite theocracy of Iran expanded its earlier system of slave *razzias* into the Christian Georgian and Armenian areas of the Caucasus. Georgian, Armenian, and Circassian inhabitants of the Caucasus were enslaved in large numbers, and thereby converted to Shia Islam. The males were made to serve as (primarily) military or administrative slaves, while the females were forced into harems. A transition apparently took place between the seventeenth and eighteenth centuries such that fewer of the slaves came from the Caucasus, while greater numbers came via the Persian Gulf, originating from Africa.[257] Ricks notes that by the reign of Shah Sultan Husayn,

> The size of the royal court had indeed expanded if the numbers of male and female slaves including white and black eunuchs are any indicators. According to a contemporary historian, Shah Sultan Husayn (d. 1722) made it a practice to arrive at Isfahan's markets on the first days of the Iranian New Year (March 21) with his entire court in attendance. It was estimated by the contemporary recorder that 5,000 male and female black and white slaves including the 100 black eunuchs comprised the royal party.[258]

Clement Huart, writing in the early twentieth century, observed that slaves continued to be the most important component of the booty acquired during jihad campaigns or *razzias*: "Not too long ago several expeditions crossed Amoû-Deryâ, i.e. the southern frontier of the steppes, and ravaged the eastern regions of Persia in order to procure slaves; other campaigns were launched into the very heart of unexplored Africa, setting fire to the inhabited areas and massacring the peaceful animist populations that lived there."[259]

Willis characterizes the timeless Islamic rationale for the enslavement of such "barbarous" African animists as follows:

> [A]s the opposition of Islam to kufr erupted from every corner of malice and mistrust, the lands of the enslavable barbarian became the favorite hunting ground for the "people of reason and faith"—the parallels between slave and infidel began to fuse in the heat of jihad. Hence whether by capture or sale, it was as slave and not citizen that the kafir was destined to enter the Muslim domain. And since the condition of captives flowed from the status of their territories, the choice between freedom and servility came to rest on a single proof: the religion

of a land is the religion of its amir (ruler); if he be Muslim, the land is a land of Islam (dar al-Islam); if he be pagan, the land is a land of unbelief (dar al-kufr). Appended to this principle was the kindred notion that the religion of a land is the religion of its majority; if it be Muslim, the land is a land of Islam; if it be pagan, the land is a land of kufr, and its inhabitants can be reckoned within the categories of enslavement under Muslim law. Again, as slavery became a simile for infidelity, so too did freedom remain the signal feature of Islam. . . . The servile estate was hewn out of the ravaged remains of heathen villages—from the women and children who submitted to Islam and awaited their redemption . . . [according to Muslim jurist] al-Wanshirisi (d. 1508), slavery is an affliction upon those who profess no Prophecy, who bear no allegiance to religious law. Moreover, slavery is an humiliation—a subjection—which rises from infidelity.[260]

Based on his study and personal observation of Muslim slave *razzias* gleaned while serving in the Sudan during the Mahdist jihad at the close of the nineteenth century, Winston Churchill wrote this description in 1899:

[A]ll [of the Arab Muslim tribes in the Sudan], without exception, were hunters of men. To the great slave markets of Jeddah a continual stream of negro captives has flowed for hundreds of years. The invention of gunpowder and the adoption by the Arabs of firearms facilitated the traffic. . . . Thus the situation in the Sudan for several centuries may be summed up as follows: The dominant race of Arab invaders was increasingly spreading its blood, religion, customs, and language among the black aboriginal population, and at the same time it harried and enslaved them. . . . The warlike Arab tribes fought and brawled among themselves in ceaseless feud and strife. The negroes trembled in apprehension of capture, or rose locally against their oppressors.[261]

All these elements of jihad slavery—its juridical rationale, employment as a method of forcible Islamization (for non-Muslims in general, and directed at sub-Saharan African animists, specifically), and its association with devshirme-like levies of adolescent males for slave soldiering—are apparent in the contemporary jihad being waged against the animists and Christians of southern Sudan by the Arab Muslim–dominated Khartoum regime.[262]

Extent and Persistence

The scale and scope of Islamic slavery in Africa are comparable to the Western transatlantic slave trade to the Americas, and as Willis has observed (somewhat wryly), the former "out-distances the more popular subject in its length of duration."[263] Quantitative estimates for the transatlantic slave trade (between the sixteenth and late nineteenth centuries) of 10.5 million (or somewhat higher),[264] are at least matched (if not exceeded by 50 percent) by a contemporary estimate for the Islamic slave trade out of Africa. Professor Ralph Austen's working figure for this composite of the trans-Saharan, Red Sea, and Indian Ocean traffic generated by the Islamic slave trade from 650 to 1905 CE, is 17 million.[265] Moreover, the plight of those enslaved animist peoples drawn from the savannah and northern forest belts of western and central Africa for the trans-Saharan trade was comparable to the sufferings experienced by the unfortunate victims of the transatlantic slave trade, as acknowledged by John Wright: "In the nineteenth century, slaves reached the ports of Ottoman Tripoli by three main Saharan routes, all so harsh that the experience of slaves forced to travel them bore comparison with the horrors of the so-called 'middle-passage' of the Atlantic."[266]

This illuminating comparison, important as it is, ignores other vast domains of jihad slavery: throughout Europe (Mediterranean and western Europe, as well as central and eastern Europe, involving the Arabs [western/Mediterranean], and later the Ottoman Turks and Tatars [central and eastern Europe]); Muscovite Russia (subjected to Tatar depredations); Asia Minor (under Seljuk and Ottoman domination); Persia, Armenia, and Georgia (subjected to the systematized jihad slavery campaigns waged by the Shiite Safavids, in particular); and the Indian subcontinent (*razzias* and jihad campaigns by the Arabs in the seventh and eighth centuries, and later depredations by the Ghaznavids, during the Delhi Sultanate, the Timurid jihad, and under the Mughals). As a cursory introduction to the extent of jihad slavery beyond the African continent, three brief examples are provided: the Seljuks in Asia Minor (eleventh and twelfth centuries); the Ottomans in the Balkans (fifteenth century); and the Tatars in southern Poland and Muscovite Russia (mid-fifteenth through seventeenth centuries).

The capture of Christians in Asia Minor by the Seljuk Turks was very extensive in the eleventh and twelfth centuries.[267] Following the seizure and pillage of Edessa, sixteen thousand were enslaved.[268] Michael the Syrian reported that when the Turks of Nur al-Din were brought into Cilicia by Mleh the Armenian, they enslaved sixteen thousand Christians, whom they sold at Aleppo.[269] A major series of *razzias* conducted in the Greek provinces of western Asia Minor enslaved thousands of Greeks (Vryonis believes the figure of one hundred thousand cited in a contemporary account is exaggerated),[270] and according to Michael the Syrian, they were sold in slave markets as far away as Persia.[271] During *razzias* conducted by the Turks in 1185 and over the next few years, twenty-six thousand inhabitants from Cappadocia, Armenia, and Mesopotamia were captured and sent off to the slave markets.[272] Vryonis concludes: "[T]hese few sources seem to indicate that the slave trade was a flourishing one. In fact, Asia Minor continued to be a major source of slaves for the Islamic world through the 14th century."[273]

The Ottoman sultans, in accord with sharia prescriptions, promoted jihad slavery aggressively in the Balkans, especially during the fifteenth-century reigns of Mehmed I (1402–1421), Murad II (1421–1451), and Mehmed II (1451–1481).[274] Alexandrescu-Dersca summarizes the considerable extent of this enslavement, and suggests the importance of its demographic effect:

The contemporary Turkish, Byzantine and Latin chroniclers are unanimous in recognizing that during the campaigns conducted on behalf of the unification of Greek and Latin Romania and the Slavic Balkans under the banner of Islam, as well as during their *razzias* on Christian territory, the Ottomans reduced masses of inhabitants to slavery. The Ottoman chronicler Ašikpašazade relates that during the expedition of Ali pasha Evrenosoghlu in Hungary (1437), as well as on the return from the campaign of Murad II against Belgrade (1438), the number of captives surpassed that of the combatants. The Byzantine chronicler Ducas states that the inhabitants of Smederevo, which was occupied by the Ottomans, were led off into bondage. The same thing happened when the Turks of Menteše descended upon the islands of Rhodes and Cos and also during the expedition of the Ottoman fleet to Enos and Lesbos. Ducas even cites numbers: 70,000 inhabitants carried off into slavery during the campaign of Mehmed II in Morée (1460). The Italian Franciscan Bartholomé de Yano (Giano dell'Umbria) speaks about 60,000 to 70,000 slaves captured over the course of two expeditions of the *akinĝis* in Transylvania (1438) and about 300,000 to 600,000 Hungarian captives. If these figures seem exaggerated, others seem more accurate: forty inhabitants captured by the Turks of Menteše during a *razzia* in Rhodes, 7,000 inhabitants reduced to slavery following the siege of Thessalonika (1430), according to John Anagnostes, and ten thousand inhabitants led off into captivity during the siege of Mytilene (1462), according to the Metropolitan of Lesbos, Leonard of Chios. Given the present state of the documentation available to us, we cannot calculate the scale on which slaves were introduced into Turkish Romania by this method. According to Bartholomé de Yano, it would amount to 400,000 slaves captured in the four years from 1437 to 1443. Even allowing for a certain degree of exaggeration, we must acknowledge that slaves played an important demographic part during the fifteenth-century Ottoman expansion.[275]

Alan Fisher has analyzed the slave *razzias* conducted by the Muslim Crimean Tatars against the Christian populations of southern Poland and Muscovite Russia from the mid-fifteenth to late seventeenth centuries (1463–1794).[276] Relying upon admittedly incomplete sources (". . . no doubt there are many more slave raids that the author has not uncovered"[277]), his conservative tabulations indicate that at least 3 million persons—men, women, and children—were captured and enslaved during this so-called harvesting of the steppe.[278] Fisher describes the plight of those enslaved:

[T]he first ordeal [of the captive] was the long march to the Crimea. Often in chains and always on foot, many of the captives died en route. Since on many occasions the Tatar raiding party feared reprisals or, in the seventeenth century, attempts by Cossack bands to free the captives, the marches were hurried. Ill or wounded captives were usually killed rather than be allowed to slow the procession. Heberstein wrote . . . "the old and infirm men who will not fetch much as a sale, are given up to the Tatar youths either to be stoned, or thrown into the sea, or to be killed by any sort of death they might please." An Ottoman traveler in the mid-sixteenth century who witnessed one such march of captives from Galicia marveled that any would reach their destination—the slave markets of Kefe. He complained that their treatment was so bad that the mortality rate would unnecessarily drive their price up beyond the reach of potential buyers such as himself. A Polish proverb stated: "Oh how much better to lie on one's bier, than to be a captive on the way to Tartary."[279]

The persistence of Islamic slavery is as impressive and unique as its extent. Slavery was openly practiced in both Ottoman Turkey[280] and Shiite (Qajar) Iran[281] through the first decade of the twentieth century. As Ehud Toledano points out regarding Ottoman Turkey, *kul* (administrative)/*harem* slavery "survived at the core of the Ottoman elite until the demise of the empire and the fall of the house of Osman in the second decade of the twentieth century."[282]

Moreover, Ricks indicates that despite the modernizing pressures and reforms culminating in the Iranian Constitutional Movement of 1905–1911, which effectively eliminated military and agricultural slavery, "The presence of domestic slaves, however, in both the urban and rural regions of Southern Iran had not ceased as quickly. Some Iranians today attest to the continued presence of African and Indian slave girls."[283]

Slavery on the Arabian Peninsula was not abolished formally until 1962 in Saudi Arabia[284] and 1970 in Yemen and Oman.[285] Writing in 1989, Murray Gordon observed that although Mauritania abolished slavery officially on July 15, 1980, "as the government itself acknowledges, the practice is still alive and well. It is estimated that 200,000 men, women, and children are subject to being bought and sold like so many cattle in this North African country, toiling as domestics, shepherds, and farmhands."[286]

Finally, as discussed earlier, there has been a recrudescence of jihad slavery since 1983 in the Sudan.[287]

An Overview of Eunuch Slavery—the "Hideous Trade"

Eunuch slaves—males castrated usually between the ages of four and twelve (due to the high risk of death, preferentially between ages eight and twelve)[288]—were in considerable demand in Islamic societies. They served most notably as super-visors of women in the harems of the rulers and elites of the Ottoman Empire, its contemporary Muslim neighbors (such as Safavid Iran), and earlier Muslim dominions. The extent and persistence of eunuch slavery—becoming prominent within two hundred years of the initial seventh-century Arab jihad conquests[289] and continuing through the beginning of the twentieth century[290]—are peculiar to the Islamic incarnation of this aptly named "hideous trade." For example, Toledano documents that as late as 1903, the Ottoman imperial harem contained between four hundred to five hundred female slaves, supervised and guarded by 194 black African eunuchs.[291]

But an equally important and unique feature of Muslim eunuch slavery was the acquisition of eunuchs from foreign "slave producing areas," that is, non-Muslim frontier zones subjected to *razzias*.[292] As David Ayalon observed, "[T]he overwhelming majority of the eunuchs, like the overwhelming majority of all other slaves in Islam, had been brought over from outside the borders of Muslim lands."[293] In stark contrast, eunuch slaves in China were almost exclusively Chinese procured locally.[294]

Jan Hogendorn has identified the three main slave-producing regions, as they evolved in importance over time, between the eighth and late nineteenth centuries: "These areas were the forested parts of central and eastern Europe called by Muslims the 'Bild as-Saqaliba' ('slave country'), the word saqlab meaning slave in Arabic (and related to the ethnic designation 'Slav'); the steppes of central Asia called the "Bilad al-Atrak" ('Turks' country' or Turkestan); and eventually most important, the savanna and the fringes of the wooded territory south of the Sahara called the country of the blacks or 'Bilad as-Sudan.'"[295]

Finally, given the crudeness of available surgical methods and absence of sterile techniques, the human gelding procedure by which eunuchs were "manufactured" was associated with extraordinary rates of morbidity and mortality. Hogendorn describes the severity of the operation, and provides mortality information from West and East Africa:

> Castration can be partial (removal of the testicles only or removal of the penis only), or total (removal of both). In the later period of the trade, that is, after Africa became the most important source for Mediterranean Islam, it appears that most eunuchs sold to the markets underwent total removal. This version of the operation, though considered most appropriate for slaves in constant proximity to harem members, posed a very high danger of death for two reasons. First was the extensive hemorrhaging, with the consequent possibility of almost immediate death. The hemorrhaging could not be stopped by traditional cauterization because that would close the urethra leading to eventual death because of inability to pass urine. The second danger lay in infection of the urethra, with the formation of pus blocking it and so causing death in a few days.
>
> [W]hen the castration was carried out in sub-Saharan West and West-Central Africa . . . a figure of 90% [is] often mentioned. Even higher death rates were occasionally reported, unsurprising in tropical areas where the danger of infection of wounds was especially high. At least one contemporary price quotation supports a figure of over 90% mortality: Turkish merchants are said to have been willing to pay 250 to 300 (Maria Theresa) dollars each for eunuchs in Borno (northeast Nigeria) at a time when the local price of young male slaves does not seem to have exceeded about 20 dollars. . . . Many sources indicate very high death rates from the operation in eastern Africa. Richard Millant's [1908] general figure for the Sudan and Ethiopia is 90%.[296]

Conclusions

Throughout the twentieth century, uniform summary assessments of the unique Muslim institution of jihad have been provided by seminal Islamic scholars. The views of ten such scholars, beginning with Clement Huart in the first decade of the twentieth century and culminating with Bassam Tibi in the final decade, are presented below.

Clement Huart (1907):

> [W]e are pointing out a permanent historic force [i.e, jihad], which is ceaselessly renewed down through the generations, independent of race, color, climate, and all external circumstances, never beaten, ever being reborn. This force is the deeply-held conviction, rooted in the soul of every Moslem without exception, that he was created to fight *on the path of God*, and that at the call of the supreme authority he *must* get up and go, not reluctantly but joyfully, so that the word of God might have the final word; so that, according to the Koranic expression, it might always be the highest. The Moslem jurists explain to us this state of soul with perfect clarity. [Jihad] Holy war is a categorical requirement, pure and simple, apart from any restrictive condition, such as, for example, the time in which it can be fulfilled or the need for an act of aggression [on the enemy's part] to provide a [suitable] occasion. It is a law of God, which is part of the worship that must be rendered to him, since the doctors [of the law] classify in the category of the *'ibâdât* or acts of adoration. The text of the Koran is explicit. It is true that the revelation of this took place only gradually. Mohammed received first the order to proclaim what he had been commanded and to turn away from the infidels (XV, 94), then to debate with them in the most persuasive manner, inviting them to follow the right path (XVI, 126); afterward, the believers were ordered to fight if someone attacked them (II, 87), at first on the condition that it not be during the four sacred months, then without conditions of any sort; and this last-mentioned text (II, 245) has governed the matter ever since, corroborated by a tradition of the Prophet which proclaims that the holy war will go on until the [final] resurrection.[297]

C. Snouck Hurgronje (1916):

> [Y]et another duty was most emphatically impressed on the Faithful; jihad, i.e., readiness to sacrifice life and possessions for the defense of Islam, understood, since the conquest of Mecca in 630, as the extension by force of arms of the authority of the Muslim state, first over the whole of Arabia, and soon after Muhammad's death over the whole world, so far as Allah granted His hosts for the victory.[298]

Henri Lammens (1929):

> The war against the non-Muslims, so frequently recommended in the Medinese suras, almost became . . . the sixth pillar of Islam. Islam owes to it her expansion,

in which "the mission" [missionary work], properly speaking, has played an insignificant role. The shari'a has always looked upon the Holy War as one of the principal duties of the Caliph. It continues to be regarded as a "required duty" (fard al-kifaya), not an individual obligation, but binding on the community as a whole. Thus if a Muslim sovereign or state consecrate themselves to it, it is considered as accomplished; but in theory the Jehad (Jihad) should know neither intermission nor end until the whole world has been conquered for Islam. This is one of the most incontestably popular concepts of the Islamic ideal. It is to this theory that we owe the geographical distinction between "dar al-harb" or "war territory," and "dar al-islam," or "the land of Islam," governed by the laws of the Qoran [Qur'an].[299]

Arthur Jeffery (1942):

The classical works on jurisprudence define it [jihad] quite baldly as "the religious duty of spreading Islam by force of arms" and lay down five propositions concerning it:

- It is a duty because such war was ordered by the Prophet
- It must continue until the whole world is under the domination of Islam
- The sovereign must be at the head of it and direct it—not some upstart, self-appointed leader
- The offer of Islam or Dhimmi status must be made before the attack is launched
- Any Muslim who dies fighting on Jihad is a shahid (martyr) and as such is assured of Paradise and in Paradise will have particular privileges.[300]

Majid Khadduri (1955 and 1966):

The universality of Islam provided a unifying element for all believers, within the world of Islam, and its defensive-offensive character produced a state of warfare permanently declared against the outside world, the world of war. Thus the jihad may be regarded as Islam's instrument for carrying out its ultimate objective by turning all people into believers, if not in the prophethood of Muhammad (as in the case of the dhimmis), at least in the belief of God. The Prophet Muhammad is reported to have declared "some of my people will continue to fight victoriously for the sake of the truth until the last one of them will combat the anti-Christ." Until that moment is reached the jihad, in one form or another will remain as a permanent obligation upon the entire Muslim community. It follows that the existence of a dar al-harb is ultimately outlawed under the Islamic jural order; that the dar al-Islam permanently under jihad obligation until the dar al-harb is reduced to non-existence; and that any community accepting certain disabilities—must submit to Islamic rule and reside in the dar al-Islam or be bound as clients to the Muslim community. The universality of Islam, in its all embracing creed, is imposed on the believers as a continuous process of warfare, psychological and political if not strictly military.

The Islamic state became necessarily an imperial and an expansionist state striving to win other peoples by conversion. At the very outset, the law of war, the jihad, became the chief preoccupation of jurists. The Islamic law of nations was essentially a law governing the conduct of war and the division of booty. This law was designed for temporary purposes, on the assumption that the Islamic state was capable of absorbing the whole of mankind; for if the ideal of Islam were ever achieved, the *raison d'être* of the law of war, at least with regard to Islam's relations with non-Islamic states, would pass out of existence.[301]

Antoine Fattal (1958):

Dhimma or dhimmi status . . . is one of the results of the *jihad* or holy war. Connected with the notion of *jihad* is the distinction between *dar al-harb* (territory or "house" of war) and *dar al-islam* (house of Islam). The latter includes all territories subject to Moslem authority. It is in a state of perpetual war with the *dar al-harb*. The inhabitants of the *dar al-harb* are *harbis*, who are not answerable to the Islamic authority and whose persons and goods are *mubah*, that is, at the mercy of Believers. However, when Moslems are in a subordinate state, they can negotiate a truce with the *harbis* lasting no more than ten years, which they are obliged to revoke unilaterally as soon as they regain the upper hand, following the example of the Prophet after Hudaibiyya.[302]

Armand Abel (1958):

For the Believer, the Koran presents the obligation to make war "in the way of God." At the time when this text was revealed, it was justified by the need to defend the community at Medina against the attacks of the "polytheists" of Mecca, and by the need to extend and enrich it at the expense of the Judeo-Christians, in particular the Jews of Khaybar. To all people, the book offered conversion as a means of making peace. To the People of the Book, it left the choice between conversion and "redemption," which at first was understood along the lines of the ancient manner in which the Arabs waged war, whereby the captive repurchased his freedom and his life at the cost of humiliation and a ransom. . . . The *hadith* that shows the Prophet writing "to" Negus, "to" Caesar," "to" Khosroès, in order to invite them to convert, is nothing but the seal of approval placed on this pretense, incorporating it into the totality of tradition that serves as a guide to the *Umma*. Together with the duty of the "war in the way of God" (or *jihad*), this universalistic aspiration would lead the Moslems to see the world as being divided fundamentally into two parts. On the one hand there was that part of the world where Islam prevailed, where salvation had been announced, where the religion that ought to reign was practiced; this was the *Dar ul Islam*. On the other hand, there was the part which still awaited the establishment of the saving religion and which constituted, by definition, the object of the holy war. This was the *Dar ul Harb*. The latter, in the view of the Moslem jurists, was not populated

by people who had a natural right not to practice Islam, but rather by people destined to become Moslems who, through impiousness and rebellion, refused to
accept this great benefit. Since they were destined sooner or later to be converted
at the approach of the victorious armies of the Prophet's successor, or else killed
for their rebelliousness, they were the rebel subjects of the Caliph. Their kings
were nothing but odious tyrants who, by opposing the progress of the saving religion together with their armies, were following a Satanic inspiration and rising
up against the designs of Providence. And so no respite should be granted them,
no truce: perpetual war should be their lot, waged in the course of the *winter and
summer ghazu*. [*razzias*] If the sovereign of the country thus attacked desired
peace, it was possible for him, just like for any other tributary or community, to
pay the tribute for himself and for his subjects. Thus the [Byzantine] Empress
Irene [d. 803] "purchased peace at the price of her humiliation," according to the
formula stated in the *dhimma* contract itself, by paying 70,000 pounds in gold
annually to the Caliph of Baghdad. Many other princes agreed in this way to
become tributaries—often after long struggles—and to see their dominions pass
from the status of *dar al Harb* to that of *dar al Sulh*. In this way, those of their
subjects who lived within the boundaries of the territory ruled by the Caliphate
were spared the uncertainty of being exposed arbitrarily, without any guarantee,
to the military operations of the summer *ghazu* and the winter *ghazu*: indeed,
anything within the reach of the Moslem armies as they advanced, being property of impious men and rebels, was legitimately considered their booty; their
men, seized by armed soldiers, were mercilessly consigned to the lot specified in
the Koranic verse about the sword, and their women and children were treated
like things.[303]

Joseph Schacht (1964):

The basis of the Islamic attitude towards unbelievers is the law of war; they must
be either converted or subjugated or killed (excepting women, children, and
slaves); the third alternative, in general, occurs only if the first two are refused. . . .
Apart from this, prisoners of war are either made slaves or killed or left alive as
free dhimmis or exchanged for Muslim prisoners of war, at the discretion of the
imam; also a treaty of surrender is concluded which forms the legal basis for the
treatment of the non-Muslims to whom it applies. It is often called *dhimma*. . . .
This treaty necessarily provides for the surrender of the non-Muslims with all
duties deriving from it, in particular the payment of tribute, i.e., the fixed poll-tax
(*jizya*) and the land tax (*kharaj*), the amount of which is determined from case to
case. The non-Muslims must wear distinctive clothing and must mark their houses,
which must not be built higher than those of the Muslims, by distinctive signs; they
must not ride horses or bear arms, and they must yield the way to Muslims; they
must not scandalize the Muslims by openly performing their worship or distinctive
customs, such as drinking wine; they must not build new churches, synagogues, or
hermitages; they must pay the poll-tax under humiliating conditions. . . . A non-
Muslim who is not protected by a treaty is called *harbi*, "in a state of war," "enemy
alien"; his life and property are completely unprotected by law.[304]

Rudolph Peters (1995):

The doctrine of the jihad, as laid down in the works on Islamic law, developed out of the Koranic prescriptions and the example of the Prophet and the first caliphs, which is recorded in the hadith. The crux of the doctrine is the existence of one single Islamic state, ruling the entire umma. It is the duty of the umma to expand the territory of this state in order to bring as many people under its rule as possible. The ultimate aim is to bring the whole earth under the sway of Islam and to extirpate unbelief: "Fight them until there is no persecution (or seduction) and the religion is God's (entirely)" [2:193 and 8:39]. Expansionist jihad is a collective duty (fard 'ala al-kifaya), which is fulfilled if a sufficient number of people take part in it. If this is not the case, the whole umma is sinning. . . . The most important function of the doctrine of jihad is that it mobilizes and motivates Muslims to take part in wars against unbelievers, as it is considered to be a fulfillment of a religious duty. The motivation is strongly fed by the idea that those who are killed on the battlefield, called martyrs (shahid, plur shuhada), will go directly to Paradise. At the occasion of wars fought against unbelievers, religious texts would circulate, replete with Koranic verses and hadiths extolling the merits of fighting a jihad and vividly describing the reward waiting in the hereafter for those slain during the fighting.[305]

Bassam Tibi (1996):

The establishment of the new Islamic polity at Medina and the spread of the new religion were accomplished by waging war. The sword became the symbolic image of Islam in the West. In this formative period of classical Islam, Islamic militancy was reinforced by the superiority of Muslims over their enemies. Islamic jurists never dealt with relations with non-Muslims under conditions other than those of "the house of war," except for the temporary cessation of hostilities under a limited truce. . . . At its core, Islam is a religious mission to all humanity. Muslims are religiously obliged to disseminate the Islamic faith throughout the world "We have sent you forth to all mankind" (Q. 34:28). If non-Muslims submit to conversion or subjugation, this call (da'wa) can be pursued peacefully. If they do not, Muslims are obliged to wage war against them. In Islam, peace requires that non-Muslims submit to the call of Islam, either by converting or by accepting the status of a religious minority (dhimmi) and paying the imposed poll tax, jizya. World peace, the final stage of the da'wa, is reached only with the conversion or submission of all mankind to Islam. . . . Muslims believe that expansion through war is not aggression but a fulfillment of the Qur'anic command to spread Islam as a way to peace. The resort to force to disseminate Islam is not war (harb), a word that is used only to describe the use of force by non-Muslims. Islamic wars are not hurub (the plural of harb) but rather futuhat, acts of "opening" the world to Islam and expressing Islamic jihad. Relations between dar al-Islam, the home of peace, and dar al-harb, the world of unbelievers, nevertheless take place in a state of war, according to the Qur'an and to the authoritative commentaries of Islamic jurists. Unbelievers who stand in the way, creating obstacles for the da'wa, are blamed for this state of war, for the da'wa can be pursued peacefully if others submit to it. In other words, those who resist Islam cause wars and are responsible for them. Only when Muslim power is weak is "temporary truce" (hudna) allowed (Islamic jurists differ on the definition of "temporary"). The notion of temporary peace introduces a third realm: territories under temporary treaties with Muslim powers (dar al-sulh or at times, dar al-'ahd). . . . The Western distinction between just and unjust wars linked to specific grounds for war is unknown in Islam. Any war against unbelievers, whatever its immediate ground, is morally justified. Only in this sense can one distinguish just and unjust wars in Islamic tradition. When Muslims wage war for the dissemination of Islam, it is a just war (futuhat, literally "opening," in the sense of opening the world, through the use of force, to the call of Islam); when non-Muslims attack Muslims, it is an unjust war ('idwan). The usual Western interpretation of jihad as a "just war" in the Western sense, is therefore a misreading of this Islamic concept. . . . According to the Western just war concept, just wars are limited to a single issue; they are not universal and permanent wars grounded on a religious worldview.[306]

In 1916 Hurgronje underscored how the jihad doctrine of world conquest remained a potent force among the Muslim masses thirteen centuries later:

[I]t would be a gross mistake to imagine that the idea of universal conquest may be considered as obliterated . . . the canonists and the vulgar still live in the illusion of the days of Islam's greatness. The legists continue to ground their appreciation of every actual political condition on the law of the holy war, which war ought never be allowed to cease entirely until all mankind is reduced to the authority of Islam—the heathen by conversion, the adherents of acknowledged Scripture by submission. Even if they admit the improbability of this at present, they are comforted an encouraged by the recollection of the lengthy period of humiliation that the Prophet himself had to suffer before Allah bestowed victory upon his arms; and they fervently join with the Friday preacher, when he announces the prayer taken from the Qur'an: "And lay not upon us, O our Lord, that for which we have not strength, but blot out our sins and forgive us and have pity upon us. Thou art our Master; grant us then to conquer the unbelievers." And the common people are willingly taught by the canonists and feed their hope of better days upon the innumerable legends of the olden time and the equally innumerable apocalyptic prophecies about the future. The political blows that fall upon Islam make less impression . . . than the senseless stories about the power of the Sultan of Stambul, that would instantly be revealed if he were not surrounded by treacherous servants, and the fantastic tidings of the miracles that Allah works in the Holy Cities of Arabia which are inaccessible to the unfaithful. The conception of the Khalifate still exercises a fascinating influence, regarded in the light of a central point of union against the unfaithful.[307]

Writing a quarter century after Hurgronje in 1942, Jeffery stressed why detailed consideration of the institution of jihad remained essential, "not merely academic," for understanding the contemporary Islamic world, for the theory of the world which it enshrines is still fundamental to the thinking of great masses of Muslim people to the present day. The troubles in India which lead up to the great Patna conspiracy trials of 1864 were due to the fact that Syed Ahmad of Oudh had preached against the Sikh cities of the Panjab a Jihad which later turned to one against all non-Muslim groups. The bloody episode of the Padri rebellion in Malaysia was due to the preaching of Jihad against the pagan Battak tribes. The Fula wars in the Hausa country [Western Sudan] in the early nineteenth century, which lead to Osman Dan Fodio's setting up the ephemeral sultanate of Sokoto, began as a jihad preached against the pagan king of Gobir. The Moplah rebellion in South India in 1921, with its massacres, forcible conversions, desecration of temples, and outrages on the hapless Hindu villagers, could be heard openly proclaimed as a Jihad in the streets of Madras.[308]

With the resurgence of jihad military campaigns and major acts of jihad terrorism literally across the globe in the last decades of the twentieth century through the present, Jeffery's additional insights from sixty-three years ago resonate prophetically:

> It is of course, easy to raise the objection that a Jihad in the old sense is impossible of realization in the modern world, for Islam is far too badly divided for anything like a general Jihad to be contemplated and far too weak in technical equipment for a Jihad to be successful even if started. This does not dispose of the fact, however, that the earlier conception of Jihad has left a deposit in Muslim thinking that is still to be reckoned with in the political relations of the Western world with Islam.[309]

In a 1999 essay, Mordechai Nisan provided a succinct recapitulation of the global resurgence of jihad campaigns during the second half of the twentieth century, affirming Jeffery's prescient observations from 1942.[310] By the mid-1960s aggressive jihad had reasserted itself, superseding those "fading and false ideological options" popular a decade earlier among the Islamic nations.[311] Indonesian Muslims, encouraged by a Sukarno regime fatwa, waged a jihad in 1965 against Indonesian Communists, exterminating some one hundred thousand to five hundred thousand.[312] Arab Muslim scholars and jurists, lamenting the failures of Arab nationalism after the crushing military defeat in the June 1967 war against Israel, convened an Islamic conference in 1968 under the aegis of the renowned Al-Azhar Academy of Islamic Research.[313] This assembly of learned Muslim speakers called for an annihilationist jihad against the Jews of Palestine. Repeated declarations expounded the classical Islamic doctrine of jihad war, focusing its bellicose energy on the destruction of Israel:

> Jihad is legislated in order to be one of the means of propagating Islam. Consequently Non-Muslims ought to embrace Islam either willingly or through wisdom and good advice or unwillingly through fight and Jihad. . . . It is

unlawful to give up Jihad and adopt peace and weakness instead of it, unless the purpose of giving up Jihad is for preparation, whenever there is something weak among Muslims, and their opponents are, on the other hand, strong. . . . War is the basis of the relationship between Muslims and their opponents unless there are justifiable reason for peace, such as adopting Islam. [Shaikh Abdullah Ghoshah, Chief Judge of the Hashemite Kingdom of Jordan]

Your honorable conference has been an Arab, Islamic and patriotic necessity in view of the present circumstances in which the Arabs and Muslims face the most serious difficulties. All Muslims expect you to expound Allah's decree concerning the Palestine cause, to proclaim that decree, in all clarity, throughout the Arab and Muslim world. We do not think this decree absolves any Muslim or Arab from Jihad (Holy War) which has now become a duty incumbent upon the Arabs and Muslims to liberate the land, preserve honor, retaliate for [lost] dignity, restore the Aqsa Mosque, the church of Resurrection, and to purge the birthplace of prophecy, the seat of revelation, the meeting-place of Prophets, the starting-point of Issa, and the scenes of the holy spirit, from the hands of Zionism—the enemy of man, of truth, of justice, and the enemy of Allah. . . . The well-balanced judgement frankly expressed with firm conviction is the first stop on the road of victory. The hoped-for judgment is that of Muslim Scholars who draw their conclusions from the Book of Allah, and the Summa of His prophet. May Allah guard your meeting, and guide your steps! May your decisive word rise to the occasion and enlighten the Arab and Muslim world, so that it may be a battle-cry, urging millions of Muslims and Arabs on to the field of Jihad, which will lead us to the place that once was ours. . . . Muslims who are distant from the battle-field of Palestine, such as the Algerians, the Moroccans, all the Africans, Saudi Arabia people, Yemeni people, the Indians, Iraqi people, the Russians, and the Europeans are indeed sinful if they do not hasten to offer all possible means to achieve success and gain victory in the Islamic battle against their enemies and the enemies of their religion. Particularly, this battle is not a mere combat between two parties but it is a battle between two religions (namely, it is a religious battle). Zionism in fact represents a very perilous cancer, aiming at domineering the Arab countries and the whole Islamic world. [Sheikh Hassan Khalid, Mufti of the Republic of Lebanon][314]

J. B. Kelly, writing in 1980, viewed the aroused spirit of jihad in the Arabian Gulf during the 1960s and 1970s—fomented by Faisal b. Abdul Azziz's implacable hatred for Israel, and the complementary doctrines of the Muslim brotherhood—as merely a return to the region's deep Islamic roots and values, following a brief dalliance with "revolutionary" ideologies:

Yet for all the anathematizing of Arab revolutionary movements by Muslim conservatives, it is extremely doubtful whether these movements are *au fond* anti-Islamic or irreligious. Marxist dogma sits very lightly and uncomfortably upon the few semi-educated peninsular Arabs who have ostensibly adopted it. Their thoughts and their lives are still shaped by Islam, they themselves are fundamentally Muslim. Nor could it be otherwise, since. . . . Islam is the only real source of moral and intellectual guidance available to Arabs of the peninsula. The present evidence of Islamic revivalism, therefore, may be a more significant indication of the drift of events in the Gulf than sporadic troublemaking by self-styled Marxist revolutionaries.[315]

Nisan maintains that the accession to power of leaders such as Mu'ammar Gadhafi in Libya (1969), Anwar Sadat in Egypt (1970), and even Hafiz al-Asad (November, 1970)—forced to acquiesce publicly to Islamic dictates by inserting a constitutional clause mandating the Syrian president be Muslim—"represented each in his own style the articulation of the Islamic idiom. . . . In these circumstances, Islam was assuming its command of the ideological high ground in the Arab world, awaiting the moment to conquer the political domain."[316]

The early successful phase of the October 1973 war against Israel, Nisan argues, marked the modern Badr (Muhammad's triumph over the pagan Meccans in 624 CE) for Sadat's Egypt, releasing the "jihadic genie" that within a decade, ironically, "led the 'Jihad Organization' in Egypt in 1981 to take his [Sadat's] life. The 'believing President' was judged a corrupter and mocker of Islamic values and principles. Jihad against Muslim heretic was a legitimate war in the name of *shari'a* and Koran."[317]

Nisan characterizes the use of the "oil weapon" by Islamic nations in the wake of the 1973 war as a "savored" exercise in "the exaction of tribute from a deflated and faltering enemy civilization."[318] The subsequent passage (November 10, 1975) of the United Nations resolution labeling Zionism as racism—initiated by the Arab-Soviet block—reflected Muslim desires to assert "leadership of the international community. The peaceful jihad against the post–Second World War Western political order was acquiring global sanction."[319]

This simmering caldron of global jihad movements was brought to full boil by two watershed events that both occurred in 1979: the restoration of a Shiite theocracy in Iran under Ayatollah Khomeini and the jihad in Afghanistan to repel the Soviet invasion. Khomeini's Iran embraced jihad "as a central pillar of faith and action,"[320] as demonstrated by the 1980–1988 war against impious, "socialist" Iraq and the unending campaign of vilification and proxy violence against the "Zionist entity" Israel. These struggles epitomized what Khomeini's Iran viewed as its "sacred struggle to cleanse the region and the world of Muslim and non-Muslim infidel blasphemy."[321] Muslim holy warriors in Afghanistan were supported by some $2 to $3 billion dollars in covert aid from the United States, augmented by Saudi funding, Iranian assistance, and Arab manpower. Following the forced withdrawal of the Soviet army from Afghanistan, "Arab Afghans," veteran jihadists from Egypt, Jordan, Saudi Arabia, and other Arab countries, openly proclaimed "the goal of establishing an International Islamic Army. Pakistan, having provided a base of operations of Afghani Muslim resistance against the Red Army, was reported to maintain 38 terrorist training centers on its territory from which fighters were sent regularly abroad to India, Bosnia, 'Palestine,' and a number of African states to further the jihad."[322]

Moved by these profound trends, the 1980s and 1990s witnessed escalating Muslim militancy and violence. During the 1980s, Nisan recounts,

A number of countries formalized the connection between *din wa dawla* (religion and state); Pakistan maintained its *shari'a* legal system while the Sudan, in 1984, adopted it; the Gulf countries radiated with tradition blended with riches; religious dress and behavior swept through Malaysia and Indonesia in ways which threatened, at least intimidated, the local Christians. The Shiite Hazballah organization demanded with its establishment in 1982 an Islamic Republic in Lebanon, while the National Islamic Front in Sudan established this type of religious polity in 1989. Libya had earlier committed itself to the injunctions of the Koran and Saudi Arabia recognized the shari'a along as its constitution.[323]

In the 1990s, Nisan observes, even two countries committed to secularism—Algeria and Turkey—faced powerful Islamic challenges:

In Algeria, the Islamic Salvation Front (FIS) promoted from the beginning of the 1990s the establishment of an Islamic republic, through the ballot box, and if not then through massive violence. . . . The Muslim militants/terrorists in Algeria conducted a war not only against the FLN regime but also against all foreign elements in the country, from tourists to foreign workers who during the 1990's were murdered in larger numbers. This was a holy war against Christendom in North Africa.

In Turkey, the legacy of Ataturk and the dogma of desacralization were challenged by the rise of the Refah Islamist Welfare/National Salvation Party, and the coming to power of its leader Necmettin Erbakan as prime minister in 1996 . . . the Islamic movement in Turkey, recovering from the Allied defeat of the Ottoman Empire in the First World War, sought a certain revenge against the West. Erbakan called for Pan-Muslim cooperation in the form of an Islamic common market to oppose the West in the world. At a minimum Turkey considered lowering its level within the NATO bloc, perhaps a step toward leaving the Western-led alliance system. Yet the military forced Erbakan from office in 1997 as the Islamic genie was pushed back into the bottle.[324]

This Islamic momentum continued unabated into the mid-1990s:

In the mid-90's the Islamic tempo rolled on. Muslims in Malaysia proposed that apostasy from Islam become a criminal offense. In India and Thailand Muslims clashed with others. In Kashmir a Muslim liberation movement challenged Indian rule. In Afghanistan the Taleban fundamentalist government advance a purist and ruthless model for an Islamic state. In West Java (Indonesia) Muslim rioters set fire to churches. Fundamentalist Islamic activity increased in Senegal and Uganda on the African continent. Muslim majorities in both Somalia and Sudan declared jihad against Christian populations.[325]

Nisan considers that at minimum, the "praxis" of Islam was to "extend the Muslim presence and role into the heart of Western civilization, after having constituted within the Muslim lands themselves a formidable strategic world position."[326] He concludes:

> The Muslim nation [umma] was by the mid-1990s numbering approximately one billion believers, possessing over 50 Muslim states, and in control of a little less than a third of United Nations membership; moreover, possessing more than 50 per cent of known crude oil resources and a combined military arsenal of conventional and non-conventional weaponry second only to the combined Western bloc of states. The international balance-of-power could not in the aftermath of the end of the Cold War ignore the Muslim civilization and its awesome pretensions to playing a dominant role in global affairs.[327]

Within several centuries of Muhammad's death in 632 CE, based upon the "proto-jihad" campaigns he waged in Arabia, Muslim jurists and theologians formulated the uniquely Islamic institution of permanent jihad war against non-Muslims for the submission of the known world to Islam. The historical record demonstrates that this jihad war theory has been put into practice by Muslims, continuously, across the globe, for more than a millennium, through present times. What remains is for the Muslim intelligentsia to acknowledge this practice, as Bat Ye'or explained in 1990:

> [T]his effort cannot succeed without a complete recasting of mentalities, the desacralization of the historic *jihad* and an unbiased examination of Islamic imperialism. Without such a process, the past will continue to poison the present and inhibit the establishment of harmonious relationships. When all is said and done, such self-criticism is hardly exceptional. Every scourge, such as religious fanaticism, the crusades, the inquisition, slavery, apartheid, colonialism, Nazism and, today, communism, are analyzed, examined, and exorcized in the West. Even Judaism—harmless in comparison with the power of the Church and the Christian empires—caught, in its turn, in the great modernization movement, has been forced to break away from some traditions. It is inconceivable that Islam, which began in Mecca and swept through three continents, should alone avoid a critical reflection on the mechanisms of its power and expansion. The task of assessing their history must be undertaken by the Muslims themselves.[328]

Finally, the great scholar of Islamic law G. H. Bousquet wrote in 1950,

> Islam first came before the world as a doubly totalitarian system. It claimed to impose itself on the whole world and it claimed also, by the divinely appointed Muhammadan law, by the principles of the *fiqh*, to regulate down to the smallest details the whole life of the Islamic community and of every individual believer. . . . [T]he study of Muhammadan law (dry and forbidding though it may appear

to those who confine themselves to the indispensable study of the *fiqh*) is of great importance to the world today.[329]

These words have even greater significance more than a half century later. Bousquet's admonition to study Islamic law, recognizing the profound importance of this endeavor, serves as a most fitting segue to the next two chapters: jihad ideology in the Muslim sacred texts, followed by extensive samples of how these motifs were incorporated into Muslim jurists' writings, which have institutionalized the jihad.

NOTES

1. Jacques Ellul, foreword to *Les Chretientes d'Orient entre Jihad et Dhimmitude. VIIe–XXe siecle* (1991); English translation in the preface to Bat Ye'or, *The Decline of Eastern Christianity under Islam* (Cranbury, NJ: Fairleigh Dickinson University Press, 1996), pp. 18–19.

2. Arthur Jeffery, "The Political Importance of Islam," *Journal of Near Eastern Studies* 1 (1942): 386.

3. Richard Bell, *The Qur'an*, vol. 1 (Edinburgh, 1937). In the preface Bell notes, with candor and humility:

> The main object has been to understand the deliverances of Muhammad afresh, as far as possible in their historical setting, and therefore to get behind the traditional interpretation. But the Moslem commentators have not been ignored. . . . It would be temerity in a European to question their understanding of the language. But dogmatic prepossessions sometimes vitiate their exegesis, and in many passages the grammatical construction is evidently difficult even to them. In these cases, one may use one's own judgment, and seek the solution of the difficulty by methods which they were precluded from adopting. (p. v)

4. Ibid., p. 171. Parenthetical insertion of the word *jihad* by El Fadl himself. Bell's "heading" and full translation of Q. 9.29 to Q. 9.35, from p. 177, are provided below:

> *People of the Book to be subdued; in preparation for the Expedition to the North, year IX.*
>
> 9:29. Fight against those who do not believe in Allah, nor in the Last Day, and do not make forbidden what Allah and His messenger have made forbidden, and do not practice the religion of truth, of those who have been given the Book, until they pay the *jizya* [Bell notes: "Tribute; later a distinction was drawn between *jizya* (poll-tax), and *kharaj* (land tax)"] off-hand [Bell notes: "The exact meaning of the phrase is uncertain."], being subdued.
>
> 9:30. The Jews say that Uzair [Ezra] is the son of Allah, and the Christians say that the Messiah is the son of Allah; that is what they say with their mouths, con-

forming to what was formerly said by those who disbelieved; Allah fight them! How they are involved in lies!

9:31. They take their scholars and their monks as Lords apart from Allah, as well as the Messiah, son of Mary, thought they were only commanded to serve one God, besides whom there is no other god; glory be to Him above whatever they associate (with him).

9:32. They would fain extinguish the light of Allah with their mouths, but Allah refuseth to do otherwise than perfect His light, though averse are the unbelievers.

9:33. He is it who hath sent His messenger with the guidance and the religion of truth, in order that he may set it above all (other) religion, though averse are the polytheists.

9:34. O ye who have believed, many of the scholars and monks consume the wealth of the people in vanity, and turn (others) aside from the way of Allah; those who treasure up their gold and silver and do not expend them in the way of Allah—to them give (thou) tidings of a painful punishment.

9:35. On the day when they [Bell notes: "i.e., their treasures"] will be made hot in the fire of Gehenna and their foreheads and their sides and their backs will be branded with them: "This is what ye treasured up for yourselves, so taste what ye have been treasuring up."

5. Jeffery, "The Political Importance of Islam," p. 386. Three decades earlier, W. R. W. Gardner (in "Jihad," *Moslem World* 2 [1912]: 348–49, 350, 354–55) had debunked, at length, similar apologetics written by Sheikh Muhammad Rida, Chiragh Ali, and others.

6. Arthur Jeffery, "Present Day Movements in Islam," *Moslem World* 33 (1943): 183.

7. Maxime Rodinson, "The Western Image and Western Studies of Islam," in *The Legacy of Islam*, ed. Joseph Schacht with C. E. Bosworth (London, 1974), p. 59.

8. Khaled Abou El Fadl, "The Place of Tolerance in Islam," in *The Place of Tolerance in Islam* (Boston, MA: Beacon Press, 2002), p. 19.

9. Khaled Abou El Fadl, "The Rules of Killing at War: An Inquiry into Classical Sources," *Muslim World* 89 (1999): 144–57.

10. Majid Khadduri, *War and Peace in the Law of Islam* (Baltimore, MD: Johns Hopkins University Press, 1955), pp. 63–64.

11. Rudolph Peters, *Jihad in Classical and Modern Islam* (Princeton, NJ: Markus Wiener, 1996), pp. 3, 5.

12. John Esposito, *Islam: The Straight Path* (New York: Oxford University Press, 1998), p. 58.

13. Bat Ye'or, *Islam and Dhimmitude*, p. 314.

14. Ibid., pp. 315–16.

15. Al-Tabari, *The History of al-Tabari (Ta'rikh al rusul wa'l-muluk)*, vol. 12: *The Battle of Qadissiyah and the Conquest of Syria and Palestine*, trans. Yohanan Friedman (Albany: State University of New York Press, 1992), p. 167.

16. "The Noble Qur'an," Muslim Students Association, University of Southern California, http://www.usc.edu/dept/MSA/quran/.

17. M. Muhsin Khan, "Translation of Sahih Bukhari," Muslim Students Association, University of Southern California, http://www.usc.edu/dept/MSA/fundamentals/hadithsunnah/bukhari/.

18. Abdul Hamid Siddiqi, "Translation of Sahih Muslim," Muslim Students Association, University of Southern California, http://www.usc.edu/dept/MSA/fundamentals/hadithsunnah/muslim/.

19. Ibn Abi Zayd al-Qayrawani, *La Risala* (*Epitre sur les elements du dogme et de la loi de l'Islam selon le rite malikite*), trans. Leon Bercher, 5th ed. (Algiers, 1960), p. 165.

20. Ibn Taymiyyah, in Peters, *Jihad in Classical and Modern Islam*, p. 49.

21. From the *Hidayah*, vol. 2, p. 140, excerpted in Thomas P. Hughes, "Jihad," in *A Dictionary of Islam* (London: W. H. Allen, 1895), pp. 243–48.

22. Al-Mawardi, *The Laws of Islamic Governance* [*al-Ahkam as-Sultaniyyah*], trans. Asadullah Yate (London: Ta-Ha, 1996), p. 60.

23. Ibn Khaldun, *The Muqudimmah: An Introduction to History*, trans. Franz Rosenthal, vol. 1 (New York: Pantheon, 1958), p. 473.

24. *Jami-i-Abbasi: yakdawrah-i fiqh-i Farsi*, trans. Baha' al-Din Muhammad ibn Husayn al-Amili (Tehran: Muasssasah-i Intisharat-i Farahani, 1980), pp. 153–54; English translation from the Farsi by Fatemeh Masjedi.

25. Harry W. Hazard, *Atlas of Islamic History* (Princeton, NJ: Princeton University Press, 1951).

26. Al-Tabari, *The History of al-Tabari* (Ta'rikh al rusul wa'l-muluk), vol. 12, *The Battle of Qadissiyah and the Conquest of Syria and Palestine*; vol. 13, *The Conquest of Iraq, Southwestern Persia, and Egypt*, trans. G. H. A. Juynboll (Albany: State University of New York Press, 1989); Al-Baladhuri, *The Origins of the Islamic State* (*Kitab Futuh al-Buldan*), trans. Philip K. Hitti (New York: Columbia University Press, 1916); Al-Kufi, *The Chachnāmah, Part I: Giving the Mussulman Period from the Arab Conquest to the Beginning of the Reign of the Kalhorahs*, trans. Mirza Kalichbeg Fredunbeg (Delhi: Delhi Reprint, 1979); H. M. Elliott and J. Dowson, *A History of India as Told by Its Own Historians*, vols. 1–8 (1867–1877; repr., Delhi: Delhi Reprint, 2001); V. S. Bhatnagar, trans., *Kanhadade Prabandha* (New Delhi, 1991; G. Roerich, trans., *Biography of Dharmasvamin* (*Chag lotsava Chos-rje-dpal*), *a Tibetan Pilgrim* (Patna, 1959); Mary Boyce, "Under the Caliphs," in *Zoroastrians—Their Religious Beliefs and Practices* (London: Routledge, 2001), pp. 145–62; Michael Morony, *Iraq after the Muslim Conquest* (Princeton, NJ: Princeton University Press, 1984), pp. 190–96, 381–82; Dimitar Angelov, "Certain aspects de la conquete des peuples balkanique par les Turcs," in *Les Balkans au moyen age. La Bulgarie des Bogomils aux Turcs* (London: Variorum Reprints, 1978), pp. 220–75; A. E. Vacalopoulos, *Origins of the Greek Nation—The Byzantine Period, 1204–1461* (New Brunswick, NJ: Rutgers University Press, 1970), pp. 59–85; Speros Vryonis Jr., *The Decline of Medieval Hellenism in Asia Minor and the Process of Islamization from the Eleventh through the Fifteenth Century* (Berkeley and Los Angeles: University of California Press, 1971), pp. 69–287; K. S. Lal, *The Legacy of Muslim Rule in India* (New Delhi: Aditya Prakashan, 1992); K. S. Lal, "Jihad under the Mughals," from *Theory and Practice of Muslim State in India* (New Delhi: Aditya Prakashan, 1999), pp. 62–68; Moshe Gil, *A History of Palestine, 634–1099* (Cambridge: Cambridge University Press, 1992), pp.

11–74; Bat Ye'or, *The Decline of Eastern Christianity under Islam* (Cranbury, NJ: Fairleigh Dickinson University Press, 1996), pp. 43–60; Demetrios Constantelos, "Greek Christian and Other Accounts of the Moslem Conquests of the Near East," in *Christian Hellenism: Essays and Studies in Continuity and Change* (New Rochelle, NY: A. D. Caratzas, 1998), pp. 125–44.

27. Al-Mawardi, *The Laws of Islamic Governance*, pp. 60, 77–78, 200–201.

28. E. W. Lane, *An Arabic-English Lexicon* (London, 1865), bk. 1, p. 422.

29. Jadunath Sarkar, "The Islamic State Church in India," in *History of Aurangzib*, vol. 3 (London: Longmans Green, 1929), pp. 283–318; S. D. Goitein, "Evidence on the Muslim Poll Tax from Non-Muslim Sources," *Journal of the Economic and Social History of the Orient* 6 (1963): 278–95; Bat Ye'or, *The Dhimmi: Jews and Christians under Islam* (Cranbury, NJ: Fairleigh Dickinson University Press, 1985), pp. 53–54; *Decline of Eastern Christianity under Islam*, pp. 77–79; *Islam and Dhimmitude: Where Civilizations Collide*, pp. 65–71.

30. Bat Ye'or, *Islam and Dhimmitude*, p. 70.

31. Goitein, "Evidence on the Muslim Poll Tax from Non-Muslim Sources," pp. 278–79.

32. Ibid., pp. 281–82; Bat Ye'or, *Decline of Eastern Christianity under Islam*, documents II.1, pp. 305–21.

33. Bat Ye'or, *Islam and Dhimmitude*, p. 70.

34. Ibid., p. 65.

35. Daniel C. Dennett Jr., *Conversion and the Poll Tax in Early Islam* (Cambridge, MA: Harvard University Press, 1950), p. 80; Goitein, "Evidence on the Muslim Poll Tax from Non-Muslim Sources," p. 279; Bat Ye'or, *Decline of Eastern Christianity under Islam*, documents II.1, pp. 305–21; Bat Ye'or, *Islam and Dhimmitude*, p. 65.

36. Bat Ye'or, *Islam and Dhimmitude*, p. 68.

37. Gil, *A History of Palestine*, p. 151; Bat Ye'or, *Decline of Eastern Christianity under Islam*, documents II.1, pp. 305–21.

38. Vryonis, *Decline of Medieval Hellenism in Asia Minor*; Ivo Andric, *The Development of Spiritual Life in Bosnia under the Influence of Turkish Rule* (Durham, NC: Duke University Press, 1990), pp. 20–38.

39. Bat Ye'or, *Islam and Dhimmitude*, pp. 70–71.

40. David Littman, "Jews under Muslim Rule in the Late Nineteenth Century," *Wiener Library Bulletin* 28 (1975): 75. Littman corrected the first name of Rabbi Elmaleh from Rabbi Abraham to Rabbi Avram (personal communication).

41. Al-Mawardi, *The Laws of Islamic Governance*, p. 211; Bat Ye'or, *Dhimmi*, p. 169; Lal, *Legacy of Muslim Rule in India*, p. 237.

42. For example, see Marghinian Ali ibn Abi Bakr, *The Hedaya, or Guide—A Commentary on the Mussulman Laws*, trans. Charles Hamilton (New Delhi, 1982), vol. 2, pp. 362–63:

> Malik and Shafi'i have said that their (i.e., the non-Muslim dhimmis) is absolutely inadmissible, because as infidels are unjust, it is requisite to be slow in believing anything they may advance. God having said (in the Koran) "When an unjust person tells you anything be slow in believing him"; whence it is that the evidence of an infidel is not admitted concerning a Mussulman; and conse-

quently that an infidel stands (in this particular) in the same predicament with an apostate. . . . Besides, a dhimmi may be suspected of inventing falsehoods against a Mussulman from the hatred he bears to him on account of the superiority of the Mussulmans over him.

And, from Joseph Schacht, *An Introduction to Islamic Law* (Oxford: Clarendon Press, 1982), p. 132:

[T]he dhimmi cannot be a witness, except in matters concerning other dhimmis.

43. W. M. Watt, trans., *The Faith and Practice of Al-Ghazali* (Oxford, 1953), p. 13.
44. Al-Ghazali, *Kitab al-Wagiz fi fiqh madhab al-imam al-Safi'i* (Beirut, 1979), pp. 186, 190–91, 199–200, 202–203, English trans. Dr. Michael Schub. Emphasis mine.
45. Ignaz Goldziher, introduction to *Islamic Theology and Law* (Princeton, NJ: Princeton University Press, 1981), p. 213.
46. Al-Majlisi, "The Treatise Lightning Bolts against the Jews," trans. V. B. Moreen, in *Die Welt des Islams* 32 (1992): 187–93.
47. Laurence Loeb, *Outcaste—Jewish Life in Southern Iran* (New York: Gordon and Breach, 1977), p. 21.
48. Al-Majlisi, *Lightning Bolts against the Jews*. The enduring nature of the fanatical *najas* regulation prohibiting *dhimmis* from being outdoors during rain and/or snow is well established. For examples, see items 4 and 5 of Israel Joseph Benjamin's list of "oppressions" in *Eight Years in Asia and Africa—From 1846–1855* (Hanover, 1859), pp. 211–13:

Item 4: "Under the pretext of their being unclean, they are treated with the greatest severity, and should they enter a street, inhabited by Mussulmans, they are pelted by the boys and mob with stones and dirt."; Item 5: "For the same reason they are forbidden to go out when it rains; for it is said the rain would wash dirt off them, which would sully the feet of the Mussulmans."

Also see item 1 of Hamadan's 1892 regulations, twenty-two in total, for its Jews, from a letter by S. Somekh, published in *The Alliance Israelite Universale*, October, 27, 1892, translated and reproduced in D. G. Littman, "Jews under Muslim Rule: The Case of Persia," *Weiner Library Bulletin* 32 (1979): 7–8:

The Jews are forbidden to leave their houses when it rains or snows [to prevent the impurity of the Jews being transmitted to the Shiite Muslims].

Regarding this condition, as well as the other twenty-one conditions, Somekh writes,

The latter [i.e., the Jews] have a choice between automatic acceptance, conversion to Islam, or their annihilation. Some who live from hand to mouth have consented to these humiliating and cruel conditions through fear, without offering resistance; thirty of the most prominent members of the community were surprised in the telegraph office, where they had gone to telegraph their grievances to Teheran. They were compelled to embrace the Muslim faith to escape from certain death. But the majority is in hiding and does not dare to venture into the streets." [p. 7]

This account was provided by the missionary Napier Malcolm (*Five Years in a Persian Town*, [New York, 1905], p. 107) who lived in the Yezd area at the close of the nineteenth century:

They [the strict Shi'as] make a distinction between wet and dry; only a few years ago it was dangerous for an Armenian Christian to leave his suburb and go into the bazaars in Isfahan on a wet [rainy] day. "A wet dog is worse than a dry dog."

Moreover, the late Persian Jewish scholar Sarah (Sorour) Soroudi ("The Concept of Jewish Impurity and its Reflection in Persian and Judeo-Persian Traditions," *Irano-Judaica* 3 [1994]: 156) related this family anecdote:

In his youth, early in the 20th century, my late father was eyewitness to the implementation of this regulation. A group of elder Jewish leaders in Kashan had to approach the head clergy of the town (a Shi'i community from early Islamic times, long before the Safavids, and known for its religious fervor) to discuss a matter of great urgency to the community. It was a rainy day and they had to send a Muslim messenger to ask for special permission to leave the ghetto. Permission granted, they reached the house of the clergy but, because of the rain, they were not allowed to stand even in the hallway. They remained outside, drenched, and talked to the mullah who stood inside next to the window.

Soroudi added this note as well:

As late as 1923, the Jews of Iran counted this regulation as one of the anti-Jewish restrictions still practiced in the country. (p. 156, n.36)

A more disconcerting twentieth-century anecdote from an informant living in Shiraz was recounted by anthropologist Laurence Loeb in *Outcaste*:

When I was a boy, I went with my father to the house of a non-Jew on business. When we were on our way, it started to rain. We stopped near a man who had apparently fallen and was bleeding. As we started to help him, a Muslim *akhond* (theologian) stopped and asked me who I was and what I was doing. Upon discovering that I was a Jew, he reached for a stick to hit me for defiling him by being near him in the rain. My father ran to him and begged the *akhond* to hit him instead. (p. 21)

Finally, Janet Kestenberg Amighi (*The Zoroastrians of Iran: Conversion, Assimilation, or Persistence* [New York: AMS Press, 1990]) has argued that the Zoroastrians were the lowest non-Muslim caste in Shiite Iran, and accordingly, subjected to the most severe *najas*-related restrictions:

In Yezd and Kerman (through the early 20th century), Moslem pollution prohibitions were strictly observed and extended to most aspects of life. A Moslem would not eat out of a dish touched by a Zoroastrian nor permit even his garment to be touched by a Zoroastrian. Zoroastrians were forbidden the use of most community facilities such as barber shops, bath houses, water fountains, and tea houses. Water and wetness were considered to be particularly strong carriers of pollution. Zoroastrians were not permitted to go to the market in the rain. They could not touch fruit when shopping in the bazaar, although the dry goods could be touched. (p. 85)

49. See Bat Ye'or's major works in English cited earlier, *Dhimmi, Decline of Eastern Christianity under Islam,* and *Islam and Dhimmitude.*

50. Jadunath Sarkar, "The Islamic State Church in India," *History of Aurangzib,* vol. 3: *Northern India, 1658–1681,* pp. 283–97. The scholar K. S. Lal records this translation, "and should the collector choose to spit into his mouth, opens the same without hesitation, so that the official may spit into it." Lal notes further that "[a]ctual spitting in the mouth of the non-Muslims was not uncommon." Lal cites a poem by Vijaya Gupta (1493–1519 CE), which includes the line, "The peons employed by the qazis tore away the sacred threads of the Brahmans and spat saliva in their mouths." From *Theory and Practice of Muslim State in India,* pp. 238–39n124.

51. Antoine Fattal, *Le Statut Legal de Musulmans en Pays' d'Islam* (Beirut, 1958), pp. 369, 372.

52. Mary Boyce, *Zoroastrians: Their Religious Beliefs and Practices* (1979; repr., London, 2001); *A Persian Stronghold of Zoroastrianism: Based on the Ratanbai Katrak Lectures, 1975* (Lanham, MD: University Press of America, 1989). During the initial jihad conquest of Persia, for example, forty thousand Zoroastrians were killed defending the royal city of Istakhr, where the religious library was housed.

53. Boyce, *Persian Stronghold of Zoroastrianism,* pp. 7–8. Napier Malcolm lived among the Zoroastrians in the central Iranian town of Yezd at the end of the nineteenth century. He documented the following in his narrative *Five Years in a Persian Town,* pp. 45–50:

Up to 1895 no Parsi (Zoroastrian) was allowed to carry an umbrella. Even during the time that I was in Yezd they could not carry one in town. Up to 1895 there was a strong prohibition upon eye-glasses and spectacles; up to 1885 they were prevented from wearing rings; their girdles had to be made of rough canvas, but after 1885 any white material was permitted. Up to 1896 the Parsis were obliged to twist their turbans instead of folding them. Up to 1898 only brown, grey, and yellow were allowed for the qaba [outer coat] or arkhaluq [under coat] (body garments), but after that all colors were permitted except blue, black, bright red, or green. There was also a prohibition against white stockings, and up to about 1880 the Parsis had to wear a special kind of peculiarly hideous shoe with a broad, turned-up toe. Up to 1885 they had to wear a torn cap. Up to 1880 they had to wear tight knickers, self-colored, instead of trousers. Up to 1891 all Zoroastrians had to walk in town, and even in the desert they had to dismount if they met a Mussulman of any rank whatsoever. During the time that I was in Yezd they were allowed to ride in the desert, and only had to dismount if they met a big Mussulman. There were other similar dress restrictions too numerous and trifling to mention.

Then the houses of both the Parsis and the Jews, with the surrounding walls, had to be built so low that the top could be reached by a Mussulman with his hand extended; they might, however, dig down below the level of the road. The walls had to be splashed with white around the door. Double doors, the common form of Persian door, were forbidden, also rooms containing three or more windows. Bad-girs [Air-shafts] were still forbidden to Parsis while we were in Yezd, but in 1900 one of the bigger Parsi merchants gave a large present to the Governor and to the chief mujtahid (Mohammedan priest) to be allowed to build one. Upper rooms were also forbidden.

Up to about 1860 Parsis could not engage in trade. They used to hide things in their cellar rooms, and sell them secretly. They can now trade in the caravanserais or hostelries, but not in the bazaars, nor may they trade in linen drapery. Up to 1870 they were not permitted to have a school for their children.

The amount of the jaziya, or tax upon infidels, differed according to the wealth of the individual Parsi, but it was never less than two tomans [a sum of money, 10,000 dinars]. A toman is now worth about three shillings and eight pence, but it used to be worth much more. Even now, when money has much depreciated, it represents a laborer's wage for ten days. The money must be paid on the spot, when the farrash [literally, a carpet sweeper. Really a servant, chiefly, outdoor], who was acting as collector, met the man. The farrash was at liberty to do what he liked when collecting the jaziya. The man was not even allowed to go home and fetch the money, but was beaten at once until it was given. About 1865 a farrash collecting this tax tied a man to a dog, and gave a blow to each in turn.

About 1891 a mujtahid caught a Zoroastrian merchant wearing white stockings in one of the public squares of the town. He ordered the man to be beaten and the stockings taken off. About 1860 a man of seventy went to the bazaars in white trousers of rough canvas. They hit him about a good deal, took off his trousers, and sent him home with them under his arm. Sometimes Parsis would be made to stand on one leg in a mujtahid's house until they consented to pay a considerable sum of money.

In the reign of the late Shah Nasiru'd Din, Manukji Limji, a British Parsi from India, was for a long while in Tehran as Parsi representative. Almost all the Parsi disabilities were withdrawn, the jaziya, the clothes restrictions, and those with regard to houses, but the law of inheritance was not altered, according to which a Parsi who becomes a Mussulman takes precedence of his Zoroastrian brothers and sisters. The jaziya was actually remitted, and also some of the restrictions as to houses, but the rest of the firman was a dead letter.

In 1898 the present Shah, Muzaffaru'd Din, gave a firman to Dinyar, the present Qalantar [Head Man] of the Parsi Anjuman, or Committee, revoking all the remaining Parsi disabilities, and also declaring it unlawful to use fraud or deception in making conversions of Parsis to Islam. This firman does not appear to have had any effect at all.

About 1883, after the firman of Nasiru'd Din Shah had been promulgated, one of the Parsis, Rustami Ardishiri Dinyar, built in Kucha Biyuk, one of the villages near Yezd, a house with an upper room, slightly above the height to which the Parsis used to be limited. He heard that the Mussulmans were going to kill him, so he fled by night to Tehran. They killed another Parsi, Tirandaz, in mistake for him, but did not destroy the house.

So the great difficulty was not to get the law improved, but rather to get it enforced. When Manukji [British Parsi and 'consul' in Tehran] was at Yezd, about 1870, two Parsis were attacked by two Mussulmans outside the town, and one was killed, the other terribly wounded as they had tried to cut off his head. The Governor brought the criminals to Yezd, but did nothing to them. Manukji got leave to take them to Tehran. The Prime Minister, however, told him that no Mussulman would be killed for a Zardushti, or Zoroastrian, and that they would only be bastinadoed. About this time Manukji enquired whether it was true that the blood-price of a Zardushti was to be seven tomans. He got back the reply that it was to be a little over.

The Yezd Parsis have been helped considerably by agents from Bombay, who are British subjects, and of late years things have improved slightly.

54. Gil, *A History of Palestine*, p. 11.

55. Ibid. See also Moshe Gil, "The Constitution of Medina: A Reconsideration," *Israel Oriental Studies* 4 (1974): 44–66. Gil concludes the following:

Through his alliance with the Arab tribes of Medina the Prophet gained enough strength to achieve a gradual anti-Jewish policy, despite the reluctance of his Medinese allies, who had formerly been those of the Jews. . . . Muslim sources have developed a tradition about a treaty between Muhammad and the Jews, be it this document or a lost one, as presumed by some modern scholars. Elsewhere, it is declared in complete sincerity that Muhammad, without invoking any treaty, simply asked the B. Qaynuqa before taking action against them, to accept Islam. . . . The document, therefore, was not a covenant with the Jews. On the contrary, it was a formal statement of intent to disengage the Arab clans of Medina from the Jewish neighbors they had been allied with up to that time. (pp. 64–65)

56. William Montgomery Watt, "Economic and Social Aspects of the Origin of Islam," *Islamic Quarterly* 1 (1954): 102–103.

57. Richard Bell, *The Origin of Islam in Its Christian Environment* (London, 1926), pp. 134–135, 151, 159–161.

58. Gil, *History of Palestine*, p. 12.

59. Ibid., p. 32.

60. Constantelos, "Greek Christian and Other Accounts of the Moslem Conquests of the Near East," p. 125.

61. Ibid., p. 126.

62. Walter Kaegi, *Byzantium and the Early Islamic Conquests* (Cambridge: Cambridge University Press, 1992), p. 274.

63. Ibn Hudayl, *L'Ornement des Ames*, trans. Louis Mercier (Paris, 1939), p. 195; English trans. Michael J. Miller.

64. Charles Emmanuel Dufourcq, *La Vie Quotidienne dans l'Europe Medievale sous Domination Arabe* (Paris: Hachette, 1978), p. 20; English trans. Michael J. Miller.

65. Bat Ye'or, *Decline of Eastern Christianity under Islam*, pp. 45–46.

66. Ibid., p. 48.

67. Hazard, *Atlas of Islamic History*, pp. 6–9.

68. Francesco Gabrieli, "Greeks and Arabs in the Central Mediterranean Area," *Dumbarton Oaks Papers* 18 (1964): 59–65.

69. Ibid.; Kenneth M. Setton, "On the Raids of the Moslems in the Aegean in the Ninth and Tenth Centuries," *American Journal of Archaeology* 58 (1954): 311–19; George C. Miles, "Byzantium and the Arabs: Relations in Crete and the Aegean Area," *Dumbarton Oaks Papers* 18 (1964): 3–32.

70. Gabrieli, "Greeks and Arabs in the Central Mediterranean Area," pp. 59, 62, 63.

71. Halil Inalcik, "The Rise of the Turcoman Maritime Principalities in Anatolia: Byzantium and the Crusades," *Byzantinische Forschungen* 11 (1986): 180–81, 184, 191–92, 197–98, 204, 210.

72. Elizabeth Zachariadou, "The Holy War in the Aegean during the Fourteenth Century," in *Latins and Greeks in the Eastern Mediterranean after 1204* (Totowa, NJ: Cass, 1989), p. 219.

73. Ibid.

74. Ibid.

75. C. Snouck Hurgronje, introduction to *The Acehnese*, vol. 1 (1906), pp. vii–viii.

76. Gil, *History of Palestine*, p. 2.

77. Ibid., pp. 14–15.

78. Ibid., p. 20.

79. Bat Ye'or, *Decline of Eastern Christianity under Islam*, pp. 44, 47; "Islam and the Dhimmis," *Jerusalem Quarterly* 42 (1987): 85.

80. Michael the Syrian, *Chronique*, ed. and trans. Jean-Baptiste Chabot, vol. 2 (Paris, 1899–1905), p. 418; English translation in Bat Ye'or, *Decline of Eastern Christianity under Islam*, p. 47.

81. Michael the Syrian, *Chronique*, vol. 2, p. 421; English trans. in Bat Ye'or, *The Decline of Eastern Christianity under Islam*, p. 47.

82. Gil, *History of Palestine*, pp. 61, 169.

83. Naphtali Lewis, "New Light on the Negev in Ancient Times," *Palestine Exploration Quarterly* 80 (1948): 116–17.

84. Gil, *History of Palestine*, p. 170.

85. Ibid., pp. 420–21.

86. Ibid., p. 477, n.50. Gil takes great exception to Claude Cahen's negationist assessment of Christian persecution during the initial 450 years of Muslim suzerainty in Palestine:

[Claude] Cahen [*Bulletin de la faculte des letters de Strasbourg* 29 (1950), 122; idem, *Past and Present* 6 (1954), 6f] claims that Muslim rule, in general, saw a period of peace and security, and that the sole persecution of the Christians recorded under Islam occurred during al-Hakim's rule. This is an apologetic and incomprehensible approach which ignores the facts.

87. Ibid., p. 473.

88. Ibid.

89. Ibid.

90. Ibid., p. 474.

91. Bat Ye'or, *Decline of Eastern Christianity under Islam*, p. 74.

92. Denys de Tell-Mahre, *Chronique*, trans. Jean-Baptiste Chabot (Paris, 1895), pt. 4, p. 112; English trans. in Bat Ye'or, *Decline of Eastern Christianity under Islam*, p. 74.

93. Gil, *History of Palestine*, pp. 474–75.

94. Ibid., p. 159.

95. Ibid. Q. 16.63: "By God, We (also) sent (Our apostles) to peoples before thee; but Satan made, (to the wicked) their own acts seem alluring: he is also their patron today, but they shall have a most grievous penalty"; Q. 5.72: "They do blaspheme who say: 'Allah is Christ the son of Mary.' But said Christ: 'O Children of Israel! worship Allah, my Lord and your Lord.' Whoever joins other gods with Allah—Allah will forbid him the garden, and the Fire will be his abode. There will for the wrong-doers be no one to help." Q. 58.19: "The devil hath engrossed them and so hath caused them to forget remembrance of Allah. They are the devil's party. Lo! is it not the devil's party who will be the losers?" In both 850 and 907–908, the Abbasid caliphs al-Mutawwakil and al-Muqtadir decreed that Jews and Christians either attach wooden images or drawings, respectively, of devils to the doors of their homes to distinguish them from the homes of Muslims. Tabari (d. 923), cited in Bat Ye'or, *The Dhimmi*, p. 186; Ibn al-Jawzi, cited in Gil, *History of Palestine*, p. 159n32.

96. Bat Ye'or, *Decline of Eastern Christianity under Islam*, p. 84.

97. Gil, *History of Palestine*, pp. 475–76.

98. Ibid., p. 375.

99. Ibid., p. 373.

100. Ibid., p. 376.

101. Moshe Gil, "Dhimmi Donations and Foundations for Jerusalem (638–1099)," *Journal of the Economic and Social History of the Orient* 37 (1984): 166–67.

102. Gil, *History of Palestine*, p. 415.

103. Ibid., p. 412.

104. Ibid., p. 415.

105. Ibid., p. 416.

106. Ibid.

107. Julius Greenstone, in his essay "The Turcoman Defeat at Cairo," *American Journal of Semitic Languages and Literatures* 22 (1906): 144–75, provides a translation of this poem [excerpted, pp. 164–65] by Solomon ha-Kohen b. Joseph (believed to be a descendant of the Geonim, an illustrious family of Palestinian Jews of priestly descent), which includes the poet's recollection of the previous Turcoman conquest of Jerusalem during the eighth decade of the eleventh century. Greenstone comments, "As appears from the poem, the conquest of Jerusalem by Atsiz was very sorely felt by the Jews. The author dwells at great length on the cruelties perpetrated against the inhabitants of the city" (p. 152).

108. Gil, *History of Palestine*, p. 420.

109. Ibid., pp. 420–21.

110. Bat Ye'or, *Decline of Eastern Christianity under Islam*, p. 46.

111. Fred M. Donner. *The Early Islamic Conquests* (Princeton, NJ: Princeton University Press, 1981), pp. 209–10.

112. Morony, *Iraq after the Muslim Conquest*, pp. 191–92.

113. Ibid., pp. 195–96.

114. Ibid., pp. 381–82.

115. Bat Ye'or, *Decline of Eastern Christianity under Islam*, p. 46.

116. P. K. Hitti, *History of the Arabs* (London, 1960), p. 165.

117. Jacques Jarry. *Hérésies et factions dans l'empire byzantin du IVe au VIIe siècle* (Le Caire, L'Institut français d'archéologie orientale, 1968).

118. John of Nikiu, *The Chronicle*, trans. R. H. Charles, from *Zotenberg's Ethiopic text* (Oxford, 1916), p. 179.

119. Ibid., 113.4–6, p. 182.

120. Ibid., 114.1, p. 182.

121. Ibid., 115.9, p. 184.

122. Ibid., 113.6, 115.6, pp. 182–84.

123. Ibid., 110.24, p. 194.

124. Ibid., 120.32, p. 195.

125. Ibid., 120.33, p. 195.

126. Constantelos, "Greek Christian and Other Accounts of the Moslem Conquests of the Near East," p. 133.

127. Ibid., p. 132.

128. Aram Ter-Ghevondian, *The Arab Emirates in Bagratid Armenia*, trans. Nina G. Garsoian (Lisbon: Livraria Bertrand, 1976), p. 20.

129. Al-Baladhuri, *The Origins of the Islamic State*, trans. Philip K. Hitti, vol. 1 (New York: Columbia University Press, 1916), p. 310.

130. Michael the Syrian, *Chronique*, vol. 2, p. 431.

131. Edouard Dulaurier, *Recherches sur la Chronologie Arménienne: Technique et Historique*, vol. 1 (Paris, 1859), p. 229; English trans. in Bat Ye'or, *Decline of Eastern Christianity*, p. 47.

132. Sebeos, seventh-century Armenian chronicler, quoted in Dulaurier, *Recherches sur la Chronologie Arménienne*, vol. 1, p. 228; English trans. in Bat Ye'or, *Decline of Eastern Christianity*, p. 47.

133. Sebeos, in Dulaurier, *Recherches sur la Chronologie Arménienne*, vol. 1, p. 231; English translation in Bat Ye'or, *Decline of Eastern Christianity*, p. 48.

134. Ter-Ghevondian, *Arab Emirates in Bagratid Armenia*, p. 20.

135. Kaegi, *Byzantium and the Early Islamic Conquests*, p. 199.

136. Ter-Ghevondian, *Arab Emirates in Bagratid Armenia*, p. 20.

137. Al-Baladhuri, *Origins of the Islamic State*, p. 322.

138. Ter-Ghevondian, *Arab Emirates in Bagratid Armenia*, pp. 20–21. For detailed additional discussion, see also Aram Ter-Ghevondian, "The Armenian Rebellion of 703 against the Caliphate," trans. Marina A. Arakelian, *Armenian Review* 36 (1983): 59–72, which is included in this collection.

139. Evariste Levi-Provencal, *Histoire de l'Espagne Musulmane*, vol. 1 (Paris, 1950); and Dufourcq, *Europe Medievale sous Domination Arabe*, see esp. chap. 1, "Les Jours de Razzia et d'Invasion."

140. Lévi-Provençal, *Histoire de l'Espagne Musulmane*, p. 150.

141. Dufourcq, *Europe Medievale sous Domination Arabe*, pp. 50, 194, 196.

142. Bat Ye'or, *Decline of Eastern Christianity*, pp. 49–50.

143. Georges Vajda, "À propos de la situation des Juifs et des Chrétiens à Séville au début du XIIe siècle," *Revue des Études Juives* 99 (1935): 127–29.

144. Roger Arnaldez, "La guerre sainte selon Ibn Hazm de Courdoue," in *Etudes d'Orientalism Dediees a la Memoire de Levi-Provencal*, vol. 2 (Paris, 1962), pp. 445–59.

145. Moshe Perlmann, "Eleventh-Century Andalusian Authors on the Jews of Granada," *Proceedings of the American Academy for Jewish Research* 18 (1948–49): 286–87.

146. Charles Emmanuel Dufourcq, "Les Mozarabes du XIIe siecle et le pretendu 'Eveque' de Lisbonne," *Revue d'Histoire et de Civilisation du Maghreb* 5 (1968): 125–26.

147. Reinhart Dozy, *Spanish Islam: A History of the Muslims in Spain* (London, 1915), pp. 721–22.

148. H. Z. Hirschberg, *A History of the Jews of North Africa*, vol. 1 (Leiden, 1974), pp. 123–29.

149. Bat Ye'or, *Dhimmi*, p. 351.

150. Michael the Syrian, *Chronique*, ed. and trans. Jean-Baptiste Chabot, vol. 3 (Paris, 1899–1905), pp. 170–71; English trans. in Bat Ye'or, *Decline of Eastern Christianity under Islam*, p. 53.

151. Michael the Syrian, *Chronique*, vol. 3, p. 176; English trans. in Bat Ye'or, *Decline of Eastern Christianity under Islam*, p. 55.

152. See the numerous primary sources cited in Dimitar Angelov, "Certains Aspects de la Conquete Des Peuples Balkaniques par les Turcs," *Byzantinoslavica* 17 (1956): 220–75; Vacalopoulos, *Origins of the Greek Nation—The Byzantine Period*; Vryonis, *Decline of Medieval Hellenism in Asia Minor*.

153. Bat Ye'or, *Decline of Eastern Christianity under Islam*, p. 55–56.

154. Paul Wittek, *The Rise of the Ottoman Empire. London* (Royal Asiatic Society of Great Britain and Ireland, 1938; repr., 1966), p. 18.

155. Vryonis, "Nomadization and Islamization in Asia Minor," *Dumbarton Oaks Publications* 29 (1975): 49.

156. Ibid.

157. Wittek, *Rise of the Ottoman Empire. London*, p. 14. Wittek includes this discussion, with a block quote from Ahmedi's text:

The chapter Ahmedi devotes in his *Iskender-name* to the history of the Ottoman sultans, the ancestors of his protector Sulayman Tshelebi, son of Bayazid I, begins with an introduction in which the poet solemnly declares his intention of writing a Ghazawat-name, a book about the holy war of the Ghazis. He poses the question: "Why have the Ghazis appeared at last?" And he answers: "Because the best always comes at the end. Just as the definitive prophet Mohammed came after the others, just as the Koran came down from heaven after the Torah, the Psalms and the Gospels, so also the Ghazis appeared in the world at the last," those Ghazis the reign of whom is that of the Ottomans. The poet continues with this question: "Who is a Ghazi?" And he explains: "A Ghazi is the instrument of the religion of Allah, a servant of God who purifies the earth from the filth of polytheism (remember that Islam regards the Trinity of the Christians as a polytheism); the Ghazi is the sword of God, he is the protector and refuge of the believers. If he becomes a martyr in the ways of God, do not believe that he has died—he lives in beatitude with Allah, he has eternal life." (p. 14)

158. Halil Inalcik, *The Ottoman Empire—The Classical Age, 1300–1600* (London: Weidenfeld and Nicolson, 1973), p. 6.

159. Vacalopoulos, *Origins of the Greek Nation—The Byzantine Period*, p. 66.

160. Speros Vryonis, "The Experience of Christians under Seljuk and Ottoman Domination, Eleventh to Sixteenth Century," in *Conversion and Continuity: Indigenous Christian Communities in Islamic Lands, Eighth to Eighteenth Centuries*, ed. Michael Gervers and Ramzi Jibran Bikhazi (Toronto, ON: Pontifical Institute of Medieval Studies, 1990), p. 201.

161. Vacalopoulos, *Origins of the Greek Nation—The Byzantine Period*, pp. 61–62.

162. Ibid., pp. 69–85; Angelov, "Certains Aspects de la Conquete des Peuples Balkaniques par les Turcs," pp. 220–75.

163. Vacalopoulos, *Origins of the Greek Nation—The Byzantine Period*, p. 77.

164. Ibid., p. 73.

165. Angelov, "Certains Aspects de la Conquete Des Peuples Balkaniques par les Turcs," pp. 236, 238–39.

166. Joseph Hacker, "Ottoman Policy toward the Jews and Jewish Attitudes toward the Ottomans during the Fifteenth Century," in *Christians and Jews in the Ottoman Empire: The Functioning of a Plural Society*, ed. Benjamin Braude and Bernard Lewis (New York: Holmes & Meier, 1982), p. 117.

167. Ibid., p. 120

168. Ivo Andric, *The Development of Spiritual Life in Bosnia under the Influence of Turkish Rule* (Durham, NC: Duke University Press, 1990), pp. 16–38.

169. Ibid., pp. 23–24.

170. Ibid., pp. 24–25.

171. Ibid., p. 78n2.

172. Ibid., p. 25.

173. Ibid., pp. 25–26.

174. Ibid., pp. 26, 80n11.

175. Ibid., pp. 26–27.

176. Ibid., p. 30.

177. Ibid., p. 30.

178. Ibid., pp. 30–31.

179. Ibid., p. 38.

180. Paul Ricaut, *The Present State of the Greek and Armenian Churches, Anno Christi 1678* (London, 1679; reprint, New York: AMS Press, 1970), pp. 1–30.

181. Vryonis, *Decline of Medieval Hellenism in Asia Minor*, pp. 340–43, 351–402.

182. Ibid., p. 342.

183. Demetrios Constantelos, "The 'Neomartyrs' as Evidence for Methods and Motives Leading to Conversion and Martyrdom in the Ottoman Empire," *Greek Orthodox Theological Review* 23 (1978): 228.

184. Ibid., pp. 217–18.

185. Ibid., p. 226.

186. Ibid., p. 227.

187. Abdolonyme Ubicini, *Lettres Sur La Turque*, vol. 2 (Paris, 1854), p. 32; English trans. in Bat Ye'or, *Decline of Eastern Christianity*, p. 181.

188. A. E. Vacalopoulos, "Background and Causes of the Greek Revolution," *Neo-Hellenika* 2 (1975): 54–55.

189. Stanford Shaw, *History of the Ottoman Empire and Modern Turkey*, vol. 1 (Cambridge, 1976), pp. 19, 24.

190. Bernard Lewis, *What Went Wrong? Western Impact and Middle Eastern Response* (New York: Oxford University Press, 2002), pp. 114–15.

191. A. E. Vacalopoulos, *The Greek Nation, 1453–1669* (New Brunswick, NJ: Rutgers University Press, 1976), p. 41; Vasiliki Papoulia, "The Impact of Devshirme on Greek Society," in *War and Society in East Central Europe*, ed. Bela K. Kiraly, vol. 2 (1982), pp. 561–62.

192. Bernard Lewis, *The Muslim Discovery of Europe* (New York: Norton, 1982), pp. 190–91. Lewis also describes the devshirme solely as a form of social advancement for Balkan Christians in both the 1968 and 2002 editions of *The Emergence of Modern Turkey* (Oxford University Press):

> [T]he Balkan peoples had an enormous influence on the Ottoman ruling class. One of the most important channels was the devshirme, the levy of boys, by means of which countless Balkan Christians entered the military and political elites of the Empire. (p. 5)

193. Speros Vryonis Jr., "Seljuk Gulams and Ottoman Devshirmes," *Der Islam* 41 (1965): 245–47.

194. Papoulia, "The Impact of Devshirme on Greek Society," pp. 554–55.

195. Ibid., p. 557.

196. Edouard Engelhardt, *La Turquie et La Tanzimat*, vol. 1 (Paris, 1882), p. 111, vol. 2, p. 171; English trans. in Bat Ye'or, *Islam and Dhimmitude*, pp. 431–342.

197. *Reports from Her Majesty's Consuls Relating to the Condition of the Christians in Turkey* (1867), pp. 5, 29. See also related other reports by various consuls and vice-consuls, in the 1860 ed., p. 58; the 1867 ed., pp. 4–6, 14–15; and the 1867 ed., pt. 2, p. 3; all cited in Vahakn Dadrian, *Warrant for Genocide: Key Elements of Turko-Armenian Conflict* (New Brunswick, NJ: Transaction, 1999), pp. 26–27n4. See also extensive excerpts from these reports in Bat Ye'or, *Decline of Eastern Christianity*, pp. 409–33.

198. Excerpts from Bulwer's report reproduced in Bat Ye'or, *Decline of Eastern Christianity*, pp. 423–26.

199. Tudor Parfitt, *The Jews of Palestine* (Suffolk, UK: Boydell Press, 1987), pp. 168, 172–73.

200. Roderick Davison, "Turkish Attitudes concerning Christian-Muslim Equality in the Nineteenth Century," *American Historical Review* 59 (1954): 848, 855, 859, 864.

201. Quoted in Andre Servier, *Islam and the Psychology of the Musulman*, trans. A. S. Moss-Blundell (London, 1924), pp. 241–42.

202. Januarius A. MacGahan, *The Turkish Atrocities in Bulgaria* (Geneva, 1976); Yono Mitev, *The April Uprising and European Public Opinion* (Sofia Press, 1978); Philip Shashko, "The Bulgarian Massacres of 1876 Reconsidered: Reaction to the April Uprising or Premeditated Attack?" *Etudes Balkaniques* 22 (1986): 18–25.

203. Vahakn Dadrian, *The History of the Armenian Genocide* (Providence, RI: Bergahn Books, 1995), pp. 113–72.

204. Ibid., pp. 219–34.

205. Oliver Warner, *William Wilberforce and His Times* (London: Batsford, 1962).

206. J. B. Kelly, *Britain and the Persian Gulf* (Oxford, 1968), pp. 588–89.

207. Christopher Lloyd, *The Navy and the Slave Trade* (London, 1949).

208. Ehud Toledano, *The Ottoman Slave Trade and Its Suppression* (Princeton, NJ: Princeton University Press, 1982), p. 260.

209. Reuben Levy, *The Social Structure of Islam* (Cambridge, 1957), p. 88.

210. E. G. Browne, *A Literary History of Persia in Four Volumes*, vol. 3: *The Tartar Domain (1265–1502)* (Cambridge: Cambridge University Press, 1928), pp. 180–206; Rene Grousset, *L'Empire Des Steppes. Attila, Gengis-Khan, Tamerlan* (Paris: Payot, 1952), trans. Naomi Walford as *The Empire of the Steppes* (New Brunswick, NJ: Rutgers University Press, 1970), pp. 409–65. A. L. Srivastava, *The Delhi Sultanate (711–1526 A.D.)* (Agra, 1950), p. 222.

211. Grousset, *Empire of the Steppes*, pp. 419–20.

212. Browne, *Literary History of Persia*, p. 181.

213. Grousset, *Empire of the Steppes*, pp. 416–17.

214. For conflicting views regarding the apocryphal nature of this work, see Browne, *Literary History of Persia*, pp. 183–84, and Elliot and Dowson, *History of India*, vol. 3, pp. 389–94.

215. Elliot and Dowson, *History of India*, vol. 3, pp. 394–95.

216. Browne, *Literary History of Persia*, p. 196.

217. Elliot and Dowson, *History of India*, vol. 3, p. 429.

218. Ibid., pp. 432–33.

219. Ibid., pp. 445–46.

220. Srivastava, *Delhi Sultanate*, pp. 222–23.

221. Ibid., p. 223.

222. Ibid., p. 223.

223. Elliot and Dowson, *History of India*, vol. 3, p. 459.

224. Srivastava, *Delhi Sultanate*, p. 223.

225. Ibid., p. 224.

226. Bar Hebraeus, *Chronography*, trans. Ernest A. Walli Budge, vol. 1 (Oxford: Oxford University Press, 1932), p. 354.

227. Grousset, *Empire of the Steppes*, p. 434. The English translation omits the word *coranique* in translating "Il tuait par piete coranique" (p. 513 of the original French, *L'Empire Des Steppes*), so that the phrase becomes, "He killed from piety" as opposed to Grousset's original, "He killed from Qur'anic piety."

228. A. L. Srivastava, "A Survey of India's Resistance to Medieval Invaders from the North-West: Causes of Eventual Hindu Defeat," *Journal of Indian History* (1965): 349–50.

229. Srivastava, *Sultanate of Delhi*, p. 127; R. C. Majumdar, ed., *The History and Culture of the Indian People*, vol. 6: *The Sultanate of Delhi* (Bombay, 1960), p. xxiii, states, for example, with regard to the Delhi sultanate:

The popular notion that after the conquest of Muhammad Ghauri, India formed a Muslim Empire under various dynasties, is hardly borne out by facts . . . barring the two very short lived empires under the Khaljis and Muhammad bin Tughlaq which lasted respectively, for less than twenty and ten years, there was no Turkish empire of India. The Delhi Sultanate, as the symbol of this empire, continued in name throughout the period under review [i.e., 1206–1526] but, gradually shorn of power and prestige, it was reduced to a phantom by the invasion of Timur at the end of the fourteenth century AD.

For discussions of the limits of the Mughal Empire, see A. L. Srivastava, *The History of India (1000 AD–1707 AD)* (Agra, 1964), pp. 674–76; and K. S. Lal, *Indian Muslims—Who Are They?* (New Delhi, 1990), pp. 122–23, 127, 136–37.

230. A. S. Beveridge, trans., *Baburnama* (Lahore: Sangmeel Publications, 1976), pp. 484, 518.

231. Vincent Smith, *The Oxford History of India* (Oxford: Oxford University Press, 1928), p. 221.

232. Al-Baladhuri, *The Origins of the Islamic State (Kitab Futuh Al-Buldan)*, trans. F. C. Murgotten (New York: Columbia University Press, 1924), pt. 2, pp. 217–24; Al-Kufi, *The Chachnama*, excerpts translated in Elliot and Dowson, *History of India*, vol. 1, pp. 157–211.

233. Al-Baladhuri, *Origins of the Islamic State*, pt. 2, p. 218.

234. R. C. Majumdar, ed., *The History and Culture of the Indian People*, vol. 3: *The Classical Age* (Bombay, 1954), p. 458.

235. Ibid., pp. 458–59.

236. From a translation of Ziauddin Barani's *Fatawa-i Jahandari*, c. 1358–59 CE, in Mohammad Habib, *The Political Theory of the Delhi Sultanate* (Allahabad: Kitab Mahal, 1961), pp. 46–47.

237. Al-Kufi, *Chachnama*, pp. 173–74.

238. Majumdar, *Classical Age*, p. 460.

239. Ibid., pp. 461–62.

240. Elliot and Dowson, *History of India*, vol. 2, appendix note D, pp. 434–84.

241. Srivastava, *Sultanate of Delhi*, p. 52.

242. Lal, *Legacy of Muslim Rule in India*, pp. 96–97.

243. Elliot and Dowson, *History of India*, vol. 2, pp. 40–41.

244. Ibid., p. 49.

245. Srivastava, *Sultanate of Delhi*, p. 59.

246. Alberuni, *Alberuni's India: An Account of the Religion, Philosophy, Literature, Geography, Chronology, Astronomy, Customs, Laws, and Astrology of India*, ed. E. C. Sachau (1888; repr., New Delhi, 1993), p. 22.

247. Srivastava, *Sultanate of Delhi*, pp. 61–62.

248. K. S. Lal, *Theory and Practice of Muslim State in India* (New Delhi: Aditya Prakashan, 1999), pp. 20–21.

249. Ibid., p. 21.

250. Srivastava, *Sultanate of Delhi*, pp. 304–305.

251. R. C. Majumdar, ed., *The Mughul Empire* (Bombay, 1974), p. xi.

252. Majumdar, *Sultanate of Delhi*, p. 623.

253. Patricia Crone, *God's Rule: Government and Islam* (New York: Columbia University Press, 2004), pp. 371–72.

254. K. S. Lal, *Muslim Slave System India* (New Delhi: Aditya Prakashan, 1994), pp. 46, 69.

255. Vryonis, *Decline of Medieval Hellenism in Asia Minor*, pp. 174–75.

256. Vasiliki Papoulia, "The Impact of Devshirme on Greek Society," in *East Central European Society and War in the Prerevolutionary Eighteenth Century*, ed. Gunther E.

Rothenberg, Béla K. Király, and Peter F. Sugar (New York: Columbia University Press, 1982), pp. 555–56.

257. Thomas Ricks, "Slaves and Slave Trading in Shi'i Iran, AD 1500–1900," *Journal of Asian and African Studies* 36 (2001): 407–18.

258. Ibid., pp. 411–12.

259. Clement Huart, "Le droit de la guerre," *Revue du monde musulman* (1907): 337.

260. John Ralph Willis, "Jihad and the Ideology of Enslavement," in *Slaves and Slavery in Muslim Africa*, vol. 1: *Islam and the Ideology of Enslavement* (Totowa, NJ: Frank Cass, 1985), pp. 17–18.

261. Winston Churchill, *The River War*, vol. 2 (London: Longmans, Green, 1899), pp. 248–50.

262. John Eibner, "My Career Redeeming Slaves," *Middle East Quarterly* 4, no. 4 (December 1999), http://www.meforum.org/article/449. Eibner notes:

[B]ased on the pattern of slave raiding over the past fifteen years and the observations of Western and Arab travelers in southern Darfur and Kordofan, conservatively puts the number of chattel slaves close to or over 100,000. There are many more in state-owned concentration camps, euphemistically called "peace camps" by the government of Sudan, and in militant Qur'anic schools, where boys train to become mujahidun (warriors of *jihad*).

263. Willis, *Slaves and Slavery in Muslim Africa*, p. vii.

264. This controversial topic is discussed in Philip D. Curtin, Roger Antsey, and J. E. Inikori, *Journal of African History* 17 (1976): 595–627.

265. Willis, *Slaves and Slavery in Muslim Africa*, p. x.

266. John Wright, "The Mediterranean Middle Passage: The Nineteenth-Century Slave Trade Between Triploi and the Levant," *Journal of North African Studies* 1 (1996): 44.

267. Vryonis, *Decline of Medieval Hellenism in Asia Minor*, p. 175n245.

268. Bar Hebraeus, *Chronography*, vol. 1, pp. 268–73; Michael the Syrian, *Chronique*, vol. 3, p. 331.

269. Michael the Syrian, *Chronique*, vol. 3, p. 331.

270. Vryonis, *Decline of Medieval Hellenism in Asia Minor*, p. 175n245.

271. Michael the Syrian, *Chronique*, vol. 3, p. 369.

272. Ibid., pp. 401–402; Bar Hebraeus, *Chronography*, vol. 1, p. 321.

273. Vryonis, *Decline of Medieval Hellenism in Asia Minor*, p. 175n245.

274. M.-M. Alexandrescu-Dersca Bulgaru, "Le role des escalves en Romanie turque au XVe siècle," *Byzantinische Forschungen* 11 (1987): 15.

275. Ibid., pp. 16–17.

276. Alan Fisher, "Muscovy and the Black Sea Slave Trade," *Canadian American Slavic Studies* 6 (1972): 575–94.

277. Ibid., p. 579n17.

278. Ibid., pp. 580–82.

279. Ibid., pp. 582–83.

280. Levy, *Social Structure of Islam*, p. 88.

281. Ricks, "Slaves and Slave Trading in Shi'i Iran," p. 408.

282. Ehud Toledano, *Slavery and Abolition in the Ottoman Middle East* (Seattle: University of Washington Press, 1998), p. 53.

283. Ricks, "Slaves and Slave Trading in Shi'i Iran," p. 415.

284. Murray Gordon, *Slavery in the Arab World* (New York: New Amsterdam, 1989), p. 232.

285. Ibid., p. 234.

286. Ibid., preface.

287. Eibner, "My Career Redeeming Slaves."

288. Jan Hogendorn, "The Hideous Trade: Economic Aspects of the 'Manufacture' and Sale of Eunuchs," *Paideuma* 45 (1999): 143, esp. n25.

289. Ibid., p. 137.

290. Ehud Toledano, "The Imperial Eunuchs of Istanbul: From Africa to the Heart of Islam," *Middle Eastern Studies* 20 (1984): 379–90.

291. Ibid., pp. 380–81.

292. Hogendorn, "Hideous Trade," p. 138.

293. David Ayalon. "On the Eunuchs in Islam," *Jerusalem Studies in Arabic and Islam* 1 (1979): 69–70.

294. Hogendorn, "Hideous Trade," p. 139n5.

295. Ibid., p. 139.

296. Ibid., pp. 143, 145–46.

297. Clement Huart, "Le droit de la guerre," pp. 332–33; English trans. Michael J. Miller.

298. C. Snouck Hurgronje, *Mohammedanism* (New York, 1916), p. 59.

299. Henri Lammens, *Islam—Beliefs and Institutions* (London, 1929), p. 62.

300. Jeffery, "Political Importance of Islam," p. 388.

301. Khadduri, *War and Peace in the Law of Islam*, pp. 63–64, and introduction to *The Islamic Law of Nations: Shaybani's Siyar* (Baltimore: Johns Hopkins University Press, 1966), p. 5.

302. Fattal, *Le Statut Legal des Non-Musulmans en Pays d'Islam*, p. 71; English trans. Michael J. Miller.

303. Armand Abel, "L'Etranger dans L'Islam Classique," *Recueils de la Societe Jean Bodin* 9 (1958): 332–33, 343–45; English trans. Michael J. Miller.

304. Schacht, *Introduction to Islamic Law*, pp. 130–31.

305. Peters, *Jihad in Classical and Modern Islam*, p. 3.

306. Bassam Tibi, "War and Peace in Islam," in *The Ethics of War and Peace: Religious and Secular Perspectives*, ed. Terry Nardin (Princeton, NJ: Princeton University Press, 1996), pp. 129–31.

307. Hurgronje, *Mohammedanism*, pp. 105–106.

308. Jeffery, "Political Importance of Islam," p. 388.

309. Ibid., pp. 388–89.

310. Mordechai Nisan, "The Islamic Assault on the West and Israel," in *Identity and Civilization* (Lanham, NY: University Press of America, 1999), pp. 127–62.

311. Ibid., p. 139.

312. B. J. Boland. *The Struggle of Islam in Modern Indonesia* (The Hague: Martinus Nijhoff, 1971), pp. 1401–46; cited in Nisan, "The Islamic Assault on the West and Israel," p. 139n44.

313. D. F. Green, ed., *Arab Theologians on Jews and Israel* (Geneva: Editions de l'Avenir, 1974).

314. These specific excerpts from the 1968 Al Azhar Conference are cited in Bat Ye'or, *Dhimmi: Jews and Christians under Islam*, pp. 391–94.

315. J. B. Kelly, *Arabia, the Gulf, and the West* (New York: Basic Books, 1980), p. 217.

316. Nisan, "Islamic Assault on the West and Israel," p. 140.

317. Ibid.

318. Ibid.

319. Ibid.

320. Ibid.

321. Ibid.

322. Ibid., p. 143.

323. Ibid., p. 141.

324. Ibid.

325. Ibid., p. 143.

326. Ibid.

327. Ibid., pp. 143–44.

328. Bat Ye'or, *The Decline of Eastern Christianity under Islam*, p. 220, and p. 469n4, dating the original statement in French to September 1990.

329. G. H. Bousquet, "Islamic Law and Customary Law in French North Africa," *Journal of Comparative Legislation and International Law* (1950): 65. Fiqh

has become the technical term for jurisprudence, the science of religious law in Islam. . . . All aspects of public and private life and business should be regulated by laws based on religion; the science of these laws is fiqh." (I. Goldziher and J. Schacht, *The Encyclopedia of Islam*, CD-ROM ed., v.1.1)

PART 2:
Jihad in the Qur'an and Hadith

2

JIHAD IN THE QUR'AN

9.5: But when the forbidden months are past, then fight and slay the pagans wherever ye find them, And seize them, beleaguer them, and lie in wait for them in every stratagem (of war); but if they repent (accept Islam) and establish regular prayers and practices regular charity then open the way for them; for God is oft-forgiving, Most Merciful.

9.29: Fight those who believe not in Allah nor the last day, nor hold that forbidden which hath been forbidden by Allah and his apostle, nor acknowledge the religion of truth even if they are the people of the book, until they pay the Jizya with willing submission, and feel themselves subdued.

9.73: O Prophet! Strive against the disbelievers and the hypocrites! Be harsh with them. Their ultimate abode is hell, a hapless journey's end.

9.111: Allah hath purchased of the believers their persons and their goods; for theirs (in return) is the garden (of Paradise): they fight in His cause, and slay and are slain: a promise binding on Him in truth, through the Law, the Gospel, and the Qur'an, and who is more faithful to his covenant than Allah? then rejoice in the bargain which ye have concluded: that is the achievement supreme.

9.123: O ye who believe! Fight those of the disbelievers who are near to you, and let them find harshness in you, and know that Allah is with those who keep their duty (unto Him).

4.74: Let those fight in the cause of Allah Who sell the life of this world for the hereafter. To him who fighteth in the cause of Allah,—whether he is slain or gets victory—Soon shall We give him a reward of great (value).

4.76: Those who believe fight in the cause of Allah, and those who reject Faith Fight in the cause of Evil: So fight ye against the friends of Satan: feeble indeed is the cunning of Satan.

Taken from "The Noble Qur'an," Muslim Students Association, University of Southern California, http://www.usc.edu/dept/MSA/quran.

4.95: O ye who believe! Shall I show you a commerce that will save you from a painful doom? You should believe in Allah and His messenger, and should strive for the cause of Allah with your wealth and your lives. That is better for you, if ye did but know. . . . Allah hath granted a grade higher to those who strive and fight with their goods and persons than those who sit (at home).

2.216: Fighting is prescribed for you, and ye dislike it. But it is possible that ye dislike a thing which is good for you, and that ye love a thing which is bad for you. But Allah knoweth, and ye know not.

2.217: They ask thee concerning fighting in the Prohibited Month. Say: "Fighting therein is a grave (offence); but graver is it in the sight of Allah to prevent access to the path of Allah, to deny Him, to prevent access to the Sacred Mosque, and drive out its members." Tumult and oppression are worse than slaughter. Nor will they cease fighting you until they turn you back from your faith if they can. And if any of you Turn back from their faith and die in unbelief, their works will bear no fruit in this life and in the Hereafter; they will be companions of the Fire and will abide therein.

2.218: Those who believed and those who suffered exile and fought (and strove and struggled) in the path of Allah,—they have the hope of the Mercy of Allah: And Allah is Oft-forgiving, Most Merciful.

2.191: And slay them wherever ye catch them, and turn them out from where they have turned you out . . . such is the reward of those who suppress faith.

8.12: . . . "I will instill terror into the hearts of the unbelievers: smite ye above their necks and smite all their finger-tips off them."

8.15, 16: O ye who believe! when ye meet the Unbelievers in hostile array, never turn your backs to them. If any do turn his back to them on such a day—unless it be in a stratagem of war, or to retreat to a troop (of his own)—he draws on himself the wrath of Allah, and his abode is Hell,—an evil refuge (indeed)!

8.39: And fight them on until there is no more tumult or oppression, and there prevail justice and faith in Allah altogether and everywhere; but if they cease, verily Allah doth see all that they do.

8.41: And know that out of all the booty that ye may acquire (in war), a fifth share is assigned to Allah,—and to the Messenger, and to near relatives, orphans, the needy, and the wayfarer,—if ye do believe in Allah and in the revelation We sent down to Our servant on the Day of Testing,—the Day of the meeting of the two forces. For Allah hath power over all things.

8.65: O Apostle ! Rouse the believers to the fight, if there are twenty amongst you, patient and persevering, they will vanquish two hundred; if a hundred, they will vanquish a thousand of the unbelievers; for these are a people without understanding.

48.20: . . . Allah promises you much booty (spoils of war) that you will capture from the defeated infidels . . .

3

CLASSICAL AND MODERN QUR'ANIC COMMENTATORS ON QUR'AN 9:29

AL-SUYUTI (D. 1505 CE)

Fight those who don't believe in God nor in the Last Day [Unless they believe in the Prophet God bless him and grant him peace] nor hold what is forbidden that which God and His emissary have forbidden [e.g., wine] nor embrace the true faith [which is firm, and abrogates other faiths, i.e., the Islamic religion] from among [for distinguishing] those who were given the Book [i.e., the Jews and Christians] until they give the head-tax [i.e., the annual taxes imposed on them] (/'an yadin/) humbly submissive, and obedient to Islam's rule.[1]

[Jizya is part of] land and slaves . . . is incumbent upon the People of the Book . . . on people who allow wine [Jews and Christians] and pig-meat [Christians]. . . . [Saaghiruuna means] submissively . . . [it means] by coercion . . . ['an yadin means] directly, not trusting the trickery of an intermediary . . . by force . . . without resistance . . . in an unpraiseworthy manner . . . while you stand and [the dhimmi] sits with the whip in front of you [you take] the money while he has dirt on his head.[2]

AL-ZAMAKHSHARI (D. 1144)

('an yadin): does this refers to the hand of the giver or the receiver? It refers to the giver, i.e. from a forthcoming rather than a withholding hand. For he who refuses and withholds doesn't proffer his hand, as opposed to the reluctant obeyer. [proverb example]—not by someone deputized, but directly from the hand of the [dhimmi]. The hand of the taker means that [when he takes it] his hand is the upper, the ruler; or, because of the benefit [to the *dhimmis*, viz. protection] because receiving the jizya from them and lowering their spirits is of benefit to them. (wa-hum Saarighuuna) it is taken from them when they are in a lowered and humbled state. [The *dhimmi*] must approach walking, not riding; the taker is standing while the giver is sitting and trembling in awe /yutaltilu taltalatan/. He is seized by his collar, and is told: "Perform the *jizya*," and is pushed on the nape of his neck /yuzakhkhu/.[3]

AL-TABARI (D. 923)

The dhimmis posture during the collection of the *jizya*—"[lowering themselves] by walking on their hands [on all fours?], reluctantly; on the authority of Ibn 'Abbas—but this is not accepted by everyone."[4]

AL-BEIDAWI (D. 1286)

... on the authority of Ibn Abbas ... that the jizya is taken from the dhimmi, [while] his neck is being hung low.[5]

IBN KATHIR (D. 1373)

The Order to Fight the People of the Scriptures until They Give the Jizyah

Allah said, *"Fight against those who believe not in Allah, nor in the Last Day, nor forbid that which has been forbidden by Allah and His Messenger, and those who acknowledge not the religion of truth among the People of the Scripture, until they pay the Jizyah with willing submission, and feel themselves subdued."* Therefore when the People of the Scriptures disbelieved in Muhammad, they had no beneficial faith in any Messenger or what the Messengers brought. Rather they followed their religions because this conformed with their ideas, lusts, and the ways of their forefathers, not because they are Allah's laws and religion. Had they been true believers in their religions, that faith would have directed them to believe in Muhammad because all Prophets gave the good news of Muhammad's advent and commanded them to obey and follow him. Yet when he was sent, they disbelieved in him, even though he is the mightiest of all Messengers. Therefore, they do not follow the religion of earlier Prophets because these religions came from Allah, but because these suit their desires and lusts. Therefore, their claimed faith in an earlier Prophet will not benefit them because they disbelieved in the master, the mightiest, the last and most perfect of all Prophets. Hence Allah's statement,

"Fight against those who believe not in Allah, nor in the Last Day, nor forbid that which has been forbidden by Allah and His Messenger, and those who acknowledge not the religion of truth among the People of the Scripture."

This honorable Ayah was revealed with the order to fight the People of the Book, after the pagans were defeated, the people entered Allah's region in large numbers, and the Arabian Peninsula was secured under the Muslims' control. Allah commanded His Messenger to fight the People of the Scriptures, Jews and Christians, on the ninth year of Hijrah, and he prepared his army to fight the Romans [Byzantines] and called the people to *Jihad* announcing his intent and destination. The Messenger sent his intent to various Arab areas around Al-Madinah to gather forces, and he collected an army of thirty thousand. Some people from Al-Madinah and some hypocrites, in and around it, lagged behind, for that was a year of drought and intense heat. The Messenger of Allah marched, heading towards Ash-Sham to fight the Romans until he reached Tabuk, where he set camp for about twenty days next to its water resources. He then prayed to Allah for a decision and went back to Al-Madinah because it was a hard year and the people were weak, as we will mention, Allah willing.

Paying Jizyah *Is a Sign of Kufr and Disgrace*

Allah said, *"until they pay the Jizyah,"* if they do not choose to embrace Islam, *"with willing submission,"* in defeat and subservience, *"and feel themselves subdued,"* disgraced, humiliated and belittled. Therefore, Muslims are not allowed to honor the people of *Dhimmah* or elevate them above Muslims, for they are miserable, disgraced, and humiliated. Muslim recorded from Abu Hurayrah that the Prophet said, *"Do not initiate the Salam to the Jews and the Christians, and if you meet them in a raod, force them to its narrowest alley."* This is why the Leader of the faithful 'Umar b. Al-Khattab, may Allah be pleased with him, demanded his well-known conditions be met by the Christians, these conditions that ensured their continued humiliation, degradation, and disgrace. The scholars of Hadith narrated from Abdur-Rahman b. Ghanm Al-Ash'ari that he said, "I recorded for 'Umar b. Al-Khattab, may Allah be pleased with him, the terms of the treaty of peace he conducted with the Christians of Ash-Sham: 'In the Name of Allah, Most Gracious, Most Merciful. This is a document to the servant of Allah, 'Umar the Leader of the faithful, for the Christians of such and such city. When you [Muslims] came to us we requested safety for ourselves, children, property and followers of our religion. We made a condition on ourselves that we will neither erect in our areas a monastery, church, or a sanctuary for a monk, nor restore any place of worship that needs restoration nor use any of them for the purpose of enmity against Muslims. We will not prevent any Muslim from resting in our churches whether they come by day or night, and we will open the doors [of our houses of worship] for the wayfarer and passerby. Those Muslims who come as guests, will enjoy boarding and food for three days. We will not allow a spy against Muslims into our churches and homes or hide deceit [or betrayal] against Muslims. We will not teach our children the Qur'an, publicize practices of *Shirk*, invite anyone to *Shirk* or prevent any of our fellows from embracing Islam, if they choose to do so. We will respect Muslims, move from places we sit in if they choose to sit in them. We will not imitate their clothing, caps, turbans, sandals, hairstyles, speech, nicknames and title names, or ride on saddles, hang swords on the shoulders, collect weapons of any kind or carry these weapons. We will not encrypt our stamps in Arabic, or sell liquor. We will have the front of our hair cut, wear our customary clothes wherever we are, wear belts around our waist, refrain from erecting crosses on the outside of our churches and demonstrating them and our books in public in Muslim fairways and markets. We will not sound the bells of our churches, except discretely, or raise our voices while reciting our holy books inside our churches in the presence of Muslims, nor raise our voices [with prayer] at our funerals, or light torches in funeral processions in the fairways of Muslims, or in their markets. We will not bury our dead next to Muslim dead, or buy servants who were captured by Muslims. We will be guides for Muslims and refrain from breaching privacy in their homes.' When I gave this document to 'Umar, he added to it, 'We will not beat any Muslim. These are the conditions that we set against ourselves and followers to our religion in return for safety and protection. If we break any of these promises that we set for your benefit against ourselves, then our *Dhimmah* (promise of protection) is broken and you are allowed to do with us what you are allowed of people of defiance and rebellion.'"[6]

SAYYID QUTB (D. 1966)

History witnessed repeated violations by the Jews of their treaties with the Muslim state in Madinah, as also their scheming against the Muslims. These violations led to the encounters with the Jewish tribes of Qaynuqa, al-Nadir and Qurayzah, and also the Battle of Khaybar. Their efforts to bring together all the forces hostile to Islam in an unholy affiance, with the aim of exterminating Islam altogether, are well known.

They have continued to scheme against Islam and the Muslim community ever since. They were instrumental in the chaotic events that led to the assassination of the third rightly-guided Caliph, 'Uthman ibn 'Affan and to the emergence of division in the Muslim community. They were the main culprits in the conflict that took place between 'Ali and Mu 'awiyah. They led the way in the fabrication of false statements attributed to the Prophet, historical reports and baseless interpretations of Qur'anic statements. They also paved the way to the victory of the Tartars and their conquest of Baghdad and the fall of the Islamic Caliphate.

In modern history, the Jews have been behind every calamity that has befallen the Muslim communities everywhere. They give active support to every attempt to crush the modern Islamic revival and extend their protection to every regime that suppresses such a revival.

History Tells Its Tale

The other people of earlier revelations, the Christians, have been no less hostile. Enmity between the Byzantines and the Persians went back for centuries. Nevertheless, as soon as the Church felt that Islam, the new faith, represented a threat to its concocted version of Christianity, which was no more than a collection of ancient pagan legends, misguided inventions and a handful of statements from the Prophet Jesus, both camps buried all their past enmity and age old-hatred to confront the new faith together.

Then the expedition to Tabuk, which is the major subject of discussion in this surah, took place, followed by the march of the army commanded by Usamah ibn Zayd. This was prepared by the Prophet and dispatched by his successor, Abu Bakr, in a demonstration of power to confront the Byzantine forces being mobilized to suppress the voice of Islam. Then the Muslims achieved a great victory in the Battle of Yarmuk against the Byzantines. This ushered in the liberation of wide areas of Syria, Egypt, North Africa and the Mediterranean from Byzantine colonialism, and the consolidation of an Islamic base in Andalusia.

These final rulings, as they are stated in this surah, deal with a specific situation that obtained in Arabia, and serve, in a sense, as a legislative prelude to the Tabuk campaign, the-central issue of the surah, which sought to confront the Byzantine mobilization close to the Arabian borders. But the attitude of the people of earlier revelations and their hostility to Islam and the Muslim community were not the result of any particular historical event, or limited to any stage. That is a permanent reality. They will continue to be at war with Islam until the Muslims have abandoned their faith altogether. This hostility and the war it launches will continue to be fed by all possible means. Hence, the rulings outlined in this surah remain in full effect, unlimited to a particular period of history.

A Fight until Submission

> Fight against those who—despite having been given Scripture—do not truly believe in God and the Last Day, and do not treat as forbidden that which God and His Messenger have forbidden, and do not follow the religion of truth, till they [agree to] pay the submission tax with a willing hand, after they have been bumbled. (Verse 29)

This verse and the ones that follow were meant to prepare the Muslims for their expedition to Tabuk and the confrontation with the Byzantines and their puppet regime of Christian Arabs, known as the Ghassanld. This suggests that the descriptions we have here were true of the people on the other side of the confrontation. They simply show the reality of those people. These descriptions are not mentioned here as conditions for fighting the people of earlier revelations, but as qualities inherent in their distorted beliefs and the actual reality of those people. Hence they provide the justification for fighting them. The ruling also applies to all those who share the same beliefs and characteristics.

This verse specifies three such characteristics. (1) They do not believe in God and the Last Day; (2) they do not treat as forbidden what God has forbidden; and (3) they do not believe in the religion of truth. The verses that follow show how these characteristics apply to them.

Firstly, the Jews claim that Ezra is the son of God, and the Christians assert that Christ is His son. These claims echo similar ones made by the pagans of former times. Hence, they are to be treated on the same basis as people who do not believe in God and the Last Day. Secondly, they treat their rabbis and their monks, as well as Jesus Christ, as their Lords, in place of God. This is in total conflict with the principles of the faith of truth which is based on total submission to God alone, who has no partners. As they make such claims they demonstrate that they are idolaters who do not follow the true faith. Thirdly, they try to put out the light of God's guidance with their mouths. In other words, they are at war with the divine faith. No one is ever at war with the divine faith if he truly believes in God. Fourthly, many of their monks and rabbis devour peoples property without any justification. They do so knowing that their claims to such property are false. Hence they do not treat as forbidden what God and His Messenger have made forbidden, whether we take this statement as referring to the Messenger sent to them or to the Prophet Muhammad.

All these characteristics were true of the Christians in Syria and the Byzantines, as well as other Christians ever since Church Synods distorted the faith preached by Jesus Christ and claimed that he was the son of God and invented the concept of the Trinity, the conflict between the different sects and churches over the concept of Trinity notwithstanding. What we have here then is a general order stating a universal rule that applies to all those among the people of earlier revelations who share the same characteristics as the Christians of Syria and Byzantium.

Aggression has been committed in the first place, against God's Lordship of the universe and against human beings who are forced to submit to deities other than God. As Islam tries to defend God's Lordship and human dignity, ignorance will try to stop it by aggression and war. This is the reality we have to realize.

This Qur'anic verse commands the Muslims to fight against those among the people of earlier revelations who "do not believe in God and the Last Day." A person who claims that Ezra or Jesus is the son of God cannot be described as a believer in God. The same applies to a person who says that the Christ is the Lord, or that God is one of a Trinity, or that He manifested Himself in Jesus. It further applies to all concepts formulated by the Synods, diverse as these concepts are.

Nor can we describe as believers in God and the Last-Day—those who say that they will suffer God's punishment only for a few days no matter what sins they may commit because God loves them as His sons and daughters, or because they are God's chosen people. The same applies to those who claim that all sins are forgiven through a holy communion with Jesus Christ, which is the only way to achieve forgiveness. Neither of these two groups can be described as believers in God or in the Last Day.

This verse also describes the people of earlier revelations as ones who do not treat as forbidden what God and His Messenger have made forbidden. Whether the term "His Messenger" refers to the Messenger whom God sent to them in particular or to the Prophet Muhammad, the import is the same. The following verses explain this by saying that they devour other people's property by false claims, an action which has been forbidden in all divine messages and by all God's messengers. Some of the clearest examples of this are usurious transactions, the sale of bonds of forgiveness by the Church, opposition to the divine faith with brutal force as well as trying to turn believers away from their faith. Another clear example is forcing people to submit to beings other than God, and forcing them to implement laws other than those revealed by God. All these examples are covered by the description: "who do not treat as forbidden what God and His Messenger have forbidden." All this applies today to the people of earlier revelations as was applicable to them when this verse was revealed.

The Qur'anic verse also describes them as not following "the religion of truth." This is clear from what we have already said. It is not part of the religion of truth to believe in the Lordship of anyone other than God, or to apply a law different from God's law, or to accept legislation enacted by any authority other than God, or to submit to anyone other than Him. All these qualities are today true of the people of earlier revelations, as it was true of them then.

The condition simply that they should pay the tribute, or the submission tax, with a willing hand and that they be utterly subdued. What is the purpose of this condition, and why is it the end at which all fighting must stop?

The answer is found in the fact that with such characteristics, the people of earlier revelations place themselves at war with the divine faith, both in belief and in practical terms. They are also at war with Islamic society because of the inherent conflict between the codes of living derived from the divine faith on the one hand and ignorance, or *jahiliyyah*, on the other. As described in these verses, the people of earlier revelations belong to *jahiliyyah* in both beliefs and practices. History also proves the nature of conflict, and the impossibility of co-existence between the two codes. The people of earlier revelations were determined in their opposition to the Islamic faith in the period preceding the revelation of this verse, and in the period following it, up to the present day.

As the only religion of truth that exists on earth today, Islam takes appropriate action to remove all physical and material obstacles that try to impede its efforts to liberate mankind from submission to anyone other than God. That submission is translated in following the religion of truth, provided that every human being is given free choice. There must be no pressure either from the religion itself or from those forces putting up the physical obstacles. The practical way to ensure the removal of those physical obstacles while not forcing anyone to adopt Islam is to smash the power of those authorities based on false beliefs until they declare their submission and demonstrate this by paying the submission tax. When this happens, the process of liberating mankind is completed by giving every individual the freedom of choice based on conviction. Anyone who is not convinced may continue to follow his faith. However, he has to pay the submission tax to fulfill a number of objectives . . . by paying this tax, known as *jizyah*, he declares that he will not stand in physical opposition to the efforts advocating the true Divine faith.[7]

AL-AZHAR, AL-MUNTAKHAB FII TAFSIIR AL-QUR'AAN AL-KARIIM, 1985:

9.28: O you believers, it is because of their polytheism that the polytheists have defiled their souls, being in error in their belief. Don't let them enter the Prohibited Mosque after this year (9AH). If you fear poverty because of cutting off your business with them, God will compensate you for this, and out of his bounty will make you rich, if He wills. Verily, God is knowledgeable about your condition, and wise to put it [back] in order.

9.29: O you believers, fight the unbelievers, namely the People of the Book who do not believe True Faith and do not accept the Resurrection and the Recompense [heaven, hell] in the true way, and do not require stopping what God and his Emissary ordered stopped; they do not embrace the True Religion, i.e. Islam. Fight until they believe, or force them to pay the jizya humbly and obediently, not grudgingly, so that they contribute to the Islamic budget [*sic*].

9.30: . . . may God curse these unbelievers and their families, out of amazement at how far they have strayed from the Truth, which is clear; but they inclined toward error.[8]

RICHARD BELL (D. 1952), *A COMMENTARY ON THE QUR'AN*

V. [verse] 29 begins somewhat abruptly, and the phrase min alladhina 'utu l-kitab comes in rather awkwardly. It is also an unusual charge against the People of the Book that they do not believe in Allah or in the Last Day. It looks as if this verse had first been used with regard to the polytheists, and later made the beginning of the declaration of war against "those who have been given the Book." *jizyah*—only here in later Muslim law was the special poll-tax levied upon non-Muslims living under Muslim rule, and was distinguished from the *kharaj* which rested on the land. But it is doubtful if this distinction was introduced before the second century [A.H.]; and probably the word here is equivalent to "tribute" in general. 'an yad, the exact meaning of the phrase is uncertain. Beidawi gives "submissively" or "in person." . . . Another possible sense is "out of hand," i.e., at once, on the spot, in ready money.[9]

NOTES

1. Suyuti wrote a famous and ubiquitous commentary, *Tafsiir al-Jalalayn*, which he composed with his teacher, Jalaal al-Diin al-MaHallii; the latter composed the second part, and then Suyuti wrote the first part to complete it, including this translation/quote for Q. 9.29. *Tafsīr al-Jalālayn*. (Beirut, 1404/1984), p. 244.

2. From Suyuti's *Durr al-Manthūr* . . . (Beirut, n.d.), vol. 3, p. 228, where Suyuti quotes various traditions.

3. Zamakhshari, *Al-Kashshaaf* . . . , ed. M. Ahmad (Cairo, 1365/1946), vol. 2, pp. 262, 263.

4. Tabari, *Jāmi 'al-Bayān* . . . , ed. M. Shākir (Beirut, 1421/2001), vol. 10, pp. 125, 126.

5. Beidawi, *Anwār al-Tanzīl* . . . , ed. H. O. Fleischer (1846–1848; repr., Osnabrueck, 1968), vol. 1, p. 383, line 25.

6. Ibn Kathir, *Tafsir Ibn Kathir* (Riyadh, 2000), vol. 4, pp. 404–407.

7. Sayyid Qutb, *In the Shade of the Qur'an*, vol. 8: Surah 9 (Leicestershire, UK, 2003), pp. 115–16, 120–23.

8. *Al-Muntakhab fii Tafsiir al-Qur'aan al-Kariim* [The Culled [correct selection from] Qur'an Commentary], 11th ed. (Cairo: Committee for the Qur'an and Sunna, 1985). Note says the jizya was a tax somewhere between 8 and 40 dirhams (p. 263 ff.).

9. Richard Bell, *A Commentary on the Qur'an,* vol. 1: *Surahs I–XXIV* (Manchester, 1991), p. 299.

4

JIHAD IN THE HADITH

SAHIH BUKHARI*

Vol. 4, bk. 52, no. 46: Narrated Abu Huraira: I heard Allah's Apostle saying, "The example of a Mujahid in Allah's Cause—and Allah knows better who really strives in His Cause—is like a person who fasts and prays continuously. Allah guarantees that He will admit the Mujahid in His Cause into Paradise if he is killed, otherwise He will return him to his home safely with rewards and war booty (*maal-e-gani-maat*)."

Vol. 4, bk. 52, no. 53: Narrated Anas bin Malik: The Prophet said, "Nobody who dies and finds good from Allah (in the Hereafter) would wish to come back to this world even if he were given the whole world and whatever is in it, except the martyr who, on seeing the superiority of martyrdom, would like to come back to the world and get killed again (in Allah's Cause)."

Vol. 4, bk. 52, no. 48: Narrated Anas: The Prophet said, "A single endeavor (of fighting) in Allah's Cause in the afternoon or in the forenoon is better than all the world and whatever is in it. A place in Paradise as small as the bow or lash of one of you is better than all the world and whatever is in it. And if a houri from Paradise appeared to the people of the earth, she would fill the space between Heaven and the Earth with light and pleasant scent and her head cover is better than the world and whatever is in it."

Vol. 4, bk. 52, no. 44: Narrated Abu Huraira: A man came to Allah's Apostle and said, "Instruct me as to such a deed as equals Jihad (in reward)." He replied, "I do not find such a deed." Then he added, "Can you, while the Muslim fighter is in the battle-field, enter your mosque to perform prayers without cease and fast and never break your fast?" The man said, "But who can do that?" Abu-Huraira added, "The Mujahid (i.e. Muslim fighter) is rewarded even for the footsteps of his horse while it wanders bout (for grazing) tied in a long rope."

---

*Excerpted from M. Muhsin Khair, "Translation of Sahih Bukhari," Muslim Students Association, University of Southern California, http://www.usc.edu/dept/MSA/fundamentals/hadithsunnah/bukhari.

Vol. 4, bk. 52, no. 49: Narrated Samura: The Prophet said, "Last night two men came to me (in a dream) and made me ascend a tree and then admitted me into a better and superior house, better of which I have never seen. One of them said, 'This house is the house of martyrs.'"

Vol. 4, bk. 52, no. 50: Narrated Anas bin Malik: The Prophet said, "A single endeavor (of fighting) in Allah's Cause in the forenoon or in the afternoon is better than the world and whatever is in it."

Vol. 4, bk. 52, no. 42: Narrated Ibn 'Abbas: Allah's Apostle said, "There is no Hijra (i.e. migration) (from Mecca to Medina) after the Conquest (of Mecca), but Jihad and good intention remain; and if you are called (by the Muslim ruler) for fighting, go forth immediately."

Vol. 4, bk. 52, no. 4: Narrated Abu Huraira: The Prophet said, "By Him in Whose Hands my life is! Were it not for some men amongst the believers who dislike to be left behind me and whom I cannot provide with means of conveyance, I would certainly never remain behind any Sariya' (army-unit) setting out in Allah's Cause. By Him in Whose Hands my life is! I would love to be martyred in Allah's Cause and then get resurrected and then get martyred, and then get resurrected again and then get martyred and then get resurrected again and then get martyred."

Vol. 4, bk. 52, no. 52: Narrated Anas bin Malik: Prophet of Allah said, "Zaid took the flag and was martyred, and then Ja'far took the flag and was martyred, and then 'Abdullah bin Rawaha took the flag and was martyred too, and then Khalid bin Al-Walid took the flag though he was not appointed as a commander and Allah made him victorious." The Prophet further added, "It would not please us to have them with us." Aiyub, a sub-narrator, added, "Or the Prophet, shedding tears, said, 'It would not please them to be with us.'"

Vol. 4, bk. 52, no. 61: Narrated Anas: My uncle Anas bin An-Nadr was absent from the Battle of Badr. He said, "O Allah's Apostle! I was absent from the first battle you fought against the pagans. (By Allah) if Allah gives me a chance to fight the pagans, no doubt. Allah will see how (bravely) I will fight." On the day of Uhud when the Muslims turned their backs and fled, he said, "O Allah! I apologize to You for what these (i.e. his companions) have done, and I denounce what these (i.e. the pagans) have done." Then he advanced and Sad bin Muadh met him. He said "O Sad bin Muadh! By the Lord of An-Nadr, Paradise! I am smelling its aroma coming from before (the mountain of) Uhud," Later on Sad said, "O Allah's Apostle! I cannot achieve or do what he (i.e. Anas bin An-Nadr) did. We found more than eighty wounds by swords and arrows on his body. We found him dead and his body was mutilated so badly that none except his sister could recognize him by his fingers."

Vol. 4, bk. 52, no. 63: Narrated Al-Bara: A man whose face was covered with an iron mask (i.e. clad in armor) came to the Prophet and said, "O Allah's Apostle! Shall I fight or embrace Islam first?" The Prophet said, "Embrace Islam first and then fight." So he embraced Islam, and was martyred. Allah's Apostle said, "A Little work, but a great reward." (He did very little (after embracing Islam), but he will be rewarded in abundance).

Vol. 4, bk. 52, no. 64: Narrated Anas bin Malik: Um Ar-Rubai'bint Al-Bara', the mother of Hartha bin Suraqa came to the Prophet and said, "O Allah's Prophet! Will you tell me about Hartha?" Hartha has been killed (i.e. martyred) on the day of Badr with an arrow thrown by an unidentified person. She added, "If he is in Paradise, I will be patient; otherwise, I will weep bitterly for him." He said, "O mother of Hartha! There are Gardens in Paradise and your son got the Firdausal-ala (i.e. the best place in Paradise)."

SAHIH MUSLIM: THE BOOK OF JIHAD AND EXPEDITION (KITAB AL-JIHAD WA'L-SIYAR), BOOK 19*

Chapter 1

No. 4292: Ibn 'Aun reported: I wrote to Nafi' inquiring from him whether it was necessary to extend (to the disbelievers) an invitation to accept (Islam) before m." ing them in fight. He wrote (in reply) to me that it was necessary in the early days of Islam. The Messenger of Allah (may peace be upon him) made a raid upon Banu Mustaliq while they were unaware and their cattle were having a drink at the water. He killed those who fought and imprisoned others. On that very day, he captured Juwairiya bint al-Harith. Nafi' said that this tradition was related to him by Abdullah b. Umar who (himself) was among the raiding troops.

Chapter 2

No. 4294: It has been reported from Sulaiman b. Buraid through his father that when the Messenger of Allah (may peace be upon him) appointed anyone as leader of an army or detachment he would especially exhort him to fear Allah and to be good to the Muslims who were with him. He would say: Fight in the name of Allah and in the way of Allah. Fight against those who disbelieve in Allah.

*Excerpted from Abdul Hamid Siddiqi, "Translation of Sahih Muslim," Muslim Students Association, University of Southern California, http://www.usc.edu/dept/MSA/fundamentals/hadithsunnah/muslim.

Make a holy war, do not embezzle the spoils; do not break your pledge; and do not mutilate (the dead) bodies; do not kill the children. When you meet your enemies who are polytheists, invite them to three courses of action. If they respond to any one of these, you also accept it and withold yourself from doing them any harm. Invite them to (accept) Islam; if they respond to you, accept it from them and desist from fighting against them. Then invite them to migrate from their lands to the land of Muhajirs and inform them that, if they do so, they shall have all the privileges and obligations of the Muhajirs. If they refuse to migrate, tell them that they will have the status of Bedouin Muilims and will be subjected to the Commands of Allah like other Muslims, but they will not get any share from the spoils of war or Fai' except when they actually fight with the Muslims (against the disbelievers). If they refuse to accept Islam, demand from them the Jizya. If they agree to pay, accept it from them and hold off your hands. If they refuse to pay the tax, seek Allah's help and fight them. When you lay siege to a fort and the besieged appeal to you for protection in the name of Allah and His Prophet, do not accord to them the guarantee of Allah and His Prophet, but accord to them your own guarantee and the guarantee of your companions for it is a lesser sin that the security given by you or your companions be disregarded than that the security granted in the name of Allah and His Prophet be violated When you besiege a fort and the besieged want you to let them out in accordance with Allah's Command, do not let them come out in accordance with His Command, but do so at your (own) command, for you do not know whether or not you will be able to carry out Allah's behest with regard to them.

Chapter 6

No. 4313: It has been narrated on the authority of Abu Huraira that the Messenger of Allah (may peace be upon him) said: Do not desire an encounter with the enemy; but when you encounter them, be firm.

No. 4314: It is narrated by Abu Nadr that he learnt from a letter sent by a man from the Aslam tribe, who was a Companion of the Holy Prophet (may peace be upon him) and whose name was 'Abdullah b. Abu Aufa, to 'Umar b. 'Ubaidullah when the latter marched upon Haruriyya (Khawarij) informing him that the Messenger of Allah (may peace be upon him) in one of those days when lie was confronting the enemy waited until the sun had declined. Then he stood up (to address the people) and said: O ye men, do not wish for an encounter with the enemy. Pray to Allah to grant you security; (but) when you (have to) encounter them exercise patience, and you should know that Paradise is under the shadows of the swords. Then the Messenger of Allah (may peace be upon him) stood up (again) and said: O Allah. Revealer of the Book, Disperser of the clouds, Defeater of the hordes, put our enemy to rout and help us against them.

Chapter 7

No. 4315: It is narrated on the authority of Ibn Abu Aufa that the Messenger of Allah (may peace be upon him) cursed the tribes (who had marched upon Medina with a combined force in 5 H) and said: O Allah, Revealer of the Book, swift in (taking) account, put the tribes to rout. O Lord, defeat them and shake them.

No. 4318: It is narrated on the authority of Anas that the Messenger of Allah (may peace be upon him) said on the day of the Battle of Ubud: O Allah, if Thou wilt (defeat Muslims), there will be none on the earth to worship Thee

Chapter 8

No. 4319: It is narrated on the authority of 'Abdullah that a woman was found killed in one of the battles fought by the Messenger of Allah (may peace be upon him). He disapproved of the killing of women and children.

No. 4320: It is narrated by Ibn 'Umar that a woman was found killed in one of these battles; so the Messenger of Allah (may peace be upon him) forbade the killing of women and children.

Chapter 9

No. 4321: It is reported on the authority of Sa'b b. Jaththama that the Prophet of Allah (may peace be upon him), when asked about the women and children of the polytheists being killed during the night raid, said: They are from them.

Chapter 10

No. 4324: It is narrated on the authority of 'Abdullah that the Messenger of Allah (may peace be upon him) ordered the date-palms of Banu Nadir to be burnt and cut. These palms were at Buwaira. Qutaibah and Ibn Rumh in their versions of the tradition have added: So Allah, the Glorious and Exalted, revealed the verse: "Whatever trees you have cut down or left standing on their trunks, it was with the permission of Allah so that He may disgrace the evil-doers" (lix. 5).

PART 3:
Muslim Theologians and Jurists on Jihad: Classical Writings

5

MUWATTA

Malik b. Anas (d. 795)

BOOK 21: JIHAD

Stimulation of Desire for Jihad

21.1.1: Yahya related to me from Malik from Abu'z-Zinad from al-Araj from Abu Hurayra that the Messenger of Allah, may Allah bless him and grant him peace, said "Someone who does jihad in the way of Allah is like someone who fasts and prays constantly and who does not slacken from his prayer and fasting until he returns."

21.1.2: Yahya related to me from Malik from Abu'z Zinad from al-Araj from Abu Hurayra that the Messenger of Allah, may Allah bless him and grant him peace, said, "Allah guarantees either the Garden or a safe return to his home with whatever he has obtained of reward or booty, for the one who does jihad in His way, if it is solely jihad and trust in his promise that brings him out of his house."

21.1.3: Yahya related to me from Malik from Zayd ibn Aslam from Abu Salih as-Samman from Abu Hurayra that the Messenger of Allah, may Allah bless him and grant him peace, said, "Horses are a reward for one man, a protection for another,

Excerpted from 'A'isha 'Abdarghman at-Tarjumana and Ya'qub Johnson, trans., *Muwatta*, by Malik b. Anas, http://www.usc.edu/dept/MSA/fundamentals/hadithsunnah/muwatta.

a burden for another. The one who has them as a reward is the one who dedicates them for use in the way of Allah, and tethers them in a meadow or grassland. Whatever the horse enjoys of the grassland or meadow in the length of its tether are good deeds for him. If it breaks its tether and goes over a hillock or two, its tracks and droppings are good deeds for him. If it crosses a river and drinks from it while he did not mean to allow it to drink it, that counts as good deeds for him, and the horse is a reward for him.

Another man uses his horse to gain self reliance and up-standingness and does not forget Allah's right on their necks and backs (i.e. he does not ill treat or over-work them). Horses are a protection for him.

Another man uses them out of pride to show them off and in hostility to the people of Islam. They are a burden on that man."

The Messenger of Allah, may Allah bless him and grant him peace, was asked about donkeys, and he said, "Nothing has been revealed to me about them except this single all-inclusive ayat, 'Whoever does an atom of good will see it, and whoever does an atom of evil, will see it'" (sura 99 ayats 7, 8).

21.1.4: Yahya related to me from Abdullah ibn Abd ar-Rahman ibn Mamar al-Ansari that Ata ibn Yasar said that the Messenger of Allah, may Allah bless him and grant him peace, said, "Shall I tell you who has the best degree among people? A man who takes the rein of his horse to do jihad in the way of Allah. Shall I tell you who has the best degree among people after him? A man who lives alone with a few sheep, performs the prayer, pays the zakat, and worships Allah without associating anything with him."

21.1.5: Yahya related to me from Malik that Yahya ibn Said said, "Ubada ibn al-Walid ibn Ubada ibn as-Samit informed me from his father that his grandfather (Ubada) said, 'We made a contract with the Messenger of Allah, may Allah bless him and grant him peace, to hear and obey in ease and hardship, enthusiasm and reluctance, and not to dispute with people in authority and to speak or establish the truth wherever we were without worrying about criticism.'"

21.1.6: Yahya related to me from Malik that Zayd ibn Aslam had said that Ubayda ibn al-Jarrah had written to Umar ibn al-Khattab mentioning to him a great array of Byzantine troops and the anxiety they were causing him. Umar ibn al-Khattab wrote in reply to him, "Whatever hardship befalls a believing slave, Allah will make an opening for him after it, and a hardship will not overcome two eases. Allah the Exalted says in His Book, 'O you who trust, be patient, and vie in patience; be steadfast and fear Allah, perhaps you will profit'" (sura 3 ayat 200).

21.18.39: Yahya related to me from Malik from Ishaq ibn Abdullah ibn Abi Talha that Anas ibn Malik had said that when the Messenger of Allah, may Allah bless him and grant him peace, went to Quba, he visited Umm Haram bint Milhan and she fed him. Umm Haram was the wife of Ubada ibn as-Samit. One day the Messenger of Allah, may Allah bless him and grant him peace, had called on her and she had fed him, and sat down to delouse his hair. The Messenger of Allah, may Allah bless him and grant him peace, had dozed and woke up smiling. Umm Haram said, "What is making you smile, Messenger of Allah?" He said, "Some of my community were presented to me, raiding in the way of Allah. They were riding in the middle of the sea, kings on thrones, or like kings on thrones." (Ishaq wasn't sure). She said, "O Messenger of Allah! Ask Allah to put me among them!" So he had made a dua for her, and put his head down and slept. Then he had woken up smiling, and she said to him, "Messenger of Allah, why are you smiling?" He said, "Some of my community were presented to me, raiding in the way of Allah. They were kings on thrones or like kings on thrones," as he had said in the first one. She said, "O Messenger of Allah! Ask Allah to put me among them!" He said, "You are among the first."

Ishaq added, "She travelled on the sea in the time of Muawiya, and when she landed, she was thrown from her mount and killed."

21.18.40: Yahya related to me from Malik from Yahya ibn Said from Abu Salih as-Samman from Abu Hurayra that the Messenger of Allah, may Allah bless him and grant him peace, said, "Had I not been concerned for my community, I would have liked never to stay behind a raiding party going out in the way of Allah. However, I do not find the means to carry them to it, nor do they find anything on which to ride out and it is grievous for them that they should stay behind me. I would like to fight in the way of Allah and be killed, then brought to life so I could be killed and then brought to life so I could be killed."

21.18.41: Yahya related to me from Malik that Yahya ibn Said said, "On the Day of Uhud, The Messenger of Allah, may Allah bless him and grant him peace, said, 'Who will bring me news of Sad ibn al-Rabi al-Ansari?' a man said, 'Me, Messenger of Allah!' So the man went around among the slain, and Sad ibn al-Rabi said to him, 'What are you doing?' The man said to him, 'The Messenger of Allah, may Allah bless him and grant him peace, sent me to bring him news of you.' He said, 'Go to him, and give him my greetings, and tell him that I have been stabbed twelve times, and am mortally wounded. Tell your people that they will have no excuse with Allah if the Messenger of Allah, may Allah bless him and grant him peace, is slain while one of them is still alive.'"

21.18.42: Yahya related to me from Malik from Yahya ibn Said that the Messenger of Allah, may Allah bless him and grant him peace, stimulated people for jihad and mentioned the Garden. One of the Ansar was eating some dates in his hand, and said, "Am I so desirous of this world that I should sit until I finish them?" He threw aside what was in his hand and took his sword, and fought until he was slain.

21.18.43: Yahya related to me from Malik from Yahya ibn Said that Muadh ibn Jabal said, "There are two military expeditions. There is one military expedition in which valuables are spent, the contributor is willing, the authorities are obeyed, and corruption is avoided. That military expedition is all good. There is a military expedition in which valuables are not spent, the contributor is not willing, the authorities are not obeyed, and corruption is not avoided. The one who fights in that military expedition does not return with reward."

The Martyrs in the Way of Allah

21.14.27: Yahya related to me from Malik from Abu'z-Zinad from al-Araj from Abu Hurayra that the Messenger of Allah, may Allah bless him and grant him peace, said, "By He in whose hand my self is! I would like to fight in the way of Allah and be killed, then be brought to life again so I could be killed, and then be brought to life again so I could be killed." Abu Hurayra said three times, "I testify to it by Allah!"

21.14.28: Yahya related to me from Malik from Abu'z-Zinad from al-Araj from Abu Hurayra that the Messenger of Allah, may Allah bless him and grant him peace, said, "Allah laughs at two men. One of them kills the other, but each of them will enter the Garden: one fights in the way of Allah and is killed, then Allah turns to the killer, so he fights (in the way of Allah) and also becomes a martyr."

21.14.29: Yahya related to me from Malik from Abu'z-Zinad from al-Araj from Abu Hurayra that the Messenger of Allah, may Allah bless him and grant him peace, said, "By He in whose hand my self is! None of you is wounded in the way of Allah—and Allah knows best who is wounded in HisWay, but that when the Day of Rising comes, blood will gush forth from his wound. It will be the colour of blood, but its scent will be that of musk."

21.14.30: Yahya related to me from Malik from Zayd ibn Aslam that Umar ibn al-Khattab used to say, "O Allah! Do not let me be slain by the hand of a man who has prayed a single prostration to You with which he will dispute with me before You on the Day of Rising!"

21.14.31: Yahya related to me from Malik from Yahya ibn Said from Said al-Maqburi from Abdullah ibn Abi Qatada that his father had said that a man came to the Messenger of Allah, may Allah bless him and grant him peace, and said, "O Messenger of Allah! If I am killed in the way of Allah, expectant for reward, sin-

cere, advancing, and not retreating, will Allah pardon my faults?" The Messenger
of Allah, may Allah bless him and grant him peace, said, "Yes." When the man
turned away, the Messenger of Allah, may Allah bless him and grant him peace,
called him—or commanded him and he was called to him. The Messenger of
Allah, may Allah bless him and grant him peace, said to him, "What did you say?"
He repeated his words to him, and the Prophet, may Allah bless him and grant him
peace, said to him, "Yes, except for the debt. Jibril said that to me."

21.14.32: Yahya related to me from Malik from Abu'n-Nadr, the mawla of Umar
ibn Ubaydullah that he had heard that the Messenger of Allah, may Allah bless
him and grant him peace, said over the martyrs of Uhud, "I testify for them." Abu
Bakr as-Siddiq said, "Messenger of Allah! Are we not their brothers? We entered
Islam as they entered Islam and we did jihad as they did jihad." The Messenger
of Allah, may Allah bless him and grant him peace, said, "Yes, but I do not know
what you will do after me." Abu Bakr wept profusely and said, "Are we really
going to out-live you!"

21.14.33: Yahya related to me from Malik that Yahya ibn Said said, "The Messenger of Allah, may Allah bless him and grant him peace, was sitting by a grave
which was being dug at Madina. A man looked into the grave and said, 'An awful
bed for the mumin.' The Messenger of Allah, may Allah bless him and grant him
peace, said, 'Evil? What you have said is absolutely wrong.'

The man said, 'I didn't mean that, Messenger of Allah. I meant being killed
in the way of Allah.' The Messenger of Allah, may Allah bless him and grant him
peace, said, 'Being killed in the way of Allah has no like! There is no place on the
earth which I would prefer my grave to be than here (meaning Madina). He
repeated it three times.'"

Things in Which Martyrdom Lies

21.15.34: Yahya related to me from Malik from Zayd ibn Aslam that Umar ibn al-
Khattab used to say, "O Allah! I ask you for martyrdom in Your way and death in
the city of Your Messenger!"

21.15.35: Yahya related to me from Malik from Yahya ibn Said that Umar ibn al-
Khattab said, "The nobility of the mumin is his taqwa. His deen is his noble
descent. His manliness is his good character. Boldness and cowardice are but
instincts which Allah places wherever He wills. The coward shrinks from
defending even his father and mother, and the bold one fights for the sake of the
combat not for the spoils. Being slain is but one way of meeting death, and the
martyr is the one who gives himself, expectant of reward from Allah."

6

[UNTITLED]

Ibn Abi Zayd al-Qayrawani

(d. 996)

Jihad is a precept of Divine institution. Its performance by certain individuals may dispense others from it. We Malikis [one of the four schools of Muslim jurisprudence] maintain that it is preferable not to begin hostilities with the enemy before having invited the latter to embrace the religion of Allah except where the enemy attacks first. They have the alternative of either converting to Islam or paying the poll tax <jizya>, short of which war will be declared against them. The jizya can only be accepted from them if they occupy a territory where our laws can be enforced. If they are out of our reach, the jizya cannot be accepted from them unless they come within our territory. Otherwise we will make war against them.

It is incumbent upon us to fight the enemy without inquiring as to whether we shall be under the command of a pious or depraved leader.

There is no inconvenience to kill white non-Arabs who have been taken prisoner. But no one can be executed after having been granted the aman <protection>. The promises made to them must not be broken. Women and non-pubescents will not be executed. One will avoid killing monks and rabbis unless they have taken part in battle. Women also will be executed if they have participated in the fighting. The aman granted by the humblest Muslim must be recognized by others [Muslims]. A Women and a non-pubescent child can also grant the aman when they are aware of its significance. However, according to another opinion, it is only valid if confirmed by the imam. The imam will retain a fifth of the booty captured by the Muslims in the course of warfare and he will share the remaining four fifths among the soldiers of the army. Preferably, the apportioning will take place on enemy ground.

Excerpted from Leon Bercher, *La Risala ou Epitre sue les elements du dogme de la loi d'Islam* (Algiers, 1945); English translation from Bat Ye'or, *The Decline of Eastern Christianity under Islam: From Jihad to Dhimmitude Seventh–Twentieth Century* (Madison, NJ: Fairleigh Dickinson University Press, 1996), p. 295.

7

BIDAYAT AL-MUDJTAHID

Averroes (d. 1198)

THE JIHAD

The most important rules concerning this subject will be dealt with in two chapters. The first will contain the most important regulations as regards warfare, the second the rules pertaining to the enemy's property when it is captured by the Moslems.[1]

The first chapter consists of seven paragraphs:

1. The legal qualification (*hukm*) of this activity and the persons who are obliged to take part in it.
2. The enemy.
3. The damage allowed to be inflicted upon the different categories of enemies.
4. The prerequisites for warfare.
5. The maximum number of enemies against which one is obliged to stand one's ground.
6. Truce.
7. The aims of warfare.

Par. 1. The legal qualification (hukm) of this activity and the persons obliged to take part in it

Scholars agree that the jihad is a collective not a personal obligation. Only 'Abd Allāh Ibn al-Hasan[2] professed it to be a recommendable act. According to the majority of scholars, the compulsory nature of the jihad is founded on [K 2:216]: "*Fighting is prescribed for you, though it is distasteful to you.*"[3] That this obligation is a collective and not a personal one, i.e., that the obligation, when it can

---

Excerpted from *Bidayat al-Mudjtahid*, in Rudolph Peters, *Jihad in Mediaeval and Modern Islam: The Chapter on Jihad from Averroes' Legal Handbook "Bidayat al-mudjtahid,"* trans. and annotated by Rudolph Peters (Leiden: Brill, 1977), pp. 9–25.

be properly carried out by a limited number of individuals, is cancelled for the remaining Moslems, is founded on [K 9:112]: *"It is not for the believers to march out all together,"*[4] on [K 4:95]: *"Though to all, Allah hath promised the good (reward),"*[5] and, lastly, on the fact that the Prophet never went to battle without leaving some people behind. All this together implies that this activity is a collective obligation. The obligation to participate in the jihad applies to adult free men who have the means at their disposal to go to war and who are healthy, that is, not ill or suffering from chronic diseases. There is absolutely no controversy about the latter restriction because of [K 48:17]: *"There is no blame upon the blind, or upon the lame, or upon the sick"*[6] and because of [K 9:91]: *"No blame rests upon the frail or upon the sick or upon those who find nothing to contribute."*[7] Nor do I know of any dissentient views as regards the rule that this obligation applies only to free men. Nearly all scholars agree that this obligation is conditional on permission granted by the parents. Only in the case that the obligation has become a personal one, for instance because there is nobody else to carry it out, can this permission be dispensed with.[8] The prerequisite of permission is based on the following authentic Tradition: *"Once a man said to the Messenger of Allah: 'I wish to take part in the jihad.' The Messenger said to him: 'Are both your parents still alive?' When he answered in the affirmative, the Messenger said: 'Then perform the jihad for their sake.'"* Scholars are not agreed whether this permission is also required of parents who are polytheists. There is controversy, too, about the question whether the creditor's permission has to be asked when a person has run into debt. An argument in favour of this can be found in the following Tradition: *"A man said to the Prophet: 'Will Allah forgive me my sins if I shall sacrifice myself patiently and shall be killed in the way of Allah (i.e., by taking part in the jihad)?' The Prophet said: 'Yes, with the exception of your debts. This Djibrīl has told me before.'"*[9] The majority of scholars do not consider it obligatory, especially not when the debtor leaves enough behind to serve as payment for his debts.

Par. 2. The Enemy

Scholars agree that all polytheists should be fought. This is founded on [K 8:39]: *"Fight them until there is no persecution and the religion is entirely Allah's."*[10] However, it has been related by Mālik[11] that it would not be allowed to attack the Ethiopians and the Turks on the strength of the Tradition of the Prophet: *"Leave the Ethiopians in peace as long as they leave you in peace."* Questioned as to the authenticity of this Tradition, Mālik did not acknowledge it, but said: "People still avoid attacking them."

Par. 3. The damage allowed to be inflicted upon the different categories of enemies

Damage inflicted upon the enemy may consist in damage to his property, injury to his person or violation of his personal liberty, i.e., that he is made a slave and is appropriated. This may be done, according to the *Consensus (idjmā)* to all poly-theists: men, women, young and old, important and unimportant. Only with regard to monks do opinions vary; for some take it that they must be left in peace and that they must not be captured, but allowed to go unscathed and that they may not be enslaved. In support of their opinion they bring forward the words of the Prophet: *"Leave them in peace and also that to which they have dedicated them-selves,"*[12] as well as the practice of Abū Bakr.[13]

Most scholars are agreed that, in his dealings with captives, various policies are open to the Imam [head of the Islamic state, caliph]. He may pardon them, kill them, or release them either on ransom or as *dhimmī* [non-Moslem subject of the Islamic state], in which latter case the released captive is obliged to pay poll-tax (*jizyah*). Some scholars, however, have taught that captives may never be slain. According to al-Hasan Ibn Muhammad al-Tamīmī,[14] this was even the *Consensus (idjmā)* of the *Sahābah* [contemporaries of Muhammad that have known him.] This controversy has arisen because, firstly, the Koran-verses contradict each other in this respect; secondly, practice [of the Prophet and the first caliphs] was inconsistent; and lastly, the obvious interpretation of the Koran is at variance with the Prophet's deeds. The obvious interpretation of [K 47:4]: *"So when ye meet those who have disbelieved (let there be) slaughter until when ye have made havoc of them"*[15] is that the Imam is only entitled to pardon captives or to release them on ransom. On the other hand, [K 8:67]: *"It was not for a prophet to have prisoners so as to cause havoc in the land,"*[16] as well as the occasion when this verse was revealed [viz. the captives of Badr] would go to prove that it is better to slay captives than to enslave them. The Prophet himself would in some cases slay captives outside the field of battle, while he would pardon them in others. Women he used to enslave. Abū Ubayd[17] has related that the Prophet never enslaved male Arabs. After him, the *Sahābah* reached unanimity about the rule that the People of the Book (*ahl al-kitāb*), both male and female, might be enslaved. Those who are of the opinion that the verse which prohibits slaying [K 47:4] abrogates the Prophet's example, maintain that captives may not be slain. Others profess, however, that this verse does not concern itself with the slaughter of captives and that it was by no means intended to restrict the number of policies possible with regard to captives. On the contrary, they say, the fact that the Prophet used to slay captives adds a supplementing rule to the verse in question [K 47:4] and thus removes the occasion for the complaint that he omitted to kill the captives of Badr. These, not, do profess that the killing of captives is allowed.

It is only allowed to slay the enemy on the condition that *amān* [safe conduct] has not been granted. There is no dissension about this among the Moslems. There is controversy, however, concerning the question who is entitled to grant *amān*. Everyone is agreed that the Imam is entitled to this. The majority of scholars are of the opinion that free Moslem males are also entitled to grant it, but Ibn Mādjishūn[18] maintains that in this case, it is subject to authorization by the Imam. Similarly, there is controversy concerning the *amān* granted by women and slaves. Ibn Mādjishūn and Sahnūn[19] hold that *amān* granted by a woman is also subject to authorization by the Imam. Abū Hanīfah[20] has taught that the *amān* granted by a slave is only valid when the slave is allowed to join in the fighting.[21] The source of the controversy is that a general rule is in conflict with the analogous interpretation of another rule. The general rule is founded on the words of the Prophet: *"The blood (money) of all Moslems is equal. Even the humblest strives for their protection. Together, they make up a unity against the others."* These words, in their universality, imply that *amān* granted by a slave is valid. The conflicting analogy is that in order to be able to grant *amān*, full legal capacity is required. Now, a slave has only partial legal capacity by the very fact of his being a slave. By analogy, the fact that he is a slave should counteract the validity of this *amān*, as it does with regard to numerous other legal acts. The general rule, then, should be restricted by analogy.

The controversy about the validity of *amān* granted by a woman owes its origin to two different readings of the words of the Prophet: *"We grant protection to those whom you have granted protection, Umm Hāni"* as well as to the question whether women are to be put on a par with men by analogy. Some read in the words of the Prophet an authorization of the *amān* granted by Umm Hāni, not a confirmation of its validity, and they infer that her *amān* would have had no legal effects had the Prophet not authorized it. Consequently, they maintain that *amān* granted by a woman is only valid when the Imam has authorized it. Others hold that the Prophet confirmed the *amān* granted by Umm Hāni in the sense that he approved something which already existed and had legal effects, not in the sense that the act was only validated by his authorization. Thus, the latter group maintains that a woman is entitled to grant valid *amān*. This view finds also favour with those who, in this respect, put women on a par with men and feel that there is no difference between them here. Others, who are of the opinion that a woman is inferior to a man, consider an *amān* granted by enslavement but only against death.[22] The controversy [about the validity of *amān* granted by women] might also be explained by the divergent opinions about the use of the male plural: does this include women or not? All this, of course, according to legal usage.

As regards injury to the person, that is, the slaying of the enemy, the Moslems agree that in times of war, all adult, able-bodied, unbelieving males may be slain. As to the question whether the enemy may also be slain after he has been captured, there is the above-mentioned controversy. There is no disagreement about the rule that it is forbidden to slay women and children, provided that they are not fighting, for then women, in any case, may be slain. This rule is founded on the fact that, according to authoritative Traditions, the Prophet prohibited the slaughter of women and children and once said about a woman who had been slain: *"She was not one who would have fought."*[23]

There is controversy about the question whether it is allowed to slay hermits who have retired from the world, the blind, the chronically ill and the insane, those who are old and unable to fight any longer, peasants, and serfs. Mālik professes that neither the blind, nor the insane, nor the hermits may be slain and that of their property not all may be carried off, but that enough should be left for them to be able to survive. Neither is it allowed, according to him, to slay the old and decrepit. Of the same opinion are Abū Hanīfah and his pupils. Thawrī[24] and Awzāī,[25] however, have taught that of these groups, only the aged may not be slain. On the other hand, Awzāī had also taught that this prohibition is also valid with regard to peasants. According to the most authoritative opinion of Shāfiī,[26] all of these categories may be slain. The source of this controversy is to be found in the fact that in a number of Traditions, rules are given which are at variance with the general rule of the authentic Tradition: *"I have been commanded to fight the people until they say: 'There is no God but Allah.'"*[27] [K 9:5]: *"Then when the sacred months have slipped away, slay the polytheists wherever ye find them"*[28] as well as the above-mentioned Tradition give as a general rule that every polytheist must be slain, whether he is a monk or not. Nevertheless, the following Traditions, among others, are brought forward in support of the prescription that the lives of the categories mentioned must be saved:

1. Dāwūd Ibn al-Hasīn[29] has related on the authority of Ikrimah[30] on the authority of Ibn 'Abbās[31] that the Prophet used to say, whenever he sent out his armies: *"Do not slay hermits."*

2. On the authority of Anas Ibn Mālik[32] it has been related that the Prophet said: *"Do not slay the old and decrepit, children, or women. Do not purloin what belongs to the spoils."* Abū Dāwūd[33] included this Tradition in his complication.

3. Mālik has related that Abū Bakr said: *"You will find people who will profess that they gave dedicated themselves entirely to God. Leave them in peace and also that to which they have dedicated themselves."*

4. *"Do not slay women, nor infants, nor those worn with age."* However, it seems to me that the chief source for the controversy about this question is that [K 2:190]: *"Fight in the way of Allah those who fight you, but do not provoke hostility; verily Allah loveth not those who provoke hostility"* is in conflict with [K 9:5]: *"Then when the sacred months have slipped away, slay the polytheists wherever ye find them."*[34] Some maintain that K 9:5 has abrogated K 2:190, because at the outset it was only allowed to slay people who were able-bodied.[35] Consequently, the latter take it that K 9:5 gives a rule without exceptions. Others are of the opinion that K 2:190

has not been abrogated and that it is valid with regard to all those categories which do not take part in the fighting. According to these, K 2:190 gives an exceptive regulation as regards K 9:5. Shāfiī, in support of his interpretation, argues that it has been related on the authority of Sumrah[36] that the Prophet commanded: *"Slay the polytheists but spare their children."* The only motive why the enemy should be put to death, according to him, is their unbelief. This motive, then, goes for all unbelievers. Those who maintain that peasants are not to be slain argue that Zayd Ibn Wahb[37] has related: *"We received a letter from 'Umar,[38] saying: Do not purloin what belongs to the spoils, do not act perfidiously, do not slay babies and be god-fearing with regard to peasants."*[39] The prohibition to slay polytheist serfs is based on the Tradition of Rabāh Ibn Rabīah: *"Once, when Rabāh Ibn Rabīah sallied forth with the Messenger of Allah, he and (the) companions of the Prophet passed by a woman who had been slain. The Messenger halted and said: 'She was not one who would have fought.' Thereupon he looked at the men and said to one of them: 'Run after Khālid Ibn al-Walīd (and tell him) that he must not slay children, serfs or women.'"* Basically, however, the source of their controversy is to be found in their divergent views concerning the motive why the enemy may be slain. Those who think that this is because they are unbelieving do not make exceptions for any polytheist. Others, who are of the opinion that this motive consists in their capacity for fighting, in view of the prohibition to slay female unbelievers, do make an exception for those who are unable to fight or who are not as a rule inclined to fight, such as peasants and serfs. Enemies must not be tortured nor must their bodies be mutilated. The Moslems agree that they may be slain with weapons. Controversy exists, however, concerning the question whether it is allowed to burn them by fire. Some consider it reprehensible to burn or to assail them with fire. This is also the opinion of 'Umar. It has been related that Mālik held a similar view. Sufyān al-Thawrī, on the other hand, considered it admissible. Others allow it only in case the enemy has started it. The source of this controversy is again in the fact that a general and a particular rule are at variance. The general rule is given by [K 9:5]: *"Slay the polytheists wherever ye find them."*[40] This does not preclude any manner of slaying. The particular rule is founded on an authoritative Tradition, according to which the Prophet said to a certain man: *"If ye should seize him, then slay him, yet do not burn him. No one is free to punish by means of fire, save the Lord of the (Hell) fire (i.e. Allah)."* Most scholars agree that fortresses may be assailed with mangonels, no matter whether there are women and children within them or not. This is based on the fact that the Prophet used mangonels against the population of al-Tā'if. Some, among whom is Awzāī, have taught that mangonels should not be resorted to when Moslem captives or children are within the [walls of the] fortress. Layth[41] on the other hand, considered it admissible. The argument of those who do not allow it, reads [K 48:25]: *"Had they been separated out, We should have inflicted upon those of them who have disbelieved a punishment painful."*[42] Those who do allow it do so, as it were, with a view to the general interest. So much for the extent to which injury may be inflicted upon the person of the enemy.

Opinions vary as to the damage that may be inflicted on their property, such as buildings, cattle, and crops. Mālik allowed the felling of trees, the picking of fruits, and the demolishing of buildings, but not the slaughter of cattle and the burning of date-palms. Awzāī disapproved of the felling of fruit-trees and the demolishing of buildings, regardless of whether the buildings in question were churches or not. According to Shāfiī, dwellings and trees may be burnt as long as the enemy have the disposal of fortresses. When that is not the case, he considers it reprehensible to demolish buildings and to fell trees. The reason why there is this divergence of opinions is that the practice of Abū Bakr was at variance with that of the Prophet who set fire to the palm-trees of Banū Nadīr. On the other hand, it has been related as an irrefutable fact that Abū Bakr said: *"Do not fell trees and do not demolish buildings."* Some are of the opinion that Abū Bakr could only have spoken thus because he knew the practice of the Prophet to have been at liberty to act in defiance of this practice had he known it. There are also those who take it that this policy of the prophet [did not give a general rule but] had reference only Banū Nadīr, since it was them who attacked him. Those who bring forward all these arguments adhere to the view of Abū Bakr. Others, however, go entirely by the practice of the Prophet. They maintain that it is impossible that anybody's words or deeds could be put forward as an argument against his practice and they consider it lawful to burn trees. Mālik makes a distinction between cattle and trees. According to him, the slaughter of cattle is torture, which is prohibited. Moreover, the Prophet is not related ever to have slain animals. So much for the extent to which it is allowed to inflict damage to the lives and property of the unbelievers.

Par. 4. The prerequisites for warfare

According to all scholars, the prerequisite for warfare is that the enemy must have heard the summons to Islam. This implies that it is not allowed to attack them before the summons has reached them. All Moslems are agreed about this because of [K 17:15]: *"We have not been accustomed to punish until We have sent a messenger."*[43] However, there is controversy about the question whether the summons should be repeated when the war is resumed. Some hold that this is obligatory, others consider it merely recommendable, while according to a third group it is neither obligatory nor recommendable [and therefore a matter of indifference]. The source of this controversy is that the words and the deeds of the Prophet are at variance. According to an authoritative Tradition, the Prophet, when he sent out his armies, used to say to the leader: *"When ye will encounter your polytheist foes, then summon them to three things. Accept that which they consent to and refrain from [attacking] them. Summon them to conversion to Islam. If they consent to that, accept it and refrain from [attacking] them. Summon them thereupon to sally forth from their territory to the Abode of the Emigrant (muhādjirūn) [i.e., Medina] and impart to them that, if they do so, they will have the same rights and duties as the Emigrants. If they are unwilling to do so, however, and prefer to remain in their own territory, impart to them thereupon that they will be like the converted Beduins, who are subject to the same supreme authority of Allah as the [other] believers, but who are not entitled to a share in the spoils, unless they join the Moslems in the war. If they refuse that, then summon them to the payment of poll-tax. If they consent to that, accept it and refrain from [attacking] them. But if they refuse it, then invoke the help of Allah and attack them."* Nevertheless it has been related irrefutably that the Prophet repeatedly made sudden attacks upon the enemy at night or at dawn. Some, consequently, maintain, and they are majority, the practice of the Prophet has abrogated his words. According to the latter, the relevant dictum dates back from an early period of Islam, before the summons had been propagated, because it contains a summons to emigration (*hidjrad*).[44] Others are of the opinion that more weight should be attached to the Prophet's words than to his deeds, because the latter are to be interpreted in the light of the particular circumstances. Those, lastly, who consider it recommendable, do so in order to reconcile both views.[45]

Par. 5. The maximum number of enemies against which one is obliged to stand one's ground

The maximum number of enemies against which one is obliged to stand one's group is twice the number [of one's own troops]. About this, everybody agrees on account of [K 8:66]: *"Now Allah hath made it lighter for you and knoweth that there is weakness among you."*[46] Ibn Mādjishūn maintains, on the authority of Mālik, that the actual force, rather than the number, is to be considered and that it might be allowed for a single man to flee before another if the latter should possess a superior horse, superior weapons, and superior physical strength.

Par. 6. Truce

The conclusion of truce is considered by some to be permitted from the very outset and without an immediate occasion, provided that the Imam deems it in the interest of the Moslems. Others maintain that it is only allowed when the Moslems are pressed by sheer necessity, such as a civil war and the like. As a condition for truce, it may be stipulated that the enemy pay a certain amount of money to the Moslems. This is not poll-tax (*djizyah*), because for that it would be required that they come under Islamic rule [which is not the case here]. Such a stipulation [the payment of a tribute], however, is not obligatory. Awzāī even considered it admissible that the Imam should conclude a truce with the stipulation that the Moslems pay a certain amount to the enemy, should this be forced upon them by emergency, such as a civil war and the like. Shāfiī's opinion is that the Moslems may never give anything to the unbelievers, unless they are normal fear of being extinguished, on account of the enemy's superiority or because they are being harassed by disasters. Among those who profess that the Imam is entitled to conclude a truce when he considers it in the interest [of the Moslems] are Mālik, Shāfiī, and Abū Hanifah. Shāfiī maintains that a truce may not be concluded for a period longer than that of the truce which the Prophet concluded with the unbelievers in the year of Hudaybiyyah.[47] The controversy about the question whether the conclusion of truce is also allowed without a compulsive reason, is rooted in the fact that the obvious interpretation of [K 9:5]: "*Slay the polytheists wherever ye find them*"[48] and that of [K 9:29]: "*Fight against those who do not believe in Allah nor in the last day*,"[49] contradict that of [K 8:61]: "*If they incline to make peace, incline thou to it, and set thy trust upon Allah*."[50] Some hold that the verse which commands the Moslems to fight the polytheists until they have been converted or until they pay poll-tax (*djizyah*) [K 9:29] abrogates the Peace-verse [K 8:61]. Consequently, they maintain that truce is only admissible in cases of necessity. Others are of the opinion that the Peace-verse [K 8:61] supplements the other two verses and they consider the concluding of truce allowed if the Imam deems it right. They also argue, in support of their view, that the Prophet acted accordingly, as the truce of Hudaybiyyah had not been concluded from necessity. According to Shāfiī, the principle is that polytheists must be fought until they have been converted or until they are willing to pay poll-tax (*djizyah*). The acts of the Prophet in the year of Hudaybiyyah are an exception to this [principle]. Therefore, says Shāfiī, a truce may never exceed the period for which the Prophet concluded truce in the case of Hudaybiyyah. Still, there is controversy about the duration of this period. According to some it amounts to four years, but according to others three or ten years. Shāfiī opts for the latter. As to the view of some, that in cases of emergency such as civil war and the like, the Moslems may conclude a truce on the stipulation that they pay the enemy a certain amount of money, this is based on the Prophet's example, for it has been related that he was seriously contemplating to bestow a third of the date-harvest of Medina upon a group of polytheists belonging to the Confederates with a view to induce them to move off. However, before he had had time to reach an agreement on the basis of the quantity of dates he had been allowed [by the people of Medina] to give away, Allah granted him the victory.[51] The opinion of those who profess that a truce may only be concluded when the Moslems are in mortal fear of extinction, is founded on analogous application of the rule that Moslem captives may be ransomed; for when Moslems have been reduced to such a state they are in the position of captives.

Par. 7. The aims of warfare

The Moslems are agreed that the aim of warfare against the People of the Book, with the exception of those belonging to the Quraysh-tribe and Arab Christians, is twofold: either conversion to Islam, or payment of poll-tax (*djizyah*). This is based on [K 9:29]: *"Fight against those who do not believe in Allah nor in the last Day, and do not make forbidden what Allah and His messenger have made forbidden, and do not practice the religion of truth, of those who have been given the Book, until they pay the jizya off-hand, being subdued."* Most lawyers likewise agree that poll-tax (*djizyah*) may also be collected from Zoroastrians (*madjūs*) on the strength of the words of the Prophet: *"Treat them like the People of the Book."* There is, however, controversy with regard to polytheists who are not People of the Book: is it allowed to accept poll-tax (*djizyah*) from them or not? Some, like Mālik, have taught that it may be collected from any polytheist. Others make an exception for the polytheist Arabs. Shāfiī, Abū Thawr,[52] and a few others maintain that poll-tax (*djizyah*) may only be accepted from People of the Book and Zoroastrians. The controversy is again brought about by the fact that a general rule conflicts with a particular one. The general rule is derived from [K 2:193 and 8:39]: *"Fight them until there is no persecution (i.e., persecution of believers by polytheists), and religion becomes Allah's,"*[53] and from the Tradition: *"I have been commanded to fight the people until they say: 'There is no god but Allah.' When they say that, then their lives and property are inviolable to me, except [in the case when] the [law of] Islam allows it [to take them]. They will be answerable to Allah."* The particular rule is founded on the Tradition mentioned earlier,[54] viz., that Mohammed used to say to the leaders of troops which he sent out to the polytheist Arabs: *"When ye will encounter your polytheist foes, then summon them to three things,"* etc. In this Tradition, poll-tax (*djizyah*) is also mentioned. Now, some scholars hold that a general rule cancels a particular one if the general rule was revealed at a later date. These do not accept poll-tax (*djizyah*) from others than People of the Book, since the verses prescribing, in general terms, to fight them are of a more recent date than Tradition mentioned; for the general command to fight the polytheists is to be found in the *Sūrat Barā'ah*[55] which was revealed in the year of the conquest of Mecca.[56] The Tradition in question, on the other hand, dates back form before the conquest of Mecca, in view of the fact that it contains a summons to emigration.[57] Others, however, maintain that general rules should always be interpreted in association with the particular rules, no matter whether this is unknown. The latter group, accordingly, accepts poll-tax (*djizyah*) from any polytheist. The People of the Book are in an exceptional position with respect to the other polytheists because they have been excluded from the general rule just mentioned, on the strength of the particular rule given in [K 9:29]: ". . . *of those who have been given the Book, until they pay the jizya off-hand, being subdued.*"[58] The poll-tax (*djizyah*) itself and the rules related to it will be dealt with in the next chapter. So much for the principles of warfare. One famous question remains to be touched upon in this connection: that whether it is prohibited to march into hostile territory carrying a copy of the Koran. Most scholars do not consider it allowed because an authoritative rule to this effect has been handed down from the prophet in an authentic Tradition. Abū Hanīfah, on the other hand, has taught that it is allowed, provided that it is done under the protection of a strong and safe army. The source of this controversy is the question: was this prohibition put in general terms in order that it might hold good universally and without exceptions, or was the prohibition put in general terms while it was nevertheless intended as a particular rule?

NOTES

1. Only the first chapter has been translated here.
2. 'Abdallah Ibn al-Hasan (d. 145/762), a traditionist.
3. As in most Islamic writings, the author assumes that the reader knows the Koran by heart, so that it was often sufficient to quote only a few words of the Koran texts. The reader was capable of completing them for himself. Here, the full text of each quotation will be given in the notes. Full text of [2:216]: "Prescribed for you is fighting, though it be hateful to you. Yet it may happen that you will hate a thing which is better for you; and it may happen that you will love a thing which is worse for you. God knows and you know not."
4. Full text of [9:112]: "It is not for the believers to go forth totally; but why should not a party of every section of them go forth, to become learned in religion, and to warn their people when they return to them, that haply they may beware." For the original meaning of this verse, which almost certainly is not referring to going to war, cf. R. Paret, "Sura 9, 122 and der Gihad," *Welt des Islam* 2 (1953): 232 ff.
5. Full text of [4:95]: "Such believers as sit at home—unless they have an injury—are not the equals of those who struggle in the path of God with their possessions and their selves. God has preferred in rank those who struggle in the path of God with their possessions and their selves over the ones who sit at home; yet to each God has promised the reward most fair."
6. Full text of [48:17]: "There is no fault in the blind, and there is no fault in the lame, and there is no fault in the sick. . . ."
7. Full text of [9:91]: "There is no fault in the weak and the sick and those who find nothing to expend, if they are true to God and His Messenger. There is no way against the good-doers—God is All forgiving, All-compassionate—."
8. The most important occurrence when the jihad becomes a personal obligation is an attack by the enemy on Islamic territory. All inhabitants of the area under attack—including women and slaves—are then obliged to expel the enemy.

9. Jibril is the Arabic name for the archangel Gabriel. According to the Islamic doctrine, God's words were revealed to Mohammed through Djibril.

10. Full text of [8:39]: "Fight them until there is no persecution and the religion is God's entirely; then, if they give over, surely God sees the things they do."

11. Malik Ibn Anas (d. 179/795), famous lawyer. The Traditions related by him were collected by his pupils in the compilation al-Muwatta'. The school founded on his doctrines, the Malikite, is still extant and counts its adherents chiefly in North Africa.

12. This Tradition can be found in Malik Ibn Anas, al-Muwatta': jihad 10. However, Averroes's suggestion that we are dealing here with words of the Prophet must be a lapsus. The Tradition in question goes back to Abu Bakr. Cf. al-Muwatta': jihad 10.

13. Abu Bakr (d. 13/634), personal friend of Mohammed and after his death in the year 11/632, his successor (caliph). During his short reign, he subdued once more the revolting tribes of the Arabian Peninsula and made a beginning with the conquest of Syria and Iraq.

14. Al-Hasan Ibn Muhammad al-Tamimi, a nonidentified traditionist.

15. Full text of [47:4]: "When you meet the unbelievers, smite their necks, then, when you have made wide slaughter among them, tie fast the bonds; then set them free, either by grace or ransom, till the war lays down its loads. So it shall be; and if God had willed, He would have avenged Himself upon them; but that He may try some of you by means of the others. And those who are slain in the way of God, He will not send their works astray."

16. Full text of [8:67]: "It is not for any Prophet to have prisoners until he make wide slaughter in the land. You desire the chance-goods of the present world, and God desires the world to come; and God is All-mighty, All-wise." This verse is generally taken to have been a reproof at the address of Mohammed for his releasing on ransom most of the captives after the Battle of Badr. The phrase "make wide slaughter in the land" goes to point out the danger that these released captives may, when occasion arises, attack the Muslims afresh.

17. Abu 'Ubayd Sacd Ibn Ubayd al-Zuhri (d. 98/716), famous traditionist.

18. Abd al-Malik Ibn 'Abd al-Aziz Ibn al-Majishun (d. c. 213/827), Malikite lawyer.

19. 'Abd al-Salam Ibn Said Ibn Habib al-Tanukhi, known as Sahnun (d. 240/854), one of the best-known early Malikite lawyers.

20. Abu Hanifa al-Nucman (d. 150/767), well-known lawyer. The school founded on his doctrines is called the Hanafite School and counts its adherents chiefly in the regions formerly belonging to the Ottoman Empire and in Central Asia.

21. He is only allowed to do this with the permission of his owner.

22. This remark is not entirely correct. In view of its singular position in the context, it is possibly an interpolation.

23. For the full text of this Tradition, see Par. 3: The Damage Allowed to be Inflicted upon the Different Categories of Enemies.

24. Sufyan al-Thawri (d. 161/778), famous traditionist and lawyer. A school founded on his doctrines existed for several centuries.

25. Al-Awzāī (d. 157/774), famous lawyer. Like the School of Thawri, his school was superseded after a few centuries by other, still extant schools.

26. Al-Shafi'i (d. 204/820), famous lawyer. He was the first to systematize the study of original sources ('ilm al-usul). The Shafi'ite School derives its name from him and obtains its widest recognition along the borders of the Arabian Peninsula, in East Africa

and in the Indian Archipelago. Occasionally, he is related to have given two different solutions for one and the same problem. Later generations of scholars decided which interpretation was the most authoritative.

27. For the full text of this Tradition, see Par. 7: The Aims of Warfare.

28. Full text of [9:5]: "Then, when the sacred months are drawn away, slay the idolaters wherever you find them, and take them, and confine them, and lie in wait for them at every place of ambush. But if they repent, and perform the prayer, and pay the alms, then let them go their way; God is All-forgiving, All-compassionate."

29. Dawud Ibn al-Hasin (d. 135/752–753), well-known traditionist.

30. 'Ikrima (d. 105/723–724), well-known traditionist. He was the slave of Ibn Abbas and many Traditions were related on his athority.

31. Abdallah Ibn al-Abbas (d. 68/686–687). One of the companions of the Prophet and one of the most important scholars among the first generation of Muslims.

32. Anas Ibn Malik (d. c. 92/710), well-known traditionist. In his youth, he was the Prophet's servant.

33. Abu Dawud (d. 275/888), author of one of the authoritative compilations of Traditions.

34. For the full text of K 9:5, see n. 28.

35. During Mohammed's life, his relations with the unbelievers manifested a gradual escalation. This escalation is reflected in the Koran. In his Meccan period, he attempted to win the unbelievers by persuasion and arguments. When this failed, it was revealed that the believers should leave the unbelievers alone. The verse determining that polytheists may only be fought if they make the first move (K 2:190) dates from the beginning of his Medinese period. At last the verses were revealed which gave the absolute command to fight the unbelievers (K 2:216, K 9:5—the verse of the Sword—and K 9:29). According to most scholars, this command cancelled all previous verses with regard to the relations with unbelievers.

36. Sumra Ibn Jundub al-Fazari (d. 59/678-9), well-known traditionist.

37. Zayd Ibn Wahb (d. 96/714–715), well-known traditionist.

38. 'Umar Ibn al-Khattab (d. 23/644), second caliph of the Islam and successor of Abu Bala (see n. 13). During his reign, which lasted for ten years (13/634–23/644), Syria, Iraq, and Egypt were conquered. He is regarded as the founder of the organization of the Islamic state.

39. This Tradition has not been included in any of the authoritative compilations.

40. For the full text, see n. 28.

41. Al-Layth Ibn Sa'd (d. 175/791–792), well-known lawyer and traditionist.

42. Full text of [48:25]: "They are the ones who disbelieve and have barred you from the Holy Mosque and the offering, detained so as not to reach its place of sacrifice. If it had not been for certain men believers and certain women believers whom you knew not, lest you should trample them, and there befall you guilt unwittingly on their account (that God may admit into His mercy whom He will), had they been separated clearly, then We would have chastised the unbelievers among them with a painful chastisement."

43. Full text of [17:15]: "Whosoever is guided, is only guided to his own gain, and whosoever goes astray, it is only to his own loss; no soul laden bears the load of another. We never chastise, until We send forth a Messenger."

44. After the Emigration (Hijra) in the year 622 it became obligatory for fresh con-

verts to Islam to emigrate to Medina and to join the other Muslims. After the conquest of Mecca in 630 this obligation fell into abeyance according to most scholars.

45. Sometimes there is controversy about the qualification of a certain act. It may, for instance, be obligatory according to some, and a matter of indifference according to others. In order to reconcile these opinions, it is often assumed that the act in question is recommendable.

46. Full text of [8:66]: "Now God has lightened it for you, knowing that there is weakness in you. If there be a hundred of you, patient men, they will overcome two hundred; if there be of you a thousand, they will overcome two thousand by the leave of God; God is with the patient." This verse has abrogated the previous one, 8:65: "O Prophet, urge on the believers to fight. If there be twenty of you, patient men, they will overcome two hundred; if there be a hundred of you, they will overcome a thousand unbelievers, for they are a people who understand not."

47. In the year 628, Mohammed concluded a peace treaty with the Meccans for a period of ten years. However, when the Meccans began to incite to rebellion some troops that were allied to Mohammed, he broke off the treaty and attacked Mecca, which he conquered in the year 630.

48. For the full text, see n. 28.

49. Full text of [9:29]: "Fight those who believe not in God and the Last Day and do not forbid what God and His Messenger have forbidden—such men as practise not the religion of truth, being of those who have been given the Book—until they pay the tribute out of hand and have been humbled."

50. Full text of [8:61]: "And if they incline to peace, do thou incline to it; and put thy trust in God; He is the All-hearing, the All-knowing."

51. In the year 627, the Meccans besieged Medina with the assistance of some Bedouin tribes, the Confederates. These tribes had come along with the Meccans in prospect of financial reward. Mohammed attempted to bribe one of these tribes into moving away. At first, this tribe, Ghatafan, demanded half of the Medinese date-harvest, but when after some negotiating they had agreed on a third, the citizens of Medina remonstrated. However, before matters had been settled, Mohammed had succeeded in expelling the Meccans and their allied tribes in the Battle of the Trench.

52. Abu Thawr (d. 240/854), well-known lawyer. A school founded on his doctrines existed for a few centuries only.

53. Full text of [8:39]: "Fight them until there is no persecution and the religion is God's entirely; then, if they give over, surely God sees the things they do."

54. See Par. 4: The Prerequisites for Warfare.

55. The ninth chapter of the Koran, called Surat Bara'a or Surat al-Tawba, is considered as the last chapter revealed.

56. In the year 8/630.

57. For the full text, see n. 44.

58. For the full text, see n. 49.

8

THE MUQADDIMAH

Ibn Khaldun (d. 1406)

In the Muslim community, the holy war is a religious duty, because of the universalism of the <Muslim> mission and <the obligation to> convert everybody to Islam either by persuasion or by force. Therefore, caliphate and royal authority are united <in Islam>, so that the person in charge can devote the available strength to both of them <religion and politics> at the same time. The other religious groups did not have a universal mission, and the holy war was not a religious duty to them, save only for purposes of defense. It has thus come about that the person in charge of religious affairs <in other religious groups> is not concerned with power politics at all. <Among them>, royal authority comes to those who have it, by accident and in some way that has nothing to do with religion. It comes to them as the necessary result of group feeling, which by its very nature seeks to obtain royal authority, as we have mentioned before, and not because they are under obligation to gain power over other nations, as is the case with Islam. They are merely required to establish their religion among their own <people>. That is why the Israelites after Moses and Joshua remained unconcerned with royal authority for about four hundred years. Their only concern was to establish their religion.

Thereafter, there were dissensions among the Christians with regard to their religion and to Christology. They split into groups and sects, which secured the support of the various Christian rulers against each other. At different times there appeared different sects. Finally, these sects crystallized into three groups, which constitute the <Christian> sects. Others have no significance. These are the Melchites, the Jacobites, and the Nestorians. We do not think that we should blacken the pages of this book with discussion of their dogmas of unbelief. In general, they are well known. All of them are unbelief. This is clearly stated in the noble Qur'an. <To> discuss or argue those things with them is not up to us. It is <for them to choose between> conversion to Islam, payment of the poll tax, or death.

Excerpted from Ibn Khaldun, *The Muqaddimah: An Introduction to History*, trans. Franz Rosenthal (New York: Pantheon, 1958), pp. 473, 480.

9

LEGAL WAR

Ibn Qudama (d. 1223)

Legal war (jihad) is an obligatory social duty (*fard-kifaya*); when one group of Muslims guarantees that it is being carried out in a satisfactory manner, the others are exempted.[1]

The jihad becomes a strictly binding personal duty (*fard-'ain*) for all Muslims who are enlisted [? *en ligne*] or whose country has been [invaded][2] by the enemy. It is obligatory only for free men who have reached puberty, are endowed with reason and capable of fighting. Jihad is the best of the works of supererogation. Abu Huraira[3] relates that "[t]he Prophet, when asked what was the best of all works, replied: Belief in God [and in His Prophet].[4]—And then? someone asked him.—War for God's cause, then a pious pilgrimage." Abu Sa'id[5] reports also that the Prophet, when asked who was the best of all men, replied, "He who fights for God's cause, personally and with his goods."

Naval expeditions are more meritorious than campaigns on land. One must fight under every leader, whether it be a respectable man or a corrupt man. Every nation must fight the enemies that are its immediate neighbors. A full stint of service in a frontier post (*ribat*) is of forty days' duration.[6] It is reported that the Prophet said: ["To mount guard for one day in a *ribat*, to serve God's cause, is more meritorious than to spend a thousand days in any other place."][7] The Prophet also said: "To mount guard for one day in a *ribat*, to serve God's cause, is more meritorious than to fast and keep watch for an entire month. To him who dies in a *ribat*, God will give his reward until the day of the resurrection, and he will protect him from the temptations of the devil."

No one can engage in jihad without the permission of his father and mother, if they are alive and Muslims, unless the jihad is an individual duty that strictly obliges. Only elderly women are permitted to venture into the war zone in order to replenish the water supply and to care for the wounded. No one should enlist the services of an infidel except in case of need. It is forbidden to engage in

Excerpted from Henri Laoust, trans., *Le précis de droit d'Ibn Qudama, jurisconsulte musulman d'é-cole hanbalite né à Jérusalem en 541/1146, mort à Damas en 620/1223*, Livre 20, "La Guerre Legale" (Beirut, 1950), pp. 273–76, 281. English translation by Michael J. Miller.

combat without the authorization of the commander in chief (*amir*), except to respond to a sudden attack or to seize a favorable opportunity. Once the army have arrived in the war zone, no one has the right to wander off unless he has permission from the commander in chief, whether it be to gather fodder, cut wood, or for any other reason.

A man in a war zone who takes possession of an article of a certain value does not have the right to keep it, except for the food and the fodder that he needs. If he sells the article, he must contribute the price of it to the sum total of the booty. Once he has returned to his country, he must give back the things obtained from the pillage that he still has with him, unless they are of little value; in that case, he is permitted to use them or give them away.

It is permitted to surprise the infidels under cover of night, to bombard them with mangonels [an engine that hurls missiles] and to attack them without declaring battle (*du'a'*). The Prophet attacked the Banu Mustaliq[8] unexpectedly, while their animals were still at the watering-place; he killed the men who had fought against him and carried off the children into captivity. It is forbidden to kill children, madmen, women, priests, impotent old men, the infirm, the blind, the weak-minded, unless they have taken part in the combat.

The chief of state decides on the fate of the men who are taken as prisoners; he can have them put to death, reduce them to slavery, free them in return for a ransom or grant them their freedom as a gift. He must choose the solution most in keeping with the common good of the Muslims. The prisoners whom the head of state decides to reduce to slavery or to liberate for a ransom are included in the sum total of the booty. The women and the children taken prisoner must not be separated when they are related by a bond of kinship which, in Islam, would constitute an impediment to marriage, unless they have already reached the age of puberty. The man who buys some prisoners, believing that they are related by close kinship, and then finds that that is not the case, must pay the surplus value that results from their separation.

The head tax (*jizya*)[9] can be demanded only from the People of the Book (*ahl-al-kitab*) and from Zoroastrians (*Magus*), who pledge to pay it and submit to the laws of the community. The People of the Book are understood to mean the Jews and those who follow the religion of the Torah, as well as the Christians and those who follow the religion of the Gospel. When People of the Book or Zoroastrians ask to pay the head tax and to submit to the laws of the community, one must grant their request, and it is forbidden to fight them. The head tax is collected at the beginning of each year. It is set at forty-eight dirhems for a rich man, at twenty-four dirhems for a man of moderate means, and at twelve dirhems for a man of lowly estate. It cannot be demanded from children who have not reached the age of puberty, from women, helpless old men, the sick, the blind, or slaves, nor from poor people who are unable to pay it. An infidel subject to the head tax who converts to Islam is free of this obligation. When an infidel dies, his heirs are responsible for the head tax.

A protected member of a minority group who goes abroad to trade is bound, when he returns, to pay one-half of the tithe. An infidel foreigner who enjoys no protection (*harbi*) and who comes to our land to trade is bound to pay the tithe (*'usr*). A protected person who violates his protection agreement,[10] whether by refusing to pay the head tax or to submit to the laws of the community, or else by fighting the Muslims or by committing some act of hostility against them, or else by fleeing to the House of Hostility, makes his person and his goods "licit" [fair game to be killed or captured by Muslims]. A breach of his own agreement does not result in a breach of the agreement benefiting his wives and children, unless he brought them with him into the House of Hostility.

NOTES

For clarification of citations, the reader is referred to the original full text, Henri Laoust, trans., "La Guerre Legale," *Le précis de driot d'Ibn Qudama, jurisconsulte musulman d'é-cloe hanbalite né à Jérusalem en 541/1146, mort à Damas en 620/1223* (Beirut, 1950), pp. 273–76, 281, English trans. Michael J. Miller.

1. Cf. the Cairo edition, pp. 152–54; Damascus MS, folios 176a–178b. On jihad itself, see Mugni, vol. 10, pp. 364–97; Sarh, vol. 10, pp. 364–25.

2. In the Cairo edition (p. 152, line 3): hasara (surrounds); in the Damascus MS (folio 176a, line 4): hadara (is present, is found in). The latter reading is also that of Sarh, vol. 10, p. 368, line 3).

3. On Abu Huraira, a traditionist who died in the year 57 or 58 (676–678 AD), see the article by Goldziher, *Encyclopédie de l'Islam*, vol. 1, p. 96.

4. Damascus MS (folio 176a, line 7): wa-birasulihi (and in His Prophet); likewise in Sarh, vol. 10, p. 369, but not found in the Cairo edition (p. 152, line 6).

5. Abu Sa'id al-Hudri, companion [of the Prophet] and traditionalist who died in the year 74 of the Hegira. Cf. Isaba, vol. 2, p. 35, no. 3, 196.

6. On the subject of staying at frontier posts, or ribat, see Mugni, vol. 10, pp. 375–81; Sarh, vol. 10, pp. 374–78.

7. This hadith is not included in the Cairo edition (p. 152, line 11); it is found in the Damascus MS (folio 176b, lines 4–5) as well as in the Mugni (vol. 10, p. 376) and the Sarh (vol. 10, p. 375).

8. The raid against the Banu Mustaliq took place at the beginning of the sixth year of the Hegira (627 AD). Cf. Ibn Kafir, *Bidaya wa-nihaya*, vol. 5, p. 156–64.

9. Cairo edition, p. 158; Damascus MS, folio 182a–182b. The jizya is studied within the framework of the protection agreement of the dhimmi; see Mugni, vol. 10, pp. 567–96; Sarh, vol. 10, pp. 587–607.

10. On the protection agreement ('aqd-ad-dhimma) and the breach of it, see in particular Sarh, vol. 10, pp. 584–611, 611–35.

10

AL-SIYASA AL-SHARIYYA

Ibn Taymiyya (d. 1328)

JIHAD

The penalties that the *Sharīa* has introduced for those who disobey God and His Messengers of two kinds: the punishment of those who are under the sway [of the imam], both individuals and collectivities, as has been mentioned before [in the chapter on criminal law], and, secondly, the punishment of recalcitrant groups, such as those that can only be brought under the sway of the Imam by·a decisive fight. That then is the jihad against the unbelievers (*kuffār*), the enemies of God and His Messenger. For whoever has heard the summons of the Messenger of God, Peace be upon him, and has not responded to it, must be fought, *"until there is no persecution and the religion is God's entirely"* (K. 2:193, 8:39).

When God sent his Prophet and ordered him to summon the people to His religion, He did not permit him to kill or fight anyone for that reason before the Prophet emigrated to Medina. Thereafter He gave him and the Muslims permission with the words:

> Leave is given to those who are fought[1] because they were wronged—surely God is able to help them—who were expelled from their habitations without right, except that they say "Our Lord is God." Had God not driven back the people, some by the means of others, there had been destroyed cloisters and churches, oratories and mosques, wherein God's name is much mentioned. Assuredly God will help him who helps Him—surely God is all-strong, all-mighty—who, if We establish them in the land, perform the prayer, and pay the alms, and bid to honour, and forbid dishonour; and unto God belongs the issue of all affairs. (K. 22:39–41)

Then, after that, He imposed fighting to them with the following words:

Excerpted from Rudolph Peters, *Jihad in Classical and Modern Islam* (Princeton, NJ: Markus Wiener, 1996), pp. 44–54.

Prescribed for you is fighting, though it be hateful to you. Yet it may happen that you will hate a thing which is better for you; and it may happen that you will love a thing which is worse for you. God knows and you know not. (K. 2:216)

He has emphasized this command and glorified jihad in many of the Medinese suras. He has criticized those who fail to participate it and called them hypocrites and sick in their hearts. God has said:

Say: "If your fathers, your sons, your brothers, your wives, your clan, your possessions that you have gained, commerce you fear may slacken, dwellings you love—if these are dearer to you than God and His Messenger, and to struggle in His way, then wait till God brings His command; God guides not the people of the ungodly." (K. 9:24)

And:

The believers are those who believe in God and His Messenger, then have not doubted, and have struggled with their possessions and their selves in the way of God; those—they are the truthful ones. (K. 49:15)

And:

Then, when a clear sura is sent down, and therein fighting is mentioned, thou seest those in whose heart is sickness looking at thee as one who swoons of death; but better for them would be obedience and words honourable. Then when the matter is resolved, if they were true to God, it would be better for them. (K. 47:20–21)

There are numerous similar verses in the Koran and equally frequent is the glorification of jihad and those who participate in it, [for instance] in Surat The Ranks (al-saff):

O believers, shall I direct you to a commerce that shall deliver you from a painful chastisement? You shall believe in God and His Messenger, and struggle in the way of God with your possessions and your selves. That is better for you, did you but know. He will forgive you your sins and admit you into gardens underneath which rivers flow, and to dwelling places goodly in Gardens of Eden; that is the mighty triumph; and other things you love, help from God and a nigh victory. Give thou good tidings to the believers. (K. 61:10–13)

And [elsewhere] He has said:

Do you reckon the giving of water to pilgrims and the inhabiting of the Holy Mosque as the same as one who believes in God and the Last Day and struggles in the way of God? Not equal are they in God's sight; and God guides not the

people of the evildoers. Those who believe, and have emigrated, and have struggled in the way of God with their possessions and their selves are mightier in
rank with God; and those—they are the triumphant; their Lord gives them good
tidings of mercy from Him and good pleasure; for them await gardens wherein
is lasting bliss, therein to dwell forever and ever; surely with God is a mighty
wage. (K. 9:19–21)

And:

O believers, whosoever of you turns from his religion, God will assuredly bring
a people he loves, and who loves Him, humble towards the believers, disdainful
towards the unbelievers, men who struggle in the path of God, not fearing the
reproach of any reproacher. That is God's bounty; He gives it unto whom He
will. (K. 5:54)

And He has said:

That is because they are smitten neither by thirst, not fatigue, nor emptiness in
the way of God, neither tread they any tread enraging the unbelievers, nor gain
any gain from any enemy, but a righteous deed is thereby written to their
account; God leaves not to waste the wage of the good-doers. Nor do they
expend any sum, small or great, nor do they traverse any valley, but it is written
to their account, that God may recompense them the best of what they were
doing. (K. 9:120–21)

Thus He has mentioned [the reward] resulting from their deeds and the deeds
they must practice.

The command to participate in jihad and the mention of its merits occur innumerable times in the Koran and the Sunna. Therefore it is the best voluntary [reli-
gious] act that man can perform. All scholars agree that it is better than the *hajj*
(greater pilgrimage) and the *umra* (lesser pilgrimage), than voluntary *salāt* and
voluntary fasting, as the Koran and Sunna indicate. The Prophet, Peace be upon
him, has said, *"The head of the affair is Islam, its central pillar is the salat and
its summit is the jihad."* And he has said: *"In Paradise there are a hundred grades
with intervals as wide as the distance between the sky and the earth. All these God
has prepared for those who take part in jihad."* There is unanimity about the
authenticity of this Tradition. Al-Bukhārī [2] has transmitted that he has said: *"Him
whose feet have become dusty I the way of God [i.e., jihad] will God save from
hellfire."* And, as indicated by Muslim,[3] he has said:

A day and a night in spent in ribāt[4] are better than one month spent in fasting and
vigils. If he dies [in the fulfillment of this task], he will receive the recompense
of his deeds and subsistence, and he will be protected from the Angel of the
Grave.[5]

It is related in the *Sunan* that *"a day spent in ribāt in the way of God is better than thousand days spent elsewhere."* He has said: *"Two eyes will not be touched by the fire: the eye that has wept out of fear for God and the eye that has spent the night on the watch in the way of God."* Al-Tirmidhī[6] has said about this tradition that it is good (*hasan*).[7] In the *Musnad* of Ahmad ibn Hanbal[8] we find: *"A night spent on the watch in the way of God is better than a thousand nights and days spent in nightly vigils and fasting."* In the *Sahīh* of al-Bukhārī as well as in the *Sahīh* of Muslim we find:

> A man said: "O Messenger of God, tell me of an act that equals jihad in the way of God." He answered: "You will not be capable of it." The man said: "Tell me anyway." The Messenger of God said, "Can you, when a jihad warrior has gone out on expedition, fast without interruption and spend the night in continuous prayer?" The man said: "No." Then the Messenger of God said: "This then is what equals jihad."

In the *Sunan* we find that Mohammed has said: *"Every community has its devotional journeys and the devotional journey of my community is jihad in the way of God."*

This is a vast subject, unequalled by other subjects as far as the reward and merit of human deeds is concerned. This is evident upon closer examination. The [first] reason is that the benefit of jihad is general, extending not only to the person who participates in it but also to others, both in a religious and a temporal sense. [Secondly,] jihad implies all kinds of worship, both in its inner and outer forms. More than any other act it implies love and devotion for God, Who is exalted, trust in Him, the surrender of one's life and property to Him, patience, asceticism, remembrance of God and all kinds of other acts [of worship]. Any individual or community that participated in it, finds itself between two blissful outcomes: either victory and triumph or martyrdom and Paradise. [Thirdly,] all creatures must live and die. Now, it is in jihad that one can live and die in ultimate happiness, both in this world and in the Hereafter. Abandoning it means losing entirely or partially both kinds of happiness. There are people who want to perform religious and temporal deeds full of hardship, in spite of their lack of benefit, whereas actually jihad is religiously and temporally more beneficial than any other deed full of hardship. Other people [participate in it] out of a desire to make things easy for themselves when death meets them, for the death of a martyr is easier than any other form of death, In fact, it is the best of all manners of dying.

Since lawful warfare is essentially jihad and since its aim is that the religion is God's entirely[9] and God's word is uppermost,[10] therefore, according to all Muslims, those who stand in the way of this aim must be fought. As for those who cannot offer resistance or cannot fight, such as women, children, monks, old people, the blind, handicapped, and their likes, they shall not be killed, unless they actually fight with words [e.g., by propaganda] and acts [e.g., by spying or otherwise assisting in the warfare]. Some [jurists] are of the opinion that all of them may be killed, on the mere ground that they are unbelievers, but they make an exception for women and children since they constitute property for Muslims. However, the first opinion is the correct one, because we may only fight those who fight us when we want to make God's religion victorious. God, Who is exalted, has said in this respect: "*And fight in the way of God with those who fight you, but aggress not: God loves not the aggressors*" (K. 2:190). In the *Sunan* it is reported from the Messenger of God, Peace be upon him:

> That he once passed by a woman who had been slain. The Messenger of God halted and said: "She was not one who would have fought." Then he said to one of [his companions]: "Catch up with Khālid ibn al-Walīd and tell him not to kill women, children and serfs."

It is also reported in the *Sunan* that he used to say: "*Do not kill very old men, nor small children or women.*" The reason is that God has [only] permitted to shed blood if that is necessary for the welfare of the creation. He has said: "*Persecution is more grievous than slaying*" (K. 2:191). This means that, although there is evil and abomination in killing, there is greater evil and abomination in the persecution by the unbelievers. Now, the unbelief of those who do not hinder the Muslims from establishing God's religion, is only prejudicial to themselves. In the same vein, the jurists have said that the one who propagates innovations (*bida*) that are contrary to the Koran and the *Sunna* must be punished much more severely than the person [who holds such beliefs but] remains silent. "*A mistake that is kept secret*," says a Tradition, "*only harms the person who has committed it, but if it becomes public and is not denounced, it harms the community.*"

The *Sharīa* enjoins fighting the unbelievers, but not the killing of those who have been captured. If a male unbeliever is taken captive during warfare or otherwise, e.g., as a result of a shipwreck, or because he lost his way, or as a result of a ruse, then the head of state (*imām*) may do whatever he deems appropriate: killing him, enslaving him, releasing him or setting him free for a ransom consisting in either property or people. This is the view of most jurists and it is supported by the Koran and the *Sunna*. There are, however, some jurists who hold that the options of releasing them or setting them free for a ransom have been abrogated. As for the People of the Book and the Zoroastrians (*Majūs*), they are to be fought until they become Muslims or pay the tribute out of hand and have been humbled.[11] With regard to the others, the jurists differ as to the lawfulness of taking tribute from them. Most of them regard it as unlawful to accept it from [heathen] Arabs.

If a rebellious group, although belonging to Islam, refuses to comply with clear and universally accepted commands, all Muslims agree that jihad must be waged against them, I order that the religion will be God's entirely.[12] Thus Abu Bakr al-Siddīq[13] and other Companions, may God be pleased with them, have fought those who refused to pay *zakāt*. Initially some of the Companions hesitated in fighting them, but eventually they all agreed. Umar ibn al-Khattāb[14] said to Abu Bakr, may God be pleased with them: "How can you fight these people? Has the Messenger of God, Peace be upon him, not said: 'I have been ordered to fight people until they profess that there is no god but God and that Mohammad is God's Messenger. If they say that, their lives and properties will be inviolable for me, unless there is a rule of law that allows taking them. [For their actions] they must render account to God.' Abu Bakr then said: "The [obligation to pay] *zakāt* is such a rule. By God, if they refuse to give me one she-kid which they used to give to the Messenger of God, Peace be upon him, I shall fight them for this refusal.' Umar said: 'Then I realized immediately that God had opened his heart for fighting and I knew that that was right.'"

There are various authentic Traditions according to which the Prophet, Peace be upon him, has ordered to fight the Kharijites.[15] In the *sahīh* of al-Bukhārī as well as in the *sahīh* of Muslim it is reported on the authority of Alī ibn Abī Tālib,[16] may God be pleased with him, that he said:

I have heard the Messenger of God, Peace be upon him, saying: "Towards the end of time a group of people will emerge, young of age and simple of minds, who will speak the most beautiful words, but whose faith does not go deeper than their throats. They will abandon the religion just like an arrow pierces and then abandons a game animal. Wherever you find them you must kill them since those who kill them will be rewarded on the Day of Resurrection."

Muslim has reported that Alī, may God be pleased with him, said:

I have heard the Messenger of God, Peace be upon him, saying: "A group of people will emerge from amongst my community, who will recite the Koran [very well]. Your recitation is nothing compared to theirs. Likewise your way of performing salāt and your way of fasting are nothing compared with theirs. They will recite the Koran believing that it[s text] supports them, whereas [in reality] it condemns them. Their recitation does not go deeper than their collarbones. They will abandon the religion just like an arrow pierces and then abandons a game animal. If the army that reaches them would know how much [reward] the Prophet has promised them, they would rely on this deed [alone and not worry about other good deeds].

In another version of this Tradition, transmitted on the authority of Abū Saīd from the Prophet, Peace be upon him, we find the following words: "*They will fight the people of faith and leave the idolaters. If I live long enough to meet them, I shall kill them in the manner the tribe of Ād[17]was killed.*" There is unanimity about the authenticity of this Tradition.

In another Tradition reported by Muslim it is said: "*My community will fall apart into two parties. From amongst them there will emerge heretics (māriqa).*

The party that is closest to truth will be in charge of killing them." These were the
people that were killed by the Commander of the Faithful Alī, when the breach
between the people of Iraq and the people of Syria took place. They were called
harūriyya.[18] The Prophet, Peace be upon him, has made it clear that both parties
into which the community had fallen apart, belonged to his community and that
the partisans of Alī were closer to the truth. He incited to fight only those heretics
that had abandoned Islam and had left the community and that had permitted the
taking of the lives and properties of the other Muslims. It has been established on
the authority of the Koran, the *Sunna*, and the Consensus of the Community, that
those who depart from the law of Islam must be fought, even if they pronounce
the two professions of faith.

The jurists disagree about the permissibility to fight rebellious groups that
abandon an established supererogatory act of worship (*sunna rātiba*), such as the
two [extra] *rakas*[19] of dawn prayer. There is, however, unanimity that it is allowed
to fight people for [not observing] unambiguous and generally recognized obligations and prohibitions, until they undertake to perform the explicitly prescribed
prayers, to pay *zakāt*, to fast during the month of Ramadan, to make the pilgrimage to Mecca and to avoid what is prohibited, such as marrying women in
spite of legal impediments, eating impure things, acting unlawfully against the
lives and properties of Muslims, and the like. It is obligatory to take the initiative
in fighting those people, as soon as the Prophet's summons with the reasons for
which they are fought has reached them. But if they first attack the Muslims, then
fighting them is even more urgent, as we have mentioned when dealing with the
fighting against rebellious and aggressive bandits.

The most serious type of obligatory jihad is the one against the unbelievers
and against those who refuse to abide by certain prescriptions of the *Sharīa*, like
those who refuse to pay *zakāt*, the Kharijites and the like. This jihad is obligatory
if it is carried out on our initiative and also if it is waged as defence. If we take
the initiative, it is a collective duty, [which means that] if it is fulfilled by a sufficient number [of Muslims], the obligation lapses for all others and the merit goes
to those who have fulfilled it, just as God, He is exalted, has said:

> Such believers as sit at home—unless they have an injury—are not the equals [of
> those who struggle in the path of God with their possessions and their selves.
> God has preferred in rank those who struggle in the path of God with their pos-
> sessions and their selves over the ones who sit at home; yet to each God has
> promised the reward most fair; and God has preferred those who struggle over
> the ones who sit at home for the bounty of a mighty wage, in ranks standing
> before Him, forgiveness and mercy.] (K. 4:95–96)

But if the enemy wants to attack the Muslims, than repelling him becomes a
duty for all those under attack and for the others in order to help them. God, He
is exalted, has said: "*Yet if they ask you for help, for religion's sake, it is your duty*

to help them." (K. 8:72) In the same vein the Prophet has ordered Muslims to help fellow Muslims. The assistance, which is obligatory both for the regular professional army and for others, must be given, according to everybody's possibilities, either in person, by fighting on foot or on horseback, or through financial contributions, be they small or large. When the Muslims were attacked by the enemy in the year of the Trench,[20] God did not permit anybody to abandon jihad, although He did allow them not to take part in jihad [after the siege was lifted] in order to pursue the enemy. At that occasion He divided them into two categories, those who sat at home and those who marched out, and He criticized those who were asking the Prophet for leave [not to take part in jihad]: "*[And a part of them were asking leave of the Prophet,] saying, 'Our houses are exposed'; yet they were not exposed; they desired only to flee*" (K. 33:13).

So the latter [form of jihad] consists in defense of the religion, of things that are inviolable, and of lives. Therefore it is fighting out of necessity. The former [type of jihad], however, is voluntary fighting in order to propagate the religion, to make it triumph and to intimidate the enemy, such as was the case with the expedition to Tabūk and the like.[21] Now, this form of punishment [i.e., jihad] must be administered to rebellious [but refuse to carry out religious duties], they must be forced to carry out their obligation such as the five fundamental duties of Islam[22] and others like the delivering of trusts to their owners and the preserving of covenants in social relations.

NOTES

1. Different from Arberry, who has: ". . . to those who fight. . . ."

2. Died 870. Famous compiler of hadīth and editor of the sahīh al Bukhārī, one of the six canonical hadīth collection.

3. Died 875. Famous compiler of hadīth and editor of the sahīh Muslim, one of the six canonical hadīth collection.

4. Ribāt is a verbal noun meaning remaining at the frontiers of Islam with the intention of defending Islamic territory against the enemies. Later it began to mean fortification and sufi establishment.

5. One of the Islamic beliefs regarding Afterlife is that someone who has died will be hard-handedly interrogated with regard to his deeds by the Angels of the Grave.

6. Died ca. 890. Famous compiler of hadīth and editor of the Sunan al-Tirmidhī, one of the six canonical hadīth collection.

7. Which means that the Tradition is widely accepted although among its transmitters there is one who is not entirely reliable.

8. Died 855. Famous jurist and traditionalist, compiler of a voluminous collection of Traditions with the title al-Musnad.

9. Cf. K. 2:189 and 8:39.

10. Cf. K. 9:40.

11. Cf. K. 9:29.

12. Cf. K. 2:189 and 8:39.

13. First caliph after Mohammed's death. Ruled from 632–634.

14. Second caliph after Mohammed's death. Ruled from 634–644.

15. An early Islamic sect that held, among other things, that the caliph is to be elected by the community of the Muslims from among the pious believers, regardless of decent and tribal affiliation, and that a Muslim ceases to be a believer if he commits a grave sin.

16. Cousin and son-in-law of Mohammed and fourth Caliph after his death. Ruled from 656–661.

17. A legendary ancient Arabian tribe, mentioned in several places in Koran. They refused to accept the message of the Prophet Hūd, whom God had sent to them, and were then destroyed by a violent gale.

18. Another name for the Kharijites.

19. Part of the ritual of salāt, consisting of a bow followed by two prostrations.

20. In the year 627 the Meccans and allied tribes attacked Medina. In order to defend the town, the Prophet had a trench dug which prevented the enemy from entering. After a siege of a few months, the enemy withdrew.

21. In 630 Mohammed led a large expeditionary force to Tabūk, located in the North, near the Gulf of 'Aqaba. This can be regarded as the beginning of the great conquests.

22. Also called the pillars, arkān, of Islam, to wit: pronouncing the profession of faith, the five daily prayers, the zakāt, fasting during the month of Ramadān and pilgrimage to Mecca for those who are capable of it.

11

KITAB AL-KHARAJ

Abu Yusuf (d. 798)

FATE OF THE ANNEXED—TERRITORIES AND THE CONQUERED PEOPLES

Umar b. al-Khattab (634—644) replies to the Muslims who demand the sharing-out of the lands of Iraq and Syria (Palestine) among the conquerors.

But I thought that we had nothing more to conquer after the land of Kesra [Persia], whose riches, land, and people Allah has given us. I have divided the personal possessions among those that conquered them after having subtracted a fifth, which under my supervision was used for the purpose for which it was intended. I thought it necessary to reserve the land and its inhabitants, and levy from the latter the *kharaj* by virtue of their land, and the capitation (*jizya*) as a personal tax on every head, this poll tax constituting a *fay*[1] in favor of the Muslims who have fought there, of their children and of their heirs. Do you think that these borders could remain without warriors to defend them? Do you think that these vast countries, Syria [-Palestine], Mesopotamia, Kufa, Basra, Misr [Egypt] do not have to be covered with troops who must be well paid? Where can one obtain their pay if the land is divided up, as well as its inhabitants? (pp. 40–41).

Umar's decision against the dividing up among the conquerors of the conquered territories, as soon as Allah had shown him the decisive passages of his Holy Book [the Koran] concerning this subject, constituted for him and his work a sign of divine protection and a blessing for all the Muslims. His resolution to levy the *kharaj*, so that the revenues could be shared among the Muslims was beneficial to all the Community [*umma*], for had it not been reserved to pay the wages and food of the warriors, the border provinces would never have been populated,

Excerpted from Edmond Fagnan, trans., *Kitab al-Kharaj (Le livre de l'impôt foncier)* (Paris, 1921). English translation in Bat Ye'or, *The Dhimmi: Jews and Christians under Islam* (Madison, NJ: Fairleigh Dickinson University Press, 1985), pp. 165–72.

the troops would have been deprived of the necessary means to carry on the holy war [jihad], and one would have been afraid that the infidels would return to their former possessions, since these would not have been protected by soldiers and mercenaries. Allah knows best where is the good! (p. 43).

The People of the Countries of War and the Bedouin Who Converted to Preserve Their Lands and Possessions

Prince,[2] you also demanded what are the rules applicable to those of the inhabitants of the countries of war[3] who convert in order to save their lives and their possessions. Their life is sacred, those belongings for whose preservation they converted remain their property, and likewise their lands, which thus become lands liable to tithes in the same way as in Medina, where the inhabitants converted at the arrival of the Prophet and whose land is liable to tithes. The same goes for Ta'if and Bahrayn, as well as for the Bedouin who converted in order to save their water-holes and their territory, which remained their land and which they continue to hold (pp. 94–95).

Every polytheistic people with whom Islam has made peace on condition that they recognize its authority, are subjected to the division of spoils and pay the *kharaj* as a tributary [people]. The land they occupy is called land of *kharaj*: it shall be taxed according to the stipulations of the treaty, but in good faith and without overcharging. All land over which the imam [sovereign] has become master by force may be apportioned—if he so decides, for he enjoys complete freedom in this respect—among those who have conquered it, whereupon it becomes tithe land; or, if he deems it preferable, it can be left in the hands of its inhabitants, as Umar b. al-Khattab did in the case of Sawad, whereupon it becomes land liable to *kharaj*, which cannot be retaken. The conquered have full possession of it, which they transfer by inheritance and by contract, and the *kharaj* that is liable on it must not exceed the capacity of its taxpayers (p. 95).

Arab territory differs from non-Arab territory in that one fights Arabs only to oblige them to embrace Islam without making them pay the poll tax: nothing but their conversion is acceptable, and their land, if it is left to them, is tithe land. If the imam does not leave it to them and decides on its division, it still remains tithe land. The decision in respect of non-Arabs is different because they are fought not only to convert them but also to oblige them to pay the poll tax, whereas only the first of these objectives applies to the Arabs since they must either convert or be put to death. We are not aware that either the Prophet or any of his companions, or any caliph since then accepted the payment of a poll tax by the idolatrous Arabs, who had only the choice between conversion or death. If they were conquered, their wives and children were reduced to slavery, which was done by the Prophet toward the Hawazin[4] at the time of the Hunayn affair; subsequently, however, he gave them back their freedom. He only acted in this manner toward those who were idolaters.

The Arabs who possess Revealed Scriptures [Jews and Christians] are treated as non-Arabs and are allowed to pay the poll tax. Umar acted in this way with regard to the Banu Taghlab [Christians][5] whose alms tithe he doubled as replacement of the *kharaj*; and [the Prophet acted in a like manner when he levied a dinar from every pubescent person in the Yemen—or its equivalent in clothes—which in our eyes is similar to (the procedure to be followed in the case of peoples) having Revealed Scriptures. He acted likewise in granting peace to the people of Najran [Christians] for a ransom.

In the case of non-Arabs: Jews or Christians, polytheists, idolaters, fire-worshippers, the poll tax is to be levied on the males. The Prophet made the mages of Hajar pay it; yet the mages are polytheists and do not possess a Revealed Scripture. We consider them to be non-Arabs and we do not marry the women of their race, neither do we eat the animals that they slaughter. Umar b. al-Khattab levied on the non-Arab male polytheists of Iraq a poll tax divided into three categories: poor, wealthy, and middle-class.

In the case of Arab and non-Arab renegades, they are to be treated as Arab idolaters: they have the choice between conversion or death and they are not liable to the poll tax (pp. 100–101). The inhabitants of villages and the countryside, as well as the towns, their inhabitants and all that they contain, can be, left on their land, their dwelling places, or houses, as the imam decides, and may continue to enjoy their property in return for the payment of the poll tax and the *kharaj* (or all may be shared out among the conquerors). The only exception is the male Arab idolaters, who are not allowed to pay the poll tax and must choose between conversion or death (p. 103).

Thus the imam has the choice between two options, each of which is equally acceptable: either divide up [the land] as did the Prophet, or leave things as they were, as was the case elsewhere than at Khaybar. Umar b. al-Khattab made no changes in the Salad [Iraq]. Most of the countryside of Syria and Egypt was taken by force and treaties were required only when negotiating with the inhabitants of fortified places. Since the countryside had been occupied by the conquerors and taken by force, Umar relinquished it to the Muslim collectivity then existing, as well as to those who would come after them. He preferred to adopt this option, and similarly the imam is free to act as he pleases, providing the necessary precautions are taken (for the security) of the faithful and of religion (Islam) (pp. 103–104).

DIFFERENCE BETWEEN TITHED LAND AND *KHARAJ* LAND

Prince of the Believers, as to your question concerning the difference between tithed land and that of *kharaj*, any land, whether Arab or non-Arab, for which the inhabitants converted, remains in their possession and is considered tithed land, following the example of Medina, whose inhabitants converted for this purpose, as did those of the Yemen. Likewise, the land of idolatrous Arabs, from whom no poll tax can be accepted and who have to choose between conversion or death, is considered tithed even if it was conquered by the imam. Indeed, after having conquered the lands belonging to the Arab populations, the Prophet left them as they were, and they will remain tithed land until the day of the Last Judgement.

Any non-Arab inhabitable place, which has been conquered by the imam and left by him to the conquered, is to be considered land liable to *kharaj* but is tithable land if he shares it among the conquerors. It is not known that the non-Arab lands conquered by Umar b. al-Khattab and left by him to the conquered owners are lands liable to *kharaj*? Any non-Arab soil, concerning which the inhabitants negotiated and became tributaries, is liable to *kharaj* (p. 104).

Thus be sure, O prince of the Believers, to choose a reliable man, trustworthy, reserved, a loyal adviser, who is a guarantee both for you and for your subjects. Entrust him with the collection of all the charitable tithes from various countries, to which, according to your instructions, he will dispatch men of his choice, after whose manners, means, and collections he will inquire, and they will remit to him the tithes of the various regions. When they have been remitted, give him instructions regarding them in accordance with what Allah has stated, so that he should then carry them out. Do not entrust the collectors of the *kharaj* with the matter of tithes, for the product of the former must not be mixed with that of the latter. I have indeed heard that the *kharaj* collectors have sent out men to collect the charitable tithes who use unjust and abusive means and make impositions that are neither legal nor acceptable. For (collecting) the tithes, only reserved and virtuous people must be chosen. . . .

The product of the *kharaj* must not be united with that of the charitable tithes or with other tithes, for the former is a *fay* for all the Muslims, whereas the charitable tithes belong to those whom Allah has designated in His Holy Book (p. 121).

In order to collect payment of the poll tax, one must not beat the taxpayers nor expose them to the sun nor resort to other such methods, or inflict upon them repulsive physical torments. They must be shown gentleness, or imprisoned in order to extract payment from them for what they owe, and they are not to be released until they have paid in full. The, *wali* [governor of a province] is not allowed to exempt any Christian, Jew, Magean, Sabaean, or Samaritan from paying the tax, and no one can obtain a partial reduction. It is illegal for one to be exempted and another not, for their lives and belongings are spared only because of payment of the poll tax, which, levied on one's possessions, replaces the kharaj [levied on the land] (p. 189).

CONCERNING THE COSTUME AND APPEARANCE OF THE TRIBUTARIES

Furthermore, you must set a seal upon their necks when the poll tax is collected and until all have been passed in review, though these seals may later be broken at their request, as did Uthman b. Hunayf. You have succeeded in forbidding any of them the freedom to resemble a Muslim by his dress, his mount, or his appearance; that all should wear a belt (*zunnar*) at the waist similar to a coarse string, which each must knot in the middle; that their bonnets be quilted; that their saddles carry, instead of a pommel, a piece of wood like a pomegranate; that their footwear be furnished with double straps. That they avoid coming face to face with Muslims; that their womenfolk do not ride on padded saddles; that they do not build new synagogues or churches within the town and restrict themselves to using, as places of worship, those which existed at the time of the treaty that transformed them into tributaries, and which were left to them without having been demolished; the same applies to the funeral pyres [of the Zoroastrians]. Their residence in the main towns and Muslim markets is tolerated and they may buy and sell there, but neither wine nor pigs, and without displaying crosses in the main towns; but their headgear will be long and coarse. Consequently, command your representatives to oblige the tributaries to respect these requirements in their appearance, as Umar b. al-Khattab had done, as he said: "in order to distinguish them from the Muslims at a glance."

I have it from Abd ar-Rahman b. Thabit b. Thawban, in the name of his father, that Umar b. Abd al-Aziz[6] wrote the following to one of his governors: "After the preliminaries [greetings], do not allow any cross to be exhibited without smashing and destroying it; no Jew or Christian may be allowed to ride upon a saddle, but must use a pack-saddle, and let none of their womenfolk use a padded saddle, but only a pack-saddle; formal decrees must be issued in this respect and the public restricted from disobeying them. No Christian may wear a *kaba*, nor a fine cloth nor a turban! It has been reported to me that several Christians under your jurisdiction have relapsed into the custom of wearing turbans, no longer wear belts at the waist, and let their hair grow freely without cutting it. Upon my life! if this happens in your entourage, it is on account of your weakness, your incompetence, and the flatteries that you heed, and these people know, in resuming their former customs, what kind of person you are. Keep a watch on all I have forbidden and do not contradict those who have done it. Peace" (pp. 195–96).

Leave that which Allah has made to return[7] to you, in the hands of those who hold it and impose upon them a poll tax, in accordance with their capacity, the produce of which is to be distributed among the Muslims. These are the people that till the soil, a task that they know well and for which they are more capable. There is no way, either for you or for the faithful who are with you, to make of it a *fay* that you could distribute, on account of the agreement that was drawn up between them and you and because you are already collecting their poll tax according to their means. This was set out both to us and to you by Allah in His Book: "Fight those that believe not in God and the Last Day and do not forbid what God and His Messenger have forbidden—such men as practice not the religion of truth, being of those who have been given the Book—until they pay the tribute out of hand and have been humbled" (Koran 9:29). When you collect their poll tax, you can reclaim nothing more, nor have you any reason to do so. Reflect thereon! Were we to take those who are subjected to it and were we to share them out, what would be left for the Muslims that will come after us? By Allah, they would find no one to address, nor any work to exploit; the Muslims of our time would eat these people as long as they remained alive; once they were dead, and we also, our sons would devour their sons indefinitely, as long as any continue to exist, and these people would remain enslaved to the followers of Islam as long as it should last! So, impose upon them the poll tax, free their women and children from bondage, prevent the Muslims from oppressing and harming them, from devouring their possessions except within the legal limits, and fulfill the conditions upon which you have agreed with them concerning that which you have conceded to them. As for the display of crosses outside the town during their festivals, do not prevent them from doing it, but without banners or flags, just as they have requested, once a year; but within the walls of the town, amongst the Muslims and their mosques, no crosses must ever be displayed! (pp. 217–18).

BATTLE PROCEDURES

It seems that the most satisfactory suggestion we have heard in this connection is that there is no objection to the use of any kind of arms against the polytheists, smothering and burning their homes, cutting down their trees and date groves, and using catapults, without, however, deliberately attacking women, children, or elderly people; that one can yet pursue those that run away, finish off the wounded, kill prisoners who might prove dangerous to the Muslims, but this is only applicable to those on the chin of whom a razor has passed, for the others are children who must not be executed.

As for the prisoners who are led before the imam, the latter has the choice of executing them or making them pay a ransom, as he pleases, opting for the most advantageous choice for the Muslims and the wisest for Islam. The ransom imposed upon them is not to consist either of gold, silver, or wares, but is only an exchange for Muslim captives.

All that the victors bring back to the camp, or the possessions and goods of their victims, becomes a *fay*, which is to be divided into five parts. One share is to be given to those numbered in the Holy Book, and the four remaining shares are distributed among the soldiers who captured the spoils in the ratio of two portions to each horseman and one to each footsoldier. If a certain territory is conquered, the decision is left to the imam as to the best course to take in the interest of the Muslims: if he decides to leave it, as did Umar b. al-Khattab, who left the Sawad [Iraq] to the indigenous people—the local inhabitants—in exchange for the *kharaj*, then he can do so; and if he thinks that it should be left to the victors, he divides the land between them after having deducted a fifth. I am inclined to believe that if he acts in this manner after having taken the necessary precautions in order to safeguard the Muslims' interest, then the act is admissible (pp. 301–302).

For my part I say that the decision concerning prisoners is in the hands of the imam: in accordance with whatever he feels to be more to the advantage of Islam and the Muslims, he can have them executed or he can exchange them for Muslim prisoners (pp. 302–303).

Whenever the Muslims besiege an enemy stronghold, establish a treaty with the besieged who agree to surrender on certain conditions that will be decided by a delegate, and this man decides that their soldiers are to be executed and their women and children taken prisoner, this decision is lawful. This was the decision of Sa'ad b. Mu'adh in connection with the Banu Qurayza (a Jewish tribe of Arabia) (p. 310).

The decision made by the chosen arbitrator, if it does not specify the killing of the enemy fighters and the enslavement of their women and children, but establishes a poll tax, would also be lawful; if it stipulated that the vanquished were to be invited to embrace Islam, it would also be valid and they would therefore become Muslims and freemen (p. 311).

. . . [I]t is up to the imam to decide what treatment is to be meted out to them and he will chose that which is preferable for religion and for Islam. If he esteems that the execution of the fighting men and the enslavement of their women and children is better for Islam and its followers, then he will act thus, emulating the example of Sa'ad b. Mu'adh. If, on the contrary, he feels that it would be more advantageous to impose the *kharaj* upon them and that this is preferable in order to increase the *fay*, which enhances the resources of the Muslims against them and the other polytheists, then he is to adopt this measure toward them. Is it not correct that Allah has said in His Book: "Fight those . . . until they pay the tribute out of hand and have been humbled" (Koran 9:29), and that the Prophet invited the polytheists to embrace Islam, or, if they refused, to pay the poll tax, and that Umar b. al-Khattab, after having subdued the inhabitants of Sawad, did not spill their blood but made of them tributaries? (p. 312).

If they offer to surrender and accept the mediation of a Muslim of their choice together with one of their number, this is to be refused, for it is unacceptable that a Believer collaborate with an infidel to arrive at a decision on religious matters. If by error, the ruler's representative accepts and a verdict is proposed by both men, the imam is not to declare it binding unless it stipulates that the enemies will be tributaries or be converted to Islam. If this condition is adopted by them, then they are reproachless and if they acknowledge that they are tributaries, then they shall be accepted as such, without there being need of a verdict (pp. 314–15).

NOTES

1. Fay, "booty." The traditional Muslim commentators derive the word from the verb afa'a "to bring back" (cf. Koran 59:7), that which belongs by right to Allah and consequently to the Muslims. It was normally the spoils of an unconditional surrender, a fifth of which went to the imam and the rest of which was apportioned among the soldiers.

2. The author, a jurist, is giving advice to the Caliph Harun al-Rashid (786809).

3. Countries of the dal al-Harb, conquered by jihad.

4. A confederation of North Arabian tribes, which were routed by Muhammad at the battle of Hunayn in 630.

5. A tribe of Christian Arabs of the Wail branch, established in Arabia.

6. Umayyad caliph (717–720).

7. See n. 1.

12

SIYAR

Shaybani (d. 803/805)

Fight in the name of God and in the "path of God" [i.e., truth]. Combat [only] those who disbelieve in God. Whenever you meet your polytheist enemies, invite them [first] to adopt Islam. If they do so, accept it, and let them alone. You should then invite them to move from their territory to the territory of the emigres [Madina]. If they do so, accept it and let them alone. Otherwise, they should be informed that they would be [treated] like the Muslim nomads (Bedouins) [who take no part in the war] in that they are subjects of God's orders as [other] Muslims, but that they will receive no share in either the ghanima (spoil of war) or in the fay. If they refuse [to accept Islam], then call upon then to pay the jizya (poll tax); if they do, accept it and leave them alone. If you besiege the inhabitants of a fortress or a town and they try to get you to let them surrender on the basis of God's judgment, do not do so, since you do not know what God's judgment is, but make them surrender to your judgment and then decide their case according to your own views.

I heard the Apostle of God in the campaign against Banu Qurayza saying: "He [of the enemy] who has reached puberty should be killed, but he who has not should be spared."

If the army [of Islam] attacks the territory of war and it is a territory that has received an invitation to accept Islam, it is commendable if the army renews the invitation, but if it fails to do so it is not wrong. The army may launch the attack [on the enemy] by night or by day and it is permissible to burn [the enemy] fortifications with fire or to inundate them with water. If [the army] captures any spoil of war, it should not be divided up in enemy territory until [the Muslims] have brought it to a place of security and removed it to the territory of Islam.

Excerpted from Majid Khadduri, trans., *The Islamic Law of Nations: Shaybani's Siyar* (Baltimore: Johns Hopkins University Press, 1966), pp. 76–77, 87, 95–96, 100–101.

THE KILLING OF CAPTIVES AND THE DESTRUCTION OF ENEMY FORTIFICATIONS

I asked: If male captives of war were taken from the territory of war, do you think that the Imam should kill them all or divide them as slaves among the Muslims?

He replied: The Imam is entitled to a choice between taking then to the territory of Islam to be divided [among the warriors] and killing them [while in the territory of war].

I asked: Which is preferable?

He replied: [The Imam] should examine the situation and decide whatever he deems to be advantageous to the Muslims.

I asked: If killing them were advantageous to the Muslims, [do you think that the Imam] should order their killing?

He replied: Yes.

I asked: If all of them became Muslims, would he be entitled to kill them?

He replied: He should not kill them if they became Muslims; they should be regarded as booty to be divided among the Muslims.

I asked: If they did not become Muslims, but they claimed that they had been given a safe-conduct and a few Muslims declared that they had given such a pledge to them, would such a claim be accepted?

He replied: No.

I asked: Why?

He replied: Because both [merely] stated their own claim.

13

THE HIDAYAH

Sheikh Burhanuddin Ali of Marghinan
(d. 1196)

The sacred injunction concerning war is . . . established as a divine ordinance, by the word of God, who said in the Qur'an, "Slay the infidels," and also by a saying of the Prophet, "War is permanently established until the Day of Judgment" (meaning the ordinance respecting war).

The destruction of the sword is incurred by infidels, although they be not the first aggressors, as appears from various passages in the traditions which are generally received to this effect.

When the Muslims enter the enemy's country and besiege the cities or strongholds of the infidels, it is necessary to invite them to embrace the faith, because Ibn 'Abbas relates of the Prophet that he never destroyed any without previously inviting them to embrace the faith. If, therefore, they embrace the faith, it is unnecessary to war with them, because that which was the design of the war is then obtained without war. The Prophet, moreover, has said we are directed to make war upon men only until such time as they shall confess, "There is no God but one God." But when they repeat this creed, their persons and properties are in protection (*aman*). If they do accept the call to the faith, they must then be called upon to pay *jizyah*, or capitation tax, because the Prophet directed the commanders of his armies so to do, and also because by submitting to this tax war is forbidden and terminated upon the authority of the Qur'an. (This call to pay capitation tax, however, respects only those from whom the capitation tax is acceptable, or, as to apostates and the idolaters of Arabia, to call upon them to pay the tax is useless, since nothing is accepted from them but embracing the faith, as it is thus commanded in the Qur'an).

If a Muslim attack infidels without previously calling them to the faith, he is an offender, because this is forbidden; but yet if he does attack them before thus inviting them and slay them, and take their property, neither fine, expiation, nor

Excerpted from *The Hidayah*, English translation in T. P. Hughes, *A Dictionary of Islam* (London, 1895), reissued 1994, pp. 244–45.

184

atonement are due, because that which protects (namely, Islam) does not exist in them, nor are they under protection by place (namely the *Daru 'l-Islam*, or Muslim territory), and the mere prohibition of the act is not sufficient to sanction the exaction either of fine or of atonement for property; in the same manner as the slaying of the women or infant children of infidels is forbidden, but if, notwithstanding, a person were to slay such, he is not liable to a fine. It is laudable to call to the faith a people to whom a call has already come, in order that they may have the more full and ample warning; but yet this is not incumbent, as it appears in the Traditions that the Prophet plundered and despoiled the tribe of al-Mustaliq by surprise, and he also agreed with Asamah to make a predatory attack upon Qubna at an early hour, and to set it on fire, and such attacks are not preceded by a call. (Qubna is a place in Syria: some assert it is the name of a tribe.) If the infidels, upon receiving the call, neither consent to it nor agree to pay capitation tax, it is then incumbent on the Muslims to call upon God for assistance, and to make war upon them, because God is the assistant of those who serve Him, and the destroyer of His enemies, the infidels, and it is necessary to implore His aid upon every occasion; the Prophet, moreover, commands us so to do. And having so done, the Muslims must then with God's assistance attack the infidels with all manner of warlike engines (as the Prophet did by the people of Ta'if), and must also set fire to their habitations (in the same manner as the Prophet fired Baweera), and must inundate them with water and tear up their plantations and tread down their grain because by these means they will become weakened, and their resolution will fail and their force be broken; these means are, therefore, all sanctified by the law.

14

AL-IMAM MUHAMMAD IBN IDRIS AL-SHAF'I'S AL-RISALA FI US UL AL-FIQH

Al-Shafi'i (d. 820)

40. Shafi'i replied: God has imposed the [duty of] jihad as laid down in His Book and uttered by His Prophet's tongue. He stressed the calling [of men to fulfill] the jihad [duty] as follows:

> God has brought from the believers their selves and their possessions against [the gift of] Paradise. They fight in the way of God; they kill, and are killed; that is a promise binding upon God in the Torah and Gospel and the Qur'an; and who fulfills his covenant better than God? So rejoice in the bargain you have made with Him. That is the mighty triumph. [Q. 9.112]

And He said:

> Fight the polytheists totally as they fight you totally; and know that God is with the godfearing. [Q. 9.36]

And He said:

> Slay the polytheists wherever you find them, and take them, and confine them, and lie in ambush for them everywhere. But if they repent and perform the prayer and pay the zakat, then set them free. God is All-forgiving, All-compassionate. [Q. 9.5]

Excerpted from Majid Khadduri, trans., *al-Imam Muhammad ibn Idris al-Shaf'i's al-Risala fi us ul al-fiqh: Treatise on the Foundations of Islamic Jurisprudence* (Cambridge: Islamic Texts Society, 1997), pp. 82–87.

And he said:

Fight those who do not believe in God nor in the Last Day, who do not forbid what God and His Apostle have made forbidden, and who do not practice the religion of truth, of those who have been give the Book, until they pay the jizya out of hand and have been humbled. [Q. 9.29]

41. Abd al-Aziz b. Muhammad as-Darawardi told us from Muhammad b. Amr b. Alqama from Abu Salama [b. Abd al-Rahman] from Abu Hurayra, who said that the Apostle of God said:

I shall continue to fight the unbelievers they say: "There is no god but God," if they make this pronouncement they shall be secured their blood and property, unless taken for its price, and their reward shall be given by God.

And God, gloried by His praise, said:

O believers, what is the matter with you, that when it is said to you: "Go forth in the way of God," you sink down to the ground? Are you so content with this present life as to neglect the Here-after? The enjoyment of this life is little in comparison with the Hereafter. If you do not go forth, He will inflict upon you a painful punishment, and instead of you He will substitute another people; and you will not hurt Him at all, for God is powerful over everything. [Q. 9.38–39]

And he said:

Go forth, light and heavy! Struggle in God's way with your possessions and yourselves! That is better for you, did you but know. [Q. 9.41]

42. Shafi'i said: These communications mean that the jihad, and rising up in arms in particular, is obligatory for all able-bodied [believers], exempting no one, just as prayer, pilgrimage and [payment of] alms are performed, and no person is permitted to perform the duty for another, since performance by one will not fulfil the duty for another. They may also mean that the duty of [jihad] is a collective (kifaya) duty different from that of prayer: Those who perform it in the war against the polytheists will fulfil they duty and receive the supererogatory merit, thereby preventing those who stayed behind from falling into error. But God has not put the two [categories of men] on an equal footing, for He said:

Such believers who sit at home—unless they have an injury—are not the equals of those who fight in the path of God with their possessions and their selves. God has given precedence to those who fight with their possessions and their selves over those who sit at home. God has promised the best of things to both, and He has preferred those who fight over those who sit at home by [granting them] a mighty reward. [Q. 4.97]

The literal meaning of this communication is that the duty is obligatory on all men.

43. He asked: Where is the proof for your opinion that if some people perform the duty, the others would be relieved of punishment?

44. Shafi'i said: It is in the communication [that I have just cited].

45. He asked: In what part of it?

46. Shafi'i replied: God said: "Yet to each God has promised the best of things."

Thus God has promised "the best of things" for those who stayed behind and could not go to the jihad, although he clearly specified his preference for those who went to the jihad over those who stayed home. If those who stayed at home were in error, while others were fighting, they would be committing a sin, unless God forgives them, rather than receiving "the best of things."

47. He asked: Is there any other [proof]?

48. Shafi'i replied: Yes, God said:

It is not for the believers to go forth all together, but why should not a party of every section of them go forth, to become learned in religion, and to warn their people when they return to them, perhaps they will beware. [Q. 9.123]

[When] the Apostle went to battle he was accompanied by some of his companions while others stayed at home; for Ali b. Abi Talib stay at home during the battle of Tabuk. Nor did God ordain that all Muslims were under obligation to go to battle, for He said: "Why should not a party of every section of them for forth?" So He made it known that going into battle was obligatory on some, not on all, [just] as knowledge of the law is not obligatory on all but on some, save the fundamental duties which should be known to all men. But God knows best.

49. Shafi'i said: In like manner are other duties, the fulfillment of which is intended to be collective; whenever they are performed by some Muslims collectively, those who do not perform them will not fall in error. If all men failed to perform the duty so that no able-bodied man went forth to battle, all I am afraid, would fall into error (although I am certain that this would never happen) in accordance with [God's] saying:

If you do not go forth, He will inflict upon you a painful punishment. [Q. 9.39]

50. He asked: What is the meaning [of this communication]?

51. Shafi'i replied: It means that it is not permissible that all men should fail to "go forth"; but that if some go forth, so that a sufficient number fulfils [the collective duty], the other do not fall into error, because the going forth by some would fulfil the [duty of] "going forth."

52. He asked: Are there examples other than the jihad?

53. Shafi'i replied: [Yes, such as] the funeral and burial prayers, the perform-

ance of which should not be neglected; but men are not all under the obligation to attend to their performance, for those who perform them will relieve those who do not from falling into error.

In the same [category falls the duty to] reply to a salutation. For God said:

> When you are greeted with a greeting, respond with a better one, or return it. Verily God keeps account of everything. [Q. 4.88]

The Apostle of God said:

> He who is standing shall greet him who is sitting. If [only] one replies to a greeting, he would fulfill [the duty] on behalf of the others.

These are merely intended to mean that a reply must be made. So the response of the few fulfils the duty for all who are obligated to reply, for the [collective] response is sufficient.

So far as I have been informed, the Muslims have continued to act as I have stated, from the time of the Prophet to the present. Only a few men must know the law, attend the funeral service, perform the jihad and respond to greeting, while others are exempt. So those who know the law, perform the jihad, attend the funeral service, and respond to a greeting will be rewarded, while others do not fall into error since a sufficient number fulfill the [collective] duty.

15

AL-AHKAM
AS-SULTANIYYAH

Al-Mawardi (d. 1058)

The amirate of jihad is particularly concerned with fighting the mushrikun. . . .

This section deals with the direction of war. The mushrikun of Dar al-Harb (the arena of battle) are of two types:

First, those whom the call of Islam has reached, but they have refused it and have taken up arms. The amir of the army has the option of fighting them in one of two ways, that is in accordance with what he judges to be in the best of interests of the Muslims and most harmful to the mushrikun: the first, to harry them from their houses and to inflict damage on them day and night, by fighting and burning, or else to declare war and combat them in ranks;

Second, those whom the invitation to Islam has not reached, although such persons are few nowadays since Allah has made manifest the call of his Messenger—unless there are people to the east and extreme east, or to the west, of whom we have no knowledge, beyond the Turks and Romans we are fighting; it is forbidden us to initiate an attack on the mushrikun while they are unawares or at night, that is, it is forbidden to kill them, use fire against them or begin to attack before explaining the invitation to Islam to them, informing them of the miracles of the Prophet and making plain the proofs so as to encourage acceptance on their part; if they still refuse to accept after this, war is waged against them and they are treated as those whom the call has reached. Allah, may He be exalted, says, "Call to the way of your Lord with wisdom and kindly admonition and converse with them by what better in argument" (Qur'an 16.125)—which means calling to the *deen* of your Lord with wisdom, about which there are two interpretations: the first, that wisdom refers to prophethood and the second, that it refers to the Qur'an, and al-Kalbi is of this view. For "kindly admonition" there are also two interpretations: the first, that it refers to the Qur'an on account of its quiet, restrained speech, and this is again al-Kalbi's view, and the second, that it refers

Excerpted from *The Laws of Islamic Governance* [*al-Ahkam as-Sultaniyyah*], trans. Asadullah Yate (London: Ta-Ha, 1996), pp. 60, 77–78, 200–201.

to the commands and interdictions therein. As for, "and converse with them by what is better in argument," it means, "explain the truth to them and make clear the proofs to them!"

If the amir initiates the attack against them before calling them to Islam or warning them by means of cogent proofs, and kills them by surprise or at night, blood money must be paid; according to the most correct judgment of the Shafi'is, it is equal to the blood money paid to Muslims, although according to other it is equal to the blood money paid to the kuffar, because of the difference of their beliefs. Abu Hanifah, however, says that no blood money is liable for killing them and their blood is shed with impunity.

A Muslim may put to death any mushrik combatant he seizes, whether or not he is involved in the fighting. There is a difference of opinion regarding the killing of old persons and monks inhabiting cells and monasteries. One view concerning them is that they are not to be killed unless they fight, as they are covered, like women and children, by treaty; another, is that they are killed even if they are not fighting, because it may be that their opinions will cause more harm to the Muslims than fighting. Durayd ibn as-Simma, who was more than one hundred years old, was killed during the battle of Hawazin at Hunayn while the Prophet, may the peace and blessings of Allah be upon him, was watching and he did not oppose his killing. . . .

It is not permitted to kill women and children in battle, nor elsewhere, as long as they are not fighting because of the prohibition of the Messenger of Allah, may the peace and blessings of Allah be upon him, forbade the killing of those employed as servants and mamlouks, that is young slaves. If women and children fight, then they are fought and killed, but only face to face, not from behind while fleeing. If they use their women and children as shields in battle, then one must avoid killing them and aim only at killing the men; if, however, it is impossible to kill them except by killing the women and children, then it is permitted. . . .

Moreover as continual perseverance in fighting is among the duties of jihad, it is binding until one of four things occur:

First, they (the enemy) become Muslims, in which case they receive the same rights as us, become responsible for the same obligations as us and they are allowed to retain any land and property they possess. The Messenger of Allah, may the peace and blessings of Allah be upon him, said, "I have been commanded to fight people until they say, 'No god but Allah.' If they say this, then their blood and their property are safe from me—except when there exists another legitimate reason." Their country becomes part of the Territory of Islam when they become Muslims during the battle—be they small or great in number—any land or wealth belonging to them in the battle-zone remains theirs. If the amir conquers the battle zone he cannot take the wealth of those who have accepted Islam. Abu Hanifah, however, says booty is taken the form of unmovable properties of land and houses, but not movable wealth or chattels. This is at variance with the sunnah: in the blockade of the Banu Qurayzhah, the two Jews Tha'labah and Asid, sons of Shaba, became Muslims and their Islam protected their wealth.

Their Islam also entails Islam for any minors amongst their children and any still in the womb. Abu Hanifah, however, says that if a kafir becomes a Muslim in the Territory of Islam, it does not entail Islam for his children who are still minors, whereas if he becomes a Muslim in Dar al-Harb (the war zone), it entails Islam for his children who are minors, but not for the foetus, for his wife and the foetus are treated as fay.

If a Muslim enters Dar al-Harb and buys land and goods therein, he is not dispossessed of these if the Muslims conquer it, as he purchaser still has more claim over them. Abu Hanifah, however, is of the opinion that any land he possess is treated as fay;

The second thing that might occur is that Allah gives victory over them but they remain mushrikun, in which case their women and children are taken prisoner, and their wealth is taken as booty, and those who are not made captive are put to death. As for the captives, the amir has the choice of taking the most beneficial action of four possibilities: the first, to put them to death by cutting their necks; the second, to enslave them and apply the laws of slavery regarding their sale or manumission; the third, to ransom them in exchange for goods or prisoners; and fourth, to show favour to them and pardon them. Allah, may He be exalted, says, "When you encounter those who deny [the Truth] then strike [their] necks" (Qur'an 47.4). There are two ways of understanding this: the first, that it refers to the striking of their necks while in battle. Then He says: "Then when you have weakened them" is wounding them, and "make the fetter tight" the taking of prisoners. "Then either grace or ransom" (Qur'an 47.4). Regarding "grace" there are two opinions: the first, that it means to pardon and setting free, just as the Messenger of Allah, may the peace and blessings of Allah be upon him, pardoned Thumamah ibn Uthal after having made him captive; the second, that it means manumission after being enslaved, and this is the opinion of Muqatil. As for "ransom": there are two opinions as to its meaning in this case: The first, that it refers to the purchase of the prisoner with wealth, or in return for the setting free of another prisoner, just as the Messenger bought back the prisoners of Badr for money, while on another battlefield he bought back one of his men for two enemy captives; the second, that is refers to the sale, and this is the opinion of Muqatil. "Until the war lays down its burdens" (Qur'an 47.4). There are two interpretations of this: the first, that it refers to the submission of the burdens of kufr to Islam and the second, to a heavy load, meaning the weapons and instruments of war. If it is taken as meaning the laying down of weapons, it refers either to the Muslims laying down their arms after the victory, or to the mushrikun abandoning their arms after their defeat. There will be a further explanation of these four rules in the section dealing with booty below.

The third possibility is that the enemy make a payment in return for peace and reconciliation. It is permitted to accept this payment and reconciliation with them in two ways:

i. Payment is made immediately and is not treated as ongoing tribute. This payment is treated as booty as it has been taken as a result of riding out on horses and camels; it is shared amongst those entitled to the booty and it represents a guarantee that those paying it will no longer be fought during this jihad; it does, however, not prevent a jihad being carried out against them in the future;

ii. They make a payment every year in which case it constitutes an ongoing tribute by which their security is established. What is taken from them in the first year is treated as booty and is shared amongst the people entitled to the fay. It is not permitted to resume the jihad against them as long as they make the payments. If one of them enters Dar al-Islam, this contract of reconciliation guarantees safety for himself and his wealth. If they refuse to make payment, however, the reconciliation ceases, their security is no longer guaranteed and war must be waged on them—like any other persons from the enemy camp. Abu Hanifah, however, says that their refusal to make the jizyah payment and that of reconciliation does not invalidate their guarantee of security, as this tax constitutes an ongoing claim against them but the contract is not broken by their nonpayment— just as in the case of contracts of debt.

As for presents which the enemy offer before hostilities, their acceptance does not mean any arrangement has been made and it is permitted to make war on the after the offer—as any such arrangement was not the result of a contract;

The fourth possibility is that the enemy request a guarantee of safety and a truce. It is permitted to make a truce of peace for a specific period with them if victory over them and taking payment from them is too difficult to obtain—as long as the Imam has given him permission to undertake this or has delegated full authority to him. The Messenger of Allah, may the peach and blessings of Allah be upon him, made a ten-year truce with the Quraysh in the year of Hudaybiyyah. It should be as short as possible and not exceed ten years; if a truce is made with them for more than this, the period in excess of this is invalidated. Their security is guaranteed until the period come to an end, and jihad is not waged against them as long as they respect the agreement; if, however, they break it, then hostilities begin again and war is made against them without warning. The Quraysh broke the treaty of Hudaybiyyah and so the Messenger of Allah, may the peace and blessings of Allah be upon him, set out on a campaign against them in the year of the Victory and conquered Makkah—as a result of the peace treaty, according to Shafi'i, but by an act of war, according to Abu Hanifah. . . .

This section concerning the rules of this type of amirate is about the action to be taken in assailing and fighting the enemy. The amir of the army may use bal-listas and catapults when besieging the enemy, for the Messenger of Allah, may the peace and blessings of Allah be upon him, set up a catapult against the inhab-itants of Ta'if. He may also destroy their homes, make night raids against them and cause fired. If, moreover, he reckons that by cutting their date-palms and their trees down it will serve to weaken them, such that they are overcome by force or are compelled to make a peace agreement, then he should do so; he should not, however, act in this way if he does not see any such benefit in it.

The Messenger of Allah, may the peace and blessings of Allah be upon him, cut down the vines of the people of Ta'if and this was a reason for their becoming Muslims. He also ordered the cutting down of the type of date-palm known as the yellow date-palm, whose date-stone can be seen through its flesh, and its flesh was dearer to them than a slave. When these palms of theirs were cut down, they were aggrieved, saying, "All the palms have either been cut down or burned down." The Jew Sammak declaimed the following verses as they were being cut down:

> Have we not inherited the Wise Book from the time of Musa and we have not strayed from it? And you people, shepherds of thin sheep on the plain of Tihama and al-Ahnaf, you regard your shepherding as a glory for you, as you have done in every age passing over you. O those of you present! Stop this injustice and these words of incitement. It may well be that the nights and the vicissitudes of time will bring down the just and upright person because of the killing and expul-sion of the Nadir tribe and the destruction of the date-palms before they have even been harvested.

Then Hassan ibn Thabit replied with the following:

> They have been given the Book and have abandoned it: they are blind to the Tawrah and are a people doomed. "You have denied the Qur'an which came to you as an affirmation of what the one who warns said," so the fire engulfing al-Buqayra (inhabited by Banu Nadir) was an insignificant thing for the nobles of Bani Lu'ayy (ascendants of the Quraysh).

When the Messenger of Allah, may the peace and blessings of Allah be upon him, did this to them, the Muslims felt ill at ease in their breasts and said, "O Mes-senger of Allah! Will we be rewarded for what we have cut and reproached for what we have left?" And the Allah revealed the following, "Whatever of the date-palms (lina) you cut down or left standing on their roots, it was by the permission of Allah and so as to bring loss to the corrupt ones" (Qur'an 59.5). As to the word *lina*, there are four interpretations: first, that it refers to any kind of date-palm, and this is according to Muqatil; second, that it refers to the best quality date-palms, according to Sufyan; third, that it refers to the offshoots as they are more supple than the date-palm itself; and fourth, that it refers to all trees because of their sup-pleness when alive.

It is also permitted to block off the supply of water to them, or to prevent them from using it, even if there are women and children amongst them, as it is one of the most potent means of weakening them and gaining victory over them, either by force or through a treaty. If a thirsty person amongst them requests a drink, the amir may either give him to drink or refuse him, just as he has the option of killing him or letting him live.

Anyone who kills one of them should hide him from the sight of others, but he is not obliged to bury him. The Messenger of Allah, may the peace and blessing of Allah be upon him, commanded that those killed at Badr should be thrown into an old well. It is not permitted to burn any of them, be they dead or alive, for it is reported that the Messenger of Allah, may the peace and blessings of Allah be upon him, said, "Do not torment the slaves of Allah with the torture of Allah." Abu Bakr, may Allah be pleased with him, did burn a group of the people who refused to pay the zakah, but it could well have been his own decision before news (of the Prophet's precedent) had reached him.

16

FATAWA-I JAHANDARI

Ziauddin Barani (d. 1357)

[Barani pleads for an all-out struggle against Hinduism.]

The Muslim king will not be able to establish the honour of theism (tauhid) and the supremacy of the Islam unless he strives with all his courage to overthrow infidelity and to slaughter its leaders (imams), who in India are the Brahmans. He should make a firm resolve to overpower, capture, enslave and degrade the infidels. All the strength and power of the king and of the holy warriors of Islam should be concentrated in holy campaigns and holy wars; and they should risk themselves in the enterprise so that the true Faith may uproot the false creeds, and then it will look as if these false creeds had never existed because they have been deprived of all their glamour. On the other hand, if the Muslim king, in spite of the power and position which God has given him, is merely content to take the poll-tax (jizya) and tribute (kharaj) from the Hindus and preserves both infidels and infidelity and refuses to risk his power in attempting to overthrow them, what differences will there be in this respect between the kings of Islam and the Rais of the infidels? For the Rais of the infidels also exact the poll-tax (jizya) and the tribute (kharaj) from the Hindus, who belong to their own false creed, and fill their treasuries with money so obtained; in fact, they collect a hundred times more taxes.

Further, if the kings of Islam, despite their royal power and prestige, are content to preserve infidels and infidelity in return for the tribute and the poll-tax, how can effect be given in this world to the following tradition of the Prophet: "I have been ordered to tight all people until they affirm 'There is no God but Allah'; but when they affirm this, their lives and properties are protected from me, subject to the law of Islam (as between Muslims)."

The Divine object in sending one hundred and twenty four thousand prophets has been to overthrow infidels and infidelity and this has also been the object of

Excerpted from a translation of Ziauddin Barani's *Fatawa-i Jahandari*, ca. 1358–59 CE, in Mohammad Habib, *The Political Theory of the Delhi Sultanate* (Allahabad: Kitab Mahal, 1961), pp. 46–47.

early and later Muslim kings. But the succession of prophets has come to an end with our holy Prophet and the liquidation of infidelity through the preachings of prophets is no longer possible. Consequently, the overthrow of infidelity and the disgrace of infidels and polytheists is now only possibly if the king, after all necessary arrangements, concentrates his courage and his high resolve on this one object in order to win the approval of God and the Prophet by establishing the supremacy of the true Faith. But if the king is content merely to take the poll-tax and the tribute from the Hindus, who are worshippers of idols and cow-dung, and the Hindus are able with peace of mine to preserve the customs of infidelity, then, of course, infidelity will not be liquidated, truth will not be establish at the centre and the True Word will not be honoured. [A paragraph which repeats the same idea in about the same words has been omitted from here.]

It is possible, nevertheless, that kings through their determined efforts may, first, put their governments in order and then with their high resolve risk their power, dignity, and prestige so that the true religion defeats and prevails over the false creeds, the traditions of Islam are elevated, and what has been designed by Providence comes to pass by the establishment of truth at the centre. But it is necessary for kings to understand what the establishment of truth at the centre means, so that they may devote their lives to striving for it, deeming it to be the main objective for the attainment of which they should be prepared to risk themselves and their supporters. The kings in reward for their efforts in this enterprise, which has been the object of prophets, caliphs, saints, and truthful men (siddiqan) as well as of the earlier and later kings of the Muslim community, will obtain in this world praises for their good deeds which will last till the Day of Judgment and in the next world they will have the status of prophets, truthful men, saints, and of those near to God (muqarribin) and a share of that Divinely promised blessing, "which the ear has not heard of and the eye has not seen." Also, by that increase of spiritual rewards that is due to kings, such rulers will be blessed in Paradise by a variety of good things, while love for them will survive in the hearts of the people of this earth and their good deeds will be recounted generation after generation. The religious perfection of the Muslim kings lies in this—they should risk themselves as well as their power and authority and strive day and night to establish truth at the centre. The sons of Mahmud and kings of Islam ought to know that in the Sunni faith the establishment of truth at the centre is both excellent knowledge and excellent action. This is the highest of all good works with the exception of the mission of the prophets.

Sons of Mahmud[1] and kings of Islam! You should with all your royal determination apply yourself to uprooting and disgracing infidels, polytheists, and men of bad dogmas and bad religions, if you wish that you may not have to be ashamed before God and his Prophets and that in your record of life—concerning what you have said and done, the clothes you have worn, and the food you have eaten—they may write good instead of evil. You should consider the enemies of God and

His Faith to be your enemies and you should risk your power and authority in overthrowing them, so that you may win the approval of God and the Prophet Mohammad and of all prophets and saints. You should not content yourself merely with levying the poll-tax and the tribute from the infidels and you should not allow infidelity to be preserved in spite of your royal power and authority. You should strive day and night for the degradation of infidelity so that (on the Day of Judgment) you may be raised (from your graves) among the prophets and be blessed with the sight of God for all eternity and "may find a seat among the truthful near the Powerful King of (God)."

The majority of religious scholars and wise men of early (Islamic) as well as later time have been sure that if Muslim kings strive with all their might and power and the power of all their supporters on this path, the following objects will be attained:—the true Faith will gain a proper ascendancy over the false creeds; the True Word will be honoured; the traditions of infidelity and polytheism will be weakened; Musalmans will be favoured and honoured; infidels and men of bad faith will be faced with destitution and disgrace; the orders of the unlawful state and the opposed creeds will be erased; the laws of the *shari'at* will be enforced on the seventy-two communities; and the enemies of God and the Prophet will be condemned, banished, repudiated, and terrorised.

NOTE

1. Mahmud of Ghazni (d. 1030), who waged devastating jihad campaigns against the Hindus in Northern India—which included extensive slaughter, pillage, mass enslavement, and forced conversions to Islam—during the first three decades of the 11th century.

17

KITAB AL-WAGIZ FI FIQH MADHAB AL-IMAM AL-SAFI'I

Al-Ghazali (d. 1111)

... [O]ne must go on jihad (i.e., warlike *razzias* or raids) at least once a year ... one may use a catapult against them [non-Muslims] when they are in a fortress, even if among them are women and children. One may set fire to them and/or drown them. ... If a person of the *ahl al-kitab* [People of the Book—Jews and Christians, typically] is enslaved, his marriage is [automatically] revoked. ... One may cut down their trees. ... One must destroy their useless books. Jihadists may take as booty whatever they decide ... they may steal as much food as they need. ...

[On the *dhimmis* subjected by jihad]

... [T]he *dhimmi* is obliged not to mention Allah or His Apostle ... Jews, Christians, and Majians must pay the *jizya* [poll tax on non-Muslims] ... on offering up the *jizya*, the *dhimmi* must hang his head while the official takes hold of his beard and hits [the dhimmi] on the protruberant bone beneath his ear [i.e., the mandible]. ... They are not permitted to ostentatiously display their wine or church bells ... their houses may not be higher than the Muslim's, no matter how low that is. The *dhimmi* may not ride an elegant horse or mule; he may ride a donkey only if the saddle[-work] is of wood. He may not walk on the good part of the road. They [the *dhimmis*] have to wear [an identifying] patch [on their clothing], even women, and even in the [public] baths ... [*dhimmis*] must hold their tongue. ...

Excerpted from *Kitab al-Wagiz fi fiqh madhab al-imam al-Safi'i* (Beirut, 1979), pp. 186, 190–91, 199–200, 202–203. English translation by Dr. Michael Schub.

18

[UNTITLED]

Sirhindi (d. 1624)

Shariat can be fostered through the sword.

Kufr and Islam are opposed to each other. The progress of one is possible only at the expense of the other and co-existence between these two contradictory faiths is unthinkable.

The honour of Islam lies in insulting *kufr* and *kafirs*. One who respects *kafirs*, dishonours the Muslims. To respect them does not merely mean honouring them and assigning them a seat of honour in any assembly, but it also implies keeping company with them or showing considerations to them. They should be kept at an arm's length like dogs. . . . If some worldly business cannot be performed without them, in that case only a minimum of contact should be established with them but without taking them into confidence. The highest Islamic sentiment asserts that it is better to forego that worldly business and that no relationship should be established with the *kafirs*.

The real purpose in levying *jizya* on them (the non-Muslims) is to humiliate them to such an extent that, on account of fear of *jizya*, they may not be able to dress well and to live in grandeur. They should constantly remain terrified and trembling. It in intended to hold them under contempt and to uphold the honour and might of Islam.

[To Lala Beg he wrote] Cow-sacrifice in India is the noblest of Islamic practices. The *kafirs* may probably agree to pay *jizya* but they shall never concede to cow-sacrifice.

The execution of the accursed *kafir* of Gobindwal [Sikh leader] is an important achievement and is the cause of great defeat of the accursed Hindus.[1] Whatever might have been the motive behind the execution, the dishonour of the *kafirs* is an act of highest grace for the Muslims. Before the execution of the *kafirs* I had

---

Excerpted from Saiyid Athar Abbas Rizvi, *Muslim Revivalist Movements in Northern India in the Sixteenth and Seventeenth Centuries* (Agra, Lucknow: Agra University, Balkrishna Book Co., 1965), pp. 247–50; and Yohanan Friedmann, *Shaykh Ahmad Sirhindi: An Outline of His Thought and a Study of His Image in the Eyes of Posterity* (Montreal, Quebec: McGill University, Institute of Islamic Studies, 1971), pp. 73–74.

seen in a vision that the Emperor had destroyed the crown of the head of *Shirk*. Verily he was the chief of the *Mushriks* and the leader of the *kafirs*.

Whenever a Jew is killed, it is for the benefit of Islam.

NOTE

1. Yohanan Friedmann (*Shaykh Ahmad Sirhindi: An Outline of His Thought and a Study of His Image in the Eyes of Posterity* [Montreal, Quebec: McGill University, Institute of Islamic Studies, 1971], pp. 73–74) offers this summary assessment of Sirhindi's attitudes toward the Hindus:

> Sirhindi follows up his utter rejection of the beliefs and practices of Hinduism with an equally outspoken statement of his attitude regarding the position of the Hindus in the Mughul empire. The honour of Islam demands the humiliation of the infidels and their false religion. To achieve this objective, *jizyah* should be mercilessly levied upon them, and they should be treated like dogs. Cows should be slaughtered to demonstrate the supremacy of Islam. The performance of this rite is, in India, the most important symbol of Islamic domination. One should refrain from dealing with the infidels unless absolutely necessary, and even then treat then with contempt. Islam and infidelity are two irreconcilable opposites. One thrives upon the degradation of the other. Sirhindi's deep-seated hatred of the non-Muslims can be best illustrated by his rejoicing at the execution in 1606 of Arjun, the fifth *guru* of the Sikhs.

19

[UNTITLED]

Shah Wali-Allah (d. 1762)

It has become clear to my mind that the kingdom of heaven has predestined that *kafirs* should be reduced to a state of humiliation and treated with utter contempt. Should that repository of majesty and dauntless courage (Nizam al-Maluk) gird his loins and direct his attention to such a task he can conquer the world. Thus the faith will become more popular and his own power strengthened; a little effort would be profoundly rewarded. Should he make no effort, they (the Marathas) would inevitably be weakened and annihilated through celestial calamities and in such an event he would gain no credit. . . . As I have learnt this unequivocally (from the divine) I spontaneously write to draw your attention to the great opportunity laid before you. You should therefore not be negligent in fighting *jihad*.

Oh Kings! *Mala a'la* urges you to draw your swords and not put them back in their sheaths again until Allah has separated the Muslims from the polytheists and the rebellious *kafirs* and the sinners are made absolutely feeble and helpless.

In his testament to 'Umar, Abu Bakr had informed him that if he feared God, the entire world would be frightened of him ('Umar). Sages and declared that the world resembled a shadow. If a man ran after his shadow it would pursue him, and if he took flight from the shadow it would still pursue him. God has chosen you as the protector of the Sunnis as there is no-one else to perform this duty, and it is crucial that at all times you consider your role as obligatory. By taking up the sword to make Islam supreme and by subordinating your own persona needs to this cause, you will reap vast benefits.

We beseech you (Durrani) in the name of the Prophet to fight a *jihad* against the infidels of this region. This would entitle you to great rewards before God the Most High and your name would be included in the list of those who fought *jihad* for His sake. As far as worldly gains are concerned, incalculable booty would fall into the hands of the Islamic *ghazis* and the Muslims would be liberated from their bonds. The invasion of Nadir Shah who destroyed the Muslims left the Marathas

---

Excerpted from Saiyid Athar Abbas Rizvi, *Shah Wali-Allah and His Times* (Canberra, Australia: Ma'rifat Publishing House, 1980), pp. 294–96, 299, 301, 305.

and Jats secure and prosperous. This resulted in the infidels regaining their strength and in the reduction of the Muslim leaders of Delhi to mere puppets.[1]

When the conquering army arrives in an area with a mixed Muslim-Hindu population, the imperial guards should transfer the Muslims from their villages to the towns and at the same time care for their property. Financial assistance should be given by governments to the deprived and the poor as well as to Sayyids and the *'ulama*. Their generosity would then become famous with prompt prayers for their victories. Each town would eagerly await the arrival of the Islamic army ("that paragon of bounty"). Moreover, wherever there was even the slightest fear of a Muslim defeat, the Islamic army should be there to disperse infidels to all corners of the earth. *Jihad* should be their first priority, thereby ensuring the security of every Muslim.

NOTE

1. Rizvi's analysis of Shah Wali-Allah's doctrine of jihad [*Shah Wali-Allah and His Times* (Canberra, Australia: Ma'rifat Publishing House), pp. 285–86] is summarized below:

According to Shah Wali-Allah the mark of the perfect implementation of the *Shari'a* was the performance of *jihad*. He compared the duties of Muslims in relation to the law to those of a favourite slave who administered bitter medicine to other slaves in a household. If this was done forcefully it was quite legitimate but if someone mixed it with kindness it was even better. However, there were people, said the Shah who indulged in their lower natures by following their ancestral religion, ignoring the advice and commands of the Prophet Muhammad. If one chose to explain Islam to such people like this it was to do them a disservice. Force, said the Shah, was the much better course—Islam should be forced down their throats like bitter medicine to a child. This, however, was only possible if the leaders of the non-Muslim communities who failed to accept Islam were killed; the strength of the community was reduced, their property confiscated and a situation was created which led to their followers and descendants willingly accepting Islam. The Shah pleaded that the universal domination of Islam was not possible without *jihad* and by holding on to the tails of cows. Not only would this be humiliating but it would make other religions more powerful.

Shah Wali-Allah was pessimistic about the real depth of faith of those converted by the sword. Such converts were in reality hypocrites and on the Day of Judgment they would be thrown to the very deepest part of Hell, together with the infidels. Islamicization by the sword, added the Shah, did not remove doubts from the minds of newly converted Muslims and it was always possible they might revert to infidelity. The Shah believed that *Imams* (here meaning rulers) should convince the people through rational argument. They should preach that other religions were worthless since their founders were not perfect, and that their practice was opposed to divine law, interpolations having made them unbelievable. The superiority of Islam should be explained in positive terms and it should be brought home to converts that Islamic laws were perfectly clear and easy to follow. What appeared confusing (literally, night) in reality was clear (literally, day).

Another means of ensuring conversions was to prevent other religious communities from worshipping their own gods. Moreover, unfavourable discriminating laws should be imposed on non-Muslims in matters of rules of retaliation, compensation for manslaughter and marriage, and in political matters.

By the time of Shah Wali-Allah's death no power in the disintegrating Mughal empire had been left to convert Hindus to Islam, but it would seem that the rising Baluch and Afghan *zamindars* and the military adventures converted Hindus to Islam in their respective areas of influence. Shah Wali-Allah's son Shah 'Abd al-Aziz claims to have Islamicized hundreds of Hindus. They might have been Hindus living between Phalit and Delhi. However, the proselytization programme of Shah Wali-Allah only included the heads of the Hindu community. The low class of the infidels, according to him, were to be left alone to work in the fields and for paying *jizya*. They, like beasts of burden and agricultural livestock, were to be kept in abject misery and despair.

20

SHARA'I'U 'L-ISLAM

Al-Hilli (d. 1277)

INFIDELS ON WHOM A TRIBUTE MAY BE IMPOSED

167. Some infidels are permitted to retain the privilege of practicing their religion, in return for a tribute; they are: the Jews, the Christians, and those whose revealed scripture is of doubtful authenticity, that is, the guebres.[1] Any infidel other than those who profess one of the three above-mentioned religions must be compelled to embrace Islam.

168. Every infidel belonging to one of the three categories mentioned in the preceding article, whatever his nationality, Arab or foreigner is permitted to practice his religion, provided that he abides by the conditions that are prescribed.

169. Every infidel who claims to belong to one of the three categories defined in article 167 is believed on the basis of his statement, without being bound to provide proof of it.

170. If it appears that the infidel has not told the truth, the treaty made with him is dissolved by that very fact.

171. The following are exempt from the tribute: infidel minors, madmen, women, and old men who have reached an advanced age. The latter point is disputed, but it is based on tradition; the same goes for infidel slaves.

172. Except for the persons mentioned in the preceding article, every infidel belonging to one of the three categories defined in article 167 is subject to the tribute, including monks and sick people.

173. The infidel who is poor is obliged to pay the tribute, too; but one should wait until he has acquired the means with which to pay.

174. If, when surrendering, the infidels stipulated that women should be allowed to pay the tribute,[2] the treaty is null.

175. If there are no men in a place under siege, the surrender requested by the

Excerpted from *Shara'i'u 'l-Islam*, in A. Querry, trans., *Droit Musulman, Recued des lois concernant les Musulmans Schyites [Collection of Laws concerning the Shiite Muslims]* (Paris, 1871), pp. 342–52. English translation by Michael J. Miller.

women, for the purpose of preserving their freedom in return for tribute, can be accepted legally. This point is disputed, and with good reason.

176. After a surrender has been arranged, it is permitted to grant to the women also, by a supplementary clause, the protection that is afforded to the men.

177. When an infidel slave has been set free, he can be compelled to leave Muslim territory or else to pay the tribute.

178. The infidel madman who has no intervals of sanity is exempt from the tribute.

179. When his madness is intermittent, the madman must pay the tribute if the interval in which he is sane is longer than that of his madness.

180. The madman who possesses the use of his mental faculties during an interval lasting a legal year (book 3, art. 54) must pay the tribute, even if his madness were to reappear later.[3]

181. An infidel minor, upon attaining maturity, must be compelled to embrace Islam or else to be subjected to the tribute; if he refuses, he is to be reckoned as an enemy and treated as such.

ON THE RATE OF THE TRIBUTE

182. The rate of the tax is not fixed and must be set by the imam according to the circumstances; the precedent provided by the imam Ali, though certainly fair in one particular case, cannot serve as an example, however.[4] Hence, for lack of a definition of [the amount of] the tribute by the Qur'an, one must take into account the necessities of the moment in order to set the rate, and consider the fact that the rate of the tribute is left to the imam's discretion as a humiliating arrangement for the infidels.

183. The tax base for the tribute must be determined either per capita by the number of infidels or else by the extent of their lands, but it cannot depend on both of these bases at once; however some jurists are correct in holding the opinion that the tribute can be levied simultaneously on persons and on lands when this condition is included in the terms of surrender.

184. It is permitted, at the time of the surrender, to stipulate that, besides paying tribute, the subject infidels will be obliged also to feed soldiers in transit, provided that the treaty specifies the quantity and quality of provisions which must be furnished.

185. When the condition of feeding soldiers in transit has not been included among the terms of the surrender, the quota of provisions to be furnished by the subject infidel must not be less than the amount of the quota for a tributary of the least heavily taxed class.

186. The annual rate of tribute owed by the subject infidel, when he happens to die after the expiration of the legal year, must be withheld from the total of his

estate. The subject infidel who embraces Islam before the expiration of the legal year and even after that time, without having paid the tribute, is exempt from it.

CONDITIONS TO WHICH THE INFIDEL TRIBUTARIES MUST BE SUBJECTED

187. The six conditions to which the infidel tributaries must be subjected are as follows:

188. First, to pay the tribute.

189. Second, not to commit any act contrary to the terms of surrender, such as rebelling against the Muslim authority, or giving aid to the enemy. Every infidel who commits an act of this nature places himself, ipso facto, outside the terms of surrender [i.e., forfeits his protection].

190. Third, not to commit any act that could be harmful to the Muslims, such as fornication or adultery with a Muslim woman, sodomy with a Muslim youth, stealing something belonging to a Muslim, giving asylum to enemy spies or spying on behalf of the enemy.

191. When the obligation to refrain from one of the acts mentioned in the preceding article is the subject of one of the terms of surrender, any infraction entails a breach [annulment] of the treaty.

192. When this obligation was not stipulated, the treaty remains valid, but the guilty parties become liable to the punishments incurred by the crime.

193. A tributary who blasphemes the Prophet must be put to death.

194. A tributary who speaks irreverently about the memory of the Prophet incurs a corporal punishment only, if the terms of the treaty did not include a prohibition of this act.[5]

195. Fourth, to abstain from committing publicly any act forbidden by Muslim law, such as consuming wine, fornication and adultery with the women and wives of their coreligionists, consuming pork, or marriage between persons related by consanguinity in the degrees prohibited among the Muslims.

196. Perpetrating one of these acts publicly results in the annulment of the treaty; some jurists, however, who do not consider this as a violation of the treaty, are of the opinion that the guilty part in this case must be punished according to the provisions of the Muslim penal code.

197. Fifth, not to build temples or to ring church bells, and not to erect houses to a height more prominent than the houses of the Muslims, under pain of corporal punishment, when the terms of surrender are silent on this subject. When, on the contrary, this prohibition is incorporated into the treaty, an infraction results in the annulment of the treaty.

198. Sixth, to abide by Muslim laws.

PARTICULAR PROVISIONS

199. When the tributary acts contrary to the laws of Islam in a Muslim country, the imam has the right to banish him. Some jurists admit the imam's right to kill the infidel in this case, to reduce him to slavery, or to impose a fine on him, but this point is disputed.

200. The infidel who is guilty of acting contrary to Muslim laws, and then converts, is exempted from the penalties incurred by the offense or the crime that he committed, except for the retaliation and corporal punishment that he may have incurred; he is, furthermore, bound to restore what he unjustly seized.

201. The infidel tributary who has acted against Muslim laws and did not convert until after being reduced to slavery or after having paid the penalty, is not set free and has no right to restitution of what he has paid.

202. After the death of the imam who concluded the treaty with the tributaries, his successor is obliged to observe the terms of surrender throughout the specified time; but if the duration was not determined by the treaty, the successor of the deceased imam can introduce changes in those terms that he deems useful to the common interest.

203. The tributary must avoid greeting a Muslim first using the formula [Arabic] *el selam eleikom.*

204. It is recommended that the tributary not stand upon the higher part of the pavement and that he yield the right of way to a Muslim.

PROVISIONS RELATING TO HOUSES AND TEMPLES USED FOR WORSHIP BY THE INFIDEL TRIBUTARIES, AND THE PROHIBITION AGAINST THEIR ENTERING PLACES CONSECRATED TO MUSLIM WORSHIP

205. It is forbidden to build in a Muslim land any church, synagogue, or temple to be used for any worship other than Muslim worship. Any newly built construction of this sort must be demolished, regardless of whether the inhabitants of this country recently and voluntarily embraced Islam, or whether the territory was conquered by military force or annexed by virtue of a surrender: All that matters is that the country is subject to Muslim rule.

206. Tributaries are permitted to keep the temples serving as their places of worship which were built before the conquest or annexation.

207. When, by virtue of a treaty, infidel tributaries retain the government and possession of their territory, they are permitted to build temples there in order to practice their religion.

208. When the religious buildings constructed before the conquest or annexation of the territory are dilapidated or in ruins, the tributaries are permitted to repair and rebuild them. This point is disputed.

209. Tributaries are forbidden to build the houses that they construct for their own use to a height surpassing that of the Muslim houses in the neighborhood; but it is probably permissible to build them to a height equal to that of the Muslim houses.

210. When a tributary buys from a Muslim a house that is taller than the neighboring Muslim houses, he is not obliged to shorten it; however, if a story is being removed, the height of that house must be lowered to the level or below the level of the other Muslim houses.

211. It is forbidden for infidels to enter the temple in Mecca under any circumstances, and in the Shiite region this prohibition extends to every other mosque; not only is it forbidden to enter that place, but also to remain there, to pass by it, to consume or to receive food there. Permission granted to an infidel to register as a member of [s'établir dans] a mosque is null and has no effect.

212. Infidels are forbidden to take up residence in the Hejaz region.[6] Some jurists restrict this prohibition to the two cities of Mecca and Medina. As for the prohibition against infidels passing by Hejaz or taking provisions from it, the point is disputed.

213. Supposing that temporary permission is granted to an infidel to live in Hejaz, the maximum duration of the stay is set at three days.

214. Infidels are forbidden to take up residence in the Arabian Peninsula,[7] that is, in the city of Mecca, in the city of Medina, in the province of Yemen, and all their [outlying] districts. According to other commentators, the Arabian Peninsula extends, lengthwise, from Aden to Riff Ebbadan, and widthwise from *Tehamet*[8] to the borders of Syria.

TRUCE WITH THE INFIDELS

215. This term is understood to mean a treaty concluded with the enemy, having as it purpose a temporary suspension of hostilities during a set period of time.

216. The imam is authorized to negotiate the suspension of hostilities with a view to the general interest, for example, in the case where the number of Muslim soldiers is too weak to be able to continue the war advantageously; when it is necessary to wait for reinforcements, or when there is the hope that, thanks to a suspension of hostilities, the infidels will convert voluntarily to Islam.

217. Except for the cases mentioned in the preceding article, and when the Muslim army is strong enough in number to pursue the war, it is not permitted to declare a truce.

218. A truce can be declared for a period of four months, but only once in any given year. Some jurists, citing the eighteenth verse of the ninth chapter of the Qur'an (article 18, note), are of the opinion that the duration of the truce cannot exceed four months; others, inspired by the sixty-eighth verse of the eighth

chapter,[9] are of the opinion that the duration of the truce can be extended beyond that term; but it is best, in this regard, to act according to the circumstances.

219. The armistice can be concluded only for a set period of time, unless the imam has reserved for himself, by the treaty, the right to revoke it whenever he wants.

220. When the treaty suspending hostilities contains a few clauses contrary to the precepts of Islam, for instance the public performance of certain acts forbidden to Muslims, or the return of women captives or refugees, one is not obliged to observe them.

221. The infidel woman who is a captive or a refugee among the Muslims must not be returned, if she has embraced Islam, or if she professed it already; but her dowry must be refunded to her husband, if it is made of things that Muslims are allowed to use; if not, the husband loses his claim to restitution in kind or in money.

222. The infidel woman captive or refugee who has embraced Islam must not be returned, even if she apostatizes, since her conversion brought her into the bosom of Islam.

223. The husband of the woman captive or refugee who has converted has a right to the restitution of the dowry if he makes his claim before the death of that woman; if not, the death overrules the claim. This last point is disputed.

224. The husband has no claim to restitution of the dowry when his captive or refugee wife, who has embraced Islam, was divorced by him without intention of returning.

225. The infidel husband who has divorced his wife with the intention of returning [to her] and also embraces Islam during the time when he has set his wife aside, has the right to take her back, in preference to any other man.

226. It is permitted to give back male prisoners, as long as there is no fear that the enemy forces will be increased by their number or by their personal importance; otherwise they must not be returned.

227. An armistice clause stipulating that all male prisoners without exception will be returned must not be accepted, because there could be in their number some who fulfill the conditions mentioned in the preceding article.

228. One is not bound to lead back the prisoners or to transport the objects when one has agreed to make restitution; one can limit one's efforts to setting the persons free and depositing the objects between the two armies.

229. The imam or his special delegate alone have the right to conclude a general armistice with the population of a country or that of a city or district.

PARTICULAR PROVISIONS

230. An infidel who embraces a religion not recognized by his coreligionists must be prevented from doing so and compelled to choose between Islam and death.

231. An infidel is permitted to embrace a religion recognized by his coreligionists; thus a Jew can convert to Christianity or Parsiism [Zoroastrianism], since these other religions are "infidel" to the same degree; however some jurists, citing the seventy-ninth verse of the thirtieth chapter of the Qur'an,[10] do not allow such tolerance.

232. An infidel who has embraced a religion other than his own, and other than Islam, remains free to adopt once more the faith of his fathers. This point is rightly disputed, and according to the second opinion, the infidel who persists must be put to death, but his children must not be reduced to slavery, since the fault of the father does not result in a change of the children's condition.

233. An infidel must not be prevented from performing acts which, although not forbidden by his religion, are nevertheless prohibited by Muslim law, as long as he does not perform them publicly.

234. An infidel who performs publicly an act that is not forbidden by his religion but which is prohibited by the precepts of Islam must be punished according to the provisions of Muslim law with respect to a Muslim.

235. An infidel who commits an act forbidden both by his religion and by Islam, such as sodomy and fornication, must be punished according to the provisions of the Muslim penal code. However, the judge can remand the delinquent to the authorities of his religion, so that they can treat him according to the provisions of their particular code.

236. The sale of a Qur'an to an infidel is null and void; some jurists admit the legality of the sale, but not of the possession of the book by the infidel, out of respect for the holy word.[11] This provision applies also to the book containing the traditions about the Prophet. Some jurists are of the more probably opinion that the sale of the latter book to an infidel does not constitute a blameworthy act.

237. A legacy made by an infidel for the construction of a building for worship in a religion other than Islam is null, since the construction of this sort of building is forbidden.

238. This provision applies also to a legacy destined to cover the expenses for copies of the Bible or the Gospel, since the original text of these two books has been altered.[12]

239. A legacy made by an infidel for the benefit of monks and priests remains valid, because he is permitted to distribute alms to these persons.

240. It is recommended that every Muslim refrain from hiring out his services for the repair of building used by infidels for their worship, whether as a mason, a carpenter, or any other job of this sort.

NOTES

1. According to the Muslim belief, the "guebres" [fire-worshippers] killed Zoroaster, the founder of their religion, and since they then burned the book of revelations that had

been written on twelve thousand hides of oxen, the book that they have today is nothing but an apocryphal work.

2. The implication being, "provided that the women preserve their freedom."

3. That is to say, the tribute is owed, in this case, only for the year during which the madman temporarily recovered his sanity.

4. After a victory over the infidels, the imam Ali, given the circumstances, had fixed the annual amount of the tribute at twelve dirhem for the poor, twenty-four dirhem for those of moderate means, and forty-eight dirhem for the wealthy; this was the equivalent of 30.24 grams, 60.48 grams, and 120.96 grams of silver, respectively; but he was rebuked by the Prophet.

5. Otherwise, the treaty can be dissolved, since it has been violated.

6. The province of which Mecca is the capital.

7. [Arabic] djeziret ol ereb. This term is understood to mean the Arabian Peninsula with the Euphrates River as its northern boundary.

8. A district bordering upon the province of Nedjd.

9. "When they demand a truce, grant it to them."

10. "Do not allow an infidel to embrace any religion other than Islam."

11. That is, an infidel can buy the Qur'an, but on the condition that he immediately resells it or gives it up.

12. According to Muslim beliefs, the present-day texts of the Bible and the Gospels are apocryphal; Christians, in turn, ascribe no authenticity to the Gospel passages [sic] that are preserved by Muslim tradition and found in the Qur'an.

21

JAMI'-I 'ABBASI: YAKDAWRAH-I FIQH-I

Muhammad al-Amili (d. 1621)

PART SIX: HOLY WAR (JIHAD)

Islamic holy war against followers of other religions, such as Jews, is required unless they convert to Islam or pay the poll tax. There are twelve conditions required in paying the poll tax. First condition: According to some *Mojtahids* those possessing Holy Scriptures, such as Christians, Jews, and Zoroastrians, living in Muslim territories are obliged to pay the poll tax, (in lieu of conversion to Islam). In this regard, Imam Ali required Jews who were poor to pay 12 *Dirham* in a year, and the average Jews to pay 24 *Dirham* a year as poll tax. The wealthy Jews, however, paid 148 *Dirham* a year. The amount of poll tax depends on [the] Imams' decision. If a Jew or any of those possessing Holy Scriptures converted to Islam, they were not obliged to pay the poll tax.

Second condition: Others possessing Holy Scriptures residing in Islamic territories must recognize and respect Islamic laws. Third condition: Those possessing Holy Scriptures are not authorized to sabotage Muslims' safety, which means they are not supposed to associate with Muslim enemies or disobey paying poll tax. Fourth condition: Those possessing Holy Scriptures are not allowed to sleep with Muslim women or marry them. Fifth condition: Those possessing Holy Scriptures must not deceive Muslims or debunk what they [the Muslims] believe in. Sixth condition: Those possessing Holy Scriptures must not be convicted of robbery. Seventh condition: Those possessing Holy Scriptures must not harbor or finance the Muslims' enemies such as spies and invaders, or reveal any intelligence information regarding Muslims to infidels. Eighth condition: Those possessing Holy Scriptures must not be convicted of murdering a Muslim. Ninth condition: Those possessing Holy Scriptures must not disrespect the Muslim Faith.

Excerpted from *Jami'-i Abbasi: Yakdawrah-i fiqh-i*, trans. Fatemeh Masjedi (Fars: Tehran, 1980), pp. 153–54, 367, 417, 423, 428–32.

Tenth condition: Those possessing Holy Scriptures are not allowed to practice any un-Islamic behavior such as drinking alcohol, eating pork, or being married to two sisters simultaneously. Eleventh condition: Those possessing Holy Scriptures must not establish any temples or churches in the Dar al-Islam (Muslim territory), preach or read their religious books loudly, ring their church bells, or build their houses higher than Muslim houses. Twelfth condition: Those possessing Holy Scriptures must be distinguished from Muslims by being attired differently. They must also ride on different animals, sit on one side of the animal [i.e., side-saddle] while riding, and are not permitted to carry any weapon or sword with them. They must also not walk on the road. They cannot hold any title nor can they reside in Mecca or Medina. They are not supposed to buy the Koran or Hadith (collections), for they won't be allowed to own them.

PART SIXTEEN: TESTIFYING

According to Islamic *sharia*, no *dhimmi* such as a Jew is allowed to testify for a Muslim. However *dhimmi* [are] allowed to testify for one another disregarding [their] religion (Christian, Jewish, Zoroastrian). Regardless of what is mentioned above, in the case of *Wasyiah* (making a will), if there is no righteous Muslim to testify, then it is possible to have *dhimmi*s testify. Some *Mojtahids* believe that a *dhimmi* might testify for a Muslim only if the Muslim is traveling and has no access to other Muslims.

Jews are allowed to testify for Christians as well.

PART NINETEEN: PUNISHMENT AND SENTENCE

Hadd Crimes (most serious): Robbery, Zena

If a Muslim is convicted of a robbery, [he] will face having one of [his] body parts cut off. But if a Muslim is convicted of a robbery of alcohol or pork from a Jew, [he] will not face the same punishment.

Zena *[unlawful sexual intercourse between a man and a woman or adultery]*

If a Jew has committed *Zena*, [he] will face the maximum sentence, which is the death penalty.

Tazir Crimes (least serious)

If a Muslim is convicted of murdering a Jew, he will face *tazir*, which is the minimum sentence.

PART TWENTY: ISLAMIC CRIMINAL CODE

A Muslim is allowed to kill the *dhimmi* unless the *dhimmi* follows the twelve conditions that are mentioned above in the *Jihad* section, or the *dhimmi* converts to Islam.

Dieh *or Blood Money*

A Muslim who is convicted of murdering [a] *dhimmi* is not liable to pay *kaffareh* (alms to be given as penance on different occasions). However he is obligated to pay *dieh*, which is called blood money in Islamic *sharia* law.

Retaliation (Qesas)

According the Islamic criminal code, a Muslim who is convicted of murdering a Jew is not liable to receive the death penalty. However he will receive retaliation or discretionary (*Tazir*) punishments that have been prescribed, according to the type of the crime committed. However, a *dhimmi* receives the death penalty if convicted of murdering another *dhimmi*.

If a *dhimmi* is convicted of murdering a Muslim, he will receive the death penalty. If an infidel who is convicted of murdering another infidel, becomes a Muslim, he will pay *dieh* or blood money and receive *Qesas* crimes (revenge crimes restitution).

22

RISALA-YI SAWA'IQ AL-YAHUD

Muhammad Al-Majlisi (d. 1699)

In the name of Allah, the Beneficent, the Merciful, praise be to God who strengthens Islam and the Muslims, who degrades Unbelief. [It is He Who] bring to the clear religion and bestows prayer upon him whom He sent as a mercy to all created beings, [upon] Muhammad and the most pure people of his household.

Know that God, the Exalted, established the *jizya* upon the People of the Book, since they are closer to [true] guidance than the rest of the infidels, because they have heard about the manners and practices of the prophets, peace be upon them, and because they have seen the descriptions of His Excellency [Muhammad] in their books. Wherever they remain for some time among Muslims and hear Qur'anic verses and the *ahadith* of the Prophet and of those of his House [the Imams], peace be upon them, and witness the true laws and perfect worship of the people of Islam, if they do not act fanatically, they will quickly arrive at the knowledge of the true claims of Islam. So if they observe the conditions of the *jizya* and live in baseness and abjectness among Muslims, bias and obstinacy will not prevent them from accepting the true religion, and they will soon accept Qur'an [9:29]: "Fight against such as those who have been given the Scripture as believe not in Allah nor the Last Day, and forbid not that which Allah hath forbidden by His messenger, and follow not the religion of truth, until they pay the tribute readily, being brought low." That is, fight against those who do not believe in God and in the Day of Resurrection, who do not prohibit the things that have been prohibited by God and His Prophet, such as wine and pork, and do not believe in the religion of truth, from among those who had been given the Book,—until they pay the *jizya*, with their own hands, while they are in a low and abased state.

Excerpted from "Risala-yi Sawa'iq al-Yahud [The Treatise Lightning Bolts against the Jews]." English translation by V. B. Moreen in *Die Welt des Islams* 32 (1992): 187–93.

THE LAWS OF *JIZYA*

It should be known that the laws of *jizya*, according to the unanimous opinion of the Shi I *ulama,* may God be pleased with them, apply only to the People of the Book, that is, to the Jews who have the Torah, the Christians who have the Gospels, and the Zoroastrians who have the like of a Book. They [the Zoroastrians] has been sent a prophet who brought a book written on twelve thousand parchments [lit., "cow skins"]. They killed their prophet and burned his book. Then Zoroaster wrote for them the *Zand* and *Pazand,* in place of the Book; it is like a Scripture for they believe it to be God's book. Their original book, together with the rest of the books of the prophets, are with His Excellency, the Twelfth Imam, may God's prayers be upon him. As for other than these three denominations, idolaters and other infidels, it is not allowed to accept the *jizya* from them. If the ruler of the Muslims [*hakim-I Musalmanan*] deems it advisable he may grant an exemption to some of them [idolaters and non-*dhimmis*] while they are within Muslim lands, whether or not by settling with them for a substitute. It is a well supported opinion that this is lawful.

The *jizya* is obligatory for mature and sane people; it is not to be taken from pre-adolescent children, from the mentally disturbed, or from women. But it is the opinion of most jurists that the *jizya* can be taken from old men, from the blind, and [from] the disabled who are unable to move. As for slaves, there is a difference of opinion [regarding the *jizya*], but the majority of the jurists maintain that the *jizya* is taken from the master on the slave's behalf. They also maintain that it should be extracted from the poor as well as from the distressed; and if they do not have it they are to be given a reprieve until they obtain it, even if it is done by begging.

It is maintained by most jurists that the *jizya* is not a fixed amount but the Imam, peace be upon him, or his deputy impose whatever they deem best. It is permissible for the *jizya* to be levied on their person <or on their land>—to determine, for example, how much they should pay for any *jarib* [acre] of land. There is a difference of opinion regarding whether or not the *jizya* can be levied on both. A tradition has come down that this is not permissible, and this [view] is more prudent. It is lawful to subject them [the *dhimmis*] to different rates of taxation as His Excellency Ali, The Commander of the Faithful, settled [a *jizya*] of 12 *dirhams* on the rich (which, in the reckoning of those days, was almost equal to 5 *ashrafis.*)

In the realization of the state of *dhimma* [protection] it is necessary that they [the *dhimmis*] should accept the *jizya* and not perpetrate deeds that are opposed to [the state of] security, such as waging war against Muslims, or aiding infidels in their war against Muslims. And some [of the jurists] said that they should commit themselves to the laws of the Muslims, and that they should not reject anything decreed upon them by a Muslim ruler in accordance with the *sharia*. And they

[also] said that it is appropriate for the Muslim ruler to impose upon them seven conditions; First, that they should not fornicate with Muslim women, nor assault their [Muslims'] children; second, that they should not marry Muslim women; third, that they should not tempt Muslims to turn away from their religion; fourth, that they should not rob Muslims; fifth, that they should not harbor the spies of infidels; sixth, that they should not help infidels attain victory over Muslims nor inform them about the state/conditions of the Muslims; seventh, that they should not kill Muslim men, women, and children. If these seven conditions have been stipulated, and they violate them, then they forfeit protection. But if the conditions have not been stipulated, [and they commit any of the above acts] they will be punished in accordance with the *sharia* of Islam, but they do not forfeit protection. Most of the "*ulama*" maintain that they should not perpetrate anything that would be to the detriment of the religion of Islam, such as maligning the Supreme God or His Excellency, the Prophet, or one of the innocent Imams, may God's prayers be upon them, and that this should [also] be a condition imposed upon them. And if they violate it they forfeit protection. And if, God forbid, they insult God, the Prophet or the Imams, peace be upon them, whoever [from among the Muslims] hears [such an insult] from the *dhimmis* must kill [them] if no harm results from it.

The following are [also] among the things that they [the *dhimmis*] must be prevented from, and provided that they are stipulated, if they violate them they forfeit protection, but if they are not stipulated they do not forfeit protection. First, that they should not openly publicize those things which are prohibited by the *sharia* but are permitted to them and there is not harm from them to the Muslims such as wine, eating pork, contracting marriages with close family members, etc.; second, that they should not erect churches, temples, or places of fire worship in the lands of Islam, but if they [already] have some, and these are in need of repair, they may repair them. If they are ruined entirely there is a difference of opinion regarding whether or not they may rebuild them in the same place; third, that they should not read out very loudly from their [holy] books, nor ring any bells. And some say that they may ring them softly so that Muslims would not hear them; fourth, that they may not build their own homes higher than the houses of their Muslim neighbors (or their part of the house), nor higher than those of the Muslims dwelling in other parts of the same house. And some say that they may not build them of the same height with them either but that they must be lower; fifth, most of the *ulama* believe that it is appropriate that the ruler of the Muslims imposed upon them clothing that would distinguish then from Muslims so that they would not resemble Muslims. It is customary for Jews to wear yellow clothes while Christians wear black and dark blue ones. Christians [also] wear a girdle on their waists, and Jews sew a piece of silk of a different color on the front part of their clothes. And some [jurists] say that they should be recognizable by their wearing different shoes than Muslims, for instance, one of their shoes be of one color and the other of another color, such as one yellow and one red. [And they also say that] they should wear a ring of iron, lead, or copper, and that they should tie a bell on their feet at the [public] baths so as to be distinguishable from Muslims. Similarly, their women should be distinguished through their clothing from Muslim women in the manner stated above or by other means; sixth, that they should not ride upon Arabian steeds, or that they should not ride any horses at all, only mules or asses, and that they should not ride upon saddles, only on pack saddles, with [both] legs on one side, and have no sword, dagger, or any [other] weapon with them, nor should they keep any of these within their homes. But foremost of these matters I found no legal basis. However, if the ruler of the Muslims deems it advisable to impose these conditions upon them, thus shall it be.

Some say that they [the *dhimmis*] should not be informed of the amount of the *jizya* so that they should live continuously, in the course of the year, in a state of anxiety and agitation. [They say that] at the time of paying the *jizya* they should stand on the ground in front of him who takes the *jizya*. [The official] should say to him: "Count it!" And he [the payer] should count the money until the Muslims speak up and say that it is enough. And some [also] say that he should lower his head while handing it over, and that he who takes the *jizya* should pull his beard and slap his face at the time of paying. But I have not seen any legal basis for these.

And it is [also] said to be recommended that if Muslims walk with them on the [same] road that they [the *dhimmis*] should not walk in the middle but rather on the side of the road. And, that they should not enter the pool while a Muslim is bathing at the public baths. At meetings, they should not be seated high[er than Muslims] nor should Muslims greet them first. And, if they greet them, Muslims should answer [only] with "Alayka" ["Upon you!"]. Muslims should not associate with them, neither should they enter into sleeping partnership with them. It is also incumbent upon Muslims that they should not accept from them victuals with which they had come into contact, such as distillates <and oils>, which cannot be purified. In something can be purified, such as clothes, if they are dry, they can be accepted, they are clean. But if they [the *dhimmis*] had come into contact with those cloths in moisture they should be rinsed with water after being obtained. As for hide, or that which has been made of hide such as shoes and boots, and meat, whose religious cleanliness and lawfulness are conditional on the animal's being slaughtered [according to the *sharia*], these may not be taken from them. Similarly, liquids that have been preserved in skins, such as oils, grape syrup, [fruit] juices, myrobalan, and the like, if they have been put in skin containers or water skins, these should [also] not be accepted from them. Other infidels, such as the Hindus and others, have such laws in common with them [the *dhimmis*], but these [infidels] are even worse.

It would also be better if the ruler of the Muslims would establish that all infidels could not move out of their homes on days when it rains or snows because they would make Muslims impure. And if Muslims should hear that they insult or hold a Muslim in contempt, they should prevent and hinder them as well as chastise them. They should never be in position of authority over Muslims. But Muslims should also be urged to show disrespect toward them [the *dhimmis*].

If a litigation breaks out between them and the Muslims, the Muslim judge should judge between them according to the *sharia*. And, if they have a litigation among themselves, it is held by most jurists that the judge of the Muslims has the choice to settle [the case] himself according to Islamic law or entrust it to their own judges. But it is better if he judges [the case] himself.

> And God favors the good and the just.
> Praise be to God, First and Last.
> May God's prayer be upon Muhammad and upon
> his Pure Family.

23

1915 OTTOMAN FATWA

OUR DUTY IS TO ATTAIN SENSIBLE SUCCESS: ALJIHAD (HOLY WAR)

"Kill their associates wherever you find them and surround them and prepare for them all sorts of tape."

"Kill them the best way that you can."

The holy war of today is obligatory on every Mussulman, and this *present moment is the only opportune one for it.* Patience and indifference in these times is a grave mistake. The massacre of unbelievers (*and only those who command us*) whether they are found in public or private places is now our duty, as it is said in God's words "Take then and kill them wherever you find them. Behold we have delivered then into your hands, and from you must issue supreme sovereignty." The slaying of one unbeliever (of those who rule over us) in public or private shall be called an additional life for Islamism, and will be well recompensed by God.

Let every Mussulman know that his reward for so doing shall be doubled by our God who created heaven and earth. It is will accounted him as a great precept, and his recompense will be greater than fasting on "Ramadan." He will be saved from the terrors of the day of Judgment—the day of the resurrection of the dead. Who is the man who refuses to enjoy such a reward? *for such a small deed?*

The faithful Mussulman with warm attachment to his faith and believing in the resurrection of the dead does not approach nor befriend the foes of Islam. Such an attitude is not according to common sense. The man who does so is far from the religion of Islam. You are astonished why we are so estranged from the unbelievers? But why are you not surprised at your own conduct towards them? by permitting yourselves to be humiliated by them? What excuse will you give not to God, but to us your brethren? If you believe in God, in his faith and apostle, hear the words of our sages as recorded by his holy prophet. "You believers take

---

Excerpted from an Ottoman fatwa believed to have been written by Sheikh Shawish, titled *Aljihad*. English translation from the American Agency and Consulate, Cairo, Egypt, in US State Department document 867.4016/57, March 10, 1915.[1]

not the Jews and Christians as friends unto you, He who loves then shall be called one of them." "God shall not foster the tyrants." You believers accept not unto you friends of these who abuse your faith and mock thereof. They are called unbelievers, and you hearken unto the words of God of you believe. Therefore if after you will put to heart to these sacred words, perhaps they have been spoken to you by God not to acquire unto us Jewish or Christian friends. From these holy words you will realize that it is forbidden us to approach those who mock our faith— Jews and Christians, for then God forbid, God forbid we shall be deemed by the almighty as one of them God forbid.

After all this how can we believe in the sincerity of your faith when you befriend and love unbelievers, and accept their Government without any rising without attempting to expel them from your country. Therefore arise and purify yourselves of such deeds. Arise to the Holy War no matter what it costs so as to carry into execution this sacred deed. It is furthermore said in the Koran, "If your fathers if children taken unto them friends of the unbelievers, estrange yourselves even from them."

Beloved you have not taken to heart these holy words, and you are following an unrighteous path, and therefore why have you pity on your religion. Arouse, Arouse, and let not this opportunity pass. You approach the unbelievers so as to enjoy of their greatness and honor, and have forgotten God's words. To thee O God belongs the strength and honour. Therefore, take to heart out holy aims for realization and honour will ultimately follow. If not we are afraid that your name will not be remembered among Mahomedans.

The Mohammedan religion enjoins us to set aside some money for Government expenses and for preparations of a Holy War. The rest of your tithes and contributions you are duty bound to send to the capital of the Caliphatic to help them to glorify the name of God, through the medium of the Caliph.

Let all Mussulmans know that the Holy War is created only for this purpose. We trust in God that the Mohammedan lands will rise from humiliation and become faithfully tied to the capital of the Caliphate, so as to be called "the lands of Islam." This is our hope and God help us to carry through our holy aims to a successful issue for the sake of our holy Prophet. Dear Brethren!

A Holy War is a sacred duty and for your information let it be known that the armies of the Caliph is ready and in three divisions, as follows: War in secret, war by word of mouth, and physical war.

1) *War in secret.* This is the easiest and simplest. In this case it is to suppose that every unbeliever is an enemy, to persecute and exterminate him from the face of the earth. There is not a Mussulman in the world who is hot inspired by this idea. However in the Koran it is said: "That such a war is not enough for a Mohammedan whether young or old, and must also participate in the other parts of the Holy War."

2) *War by word of mouth.* That is to say fighting by writing and speaking. This kind of war for example should pertain to the Mahomedans of the Caucasus. They should have commenced this war three or four months ago, because their actual position does not permit them to but the carrying on of such warfare. Every Mahomedan is in duty bound to write and speak against the unbelievers when actual circumstances do not permit him to assume more stringent measures, as for instance in the Caucasus. Therefore every writer must use his pen in favor of such a war.

3) *Physical war.* This means actual fighting in the fullest sense of the word. This kind of war is also subdivided into two parts, viz: The lesser and greater war.

   a) *The lesser war,* is when a certain section of Mahomedans rise to fight against their enemies in combination with their compatriots in the war sphere only, without summonsing the aid of Mahomedans of other lands. For example the Sinoussians war with the Italians in Tripoli. Even in such a case every Mussulman should offer material and moral help and not follow the course of the Egyptian Government took in the Italian war when acting under the advise of the unbelieving English they declared themselves neutral. This sin shall never be forgiven them. However our Egyptian brethren have helped us to a certain degree financially and morally in the last two wars and in spite of their unbelieving rulers forwarded their collections on our behalf to the Capital of the Caliphate.

Every provincial governor may proclaim a lesser Holy War, nevertheless for prestige sake it is necessary to obtain the permission of the Caliph for so doing, as the late Sheikh Vaadi did when he declared a lesser holy war on the French. *A greater Holy War* is that which is proclaimed by the whole of Islam in union with all the Mahomedans throughout the world, such a war can only be called out by the Caliph himself, and as soon as a Mohammedan hears this call he must hasten to his brethren's assistance, an example, our proclamation of today. There is no doubt at all that he who shall assist in this great and Holy War, shall be doubly recompensed by heaven. He who shall fall in this war shall die a hero's death on the battlefield for sanctifying God's name and that of the Prophet.

Thou O God pour out thy mercy to arouse the hearts of the Mussulmen children to this holy proclamation. Give ample reward to the victims that shall fall in glorifying thy name and that of thy prophet, for thou art the hoard of righteousness.

Now let us mention here the means to be adopted in carrying on this holy war, as follows:

Every private individual can fight with deadly weapons, as for example. Here is the following illustration of the late Egyptian Verdani who shot the unbelieving

Butros Gal Pacha the friend of the English with a revolver. The murder of the English police Commissioner Bavaro in India by one of our Indian brethren. The killing of one of the officials of Kansch on his coming from Mecca by the Prophet's friend "Abu Bazir El Pachbi," peace be unto him! Abdallah ibn Aatick and four colleagues killed "Abu Raafah Ibn El Hakiki." The leader of the Jews Khaybar so famous for his enmity to Islamism. This was executed by our Prophet's command, so did Avrala Ibn Ravacha and his friends whey they killed Oscher Ibn Dawas one of the Jewish dignitaries. There are many instances of similar cases. Lord of the Universal What fails us now, and why should not some of us go forth to fight this sacred war for exalting thy glorious name? What could not happen were some individuals among us men of courage and stout hearted kill the principal Christian men of the Triple Alliance, the foes of Islam. By so doing they would wipe their names from the face of the earth. Thou O God art responsible if you wilt not inspire every Mussulman with this holy spirit, to fight in this holy war. The second method is to fight this war secretly and deceitfully. This method is well known to every Mussulman. This system has special advantages, where the number of Mussulman is inferior to that of the unbelievers. When the prophecy of God inspired our Prophet, "Fight for God, with those who fight against you," he began to do so in secret, and in this way. At first he sent some of his soldiers accompanied by an officer to fight his enemies. Of course only men of exceptional bravery were chosen by the prophet to carry on these expeditions. They formed several secret expeditions which ultimately numbered fifty or sixty which harassed and fought the enemy. Of the first were the expeditions of Hamsha Ibn Abed El Matlav, Abidu Ibn Charat, Saad Habas, Gzid ibn Chartah, Abu Maslaam Asham ibn Taabet, Manzur ibn Omar, Abed el Rahman ven Oof and Abou Taleb.

It is also the duty o the Mahomedans of today to follow this method—to arm small riding parties which we hope will bring much use and advantage at this present moment particularly in the towns of Caucasus, Turkistan, India, and Java. Perpetually harassing the enemy by such means brings great advantage. To prepare such expeditions in our days there are many facilities, but what is certain to us is that these secret raids bring much benefit. Therefore every individual should endeavor to organize such raids, and perhaps in the same way as our holy Prophet did when he entered "Bachlaf El Fazul."

The third method is actual war in the offensive. The commander in Chief in such a war is to be the Caliph of all Mussulmen or his substitute as it was in the battles of "Badr" and "Uhud." In thee battles our prophet personally was in command of the forces. As it is well known to you, dear brethren, that the participation in the great holy war is obligatory upon every Mussulman, so you should know the ways how to prosecute it. Therefore, dear brethren, arouse and trust in God, and choose the method most appropriate for you according to the requirements of your places. Do not delay a moment, the time has ultimately arrived for this matter. As the center of the Caliphate has not the power to send armed forces to help you in your respective places, therefore you yourselves must arm and prepare and unite as one man with some powerful nation if it be necessary, and to commence the holy war. Support yourselves on God's mercy, observe and guard over all the precepts of Islamism, and do not estrange yourselves from politics. If any political difficulties shall confront you, bring them to the notice of your diplomatic brethren in the capital of the Caliph, from whom you will receive the necessary advice. And whereas our Muslim code enjoins us and compels us to fight in the holy war, it also commands us to *distinguish between those who love Islam and the Caliph, for they are virtuous, just, powerful and on good terms with us, and though of a different faith to ours, we are commanded to protect them.*

The holy war is proclaimed only against those who rule over Islamic countries, and it is they who have us and the Caliph. Therefore our holy war is not against all unbelievers. We respect again and again, know how to distinguish between foe and friend. Let our holy faith be your guide book, as it is said in the Koran, "Those who do not believe accept not for friends," so that they rule not over you, and if they will govern you, kill them wherever you will find them, and protect those who shall not fight against you, nor rule you.

In conclusion, I might remind you of these sacred words: "He of the believers who shall return from his path, God will bring him to a friendly people who shall love him, and fight against the unbelievers. God's help is magnanimous, and he who is near to God and his Propjet, his path shall prosper, and success will attend his undertakings. Multiply precepts, charity, and prayer to God and his prophet and he who shall believe in God and his prophet shall conquer. Peace be to the apostle of God, and praise to the Creator of the Universe.

NOTE

1. An official statement attached to this document indicates, "It was undoubtedly this and similar pamphlets which inspired the Jewish community of Alexandria" to contact the United States Consul General's office in Cairo. Sheikh Shawish, *Aljihad*, trans. American Agency and Consulate, Cairo, Egypt, in US State Department document 867.4016/57, March 10, 1915.

24

[UNTITLED]

Ayatollah Ruhollah Khomeini (d. 1989)

ISLAM IS NOT A RELIGION OF PACIFISTS (1942)

Islam's *jihad* is a struggle against idolatry, sexual deviation, plunder, repression, and cruelty. The war waged by [non-Islamic] conquerors, however, aims at promoting lust and animal pleasures. They care not if whole countries are wiped out and many families left homeless. But those who study *jihad* will understand why Islam wants to conquer the whole world. All the countries conquered by Islam or to be conquered in the future will be marked for everlasting salvation. For they shall live under [God's law]. . . .

Those who know nothing of Islam pretend that Islam counsels against war. Those [who say this] are witless. Islam says: Kill all the unbelievers just as they would kill you all! Does this mean that Muslims should sit back until they are devoured by [the unbelievers]? Islam says: Kill them [the non-Muslims], put them to the sword and scatter [their armies]. Does this mean sitting back until [non-Muslims] overcome us? Islam says: Kill in the service of Allah those who may want to kill you! Does this mean that we should surrender [to the enemy]? Islam says: Whatever good there is exists thanks to the sword and in the shadow of the sword! People cannot be made obedient except with the sword! The sword is the key to paradise, which can be opened only for holy warriors!

There are hundreds of other [Koranic] psalms and *hadiths* [sayings of the Prophet] urging Muslims to value war and to fight. Does all that mean that Islam is a religion that prevents men from waging war? I spit upon those foolish souls who make such a claim.

Excerpted from "Islam Is Not a Religion of Pacifists" (1942), "Speech at Feyziyeh Theological School" (August 24, 1979), and "On the Nature of the Islamic State" (September 8, 1979). English translations in Barry Rubin and Judith Colp Rubin, *Anti-American Terrorism and the Middle East* (Oxford: Oxford University Press, 2002), pp. 29, 32–36.

SPEECH AT FEYZIYEH THEOLOGICAL SCHOOL (AUGUST 24, 1979)

Islam grew with blood. The great religions of the preceding prophets and the momentous religion of Islam, while clutching divine books for the guidance of the people in one hand, carried arms in the other. Abraham . . . in one hand carried the books of the prophets; in the other, an ax to crush the infidels. Moses, the interlocutor of God . . . in one hand carried the Pentateuch and in the other a staff, which reduced the pharoahs to the dust of ignominy, a staff that was like a dragon swallowing up the traitors.

The great prophet of Islam in one hand carried the Koran and in the other a sword; the sword for crushing the traitors and the Koran for guidance. For those who could be guided, the Koran was their means of guidance, while as for those who could not be guided and were plotters, the sword descended on their heads. . . . Islam is a religion of blood for the infidels but a religion of guidance for other people.

We have sacrificed much blood and many martyrs. Islam has sacrificed blood and martyrs.

We do not fear giving martyrs. . . . Whatever we give for Islam is not enough and is too little. Our lives are not worthy. Let those who wish us ill not imagine that our youths are afraid of death or of martyrdom. Martyrdom is a legacy which we have received from our prophets. Those should fear death who consider the aftermath of death to be obliteration. We, who consider the aftermath of death a life more sublime than this one, what fear have we? The traitors should be afraid. The servants of God have no fear. Our army, our gendarmerie, our police, our guards have no fear. Our guards who were [killed] . . . have achieved eternal life. . . .

These people who want freedom, who want our youth to be free, write effusively about the freedom of our youth. What freedom do they want? . . . They want the gambling casinos to remain freely open, they want heroin addicts to be free, opium addicts to be free. They want the seas [reference to mixed bathing] to be free everywhere for the youth.

Our youth should be free to do whatever they want. To be dragged into any form of prostitution they want. This is something dictated by the West. This is something by which they want to emasculate our youth, who could stand up to them. We want to take our youth from the bars to the battlefield. . . .

We want to take our young people from these [movie theaters] that were designed and made to drag them to corruption, and to take them by the hand to places where they will be of some use to the nation. This freedom that these people want is freedom that the powerful have dictated, and our writers are either unaware of this or are traitors. . . .

The safeguarding of the realm cannot be effected with the freedom that you proclaim. This freedom fragments and ruins the realm. This freedom that you want is a freedom dictated by others so that they can devour the realm and deprive us of young people who could administer a rebuff; this is how we have seen them act, and we have seen the consequences. Calamities have been inflicted on our realm because they dragged our youth into corruption.

We want to release our youths from the opium pipe and place machine guns in their hands. We want to release our youths from the opium pipe and dispatch them to the battlefield. You want us to let things be free and easy so that our youth may become corrupt and so that your masters may reap the profits.

Yes, we are reactionaries, and you are enlightened intellectuals: You intellectuals do not want us to go back 1,400 years. You are afraid lest we bring up our youth in the same way as 1,400 years ago, when just a small number of them were able to relegate to oblivion two great empires. We are reactionaries! You who want to drug our youth into Western teachings and not the teachings that they possess, the teachings of the Islamic countries, you are intellectuals! You, who want freedom, freedom from everything, the freedom of parties, you who want all freedoms, you intellectuals: freedom that will corrupt our youth, freedom that will pave the way to the oppressor, freedom that will drag our nation to the bottom. This is the freedom that you want; and this is a dictate from abroad that you have imposed. You do not believe in any limits to freedom. You deem license to be freedom. . . .

In the name of democracy, in the name of liberalism, in the name of intellectualism—in various names—the traitors in this realm embarked on their activities and machinations with a free hand. . . . Of course, a freedom that will culminate in corruption, that will result in the fragmentation of the nation, the dissolution of the state, we cannot grant such a freedom, this freedom that you want, this freedom whereby you wish to bring up our youth to indifference, whereby everything could happen anywhere and whereby everyone will do what he wants, whereby the great powers will take away all our revenues and will enjoy life. . . .

Those who saved our realm are none other than the masses of the people. . . . It was these youths, these workers, these farmers who saved our realm; and now the likes of you, entertaining the thought of freedom, liberalism, democracy, and similar things, now want to return them to their former condition.

. . . Let these people be free to do whatever they want, so that in another generation not a single committed man may be found—this is the freedom you want, and this is the same freedom that inspires you from abroad.

We do not accept this imported freedom. We must safeguard this nation. We must safeguard these youths. We must take these young people away by the hand from dissolution and render them powerful. We need a militant man.

. . . We do not need intellectual, those intellectuals. Of course, there are a great many good people among the intellectuals, among the educated. But these people who are using their pens so effusively against the nation and are now taking steps against the nation and are threatening the people, shall be crushed. [*Cheers*] . . .

ON THE NATURE OF THE ISLAMIC STATE
(SEPTEMBER 8, 1979)

. . . I would like to see everyone believe that our movement . . . for which considerable efforts were made, sacrifices given, young people killed, and families
ruined . . . was only for Islam. I cannot believe, I do not accept that any prudent
individual can believe that the purpose of all these sacrifices was to have less
expensive melons, that we sacrificed our young men to have less expensive
housing. No one in his right mind would lose young men simply to acquire less
expensive housing. There is a false logic promoted perhaps by some self-seeking
individuals, that, as it were, the aim of our sacrifices is to improve agriculture. No
one would give his life for better agriculture. . . .

Liberals and intellectuals keep complaining that there is no freedom. Indeed,
what happened when this freedom was lost? The taverns have been destroyed,
houses of disrepute have been closed—actually, I am not sure whether all of them
have been closed. We no longer allow boys and girls to undress and go bathing in
the sea. To these people this is a freedom they want—a freedom designed for us
by the West, rather than a freedom they want—a freedom designed for us by the
West, rather than a freedom planned by us. This freedom has been dictated by
colonist countries. These freedoms are imported. Now these unfair and so-called
supporters of human rights, these unfair so-called writers—not all of them, of
course—these unfair liberals are making propaganda in support of this type of
freedom. This is a freedom that would lead our country to destruction. A country
depends on its young men, on its manpower. What wastes the manpower destroys
the country. Any country without manpower will fail.

The point is that those who plan to plunder our wealth wish to do so without
obstacles. They say to themselves: . . . The thing to do is to facilitate ways of rev-
elry for these young men . . . while we are busy plundering their resources. This
is what has been happening during the past fifty years. They were encouraging our
men to corruption, to indifference.

Islam has put an end to means that lead our young men to corruption. Islam
wants fighters to stand up to the unbelievers, to those attacking our country. Islam
want to create *mujahid*; it has no intention of making revelers, so that while they
are engaged in having a good time, others denigrate and dishonor them. Islam is
a serious religion. There is no debauchery in Islam. . . . The only games allowed
by Islam are shooting and horse racing, and only for fighting. . . .

However, the West wants to keep us as before. . . .We must try to implement
the true nature of the Islamic Republic, adhere to Islam. Certain drastic and profound changes have taken place that give rise to hopefulness. . . .

25

JIHAD IN THE CAUSE OF GOD

Sayyid Qutb (d. 1966)

The great scholar Ibn Qayyim, in his book *Zad al-Mitad*, has a chapter entitled "The Prophet's Treatment of the Unbelievers and the Hypocrites from the Beginning of His Messengership until His Death." In this chapter, this scholar has summed up the nature of Islamic Jihaad.

> The first revelation from God which came to the Prophet—peace be on him—was "Iqraa, bisme Rabbika alladhee . . ." ("Read, in the name of Your Sustainer, Who created . . ."). This was the beginning of the Prophethood. God commanded the Prophet—peace be on him—to recite this in his heart. The commandment to preach had not yet come. Then God revealed "Ya ayyuha al-Muddathir, qum fandhir" ("O you who are enwrapped in your mantle, arise and warn"). Thus, the revelation of "Iqraa" was his appointment to Prophethood, while "Ya ayyuha al-muddathir" was his appointment to Messengership. Later God commanded the Prophet—peace be on him—to warn his near relatives, then his people, then the Arabs who were around them, then all of Arabia, and finally the whole world. Thus for thirteen years after the beginning of his Messengership, he called people to God through preaching, without fighting or Jizyah [a tax levied by Muslims on non-Muslim men in areas governed by Muslims, in lieu of military service], and was commanded to restrain himself and to practice patience and forbearance. Then he was commanded to migrate, and later permission was given to fight. Then he was commanded to fight those who fought him, and to restrain himself from those who did not make war with him. Later he was commanded to fight the polytheists until God's religion was fully established. After the command for Jihaad came, the non-believers were divided into three categories: one, those with whom there was peace; two, the people with whom the Muslims were at war; and three, the Dhimmies. [Literally meaning "responsibility," Dhimmies refers to the non-Muslim peoples residing in a Muslim state for whose protection and rights the

Excerpted from Sayyid Qutb, "Jihaad in the Cause of God," in *Milestones* (Cedar Rapids, IA: Mother Mosque Foundation, 1993), pp. 53–76.

Muslim government was responsible.] It was commanded that as long as the non-believers with whom he had a peace treaty met their obligations, he should fulfill the articles of the treaty, but if they broke this treaty, then they should be given notice of having broken it; until then, no war should be declared. If they persisted, then he should fight with them. When the chapter entitled "'Bra't" was revealed, the details of treatment of these three kinds of non-believers were described. It was also explained that war should be declared against those from among the "People of the Book" [Christians and Jews] who declare open enmity, until they agree to pay Jizyah or accept Islam. Concerning the polytheists and the hypocrites, it was commanded in this chapter that Jihaad be declared against them and that they be treated harshly. The Prophet—peace be on him—carried on Jihaad against the polytheists by fighting and against the hypocrites by preaching and argument. In the same chapter, it was commanded that the treaties with the polytheists be brought to an end at the period of their expiration. In this respect, the people with whom there were treaties were divided into three categories: The first, those who broke the treaty and did not fulfill its terms. He was ordered to fight against them; he fought with them and was victorious. The second were those with whom the treaty was made for a stated term; they had not broken this treaty nor helped anyone against the Prophet—peace be on him. Concerning them, God ordered that these treaties be completed to their full term. The third kind were those with whom there was neither a treaty nor were they fighting against the Prophet—peace be on him—or those with whom no term of expiration was stated. Concerning these, it was commanded that they be given four months' notice of expiration, at the end of which they should be considered open enemies and fought with. Thus, those who broke the treaty were fought against, and those who did not have any treaty or had an indeterminate period of expiration were given four months' period of grace, and terms were kept with those with whom the treaty was due to expire. All the latter people embraced Islam even before the term expired, and the non-Muslims of the state paid Jizyah.

Thus, after the revelation of the chapter "'Bra't," the unbelievers were of three kinds: adversaries in war, people with treaties, and Dhimmies. The people with treaties eventually became Muslims, so there were only two kinds left: people at war and Dhimmies. The people at war were always afraid of him. Now the people of the whole world were of three kinds: One, the Muslims who believed in him; two, those with whom he had peace and three, the opponents who kept fighting him. As far as the hypocrites were concerned, God commanded the Prophet—peace be on him—to accept their appearances and leave their intentions to God, and carry on Jihaad against them by argument and persuasion. He was commanded not to pray at their funerals nor to pray at their graves, nor should he ask forgiveness from God for them, as their affair was with God. So this was the practice of the Prophet—peace be on him—concerning his enemies among the non-believers and the hypocrites.

In this description we find a summary of the stages of Islamic Jihaad presented in an excellent manner. In this summary we find all the distinctive and far-reaching characteristics of the dynamic movement of the true religion; we should ponder over them for deep study. Here, however, we will confine ourselves to a few explanatory remarks.

First, the method of this religion is very practical. This movement treats people as they actually are and uses resources which are in accordance with practical conditions. Since this movement comes into conflict with the Jahiliyyah which prevails over ideas and beliefs, and which has a practical system of life and a political and material authority behind it, the Islamic movement had to produce parallel resources to confront this Jahiliyyah. This movement uses the methods of preaching and persuasion for reforming ideas and beliefs and it uses physical power and Jihaad for abolishing the organizations and authorities of the Jahili system which prevents people from reforming their ideas and beliefs but forces them to obey their erroneous ways and make them serve human lords instead of the Almighty Lord. This movement does not confine itself to mere preaching to confront physical power, as it also does not use compulsion for changing the ideas of people. These two principles are equally important in the method of this religion. Its purpose is to free those people who wish to be freed from enslavement to men so that they may serve God alone.

The second aspect of this religion is that it is a practical movement which progresses stage by stage, and at every stage it provides resources according to the practical needs of the situation and prepares the ground for the next one. It does not face practical problems with abstract theories, nor does it confront various stages with unchangeable means. Those who talk about Jihaad in Islam and quote Qur'anic verses do not take into account this aspect, nor do they understand the nature of the various stages through which this movement develops, or the relationship of the verses revealed at various occasions with each stage. Thus, when they speak about Jihaad, they speak clumsily and mix up the various stages, distorting the whole concept of Jihaad and deriving from the Qur'anic verses final principles and generalities for which there is no justification. This is because they regard every verse of the Qur'an as if it were the final principle of this religion. This group of thinkers, who are a product of the sorry state of the present Muslim generation, have nothing but the label of Islam and have laid down their spiritual and rational arms in defeat. They say, "Islam has prescribed only defensive war!" and think that they have done some good for their religion by depriving it of its method, which is to abolish all injustice from the earth, to bring people to the worship of God alone, and to bring them out of servitude to others into the servants of the Lord. Islam does not force people to accept its belief, but it wants to provide a free environment in which they will have the choice of beliefs. What it wants is to abolish those oppressive political systems under which people are prevented from expressing their freedom to choose whatever beliefs they want, and after that it gives them complete freedom to decide whether they will accept Islam or not.

A third aspect of this religion is that the new resources or methods which it uses during its progressive movement do not take it away from its fundamental principles and aims. From the very first day, whether the Prophet—peace be on him—addressed his near relatives, or the Quraish, or the Arabs, or the entire world, his call was one and the same. He called them to the submission to One God and rejection of the lordship of other men. On this principle there is no compromise nor any flexibility. To attain this purpose, it proceeds according to a plan, which has a few stages, and every stage has its new resources, as we have described earlier.

A fourth aspect is that Islam provides a legal basis for the relationship of the Muslim community with other groups, as is clear from the quotation from Zad al-Mitad. This legal formulation is based on the principle that Islam—that is, submission to God—is a universal message which the whole of mankind should accept or make peace with. No political system or material power should put hindrances in the way of preaching Islam. It should leave every individual free to accept or reject it, and if someone wants to accept it, it should not prevent him or fight against him. If someone does this, then it is the duty of Islam to fight him until either he is killed or until he declares his submission.

When writers with defeatist and apologetic mentalities write about "Jihaad in Islam," trying to remove this "blot" from Islam, then they are mixing up two things: first, that this religion forbids the imposition of its belief by force, as is clear from the verse, "There is no compulsion in religion" (2.256), while on the other hand it tries to annihilate all those political and material powers which stand between people and Islam, which force one people to bow before another people and prevent them from accepting the sovereignty of God. These two principles have no relation to one another nor is there room to mix them. In spite of this, these defeatist-type people try to mix the two aspects and want to confine Jihaad to what today is called "defensive war." The Islamic Jihaad has no relationship to modern warfare, either in its causes or in the way in which it is conducted. The causes of Islamic Jihaad should be sought in the very nature of Islam and its role in the world, in its high principles, which have been given to it by God and for the implementation of which God appointed the Prophet—peace be on him—as His Messenger and declared him to be the last of all prophets and messengers.

This religion is really a universal declaration of the freedom of man from servitude to other men and from servitude to his own desires, which is also a form of human servitude; it is a declaration that sovereignty belongs to God alone and that He is the Lord of all the worlds. It means a challenge to all kinds and forms of systems which are based on the concept of the sovereignty of man; in other words, where man has usurped the Divine attribute. Any system in which the final decisions are referred to human beings, and in which the sources of all authority are human, deifies human beings by designating others than God as lords over men. This declaration means that the usurped authority of God be returned to Him and the usurpers be thrown out—those who by themselves devise laws for others to follow, thus elevating themselves to the status of lords and reducing others to the status of slaves. In short, to proclaim the authority and sovereignty of God means to eliminate all human kingship and to announce the rule of the Sustainer of the universe over the entire earth. In the words of the Qur'an:

"He alone is God in the heavens and in the earth." (43.84)

"The command belongs to God alone. He commands you not to worship anyone except Him. This is the right way of life."(12.40)

"Say: O People of the Book, come to what is common between us: that we will not worship anyone except God, and will not associate anything with Him, and will not take lords from among ourselves besides God; and if they turn away then tell them to bear witness that we are those who have submitted to God." (2.64)

The way to establish God's rule on earth is not that some consecrated people—the priests—be given the authority to rule, as was the case with the rule of the Church, nor that some spokesmen of God become rulers, as is the case in a "theocracy." To establish God's rule means that His laws be enforced and that the final decision in all affairs be according to these laws.

The establishing of the dominion of God on earth, the abolishing of the dominion of man, the taking away of sovereignty from the usurper to revert it to God, and the bringing about of the enforcement of the Divine Law (Shari'ah) and the abolition of man-made laws cannot be achieved only through preaching. Those who have usurped the authority of God and are oppressing God's creatures are not going to give up their power merely through preaching; if it had been so, the task of establishing God's religion in the world would have been very easy for the Prophets of God! This is contrary to the evidence from the history of the Prophets and the story of the struggle of the true religion, spread over generations.

This universal declaration of the freedom of man on the earth from every authority except that of God, and the declaration that sovereignty is God's alone and that He is the Lord of the universe, is not merely a theoretical, philosophical, and passive proclamation. It is a positive, practical, and dynamic message with a view to bringing about the implementation of the Shari'ah of God and actually freeing people from their servitude to other men to bring them into the service of God, the One without associates. This cannot be attained unless both "preaching" and "the movement" are used. This is so because appropriate means are needed to meet any and every practical situation.

Because this religion proclaims the freedom of man on the earth from all authority except that of God, it is confronted in every period of human history— yesterday, today, or tomorrow—with obstacles of beliefs and concepts, physical power, and the obstacles of political, social, economic, racial, and class structures.

In addition, corrupted beliefs and superstitions become mixed with this religion, working side by side with it and taking root in peoples' hearts. If through "preaching" beliefs and ideas are confronted, through "the movement" material obstacles are tackled. Foremost among these is that political power which rests on a complex yet interrelated ideological, racial, class, social, and economic support. Thus these two—preaching and the movement—united, confront "the human situation" with all the necessary methods. For the achievement of the freedom of man on earth—of all mankind throughout the earth—it is necessary that these two methods should work side by side. This is a very important point and cannot be overemphasized.

This religion is not merely a declaration of the freedom of the Arabs, nor is its message confined to the Arabs. It addresses itself to the whole of mankind, and its sphere of work is the whole earth. God is the Sustainer not merely of the Arabs, nor is His providence limited to those who believe in the faith of Islam. God is the Sustainer of the whole world. This religion wants to bring back the whole world to its Sustainer and free it from servitude to anyone other than God. In the sight of Islam, the real servitude is following laws devised by someone, and this is that servitude which in Islam is reserved for God alone. Anyone who serves someone other than God in this sense is outside God's religion, although he may claim to profess this religion. The Prophet—peace be on him—clearly stated that, according to the Shari'ah, "to obey" is "to worship." Taking this meaning of worship, when the Jews and Christians "disobeyed" God, they became like those who "associate others with God."

Tirmidhi has reported on the authority of 'Adi bin Hatim that when the Prophet's message reached him, he ran away to Syria (he had accepted Christianity before the Prophet's time), but his sister and some of the people of his tribe became prisoners of war. The Prophet—peace be on him—treated his sister kindly and gave her some gifts. She went back to her brother and invited him to Islam, and advised him to visit the Prophet—peace be on him. 'Adi agreed to this. The people were very anxious to see him come to Medina. When he came into the presence of the Prophet, he was wearing a silver cross. The Prophet—peace be on him—was reciting the verse: "They (the People of the Book) have taken their rabbis and priests as lords other than God." 'Adi reports: "I said, 'They do not worship their priests.'" God's Messenger replied, "Whatever their priests and rabbis call permissible, they accept as permissible; whatever they declare as forbidden, they consider as forbidden, and thus they worship them."

This explanation of the above verse by the Prophet—peace be on him—makes it clear that obedience to laws and judgments is a sort of worship, and anyone who does this is considered out of this religion. It is taking some men as lords over others, while this religion has come to annihilate such practices, and it declares that all the people of the earth should become free of servitude to anyone other than God.

If the actual life of human beings is found to be different from this declaration of freedom, then it becomes incumbent upon Islam to enter the field with preaching as well as the movement, and to strike hard at all those political powers which force people to bow before them and which rule over them, unmindful of the commandments of God, and which prevent people from listening to the preaching and accepting the belief if they wish to do so. After annihilating the tyrannical force, whether it be in a political or a racial form, or in the form of class distinctions within the same race, Islam establishes a new social, economic, and political system, in which the concept of the freedom of man is applied in practice.

It is not the intention of Islam to force its beliefs on people, but Islam is not merely "belief." As we have pointed out, Islam is a declaration of the freedom of man from servitude to other men. Thus it strives from the beginning to abolish all those systems and governments which are based on the rule of man over men and the servitude of one human being to another. When Islam releases people from this political pressure and presents to them its spiritual message, appealing to their reason, it gives them complete freedom to accept or not to accept its beliefs. However, this freedom does not mean that they can make their desires their gods, or that they can choose to remain in the servitude of other human beings, making some men lords over others. Whatever system is to be established in the world ought to be on the authority of God, deriving its laws from Him alone. Then every individual is free, under the protection of this universal system, to adopt any belief he wishes to adopt. This is the only way in which "the religion" can be purified for God alone. The word "religion" includes more than belief; "religion" actually means a way of life, and in Islam this is based on belief. But in an Islamic system there is room for all kinds of people to follow their own beliefs, while obeying the laws of the country which are themselves based on the Divine authority.

Anyone who understands this particular character of this religion will also understand the place of *Jihaad bis saif* (striving through fighting), which is to clear the way for striving through preaching in the application of the Islamic movement. He will understand that Islam is not a "defensive movement" in the narrow sense which today is technically called a "defensive war." This narrow meaning is ascribed to it by those who are under the pressure of circumstances and are defeated by the wily attacks of the orientalists, who distort the concept of Islamic Jihaad. It was a movement to wipe out tyranny and to introduce true freedom to mankind, using resources according to the actual human situation, and it had definite stages, for each of which it utilized new methods.

If we insist on calling Islamic Jihaad a defensive movement, then we must change the meaning of the word "defense" and mean by it "the defense of man" against all those elements which limit his freedom. These elements take the form of beliefs and concepts, as well as of political systems, based on economic, racial, or class distinctions. When Islam first came into existence, the world was full of such systems, and the present-day Jahiliyyah also has various kinds of such systems. When we take this broad meaning of the word "defense," we understand the true character of Islam, and that it is a universal proclamation of the freedom of man from servitude to other men, the establishment of the sovereignty of God and His Lordship throughout the world, the end of man's arrogance and selfishness, and the implementation of the rule of the Divine Shari'ah in human affairs.

As to persons who attempt to defend the concept of Islamic Jihaad by interpreting it in the narrow sense of the current concept of defensive war, and who do research to prove that the battles fought in Islamic Jihaad were all for the defense of the homeland of Islam—some of them considering the homeland of Islam to be just the Arabian peninsula—against the aggression of neighboring powers, they lack understanding of the nature of Islam and its primary aim. Such an attempt is nothing but a product of a mind defeated by the present difficult conditions and by the attacks of the treacherous orientalists on the Islamic Jihaad.

Can anyone say that if Abu Bakr, 'Umar, or 'Othman had been satisfied that the Roman and Persian powers were not going to attack the Arabian peninsula, they would not have striven to spread the message of Islam throughout the world? How could the message of Islam have spread when it faced such material obstacles as the political system of the state, the socio-economic system based on races and classes, and behind all these, the military power of the government?

It would be naive to assume that a call is raised to free the whole of humankind throughout the earth, and it is confined to preaching and exposition. Indeed, it strives through preaching and exposition when there is freedom of communication and when people are free from all these influences, as "[t]here is no compulsion in religion"; but when the above-mentioned obstacles and practical difficulties are put in its way, it has no recourse but to remove them by force so that when it is addressed to peoples' hearts and minds they are free to accept or reject it with an open mind.

Since the objective of the message of Islam is a decisive declaration of man's freedom, not merely on the philosophical plane but also in the actual conditions of life, it must employ Jihaad. It is immaterial whether the homeland of Islam—in the true Islamic sense, Dar al-Islam—is in a condition of peace or whether it is threatened by its neighbors. When Islam strives for peace, its objective is not that superficial peace which requires that only that part of the earth where the followers of Islam are residing remain secure. The peace which Islam desires is that the religion (i.e., the Law of the society) be purified for God, that the obedience of all people be for God alone, and that some people should not be lords over others. After the period of the Prophet—peace be on him—only the final stages of the movement of Jihaad are to be followed; the initial or middle stages are not applicable. They have ended, and as Ibn Qayyim states, "Thus, after the revelation of the chapter 'Bra't,' the unbelievers were of three kinds: adversaries in war, people with treaties, and Dhimmies. The people with treaties eventually became

Muslims, so there were only two kinds left: people at war and Dhimmies. The people at war were always afraid of him. Now the people of the whole world were of three kinds: one, the Muslims who believed in him; two, those with whom he had peace (and from the previous sentence we understand that they were Dhimmies); and three, the opponents who kept fighting him."

These are the logical positions consonant with the character and purposes of this religion, and not what is understood by the people who are defeated by present conditions and by the attacks of the treacherous orientalists.

God held back Muslims from fighting in Mecca and in the early period of their migration to Medina, and told them, "Restrain your hands, and establish regular prayers, and pay Zakat." Next, they were permitted to fight: "Permission to fight is given to those against whom war is made, because they are oppressed, and God is able to help them. These are the people who were expelled from their homes without cause." The next stage came when the Muslims were commanded to fight those who fight them: "Fight in the cause of God against those who fight you." And finally, war was declared against all the polytheists: "And fight against all the polytheists, as they all fight against you"; "Fight against those among the People of the Book who do not believe in God and the Last Day, who do not forbid what God and His Messenger have forbidden, and who do not consider the true religion as their religion, until they are subdued and pay Jizyah." Thus, according to the explanation by Imam Ibn Qayyim, the Muslims were first restrained from fighting; then they were permitted to fight; then they were commanded to fight against the aggressors; and finally they were commanded to fight against all the polytheists. With these verses from the Qur'an and with many Traditions of the Prophet—peace be on him—in praise of Jihaad, and with the entire history of Islam, which is full of Jihaad, the heart of every Muslim rejects that explanation of Jihaad invented by those people whose minds have accepted defeat under unfavorable conditions and under the attacks on Islamic Jihaad by the shrewd orientalists.

What kind of a man is it who, after listening to the commandment of God and the Traditions of the Prophet—peace be on him—and after reading about the events which occurred during the Islamic Jihaad, still thinks that it is a temporary injunction related to transient conditions and that it is concerned only with the defense of the borders?

In the verse giving permission to fight, God has informed the Believers that the life of this world is such that checking one group of people by another is the law of God, so that the earth may be cleansed of corruption. "Permission to fight is given to those against whom war is made, because they are oppressed, and God is able to help them. These are the people who were expelled from their homes without cause, except that they said that our Lord is God. Had God not checked one people by another, then surely synagogues and churches and mosques would have been pulled down, where the name of God is remembered often." Thus, this struggle is not a temporary phase but an eternal state—an eternal state, as truth and falsehood cannot co-exist on this earth.

Whenever Islam stood up with the universal declaration that God's Lordship should be established over the entire earth and that men should become free from servitude to other men, the usurpers of God's authority on earth have struck out against it fiercely and have never tolerated it. It became incumbent upon Islam to strike back and release man throughout the earth from the grip of these usurpers. The eternal struggle for the freedom of man will continue until the religion is purified for God.

The command to refrain from fighting during the Meccan period was a temporary stage in a long journey. The same reason was operative during the early days of Hijra, but after these early stages, the reason for Jihaad was not merely to defend Medina. Indeed, its defense was necessary, but this was not the ultimate aim. The aim was to protect the resources and the center of the movement—the movement for freeing mankind and demolishing the obstacles which prevented mankind from attaining this freedom.

The reasons for refraining from fighting during the Meccan period are easily understood. In Mecca preaching was permitted. The Messenger—peace be on him—was under the protection of the Banu Hashim and hence he had the opportunity to declare his message openly; he had the freedom to speak to individuals as to groups and to appeal to their hearts and minds. There was no organized political power which could prevent him from preaching and prevent people from listening. At this stage there was no need for the use of force. Besides this, there were other reasons and I have detailed these reasons in my commentary, *In the Shades of the Qur'an*, in explanation of the verse, "Have you seen the people to whom it was said, 'Restrain your hands, and establish regular prayers, and pay Zakat'?" (3:77) It may be useful to reproduce parts of this explanation here.

A reason for prohibiting the use of force during the Meccan period may have been that this was a stage of training and preparation in a particular environment, for a particular nation and under particular conditions. Under these circumstances, an important factor in training and preparation was to train the individual Arab to be patient under oppression to himself or to those he loved, to conquer his pride, and not to make personal revenge or revenge for one's dear ones the purpose of one's life. Training was also needed so that he could learn control of his nerves, not lose his temper at the first provocation as was his temperament—nor get excited at the first impulse, but so that he could develop dignity and composure in his temperament and in his action. He was to be trained to follow the discipline of a community which is under the direction of a leader, and to refer to this leader in every matter and to obey his injunctions even though they might be against his habit or taste. The aim was to develop individuals of high character who would constitute the Muslim community, who would follow the directions of the leader, and who would be civilized and progressive, free of wild habits and tribalism.

Another reason for it may have been that the Quraish were proud of their lineage and honor, and in such an environment only persuasion could be most appealing and effective. At this stage, fighting would have resulted in kindling the fires of revenge. There was already much tribal warfare based on blood feuds, such as the wars of Dahis, Gabra and Basus, which continued for years and annihilated tribe after tribe. If blood feuds were to become associated in their minds with Islam, then this impression would never have been removed. Consequently, Islam, instead of being a call toward the true religion, would have become an unending sequence of tribal feuds and its basic teachings would have been forgotten at the very beginning.

Another reason may have been to avoid sowing the seed of discord and bloodshed in every household. At that time, there was no organized government which was torturing and persecuting the Believers; the Believer was persecuted, tortured and taught a lesson by his own patrons. Under these circumstances, permission to fight would have meant that every house would have become a battlefield. The people would have said, "So, this is Islam!" In fact, this was said about Islam, even though fighting was not permitted. During the season when the people of Arabia came to Mecca for pilgrimage and commerce, the Quraish would have gone to them and would have said, "Muhammad is not only dividing his nation and his tribe; he is even dividing sons from fathers! What kind of a thing is this which incites the son to kill his father, the slave to kill his master, in every house and in every locality?"

Another reason may have been that God knew that a great majority of those who persecuted and tortured the early Muslims would one day become the loyal soldiers of Islam, even its great leaders. Was not 'Umar Ibn al-Khattab one of them?

Another reason may have been that the sense of honor of the Arabs, especially in a tribal framework, comes to the help of the person who is persecuted yet does not concede defeat, especially if the persecuted are honored by the people. Several such incidents can be quoted to support this thesis. When Abu Bakr, who was an honorable man, left Mecca in order to migrate to some other place, Ibn al-Daghna could not bear it and restrained him from leaving because he considered it a disgrace to the Arabs; he offered Abu Bakr his own protection. The best example of such an incident is the tearing up of the contract under which the Banu Hashim were confined to the Valley of Abu Talib when the period of their hunger and privation seemed unreasonably long. This chivalry was a peculiarity of the Arabs, while in ancient "civilizations" which were accustomed to seeing people humiliated, those who suffered and were persecuted were laughed at, ridiculed and treated with contempt, and the oppressor and the tyrant were respected.

Another reason may have been that the Muslims were few in number and they lived only in Mecca, as the message of Islam had not reached other parts of Arabia or had reached only as hearsay. Other tribes considered it as a domestic quarrel of the Quraish; they were watching for the outcome of this struggle. Under these circumstances, if fighting had been allowed, this limited warfare would have resulted in the complete annihilation of the Muslims; even if they had killed a great number of their opponents, they would still have been completely annihilated. Idolatry would have continued and the dawn of the Islamic system would never have arrived and would never have reached its zenith, while Islam is revealed to be a practical way of life for all mankind.

In the early Medinite period fighting was also prohibited. The reason for this was that the Prophet—peace be on him—had signed a pact with the Jews of Medina and with the unbelieving Arabs in and around Medina, an action which was necessary at this stage.

First, there was an open opportunity for preaching and persuasion. There was no political power to circumscribe this freedom; the whole population accepted the new Muslim state and agreed upon the leadership of the Prophet—peace be on him—in all political maners. In the pact it was agreed by all parties that no one would make a treaty of peace or declare war or establish relations with any outsider without the express permission of the Prophet—peace be on him. Thus, the real power in Medina was in the hands of Muslim leadership. The doors were also open for preaching Islam and there was freedom of belief.

Secondly, at this stage the Prophet—peace be on him—wanted to conserve all his efforts to combat the Quraish, whose relentless opposition was a great obstacle in spreading Islam to other tribes which were waiting to see the final outcome of the struggle between the two groups of the Quraish. That is why the Prophet—peace be on him—hastened to send scouting parties in various directions. The first such party was commanded by Hamza bin Abdul Muttalib, and it went out during the month of Ramadan, only six months after the Immigration.

After this, there were other scouting parties, one during the ninth month after Hijra, the next in the thirteenth month, the third sixteen months after Hijra, and in the seventeenth month he sent a party under the leadership of Abdullah bin Jahash. This party encountered some resistance and some blood was shed. This occurred during the month of Rajab, which was considered a sacred month. The following verse of Chapter Baqara refers to it:

> They ask you about fighting in the sacred months. Say: Fighting in them is a great sin, but to prevent people from the way of God, and to reject God, and to stop people from visiting the Sacred Mosque, and to expel people from their homes are a much greater sin, and oppression is worse than killing. (2.217)

During Ramadan of the same year, the Battle of Badr took place, and in Chapter Anfal this battle was reviewed. If this stage of the Islamic movement is viewed in proper perspective, then there is no room to say that the basic aim of the Islamic movement was "defensive" in the narrow sense which some people ascribe to it today, defeated by the attacks of the treacherous orientalists! Those who look for causes of a defensive nature in the history of the expansion of Islam are caught by the aggressive attacks of the orientalists at a time when Muslims possess neither glory nor do they possess Islam. However, by God's grace, there are those who are standing firm on the issue that Islam is a universal declaration of the freedom of man on the earth from every authority except God's authority, and that the religion ought to be purified for God; and they keep writing concerning, the Islamic Jihaad.

But the Islamic movement does not need any arguments taken from the literature, as it stands on the clear verses of the Qur'an:

> They ought to fight in the way of God who have sold the life of this world for the life of the Hereafter; and whoever fights in the way of God and is killed or becomes victorious, to him shall We give a great reward. Why should not you fight in the way of God for those men, women and children who have been oppressed because they are weak and who call "Our Lord! Take us out of this place whose people are oppressors, and raise for us an ally, and send for us a helper." Those who believe fight in the cause of God, while those who do not believe fight in the cause of tyranny. Then fight against the friends of Satan. Indeed, the strategy of Satan is weak. (3.74–76)
>
> Say to the unbelievers that if they refrain, then whatever they have done before will be forgiven them; but if they turn back, then they know what happened to earlier nations. And fight against them until there is no oppression and the religion is wholly for God. But if they refrain, then God is watching over their actions. But if they do not, then know that God is your Ally and He is your Helper. (8.38–40)
>
> Fight against those among the People of the Book who do not believe in God and the Last Day, who do not forbid what God and His messenger have forbidden, and who do not consider the true religion as their way of life, until they are subdued and pay Jizyah. The Jews say: "Ezra is the Son of God," and the Christians say: "The Messiah is the Son of God." These are mere sayings from their mouths, following those who preceded them and disbelieved. God will assail them; how they are perverted! They have taken their rabbis and priests as lords other that God, and the Messiah, son of Mary; and they were commanded to worship none but One God. There is no deity but He, glory be to Him above what they associate with Him! They desire to extinguish God's light with their mouths, and God intends to perfect His light, although the unbelievers may be in opposition. (9.29–32)

The reasons for Jihaad which have been described in the above verses are these: to establish God's authority in the earth; to arrange human affairs according to the true guidance provided by God; to abolish all the Satanic forces and Satanic systems of life; to end the lordship of one man over others since all men are creatures of God and no one has the authority to make them his servants or to make arbitrary laws for them. These reasons are sufficient for proclaiming Jihaad. However, one should always keep in mind that there is no compulsion in religion; that is, once the people are free from the lordship of men, the law governing civil affairs will be purely that of God, while no one will be forced to change his beliefs and accept Islam.

The Jihaad of Islam is to secure complete freedom for every man throughout the world by releasing him from servitude to other human beings so that he may serve his God, Who is One and Who has no associates. This is in itself a sufficient reason for Jihaad. These were the only reasons in the hearts of Muslim warriors. If they had been asked the question "Why are you fighting?" none would have answered, "My country is in danger; I am fighting for its defense," or "The Persians and the Romans have come upon us," or "We want to extend our dominion and want more spoils.'"

They would have answered the same as Rabati bin 'Amer, Huzaifa bin Muhsin, and Mughira bin Shtuba answered the Persian general Rustum when he asked them one by one during three successive days preceding the battle of Qadisiyyah, "For what purpose have you come?" Their answer was the same: "God has sent us to bring anyone who wishes from servitude to men into the service of God alone, from the narrowness of this world into the vastness of this world and the Here-after, and from the tyranny of religions into the justice of Islam. God raised a Messenger for this purpose to teach His creatures His way. If anyone accepts this way of life, we turn back and give his country back to him, and we fight with those who rebel until we are martyred or become victorious."

These are the reasons inherent in the very nature of this religion. Similarly, its proclamation of universal freedom, its practical way of combatting actual human conditions with appropriate methods, its developing new resources at various stages, is also inherent in its message from the very beginning—and not because of any threat of aggression against Islamic lands or against the Muslims residing in them. The reason for Jihaad exists in the nature of its message and in the actual conditions it finds in human societies, and not merely in the necessity for defense, which may be temporary and of limited extent. A Muslim fights with his wealth and his person "in the way of God" for the sake of these values in which neither personal gain nor greed is a motive for him.

Before a Muslim steps into the battlefield, he has already fought a great battle within himself against Satan—against his own desires and ambitions, his personal interests and inclinations, the interests of his family and of his nation; against that which is not from Islam; against every obstacle which comes into the way of worshipping God and the implementation of the Divine authority on earth, returning this authority to God and taking it away from the rebellious usurpers.

Those who say that Islamic Jihaad was merely for the defense of the "homeland of Islam" diminish the greatness of the Islamic way of life and consider it less important than their "homeland." This is not the Islamic point of view, and their view is a creation of the modern age and is completely alien to Islamic consciousness. What is acceptable to Islamic consciousness is its belief, the way of life which this belief prescribes, and the society which lives according to this way of life. The soil of the homeland has in itself no value or weight. From the Islamic point of view, the only value which the soil can achieve is because on that soil

God's authority is established and God's guidance is followed; and thus it becomes a fortress for the belief, a place for its way of life to be entitled the "homeland of Islam," a center for the movement for the total freedom of man.

Of course, in that case the defense of the "homeland of Islam" is the defense of the Islamic beliefs, the Islamic way of life, and the Islamic community. However, its defense is not the ultimate objective of the Islamic movement of Jihaad but is a means of establishing the Divine authority within it so that it becomes the headquarters for the movement of Islam, which is then to be carried throughout the earth to the whole of mankind, as the object of this religion is all humanity and its sphere of action is the whole earth.

As we have described earlier, there are many practical obstacles in establishing God's rule on earth, such as the power of the state, the social system and traditions, and, in general, the whole human environment. Islam uses force only to remove these obstacles so that there may not remain any wall between Islam and individual human beings, and so that it may address their hearts and minds after releasing them from these material obstacles, and then leave them free to choose to accept or reject it.

We ought not to be deceived or embarrassed by the attacks of the orientalists on the origin of Jihaad, nor lose self-confidence under the pressure of present conditions and the weight of the great powers of the world to such an extent that we try to find reasons for Islamic Jihaad outside the nature of this religion, and try to show that it was a defensive measure under temporary conditions. The need for Jihaad remains, and will continue to remain, whether these conditions exist or not!

In pondering over historical events, we should not neglect the aspects inherent in the nature of this religion, its declaration of universal freedom, and its practical method. We ought not to confuse these with temporary needs of defense. No doubt this religion must defend itself against aggressors. Its very existence in the form of a general declaration of the universal Lordship of God and of the freedom of man from servitude to any being other than God, and its organizing a movement under a new leadership other than the existing *jahili* leadership, and its creating a distinct and permanent society based on the Divine authority and submission to One God, is sufficient cause for the surrounding *jahili* society, which is based on human authority in some form or another, to rise against it for its own preservation and for the suppression of Islam. Clearly, under these conditions, the newly organized Islamic community will have to prepare itself for defense. These conditions inevitably occur and come into existence simultaneously with the advent of Islam in any society. There is no question of Islam's liking or disliking such a situation, as the struggle is imposed upon Islam; this is a natural struggle between two systems which cannot co-exist for long. This is a fact which cannot be denied, and hence Islam has no choice but to defend itself against aggression.

But there is another fact which is much more important than this fact. It is in the very nature of Islam to take initiative for freeing the human beings throughout the earth from servitude to anyone other than God; and so it cannot be restricted within any geographic or racial limits, leaving all mankind on the whole earth in evil, in chaos and in servitude to lords other than God. It may happen that the enemies of Islam may consider it expedient not to take any action against Islam, if Islam leaves them alone in their geographical boundaries to continue the lordship of some men over others and does not extend its message and its declaration of universal freedom within their domain. But Islam cannot agree to this unless they submit to its authority by paying Jizyah, which will be a guarantee that they have opened their doors for the preaching of Islam and will not put any obstacle in its way through the power of the state.

This is the character of this religion and this is its function, as it is a declaration of the Lordship of God and the freedom of man from servitude to anyone other than God, for all people. There is a great difference between this concept of Islam and the other, which considers it confined to geographical and racial limits, and does not take any action except out of fear of aggression. In the latter case, all its inherent dynamism is lost.

To understand the dynamism of Islam with clarity and depth, it is necessary to remember that Islam is a way of life for man prescribed by God. It is not a man-made system, nor an ideology of a group of people, nor a way of life peculiar to a given race. We cannot talk about external reasons for Jihaad unless we overlook this great truth and unless we forget that the fundamental question here is the sovereignty of God and the obedience of His creatures; it is impossible for a person to remember this great truth and still search for other reasons for Islamic Jihaad. The true estimate of the difference between the concept that war was forced upon Islam by Jahiliyyah because its very nature demanded that *jahili* societies would attack it, and the concept that Islam takes the initiative and enters into this struggle, cannot be made in the early stages of its movement.

In the early stages of the Islamic movement it is difficult to discriminate between these two concepts, because in either case Islam will have to do battle. However, in the final stages, when the initial battles are won, the two concepts make a great difference—a great difference in understanding the purposes and the significance of the Islamic message. And here lies the danger.

There is also a great difference in the idea that Islam is a Divinely ordained way of life and in the idea that it is a geographically bounded system. According to the first idea, Islam came into this world to establish God's rule on God's earth, to invite all people toward the worship of God, and to make a concrete reality of its message in the form of a Muslim community in which individuals are free from servitude to men and have gathered together under servitude to God and follow only the Shari'ah of God. This Islam has a right to remove all those obstacles which are in its path so that it may address human reason and intuition with no interference and opposition from political systems. According to the second idea, Islam is merely a national system which has a right to take up arms only when its homeland is attacked.

In the case of either concept, Islam has to strive and to struggle; but its purposes and its results are entirely different, both conceptually and practically. Indeed, Islam has the right to take the initiative. Islam is not a heritage of any particular race or country; this is God's religion and it is for the whole world. It has the right to destroy all obstacles in the form of institutions and traditions which limit man's freedom of choice. It does not attack individuals nor does it force them to accept its beliefs; it attacks institutions and traditions to release human beings from their poisonous influences, which distort human nature and which curtail human freedom.

It is the right of Islam to release mankind from servitude to human beings so that they may serve God alone, to give practical meaning to its declaration that God is the true Lord of all and that all men are free under Him. According to the Islamic concept and in actuality, God's rule on earth can be established only through the Islamic system, as it is the only system ordained by God for all human beings, whether they be rulers or ruled, black or white, poor or rich, ignorant or learned. Its law is uniform for all, and all human beings are equally responsible within it. In all other systems, human beings obey other human beings and follow man-made laws. Legislation is a Divine attribute; any person who concedes this right to such a claimant, whether he considers him Divine or not, has accepted him as Divine.

Islam is not merely a belief, so that it is enough merely to preach it. Islam, which is a way of life, takes practical steps to organize a movement for freeing man. Other societies do not give it any opportunity to organize its followers according to its own method, and hence it is the duty of Islam to annihilate all such systems, as they are obstacles in the way of universal freedom. Only in this manner can the way of life be wholly dedicated to God, so that neither any human authority nor the question of servitude remains, as is the case in all other systems which are based on man's servitude to man. Those of our contemporary Muslim scholars who are defeated by the pressure of current conditions and the attacks of treacherous orientalists do not subscribe to this characteristic of Islam. The orientalists have painted a picture of Islam as a violent movement which imposed its belief upon people by the sword. These vicious orientalists know very well that this is not true, but by this method they try to distort the true motives of Islamic Jihaad. But our Muslim scholars, these defeated people, search for reasons of defense with which to negate this accusation. They are ignorant of the nature of Islam and of its function, and that it has a right to take the initiative for human freedom.

These research scholars, with their defeated mentality, have adopted the Western concept of "religion," which is merely a name for "belief" in the heart, having no relation to the practical affairs of life, and therefore they conceive of religious war as a war to impose belief on peoples' hearts. But this is not the case with Islam, as Islam is the way of life ordained by God for all mankind, and this way establishes the Lordship of God alone—that is, the sovereignty of God—and orders practical life in all its daily details. Jihaad in Islam is simply a name for striving to make this system of life dominant in the world. As far as belief is concerned, it clearly depends upon personal opinion, under the protection of a general system in which all obstacles to freedom of personal belief have been removed. Clearly this is an entirely different matter and throws a completely new light on the Islamic Jihaad.

Thus, wherever an Islamic community exists which is a concrete example of the Divinely ordained system of life, it has a God-given right to step forward and take control of the political authority so that it may establish the Divine system on earth, while it leaves the matter of belief to individual conscience. When God restrained Muslims from Jihaad for a certain period, it was a question of strategy rather than of principle; this was a matter pertaining to the requirements of the movement and not to belief. Only in the light of this explanation can we understand those verses of the Holy Qur'an which are concerned with the various stages of this movement. In reading these verses, we should always keep in mind that one of their meanings is related to the particular stages of the development of Islam, while there is another general meaning which is related to the unchangeable and eternal message of Islam. We should not confuse these two aspects.

26

[UNTITLED]

Yusuf al-Qaradawi (1926–)

THE PROPHET MUHAMMAD AS A *JIHAD* MODEL

. . . Allah has also made the prophet Muhammad into an epitome for religious warriors [*Mujahideen*] since he ordered Muhammed to fight for religion.[1] . . . The youth who wish to hurry to establish an Islamic state with an Islamic rule seek clashes with the existing regimes in the Arab states despite the fact that they don't have sufficient strength; they don't have military strength and not even the mental strength to establish an Islamic rule. . . . There are various ways to prepare for Jihad: there is mental preparation, there is physical preparation, and there is material preparation, meaning the preparation of the weapons. The messenger [Muhammad] prepared all his friends first mentally since equipment and weapons cannot fight by themselves, but rather need hands to operate them, and those hands must also have a purpose. . . .

Why were we defeated in 1967? Officers stated that we had vast amounts of weapons but we did not provide the warrior with mental preparation. We did not prepare him to fight for religious belief and for defending religious sanctuaries. . . . He who got killed is a [Shahid] in heaven . . . the first assignment is to prepare the hero who is willing to put his life in his own hands for Allah's sake, and he who does not care whether he encounters death or death encounters him. . . . He [i.e., a self-immolating bomber] kills the enemy while taking self-risk, similarly to what Muslims did in the pas. . . . He wants to scare his enemies, and the religious authorities have permitted this. They said that if he causes the enemy both sorrow and fear of Muslims . . . he is permitted to risk himself and even get killed.

From Yusuf al-Qaradawi, "The Prophet Muhammad as a *Jihad* Model," Middle East Media Research Institute, Special dispatch no. 246, July 24, 2001, http://memri.org/bin/articles.cgi?Page=archives&Area=sd&ID=SP24601; and "Al-Qaradawi Speaks in Favor of Suicide Operations at an Islamic Conference in Sweden," Middle East Media Research Institute, Special dispatch no. 542, July 24, 2003, http://memri.org/bin/articles.cgi?Page=archives&Area=sd&ID=SP54203.

THOSE WHO OPPOSE MARTYRDOM OPERATIONS AND CLAIM THAT THEY ARE SUICIDE ARE MAKING A GREAT MISTAKE

It has been determined by Islamic law that the blood and property of people of *Dar Al-Harb* [the Domain of Disbelief where the battle for the domination of Islam should be waged] is not protected. Because they fight against and are hostile towards the Muslims, they annulled the protection of his blood and his property . . . in modern war, all of society, with all its classes and ethnic groups, is mobilized to participate in the war, to aid its continuation, and to provide it with the material and human fuel required for it to assure the victory of the state fighting its enemies. Every citizen in society must take upon himself a role in the effort to provide for the battle. The entire domestic front, including professionals, laborers, and industrialists, stands behind the fighting army, even if it does not bear arms. Therefore the experts say that the Zionist entity, in truth, is one army. . . . What weapon can harm their enemy, can prevent him from sleeping, and can strip him of a sense of security and stability, except for these human bombs—a young man or woman who blows himself or herself up amongst their enemy. This is a weapon the likes of which the enemy cannot obtain, even if the U.S. provides it with billions [of dollars] and the most powerful weapons, because it is a unique weapon that Allah has placed only in the hands of the men of belief. It is a type of divine justice on the face of the earth. . . . Those who oppose martyrdom operations and claim that they are suicide are making a great mistake. The goals of the one who carries out a martyrdom operation and of the one who commits suicide are completely different. Anyone who analyzes the soul of [these two] will discover the huge difference between them. The [person who commits] suicide kills himself for himself, because he failed in business, love, an examination, or the like. He was too weak to cope with the situation and chose to flee life for death. . . . In contrast, the one who carries out a martyrdom operation does not think of himself. He sacrifices himself for the sake of a higher goal, for which all sacrifices become meaningless. He sells himself to Allah in order to buy Paradise in exchange. Allah said: "Allah has bought from the believers their souls and their properties for they shall inherit Paradise. . . . While the [person who commits] suicide dies in escape and retreat, the one who carries out a martyrdom operation dies in advance and attack. Unlike the [person who commits] suicide, who has no goal except escape from confrontation, the one who carries out a martyrdom operation has a clear goal, and that is to please Allah."[2]

NOTES

1. For example, see D. S. Margoliouth, *Mohammed and the Rise of Islam* (London, 1905; repr., New Delhi, 1985), pp. 362–63. Professor Margoliouth explains the lasting

implications of the aggressive jihad campaign Muhammad launched against the Jewish farmers of the Khaybar oasis:

> The taking of Khaibar marks the stage at which Islam became a menace to the whole world. True, Mohammad had now for six years lived by robbery and brigandage: but in plundering Meccans he could plead that he had been driven from his home and possessions: and with the Jewish tribes of Medina he had in each case some outrage, real or pretended, to avenge. But the people of Khaibar, all that distance from Medinah, had certainly done him and his followers no wrong: for their leaving unavenged the murder of one of their number by his emissary was no act of aggression. Ali, when told to lead the forces against them, had to enquire for what he was fighting: and was told that he must compel them to adopt the formulae of Islam. Khaibar was attacked because there was booty to be acquired there, and the plea for attacking it was that its inhabitants were *not Moslems*. That plea would cover attacks on the whole world outside Medinah and its neighborhood: and on leaving Khaibar the Prophet seemed to see the world already in his grasp. . . . Now the fact that a community was idolatrous, or Jewish, or anything but Mohammedan, warranted a murderous attack upon it: the passion for fresh conquests dominated the Prophet.

2. Al-Qaradawi's views are supported by the research of Professor Franz Rosenthal. In his seminal essay "On Suicide in Islam," *Journal of the American Oriental Society* 66 (1946): 243, 256, Rosenthal observed:

> While the Qur'anic attitude toward suicide remains *uncertain*, the great authorities of the hadith leave no doubt as to the official attitude of Islam. In their opinion suicide is an unlawful act. . . . *On the other hand, death as the result of "suicidal" missions and of the desire of martyrdom occurs not infrequently, since death is considered highly commendable according to Muslim religious concepts. However, such cases are no[t] suicides in the proper sense of the term.* (Emphasis added.)

John Paul Jones, in a letter to Prince Potemkin dated June 20, 1788, while Jones commanded Russian naval ships, wrote about a naval engagement with the Turkish fleet (outside Kimbourn) involving an unsuccessful martyrdom operation planned by the Muslim sailors [from John H. Sherburne, *Life and Character of John Paul Jones—A Captain in the Navy of the United States* (New York: Adriance, Sherman, 1825), p. 308]:

> [F]or it was the intention of the Turks to attack us and board us, and if we had been only three versts further the attempt would have been made on the 16th [June 1788] (before the vessel of the Captain Pacha ran aground in advancing before the wind with all his forces to attack us,), God only knows what would have been the result. . . . The Turks had a very large force, and we have been informed by our prisoners that they were resolved to destroy us, even by burning themselves, (in setting fire to their own vessels after having grappled with ours.) [Note added by Jones: Before their departure from Constantinople, they swore by the beard of the Sultan to execute this horrible plan . . . if Providence had not caused its failure from two circumstances which no man could forsee.]

PART 4

Jihad—Overviews from Important Twentieth-Century Scholars

27

THE JIHAD OR HOLY WAR ACCORDING TO THE MALIKITE SCHOOL

Edmond Fagnan

1. THE NATURE OF THIS DUTY; CASES OF EXEMPTION

The holy war[2] conducted each year on the most dangerous front, even if there is risk of an attack by bandits, constitutes, just like the visit of the Ka'ba [i.e., being stationed at 'Arafat], a duty of showing solidarity,[3] which is incumbent on every free male who has attained the age of puberty and is of sound mind and body.

It is likewise a duty of solidarity to devote oneself to the religious sciences, to render judicial opinions; to ward off what might cause harm to Muslims, to fulfill the responsibilities of a judge; to act as a witness; to accept the position of imam [whether that of the supreme imam or for the purposes of prayer]; to com-

Edmond Fagnan, *Le djihad ou guerre sainte selon l'école malikite* (Algiers, 1908).[1] English translation by Michael J. Miller.

mand what is good; to carry on the basic, indispensable trades; to respond to a greeting; to pay one's last respects to the dead; and to free captives.[4]

In the case of a sudden invasion, holy war becomes a personal duty, even for a woman or for the neighbors [of the believers who are being attacked], if they (i.e., the latter) are too weak, as well as for those who hold the title of imam.

A person is exempted by sickness, extreme youth (i.e., not having attained puberty), insanity, blindness, lameness, sex (i.e., being a woman), the inability to obtain what is needed in order to participate, being in a state of servitude, the existence of a demandable debt, the refusal of the father and mother [or of one of them]—but not of a grandparent—to give permission to fulfill a duty of solidarity.

2. HOW CONQUERED INFIDELS ARE TREATED

Infidels living in a place where there is nothing to fear from their bad faith are invited to embrace Islam, or else to pay the head tax. If they refuse, they are to be fought and can be killed, except for: a woman, provided that she does not participate [armed] in the fight; a child or someone who is weak-minded; and also—provided that they do not interfere by stating their opinions—an old man who is bald, someone who is infirm, a blind man, and a monk who lives secluded in a monastery or a hermitage. To these [individuals whose life or freedom is respected] one should leave only something to live on. The believer who [unduly] kills an enemy [other than a monk] has only to repent [without paying the price of blood], just as for the murder of someone who [even outside of a holy war] has not received the invitation to convert; if he kills one of those who have fallen into our hands, he owes the value of that individual [which is added to the sum total of the booty]. As for the monk and the nun, they remain at liberty.

3. PERMISSIBLE AND FORBIDDEN METHODS OF FIGHTING

Let those who fight employ flooding (*l'interception de l'eau*), any and all sorts of weapons, and, when all else fails, and when there are no Muslims among the enemy, let them use fire, even at sea.

In attacking a fortress containing children [or women], recourse is not had to burning or flooding. If the enemy shields himself behind his children, leave him alone, unless he is too dangerous; if he uses Muslims in this way, [fight him] without aiming at this (human) shield, provided that there is not too great a risk for most of the Muslims.

It is forbidden to use poisoned arrows, to ask polytheists to assist except in rendering auxiliary services, to send them the Qur'an or to take it on a journey in an enemy country, and also to take a woman there except in an army that provides complete safety; to flee if the Muslims are outnumbered only two-to-one by the enemy or if there are more than twelve thousand of them, unless it is a question of a feigned flight or of a regrouping at a perilous juncture;[5] to inflict [undue] punishment [on those who are conquered] by way of example; to carry the enemies' heads to another country or to the general.

It is also forbidden for a captive [Muslim] to betray the trust of his infidel master which he has freely accepted, be it with regard [to the master's material goods or] to his own person.

Likewise forbidden is the misappropriation of a portion of the booty that has not yet been divided up—an action which, once proven, makes the guilty party liable to an arbitrary punishment [unless he repents].[6]

4. LIBERTIES THAT ARE TOLERATED IN TIME OF WAR; REPLACEMENT; SINGLE COMBAT

It is permissible for a combatant who needs them to take shoes, belts (or "straps"), needles, or food, even in the form of livestock and fodder; provided he intends to make restitution, clothing, weapons, or a mount (e.g., horse, donkey) may be taken as well. Anything of value [be it a half dinar] that is left of all these objects is returned [to the local inhabitants]; if that is too difficult, it is given as an alms.

Combatants may exchange these objects with one another.

In enemy territory [the imam] can establish written penal law.[7] Dwellings may be destroyed, palms [and other trees] may be cut down and burned, if that harms the infidels or if there is no hope of dominating them; in the absence of that hope, destroying these things is recommended, according to Ibn Rushd (Averroes, d. 1198), just as it is recommended to refrain from destruction if such hope exists.

The Muslim who has been taken captive can cohabit with his wife or his slave woman [who have also been captured], provided that they have not cohabited with the infidel.

It is permissible to slaughter animals [belonging to the enemy for which one has no use] or to hamstring them and then finish them off. As for bees, if [they constitute a valuable resource because they are] numerous, and one does not intend to seize their honey, there are two versions.[8] These creatures should be burned afterward, if the enemy eats such dead animals. Similarly, one can also destroy objects that cannot be carried off.

The imam can set up a *diwan* [or registry of enlisted soldiers arranged by country of origin], and, by paying him a price, one believer can remain (at home) while another replaces him in battle, as long as both men are part of the same *diwan*.

Soldiers [who are on guard duty] can say the "*Allah akbar*" in a loud voice, but it is blameworthy to intone it. It is permissible to kill a spy, even one who is welcomed under safe conduct, and a Muslim is treated in this regard as an atheist. The imam can accept gifts from the enemy, which become his when someone presents them to him, for instance, because they are neighbors; these gifts, on the contrary, are placed in the public treasury when they are sent to him by the king of the infidels and he has not set foot on their territory.

It is permissible to fight against the Nubians[9] and the Turks, to argue against them with the help of the Qur'an, to send them a letter containing one or more verses.

One Muslim can, according to Ibn Rushd, break ranks in order to fight several infidels alone, provided that he is not motivated by the [sole] desire to show his bravery.[10]

One can choose one sort of death rather than another, and he is obliged to do so if he hopes thus either to save or to prolong his life.

5. THE FATE INTENDED FOR THE CONQUERED; *AMAN*

The imam must also investigate, with regard to combatants taken prisoner, whether he should put them to death, or set them free, or ransom them, or impose the head tax (*jizya*) upon them, or reduce them to slavery.

Pregnancy caused by a Muslim man does not prevent the [infidel] mother from becoming a slave, and the child is born a slave if the father was an infidel when it was conceived.

One must fulfill the conditions according to which an enemy has made it possible for us to conquer, and keep absolutely the promise of clemency made by the imam. [The same good faith is obligatory] vis-à-vis the adversary for someone who engages in single combat;[11] if the adversary receives help and he consents to it, he is to be killed, along with his helper. It is permissible for one Muslim in a group fighting against an equal number of enemies to come to the aid [of a comrade] when he himself has dispatched [his adversary].

Infidels who leave their city when it is besieged [or who come among us to trade] and rely upon the decision [of a Muslim] are required to abide by it if that arbiter is a respectable person acquainted with the interests of Muslims; if not, the imam will be the judge, just as he is also in the case where someone other than he grants the *aman* to an entire region.

But if it is not a question of a region, is the *aman* valid—this is the majority opinion—or is it acceptable, since it comes not from a tributary or from someone acting out of fear, but rather from an individual endowed with discernment, even a minor or a slave or someone of the female sex, or someone in rebellion against the imam? There are two interpretations [of the text of the *Modawwana*].

The right to put to death is withdrawn by the grant of the *aman*, even if the agreement is made after military victory. [The *aman*, which is manifested] by the use of a verbal expression or of an intelligible sign, must not be injurious to Muslim interests. If an enemy, believing that there is an *aman*, presents himself to us, or if the imam's prohibition against granting it is violated or forgotten by his men or unknown to them, or if the enemy does not know whether the one whom he is addressing is Muslim—as opposed to the case where he knows him to be non-Muslim but is unaware that this *aman* would therefore require ratification— then either the *aman* is ratified [by the imam] or else the enemy is sent back to his country. If he is captured on his territory while advancing upon us and he says, "I am coming to ask you for the *aman*,"—or on our territory and he says, "I thought that you did not arrest merchants,"—or somewhere between the two territories, then he is sent back to a safe place. If there is some circumstance [that would indicate his intentions], one acts accordingly.

Someone who, having obtained the *aman*, is driven back by (adverse) winds [or by some other obstacle] enjoys this right until he arrives home.

6. INFIDELS AUTHORIZED TO TAKE UP RESIDENCE; QUESTIONS OF PROPRIETY

If a domiciled infidel [i.e., who has been admitted under safe conduct][12] dies on our territory, his goods belong to the treasury if he has no heir and did not come among us in order to settle some business matter. Otherwise [i.e., if he is not a permanent resident—Derdir], these valuables are sent back to his heir and [if there is reason for it] the price of blood, as well as any deposits belonging to the deceased. Does [this return of deposits] take place even if the foreigner is killed while fighting believers, or is the sum put into the treasury? There are two opinions. In the case where this authorized foreigner is taken captive [for violating his obligations] and then put to death, his goods devolve on the one who kills him.

[If he imports spoils that had been taken from believers], it is blameworthy that the purchase of them should be made by anyone other than the original owner, but the latter loses these goods when they are sold or given [to any Muslim or tributary]. According to Ibn Rushd, objects stolen [by an authorized foreigner] and [later] reimported are to be confiscated, but not Muslims who were originally free [but were taken captive] who are reimported.

By his conversion, an infidel becomes the full proprietor [of everything that he was able to gain by pillage], except from a free Muslim, with the following reservations: a concubine-mother must be redeemed [by her former master]; a slave who is to be freed posthumously must be redeemed with the help of the available third part of the estate of his former master; the indentured servant [*l'affranchi à terme*] must be set free upon the completion of the term, and no one shall have any reason to be troubled about it. [If the slave who is supposed to be freed after his master's death comes to be owned in this way by another, and is freed only partially or not at all at the death of his former master,] the heir does not have a choice [between losing all his rights over this freed man and paying the sum necessary to make up the slave's value].

The written penal law[13] is applied to the believer who, after the sum total of the booty has been established, has illicit relations [with a captive woman] or steals some part of the booty.

7. OWNERSHIP OF THE LAND; BOOTY; ADDITIONAL SHARES OF THE BOOTY

The land [except for unproductive lands] is converted into real estate [for the benefit of the Muslim community], following the example of what Umar b. al-Khattab did with the land of Egypt, Syria, and Iraq,[14] and the remainder of the things that have been seized is divided into five shares [in either case], if dominion over them has been acquired by means of hostilities.

The income from the land tax, from the fifth, from the head tax, [etc.,] is used for the needs of the Prophet's family and then for those of the community, providing first for those in the country from which these sums have been appropriated; after that, the lion's share goes for those of a more needy country.

The imam can, for a pragmatic reason, give up an additional share deducted from the fifth. He is not permitted to say, while the fight is not yet finished, "The one who kills [an enemy] will receive his spoils"; nevertheless this promise, [although illicit,] is valid if he does not revoke it before the booty is seized. [In that case] only a Muslim can take the usual spoils [of a warrior], which do not include a bracelet, cross, or precious metal, or mount [other than the one that belonged to the dead man]. It is possible that the beneficiary has not even heard about this promise, and [the spoils can be those of] several enemies, if the leader did not address one combatant individually; whereas, if he was speaking to a particular warrior, the latter has a right only to the spoils of the first of his victims. The spoils in question cannot be those of a woman, [of an old man, etc.] if she does not fight. The imam himself can also [have a right to the spoils of a dead man] if, in his promise, he did not say "anyone among you" or (even) if he has not reserved that right for himself.

The conquering warrior has a right to the mule [or the camel, etc. of his victim] if the imam has spoken [about an enemy mounted] upon a mule, [a camel, etc.]. The mount that is in the hands of a servant is not [regarded as being part of the spoils].

8. DIVIDING THE SPOILS

The imam divides the four[-fifths remaining] among the Muslim men who are free, endowed with the use of reason, postpubertal, and present at the battle, and also among the merchants and journeymen who have fought or made a sortie with the intention of going to war. Those who do not have all these qualifications, even if they did fight, have no share in the division (of the spoils); however, there is a difference of opinion as to a minor who was authorized to fight and actually did so. They receive nothing from the reserved fifth, either. Similarly [the following have no share either in the spoils or in the distribution of the fifth:] anyone who dies before the battle, is blind, lame, or one-handed; anyone who remains behind for a reason unconnected with military service, or loses his way, even as a result of a contrary wind, within a Muslim country. On the contrary, the following do have a share in the spoils: someone who goes astray in enemy territory, the sick man who helps [in combat and makes himself useful], the wounded horse, [any man or horse] that has fallen sick at the time when the booty is gathered. In the case of an illness that began at some other moment, there are two opinions.

9. PROPORTION OF THE SHARES OF BOOTY

A horse has twice the share allotted to his rider, even if it was on board a ship or is a draft horse, a half-breed, or a young animal, provided that it can be used to charge and retreat; [this same proportion is allotted] to the sick horse with a hope of recovery, to one that is the object of a *wakf*, to one that was set apart in advance from the spoils or seized from someone outside the army, or even taken from a military man, though in this last case the double share goes to the horse's master.

Nothing is allotted to a horse that is gaunt and weak, or too old to be of any use, to a mule, a camel, or the spare horse [of the same cavalier].

[The double share that goes] to a horse that is owned jointly is paid to the combatant, who pays the reward or hire (in French, *loyer*) for the animal to the coowner.

[Booty amassed by detachments] that rely on the main body of the army is treated like the booty taken by the latter; otherwise, it belongs to the one who seizes it, to the plunderer, for example. However, even then, according to Ibn el-Kasim, he owes the fifth if he is a Muslim, even a slave, but not if he is a tributary—nor is the Muslim obliged if he makes a saddle or arrows [with material from the booty].

10. THE PLACE OF THE DIVISION; OBJECTS RECOGNIZED AS BELONGING TO MUSLIMS

The [traditional] way of doing it is to go ahead and divide the spoils in enemy territory. If it is necessary to sell in order to make the division, there are two opinions. According to Ibn Younos, various sorts of objects are divided, if possible, into portions.

A known individual, even a tributary, can take back, before the division and without cost, what is known to belong to him, provided that he declares on oath his right of ownership. [When he is absent,] the object is forwarded to him or is sold and the profits given to him, depending on which alternative is the more advantageous for him.

The act of including an object [whose owner is known] in the spoils to be divided is not valid, unless it is based upon an interpretation of documents,[15] according to what Ibn 'Abd es-Selam says. But an object whose owner has not been determined is included in the spoils to be divided—contrary to what happens in the case of an unclaimed object [bearing a suitable inscription and found among the enemies; such an object is sequestered].

11. SLAVES INCLUDED IN THE BOOTY AND RECOGNIZED AS MUSLIM PROPERTY

The services of a slave with a term of indenture or of one who is supposed to be freed posthumously [whose master has not been determined and who is found among the enemies] can be put up for sale, as well as the contract of enfranchisement, but not the services of a concubine-mother. After the distribution, the owner [once he is discovered] can take back his property by depositing the price that was paid, or the first price, if there have been several sales in succession. As for the concubine-mother [unwittingly included in the spoils to be divided, her former master] is compelled to take her back at the price [of the sale or of her appraisal] and, if he is poor, he is prosecuted under law to this effect; this obligation ceases at the death of the slave or of the master. As for the indentured servant and the slave to be emancipated posthumously [who has unwittingly been included in the spoils], their former master can choose either to pay their ransom so as to bring them back to their former status, or else let them go, relinquishing their services to their new master.

If the first master of the slave to be emancipated posthumously dies before the latter has paid off [the price of his redemption or of his appraisal], this slave goes free if the available third of the estate is sufficient, but he is prosecuted [by the second master] for the portion that he still owes. Legal action is brought in the same way against the Muslim or the tributary [mistakenly] included in the spoils to be divided and who have no good excuse for having remained silent.

[If, in the case under consideration, the available third is sufficient to buy] in part [the freedom of the slave to be emancipated posthumously], he remains a slave for the remainder (of the time). The heir then has no choice [between redeeming or relinquishing said slave], whereas he does have a choice in the case [where the testator relinquished the slave because] of damages that were done.

The contract servant (*l'affranchi contractuel*) who [having been sold or included in the division of the spoils by mistake or unwittingly] pays his purchase price, reverts to his previous status; if he cannot pay it, he is a slave pure and simple, regardless of whether he is handed over [to his purchaser] or redeemed [by his former master].

Anyone who receives an object that comes from the booty and knows that it belongs to a certain person must not dispose of it, in order that the latter may have the choice [of paying for it or relinquishing it]. But if he does dispose of it, his act is valid, and the same goes for someone who buys something from an enemy [in a Muslim country] and, for example, impregnates a slave woman, if he did not buy that object with the intention of restoring it to its master. If he did have that intention, there are two opinions. There is doubt as to the validity of freeing an indentured servant (*d'un affranchiseement à terme*).

Either a Muslim or a tributary can, without indemnity, recover an object given [or sold] by the enemy on his territory, by means of a reimbursement of the amount that was given in exchange, before this object is sold again. [If there was a sale], it is valid, and the former owner receives the price or the surplus [over and above what was given in exchange for the object, as the case may be]. The best thing to do about an object recovered from a thief by means of a ransom, is for the owner to reimburse the amount to the one who paid the ransom.

When a slave who is to be freed upon his master's death or the like is relinquished [by his master] to someone who has paid what was necessary to set him free, his services in their entirety are acquired by the latter (master). But [if by the time of the death of the one who manumitted him he has not worked off the amount] that would set him free, will he be prosecuted for the entire sum, or for what remains to be paid off? There are two opinions.

12. SLAVES OF INFIDELS; BREAKUP OF A MARRIAGE AS A RESULT OF CAPTIVITY

The slave of an infidel becomes free, whether [or not] he converts, when he flees to our territory or when he [having converted] remains in enemy territory until he is taken as booty—but not if he flees after his master's conversion or by the simple fact that he himself, the slave, converts.

The fact of being taken captive annuls marriage [between infidels], unless the wife who has been taken prisoner converts after her husband.

The child and the belongings of a converted captive are, in any case, considered as booty, but not the minor child of an enemy by a Jewish, Christian, or Muslim wife who was born free.

But do the children of this Muslim woman who was born free become part of the booty when they grow up, or does that happen only in the case where they fight? There are two interpretations.

The child of a slave women [who has been taken captive and has fallen again into our hands] belongs to her [Muslim or tributary] owner.

13. RATE AND MANNER OF LEVYING THE HEAD TAX

The obligation to pay the head tax results from a grant made by the imam to an infidel—who has been taken captive legitimately, who has attained puberty, is a free man, capable of paying, leading a secular life, and has not been set free by a Muslim [in a Muslim country]—of permission to live in a place other than Mecca, Medina [or the surrounding territories] or Yemen—places through which he may travel, however—in return for a payment once every lunar year which consists, for someone who is subdued by main strength, of four dinars or forty dirhems [in legal currency]. This payment, according to Ibn Rushd, is made at the end of the year. The poor man is relieved of the tax in proportion to his circumstances, and his tax is not raised [if he becomes richer].

For someone who surrenders militarily, the rate of the head tax is the one stipulated or, if there was no discussion of it, the same as in the preceding case. According to Ibn Rushd, if the taxpayer pays this last-mentioned rate, the imam can no longer fight against him.[16]

The collection of the head tax should be done in a degrading manner. But this tax and these degrading methods cease once an individual has converted; the same goes[17] for the supplies of food provided to Muslims and the three-day hospitality that is to be offered to a traveling Muslim, because they are by nature unfair.[18]

14. THE STATUS OF THE TRIBUTARY

The infidel, whether he was subjected by main strength [or by surrender, pays the head tax, but] is free. When he dies or is converted, his land alone belongs to the Muslims [and not his movable goods].

For those who subjected themselves by surrendering [there are four cases]: 1. If the head tax is one fixed lump sum [without distinction as to persons or real estate], the ground belongs to them, and they can dispose of their goods by testament and inherit land; 2. If the head tax is reckoned per capita, the ground belongs to them [with full ownership], but in the case of death without an [infidel] heir, it reverts [along with the movable goods] to the Muslims, and it can be disposed of by testament only by the third party; 3. and 4. If the head tax is reckoned by parcels of land, or both by parcels and per capita, the land can be sold, but the amount of the head tax is owed by the seller.

The infidel who has been subjected by force can build a church if that is stipulated (in the *dhimma* contract); if not, then he cannot. The same goes for restoring a church that has fallen into ruins. Someone who has surrendered can erect a church and sell the site on which it stands or the lands belonging to it. This is not permitted [in either case] in a country which is Muslim, strictly speaking, unless it is done to avoid a greater evil.[19]

It is forbidden [for any tributary] to ride a horse or a mule, to use a saddle, to take the middle of the road; he must wear distinctive clothing.[20] He is punished if he fails to wear his characteristic belt, if he makes a public display of himself in a drunken state, if he manifests his religious opinions, if he speaks in a disrespectful manner; let the wine be poured out [which is displayed publicly] and let the rattle [used to call people to religious services] be broken.

15. BREACH OF THE HEAD TAX CONTRACT

The protection agreement is breached in the following cases: when the tributary fights against the Muslims, when he refuses to pay the head tax, when he opposes legal decisions, when he kidnaps a free Muslim woman [and has relations with her], when he deceives her [by posing as a Muslim so as to marry her], when he informs the enemy of the weak points in Muslim territory, when he insults a prophet using expressions permitted by his faith, such as the following that has been reported: "He is not a prophet, God did not send him—the Qur'an was not revealed to him—he's the author of it—Jesus created Muhammad—Muhammad is a poor man: he tells you that he is in paradise, but why, then, could he not defend himself from the biting dogs?"[21] The guilty party [in this last case] is put to death if he does not convert.

The fate of the tributary who flees to an enemy country and is recaptured [is determined by the imam]; more particularly, he can be reduced to slavery, as long as his flight was not provoked by abusive acts, since in this case he is regarded as being guilty of highway robbery. If a band [of converted infidels] apostatizes and indulges in highway robbery, the individuals who make up the group are treated as [Muslim] apostates.

16. TRUCES

To the imam alone belongs the right to declare a truce, provided that it is for a useful purpose and there there are no conditions such as keeping Muslims in captivity. A payment can be stipulated. But fear [of a greater evil] precludes these considerations.

There is no limit to the duration, but it is recommended that it not exceed four months. If he foresees treachery on the part of the enemy, he denounces the treaty and advises him of it.

The stipulated conditions must be carried out, even that of returning hostages who have meanwhile become Muslim, as well as [that of returning] those who converted [and fled to our territory], even if they come as envoys; all of this being understood of males only.

17. REDEMPTION OF CAPTIVES

The ransom [of a Muslim captive] is paid from the public treasury or, by default, from the property of believers [while taking into account ties of blood and of dwelling place] or, as a last recourse, from his personal property. [When a certain individual], not acting out of charity, pays a ransom, given that redemption is only possible at that price, he has legal recourse against the captive who has been freed, whether the latter is well-off or not, for the equivalent of the fungible items given in payment for him, or else, if it is a question of nonfungible items, for their value. However he cannot exercise this right of recourse against a relative of a specified degree of consanguinity, or against a spouse, when their status is known to him [at the time of the redemption], nor can he do so against someone whom he would be obliged to deliver, unless the captive demanded this redemption and declared that he would be responsible for it. The right to this sort of debt has precedence over all others, and the amount is recovered [whatever Ibn el-Mawwaz may say] even from the goods of the freed man, other than those of which he is the bearer.

[Ransom paid in a lump sum to redeem several captives is divided equally among them and] per capita if [the enemy] does not know their respective worth. The statement [under oath] of the liberated captive is proof of the total or partial amount of the ransom, even if, [despite the opinion of Sohnoun], the freed man is still in the hands of his redeemer.

The ransom can consist of infidel captives who are fit for combat or, according to Ibn 'Abd es-Selam, of wine, pigs, etc. In this case, the redeemer, if he is Muslim, has no legal recourse [except for the amount that he has devoted to the purchase of these things].

On the question as to whether or not it is permissible for the ransom to consist of horses or military gear, there are two opinions.

18. HORSE RACES AND MILITARY COMPETITIONS[22]

Speed races can be organized between horses, between camels, or between animals of these two sorts, or shooting matches, offering a prize consisting of an object that can be sold legitimately.

The following things must be determined: the starting point and the point of arrival, the mount, the marksman, the number of times that the target must be hit and the manner of hitting it, whether the arrow must pass through it without remaining fixed therein, or otherwise.

The prize consists of a gift given gratuitously by a third party, or else it is assigned by one of the two contestants; in the latter case, if the challenger is victorious, he receives the prize, which on the other hand is distributed to the spectators if the donor wins. It is not permissible for two contestants to assign one prize each and for the winner to take all, even if there were a third contestant who could win, in order to lend an appearance of legitimacy to the contest.

There should be no specifications as to the arrow or the bowstring to be used, each one being free in this regard, nor is it necessary that the speed of the mount or (the identity? the skill? of) the rider be known.

A boy who has not reached puberty must not compete; [that is reprehensible].

It is not necessary that the prize be of equal importance [to each of the two contestants], nor that the target to be hit be the same, nor that both contestants have the same distance to cover or the same number of successful hits to make.

If some obstacle stops the arrow, or if it breaks, or if the horse is, [for example], struck in the face, or if the whip is wrested from the rider, the contestant who is handicapped in that way is not declared the loser; the contrary is so in the case where the whip is lost [or broken], or the horse is shy.

Contests other than the aforementioned are permitted, but without stakes.

While shooting arrows, one may speak in praise of himself, recite verses, pronounce his own name, or cry out; the best thing is for the shooter to declare the name of God, without saying anything else.

The contest is an indented deed (i.e., a reciprocal contract), just like hiring or renting.[23]

NOTES

For clarification of any citations, the reader is referred to the original text, Edmond Fagnan, *Le djihad ou guerre sainte selon l'école Malikite* (Algiers, 1908), English trans. Michael J. Miller.

1. This subject has been dealt with repeatedly by European authors, and I will limit myself to citing the work by Haneberg, "Das muslimische Kriegsrecht," *Bayerische Akten der Wissenschaft* 12 (1871), which consists of a commentary on the chapter from the Wikâya, with the text and a translation. For the Malikite rite, we must refer principally to

Sidi Khalil (who died in 767 H/1365–1366 AD), using the French version by Perron, a monumental work which needs to be retouched somewhat for the sake of a little more clarity. This is what I have tried to do by translating, with the help of several commentaries, the chapter dedicated to holy war by the author of the *Compendium*—a work which, ever since its appearance, has been authoritative for adherents of the Malikite rite. Thus we will be able to appreciate, based on the texts themselves, what the theory of this "holy war" entails, which is so often discussed in relation to current events [as of 1908] in Morocco. We must not overlook the fact that the Muslim jurists, whose thought is subtle and even hair-splitting, divide and subdivide the matter at hand almost to infinity, and quite often devote themselves to discussions which are scarcely more than intellectual games or intra-mural academic controversies.

Because it was meant to be learned by heart, Khalil's text is extremely dense; it could almost be compared to a series of algebraic formulas, and it becomes intelligible only with the help of commentaries. The words added in brackets come from those commentaries, and the succinct character of my translation makes the addition of these glosses indispensable for the Western reader. (Words within parentheses in the body of the text have been added by the English translator for the sake of clarity.)

2. So it is defined by Ibn 'Arafa (according to the commentary by Kharachi): "It is the Moslem's act of fighting the infidel with whom there is no treaty, for the purpose of exalting the word of Allah, or else the act of assisting in this war or of penetrating enemy territory to this end." This is the proper meaning of jihad, a word which is also used to express the following actions: combating one's passions, preaching good and dissuading from evil, the repression by leaders of forbidden acts by means of blows and chastisements (cf. the same commentary; also Ismail Hakkl's commentary on the Qur'an, etc.).

3. This expression, for lack of a more precise one, designates the duties incumbent upon the faithful as a whole; the fulfillment of these duties by some of them suffices to dispense the others from them. They are contrasted with individual or personal duties, such as prayer, fasting, etc., which are incumbent on each believer individually.

4. This new paragraph, which is unrelated to the subject of the chapter, enumerates duties of solidarity other than the jihad, which, however, are suggested by it. The comparison drawn by the text, therefore, is purely a formality, something that happens frequently in the works of the writer we are considering and of others as well.

5. Cf. Qur'an 8.16.

6. Arbitrary punishment consists in any punishment, be it a simple reprimand, left to the discretion of the imâm or the judge. It is in contrast with a punishment determined by law, which is referred to as h'add, literally "limit," i.e., a case where the judge does not have to weigh options, where his power is limited by the legal texts.

7. See the preceding note.

8. This expression and others with an analogous meaning that will be found further on ("statements," "doubt," etc.) are conventionally used by our author [i.e., Sidi Khalil in the Perron translation] to refer to the opinion of certain jurists or of certain classes of jurists.

9. This reading is certainly preferable to the reading Roûm given by Derdir and the author of the gloss of Kharachi.

10. See a few lines further on.

11. It is a question here of battles waged on the front line of two opposing armies,

following challenges issued by one side or the other, between two champions or two groups of champions. The name of Cid Campeador evokes the memory of these chivalrous contests.

12. This word mosta'min is defined in this way in Bianchi's *Dictionnaire turc*: "every foreigner who finds himself in the Ottoman Empire under the terms of treaties or of the law of nations, whether as a traveler or as a resident." The word is not used by Khalil but has been supplied by the commentators. According to its grammatical form it signifies "one who requests or solicits the amân," as Ça'ldi points out, but the term has acquired a special technical meaning.

13. That is, the h'add discussed above, by virtue of which a thief, for example, is punished by amputation.

14. On this question of the ownership of land conquered by storm, see Van Berchem, *La propriété territoriale et l'impôt foncier*; compare the commentaries on Khalil d'Abd el-Baki, MS 1178 of Algiers, 1. 41 v., and especially the one by Derdir, I, 268.

15. According to Awza'i, the founder of a legal school of thought which did not develop and about which we know little more than the name, the infidel can validly become the owner of a thing belonging to a Muslim. Malik himself shared this opinion, according to Ibn Wahb (Derdir and Desouki).

16. These rates are not fixed and represent a maximum. The taxpayer's financial situation at the time of the payment is taken into account, and no mention is made of the tax from the preceding year in the case of someone who at that time was insolvent. The payment is reckoned in dinars, or gold coins, and by dirhems, or silver coins, according to whether one is dealing with men of gold or men of silver, expressions that are found frequently and which Van Berchem (*Propriété territoriale*, p. 60) translates as "people of great or moderate wealth," a meaning that I can hardly accept. However we read in Derdir (*Commentaire*, vol. 1, p. 274, line 13: "The inhabitants of Egypt are men of gold, although silver is used in their transactions"; and the same thing is repeated by Ça'ldi in his glosses upon Aboû 'l-Hasan, *ad Risala*, vol. 1, p. 341, line 24. In Kharchi (vol. 4, p. 381, line 2 below) the men of gold are contrasted with the men of camels, which is to say that, for the peoples which make little or no use of coinage, the camel serves as a sign representing worth.

17. An allusion to the abrogation of the additional levies that are discussed further on, through obsolescence or some other reason, since the commentaries set no date.

18. According to Malik, the commentaries report the following: "'Omar ben el-Khattab had imposed, besides the head-tax in silver, additional monthly per capita contributions of two modd of grain and three kist of oil for the tributaries of Syria and Hira; for those of Egypt, of one ardeh of grain and of some quantity, unknown to me, of grease, honey, and clothing. Besides that, they all had to provide three days of hospitality to traveling Moslems. In Iraq he imposed 15 ça of dates per capita per month, besides certain garments, I do not know how many, which he would use to clothe people." The author of the gloss of Kharachi adds: "Instead of two modd, Tatâ'l says one ça, and Mawwak, two mody, a measure equivalent to 17 [or 17.5] ça. The kist is made up of three ritl or Syrian pounds, or, according to other sources, nine ritl." On these equivalences, see Perron's translation of Sidi Khalil, vol. 1, p. 561. These supplementary contributions have also been mentioned by Kremer, Culturgeschichte, vol. 1, p. 61.

But Lakhmi (died 478 H/1085–1086 AD), who is cited by Ibn 'Arala, could already say: "I do not see that people in the West today are surprised by these levies, since no violence is used in their regard" (Hattab, MS 1175 of Algiers, l. 113 v.). Derdir (died 1201 H/1786–1787 AD) says for his part: "The governors of Egypt have strengthened their influence by taking in the scribes that they need, and they have entrusted to them their own goods and wives" (vol. 1, p. 274). The commentaries, supplementing the text of this passage by Khalil, add that tributary merchants who import merchandise into a Muslim land must pay a duty of one tenth of its value.

19. Here is how Derdir puts it—an author who rarely misses an occasion to display his orthodox rigidity (Akrab el-mesalik, vol. 1, p. 205): "The infidel who has surrendered can construct or repair a religious building, whether he has stipulated this or not, upon his territory, but not in a city founded by Moslems, such as Cairo, unless, however, there is good reason to avoid a greater evil. But the rulers in Egypt, thanks to the tepidity of their faith, have authorized them to do so, and no learned man has been able to show his disapproval except in his heart or in his words, and not by force. The emirs of our era have done even more: they have exalted the infidels and have given them superiority over the Moslems. Would to heaven that something like the tenth of the tributaries were levied upon them (i.e., those Moslems)! One frequently hears the believers exclaim: How we would like to see the emirs impose the head-tax upon us, like the Christians and the Jews, and then have no more to do with us than with these infidels! But those who have mistreated others will find out what treatment they will have to undergo (Koran 26.228)."

20. The chroniclers recall on more than one occasion the sorts of harassment that the Christians and Jews were subjected to; see for example my partial translation of En-Nadjoûm ez-Zahira, p. 103; Merrakechi, *Histoire des Almohades*, p. 264 of the French translation, etc.

21. One might be led to believe that there is an allusion here to some episode from the life of the Prophet; but it seems quite clear from the commentaries, which at any rate are not very explicit on this point, that it is a simple recollection of words that had been pronounced publicly, the insulting nature of which had prompted a request for a juridical consultation or fetwa.

22. Horse-races and other military exercises, because they serve as preparation and training for the holy war, are considered to be connected with it.

23. The text Aeoll p. 1, is explained as follows: "That is to say that the contract, by the mere fact that it comes into being, becomes idzim (indissoluble), by the same title as the rental contract, in such manner that it can be dissolved only with the agreement of both parties at once."

28

THE HOLY WAR ACCORDING TO IBN HAZM OF CORDOVA

Roger Arnaldez

In the legal teachings of Ibn Hazm there is a latent contradiction that is resolved by a sort of challenge to history. The Zahirite jurist has the ideal of reconstructing literally what Muslim law was at the time of the Prophet and his Companions. He denies any possibility that the *fiqh* may have evolved: the truth of the law must have burst forth at the very beginnings of Islam. There is good reason, therefore, to question history, whether it is reported in traditions that were transmitted from one man to another, or included in the general knowledge that is handed down from one generation to the next. But once he has determined what the Prophet said or did in a given situation, once he has elucidated, in relation to those circumstances, the meaning and application of the words, actions, and silences of the Messenger of God, Ibn Hazm repudiates all the historical contexts upon which he has based his conclusions, for fear that they might limit the value of the traditional texts to particular times and places. Only a text [from the Qur'an] can particularize the value of another. Indeed, man speaks and acts only in particular situations, which can shed light on what he wanted to say and do, but which must not confine the intended meaning; otherwise no one would ever express general ideas and rules, and one could not formulate laws.

In turning to the past, therefore, Ibn Hazm is not dreaming of bringing it back to life as past history. He knows, better perhaps than many of his contemporaries, that changes take place, not to mention evolutions. He knows that the Islam of his day, which extended from Spain to the East Indies, was no longer at the same stage of development as the Islam of the Prophet and the first caliphs. He recog-

Roger Arnaldez, "La guerre sainte selon Ibn Hazm de Cordoue," in *Études d'Orientalism dediees a la memoire de Levi-Provencal* (Paris: Masionneuve and Larose, 1962), vol. 2, pp. 445–59. English translation by Michael J. Miller.

nizes this with respect to the problems of consensus within the community. What interests him about the past is a privileged moment of history at which the law eternally intended by God was revealed in universal and definitive formulations. Despite the most obvious evidence, the commandments given to the Prophet are not, in his view, relative to the Prophet's time, in such manner that one would have to adapt them to the demands of other times in order to apply them. These commandments, rather, are valid as such for all times. Now one of the most serious consequences of Hazmian Zahirism is that the general import of the judgments of the law is entirely contained within the meaning of the words and the construction of the Arabic sentences that express it. Therefore, if languages evolve—something that Ibn Hazm explicitly recognizes—it is necessary to adhere to the Arabic of the Qur'an and of the Prophet in order to understand the will of God. But there is no denying that, at a given stage of the history of a language, the possibilities for expression are always bound up with what is expressible, which in turn is closely connected with a particular civilization. This is where the contradiction appears. The exegetes who allow for a spiritual sense, which each generation explores more profoundly [approfondit] according to the demands of their own spirit, easily manage to detach the texts from their historical background. But believers in the literal sense are inevitably bound to the contingent milieu beyond which the letter of the law no longer has a precise meaning.

Consequently, whatever he may claim, Ibn Hazm, in defining everything with reference to the initial period of Islam, in seeking what the revelations signified for the Prophet and his Companions, could only perceive a body of laws that reflected the characteristics of that ancient society. How, then, should it be considered as valid for all times and all places?

To tell the truth, Ibn Hazm did not ask himself that question directly. He does, however, provide the basic elements of an answer. The law is applicable only in a place where the real situation allows it to be applied. A country that produced only rice, which is not mentioned by any authentic text, would avoid the *zakat* on agricultural commodities. When a development has made it impossible to put a regulation into practice, the regulation automatically lapses (without being revoked), since man does not have the right to modify it to suit a new form of life. Only a text can bring about an obligation.

A dangerous position, no doubt. But could Ibn Hazm foresee that human society would be transformed to the point where almost the entirety of Muslim law, understood in that way, would be inapplicable? Not very likely. Be that as it may, the inapplicability of a law renders it null and void in practice, although it retains all of its validity as law and must be put back in force as soon as circumstances permit.

As for holy war, it is clear that we do not find in Ibn Hazm's writings any attempt to spiritualize the notion. For him, the jihad remains essentially a war waged with arms, even though he is aware of a more general meaning of the term.

Only it is a war that retains the archaic characteristics of the *razzias* between the Bedouin tribes. In the texts that he cites, the word *ghazwa* [plural, *ghazawat*— military expedition, foray, raid] occurs several times. The opposition between the Dar al-Harb and the Dar al-Islam still reflects something of the instability of the boundaries between the pasturelands where rival nomadic clans grazed their flocks. The question of sharing booty is the subject of a long development. Then too, in a certain sense, the defense of the House of Islam against the infidels resembles in many aspects the defense of the urban populations or the agricultural settlements of Arabia against the pillagers from the desert. In passages that speak of frontier towns, the reference seems to be to the strongholds, like those at Medina, that protected the settled inhabitants against the nomads. It is within these narrow parameters that relations between Muslims and non-Muslims are studied. It would not be in keeping with the thought of Ibn Hazm to generalize what he says in this regard and to see in it the principles of a law capable of reg- ulating, from the Muslim point of view, the complexity of contemporary interna- tional relations. The conditions for the jihad, as Ibn Hazm sees them, are certainly not fulfilled in our days [1962], either on the military level or in the economic or political arena. But if the right conditions presented themselves in a particular spot somewhere in the world, the rules about the holy war would have to come into play immediately.

How did things stand during Ibn Hazm's lifetime? Without speaking of the Near East, we might think that in Spain the situation lent itself well enough to the jihad, with a movable frontier between the lands conquered by the Muslims and the rest of Christian territory, with annual expeditions and guerilla warfare, alter- nating with truces and agreements. Two elements, however—which no doubt always existed, even in the Prophet's time, but which have acquired a singular importance—already change the ideal schema of the holy war theory. On the one hand, the Dar al-Islam is no longer unified; there are wars between Muslims and, worse yet, some Muslims ally themselves occasionally with the infidels against their brothers in religion. On the other hand, the war takes on a more decidedly political character, and although it is still waged in the name of a religious cause, its real nature as a human enterprise clearly gains the ascendancy. But isn't it because the Muslims have modified the original purity of Islam? Of this, Ibn Hazm is most certain. This reformer is unsparing in his condemnation of any devi- ation, however slight it may be; in his opinion, the authentic religion preached by the Messenger of God must be rediscovered. Although there are some unavoid- able transformations, which Ibn Hazm easily takes in stride, other more serious changes are due to the infidelity of the Muslims, who have innovated by bor- rowing from foreign civilizations, who have been too unmindful of the rights of God and have behaved like one nation among the others, who have renounced the Arab virtues that Islam had set upon such a magnificent career, and who, by losing the interior tension of the *Umma* that placed them far above other peoples, have given weapons to their enemies. Ibn Hazm has deep-seated motives for his attachment to the Umayyad Dynasty. Despite its faults, it represents the Arab spirit, and because of that it is closer to the Prophet than all those dynasties that allowed Islam to be changed by non-Arab influences, both in the East and in the West. Zahirism leads logically to Arabism. And so we think that in this paleographic [*archaïsant*—backward looking] treatise on jihad, Ibn Hazm's essential purpose was not to define the regulations relating to the holy war, as though they were still immediately applicable, but rather to recall what ought to have been the conduct of the Muslim community, since the golden age of Muhammad, Abu Bakr and 'Umar, so as to remain worthy of its founder and to maintain the impetus that had led it to conquer half of the known world. Was he hoping that one day, thanks perhaps to his clarion call, the conditions of a genuine jihad would recur and Islam would complete its conquest of the whole earth? He says nothing about it. But we have reason to think that his sad experience with men and with politics, the lamentable result of the course of action that he had taken, left him with few illusions. At the time when he was writing the *Kitab al-Muhalla*, he had become a man who imperturbably says what ought to be, proudly refusing to take into consideration what actually is or can be. And so his legal writings in their entirety, and in particular his treatise on the jihad, can be interpreted as the implacable condemnation of men and history. So much the worse for men and for history, since ultimately it is the law—as found in the texts, as he explains it by the texts—which will judge the world.

We do not believe that we are misstating the thought of Ibn Hazm in concluding that, for him, the law can be applied only if the Muslim community is founded upon a strict obedience to God's commands, that is to say, a Zahirite obedience. In a place where there are no longer any true Muslims, there cannot be a true jihad. Consequently, the jihad supposes that the Muslims are—not only de jure but de facto—*different* from their adversaries, on a level of their own, and impervious to the slightest compromise. The holy war is regulated as a religious ritual.

Jihad is an obligation incumbent upon all Muslims. But when some of them fulfill it, drive back the enemy and bring the war (*gazwa*) to his home territory, when they defend the frontier towns, the others are relieved of this obligation. It is therefore a *fard kifaya*. Nevertheless, in the case of an emergency, every believer who has no serious impediment can be called up to fight. The Muslim in the Dar al-Harb who receives orders to fight must obey, unless he has a valid excuse. Ibn Hazm does not mean that the Muslims, even those who are in fact relieved of the obligation, should dissociate themselves from the jihad on the pretext that it is not a personal requirement in the highest degree (*fard 'ayn*). The texts that he cites are typical of this concern for keeping the believers involved. The Qur'an, in many verses, insists on this duty: Offer your help, whether you have little or much weight, wage jihad by enlisting your property and your persons. Now Ibn Hazm says that this is a "general" command, since there is no one who is not "either light or heavy." According to one hadith, "he who dies without having waged war (*wa lam yagzu*) or without having harbored the hope of doing so (*wa lam yuhaddith bihl nafsahu*), dies in a sort of hypocrisy." According to another, the Prophet declared: "No abandonment [of the cause] after victory, but jihad and steadfast resolve (*niyya*). And if you are called, come to their aid." It seems, therefore, that besides the war, strictly speaking, there is something like a permanent psychological preparedness for war. In this latent form, the jihad must not cease.

It is not permitted, however, to go to war without the permission of father and mother, unless the enemy has invaded Muslim territory. Then there is an obligation, for all who are able, to give assistance to those who are attacked, whether the parents allow it or not, unless the departure of their son would place either one or both of them in danger of perishing. A hadith confirms this regulation. Abu Tabit heard Abu'l-'Abbas say that he had heard this account from 'Abd Allah ben 'Amr: "A man went to the Prophet and asked him for permission to wage holy war. The Prophet said to him: Are your father and mother alive? Yes, the man replied. The Prophet said, it is with regard to them, therefore, that you must wage the jihad." This text is interesting because it shows the antiquity of a very broad concept of the jihad, which consists of making a fundamental commitment to obey God in everything. In the book about the Pilgrimage, Ibn Hazm cites another tradition in which the *hajj* is also described, with respect to the *'umra* [lesser pilgrimage], as jihad. The point is that every worship of God in obedience is a service (*'ibada*) comparable to armed service, which has a privileged place. War against the infidels makes the believer who loses his life therein a martyr to whom Paradise is promised. However war in itself does not bring this advantage with it; the jihad must be just, that is, it must be a true jihad [conducted] entirely along the path of God, subject to the comprehensive observance of the divine Commandments. Consequently this true jihad, in the strong sense of the word, could not exclude other duties, other jihad in the broad sense, which can take precedence (except in emergencies), such as duties toward parents. To obey the leader who calls one to the holy war, without taking into account the other requirements of the Law, is therefore not giving proof of valid obedience. To hear an order and to obey it, says one hadith, is just, as long as it does not command rebellion against God; if it does, then it should not be listened to or obeyed. 'Ali ben Abi Talib has said that there is no obedience except in doing good. By means of these traditions and others as well, Ibn Hazm, after exalting the holy war, shows that normally it cannot dispense from duties imposed by God and that it cannot be an excuse for someone who would neglect them. It is not the jihad that sanctifies a man and makes him a good Muslim, but rather only a good Muslim can conduct a true jihad. Ibn Hazm was acquainted with the brutality of men, their bellicose and covetous instincts, and he wanted to emphasize at the outset of his study that it is not enough to be a mercenary run amok in order to enter Paradise.

Then follow general rules concerning conduct in combat. It should be noted that Ibn Hazm makes no appeal here to any military virtue. He might have praised courage but doesn't say a word about it. The point is that human virtues do not count unless they are within the framework of obedience. Then, too, the emphasis is on the divine command. It is absolutely forbidden for a Muslim to flee from the infidels (*mushrik*) [associators, term for Christians of Western trinitarian theology, which associated Jesus to God, thus deifying him] or from several, even if they are very numerous. However, he has the right to retreat, provided that the purpose is to return to the attack or to rally the main body of the Muslim forces. He who merely intends to flee in turning his back on the enemy is a villain who strays from God's precepts and who must repent or else go to hell. Ibn Hazm bases this statement upon the Sura on Booty, 8.15–16.

Some claim that one man is allowed to flee from three or more enemies. They derive their argument from verse 66 of the same sura: "Now God is easing your burden; He knows that there is weakness within you. If one hundred of your men are capable of holding fast, they will conquer two hundred enemies; if there are a thousand, they will conquer two thousand enemies with the help of God; God is with those who support the cause." Ibn 'Abbas said: "Anyone who flees from two men is a fugitive; someone who flees from three is not a fugitive."

Ibn Hazm considers the hadith of Ibn 'Abbas to have little value and no authority. As for the verse [from the Qur'an], he says that it contains nothing pertinent to the claim of his adversaries, since it presents neither a text nor any indication (*dalil*) concerning the permissibility of flight from that number of enemies. It simply declares that God knows human weakness and that He lightens the burdens that He imposes, because He is merciful. With His help, 100 believers capable of supporting the effort (*sabirun*) will manage to deal with 200 adversaries. But the verse does not say that they will not conquer more of them or fewer. The method that Ibn Hazm applies here is inspired by his criticism of the rhetorical argument (*dalil al-kitab*), which supposes that every judgment connected with a specification of time, place, number, or some other factor, is no longer true apart from that specification. This leads to the belief that one is entitled to derive from the literal meaning of the text something that is not expressed, and that is an error. For example, to say that 100 will carry the day against 200 does not imply in the least that they will not carry the day against 150 or against 300. Furthermore, Ibn Hazm supports his argument from reason, as always, with a scriptural argument. Indeed, God has said: "How many times a very small band has conquered a numerous troop with God's permission!" Here there is no question of number.

Then Ibn Hazm employs irony. He questions his adversaries concerning the case of a Muslim horseman who is brave and strong, armed from head to toe, who meets three Jewish enemies, decrepit old men who are sick and unarmed, on foot or mounted on donkeys. Is he allowed to run away from them? Similarly, are a thousand elite horsemen who are well armed, noble, and experienced going to take flight when they meet a rabble consisting of three thousand enfeebled Christians on foot?

It is reported that al-Hasan said that flight from an enemy army is not numbered among the great faults (*min al-kaba'ir*), except in the particular case of the Battle of Badr. This, Ibn Hazm comments, is a specification without proof. On the contrary, according to an acceptable tradition, 'Uthman said to Ibn 'Abbas that the Sura on Booty had been one of the first to be revealed at Medina, and thus before the Battle of Badr. A hadith of the Prophet informs us, besides, that there are seven perils to avoid, among which is flight on a day of military action. This saying of the Prophet is general in scope and indisputably shows the seriousness of flight. Another account reports that he said, "O men, do not desire an encounter with the enemy. . . . But if you meet with it, hold firm, and know that Paradise is in the shadow of the swords."

But must a Muslim risk his life against forces that are too formidable? Abu Ayyub al-Ansari and Abu Musa al-As'ari do not repudiate the man who attacks alone a numerous, well-equipped army (*al-'askar al-jarrar*) and who steadfastly resists them until death. Against this, some assert the hadith, transmitted by al-Hasan, in which the Prophet says to a man who wanted to hurl himself against an enemy troop: "Do you think that you will kill them all? Be calm. If your companions arise, then arise; if they attack, then attack." But this hadith is not acceptable because it is *mursal*. On the other hand, an authentic account informs us that a man from the Prophet's entourage asked him what pleased God the most on the part of His servants. "That he should plunge into the enemy ranks without helmet or breastplate," the Messenger replied. Then the man took off his coat of mail and penetrated the enemy formations until he was killed.

Ibn Hazm, no doubt, would not go so far as to encourage martyrdom, since he, along with the texts, allows for strategic retreat. Yet, likewise in keeping with the texts, he does not forbid these acts of pure bravura that leave to God the outcome of the combat and do not hesitate to make a useless sacrifice—a reminiscence, no doubt, of the obligations of the ancient Arabs to uphold their honor. Carried over into the framework of Islam, like so many other Bedouin virtues, these obligations would exalt, among the believers, their sense of having a worth that no infidel could possibly share with them.

After the systematic rules about combat come regulations concerning acts of war. In enemy territory it is permissible to burn the produce of the land, the trees and the vineyards. One can also burn down the houses or demolish them. The Prophet set fire to the palm groves of the Banu 'l-Nadir, a Jewish tribe of Medina. And yet the Prophet knew that these palm trees would revert to the Muslims that very day or the next. Nevertheless it is reported that Abu Bakr was of a different opinion: Cut down no fruit tree and do not devastate cultivated lands, he recommended. Ibn Hazm replies that he forbade this by his own free decision, and that he had a right to do so, since the destruction of harvests is not commanded but simply permitted. The Prophet himself did not cut down the palm trees of Khaybar. All these courses of action are equally good.

In contrast, it is not permitted either to wound or to kill the animals raised by the infidels—camels, cattle, sheep, horses, chickens, pigeons, geese, or ducks—unless it be to supply food as needed. There is one exception: a pig should be killed. A war horse can also be killed. One must not drown bees or burn their hives. The Hanifites and the Malikites permit the killing of all these animals. Camels, cattle, and sheep should be killed and burned, because the infidels eat them when they find them dead (whereas Muslims eat only the meats of animals that are slaughtered ritually). Horses, mules, and donkeys, which the infidels do not eat, should simply be killed. It is evident what inspired these measures: war should bring destruction upon the enemy, and everything that is not consumed by the Muslim invader must be rendered unusable.

The response of Ibn Hazm is twofold. He speaks ironically about the division of livestock into two categories, to show that it is baseless. Since when, he asks, have Christians, Zoroastrians, and idol worshippers abstained from donkey and mule meat and limited themselves to beef and mutton? Their law permits them to eat "dead" meats, and for them no animal is forbidden. As for the Jews, they touch nothing that has been killed by a non-Jew. Therefore all of these specifications, which are not based on any text [in the Qur'an], are futile. But it is in their fundamental presuppositions that the difference between Ibn Hazm and his adversaries appears. For him, the jihad is not an ordinary war, the sole purpose of which is to destroy the enemy's power and resources. It has a higher end and must use only those methods that God wills. We find here again the idea that the holy war does not justify everything. Ibn Hazm drives this home by posing a question which carries to its logical extremes the viewpoint of the schools that he is criticizing. If you want to harm your enemies, don't you kill their women and children as well? That would be much worse for them than the loss of their livestock. It is necessary to answer that God has forbidden the massacre of children and women. He then replies: But it is likewise forbidden to kill animals if they are not to be eaten. According to one hadith, the Prophet said: "No man kills a sparrow or any more important animal in violation of their right, without God demanding of him an accounting for it. Someone asked him what their [i.e., the animals'] right was. He said: to be slaughtered ritually and eaten." According to another account, he forbade killing beasts of burden in cold blood (*sabr*^{an}; the expression *qutila sabr*^{an} is used in speaking of someone who was not killed in combat, but massacred after having fallen into the hands of the conqueror). We should add, among the other traditions cited, this warning of the Prophet: "Do not imitate the wild beasts." As on the subject of duties toward parents, we see here that the jihad does not do away with the other commandments of God. The only thing that can momentarily suspend them is urgency. But urgency has to do with the direct and immediate interest of Muslims; it is not at all concerned with strategic calculations.

As for pigs, they are to be killed. Ibn Hazm refers on this subject to a curious tradition about the return of the Messiah. 'Isa will come down from heaven, go to Jerusalem, pray the Muslim prayer behind the imam, and then he will kill the pig, shatter the cross, and destroy all the churches.

The lives of women and children must be spared, at least when they are not fighting in the ranks with the men. If they are struck down in the course of a night-time attack (*bayat*) or unintentionally in the fray, there is no crime. Apart from these two exceptions, it is permitted to kill all infidels, whether combatants or not: merchants, hired servants or common laborers, old men, peasants, bishops, priests or monks, the blind or the lame, without a single exception. Some authors cite various hadiths in favor of other exceptions: old men, monks, merchants. Ibn Hazm rejects them all. Nor does he admit that the permission to kill is limited to combatants. As a justification for his thesis, he recalls the Prophet's extermination of all the men in the Jewish tribe of Banu Qurayza, who were put to death without exception, while the women and the children were sold as slaves. As for the elderly, they enjoy no favorable treatment, as demonstrated by the account of the death of the Arab poet Durayd ben al-Simma. He was quite advanced in age, to the point where his mind was failing, he had not made *islam* [submission?] and was killed by Rabi' after the battle of Hunayn. The Prophet did not repudiate the murder: a silence that has the force of law.

What should be the qualities of the leader who conducts the holy war? It is not necessary that he be a good Muslim, provided that he orders nothing contrary to the law of God, and the believer must fight under such a leader as he would fight under the orders of the Imam. God is quite capable of strengthening Islam while making use of a libertine. The essential thing, therefore, is attaining the goal of jihad, and this goal is to destroy unbelief (*kufr*). Ibn Hazm does not conceal the fact that this inevitably involves killing infidels, destroying their dwellings and their cultivated lands, taking their women and children into captivity. No one can dispense himself from this duty on the pretext that the leader is immoral; he alone will have to render an account of it to God. But, it is clear, the enemy to be beaten is less the infidel than unbelief. What one must have in view, above and beyond the ruination of war, is "to make the *kafir* emerge from the darkness of *kufr*, to bring him into the light of Islam." Does this expression mean that for Ibn Hazm the ultimate end of the jihad is missionary and concerns the good of souls? It does not seem that that is his thought. He has in mind instead the triumph of Islam; in order that the darkness of unbelief be vanquished, it is necessary for the light of Muslim law to reach an ever growing number of men, or at least for those who resist it to disappear. The jihad serves God's interests more than those of men.

The systematic regulation of the relations between the infidels of the Dar al-Harb, the *Ahl al-kufr*, and the Muslims is as simple as can be. The infidel, practically speaking, has no rights; the Muslim has all the rights (these rights, in either case, being those defined by the law of Islam). The non-Muslim who agrees to pay tribute (*jizya*) acquires the status of a protected person (*dhimmi*), and the Muslim community recognizes that he has several rights, which it guarantees. Thus Muslims can have duties that are sacred toward non-Muslims whom they protect.

Infidels can never own as property the goods of a Muslim or of a *dhimmi*, except as the result of a valid sale, a valid gift, an inheritance from a *dhimmi*, or, in general, a transaction recognized by the Muslim religion. Booty that they take from the goods of a *dhimmi* or of a Muslim, and the slave of a Muslim who flees to their territory, remain the property of their original master, and as soon as it is possible to take them back by war, they return to their lawful owner, before or after the division of the booty of which they form a part materially, without legally constituting a share of that booty, whether or not they have been transported to the Dar al-Harb. The owner who reacquires them does not have to give any compensation for them nor pay their price. But the leader compensates the man to whose lot they had fallen when the division was made, by deducting whatever is necessary from the holdings of the community. The legal designation of these goods that are divided up with the booty, when they in fact have an owner, is that of usurped goods which one Muslim has seized by force from another Muslim. This is the teaching of Ibn Hazm, which he shares with the imam al-Safi'i and Abu Sulayman.

Among the ancient commentators there are three other teachings on this question. According to the first, no return is made: the item belongs to the one who receives it in his share when the booty is divided up. One hadith reports that 'Ali ben Abi Talib considered that Muslim property preserved in good condition by an infidel of the Dar al-Harb is counted among the goods of that infidel. Al-Hasan al-Basri rendered judgments according to this principle. Qatada relates that a *mukatab* was taken prisoner by an enemy of Islam. A Muslim bought him and consulted 'Ali on the subject. 'Ali told him: "If his master has redeemed him from captivity, this slave finds himself again under the conditions of his contract of redemption (*kitaba*),[1] but if he refuses to redeem him, he belongs to the man who has bought him." Consequently, in falling into enemy hands, the *mukatab* again becomes a simple slave belonging to a new master, with whom he has not arranged any contract to redeem himself. If this new master sells him, he belongs legally to the buyer. But if the first master buys him back, the old contract is in force again. Ibn Hazm quotes several traditions cited by those who hold this teaching: "What the enemy has preserved in good condition (*ma ahrazahu*) is Muslim booty and does not return to its first owner." And again: "What the infidels have preserved in good condition belongs to the Muslims when they succeed in taking it back, unless it is a question of a free man or of an ally" (who would have been taken prisoner and reduced to slavery by the enemies; he is not part of the booty when he is retaken by the Muslims).

According to the second teaching, if the legal owner is able to seize his property before the booty is divided, the property returns to him. But after the division, it belongs to the one to whose share it has fallen. It does not return to its first owner, even if he pays the price of it. Obviously a friendly arrangement can always be made. This teaching is interesting because it shows the importance that the Muslims attributed to the division of booty, over and above any other consideration. There is a hadith along these lines that goes back to 'Umar ben al-Hattab. If someone finds his *own* property again before the distribution of the shares, he has a greater claim than anyone else to take possession of it (*fahuwa ahaqqu bihi*); if not, he no longer has any right after the division. Note that this case concerns only his own property (*bi'aynihi*), found to be such after the victory over an enemy who has preserved it in good condition. No one can hope to be compensated, from the booty, for property that the infidels may have taken from him but which has perished or disappeared, or even that he may have found again in poor condition.

One tradition relates that a servant girl belonging to a Muslim fled to enemy territory, and then she was seized by the believers as part of the booty. Abu 'Ubayda ben al-Jarrah wrote to 'Umar in her regard. 'Umar replied that if she had not yet been put into the fifths (booty was divided up into five parts), nor assigned as part of a share, she should return to her master. "If not, let her go her way."

According to the third teaching: before the division, the property returns to its first owner. After the division, that owner has more right than anyone else to own it, on the condition that he pays the value of it. Ibn Hazm gives only the names of those who transmitted this teaching, without citing the texts.

In his critique, Ibn Hazm begins by disputing the value of the traditions upon which these three teachings are based. We are not going to insist on it. We simply mention a hadith cited by the proponents of the first view: [ma'ahraza al'adu fahuwa ja'iz]. Here Ibn Hazm attacks the *matn* itself. He says that we do not understand the meaning of *fahuwa ja'iz*. Perhaps it means that the lawful owner of property is allowed to take back the item "when he puts his hand over it" (*ida zafira bihi*). This would restrict the scope of the teaching: if, in the course of combat, a Muslim can personally take possession of property that had been stolen from him, he has the right to do so. The item does not form part of the booty—a particular slant on the subject that converges with Ibn Hazm's point of view, since for him the law of booty, as sacred as it may be, must yield to the law of personal property, which is fundamental in Islam and especially in Hazmian Zahirism.

After the critique of the traditions comes the rational critique. The author aims it initially at the third teaching, which is that of Malik. One of two things is true: either the enemy warriors lawfully own as property what they have taken from the Muslims, or else they do not have legal ownership of it. If they do not— and this is Ibn Hazm's thesis—it is necessary for the item to return to its sole true owner, and this is so in all circumstances, after the division as well as before, and without paying any price. If, on the contrary, the enemies legitimately own the item as property, the one from whom it was stolen has no recourse: he cannot have it back either before or after the division, neither by paying nor without paying, since the item then has the same status as the rest of the booty. Similar reasoning applies to the Muslim who receives this item in his share of the booty. Either he is not the owner of it, and he must give it to the one from whom it had been stolen; or else he is the owner of it, and then it is not permissible to force him to part company with it [*s'en séparer*], as the teaching maintains, in return for repayment of its price. No one can be dispossessed of something, even in return for compensation, without his consent.

Against the second teaching, Ibn Hazm is satisfied with saying that it has in its favor no proof that would lend it authority. In contrast, he goes to great lengths in criticizing the first teaching. Of the three doctrines, this is the one that contradicts itself the least. Its premise is that enemies have full possession of the goods that they have seized from the Muslims. If this premise is granted them, then their thesis will be truth itself. But can it be admitted that infidels legitimately lay hold of goods belonging to Muslims? Does God give them permission to appropriate them? Are they just or unjust when they make themselves masters of them? Are they then following the commands of God and of the Prophet, or are they deviating from them? Or is it perhaps that Muslim law does not oblige them? Won't they be in hell eternally for having strayed from it? It would quite obviously be an act of *kufr* to maintain that they act justly in such a case and that they do not come under the jurisdiction of Islam. The very important thing about these indignant reactions is that Ibn Hazm affirms therein that only Muslim law counts, even when it is a question of non-Muslims.

His conclusion is worth noting as well. Everyone in Islam agrees in recognizing that the free man who is taken prisoner by an infidel does not legitimately become his slave, and that therefore he cannot form part of the Muslims' booty. Now what difference is there, Ibn Hazm asks, between claiming to own a free believer and appropriating Muslim property? This strict parallelism between the two cases of persons and goods demonstrates the extent to which Ibn Hazm has a personalist concept of property.

In the questions that follow, the author draws out the consequences of his own teaching and applies them to all sorts of situations. We will not dwell on this material, however interesting it may be.

If some infidels arrange with a Muslim prisoner to give him back his freedom on the condition that he pays a ransom, it is not permissible for that Muslim to go back to their territory or to give them anything at all. The agreement and the oath have no validity, first because it is unjust to keep a believer prisoner, then because one must consider that there was coercion. But if there is no other way of snatching a believer from captivity in the Dar al-Harb than to pay his ransom, it is a duty to pay it, by virtue of this hadith of the Prophet: "Feed the hungry and procure liberty for the captive." Besides, it is an abomination for a Muslim to remain among the infidels, exposed to their pernicious laws and customs. It is as though he were detained among a people who conducted themselves in the manner of Lot's people [cf. Genesis 19]. Could anyone let him live among such filth?

A captive Muslim can be ransomed only with property belonging to an infidel or with a captive unbeliever. But it is forbidden to send back into the Dar al-Harb a young prisoner, still a minor, for the law of Islam stipulates that Muslims have a title to him [un droit sur lui], and that his situation is just like that of the children of Muslims, without any distinction.

Infidels have ownership of their goods as long as it is a question of goods that have never belonged to Muslims. They can therefore sell them or make gifts of them, and a Muslim can buy them or receive them. The question arises for merchants who travel in infidel territory, or for the ambassadors who are sent there and might receive gifts. But the only reason that God instituted the property rights of infidels over their goods was in view of the institution of booty for the Muslims.

When an infidel from the Dar al-Harb makes islam [submission], whether he does so in the Dar al-Harb (and remains there or comes then into the Dar al-Islam), or comes first to the House of Islam so as to become a Muslim there, all of these cases are equivalent. His goods, wherever they may be, of whatever sort they may be (provided that ownership of them is licit according to God's law), all belong to him without exception, and no one [else] has any title to them. They cannot be considered booty for Muslims. His heirs inherit them after his death. His children, if they are still young minors, are Muslims, as well as the child that his wife is still carrying in her womb. But his wife and his children who have attained majority, if they are taken prisoners, form part of the booty. He remains married to his wife and she becomes the slave of the man to whose share she is allotted.

Indeed, marriage between infidels is valid, since the Prophet recognized it. He himself was born of a marriage between infidels and could only have been born of a valid marriage. Consequently the two spouses remain married.

The thesis of Ibn Hazm is opposed in particular to that of Abu Hanifa, who introduces distinctions that are inadmissible, from the standpoint of the texts as well as from the standpoint of common sense. Here is what Abu Hanifa teaches: if this man makes islam in the Dar al-Harb and remains there until the Muslims occupy it, he remains free and all of his wealth belongs to him. No one can take it as booty. His minor children are Muslims and free. But an exception is made for his land and for the child that his wife is carrying in her womb: even though the fetus is Muslim, it forms part of the booty. If he makes islam in the Dar al-Harb and then comes into the Dar al-Islam, everything that he leaves behind in the Dar al-Harb—lands, premises, personal property, livestock—all that is fay and can be taken as booty by the Muslims. The same goes for the infant that his wife is carrying in her womb, even though it is Muslim. If he travels to the House of Islam as an infidel and there becomes a Muslim, he is free and Muslim. But all that he left behind in the Dar al-Harb—lands, premises, personal property, livestock, minor children—are considered spoils. These children and these goods do not become Muslim through his submission [conversion].

Ibn Hazm objects that this teaching is contrary to reason, since it is tantamount to favoring someone who remains in the midst of the infidels, which is as absurd as it is abominable, since it is a well established fact that one must always snatch believers from the atmosphere of the lands of *kufr*. Besides, it is contrary to the *ijma'*, since no one doubts that the Companions of the Prophet belonged to different categories: some, like Abu Bakr, 'Umar, and 'Utman, made *islam* at Mecca and then fled from that city; others left Mecca as infidels and then became Muslims, like 'Amr ben al-'Asi, who made *islam* while among the Negus, and like Abu Sufyan, who made his submission in the Prophet's army. Some made *islam* and remained in Mecca, like the entire group of women who had been deemed too weak to leave. And yet when the Prophet took possession of Mecca, all of those people regained or kept their property without exception.

Every woman who becomes Muslim while having a husband who is a *kafir* or a *dhimmi* dissolves her marriage at the very moment that she makes *islam*, even if the husband makes *islam* a twinkling of the eye after her. Once he is Muslim, he can return to her by a new marriage subsequent to her free consent. If they make *islam* together, they remain married. If the husband of a *kitabiyya* becomes Muslim, his marriage remains valid. But if his wife is not a *kitabiyya*, his marriage is dissolved at the very moment that he makes *islam*. The thesis that Ibn Hazm defends here is shared by almost all Muslim jurists. However, his formulation of it is quite peremptory, which leads him to take up the cudgels against some adversaries who are less strict. But we will not dwell upon these disputes, the complexity of which would require a separate study.

To conclude, we note the same extreme rigidity concerning the treatment of those who refuse [to convert to] Islam. Except for the People of the Book, that treatment is death, and on this point there is *ijma'*. The lives of Jews, Christians, and Zoroastrians are to be spared if they agree to pay the tribute. But Ibn Hazm specifies that the *jizya* can be accepted only from groups of people who recognize that Muhammad is God's Messenger to the Arabs and to those who make *islam*. This, he says, is the teaching of Malik: "The protected people who say that Muhammad was sent to us but not to them will not suffer any penalty. Those who say that he is not a prophet will be put to death."

These are a few of the questions treated in the *kitab al-Jihad*. The reader recognizes therein the inflexible method of the Cordovan jurist, his rigidity, his passion, his angry outbursts, his frequent indignation, his irony, his dauntlessness, which never balks from drawing a conclusion, however extreme it may be. We find here, to be sure, a very vigorous form of legal speculation. But it does not seem to be directed toward institutions. Lost in the task of reconstituting and meditating upon an eternal law, the thought of Ibn Hazm nevertheless remains on earth, where it hurls its invectives in the manner of the ancient diatribe. And indeed, is not its purpose to jolt and rouse a Muslim world that he considers to have fallen completely into religious decadence and which he seems to hope will thereby hear some anticipatory notes of what will be the trumpet at the Last Judgment—rather than to compose a serene scholarly work, or to set up a system of legislation for a society that, in its current state, inspired in him the most profound disgust?

NOTE

1. The *kitaba* is a contract whereby a slave purchases his freedom for a certain price, which is withheld from his earnings; he pledges, however, to serve his master until it has been paid in its entirety. This sort of slave has the name *mukatab*.

29

THE LAW OF WAR

Clement Huart

Among the unconditional duties imposed on the conscience of a Muslim there is one that is of capital importance for those men who are not an integral part of the Muslim *nation*, who are outside of the society made up of the followers of Islam, and who do not accept the two inseparable foundations of the Islamic faith: the oneness of God and the mission of Muhammad. That duty is jihad, holy war—not just any war, but war with a view to compelling nonbelievers to embrace their unitarian doctrines, unless they belong to the religion of Moses or that of Christ, in which case they are permitted (in return for the payment of a security tax) to retain the right of attending the ceremonies of their own cult in a land that has become Muslim through conquest. That is the theory: history teaches us how it was in practice. When was there ever a war that was not said to be a holy war? Either the war was conducted outside the limits of Muslim territory, which is indeed a holy war, since it is theoretically waged to bring the infidels into the bosom of the true faith; or else it took place on Muslim territory itself, in which case it is still a holy war, since it is a question of putting down rebellion against the supreme authority, against the man to whom have been entrusted the rights the Prophet received from God himself, against his vicar or caliph, a figure who in theory is called the imam, because his principal office is to preside over the canonical prayer of the assembled believers.

Wars of Muslims against infidels or rebels are therefore holy wars. When the Arabs invaded Syria (which was feebly guarded by the Roman Legions of the Byzantine Empire), Egypt (which by then only nominally recognized the *autocrator* of Constantinople), and Persia (which was defended with unfortunate persistence by the last of the Sassanids, the ill-fated Yezdeguerd III); when they launched raids into Turkestan and the region of the Indus; when they conquered North Africa and brought down the kingdom of the Goths in Spain; when they established a foothold in Septimania and from there sent out daring military expeditions even into the Loire and Rhone valleys; when, later on, the Turkish Seljuks,

---

Clement Huart, "Le droit de la guerre,"[1] *Revue du monde musulman* 2 (1907): 331–46. English translation by Michael J. Miller.

infiltrating the high plateaus of Asia Minor, founded there a Muslim state that battled the remnants of the Greek Empire; when the Turkish Ottomans after them
seized control of the Balkan Peninsula, then Constantinople and Hungary and
were about to lay siege to Vienna; when they tried in vain to retake Egypt from
General Bonaparte; when the pirates of the Barbary States conducted *razzias*, not
only on the high seas, but also in the cities on the shores of the Mediterranean;
when Abd-el-Kader incited against us [i.e., early to mid-nineteenth-century
Frenchmen] the peoples of Algeria, and Morocco, in a fruitless enterprise—it is
always a holy war. Having been victims of it [jihad] ourselves, we are pointing
out a permanent historic force, which is ceaselessly renewed down through the
generations, independent of race, color, climate, and all external circumstances,
never beaten, ever being reborn. This force is the deeply held conviction, rooted
in the soul of every Muslim without exception, that he was created to fight *on the
path of God*, and that at the call of the supreme authority he *must* get up and go,
not reluctantly but joyfully, so that the word of God might have the final word; so
that, according to the Qur'anic expression, it might always be the highest.

The Muslim jurists explain to us this state of soul with perfect clarity. Holy
war is a categorical requirement, pure and simple, apart from any restrictive condition, such as, for example, the time in which it can be fulfilled or the need for
an act of aggression [on the enemy's part] to provide a [suitable] occasion. It is a
law of God, which is part of the worship that must be rendered to him, since the
doctors [of the law] classify in the category of the *'ibadat* or acts of adoration. The
text of the Qur'an is explicit. It is true that the revelation of this took place only
gradually. Muhammad received first the order to proclaim what he had been commanded and to turn away from the infidels (15.94), then to debate with them in
the most persuasive manner, inviting them to follow the right path (16.126); afterward, the believers were ordered to fight if someone attacked them (2.87), at first
on the condition that it not be during the four sacred months, then without conditions of any sort; and this last-mentioned text (2.245) has governed the matter ever
since, corroborated by a tradition of the Prophet that proclaims that the holy war
will go on until the [final] resurrection.

Later, upon reflection, the Muslim casuists had scruples, and they adopted
an explanation that is found in the specialized treatises. War is evil in itself,
because it involves two consequences that are undoubtedly evil: the destruction
of the human body and the devastation of entire provinces. The human body is
the work of God, who fashioned it himself with clay taken from the earth; the
country inhabited by man, and which he needs for his food, was granted to him
by divine providence. To deprive man of life and the means of sustaining it is to
go against the will of God, to incur his reprobation and the malediction of his
Prophet. War is therefore an evil, and the worst of evils; how, then, did it become
a good thing and, as such, something incumbent on men? The answer is: in light
of its purpose. Since this purpose is the exaltation of the true faith and the repres-

sion of the infidels' iniquity (since true equity exists, theoretically, only in Muslim society), it is understood that holy war is a necessary evil, as long as there will be on earth minds which will not surrender to the evidence or to persuasion. And so the casuists ended up classifying holy war among the *accidental* acts of piety, and they ranked it after faith, prayer, fasting, and pilgrimage, which are *essentially* acts of piety.

Such is the theory of the theologians, but the common people do not go so far to fetch their interpretation. In reality, the Muslim places holy war on the same footing as the other primordial duties of his religion. He is trained to do so by the custom of bloody sacrifices, consummated by his own hand at certain times of the year. The fanaticism that has its foundations in these deep strata, in that shadowy underworld of consciousness that [the nineteenth-century French philosopher] Taine has spoken of, is stronger than all the fine arguments of the doctors. Finally there is a powerful enticement—the lure of gain—that has always made the Muslim states capable of finding more men than they needed to serve their ambitions. The booty seized in war has its legal function in Muslim society. This powerful motive of self-interest is the one that has stirred up entire populations, even at the beginning, when the faith was all-powerful, and especially later on, when men no longer fought to merit a paradise full of pleasures by dying with their weapons in hand. In the Muslim states and among the Muslim peoples, therefore, this incentive plays a powerful sociological role that deserves close study.

I

Originally Muslims formed a close-knit association, based on their common religion and a community of material interests. The purpose of this association was the propagation of Islam. The method employed was conquest. Each member of the community received his share of the benefits granted by God, that is to say, gained by conquest. From this principle are derived two facts of prime importance with respect to the goods acquired by this means:

1. The immediate division, pursuant to the law of war, of the goods of every kind that are obtained in armed conflict, among those who took part in the battle; these goods make up the booty (*ghanima*);

2. The right of the entire community to the goods acquired by a peace treaty, whether subsequent to a battle or after a voluntary surrender.

In these terms Max van Berchem[2] has provided an excellent formulation of the principles that govern the matter. We will concern ourselves here only with the goods that make up the first category, the booty, which is the one kind of goods that can mobilize individual self-interest; for it is quite clear that no one will find motives for enriching the community as a whole that are as strong as the incentives to increase one's own fortune.

Everything that belongs to the defeated party—women, children, personal property, and real estate—becomes the property of the victorious party: It is understood that all of the individual booty, without exception, is subject to a proportional contribution to the mass of the booty; first, one-fifth of this total is set aside, which is God's share, as determined by two precise texts from the Qu'ran (59.7, and later on 7.42); this share belonging to God, which the Prophet and then his vicar are to administer, remains undivided and constitutes a fund for the support of the Prophet's relatives, orphans, the poor, and travelers. Furthermore, it is absolutely forbidden to object to the manner in which these revenues are divided: "Accept what the Prophet gives you, and claim nothing further," says the sacred text. Nothing must be concealed and withheld from the mass; it is forbidden for any combatant to take possession of any item of personal property before the division and the specific designation that makes him the legitimate owner of the share granted to him by the higher authority; at the most, it is permissible to set aside in advance some food and what is required to feed the combatant's mount [e.g., horse or donkey], according to the principle of necessity.

There is, however, a category of items than cannot be part of the booty: things which Muslims are forbidden to own, such as pork, which *must* be destroyed, and wine, which *may* be turned into vinegar.

Before proceeding to the division [of the booty], it is required to set aside a certain amount for common expenses, which must be paid off by the mass; the only question that arises is whether these common expenses must be deducted from the mass before it is reduced by 20 percent by the setting aside of the fifth, or after the reduction of the mass to four-fifths of the total. The second theory has in its favor the letter of the Qur'anic text; the first, nevertheless, has been adopted by most of the jurisconsults [experts in the law]. What are these common expenses? The individual rewards promised by the army leader for an objective that is generally useful, for instance, for information about ways of gaining access to a place; the separate assignment in advance, to those who have killed enemy soldiers, of the clothing and arms of those enemies, but only if this condition was stipulated before the battle; necessary expenses for transporting and guarding the booty, and the salary for the guards and the escorts; a small bonus—at any rate, less than the share of a combatant—for the women, the slaves, and the infidels who have taken part in the battle with the authorization of the commander in chief or of his delegate.

After the fifth has been set aside, the remaining four-fifths are divided among the combatants and all persons of the male sex who were present at the battle, even if they did not participate, such as underage children and auxiliary forces who arrived with the intention of coming to the aid of the Muslims, provided that those in the first case are born and those in the second case met up with the other troops at latest during the interval between the pillage and the division.

The foot soldier has the right to one share of the booty, the horseman to two shares, if he has only one horse, but to four shares, if he has two or more horses. Grouped under the category of foot soldier are the infantryman who is mounted on a camel, a donkey, or a mule, and the horseman who rides a horse that is worn out, hackneyed, or too young; the sailor is classified as a horseman with two shares.

The division of the booty must be made on the battlefield; one should avoid postponing it except out of absolute necessity.

Slaves make up the most important part of this booty. Not too long ago several expeditions crossed Amoû-Deryâ, that is, the southern frontier of the steppes, and ravaged the eastern regions of Persia in order to procure slaves; other campaigns were launched into the very heart of unexplored Africa, setting fire to the inhabited areas and massacring the peaceful animist [*fétichistes*] populations that lived there. The rule of law is explicit: "It is permissible to reduce to slavery any infidel belonging to a nation with which the Muslim community is at war, except for Jews and Christians, who are allowed to surrender and who will declare themselves tributaries; but, if they violate [the terms of] the surrender, they are to be classified as enemies of the community and can be reduced to servitude." The status of slave is presumed until the contrary is proved; anyone who declares himself to be a slave will be believed on his word, if it cannot be determined that he is a freeman. This regulation applies to every child found in enemy territory.

Conversion to Islam does not alter that status, since it is legal to own Muslim slaves. One can be discharged only by emancipation (or "manumission"), of which there are several kinds, enumerated in the special treatises; to examine this question is beyond the scope of this article.

In former times, regular conquest procured real estate properties for the Muslim community, while the plundering of personal property enriched the soldiers of the caliphs. For many centuries the pursuit of slaves maintained the fighting spirit of the Muslims and was the motive for unceasing expeditions beyond their frontiers: the raids of the Turkish *aqyndjis* into Hungary and the Friuli region, the Mediterranean cruises of the galleys from the Barbary States. After the battle of Isly, when the French army seized in the Moroccan camp those iron collars which are preserved today in the Artillery Museum, the artifacts that they confiscated were not so much restraints prepared for eventual prisoners of war as they were shackles intended for future slaves.

II

The theorists of Muslim law have codified the rights and duties of commanders in chief. The generalissimo, who is vested with full powers by delegation from the supreme authority of the nation (the caliph of imam), is bound by seven obligations towards his troops: the first is to maintain, on the march, a moderate speed and to gauge the pace according to that of the poorest marcher (which recalls the old naval tactic from the days of sailing ships, whereby one was obliged by the very nature of things to set the speed according to that of the worst sailing vessel, so as not to allow a gap to form in the naval line through which the enemy could slip through easily). In order to explain this bad strategy, commentators invoke humanitarian reasons based on some of the Prophet's hadiths. The weakest soldier must be able to follow along, and the strongest one must not exhaust his strength. The leader's solicitude extends not only to the men, but even to the animals that they ride. "The man on a bad mount leads the army," said Muhammad, formulating in a concise proverb the maritime rule that I just mentioned.

The general should inspect the horses, both the mounts and the beasts of burden; test their toughness and staying power rather than their height and weight; he must categorically reject horses that are sickly, worn out by age, or raw boned; as for the beasts of burden, he will make sure that they are not loaded with more than they can carry, less out of compassion or pity than because animals in poor condition would contribute to [military] inferiority. He is responsible for appointing officers for the various categories of soldiers that he has under his command, and for supervising the disbursement of their pay. In the days of the Abbassid caliphs, according to Mâwardi, the army consisted of (1) regular soldiers who were enrolled in the administration's registers and paid by the treasury out of the revenues from the head tax and the land tax upon the tributaries (*kharadj*), and (2) volunteers who were not obliged to perform any military duties, a group which was made up either of Bedouins or of the settled inhabitants of towns and villages who spontaneously joined in when the holy war was proclaimed; those in the latter group [i.e., the volunteers] were recompensed from the alms-tithe that was paid into the treasury by Muslims only.

The institution of a rallying cry and the close supervision of the army by means of officers which he himself has selected, so as to expel those who incite others to defect, spread fear, or spy on behalf of the enemy, are duties of the army general upon which there is no need to elaborate. Yet it is interesting to note that the seventh duty of the commander is to avoid showing partiality to his relatives—a condemnation of nepotism that probably is entirely Platonic [theoretical]—and also to avoid favoring someone who shares his opinion or follows his teaching, to the prejudice of a capable soldier who might not have joined forces with him or who may have held a different opinion. These rules are very wise, but surely they were never followed.

What are the rights of the commander in chief with regard to the enemy, in the case of a holy war? We must make distinctions. There are two sorts of infidels, those who have received the invitation to embrace Islam and have refused it and prove to be recalcitrant, and those who have not heard of this invitation. Against the first sort, everything is permissible: the general is at liberty to fight them "in the manner that he finds most advantageous for the believers and the most harmful for the infidels," for instance, by devastating the enemy territory, putting it to the sword, and setting fire to it in surprise raids by night and day,[3] or else in pitched battle. No limit is set thereby to the destruction: state property, the property of individuals, the lives of city dwellers (there are none in the Asiatic states, but there were in the Middle Ages, in many cities that were organized on the Roman model), everything is at the mercy of the conqueror, who without any previous declaration of war can invade the land of peaceful populations which are guilty of preferring their old beliefs to the new religion that is being preached. Observing the principle that a war should be declared in advance is recommended only if the populations about to be attacked have not yet been challenged to accept Islam; according to the imam Al-Shafi'i, one should preach Islam to them, but if they refuse to be convinced, they are the ones who place themselves in the position of the first sort of enemies, that is to say, they run the risk of seeing their territory attacked in surprise raids, their properties burned, and their people slaughtered, on no other grounds [sans autre sommation] than the summons to embrace Islam. The imam Malik distinguishes between the infidels whose land is near Muslim states, whom he considers to be sufficiently informed by preaching, and those whose land is distant; the latter must be summoned before the attack, because there is doubt as to whether they have sufficient acquaintance with the preaching. Abu-Hanifa, following the example given by the Prophet himself, finds it praiseworthy to summon [the enemy] in advance in all cases.

A prisoner of war cannot imagine that he has any hope of saving his life, because it is permissible to kill able-bodied infidels who fall into the power of the Muslims, whether these infidels are actually combatants or not. This is a general rule, and it can be said that it dominates the history of Muslim wars. The only exceptions are for women, children, free servants and slaves; if they fight, they can be killed as long as they confront [the Muslim forces], but not if they turn their backs to flee. As for old men and the monks of the infidel peoples, there is a controversy: some group them in the category of women and children and admit that one can kill them only if they participate in the battle; others teach that it is licit to put them to death, even if they do not fight, because of the opinions, harmful to the true believers, that they would be capable of imparting to their coreligionists.

In matters of strategy and tactics, the general has several additional duties toward his own army: Mawardi counts ten of them and enumerates them as follows: the general must avoid ambushes and see to it that the troops are well guarded; choose favorable terrain for the battle; procure provisions of food and fodder; obtain information about enemy positions and strive to discern its movements; deploy his army in battle array and send reinforcements as needed to the point where the enemy is attacking; give speeches designed to arouse a fighting spirit in his soldiers, by convincing them that the enemy that they are confronting is insubstantial, by recalling their religious obligations, the rewards of the next life and those which are to be expected more immediately from the booty; [he must also] hold a council of war concerning the difficulties that arise; see to it that the precepts of the religious law are obeyed; and prevent his soldiers from becoming involved in commerce or agriculture, so that they will not be distracted from their military duty.

What is this military duty? To hold the line against the enemy and not to take flight in the face of forces that outnumber them two-to-one (it is admitted that the soldiers can flee when they are more heavily outnumbered); to have as one's intention the triumph of religion (for if a soldier were to think only of the booty, he would be deprived of the merits connected with the holy war); to bring back intact to the common mass the booty that falls into his hands, without taking anything from it, since legally it is only a deposit in trust; and not to betray the rights of God, which are superior to all others, by showing weakness toward any relatives or friends that he may have in the ranks of the infidels.

III

One should not think that, once a holy war has been started, it is possible to conduct it on the cheap and be content with a modicum of success, which could be merely superficial. The Qur'an (3.200) demands perseverance, endurance, and steadfastness. As interpreted by Zéïd ben Aslam, an exegete from Medina, these words refer to the holy war and apply exclusively to it. Now the Medina school echoes a tradition going back to the Ansars, both in [Qur'anic] interpretation and jurisprudence, and it represents more faithfully than the rival schools the true thinking of the Prophet's companions and, consequently, is more likely to reflect the Prophet's real ideas. El-Hasan of Bassora, whose mystical tendencies are well known, understands these words to refer only to endurance and steadfastness in submitting to God, in the way of God; Mohammed ben Ka'b, who was from Koufa, understands the verse in almost the same way and sees it as advice concerning a merely passive moral stance. Mâwerdi adopts the opinion of the Medina school.

If holy war is to be waged with endurance and perseverance, then when is it over? If it is to be conducted with unflagging energy, even against protracted resistance (for the believer must never turn his back on the enemy, as long as he has any strength remaining), then when does it stop? The war can end in four ways: by the conversion of the enemy to Islam, by the total conquest of the enemy country, by a peace agreement, or by a truce. The first of these solutions is unquestionably the most favorable. Having become Muslims, the enemies remain in possession of their lands and their goods; the Islamic laws can be applied to them, they have become the brethren of their conquerors and are treated as such by them. But if the enemies refuse to join the victorious religion, then their women and children are to be led off into slavery, their belongings are taken as booty, and the men who are not kept as prisoners (destined to be sold as slaves) are put to death, unless they are set free in return for the payment of a ransom, or exchanged for other prisoners, or else set free pure and simple; but it must be noted that Al-Shafi'i is the only commentator to suggest the last two alternatives, and that Abu Hanifa, Malik, and Ibn-Hanbal, or at least their disciples, allow only for death or slavery.

Peace can be granted to the enemy in return for payment of a sum of money, which can be handed over once and for all (in which case the safeguard, the *aman*, is valid only for the campaign in progress), or paid annually, thus constituting a perpetual tribute in return for a safeguard that is likewise perpetual; the agreement is broken by the interruption of the regular payment. If a peace agreement is made stipulating a tribute, then it is no more than a truce, the duration of which shall not exceed ten years; this derogates [detracts] from the principle of eternal struggle against the infidel, but it can be allowed in cases of necessity; otherwise there can be only an armistice, a delay of not more than four months.

IV

How is the war to be conducted? Is it permissible to destroy the enemy's livelihood, for instance, vineyards or palm groves? Yes, as soon as the general sees this as a way of weakening the enemy and forcing him to come to terms; no, if he sees no advantage to be gained from it, because that would be needless destruction. The Prophet himself had the grapevines belonging to the inhabitants of Tâïf cut down, which was decisive in bringing them around to adhere to the new doctrines; he also had his men cut down the beautiful date plantations the Jewish tribe of the Banu-Nadîr owned on the plain of Medina, and which yielded a yellow, transparent date, with the seed visible through the pulp; the Muslims themselves carried out these orders reluctantly; and so it became necessary for a verse from the Qur'an (59.5) to justify the Prophet's decision that he was obliged to take such a terrible course of action in order to subdue his adversaries.

As a way of compelling the enemy, one can also cut off the waterways that supply the towns and fortresses, even if women and children are in them; this method is regarded as an excellent one of bringing about either an armed victory or a surrender.

V

Aside from the holy war strictly so-called, the commentators recognize three additional categories of war: against apostates, against schismatics, and against rebels. This distinction, which was of capital importance during the first centuries of the Hegira, is no longer applicable at the present time. From our [contemporary] perspective, the war against the rebels is, instead, an application of the penal code, and the general in charge of conducting hostilities is vested with the power to punish according to the degree of the fault, which actually sets him up as a judge. Rebels are considered as highway robbers and are treated as such.

The war against the infidels is, on the contrary, a contemporary issue, in all places where Europe is in contact with Muslim populations, whether they are reduced to the status of subjects, or still form neighboring states, be they independent or colonial dependencies [vassaux]. By subjecting themselves to a [civil] authority with a different religion from theirs, the Muslims have only yielded to force; at the slightest pretext, at the random call of a convinced preacher, they will arise, take up arms, and put the laws of the holy war into practice. The international conventions that have limited the exercise of the right to wage war have no influence over the Muslim soul, to which pacifism is and always will be foreign. The state of peace has been imposed on it by force; the Muslim soul tolerates it but does not recognize it, and cannot recognize it as long as there are unbelievers on earth to convert. If that [civil] authority should weaken, as a result of external disasters or a weakening of the will in conducting internal affairs, the imperious duty awakens, acts upon the conscience of the believer and drives him to troublesome extremes of violence. What does it matter if he is not the stronger one? He has at least carried out his duty, and if he must die, he dies content.

*   *   *

Is there any way of preventing the explosion of such a deep-rooted and powerful sentiment? I think so. Our friends in the Muslim press can perform a great service for the cause of civilization. The believer [in Islam] could not possibly consider those who do not profess the same faith as brethren, but one can appeal to a sense of solidarity, firmly based on the instinct for self-preservation. Of course, it is in the interest of the Muslim peoples to welcome those who, out of pure altruism [dévouement], or in order to make a living, come to offer them what they themselves do not yet have: the inventions of modern mechanics, the benefits of medicine and surgery, the powerful means of economic progress provided by the accumulation of capital, scientific methods of exploiting natural resources, which alone are capable of obtaining for them a bit of well-being and tranquility. The hatred every uncivilized person feels for all that is strange and new must disappear and make room for better sentiments. Schools can only provide instruction; the moral progress that I am speaking about must come about through the diffusion of the press, of course, on the condition that journalists understand their educational duty instead of limiting themselves to reflecting the passions of their readers. One could not expect less of a host of fair-minded individuals [une foule *de bons esprits*], who will ask for nothing better than to contribute to a paramount peacemaking effort: the education of the Muslim mind.

NOTES

1. *El-Ahkâm es-Soulthânîya*, a treatise on Muslim public law, by Aboul-Hassan el-Mâwardî, trans. Count Léon Ostrorog, vol. 2, part 1 (Paris: Leroux, 1906); El-Boukhârî, *Sahîh, livre LVI: les Traditions islamiques*, trans. Houdas and Marçais, vol. 2, pp. 280–379.

2. Max van Berchem, *La Propriété territoriale et l'Impôt foncier sous les premiers califes* (Geneva: Thesis of Leipzig, 1886), p. 8.

3. Mâwardî, trsl. Ostrorog, vol. 2, p. 16.

30

JIHAD

W. R. W. Gardner

The question of jihad is one which has exercised to no small extent the minds of many Moslems, in Egypt at least, since the outbreak of the Italo-Turkish war, and not a few have felt it to be their duty, in spite of the enforced neutrality of Egypt, to proceed to the seat of war, and there fight "in the way of God" against what they naturally regard as an unprovoked and unwarrantable attack on a Moslem country; while those who cannot go to Tripoli have subscribed freely for the support of the army, or by their writings and manifest sympathy have done much to encourage their brethren in the faith who are on active service.

Sheikh Muhammad Reshéd Ridá, wrote an article in the January issue of *El Manár*, in which he claimed that Christians have completely misunderstood the word jihad, and do not intend, when they use the word, the same thing as is intended by Moslems when they employ it. Jihad, he pointed out, is etymologically connected with a root which expresses simply the doing of anything with energy and wholeheartedness. It implies strenuous exertion and endeavour in the carrying out of any action. And he denied that the word jihad refers primarily to war or warlike action. Jihad, he further claimed, when employed by Mohammedan writers, expresses very often moral and ethical endeavour alone, and corresponds very much with the meaning of the Apostle Paul when he exhorts those to whom he is writing to fight the good fight of faith. All the endeavour of a Moslem to fulfill the duties of his religion with wholehearted devotion is jihad; and that part of his endeavour which has to deal with the fight against the world, the flesh, and the devil, is in special jihad. This, indeed, is the greater jihad, while it is to the lesser jihad (actual warfare) that non-Mohammedan writers and speakers have limited their use of the word. Even in this limited use of the word, however, he claimed that non-Mohammedan writers have erred. For even this lesser jihad does not mean war for the propagation of the Faith, but war for the support of the Faith when that Faith is attacked. He then went on to state that there is nothing in the teaching of the Koran, or in that of the Moslem doctors, to support the view which is held by many Westerners that jihad is war against non-

W. R. W. Gardner, "Jihad," *Moslem World* 2 (1912): 347–57.

Moslems merely because they are non-Moslems. And, further, he claimed that in the case of war between Moslems and non-Moslems, the teaching of the Koran and the practice of Moslems has been to show consideration and kindness to the non-combatants and to those who have been taken prisoners. Instances to the contrary he would explain as being due to disregard of the clear injunctions of the Koran, and as arising from the fact that in war the passions of men are so aroused that they often break all bounds and act with horrible cruelty. But he desired it to be understood that such actions are not commended and approved by the majority of Moslems, and are quite contrary to the spirit of the teaching of the Koran, as to the methods to be employed in war and the manner in which the enemy is to be treated.

There is undoubtedly a feeling, if not a belief, among many Westerners that a Moslem regards it as a duty binding on him in accordance with the literal command of the Koran, to kill any and every unbeliever whom he may meet when once jihad has been proclaimed. Sheikh Ridá acknowledges that this conception of the duty of a Moslem during jihad may have been in the past, and may even now be that which is common among the ignorant or less educated Moslems, but he says that much of this feeling has been the result of mixing with foreigners (non-Moslems), who have had a mistaken idea of what Moslems mean by jihad, and that this mistaken idea of these non-Moslems has crept into Moslem minds, and has thus given apparent support to the belief that this is really a Mohammedan conception of one's duty in jihad.

Let us note here that it is because this conception of the duty of a "believer" in time of jihad is, as a matter of fact, the common belief of the ignorant Moslems (as the Sheikh admits, and for practical purposes it matters not how it arose), and because the ignorant Moslems form the greater part of the population in any Mohammedan land, that the non-Moslem subjects and residents in any land under Moslem rule have come to fear the word "jihad," and appeal to the more enlightened Moslems to be careful in their use of it. For they know that, however it may be used by educated writers, the common people understand by it, attack on non-Moslems, and believe that it is their duty to destroy as many as possible of these unbelievers. Further, they know well how easy it is for an ignorant mob to get out of hand, especially when, rightly or wrongly, it believes that any action which has as its object the glory of God and the better establishment of the true religion, would be looked upon by those in authority with a lenient eye, if not with actual sympathy.

Much that the learned Sheikh claims may be conceded. It is true that the word, jihad, is employed in the Koran and by Moslem writers with a double meaning. There are passages in which it refers to the strenuous exertion or endeavour of the believer to fight the good fight of faith, especially as regards the conquest of himself and his passions, and the fulfilment of all his ceremonial obligations which undoubtedly involves a not inconsiderable struggle with carelessness, indifference, and what may be called the natural disinclination of mankind in general to do more than is absolutely necessary in religious matters (e.g., 29.5, 31.14, 29.69, 5.59). It is also more than possible that Sheikh Ridá, is right in claiming that the verse, "When ye encounter the unbelievers, strike off their heads, until ye have made a great slaughter among them; and bind them in bands; and either give them a free discussion afterwards, or exact a ransom; until the war shall have laid down its arms" (47.4), and similar verses, do not refer to the attitude to be adopted by Moslems towards non-Moslems in general during war, but are simply directions as to how the actual fighting is to be carried on. According to this interpretation of the verse (and similar verses), the injunction to kill the unbelievers refers solely to actual battle, and means simply that the attack is to be carried out with energy, and slaughter of the opposing enemy. It corresponds to the modern dictum that an attack must be pressed home, and a victory followed up, so that the advantage gained may not be lost. The fleeing enemy must be pursued till all opposition ceases. Let us even concede that the Sheikh may be right in claiming that the Koran teaches not merely moderation but humanity in the treatment of the wounded and the non-combatants, especially the aged, and defenceless women and children.

Yet however interesting all this may be, it is rather away from the point at issue. For the question of what jihad is cannot be settled by reference alone to the etymology of the word jihad. The Koran plainly teaches in many passages, notwithstanding the claims put forward by Maulavi Chirágh 'Ali,[1] the duty of fighting for the Faith or "in the way of God," by using the word qátala, and El Zamakhshary, commenting on 2.186, 7, says, "Fighting in the way of God is jihad for the glorifying of his word and the strengthening of the Religion." And whatever may be the etymological meaning of the word jihad, there can be no gainsaying the fact that it is sometimes used in the Koran in the sense of warlike actions, a warfare for the sake of the Faith. And when one asks what the teaching of Mohammedanism is concerning jihad, the word is employed in this latter sense. In fact, when we ask the questions, What is jihad? and what are the duties of the Moslem with regard to jihad? The real point of the question is, What does the Koran mean when it teaches, and what do Moslem doctors mean when they teach that the taking up of arms on behalf of the Faith is the duty of every Moslem unless circumstances prevent him? And, further, is this war necessarily one of defence alone, or is it for the establishment and propagation of Islam?

Sheikh Ridá claims that Islam knows nothing of religious wars, and by this he means wars carried on for the propagation of the Faith, or for the establishment of certain religious principles. He admits, however, as all Mohammedans must who do not absolutely throw over the teachings of the Koran or explain them away more or less plausibly, as does Maulavi Chirágh 'Ali, that it is the absolute duty of Moslems to fight in defence of the faith when it is attacked. With regard, then, to the question, what is jihad? he would say, jihad is the taking up of arms in defence of Islam when an attack is made on it, and jihad is lawful only when such an attack is made. We see, then, that the question, When is jihad lawful? thus turns on the point of what constitutes an attack on Islam.

Dr. Muhammad Badr, an eager exponent of the New Islam, takes up an extreme position with regard to jihad. He would make the individual believer absolute judge of what constitutes an attack on Islam, and denies that an attack, however unprovoked, which has as its object only the infringement of the territorial rights of a Mohammedan power, can be regarded as an attack on Islam. He writes, "If the Sultan or Khalif call on believers to defend the Faith, the men called on are judges of the righteousness of the command, whether it is to the defence of Islam they are called, or to the help of the Sultan's special territory. . . . A 'Holy War' (jihad) could only be proclaimed against an enemy who had obviously determined on the extermination of Islam. The infringements of territorial rights, even to the extent of unmistakable aggressions and injuries, does not enter into the sphere of the Khalif's power."[2] In writing thus, Dr. Badr, however much we may sympathize with his position and hope that it will ultimately be recognized as the only possible position which can be taken up by Mohammedans if they desire to be free from the imputation of fanaticism, is, we fear, far ahead of the general Mohammedan opinion at the present day. He appears to believe that because with his European education he has come to distinguish between religions and political or social questions, others of his fellow-believers do the same. He has apparently forgotten, when he penned these lines, what he acknowledges elsewhere, that "Islam was not only a religion, but a system wherein a highly complex code of laws regulated the daily life of the believers. These laws are remarkably framed to. meet the eventualities of ordinary life. They are decidedly the work of a far-sighted teacher, to say the least. Their divine inspiration-is claimed."[3]

If Dr. Badr's position were generally acknowledged by Mohammedans, there could be no question about the lawfulness or unlawfulness of jihad against Italy. Unless it could be proved that Italy intended to exterminate Islam, jihad would be unlawful. Few Mohammedans, however, at the present day, will agree with Dr. Badr. In the concrete case before us, Italy has attacked a Mohammedan power, and while the Italian Government has issued a proclamation stating that the religion and the religious customs and practices of the inhabitants of the country attacked will not, in any way, be interfered with, all Mohammedan writers insist that the war against Italy is jihad—a Holy War in defence of the Faith. Sheikh Ridá maintains, as we saw, that jihad is defensive—a war in defence of Islam, and so, to show that the present war is true jihad, he asserts, in spite of the statement of the Italian Government referred to above, that Islam is attacked. His words are, "These Italians desire to do away with the laws of the Koran in this land, and to bring the Moslems into subjection to their own (Italian) laws, to destroy their power. . . ."[4]

The only ground on which such a statement can be made with even the slightest claim to truth is, that it is impossible to distinguish between religious and social laws and customs. And from the point of view of orthodox Mohammedan belief, he is right. But he ought to acknowledge that just because this is so, jihad is religious war; for a religious war does not mean simply a war for the propagation of any certain religion, but a war, for the support of which, religious motives are used and urged. It is, then, the impossibility on the part of orthodox Mohammedans to distinguish between religious and political in social questions, which makes it difficult for them to regard any war in which Mohammedan power is engaged as other than jihad. In other words, any war between Moslems and non-Moslems, in which the non-Moslems are the aggressors, must inevitably become a Holy War, a jihad, whether it actually be proclaimed as such or not: for anything which interferes with the social and civil institutions and customs of Islam is an attack on Islam itself, and therefore war in defence of these is jihad. Church and State in Islam are indissolubly one.

In the present war between Italy and Turkey, the non-Moslem subjects of the Turkish Empire, almost without exception, sympathize with Turkey, and support the Ottoman cause. Many of them are filled with indignation at the action of Italy in making war on what was considered the defenceless province of a tottering empire. But, on the part of the Moslem subjects of Turkey, while the unwarrantableness of the attack has aroused equal indignation, it is the religious feeling that Islam is attacked, which forms the main ground of their support of the Ottoman cause. They feel that not merely has their country been attacked, but that the Faith has been insulted and challenged, if not threatened, that a Moslem land has been attacked by a non-Moslem power.

We do not here enter into the academic question of whether jihad ought to be proclaimed by a properly constituted authority. This side of the question is purely theoretical. In the case of the present war between Italy and Turkey, the question is never asked, Has jihad been lawfully proclaimed or not? Orthodox Mohammedans universally regard the war as jihad; it is so described in their newspapers; those who take part in it are Mujahidin: every one killed in it is a Shahid and the proclamation or letter of Sidi Ahmed El Sennusi to the inhabitants of Tripoli is not the proclamation of a jihad, but an appeal to those who are fighting, to realize that the war is a jihad, and to quit them like good and true Moslems for the glory of God and the honour of the Faith. That the war is jihad he takes for granted.

We must now pass to consider another point. So far we have seen that, among the more recent Moslem apologists, jihad is regarded as war in defence of Islam, but we have been forced to the conclusion that any war in which a non-Moslem power is the aggressor must inevitably be regarded by Moslems as involving on their part jihad. The point we have now to consider is, what is the teaching of Mohammedanism as to wars of aggression. Is a war for the extension of Islamic rule also jihad?

In considering this point, not much light is to be got from the writings of the more recent Moslem authors, such as those we have quoted. They simply deny that it is a principle of Islam that jihad may include wars of aggression. By denying this, however, they do not prove anything; and, in order to get light on this part of the question before us, we must look at the Koran itself through those explanations of it which up to the present time pass as authoritative. This does not, of course, mean that these explanations are necessarily correct. Maulavi Chirágh 'Ali, for example, denies that they are correct. To quote his opinion as given in Sells's *The Faith of Islam*, "All fighting injunctions in the Koran are, in the first place, only for self-defence, and none of them has any reference to making war offensively. In the second place, they are transitory in their nature. The Mohammedan Common Law is wrong on this point where it allows unbelievers to be attacked without provocation."[5] We do not desire here to discuss this question as to whether the Common Law is right or wrong, that is, whether orthodox Mohammedanism is a fine representation of the spirit and teaching of the Koran, or whether a better and truer representation of the conception of Mohammed and of his teachings might not have been given in a system of doctrine, developed from the point of view of Maulavi Chirágh 'Ali and such Moslems as he.

These reformers of Islam may be right. The intention of Mohammed, in what he said of jihad, may have been misunderstood and misrepresented. But into this question we do not desire to go. For what we are considering is, what Mohammedanism is and has been—that is, what orthodox Mohammedanism teaches concerning jihad, founding its doctrine on a certain definite interpretation of those passages in the Koran which speak of jihad. Until the newer conceptions, as to what the Koran teaches as to the duty of the believer towards non-believers, have spread further and have more generally leavened the mass of Moslem belief and opinion, it is the older and orthodox standpoint on this question which must be regarded by non-Moslems as representing Mohammedan teaching and as guiding Mohammedan action.

We may sympathize strongly with the newer ideas; we may even believe that they are such as would be approved by the founder of Islam were he to return to direct the believers in the altered circumstances in which they find themselves in these latter days; we may hope that those who advance these ideas may succeed in having them generally accepted by Mohammedans; but we repeat, it is the older and narrower orthodox conception of Mohammed's teaching alone, which we can as yet regard as representing the views and practice of Islam with regard to jihad on this question of aggressive war. And the words of Maulavi Chirágh 'Ali are such that we need not spend any time in trying to prove that orthodox Mohammedanism believes and teaches that, according to the Koran, it is the nature of jihad to be aggressive. Let us quote his words again: "The Mohammedan Common Law is wrong on this point when it allows unbelievers to be attacked without provocation."

We take then as proved, the statement that Mohammedan Common Law allows unbelievers to be attacked without provocation: and we know that this position need not surprise us, if we remember the ideas prevalent among Semitic races and the genius of Semitic religions. But, first, we must distinguish between the extension of Islamic rule and the propagation of Islamic Faith. The two are not the same, however closely they may be at times united. It is easy to see that wars might be waged for the extension of Islamic rule, which were in no sense wars for the propagation and extension of Islam as a religion, though the ulterior motive in such wars may have been the conviction that the inhabitants of lands thus coming under the influence of Islam would, in course of time, accept as their own the common or general faith of the country in which they lived.

It may thus be true that the object of jihad, as prescribed and enjoined in the Koran, was not the direct propagation of the Faith: but there can be little doubt that the extension of Islamic rule was one of its main objects. With regard to Arabia itself, there is no questioning the fact that war was enjoined on the Moslems till Arabia became wholly believing. Whether the motives which lay at the back of the conquest of Arabia for Islam by force of arms, were religious or were political, the fact remains that the Arabs were given the alternative of Islam or the sword. No tribute was to be accepted from an Arab, and any Arab apostatising was to be killed off-hand. It is an easy method of apologetics to maintain now that such commands were given in special circumstances and that their force was temporary: but such is not teaching of the earlier commentators, whose views are still regarded as authoritative by all orthodox Moslems. In fact, it was just the other way. "Let there be no compulsion in religion" preceded and was abrogated by the verse of the Sword. And the command in 2.186–87 to fight against those who fight, but not to transgress by attacking first, was, according to Zamakhshary and others, abrogated by the command, "Fight against all the idolaters" (9.36).[6]

That jihad is thus enjoined in the Koran for the establishment or extension of Islamic rule is, we have said, not surprising. One is almost inclined to say that it could scarcely have been otherwise with a Semitic race. Among all Semites, the idea that war was, or could be, dissociated from religion, may be said to have been almost unthinkable. We are not maintaining that war was commanded for the propagation of the faith; but we can certainly maintain that it was for the overthrow of opposing error and the destruction of the power of the unbeliever. Thus, for instance, not merely was Jehovah the God of the hosts of heaven but He was regarded as the God of the armies of Israel, and it was inconceivable that Israel should make war which was not a war for the overthrow of His enemies, the extension of His rule and the glory of His name. That this was understood by Mohammed, and that in his eyes the wars of Israel were for the religion of God, may be seen from the following passage: "Hast thou not considered the assembly of the children of Israel, after the time of Moses, when they said unto their prophet (Samuel), Set a king over us, that we may fight far the religion of God?" (2.247) Similarly the wars of the Semitic tribes who surrounded Israel, were wars for the glory of their gods (cf., the inscription of Mesha). And the same may be held to have been true with regard to the Arabs in pre-Mohammedan times. That this conception was not cast away by Mohammed, but was only altered to suit the altered circumstances, is quite apparent. Allah is no tribal God, but the maker of heaven and earth—the one and only God: war in His name and for His glory does not, then, necessarily imply the destruction of the people of the other—the false gods: but it does imply their submission at least to His rule, though not their acceptance of His service. Allah, the ruler over all, had, in accordance with His own wise providence, not yet exerted His power and extended His dominion over all the earth; but He was now about to do so through His prophet, Mohammed, and His religion, Islam, and one of the chief means whereby Mohammed apparently conceived Him as doing this was war. Those against whom the war was carried on were offered the alternative of coming over peaceably and accepting His religion or of taking the chances of war. It may be true that they were not compelled to accept Islam, but they were compelled, except where they succeeded in resisting by force of arms, to recognize Islam as their master and to submit to whatever laws it laid upon them.

NOTES

1. Sells, *The Faith of Islam*, pp. 411 ff.
2. Muhammad Badr, "The Truth about Islam," p. 45.
3. Ibid., p. 43.
4. Muhammad Reshéd Ridá, *El Manár* 14:928.
5. Sels, *The Faith of Islam*, p. 411.
6. See Zamakhshary.

31

CLASSIFICATION OF PERSONS

Nicolas P. Aghnides

According to Mohammedan theory the world at large falls into two parts, the world of Moslems (*dar al-Islam*) and the world of foes, the *harbis* (*dar al-harb*).[2] An intermediate position may be assigned to the world of allies (*dar al-'ahd*), although strictly speaking the ally world is only a temporary stage, since theoretically Moslems are under obligation (*fard*) to engage in holy war until all infidels shall have accepted Islam or the status of *dhimmis*.[3] Indeed the *imam* may break the truce he may have entered into with the infidels on condition of payment by them of *kharaj* and *jizyah*, if such a course is required by the best interests of Islam, provided however he gives them due notice. Normally therefore the Moslem world is in a state of war with the *harbis* unless this state has been terminated in one of these three ways; namely, conversion to Islam, taking of refuge in the Sanctuary (*haram*), and the giving of *aman*. Of these three ways, only the last need be discussed here. The giving of *aman* consists in pledging security and protection to the *harbis* and may be temporary or perpetual.

THE TEMPORARY AMAN (*AMAN MUWAQQAT*)

This is of two kinds: the well-known (*ma'ruf*) or informal, and the formal (*muwada'ah*).

The Well-known Aman[4]

Any freeborn Mohammedan, man or woman, may give pledge of protection (*aman*) to a *harbi* or a group of *harbis* or even the entire defensive force of a

---

Nicolas P. Aghnides, "Classification of Persons,"[1] in *Mohammedan Theories of Finance* (New York: Columbia University Press, 1916), pp. 354–59.

fortress, and thereupon the *harbis* become *musta'mins* and are not molested, provided they can prove by two witnesses that they have been given *aman*. The *imam* however may repudiate such an *aman* and even punish the Moslem who gave it, if the latter was mistaken in thinking that Moslem interests required such a course.

The Formal Aman or Truce Pact (*muwada'ah*)[5]

It is allowed to the *imam* or to a group of Moslems without the *imam*'s permission to make truce with the *harbis* (enemy) on condition of payment by them of a certain sum of money or goods, unless they are renegades; such are not given quarter, but have to choose between the sword and Islam. The money received from the enemy is considered as *jizyah* if the enemy agreed to pay it before the beginning of hostilities; otherwise it is treated as spoils. It is even allowed to conclude a truce pact on condition of payment on the part of Moslems, if such course is indispensably necessary for the furtherance of the Moslem interests. The legal result of the pact is like that of the informal *aman*, namely, the enemy enjoys security from death and captivity, and security of property on the part of Moslems. If a person residing in the country with which the pact has been made, enters the country of the *harbis* and subsequently the latter country is conquered by the Moslems, that person is treated as a *musta'min*. Likewise a *harbi* entering the country of pact with *aman*, is considered a *musta'min* with regard to the Moslem country also if he has not meanwhile returned to the *dar al-harb*. The *imam* may repudiate the pact made if that is conducive to the interests of Islam, provided the enemy is duly notified about it, and in such case there is returned to the enemy a proportionate part of the tribute paid by them. This is based on the precedent of the Prophet, who broke the agreement made between him and the Meccans.[6]

According to the Shafiites, a valid *aman* of either kind may not be annulled by the *imam* unless he suspects treachery.[7] The Malikites agree with the Shafiites as regards the formal *aman* only.[8] The dissolution of the pact takes place at the time set if one has been set. If no time has been set, the pact ends in two ways, namely, by express dissolution by either side, or implicitly, if, for instance, the *harbis* go out on the highways with the permission of their ruler in order to rob Moslems. If the pact is made with the condition that in the country of the enemy the laws of Islam will be enforced, it is equivalent to giving the perpetual *aman*.

THE PERPETUAL AMAN CALLED *'AQD DHIMMAH*

This consists in the acquisition of the status of the *dhimmi*, and may be expressed or implicit, as, for instance, when the *harbi* enters the Moslem state by a temporary *aman*, and exceeds the time limit set by the *imam*, or if no limit has been set, according to the *Mabsut*,[9] when he resides in the Moslem state a year, but according to others, only after a time has been set and has elapsed. Indeed, when a *harbi* enters the Moslem state by virtue of an *aman* the *imam* should notify him, that should he reside a year or more, he would be considered as a *dhimmi* and would be subject to the *jizyah* and the *kharaj*. The author of the *Majma'* approves of the policy of allowing the *harbis* a short stay because in the contrary case trade would stop and the Moslems would suffer by it. If a *harbi* buys a *kharaj* land he becomes *dhimmi* from the time the *kharaj* has been assessed on the land, even if the time previously set has not elapsed. The effect of becoming a *dhimmi* is security of property and life. Indeed in the field of civil transactions the *dhimmis* enjoy the same rights as the Moslems.[10]

In reply to the following question put by certain Moslems, "How may the *dhimmis* be allowed to persist in what is the worst of crimes, i.e., unbelief, by payment of a monetary consideration?" al-Sarakhsi says that the object is not the monetary consideration, but their invitation to the Faith in the most beautiful way. In fact, as a result of the act of covenant (*'aqd al-dhimmah*) the *dhimmi* abandons fighting, and the person who does not fight may not be attacked. Then, too, "the *dhimmi* by living among the Moslems sees the beauties of the Moslem faith and is exhorted to, and often does, accept Islam."[11]

It is not within the power of the Moslem state to break of its own accord the pact of *dhimmah*, but the pact is not binding (*lazim*) as regards the *dhimmis*.[12] The pact is considered dissolved in three ways: If the *dhimmi* becomes Moslem, because the reason in giving him the status of *dhimmi* was the possibility of his conversion to Islam, and the object in this case has been secured; or if the *dhimmi* returns to the land of *harbis*, for by so doing he becomes like the renegades; except that if he is captured he is made a slave, which is not true of the renegades; or, thirdly, if the *dhimmi* fights the Moslems.

The pact is not broken, however, if the *dhimmis* do not pay the taxes, for it may be due to their poverty; or if they slander the Prophet, for this would only amount to an increase of unbelief, but unbelief was not an obstacle to their acquisition of the status of *dhimmi* in the first place.

The refusal of a dhimmi to pay the jizyah is not construed as a breach on his part of the pact of *dhimmah* by virtue of which he acquired the status of *dhimmi*, because the object in view is the *dhimmi*'s acceptance of the obligation to pay the *jizyah*, but not its payment *per se*, and so when he refuses to pay the tax, his previous acceptance and the humiliation attendant on it are still there.

In the *Durar* it is stated that there is a difficulty involved in this view, because to refuse to pay the *jizyah* is virtually to state expressly that it will not be paid, as if one said: "I will not pay the *jizyah* in the future," and it is evident that this makes impossible the continuation of the acceptance unless refusal be construed to mean delay and offer of excuses, in which case the difficulty is removed. It may, however, be replied that in consequence of the *dhimmi*'s acceptance of the obligation the *jizyah* becomes a debt, as in case of suretyship for wealth, and therefore if the *dhimmi* later says: "I will not pay the *jizyah*," it has no legal effect beyond entailing his imprisonment, as in the case of other debts.[13]

According to the Shafiites,[14] the pact is broken if the *dhimmis* fight the Moslems, or if they refuse to pay the *jizyah* or to obey the Moslem laws, but, unless expressly stipulated, not if they debauch Moslem women or slander the Prophet. Finally, according to the Malikites,[15] the pact is broken in all the four cases mentioned.

Corresponding to the three "worlds," the Moslem, the ally, and the enemy, there are the three classes of persons designated as Moslems, allies (*mu'ahid*), and enemies (*harbi*); besides, there are the classes of *dhimmis* and *musta'mins*. The *dhimmis* are, as already explained, the *harbis* who have definitely committed themselves to the protection of the Moslems, whereas the *musta'mins* are persons who have come under that protection only temporarily.

NOTES

For clarification of these citations, the reader is referred to the original source, Nicolas P. Aghnides, "Classification of Persons," in *Mohammedan Theories of Finance* (New York: Columbia University Press, 1916), pp. 354–59.

1. Kasani, vol. 7, p. 102.

2. For details concerning definitions and as to when *dar al-harb* becomes *dar al-Islam*, and *vice versa*, consult al-Kasani (vol. 7, p. 130), the *'Alamkiriyyah* (vol. 2, p. 330), and the *Technical Dictionary* (p. 466); also al-Mawardi (p. 239). Suffice it to say that the expression *dar al-Islam* applies to every land where the *imam* (ruler) of the Moslems holds sway and the Moslems enjoy security, and that the enemy world (*dar al-harb*) becomes Moslem world when the *shari'ah* prescriptions are enforced in it. There is divergence of opinion as to when the Moslem world becomes enemy world.

3. Cf. *Umm*, vol. 4, p. 91; *Wajiz*, vol. 2, p. 186; *Minhaj*, vol. 3, p. 255; *Kanz*, vol. 2, p. 253, no. 5393; *Kharashi*, p. 406. According to the *Mugni* (vol. 4, p. 193) the obligation of holy war should be fulfilled at least once a year. The "holy war," however, may be only negative and consist in the strengthening of defences [*sic*] instead of in actual aggression.

4. Cf. *Wajiz*, vol. 2, p. 194; *Minhaj*, vol. 3, p. 271; *Kharashi*, p. 420.

5. The Shafiites and Malikites instead of *muwada'ah* use *muhadanah* and *hudnah*.

6. *Majma*, p. 498.

7. *Minhaj*, vol. 3, pp. 272, 290.

8. *Kharashi*, p. 449.

9. *Majma*, p. 519.

10. Cf. *Wafts*, vol. 2, p. 201; *Minhaj*, vol. 3, p. 283.

11. *Mabsuf*, part 10, p. 77.

12. Cf. *Wajiz*, vol. 2, p. 197; *Kharashi*, p. 447.

13. *Majma*, p. 519.

14. *Minhaj*, vol. 3, p. 286; *Wajiz*, vol. 2, p. 203.

15. *Kharashi*, p. 447.

32

THE LAW OF WAR: THE JIHAD

Majid Khadduri

INTRODUCTION

"Had thy Lord pleased, He would have made mankind one nation; but those only to whom thy Lord hath granted his mercy will cease to differ . . ."
—Qur'an 11.120

The state which is regarded as the instrument for universalizing a certain religion must perforce be an ever expanding state. The Islamic state, whose principal function was to put God's law into practice, sought to establish Islam as the dominant reigning ideology over the entire world. It refused to recognize the coexistence of non-Muslim communities, except perhaps as subordinate entities, because by its very nature a universal state tolerates the existence of no other state than itself. Although it was not a consciously formulated policy, Muhammad's early successors, after Islam became supreme in Arabia, were determined to embark on a ceaseless war of conquest in the name of Islam. The jihād was therefore employed as an instrument for both the universalization of religion and the establishment of an imperial world state.[1] The mission of Islam was rapidly and successfully carried out during the first century of the Islamic era—although the peaceful penetration of Islam continued—and the empire extended over a large portion of the Old World and became as large as the Roman Empire.

But the expanding Muslim state, not unlike other universal states, could not extend ad infinitum. The hitherto victorious Muslim warriors were defeated in the West at Tours (A.D. 732) and in the East found they could not proceed further than the Indian borders.[2] Thus the wave of Muslim expansion, strong as it was, could

Majid Khadduri, "Introduction" and "The Doctrine of Jihad," in *War and Peace in the Law of Islam, Book 2: The Law of War: The Jihad* (Baltimore: Johns Hopkins University Press, 1955), pp. 49–73.

not complete the Sun's circle; it imperceptibly subsided where it reached its utmost limits at the Pyrenees and the Indus.[3] The Muslim (world) state consequently did not correspond to the then known world. Outside it there remained communities which the Muslim authorities had to deal with, though in theory only temporarily, throughout all the subsequent history of Islam.

The world accordingly was sharply divided in Muslim law into the dār al-Islām (abode or territory of Islam) and the dār al-harb (abode or territory of war). These terms may be rendered in less poetic words as the "world of Islam" and the "world of War." The first corresponded to the territory under Muslim rule. Its inhabitants were Muslims, by birth or conversion, and the communities of the tolerated religions (the dhimmīs) who preferred to hold fast to their own cult, at the price of paying the jizya (poll tax). The Muslims enjoyed full rights of citizenship; the subjects of the tolerated religions enjoyed only partial rights, and submitted to Muslim rule in accordance with special charters regulating their relations with the Muslims.[4] The dār al-harb consisted of all the states and communities outside the world of Islam. Its inhabitants were often called infidels, or, better, unbelievers.[5]

On the assumption that the ultimate aim of Islam was worldwide, the dār al-Islām was always, in theory, at war with the dār al-harb. The Muslims were required to preach Islam by persuasion, and the caliph or his commanders in the field to offer Islam as an alternative to paying the poll tax or fighting; but the Islamic state was under legal obligation to enforce Islamic law and to recognize no authority other than its own, superseding other authorities even when non-Muslim communities had willingly accepted the faith of Islam without fighting. Failure by non-Muslims to accept Islam or pay the poll tax made it incumbent on the Muslim State to declare a jihād (commonly called "holy war") upon the recalcitrant individuals and communities. Thus the jihād, reflecting the normal war relations existing between Muslims and non-Muslims, was the state's instrument for transforming the dār al-harb into the dar al-Islām. It was the product of a warlike people who had embarked on a large-scale movement of expansion. Islam could not abolish the warlike character of the Arabs who were constantly at war with each other;[6] it indeed reaffirmed the war basis of intergroup relationship by institutionalizing war as part of the Muslim legal system and made use of it by transforming war into a holy war designed to be ceaselessly declared against those who failed to become Muslims. The short intervals which are not war—and these in theory should not exceed ten years—are periods of peace.[7] But the jihād was not the only legal means of dealing with non-Muslims since peaceful methods (negotiations, arbitration, and treaty making) were applied in regulating the relations of the believers with unbelievers when actual fighting ceased.

The Muslim law of nations was, accordingly, the product of the intercourse of an ever-expanding state with its neighbors which inevitably led to the development of a body of rules and practices followed by Muslims in war and peace. The practices followed by the Arabs before Islam in their intertribal warfare were regarded as too ungodly and brutal, because they were motivated by narrow tribal interests. Islam abolished all war except the jihād and the jurist-theologians consciously formulated its law subordinating all personal considerations to ration d'état, based on religious sanction.

THE DOCTRINE OF JIHĀD

"Every nation has its monasticism, and the monasticism of this [Muslim] nation is the jihād." —a hadīth.

The Meaning of Jihād

The term jihād is derived from the verb jāhada (abstract noun, juhd) which means "exerted";[8] its juridical-theological meaning is exertion of one's power in Allah's path, that is, the spread of the belief in Allah and in making His word supreme over this world. The individual's recompense would be the achievement of salvation, since the jihād is Allah's direct way to paradise. This definition is based on a Qur'ānic injunction which runs as follows:

> O ye who believe! Shall I guide you to a gainful trade which will save you from painful punishment? Believe in Allah and His Apostle and carry on warfare (jihād) in the path of Allah with your possessions and your persons. That is better for you. If ye have knowledge, He will forgive your sins, and will place you in the Gardens beneath which the streams flow, and in fine houses in the Gardens of Eden: that is the great gain.[9]

The jihād, in the broad sense of exertion, does not necessarily mean war or fighting, since exertion in Allah's path may be achieved by peaceful as well as violent means. The jihād may be regarded as a form of religious propaganda that can be carried on by persuasion or by the sword. In the early Makkan revelations, the emphasis was in the main on persuasion. Muhammad, in the discharge of his prophetic functions, seemed to have been satisfied by warning his people against idolatry and inviting them to worship Allah. This is evidenced by such a verse as the following: "He who exerts himself (jāhada), exerts only for his own soul,"[10] which expresses the jihād in terms of the salvation of the soul rather than a struggle for proselytization.[11] In the Madīnan revelations, the jihād is often expressed in terms of strife, and there is no doubt that in certain verses the conception of jihād is synonymous with the words war and fighting.[12]

The jurists, however, have distinguished four different ways in which the believer may fulfill his jihād obligation: by his heart; his tongue; his hands; and by the sword.[13] The first is concerned with combating the devil and in the attempt to escape his persuasion to evil. This type of jihād, so significant in the eyes of the

Prophet Muhammad, was regarded as the greater jihād.[14] The second and third are mainly fulfilled in supporting the right and correcting the wrong. The fourth is precisely equivalent to the meaning of war, and is concerned with fighting the unbelievers and the enemies of the faith.[15] The believers are under the obligation of sacrificing their "wealth and lives" (Q. 61.11) in the prosecution of war.[16]

The Jihād as Bellum Justum

War is considered as just whether commenced and prosecuted in accordance with the necessary formalities required under a certain system of law, or waged for justifiable reasons in accordance with the tenets of the religion or the mores of a certain society. In Islam, as in ancient Rome, both of these concepts were included in their doctrine of the *bellum justum* since a justifiable reason as well as the formalities for prosecuting the war were necessary. In both Islam and ancient Rome, not only was war to be *justum*, but also to be *pium*, that is, in accordance with the sanction of religion an the implied commands of gods.[17]

The idea that wars, when institutionalized as part of the mores of society, are just may be traced back to antiquity. It was implied in the concept of vendetta as an act of retaliation by one group against another. In the *Politics*, Aristotle refers to certain wars as just by nature.[18] The Romans instituted the *jus fetiale*, administered by a *collegium fetialium* (consisting of twenty members, presided over by *magister fetialium*), embodying the proper rules of waging war in order to be just.[19] In medieval Christendom, both St. Augustine and Isodore de Seville were influenced in their theory of just war by Cicero. St. Thomas Aquinas, who was acquainted with Muslim writings, formulated his theory of just war along lines similar to the Islamic doctrine of the jihād.[20] St. Thomas and other medieval writers influenced in their turn the natural law theories of the sixteenth, seventeenth, and eighteenth centuries. Grotius, the father of the modern law of nations, developed his system under the impact of the natural law theory of just war, and his ideas remained predominant until the end of the eighteenth century.[21] Although the doctrine of war during the nineteenth century was by far less influenced by natural law than in previous centuries, the concept of just war reappeared after the First World War in the form of a doctrine of outlawing war, save that against an aggressor.

Recurring as a pattern in the development of the concept of war from antiquity, it assumed in Islam a special position in its jural order because law and religion formed a unity; the law prescribed the way to achieve religious (or divine) purposes, and religion provided a sanction for the law.

In Muslim legal theory, Islam and shirk (associating other gods with Allah) cannot exist together in this world; it is the duty of the imām as well as every believer not only to see that God's word shall be supreme, but also that no infidel shall deny God or be ungrateful for His favors (*ni'am*).[22] This world would ultimately be reserved for believers;[23] as to unbelievers, "their abode is hell, and evil is the destination."[24] The jihād, in other words, is a sanction against polytheism and must be suffered by all non-Muslims who reject Islam, or, in the case of the *dhimmis* (Scripturaries), refuse to pay the poll tax. The jihād, therefore, may be defined as the litigation between Islam and polytheism; it is also a form of punishment to be inflicted upon Islam's enemies and the renegades from the faith.[25] Thus in Islam, as in Western Christendom, the jihād is the *bellum justum*. [26]

In Islam, however, the jihād is no less employed for punishing polytheists than for raison d'état. For inherent in the state's action in waging a jihād is the establishment of Muslim sovereignty, since the supremacy of God's word carries necessarily with it God's political authority. This seems to be the reason why the jihād, important as it is, is not included—except in the Khārijī legal theory— among the five pillars of Islam. The reason is that the five pillars are not necessarily to be enforced by the state; they must be observed by the individuals regardless of the sanction of authority. The jihād, in order to achieve raison d'état, must, however, be enforced by the state. In the technical language the five pillars—the basic articles of the faith—are regarded as individual duties (*fard 'ayn*), like prayer or fasting, which each believer must individually perform and each is held liable to punishment if he failed to perform the duty. The jihād, on the other hand—unless the Muslim community is subjected to a sudden attack and therefore all believers, including women and children, are under the obligation to fight—is regarded by all jurists, with almost no exception, as a collective obligation of the whole Muslim community.[27] It is regarded as *fard al-kifāya*, binding on the Muslims as a collective group, not individually. If the duty is fulfilled by a part of the community it ceases to be obligatory on others; the whole community, however, falls into error if the duty is not performed at all.[28]

The imposition of the jihād duty on the community rather than on the individual is very significant and involved at least two important implications. In the first place, it meant that the duty need not necessarily be fulfilled by all the believers. For the recruitment of all the believers as warriors was neither possible nor advisable.[29] Some of the believers were needed to prepare food and weapons, while the crippled, blind, and sick would not qualify as fighters.[30] Women and children were as a rule excused from actual fighting, although many a woman contributed indirectly to the war effort.

In the second place, the imposition of the obligation on he community rather than on the individual made possible the employment of the jihād as a community and, consequently, a state instrument; its control accordingly, is a state, not an individual, responsibility. Thus the head of the state can in a more effective way serve the common interest of the community than if the matter is left entirely to the discretion of the individual believer. Compensation for the fulfillment of such an important public duty has been amply emphasized in both the authoritative sources of the creed[31] and in formal utterances of public men.[32] All of them give lavish promises of martyrdom and eternal life in paradise immediately and without trial on resurrection and judgment day for those who die in Allah's path. Such martyrs are not washed but are buried where they fall on the battlefield, not in the usual type of grave, after washing in a mosque. It is true that a promise of paradise is given to every believer who performs the five basic duties, but none of them would enable him to gain paradise as surely as participation in the jihād.[33]

The Jihād as Permanent War

War, however, was not introduced into Arabia by Islam. It was already in existence among the Arabs; but it was essentially a tribal war. Its nature was peculiar to the existing social order and its rules and procedure were thoroughly integrated as part of the sunna. Since the tribe (in certain instances the clan) was the basic political unit, wars took the form of raids; mainly for robbery or vendetta (tha'r). This state of affairs had, as observed by Ibn Khaldūn, developed among the Arabs a spirit of self-reliance, courage, and co-operation among the members of the single tribe.[34] But these very traits intensified the character of warfare and rivalry among the tribes and created a state of instability and unrest.

The importance of the jihād in Islam lay in shifting the focus of attention of the tribes from their intertribal warfare to the outside world; Islam outlawed all forms of war except the jihād, that is, the war in Allah's path. It would, indeed, have been very difficult for the Islamic state to survive had it not been for the doctrine of the jihād, replacing tribal raids, and directing that enormous energy of the tribes from an inevitable internal conflict to unite and fight against the outside world in the name of the new faith.

The jihād as such was not a casual phenomenon of violence; it was rather a product of complex factors while Islam worked out its jural-doctrinal character. Some writers have emphasized the economic changes within Arabia which produced dissatisfaction and unrest and inevitably led the Arabs to seek more fertile lands outside Arabia.[35] Yet this theory—plausible as it is in explaining the outburst of the Arabs from within their peninsula—is not enough to interpret the character of a war permanently declared against the unbelievers even after the Muslims had established themselves outside Arabia. There were other factors which created in the minds of the Muslims a politico-religious mission and conditioned their attitude as a conquering nation.

To begin with, there is the universal element in Islam which made it the duty of every able-bodied Muslim to contribute to its spread. In this Islam combined elements from Judaism and Christianity to create something which was not in either: a divine nomocratic state on an imperialistic basis. Judaism was not a missionary religion, for the Jews were God's chosen people; a holy war was, accordingly, for the defense of their religion, not for its spread. Christianity on the other hand was a redemptive and, at the outset, a non-state religion. Even when it was associated with politics, the Church and state remained apart. Islam was radically different from both. It combined the dualism of a universal religion and a universal state. It resorted to peaceful as well as violent means for achieving that ultimate objective. The universality of Islam provided a unifying element for all believers, within the world of Islam, and its defensive-offensive character produced a state of warfare permanently declared against the outside world, the world of war.

Thus the jihād may be regarded as Islam's instrument for carrying out its ultimate objective by turning all people into believers, if not in the prophethood of Muhammad (as in the case of the dhimmis), at least in the belief in God. The Prophet Muhammad is reported to have declared "some of my people will continue to fight victoriously for the sake of the truth until the last one of them will combat the anti-Christ."[36] Until that moment is reached the jihād, in one form or another, will remain as a permanent obligation upon the entire Muslim community. It follows that the existence of a dār al-harb is ultimately outlawed under the Islamic jural order; that the dār al-Islām is permanently under jihād obligation until the dār al-harb is reduced to nonexistence; and that any community which prefers to remain non-Islamic—in the status of a tolerated religious community accepting certain disabilities—must submit to Islamic rule and reside in the dār al-Islām or be bound as clients to the Muslim community. The universalism of Islam, in its all-embracing creed, is imposed on the believers as a continuous process of warfare, psychological and political if not strictly military.

Although the jihād was regarded as the permanent basis of Islam's relations with its neighbors, it did not at all mean continuous fighting. Not only could the obligation be performed by nonviolent means, but relations with the enemy did not necessarily mean an endless or constant violent conflict with him. The jihād, accordingly, may be stated as a doctrine of a permanent state of war, not a continuous fighting. Thus some of the jurists argued that the mere preparation for the jihād is a fulfillment of its obligation.[37] The state, however, must be prepared militarily not only to repel a sudden attack on Islam, but also to use its forces for offensive purposes when the caliph deems it necessary to do so.

In practice, however, the jihād underwent certain changes in its meaning to suit the changing circumstances of life. Islam often made peace with the enemy, not always on its own terms. Thus the jurists began to reinterpret the law with a view to justifying suspension of the jihād, even though temporarily. They seem to have agreed about the necessity of peace and the length of its duration.[38] When Muslim power began to decline, Muslim publicists seem to have tacitly admitted that in principle the jihād as a permanent war had become obsolete; it was no longer compatible with Muslim interests. The concept of the jihād as a state of war underwent certain changes. This change, as a matter of fact, did not imply abandonment of the jihād duty; it only meant the entry of the obligation into a period of suspension—it assumed a dormant status, from which the imām may revive it at any time he deems necessary. In practice, however, the Muslims came to think of this as more of a normal condition of life than an active jihād.

The shift in the conception of the jihād from active to dormant war reflects a reaction on the part of the Muslims from further expansion. This coincided with the intellectual and philosophical revival of Islam at the turn of the fourth century of the Muslim era (tenth century A.D.), when the Muslims were probably more stirred by the controversy between orthodoxy and rationalism than by fighting Byzantine encroachments on the frontiers. To certain Muslim thinkers, like Ibn Khaldūn (d. 1406),[39] the relaxation of the jihād marked the change in the character of the nation from the warlike to the civilized stage. Thus the change in the concept of the jihād was not merely an apologia for weakness and failure to live up to a doctrine, but a process of evolution dictated by Islam's interests and social conditions.

The Shī'ī and Khārijī Doctrines of the Jihād

Generally speaking, the Shī'ī law of the jihād is not different from the Sunnī; but in linking the special duty of prosecuting the jihād with the doctrine of *walāya* (allegiance to the imām), the concept of jihād assumed in Shī'ism a special doctrinal significance.[40] In Shī'ī legal theory, not only would the failure of a non-Muslim to believe in Allah justify waging a jihād, but also the failure of a Muslim to obey the imām would make him liable for punishment by a jihād.[41] While to a Sunnī the jihād is the sure way to Heaven, a jihād without an allegiance to the imām would not constitute an imān (a necessary requirement for salvation) in the Shī'ī creed.

The jihād is regarded as one of the chief functions of the imāmate, the performance of which would fulfill one of the requirements for the best (*afdal*) qualified person for this position. If the imām fails to fulfill the jihād obligation, he disqualifies his claim as the best candidate, according to the Zaydī creed.[42] The imām, as an infallible ruler, is the only one who can judge when the jihād should be declared and under what circumstances it would be advisable not to go to war with the enemy. If the imām finds it necessary to come to terms with the enemy, he may do so; he may even deem it necessary to seek the support of non-Muslims (including polytheists) in order to avoid risking defeat by the enemy.[43] Under no circumstances, however, should the imām risk a jihād if he considers the enemy too powerful for him to win a victory, namely, if the enemy is at least twice as powerful as the Muslims.[44]

The disappearance of the imām, however, has left the duty of declaring the jihād unfulfilled.[45] Opinion differed as to the capacity of the mujtahids to act in the name of the imām in fulfilling the jihād obligation; but since the duty of calling the believers to battle is a matter in which an infallible judgment is necessary—since the interest of the entire community would be at stake—only an imām is capable of fulfilling such a duty. Further, it is deemed impossible to combat evil during the absence of the imām; the jihād, accordingly, is regarded unconsequential. Thus in the Shī'ī legal theory, the jihād has entered into a dormant stage—it is in a state of suspension. In contrast to the Sunnī doctrine which requires the revival of the dormant jihād when Muslim power is regained, the resumption of the jihād in the Shī'ī doctrine would be dependent on the return of the imām from his *ghayba* (absence), in the capacity of a Mandī, who will triumphantly combat evil and re-establish justice and righteousness.[46]

In contrast to the Shī'ī doctrine of the jihād, the Khārijīs maintain that the jihād is a fundamental article of the faith which could not possibly be abandoned or relaxed. To them the jihād is a sixth pillar of the faith, binding individually on every believer and on the community as a whole.[47] They also go as far as to enforce imān on all who do not accept their version of Islam, Muslims as well as non Muslims, by the jihād; for, they argue, that since the Prophet Muhammad had spent almost all his life in war, all true believers must also do so. Their strict belief in their religion and their fanaticism made them uncompromising in the fulfillment of their jihād duty. Thus their conception of the state was that of a garrison state; an ever-ready community, led by its imām, to wage war on the enemies of the faith. Even if the imām does not lead in war, the jihād is incumbent on each believer to fulfill by himself, for he falls in error if he fails to do so.

The Khārijīs' conception of the jihād, in contrast to the Sunnī doctrine is that of violence rather than strife or religious propaganda.[48] To them true belief is a matter of conviction which should be imposed on reluctant individuals, not a subject of debate and argumentation; for, if evil is to be exterminated and justice re-established, obstinate heretics must be either forced to believe or be killed by the sword. This is based on a hadīth in which the Prophet Muhammad is reported to have said: "My fate is under the shadow of my spear."[49]

Strict and fanatical, the Khārijīs were as fierce and brutal in war as their desert life was austere and puritanical. The humane and moral aspect of religion made little impact on their tribal character. In war they killed women and children and condemned to death prisoners of war. Although these rules were not always followed, the extremist Khārijīs, such as the followers of Nāfi' ibn al-Azraq (A.H. 686), insisted that they should always be enforced.[50]

The Jihād and Secular War

Islam, it will be recalled, abolished all kinds of warfare except the jihād. Only a war which has an ultimate religious purpose, that is, to enforce God's law or to check transgression against it, is a just war. No other form of fighting is permitted within or without the Muslim brotherhood.

Throughout the history of Islam, however, fighting between Muslim rulers and contending parties was as continuous as between Islam and its external enemies. The *casus foederis* of a jihād was frequently invoked on the grounds of suppressing innovations and punishing the leaders of secession from the faith. Not infrequently the naked ambition of opposition leaders who resorted to war for the sake of a throne or high political offices was too apparent to be ignored. When the caliph's prestige and power declined, lack of respect for and opposition to the central authority became fashionable among local rulers. This state of affairs accentuated the struggle for power and created instability and anarchy in the world of Islam. Ignoring existing realities, the jurists continued to argue—following the example of al-Māwardī—that ultimate authority belonged to the caliph and that no one else had the right to renounce it even if the caliph proved to be unjust and oppressive, since tyranny, it was then contended, was preferable to anarchy[51]—a sad comment on existing conditions.

A few publicists, in their reflections on the state of affairs as they then existed, have said that wars, in forms other than the jihād, had often recurred in the Islamic society. Paying lip service to the jihād as a religious duty, they looked upon wars as dangers which Muslim rulers should avoid. Al-Tartūshī (died A.H. 520) described "war crises" as social anomalies[52] and al-Hasan ibn 'Abd-Allah compared them to diseases of society.[53] Both of these writers, who expatiated on the ways and means of conducting fighting, advised their rulers that the best way to win wars, if they found it impossible to avert them, was to be adequately prepared militarily. Thus Muslim publicists, like their Roman predecessors, seemed to have been convinced that *si vis pacem, para bellum* [If you wish (for) peace, prepare for war].

It was, perhaps, Ibn Khaldūn (A.D. 1332–1406) who for the first time recognized that wars were not, as his Muslim predecessors thought, casual social calamities. He maintained that war has existed in society ever since "Creation." Its real cause, which accounts for its persistence in society, is man's will-to-revenge. Man, in other words, is by nature warlike. He is forever moved to fight either for his own selfish interests or by such emotional motives as jealousy, anger, or a feeling of divine guilt. Thus the members of one group or nation, in order to attain their objectives, combined against others and the inevitable result was war.

Wars, according to Ibn Khaldūn, are of four kinds. First is the tribal warfare, such as that which existed among the Arabian tribes; second, feuds and raids which are characteristic of primitive people; third, the wars prescribed by the sharī'a, i.e., the jihād; fourth, wars against rebels and dissenters. Ibn Khaldūn contends that the first two are unjustified, because they are wars of disobedience; the other two are just wars (*'adl*).

Ibn Khaldūn was not of the opinion, as Tartūshī contended, that victory could be attained by sheer military preparedness. He believed that there are always deeper causes for victory—more important than arms and armaments—which he called *al-asbāb al-khafiyya*, that is, the hidden causes. He does not mean, however, by *khafiyya* the morale of the army (although he regards this as absolutely necessary); but rather the application of certain skills and tactics which enable an army to attain victory, such as making use of certain highlands which helps to start an offensive, and deceiving tactics which tend to mislead the enemy.[54]

It is to be noted that Muslim thinkers, from the rise of Islam to the time of Ibn Khaldūn, regarded secular wars as an evil to be avoided since they were inconsistent with God's law which prohibited all forms of war except those waged for religious purposes. A close examination of society taught Muslim thinkers that secular wars were not easily avoided by fallible human beings; peace within the Muslim brotherhood needed the inspiring influence of a Prophet or the prestige and power of an 'Umar I. When the caliphs departed from the sunna of the Prophet, holy wars were no longer the only kind of warfare waged; nor were they always devoid of secular purposes. A war, called *harb*, in distinction from a holy war (jihād), was looked upon as an unnatural phenomenon which befell society only because of man's carelessness and sins. Ibn 'Abd-Allah, it will be remembered, described wars as diseases; but Ibn Khaldūn thought that their frequency in society, arising from the very nature of man, makes their recurrence as permanent as social life itself. Ibn Khaldūn based his conclusions not only on his own personal observations on the state of constant warfare that existed among the petty Muslim states in North Africa, but also on the experiences of various nations with whose history he was acquainted. Ibn Khaldūn's observation, which shows keen insight in understanding human society, is corroborated by modern research, which has demonstrated that early societies tended to be more warlike and that peace was by no means the normal state of affairs.[55] As Sir Henry Maine stated, "It is not peace which was natural and primitive and old, but rather war. War appears to be as old as mankind, but peace is a modern invention."[56] Islam, unlike Christianity, sought to establish the Kingdom of Heaven on earth; but, like Christianity, could not produce that world brotherhood and God-fearing society which would live permanently in peace. War was as problematic to our forefathers as to ourselves; they sought earnestly to abolish it by the faiths they honored no less than we do by our own faith in the scientific approach.

NOTES

For clarification of any citations, the reader is referred to the original, Majid Khadduri, *War and Peace in the Law of Islam, Book 2: The Law of War: The Jihad* (Baltimore: Johns Hopkins University Press, 1955), pp. 49–73.

1. See the section "The Doctrine of Jihad."

2. The Muslims suffered another defeat before the battle of Tours at Constantinople (AD 717–718).

3. Edward Gibbon maintains that had the Muslims been successful at Tours the Qur'ān would have been taught at Oxford and Cambridge instead of the Bible (*History of*

the Decline and Fall of the Roman Empire, ed. Bury [London, 1898], vol. 6, p. 15); but in fact the Muslim Empire, due to internal forces, reached its utmost limits.

4. See "Status of the Dhimmis," in *War and Peace in the Law of Islam*, bk. 2, pp. 175–201.

5. For more precise definitions of dār al-Islam and dār al-harb, see pp. 155–57, 170–71, below.

6. "The primitive nomad of the desert and steppes," says Quincy Wright, "has a hard environment to conquer. . . . His terrain, adapted to distant raids and without natural defenses, leads him to institutionalize war for aggression and defense" (*A Study of War* [Chicago, 1942], vol. 1, p. 64).

7. The idea that intergroup relationships were normally unpeaceful goes back to Antiquity (Plato, *The Laws*, bk. 1, 2) and it recurred in the writings of medieval and modern thinkers. See Ibn Khaldūn, *al-Muqaddima*, ed. Quatremère (Paris, 1858), vol. 2, pp. 65–79; Thomas Hobbes, *Leviathan*, chap. 13; *Elements of Law*, part 1, chap. 14, 2. See also Wright, *A Study of War*, vol. 1, chaps. 6 and 7.

8. For the literal meaning of jihād, see Fayrūzabādī, *Qāmūs al-Munīt* (Cairo, 1933), vol. 1, p. 286. For the Quar'ānic use of jihād in the sense of exertion see Q. 6.108, 22.77.

9. Q. 61.10–13. See also Jurjānī, *Kitāb al-Ta'rīfāt*, ed. Gustavus Fülgel (Leipzig, 1845), p. 84.

10. Q. 29.5.

11. See Shāfi'ī, *Kitāb al-Umm* (Cairo, 1321 H), vol. 4, pp. 84–85; 'Abd al-Qāhir al-Baghdādī, *Kitāb Usūl al-Dīn* (Istanbul, 1928), vol. 1, p. 193; Shaybānī, *al-Siyar al-Kabīr*, with Sarakhsī's commentary (Hyderabad, 1335 H), vol. 1, p. 126.

12. See Q. 2.215, 9.41, 49.15, 61.11, 66.9.

13. See Ibn Hazm, *Kitāb al-Fasl fī al-Milal wa'l-Ahwā' wa'l-Nihal* (Cairo, 1321 H), vol. 4, p. 135; Ibn Rushd, *Kitāb al-Mugaddimāt al-Mumahhidāt* (Cairo, 1325 H), vol. 1, p. 259; Buhūtī, *Kashshāf al-Qinā' 'An Matn al-Ignā'* (Cairo, 1366 H), vol. 3, p. 28.

14. Ibn al-Humām, *Sharh Fath al-Qadīr* (Cairo, 1316 H), vol. 4, p. 277.

15. Ibn Hazm distinguishes between the jihād by the tongue and the jihād by ra'y and tadbīr (i.e., reason) and he maintains that the Prophet Muhammad showed preference for reason over the sword. Ibn Hazm, *Kitāb al-Fasl fī al-Milal wa'l-Ahwā' wa'l-Nihal*, vol. 4, p. 135.

16. Bukhārī, *Kitāb al-Jāmi' al-Sahīh*, ed. Krehl (Leiden, 1864), vol. 2, p. 199; Abū Dā'ūd, *Sunan* (Cairo, 1935), vol. 3, p. 5; Dārimī, *Sunan* (Damascus, 1349 H), vol. 2, p. 213.

17. See J. Von Elbe, "The Evolution of the Concept of the Just War in International Law," *American Journal of International Law* 33 (1939): 665–88; and Coleman Phillipson, *The International Law and Custom of Ancient Greece and Rome* (London, 1911), vol. 2, p. 180.

18. Plato, *Politics*, bk. 1, chap. 8.

19. In the *Offices*, Cicero, who may be regarded as the representative legal philosopher of ancient Rome, has discussed the rules and formalities that constitute the bellum justum. See Cicero, *Offices, Essays and Letters* (Everyman's ed.), bk. 1, sec. 11–12.

20. See A. P. D'Entreves, *Aquinas: Selected Political Writings* (Oxford, 1948) pp. 59–61; John Epstein, *The Catholic Tradition of the Law of Nations* (London, 1935); William Ballis, *The Legal Position of War: Changes in Its Practice and Theory* (The Hague, 1937), pp. 32–60.

21. Hugo Grotius, *De Jure Belli ac Pacis* (1625; repr., Oxford, 1925).

22. The Prophet Muhammad is reported to have said: "I am ordered to fight polytheists until they say: 'there is no god but Allah.'" The validity of the rule of fighting polytheists is also based on a Qur'ānic injunction, in which Allah said to His Apostle, as follows: "slay the polytheists wherever you may find them" (Q. 9.5). See also Tāj al-Dīn al-Subkī, *Kitāb Mu'īd al-Ni'am wa Mubīd al-Niqam*, ed. David W. Myhrman (London, 1908), p. 27.

23. The idea that Islam would ultimately replace other religions (except perhaps the tolerated religions) is not stated in the Qur'ān, but it is implied in the objective of the jihād and expressed in the hadīth. See n22, above.

24. Q. 9.74.

25. For the forms or types of jihād, see chap. 6 in Khadduri, *War and Peace in the Law of Islam*.

26. Bassam Tibi, in an essay included in this collection (p. 331), "War and Peace in Islam," from *The Ethics of War and Peace: Religious and Secular Perspectives*, ed. Terry Nardin (Princeton, NJ: Princeton University Press, 1996), rejects the assessment by Khadduri that jihad comports with the Western notion of bellum justum, citing Khadduri's own words, and stating:

> I disagree, for example, with Khadduri's interpretation of the jihad as bellum justum. As Khadduri himself observes:
> "The universality of Islam provided a unifying element for all believers, within the world of Islam, and its defensive-offensive character produced a state of warfare permanently declared against the outside world, the world of war. Thus jihad may be regarded as Islam's instrument for carrying out its ultimate objective by turning all people into believers."
> According to the Western just war concept, just wars are limited to a single issue; they are not universal and permanent wars grounded on a religious worldview.

27. Sa'īd ibn al-Musayyib said that the jihād duty is fard'ayn. Awzā'ī and Thawrī, however, advocated a defensive jihād (Shaybānī, *al-Siyar al-Kabār*, vol. 1, p. 125) and an extremely pacifist sect, known as the Māziyāriyya, dropped both the jihād against polytheists and fasting from the articles of faith. See 'Abd al-Qāhir al-Baghdādī, *Mukhtasar Kitāb al-Farq Bayn al-Firaq*, summarized by al-Ras'anī and ed. Hitti (Cairo, 1924), p. 163.

28. For a definition of this term, see Suyūtī, *al-Ashbāh wa'l-Nazā'ir* (Cairo, 1938), pp. 496–503; Ibn Qudāma, *al-Mughnī*, ed. Rashīd Rida (Cairo, 1367 H), vol. 8, pp. 345–46; Ibn al-Humām, *Sharh Fath al-Qadīr*, p. 278.

29. Q. 9.123: "The believers must not march forth all to war."

30. Q. 24.60: "There is no blame on the blind man, nor on the lame, nor on the sick."

31. Q. 3.163: "Count not those who are killed in the path of Allah as dead; they are alive with their Lord." A woman complained to Muhammad about the death of her son in the battle of Badr, and then she asked whether her son went to hell or paradise, Muhammad replied: "Your son is in the higher Paradise" (Bukhārī, *Kitāb al-Jāmi' al-Sahīh*, vol. 2, p. 202.) Another hadīth runs as follows: "There are one hundred stages in Paradise that are provided by Allah for those who fight in His path" (ibid., p. 200). See also Ibn Hudhayl, *Tuhfat al-Anfus wa Shi'ar Sukkān al-Andalus*, ed. Louis Mercier (Paris, 1936), chaps. 10 and 20.

32. See a speech given by Caliph Abū Bakr to Syrian expedition in Tabarī, *Ta'rīkh*, ed. de Goeje (Leiden, 1890), series 1, vol. 4, p. 1850.

33. Shaybānī, *al-Siyar al-Kabīr*, vol. 1, p. 20; and Herman Theodorus Obbink, *De Heilige Oorlog Volgen den Koran* (Leiden, 1901), pp. 110–11.

34. Ibn Khaldūn, *al-Muqaddima*, vol. 2, pp. 220–21.

35. The economic factors are discussed by Carl H. Becker in *The Cambridge Medieval History* (Cambridge, 1913), vol. 2, pp. 329 ff.; Henri Lammens, *Le Berceau de l'Islam* (Rome, 1914), vol. 1, pp. 114 ff.; the Semitic migratory theory is discussed in Prince Caetani, *Annali dell'Islam* (Milan, 1907), vol. 2, pp. 831–61.

36. Abū Dā'ūd, *Sunan*, vol. 3, p. 4.

37. Ibn Hudhayl, *Tuhfat al-Anfus wa Shi'ar Sukkān al-Andalus*, p. 15.

38. See chap. 13 in Khadduri, *War and Peace in the Law of Islam*.

39. Ibn Khaldūn, *al-Muqaddima*, vol. 1, pp. 309 ff.

40. For an exposition of the Shī'ī law of the jihād, see Tūsī, *Kitāb Masā'il al-Khilāf* (Tehran, 1370 H), vol. 2, pp. 196–99; and Qāḍī Nu'mān, *Da'ā'im al-Islām*, ed. Āsif ibn 'Alī Faydī (Fyzee) (Cairo, 1951), vol. 1, pp. 399–466. For a translation of the Shī'ī law of the jihād, see A. Querry, *Recueil de lois concernant les Musulmans Schyites* (Paris, 1881), vol. 1, pp. 321–53.

41. 'Abd-Allah ibn Muftāh, *Sharh al-Azhār* (Cairo, 1358 H), vol. 5, p. 525.

42. See R. Strothmann, *Das Staatrecht de Zaiditen* (Strassburg, 1912), p. 61.

43. Ibid., p. 105.

44. Qāḍī Nu'mān, *Da'ā'im al-Islām*, vol. 1, p. 434; Hillī, *Tabsirat al-Muta'allimīn fī Ahkām al-Dīn* (Damascus, 1342 H), p. 103; Strothmann, *Das Staatrecht de Zaiditen*, p. 91.

45. This situation has not arisen among the Zaydis, since they technically elect their imāms.

46. For an exposition of the Shī'ī doctrine of Mahdism, see Dwight M. Donaldson, *The Shiite Religion* (London, 1933), chap. 21.

47. The Khārijīs do not actually add a sixth pillar to the already recognized five pillars of the Sunnīs, because they substitute jihād for imān (which to them is synonymous with Islam) and thus the number of the pillars is not increased.

48. See note 27, above.

49. Bukhārī, *Kitāb al-Jāmi' al-Sahīh*, vol. 2, p. 227.

50. Shahrastānī, *Kitāb al-Milal wa'l-Nihal*, ed. Cureton (London, 1840), pp. 90, 93; and Ras'anī's *Mukhtasar*, pp. 73, 80, 97.

51. Badr al-Dīn Ibn Jamā'a, "Tahrīr al-Ahkām fī Tadbīr Ahl al-Islām," ed. H. Koefler, *Islamica* 6 (1934): 365.

52. Tartūshī, *Sirāl al-Mulūk*, pp. 150–53.

53. Ibn 'Abd-Allah, who wrote his book in 708 H, gives seven reasons for the recurrence of war in society: First, for the establishment of a new state (dawla) or dynasty; second, for the consolidation of an already established state or dynasty; third, the wars of a just state (dawla 'ādila) against rebels and dissenters; fourth, wars between two nations or tribes in the form of raids; fifth, the annexation of one state by another, regardless of whether the latter was just or unjust; sixth, wars for the purpose of mere robbery, not for any political purpose; seventh, intertribal warfare as those existed in pre-Islamic Arabia. Al-Hasan ibn 'Abd-Allah, *Āthār al-Uwal fī Tartīb al-Duwal* (Cairo, 1295 H), pp. 167–68.

54. Ibn Khaldūn, *al-Muqaddima*, vol. 2, pp. 65–79.

55. Ibn Khaldūn is not the first thinker who said that warfare is the normal state in society, but he was the first Muslim thinker to say so. Plato (*The Laws*, bk. 1, 2) before him as well as others after in medieval and modern times have expressed similar ideas. Hobbes, in an often quoted statement, said: "Hereby it is manifest, that during the time men live without a common power to keep them all in awe, they are in that condition which is called war; and such a war, as is of every man, against every man. For war, consisteth not in battle only, or the act of fighting; but in a tract of time, wherein the will to contend by battle is sufficiently known: and therefore the notion of time, is to be considered in the nature of war; as it is in the nature of weather. For as the nature of foul weather, lieth not in a shower or two of rain; but in an inclination thereto of many days together: so the nature of war consisteth not in actual fighting; but in the known disposition thereto, during all the time there is no assurance to the contrary. All other time is peace." (Hobbes, *Leviathan*, chap. 13). See also Leo Strauss, *The Political Philosophy of Hobbes* (Oxford, 1936), pp. 160–63.

56. Sir Henry Maine, *International Law* (London, 1888), p. 8. See also Quincy Wright, *A Study of War*, vol. 1, chaps. 6 and 7, appendixes 6, 8, 9, and 10.

33

JIHAD:
AN INTRODUCTION

Rudolph Peters

The Arabic word *jihad* (verbal noun of the verb *jahada*) means to strive, to exert oneself, to struggle. The word has a basic connotation of an endeavour towards a praiseworthy aim. In a religious context it may express a struggle against one's evil inclinations or an exertion for the sake of Islam and the *umma*, e.g., trying to convert unbelievers or working for the moral betterment of Islamic society ("jihad of the tongue" and "jihad of the pen"). In the books on Islamic law, the word means armed struggle against the unbelievers, which is also a common meaning in the Koran. Sometimes the "jihad of the sword" is called "the smaller jihad," in opposition to the peaceful forms named "the greater jihad." Nowadays, it is often used without any religious connotation, more or less equivalent to the English word crusade ("A crusade against drugs"). If used in a religious context, the adjective "Islamic" or "holy" is currently added to it (*al jihad al-Islam i or al-jihad al-muqaddas*).

The origin of the concept of jihad goes back to the wars fought by the Prophet Mohammed and their written reflection in the Koran. It is clear that the concept was influenced by the ideas of war among the pre-Islamic Northern Arabic tribes. Among these, war was the normal state, unless two or more tribes had concluded a truce. War between tribes was regarded as lawful and if the war was fought as a defence against aggression, the fighting had an additional justification. Ideas of chivalry forbade warriors to kill non-combatants like children, women and old people. These rules have become incorporated into the doctrine of jihad which was fixed in the latter half of the second century of the Hijra era.

The Koran frequently mentions jihad and fighting (*qit'il*) against the unbelievers. K. 22.39 ("Leave is given to those who fight because they were

Rudolph Peters, "Jihad: An Introduction," in *Jihad in Classical and Modern Islam* (Princeton, NJ: Markus Wiener, 1996), pp. 1–8.

wronged—surely God is able to help them—who were expelled from their habitations without right, except that they say 'Our Lord is God.'"), revealed not long after the Hijra, is traditionally considered to be the first verse dealing with the fighting of the unbelievers. Many verses exhort the believers to take part in the fighting "with their goods and lives" (*bi-amwalihim wa-anfusihim*), promise reward to those who are killed in the jihad (K. 3.157–58, 169–72) and threaten those who do not fight with severe punishments in the hereafter (K. 9.81–82, 48:16). Other verses deal with practical matters such as exemption from military service (K. 9.91, 48.17), fighting during the holy months (K. 2.217), and in the holy territory of Mecca (K. 2.191), the fate of prisoners of war (K. 47.4), safe conduct (K. 9.6), and truce (K. 8.61).

It is not clear whether the Koran allows Muslims to fight the unbelievers only as a defense against aggression or under all circumstances. In support of the first view a number of verses can be quoted justifying fighting as a reaction against aggression or perfidy on the part of the unbelievers (e.g., "*And fight in the way of God with those who fight you, but aggress not: God loves not the aggressors,*" [K. 2.190] and "*But if they break their oaths after their covenant and thrust at your religion, then fight the leaders of unbelief.*" [K. 9.12]). In those verses that seem to order the Muslims to fight the unbelievers unconditionally, the general condition that fighting is only allowed by way of defense could be said to be understood (e.g., "*Then, when the sacred months are drawn away, slay the idolaters wherever you find them, and take them, and confine them, and lie in wait for them at every place of ambush,*" [K. 9.5] and "*Fight those who believe not in God and the Last Day and do not forbid what God and His Messenger have forbidden—such men as practise not the religion of truth, being of those who have been given the Book—until they pay the tribute out of hand and have been humbled.*" [K. 9.29]). Classical Muslim Koran interpretation, however, did not go into this direction. It regarded the Sword Verses, with the unconditional command to fight the unbelievers, as having abrogated all previous verses concerning the intercourse with non-Muslims. This idea is no doubt connected with the pre-Islamic concept that war between tribes was allowed, unless there existed a truce between them, whereby the Islamic *umma* took the place of a tribe.

During the second half of the eighth century the first comprehensive treatises on the law of jihad were written by al-Awza'i (d. 774) and Muhammad al-Shaybani (d. 804). The legal doctrine of jihad was the result of debates and discussions that had been going on since the Prophet's death and through which the doctrine had been developed. The period in which the doctrine of jihad was gradually formulated coincided with the period of the great conquests, in which the Muslim conquerors were exposed to the cultures of the conquered peoples. With regard to the doctrine of jihad, there may have been some influence from the Byzantine Empire, where the idea of religious war and related notions were very much alive. It is, however, very difficult to identify these influences. If there are similarities, they are not necessarily the result of borrowing and may be due to parallel developments.

The doctrine of jihad, as laid down in the works on Islamic law, developed out of the Koranic prescriptions and the example of the Prophet and the first caliphs, which is recorded in the hadith. The crux of the doctrine is the existence of one single Islamic state, ruling the entire *umma*. It is the duty of the *umma* to expand the territory of this state in order to bring as many people under its rule as possible. The ultimate aim is to bring the whole earth under the sway of Islam and to extirpate unbelief: "*Fight them until there is no persecution (or: seduction) and the religion is God's (entirely).*" (K. 2.193 and 8.39). Expansionist jihad is a collective duty (*fard 'ala al-kifaya*), which is fulfilled if a sufficient number of people take part in it. If this is not the case, the whole *umma* is sinning. Expansionist jihad presupposes the presence of a legitimate caliph to organize the struggle. After the conquests had come to an end, the legal specialists laid down that the caliph had to raid enemy territory at least once a year in order to keep the idea of jihad alive.

Sometimes jihad becomes an individual duty. This is the case when the caliph appoints certain persons to participate in a raiding expedition or when someone takes an oath to fight the unbelievers. Moreover, jihad becomes obligatory for all people capable of fighting in a certain region if this region is attacked by the enemy. In this case, jihad is defensive.

Sunnite and Shi'ite theories of jihad are very similar. However, there is one crucial difference. The Twelver Shi'ites hold that jihad can only be waged under the leadership of the rightful *Imam*. After the Occultation of the last one in 873, theoretically no lawful jihad can be fought. This is true for expansionist jihad. However, as defence against attacks remains obligatory and the *'ulama* are often regarded as the representatives of the Hidden Imam, several wars between Iran and Russia in the 19th century have been called jihad.

War against unbelievers may not be mounted without summoning them to Islam or submission before the attack. A *hadith* lays down the precise contents of the summons:

> Whenever the Prophet appointed a commander to an army or an expedition, he would say: ". . . When you meet your heathen enemies, summon them to three things. Accept whatsoever they agree to and refrain then from fighting them. Summon them to become Muslims. If they agree, accept their conversion. In that case summon them to move from their territory to the Abode of the Emigrants [i.e., Medina]. If they refuse that, let them know that then they are like the Muslim bedouins and that they share only in the booty, when they fight together with the [other] Muslims. If they refuse conversion, then ask them to pay poll-tax (*jizya*). If they agree, accept their submission. But if they refuse, then ask God for assistance and fight them. . . ." (*Sahih* Muslim)

This *hadith* also neatly sums up the aims of fighting unbelievers: conversion or submission. In the latter case, the enemies were entitled to keep their religion and practice it, against payment of a poll-tax (*jizya*) (cf. K. 9.29, quoted above). Although the Koran limits this option to the People of the Book, i.e., Christians and Jews, it was in practice extended to other religions, such as the Zoroastrians (*Majus*).

Whenever the caliph deems it in the interest of the *umma*, he may conclude a truce with the enemy, just as the Prophet did with the Meccans at al-Hudaybiyya. According to some law schools a truce must be concluded for a specified period of time, no longer than ten years. Others hold that this is not necessary, if the caliph stipulates that he may resume war whenever he wishes to do so. The idea behind it is that the notion of jihad must not fall into oblivion.

The books on law contain many practical rules concerning warfare, dealing, e.g., with exemptions from the obligation to fight, the protection of the lives of noncombatants, lawful methods of warfare, treatment of prisoners of war, safe-conduct to enemy persons, and the division of the spoils.

The most important function of the doctrine of jihad is that it mobilizes and motivates Muslims to take part in wars against unbelievers, as it is considered to be the fulfillment of a religious duty. This motivation is strongly fed by the idea that those who are killed on the battlefield, called martyrs (*shahid*, plur. *shuhada'*), will go directly to Paradise. At the occasion of wars fought against unbelievers, religious texts would circulate, replete with Koranic verses and *hadiths* extolling the merits of fighting a jihad and vividly describing the reward waiting in the hereafter for those slain during the fighting.

Another function was to enhance the legitimation of a ruler. After the year 750, the political unity of the *umma* was lost, never to be restored again. Several rulers would govern different regions of the Muslim world. One of the ways to acquire greater legitimacy was to wage jihad against unbelievers, which is one of the main tasks of the lawful caliph.

A final function of the jihad doctrine was that it provided a set of rules governing the relationship with the unbelieving enemies and behaviour during actual warfare. Muftis could invoke this set of rules and give fatwas showing that a ruler's foreign policy was in conformity with the rules of Islamic law. These rules could be moulded to fit the circumstance. A case in point is that, due to the collapse of Islamic political unity, often two Muslim states would be at war with one another. In such situations rnuftis would usually find cause to label the enemies either as rebels or as heretics, thus justifying the struggle against them.

During Islamic history, but especially in the 18th and 19th centuries, radical movements striving for a purification of Islam and the establishment of a purely Islamic society proclaimed jihad against their opponents, both Muslims and non-Muslims. To justify the struggle against their Muslim adversaries, they would brand them as unbelievers for their neglect to adhere to and enforce the strict rules of Islam.

For some Muslim intellectuals the colonial experience affected their outlook on jihad. Some would argue that in view of the military superiority of the colonizer, jihad was not obligatory anymore on the strength of K. 2.195 (". . . and cast not yourselves by your own hands into destruction . . ."). Others, however, elaborated new interpretations of the doctrine of jihad.

The first one to do so was the Indian Muslim thinker Sayyid Ahmad Khan (1817–1898). When after the Mutiny of 1857 the British, arguing that the Muslims wanted to restore Moghul rule and that the doctrine of jihad made them fight the British, began favouring the Hindus in the army and in government service, Sayyid Ahmad Khan wanted to show that Islam did not forbid cooperation with the British colonial government. In this he was motivated by his desire to safeguard employment for the young Muslims from the middle and higher classes. In order to demonstrate that the Indian Muslims were not obliged to fight the British and could be loyal subjects, he gave a new interpretation of the jihad doctrine. On the basis of a new reading of the Koran, he asserted that jihad was obligatory for Muslims only in the case of "positive oppression or obstruction in the exercise of their faith . . . impair[ing] the foundation of some of the pillars of Islam." Since the British, in his opinion, did not interfere with the practising of Islam, jihad against them was not allowed.

Middle Eastern Muslim reformers like Muhammad 'Abduh (1849–1905) and Muhammad Rashid Rida (1865–1935) did not go as far as Sayyid Ahmad Khan. On the strength of those Koranic verses that make fighting against the unbelievers conditional upon their aggression or perfidy, they argue that peaceful coexistence is the normal state between Islamic and non-Islamic territories, and that jihad is only allowed as defensive warfare. This, however, left the way open to proclaim jihad against colonial oppression, as the colonial enterprise was clearly an attack on the territory of Islam. A recent development in this line of thinking is the presentation of the jihad doctrine as a form of Muslim international law and the equation of jihad with the concept of *bellum justum*. Those who have elaborated this theory proudly point out that Muhammad al-Shaybani (d. 804) had formulated a doctrine of international public law more than eight centuries before Hugo Grotius.

Present-day thinking about jihad, however, offers a wider spectrum than only the modernist interpretation mentioned here. Apart from the conservatives, who adhere to the interpretation as given in the classical books on Islamic law, there are the ideologues of the radical Islamic opposition, who call for jihad as a means to spread their brand of Islam. Some of these radical groups call for the use of violence in order to defeat the established governments. However, they are faced with a serious doctrinal problem, as they preach an armed revolution against Muslim rulers, whereas Islamic law allows revolt only in very rare circumstances. One of these is when a ruler abandons his belief. Since the apostate deserves capital punishment, fighting against him is allowed. Throughout Islamic history, governments and opposition movements have declared their Muslim adversaries to be heretics or unbelievers (*takfir*, declaring someone to be a *kafir*, unbeliever) in order to justify their struggle against them. It is this line of reasoning that is used by contemporary radical Islamic groups to give legitimacy to their use of arms against rulers who are to all appearances Muslims. In modern times these views were first propagated by fundamentalists like Sayyid Qutb (d. 1966) and Abu al-Adla al-Mawdudi (1903–1979).

The most eloquent and elaborate statement of this view can be found in a pamphlet published by the ideologue of the Jihad Organization, whose members, in 1981, assassinated President Sadat of Egypt. It is called *al-Farida al-Gha'iba*, or "The Absent Duty" referring to the duty to wage jihad, which, according to the author, 'Abd al-Salam Faraj, is not fulfilled anymore. The author borrows his arguments from two fatwas issued by the fundamentalist author Ibn Taymiyya (1263–1328), whose opinion was sought regarding the legitimacy of Mongol rule in the Middle East. The prop of Ibn Taymiyya's reasoning is the fact that they apply their own law instead of the Shari'a. This, in his opinion, is sufficient cause to regard them as unbelievers, even if they pronounce the profession of faith. However, even if this argument is not accepted, then they still have forfeited their right to demand the obedience of their Muslim subjects and they may be fought.

The author of "The Absent Duty" argues that the situation Ibn Taymiyya describes is very similar to the Egyptian situation, as Egyptian law, with the exception of family law and the law of succession, is based on codes of Western inspiration. Observing that in spite of the vocal demands of the Islamist groups the government has always refused to introduce the Shari'a, the author concludes that such a government cannot be regarded as Islamic and that it is an individual duty of all Muslims to rise in armed rebellion against this heathen regime in order to replace it with an Islamic one.

34

WAR AND PEACE IN ISLAM

Bassam Tibi

Islam is a system of moral obligations derived from divine revelation and based on the belief that human knowledge can never be adequate. It follows that believers must act on the basis of Allah's knowledge, which is the exclusive source of truth for Muslims. Ethics in Islam, though concerned with man's actions, always relates these actions to the word of God as revealed to the Prophet, Muhammad, and as collected in the Qur'an. This understanding of ethics is shared by all Muslims, Sunni or Shi'i, Arab or non-Arab.[1]

In this chapter, I first identify the Qur'anic conceptions of war and peace that are based on this ethical foundation. I then consider several Islamic traditions pertaining to the grounds for war, the conduct of war, and the proper relation of Islam to the modern international system. I conclude that the Islamic worldview is resistant to change and that there are many obstacles to the development of an ethic of war and peace compatible with the circumstances of the modern age.

The basic scriptures of Islam, the Qur'an and the hadith, are written in Arabic. My effort here to understand Islamic thinking on war and peace focuses on the Qur'an and on interpretations of Islamic tradition in contemporary Sunni Islam. Because the most important trends in Sunni Islam have been occurring in the Arab world (all Sunni Muslims are, for example, bound by the fatwas of the Islamic al-Azhar University in Cairo), my references to the Arabic Qur'an, to the teachings of al-Azhar, and to authoritative sources for Islamic fundamentalism reflect not Arab centrism but the realities of Islam.

CONCEPTIONS OF WAR AND PEACE

The Qur'an chronicles the establishment of Islam in Arabia between the years 610 and 632 CE. In early Meccan Islam, before the founding of the first Islamic state at Medina, in a Bedouin culture hostile to state structures, one fails to find

Bassam Tibi, "War and Peace in Islam," in *The Ethics of War and Peace: Religious and Secular Perspectives*, ed. Terry Nardin (Princeton, NJ: Princeton University Press, 1996), pp. 128–45.

Qur'anic precepts related to war and peace. Most Meccan verses focus on spiritual issues. Following their exodus (*hijra*) from Mecca in 622, the Prophet and his supporters established in Medina the first Islamic political community (*umma*). All Qur'anic verses revealed between 622 and the death of the Prophet in 632 relate to the establishment of Islam at Medina through violent struggle against the hostile tribes surrounding the city-state.

Most debate among Muslims about the Islamic ethics of war and peace is based on literal readings of the Qur'anic verses pertaining to early Medina. Muslims believe in the absolutely eternal validity of the Qur'an and the hadith (the sayings and deeds of the Prophet). Muslims believe that human beings must scrupulously obey the precepts of the Qur'an. In addition, Muslims are generally reluctant to take a historical view of their religion and culture. Quotations from the Qur'an serve as the point of departure for discussions of war and peace.[2]

Qur'anic traditions of war are based on verses related to particular events. At times, they contradict one another. It is not possible, therefore, to reconstruct from these verses a single Islamic ethic of war and peace.[3] Instead, there are a number of different traditions, each of which draws selectively on the Qur'an to establish legitimacy for its view of war and peace.

The common foundation for all Islamic concepts of war and peace is a worldview based on the distinction between the "abode of Islam" (*dar al-Islam*), the "home of peace" (*dar al-salam*) (Q. 10.25), and the non-Muslim world, the "house of war" (*dar al-harb*).[4] This distinction was the hallmark of the Islamic system before the globalization of European society and the rise of the modern international system.[5] In fact, however, the division of the world in early Islam into the abode of peace and the world of unbelievers clashed with reality long before the intrusion of Europe into the Muslim world. Bernard Lewis, for example, argues that by the Middle Ages, the dar al-Islam was dismembered into a "multiplicity of separate, often warring sovereignties." Lewis also holds that "in international . . . matters, a widening gap appeared between legal doctrine and political fact, which politicians ignored and jurists did their best to conceal."[6] As we shall see, this refusal to come to terms with reality remains a hallmark of Islamic thought today.

The establishment of the new Islamic polity at Medina and the spread of the new religion were accomplished by waging war. The sword became the symbolic image of Islam in the West.[7] In this formative period as well as during the period of classical Islam, Islamic militancy was reinforced by the superiority of Muslims over their enemies. Islamic jurists never dealt with relations with non-Muslims under conditions other than those of "the house of war," except for the temporary cessation of hostilities under a limited truce.

The military revolution that took place between the years 1500 and 1800 signaled the start of modern times and, ultimately, the rise of the West and the concomitant decline of the world of Islam. Since the beginning of the seventeenth century, Muslims have tried to establish armies on the European model to offset the increasing weakness of the "abode of Islam."[8] The rise of the West as a superior military power ultimately led to the globalization of the European model of the modern state. The changed historical balance presented Muslims with a major challenge, for the dichotomy between dar al-Islam and dar al-harb is incompatible with the reality of the world of nation-states. Each of these changes created pressure for Muslims to rethink their holistic worldview and their traditional ethics of war and peace. But despite its incompatibility with the current international system, there has yet to be an authoritative revision of this worldview.

At its core, Islam is a religious mission to all humanity. Muslims are religiously obliged to disseminate the Islamic faith throughout the world: "We have sent you forth to all mankind" (Q. 34.28). If non-Muslims submit to conversion or subjugation, this call (*da'wa*) can be pursued peacefully. If they do not, Muslims are obliged to wage war against them. In Islam, peace requires that non-Muslims submit to the call of Islam, either by converting or by accepting the status of a religious minority (*dhimmi*) and paying the imposed poll tax, *jizya*. World peace, the final stage of the *da'wa*, is reached only with the conversion or submission of all mankind to Islam.

It is important to note that the expression "dar al-harb" (house of war) is not Qur'anic; it was coined in the age of Islamic military expansion. It is, however, in line with the Qur'anic revelation dividing the world into a peaceful part (the Islamic community) and a hostile part (unbelievers who are expected to convert to Islam, if not freely then through the instrument of war). In this sense, Muslims believe that expansion through war is not aggression but a fulfillment of the Qur'anic command to spread Islam as a way to peace. The resort to force to disseminate Islam is not war (*harb*), a word that is used only to describe the use of force by non-Muslims. Islamic wars are not *hurub* (the plural of *harb*) but rather *futuhat*, acts of "opening" the world to Islam and expressing Islamic *jihad*.

Relations between dar al-Islam, the home of peace, and dar al-harb, the world of unbelievers, nevertheless take place in a state of war, according to the Qur'an and to the authoritative commentaries of Islamic jurists. Unbelievers who stand in the way, creating obstacles for the *da'wa*, are blamed for this state of war, for the *da'wa* can be pursued peacefully if others submit to it. In other words, those who resist Islam cause wars and are responsible for them. Only when Muslim power is weak is "temporary peace" (*hudna*) allowed (Islamic jurists differ on the definition of "temporary"). The notion of temporary peace introduces a third realm: territories under temporary treaties with Muslim powers (*dar al-sulh* or, at times, *dar al-'and*).[9]

The attitude of Muslims toward war and nonviolence can be summed up briefly: there is no Islamic tradition of nonviolence and no presumption against war. But war is never glorified and is viewed simply as the last resort in responding to the da'wa to disseminate Islam, made necessary by the refusal of unbelievers to submit to Islamic rule. In other words, there is no such thing as Islamic pacifism.

THE GROUNDS FOR WAR

The Western distinction between just and unjust wars linked to specific grounds for war is unknown in Islam. Any war against unbelievers, whatever its immediate ground, is morally justified. Only in this sense can one distinguish just and unjust wars in Islamic tradition. When Muslims wage war for the dissemination of Islam, it is a just war (*futuhat*, literally "opening," in the sense of opening the world, through the use of force, to the call to Islam); when non-Muslims attack Muslims, it is an unjust war (*'idwan*).

The usual Western interpretation of jihad as a "just war" in the Western sense is, therefore, a misreading of this Islamic concept. I disagree, for example, with Khadduri's interpretation of the jihad as *bellum justum*. As Khadduri himself observes:

> The universality of Islam provided a unifying element for all believers, within the world of Islam, and its defensive-offensive character produced a state of warfare permanently declared against the outside world, the world of war. Thus jihad may be regarded as Islam's instrument for carrying out its ultimate objective by turning all people into believers.[10]

According to the Western just war concept, just wars are limited to a single issue; they are not universal and permanent wars grounded on a religious worldview.

The classical religious doctrine of Islam understands war in two ways. The first is literal war, fighting or battle (*qital*), which in Islam is understood to be a last resort in following the Qur'anic precept to guarantee the spread of Islam, usually when non-Muslims hinder the effort to do so. The other understanding is metaphorical: war as a permanent condition between Muslims and nonbelievers. The Qur'an makes a distinction between fighting (*qital*) and aggression (*'idwan*) and asks Muslims not to be aggressors: "Fight for the sake of Allah against those who fight against you but do not be violent because Allah does not love aggressors" (al-Baqara 2.190). The same Qur'anic passage continues: "Kill them wherever you find them. Drive them out of places from which they drove you. . . . Fight against them until idolatry is no more and Allah's religion reigns supreme" (al-Baqara 2.190–92). The Qur'anic term for fighting is here qital, not jihad. The Qur'an prescribes fighting for the spread of Islam: "Fighting is obligatory for you, much as you dislike it" (al-Baqara 2.216). The qital of Muslims against unbelievers is a religious obligation: "Fight for the cause of Allah . . . how could you not fight for the cause of Allah? . . . True believers fight for the cause of Allah, but the infidels fight for idols" (al-'Nisa 4.74–76).

As noted above, Muslims tend to quote the Qur'an selectively to support their own ethical views. This practice has caused a loss of specificity in the meaning of jihad, as Saddam Hussein's use of the term during the Gulf War illustrates.[11] The current dissension about the concept of jihad dates from the rise of political Islam and the eruption of sectarian religious strife. Present-day Islamic fundamentalist groups—groups whose programs are based on the revival of Islamic values—often invoke the idea of jihad to legitimize their political agendas. The reason for this misuse of the concept is simple: most fundamentalists are lay people who lack intimate knowledge of Islamic sources and who politicize Islam to justify their activities. Before the Gulf War, for example, this occurred in Egypt, during the Lebanon War, and in the civil war in Sudan.[12] Through such overuse and misuse, the concept of jihad has become confused with the related Islamic concept of "armed fighting" (qital). Therefore, there is a great need for a historical analysis of the place of scripture in Islamic tradition. Although Islamic ethics of peace and war are indeed mostly scriptural, scriptural references can be adequately interpreted only in a historical context.

As we have seen, Islam understands itself as a mission of peace for all humanity, although this call (da'wa) can sometimes be pursued by war. In this sense, the da'wa is an invitation to jihad, which means fundamentally "to exert one's self" and can involve either military or nonmilitary effort.[13] Jihad can become a war (qital) against those who oppose Islam, either by failing to submit to it peacefully or by creating obstacles to its spread. Although Islam glorifies neither war nor violence, those Muslims who fight and die for the da'wa are considered blessed by Allah.

During the very beginnings of Islam (that is, before the establishment of the city-state at Medina in 622), the revealed text was essentially spiritual and contained no reference to war. In the Meccan chapter al-Kafirun ("the unbelievers"), the Qur'an asks supporters of the new religion to respond to advocates for other faiths in this manner: "You have your religion and I have mine" (al-Kafirun 109.6). In another Meccan chapter, the Qur'an simply asks believers not to obey unbelievers. Qur'anic verses from this period use the term jihad to describe efforts to convert unbelievers, but not in connection with military action. There is no mention of qital in the Meccan Qur'an. The Muslims then were, in fact, a tiny minority and could not fight. The verse "Do not yield to the unbelievers and use the Qur'an for your jihad [effort] to carry through against them" (al-Furqan 25.52) clearly illustrates this persuasive rather than military use of the word jihad: in Mecca, the only under-taking the Qur'an could ask of believers was the argument.

After the establishment of the Islamic state at Medina, however, the Qur'an comes gradually to offer precepts in which jihad can take the form of qital (fighting). Although the Qur'an teaches the protection of life as given by God and prohibits killing, this norm has an exception: "You shall not kill—for that is forbidden—except for a just cause" (al-An'am 6.151). But it is misleading to interpret this verse as a Qur'anic expression of just war because, as noted above, the distinction between just and unjust war is alien to Islam. Instead, the verse tells Muslims to remain faithful to morality during the qital.

THE CONDUCT OF WAR

When it comes to the conduct of war, one finds only small differences between Islam and other monotheistic religions or the international laws of war. Islam recognizes moral constraints on military conduct, even in wars against non-Muslims. As in other traditions, two categories of restrictions can be distinguished: restrictions on weapons and methods of war, and restrictions on permissible targets. And, just as other traditions sometimes permit these constraints to be set aside in extreme situations, in Islamic law (*shari'a*) we find the precept "Necessity overrides the forbidden" (*al-darura tubih al-mahzurat*). This precept allows moral constraints to be overridden in emergencies, though the criteria for determining whether an emergency exists are vague.

Islamic doctrine regarding the conduct of war developed in an age in which the destructive weapons of industrial warfare were not yet available. The Qur'anic doctrine on the conduct of war is also shaped by pre-Islamic tribal notions of honor. The Qur'an asks believers to honor their promises and agreements: "Keep faith with Allah, when you make a covenant. . . . Do not break your oaths" (al-Nahl 16.19). And: "Those who keep faith with Allah do not break their pledge" (al-R'ad 13.19). It also prescribes that the enemy be notified before an attack.

Regarding permissible targets of war, Qur'anic doctrine is in line with the pre-Islamic norm of "man's boldness" (*shahama*) in strictly prohibiting the targeting of children, women, and the elderly. Consistent with this prohibition, as well as with the pre-Islamic tribal belief that it is not a sign of honor for a man to demonstrate his power to someone who is weaker, is the precept that prisoners be fairly treated (al-Insan 76.8–9). And because the goal of war against unbelievers is to force them to submit to Islam, not to destroy them, the rules of war forbid plundering and destruction.

ISLAM IN THE AGE OF THE TERRITORIAL STATE

Like any text, Islamic scripture permits divergent readings or interpretations (*ta'wil*). I wish to turn now to a discussion of three divergent patterns of Islamic thinking about war and peace, each characteristic of a different period in Islamic history: the conformism of the Islamic scholar Ahmad Ben Khalid al-Nasiri; the more recent conformism of al-Azhar; and finally, the contemporary fundamentalist reinterpretation of the concepts of jihad and *qital*. Conformism seeks to perpetuate, in an altered world, the traditional ethics and the religious doctrine on which it rests, whereas fundamentalism insists on the absolute truth of the religious doctrine.

The pattern of conformism is illustrated in Moroccan thought. Unlike most Islamic states, Morocco has been independent for more than three centuries.

Moroccan dynastic history is state history, and is thus a good example of Islamic conformism. Morocco was the only Arab country the Turks failed to subordinate. Political rule in Morocco was legitimized by Sunni Islam in the sultanate (*Makhzan*), just as Ottoman rule was legitimized by Sunni Islam in the caliphate. Though nineteenth-century Muslim thinkers in general were confused by the changing global balance of power, those Muslim '*ulama* who stood in the service of the Moroccan sultan were in a better position to face the new reality. Ahmad Ben Khalid al-Nasiri (1835–1897) was the first Muslim '*alim* (man of learning) of his age to acknowledge the lack of unity in the Islamic community (*umma*), as well as Islam's weakness in the face of its enemies.

Al-Nasiri provided the legitimizing device for the politics of his Moroccan sultan Hassan I, even though he was reluctant to legitimize the quasi-sovereign Moroccan state and to repudiate the duty of waging war against unbelievers. Conformism like that of al-Nasiri remains the typical pattern among Muslim statesmen and their advisors, many of whom do not even know of al-Nasiri. This pattern is characterized by submission to international standards of law and conduct and acceptance of peaceful relations with non-Islamic countries. But it retains the traditional Islamic belief in the superiority of Islam and the division of the world into Islamic and non-Islamic realms.[14] Al-Nasiri continually refers to the "abode of Islam" (*dar al-Islam*), even though he has only his own country, Morocco, in mind.

Al-Nasiri based his case on two arguments, one scriptural and one expediential. He selectively and repeatedly refers to the Qur'anic verse "If they incline to peace, then make peace with them" (al-Anfal 8.61), which becomes the normative basis for the peace established between Morocco and Europe. Al-Nasiri's expediential argument pertains to the conditions of the Islamic community (*umma*):

> No one today can overlook the power and the superiority of Christians. Muslims . . . are in a condition of weakness and disintegration. . . . Given these circumstances, how can we maintain the opinion and the politics that the weak should confront the strong? How could the unarmed fight against the heavily armed power?[15]

Despite these insights, al-Nasiri maintains that Islam is equally a "shari'a of war" and a "shari'a of peace." He argues that the Qur'anic verse "If they incline to peace, then make peace with them" rests on the notion of "Islamic interest" (*al-maslaha*). Under contemporary conditions, in al-Nasiri's view, the interest of Islam forbids Muslims to wage war against unbelievers:

> The matter depends on the Imam who is in a position to see the interest of Islam and its people in regard to war and peace. There is no determination that they must fight forever or accept peace forever. . . . The authority that cannot be contested is the opinion of the Imam [Sultan Hassan I]. . . . Allah has assigned him to fix our destiny and authorized him to decide for us.[16]

The neo-Islamic notion of *maslaha* is strongly reminiscent of the Western idea of the "national interest" of the modern state.

This pragmatic but submissive fatwa by a leading *'alim* is reflected in the position of most contemporary *'ulama* regarding war and peace. Their ethic of peace is implicitly determined by their view that non-Muslims are enemies with whom Muslims can, at best, negotiate an armistice (*muhadana*). The belief that true peace is only possible among Muslims persists, even though it runs counter to the idea of a pluralist, secular international society.

Today there are two contrary positions on the ethics of war and peace in Islam. The Sunni Islamic establishment, as reflected in the scholarship produced at al-Azhar University, continues the tradition of Islamic conformism, reinterpreting the Islamic notion of jihad to discourage the use of force. In contrast to this peaceful interpretation of Islamic ethics, contemporary Islamic fundamentalists have emphasized the warlike aspect of jihad, while also emphasizing the dichotomy between the dar al-Islam and the dar al-harb.

The authoritative textbooks of al-Azhar contain an ethic of war and peace characterized both by selective use of the sacred text and by free interpretation. Al-Azhar does not offer either a redefinition or a rethinking of the traditional ethics of war and peace in Islam; it simply offers one variety of Islamic conformism.

In the most authoritative textbook of this school, Shaykh Mahmud Shaltut asserts that Islam is a religion for all mankind, but acknowledges that it is open to pluralism.[17] Shaltut quotes the Qur'anic verse "We have created you as peoples and tribes to make you know one another" (al-Hujrat 49.13) to support the legitimacy of interpreting scripture at the service of pluralism. He also rejects the notion that Islam must resort to war to spread its beliefs, again quoting the Qur'an: "Had Allah wanted, all people of the earth would have believed in Him, would you then dare force faith upon them?" (Jon. 10.99). War, he argues, is not a proper instrument for pursuing the call to Islam (*da'wa*). Because "war is an immoral situation," Muslims must live in peace with non-Muslims. Shaltut takes pride in the fact that centuries ago Islam laid the foundations for a peaceful order of relations among nations, whereas

> the states of the present [that is, Western] civilization deceive the people with the so-called public international law. . . . Look at the human massacres which those people commit all over the world while they talk about peace and human rights!

Peaceful coexistence should be sanctioned by treaties that "do not impinge on the essential laws of Islam."[18]

A two-volume textbook edited by the former shaykh of al-Azhar, Jad al-Haqq 'Ali jad al-Haqq, continues the effort to establish the centrality of peace in Islamic ethics and offers a significant reinterpretation of the concept of jihad.[19] But, in line with Islamic tradition, there is no mention of states: at issue is the Islamic community (*umma*) as a whole on the one hand, and the rest of the world on the other.

In a chapter on jihad in the first volume of his textbook, Jad al-Haqq emphasizes that jihad in itself does not mean war. If we want to talk about war, he
argues, we must say "armed jihad" (*al-musallah*), to distinguish between this
jihad and the everyday "jihad against ignorance, jihad against poverty, jihad
against illness and disease. . . . The search for knowledge is the highest level of
jihad." Having made this distinction, the Azhar textbook downgrades the importance of armed jihad, since the *da'wa* can be pursued without fighting:

> In earlier ages the sword was necessary for securing the path of the da'wa. In our
> age, however, the sword has lost its importance, although the resort to it is still
> important for the case of defense against those who wish to do evil to Islam and
> its people. However, for the dissemination of the da'wa there are now a variety
> of ways. . . . Those who focus on arms in our times are preoccupied with weak
> instruments.[20]

Jad al-Haqq also avoids interpreting the *da'wa* as requiring the imposition of
Islam on others: "The da'wa is an offer to join in, not an imposition. . . . Belief is
not for imposition with force." Earlier Meccan verses are quoted again and again
in an effort to separate the *da'wa* from any notion of *qital* or armed jihad. "Islam
was not disseminated with the power of the sword. The qital (fighting) was an
exception only for securing and also for the defense of the da'wa (call) to Islam."
Despite this substantial reinterpretation, however, the textbook insists on the traditional view of Islam as a mission for all of humanity; quoting the Qur'an: "We
have sent you forth as a blessing to mankind" (al-Anbiya 21.107).[21]

The Al-Azhar believes that in the modern age, communication networks offer
a much better medium than armed conflict for the pursuit of the *da'wa*. Jad al-
Haqq does not work out the details, however. He does not resolve the question of
treaties between Muslims and non-Muslims, nor does he mention territorial states.
Jad al-Haqq quotes the classical al-Qurtubi commentary on the Qur'an.[22]
According to this commentary, treaties creating an armistice (*hudna*) between
Muslims and non-Muslims can be valid for a period of no more than ten years.
The model here is the treaty of Hudaybiyya, negotiated by the Prophet with the
Quraysh in a state of war: it was a limited truce. If the Muslims are powerful, they
may not hold an armistice for more than one year; if they are militarily inferior,
an armistice of ten years is allowed. There is no discussion of what occurs after
that time, which implies that it is seen as heretical to revise classical doctrine and
that there is no desire to review this doctrine in the light of changed international
circumstances. The result is conformity or acquiescence to the new international
system, but no effort to alter the classic categories.

Unlike al-Azhar conformists, who seek to read scripture in the light of
present realities, Islamic fundamentalists are inclined to reverse the procedure: a
true Muslim has to view reality in the light of the text. Islamic fundamentalism as
a mass movement dates back to the 1970s, though its intellectual and organiza-

tional roots can be traced to 1928, when the Muslim Brotherhood (*al-Ikhwan al-Muslimun*) was created in Egypt.[23] The leading authorities on the political thought of Islamic fundamentalism are Hasan al-Banna, the founder of this movement, and Sayyid Qutb, its foremost ideologue. But they speak only for fundamentalism, which, because it is a recent trend within Islam, cannot be seen as representative of Islam as a whole—a mistake often made in the Western media.

In his treatise on jihad, Hasan al-Banna makes literal use of the Qur'an and hadith to support conclusions opposed to those of the Islamic conformists quoted above. According to al-Banna, the jihad is an "obligation of every Muslim" (*farida*).[24] *Jihad* and *qital* are used interchangeably to mean "the use of force," whether in the pursuit of resistance against existing regimes or in waging war against unbelievers. Fundamentalists follow the Islamic tradition of not considering states in the context of war and peace; the term "war" is used here to mean fighting among loose parties of believers and unbelievers, no matter how they are organized politically. And in contrast to traditionalists, who distinguish between the use of force to further Islam and wars of aggression ('*idwan*), fundamentalists apply the word jihad indiscriminately to any use of force, whether against unbelievers or against fellow believers whom they suspect of being merely nominal Muslims.

Al-Banna begins his treatise by quoting the al-Baqara verse referred to above: "Fighting is obligatory for you, much as you dislike it" (2.216). He continues with another quotation from the Qur'an: "If you should die or be slain in the cause of Allah, his mercy will surely be better than all the riches you amass" ('Imran 3.158). And, "We shall richly reward them whether they die or conquer" (al-Nisa' 4.74). These and similar quotations serve as the basis for al-Banna's glorification of fighting and death in "the cause of Allah."

But al-Banna does not cite the tolerant Qur'anic verse from al-Kafirun, "You have your religion and I have mine," preferring instead to extend the obligation of the *qital* even against the "People of the Book" (*ahl al-kitab*)—Christians and Jews—with the verse "Fight against those who neither believe in Allah nor in the Last Day . . . until they pay tribute out of hand and are utterly subdued" (al-Tauba 9.29). Allah, he concludes, "has obliged Muslims to fight . . . to secure the pursuit of *al-da'wa* and thus of peace, while disseminating the great mission which God entrusted to them."[25]

With a few exceptions, the al-Azhar textbook does not treat the armed *jihad* (*jihad al-musallah*) as a duty for Muslims in the modern age. It downgrades the status of fighting (*qital*) while it upgrades the nonmilitary jihad against such evils as ignorance, poverty, and disease. In contrast, al-Banna draws a distinction between "low jihad" (*al jihad al-asghar*) and "high jihad" (*al jihad al-akbar*), ridiculing those Muslims who consider the *qital* to be a "low jihad." He considers this denigration of *qital* to be a misunderstanding of *qital* as the true essence of jihad: "The great reward for Muslims who fight is to kill or be killed for the sake of Allah." Al-Banna's treatise is in fact permeated with rhetoric glorifying death, which seems to legitimize the suicidal terrorist acts often committed by Islamic fundamentalists:

> Allah rewards the umma which masters the art of death and which acknowledges the necessity of death in dignity. . . . Be sure, death is inevitable. . . . If you do this for the path of Allah, you will be rewarded.[26]

It is clear that for al-Banna, peace is possible only under the banner of Islam. Non-Muslims should be permitted to live only as members of protected minorities under Islamic rule. In all other cases, war against unbelievers is a religious duty of Muslims.

The other leading fundamentalist authority, Sayyid Qutb, has revived the dichotomous Islamic division of the world into "the house of peace" (dar al-Islam) and "the house of war" (dar al-harb). He employs this dichotomy to establish that war against "unbelievers" is a religious duty for Muslims. Giving the old dichotomy a new twist, he coins the expressions "the world of believers" and "the world of neo-jahiliyya" (jahiliyya is the Islamic term for the pre-Islamic age of ignorance). For Qutb, modernity is nothing more than a new form of jahiliyya. Qutb claims that "the battle lying ahead is one between the believers and their enemies. . . . Its substance is the question kufr aw iman? (unbelief or belief?), jahiliyya aw Islam? (ignorance or Islam?)."[27] The confrontation, then, is "between Islam and the international society of ignorance"[28]—a confrontation in which victory is reserved for Islam.[29]

The large number of pamphlets industriously produced by Islamic fundamentalists during the past two decades seldom go beyond quoting passages from al-Banna and Qutb. Contemporary fundamentalists often cite passages like this from Qutb:

> The dynamic spread of Islam assumes the form of jihad by the sword . . . not as a defensive movement, as those Muslim defeatists imagine, who subjugate to the offensive pressure of Western orientalists. . . . Islam is meant for the entire globe.[30]

Qutb's repudiation of the mainstream conformist view that Islam resorts to war only for the defense of Muslim lands is central to fundamentalist thinking.

Qutb's influence is illustrated in Muhammad Na'im Yasin's 1990 book on jihad. The book develops an understanding of war between believers and unbelievers as a gradual process in which, in the last stage, "regardless of an attack of the Muslim lands by unbelievers, . . . fighting of Muslims against them ought to take place." Yasin then quotes the Qur'anic verse "Fight against the unbelievers in their entirety as they fight against you in your entirety" (9.36), commenting on the verse as follows: "The duty of jihad in Islam results in the necessity of qital against everyone who neither agrees to convert to Islam nor to submit himself to Islamic rule." He concludes that the ultimate "return to Allah cannot be pursued through wishful thinking but only through the means of *jihad*."[31] According to Colonel Ahmad al-Mu'mini, an officer in the Jordanian army, this offensive view of jihad must determine the military policies of all Islamic states.[32] Al-Mu'mini's views have been widely circulated.

As we have seen, some Muslims have made the effort to adapt Islamic doctrine to the modern international system, but many go only so far as to make pragmatic adjustments to the doctrine that mankind must either accept Islam or submit to Muslim rule. It is true that Islamic states subordinate themselves to international law by virtue of their membership in the United Nations. But although international law prohibits war, Islamic law (the *shari'a*) prescribes war against unbelievers.[33] Does the recognition of international law by Islamic states really indicate a revision of Islamic ethics regarding war and peace? Or does this recognition indicate no more than outward conformity of the Muslim world to international society?

Most Western authors on war and peace in Islam overlook the fact that there is no concept of the territorial state in Islam.[34] Therefore, Islamic thinkers view war as a struggle, not between states, but between Muslims as a community (*umma*) and the rest of the world inhabited by unbelievers (*dar al-harb*). In contrast, the classic treatise on Islamic "international law" by the Muslim legal scholar Najib Armanazi acknowledges that the international order established by the treaty of Westphalia—in which relations among states are organized on the basis of the mutual recognition of each other's sovereignty—is contradicted by the intention of the Arab conquerors to impose their rule everywhere. But despite this contradiction, Armanazi argues, Muslims do in practice recognize the sovereignty of states with whom they conduct relations on the basis of "the *aman*, customary law or the rule of honoring agreements (*'and, 'uhud*)." Nevertheless, "for Muslims war is the basic rule and peace is understood only as a temporary armistice. . . . Only if Muslims are weak [are their adversaries] entitled to reconciliation." And, he continues, "for Muslim jurists peace only matters when it is in line with the *maslaha* (interest) of Muslims."[35] Between Muslim and non-Muslim, peace is only a temporary armistice and war remains the rule.

In short, Muslim states adhere to public international law but make no effort to accommodate the outmoded Islamic ethics of war and peace to the current international order. Thus, their conduct is based on outward conformity, not on a deeper "cultural accommodation"—that is, a rethinking of Islamic tradition that would make it possible for them to accept a more universal law regulating war and peace in place of Islamic doctrine. Such a "cultural accommodation" of the religious doctrine to the changed social and historical realities would mean a reform of the role of the religious doctrine itself as the cultural underpinning of Islamic ethics of war and peace.[36] If this is correct, then Mayer's conclusion that

"Islamic and international legal traditions, long separated by different perspectives, are now starting to converge in areas of common concern"[37] is far too optimistic. The convergence is limited to practical matters and does not reach to basic conceptions of war and peace.[38]

On the contrary, what we have seen, instead of convergence with Western ideas, is a revival of the classical doctrine of the dichotomy between dar al-Islam and dar al-harb. Muslim writers today commonly describe all the wars involving Muslim lands since 1798 (when Napoleon invaded Egypt) down to the Arab-Israeli wars and the Gulf War as "unjust wars" undertaken by the "crusaders" against the world of Islam.[39]

For Muslims, the modern age is marked by a deep tension between Islam and the territorial state.[40] In fact, there is no generally accepted concept of the state in Islam; the "community of believers" (*umma*), not the state, has always been the focus of Islamic doctrine. With a few exceptions, Islamic jurists do not deal with the notion of the state (*dawla*). As the Moroccan scholar 'Abd al-Latif Husni writes in his study of Islam and international relations, recent defenders of the classical Islamic division of the world

> confine themselves to quoting classical Islamic jurists. In their writings we do not even find the term "state." This deliberate disregard indicates their intention to ignore the character of the modern system of international relations. They refuse to acknowledge the multiplicity of states which are sovereign and equal in maintaining the notions of *dar al-Islam* and *dar al-harb*.[41]

Though the Islamic world has made many adjustments to the modern international system,[42] there has been no cultural accommodation, no rigorously critical rethinking of Islamic tradition.[43]

CONCLUSION

In discussing the basic concepts of the Islamic tradition of war and peace, and their understanding by Muslims at the present, my focus has been on Muslim attitudes toward war. The ground for war is always the dissemination of Islam throughout the world. And in conducting war, Muslims are to avoid destruction and to deal fairly with the weak. Muslims do not view the use of force to propagate Islam as an act of war, given their understanding of the *da'wa* as an effort to abolish war by bringing the entire world into the "house of Islam," which is the house of peace. For this reason, as we have seen, Islamic conquests are described by Islamic historians not as wars (*hurub*) but as "openings" (*futuhat*) of the world to Islam.

Despite the universal religious mission of Islam, the world of Islam was a regional, not a global, system.[44] The only global system in the history of mankind is our present international system, which is the result of the expansion of the European model. As we have seen, this modern international system has placed strain on the ethics of war and peace in Islam, generating the divergent responses of conformism and fundamentalism.

Islamic war/peace ethics is scriptural and premodern. It does not take into account the reality of our times, which is that international morality is based on relations among sovereign states, not on the religions of the people living therein. Though the Islamic states acknowledge the authority of international law regulating relations among states, Islamic doctrine governing war and peace continues to be based on a division of the world into dar al-Islam and dar al-harb. The divine law of Islam, which defines a partial community in international society, still ranks above the laws upon which modern international society rests.

The confrontation between Islam and the West will continue, and it will assume a most dramatic form.[45] Its outcome will depend on two factors: first, the ability of Muslims to undertake a "cultural accommodation" of Islamic religious concepts and their ethical underpinnings to the changed international environment; and second, their ability to accept equality and mutual respect between themselves and those who do not share their beliefs.

NOTES

1. George Makdisi, "Ethics in Islamic and Rationalist Doctrine," in *Ethics in Islam*, ed. Richard G. Hovannisian (Malibu, CA: Udena Publications, 1985), p. 47. On the concept of knowledge in Islam, see Bassam Tibi, *Islamischer Fundamentalismus, moderne Wissenschaft and Technologic* (Frankfurt am Main: Suhrkamp Verlag, 1992), pp. 80–93; and "Culture and Knowledge," *Theory, Culture, and Society* 12 (1995): 1–24.

2. Representative of this method, and equally authoritative, is a book by the former shaykh of al-Azhar, 'Abd al-Halim Mahmud, *Al-Jihad wa al-nasr* (Cairo: Dar al-Katib al-'Arabi, 1968). This work is the point of departure for the other books published in Arabic that are cited here.

3. On this point, I disagree with Muhammad Shadid, *Al-Jihad fi al-Islam*, 7th ed. (Cairo: Dar al-Tawzi' al-Islamiyya, 1989), the most widely known and authoritative study in Arabic on this topic, and with Majid Khadduri, *War and Peace in the Law of Islam* (Baltimore: Johns Hopkins University Press, 1955). Both authors suggest, though from different points of view, that a consistent concept of jihad can be found in the Qur'an. My reading of the Qur'an does not support this contention.

4. Qur'anic references are to the Arabic text in the undated Tunis edition published by Mu'assasat 'Abd al-Karim b. 'Abdallah. I have checked my translations against the standard German translation of Rudi Paret (Stuttgart: Kohlhammer Verlag, 1979), the new German translation by Adel Th. Khoury (Giitersloh: Gerd Mohn Verlag, 1987), and the often inadequate English translation by N. J. Dawood, 4th ed. (London and New York: Penguin, 1974).

5. See Bernard Lewis, "Politics and War," in *The Legacy of Islam*, ed. Joseph

Schacht and C. E. Bosworth, 2nd ed. (Oxford: Clarendon Press, 1974); Marshall G. S. Hodgson, *The Venture of Islam*, 3 vols. (Chicago: University of Chicago Press, 1974); Adam Watson, *The Evolution of International Society* (London: Routledge, 1992), pp. 113 ff.; and Hedley Bull, "The Revolt against the West," in *The Expansion of International Society*, Hedley Bull and Adam Watson (Oxford: Clarendon Press, 1984), pp. 217–28.

   6. Lewis, "Politics and War," pp. 173, 176.

   7. See, for example, Beate Kuckertz, ed., *Das Grune Schwert: Weltmacht Islam* (Munich: Heyne Verlag, 1992).

   8. See David B. Ralston, *Importing the European Army: The Introduction of European Military Techniques and Institutions into the Extra-European World, 1600–1914* (Chicago: University of Chicago Press, 1990), esp. chaps. 3 and 4.

   9. See Sabir Tu'ayma, *Al-Shari 'a al-Islamiyya fi 'asr al-Um* (Beirut: Dar al-Jil, 1979), pp. 217, 223 ff.

   10. Khadduri, *War and Peace*, pp. 63–64. Khadduri concludes, I think prematurely, that "at the present it is not possible to revive the traditional religious approach to foreign/affairs. . . . The jihad has become an obsolete weapon" (p. 295). See the more recent survey by John Kelsay, *Islam and War: A Study in Comparative Ethics* (Louisville, KY: Westminster/John Knox Press, 1993).

   11. See the Arabic text of the first call by Saddam Hussein to jihad in *Al-Muntada* (Amman) 5 (September 1990): 21–22. The concept of jihad is considered by Kenneth L. Vaux, *Ethics and the Gulf War: Religion, Rhetoric, and Righteousness* (Boulder, CO: Westview Press, 1992), pp. 63–86. See also James Piscatori, ed., *Islamic Fundamentalisms and the Gulf Crisis* (Chicago: American Academy of Arts and Sciences, 1991), esp. the entry for jihad in the index (p. 259). Earlier, Islamic jihad had been interpreted in Western terms as a war of liberation grounded in the right of self-determination against colonial rule. On this topic, see Rudolph Peters, *Islam and Colonialism: The Doctrine of Jihad in Modern History* (The Hague: Mouton, 1979); Bassam Tibi, "Politische Ideen in der 'Drifter Welt' wahrend der Dekolonisation," in *Pipers Handbuch der politischen Ideen*, vol. 5, ed. Iring Fetscher and Herfried Miinkler (Munich: Pipers Handbuch, 1987), pp. 363–402; and Jean-Paul Charnay, *L'Islam et la guerre: De la guerre juste a la revolution sainte* (Paris: Fayard, 1986).

   12. On Egypt, see Nabil 'Abd al-Fattah, *Al-Mashaf wa al-saif* (Cairo: Madbuli, 1984), and Na'mat-Allah Janina, *Tanzim al jihad* (Cairo: Dar al-Huriyya, 1988); on Lebanon, see Martin Kramer, "Hizbullah: The Calculus of Jihad," in *Fundamentalisms and the State*, ed. Martin Marty and Scott Appleby (Chicago: University of Chicago Press, 1993); and on Sudan, see Bassam Tibi, *Die Verschworung: Das Trauma arabischer Politik* (Hamburg: Hoffmann and Campe, 1993), pp. 191–208.

   13. See Shadid, *Al-Jihad fi al-Islam*.

   14. The work of al-Nasiri has been republished in nine volumes: Ahmad bin Khalid al-Nasiri, *Al-Istigsa' fi akhbar al-Maghrib al-agsa* (Casablanca: Dar al-Kitab, 1955). I am relying on the comprehensive study by 'Abd al-Latif Husni, *Al-Islam wa al-'alaqat al-duwaliyya: Namudhaj Ahmad bin Khalid al-Nasiri* (Casablanca: Afriqya al-Sharq, 1991), which examines al-Nasiri's work in its entirety. See also Kenneth Brown, "Profile of a Nineteenth-Century Moroccan Scholar," in *Scholars, Saints, and Sufis: Muslim Religious Institutions in the Middle East since 1500*, ed. Nikki Keddie (Berkeley and Los Angeles: University of California Press, 1972), pp. 127–48.

15. Quoted in Husni, *Al-Islam*, p. 141.

16. Ibid., pp. 149, 150.

17. Mahmud Shaltut, *Al-Islam 'aqida wa shari a*, 10th ed. (Cairo: Dar al-Shuruq, 1980).

18. Ibid., pp. 404, 409, 406.

19. Jad al-Haqq 'Ali Jad al-Haqq, for *al-Azhar, Bayan ila al-nas,* 2 vols. (Cairo: al-Azhar, 1984–88).

20. Ibid., 1: 277, 278–79.

21. Ibid., 1: 281; 2: 268; 1: 280.

22. Ibid., 2: 371.

23. See Richard Mitchell, *The Society of Muslim Brothers* (Oxford: Oxford University Press, 1969).

24. Hasan al-Banna, *Majmu'at rasail al-imam al-Shahid Hasan al-Banna*, new legal ed. (Cairo: Dar al-Da'wa, 1990), p. 275.

25. Ibid., pp. 275, 287.

26. Ibid., pp. 289, 291.

27. See Sayyid Qutb, *Ma alim fi al-tariq*, 13th legal ed. (Cairo: Dar al-Shuruq, 1989); the quotation is from p. 201. For a commentary on Qutb's view, see Tibi, *Islamischer Fundamentalismus*.

28. Sayyid Qutb, *Al-Islam wa mushiklat al-hadarah,* 9th legal ed. (Cairo: Daral-Shuruq, 1988), p. 195. See also his *Al-Salam al-alami wa al-Islam*, 10th legal ed. (Cairo: Dar al-Shuruq, 1992).

29. Sayyid Qutb, *Al-Mustaqbal li hadha al-din* (Cairo: Dar al-Shuruq, 1981).

30. Sayyid Qutb, *Ma'alim fi al-tariq*, p. 72.

31. Muhammad N. Yasin, *Al-Jihad: Mayadinahu wa asalibahu* (Algiers: Dar al-Irshad, 1990), pp. 76, 77, 81.

32. Colonel (al-Mugaddam) Ahmad al-Mu'mini, *Al-Tabi'a al jihadiyya fi al-Islam* (Constantine, Algeria: Mu'assasat al-Isra', 1991).

33. For an interpretation of the shari'a, see Ann E. Mayer, "The Shari'a: A Methodology or a Body of Substantive Rules?" in *Islamic Law and Jurisprudence*, ed. Nicholas Heer (Seattle: University of Washington Press, 1990), pp. 177–98; and Bassam Tibi, *Islam and the Cultural Accommodation of Social Change* (Boulder, CO: Westview Press, 1990), pp. 59–75.

34. The concept of an "Islamic state" (dawla islamiyya) is not found in the classical sources; it is a new idea related to the concerns of Islamic fundamentalism. See, among others, Muhammad Hamidullah, *The Muslim Conduct of State* (Lahore: Sh. Muhammad Ashraf, 1977); Abdulrahman A. Kurdi, *The Islamic State* (London: Mansell Publishers, 1984); and Bassam Tibi, *Die fundamentalistische Herausforderung: Der Islam und die Weltpolitik* (Munich: C. H. Beck, 1992). A more detailed discussion of the confusion between the terms *community* (umma) and *nation* may be found in Tibi, "Islam and Arab Nationalism," in *The Islamic Impulse*, ed. Barbara F. Stowasser (Washington, DC: Center for Contemporary Arab Studies, 1987), pp. 59–74.

35. Najib al-Armanazi, *Al-Shan'al-duwali fi al-Islam* (1930; repr., London: Riad El-Ray-yes Books, 1990), pp. 226, 157, 163.

36. See Tibi, *Islam and the Cultural Accommodation of Social Change*.

37. Ann E. Mayer, "War and Peace in the Islamic Tradition: International Law,"

mimeo, ref. no. 141 (Philadelphia: University of Pennsylvania, Wharton School, Department of Legal Studies, n.d.), p. 45.

38. Because the Islamic perception of non-Muslims either as dhimmi (Christians and Jews as protected minorities) or as kafirun (unbelievers) is untenable in the international system, there is an urgent need to revise the shari'a in the light of international law. See Abdullahi Ahmed an-Na'im, *Toward an Islamic Reformation: Civil Liberties, Human Rights and International Law* (Syracuse, NY: Syracuse University Prss, 1990). This Islamic view of non-Muslims is incompatible with the idea of human rights, as an-Na'im clearly shows; on this point, see Ann E. Mayer, *Islam and Human Rights: Tradition and Politics* (Boulder, CO: Westview Press, 1991); and Bassam Tibi, "Universality of Human Rights and Authenticity of Non-Western Cultures: Islam and the Western Concept of Human Rights" (review article), *Harvard Human Rights Journal* 5 (1992): 221–26.

39. See Bassam Tibi, *Conflict and War in the Middle East* (New York: St. Martin's Press, 1993); and *Die Verschworung*, pp. 273–326.

40. For a different view, see James Piscatori, *Islam in a World of Nation-States* (Cambridge: Cambridge University Press, 1986), pp. 40 ff. I discuss this view in the introductory chapter of *Arab Nationalism: A Critical Inquiry*, 2nd ed. (London: Macmillan, 1990).

41. 'Abdullatif Husni, *Al-Islam*, p. 59.

42. See the discussion above of the conformism of al-Nasri and Al-Azhar.

43. Bassam Tibi, *The Crisis of Modern Islam: A Preindustrial Culture in the Scientific-Technological Age* (Salt Lake City: University of Utah Press, 1988); Fazlur Rahman, *Islam and Modernity* (Chicago; University of Chicago Press, 1982); and Montgomery Watt, *Islamic Fundamentalism and Modernity* (London: Routledge, 1988).

44. Watson, *Evolution of International Society*, pp. 112–19, 214–18.

45. See Samuel P. Huntington, "The Clash of Civilizations?" *Foreign Affairs* 72 (1993): 22–49; and Bassam Tibi, *Der Kreig der Zivilisationen* (Hamburg: Hoffmann and Campe, 1995), esp. chap. 4.

35

JIHAD AND THE IDEOLOGY OF ENSLAVEMENT

John Ralph Willis

It is an apparent paradox that the *jihad*,[1] in its effort to free men from unbelief, should become a device to deprive men of freedom. For the contradictions of liberty[2] and servitude both rest in the ideology of struggle in the path of Allah. As the jihad seeks to ennoble the spirit in Islam—to release the spirit from the bondage of unbelief—conversion is no sanctuary from the servile condition. And if the jihad frees men from unbelief and deprives men of freedom, so also does the humiliation and subjection of enslavement serve to remove men from infidelity.[3] Hence, jihad brings death to the infidel: while it vanquishes *kufr*, it annihilates the dignity, the essence—indeed the legal existence of the person who sustained it. In order to recapture his identity (*nasab*),[4] the slave must incarcerate his spirit in Islam, and it is only through manumission that the process is sustained.

In the Muslim view, the two dislikes, Islam and infidelity, are sundered into opposing camps. Out of the womb of this cleavage are born the categories of the enslavable under Islam. Whether the cleavages of mankind are sharpened by criteria of religion—widened by notions of observed behavior—there is a remarkable concordance in the sources on the conditions which unchain the animosities between belief and unbelief.

It is on the level of a closely defined monotheism that the issue between Islam and its opponents is joined. *Shirk* (polytheism) and *kufr* (unbelief) are pollutions to be scoured from the earth by jihad.[5] Yet the "lower monotheisms," Judaism and Christianity, are allowed to cover their deficiency in return for a recognition of the superior position of Islam. Hence, Jews and Christians are excused from the categories of the enslavable by a concession which acknowledges their place in the ascending line of prophecy culminating in the revelations of Islam. But they must

John Ralph Willis, "Jihad and the Ideology of Enslavement," in *Slaves and Slavery in Muslim Africa*, vol. 1: *Islam and the Ideology of Enslavement* (Totowa, NJ: Frank Cass, 1985), pp. 16–26.

suffer a diminution in their condition—pay the *jizya* as a sign of subjection and contempt. They become *ahl al-dhimma*, endowed with a legal personality (*dhimma*)[6] by which they are viewed a proper subject of Muslim law. Though they are left in a weakened state—open to censure, dispraise, and rebuke—the *dhimma* in their person becomes the foundation for rights and obligations between those who enter the pact. Thus, the *ahl al-dhimma* cannot be forced to Islam. It is the *jizya*, the sign of humiliation, that allows them to adhere to their beliefs—to ransom their person and their wealth:

> The *'Anwi* [captive], after the levying of the *jizya*, is free. Do not confiscate his wealth. If he should die without an heir, [his wealth] goes to the Muslims; [and again]. . . . The Anwi can bestow his wealth as presents, and [he is free to] make a will, even for all of his wealth. If all of this is understood, it appears that the dhimmi, after the jizya is levied upon him, is immune—he has freed himself and his wealth.[7]

Again, according to prescribed conditions and legally enunciated principles, further concessions are bestowed upon the *halif*, *mawla*, and *jar*. These are brought within the confines of the "protected" or *dhimmi* category, and their rights and privileges sanctioned by custom and law.[8]

If the animosity between Islam and the lower monotheisms is softened by condescendences of respect, no such understanding can close the rift between Islam and the more blatant manifestations of *kufr*. Under Islam, the settled existence becomes the highest expression of human life, and its central figure, agriculture, the natural ground for stable and orderly rule.[9] From this point of vantage Muslims were able to look with disfavor upon those who disavowed the settled state—who lived close to the condition of wild beasts (*sa'iba*);[10] who lacked the requisites for civilised life;[11] who disdained recognized authority and the fixed boundaries of the urban genre.

JIHAD AND THE CATEGORIES OF ENSLAVEMENT

Thus, as the opposition of Islam to *kufr* erupted from every corner of malice and mistrust, the lands of the enslavable barbarian became the favorite hunting ground for the "people of reason and faith"—the parallels between slave and infidel began to fuse in the heat of jihad. Hence whether by capture or sale, it was as slave and not citizen that the *kafir* was destined to enter the Muslim domain. And since the condition of captives flowed from the status of their territories, the choice between freedom and servility came to rest on a single proof: the religion of a land is the religion of its *amir* (ruler); if he be Muslim, the land is a land of Islam (dar al-Islam); if he be pagan, the land is a land of unbelief (dar al-kufr). Appended to this principle was the kindred notion that the religion of a land is the religion of its majority; if it be Muslim, the land is a land of Islam; if it be pagan, the land is a land of *kufr*, and its inhabitants can be reckoned within the categories of enslavement under Muslim law.[12] Again, as slavery became a simile for infidelity, so too did freedom remain the signal feature of Islam.

With the opening of the seventeenth century, the practice of securing slaves from the Sudan had begun to clash with the reality that many of these captives stemmed from lands in which the Shari'a held sway—in which the political authorities and the majority of inhabitants had embraced the religion of Islam. In a series of pronouncements which were to clear the doctrinal ground, Shaykh Ahmad Baba of Timbuctu points a contrast between those lands known to have come over to Islam, such as Bornu, Kano, Mali, Songhai, Gobir, Katsina, and Gao,[13] and those which remained under the threat of jihad, such as Mossi, Gurma, Bobo, Busa, Dogon, and Yoruba.[14] As regards the first category, the assumption was in favor of freedom, and it was advised against the ownership of any captives stemming from these lands. As regards the second, assumption weighed in favor of enslavement, as these had long been in opposition to Muslim rule. Between these extremes lay a vast abyss of doubt—a wilderness of territories in which the status of inhabitants remained obscure. Here, Ahmad Baba ranged himself with those who voiced a defence of the captive of doubtful status—who threw the burden of proof on those who bought.[15]

From this early text, we gain a glimpse of the assumptions which seized the slaveholders of the time. It can be seen that descent from the biblical Ham, a reference which returns each time in a different dress, condemned Sudanis to low esteem and awoke strong feelings of reproach among those who saw in their hue a sure sign of disrepute. Thus the people of Tuwat, who placed this petition before the Shaykh, were caused to assume that the Sudan had come to Islam through conquest and not belief; that it formed a vein of human resource for the slave-miners of the Muslim world; that conversion after conquest had no effect on the servile state. Hence, a caste-like permanency is presumed for the people of the Sudan, as the hereditary principle invades the ideology of enslavement under Islam.[16] Into these assumptions Ahmad Baba inflates the reality of Muslim law; the cause of slavery is non-belief, and the Sudan in no way constitutes a special case.[17]

Categories of the Free

Ahmad Baba's list	Usuman dan Fodio's list
Barnu [Bornu]	Barnu [Bornu]
'Afnu [Hausa]	
Kanaw [Kano]	Kanu [Kano]
Kaghu [Gaol]	
Kashna [Katsina]	Kashina [Katsina]

Sughay [Songhay]   Sughay [Songhay]
Mali
Kabru [Gobir], Kubur
Fullani   Fullani
                                    Zakzak

Categories of the Enslavable

Ahmad Baba's list   *Usuman dan Fodio's list*

Mushi [Mossi]   Mushi [Mossi]
Kurma [Gurma]   Ghurma [Gurma]
Busa   Busa
Yurku [Yorko]
Kutukuli   Kutukuli
Yurba [Yoruba]   Yuruba [Yoruba]
Tanbughu   Tabanghu
Bubu [Bobo]   Bubuli [Bobo]
Kurmu
Kunbay

                                    Barghu [Borgu]
                                    Daghumba [Daghomba]
                                    Ghambiya [Gambia]

The arrival of the nineteenth century and its polarization of Muslim sympa-thies[18] exposed the frailness of Ahmad Baba's categories and inspired a desertion of his dichotomy in favor of a closer delineation of the boundaries of faith. Between the terminals of belief and unbelief lay a circuit of controversy. While Usuman dan Fodio's *Tahqiq alis'ma*[19] does not appear to offend against the basic principles set down by the Timbuctu *faqih*, the Shehu's Bayan *wujub al-hijra* takes flight from the easy categorization that sets the tone for the earlier text.

Though the *Tahqiq* and the *Bayan* address different themes, and while Ahmad Baba's *Mi'raj*[20] remains central to both, the *Bayan*, written three years after the commencement of the Shehu's jihad, retains the strident tone of the years of stress. Hence, its extra severity on questions of faith is in sharp contrast to the mild pronouncements of the *Tahqiq*, issued it would seem in a period of relaxed duress. The theme of the *Tahqiq* focuses upon the problem of female slavery, and it was written to warn against the reduction of concubinage of women whose reli-gious affiliation and point of origin remained unknown. Thus, the weight of the *Mi'raj* is brought to bear upon the categories of the enslavable, and the dichotomy between dar al-harb and dar al-Islam is undissolved. Indeed the classification enunciated some two hundred years before undergoes no appreciable change.

Bornu, Kano, Katsina, and Songhay occupy their usual place as lands which acknowledge Islam,[21] and Mossi, Gurma, Bobo, Yoruba, and Busa remain under the threat of jihad.[22] As regards the first category, the assumption is in favor of freedom, and it was advised against taking as concubines women who stemmed from these lands. As regards the second, assumption continued to weigh in favor of enslavement, and concubinage became permissible upon the woman's conversion to Islam. Again, permissibility for concubinage was seen to extend from permissibility to enslave.[23]

The *Bayan* catches the Shehu in a contentious mood. Here, he is at pains to press the need for *hijra* and *jihad*. Chapter 1, "on the obligation of emigrating from the lands of the unbelievers,"[24] stirs the controversy between belief and unbelief, as it topples the categories of enslavement erected by Ahmad Baba in his *Mi'raj*:

> Our master [Sidi al-Mukhtar] al-Kunti[25] said in his *Nasiha*: "The Sudan is a land where unbelief prevails among the majority of its people and all the Muslims there are under the domination of the unbelievers whom they have recognized as rulers. And people generally adopt the behavior of their ruler remaining in the darkness of ignorance, willfulness and unbelief. . . ." I have read in the writings of a certain scholar [a statement] which reports that there are absolutely no lands of Islam in Bilad al-Sudan. He says therein: "The sultans of Bilad al-Sudan, which are lands of unbelief having nothing in common with lands of Islam, have all, one after another, rendered the Shari'a of our Prophet Muhammad ineffective." And God knows best.[26]

Thus, in a single stroke, the canonical view of enslavement which had stood firm for two hundred years is upset—the dichotomy between belief and unbelief becomes a dichotomy by contradiction only; Sudanis are either Muslims of the Jama'a or *kafir*; the circuit of controversy can be compassed by hijra or jihad.

HIJRA[27] AND THE IDEOLOGY OF ENSLAVEMENT

For the *kafir* who embraces Islam, *hijra* points the path to freedom; for the *kafir* who defies Islam, jihad points the path to bondage. These are the only means by which the controversy between belief and unbelief can be closed. Again, for the slave from dar al-harb who flees to dar al-Islam, *hijra* is the sanctuary from the servile condition. Hence, "flight" brings life to the infidel: while it vanquishes *kufr*, it confirms the dignity, the essence—indeed the legal existence—of the person who sustained it. It is as though the slave has recaptured his own identity, in al Karashi's phrase, "seized himself as spoil"[28]—become the master of himself. Moreover, it means that a belligerent's slave becomes free by his fleeing to the land of the Muslims before his master has accepted Islam. . . . It makes no difference whether he comes over already a Muslim or not [provided, it seems, he becomes a Muslim as soon as he has crossed over]. . . . If he comes over bringing any property, it belongs to him and he does not have to give up the *khums*. He also becomes free if he accepts Islam and stays on with his master in the non-Muslim territory until he is captured by Muslims as booty, while his master is still a polytheist.[29]

Here, the pattern of enslavement takes an ironic twist: a free man, whose conversion is after the triumph of jihad, sinks in status beneath his former slave whose conversion precedes the coming of Islam. And, depending on the web of circumstance, masters might become slaves and slaves masters. Still again, crossing these threads of legal irony is the warp of the *dhimmi* condition; though the *ahl al-dhimma* cannot be forced to Islam, they can be constrained to set free those slaves who have embraced Islam:

And as for those slaves of the ahl-al-dhimma who were converted to Islam or who fled to the Muslims, let it be known that the dhimmi, if his slave should be converted, he can no longer remain under his control [but he can be forced to] turn over the slave to Islam or grant the slave his ultimate freedom. [and in another place] . . . or the ruler sells him if the master is absent over a prolonged period.[30]

Yet the master-slave connection cannot be disjoined at every seam. For the slave who comes to Islam after the Islamization of his master or synchronous with the conversion of his lord, *hijra* is no sanctuary from the servile condition:

If [the slave] comes to us after the Islamization of his master . . . , or if he comes to us as a Muslim or as an unbeliever after the Islamization of his master, it [i.e., the situation] is different—even if the Islamization of the one has preceded the Islamization of the other, or if the one has been Islamized at the same time as the other; the circumstance turns on the fact of his fleeing after the Islamization of his master.[31]

Thus the condition of the slave is to be judged in accordance with the condition of the master at the time of Islamization, and the direction of loyalty pursues the path of conversion and flight.

JIHAD AND THE IDEOLOGY OF ENSLAVEMENT

With the declaration of jihad, the issue between belief and non-belief is joined the line of demarcation drawn between combatants of contending sides. Among the

Muslims, jihad is the affair of the people of praise and identity—the males of *ism*, *laqab*, and *nisba*.[32] Within the ranks of the *mujahidin*, the encumbered have no place: slaves, with the heavy lien on their person; women, whose dependence rests on their husbands; children, under the charge of their parents. And so it is with the sick, the lame, and deranged—with debtors unable to disembarrass themselves of their debts.

In the same spirit came the view that the weakened were unworthy of engagement—that jihad was a conflict between warriors of strength. Hence, the admonition of al-Maghili preechoed in all the legal texts: "[M]ake jihad against the infidels, kill their men, make captive their women and children, seize their wealth. . . ."[33] Thus, encumbrance was no sanctuary from the servile condition; with the elimination of the men, the net of enslavement slipped over the remnants of the *kafir* camp, round the women and children who became spoil in the path of Allah. The ideology of enslavement in Islam then, becomes that ideology which seeks to repair the losses of jihad. Women and children are the *diya*,[34] the *jizya*—the reparation and plunder for lives pledged in jihad. Hence again, spoil[35] becomes a kind of compensation—a collateral security which appreciates to the good of the *jama'a*. But collateral increased through the proxy of female slaves was not to be mistaken for the original pledge—the progeny of spoil matured in an inferior line. It is this anomaly which led Schacht to observe:

> The master's right to take his slave-girls as concubines was recognised by Muhammad in continuation of a general practice of Arab paganism. In regard to the position of the children of such unions a change of view had been perceptible among the Arabs in the period just before the coming of Islam. In place of the previous unrestrictedness in marriage and concubinage a certain [*sic*] decree of regulation had grown up, and a higher value began to be attached to marriage with free women and to good birth on the mother's side also; corresponding to this however, the position of the children of slaves become worse; they were as a rule called only after their mother and not after their father, and only received their freedom when expressly recognised by their father . . . and even then were not fully privileged: the slave-girl, it was argued, must not give birth to her future master as the son would reveal the qualities of the slave like his mother. The position of such a slave was not at all a privileged one. Even her designation *umm al-walad* ("mother of children") is in contrast to *umm al-banin* ("mother of sons") as the name for a free woman.[36]

The distinction between concubinage and marriage—between collateral and lineal—became a constant ingredient of canon law, as the "mother of sons" refused to be edged out by the "spoil" of jihad.

In summary, it can be said that the jihad, in its effort to banish the humiliation of *kufr*, inflicted the shame of servility, and set in tandem a series of legal relations which fixed the bond between master and slave. Slavery became a means of extinguishing the guilt of *kufr*—an expiation for the blood of Muslims spilt in jihad. Moreover, slavery was a grave debt as well as a deep humiliation, and it was only upon atonement of the debt that the humiliation could be removed. Thus the master was cast in the role of creditor, and the slave or *dhimmi* assumed the guise of debtor. Neither the Christian nor the Jew could break out of the limits of humiliation—the guilt of *shirk* could only be satisfied by the shame of submission (*jizya*, a kind of compensation for their not being slain,[37] a form of ransom for their failure to convert to Islam). Even the intimate connection between owner and concubine can be viewed from the perspective of the debtor-creditor bond. *Ghanima* (spoil) exonerated the debt incurred through the spilling of Muslim blood in jihad, though (in most cases) only birth or death could remove the debt of humiliation suffered upon female slaves. In the interim between the birth of an infant and the death of a master,[38] the woman's sexual favors—her service in domestic life—served to amortize the legacy of humiliation and defeat.

NOTES

For clarification of any citations, the reader is referred to the original, John Ralph Willis, "Jihad and the Ideology of Enslavement," in *Slaves and Slavery in Muslim Africa*, vol. 1: *Islam and the Ideology of Enslavement* (Totowa, NJ: Frank Cass, 1985), pp. 16–26.

1. For other aspects of the *jihad* theme, see my *"Jihad fi sabil Allah*—Its Doctrinal Basis in Islam and Some Aspects of Its Evolution in Nineteenth-Century West Africa," *Journal of African History* 8, no. 3 (1967): 395–415.

2. On the concept of "liberty" ("freedom," *hurriyya*) in Islam, see F. Rosenthal, *The Muslim Concept of Freedom* (Leiden, 1960), and the same author's "Hurriyya," *E.I.* (2), vol. 3: 589.

3. Al-Wansharisi [Abu'l-'Abbas Ahmad b. Yahya b. Muhammad b. 'Abd al-Wahid b. 'Ali al-Tilimsani al-Wansharisi] (d. 914/1508) Brockelmann, *GAL*, II, 248, *Kitab al-Mi'yar al-mughrib wa'l-jami 'al-mu 'rib amma tadammanahu Fatawi 'Ulama' Ifrigiya wa'l-Andalus wa'l-Maghrib*, 12 vols. (Fas), A.H.1315 (vol. 9 trans. and ed. E. Amar, "Consultations juridiques des fakihs du Maghreb," *Archives Marocaines* [Paris, 1908], pp. 426–28).

4. Perhaps one should say, "acquire," as it was the Islamic view that slaves were without (or were deprived of) *nasab*, that is, "rank," "station," [known] "ancestry" (or, in any case, illustrious ancestry). It is interesting to note that the term *sa'iba*, "wild" (see p. 10, note 7), often applied to horses, was used in counterdistinction to the well-bred "noble" beasts with a known pedigree. It is the *mawla* (freedman) who acquires the nasab of his master, and it is in that sense that he takes on an "identity," becomes "personified": Cf. "Hasab wa-nasab" [The Twin Aspects of Nobility], in *E.I.* (2), vol. 3, pp. 238–39; and W. Montgomery Watt, "Badw," *E.I.* (2), p. 890. (Cf. the term *Haratin*—"mixed breed" applied to horses and men.)

5. I. Melikoff, "Ghazi," *E.I.* (2), vol. 2, pp. 1043–45, wherein is given the following definition of the *ghazi* (he who distinguishes himself in the *ghazwa*): one who "is the instrument of the religion of God, a servant of God who cleans the earth from the defilement of polytheism; a ghazi is the sword of God, he is the protector and the refuge of the

Believers; if he becomes a martyr while following the paths of God, do not think him dead, he lives with God as one of the blessed, he has Eternal Life." Here, the notions of jihad and ghazwa are joined.

6. Chafik Chehata, "Dhimma," *E.I.* (2), vol. 2, p. 231.

7. 'Umar b. Sa'id, *Fatwa*, f.3 (see Willis, "The Writings of al-Hajj 'Umar al-Futi and Shaykr Mukhtar b. Wadi'at Allah: Literary Themes, Sources and Influences," in *Studies*, vol. 1, p. 199). Cf. Uthman b. Fudi, *Bayan Wujub al-Hi jra 'ala'l-'Ibad*, ed. and trans. F. H. el Masri (Khartoum and Oxford,1978): trans. pp. 126–27; text, pp. 105–106), where two kinds of jizya are discussed: the jizya of "agreement" (*sulhi*) and the jizya of "compulsion" (*'anwi*).

8. Watt, "Badw," p. 890: "[A] person not related to [an Arab] group by blood (not a sahih or samim) could enjoy some of the privileges of membership, above all protection. He might do so as an 'ally' (halif); a 'protected neighbour' (djar), or a 'client' (mawla)." (See Pipes, in *Slaves and Slavery in Muslim Africa*, p. 202.)

9. See, for example, A. K. S. Lambton, "Filaha," "agriculture" (part 3), *E.I.* (2), vol. 2, p. 902; and Y. Linant de Bellefonds, "Ihya" [i.e., "putting a piece of land to use"], *E.I.* (2), vol. 3, pp. 1053–54.

10. The Muslim jurist and jihad theorist Muhammad b. 'Abd al-Karim b. Muhammad al-Maghili al-Tilimsani (d. 1503–1504) employs the term *sa'iba* to mean a country without centralized control (Joseph M. Cuoq, *Recueildes sources arabes concernant l'Afrique Occidentale du Vllle au XVIe Siecle* [Paris: Bilad al-Sudan, 1975], p. 418). (Cf. Pipes, infra, p. 203, where sa'iba designates an individual without affiliation (i.e., wala') to the group.)

11. Cf. Hilliard, infra (appendix), p. 175, and Ibn Khaldun, *Muqaddima*, vol. 1, p. 172.

12. Authorities for this dictum range from Al-Maghili and Ahmad Baba (cited by al-Hajj'Umar and Usuman dan Fodio) to al-Nasiri (see infra, p.177). Cf. Willis, "Jihad fi Sabil Allah" (p. 413 n68), and 'Uthman b. Fudi, Bayan Wujub al-Hijra (editor's note, p. 50 n1).

13. Infra, p. 130.

14. Infra, p. 137.

15. Infra, p. 130.

16. For the controversy over the so-called Zanj, see the following: J. O. Hunwick, "Some Notes on the Term 'Zanj' and Its Derivatives in a West African Chronicle," Centre of Arabic Documentation (Ibadan), *Research Bulletin* 4, nos. 1 and 2 (December 1968): 41–52; Nehmia Levtzion, "A Seventeenth-Century Chronicle by Ibn al-Mukhtar: A Critical Study of Ta'rikh al-Fattash," *BSOAS* 34 (1971): 517–93; John Ralph Willis, review of N. Levtzion, *Ancient Ghana and Mali*, *International Journal of African Historical Studies* 8, no. 1: 181. Al-Maghili ruled that certain of the Zanj could be passed from generation to generation as "*hubs*" (Hunwick, "Some Notes on the Term 'Zanj,'" p. 51); in Islam, slaves could become part of an endowment (waqf), the "yield" of the labor to be used for good purposes (see E. I. Heffening (1), 1096–1103). In the *Ta'rikh al-Fattash*, the term *tilad* is used to refer to slaves "born of the house of the master," or "long possessed property inherited from parents" (text, p. 14; trans. p. 21).

17. Infra, p. 134.

18. The most rancorous of these exchanges can be seen in the correspondence between Muhammad Bello and al-Kanimi (Murray Last, *Sokoto Caliphate* [London, 1967]); between al-Hajj 'Umar and al-Kanimi, and the former and Ahmad b. Ahmad (Willis, *Studies*, vol. 1, pp. 183, 186), and Ahmad al-Bakka'i al-Kunti (ibid., p. 187).

19. *Tahqiq al-isma li-Jami' Tabaqat hadihi 'l-umma*, Arabic manuscript, Centre of Arabic Documentation, Insititute of African Studies, Ibadan, C.A.D./20, 14 ff.), undated; for other copies, see Last, *Sokoto*, p. 239.

20. Infra, the chapter by Barbour and Jacobs.

21. Usuman dan Fodio, *Tahqiq*, fol. 2(b).

22. Ibid., fol. 2(a). For a comparison of Ahmad Baba's list with that of the Shehu, see diagrams I and II. It will suffice here to note the omission of Hausa ['Afnu] and Gobir from the original list of the free, and the addition of Borgu, Daghomba, and Gambia to the categories of the enslavable. Again, the Fulani are given special notice, as in the list of Ahmad Baba, because of the "change of heart" their *qaba'il* observed with respect to Islam. Hence the Shehu's admonitory statements with regard to the sale and subsequent enslavement of Fulbe women. Cf., the Shehu's *Bayan. wujub al-hijra*, p. 49.

23. Usuman dan Fodio, *Tahqiq*, fol. 3(b).

24. Usuman dan Fodio, *Bayan wujub al-hijra*, p. 51.

25. Mukhtar al-Kunti (1729–1811) was the titular head of the Qadiriyya brotherhood—a spiritual leadership which extended to the Shehu's sphere of influence. See John Ralph Willis, "The Western Sudan from the Moroccan Invasion (1591) to the Death of Mukhtar al-Kunti (1811)," in *A History of West Africa*, ed. Jacob Ajayi and Michael Crowder (1971), vol. 1, pp. 441–85.

26. Usuman dan Fodio, *Bayan wujub al-hijra*, p. 51.

27. *Hijra*, often rendered "flight," denotes a break-off of relations with one's clansmen—this was its meaning in the Prophet's time, and Muslims of every era were apt to imitate his Sunna (model). See Willis, "Jihad fi sabil Allah," p. 399. Again, the act of *hijra* set in tandem new links of kinship among arriving groups who swore allegiance to the leader of the "migration." See W. Montgomery Watt, "Hidjra," *E.I.* (2), where arriving groups become the *mawali* of Muhammad (pp. 366–67), and John Ralph Willis, "The Torodbe Clerisy: A Social View," *Journal of African History* 19, no. 2 (1978): 195–213, where *hijra* from *dar al-harb* becomes a means of refuge for slaves seeking a new life in Islam.

28. Usuman dan Fodio, *Bayan wujub al-hijra*, p. 117; cf. 'Umar b. Said, *Fatwa*, fol. 5, where this saying is attributed to Ibn al-Qasim [Abu 'Abd Allah 'Abd al-Rahman b. al-Qasim al-'Utaqi, d. 191/806; *GAL* 1: 176–77], and elsewhere (ibid.) to al-Shabrakhiti [Burhan al-Din Ibrahim b. Mari, d. 1106/1697; *GAL* 2: 318; SII, p. 438] and Ibn Dardir [Abu al-Barakat Ahmad b. Muhammad, 1127/1715–1201/1786, *GAL* 2: 353; SII, pp. 479–80], fol. 4. Everywhere it is stressed that it is the slave's seizing himself as spoil (and not solely his conversion to Islam) that sets the stage for freedom. Hence it is on the element of reparation or compensation that the slave's status turns. According to Ibn al-Qasim, "it is the same as when the unbeliever freed his Muslim slave." Thus the manumission principle waxes stronger than the conversion principle, as the problem of compensation is satisfied by the act of seizure itself.

29. Usuman dan Fodio, *Bayan wujub al-hijra*, p. 117.

30. 'Umar b. Said, *Fatwa*, fol. 5.

31. Ibid., fol. 4. Cf., Usuman dan Fodio, *Bayan wujub al-hijra*, p. 117.

32. *Ism* denotes the fame, renown, or reputation of a person (especially in relation to something praiseworthy); *laqab* is an appellation or "nickname" of praise; *nisba* suggests the pedigree or lineage of a person.

33. Cuoq, *Recueil*, p. 415.

34. Properly speaking, *diya* is the compensation (fixed by custom and law) to be paid by an offending party to an offended party. Since these arrangements obtained normally among nomadic Arabs especially (and was carried over into the Islamic period with certain modifications), it may be stretching its significance to apply the term *diya* to the settlement of offenses between Muslims and non-Muslims. Nevertheless, the notion would seem to sustain that a kind of compensation is called for when "blood" is spilt in jihad.

35. "Spoil" (*ghanima*) division in *jihad* is very carefully governed by custom and law (see F. Lekkegaard, "Ghanima," *E.I.* (2), pp. 1005–1006).

36. J. Schacht, "Umm al-Walad," *E.I.* (1), p. 1012.

37. E. W. Lane, "Jizya," *An Arabic English Lexicon* (London, 1865), bk. 1, part 2, p. 422.

38. Schacht, "Umm al-Walad," p. 1012.

36

THE INFLUENCE OF ISLAM

Jacques Ellul

Stress has seldom been laid upon the influence of Islam on Christianity, that is, on the deformation and subversion to which God's revelation in Jesus Christ is subjected. Yet this influence was considerable between the ninth and eleventh centuries. We have been brought up on the image of a strong and stable Christianity that was attacked and besieged in some sense by Islam. Engaged in unlimited conquest, with a universal vocation similar to that claimed by Christianity, Islam was expanding its empire in three directions: to the south, especially along the coasts into black Africa, and reaching as far as Zanzibar by the twelfth century; to the northwest, with the conquest of Spain and the invasion of France up to Lyons on the one side and Poitiers on the other; and to the northeast into Asia Minor and as far as Constantinople. With the Turks Islam would then continue incessantly to threaten the Balkans, Austria, Hungary, etc. The picture is a Manichean and warlike one; as it is hard to conceive of profound contacts between warring enemies, how can Islam have influenced Christianity in this permanent state of war?

The fine book by H. Pirenne, *Mahomet et Charlemagne*,[2] has admirably shown what were the economic and political consequences of this permanent military threat. But it has often been emphasized that we lack any study of relationships. This is the more surprising in that elsewhere, in the domain of philosophy we know perfectly well that Aristotle's thought came into Europe thanks to the translations and commentaries of the Arab philosopher Averroes (twelfth century), and we can also point to the influence of Avicenna from the eleventh century. It is also recognized that Arab influence was great in scientific fields such as mathematics, medicine, agronomy, astronomy, and physics. All this is conceded and generally known.

A little later Arab influence may be seen incontestably in the black arts, in magic, the various "-mancies," alchemy, the search for the philosopher's stone, and also music (twelfth century). It is also well understood that the Arabs had considerable military influence (e.g., upon cavalry, etc.) and that some technical fields

Jacques Ellul, "The Influence of Islam,"[1] in *The Subversion of Christianity*, trans. Geoffrey Bromiley (Grand Rapids, MI: Eerdmans, 1986), pp. 95–112.

(irrigation) and architecture felt their impact. Finally, it is constantly stressed that through the Crusades and the contacts of the Crusaders with the Arabs many changes came about in various areas, such as the bringing of certain fruit trees (cherries and apricots) into France. All this is very banal. But it does at least tell us beyond a doubt that even between enemies who are depicted as irreconcilable there were cultural and intellectual relations. Exchanges took place and knowledge circulated. In truth, knowledge seems to have circulated in only one direction, coming from Islam and the Arab world to the West, which was much more backward and "barbarian."[3]

There are two areas that to my knowledge have not yet been studied in such surveys, those of law and theology. But how can we believe or admit or think that exchanges took place in the intellectual, commercial, and economic fields without affecting these disciplines in any way? It is recognized, for example, that the bill of exchange was almost certainly invented by the Arabs and then adopted in the West to facilitate maritime trade. But other areas of law must have been influenced as well. I am inclined to think, for example, that the law of serfdom is a Western imitation of the Muslim *dhimmi*. Religious law is also important. I am convinced that some parts of canon law have their origin in Arab law. And this leads us, in effect, to Christianity.

How can we imagine that there was a well-known and admitted influence on philosophy that did not have theological repercussions? Everyone knows that the problem solved by Thomas Aquinas was precisely that of the confrontation between classical theology and Aristotle's philosophy. But the bridge is by way of the Arabs. We speak of Greek philosophy and Christian theology. But this Greek philosophy was faithfully transmitted by Arab interpreters. It was by way of Arab-Muslim thinking that the problem came to be addressed at this time. We can hardly think that the Arab influence was nil except in matters concerning Aristotle.

Furthermore, it is readily perceived that Christianity and Islam had certain obvious points in common or points of meeting. Both were monotheistic and both were based on a book. We should also note the importance that Islam accords to the poor. Certainly Christians reject Allah because of the denial that Jesus Christ is God's Son, and they do not allow that the Koran is divinely inspired. On the other hand, Muslims reject the Trinity in the name of the unity, and they make the whole Bible a mere preface or introduction to the Koran. At root, Muslims do with the whole Bible what Christians do with the Hebrew Bible. But on this common foundation there are necessarily encounters and debates and discussions, and hence a certain openness. Even where there is rejection and objection, there can be no evading the question that is put.

It seems that the Muslim intellectuals and theologians were much stronger than their Christian counterparts. It seems that Islam had an influence, but not Christianity. Our interest here is not in the philosophical problem or in theological formulations, which were necessarily restricted to a small intellectual circle, but in the way in which Islamic influences change practices, rites, beliefs, attitudes toward life, all that belongs to the domain of moral or social belief or conduct, all that constitutes Christendom. Here again, everyone knows that the Frankish kingdom of Jerusalem, the French knights installed in Palestine, rapidly adopted many manners and customs that originated in Islam. But the exceptional case is not important. What counts is what is imported into Europe. It is the fact of unwitting imitation. It is the fact of being situated on the chosen territory and being delimited by those whom one wants to combat. I will thus leave on one side theology in the pure sense, the difference between Thomas Aquinas and biblical theology, and the influence of Aristotle. I will concern myself with other problems.

I believe that in every respect the spirit of Islam is contrary to that of the revelation of God in Jesus Christ. It is so in the basic fact that the God of Islam cannot be incarnate. This God can be only the sovereign judge who ordains all things as he wills. Another point of antithesis lies in the absolute integration of religious and political law. The expression of God's will inevitably translate itself into law. No law is not religious, inspired by God. Reciprocally, all God's will must translate itself into legal terms. Islam pushed to an extreme a tendency that is virtual in the Hebrew Bible, but there it is symbolic of the spiritual and is then transcended by Jesus Christ; with Islam we come back to legal formulation as such.

I have shown elsewhere that the twofold formulation of "having a law" and of "objective law" is contrary to revelation. This can naturally be contested only by champions of natural law and classical theology. My conviction is that this revelation of love, seeking to set up a relationship of love (alone) among us, and thus basing everything on grace and giving us a model of exclusively gracious relationships, is in fact the exact opposite of law, in which everything is measured by debits and credits (the opposite of grace) and duties (the opposite of love).

To the extent that we are not in the kingdom of God, we certainly cannot achieve this pure relation of love and grace, this completely transparent relation. Hence law has a necessary existence. Yet we have to view it merely as a matter of expediency (because we cannot do better) and a necessary evil (which is always an evil). This understanding has nothing in common with that which contrariwise greatly exalts law, making it the expression of God's will and the legal formulation of the "religious" world. On this view law is a preeminent value. In taking this approach Christians were greatly influenced by their Roman background. They could not exclude or minimize the value of Roman law, as we have seen. There then comes a great rebound with the Arabs. We now have an intimate union between law and the will of God.

The jurist is the theologian. Theology becomes no less legal than philosophical. Life is set in law no less and even more than in ethics. Everything religious becomes legal. Judges handle religious matters, and jurisprudence becomes theology. This gives an enormous boost to the juridicizing of Christendom. Canon law expands after the pattern found in Islam. If everything is not included in it, it is because the feudal lords and monarchs are very hostile to the growing power of the church and because (lay) customs put up firm opposition to this sanctification. But the legal spirit penetrates deeply into the church, and I maintain that this is both under the influence of Islam and in response to the religious law of Islam. The church had to follow suit.

Furthermore, law set up ecclesiastical courts and gave them means of ruling. They would have liked to have seen everything referred to canon law and their courts, as in the Muslim world. The church would have liked sole power. But in Islam there was an indissoluble correlation between religious law and political power. In this field, too, what was introduced with Constantinianism, as we have seen, received a new impulse from Islam. Every political head in Islam is also the ruler of believers. There is no separation between the church and political power. The political head is the religious head. He is a representative of Allah. His political and military acts, etc., are inspired.

Now this is all familiar in Europe. The king or emperor does not merely claim to be the secular arm of the church but the one who has spiritual power. He wants it to be recognized that he personally is chosen by God, elected by the Almighty. He needs a prophetic word and the power to work miracles. His word and person have to be sacred.

Naturally some of this was already present prior to Islam. It was not for nothing, however, that this theology, liturgy, and imperial understanding developed first at Byzantium on the first contact with Islam, and only later spread to the West. Royal power becomes religious not merely in an alliance with the church but under the influence of Islam, which was much more of a theocracy than the West ever was: a theocracy in which God is indeed the sole king, but the true representative of God on earth is the political head, so that we have what has rightly been called "lay theocracy" with no religious organization, clergy, no ecclesiastical institution—a situation in which to rejoice, for it implies that only, the political power is religious. Islam does not know the duality of church and state with conflicts and also with the limitation that it entails for the political power.

We can thus understand perfectly the wish or desire or temptation of Western kings and emperors to be themselves sole representatives of God on earth and thus to go much further than Constantine. The formula according to which the emperor is "the bishop on the outside" did not suffice for them. I am certain that the Islamic model acted in favor of the emancipation of kings and their attempt from the fourteenth century to create a church that would be wholly dependent on the political power. Certainly in the big debate they were not able to advance this argument. What an admission it would be to say that they were taking those terrible unbelievers as a model!

In tandem with this great importance of the political power there is, of course, the importance and glorification of war as a means of spreading the faith. Such war is a duty for all Muslims. Islam has to become universal. The true faith, not the power, has to be taken to every people by every means, including by military force. This makes the political power important, for it is warlike by nature. The two things are closely related. The political head wages war on behalf of the faith. He is thus the religious head, and as the sole representative of God he must fight to extend Islam. This enormous importance of war has been totally obliterated today in intellectual circles that admire Islam and want to take it afresh as a model. War is inherent in Islam. It is inscribed in its teaching. It is a fact of its civilization and also a religious fact; the two cannot be separated. It is coherent with its conception of the Dhar al harb, that the whole world is destined to become Muslim by Arab conquests. The proof of all this is not just theological; it is historical: hardly has the Islamic faith been preached when an immediate military conquest begins. From 632 to 651, in the twenty years after the death of the prophet, we have a lightning war of conquest with the invasion of Egypt and Cyrenaica to the west, Arabia in the center, Armenia, Syria, and Persia to the east. In the following century all North Africa and Spain are taken over, along with India and Turkey to the east. The conquests are not achieved by sanctity, but by war.

For three centuries Christianity spread by preaching, kindliness, example, morality, and encouragement of the poor. When the empire became Christian, war was hardly tolerated by the Christians. Even when waged by a Christian emperor it was a dubious business and was assessed unfavorably. It was often condemned. Christians were accused of undermining the political force and military might of the empire from within. In practice Christians would remain critical of war until the flamboyant image of the holy war came on the scene. In other words, no matter what atrocities have been committed in wars waged by so-called Christian nations, war has always been in essential contradiction to the gospel. Christians have always been more or less aware of this. They have judged war and questioned it.

In Islam, on the contrary, war was always just and constituted a sacred duty. The war that was meant to convert infidels was just and legitimate, for, as Muslim thinking repeats, Islam is the only religion that conforms perfectly to nature. In a natural state we would all be Muslims. If we are not, it is because we have been led astray and diverted from the true faith. In making war to force people to become Muslims the faithful are bringing them back to their true nature. Q.E.D. Furthermore, a war of this kind is a jihad, a holy war. Let us make no mistake, the word jihad has two complementary senses. It may denote a spiritual war that is moral and inward. Muslims have to wage this war within themselves in the fight against demons and evil forces, in the effort to achieve better obedience to God's will, in the struggle for perfect submission. But at the same time and in a wholly consistent way the jihad is also the war against external demons. To spread the faith, it is necessary to destroy false religions. This war, then, is always a religious war, a holy war.

At this point we have two very strong direct influences exerted by Islam on Christianity. Prior to the eighth century Christianity hardly ever stated that revelation conforms to nature. Tradition, based on the Bible, took the contrary view. Nature is fallen, the flesh is wicked, people in themselves, in their natural state, are sinners and unbelievers. Naturally I realize that the church fathers had already run into the problem of the contradiction between the biblical statements and, for example, Greek philosophy, which in certain streams presents nature as the model that one should follow. But nature was never confused with the biblical revelation. Even those who allowed some positive value to nature always had reservations about corrupted nature. I believe that it is the Muslim identification of nature and Islam that poses for Christians in an urgent way the question whether one could let infidels get away with this, whether one had not to say something similar.

As is well known, theologies from the eleventh century onward tend to bring nature and revelation together, to find in nature a source of revelation (as in the ambiguous statements of Denis about light), to elaborate a "natural" theology, to show that the Fall is not radical or total, and then to coordinate the two in a nature completed by grace as supernature. Thus the great deviation of Christian thought and theology from the biblical revelation in this matter of nature has at least two sources: the Greek and the Arab. The latter, in my opinion, is finally the more important. This orientation leads at once to the same conclusions we have noted in Islam. If there is a coincidence of nature and revelation, then only damnable blindness leads to the nonrecognition of God (the Christian God, of course!). For one has only to open one's eyes and look at nature to see God. One has only to know oneself to discern the true religion. If one will not do such simple things, one is culpable. As soon as Christianity becomes a religion that conforms to nature, then it becomes necessary to force people to become Christians. In this way they will come back to their true nature. Forced conversions begin to take place.

The famous story of Charlemagne forcing the Saxons to be converted on pain of death simply presents us with an imitation of what Islam had been doing for two centuries. But if war now has conversions to Christianity as its goal, we can see that very quickly it takes on the aspect of a holy war. It is a war waged against unbelievers and heretics (we know how pitiless was the war that Islam waged against heretics in its midst). But the idea of a holy war is a direct product of the Muslim jihad. If the latter is a holy war, then obviously the fight against Muslims to defend or save Christianity has also to be a holy war. The idea of a holy war is not of Christian origin. Emperors never advanced the idea prior to the appearance of Islam.

For half a century historians have been studying the Crusades to find explanations other than the silly theory that was previously held and conforms to addresses and sermons, that claims their intention was to secure the holy places. It has been shown that the Crusades had economic objectives, or that they were stirred up by the popes for various political motives such as that of securing papal preeminence by exhausting the kingdoms, or reforging the weakening unity of the church, or again that they were a means whereby the kings ruined the barons who were challenging their power, or again that the bankers of Genoa, Florence, and Barcelona instigated them so as to be able to lend money to the Crusaders and make fabulous profits, etc. One fact, however, is a radical one, namely, that the Crusade is an imitation of the jihad. Thus the Crusade includes a guarantee of salvation. The one who dies in a holy war goes straight to Paradise, and the same applies to the one who takes part in a Crusade. This is no coincidence; it is an exact equivalent.

The Crusades, which were once admired as an expression of absolute faith, and which are now the subject of accusations against the church and Christianity, are of Muslim, not Christian, origin. We find here a terrible consequence and confirmation of a vice that was eating into Christianity already, namely, that of violence and the desire for power and domination. To fight against a wicked foe with the same means and arms is unavoidably to be identified with this foe. Evil means inevitably corrupt a just cause. The nonviolence of Jesus Christ changes into a war in conflict with that waged by the foe. Like that war, this is now a holy war. Here we have one of the chief perversions of faith in Jesus Christ and of the Christian life.

But we must take this a step further. Once the king is the representative of God on earth and a war is holy, another question necessarily arises. If a war is not holy, what is it? It seems that the Christian emperors of Rome did not ask this question. They had to defend the empire. That was all. Naturally it did not arise in the period of the invasions and the Germanic kingdoms either. War was then a fact, a permanent state. No one tried to justify it. But with the Muslim idea of a holy war the idea is born that a war may be good even if it is not motivated by religious intentions so long as it is waged by a legitimate king. Gradually the view is accepted that political power has to engage in war, and if this power is Christian, then a ruler has to obey certain precepts, orientations, and criteria if he is to act as a Christian ruler and to wage a just war. We thus embark on an endless debate as to the conditions of a just war, from Gratian's decree to St. Thomas. All this derives from the first impulse toward a holy war, and it was the Muslim example that finally inspired this dreadful denial of which all Christendom becomes guilty.

We have still to examine a very different subversion. It concerns piety, the relation to God. We see in it an influence that we have already mentioned in passing. Every infant is supposedly born a Muslim, for Islam is perfect conformity to nature. Scholars, then, argue that it is through a bad influence or the "cultural" setting that this baby, who is by nature a Muslim, deviates from the truth and becomes a Jew or a Christian or a pagan. Evangelical thinking takes exactly the opposite view. One becomes a Christian only by conversion. Our old being, which is by nature corrupt, is changed by the action of the Holy Spirit, who makes of us new beings. Conversion alone, conscious and recognized, so that there is confession with the lips as well as faith in the heart, produces the Christian. This new birth, the opposite of natural birth, is confirmed by the outward sign of baptism, which seems to imply an express acknowledgment of faith. But progressively this strict view weakens. The church fathers analyze the sacraments, and the tendency toward an opus operatum understanding develops. The sacrament is intrinsically efficacious. Baptism ceases to be a sign of converting grace and becomes in itself an instrument of salvation. Hence, if we desire that infants, who are naturally damned due to the transmission of original sin, should be saved, we must baptize them immediately at birth so as to avoid the risk of their dying first. Salvation, then, comes almost at the moment of birth. At the same time that we reevaluate nature, which is now not radically bad, the conviction gains ground that the soul is "naturally" good and saved, that there is only a hindrance, a flaw, and that original sin is merely an obstacle that baptism overcomes.

Very quickly the formula spreads that the soul is by nature Christian, which is the counterpart of the Muslim view. Now the idea that faith is natural, that one is put in a Christian state by heredity, that being a Christian is indeed a kind of status in society, that it involves at the same time membership in both the church and society (just as excommunication is exclusion from both the church and society), is the very opposite of the work of Jesus Christ. We have to insist that Christendom in this sense is superimposed upon the church and that it duplicates exactly what is taught by Islam. Once the theory of "the soul by nature Christian" is accepted, society has to be made up of Christians. There is no alternative. Already with the Christian emperors there was a thrust in this direction. But it was the Muslim example that proved decisive. Each time we find the same refrain. There is a need to outdo Islam, and that means imitating it.

Now we have to say that this is the very opposite of what may be seen in the Gospels and in Paul. It negates the unique redemptive worth of the death of Jesus Christ. If human nature is not totally incapable of having access to God, if it is naturally in harmony with the will of God, what is the point of the death of Jesus Christ? It was not at all necessary that God should come among us, that Jesus should obey his Father's will even to the point of accepting death by reason of the evil that holds sway in the human race. The impossibility of our being able to be in harmony with God is shown by the fact that we reject the holy and the good, love and truth, in the person of Jesus. Unwittingly the imitation of Islam robs the death of Jesus Christ of its ultimate seriousness.

In this field of the relation to God, Christianity discloses the influence of Islam at two other points as well: mysticism and obedience. Mysticism is not essentially Christian. I would even say that in its final form it is more anti-Christian. I know that this will cause pain and anger in some circles. Yet when I look at the Bible I find hardly any examples of mystics. Paul alludes to his own experience; he knew a man who was lifted up to the third heaven, and he could not say whether this was with or without the body. But he was not intentionally seeking union with God. He did not engage in a movement of ascent. He was caught up or taken up by an external force like the chariot of fire that catches up Elijah or the hand of God that lifts tip Daniel. Nothing more. We find prophets in the Old Testament and apostles in the New. In the enumeration of spiritual gifts there is no mention of mystical gifts. We are told to imitate Jesus Christ but not to achieve union with God by a mystical ascent.

When the apostles are invested with spiritual power, it is by tongues of flame that come down from heaven. There is no question of union with God. Jesus alone is in total union with God. Such union is brought about by the fact that God comes (down) to us, not by our spiritual intensity or psychological action or by any attempt to climb up to him. The idea of a possible union with God is ruled out by the revelation of cherubim guarding against any return to Paradise. As I have often said, there is no possible ascent to God, or access to him. But this is what mystics passionately seek. They want union with God. They have a discipline. They follow a path to the inner void where the soul is filled by the Holy Spirit and access opens up to God. This is the exact opposite of what the Bible teaches.

The antithesis is even more radical if one accepts the common etymology whereby "mystic" comes from muein, to be mute or speechless. How can this be when God's work is wholly that of the Word? God himself speaks, and he calls upon us to bear witness by the Word. There could hardly be a greater contradiction. In fact all mystical experiences are ineffable, and Paul is totally against anything of this kind. If we follow Jesus, it is not a matter of looking up to heaven ("Why do you look up to heaven?" etc.) but of being on earth and concretely living out the will of God that was done in Jesus Christ.

But mysticism is a fundamental aspect of the Muslim religion. There is undoubtedly some correlation with the Orient here. We know to what extent people seek ecstatic and mystical phenomena, using drugs and somatic techniques to achieve this abstract knowledge, this fusion with God. Fasts, exhausting dances, absolute silence, hashish, etc.—all things are good that lead to merger with God. Great Muslim mystics abound. Once again, prior to the relation with Islam, one may perceive certain mystical tendencies in Christianity, especially the trend that derives from Gnosticism and neo-Platonism. But this trend was regarded with suspicion and did not form any glorious part of the Christian life or the church. In contrast, mysticism is directly linked with Islam; it forms part of its spiritual development. Let us make no mistake; when I speak about the desire to mount up to God, this does not mean pride and conquest, for mystics view themselves as objects that are annihilated in God. But here again the biblical orientation is very different. Furthermore, I am not saying that the influence of Islam is the only one in this regard. My point is that it was decisive in the development of mysticism as an expression of Christian faith.

The second aspect seems to me to be the essential one, and it is not at all alien to the first. Islam means submission (to God's will). Just as mystics negate themselves to give place to God, so Muslims have the same religious orientation. Not just obedience but submission is involved. At a first glance this seems to be in full conformity with the biblical revelation. We know how important a role is played in current piety by the formula *mektoub*, it was written. We have to submit to the sovereign, preexistent, eternal, and immutable will of God. All history, all the events of history, all the things that come to pass in each individual life have already been decreed and fixed in advance and written by God. In reality this is the very reverse of what we are told about the biblical God, who opens up freedom for us, who lets us make our own history, who goes with us on the more or less unheard-of adventures that we concoct. This God is not "providence" (which is never a biblical word). He is never a determinative cause or an irreducible conductor of events. The biblical God is he who unceasingly reestablishes our human liberty when we keep falling into bondage. He unceasingly enters into dialogue with us, but only so as to warn us about what is good, to set us on guard, to associate us with his will; never to force us. Here again the tendency to believe in a God who because he is omnipotent is also omniscient (which presupposes that everything is already said) was already present in Christian thinking when it was invaded by certain elements in Greek thought. Yet at first the themes of salvation and love were always dominant. I believe that it was the strictness of Muslim piety that really led Christians along this path.

If we make God's omnipotence dominant over his love and autonomy, his transcendence over the incarnation and liberation, then we think of his omniscience as an inscribing of history and events in a nexus of events that has already been established that is unchangeable and immutable, and that all takes place at a stroke. Then we do not have to enter into a dialogue with God, or into a monologue that, like Job's, demands a response from God, but simply have to submit to the unchanging and, in a true sense, inhuman will of God. The whole Bible, whether in the Old Testament or the Gospels, tells us that there is no such thing as destiny or fate. All this is replaced by love, and hence the joyful freedom that the first Christians experience. But gradually, and insidiously, fate stages a comeback.

I admit that here again popular beliefs perpetuated the Roman idea of fatum and that the idea of liberation from destiny had hard work making its way. I also admit that philosophical thought inclined theologians toward problems of this type: If God is omnipotent, it is he who does all things (cf. the error in translating Matt. 10:29), he is not just the causa sui but the cause of causes . . . and the future as well as the past is before him. Hence our future is already there for God. We live out nothing, construct nothing, and can change nothing. It must be understood, however, that these are logical questions that have nothing whatever to do with what the Bible reveals to us. This logic tends to assimilate the biblical God to Roman ideas of God. To unite the relics of popular belief and philosophical deductions only some new input was needed, and I think that Islam supplied this with its specific conception of the omnipotent God who retains only one aspect of the Hebrew God and absolutizes it.

From now on destiny and divine omniscience are conjoined. Believers can live in perfect peace because they know that everything was written in advance and they can change nothing. The very formula "It was written" could come only from a religion of the book. Yet the Hebrew Bible and the Gospels never use such a formula. Thanks to it, the idea of predestination that was already haunting philo-sophical and Christian thinking received confirmation, forcibly established itself, and came to include double predestination (in Calvin), which, whether we want it or not, transforms the biblical God into destiny, Ananke, etc. And this derives from Muslim thinking. For it is not just historical events that were written in advance; it is also eternal salvation (or rejection). Ultimately this conviction came to dominate a good part of Christendom, and paganism rejoins it with its belief in the god of fate.

Finally, we have to take into account some rather different contributions of Islam, not directly in the theological field but with reference to some social impli-cations of belief that are at every point inconsistent with Christian ethics. We have already met one of these: the holy war. A second on which I shall not expand, having studied it already, is the status of women. Another difficulty that arises in Islam in this regard is that modern Muslims claim that women are in every way equal to men and completely free, that Islam has been a movement of feminine emancipation. Yet one can go so far as to say that nowhere have women been more fully subject than on Muslim territory.[4] Marriages are arranged for young girls, women are reduced to being the slaves of men in poor families and are put in the harems of the wealthy; women have no rights, having no property—all this is beyond dispute. Furthermore, the well-known question whether women have souls (the church has run into trouble for asking this question, and some have wrongly alleged that in the eleventh and twelfth centuries it said women had no souls) is a question that was in reality posed by Muslim theologians. Before Arab theologians raised the issue, no one in the Christian world had any doubts about the matter. Indeed, in spite of the anti-Christian fable that is spread abroad with such satisfaction, the famous Council of Macon in particular (585), to which ref-erence is often made, did not deal with the matter, as H. Leclercq has shown incontrovertibly in his article in the *Dictionnaire d'archeologie chretienne*. The polemical legend rests solely on some misunderstood lines of Gregory of Tours on the subject, in which the question is a purely grammatical one, namely, whether the word homo is a generic term that may also apply to women (the answer being in the affirmative), and not a theological one, whether women are human beings furnished with souls. Neither Christianity nor the church ever denied that women have souls. Furthermore, it was certainly only in those Western lands subject to Muslim domination that the position of women deteriorated. A detailed study is impossible, but an answer to the question would have to be along the lines that I have indicated.

I have to admit that Christian history took an incredibly sad turn in two other areas. The first concerns slavery. Not all at once but progressively under Christian influence (and not because of technical improvements, as is often stated today), slavery disappeared in the Roman Empire. It persisted, however, in remote corners of the Carolingian Empire. We may note, meanwhile, two currents: the one from the North (the Slavs), the other from the Mediterranean. Yet the incidence of this is negligible and episodic. The general thesis that there was no more slavery in Christendom is true. Thus the proclamation that "everyone in the kingdom of France is free" was correct, and it was even allowed (although perhaps theoretically) that the moment slaves arrived in France, the mere fact of setting foot on French soil made them free. This was wholly in keeping with Christian thinking.

Nevertheless, from the fifteenth century, with the development of a knowledge of Africa, and then especially in the seventeenth and eighteenth centuries, we have the familiar and dreadful history of the enslaving of Africans, who were torn from their own country and transported to America. What accusations have been made against "Christianity" and Western civilization! And rightly so! How lightly the revelation in Christ was taken, which would have totally and radically and unreservedly forbidden slavery. In the Middle Ages the traffic in slaves would undoubtedly have led to excommunication. It is a curious fact, however, that apart from some conscientious historians no one has put the elementary question how it was that a few Western navigators could round up thousands of slaves from among peoples who were by no means sheeplike. Could a hundred French sailors, even though armed with muskets, attack a tribe of several hundred hardy warriors and seize a cargo of slaves? Such an idea is pure fiction. For centuries the Muslims had regularly cropped the black continent for slaves. Seizing Africans as slaves was a Muslim practice from at least the tenth century. The African tribes were in this case attacked by considerable armies, in veritable invasions, of which we shall have to speak later.[5]

The Muslims carried off to the East far more black slaves than the Westerners ever did. In the eleventh century fifteen great slave markets were set up by the Arabs in black Africa. In the east they extended as far as across from Madagascar [present-day Mozambique], and in the west as far as the Niger [present-day Guinea River]. Slaves were the main item in Muslim trade from the tenth century to the fifteenth. Furthermore, the Muslims began to use political methods by which the Western merchants profited. They played off the African chiefs against one another in such a way that a chief would take prisoners from neighboring tribes and then sell them to the Arab merchants. It was by following this practice, which had been established for many centuries, that the Western sailors obtained slaves so easily. Naturally, the reality itself is terrible and anti-Christian, but we see here the direct influence of Islam on the practice of Westerners who were

Christian only in name. One should also remember, as the United Nations has pointed out, that trading in black slaves by Arab merchants still goes on in countries around the Gulf of Oman.

Finally, a last point: colonizing. Here again, for the last thirty years some have attacked Christianity for instigating colonialism. Christians are accused of invading the whole world and justifying the capitalist system. It has become a traditional belief that missionaries pioneered the way for merchants. Undoubtedly there is some truth in all this. Undoubtedly serious and conscientious Christians should never have acquiesced in the invasion of "Third World" peoples, in the seizing of their lands, in their reduction to semi-slavery (or their extermination), in the destruction of their cultures. The judgment against us is a crushing one. Las Casas is entirely right. But who invented colonizing? Islam. Incontestably so!

I will not discuss again the question of war or the establishment in Africa of kingdoms dominated by the Arabs. My theme is colonizing, the penetration by other than military means, the reduction of subject peoples by a sort of treaty that makes them do exactly as the rulers want. In Islam we find two methods of penetration, commercial and religious. Things are exactly the same as they will be among the Westerners five centuries later. Muslim missionaries convert the Africans to Islam by every possible means. Nor can one deny that their intervention has just the same effects as that of Christian missionaries: the destruction of the independent religions and cultures of the African tribes and kingdoms. Nor must we back the stupid argument that it was an internal affair of the African world. The Muslims came into the north by conquest, and the Arabs are white. Muslim missionaries went as far as Zanzibar, and in Angola they brought within the Muslim orbit African peoples that had not been conquered or subjugated.

The other method is that of commerce. The Arab merchants go much further afield than the soldiers. They do much the same as the Westerners will do five centuries later. They set up trading posts and barter with the local tribes. It is not without interest that one of the commodities they were seeking in the tenth and eleventh centuries was gold. Trading in gold by the Arabs took place in Ghana, to the south of the Niger, and on the east coast down toward Zanzibar. When it is said that the desire for gold prompted the Westerners in the fifteenth century, they were simply following in the footsteps of Islam. Thus the Arab mechanism of colonizing serves as a model for the Europeans.

In conclusion, let me make it clear that I have not been trying to excuse what the Europeans did. I have not been trying to shift the "blame," to say that the Muslims, not the Christians, were the guilty party. My purpose is to try to explain certain perversions in Christian conduct. I have found a model for them in Islam. Christians did not invent the holy war or the slave trade. Their great fault was to imitate Islam. Sometimes this was direct imitation by following the example of Islam. Sometimes it was inverse imitation by doing the same thing in order to combat Islam, as in the Crusades. Either way, the tragedy was that the church completely forgot the truth of the gospel. It turned Christian ethics upside down in favor of what seemed to be very obviously a much more effective mode of action, for in the twelfth century and later the Muslim world offered a dazzling example of civilization. The church forgot the authenticity of the revelation in Christ in order to launch out in pursuit of the same mirage.

NOTES

1. See, among other works, D. Sourdel, *L'Islam medievel* (Paris: PUF, 1979), and on Muslim mysticism M. Eliade, *Histoire des croyances et des idees religieuses* (Paris: Payot, 1983), 3: 283; *Islam et Christianisme*, a special issue of *Foi et Vie* (1983).

2. H. Pirenne, *Mahomet et Charlemagne* (Paris: Payot, 1937).

3. This has led some fervent supporters of Islam to regret that the Arabs were finally defeated and repulsed. What a wonderfully civilized empire would have been set up if all Europe had been invaded! This position, the opposite of the prevailing one in history up to about 1950, leads people to forget the horrors of Islam, the dreadful cruelty, the general use of torture, the slavery, and the absolute intolerance notwithstanding zealous apostles who underline Islam's toleration. We shall come back to this. It is enough to point out that wherever Islam gained a hold strong and vital churches like those of North Africa and Asia Minor simply disappeared. And all native cultures that were different, that the Romans and Germans had respected, were exterminated in areas conquered by the Arabs.

4. Cf. the fine study by G. Bousquet, *L'Ethique sexuelle de l'Islam* (Paris: Maisonneuve, 1966). The Prophet's own practice was also not particularly edifying for women, and Muslims are told to copy him in all things.

5. Apart from the wars, we also find brutal expeditions that were mounted solely to seize prisoners as slaves or to carry off herds and women. For these the word is razzia, a good Arab term.

PART 5
Jihad, Seventh through Eleventh Centuries: Summary Text

Please refer to the photo insert for these maps.

SEVENTH CHRISTIAN CENTURY/ FIRST ISLAMIC CENTURY

In Europe

Balkans: Constantinople attacked by Umayyads of Syria in 669 and in 674–680.

Daghestan: Under Sāsānids until 644; orthodox caliphs, 644-661; and Umayyads after 661.

In the Mediterranean

Sicily: Under Byzantine emperors (pillaged by Muslims in 652 and 668).

Crete: Under Byzantines (occupied briefly by Umayyads of Syria in 674).

Rhodes: Under Byzantines (attacked by Muslims in 654, occupied 672–679).

Cyprus: Under Byzantines until 649; disputed between Byzantines and Muslims after 649.

In Africa

Morocco and Algeria: Coast under Byzantines until 699 (raided by 'Uqbah ibn-

---

From Harry W. Hazard, comp., *Atlas of Islamic History*, maps executed by H. Lester Cooke Jr. and J. McA. Smiley (Princeton, NJ: Princeton University Press, 1951). Text: pp. 6, 8, 10, 12, 14; Maps: pp. 7, 9, 11, 13, 15.

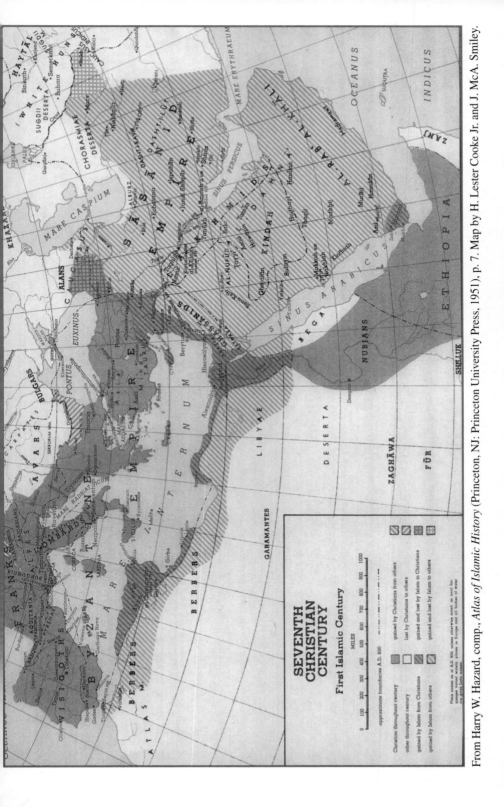

From Harry W. Hazard, comp., *Atlas of Islamic History* (Princeton, NJ: Princeton University Press, 1951), p. 7. Map by H. Lester Cooke Jr. and J. McA. Smiley.

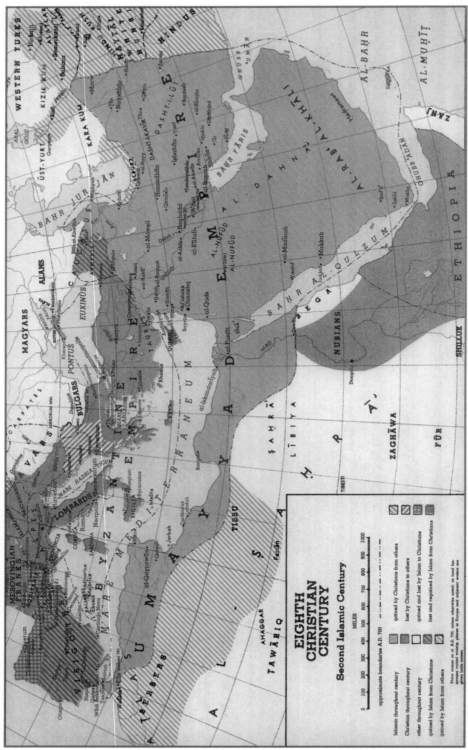

From Harry W. Hazard, comp., *Atlas of Islamic History* (Princeton, NJ: Princeton University Press, 1951), p. 9. Map by H. Lester Cooke Jr. and J. McA. Smiley.

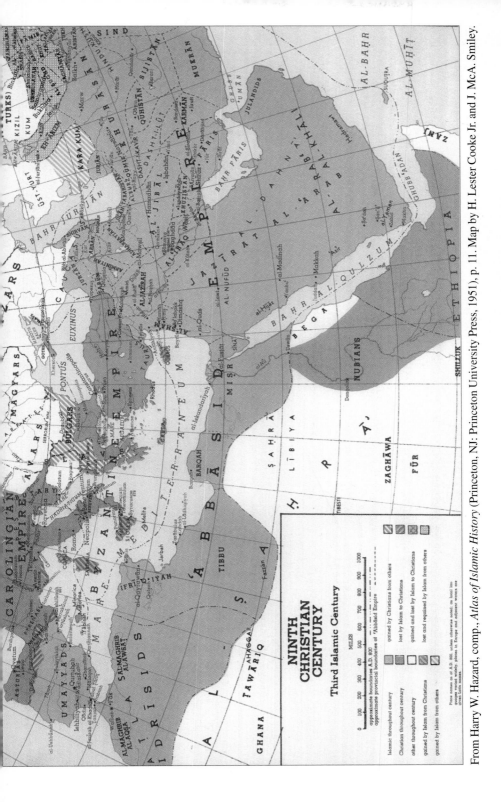

From Harry W. Hazard, comp., *Atlas of Islamic History* (Princeton, NJ: Princeton University Press, 1951), p. 11. Map by H. Lester Cooke Jr. and J. McA. Smiley.

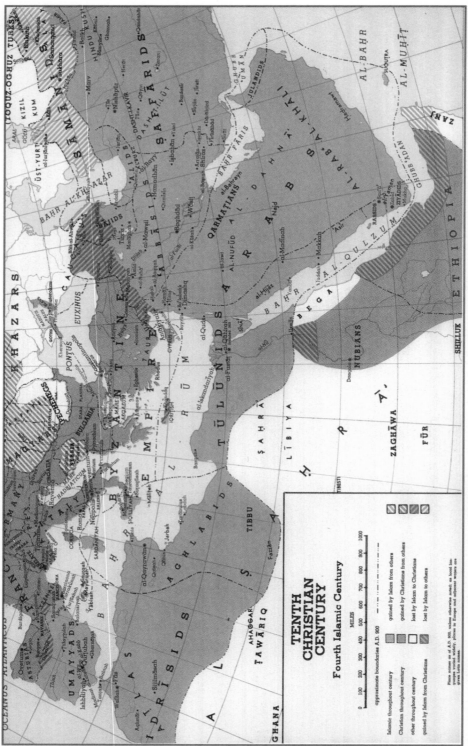

From Harry W. Hazard, comp., *Atlas of Islamic History* (Princeton, NJ: Princeton University Press, 1951), p. 13. Map by H. Lester Cooke Jr. and J. McA. Smiley.

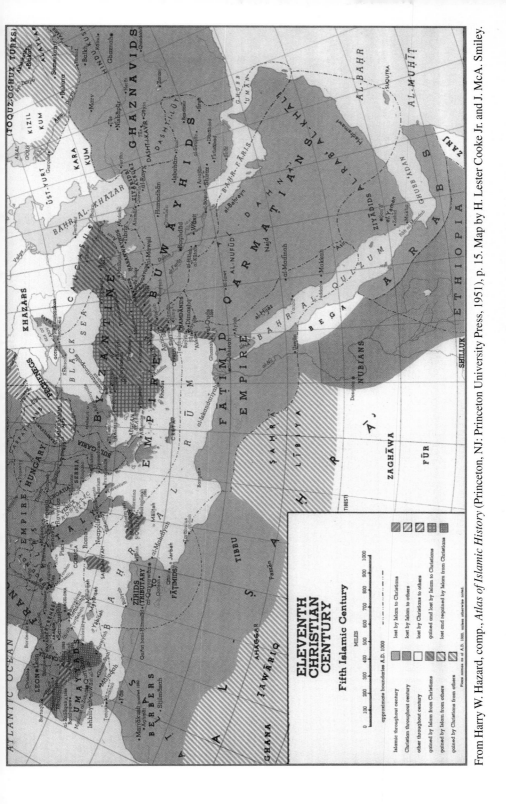

From Harry W. Hazard, comp., *Atlas of Islamic History* (Princeton, NJ: Princeton University Press, 1951), p. 15. Map by H. Lester Cooke Jr. and J. McA. Smiley.

RECRUITMENT OF TRIBUTE CHILDREN
(folio 3 rb) Painters A and E

This unique scene illustrating the recruiting of the devshirme children takes place in a Christian town in one of the western provinces. The devshirme *emini* (officer in charge of recruitment) wears a tall hat topped by a plume and sits on a red rug spread on a brick platform. He is counting the money given to the recruits as travel expenses from their hometown to the capital. His assistant records the town, province, parents, and birthdates of the children in a ledger; a copy of the record, which was required by the state, is on the rug. In the foreground, guarded by an officer, are six of the recruits, attired in their new red garments and caps, carrying bags that hold their only earthly possessions. The men, women, and children of the town gather in front of an elaborate architectural setting with arches and high, sloping roofs that represent non-Ottoman structures. A mother, most likely asking questions about her son's welfare, confronts a janissary, himself once a devshirme child. Next to her is a priest or monk wearing a dark robe and hat, equally apprehensive. Another woman, standing behind to the right of the devshirme *emini*, appears quite despondent, her young daughter clinging to her for comfort. (From Esin Atıl, *Süleymanname: The Illustrated History of Süleyman the Magnificent* [New York: Harry N. Abrams, 1986], p. 95.)

SULEYMAN ARRIVING AT RHODES
(folio 143a) Painter B

The battle of Rhodes, which lasted almost five months, was possibly the most strenuous of all Suleyman's campaigns. This critical campaign is represented by three consecutive scenes that narrate different events. The first depicts the arrival of the sultan and the preparations for the siege of the fortress. The fortress of Rhodes rises in the background, manned by soldiers wearing different types of armor and headdress. The Ottomans, gathered in the hilly terrain outside the stronghold, have begun the siege. Suleyman, accompanied by his *peyks*, *solaks*, and Has Oda *agas*, approaches the fortress on horseback and instructs the miners, who have started to dig tunnels under the structure. The janissaries have taken their position behind the trenches and are ready to open fire with their rifles. The cavalry, holding maces and banners, lines up behind a hill on the far right. In the foreground are attendants leading the sultan's spare horses. (From Esin Atıl, *Süleymanname: The Illustrated History of Süleyman the Magnificent* [New York: Harry N. Abrams, 1986], p. 119.)

SIEGE OF BUDAPEST
(folio 282a) Painter B

The painting representing the second conquest of Budapest shows the inner fortress in the background. The fortress offers protection to several Hapsburg soldiers wearing helmets and short-brimmed caps with white feathers. A guard stationed at the top of the observation tower scrutinizes a group of mace-bearing Ottoman cavalry officers, who advance toward the structure. In the center of the painting is the outer fortress, which has been demolished by explosives that have thrown a number of men from its walls. The soldiers fall upside down, flinging their arms and legs and dropping their hats. Two of the men have landed in the foreground; one clutches his leg, and the other, still in a swan-dive position, spreads his hands, surrendering to the officer on the lower right, who threatens him with a spear. Opposite are other cavalrymen, ready to take prisoners. Painter B portrays the enemy soldiers in a whimsical manner, representing their demise with a touch of frivolity. Even the animated rocks on the upper right appear to be amused by their clumsiness. (From Esin Atıl, *Süleymanname: The Illustrated History of Süleyman the Magnificent* [New York: Harry N. Abrams, 1986], p. 150.)

Nāfiʿ 682–683), conquered by Mūsa ibn-Nusayr 699–705; hinterland under Berber chiefs.

Tunisia: Under Byzantines until 670 (invaded by ʿAbd-Allāh ibn-Saʿd in 647); conquered by ʿUqbah ibn-Nāfiʿ 670–683; lost to Berbers and Byzantines 683–693; reconquered by Hassān ibn-al-Nuʿmān 693–698; under Umayyads of Syria after 698.

Tripolitania Cyrenaica: Coast under Byzantines until 642, conquered by ʿAmr ibn-al-ʿĀs 642–647, under orthodox caliphs 647–661, under Umayyads of Syria after 661. Hinterland held by pagan Berber and Tibbu tribes.

East Africa: Nubia frequently raided from Egypt; treaty in 652 established tribute.

Egypt: Nile and delta under Byzantines until 639 (attacked by Sāsānids 619–628), deserts held by pagan tribes; conquered by ʿAmr ibn-al-ʿĀs 639–642; under orthodox caliphs 642–661 (in revolt 655–656, 659–661); under Umayyads of Syria after 661 (disputed with ʿAbd-Allāh ibn-al-Zubayr of Arabia 680–684).

In Asia

Arabia: Disputed among Arab tribes including Ghassānid allies of Byzantines, Lakhmid allies of Persians, Himyar allies of Axumites of Ethiopia, and Kindah until 622; subjected by Muhammad, 622–632, and orthodox caliphs at Medina (al-Madīnah), 632–656:

    (1) 632–634, abu-Bakr ibn-ʿUthmān (father of Muhammad's wife ʿĀ'ishah),
    (2) 634–644, ʿUmar ibn-al-Khattab (father of Muhammad's wife Hafsah),
    (3) 644–656, ʿUthmān ibn-ʿAffān (husband of Muhammad's daughter Ruqayyah); disputed among ʿAli ibn-abi-Tālib, al-Zubayr ibn-al-ʿAwwām, and Talhah ibn-ʿAbd-Allāh in 656 and between ʿAli and Muʿāwiyah in 656–661; under Umayyads of Syria after 661 (disputed by al-Husayn ibn-ʿAli in 680 and ʿAbd-Allāh ibn-al-Zubayr in 680–690).

Syria: Under Byzantine until 634 (disputed by Sāsānids 608–628); conquered by Khālid ibn-al-Walīd 634–640; under orthodox caliphs at Damascus (Dimashq) after 661:

    (1) 661–680, Muʾāwiyah I ibn-abi-Sufyān (distant cousin of Muhammad),
    (2) 680–683, Yazīd I (son of no. 1),
    (3) 683–684, Muʾāwiyah II (son of no. 2; ʿAbd-Allāh ibn-al-Zubayr),
    (4) 684–685, Marwān I ibn-al-Hakam (second cousin of no. 1),
    (5) 685–705, ʿAbd-al-Malik (son of no. 4).

Anatolia: Under Byzantines (disputed by Sāsānids 608–628; subjected to annual raids and intermittent invasions by Syrian Muslims after 637).

Transcaucasia: Disputed between Byzantines and Sāsānids until 644 (attacked by ʿIyād ibn-Ghanm in 640); conquered by Habīb ibn-Maslamah, 644–652; under orthodox caliphs, 652–661; under Umayyads of Syria, 661–680; divided between Umayyads and kings of Armenia after 680.

Mesopotamia: Disputed between Byzantines and Sāsānids until 634; conquered by Saʿd ibn-abi-Waqqās, 634–641; under orthodox caliphs, 641–661, including, at al-Kūfah:

> (4) 656–661, ʿAli ibn-abi-Tālib (husband of his cousin Muhammad's daughter Fātimah); under Umayyads of Syria after 661 (disputed by ʿAbd-Allāh ibn-al-Zubayr, 680–690).

Persia: Under Sāsānids until 637; all except Tabaristān (held by local nobles after 637) conquered by Saʿd ibn-abi-Waqqās, 637–650, under Orthodox caliphs, 650–661, under Umayyads of Syria after 661 (disputed by ʿAbd-Allāh ibn-al-Zubayr, 680–690).

Khurasan: Under Sāsānids until 637; under local Iranian princes, 637–651; conquered by ʿAbd-Allāh ibn-ʿĀmir in 651; under orthodox caliphs, 651–656; in revolt against ʿAli and Muʿāwiyah, 656–663; reconquered, 663–671; under Umayyads of Syria after 671.

Afghanistan: Disputed between Sāsānids and local Turkish and White Hun chiefs until 637; under local chiefs, 637–661 (Heart area invaded by Aws ibn-Thaʿlabah in 652, Balkh area by al-Ahnaf ibn-Qays in 653); divided between Umayyads of Syria and local chiefs after 661 (Kabul [Kâbil] raided by ʿAbd-al-Rahmān ibn-Muhammad, 699–700).

Transoxiana: Under Turkish and White Hun chiefs (Bukhara [Buhara] raided by Saʿīd ibn-ʿUthmān in 674, Samarkand [Semerkant] in 676).

EIGHTH CHRISTIAN CENTURY/SECOND ISLAMIC CENTURY

In Europe

Spain: Under Visigothic kings until 711; conquered by Tāriq ibn-Ziyād and Mūsa ibn-Nusayr, 711–718; disputed between Christians and Umayyads of Syria, 718–750, between Christians and 'Abbāsids, 750–756; disputed among Christians, rebellious Muslims (Yemenites and Shī'ites instigated by 'Abbāsids; Berbers), and Umayyads at Cordova (Corduba) after 756:

(1) 756–788, 'Abd-al-Rahmān I ibn-Mu'āwiyah (grandson of Syrian Umayyad no. 10) (abortive invasion by Charlemagne in 776 stopped at Saragossa [Caesaraugusta, Saraqustah], retreating rear-guard defeated at Roncesvalles),

(2) 788–796, Hishām I (son of no. 1),

(3) 796–822, al-Hakam I (son of no. 2).

France: Invaded by al-Hurr ibn-'Abd-al-Rahmān 717–718, Narbonne (Narbona) taken by al-Samh ibn-Mālik in 720; Toulouse (Tolosa) attacked in 721; Carcassonne (Carcaso) captured in 725; Bordeaux (Burdigala) pillaged by 'Abd-al-Rahmān ibn-'Abd-Allāh in 732; 'Abd-al-Rahmān defeated by Charles Martel between Tours (Turoni) and Poitiers (Pictavi) in October 732; Avignon (Avenio) sacked in 734; Lyons (Lugdunum) pillaged in 743; Narbonne lost in 759, forcing Arabs to withdraw to Spain.

Italy: Coast raided by Muslim corsairs.

Balkans: Constantinople attacked by Maslamah (son Syrian Umayyad no. 5), 717–718; threatened by Hārūn (later 'Abbāsid no. 5) in 782.

Daghestan: Under Umayyads of Syria until 749; under 'Abbāsids after 749.

Baleares: Under Byzantine emperors until 754 (raided by 'Abd-Allāh ibn-Mūsa 707–708); under Franks 754–798; Iviza (Ebusus) conquered by Umayyads of Spain in 798.

Corsica: Under Byzantines until 774; under Franks after 774 (raided by Muslims).

Sardinia, Sicily, and Malta: Under Byzantines (frequently raided by Muslim corsairs).

Rhodes: Under Byzantines (occupied by Syrian Muslims, 717–718).

Cyprus: Disputed with Byzantines by Umayyads until 750, by 'Abbāsids after 750.

In Africa

Morocco and Western Algeria: Coast conquered by Mūsa ibn-Nusayr 699–705; under Umayyads of Syria, 705–750; under 'Abbāsids, 750–789; under Idrīsids at Walīlah after 789; hinterland held by Berbers (converted and partially subjected by Idrīsids).

Eastern Algeria, Tunisia, Tripolitania, and Cyrenaica: Under Umayyads of Syria until 750; under 'Abbāsids, 750–800; Aghlabids at Kairouan (al-Qayrawān) after 800.

Sahara: North held by Berber and Tibbu tribes (converted and partially subjected).

East Africa: Nubians on Nile and coastal Ethiopians in contact with Arab traders.

Egypt: Under Umayyads of Syria until 750; under 'Abbāsids after 750.

In Asia

Arabia: Under Umayyads of Syria until 750; under 'Abbāsids after 750.

Syria: Umayyads at Damascus (Dimashq) until 750:
 (5) 685–705, 'Abd-al-Malik (son of no. 4),
 (6–7) 705–717, al-Walīd I (to 715) and Sulaymān (sons of no. 5),
 (8) 717–720, 'Umar ibn-'Abd-al-'Azīz (grandson of no. 4),
 (9–10) 720–743, Yazīd II (to 724) and Hishām (son of no. 5),
 (11) 743–744, al-Walīd II (son of no. 9),
 (12–13) 744–744, Yazīd III and Ibrāhīm (sons of no. 6),
 (14) 744–750, Marwān II ibn-Muhammad (grandson of no. 4); under 'Abbāsids after 750.

Anatolia: Under Byzantine emperors (frequently invaded by Syrian Muslims).

Transcaucasia: Divided between kings of Armenia and Umayyads of Syria until 717; under Umayyads, 717–750; under 'Abbāsids after 750.

Mesopotamia: Under Umayyads until 749; 'Abbāsids at al-Anbār and Baghdad after 749:
(1) 749–754, 'Abn-Allāh al-Saffāh ibn-Muhammad (distant cousin of Muhammad),
(2) 754–775, 'Abd-Allāh al-Mansūr (brother of no. 1),
(3) 775–785, Muhammad al Mahdi (son of no. 2),
(4–5) 785–809, Mūsa al-Hādi (to 786) and Hārūn al-Rashīd (sons of no. 3).

Persia: All except Tabaristān under Umayyads until 748; disputed between Umayyads and 'Abbāsids 748–749; under 'Abbāsids after 749; Tabaristān annexed about 765.

Khurasan: Under Umayyads until 747; 'Abbāsid revolt under abu-Muslim al-Khurāsāni, 747–749; under 'Abbāsids after 749.

Afghanistan: Disputed between Umayyads and Turkish and White Hun chiefs until 749 (Balkh [Belh] reconquered by Qutaybah ibn-Muslim in 705); invaded several times and loosely held by 'Abbāsids after 749.

Transoxiana: Under Turkish and White Hun chiefs until 706; conquered by Qutaybah ibn-Muslim, 706–715; held loosely by Umayyads, 715–738; conquest consolidated by Nasr ibn-Sayyār, 738–740; under Umayyads, 740–748; under 'Abbāsids after 748 (Tashkent [Binkath] taken in 751; revolts frequent).

NINTH CHRISTIAN CENTURY/
THIRD ISLAMIC CENTURY

In Europe

Spain: Divided between Christians (N 25%) and Umayyads at Cordova (Qurtubah):
(3) 796–822, al-Hakam I (son of no. 2; Barcelona lost to Charlemagne in
        801),
(4) 822–852, 'Abd-al-Rahmān II (son of no. 3),
(5) 852–886, Muhammad I (son of no. 4),
(6–7) 886–912, al-Mundhir (to 888) and 'Abd-Allāh (sons of no. 5).

France: Coasts raided by Muslim corsairs, who occupied coast of Provence after
890.

Italy: Under steady attack by Muslims from Sicily and Tunisia; Brindisi (Brundisium) occupied 836, 840–870; Naples (Neapolis) relieved, 837; Calabria raided, 838; Capua razed, 840; Taranto (Tarentum) occupied, 840–880; Bari (Barium) occupied, 841–871; Benevento (Beneventum) subjected, 842–847, 849–852; Rome (Roma) attacked, 846; Campagna ravaged, 876–877; Monte Cassino burned, 883; northern Italy raided by Umayyads of Spain, who penetrated Alps as far as Switzerland.

Daghestan: Under 'Abbāsids until 898; under Sājids of Azerbaijan after 898.

In the Mediterranean

Baleares: Iviza (Yābisah) held by Umayyads; Majorca and Minorca under Franks (frequently attacked by Muslim corsairs).

Corsica: Held by Franks (disputed by Aghlabid corsairs after 809).

Sardinia: Under Byzantine emperors (disputed by Aghlabid corsairs after 809).

Sicily: Under Byzantines until 827; gradually conquered by Aghlabids, 827–902, with only Taormina (Taurominium) in Byzantine hands in 900.

Malta: Under Byzantine emperors until 824; attacked by Aghlabids, 824–869; under Aghlabids after 869.

Crete: under Byzantines until 825; conquered in 825 by 'Umar ibn-'Īsa and refugees from Andalusia; under local Muslim emirs after 825.

Cyprus: Disputed by Byzantines after 876 (frequently raided by Muslims).

In Africa

Morocco and Western Algeria: Idrīsids at Walīlah and Fez (Fās).

Eastern Algeria, Tunisia, Tripolitania: Aghlabids at Kairouan.

Sahara: Northern part held by Muslim Berber and Tibbu tribes under loose control of Idrīsids and Aghlabids.

East Africa: Nubians on Nile and coastal Ethiopians in contact with Arab traders.

Cyrenaica and Egypt: Under 'Abbāsids until 868; nominally under 'Abbāsids but actually ruled by Tūlūnids at al-Fustāt after 868.

In Asia

Arabia: Disputed between 'Abbāsids and local Arab chiefs, particularly Ziyādids of Zabīd (after 820), Ya'furids of San'ā' (after 861), and Rassids of Sa'dah (after 893), all in Yemen (al-Yaman), and Julandids of Oman ('Umān); Hejaz (al-Hijāz) and Asir ('Asīr) under Tūlūnids after 868; Qarmatian revolt in 899.

Syria: Under 'Abbāsids (actually ruled by Tūlūnids after 877).

Anatolia: Under Byzantine emperors (raided annually by Muslim, invaded in 806, 838).

Transcaucasia: Under 'Abbāsids until 889–890; eastern half under Sājids at Marāghah after 889–890.

Mesopotamia: 'Abbāsid caliphs at Baghdad and (836–892) Sāmarra:
    (5) 786–809, Hārūn al-Rashīd (son of no. 3),
    (6–7) 809–833, Muhammad al-Amīn (to 813) and 'Abn-Allāh al-Ma'mūn
            (sons of no. 5),
    (8) 833–842, Muhammad al-Mu'tasim (son of no. 5),
    (9–10) 842–861, Hārūn al-Wāthiq (to 847) and Ja'far al-Mutawakkil (sons of
            no. 8),
    (11) 861–862, Muhammad al-Muntasir (son of no. 10),
    (12) 862–866, Ahmad al-Musta'īn ibn-Muhammad (grandson of no. 8),
    (13) 866–869, Muhammad al-Mu'tazz (son of no. 10),
    (14) 869–870, Muhammad al-Muhtadi (son of no. 9),

(15) 870–892, Ahmad al-Mu'tamid (son of no. 10) (Zanj slave revolt at al-
       Basrah, 870–883),
(16) 892–902, Ahmad al-Mu'tadid ibn-al-Muwaffaq (grandson of no. 10).

Persia: Under 'Abbāsids until 864; disputed among 'Abbāsids and 'Alids of
Tabaristān (after 864), Saffārids of Sijistān (after 867), and Sājids of Azerbaijan
(after 889–890).

Khurasan: Under 'Abbāsids until 820; nominally under 'Abbāsids but actually
ruled by Tāhirids at Merv (Marw) and Nishapur (Naysābūr), 820–872; under Saffārids, 872–900.

Afghanistan: Under 'Abbāsids until 869; under Saffārids after 869.

Transoxiana: Under 'Abbāsids until 819–820; nominally under 'Abbāsids but
actually ruled by a noble Persian vassal Ahmad ibn-Asad 819–874; independent
under Sāmānids at Bukhara after 874:
    (1) 874–892, Nasr I (son of Ahmad ibn-Asad),
    (2) 892–907, Ismā'īl (brother of no. 1).

TENTH CHRISTIAN CENTURY/
FOURTH ISLAMIC CENTURY

In Europe

Spain: Disputed between Christians (N 30%) and Umayyads at Cordova (Qurtubah):
- (7) 888–912, 'Abd-Allāh (son of no. 5),
- (8) 912–961, 'Abd-al-Rahmān III ibn-Muhammad (grandson of no. 7; caliph after 929),
- (9) 961–976, al-Hakam II (son of no. 8),
- (10) Hishām II (son of no.; until 1002 under chamberlain al-Mansūr).

France: Muslim corsairs held coast of Provence and raided inland, expelled in 975.

Italy: Coasts raided from Sicily; Genoa (Genua) sacked by Fātimid fleet in 934–935.

Daghestan: Held by Sājids until 930; under local mountain chieftains after 930.

In the Mediterranean

Baleares: Under Franks (except Iviza) until conquered by 'Isām al-Khawlāni in 903; under Umayyads of Spain after 903.

Corsica: Under Byzantine (disputed by Aghlabids until 909, by Fātimids 909–930).

Sardinia: Disputed with Byzantines by Aghlabids (until 909), by Fātimids (after 909).

Sicily: Under Aghlabids until 909 (Taormina taken 902); under Fātimids after 909 (in revolt under Ahmad ibn-Qurhub 912–916; Kalbid governors partially independent after 948; Taormina lost to Byzantines 965; Byzantine invasion repulsed after 909).

Malta: Under Aghlabids until 909; under Fātimids after 909.

Crete: Under mirs until 961; under Byzantine emperors after 961.

Cyprus: Under Byzantines (disputed by Tūlūnids until 905, by 'Abbāsids 905–964).

In Africa

Morocco and Western Algeria: Disputed among Idrīsids at Walīlah and Fez (Fās) (until 985), Fātimids of Tunisia (909–972), Umayyads of Spain, and local Berber tribes.

Eastern Algeria, Tunisia, Tripolitania: Aghlabids at Kairouan (al-Qayrawān) until 909; Fātimids at Kairouan 909–972:
  (1) 909–934, Sa'īd 'Ubayd-Allāh al-Mahdi ibn-Husayn (descendant of Muhammad),
  (2) 934–946, Muhammad al-Qā'im (son of no. 1),
  (3) 946–952, Ismā'il al-Mansūr (son of no. 2),
  (4) 952–975, Ma'add al-Mu'izz (son of no. 3; moved to Egypt in 972); Zīrids, governing in the name of Fātimids of Egypt, at Kairouan after 972.

Sahara: North held by Berber and Tibbu tribes under loose control of coastal rulers.

East Africa: Nile valley to second cataract and coastal region occupied by Arabs.

Cyrenaica and Egypt: Tūlūnids at al-Fustāt until 905; under 'Abbāsids, 905–935; Ikhshīdids at al-Fustāt, 935–969; Fātimid conquest, 969–972, at Cairo after 972:
  (5) 975–996, Nizār al-'Azīz (son of no. 4),
  (6) 996–1021, al-Mansūr al-Hākim (son of no. 5).

In Asia

Arabia: Disputed among 'Abbāsids, Tūlūnids, Ikhshīdids, and Arabs, particularly Ziyādids at Zabīd, Julandids in Oman, and Qarmatians, who subjected most of Arabia.

Syria: Under Tūlūnids until 905; 'Abbāsids, 905–941, Ikhshīdids, 941–944; divided with Hamdānids at Aleppo (Halab) by Ikhshīdids, 944–969; and by Fātimids after 969 (Byzantines recovered large border areas including Tarsus, Antioch, and Malatya).

Anatolia: Under Byzantines (occasionally raided by Hamdānids, usually on offensive).

Transcaucasia: Divided between 'Abbāsids and Sājids until 930; Christian after 930.

Mesopotamia: 'Abbāsids at Baghdad (ruled until 929, divided with Hamdānids at Mosul [al-Mawsil], 929–945, only nominal after 945); divided between Hamdānids and Buwayhids, 945–991; after 991 disputed among Buwayhids, Marwānids, and 'Uqaylids.

Persia: Disputed among 'Abbāsids (until 945), 'Alids of Tabaristān (until 928), Saffārids of Sijistān (until 903), Sājids of Azerbaijan (until 930), Sāmānids of Transoxiana (903–944), Ziyārids of Tabaristān (after 928), Buwayhids (after 932), Hasanwayhids of Kurdistan (after 959), and Ghaznavids of Afghanistan (after 994).

Khurasan: Under Sāmānids, 900–994; under Ghaznavids after 994.

Afghanistan: Under Saffārids until 908; disputed between Sāmānids and native princes, 908–962; Ghaznavids at Ghaznah after 962.

Transoxiana: Sāmānids at Bukhara until 999; under Kara-Khanid Īlek Khāns after 999.

ELEVENTH CHRISTIAN CENTURY/ FIFTH ISLAMIC CENTURY

In Europe

Spain: Disputed among Christians, Umayyads at Cordova (Qurtubah; until 1031), petty Muslim emirs (*mulūk al-tawā'if*; after 1012), and Murābits (Almoravids; after 1086).

Italy: Pisa sacked by Muslim corsairs in 1002; Salerno besieged in 1015.

Balkàns: Coasts of Dalmatia and Thrace raided by Fātimid fleet.

In the Mediterranean

Baleares: Under Umayyads of Spain until 1022; under local Muslim emirs after 1022.

Sardinia: Disputed by Byzantines and Fātimids until 1003; under Umayyads, 1003–1031; under local Muslim emirs conquest by Genoa and Pisa, 1016–1050.

Sicily: Kalbid governors for Fātimids until 1060 (invaded by Normans in 1025, by Byzantines and Normans, 1038–1042); disputed among Fātimids, Sicilian Muslims, and Normans, 1060–1091 (Palermo [Balarm] taken by Normans in 1070); held by Normans after 1091.

Malta: Under Fātimids until 1090; under Normans after 1090.

Aegean Islands: Cyclades raided by Fātimid fleet about 1030.

In Africa

Morocco and Western Algeria: Under Berber chiefs until 1056; conquered by Murābits, 1056–1084; Murābits at Sijilmāsah and Marrākush after 1084:
   (1) 1056–1087, abu-Bakr ibn-'Umar (Lamtūni chieftain, follower of ibn-Yāsīn),
   (2) 1087–1106, Yūsuf ibn-Tāshfīn (cousin of no. 1; independent after 1061).

Eastern Algeria: Under Zīrids (as governors for Fātimids) until 1014; Hammādids at Qal'at bani-Hammād and Bougie (Bijāyah) after 1014 (disputed by Arabs after 1058).

Tunisia and Tripolitania: Zīrids at Kairouan (al-Qayrawān) (as governors for Shī'ite Fāṭimids until 1049; as independent Sunnites after 1049); overrun by Arab nomads (banu-Hilāl, banu-Sulaym, and others) after 1052; with Zīrids restricted to al-Mahdīyah.

Cyrenaica: Loosely held by Fāṭimids until 1052; under Arab nomads after 1052.

Sahara: West divided among Muslim Berbers, pagan Negroes of Ghana, and Tawāriq (Touareg) until Murābit conquest after 1056; northeast overrun by Arab nomads after 1052.

East Africa: Coastal strip south to Mogadiscio occupied by Arab and Persian traders.

Egypt: Fāṭimids at Cairo (al-Qāhirah).

In Asia

Arabia: Interior held by Qarmatians; Hejaz tributary to Fāṭimids until 1070, to Seljüks after 1070; Yemen under Ziyādids until 1018, Najāhids after 1021, Sulayhids, 1037–1098, Hamdānids after 1098; Oman under Buwayhids until 1010, Julandids after 1010.

Syria: Under Fāṭimids until 1070 (Byzantines at Antioch; Hamdānids at Aleppo [Halab] until 1003; Mirdāsids at Aleppo, 1024–1037, 1042–1057, 1060–1079); disputed in 1070–1094 among Byzantines (at Antioch until 1084), Fāṭimids, Seljüks, Mirdāsids (at Aleppo until 1079), 'Uqaylids (held Aleppo 1079–1094), and other local dynasties (Shayzar independent after 1081, Tripoli [Tarābulus] after 1089); disputed after 1094 among local Seljüks, Fāṭimids (coastal cities after 1089, Jerusalem, 1089–1099), Assassins, and Crusaders.

Anatolia: Under Byzantines until defeat by Seljüks at Manzikert (Malāzjird) in 1071; under Seljüks, 1071–1077, and Seljüks of Rūm, 1077–1097 (at Nicaea [Īznik] [to 1084] and Iconium [Konya]); coast restored to Byzantines by crusaders after 1097, with Armenian Cilicia free, Seljüks of Rūm in interior, and Dānishmandids ruling eastern highlands.

Transcaucasia: Under local Christians until 1064; under Seljüks after 1064.

Mesopotamia: Disputed among Buwayhids (until 1055), Marwānids at Āmid (Diyār-Bakr) (until 1096), 'Uqaylids at Mosul (until 1096), Mazyadids at al-Hillah (after 1012), Seljüks (after 1055), Fāṭimids (1058–1060), and crusaders at Edessa (al-Ruhā'; after 1098).

Persia: Disputed among Buwayhids at Shīrāz (until 1055), Ziyārids of Tabaristān (until 1042), Hasanwayhids of Kurdistan (until 1015), Kakwayhids of Kurdistan (1007–1051), and Ghaznavids; all except Indian Ocean coast (under Ghaznavids) conquered by Seljüks, 1037–1055, and under Seljüks after 1055 (Assassins at Alamūt after 1090):

(1) 1037–1063, Tughril (capital Merv [Marv]),

(2) 1063–1072, Alp Arslān (nephew of no. 1; at Isfahan [Isbahān]),

(3) 1072–1092, Malik Shāh (son of no. 2; at Isfahan [to 1091] and Baghdad),

(4–5) 1092–1104, Mahmūd (to 1094) and Barkiyāruq (sons of no. 3).

Khurasan: under Ghaznavids until 1035; in dispute, 1035–1040; under Seljüks after 1040.

Afghanistan: Ghaznavids at Ghaznah:

(3) 998–1030, Mahmūd ibn-Subuktigīn.

Transoxiana: Under Kara-Khanid Īlek Khāns until 1016; under Ghaznavids, 1016–1037; loosely held by Seljüks, 1037–1089; under Seljüks after 1089.

PART 6

Jihad in the Near East, Europe, and Asia Minor and on the Indian Subcontinent

37

GREEK CHRISTIAN AND OTHER ACCOUNTS OF THE MUSLIM CONQUESTS OF THE NEAR EAST

Demetrios Constantelos

In order to present a revised historical assessment of early Islam and its long-term impact upon the conquered Christian populations of the Near East, this essay attempts to examine the evidence of all the significant Greek sources of the seventh and eighth centuries and to coordinate their testimony with several authoritative non-Greek writings.

The Greek sources under examination consist of: first, texts which describe the Arabs and their invasions as well as the impressions they made upon conquered populations; second, treaties which reveal the relations between the victorious Arabs and the occupied states; and third, theological and apologetic writings which review Islam as a religion.

Demetrios Constantelos, "Greek Christian and Other Accounts of the Muslim Conquests of the Near East," in *Christian Hellenism: Essays and Studies in Continuity and Change* (New Rochelle, NY: A. D. Caratzas, 1998), pp. 125–44.

The texts include histories, chronicles, sermons, apocalyptic or eschatological treatises, hagiographical texts, and theological essays written within two centuries after the emergence of Islam. These texts, being limited, sometimes one-sided, and fragmentary, require corroboration by other, non-Greek sources to enable the reader to form an opinion concerning the nature and the impact of the Muslim conquest in the Near East. My task is to let the sources speak for themselves.

The Arab conquests under discussion took place during a period of 118 years, that is, from the year of Mohammed's death in AD 632 under Abu-Bakr, to 750 when Marwan II, the last caliph of the Umayyad Dynasty, died.

Within thirty years after Mohammed's death Islam achieved the most spectacular expansion in its history. During the caliphate of Mohammed's immediate successors from 632 to 661, Islam conquered the whole Arabian peninsula and invaded territories which had been in Greco-Roman hands since the reign of Alexander the Great.

The first phase of Islamic expansion ended with a civil war among the Arabs, at the conclusion of which a new era in Islamic history was inaugurated. The Umayyad Dynasty (661–750) which followed was just as eager for conquest. What the Arabs subjugated, however, was foreign to them both technologically and religiously. The populations of the cities and of the seacoast of Syria, Palestine, Egypt, and Cyrene were predominantly Greek or Hellenized. The Greek domination of those lands for over nine hundred years (since the conquests of Alexander the Great) had affected not only numerous Syrians, Egyptians, and Jews of urban areas, but other indigenous populations of the interior. The Roman conquest did not alter the Greek or Hellenistic character of the Near East, which was at that time under the rule of the Byzantine Empire. Not only Antioch, Gaza, Alexandria, and Ptolemais, but even cities of the interior such as Edessa claimed to be as Greek as Athens itself. Nevertheless, in the seventh and eighth centuries both Hellenism and Christianity were eliminated as major ethnic, religious, and cultural forces in the Near East—save in Asia Minor and Cyprus.

Let us note briefly some of the major Arab conquests. Damascus fell in 635. Jerusalem was captured in 638. In the same year, Antioch fell, and the other great Hellenistic capital, Alexandria, became a permanent Arab possession in 646. Coastal cities in Syria, Palestine, and Egypt, as well as the island of Cyprus were successively occupied by the Arabs in a short period of time.

I

The rapid advance of Islam spread panic and consternation among the Christians in the Greek Near East and became associated with eschatological events, as indicated in the earliest accounts of the Islamic conquest, in which the Arab conquerors are described as "wild and untamed beasts," "blood-thirsty," "beastly and barbarous enemies." Of course, Greek views of the Saracens before the seventh century were not much different.[1] The term "barbarian" was used excessively by Greek authors of the seventh and the eighth centuries to describe their enemies. The word "barbarian" so used was sometimes merely a synonym for "non-Christian," but as a rule the term primarily connoted belligerence, ferocity, brutality and cruelty, that is, warlike habits.

Fifth- and sixth-century texts as well as manuscript miniatures show that Arab raids on Christian communities, monasteries in particular, were both destructive and cruel even before the onset of the Islamic wars. For example, the narrations of St. Nilos[2] and Ammonios,[3] while they have been exploited for propagandistic purposes to depict the Arabs as barbarians, in many ways reflect the nature of Saracen raids and the conditions of the pre-Islamic era.[4] The narrations of St. Nilos are attributed today to an unknown author of later times and may be considered as a genuine reflection of prevailing Byzantine notions concerning the Arabs, who are described as a people caring neither for trade and the crafts nor for agriculture, but only for robbery and warfare, living a nomadic "beastly and blood-thirsty life."[5]

The Greek writers of the period under discussion unanimously condemned the Arabs, who destroyed their freedom, burned down their cities, and enforced a new way of life. The Arabic wars against the Greeks were not only political and economic wars, but holy wars of Islam against Christianity. The Arabs were especially severe toward the churches in communion with Constantinople, such as the Orthodox patriarchates of Antioch, Jerusalem, and Alexandria.

The Arab conquerors regarded the Byzantine Empire as their principal enemy. More than once they attempted to capture Constantinople itself. The relations of the caliphate with Constantinople determined the fate of the Christians under Islam. In times of peace between the Arabs and Greeks, the Christians under Islam enjoyed prosperity and were tolerated, but during the almost constant state of warfare between the two states, persecution of the Christians by Islam was rather common.

The Greek sources indicate that the Arabs enjoyed a very poor reputation among the conquered Christian populations of Syria, Palestine, and Egypt. The first author to write about the advance of Islam and its impact upon the Christians of Palestine was Sophronios of Jerusalem. Some fifty years ago, the Greek historian John Phokylides published an important Christmas sermon delivered by Patriarch Sophronios in 634.

Sophronios described "the sword of the Saracens" as "beastly and barbarous . . . filled with every diabolic savagery." The Arabs had already conquered Bethlehem, the birthplace of Christ, and one of the most important places of pilgrimage in Palestine. The patriarch wished to go there and celebrate the Feast of the Nativity but fear confined him to Jerusalem.[6] The joy of a visit to Bethlehem, Sophronios states, was denied Christians because of their sins. Fear of the Saracens inflicted upon them sorrow and misery.[7] Sophronios likened the state of the Christians to that of Adam expelled from Paradise, and their sorrows paralleled his sorrows. As Adam was expelled from Paradise and could look into it only from a distance, because the flaming sword guarded the holy garden, likewise Sophronios and his flock, though neighbors of the nativity site, could not visit it because of the Saracens' sword there. Sophronios, however, believed that lost territories could be recovered, that repentance and reconciliation with God could dispel the Saracen menace and eventually lead the Christians to Bethlehem.[8] Nothing is more depressing than to have the desirable good nearby and yet be unable to enjoy it.[9] The Arabs are "godless foreigners" who threaten with massacres and destruction; their sword is "bloodthirsty," thus no one dares to approach the birthplace of Jesus.[10]

The Arab conquests between 632 and 637 must have been very violent as well as decisive. Sophronios, in a later sermon which he delivered in the Church of the Theotokos in Jerusalem on Epiphany Day in the year 637, celebrating the baptism of Christ, describes how the advancing troops of the Saracens left behind them a train of destruction and havoc, with bloodshed everywhere and abandoned human bodies devoured by the wild birds of Palestine's deserts. He writes of the "villainous and God-hating Saracens," who run through places and capture cities, who reap or destroy the crops of the fields, who burn down towns and set churches on fire, who attack monasteries and defeat Byzantine armies, winning one victory after another. He claimed that God had allowed so many calamities to befall the Christians because of the moral decline of his flock. As in his sermon of 634, he appealed for repentance and reconciliation with God in order to avert further misfortunes.[11]

Sophronios proved himself both an able theologian and hierarch and a man of wide experience and broad knowledge of political conditions and events. Upon his election to the patriarchal throne of Jerusalem in 634, he anticipated the catastrophe that was coming upon his flock. In a synodal encyclical directed to Patriarch Sergios of Constantinople, Sophronios laments the progress of the Arabs, whose ways were "furious and brutal," "godless and impious," and again attributes the advance of the Arabs to the sins of the Christians.[12] There is a sense of eschatological urgency in Sophronios's sermons.

The second Greek writer of the seventh century is the author of an apocalypse attributed to Methodios, Bishop of Patara. It speaks not only of the Arab victories against the Romans [Byzantines], but also of the Saracens' eventual decline and the coming of the end of the world. It is not because God loves the descendants of Ishmael's seed that the Arabs conquer one Byzantine land after another, but because of the sinfulness of the Christians. Thus Cappadocia, Sicily, Hellas, and all of Asia Minor will suffer from the Saracens' invasions. The islands will not be spared the Arab sword either. Nevertheless, Egypt and Syria will suffer seven times more than the other Byzantine territories because of the heavy taxation imposed upon them. The wisdom and experience of the captive peoples will prove inadequate to avert the wrath of the Arabs, for they have no respect for education or political and civic institutions and pride themselves only on the art of warfare.[13] Of course this is an exaggeration, for we know that the Arabs displayed respect for Greek institutions, which they tried to emulate even at this early date.

The Pseudo-Methodian apocalypse adds:

> The barbarians who conquered and governed tyrannically were not humans but sons of the desert, corrupted, bringing dissolution, personifying hate. They have no respect for old age, orphans, the poor, pregnant women, or priests, whose holy altars they defile.

This too seems to be hyperbole. Other such horrors are described in the apocalypse. But what is the reason, asks the author, for all these rapacious and barbarous acts? Why does God allow such a multitude of calamities to fall upon the Christians? He answers: "not all who call themselves Christians are truly Christians." He implies that, under the circumstances, many will deny "the true faith, the life-giving cross and the holy mysteries and, with no coercion or punishment, will deny Christ and join the apostates."[14] All these are eschatological signs, according to the apocalypse. God allows all these evils to take place in order that true Christians may be separated from nominal believers.[15]

Of lesser significance than Sophronios or Pseudo-Methodios are four other brief references to the Arabic invasions. Antonios Chozebites, in his life of his master, St. George Chozebites (d. ca. 638), speaks first of the Persian penetration into Palestine. He writes in great fear of imminent catastrophes, which he attributes to the existence of superstition and moral laxity, and calls for repentance in order to avert "impending disasters" from the people of Palestine.[16] Antonios writes also of the Saracens, who invaded the area where the Laura of Chozeba lay and put several monks to death. Yet because there is no direct reference to Islam, he might have mistaken the Saracens for the Persians.

Though he, too, omits the name of Islam, St. Maximos the Confessor describes the Arab invaders as a barbarous people, sons of the desert, overrunning civilized lands as if they were their own.[17] They have the form of men but they behave like wild and untamed beasts, he writes. The writings of St. Anastasios Sinaites also make reference to the Arabic capture and burning of Palestinian cities, including Caesarea and Jerusalem, as well as destruction in Egypt and other Mediterranean lands and islands. In a sermon which he delivered some time during the second half of the seventh century, Anastasios attributed the Byzantine defeats at Yarmouk (636) and Dathemon; the fall of Palestine, including Caesarea and Jerusalem; the conquest of Egypt and of other lands and islands, and the capture of Christians in Asia Minor to mistreatment of the Orthodox by Emperor Constans II (641–668), who had favored the Monothelites.[18] Even though Anastasios erroneously attributed the defeat at Yarmouk to Constans, his awareness of the dramatic progress of Islam and his interpretation of the Arabic conquests as a divine punishment provide another example of the usual Byzantine explanation for the advance of Islam.

Anastasios's information is confirmed in the biography of another saint. In 1886 the Russian Byzantinist V. Vasilievskij published a fragment from the Greek text of the life of Theodore of Edessa (ninth century) concerning the conditions of Christians and their shrines in Palestine immediately after its conquest by the Arabs. In this text, the Arab conquests of Phoenicia and Palestine were attributed to the sinfulness and impiety of Emperor Constans, who is presented as having embraced Monothelitism. Constans had committed several other crimes: he had killed his brother Theodosios, had mutilated the great confessor Maximos, and had exiled Martin, the bishop of Rome, to Cherson. Because of this, not only had the Arabs conquered Christian lands, but they had also deified Christian churches and oppressed Christian populations.[19]

A serious attack upon the island of Crete is mentioned briefly in the life of St. Andrew, Archbishop of Gortyn and of all Crete.[20] No date is given, but since Andrew was elected archbishop of Crete soon after 692, the attack could be dated after that year, perhaps between 705 and 715. These years seem probable because the Arabic chronicle of al-Baladhuri records that an attack was made against Crete during the caliphate of Al-Walid (705–715).[21] The life of St. Andrew states that the Arabs made a serious attempt to land on the island but that they were crushed by the Byzantine armies at the fort of Drimeos.[22] After this defeat, the Arabs made no other effort to capture the island until late in the caliphate of Harun al-Rashid,[23] succeeding eventually in gaining control of Crete in 827 or 828.[24]

Theophanes the Confessor has preserved perhaps more valuable information about early Islam than any other Greek writer of the period under discussion. Though he wrote in the first quarter of the ninth century (ca. 813), there is no reason to dismiss his significance. It seems that his views of Islam, which influenced the Byzantines a great deal, were borrowed from previous writings, no longer extant.

After describing the early years of Mohammed, the "pseudo-prophet," Theophanes adds that Mohammed taught his followers that anyone who kills or is killed by an enemy enters paradise. The Muslim paradise is described as a place where the faithful can fulfill every carnal desire: eating, drinking, and sexual indulgence. In paradise flows a river of wine, honey, and milk. There extraordinary women are found in abundance, sexual intercourse is of long duration and hedonistic enjoyment is continuous. Theophanes ridicules Mohammed's teachings about paradise as stupid. He also knows of Mohammed's ethical teachings, which command the faithful to have sympathy for one another and to assist those who suffer from injustices.[25] But he stresses the negative aspects of Islamic religion.

Theophanes reports that when Abu-Bakr succeeded to the caliphate after Mohammed's death, everyone became fearful. An earthquake in Palestine in 635 and the appearance of a comet during Abu-Bakr's short caliphate were interpreted as omens of the approaching occupation of Palestine by the Arabs.[26] The fall of Jerusalem to Omar some time after Christmas in 637 (probably in February 638) was viewed as the fulfillment of Daniel's prophecy: the setting up of "the abomination of desolation" (Dan. 12:11). Patriarch Nikephoros also identified the emergence of the Arabs and their conquests with devastation and total catastrophe.[27]

Theophanes is not always accurate and his chronicle is very general. Nevertheless, it is a valuable account of the Arabic conquest of Syria and Palestine, as well as a reliable record of Greco-Arabic relations. Much of what he has preserved is confirmed by other sources, including some in Arabic.

According to Theophanes, who emphasized the greed, barbarism, and cruelty of the conquerors, after the fall of Damascus, the Arabs moved against Egypt. Patriarch Kyros of Alexandria, knowing of their rapacity, offered the Arabs 120,000 dinars to conclude peace with them. His offer saved Byzantine Egypt for three years, but Kyros was accused of being very extravagant in his truce terms and depleting the imperial treasury. Thus Manuel, the imperial representative, refused to honor the terms of the truce. This resulted in a bitter war between the Arabs and the Byzantines, in which Egypt fell to the Arabs "forever."[28]

The Arabs' behavior in Egypt was not much different from their conduct in Palestine or Syria. Their attitude toward the Orthodox Church was determined by the relations between the caliphate and Constantinople. Their tolerance in peacetime changed during hostilities into violent outbursts which resulted in persecutions, the death of many Christians and the destruction of churches and other ecclesiastical institutions. For example, when the Arabic armies suffered repeated defeats during the reign of Emperor Tiberios II (698–705), Abd-al-Aziz, governor of Egypt and brother of Caliph Abd-al-Malik (685–705), unleashed a persecution against the Orthodox in Alexandria in 704. The mobs attacked the Christians, and Abd-al-Aziz ordered that all crosses be removed from Christian churches and that "Mohammed is the Great Apostle of God" and "God is neither born nor does He give birth" be written on their doors. The persecution was especially severe against monks and lasted for several years. The ecclesiastical administration of the Orthodox (Chalcedonian) patriarchate in Egypt was abolished for ninety-one years. Only two patriarchs (Kyros and Kosmas) governed in the early years of the Arabic occupation.[29] From 651 to 742 there were only a few *locum tenenes* in the Orthodox patriarchate, while vacancies existed for several years even in the Coptic patriarchate.

Philip Hitti's account, on the basis of the Arab chronicler Abd-al-Hakam (d. 871), asserts: "The native Copts of Egypt . . . were instructed from the very beginning by their bishop of Alexandria to offer no resistance to the invaders . . . in view of the religious persecution to which they as Monophysites had been subjected" by the Orthodox Church in Egypt and the imperial government in Constantinople.[30] But this is contradicted by the testimony of John, the Monophysite bishop of Nikiu, who wrote his Chronicle around the year 700, some 150 years earlier than Hitti's source.

John of Nikiu speaks of the early invasions of the Arabs in Egypt as merciless and brutal. Not only did the invaders slay the commander of the Byzantine troops and all his companions when they captured the city of Bahnasa, but "they put to the sword all that surrendered, and they spared none, whether old men, babes, or women."[31] They perpetrated innumerable acts of violence and spread panic everywhere.[32]

In fact, John of Nikiu castigates those "Egyptians who had apostasized from the Christian faith [Monophysites] and embraced the faith of the beast." He adds that many Christian Copts had fled the Arabic invasions.[33] It is true that the Copts of certain cities, such as Antinoe, because of their hostility to the Emperor Herakleios (610–641) and Patriarch Kyros of Alexandria, cooperated with the invaders and submitted to the Muslims, paying them tribute.[34] But the same authority indicates that the fall of Alexandria and of Egypt was mainly due to the impotence of Patriarch Kyros, who served as prefect there, as well as the weak position of the Byzantine government after the death of Herakleios. Many Copts refused to submit, and at times "a panic fell on all the cities of Egypt, and all their inhabitants took flight."[35] Not only the Greeks, but a multitude of Copts were horrified and were ready for battle against the Arabs when they saw them in Alexandria after its surrender.[36] The Copts prayed to God to deliver them from "the enemies of the cross who plundered the country and took captives in abundance." They saw the Islamic conquest as a yoke "heavier than the yoke which had been laid on Israel by Pharaoh"[37] and prayed to the Almighty to do "unto them as He did aforetime unto Pharaoh."[38] It is certain that because of fear or expediency many Christians, Orthodox and Copt, adopted Islam. How many of them abjured or remained crypto-Christians is unknown.

Elsewhere, the Arabs proved extremely vicious toward certain cities and forts which resisted their invasion. For example, when they took the city of Daras (640) by storm, they put many of the inhabitants to the sword.[39] Caesarea in Palestine had a similar fate. After seven years of siege, the Arabs captured the city in 643 and put to death 7,000 Greeks. Cyprus was ravaged when it fell to the Arabs in 650, and the small city of Arados on the island of Arados was totally destroyed by fire in 651 and its walls demolished. Those of the inhabitants who did not meet death were forced to evacuate the island (which lies dose to the shores of Syria) and moved anywhere they could. Other towns and villages were either sacked or depopulated.

Theophanes indicates that the more the Arabs advanced, the more atrocious they became. For example, when they invaded the district of Isauria in 650 they put to death many inhabitants and returned to Damascus with 5,000 captives as slaves.[40]

With some interruptions in the military conflicts, after the year 695 the Arabs became more audacious in their raids. For example, in the year 705, during the caliphate of Abd-al-Malik (685–705), the Arabs penetrated Armenia, where they captured all the magnates and leaders of the people, brought them together, and burned them alive.

Persecutions of the Christian populations were resumed under Caliph al-Walid I (705–715) and especially under his brother, Suleiman (715–717). When the Arabs captured the city of Tyana in 708, they put many to the sword, while numerous Christians were converted to Islam.[41] Suleiman's tax collector, Usamah b. Zayd, used particularly barbarous means to extract money from the Christians. With hot iron bars he impressed a symbol on the body of each taxpayer. If a monk or a Christian layman was discovered without the sign, Usama first amputated the victim's arms and then beheaded him. Many Christians converted to Islam in order to avoid punishment as well as to be freed of tribute. Islamic scholars agree that there were strong economic motives for conversion.[42]

Even though savage practices were discontinued under Omar II (717–720), persecutions of the Christians became more frequent from then on.[43] For example, in the year 718 Caliph Omar II inaugurated a systematic policy to convert the Christians of Syria to Islam. Those who refused were put to death. Christians were forbidden to stand as witnesses against Muslims. Theophanes, the source of this information, adds that as a result of Omar's coercion many became martyrs[44] and many more, we assume, were converted to Islam.

Theophanes' account of Omar's coercion of his Christian subjects is supported by two non-Greek sources. Michael Syrus confirms that Omar used all possible means to convert Christians to Islam. His legislation was intended to ease the position of those who were willing to embrace Islam as well as to increase the disabilities of those reluctant to deny their Christian faith. Bar Hebraeus, another non-Greek source, bears witness to this also.[45] Omar's measures, as well as his correspondence with several foreign rulers, inviting them to embrace Islam, indicate that the caliph was very zealous in his faith. He was even more interested in the propagation of Islam than in the welfare of his treasury. Among other measures, he instructed the governors in Khurasan to relieve the condition of the captive people there in order to attract them to Islam. To those Arabs who objected to his measures, Omar replied that "Allah had sent His Prophet as a Missionary, not as a tax-collector."[46] It was the duty of the caliph to pursue the Holy War, as Omar II had done, in order to prove that he was a faithful successor to the prophet. Apparently, many Christians who refused to be converted were executed.

During the first quarter of the eighth century, a group of seventy young Christians from Iconium, all wealthy and socially prominent, decided to make a pilgrimage to Jerusalem and other religious sites in Palestine. For several years their desire could not be fulfilled because of the iconoclastic policy of Emperor Leo III, who presumably discouraged pilgrimages and attacked traditional religious practices. But the opportunity was eventually given during Leo's reign, and the seventy found themselves in the Holy Land.

While in Jerusalem, the pilgrims were captured by the Arabs, "the untamed and beastly, illogical in mind and maniacs in their desires." They were taken to the Muslim governor in Caesarea, where they were accused of being spies. Despite their protests and denials of the accusations, they were given the option of becoming Muslims or they were to be condemned to death. Seven of them yielded to the coercion and tortures and adopted Islam. The other sixty-three died as Christian martyrs.[47]

Under the caliphate of Yazid II in 723, sixty visitors from Amorion who made a pilgrimage to the Holy City were put to death. They were confined in a prison in Caesarea, where they were ordered to deny Christianity and adopt Islam. When they refused, they were condemned to be crucified, which was done in Jerusalem.[48] This account was written in the eighth century in Syriac and was translated later into Greek. Both the Syriac and the Greek sources refer to the same event, even though they do not agree on place of origin and the number of martyrs.

The systematic persecutions of the first quarter of the eighth century can be understood in the light of the belligerent relations between the Byzantine Empire and the caliphate. Many Christians of Palestine, Syria, and other provinces were converted to Islam either voluntarily or by coercion when the Arabs were engaged in warfare with Constantinople.[49] For example, during the caliphate of Hisham (724–743), Christian populations or prisoners of war in the frontier regions were forced to deny Christianity. Among many who became martyrs to their Christian faith in the year 740 was Eustathios, the son of a prominent patrician named Marianos. He became a martyr in the city of Harran in Mesopotamia, or northern Syria, not far from Edessa and Samosata.[50]

While the Arabs exerted every effort to convert Christians to Islam either willingly or unwillingly, Theophanes reports that there were indeed clergymen who not only defended their faith but also tried to refute Islamic theology. But those who made attempts to convert Arabs to Christianity were put to death, for Islamic law severely condemned Christians who converted Arabs. When Metropolitan Peter of Damascus challenged the validity of Islamic religion during the caliphate of Walid II (743–744), the caliph ordered that his tongue be cut out and that he be exiled to South Arabia, where he was eventually put to death.

Another Peter, the bishop of Maiuma, invited many prominent Arabs to denounce the "pseudo-prophet" Mohammed, the forerunner of the anti-Christ, and to believe in the Holy Trinity. Peter was beheaded for his blasphemy. St. John of Damascus wrote an encomium of the bishop of Maiuma, and he dedicated his Libellus de recta sententia to the memory of Petros of Damascus.[51]

The lot of Christians in Syria, on the other hand, improved under the caliphate of Marwan ibn-Muhammad, or Marwan II (744–750). When the

Orthodox patriarch Stephen died, Marwan allowed a prompt election of his successor, and the caliph courteously issued a decree commanding all Arabs to honor the new patriarch Theophylaktos. Theophanes adds that Marwan put to death a Saracen chieftain named Abbas, who had exterminated or imprisoned many Christians.[52] Marwan's example reveals that there were caliphs capable of tolerance and clemency.

Greek sources of the eighth century speak also of the savagery of Saracen robbers who raided various monasteries, killing and plundering. For example, during the caliphate of Harun al-Rashid (786–809), the monasteries of Palestine suffered from numerous raids. Many monks were put to death. The monastery of St. Sabbas was invaded in 786 and several monks were slaughtered.[53]

Raids upon Christian communities and monasteries were not uncommon when there were disturbances such as civil wars in the caliphate. During the early years of Harun al-Rashid, civil wars were common among Saracen tribes in Palestine and Syria.[54] Several Christian communities were persecuted by the warring factions. An eyewitness writes that in the year 788 the Arabs in Palestine were engaged in ferocious factional wars. In addition to the tribal divisions, there were robber groups which mercilessly attacked the country people and monastic communities. It seems that from 786 to 796, when the armies of Harun could not suppress the Bedouin robbers, the Christians of Palestine and Syria suffered brutal persecutions.

During those years of domestic strife, there was much blood shed and several towns and villages were devastated, including Ascalon, Gaza, and Sariphaia.[55] The city of Eleutheropolis, which lay some 25 miles from Jerusalem on the road to Gaza, was totally destroyed and left uninhabited. This destruction occurred during the regime of the Orthodox patriarch Elias (787–797),[56] a date which coincides with the views of modern archaeology.[57]

While the cities were destroyed by warring tribes, Saracen robbers and Bedouin raiders plundered the monasteries. Documents indicate that the Laura of Chariton and the Great Laura of Sabbas suffered more than others.[58] The Arabs not only laid waste to the countryside and brought destruction upon monasteries and their institutions, but put many Christians, including monks, to death. The description by an eyewitness is so vivid and concrete—the author gives names, dates, and places—that it leaves little room for doubt. Several Christians became martyrs during those years, such as St. Christopher, St. John the Palaiolaurites, and St. Elias the Younger, who was tortured and eventually crucified.[59]

During the same period, Harun al-Rashid issued a decree (797) ordering the destruction of Christian churches; he also imprisoned several bishops. Harun was not an exception; several caliphs were especially intolerant toward churches and monasteries. When Marwan II fled before the Abbasid troops, he plundered and destroyed many churches and monasteries in Egypt. A Muslim historian reports that over 30,000 churches "which had been built by the Greeks" were destroyed in Egypt, Syria, and elsewhere. Bar Hebraeus is less specific on this but he, too, writes that the Arabs destroyed thousands of churches. When Christians were suspected of helping the Greeks, they suffered persecution, death and destruction of their churches by the Muslims. For example, Harun al-Rashid ordered the destruction of several churches in the frontier province of al-Awasim because he suspected the local Christians of collaboration with the Greeks.[60]

Thus, according to the Greek sources as well as other accounts, the conquests of the Arabs resulted not only from political and economic factors and Byzantine exhaustion from conflicts with the Persians. The desire of many caliphs to convert the Christians was a decisive factor in the victories of the Arabs. On the other hand, the ease with which Christians were converted to Islam and the moral laxity of the Christian populations in the Near East, of which Sophronios, Pseudo-Methodios, Antonios Chozebites, and others speak, indicate that the influence of Christianity upon the Christian populations there may have been weak. It seems that the average Christian was more concerned with his physical survival and material well-being than with the defense and preservation of his religion. The martyrs referred to earlier were the exception to the rule.

II

The second type of source materials, those which deal with the relations between the conqueror and the conquered, indicate that it was not uncommon for the Arabs to interfere in the internal affairs of Christian churches. The ecclesiastical sees of Antioch, Jerusalem, and Alexandria, as well as of other cities, remained vacant because the Arabs prevented the election of patriarchs. The Orthodox see of Antioch was vacant for forty years, until Stephanos was elected in 742.[61] During years of war between the Byzantine Empire and the Arabs, the latter exerted every effort to weaken the subject Orthodox churches, while their treatment of the adherents of the Jacobite Church was at times more tolerant.

The caliphs also interfered in the administration and affairs of lesser churches. Bar Hebraeus relates that the Nestorian Patriarch George (660–680) was imprisoned by an Arab governor in order to extort money,[62] while Abd-al-Malik imprisoned the Nestorian Patriarch Khnanishu (685–699) in order to elevate a rival named John, who was himself later imprisoned by the same caliph.[63]

Orthodox Chalcedonian patriarchs were treated severely: patriarchs of Antioch such as Alexander II (695–702) and Christopher (960–966) were executed by the caliphs. The Greek sources' claim that the patriarchate of Antioch was vacant for forty years is confirmed by Bar Hebraeus, who writes that after the death of George III no one occupied the patriarchal throne on account of the caliphate's opposition.[64]

Other writers indicate that the Orthodox patriarchs of Jerusalem did not receive better treatment than those of Antioch and Alexandria. The religious life of Jerusalem's Orthodox patriarchate was disrupted and its throne remained vacant for sixty-seven years (638–705) after the death of Sophronios because of Arab hostility there. Caliphs persecuted patriarchs even after the critical years of conquest. An example is Patriarch Elias II (787–797), who was accused unjustly, exiled and suffered merciless treatment for several years. The monk Stephanos (d. 794) and Abbot Christopher of the St. Sabbas monastery discussed the possibility of trying to obtain the patriarch's release, but two monks reached the conclusion that such attempts would be futile because the Arabs "were insulting and impious tyrants."[65] When al-Mansur (754–775) imprisoned three patriarchs,[66] many Christians embraced Islam out of fear.[67]

Bar Hebraeus relates that Caliph al-Mahdi (775–785) forcefully converted 5,000 Christians of Aleppo.[68] It was not only the caliphs, however, who often resorted to violent means against the hierarchs of the churches. Bar Hebraeus reports that mobs often assailed the Christians whenever the government was weak or reluctant to punish the Christians. A certain Christian was caught in adultery with an Arab woman; he was tortured by the mob, all his goods were confiscated and a church he had built was converted into a mosque. When a monk apostatized to Islam, then later repented and fled to Jerusalem, the Christians of Mardin, and especially the monk's brothers, suffered severe exactions.[69] Mob action became very frequent in the eighth century.

The sources cited above are primarily Greek, with a few references to the Jacobite Syrian bishop and philosopher Bar Hebraeus (1226–1286). How reliable are these Greek sources? Are there any major contradictions in Arabic or other sources? It is not possible to examine here every non-Greek text of the East and compare it with the Greek sources, but it is a fact that what the Greek chroniclers stress is confirmed by non-Greek authors, including the Armenian historian Sebeos (late seventh century) and the Arab historian al-Baladhuri (ninth century).

Sebeos tells of the "horror of the invasion of the Ishmaelites [Arabs] who conquered land and sea."[70] He too saw in the Arab conquests the fulfillment of Daniel's prophecy.

Al-Baladhuri is much more detailed. But as the Greek sources may be considered biased on the Byzantine side, so the Arab historians may be considered favorable to the Arabic cause. It is true that al-Baladhuri, in his description of the fall of Damascus in September of 635, depicts the Arab conquerors as compassionate and merciful. He reports that during the seige of Damascus the Arab leader Khalid ibn-al-Walid ("the sword of Allah") promised to give the captives "security for their lives, property, and churches." Furthermore, he pledged that

> their city wall shall not be demolished, neither shall any Moslem be quartered in their houses. Thereunto we give to them the pact of Allah and the protection of His Prophet, the Caliphs and the believers. So long as they pay the poll tax, nothing but good shall befall them.[71]

Those who see religious freedom and toleration in this or other Arabic sources should remember that these principles were guaranteed only in theory; in practice both virtues often proved illusory. Persecution of Christians in the early period under discussion was common and has been recorded even by Arabic sources. Despite the "tolerant" nature of the treaty between Omar (634–644) and Patriarch Sophronios, the caliph forbade the employment of Christians in public offices, his soldiers were allowed to break crosses on the heads of Christians during processions and religious litanies, and were permitted, if not encouraged, to tear down newly erected churches and to punish Christians for insignificant reasons.[72]

The theory of early Islamic toleration cannot be sustained even by relying on the constitution or ordinance of Omar I, because this measure forced the Christians to fulfill several self-destructive obligations, such as not to erect any new churches, monasteries, or hermitages, not to repair any ecclesiastical institutions that fell into ruin, nor to rebuild those that were situated in the Muslim quarters of a town. Not only did Omar impose limitations upon the Christians aimed at their ultimate destruction by attrition, but he apparently introduced fanatical elements into Islamic culture which became characteristic of other caliphates after his.[73] The Arab historian al-Baladhuri indicates that Omar deported Christians who refused to apostatize and embrace Islam, and that he obeyed the order of the prophet who advised: "there shall not remain two religions in the land of Arabia."[74]

During the caliphate of Omar neither cities nor monasteries were spared if they resisted Arabic goals. For example, when the Greek garrison of Gaza refused to submit and convert to Islam, all were put to death. In the year 640, sixty Greek soldiers who refused to apostatize became martyrs,[75] while in the same year that Caesarea, Tripolis, and Tyre fell to the Arabs hundreds of thousands of Christians converted to Islam, many, if not most, out of fear.[76] Of course, the early intolerance of the Arabs is understandable in the light of their values as a people who considered the pursuit of knowledge and other refinements of life contemptible, placing above all other values of civilization the art of war. This is confirmed by the writings of Arab historians, who concerned themselves primarily with political and military history, displaying utter disregard for social or other aspects of life.[77]

III

Theological and apologetic sources indicate that the Byzantines did not know much about Islam.[78] In fact, the Greeks were just as arrogant theologically as the Arabs were intolerant and determined in their militancy.[79] The Greek sources degrade Islam as a religion, claiming that Islam presented no theological presuppositions, no prophets, no miracles, no martyrs, no witnesses, and no sacraments, and advocated immorality, a warlike attitude, hatred, and cruelty.[80]

Moreover, the Byzantines may not have sufficiently understood the impact of the new religion upon the conquered lands. The Byzantine emperor Leo III, in his letter to Omar II, wrote that he knew of the essentials of Islam from the writings of Byzantine theologians, writings apparently in circulation in the first quarter of the eighth century.

> We are now for the first time learning about the substance of your [Omar's] beliefs, for we have been commanded by God to examine all and hold fast to that which is good. [Leo apparently refers to I Thess. 5:21]. So we possess historical documents composed by our blessed prelates who were living at the same epoch as your legislator Muhammad, and these writings make it unnecessary for us to importune you on the subject of your religion.[81]

It is not known what these writings were. A monk named Abraham, of the monastery of Beth Khale, wrote a polemical treatise against Islam not later than the year 670, but nothing else about him or his writings is known.[82]

The Doctrina Jacobi *nuper baptizati*,[83] a dialogue between a convert to Christianity and several Jews, which was held on July 13, 634, is perhaps the first extant literary text that mentions Islam's prophet. It refers to Islam's founding "prophet" without mentioning his name, adding that the "prophet's" name is associated with "human bloodshed."[84] But this source is more important as a reflection upon the moral conditions in the Byzantine Empire than for factual information concerning Islam.

Among the eighth-century Byzantine theologians who dealt, however briefly, with Islam as a religion was Patriarch Germanos (d. 733) of Constantinople. In a letter to Bishop Thomas of Klaudioupolis, the patriarch ridiculed the "Saracens," for directing their prayers to the shrine of Kaaba wherever they happened to find themselves. This ritual was known to the Byzantines as Habar, or Hober, derived from the Arabic *gabr*.[85]

More important than Patriarch Germanos were St. John of Damascus and Bishop Theodore Abuquarra, both significant theologians and critics of Islam in the period under discussion, but the Byzantines were slow in grasping the religious nature of Islam and its theology, as is evident even in the writings of these two serious theologians. A treatise attributed to St. John of Damascus [86] describes Islam as a mixture of the teachings of Christian scripture and Arianism. "After having read the Old and the New Testament and having talked with an Arian monk [Mohammed] instituted his own heresy."[87] Henri Gregoire maintained that it was not so much Arianism as Monophysitism that contributed to the formulation of the new monotheistic religion.[88] But whether Arianism or Monophysitism, John of Damascus considered Islam a Christian heresy and Mohammed a "pseudo-prophet."[89]

Bishop Theodore Abuquarra's information about Islamic religion is similar to that attributed to John of Damascus. Mohammed is an Arianizing pseudo-prophet and Islam a Christian, non-Trinitarian heresy.[90] But Abuquarra is less polemical against Islam than his mentor John of Damascus. Through his theological efforts, Orthodox Christian theology of the Byzantine era probably exerted an influence upon Muslim theology (Kalam).[91]

One of the early attackers of Islam is the Byzantine emperor Leo III. The eighth-century Armenian writer Ghevond (Leontios) has preserved Leo's reply to a letter from Caliph Omar II, inviting the Christian emperor to denounce Christianity and embrace Islam. Leo's reply is an extensive and well-written defense of the major tenets of the Christian religion. In it the Byzantine emperor, who was as zealous in his Christian faith as Omar was in his, refuted Islam on the basis of the Christian Gospel as well as on the basis of the Koran.[92]

Ghevond's account has been preserved by other Oriental sources. The Syrian bishop Mahbub (Agapios) relates in his Arabic World History (*Kitab al-Unwan*) that Omar II invited Leo to become a Muslim but that the Byzantine emperor refuted the caliph's arguments, using reason, the Bible and Islam's Holy Book.[93] Similar information has been recorded by other Armenian writers. Thoma Ardzruni (ca. 936) and Kirakos of Gandzac (d. 1272), referring to the correspondence between the Byzantine emperor and the Arab caliph, emphasized that Leo influenced Omar to the extent that the latter adopted a more benevolent policy toward his Christian subjects.[94]

Of course, weaknesses in the Greek administration in Egypt, Palestine, and Syria contributed to the ease with which those provinces fell to the Arabs, as did the partial dissatisfaction of some of their population with Constantinople.[95] The Arabs were invariably victorious because they were unified and bent on conquest, whereas their enemies were internally divided and exhausted from some twenty-five years of wars with the Persians.[96] The Byzantine defeat of the Persians was only a Pyrrhic victory, because an atmosphere of atony and pessimism fell upon the Byzantines—on the army as well as on the populace—paralyzing their morale and rendering them incompetent to deal with an organized, vigorous enemy.[97] With the collapse of Persia, the Byzantines remained the Arabs' enemy *par excellence.* After the emergence of Islam, "the Greeks, the Rum, are simply the enemy." H. A. R. Gibb has indicated that on the cultural level the situation altered subtly during the Umayyad Dynasty. Nevertheless,

> the Greeks are still the enemy, and Arab armies and fleets push their way through to the gates of Constantinople. . . . All this is the formal and indispensable public duty of the Caliphs, the Commanders of the Faithful, who are bound by the conditions of their office to pursue the Holy War against the Unbelievers and who must justify their claim to be the successors of the Prophet in the eyes of their Muslim subjects by visibly striving for the extension of Islam.[98]

The idea of the holy war (jihad) and indeed Islam's early intolerance derived from Mohammed's own aggressive precepts. To fight for Allah and to exterminate or humiliate the infidels was a sacred duty.

> When ye encounter the unbelievers, strike off their heads, until ye have made a great slaughter among them; and bind them in bonds . . . he [Allah] commandeth you to fight his battles that he may prove the one of you by the other. And as to those who fight (or those who are slain) in defense of God's true religion [Islam], God will not suffer their works to perish—he will lead them into paradise, of which he hath told then, O true believers, if ye assist God by fighting for his religion, he will assist you against your enemies . . . as for infidels, let them perish—catastrophe awaiteth the unbelievers.

These and similar admonitions occur repeatedly in the Koran.[99] The Arabs, and later the Turks, were led to believe that to combat the enemies of Islam, to engage in warfare and win victories over the infidel, was proof of Islam's superiority and truth.

After the middle of the ninth century, a balance in power, diplomatic activity, and cultural interaction [100] greatly improved the relations between the two major adversaries in the eastern Mediterranean. Peace between the two worlds contributed to a symbiosis between Muslims and Christians in the Islamic world, at least during the reign of the Macedonian dynasty, but the crusading spirit of the holy war became intense once again after the eleventh century.

NOTES

For clarification of any references, the reader is referred to the original, Demetrios Constantelos, "Greek Christian and Other Accounts of the Muslim Conquests of the Near East," in *Christian Hellenism: Essays and Studies in Continuity and Change* (New Rochelle, NY: A. D. Caratzas, 1998), pp. 125–44.

　　1. V. Christides, "Arabs as 'Barbaroi' before the Rise of Islam," *Balk. St.* 10 (1969): 324. Cf. W. R. Jones, "The Image of the Barbarian in Medieval Europe," *Comparative Studies in Society and History* 13 (1971): 392–94.

　　2. Nilos Eremites, *Narrationes 2, PG,* 79 589 ff.

　　3. F. Combefis, *Illustrium Christi martyrum lecti triumphi* (Paris, 1660).

　　4. V. Christides, "Pre-Islamic Arabs in Byzantine Illuminations," *Le Museon* 83 (1970): 173.

　　5. S. Nilos, *Narrationes* 3.

　　6. H. Usener, ed., "Weihnachtspredigt des Sophronios," *RhM* 4 (1886): 500–16.

　　7. Ioannes Phokylides, *EkklPhar* 17 (1918): 369–84. The same sermon in Latin PG 87, 3201–11; cf. Kallistos Meliaras, *Hoi Hagion Topoi en Palestine* (Jerusalem, 1928), 1: 182–83; W. E. Kaegi Jr., "Initial Byzantine Reactions to the Arab Conquests," *ChHist* 38 (1969): 139–49.

　　8. Usener, "Weihnachtspredigt des Sophronios," pp. 508–509.

9. Ibid., p. 513.

10. Ibid., pp. 514–15.

11. Sophronios, "Logos eis to hagion Baptisms," in *Analekta Ierosolymitikes Stachyologias*, ed. A. Papadopoulos-Kerameus (St. Petersburg, 1888; repr., Brussels, 1963), vol. 5, pp. 166–67; Chr Papadopoulos, *Historia tes Ekklesias Hierosolymon* (Jerusalem and Alexandria, 1910), p. 248.

12. Sophronios, *PG*, 87.3, 3197D.

13. B. M. Istin, ed., "Otkrovenie Mefodiia Patarskago i Apokrificheskiia Videnia Daniela v Vizantiiski i Slaviano-Russkoi Literaturakh," *Chteniia v Imperatorskom Obschchestvie Istorii i Drevnostei Rossiskikh pri Moskovskom Universitetie*, 193 (Moscow, 1897), pp. 27–31.

14. Ibid., pp. 33–34.

15. Ibid., p. 36.

16. "Vita S. Georgii Chozebitae," 18, 31, AB 7 (1888): 117–18, 129–30; Koikylides, *Ta kata ten Lauran kai ton Cheimaron tou Houzinba* (Jerusalem, 1901), unavailable to me, but cf. *Peri ton en Palaistine Archaion kai Neoteron Hellenikon Monasterion* (Jerusalem, 1906), pp. 26–27.

17. Maximos the Confessor, *Ep. XIV ad Petrum Illustrem, PG* 91, 540A.

18. Anastasios Sinaites, "Sermon no. 3," *PG* 89, 1156C.

19. B. G. Vasilievskij, *PPSb.* (1886): 264–65; I. Pomjalovskij, *Zitie ize vo sv. otca nasege Theodora akrchiep. edeskago* (St. Petersburg, 1892), pp. 15–17.

20. Papadopoulos-Kerameus, *Analekta Ierosolymitikes Stachyologias*, vol. 5, p. 177. Cf. G. K. Spyridakes, "To Thema tes Kretes pro tes katakteseos tes nesou Wct ton Arabon," *EBBS* 21 (1951): 67–68.

21. Al-Baladhuri, *The Origins of the Islamic State*, trans. Philip K. Hitti (Beirut, 1966), p. 376.

22. Papadopoulos-Kerameus, *Analekta Ierosolymitikes Stachyologias*, vol. 5, p. 177.

23. Al-Baladhuri, *Origins of the Islamic State*, p. 376.

24. N. M. Panagiotakes, "Zetemata tes katakteseos tes Kretes hypo ton Arabon," *KretChron* 15–16 (1961–62): 74–83; N. Tomadakes, "Problemata tes en Krete Arabokratias (826–961)," *EEBS* 30 (1960): 1–38; G. C. Miles, "Byzantium and the Arabs: Relations in Crete and the Aegean Area," *DOP* 18 (1964): 10.

25. Theophanes, *Chronographia*, ed. K. de Boor (Leipzig, 1883–85), vol. 1, p. 334.

26. Ibid., vol. 1, pp. 333–36.

27. Ibid., vol. 1, p. 339. Nikephoros, *Chronographikon Syntomon*, in *Nicephori Archiepiscopi Constantinopolitani Opuscula Historica*, ed. K. de Boor (Leipzig, 1880), p. 99.

28. Theophanes, *Chronographia*, vol. 1, p. 338. Cf. Nikephoros, *Chronographikon Syntomon*, pp. 24–25.

29. Eutychios of Alexandria, *Annales, PG* 3, 1123A; Al-Makine, *Chronikon*, in *Palestine from the Arabic Conquest to the Crusades According to the Arabic Sources* (in Russian), ed. N. A. Miednikow, vol. 2, p. 550, as cited by Chr. Papadopoulos, *Historia tes Ekkksias Alexandreias* (Alexandria, 1935), pp. 505–506. V. Grumel, *La chronologie* (Paris, 1958), pp. 443.

30. P. K. Hitti, *History of the Arabs* (London, 1960), p. 165. Against this see A. H. M. Jones, "Were Ancient Heresies National or Social Movements in Disguise?" *JThST* 10 (1959): 288–89.

31. John of Nikiu, *The Chronicle*, 111.540, trans. R. H. Charles from *Zotenberg's Ethiopic Text* (Oxford, 1916), p. 179.

32. Ibid., 113.4–6, trans. p. 182.

33. Ibid., 114.1, trans. p. 182.

34. Ibid., 115.9, trans. p. 184.

35. Ibid., 113.6, 115.6, trans. pp. 182–84.

36. Ibid., 110.24, trans. p. 194.

37. Ibid., 120.32, trans. p. 195.

38. Ibid., 120.33, trans. p. 195.

39. Theophanes, *Chronographia*, vol . 1, pp. 341–44; cf. Constantine Porphyrogennitos, *De Administrando Imperio* 20, ed. and trans. G. Moravcsik and R. J. H. Jenkins (Washington, DC, 1967), p. 84.

40. Theophanes, *Chronographia*, vol. 1, p. 344.

41. Ibid., vol. 1, p. 372: "He gathered all the leading people of the Armenians and burned them alive." Nikephoros, *Chronographikon Syntomon*, pp. 43–44; cf. p. 48.

42. John Monachos, *Narratio* PG 109, col. 517.2. Cf. D. C. Dennett, *Conversion and the Poll Tax in Early Islam* (Cambridge, MA, 1950), pp. 3–5; J. Wellhausen, *The Arab Kingdom and Its Fall*, trans. M. G. Weir (Calcutta, 1927), pp. 28–29, 87.

43. Miednikow, *Palestine from the Arabic Conquest to the Crusades according to the Arabic Sources*, vols. 1, p. 156; 2.1, p. 317; 2.2, pp. 1317, 1319, 1327, as cited by Chr. Papadopoulos, *Historia tes Ekkksias Alexandreias*, pp. 176–78.

44. Theophanes, *Chronographia*, vol. 1, p. 399.

45. M. Syros 11.19, in *Chronique de Michelle Syrien*, ed. and trans. J. B. Chabot (Brussels 1963), vol. 2, pp. 488–89; Bar Hebraeus, *The Chronography*, trans. E. A. Wallis Budge (London, 1932), vol. 1, p. 108–109; A. Jeffery, "Ghevond's Text of the Correspondence between Omar II and Leon III," *HThR* 37 (1944): 269 and n. 3.

46. Tabari, *Annales*, vol. 2, 1354; Ibn-al-Athir Kamil, ed. Tornberg, V, 37, cited by A. Jeffery, "Ghevond's Text of the Correspondence between Omar II and Leon III," p. 271.

47. A. Papadopoulos-Karameus, ed., "Martyrion ton hagion endoxon Martyron tou Christou exekonta kai trion," *PPSb* 19 (1907): 151–69. It was not uncommon that pilgrims were accused as spies. For example the English pilgrim to the Holy Land, Willibald, and several fellow countrymen were imprisoned there as spies around the year 754 CE. The British pilgrims found themselves "in the midst of spears and instruments of war, among barbarians and warriors, in prisons and bands of rebels." See Canon Brownlow, trans., *The Hodoeporicon of Saint Willibald* (London, 1895), p. 13; cf. p. 42.

48. *AASS*, October VIII, p. 360; A. Papadopoulos-Karameus, "Martyrion ton hagion exekonta neon Martyron," *PPSb* 12 (1892): 4–7.

49. Miednikow, *Palestine from the Arabic Conquest to the Crusades according to the Arabic Sources*, vol. 1, pp. 68, 705–19, cited by Chr. Papadopoulos, *Historia tes Ekklesias Antiocheias* (Alexandria, 1951), pp. 754, 757.

50. Theophanes, *Chronographia*, vol. 1, p. 414.

51. Ibid., p. 416: Papadopoulos, *Hstoria Ekklesias Antiochias*, p. 758; John of Damascus, PG 94, 1421–32.

52. Theophanes, *Chronographia*, vol. 1, p. 421.

53. *AASS* March, vol. 3, pp. 2–12.

54. Cf. C. Brockelmann, *History of the Islamic Peoples*, trans. J. Carmichael and M. Perlmann (New York, 1960), pp. 115–16.

55. A. Papadopoulos-Kerameus, "Exegesis etoi Martyrion ton hagion Pateron ton Anairethenton hypo . . . Sarakenon," *PPSb* 19 (1907): 3.

56. Ibid., p. 3; cf. V. Grumel, *La chronologie* (Paris, 1958), p. 452.

57. R. A. S. MacAlister, who conducted excavations in Palestine, placed the destruction of Eleutheropolis in 796. See his article in *Encyclopaedia Britannica*, 11th ed. (Cambridge, UK: Encyclopaedia Britannica, 1910), vol. 9, p. 263.

58. Papadopoulos-Kerameus, "Exegesis," pp. 2–13.

59. A. Papadopoulos-Kerameus, ed., "Hypomnema kath' historian tes athleseos tou hagiou . . . Ella tou Neou," *PPSb* 19 (1907): 42–59; for Elias's crucifixion, see p. 55.

60. Theophanes, *Chronographia*, vol. 1, p. 313; *AASS* March III, 160; July VII; 378. The Arabic accounts of persecutions and the destructions of churches have been summarized by A. S. Tritton in *The Caliphs and Their Non-Muslim Subjects* (London, 1930), pp. 54–55. For Harun's persecution of Christians in the frontier, Tritton cites Tabari and Michael Syros, p. 49.

61. Theophanes, *Chronographia*, vol. 1, p. 416; Papadopoulos, *Historia tes Ekklesias Antiocheias*, p. 773. For Arabic accounts of the Caliphs' interference in the affairs of the churches, see Tritton, *The Caliphs and Their Non-Muslim Subjects*, pp. 78–88.

62. Bar Hebraeus, *Chronicon Ecclesiasticum*, ed. J. B. Abbeloos and Thomas J. Lamy (Paris and Rome, 1877), sec. 2.17, vol. 3, pp. 130–32.

63. William A. Shedd, *Islam and the Oriental Churches* (Philadelphia, 1904), p. 241.

64. Bar Hebraeus, *Chronicon Ecclesiasticum*, vol. 1, sect. 1.57, p. 304; Shedd, *Islam and the Oriental Churches*, p. 243.

65. *Vita S. Stephani Sabaitae, AASS*, July III, (Paris and Rome, 1867), p. 511DF. Cf. pp. 522c, 524b.

66. Shedd, *Islam and the Oriental Churches*, p. 152.

67. Josepho Aloysio Assemani, *De Catholicis seu patriarehis Chaldaeorum et Nestorianorum Commentarius bistoricocbronologicus* (Rome, 1775), pp. 67–69.

68. Bar Hebraeus, *Chronography*, p. 117.

69. Bar Hebraeus, *Chronicon Ecclesiasticum*, vol. 1, sect. 1.90, pp. 562–64. For other cruel means of punishment by the Arabs, see Nikephoros, *Chronographikon Syntomon*, p. 23.

70. Sebeos, *Histoire d'Heraclius*, trans. F. Mader (Paris, 1904), p. 104.

71. Al-Baladhuri, *Origins of the Islamic State*, p. 187.

72. Miednikow, *Palestine from the Arabic Conquest to the Crusades according to the Arabic Sources*, vol. 2, pp. 1, 395, 396, 400, 401; vol. 2, pp. 1348, 1350, 1377, cited by Papadopoulos, *Historia tes Ekklesias Hierosolymon*, 264; Bar Hebraeus, *Chronography*, pp. 94–96.

73. Cf. A. von Kremer, *Gescbicbte des herrschenden Ideem des Islams* (Leipzig, 1868), pp. 333; Tritton, *Caliphs and Their Non-Muslim Subjects*, pp. 5–17.

74. Al-Baladhuri, *Origins of the Islamic State*, p. 103.

75. H. Deleyaye, "Passio sanctorum sexaginta martyrum," *AB* 23 (1904): 289–307.

76. C. Paparrigopoulos, *Historia tou Hellenikou Ethnous* (Athens, 1925), vol. 3, pp. 217–19.

77. P. K. Hitti, *Origins of the Islamic State* (Beirut, 1966), p. 2.

78. Cf. Al-Baladhuri, *Origins of the Islamic State*, pp. 63–64, 168–71, 174–77; Wellhausen, *Arab Kingdom and Its Fall*, p. 29.

79. Al-Baladhuri, *Origins of the Islamic State*, pp. 58, 171.

80. See A. T. Khoury, *Der theologische Streit der Byzantiner mit dem Islam* (Paderborn, 1959); W. Eichner, "Die Nachrichten fiber den Islam bei den Byzantinern," *Der Islam* 23 (1936): 133–62, 197–44.

81. Jeffery, "Ghevond's Text of the Correspondence between Omar II and Leon III," p. 282.

82. F. Nau, "Abraham de Beit-Hale," *DHGE* 1 (Paris, 1912), col. 165, no. 20.

83. N. Bonwetsch, ed. "Doctrina Jacobi nuper baptizati," *Abhandlungen der Koniglicben Gesellschaft der Wusenscbaften zu Gottingen*, Philologisch-historiche Klasse, 12.3 (1910): 86–87; cf. K. Dyobouniotes "Iakobos o Neobaptistos," *Hieros Syndermos* 7.183 (Athens, 1911), pp. 5–6; Papadopoulos, *Historia tes Ekklesias Antiocbeias*, p. 732.

84. Bonwetsch, "Doctrina Jacobi nupper baptist," pp. 86–87; Kaegi, "Initial Byzantine Reactions to the Arab Conquests," p. 142.

85. Germanos, *PG* 98, 168c.

86. A. Abel, "Le Chapitre CI du Livre des Heresies de Jean Damascene: Son inauthenticite," *Stadia Islamica* 19 (1963): 5–25.

87. John of Damascus, *De Haeresibus, PG* 94, 765A; J. Meyendorff, "Byzantine Views of Islam" *DOP* 18 (1964): 115–32.

88. Cf. H. Gregoire, "Mahomet et le Monophysisme," *Melanges Diehl* 1 (1930): 107.

89. John of Damascus, *De Haeresibus, PG* 94, 764B.

90. Theodore Abuquarca, *PG* 97, 1528–29, 1544–61; Meyendorff, "Byzantine Views of Islam," pp. 120–21.

91. A. T. Khoury, *Les Theologiens Byzantins et l'Islam: Textes et auteurs (VIIIe–XIIIe siecles)* (Louvain and Paris, 1969), pp. 82–92.

92. Jeffery, "Ghevond's Text of the Correspondence between Omar II and Leon III," pp. 281–330.

93. A. A. Vasiliev, ed., "Kitab al-Unwan," *PO* 8.3 (Paris, 1912), S03.

94. Jeffery, "Ghevond's Text of the Correspondence between Omar II and Leon III," pp. 270.

95. See for example John of Nikiu, *The Chronicle*, trans. R. H. Charles (Oxford, 1916), pp. 194–95, who relates that the Christians of Egypt, including the Copts, viewed the Arabic conquests with horror. They had prayed to God to destroy the enemies of the cross who plundered their country and took captives in abundance. Compare also the testimony of Sebeos, Michael Syros, Al-Baladhuri, Bar-Hebraeus and other non-Greek sources cited in the present study.

96. J. B. Glubb, *The Life and Times of Muhammad* (New York, 1970), pp. 392, 399. Cf. Khoury, *Der theologische Streit der Byzantiner mit dem Islam*, pp. 30–38, 310–18; A. N. Stratus, *To Byzantio ston 7on Aiona* (Athens, 1969), vol. 3, pp. 127–43.

97. Cf. W. Montgomery Watt, *Muhammad: Prophet and Statesman* (Oxford, 1961), pp. 217–28.

98. H. A. R. Gibb, "Arab-Byzantine Relations under the Umayyad Caliphate," *DOP* 12 (1958): 219–33, esp. p. 222.

99. George Sale, trans., *The Koran: Commonly Called the Alkoran of Mohammed*,

Surah XLVII (London, n. d.), p. 375. See also Surahs IV and VIII, pp. 62, 132. Cf. Watt, *Muhammad*, p. 222.

100. For a comprehensive survey of Byzantino-Islamic cultural relations, see the penetrating article of Speros Vryonis Jr., "Byzantium and Islam: Seventh–Seventeenth Century," *East European Quarterly* 2 (1968): 205–40.

38

THE ARMENIAN REBELLION OF 703 AGAINST THE CALIPHATE

Aram Ter-Ghevondian

The rebellion of 703 is a known fact in the history of Armenia in the Middle Ages, yet the recent discovery of different source materials calls for a reexamination of events leading to this important movement. To understand the turbulence associated with the beginning five years of the eighth century, particularly the upheavals of 703, it is necessary to glance at the preceding decade.

In 685 the Umayyad Abd-al-Malik became the Caliph, while in Byzantium Justinian II ascended the throne. In 689 the Byzantine state provoked the Amanos mountaineers (the Madraids or Jarajima)[1] to rebel against the Caliphate. To escape the mountaineers' assaults and the Byzantine intrigues, the hard-pressed Caliph signed a treaty with the Eastern Roman Empire, whereby the former agreed to pay the latter a thousand dinar a week. During the same year the Byzantine forces attacked Armenia (as well as Cyprus)[2] and appointed an Armenian nobleman, Nerseh Kamsarakan,[3] as a replacement for the slain prince Ashot Bagratuni, who had perished fighting the Arabs.

Abd-al-Malik had to suppress several other rebellions: Abdullah-ibn-al-Zubayr had declared himself the Caliph of Hejaz; Iraq was being ruled by Mukhtar, who had gathered supporters among the Shi'a Muslims, but was killed in 697 by Ibn-al-Zubayr's brother Musaab; in 691 Musaab in turn was killed in the battle of Dayr-al-Jasalik by the Caliph's brother, Muhammad-ibn-Marwan. In 692 the viceroy of Iran and Iraq, Hajjaj, crushed Ibn-al-Zubayr's movement in Hejaz.[4] This turn of events allowed the Caliph an opportunity to settle differences with Justinian. But the latter, forestalling Malik's plans, himself abrogated the treaty of 689 and invaded the Arab Empire. In 692 Byzantine armies were defeated in the battle of Sebastopol while advancing toward Assyria.[5]

Aram Ter-Ghevondian, "The Armenian Rebellion of 703 against the Caliphate," trans. Marina A. Arakelian, *Armenian Review* 36 (1983): 59–72.

This defeat sealed the fate of Armenia. In 693, Muhammad-ibn-Marwan, the brother of the Caliph, was appointed the viceroy of Armenia, Jazirah, and Azerbaijan.[6] The brothers, however, had personal conflicts—ibn-Marwan hoped to capture the Caliphate, while the Caliph, aware of the former's aspirations, made conscious efforts to please his brother.[7]

The Armenian prince of the time, Smbat Bagratuni, proclaimed allegiance to the Arabs, although his territory, the Fourth Haik, was still under Byzantine control.[8] A palace coup in 695 in Byzantium overthrew the belligerent Justinian and sent him to exile. His successor, Leo, was easier to contend with. During the following two years (695–696), Arabs overwhelmed the Fourth Haik and made considerable advances toward Asia Minor.[9] Another coup, in 698, ended Leo's reign. The former admiral Absimaros became the new Emperor Tiberius III (698–705). He dispatched Byzantine troops to the interior of Armenia and was met by Smbat Bagratuni at the valley of Paik, whom he defeated.[10] In about 699 another wave of Arab armies invaded Armenia and encountered strong resistance in some regions, one of which was the Isle of Sevan that managed to withstand for two years.[11]

According to Ghevond,[12] Muhammad-ibn-Marwan undertook a major assault against Armenia in 701, during the sixteenth anniversary of Abd-al-Malik's rule. An Arab historian, Ibn-al-Athir,[13] agrees that in the Islamic year of 81 (26 February, 700–14 February, 701) Ubaydullah, the son of the Caliph, had captured the city of Karn (Kalikala) and in 82 (15 February, 701–3 February, 702) ibn-Marwan entered Armenia. "That year," writes the chronicler, "Muhammad ibn-Marwan invaded Armenia and conquered it. The Armenians sued for peace, which he granted. He also appointed Abu Shaykh-ibn-Abdullah as governor."

The invasion of Muhammad-ibn-Marwan took place probably in the spring of 701, and based on the accounts of the chroniclers, it lasted a long while. He went to Djermadzor, whose inhabitants had taken refuge in the fortresses, and he guaranteed their security. But as they descended, the fighters were murdered, while the women and children were enslaved. In the monastery of Saint Gregory in Bagrevand, he treated the monks with extreme cruelty and looted the establishment.[14] He captured Dvin where he left a battalion. From there he proceeded to the beseiged Isle of Sevan and not being able to subdue it, he moved east. Simultaneously, Armenians recaptured Dvin and massacred the Arabs, while Muhammad, returning to Sevan, conquered it and massacred the defenders.[15] He came back to Dvin, seized it, and also captured the Fourth Haik, whose prince, Vahan of Yotedevyan (of seven devils) submitted as well.[16] Henceforth Muhammad was in full control of Armenia. Annexing the conquered territories of Virk, Aghvank, the region around the Caspian (Shirvan), and Darband, he created the state of Arabian Armenia, and as was mentioned earlier, designated Abu-Shaykh-ibn-Abdullah to govern the area. Ghevond recounts that after subjugating Armenia, Muhammad returned to Assyria.[17] In fact, in 702 he was in Iraq and took part in the skirmishes, where the rebel Abd-al-Rahman was defeated.[18]

Muhammad came back to Mosul after the battle of Dayr-al-Jamajima (near Basra).[19] It was here, in June of 702, that the self-proclaimed Caliph, formerly general, was beaten. In Armenia Muhammad had shown such brutality that after his retreat Ghevond describes the situation of the country thus:

> [T]he population was left as if scorched by a smoking fire, and like a tuft of wheat trampled upon by swine.[20]

Catholicos Hovhannes Draskhanakertsi writes about the governor appointed by Muhammad: "And after Mahmet a new governor was sent to Armenia, Abdullah, a cruel, lustful, and unrestrained man," who detained and tortured princes and freemen.[21] Vahan Goghtnatsi also mentions that "the leader left in Armenia, Abdullah, [was] vile and vicious."[22] Ghevond testifies: "He [Abdullah] decided to eliminate the independent Armenian seignorial families and their horsemen."[23] This was simply a political decision to annihilate the leading families and their troops, since according to Abd-al-Malik, they were seen as obstacles to the entrenchment of Umayyad rule in Armenia. To accomplish this objective, Prince Smbat Bagratuni and Catholicos Sahak Dzoraporetsi[24] were arrested and sent to Damascus. Religious persecutions began (for example, the crucifixion of David Devnatsi).[25] This of course was not an isolated incident as there had been demands made for a general conversion; we know it because in 703 Sahak Dzoraporetsi was asking the Arabs to grant religious freedom.[26]

During Abd-al-Malik's reign the Caliphate's yoke was especially onerous. The already burdened government was cleansed from enemies; reforms were instituted; Arabic became the only official language, replacing Greek and Persian. In 695 the first currency with Arabic inscriptions was issued.[27] Non-Muslim employees were displaced by Muslim Arabs. The most difficult aspect, however, was the burden of taxes, especially the head-count tax (*jizia*) which was forced upon the *Zimi* (non-Muslim) population. The differentiation between land tax (*Kharaj*) and head tax (*jizia*) was finalized, whereby the latter was by far the heavier of the two. An Assyrian historical work written in the eighth century and attributed to Dionisius Tell Mahre, describes the condition of the Christians living in the Upper Mesopotamia (Jazirah):

> In 691–692 Abd-al-Malik made a recount, meaning he imposed a tax on the Assyrians. He issued a decree, stating that each man must return to his country, his native village, where he must register his name, his father's name, his children's names, and all that he owns, including the numbers of grape vines and olive trees. This was the beginning of the head count and the spread of evil for the Christian populations. Hitherto kings had taxed the land, not the people. Henceforth the Children of Hagar (Arabs) imposed Egyptian slavery on the Aramaean. Woe to us, for we have sinned and are being governed by slaves. This was the first census enacted by the Arabs.[28]

The hardships described by the Assyrian historian applied to Armenia as well. Here the restrictions became so stringent that Ibn-Marwan even forbade fishing in Lake Van, where previously it had been freely permissible. Ibn-al-Fakih, the ninth-century geographer, testifies to the same: "Regarding lake Tirekh, it has always been permissible [to fish] until after Muhammad Ibn-Marwan Ibn-al Hakam became the governor of Jazirah and Armenia, and banned it."[29] The same is repeated by a thirteenth-century chronicler, who adds: "He who enacts a bad law, is responsible for it, as he is for all those who maintain it until the last day of Resurrection, while their own responsibility is by no means diminished."[30] If the Muslim historian is so upset, how much anger must the inhabitants residing around Lake Van have felt in regard to this ruling?

Thus the harsh taxes, numerous restrictions, religious persecution, and the plan to exterminate the seignorial families and their troops offended all levels of the population—the aristocracy, the clergy, and the peasantry.

As was mentioned earlier, Muhammad had left Armenia after the invasion of 701, while Smbat Bagratuni and Sahak Dzoraporetsi had been sent to Damascus.[31] Apparently, while in 702 the Caliphate was experiencing serious problems from the rebellious contender to the throne Abd-al-Rahman-ibn-Muhammad-ibn-al-Ashaas,[32] the Armenian prince and the Catholicos left Damascus to return home. It was in this chaotic time, probably toward the end of 702, that the Arab governor (*vostikan*) of Armenia was assassinated. Ibn-al-Athir attests: "It is said that he was assassinated in the year 83 [4 February, 702–23 January, 703]."[33]

Ghevond confirms that Smbat Bagratuni was aware of the Arab governor's deceitful policies from the beginning, and although he [Smbatj] had fought against Byzantium,[34] his bitter experiences had shown him the true nature of Abd-al-Malik's policies. The Armenian prince invited the notables to a secret meeting (probably in his castle of Daruynk in Kogovit). Smbat, son of Ashot; Vard, son of Theodoros Rshtuni; his brother Ashot; and other members of the nobility attended. Seeing no alternative, the notables decided to depart to Byzantium.[35] They crossed the southeast end of Mount Ararat and arrived at the village of Akor. Learning of their departure, the Arab army of eight thousand strong stationed at Nakhjavan pursued them,[36] while the Armenian nobility's army had already stopped at the village of Vardanakert, located at the west bank of the river Arax. They informed the Arabs that they had no intention of rebelling, and were merely leaving, but the enemy, realizing the disparity in numbers—8,000 versus 2,000 Armenians—was not willing to negotiate.

Throughout the night, the Armenian troops fortified the streets of the town. At dawn, Armenians, separated in regiments, massacred their pursuers who had grown numb in the cold, snowy night. The children of the desert, thrown in the frozen river Arax, were drowned as the ice gave way. The enemy was so severely thrashed that only 300 of the original 8,000 escaped alive. They appealed to Princess Shushanik for mercy. The magnanimous princess was able to persuade

Smbat, son of Ashot, and his fighters to spare the lives of the survivors. She tended their wounds, gave them pack horses, and sent them to the Caliph. The battle of Vardanakert took place approximately in January/February 703.[37] Although victorious, the nobility remained faithful to its original plan and left the country. They forwarded various gifts, such as Arabian horses, to Emperor Tiberius. The Emperor in turn granted the title of military governor to Smbat Bagratuni. This kind gesture indicated that the Emperor was in favor of anti-Arab movements. Smbat and the other nobility went and settled in the castle of Tukhart at Dayk.

The departure of this particular group of nobility did not prevent the population from revolting. In the province of Rshtunik, village of Gukark, the insurgents, along with the regular troops, attacked an Arab garrison and slew them with swords. Only 280 Arabs escaped, and found sanctuary in a church. The insurgents were about to burn the church with the Arabs inside, but Smbat, son of Ashot, prince of Vaspurakan, did not allow them to execute their plan. At last, the Arabs were persuaded to leave the church, and as they did, every single one of them was killed.[38] The same was repeated in the province of Vanang, where the Arab general Ogba and his army were attacked by Prince Kamsarakan, accompanied by an army of freemen. The Armenians annihilated the Arabs, except for General Ogba, who barely escaped to Assyria and told his tale to the Caliph.[39] The Caliph immediately dispatched an army headed by Muhammad-ibn-Marwan. General Ogba also went along. Although Hovhannes Draskhanakertsi considers Ogba as the commander of the army, according to Ibn-al-Athir [sic], in 84 (24 January, 703–13 January, 704) Muhammad invaded Armenia, which confirms Ghevond's assertion that Muhammad was the commander.[40] Actually, in 703 Muhammad was preparing for an invasion, but en route he was stopped by Catholicos Sahak Dzoraporetsi's delegation.[41]

In fact, the Armenian nobility who had not participated in the original uprising, realizing that the vengeful Arabs were on their way, asked Catholicos Sahak, who had by then returned, to intervene diplomatically and try to stop the advancing general. Ghevond describes Sahak's passage through Armenia. Catholicos and the bishops arrived at Kharan. Aware of his impending death, [Catholicos Sahak] left a strong note to be delivered to General Muhammad. The note implored the general to spare the country from bloodshed, to allow religious freedom rather than forced conversions, and, in return, Sahak promised that the Armenians would be obedient.[42] For a variety of reasons[43] Muhammad accepted this unique plea, agreed to it in writing, and gave the document to the traveling companions of the late Catholicos. In Armenia, the existence of this document calmed everyone.[44]

This document, given by the representative of the Caliphate to the Armenian Church, only assured the toleration of religion and perhaps some other church-related rights. It did not concern itself with the issue of the nobility's rights in land inheritance. This required a special agreement, which was granted a few years later. The reference by Hovhannes Draskhanakertsi to "a letter written to the Armenian nobility" does not indicate that the rights of the nobility were discussed.

Later, Ghevond adds: "In the eighteenth year of Abd-al-Malik's reign (703) General Muhammad entered Armenia for the second time. For three years[45] he waited patiently, while no one ever uttered a negative remark about the events of Vardanakert rather, he (Muhammad) faithfully kept his written promise, while secretly watching the Armenian nobility."[46] The above is partially confirmed by Ibn-al-Athir: "That year (85 Hedjri 704) Mohammed Ibn-Marwan invaded Armenia, where he spent the summer and winter."[47]

A recently discovered multivolume manuscript (*Kitab-al-Futuh* or Book of Victories),[48] written by a tenth-century Arab historian, contains interesting information about Armenia. All we know about the author, Muhammad ibn-Abdullah-ibn-Aasam-al Kufi,[49] is that he died approximately in 926. Regarding the insurrection of 703, he writes:

> There were wars in Jazirah, Armenia, and Azerbaijan. Then Abd-al-Malik-ibn-Marwan called his brother Muhammad-ibn-Marwan and ordered him with regard to the governorship of Jazirah, Armenia, and Azerbaijan, and also gave him a large army. Muhammad-ibn-Marwan and his troops left Assyria (Sham) accompanied by Maslama-ibn-Abd-al-Malik-ibn-Marwan, until they reached Jazirah. Then he called one of his fellow soldiers, whose name was Abdullah-ibn-Abu-Shaykh-al-Avio, gave him 10,000 of his Assyrian soldiers and ordered him to go to Armenia to fight against the Khazars and other infidels. Abdullah-ibn-Abu-Shaykh and his troops entered the country of Armenia and when its people found out about this, they gathered together, against the Muslims, a very large crowd (army) of over a hundred thousand people; they killed every one—no individual survived—and confiscated all their belongings and weapons. Everything was taken. [50]

The most interesting aspect of Kufi's information is the name of the Arab general or governor, Abdullah-ibn-Abu-Shayk-ibn-Abdullah, whereas in the Armenian sources, starting with Hovhannes Draskhanakertsi, only a simple Abdullah is mentioned—the same as used in Kufi's original manuscript. To resolve this discrepancy, H. Nalbandian had assumed that the Abdullah mentioned by the Armenian chroniclers and the Abu-Shaykh-ibn-Abdullah used by Ibn-al-Athir were two different personalities.[51] Yet we had always maintained that these two personalities were in reality a distorted version of the same name.[52] Now, Nalbandian's viewpoint must be reevaluated based on data provided by Kufi.

In fact, according to Kufi, the general in question was not present during the insurrection as was attested to by the Armenian sources and by Ibn-al-Athir, Rather, Muhammad dispatched him after the news of the insurrection. Therefore, it is possible to assume, with reservations, that the Abu-Shaykh-ibn-Abdullah mentioned by

Ibn-al-Athir was a governor, whereas the Abdullah-ibn-Abu-Shaykh alluded to by Armenians and also Kufi, was a general who was later sent to Armenia.

The gathering of a hundred thousand (meaning large numbers) Armenians, who attacked and destroyed the entire Arab forces without leaving a single survivor, is a remarkable revelation. If that is the case, Abdullah-ibn-Abu-Shaykh must also have perished. This corresponds with Ibn-al-Athir's affirmation that the Armenians killed the governor. Armenian sources do not specify that Abdullah was killed. M. Chamchian, while referring to the massacre of Arabs in Vardanakert, writes: "And only the governor Abdullah escaped along with a few men," without specifying his source.[53] Similarly, Theophanes narrates the insurrection of 703 and agrees that the Armenians murdered all of the Arabs: "In that year the Armenian nobility rebelled against the Saracens [Arabs] and massacred all of the Saracens in Armenia."[54] In Kufi's work the citing of Armenian victory naturally echoes the effects of Arab defeat in Vardanakert, and to a lesser extent in Rshtunik and Vanand.

After the insurrection of 703, due to the intervention of Catholicos Sahak, the reentering Arab army did not engage in bloodshed (at least temporarily). Nevertheless, they were watching the Armenian nobility and were waiting for an opportune moment to take revenge. And the occasion was offered.

In 705 the exiled Byzantine Emperor Justinian II returned and recaptured his throne. Smbat Bagratuni, residing in the castle of Tukhark, immediately wrote a letter asking Justinian's help to invade Arabian Armenia. The Emperor offered an army of fifty thousand led by a general who, along with Smbat, entered the province of Vanand and camped near the village of Drashpet. They were met by Muhammad-ibn-Marwan, who after subduing them, massacred a great majority of the Greek and Armenian fighters and returned to Dvin.[55]

The Caliphate no longer let the opportunity pass. Muhammad was ordered to swiftly execute the long-standing plan to eliminate the Armenian nobility. He ordered his subordinate, Kasim, to invite the nobility under the pretext of some business transactions that there should be an accounting for the purpose of compensating the Armenian cavalry. They were disarmed and arrested upon arrival.[56] Some were forced into the church of Nakhjavan, and others in Khram.[57] The Arabs set the wooden roofs of both churches on fire. The burning beams and tiles fell over the heads of the noblemen; the smoke-filled fire burnt them alive.[58] Another group of important noblemen were put in shackles and tortured. They were forced to turn in their wealth (gold and silver) in return for freedom; yet after being looted, they were hung from wooden beams.[59] In the provinces of Nakhjavan and Khram numerous members of the nobility[60] were killed, including Smbat, son of Ashtot Bagratuni; Grigor and Koryun Ardsrunis; and Varag Shapuh and his brother of the Amatuni house. Subsequently, the families of the burnt nobility were taken to Dvin, where they were enslaved and shipped to Damascus[61] while their estates were plundered.[62]

Kufi has interesting observations regarding the bloody events of 705. Immediately following his description of the rebellion, he says:

> The news reached Muhammad-ibn-Marwan; he was saddened (to hear) what had happened to the Muslims, and became terribly uneasy. Then he called his troops, 40,000 strong, and led them personally. When he reached the interior of Armenia, a massive crowd of Romans and Armenians met him, and Muhammad waged such fierce battles against them [because] he was afraid he would be vanquished and dishonored, since the unbelievers (*Kufar*) had a great numerical [advantage] against him. But Allah defeated the heathen (*Mushrik*) and allowed the Muslims to conquer them. Most were massacred and enslaved, their country and possessions were occupied.[63] Afterward Muhammad-Ibn-Marwan sent a message to their leaders and freemen (*ahrar*), promising that he would be generous and personally give whatever they wanted and appoint a man of their choice as governor. He [Ibn-Marwan] was able to convince them; they trusted him and came to him. They reached an agreement (with some conditions) on some issues and satisfied them. Then he said he did not trust them, therefore they should enter their church and take an oath, so that they would not transgress their obligations. Then they should give him hostages and return to their country. They agreed and entered their churches to take the oath. But when he knew they were inside, he had the doors shut, and set the churches with the people inside on fire by kerosene. These churches are still called the burnt ones (*Muhtarika*).[64]

Like Kufi, the preceding Arab historians have also linked the insurrection of 703 with the events of 705, but they have confused the periods. For example, Baladhuri (d. 892) testifies:[65]

> When the agitation of Ibn-al-Zubayr began, Armenia rebelled; her freemen (*ahrar*) and their follower mutinied. When Abd-al-Malik appointed his brother Muhammad-ibn-Marwan the governor of Armenia, he [Ibn-Marwan] fought against them [the Armenians] and won, massacred, enslaved, and subjugated the country. Then he promised to give honors to all the surviving (freemen) and gathered them to the Province of Khlam (Khlat) [put them] inside the churches, closed the doors, assigned guards to the doors and frightened them.[66]

Almost the same is repeated by Yaqubi (d. 897) who, describing Muhammad's activities around the year 73 (692–693), says:

> Then he invaded Armenia whose population had rebelled. He massacred, enslaved and wrote a letter to the nobility (*Ashraf*) who are called freemen (*ahrar*), gave guarantees and promised to give honors. Hence they gathered in their churches, in the province of Khlat (Khram) and he ordered to encircle the churches with fire-wood, closed the doors on them and burnt all of them.[67]

The chronicler Abu-l-Mahasin-Ibn-Taghri-Birdi (1411–1469) writes about the year 84 (703–764):

> That year Muhammad-ibn-Marwan invaded Armenia and defeated them, then burnt their churches and this is called the year of the fire (*sanad-al-harik*).[68]

The Byzantine historian Theophanes (d. 818) also connects the insurrection to the incidents of 705. After recounting the insurrection, he quickly adds:

> They hastily appealed to Apsimtros and brought the Romans to their country. Muhammad attacked them, massacred many, subjugated Armenia to the Saracens and, gathering the Armenian nobility in one place, burnt them alive.[69]

Kufi reveals other interesting information. Arab and Armenian historians maintain that the Arabs invited the Armenian nobility and forced them to enter the churches and burnt them. Kufi, on the other hand, says that the Arabs persuaded the Armenians to enter the churches in order to take the oath and then the doors were closed. This issue is raised in the Armenian biographical literature. In the second volume of the *Soperk Haykakank* series edited by Vahan Goghtnatsi, a reference is made to this topic: "The soldiers took their weapons and gathered them in a place of worship, the House of God, so that they could take the oath to remain loyal to the rulers of the land."[70] In the series published by M. Avgerian this information is repeated with an addition: ". . . then the doors were closed on them."[71] Vahan Goghtnatsi too notes, ". . . their weapons were taken deceitfully, they were brought in the church to take an oath of loyalty to the Arab rulers."[72]

After these tragic events the Armenian nobility, who had sought refuge in the castle of Tukhark in Taik province, abandoned their hope of returning to their homeland. They asked Emperor Justinian II to provide shelter for themselves and grazing land for their herds. The Emperor gave the town of Puyt (Poty) to them, where they lived for six years.[73]

The insurrection of 703 was directed against the harsh policies of the Caliphate. It was a popular revolt, as it involved the entire citizenry. Although it was suffocated in blood, it nevertheless left a distinct mark. For, during the reign of Caliph Walid, the policies of the Umayyads had changed in Armenia, in spite of the bloody events of the first few years. One of the main reasons for this change was undoubtedly the insurrection of 703.

NOTES

For clarification of any citations, particularly those with Armenian text (which was not reproduced here), the reader is referred to the original essay, Aram Ter-Ghevondian, "The

Armenian Rebellion of 703 against the Caliphate," trans. Marina A. Arakelian, *Armenian Review* 36 (1983): 59–72.

1. Beladsori (Baladhuri), *Liber expugnationis regionum* (Lugd. Bat., 1856), p. 160; Tabari, *Tarikh* (Cairo, 1964), vol. 6, p. 150. Ph. Hitti, *History of the Arabs* (London, 1958), pp. 204–205.

2. *Istoria Vizantii* (Moscow, 1967), vol. 2, pp. 41–42.

3. *Stepanosi Taronetsvo Asogilkan Patrautiun Tiezerakan* [The Universal History of Stepanos Asoghik of Tarim] (St. Petersburg, 1885), pp. 100–101.

4. K.V. Zettersteen, "Abd-al-Malik," in *Encyclopaedia of Islam* (Leyden and London, 1960), vol. 1, pp. 48–49.

5. *Istorii Vizantii*, vol. 2, p. 42.

6. lbn al-Athir, *al-Ramil fi-t-tarikh* (Cairo, 1934–1935), vol. 4, p. 28; Ibn al-Asir (Armenian text) (Erevan, 1981), p. 28.

7. Ibn al-Athir, *al-Ramil fi-t-tarikh*, vol. 4, pp. 167–68; lbn al-Asir (Armenian text), pp. 167–68.

8. A. Ter-Ghevondian, *Armensk i arabskii khalifat* (Erevan, 1977), p. 72.

9. Yaqubi, *Tarikh* (Beirut, 1960), vol. 2, p. 281.

10. S. Malkhasiants, ed., *Ghevondia Patmutiun Medal Vartapeti Hayots* [History of Armenians by Ghevond, the Great Vardapet] (St. Petersburg, 1887), p. 19.

11. *Patmutiun Movseq Kaghankatvatso* [History of Movses Caghankatvetsi] (Tiflis, 1912), p. 366; this source specifies a period of three years. *Patmutiun Hovhanu Katoghikosi* [History of Hovhan Catholicos] (Jerusalem, 1867), p. 119.

12. Malkhasiants, *Ghevondia Patmutiun*, p. 20.

13. Ibn al-Athir, *al-Ramil fi-t-tarikh*, vol. 4, pp. 75–84; Ibn al-Asir (Armenian text), p. 65. *Patmutiun Hayots* [History of the Armenians] (Venice, 874), vol. 2, p. 378; and Gh. Injijian, *Hnakhosutiun Ashkharhagrakar; Hayastaneata Ashkharhi* [Geographic Archaeology of Armenia] (Venice, 1835), vol. 1, p. 445, consider 694 as the date of the final Arab conquest of Armenia, as well as the year of the battle of Vardanakert. These two events are further tied to the death of David Dvnetsi, since the latter was martyrized on March 31, 693, according to *Liakatar Vark ev Vkayabanutiun Srbots* [Complete Hagiography and Martyrology of the Saints] (Venice, 1813), vol. 6, p. 228. The year 693 is correct as far as the appointment of Mohammad-ibn-Marwan as the viceroy of Armenia and Jazirah is concerned (lbn al-Asir (Armenian text), p. 62). But the invasion, which ended by the conquest of Armenia, came later. According to A. Muller (*Istoria Islama* [1895], p. 91) by 700 Armenia was already conquered. Leo (*Hayots Patmutiun* [History of the Armenians] [Erevan, 1967], vol. 2, p. 325) has the same opinion. M. Ormanian (*Azgapatum* [Beirut, 1959], vol. 1, p. 56) and B. Arakelian ("Hayeri Apestambutiune Arabakan Ldsi Dem" [The Insurrection of Armenians against Arab Yoke, 703], *Teghekagir* 5–6 [1941]: 55–62) point out that Armenia was subjugated during 698–700. J. Laurent is undecided about the year 698, *L'Armenie entre Byzance et l'Islam* ([Lisbon, 1980], p. 243). H. Nalbandian ("Arabatsi Vostikannere Hayastanum" [Arab Governors in Armenia], *Teghekagir* 8 [1956]: 107) also agrees that the subjugation of Armenia took place between 698 and 700. But based on the correct information provided by Ibn al-Athir, Muhammad invaded Armenia in the year 82 (February 15, 701–February 3, 702); thus the date cannot be earlier than 701. Similarly, the invasion could not have begun in 698, since it was Byzantium that invaded that year. Therefore, the Arab invasion must have occurred in 699. Consequently, the subjugation happened from 699 to 701.

14. Malkhasiants, *Ghevondia Patmutiun*, pp. 20–21.

15. *Patmutiun Movseq Kaghankatvatso*, pp. 366–67.

16. Theophanes, *Chronographia* (Bonnae, 1839), vol. 1, p. 569. According to M. Chamchian, the Greeks called him Yotedevian (of seven devils) because he had surrendered to the Arabs (ibid., vol. 2, pp. 382–83).

17. Malkhasiants, *Ghevondia Patmutiun*, p. 2.3.

18. Tabari, *Tarikh*, vol. 6, p. 363.

19. Ibid., p. 364.

20. Malkhasiants, *Ghevondia Patmutiun*, p. 7.2.

21. *Patmutiun Hovhanu Katoghikosi*, p. 120.

22. *Liakatar Vark ev Vkayabanutiun Srbots*, vol. 19, p. 89.

23. Malkhasiants, *Ghevondia Patmutiun*, p. 23.

24. *Patmutiun Hovhanu Katoghikosi*, p. 120.

25. David was originally a Persian named Surhan. He had been to Armenia during the reign of Prince Grigor Mamikonian; there he accepted Christianity and was christened as David. In *Liakatar Vark* (p. 228) his martyrdom is placed in 693, which certainly is not correct. E. Abuladze places the event on January 22, 703 while M. Darbinian-Melikian has accepted March 31, 704 ("Ditoghutiunner Hovhannes Draskhanakerttsu Patmutian Veraberial" [Observations on the History of Hovhannes Draskhanakerttsi], *Patma-Banasirakan-Handes* 3 [1981]: 155, particularly line 7). M. Ormanian's (*Azgapatum*, vol. 1, p. 777) date, April 4, 701, is preferable, since according to the chroniclers, the martyrdom took place immediately following the invasion. Even 702 is plausible.

26. Malkhasiants, *Ghevondia Patmutiun*, p. 29.

27. Hitti, *History of the Arabs*, p. 217.

28. *Chronique de Denys de Tell-Mahre* (Paris, 1895), p. 10.

29. Ibn al-Fakih, *Kitab al-Buldan* (Lugd Bat, 1885), vol. 5, p. 292.

30. Ibn al-Athir, *al-Ramil fi-t-tarikh*, vol. 4, p. 28; Ibn al-Asir (Armenian text), p 62.

31. *Patmutiun Hovhanu Katoghikosi*, p. 120.

32. J. Wellhausen, *The Arab Kingdom and Its Fall* (London, 1973), pp. 232–48.

33. Ibn al-Athir, *al-Ramil fi-t-tarikh*, vol. 4, p. 84; Ibn al-Asir (Armenian text), p. 65.9.

34. Laurent, *L'Armenie entre Byzance et l'Islam*, pp. 243–45.

35. Malkhasiants, *Ghevondia Patmutiun*, pp. 34–35. Ghevond recounts that, before going to the valley of Arax in a place called Arestakoghm in Vaspurakan, the nobility had consulted a hermit who foresaw the loss of the country and the massacre of the nobility and advised them to be cautious.

36. M. Chamchian maintains that Governor Abdullah was the head of the troops and that the Armenian nobility, with the help of the Byzantine army, attacked the governor and his troops, massacred all, and only the governor barely escaped (II, 378).

37. Samuel Anetsi, in his *Havakmunk i grots patmagrats* [Collection of the Writings of Historians] (Vagharshapat, 1893), p. 85, considers 702 as the date of the battle of Vardanakert, while David Baghishetsi, in his *Manr Zhamanakagrutiunner* [Minor Chronicles] (Erevan, 1956), vol. 2, p. 333, marks the Armenian year 151 (June 4, 702–June 3, 703) as the year of Vardanakert and related events. Theophanes asserts that the insurrection took place in the year 6195 of the creation, or 703. This coincides with the fifth anniversary of Apsimarus's (Tiberius) rule, which is the same as 703 in *The Chronicle of Theophanes* (trans. H. Bartikian, p. 97 of unpublished manuscript). In Ibn al-Asir's (Armenian text)

work, the invasion of Muhammad-ibn-Marwan in the year 84 (24 January 703–13 January 704) relates to this rebellion (p. 65). In recent times, the first to mention 703 is M. Saint Martin, *Memoires Historiques et Geographiques* (Paris, 1818), vol. 1, p. 155. He is followed in this assertion by Muller (*Istoria Islama*, vol. 2, p. 91); Laurent (*L'Armenie entre Byzance et l'Islam*, p. 224), Ormanian (*Azgapatum*, vol. 1, p. 781), Arakelin ("Hayeri Apestambutiune Arabakan Ldsi Dem," pp. 55–62), and H. Nalbandian ("Arabatsi Vostikannere Hayastanum," p. 107). The assumption of Laurent and Nalbandian that the battle occurred in December or at the end of 703 is improbable, since in Armenia rivers do not freeze in December, whereas that is a possibility in January or February. The first to argue that the battle occurred in January 703 is Ormanian. Leo argued in favor of the same date in *Hayots Patmutiun* (vol. 2, p. 372).

As far as Lady Shushanik is concerned, there is evidence that the Arabs "rewarded" her magnanimity by forcibly taking her to Kheran after the carnage of 705 and insisting that she renounce her Christianity. She refused and in 706 was murdered by torture: When the news of her martyrdom reached her brother Gagik Kamsarakan who at the time was completing the building of a church in Vardanakert in honor of the victory in the battle, he glorified her name by joining it to the day of consecration of the new church (M. Chamchian, II, 382; Gh. Alishan, *Ayrarat* (Venice, 1890), p. 56; Ormanian, *Azgapatum*, vol. 1, p. 807; H. Adjarian, *Andsnanunneri Bararan* [Dictionary of Names] (Erevan, 1948), p. 181.

38. Malkhasiants, *Ghevondia Patmutiun*, pp. 26–28.

39. *Patmutiun Hovhanu Katoghikosi*, pp. 121–22.

40. Malkhasiants, *Ghevondia Patmutiun*, p. 28.

41. Ibid., pp. 28–31.

42. Ibid., p. 29.

43. Actually, Abd-al-Rahman's rebellion had not been totally subdued in 703; he was killed in 704. According to Leo, the Caliphate complied because Abd al-Malik had grown tolerant of the Christians by the end of his life (*Hayots Patmutiun*, vol. 2, pp. 374–75).

44. Hovhannes Draskhanakensi presents Sahak Dzoraporetsi's mission somewhat differently. According to Hovhannes, the Catholicos heard about the events while still in Damascus. He journeyed to Kharan with the intention of averting disaster. He became ill, and was aware of his imminent death; he wrote a letter to be delivered to General Ogba, and asked that it be placed In his right hand, while he, the Catholicos, is placed in his coffin. Ogba entered and greeted him in Arabic. The deceased extended his hand and gave the note to Ogba. The general was overwhelmed by this phenomenon; he read the letter, agreed to honor the request, and wrote the [conciliatory] letter to the nobility, sending it with the traveling companions of the late Catholicos (*Patmutiun Hovhanu Katoghikosi*, pp. 122–24).

45. It is impossible to believe that Muhammad waited patiently in Armenia for three years, because the events of Nakhjavan occurred obviously in 705. The phenomenon is comprehensible if he continued to remain in Armenia after 705 as well.

46. Malkhasiants, *Ghevondia Patmutiun*, p. 31.

47. Ibn al-Athir, *al-Ramil fi-t-tarikh*, vol. 4, p. 102; Ibn al-Asir (Armenian text), p. 66.

48. Kufi, *Kitab al-Futuh*, 8 vols. (Haydarabad, 1968, 1975) is published based on the manuscripts of Gota (Germany) and Constantinople.

49. C. Brockelmann, *Geshichte der Arabischen Litteratur* (Leiden, 1937), p. 220; F. Sezgin, *Geschichte der Arabischen Schrifttums* (Leiden, 1967), vol. 1, p. 309.

50. Kufi, *Kitab al-Futuh*, vol. 6, p. 293.

51. Nalbandian, "Arabatsi Vostikannere Hayastanum," p. 107.

52. A. Ter Ghevondian, "Arminiya Vostikanneri Zhamanakagrutiune" [The Chronology of Governors of Arminiya], *Patma-Banasirakan Handes* 1 (1977): 119.

53. M. Chamchian, I, 378.

54. Theophanes, *Chronicle of Theophanes*, p. 97.

55. Malkhasiants, *Ghevondia Patmutiun*, p. 32.

56. Ibid., p. 33.

57. According to Movses Kaghankatvatsi (*Patmutiun Movseq Kaghankatvatso*, p. 367) and other historians following him, there were 800 casualties in Nakhjavan, and 400 in Khram. Ghevond and Hovhannes Draskhanakertsi do not cite numbers.

58. *Patmutiun Hovhanu Katoghikosi*, p. 125.

59. Malkhasiants, *Ghevondia Patmutiun*, pp. 34–35.

60. In the Armenian sources the date of the bloody events of 705 varies. Vardan places it on the 150th year of the Armenian calendar, meaning in 701 (*Tiezerakan Patmutiun* [Universal History] [Moscow, 1861], p. 99); the *Haysmavurk* [Lectionary], "on the 152nd year of the Armenian calendar" or 703 (*Haysmavurk*, March 28); Hovhannes Draskhanakertsi, "on their eighty-fifth year" or 704 (ibid., p. 124); Stepanos Taronetsi Asoghik, the 153rd year of the Armenian calendar (ibid., p. 125), which corresponds to July 3, 704–July 2, 705, of the Julian Calendar (H. Badalian, *Oratsuytsi Patmutiun* [History of the Calendar] [Erevan, 1970], p. 326), or to July 16, 704–July 15, 705, of the Gregorian calendar; M. Chamchian (p. 381), 704 by simply adding 153 to 551 (the beginning of the Armenian calendar); M. Saint-Martin, the same (I, 416); Alishan, 705 (*Ayrarat*, p. 562); Leo, 706 (*Hayots Patmutiun*, vol. 2, p. 375); Laurent, 705 (*L'Armenie entre Byzance et l'Islam*, p. 244); and H. Nalbandian, midway through 705 ("Arabatsi Vostikannere Hayastanum," p. 198). Ghevond is certain that the events occurred soon after the return of Justinian and the ascension of Walid to the Caliphate. Similarly, according to historian Andrea Stratos, *Seventh-Century Byzantium* (Athens, 1977), vol. 6, p. 130), whose work has been introduced to the author by H. Partikian, Justinian returned from exile and captured the throne in July-August 705 and was reconsecrated during the first few days of Walid's reign. The latter took office on October 10, 705, or in the middle of the month of Shaval, year 66 (Yaqubi, *Tarikh*, vol. 2, p. 283). Therefore, Smbat could have asked Justinian's assistance at the end of the summer of 705, and the events immediately following Nakhjavan and Khram could have taken place in the autumn (November) of that year.

61. *Patmutiun Hovhanu Katoghikosi*, p. 12.5.

62. "Vkayapanutiun Vahana Goghtnatsvo" [Martyrology of Vahan Goghtnatsi], *Soperk Haykakank* 13. Among the hostages special mention is made of Vahan Goghtnatsi, . . . the son of Prince Khosrov of Goghtn. Vahan later returned to his native land, and again professed the faith of his ancestors—Christianity—and was hence martyrized.

63. The information about the military confrontation between Muhammad and Armenian and Byzantine forces is probably an echo of the battle of Drashpet, since in Drashpet too Smbat Bagratuni was accompanied by Armenian and Byzantine units in his fight against the Arabs. This fight, however, did not happen right after the insurrection; rather, it took place two years later. The same confusion occurs in Movses Kaghankatvatsi who, immediately after mentioning Muhammad's invasion of 701, states that Armenian and Byzantine forces fought together and adds that Muhammad then gathered the Armenian nobility and burned them (*Patmutiun Movseq Kaghankatvatso*, p. 366).

64. Kufi, *Kitab al-Futuh*, vol. 6, pp. 294–95.

65. There is a major confusion in Baladhuri's testimony. Abdullah Ibn-Zubayr did rebel in 680, when Armenia had rebelled as well, but there is no connection between these and the movement of 703. Moreover, Muhammad was appointed governor of Armenia and other areas in 693. Baladhuri assumes that the burning of Armenian nobility took place in the same year.

66. Baladhuri, p. 205. Yaqubi clearly says Muhammad "burned" (*harraktum*) the princes; Baladhuri's usage of the word *frightened* (*khawaftum*) clearly indicates a writing error—a difference of a few dots.

67. Yaqubi (II, 272). For both contemporary historians (Yaqubi and Baladhuri) the name Khram has undergone a graphic change to Khelt.

68. Abu-I-Mahasin Ibn Taghre Birdi, *al-Nujum al-Zahira* (Cairo, 1929), vol. 1, p. 207.

69. Amazingly, both Kull and Theophanes emphasize that in 703 Armenians asked and received assistance from Byzantium. Theophanes even mentions the name of Apsimaros. As we have seen, M. Chamchian attests to the same. This is indeed an unclarified issue.

70. *Soperk Haykakank*, XIII, 63.

71. *Liakatar vark ev vkayapanutiun hayots*, vol. 1, p. 191.

72. Haysmavurk, March 28.

73. Malkhasiants, *Ghevondia Patmutiun*, p. 35. It is essential to emphasize that the evidence missing from Armenian historical sources yet mentioned in the hagiographic literature is attested to by the Arab historian. Unfortunately there is a degree of skepticism toward the reliability of hagiographic sources. Even Archbishop Ormanian, who certainly would not question the value of hagiographies, hesitates regarding the forced church entry of the nobility—"perhaps (it was) for the oath of loyalty," he writes with regard to the events of 705, using M. Chamchian as his sole source of reference [*Azgapatum*, I, 8031]. A serious study of hagiographies, martyrologies, and the *Haysmavurk* can enlighten many important historical issues.

39

THE DAYS OF *RAZZIA* AND INVASION

C. E. Dufourcq

As the Benedictine historians of Languedoc, Dom Devic and Dom Vessete have noted insightfully, "The Arab conquerors carefully distinguished incursions for the purpose of plundering from expeditions undertaken with a genuine goal of conquest."[1] Yet these two different modes of penetrating into enemy territory have always been connected. In principle, the Arabs never attempted to annex lands when they launched an initial attack against a new objective; they would always begin with a reconnaissance mission—a raid or a landing by night. That way they carried off some booty, sounded out a region, determined whether or not they had an interest in returning there to establish their dominion, and then reckoned the effective military force needed for that eventual enterprise of conquest, according to the degree of resistance that they had met. Thus they fulfilled, as warriors for the faith, the commandments in two verses of the Qur'an, the one in which Allah declares: "What cities we have destroyed!" (the cities of the impious, the infidels), and the one in which He says to His believers: "We have given you a place on earth."[2]

Under the repeated blows of these Arab reconnaissance raids, zones were created in the interior of the countries that were exposed to these cavalcades (*algara*)—zones that shifted and changed their geographic location over the course of the centuries, but where anxiety always reigned and emptiness spread: properties there were abandoned, cultivated fields were left to lie fallow, the populations took refuge in the walled cities. The Grenadan author Ibn Hudayl, who lived at the end of the fourteenth century, has explained this procedure and his methods:

> It is permissible to set fire to the lands of the enemy, his stores of grain, his beasts of burden—if it is not possible for the Muslims to take possession of them—as well as to cut down his trees, to raze his cities, in a word, to do everything that

C. E. Dufourcq, "Les jours de razzia et d'invasion," in *La vie quotidienne dans l'europe medievale sous domination arabe* (Paris: Hachette, 1978), pp. 15–34. English translation by Michael J. Miller.

might ruin and discourage him, provided that the imam (i.e., the religious "guide" of the community of believers) deems these measures appropriate, suited to hastening the Islamization of that enemy or to weakening him. Indeed, all this contributes to a military triumph over him or to forcing him to capitulate.[3]

CAVALCADES AND LANDINGS

We have many testimonies concerning the tragic and monotonous mechanism of these *razzias* (raids) on the Dar al-Harb, that is, in foreign, non-Muslim lands. Here are a few episodes pertaining to France: Once they made their way to the Pyrenees, after having established their dominion on the Iberian Peninsula, the invaders were attracted by the lands that extended beyond the northern foothills of the mountain range. Passing through the Segre Valley in Aragon, squadrons explored the valley of the Ariège River; in 721 [CE] they conducted a raid aimed at Toulouse, but Eudes, the Duke of Aquitaine, drove them back. Further to the east, they had already advanced through the regions of Cerdagne and Rousillon to the land of Languedoc, by taking the old Roman road that was now controlled by the Visigoths, the one that geographers call the path of the precoastal depression. Before 720, they had launched raids against Narbonne and, in 725, they seized Carcassonne. As of their first attack against Narbonne—which they had plans to take also, at the latest in 720—they succeeded in entering the city, sacked its churches, and carried off from one of them in particular seven superb statues made of solid silver, which were the pride of the city, and which they rightly reckoned as the most remarkable booty that they took there; moreover they led out as slaves great numbers of women, many children and a few men.[4]

Once they had made their way to the Lower Rhône Valley and were masters of Nîmes, advance parties ascended through the river valley in a bold offensive, and perhaps set up strongholds on the right bank, one of them situated between the Lower Ardèche and the site of present-day Viviers, at the place that is still called "Les Sarrasins" ["The Saracens" (at the summit of the Dent de Rez)], the other much farther north, in Vivarais, near Andance, on top of the hill of Castellet, which is also called "La Sarrasinière." After passing close by Lyons, following the course of the Saône River, and ravaging the regions of Mâcon and Chalon, on an indeterminate date that is believed to have been August 21, 725, but which some scholars think was in the summer of 731, they reached Autun, which they sacked and burned down, while another group was charging upon Dijon and, from there, upon Langres. Then they galloped as far as Sens, where they were driven back, to a great extent thanks to the heroic [Benedictine] Metropolitan (i.e., archbishop) of the city, Saint Ebbo (731). They were about a hundred kilometers away from Paris. The nasty affair at Autun was the most resounding episode of that expedition. As the erudite Bruzon de la Martinière wrote in 1768, it remained present in the minds of the city's inhabitants for centuries, inasmuch as "Autun has never been able to return to its former state since that destruction."[5]

While descending the slopes of the Pyrenees, the Arabs also overran Aquitaine. In 732, having conquered Duke Eudes, they entered Bordeaux, where they burned down all the churches, and advanced as far as the gates of Poitiers, setting fire to the Basilica of Saint Hilary Outside the Walls. Then they set out for the capital of Gaulish Christendom, that is, Tours, their objective being both spiritual and material: to strike a blow against the prestige of Saint Martin and to lay hold of the riches in his shrine. But they did not reach their goal: one Saturday in October, the Frankish commander Charles Martel stopped them not far from Poitiers.[6]

Besides, they found the Mediterranean regions more attractive. Around 734 or 735 they stormed and took Arles and Avignon. From the coast of Provence and in Italy, their sailors preceded the cavalry or substituted for them. In 846 they disembarked at the mouth of the Tiber, seized Ostia, went up the river, refrained from attacking the wall of Rome, but pillaged the basilicas of Saint Peter and Saint Paul, which at that time were both outside the walls.[7] This alarm prompted, as a countermeasure, the construction of a new Roman enclosure encompassing Saint Peter's and rejoining the old one at the Castello Santangelo, the old mausoleum of the Emperor Hadrian. In 849 the Muslims attempted a new landing at Ostia; then, every year from around 857 on, they threatened the Roman seaboard.

In order to get rid of them, Pope John VIII decided in 878 to promise them an annual payment of several thousand gold pieces; but this tribute of the Holy See to Islam seems to have been paid for only two years; and from time to time until the beginning of the tenth century, the Muslims reappeared at the mouth of the Tiber or along the coast nearby.

Marseilles, for its part, was also hit: in 838 the Arabs landed there and devastated it; Saint Victor's Abbey, outside the walls, was destroyed, and many inhabitants of the city were carried off in captivity; ten years later a new raid occurred, the Old Port was again sacked. And this perhaps was repeated once more around the year 920.

The whole Italian peninsula was similarly exposed: around 840 Muslim ships followed the Adriatic coasts as far as the Dalmatian archipelago and the mouth of the Pô River. Then, returning south, they dared to attack a city, Ancona, some two hundred kilometers northwest of Rome; a sort of commando dashed ashore: the city was devastated and set on fire.

During their conquest of Sicily, when they took Syracuse in 878, after a deadly attack, they were exasperated by the resistance that they met with. When they rushed into the city, they found along their way the Church of the Holy Savior, filled with women and children, the elderly and the sick, clerics and slaves, and they massacred them all. Then, spreading out through the city, they continued the slaughter and the pillage, had the treasure of the cathedral handed over to them; they also took many prisoners and gathered separately those who were armed. One week later all of the captives who had dared to fight against them were butchered (four thousand in number, according to the chronicle *al-Bayyan*).[8]

In 934 or 935, they landed at the other end of Italy, at Genoa, killed "all the men" they found there, and then left again, loading onto their ships "the treasures of the city and of its churches." A few years later they settled for a time, it seems, in Nice, Fréjus, Toulon.[9]

One could list many other similar facts. Generally speaking, in these Arab raids carried out by a cavalcade or after a landing, the churches were especially targeted, because the assailants knew that they would find there articles used in worship that were made of gold or silver, sometimes studded with precious stones, as well as costly fabrics. And because the churches were considered to be an offense against God, the One God, given that they were consecrated to the "polytheistic" belief in the Trinity, they were then burned down. The bells were the object of particular animosity, because they dared to amplify the call to infidel prayer by resounding through the skies, toward heaven; therefore they were always broken.[10]

A "GREAT FEAR"

It is not difficult to understand that such expedition sowed terror. The historian al-Maqqari, who wrote in seventeenth-century Tlemcen in Algeria, explains that the panic created by the Arab horsemen and sailors, at the time of the Muslim expansion in the zones that saw those raids and landings, facilitated the later conquest, if that was decided on: "Allah," he says, "thus instilled such fear among the infidels that they did not dare to go and fight the conquerors; they only approached them as suppliants, to beg for peace." Indeed, following Islamic law, the Muhammadans spared the lives and goods of those who did not have "the audacity to set themselves in opposition to God," that is, to those who did not struggle against them, "the champions of the Faith."

The distress that spread through the populations that were attacked was not simply the result of some lack of preparation or of a tendency to cowardice. The clerics and all the pious souls had one obsession: to avoid the profanation of the relics that were found in the churches and the monasteries. Many chroniclers relate how, when they learned that a Muslim band was approaching, the bishops had only one concern: to bring these precious relics to safety. And, often enough, the prelate himself fled with them. This was the case in 718, for example, with Metropolitan Prosper of Tarragone; he thus escaped death as well: the sack of the city was terrible; it was left completely in ruins, and it took centuries for this ancient capital of a magnificent Roman province to recover from that disaster.

As for the cities that opened their gates to the Arabs and then revolted against them—woe to them! From the very beginning of the Muslim expansion in

Europe, Toledo served as an example in this regard. The capital of the Visigoth kingdom had been handed over to the newcomers, without a fight, as of 711 or 712, for they presented themselves as enemies of the regent, Rodrigo, who was being opposed by the followers of the pretender to the throne, Akhila, the son of the late King Vittiza. In 713, when the people of Toledo realized that Akhila would not be restored to his father's throne, and that their Arab "allies" had become their masters, they declared that they were rejecting that government.

Shortly thereafter the chastisement struck them: from 713 on, their city was under attack; the Metropolitan, Sindered, had time to flee (he made it to Rome), but all the leading citizens who were not able to do that were slaughtered, and everything was pillaged.[11] The Arab general took possession, in particular, of the splendid "Solomon's table"; so they called a sort of bench or seat, raised on a dais like a throne, made entirely of gold and inlaid with gems, which was found in the cathedral. The other towns of Spain which, in the confusion of the Visigoth civil war, had welcomed the Arabs as a type of mercenaries in the service of Vittiza's son, became aware too late of the reality of Muslim domination, and they did not dare to imitate Toledo by rebelling in turn. Once given, the lesson stuck. Fear seized the people and their leaders. In the frontier regions in northern Spain, where Islamic rule was not or not yet firmly established, panic set in, just as in the territories that were raided: in 730, for example, the Arabs ravaged Cerdagne and, as a warning to others, burned a bishop alive.[12]

That is how, in Spain itself, entire regions became uninhabited. A no-man's-land was taking shape, which was especially broad and long-lasting in the western half of the Iberian Peninsula. As of the middle of the eighth century, the Arabs evacuated the entire northwest of *Hispania*; the land that extended from the Cantabrian Mountains in the north to the Duero Valley in the south remained almost deserted for a long time: no one dared to remain in the area, and no one dared to settle there.

STRATEGY AND TACTICS

For the Christian regions extending beyond the no-man's-land, the critical months were those with milder weather. Indeed, from February on, the Muslims began to recruit and train the troops that would carry out the raids in infidel territory. As Jean Gautier-Dalché, the best contemporary French historian of medieval Castille, has written about the ninth and tenth centuries:

> When spring arrived, the Galicians, Asturians, Castilians and Basques lived in expectation of the *sa'ifa* (the summer campaign) of the Muslims. . . . No doubt these campaigns did not follow a regular cycle; sometimes they were separated by intervals of several years, sometimes they occurred every year, but the threat that they represented and the fear that they inspired were constant. The raiders pil-

laged, carried off livestock; anyone who fought and lost was massacred, men fit to bear arms were killed or sold into slavery, along with the women and children.[13]

Thus, when their sallies brought them as far as the Cantabrian Mountains and they penetrated the mountainous area, the Arabs began launching raids in Asturias—for instance, their capture of Oviedo in 794, a great *razzia* followed by their withdrawal.

To be sure, the forces employed in these cavalcades were small, and each incursion took place along a narrow front; the destruction was limited to a restricted area along the path followed by the troop. Furthermore, thanks to the network of castles which was gradually built up, more and more men and livestock could flee to safety. But even when there was a respite, the inhabitants of the zones that were hit by the cavalcades did not know how long it would last.

In the unfolding of each military operation, as in the overall strategy of the raids, the Arab method put the nerves and the patience of the enemies sorely to the test. In actual combat, the tactic is that of "attack and withdrawal," *al-karr wa-l-farr*, literally "attack and flight." One poem sings in celebrated verses the Bedouin horseman in battle: "He attacks, he flees, he comes back, he goes away, he returns again." And when, at last, he comes to win the ultimate advantage: "He is like a rock that the waters hurl down from the mountain heights."[14] Another tactic, which was sometimes combined with the raids, is described by "Anonymous of Cordova," a Christian who lived in Andalusia in the second half of the eighth century: "The Arabs often lie in ambush for the Europeans by hiding behind the footpaths."[15] This passage from a poem in Latin is characteristic, for the author correctly uses the word *Europenses* (Europeans) to designate those whom the Muslims attack, while he speaks of the latter as being "Arabs" and "Ishmaelites"; the terms suggest that the parties to this conflict are larger collectives. And never, at no time of year, was the Christian West certain of being safe from Muslim onslaughts, for although the *razzias* of the horsemen usually took place in the form of the summer campaigns (*sa'ifa*) that we mentioned, and the landings generally took place between April and October,[16] sometimes the "champions for the faith" launched an impromptu winter campaign: a *shatiya*.

THE COASTAL ISLANDS AND THE LAIRS

As the years went by, and the zones afflicted by these expeditions were reduced to certain parts of the Iberian Peninsula, the struggle took on a new aspect: the islands and landmarks along the coastlines, often set up on peninsulas, became for the Arabs, after being subjected to their control, their preferential points of departure for their incursions into the land of the infidels. The method, however, did not change: they arrived at night, made their way stealthily into the estates and the houses, and massacred those whom they found there or else carried them off into captivity.[17]

For decades they landed this way on the Balearic Islands, ravaging them and departing after obtaining a promise of tribute. They would then come back each year to collect it, and they went back on the offensive if the inhabitants were unwilling to pay. After an initial raid dating back, it seems, to 707, they returned often, then settled on the islands, in the year 902 or 903, to remain for more than three centuries. In the same way, from around 650 and repeatedly during the second half of the seventh century, and then during the eighth, they assailed Sicily, taking with them each time captives and booty. Then they conquered the island slowly, place by place, from 827 to 902, the year in which they seized Taormina, the last spot on the island that had eluded their grasp. During this time, starting in 806, they invaded the island of Pantelleria, where they took many prisoners, among them dozens of monks, whom they sold in Muslim Spain;[18] furthermore, in 870, they captured Malta. From 710 on, if not already in 707, they attacked Sardinia, which over the course of the eighth and ninth centuries suffered the same fate as the Baleares. Yet at the beginning of the tenth century, it had still not been incorporated into the Dar al-Islam and remained a zone subject to naval *razzias*. Only in 1015 did a Muslim troop effect a genuine conquest of this island, but it was not able to keep control there for more than a year.[19] Little is known about what happened on Corsica. Perhaps it was attacked beginning in 710, but it seems to have been the object of few raids throughout the eighth century; on the other hand, at the beginning of the eighth century it was invaded so often that the pope urged the Corsicans to abandon their island and invited them to take refuge in Rome. According to the *Liber pontificalis*, four thousand Corsican families reportedly arrived in this way in the Eternal City shortly before the year 829; but Moorish dominion is said to have lasted only a few decades, and before the end of the ninth century Roman noblemen, acting in the name of the pope, reportedly restored the island to Christendom.[20]

Increasingly, the little islands along the coasts served as Arab bases en route to the continent; occasionally they served also as strategic beachheads. In this way they captured the island of Ischia, opposite Naples, the first time in 812, then again around 844, as well as the promontory of Misena, on the western shore of the Bay of Naples. From there, they conquered Naples in 856. In similar fashion they took up positions on the point of Licosa, which closes off the Gulf of Salerno to the south, and around 845 on the Pontine Islands (the Archipelago of Ponza, *isole Ponziane*), off Gaeta, then on the coast of the peninsula itself, south of the town, at the mouth of the Garigliano, in a zone where they would remain entrenched approximately from 880 to 916. At the very southern tip of the Italian boot, they often landed in Calabria, gaining a foothold there in 813; they occupied it at least from 840 to 885, and landed there once more at the beginning of the tenth century. They took up positions in Tarento from 840 to 880, and in Bari from 841 to 871, and by means of these two bases controlled Puglia.

In Provence, during the period from around 890 to 973, they were masters of the mountains aptly named "*des Maures*" [of the Moors], as well as of the coast-line of the Gulf of Saint-Tropez, with maybe five tower-strongholds (Grimaud, Cogolin, Ramatuelle, Notre-Dame de Miremar, Gassin) and a control center in a fortified camp at La Garde-Freinet.[21] We have some good descriptions of this bastion of the Dar al-Islam: a forest overgrown with thorny trees and tangled brambles having sharp points. Far from cultivating the land and reclaiming the wilderness, the Arabs expanded the thickets and encouraged the spread of sharp-bladed grasses that grow in clumps, thus creating an impenetrable net of vegetation. If the inhabitants of Provence tried to attack that site, they had to contend with these plants, and could only make progress with difficulty, or else retrace their steps. The only access to and from this lair that the Arabs maintained was a narrow foot-path. They kept this sole pathway under constant surveillance and used it to carry out their raids.[22] Archaeological evidence suggests that the center of the outpost consisted of a stronghold with a floor plan in the shape of a half-moon; the main building was protected by defenses incorporated into the mountainous terrain and was partially surrounded by a moat, in places where the natural obstacles were insufficient.[23] At the same time they had at their disposal an additional base in Camargue, which they controlled as an island since 869. Furthermore their connections by sea extended as far as Muslim Spain, from which reinforcements arrived and to which a part of the booty taken in Provence was destined. In the area around Alicante and Cartagena, as well as at Alméria—which was then called Pechina—privateer bases were set up, run by especially enterprising sailors.[24]

This Moorish bastion in Provence illustrates very well how the Arab threat penetrated deeply into Christian territory. On every side, Provence was continually being ransomed, as it had already been during the few years in the eighth century when the first Arabs who arrived in Europe had controlled the Rhône River between Arles and Avignon and had built on its banks fortresses from which they sallied forth, harrowing the lands situated to the east of the river. Now, from Camargue and *des Maures*, they spread out in all directions. They reached the basin of Aix-en-Provence (whereupon the bishop fled)[25] and, as of 869, the region of Arles, whose archbishop they captured; they brought him to Camargue, negotiated his ransom, collected it, and returned a corpse belonging to the prelate, who had died meanwhile.[26] Toward the north, the east, and the northeast, they reached Gap and Grenoble (which they would seize for almost twenty years in the middle of the tenth century), advanced as far as the mountain passes in the Alps, which they controlled, making everyone who traveled through them pay a tax, in particular at the Grand-Saint-Bernard. From there, to the north, they arrived in Le Valais, up to the Abbey of Saint Gall, which has prompted some historians to say that they were "the masters of Switzerland" for a decade or so. Toward the east, they reached the Valley of Suse, then the Piedmont as far as Asti, and Liguria. In this way they captured, in 972, the great Abbot of Cluny, Saint Mayeul, who was returning from a trip to Rome, and they did not release him until they had received an enormous ransom hastily collected by the monks of Cluny.[27] Anyone who knows the significance that this religious order then had for Christendom can easily guess the repercussions that such an exploit would have had throughout the West.

In the same way, starting from the Gulf of Gaeta in 881, other Muslims had destroyed the inland monastery of Saint Vincent of Volturno, and most importantly, the ancient and prestigious Benedictine Abbey of Monte Cassino which, during a previous attack in 858, had managed to have itself spared by agreeing reluctantly to paying a large sum.

Thus, two and three centuries after their arrival in Spain, the Mohammedans were still making their presence and their power felt in many other areas of Europe.

THE MILITARY VALOR AND TECHNIQUE OF THE INVADERS

The prowess of the Arabs, terrifying as it was, also conferred upon them a certain prestige. That, no doubt, is why the history of their military dealings with the Westerners are sometimes embellished with strange stories of individual combat, series of challenges that such and such a champion of Islam and this or that valiant Christian warrior hurled at each other. These sorts of duels, which from time to time played themselves out along the front as enemy forces faced off, before they joined battle, reveal attitudes of a chivalrous type, some similarities in mentality and conduct between the Arabs and those of European stock.

The courage of the Muslims is evident, accentuated moreover by the certitude of the Koran: the man who dies fighting for the faith is assured of avoiding trial at the Last Judgment and of going directly to Paradise, whatever his sins may have been. In addition, their armaments were of top quality; it was modified, to be sure, over the course of the centuries, now resembling, now distinguishing itself from that of the Christian forces. But always the Muslim warrior—be he a cavalier or a foot soldier—knows very well how to wield the lance and the sword, the dagger or the cutlass, or else a double-bladed battle-ax, javelins and darts, sometimes a sling or a mace, a bow, and then the crossbow, and—during sieges—catapults. Rather than genuine armor, he wore a sort of mantle made out of metal plates and protected himself with an excellent shield. The best bucklers were made from the skin of the African antelope.[28]

As for the ships: they often transported horses so that the landing could be followed by a cavalry raid, but first and foremost they were well equipped. From the ninth century on, the arsenal of Seville provided them with naphtha jars. The highly flammable liquid was poured in, with a wick that was soaked in sulfur and saltpeter. These were veritable firebombs—one of them was discovered in the town of Hyères. The naphtha spread on impact and set fire to the enemy ship that was hit. It resembled even more the Greek fire of the Byzantines: aimed at the hostile vessels by means of siphons, it burned on the surface of the water. As one late-tenth-century Arab writer describes it: "It bursts from the vessel that throws it like a deep red fire; this flame seems to be a swift courser, dragging its tail over the waves . . . the flame collects in the troughs between the waves [*accolant les vagues*], as though they were made of oil and wicks were being dipped into it."[29]

UNEXPECTED ATTACKS

As Arab supremacy on the seas decreased, then gradually started to disappear from the eleventh century on, another period began: the Christian reconquest, which took all the islands from Islam by force, destroyed its coastal lairs, and reduced its presence in Europe, in the thirteenth century, to a modest one-twentieth of the Iberian Peninsula: the sultanate of Granada. Nevertheless, the danger at sea still threatened. The island of Majorca, which became Christian again in 1230, was often targeted by the believers in Allah: just as in the period when they reigned on the Mediterranean, so too in the thirteenth century and later, the Arabs carried out landings at night along the craggy, winding coastlines and slipped—on foot, now—across fields towards isolated houses. An impressive series of documents, recently discovered, establishes the fact that from 1380 to 1400, almost every year and in general several times a year, the alert was sounded on the southern coast of Majorca because Muslim ships were sighted; each time that they succeeded in eluding the notice of the lookout men who scanned the horizon from the top of the watchtowers, they neared the shore and several men landed, who carried out a *razzia* [raid], usually two or three hours before sunrise.[30]

The coastline of the peninsula, too, was still exposed. Around 1320, for example, a ship travelling from Collioure to Barcelona, which was carrying pilgrims from Roussillon to the Marian shrine of Montserrat, was captured. In 1397, a village on the coast of Valencia, Torreblanca, was devastated, more than one hundred of its inhabitants were led away as slaves, the church was profaned, the Muslims carrying off in particular of a silver ciborium filled with consecrated hosts, which sent shock waves through Christian Spain.[31] In 1543 the port of Palamos on the Costa Brava of Catalonia was completely destroyed, and so on. France, too, was sometimes attacked: at Agde, for example, in 1406, whereas in 1475 Fréjus was sacked, and fishermen from Provence were often captured by Islamic privateers, who now were beginning to be called "Barbary pirates." As for the Italian coasts and waters, they were even more frequently the scene of the bold adventures of these seamen who were very much drawn by Sicily, a land which had belonged to their ancestors for more than two centuries. In 1393 they landed at Syracuse and captured several of the inhabitants, among them the bishop; in the fifteenth century they returned there more than once. But they had many other destinations for their *razzias*, for example Capri in 1428, Malta in 1429, the island of Elba in 1443, and so on.

In summary, for more than half a millennium several European populations that had already been exposed to Muhammadan attacks in the eighth and ninth centuries, if not from as early as the seventh, had to suffer these bloody and destructive military strikes, which took place without warning, without anything resembling a "declaration of war."

THE RESPONSE OF THE EUROPEANS

The picture that we have been sketching until now has been unilateral, because we are trying to show the history of the effects of the Islamic invasion of Europe. But anyone who seeks a fuller understanding of the sufferings endured by the lands that were the object of these confrontations, should not forget that they were not due solely to the successive waves of Arabs; they were also caused by the response.

Now this response was launched sometime in the eighth century and only ended with the total victory in the southeast of Spain, in the late fifteenth century. Initially it was undertaken by the Franks, not only in Gaul (which became France), but also in Spain, where they were quickly seconded by Asturians and men of Navarre and Leon, Galicians, Catalans, and soldiers from Castile, Aragon, and Portugal, whereas in Italy this reaction was the work of the Normans rather than that of the Byzantines and the Lombards. Immediately after his victory in Poitiers in 732, Charles Martel turned back against the other line of Muslim expansion in Gaul: in 737 he took back Avignon from the Arabs and tried in vain to seize Narbonne from them. This was the beginning of a sorrowful road to Calvary for the region of Languedoc, as the French attacked and the Muhammadans resisted. After 750, Pepin the Short reconquered Nîmes, Maguelonne, Agde, and Béziers, conducted several unsuccessful campaigns against Narbonne, but finally entered the city in 759 at the latest. The inhabitants of Narbonne suffered much from the battles around their city and from the final siege, which lasted over a year. A certain solidarity even united at that time the native Christians and the Arab rulers, for the land viewed the Franks as new invaders; their Catholicity, no doubt, was not enough of a key to unlock the hearts of their coreligionists whom they had just rid of the Muslims. The Christians of Narbonne asked Pepin the Short to preserve the customary Visigoth law that had been theirs before the Islamic conquest, since the kingdom of the Visigoths had covered not only the Iberian Peninsula, but all of Languedoc. It had remained their legal code under Muslim rule, and the King of the Franks consented to letting them keep it. Afterward, the Arabs tried quite often to retake Narbonne; they arrived again at its gates by means of raids conducted throughout Cerdagne and Roussillon in 793, 794, and again in 841.[32]

The Franks, however, had already arrived south of the Pyrenees, in Girona, perhaps as early as 785. Charlemagne, in any case, appeared in person beneath the walls of Saragossa and at Pamplona, and during his lifetime his son Louis the Pious conquered Ausona-Vic in Catalonia, Huesca in Aragon, and finally Barcelona in 801, amidst some anti-Frankish hesitation manifested by adherents to the Visigoth tradition. The Arabs counterattacked everywhere. In 934 they returned to Barcelona,[33] temporarily recaptured it in 985, overran Catalonia once more around the year 1000, then in 1038 and again in 1045. Navarre, too, experienced new waves of Muslims during the first half of the tenth century. At the beginning of the eleventh, an Islamic influx reached as far as distant Galicia, which the first Arab conquerors had evacuated 250 years earlier! Nothing, however, was more terrible than the duel that pitted Normans against Arabs from 1060 to 1091, during the long Christian reconquest of Sicily. From the eleventh to the fourteenth century, while the Islamo-Christian front across the Iberian Peninsula was slowly shifting toward the south, interrupted by retreats to the north, the destructive cavalcades continued in one place or another—conducted by the champions of the Cross, now, as well as by the defenders of the Crescent. Sometimes new Islamic waves arrived from Africa and dashed themselves upon Europe. In the mid-twelfth century, for example, forces from Maghreb, united by the puritan Almohad movement, landed in Spain to reinforce the Muslim government there and to put an end to its weakness and its excessive tolerance toward the Christians. Thus in 1154 they seized the Andalusian town of Niebla, which still had a bishop—more than four centuries after the Arab conquest—and which had just put up a long resistance; they massacred the men of that unfortunate city and sold the women and children as slaves.[34]

THE OBSESSION OF THE WEST

During those centuries the West was obsessed by the possibility of a new Arab offensive and by the memory of their sustained struggles against them. Christendom was constantly tempted to repeat the words spoken in the seventh century by a Byzantine bishop: "Who could recount, therefore, the horror of an invasion by the Ishmaelites, [blasting Europe] like a burning, deadly *simoom* [a violent, dust-laden wind from African and Asian deserts]?"[35]

Profound echos of these tumultuous events, arrayed over several centuries, can be heard in the French *chansons de geste* [medieval epic poems], especially in the cycle about Guillaume d'Orange, *Orange-lez-Rhône*—poems twelfth-century Frenchmen loved ardently and sang passionately. We find in them a trace of uneasiness about the fate of the prisoners: "Not a day goes by without the Saracens buffeting and torturing them!" But above all, they repeat heart-stopping rumors about the arrival of the Muhammadans, sometimes by land, sometimes by sea: "Hark! Is that not horns and tambourines, flutes and trumpets?" And behold, "suddenly, the pagan fleet appears: its sails are so white, its keels so golden that the waves glow beneath them." In this poem resounds the uproar of the battles: a Muslim chief has just challenged a Christian baron and presents himself wearing a new *hauberk* [chainmail tunic], a pointed helmet firmly laced upon his head, and, hanging from his neck, a strong shield in which is carved a dragon with outspread wings; he carries at his side a broad sword and holds in his hand a lance "with an iron point poisoned with the venom of an asp. . . ." But then the battle breaks loose: the Saracen archers leap to the shore, and the Christians are struck with mortal wounds: "The javelins fall upon them like a heavy April rain." Soon many of them lie pierced by long arrows or sharp darts, while their horses stray without riders. . . . Then, the next day, a long convoy of Christian prisoners in shackles moves forward, driven by horsemen who tear at them with whips. And the poem utters its great rallying cry to the collective conscience of the West: "The Saracens now cover all the beaches. Will Christianity perish?"[36]

NOTES

For clarification of any citations, the reader is referred to the original, C. E. Dufourcq, "Les jours de razzia et d'invasion," in *La vie quotidienne dans l'europe medievale sous domination Arabe* (Paris: Hachette, 1978), pp. 15–34.

1. Devic (Dom) and Vessete (Dom), *Histoire générale du Languedoc* (Toulouse: Éd. Privat, 1882), vol. 1, p. 777n2.

2. Qur'an 7.4 and 10 (alternate numbering 7.3 and 9).

3. Ibn Hudayl, *L'ornement des âmes*, trans. Louis Mercier (Paris, 1939), p. 195. About this author, see Rachel Arié, *L'Espagne musulmane au temps des Nasrides* (Paris: Édit. E. de Boccard, 1973), p. 229n4.

4. Devic and Vessete, *Histoire générale du Languedoc*, vol. 1, p. 779; Millas Vallicrosa and José-Maria, "La Conquista musulmana de la región pirenaica," in Pirineos (1946), vol. 2, pp. 53–67.

5. J. Lacam, *Les Sarrasins dans le haut Moyen Age français* (Paris: Maisonneuve et Larose, 1965), p. 87; Bruzon de la Martinière, *Dictionnaire géographique et historique* (Paris, 1768), vol. 1, p. 554.

6. See Michel Rouche, "Les Aquitains ont-ils trahi avant la bataille de Poitiers?" *in Le Moyen Age* (1968), pp. 6–26.

7. Michele Amari, *Storia dei Musulmani di Sicilia* (Catane, 1933–1939), vol. 1, p. 506.

8. Ibid., pp. 544–45.

9. Ossian de Negri, *Storia di Genova* (Milan: Edizioni Aldo Martello, n.d.), p. 160; Lacam, *Les Sarrasins dans le haut Moyen Age français*, pp. 16–17.

10. Francisco-Javier Simonet, *Historia de los Mozarabes de España* (Madrid, 1897–1903; new ed., Amsterdam, 1967), p. 127.

11. Ibid., p. 163.

12. Ibid., p. 176.

13. Charles-Emmanuel Dufourcq and J. Gautier-Dalché, *Histoire économique et sociale de l'Espagne Chrétienne au Moyen Age* (Paris: Armand Colin, 1976), p. 21. Cf. Charles Pellat, trans., *Calendrier de Cordoue de l'an 961* (Leyde, 1961), p. 48.

14. Information kindly shared by Atallah Dhina, assistant professor of medieval history at the University of Algiers.

15. L'anonyme de Cordoue [The Anonymous Author of Cordova], (Paris: Éditions Tailhan, 1885), p. 40.

16. Claire Poussy, *La Conquête de la mer par les Arabes en Méditerranée occidentale* (master's thesis, University of Paris-Nanterre, 1975), p. 158.

17. Liutprand de Crémone, *Chronique* (Édition Petz [Monumenta Historica Germanica], 1839), p. 7.

18. Mohammed Talbi, *L'Émirat aghlabide* (Paris, 1966), p. 390.

19. Poussy, *La Conquête de la mer par les Arabes en Méditeranée occidentale*, p. 63.

20. Ibid., p. 57; cf. Taviani, *Histoire de la Corse*, pp. 143–45.

21. Lacam, *Les Sarrasins dans le haut Moyen Age français*, pp. 102, 141.

22. Liutprand, *Chronique*, p. 7.

23. Lacam, *Les Sarrasins dans le haut Moyen Age français*, p. 141.

24. Lévi-Provençal, *Histoire de l'Espagne musulmane* (Paris-Leyde, 1950–1953); the notes refer to the Spanish translation: vols. 4 and 5 of *Historia de España*, ed. Ramon Menendez Pidal (Madrid, 1950, 1957). The citation is from vol. 4, p. 226.

25. Cf. Paul-Albert Février, Paul-Albert, *Le Développement urbain en Provence, de l'époque romaine à la find du XIVe siècle* (Paris: Éditions E. de Boccard, 1964), p. 90.

26. Lacam, *Les Sarrasins dans le haut Moyen Age français*, pp. 16–17.

27. *Recueil des Historiens des Gaules et de la France* (Dom Bouquet, vol. 7, pp. 107, 131; vol. 8, pp. 186, 195).

28. The best recent study on the armament of the last Muslim armies in Spain—those of Granada—is found in Arié, *L'Espagne musulmane au temps des Nasrides*, pp. 250–56.

29. Marius Canard, "Textes relatifs à l'emploi du feu grégeois par les Arabes," *Bulletin des Études arabes, Algiers* 26 (1946): 6.

30. Alvaro Santamaria, "Olfo de Procida," in *Hispania* 25 (1965); Sevillano Colom, "Mercaderes y navegantes," in *Historia de Mallorca*, ed. Mascaro (Palma, 1971), p. 506; Font Obrador, *Historia de Llucmayor*, (Palma, 1972), vol. 1, pp. 350–63.

31. Ivars, *Dues creudades valenciano-mallorquines* (Valence, 1921), pp. 39–42.

32. Francisco Codera, "Narbona, Gerona y Barcelona bajo la dominación musulmana," in *Anuari—Institut d'Estudìs Catalans* (Barcelona, 1909–1910); Luis de Garcia Valldeavellano, *Historia de España*, 2nd ed. (Madrid, 1955), vol. 1, p. 433.

33. Pedro Chalmeta, Pedro, speech given at the Congrès d'Études sur les Cultures de la Méditerranée occidentale, Barcelona, September/October 1975.

34. Bishop Sébéos, cited by Alain Ducellier, *Le Miroir de l'Islam*, Julliard, collection "Archives" (Paris, 1971), pp. 23–24.

35. Simonet, *Historia de los Mozarabes de España*, p. 763.

36. Cf. the modern French adaptation of *La Légende de Guillaume d'Orange* by Paul Tuffrau (Paris: Éditions Piazza, 1920), pp. 83, 90, 101, 114, 123, etc.

40

MUSLIMS INVADE INDIA

K. S. Lal

My principal object in coming to Hindustan . . . has been to accomplish two things. The first was to war with the infidels, the enemies of the Mohammadan religion; and by this religious warfare to acquire some claim to reward in the life to come. The other was . . . that the army of Islam might gain something by plundering the wealth and valuables of the infidels: plunder in war is as lawful as their mothers' milk to Musalmans who war for their faith.

—Amir Timur

While studying the legacy of Muslim rule in India, it has to be constantly borne in mind that the objectives of all Muslim invaders and rulers were the same as those mentioned above. Timur or Tamerlane himself defines them candidly and bluntly while others do so through their chroniclers.

After its birth in Arabia, Islam spread as a conquering creed both in west and east with amazing rapidity. In the north and west of Arabia Muslim conquest was swift. The Byzantine provinces of Palestine and Syria were conquered by the newly converted Arabs after a campaign of six months in 636–637 CE. Next came the turn of the Sassanid empire of Persia which included Iraq, Iran and Khurasan. The Persians were defeated decisively in 637 and their empire was so overrun in the next few years that by 643 the boundaries of the Caliphate touched the frontiers of India. In the west the Byzantine province of Egypt had fallen in 640–641. and territories of Inner Mongolia, Bukhara, Tashkand, and Samarqand were annexed by 650. The Arab armies marched over North Africa and crossed into Spain in 709 CE. Thus within a span of about seventy years (637–709) the Arabs achieved astounding success in their conquests. Still more astounding was the fact that the people of these conquered lands were quickly converted to Islam and their language and culture Arabicised.

Naturally India, known to early Arabs as Hind va Sind, too could not escape Muslim expansionist designs, and they sent their armies into India both by land and sea. They proceeded along the then known (trade) routes—(1) from Kufa and

K. S. Lal, "Muslims Invade India," in *The Legacy of Muslim Rule in India* (New Delhi: Aditya Prakashan, 1992), pp. 80–114.

Baghadad, via Basra and Hormuz to Chaul on India's west coast; (2) from West Persian towns, via Hormuz to Debal in Sind; and (3) through the land route of northern Khurasan to Kabul via Bamian. But progress of Muslim arms and religion in India was slow, very slow. For, the declarations of objectives of Muslim invaders had not taken into account the potentialities of Indians' stiff and latent resistance. Caliph Umar (634–644 CE) had sent an expedition in 636–637 to pillage Thana on the coast of Maharashtra during the reign of the great Hindu monarch Pulakesin II. This was followed by expeditions to Bharuch (Broach) in Gujarat and the gulf of Debal in Sind. These were repulsed and Mughairah, the leader of the latter expedition, was defeated and killed. Umar thought of sending another army by land against Makran which at that time was part of the kingdom of Sind but was dissuaded by the governor of Iraq from doing so. The next Caliph Uthman (644–656) too followed the same advice and refrained from embarking on any venture on Sind. The fourth Caliph, Ali, sent an expedition by land in 660 but the leader of the expedition and most of his troops were slain in the hilly terrain of Kikanan (42 H/662 CE). Thus the four "pious" Caliphs of Islam died without hearing of the conquest of Sind and Hind.

The reason why the Arabs were keen on penetrating into Sind and always bracketed it with Hind, was that Sind was then a big "country"—as big as Hind in their eyes. According to the authors of Chachnama and Tuhfatul Kiram, the dominion of Sind extended on the east to the boundary of Kashmir and Kanauj, on the west to Makran, on the south to the coast of the sea and Debal, and on the north to Kandhar, Seistan, and the mountains of Kuzdan and Kikanan.[1] It thus included Punjab and Baluchistan, parts of Northwest Frontier Province and parts of Rajasthan. Muawiyah, the succeeding Caliph (661–680), sent as many as six expeditions by land to Sind. All of them were repulsed with great slaughter except the last one which succeeded in occupying Makran in 680. Thereafter, for twenty-eight years, the Arabs did not dare to send another army against Sind. Even Makran remained independent with varying degrees of freedom commensurate with the intensity of resistance so that as late as 1290 Marco Polo speaks of the eastern part of Makran as part of Hind, and as "the last Kingdom of India as you go towards the west and northwest."[2] The stubborn and successful opposition of Makran to the invaders was simply remarkable.

Meanwhile the Arabs had started attacking Hind from the northwest. Emboldened by their success in annexing Khurasan in 643 CE, the first Arab army penetrated deep into Zabul by way of Seistan which at that time was part of India, territorially as well as culturally. After a prolonged and grim struggle the invader was defeated and driven out. But in a subsequent attack, the Arab general Abdul Rahman was able to conquer Zabul and levy tribute from Kabul (653 CE). Kabul paid the tribute but reluctantly and irregularly. To ensure its regular payment another Arab general Yazid bin Ziyad attempted retribution in 683. But he was killed and his army put to flight with great slaughter. The war against Kabul was renewed in 695, but as it became prolonged it bore no fruitful results. Some attempts to force the Hindu king of Kabul into submission were made in the reign of Caliph Al-Mansur (745–775 CE), but they met only with partial success and the Ghaznavid Turks found the Hindus ruling over Kabul in 986 CE.

THE FIRST INVASION

In the south, attempts to subjugate Sind continued through land and sea. And in 712 a full-fledged invasion was launched after prolonged negotiations. The genesis of war was this. The king of Ceylon had sent to Hajjaj bin Yusuf Sakifi, the governor of the eastern provinces of the Caliphate, eight vessels filled with presents, Abyssinian slaves, pilgrims, and the orphan daughters of some Muslim merchants who had died in his dominions. These ships were attacked and plundered by pirates off the coast of Sind. Hajjaj demanded reparations from Dahir, the king of Sind, but the latter expressed his inability to control the pirates or punish them. At this Hajjaj sent two expeditions against Debal (708 CE), the first under Ubaidulla and the other under Budail. Both were repulsed, their armies were routed and commanders killed. Deeply affected by these failures, Hajjaj fitted out a third and grandiose expedition. Astrological prediction and close relationship prompted him to confer the command of the campaign on his seventeen-year-old nephew and son-in-law Imaduddin Muhammad bin Qasim.

It was the heyday of Arab power. Wherever Muslim armies went they earned success and collected spoils. "The conquest of Sind took place at the very time in which, at the opposite extremes of the known world, the Muhammadan armies were subjugating Spain, and pressing on the southern frontier of France, while they were adding Khwarizm to their already mighty empire."[3]

Under the auspices of Hajjaj, who, though nominally governor only of Iraq, was in fact ruler over all the countries which constituted the former Persian Empire, the spirit of more extended conquest arose. By his orders, one army under "Kutaiba penetrated . . . to Kashgar, at which place Chinese ambassadors entered into a compact with the invaders. Another army . . . operated against the king of Kabul, and a third (under Muhammad bin Qasim) advanced towards the lower course of the Indus through Mekran."[4] The reigning Ummayad Caliph Walid I (86–96 H/705–715 CE) was a powerful prince under whom the Khilafat attained the greatest extent of dominion to which it ever reached. But because of earlier failures of Ubaidulla and Budail, he was skeptical about the outcome of the venture. He dreaded the distance, the cost, and the loss of Muhammadan lives.[5] But when Hajjaj, an imperialist to the core, promised to repay the Caliph the expenses of the enterprise, he obtained permission for the campaign. That is how Muhammad bin Qasim came to invade Sind. The aims of the campaign were three: (1) Spreading the religion of Islam in Sind, (2) Conquest of Sind and extension of the territory of Islam, and (3) Acquisition of maximum wealth for use by Hajjaj and payment to the Caliph.[6]

The knowledge of Hajjaj and Muhammad bin Qasim about Sind and Hind was naturally not extensive. It was confined to what the sea-and-land traders had told about the people and wealth of what was known to them as Kabul va Zabul and Hind va Sind. About India's history, its hoary civilisation, its high philosophy, its deep and abiding faith in spiritualism and non-violence, they knew but little. One thing they knew was that it was inhabited by infidels and idol worshippers. And they knew their religious duty towards such unbelievers. Instruction and inspiration about this duty came to them from three sources—the Quran, the Hadis [Hadith], and the personal exploits of the Prophet. Every Muslim, whether educated or illiterate knew something about the Quran and the Hadis. The learned or the Ulama amongst them usually learnt the Quran by heart and informed their conquerors and kings about its teachings and injunctions. The Prophet's deeds, even the most trivial ones, too were constantly narrated with reverence. The one supreme duty the Quran taught them was to fight the infidels with all their strength, convert them to Islam and spread the faith by destroying their idols and shrines.

In Surah (Chapter) 2, ayat (injunction) 193, the Quran says, "Fight against them (the mushriks) until idolatry is no more, and Allah's religion reigns supreme." The command is repeated in Surah 8, ayat 39. In Surah 69, ayats 30–37 it is ordained: "Lay hold of him and bind him. Bum him in the fire of hell." And again: "When you meet the unbelievers in the battlefield strike off their heads and, when you have laid them low, bind your captives firmly" (47.4). "Cast terror into the hearts of the infidels. Strike off their heads, maim them in every limb" (8.12). Such commands, exhortations and injunctions are repeatedly mentioned in Islamic scriptures. The main medium through which these injunctions were to be carried out was the holy Jihad. The Jihad or holy war is a multi-dimensional concept. It means fighting for the sake of Allah, for the cause of Islam, for converting people to the "true faith" and for destroying their temples. Iconoclasm and razing other people's temples is central to Islam; it derives its justification from the Quranic revelations and the Prophet's Sunnah or practice. Muhammad had himself destroyed temples in Arabia and so set an example for his followers. In return the mujahid (or fighter of Jihad) is promised handsome reward in this world as well as in the world to come. Without Jihad there is no Islam. Jihad is a religious duty of every Muslim. It inspired Muslim invaders and rulers to do deeds of valour, of horror and of terror. Their chroniclers wrote about the achievements of the heroes of Islam with zeal and glee, often in the very language they had learnt from their scriptures.

Inspired by such belligerent injunctions, Muhammad bin Qasim (and later on other invaders) started on the Indian expedition with a large force. On the way the governor of Makran, Muhammad Harun, supplied reinforcements and five catapults. His artillery which included a great ballista known as "the Bride," and was worked by five hundred men, had been sent by sea to meet him at Debal.[7] Situated on the sea-coast the city of Debal was so called because of its Deval or temple. It contained a citadel-temple with stone walls as high as forty yards and a dome of equal height. Qasim arrived at Debal in late 711 or early 712 CE with an army of at least twenty thousand horse and footmen.[8] Add to this the Jat and Med mercenaries he enlisted under his banner in India.[9]

A glance at the demographic composition of Sind at this time would help in appraising the response of the Sindhians to Muhammad's invasion. At the lower rung of the social order were Jats and Meds. Physically strong and thoroughly uneducated they flocked under the standard of the foreigner in large numbers in the hope of material gain. They also supplied Muhammad with information of the countryside he had come to invade.[10] The majority of the Sindhi population was Buddhist (Samanis of chronicles), totally averse to fighting. Their religion taught them to avoid bloodshed and they were inclined to make submission to the invader even without a show of resistance. Then there were tribal people, like Sammas, to whom any king was as good as any other. They welcomed Muhammad Qasim "with frolicks and merriment."[11] Thus the bulk of population was more or less indifferent to the invasion. In such a situation it were only Raja Dahir of Sind, his Kshatriya soldiers and Brahman priests of the temples who were called upon to defend their cities and shrines, citadels and the countryside. This is the Muslim version and has to be accepted with caution.

When Muhammad began the invasion of Debal, Raja Dahir was staying in his capital Alor about 500 kilometers away. Dabal was in the charge of a governor with a garrison of four to six thousand Rajput soldiers and a few thousand Brahmans, and therefore Raja Dahir did not march to its defence immediately. All this while, the young invader was keeping in close contact with Hajjaj, soliciting the latter's advice even on the smallest matters. So efficient was the communication system that "letters were written every three days and replies were received in seven days,"[12] so that the campaign was virtually directed by the veteran Hajjaj himself.[13] When the siege of Debal had continued for some time a defector informed Muhammad about how the temple could be captured. Thereupon the Arabs, planting their ladders stormed the citadel-temple and swarmed over the walls. As per Islamic injunctions, the inhabitants were invited to accept Islam, and on their refusal all adult males were put to the sword and their wives and children were enslaved. The carnage lasted for three days. The temple was razed and a mosque built. Muhammad laid out a Muslim quarter, and placed a garrison of 4,000 in the town. The legal fifth of the spoil including seventy-five damsels was sent to Hajjaj, and the rest of the plunder was divided among the soldiers.[14] As this was the pattern of all future sieges and victories of Muhammad bin Qasim—as indeed of all future Muslim invaders of Hindustan—it may be repeated. Inhabitants of a captured fort or town were invited to accept Islam. Those who converted were spared. Those who refused were massacred. Their women and children were enslaved and converted. Temples were broken and on their sites and with their materials were constructed mosques, *khanqahs*, *sarais*, and tombs.

Muhammad bin Qasim next advanced towards Nirun, situated near modern Hyderabad. The people of Nirun purchased their peace. Notwithstanding its voluntary surrender, Muhammad destroyed the "temple of Budh" at Nirun. He built a mosque at its site and appointed an Imam.[15] After placing a garrison at the disposal of the Muslim governor, he marched to Sehwan (Siwistan), about 130 kilometres to the northwest. This town too was populated chiefly by Buddhists and traders. They too surrendered to the invader on condition of their remaining loyal and paying jiziyah.

Nirun's surrender alarmed Raja Dahir and he and his men decided to meet the invader at Aror or Rawar. Qasim was bound for Brahmanabad but stopped short to engage Dahir first. In the vast plain of Rawar the Arabs encountered an imposing array of war elephants and a large army under the command of Dahir and his Rajput chiefs ready to give battle to the Muslims. Al Biladuri writes that after the battle lines were drawn, a dreadful conflict ensued such as had never been seen before, and the author of the Chachnama gives details of the valiant fight which Raja Dahir gave "mounted on his white elephant." A naptha arrow struck Dahir's *howdah* [a seat or covered pavilion on the back of an elephant] and set it ablaze. Dahir dismounted and fought desperately, but was killed towards the evening, "when the idolaters fled, and the Musulmans glutted themselves with massacre." Raja Dahir's queen Rani Bai and her son betook themselves into the fortress of Rawar, which had a garrison of 15,000. The soldiers fought valiantly, but the Arabs proved stronger. When the Rani saw her doom inevitable, she assembled all the women in the fort and addressed them thus: "God forbid that we should owe our liberty to those outcaste cow-eaters. Our honour would be lost. Our respite is at an end, and there is nowhere any hope of escape; let us collect wood, cotton and oil, for I think we should burn ourselves and go to meet our husbands. If any wish to save herself, she may."[16] They entered into a house where they burnt themselves in the fire of jauhar thereby vindicating the honour of their race. Muhammad occupied the fort, massacred the 6,000 men he found there and seized all the wealth and treasures that belonged to Dahir.

Muhammad now marched to Brahmanabad.[17] On the way a number of garrisons in forts challenged his army, delaying his arrival in Brahmanabad. The civil population, as usual, longed for peace and let the Muslims enter the city. Consequently, it was spared, but Qasim "sat on the seat of cruelty and put all those who had fought to the sword. It is said that about six thousand fighting men were slain, but according to others sixteen thousand were killed."[18] Continuing his ravaging march northward, he proceeded to Multan, the chief city of the upper Indus with its famous Temple of Sun. Multan was ravaged and its treasures rifled. During his campaigns Muhammad bin Qasim concentrated on collecting the maximum wealth possible as he had to honour the promise he and his patron Hajjaj had made to the Caliph to reimburse to the latter the expenses incurred on the expedition. Besides the treasure collected from the various forts of the Sindhi King, freedom of worship to the Hindus could bring wealth in the form of pilgrim tax, jiziyah, and other similar *cesses* [taxes]. Hence, the temple of Brahmanabad was permitted to be rebuilt and old customs of worship allowed.[19] In Multan also temple worship more or less went on as before. The expenses of the campaign had come to 60,000 silver dirhams. Hajjaj paid to the Caliph double the amount— 120,000 dirhams.[20]

Muhammad bin Qasim set about organising the administration of the conquered lands like this. The principal sources of revenue were the jiziyah and the land-tax. The Chachnama speaks of other taxes levied upon the cultivators such as the *baj* and *ushari*. The collection of jiziyah was considered a political as well as a religious duty, and was always exacted "with vigour and punctuality, and frequently with insult." "The native population had to feed every Muslim traveller for three days and nights and had to submit to many other humiliations which are mentioned by Muslim historians."[21]

Muhammad bin Qasim remained in Sind for a little over three years.[22] Then he was suddenly recalled and summarily executed, probably by being sewn in an animal's hide, on the charge of violating two Sindhi princesses meant for the harem of the Caliph. Such barbaric punishments to successful commanders by their jealous masters were not uncommon in Islamic history.[23] However, the recall of Qasim was a God-sent relief to the Sindhis. After his departure the Arab power in Sind declined rapidly. Most of the neo-converts returned to their former faith. The Hindus had bowed before the onrush of the Muslim invasion; but they reasserted their position once the storm had blown over.[24] Denison Ross also says that after the recall of Muhammad bin Qasim, the Muslims retained some foothold on the west bank of the river Indus, but they were in such small number that they gradually merged into Hindu population. In Mansura (the Muslim capital of Sind) they actually adopted Hinduism.[25]

But Muslims or Islam did not disappear from Sind. A dent had been made in India's social fabric, and its wealth looted. Muslims who continued to retain the new faith remained confined mostly to cities, particularly Multan,[26] and Multan according to Al Masudi (writing about 942 CE) remained one of the strongest frontier places of the Musulmans.[27] Ibn Hauqal, who finished his work in 976 CE, also calls Multan a city with a strong fort, "but Mansura is more fertile and prosperous." He also says that Debal "is a large mart and a port not only of this but neighbouring regions." It would thus appear that by the tenth century the Muslim population had stabilized and integrated with the people of Sind. Ibn Hauqal writes: "The Muslims and infidels of this tract wear the same dresses, and let their beards grow in the same fashion. They use fine muslin garments on account of the extreme heat. The men of Multan dress in the same way. The language of

Mansura, Multan and those parts is Arabic and Sindian. . . ."[28] This, in brief, was the social change brought about in Sind after the introduction of Islam there.

Before closing the discussion on the Arab invasion of Sind, a few aspects of the campaign may be evaluated. As Andre Wink points out, "In contrast to Persia . . . there is no indication that Buddhists converted more eagerly than brahmans. The theory that Muslim Arabs were 'invited' to Sind by Buddhist 'traitors' who aimed to undercut the brahmans' power has nothing to recommend itself with. If Buddhists collaborated with the invaders, the brahmans did so no less. . . . There was in short, no clear-cut religious antagonism that the Arabs could exploit." At the same time, points out Gidumal, "It is extremely doubtful if Sind could have been conquered at all, had these (Sindhi) chiefs remained true to their king, and, curious as it may seem, it was ostensibly astrology that made traitors of them. For they said: 'Our wise men have predicted that Sind will come under the sway of Islam. Why then should we battle against fate?' " And lastly, the misleading belief in the tolerance and kindness of Muhmamad bin Qasim stands cancelled on a study of the campaign in depth. The statement of Mohammad Habib that "[a]lone among the Muslim invaders of India Muhammad Qasim is a character of whom a concentious Musalman need not be ashamed," and similar conclusions do not hold ground if his massacres, conversions and iconoclasm detailed in the Chachnama alone are any indicator.[29]

SECOND INVASION

A more terrifying wave of Islamic invasion came with Mahmud of Ghazni, three hundred years after the Arab invasion of Sind. During this period Islam was spreading in various regions outside India with varying degrees of success. Furthermore, the newly converted Turks, the slave protectors of the pious Caliphs, had carved out their own kingdoms at the expense of the Caliph's "empire." But to ensure their legitimacy as rulers they kept up a relationship of formal loyalty towards the Caliph. Such were the slave rulers Alaptigin and Subuktigin.

Amir Subuktigin (977–997 CE) made frequent expeditions into Hindustan, or more precisely into the Hindu Shahiya Brahman kingdom of Punjab which extended up to Kabul, "in the prosecution of holy wars, and there he conquered forts upon lofty hills, in order to seize the treasures they contained." When Jayapal, the ruling prince of the dynasty, had ascertained from reports of travellers about the activities of Subuktigin, he hastened with a large army and huge elephants to wreak vengeance upon Subuktigin, "by treading the field of Islam under his feet."[30] After he had passed Lamghan, Subuktigin advanced from Ghazni with his son Mahmud. The armies fought successively against one another. Jayapal, with soldiers "as impetuous as a torrent," was difficult to defeat, and so Subuktigin threw animal flesh (beef?) into the fountain which supplied water to the

Hindu army.[31] In consequence, Jayapal sued for peace. But for greater gains, Subuktigin delayed negotiations, and Jayapal's envoys were sent back. Jayapal again requested for cessation of hostilities and sent ambassadors, observing: "You have seen the impetuosity of the Hindus and their indifference to death, whenever any calamity befalls them, as at this moment. If, therefore, you refuse to grant peace in the hope of obtaining plunder, tribute, elephants and prisoners, then there is no alternative for us but to mount the horse of stern determination, destroy our property, take out the eyes of our elephants, cast our children into the fire, and rush on each other with sword and spear, so that all that will be left to you, is stones and dirt, dead bodies, and scattered bones."[32]

Jayapal's spirited declaration convinced Subuktigin "that religion and the views of the faithful would be best consulted by peace." He fixed a tribute of cash and elephants on the Shahiya king and nominated officers to collect them. But Jayapal, having reflected on the ruse played by the adversaries in contaminating the water supply leading to his discomfiture, refused to pay anything, and imprisoned the Amir's officers. At this Subuktigin marched out towards Lamghan and conquered it. He set fire to the places in its vicinity, demolished idol temples, marched and captured other cities and established Islam in them. At last Jayapal decided to fight once more, and satisfy his revenge. He collected troops to the number of more than one hundred thousand, "which resembled scattered ants and locusts." Subuktigin on his part "made bodies of five hundred attack the enemy with their maces in hand, and relieve each other when one party became tired, so that fresh men and horses were constantly engaged. . . . The dust which arose prevented the eyes from seeing. . . . It was only when the dust was allayed that it was found that Jayapal had been defeated and his troops had fled leaving behind them their property, utensils, arms, provisions, elephants, and horses."[33] Subuktigin levied tribute and obtained immense booty, besides two hundred elephants of war. He also increased his army by enrolling those Afghans and Khaljis who submitted to him and thereafter expended their lives in his service.

Subuktigin's son Mahmud ascended the throne at Ghazni in 998 CE and in 1000 he delivered his first attack against India in continuation of the work of his ancestor. During the three hundred years between Muhammad bin Qasim and Mahmud Ghaznavi, Islamic Shariat had got a definite and permanent shape in the four well-defined schools of Muslim jurisprudence—Hanafi, Shafii, Hanbali, and Malaki. The Quran and the six orthodox collections of Hadis were also now widely known. Mahmud himself was well-versed in the Quran and was considered its eminent interpreter.[34] He drew around himself, by means of lavish generosity, a galaxy of eminent theologians, scholars, and divines so that on his investiture, when he vowed to the Caliph of Baghdad to undertake every year a campaign against the idolaters of India, he knew that "jihad was central to Islam and that one campaign at least must be undertaken against the unbelievers every year." Mahmud could launch forth seventeen expeditions during the course of the next thirty years and thereby fulfilled his promise to the Caliph both in letter and in spirit of Islamic theology. For this he has been eulogized sky-high by Muslim poets and Muslim historians. He on his part was always careful to include the Caliph's name on his coins, depict himself in his Fateh-namas as a warrior for the faith, and to send to Baghdad presents from the plunder of his Indian campaign.[35] The Caliph Al-Qadir Billah in turn praised the talents and exploits of Mahmud, conferred upon him the titles of Amin-ul-millah and Yamin-ud-daula (the Right hand) after which his house is known as Yamini Dynasty.

Let us very briefly recapitulate the achievements of Sultan Mahmud in the usual fields of Islamic expansionism, conversions of non-Muslims to Islam, destruction of temples and acquisition of wealth in order to appreciate the encomiums bestowed upon him as being one of the greatest Muslim conquerors of medieval India. In his first attack of frontier towns in 1000 CE Mahmud appointed his own governors and converted some inhabitants. In his attack on Waihind (Peshawar) in 1001–1003, Mahmud is reported to have captured the Hindu Shahiya King Jayapal and fifteen of his principal chiefs and relations some of whom, like Sukhpal, were made Musalmans. At Bhera all the inhabitants, except those who embraced Islam, were put to the sword. At Multan too conversions took place in large numbers, for writing about the campaign against Nawasa Shah (converted Sukhpal), Utbi says that this and the previous victory (at Multan) were "witnesses to his exalted state of proselytism."[36] In his campaign in the Kashmir Valley (1015) Mahmud "converted many infidels to Muhammadanism, and having spread Islam in that country, returned to Ghazni." In the later campaign in Mathura, Baran, and Kanauj, again, many conversions took place. While describing "the conquest of Kanauj," Utbi sums up the situation thus: "The Sultan levelled to the ground every fort . . . and the inhabitants of them either accepted Islam, or took up arms against him." In short, those who submitted were also converted to Islam. In Baran (Bulandshahr) alone 10,000 persons were converted including the Raja. During his fourteenth invasion in 1023 CE Kirat, Nur, Lohkot and Lahore were attacked. The chief of Kirat accepted Islam, and many people followed his example. According to Nizamuddin Ahmad, "Islam spread in this part of the country by the consent of the people and the influence of force."

According to all contemporary and later chroniclers like Qazwini, Utbi, Farishtah, and so on, conversion of Hindus to Islam was one of the objectives of Mahmud. Wherever he went, he insisted on the people to convert to Islam. Such was the insistence on the conversion of the vanquished Hindu princes that many rulers just fled before Mahmud even without giving a battle. "The object of Bhimpal in recommending the flight of Chand Rai was that the Rai should not fall into the net of the Sultan, and thus be made a Musalman, as had happened to Bhimpal's uncles and relations, when they demanded quarter in their distress."[37]

Mahmud broke temples and desecrated idols wherever he went. The number of temples destroyed by him during his campaigns is so large that a detailed list is neither possible nor necessary. However, he concentrated more on razing renowned temples to bring glory to Islam rather than waste time on small ones. Some famous temples destroyed by him may be noted here. At Thaneshwar, the temple of Chakraswamin was sacked and its bronze image of Vishnu was taken to Ghazni to be thrown into the hippodrome of the city. Similarly, the magnificent central temple of Mathura was destroyed and its idols broken. At Mathura there was no armed resistance; the people had fled, and Mahmud had been greatly impressed with the beauty and grandeur of the shrines.[38] And yet the temples in the city were thoroughly sacked. Kanauj had a large number of temples (Utbi's "ten thousand" merely signifies a large number), some of great antiquity. Their destruction was made easy by the flight of those who were not prepared either to die or embrace Islam. Somnath shared the fate of Chakraswamin.[39]

The sack of Somnath in particular came to be considered a specially pious exploit because of its analogy with the destruction of idol of Al Manat in Arabia by the Prophet. This "explains the idolization of Mahmud by Nizam-ul-Mulk Tusi,[40] and the ideal treatment he has received from early Sufi poets like Sanai and Attar, not to mention such collectors of anecdotes as Awfi."[41] It is indeed noticeable that after the Somnath expedition (417 H/1026 CE), "a deed which had fired the imagination of the Islamic world," Caliph al-Qadir Billah himself celebrated the victory with great eclat. He sent Mahmud a very complimentary letter giving him the title of Kahf-ud-daula wa al-Islam, and formally recognizing him as the ruler of Hindustan.[42] It is also significant that Mahmud for the first time issued his coins from Lahore only after his second commendation from the Caliph.

Mahmud Ghaznavi collected a lot of wealth from regions of his visitations. A few facts and figures may be given as illustrations. In his war against Jayapal (1001–1002 CE) the latter had to pay a ransom of 250,000 dinars for securing release from captivity. Even the necklace of which he was relieved was estimated at 200,000 dinars (gold coin) "and twice that value was obtained from the necks of those of his relatives who were taken prisoners or slain. . . ."[43] A couple of years later, all the wealth of Bhera, which was "as wealthy as imagination can conceive," was captured by the conqueror (1004–1005 CE). In 1005–1006 the people of Multan were forced to pay an indemnity of the value of 20,000,000 (royal) dirhams (silver coin). When Nawasa Shah, who had reconverted to Hinduism, was ousted (1007–1008), the Sultan took possession of his treasures amounting to 400,000 dirhams. Shortly after, from the fort of Bhimnagar in Kangra, Mahmud seized coins of the value of 70,000,000 (Hindu Shahiya) dirhams, and gold and silver ingots weighing some hundred maunds, jewellery, and precious stones. There was also a collapsible house of silver, thirty yards in length and fifteen yards in breadth, and a canopy (mandapika) supported by two golden and two silver poles.[44] Such was the wealth obtained that it could not be shifted immediately, and Mahmud had to leave two of his "most confidential" chamberlains, Altuntash and Asightin, to look after its gradual transportation.[45] In the succeeding expeditions (1015–1020) more and more wealth was drained out of the Punjab and other parts of India. Besides the treasures collected by Mahmud, his soldiers also looted independently. From Baran Mahmud obtained 1,000,000 dirhams and from Mahaban a large booty. In the sack of Mathura five idols alone yielded 98,300 misqals (about 10 maunds) of gold.[46] The idols of silver numbered two hundred. Kanauj, Munj, Asni, Sharva, and some other places yielded another 3,000,000 dirhams. We may skip over many other details and only mention that at Somnath his gains amounted to 20,000,000 dinars.[47] These figures are more or less authentic as Abu Nasr Muhammad Utbi, who mentions them, was the Secretary to Sultan Mahmud, so that he enjoyed excellent opportunities of becoming fully conversant with the operations and gains of the conqueror. He clearly notes the amount when collected in Hindu Shahiya coinage or in some other currency, and also gives the value of all acquisitions in the royal (Mahmud's) coins. A little error here or there does in no way minimise the colossal loss suffered by north India in general and the Punjab in particular during Mahmud's invasions.

The extent of this loss can be gauged from the fact that no coins (*dramma*) of Jayapal, Anandpal, or Trilochanpal have been found.[48] The economic effects of the loss of precious metals to India had a number of facets. The flow of bullion outside India resulted in stabilizing Ghaznavid currency[49] and in the same proportion debasing Indian. Consequently, the gold content of north Indian coins in the eleventh and twelfth centuries went down from 120 to 60 grams.[50] Similarly, the weight and content of the silver coin was also reduced. Because of debasement of coinage Indian merchants lost their credit with foreign merchants.[51]

Outflow of bullion adversely affected India's balance of trade in another way. India had always been a seller of raw and finished goods against precious metals. She had "swallowed up precious metals, both from the mineral resources of Tibet and Central Asia and from trade with the Islamic world. . . ."[52] Now this favourable position was lost. Indian merchants were even unable to ply their trade because of disturbed political conditions. One reason which had prompted Anandpal to send an embassy to Mahmud at Ghazni with favourable terms to the Sultan (c. 1012) was to try to normalize trade facilities, and after an agreement "caravans (again) travelled in full security between Khurasan and Hind."[53] But the balance of trade for many years went on tilting in favour of the lands west of the Indus.

Besides, the Ghaznavids collected in loot and tribute valuable articles of trade like indigo, fine muslins, embroidered silk, and cotton stuffs, and things prepared from the famous Indian steel, which have received praise at the hands of Utbi, Hasan Nizami, Alberuni, and many others. For example, one valuable commodity taken from India was indigo. From Baihaqi, who writes the correct Indian word *nil* for the dyestuff, it appears that 20,000 mans (about 500 maunds) of indigo was taken to Ghazna every year. According to Baihaqi, Sultan Masud once sent 25,000 mans (about 600 maunds) of indigo to the Caliph at Baghdad, for "the Sultans often reserved part of this (valuable commodity) for their own usage, and often sent it as part of presents for the Caliph or for other rulers."[54]

Mahmud's jihad, or the jihad of any invader or ruler for that matter, was accompanied by extreme cruelty. The description of the attack on Thanesar (Kurukshetra) is detailed. "The chief of Thanesar was . . . obstinate in his infidelity and denial of Allah, so the Sultan marched against him with his valiant warriors, for the purpose of planting the standards of Islam and extirpating idolatry. . . . The blood of the infidels flowed so copiously that the stream was discoloured, and people were unable to drink it. . . . Praise be to Allah . . . for the honour he bestows upon Islam and Musalmans."[55] Similarly, in the slaughter at Sirsawa near Saharanpur, "The Sultan summoned the most religiously disposed of his followers, and ordered them to attack the enemy immediately. Many infidels were consequently slain or taken prisoners in this sudden attack, and the Musalmans paid no regard to the booty till they had satiated themselves with the slaughter of the infidels. . . . The friends of Allah searched the bodies of the slain for three whole days, in order to obtain booty. . . ."[56] With such achievements to his credit, there is little wonder that Mahmud of Ghazni has remained the ideal, the model, of Muslims—medieval and modern.

Mahmud Ghaznavi had destroyed the Hindu Shahiya dynasty of Punjab. Alberuni, who witnessed its extinction, says about its kings that "in all their grandeur, they never slackened in their ardent desire of doing that which is right, . . . they were men of noble sentiments and noble bearing."[57] On the other hand, the Ghaznavid rule in the Punjab was essentially militarist and imperialist in character, "whose sole business was to wage war against the Thakurs and Rajas (whereby) Mahmud sought to make the plunder of Hindustan a permanent affair."[58] The susceptibilities of the Indians were naturally wounded by an "inopportune display of religious bigotry," and indulgence in women and wine.[59] In such a situation, "Hindu sciences retired away from those parts of the country conquered by us, and fled to Kashmir, Benaras and other places."[60]

Sultan Mahmud's acts of Islamic piety like iconoclasm and proselytization were continued by future Muslim invaders and rulers and became a legacy of Muslim rule in India.

Mahmud was present with Subuktigin when the latter received the letter of Jayapal, cited above, emphasising the impetuosity of the Hindu soldiers and their indifference to death, and the Ghaznavids were convinced of their bravery and spirit of sacrifice. Years later Hasan Nizami, the author of Taj-ul-Maasir, wrote about them like this: "The Hindus . . . in the rapidity of their movements exceeded the wild ass and the deer, you might say they were demons in human form."[61] Mahmud Ghaznavi therefore employed Hindu soldiers and sent them, along with Turks, Khaljis, Afghans, and Ghaznavids against Ilak Khan when the latter intruded into his dominions.[62] We learn from Baihaqi's Tarikh-i-Subuktigin and "from other histories" that "even only fifty days after the death of Mahmud, his son dispatched Sewand Rai, a Hindu chief, with a numerous body of Hindu cavalry, in pursuit of the nobles who had espoused the cause of his brother. In a few days a conflict took place, in which Sewand Rai and the greatest part of his troops were killed; but not till after they had inflicted a heavy loss upon their opponents. Five years afterwards we read of Tilak, son of Jai Sen, commander of all the Indian troops in the service of the Ghaznavid monarch, being employed to attack the rebel chief, Ahmad Niyaltigin. He pursued the enemy so closely that many thousands fell into his hands. Ahmad himself was slain while attempting to escape across a river, by a force of Hindu Jats, whom Tilak had raised against him. This is the same Tilak whose name is written in the Tabqat-i-Akbari as Malik bin Jai Sen, which, if correct, would convey the opinion of the author of that work that this chief was a Hindu convert. Five years after that event we find that Masud, unable to withstand the power of the Seljuq Turkomans, retreated to India, and remained there for the purpose of raising a body of troops sufficient to make another effort to retrieve his affairs. It is reasonable therefore to presume that the greater part of these troops consisted of Hindus. "Bijai Rai, a general of the Hindus . . . had done much service even in the time of Mahmud."[63] Thus, employment of Hindu contingents in Muslim armies, was a heritage acquired by the Muslim rulers in India.

Another inheritance was acquisition of wealth from Indian towns and cities whenever it suited the convenience or needs of Muslim conquerors, raiders, or rulers. "It happened," writes Utbi, "that 20,000 men from Mawaraun nahr and its neighbourhood, who were with the Sultan (Mahmud), were anxious to be employed on some holy expedition in which they might obtain martyrdom. The Sultan determined to march with them to Kanauj. . . ."[64] In other words, the Ghazis, to whom the loot from India had become an irresistible temptation, insisted on Mahmud to lead them to India for fresh adventures in plunder and spoliation. Even when Muslim Sultanate had been established, Muhammad Ghauri determined on prosecuting a holy war in Hind in 602 H (1205 CE), "in order to repair the fortunes of his servants and armies; for within the last few years, Khurasan, on account of the disasters it had sustained, yielded neither men nor money. When he arrived in Hind, God gave him such a victory that his treasures were replenished, and his armies renewed."[65]

In brief, Mahmud was a religious and political imperialist through and through.[66] It took him more than twenty years to extend his dominions into Punjab. But he was keenly interested in acquiring territory in India,[67] and he succeeded in his aim. It is another matter that the peace and prosperity of Punjab was gone as suggested by Alberuni's encomiums of the Hindu Shahiya kings,[68] and it was superseded by despotism and exploitation.[69] Later chroniclers write with a tinge of pride that fourteen Ghaznavids ruled at Lahore and its environs for nearly two hundred years.[70] But there was progressive deterioration in their administration. However, the importance of his occupation of most part of the Punjab lies in the fact that Muslims had come to stay in India. And these Muslims helped in the third wave of Muslim onrush which swept northern India under Muhammad Ghauri.

THIRD INVASION

Muhammad Ghauri's invasion was mounted 150 years after the death of Mahmud Ghaznavi. How the Ghauris rose on the ashes of the Ghaznavids may be recapitulated very briefly. Sultan Mahmud died in Ghazni on 20 April 1030 at the age of sixty, leaving immense treasures and a vast empire. After his death his two sons, Muhammad and Masud, contested for the throne in which the latter was successful. Masud recalled Ariyaruk, the oppressive governor of Punjab, and in his place appointed Ahmad Niyaltigin. Niyaltigin marched to Benaras to which no Muslim army had gone before. The markets of the drapers, perfumers, and jewellers were plundered and an immese booty in gold, silver, and jewels was seized. This success aroused the covetousness of Masud who decided to march to Hindustan in person for a holy war. He set out for India by way of Kabul in November 1037. Hansi was stormed and sacked in February the next year, but the Sultan on return realised that the campaign had been counterproductive. During his absence Tughril Beg, the Seljuq, had sacked a portion of Ghazni town and seized Nishapur in 1037. Khurasan was rapidly falling into the hands of the Seljuqs and western Persia was throwing off the yoke of Ghazni. On the Indian side an army of 80,000 Hindus under Mahipal seized Lahore in 1043, but hastily withdrew on the approach of forces from Ghazni. But curiously enough it was neither the Seljuq danger nor the threat from the Indian side that uprooted the Ghaznavids. The Seljuqs were not interested in the hilly terrain of what is now called Afghanistan, and were spreading westward to Damascus and the Mediterranean. The power that actually ousted the Ghaznavids comprised the almost insignificant tribesmen of the rugged hills of Ghaur lying between Ghazni and Herat, with their castle of Firoz Koh (Hill of Victory). They had submitted to Mahmud in 1010 CE and had joined his army on his Indian campaigns. But when the power of the Ghaznavids declined they raised their head. To take revenge of the death of two brothers at the hands of the Ghazni ruler, a third, Alauddin Husain, carried fire and sword throughout the kingdom. The new Ghazni which had been built by Sultan Mahmud at the cost of seven million gold coins was burnt down by Husain (1151), which earned him the title of Jahan-soz (world burner). The very graves of the hated dynasty were dug up and scattered, "but even Afghan vengeance spared the tomb of Mahmud, the idol of Muslim soldiers." Near the modern town of Ghazni that tomb and two minarets (on one of which may still be read the lofty titles of the idol breaker) alone stand to show where, but not what, the old Ghazni was.

Alauddin, the world burner, died in 1161, and his son two years later, where-upon his nephew, Ghiyasuddin bin Sam, became the chief of Ghaur. He brought order to Ghazni and established his younger brother Muizuddin on the ruined throne of Mahmud (1173–1174). Ghiyasuddin ruled at Firoz Koh and Muizuddin at Ghazni. The latter is known by three names as Muizuddin bin Sam, Shi-habuddin Ghauri, and Muhammad Ghauri. Muhammad Ghauri, entered upon a career of conquest of India from this city.

Muhammad Ghauri was not as valiant and dashing as Mahmud, but his knowledge about India and about Islam was much better. He now possessed Alberuni's India and Burhanuddin's Hidaya, works which were not available to his predecessor invaders. Alberuni's encyclopaedic work provided to Islamic world in the eleventh century all that was advantageous to know on India.[71] It pro-vided information on Hindu religion, Hindu philosophy, and sources of civil and religious law. Hindu sciences of astronomy, astrology, knowledge of distance of planets, and solar and lunar eclipses, physics, and metaphysics are all discussed by him. Ideas on matrimony and human biology are not ignored. Hindu customs and ceremonies, their cities, kingdoms, rivers, and oceans are all described. But such a treatise, written with sympathetic understanding, evoked little kindness for the Indian people in the Muslim mind, for to them equally important was the Hidaya, the most authentic work on the laws of Islam compiled by Shaikh Burhanuddin Ali in the twelfth century. The Shaikh claims to have studied all ear-lier commentaries on the Quran and the Hadis belonging to the schools of Malik, Shafi, and Hanbal besides that of Hanifa.[72] These and similar works and the mil-itary manuals like the Siyasat Nama and the Adab-ul-Harb made the Ghauris and their successors better equipped for the conquest and governance of non-Muslim India. There need be no doubt that such works were made available, meticulously studied, and constantly referred to by scholars attached to the courts of Muslim conquerors and kings. Muhammad Ghauri led his first expedition to Multan and Gujarat in 1175. Three years later he again marched by way of Multan, Uchch, and the waterless Thar desert toward Anhilwara Patan in Gujarat, but the Rajput Bhim gave him crushing defeat (1178–79).[73] The debacle did not discourage Muhammad's dogged tenacity. It only spurred him to wrest Punjab from the Ghaznavid, and make it a base of operations for further penetration into Indian territory. He annexed Peshawar in 1180 and marched to Lahore the next year. He led two more expeditions,[74] in 1184 and 1186–87, before Lahore was captured. By false promise Khusrau Malik, a prince of the Ghaznavid dynasty, was induced to come out of the fortress, was taken prisoner and sent to Ghazni. He was murdered in 1201. Not a single member of the house of Mahmud Ghaznavi was allowed to survive and the dynasty was annihilated.

With Punjab in hand, Muhammad Ghauri began to plan his attack on the Ajmer-Delhi Kingdom. Muhammad bin Qasim had fought against the Buddhist-Brahmin rulers of Sind, and Mahmud of Ghazni against the Brahman Hindu

Shahiyas of the Punjab. But now fighting had to be done with the Rajputs who had by now risen everywhere to defend their motherland against the repeated invasions of foreign freebooters. Muhammad Ghauri had already tasted defeat at the hands of Solanki Rajputs in Gujarat. Therefore, he made elaborate preparations before marching towards the Punjab in 587 H/1191 CE. He captured Bhatinda, which had been retaken by the Rajputs from the possession of its Ghaznavid governor, and placed it in charge of Qazi Ziyauddin Talaki with a contingent of 1,200 horse. He was about to return to Ghazni when he learnt that Prithviraj Chauhan, the Rajput ruler of Ajmer-Delhi, was coming with a large force to attack him. He turned to meet him and encountered him at Tarain or Taraori, about ten kilometers north of Karnal. The Rajput army comprised hundreds of elephants and a few thousand horse. The Muslims were overwhelmed by sheer weight of numbers and their left and right wings were broken. In the centre, Muhammad Ghauri charged at Govind Rai, the brother of Prithviraj, and shattered his teeth with his lance. But Govind Rai drove his javelin through the Sultan's arm, and had not a Khalji Turk come to his immediate assistance, Muhammad would have lost his life.[75] His rescue and recovery helped save his army, which continued its retreat in good order. Prithviraj besieged Bhatinda but the gallant Ziyauddin held out for thirteen months before he capitulated.

At Ghazni, Muhammad severely punished the Ghauri, Khalji, and Khurasani amirs,[76] whom he held responsible for his defeat. Wallets full of oats were tied to their necks and in this plight they were paraded through the city. The Sultan himself was overcome with such shame that he would neither eat nor drink nor change garments till he had avenged himself. Next year he again started from Ghazni towards Hindustan with full preparations and with a force of 102,000 Turks, Persians, and Afghans. On reaching Lahore, he sent an ambassador to Ajmer and invited Prithviraj to make his submission and accept Islam. The arrogant message met with a befitting retort, and the armies of the two once more encamped opposite each other on the banks of Saraswati at Tarain, 588 H/1192 CE. The Rajput army was far superior in numbers. Prithviraj had succeeded in enlisting the support of about one hundred Rajput princes who rallied round his banner with their elephants, cavalry, and infantry. To counter such a vast number Muhammad Ghauri "adopted a tactic which bewildered the Rajputs." "Of the five divisions of his army, four composed of mountain archers, were instructed to attack (by turns) the flanks and, if possible, the rear of the Hindus, but to avoid hand to hand conflicts and, if closely pressed, to feign flight."[77] He delivered a dawn attack when the Indians were busy in the morning ablutions; the Hindus had to fight the invaders on empty stomach. Explaining the reason for the empty stomach Dr. Jadunath Sarkar writes: "It was the Hindu practice to prepare for the pitched battle by waking at 3 o'clock in the morning, performing the morning wash and worship, eating the cooked food (*pakwan*) kept ready before hand, putting on arms and marching out to their appointed places in the line of battle before sunrise. . . . But in the second battle of Naraina (also called Tarain, Taraori) the Rajputs could take no breakfast; they had to snatch up their arms and form their lines as best as they could in a hurry. . . . In vain did they try to pursue the Turko-Afghan army from 9 o'clock in the morning to 3 o'clock in the afternoon at the end of which the Hindus were utterly exhausted from the fighting, hunger and thirst."[78]

When Muhammad found that the Rajput army was sufficiently wearied, he charged their centre with 12,000 of the flower of his cavalry. The Rajputs were completely routed. Govind Rai was killed. Prithviraj was captured[79] in the neighbourhood of the river Saraswati and put to death. Enormous spoils fell into the hands of the Muslim army. With the defeat and death of Prithviraj Chauhan, the task of the invader became easy. Sirsuti, Samana, Kuhram, and Hansi were captured in quick succession with ruthless slaughter and a general destruction of temples and building of mosques. The Sultan then proceeded to Ajmer which too witnessed similar scenes. Through a diplomatic move, Ajmer was made over to a son of Prithviraj on promise of punctual payment of tribute. In Delhi an army of occupation was stationed at Indraprastha under the command of Qutbuddin Aibak, who was to act as Ghauri's lieutenant in Hindustan.[80]

Further extension of territory was in the logic of conquest. After Prithviraj, the power of Jayachandra, the Gahadvala chief, was challenged. Jayachandra had not come to the aid of Prithviraj hoping, perhaps, that after the defeat of the Chauhan ruler he himself would become the sole master of Hindustan. He was old and experienced, his capital was Kanauj, his dominion extended as far as Varanasi in the east, and he was reputed to be a very powerful prince of the time. The Sultan himself marched from Ghazni in 1193 at the head of fifty thousand horse and gave a crushing defeat to Jayachandra on the Jamuna between Chandwar and Etah, and Kanauj and Varanasi became part of Muhammad Ghauri's dominions. The usual vandalism and acts of destruction at Varanasi struck terror into the hearts of the people about the cruelty of the "Turushkas."

INCIDENTAL FALLOUT

The three waves of invasions under Muhammad bin Qasim, Mahmud of Ghazni, and Muhammad of Ghaur, took about five hundred years to establish Muslim rule in India. For another five hundred years Muslim sultans and emperors ruled over the country. Invaders are cruel and unscrupulous by nature and profession, and there is nothing surprising about the behaviour of these Muslim invaders. But what is unusual is that these invaders left almost a permanent legacy of political and social turmoil in India because their aims and methods were continued by Muslims even after they had become rulers.

It was the practice of the invaders to capture defenceless people and make them slaves for service and sale. We shall deal with this phenomenon by Muslim conquerors and rulers in some detail later on. Here we shall confine to the taking of captives in the early years of Muslim invasions and how it led to rather strange occurrences. Many captives taken by conquerors like Mahmud of Ghazni were sold as slaves in Transoxiana, and the Arab Empire. But many people also fled the country to save themselves from enslavement and conversion. Centuries later they are today known as Romanies or Gypsies and are found in almost all European countries like Turkey, Yugoslavia, Hungary, Italy, Austria, Germany, Spain, and Britain and even in America. In spite of being treated as aliens in Europe, in spite of persistent persecution (as for example in Germany under Hitler), they are today around 6 million.[81]

Their nomenclature is derived from *roma* or man. They also call themselves *Roma chave* or sons of Rama, the Indian God. Gypsy legends identifying India as their land of origin, Baro Than (the Great Land), are numerous and carefully preserved.[82] Researches based on their language, customs, rituals, and physiogonomy affirm that it is Hindus from India who form the bulk of these people in Europe. "They are remarkable for their yellow brown, or rather olive colour, of their skin; the jet-black of their hair and eyes, the extreme whiteness of their teeth, and generally for the symmetry of their limbs."[83]

It is believed that the first exodus of the Roma out of India took place in the seventh century which coincides with the Arab invasion of Sind. In about 700 CE they are found serving as musicians of the Persian court.[84] Mahmud Ghazni took them away in every campaign. Their biggest group, according to Jan Kochanowski, left the country and set off across Afghanistan to Europe in the twelfth and thirteenth centuries after the defeat of Prithviraj Chauhan at the hands of Muhammad Ghauri.[85] Even today "a visit to the new community of Romanies (Gypsies) in Skojpe in the southeastern part of Yugoslavia is like entering a village in Rajasthan."[86] "With regard to their language, a large number of the words in different dialects are of Indian origin . . . as their persons and customs show much of the Hindu character."[87] They are freedom loving and prefer tent life. Their marriages are simple, Indian type. There is no courtship before marriage. Taking *parikrama* (rounds) around the fire is wholly binding, just as in India. Originally they were vegetarians. Holi and other Hindu festivals are celebrated in Serbia and Spain. Most of them have converted to Christianity but maintain Shiva's Trisula (trident)—symbol of God's three powers of desire, action, and wisdom. Gypsies are divided into caste groups who live in separate areas or mohallas. There are 149 sub-castes among the Bulgarian gypsies. Their professions comprise working in wood and iron; making domestic utensils, mats, and baskets and practising astrology; telling fortunes and sometimes indulging in tricks. Their talent for music is remarkable.[88] Their dance and music is voluptuous, of the Indian *dom-domni* type. A classic example is the Gypsy women's snake dance, which is still performed in Rajasthan. Their language has many

Indian words. They have *manush* for man, *zott* for Jat, *Yak, dui, trin* for ek, *do, tin*. They have *lovari* for *lohari* (smith), *Sinti* for *Sindhi, sui* for needle, *sachchi* for true, and *duur ja* for go away. We may close with the old Gypsy saying: "Our caravan is our family, and the world is our family which is a direct adaptation of the Sanskrit saying Vasudhaiva Kutumbakam."[89]

The Romanies or Gypsies left India or were taken away from here centuries ago. Their history comes down to our own times and is extremely absorbing. But their transplantation cannot now be counted as a legacy of Muslim conquest or rule in India. However, there are other activities of Muslim conquerors and rulers like converting people to Islam or breaking idols and temples which are still continuing and which therefore form part of Muslim heritage. We shall now turn to these.

NOTES

For clarification of any citations, the reader is referred to the original, K. S. Lal, "Muslims Invade India," in *The Legacy of Muslim Rule in India* (New Delhi: Aditya Prakashan, 1992), pp. 350–366.

1. Chachnama, trans. Mirza Kalichbeg Fredenbeg (Karachi, 1900), p. 11 and n.

2. Sir Henry Yule and H. Cordier, *The Book of Sir Marco Polo*, 2 vols. (New York, 1903), vol. 2, pp. 334–36, 359; Alberuni, *Alberuni's India*, English trans. Edward Sachau, 2 vols. (London, 1910), vol. 1, p. 208; Biladuri, E and D, vol. 1, p. 456.

3. Muhammad Qasim Hindu Shah Farishtah, a seventeenth-century historian, basing his researches (Khama-i-Tahqiq) on the works of Khulasat-ul-Hikayat, Hajjaj Nama, and the history of Haji Muhammad Qandhari, says that before the advent of Islam Indian Brahmans used to travel to and fro by sea to the temples of Ka'aba to administer worship of the idols there, and there was constant movement of people between Ceylon, India, and the countries of what is now called West Asia (Farishtah, vol. 2, p. 311); Biladuri, *Futuh-ul-Buldan*, E and D, vol. 1, pp. 118–19; Elliot, appendix, E and D, vol. 1, pp. 414–84, citing Chachnama, p. 432.

4. Elliot, appendix, pp. 428–29.

5. Ibid., p. 431, citing Abul Fida, Chachnama, and Tuhfat-ul-Kiram.

6. Al Biladuri, p. 123; Chachnama, p. 206.

7. Al Biladuri, *Futuh-ul-Buldan*, trans. E and D, vol. 1, pp. 119–20.

8. For details see K. S. Lal, *Early Muslims in India*, p. 14.

9. Al Biladuri, *Futuh-ul-Buldan*, p. 119. Also E and D, vol. 1, appendix, p. 434.

10. Elliot, appendix, E and D, p. 435.

11. Chachnama, p. 191.

12. Al Biladuri, p. 119; Elliot, appendix, p. 436.

13. Chachnama, E and D, vol. 1, pp. 188, 189.

14. W. Haig, C.H.I., vol. 3, p. 3.

15. Al Biladuri, p. 121; Chachnama, pp. 157–58; Elliot, appendix, E and D, I, p. 432. See Chachnama, pp. 85, 113, 128, for forcible conversions; pp. 83, 87, 155, 161, 173–74, for massacres; pp. 190, 196, for enslavement; pp. 92, 99, 100, 190, for destruction of temples and construction of mosques at their sites.

16. Chachnama, pp. 122, 172.

17. Elliot's note on Brahmanabad is worthy of perusal (appendix, E and D, vol. 1, pp. 369–74).

18. Mohammad Habib, "The Arab Conquest of Sind," in *Politics and Society During the Early Medieval Period being the collected works of M. Habib*, ed. K. A. Nizami, vol. 2, pp. 1–35. Al Biladuri, p. 122 has 8,000 or 26,000.

19. Chachnama, pp. 185–86.

20. Chachnama, p. 206. Al Biladuri, however, has 60 million and 120 million, respectively (E and D, vol. 1, p. 123). See also Elliot, appendix, vol. 1, p. 470 and n.

21. Ishwari Prasad, *Medieval India* (1940 ed.), p. 63.

22. Chachnama, pp. 185–86.

23. Exactly at this very point of time a similar story of success and punishment was being enacted at the other end of the then known world. Musa, the governor of North Africa, sent his commander Tariq with 7,000 men to march into the Iberian peninsula. Tariq landed at Gibraltar and utterly routed the armies of Visigothic King Roderick in July 711. He then headed towards Toledo, the capital, and attacked Cordova. Jealous of the unexpected success of his lieutenant, Musa himself with 10,000 troops rushed to Spain in June 712. It was in or near Toledo that Musa met Tariq. Here he whipped his subordinate and put him in chains for refusing to obey orders to halt in the early stage of the campaign. Musa nevertheless continued with the conquest himself. Ironically enough, in the autumn of the same year the Caliph Al-Walid in distant Damuscus recalled Musa. Musa entered Damascus in February 715. Al-Walid was dead by then, and his brother and successor Sulaiman humiliated Musa, made him stand in the sun until exhausted, and confiscated his property. The last we hear of the aged conqueror of Africa and Spain ("he affected to disguise his age by colouring with a red powder the whiteness of his beard"), is as a beggar in a remote village near Mecca (P. K. Hitti, *The Arabs: A Short History* [London, 1948], pp. 62–67; Edward Gibbon, *Decline and Fall of the Roman Empire*, Everyman's Library ed., 2 vols. [n.d.], vol. 2, pp. 769–79).

24. Al Biladuri, p. 126. Also cf. Idrisi, p. 89.

25. Denison Ross, *Islam*, p. 18. Also K. S. Lal, *Indian Muslims: Who Are They?* (New Delhi, 1990), pp. 3–4.

26. K. S. Lal, *Growth of Muslim Population in Medieval India* (Delhi, 1973), p. 99.

27. Muruj-ul-Zuhab, p. 20. Also Idrisi, *Nuzhat-ul-Mushtaq*, p. 82.

28. Ashkalal-ul Bilad, pp. 36, 37.

29. Andre Wink, *Al-Hind*, vol. 1, p. 151, and reference. Dayaram Gidumal's introduction to Chachanama, trans. Kalichbeg, p. vii; M. Habib, *Collected Works*, ed. K. A. Nizami, vol. 2, pp. 1–35, esp. p. 32; Lal, *Early Muslims in India*, pp. 21–25.

30. Utbi, Tarikh-i-Yamini, E and D, vol. 2, pp. 20–21.

31. Ibid., p. 20; Ufi, *Jamiul Hikayat*, p. 181. Elliot, appendix, on the authority of Abul Fazl, specifically mentions animal's flesh, p. 439. The trick was common. The Fort of Sevana was captured by Alauddin Khalji by contaminating the fort's water supply by throwing a cow's head into the tank. See Lal, *Khaljis*, p. 115.

32. Utbi, op. cit., p. 21.

33. Ibid., pp. 22–23.

34. C. E. Bosworth, *The Ghaznavids* (Edinburgh, 1963), p. 129; Utbi, *Kitab-i-Yamini*, trans. James Reynolds (London, 1885), pp. 438–39 and n.

35. S. H. Hodivala, *Studies in Indo-Muslim History* (Bombay, 1939).

36. For conversions at various places under Mahmud, see Utbi, *Kitab-i-Yamini*, pp. 451–52, 455, 460, 462–63; and *Tarikh-i-Yamini*, E and D, vol. 2, pp. 27, 30, 33, 40, 42, 43, 45, 49. Also appendix in E and D, vol. 2, pp. 434–78.

37. No reference (omitted in original text).

38. Utbi, E and D, p. 44; Farishtah, vol. 1, p. 29, for temples at Mathura.

39. Alberuni, vol. 2, p. 103.

40. Siyasat Nama (ed. Shefer), pp. 77–80, 138–56.

41. Aziz Ahmad, *Studies in Islamic Culture in the Indian Environment* (Oxford, 1964), p. 79. Shah Waliullah considered Mahmud as the greatest ruler after Khilafat-i-Khass. He argues that "in reference to Mahmud historians failed to recognize that his horoscope had been identical to the Prophet's and that this fact had abled him to obtain significant victories in wars to propagate Islam" (Rizvi, *History of Sufism*, vol. 2, p. 382, citing from Shah Waliullah, *Qurrat al-aynain fi tafil al-shaykhayan* [Delhi, 1893], p. 324).

42. Farishtah, vol. 1, pp. 30, 35.

43. Utbi, E and D, Reynolds, p. 282.

44. The house was quite large, covering an area of about a thousand square feet. Hodivala also says that the canopy must have been what the old annalists of Gujarat call a Mandapika. It was a folding pavilion for being used in royal journeys, and not a throne (S. H. Hodivala, *Studies in Indo-Muslim History* [Bombay, 1939], p. 143).

45. On return to Ghazni Mahmud ordered this impressive treasure to be displayed in the court-yard of his palace. "Ambassadors from foreign countries including the envoy from Taghan Khan, king of Turkistin, assembled to see the wealth . . . which had never been accumulated by kings of Persia or of Rum" (Utbi, Reynolds, pp. 342–43; E and D, vol. 2, p. 35).

46. Utbi, E and D, vol. 2, p. 45, Reynolds, pp. 455–57. I have elsewhere calculated that 70 misqals were equal to one seer of 24 tolas in the Sultanate period. See my *History of the Khaljis*, 2nd ed. (Bombay, 1967), pp. 199–200. On the basis of the above calculation the weight of five gold idols comes to 10.5 maunds, each idol being of about 2 maunds.

47. Bosworth, *The Ghaznavids*, p. 78.

48. A. Cunningham, *Coins of Medieval India* (London, 1894; repr., Varanasi: Indological Book House, 1967), p. 65.

49. *J.R.A.S.* (1848): 289, 307, 311; *J.R.A.S.* (1860): 156; Bosworth, pp. 78–79.

50. A. S. Altekar in *Journal of the Numismatic Society of India*, II, p. 2.

51. Muhammad Ufi, *Jami-ul Hikayat*, E and D, vol. 2, p. 188; Thomas in *J.R.A.S.* 17: 181.

52. Bosworth, op. cit., pp. 79, 149–52. Also Khurdadba, E and D, vol. 1, p. 14, and Jami-ul-Hikayat, E and D, vol. 2, p. 68.

53. Utbi, op. cit., Reynolds, p. 362; E and D, vol. 2, p. 36.

54. Bosworth, op. cit., pp. 76, 120, 126; Hodivala, op. cit., pp. 139–40, 176; Alberuni, vol. 1, p. 61; Fakhr-i-Mudabbir, *Adab-ul-Harb*, trans. in Rizvi, *Adi Turk Kalin Bharat* (Aligarh, 1965), p. 258; Utbi, op. cit., p. 33; Taj-ul-Maasir, E and D, vol. 2, p. 227.

55. Utbi, E and D, vol. 2, pp. 40–41.

56. Ibid., pp. 49–50.

57. Alberuni, vol. 2, p. 13.

58. M. Habib, *Mahmud of Ghaznin*, p. 95.

59. C.H.I., vol. 3, p. 28.
60. Alberuni, vol. 1, p. 22.
61. E and D, vol. 2, p. 208.
62. Utbi, op. cit., p. 32.
63. E and D, vol. 2, p. 60.
64. Utbi, E and D, vol. 2, p. 41; Reynolds, p. 450.
65. Juwaini, *Tarikh-i-Jahan Kusha*, E and D, vol. 2, p. 389.
66. Hasan Nizami, *Taj-ul-Maasir*, E and D, vol. 2, pp. 215–17.
67. Utbi, Reynolds, p. xxv.
68. Alberuni, vol. 2, p. 13.
69. Bosworth, op. cit., p. 59; M. Habib, Sultan Mahmud of Ghaznin, p. 95.
70. Badaoni, *Muntakkab-ut-Tawarikh*, Bib. Ind. Text (Calcutta, 1868–69), vol. 1, p. 8; Farishtah, vol. 1, p. 21.
71. Hazard, *Atlas of Islamic History*, p. 42.
72. It was translated into English by Charles Hamilton of the East India Company and published in England in 1791. It is easily available in a recent reprint.
73. Minhaj, p. 116; *Indian Antiquary* (1877): 186–89.
74. Habibullah, *The Foundation of Muslim Rule in India*, p. 57.
75. Minhaj, p. 118; Farishtah, vol. 1, p. 57.
76. Habibullah, op. cit., pp. 60–61.
77. C.H.I., vol. 3, p. 40; Farishtah, vol. 1, p. 58.
78. *Hindustan Standard*, March 14, 1954, later reproduced in Jadunath Sarkar, *Military History of India*.
79. Minhaj, *Tabqat-i-Nasiri*, p. 120.
80. Fakhr-i-Mudabbir, *Tarikh-i-Fakhruddin Mubarakshak*, p. 23; Farishtah, p. 58. Hasan Nizami's account in *Taj-ul-Maasir* is detailed.
81. D. P. Singhal, *India and the World Civilization* (Delhi, 1972), vol. 1, p. 234.
82. Ibid., p. 246.
83. *Modern Cyclopaedia*, vol. 4, p. 319.
84. *Hinduism Today*, Malaysia ed., August 1990, p. 17.
85. Cited in Singhal, op. cit., p. 241.
86. Rakesh Mathur in *Hinduism Today*, August 1990, p. 1.
87. *Modern Cyclopaedia*, vol. 4, p. 319.
88. Arnold, *The Legacy of Islam*, p. 17.
89. Singhal, *India and the World Civilization*, pp. 234–66, esp. pp. 249, 255, 266; Rakesh Mathur, "Hindu Origins of Romani Nomads," in *Hinduism Today*, August/September 1990.

41

JIHAD UNDER THE TURKS AND JIHAD UNDER THE MUGHALS

K. S. Lal

JIHAD UNDER THE TURKS

The chroniclers of the early Turkish rulers of India take pride in affirming that Qutbuddin Aibak was a killer of *lakhs* [i.e., one hundred thousand] of infidels. Leave aside enthusiastic killers like Alauddin Khalji and Muhammad bin Tughlaq, even the "kind-hearted" Firoz Tughlaq killed more than a *lakh* of Bengalis when he invaded their country. Timur Lang or Tamerlane says he killed a hundred thousand infidel prisoners of war in Delhi.[1] He built victory pillars from severed heads at many places. These were acts of sultans. The nobles were not lagging behind. One Shaikh Daud Kambu is said to have killed 20,000 with his dagger.[2] The Bahmani sultans of Gulbarga and Bidar considered it meritorious to kill a hundred thousand Hindu men, women, and children every year.[3] These wars were fought in the true spirit of Jihad—the total annihilation or conversion of the non-Muslims. It was in this spirit that some ulema requested Sultan Iltutmish (1210–1236) to confront the Hindus with a choice between Islam and death.

He advised them patience as dictated by the compulsions of the situation. Iltutmish fought against Nasiruddin Qubacha and Tajuddin Yaldoz. But his wars against them are not called Jihad. Jihad was against non-Muslims. Hence the insistence of the ulema on this religious duty. In a hundred years' time Muslim ambition paved the way for confident optimism. During the reigns of Nasiruddin Mahmud and Ghiyasuddin Balban (1246–1286) extensive campaigns in southern Uttar Pradesh, Bundelkhand, and Baghelkhand as well as Gwalior, Narwar, Chanderi, and Malwa were undertaken. In Katehar and Mewat there were systematic

"Jihad under the Turks" and "Jihad under the Mughals," from *Theory and Practice of Muslim State in India* (New Delhi: Aditya Prakashan, 1999), pp. 62–68.

massacres of Rajputs and Mewatis in the true spirit of Jihad. While the numbers of the enslaved boosted Muslim demography, massacres were ordered on selective basis—only of Hindus.[4] Similar scenes were witnessed during Alauddin Khalji's invasion of Gujarat in 1299, where massacres by his generals in Anhilwara, Cambay, Asavalli, Vannanthali, and Somnath earned him, according to Rasmala, the sobriquet of Khuni. Also in Chittor, where Alauddin ordered a massacre of 30,000 Hindus. The comment of Amir Khusrau on this genocide (keeping in mind the population of the period) is significant. "Praise be to God!" writes he in his Khazain-ul-Futuh (completed in 1311 CE),

> that he (the sultan) so ordered the massacre of all the chiefs of Hindustan out of the pale of Islam, by his infidel-smiting sword, that if in this time it should by chance happen that a schismatic should claim his right, the pure Sunnis would swear in the name of this Khalifa of God, that heterodoxy has no right.[5]

Shorn of its verbosity his comment on the horrible massacre only points to the fact that except for Sunni Muslims no other people could be permitted to live in India. Four years later he wrote in his *Ashiqa*—

> Happy Hindustan, the splendour of Religion, where the Law finds perfect honour and security. The whole country, by means of the sword of our holy warriors, has become like a forest denuded of its thorns by fire. . . . Islam is triumphant, idolatry is subdued. Had not the Shariat Law granted exemption from death by the payment of poll-tax, the very name of Hind, root and branch, would have been extinguished.[6]

Ziyauddin Barani, a contemporary of Amir Khusrau, writes in a similar spirit. He quoted the disposition of Qazi Mughisuddin before Alauddin that the Hindus were the greatest among the enemies of God and the religion of the Prophet [7] and so needed to be eliminated. It is in a similar vein that he advocates an all-out Jihad against the Hindus in his *Fatawa-i-Jahandari*.[8] So whether it was a Sufi of the stature of Amir Khusrau about whose liberal credentials every secularist swears, or it was an orthodox Maulana like Ziyauddin Barani, the position of the Hindu idolaters in the Islamic law was given by them fairly correctly.[9] They deserved to be exterminated through Jihad. If the sultans conceded to the Hindus the status of Zimmis, it was because of the compulsion of the Indian situation.

That is how wars against Hindus were no ordinary wars, casualties no common casualties, and massacres were massacres of extermination. This thirst for extermination was also whetted by the resistance of "the enemies of God" with their determination for survival. The rite of Jauhar killed the women, the tradition of not deserting the field of battle made Rajputs and others die fighting in large numbers. When Malwa was attacked (1305), its Raja is said to have possessed 40,000 horse and 100,000 foot.[10] After the battle, "so far as human eye could see, the ground was muddy with blood." Many cities of Malwa like Mandu, Ujjain, Dharanagri, and Chanderi were captured after great resistance. The capitulation of Sevana and Jalor in Rajasthan (1308, 1311) were accompanied by massacres after years of prolonged warfare. In Alauddin's wars in the South, similar killings took place, especially in Dwarsamudra and Tamil Nadu.[11] His successor Mubarak Khalji once again sacked Gujarat and Devagiri.

Under Muhammad Tughlaq, wars and rebellions knew no end. His expeditions to Bengal, Sindh, and the Deccan, as well as ruthless suppression of twenty-two rebellions, meant only depopulation in the thirteenth and first half of the fourteenth century.[12] For one thing, in spite of constant efforts no addition of territory could be made by Turkish rulers from 1210 to 1296; for another the Turkish rulers were more ruthless in war and less merciful in peace. Hence the extirpating massacres of Balban, and the repeated attacks by others on regions already devastated but not completely subdued. Bengal was attacked by Bakhtiyar, by Balban, by Alauddin, and by all the three Tughlaqs—Ghiyas, Muhammad, and Firoz. Malwa and Gujarat were repeatedly attacked and sacked. Almost every Muslim ruler invaded Rantambhor until it was subjugated by Alauddin Khalji (1301, again temporarily). Gwalior, Katehar, and Avadh regions were also repeatedly attacked. Rajputana, Sindh, and Punjab (also because of the Mongol invasions) knew no peace. In the first decade of the fourteenth century Turkish invaders penetrated into the South, carrying death and destruction. Later on Bahmani and Vijayanagar kingdoms also came to grips with each other. Mulla Daud of Bidar vividly describes the war between Muhammad Shah Bahmani and the Vijayanagar King in 1366 in which "Farishtah computes the victims on the Hindu side alone as numbering no less than half a million."[13] Muhammad also devastated the Karnatak region with vengeance.[14]

JIHAD UNDER THE MUGHALS

The Mughals came with new weapons and new strategy of war, but their religious ideology of Jihad and zeal remained as of old. This is borne out by the difference in Babur's attitude and actions in his two wars, one against the Muslim Ibrahim Lodi and the other against the Hindu Rana Sanga. Babur's war against Ibrahim Lodi was only a war, against Rana Sangram Singh it was Jihad. After the defeat of the Lodi Sultan in the First Battle of Panipat in April 1526, according to Ahmad Yadgar, Babur praised the slain King, and his corpse was given a decent burial at the command of the victor.[15] On the other hand, the story of the Battle of Khanwa against Rana Sanga in March 1527 has been described in the royal memoirs in an entirely different idiom. In it Rana Sanga is repeatedly called a pagan (Kafir) with studied contempt. His nobles and soldiers are similarly abused repeatedly. On account of Sanga's large army and reputation for bravery, Babur renounced wine as a measure of seeking God's grace. And how?—cups and flagons were "dashed in pieces, as God willing! soon will be dashed the gods of the idolaters."[16] The whole narrative of Babur as well as Shaikh Zain's Fateh Nama is laced with quotations from the Quran for wishing victory against the infidels, for "adequate thanks cannot be rendered for a benefit than which none is greater in the world and nothing is more blessed in the world to come, to wit, victory over most powerful infidels and dominion over wealthiest heretics, 'these are the unbelievers, the wicked.'" All the Hindu chiefs killed in battle "trod the road to Hell from this house of clay to the pit of perdition." When they were engaged in battle, they were "made to descend into Hell, the house of perdition. They shall be thrown to burn therein, and an unhappy dwelling shall it be."[17] In Babur's memoirs his narrative of Jihad is laced with quotations from the Quran in dozens which shows that he was, like Mahmud Ghaznavi, a scholar of Quran and Hadis and no simple secular warrior.

After the victory over Rana Sanga, Babur took the title of Ghazi or victor in holy war. As trophy of victory "an order was given to set up a pillar of pagan heads."[18] A similar tower of pagan heads was piled up after the success at Chanderi against Medini Rai.

> We made general massacre of pagans in it. A pillar of pagan heads was ordered set up on a hill northwest of Chanderi (and) converted what for many years had been a mansion of hostility, into a mansion of Islam. [19]

Such language is used, such towers of heads of the slain are piled up, only in the case of Hindus. Similar ideas and actions are not found in Babur's description of wars against the Muslims in India. The language betrays the psychology developed by the ideology of Jihad contained in Islamic scriptures. The ideology is not of universal brotherhood. Its brotherhood is confined to Muslims only.

Even in emperor Akbar's "secular" reign the religious spirit of Jihad was not lost. Abdul Qadir Badaoni who was then one of Akbar's court chaplains or imams, states that he sought an interview with the emperor when the royal troops were marching against Rana Pratap in 1576, begging leave of absence for "the privilege of joining the campaign to soak his Islamic beard in Hindu infidel blood." Akbar was so pleased at the expression of allegiance to his person and to the Islamic idea of Jihad that he bestowed a handful of gold coins on Badaoni as a token of his pleasure.[20] It may be recalled that as an adolescent, Akbar had earned the title of Ghazi by beheading the defenseless infidel Himu. Under Akbar and Jahangir "five or six hundred thousand human beings were killed," says Emperor Jahangir.[21] The figures given by these killers and their chroniclers may be a few thousand less or a few thousand more, but what bred this ambition of cutting down human beings without compunction was the Muslim theory, practice and spirit of Jihad, as spelled out in Muslim scriptures and rules of administration. Under Aurangzeb every chronicler avers that wars against infidels were fought in the spirit of Jihad. In short, Jihad was never given up in India from the time of Muhammad bin Qasim to that of Aurangzeb and beyond, so long as Muslim rule lasted.

We may close this discussion on the theory and practice of Jihad by pointing out that the prophet of Islam was a very practical man. He advocated Jihad or aggressive wars against non-Muslims till eternity because he did not visualize a world without Kafirs and people of other faiths. But he could not be sure of success always. Muhammad himself sometimes got Muslim prisoners of war released by giving in exchange beautiful slave girls to the strong adversary at Medina.[22]

Therefore, in many ahadis he recommended that if infidels harass the Muslims, and offer them peace in return for property the Imam must not accede thereto as far as possible, as this would be a degradation of the Muslim honour. But if destruction is apprehended, purchasing peace with property is lawful, because it is a duty to repel destruction in every possible way.[23] Muslims also repelled destruction in this wise in Hindustan from the time of Iltutmish to that of Aurangzeb. Aurangzeb, ever keen on Jihad as stressed in his Fatawa-i-Alamgiri, used to surrender forts to the Marathas when destruction stared him in the face. Rajputs too used to recover their forts and properties from Muslim rulers throughout the medieval period. But Jihad was a religious duty for Muslims till eternity for the annihilation of non-Muslims. It was carried out in India to the best of the competence and strength of Muslim invaders and rulers throughout the medieval period.

NOTES

For clarification of any citations, the reader is referred to the original, K. S. Lal, *Theory and Practice of Muslim State in India* (New Delhi: Aditya Prakashan, 1999), pp. 366–75.

1. "Tamerlane systematically destroyed the Christians, and as a result the Nestorians and Jocobites of Mesopotamia have never recovered. At Sivas, 4,000 Christians were buried alive; at Tus there were 10,000 victims. Historians estimate the number of dead at Saray to be 100,000; at Baghdad 90,000; at Isfahan 70,000." Ibn Warraq, *Why I Am Not a Muslim* (Amherst, NY: Prometheus Books, 1995), p. 235.

2. E.D. vol. 4, p. 547n.

3. Muhammad Qasim Hindu Shah Farishtah, *Tarikh-i-Farishtah*, Persian text (Lucknow, 1865), vol. 1, p. 295; Robert Sewell, *A Forgotten Empire*, pp. 30–31, 38.

4. Amir Khusrau, *M fah-ul Futuh*, Aligarh text (1954), p. 22; K. S. Lal, *History of the Khaljis* (New Delhi, 1950, 1980), p. 250 and footnote.

5. Amir Khusrau, *Kuazain-ul-Futuh*, trans., in E.D., vol. 3, p. 77.

6. Amir Khusrau, *Ashiqa* (Aligarh, 1917), p. 46.

7. Barani, pp. 216–17, also pp. 41–42, 44, 72–75.

8. Barani, *Fatawa-i-Jahandari*, pp. 46–48, also introduction, p. v.

9. *Encyclopaedia of Islam*, vol. 1, p. 958.

10. Abu Yusuf, *Kitab-ul-Kharaj*, cited in R. P. Tripathi, *Some Aspects of Muslim Administration* (Allahbad, 1936), p. 340.

11. Lal, *Khaljis*, p. 113.

12. Ibid., pp. 252–53.

13. Mandi Husain, *Tughluq Dynasty* (Calcutta, 1963), pp. 195–257.

14. Robert Sewell, *A Forgotten Empire* (repr., Delhi, 1966), pp. 30–31.

15. Farishtah, vol. 1, p. 295. Also Sewell, p. 38.

16. Babur Nama, pp. 474–75 and n.; Ahmad Yadgar, *Tarikh-i-Salatin-iAfgbana*, pp. 98 ff., and trans. in E.D. vol. 5, p. 30; K. S. Lal, *Twilight of the Sultanate* (New Delhi, 1963), pp. 224–25.

17. Babur Nama, pp. 554–55.

18. Ibid., pp. 550–73. These pages in particular are full of quotations from the Qu'ran.

19. Ibid., pp. 574, 576.

20. Ibid., pp. 483–84, 596.

21. Badaoni, *Muntakhah-ut-Tawarikh*, vol. 2, p. 383; V. A. Smith, *Akbar the Great Mogul* (repr., Delhi, 1962), p. 108.

22. Tarikb-i-Salim Shahi, trans. Price, pp. 225–26.

23. Sunan ibn Majab, vol. 2, p. 185, badis 624; p. 585, ahadis 2092–95. Also Sunan Abu Daud, vol. 2, p. 364; Hughes, *Dictionary of Islam*, p. 248; Hitti, *The Arabs*, pp. 23–26.

42

CERTAIN PHASES OF THE CONQUEST OF THE BALKAN PEOPLES BY THE TURKS

Dimitar Angelov

Numerous studies have already been devoted to the conquest of the Balkan peoples by the Turks, and their number has increased especially during these past three years, on the occasion of the five hundredth anniversary of the fall of Constantinople. One could say that, as a result of a series of general studies and specialized monographs, the military history of the conquest has been set forth clearly, to a great extent, although certain questions still remain, particularly concerning the chronology of the events which are the cause of controversies. The political situation, during the period when the feudal Turks invaded the Balkan Peninsula and carried out their plans of conquest, has also been clarified to a great extent. Bourgeois historiography has no doubt contributed to a very considerable extent in clarifying the political and military history of the conquest. But this historiography has not been and is not capable of uncovering for us, through an application of the scientific method, the deeper causes of the conquest of the Balkan peoples by the Turks, nor of providing an exact and more in-depth analysis of the character of that conquest and of the resulting consequences. It is only quite recently that certain Marxist historians have made a serious attempt to throw additional light on this problem, to analyze the economic and social situation of the Balkan peoples in the fourteenth and fifteenth centuries (which facilitated the Turkish operations of conquest), to examine more closely the resistance that the Balkan peoples put up to the invaders, and to bring to light the devastating and

Dimitar Angelov, "Certain aspects de la conquete des peuples balkanique par les Turcs," in *Les Balkans au moyen age. La Bulgarie des Bogomils aux Turcs* (London: Variorum Reprints, 1978), pp. 220–75. English translation by Michael J. Miller.

predatory character of that conquest. Studies and articles of varying lengths have been devoted to all these problems.[1] We must emphasize, however, that they are initial studies, which take constitute only the first step in the investigation of a vast and relatively little-known problem.

The present study proposes to continue the work that has been undertaken in this field, and to present new, systematically organized materials on the character of the Turkish conquest and the resulting consequences. By referring to numerous sources (of Turkish, Byzantine, Slavic, and Western origin), we have tried to shed a fuller light on various questions concerning the fall of Byzantium and of the Balkan peoples under Turkish rule, in particular: the decline of productivity in the conquered regions (the destruction of towns, economic disorganization), the massacres and mass enslavement of the population on the peninsula, and Turkish colonization in the occupied countries. All of these questions have already been partially treated in the general studies on the conquest of Asia Minor and the Balkan Peninsula and in several monographs. In any case, the topics are not treated there in a systematic manner, and the findings are not based on a large number of facts drawn from the sources. Nevertheless it is important to have recourse to a greater number of facts in order to paint a complete picture of the conquest, to demonstrate convincingly the destructive character of the campaigns of the feudal Osmanlis [= Ottomans] and the countless evils that the conquest inflicted upon the peoples of the peninsula. This task is even more important today, given that certain representatives of Turkish bourgeois historiography have recently endeavored to present the events relating to the conquest in a false light, to underestimate the degree of civilization that the Balkan peoples had attained during the Middle Ages, to idealize the economic and social regime of the conquerors, and so on. The systematic and impartial use of the sources gives the lie to all those unfounded assertions and proves incontestably that the conquest by the Turks had disastrous consequences for the Balkan peoples and for centuries trammeled their normal economic and social development.

The territories that Byzantium possessed in Asia Minor were the first objectives of the Turkish conquests.[2] Different Turkish tribes began to invade these territories beginning in the sixtieth year of the thirteenth century, during the reign of Michael VIII Paleologus (1261–1282). Taking advantage of the political fragmentation of the country, the hesitance of certain provincial aristocrats and the demoralization that had seized the military settlers (the *acrilytes* [French spelling]) who were posted in the frontier regions, several Turkish emirs managed to seize vast regions in Paphlagonia, Caria, and so on. The pressure from the Turks became extremely strong at the end of the thirteenth and the beginning of the fourteenth century. The last attempts that Byzantium made to halt the invaders by resorting to *Alain* and *Catalan* mercenaries [from Alai, mountainous region of southwest Kyrgyzstan and Catalonia, northwest Spain] were ineffective. Between 1302 and 1310, all of Asia Minor fell into the hands of the invaders, with the exception of a few cities on the coast and in the interior of the country (*Brousse* [Fr.], Nicea, Nicomedia, etc.). But these cities, too, did not resist the conquerors for long. Brousse [Burgas in Bulgaria] was taken in 1326, Nicea in 1331 and Nicomedia in 1337. Byzantium retained only Philadelphia, a fortified town that did not fall into the hands of the invaders until 1391.

In the territories thus conquered a certain number of emirates were established, governed by emirs who maintained only rather weak relations with their neighbors and often even made war with one another. According to the testimonies of Nicephorus Gregoras[3] relative to the beginning of the fourteenth century, Phrygia and the region around Philadelphia and Antioch were occupied by the emir Karaman Alisour. Sarkhan settled in the region surrounding Smyrna. The cities of Magnesia, Priène, and Ephesus were incorporated into the emirate of Sassan. The emir Khalan governed Lydia and Aeolia as far as the Sea of Marmara. Among the great and powerful emirates that were founded in Asia Minor, the one that occupied Bythinia and the region extending around Olympus held an important place at first. This was the emirate of the Turks who were called Osmanlis, created following the conquests carried out by Ertoghroul—and especially by his son Osman (1288 to 1326) and his grandson Orkhan (1326–1359).

The conquest of Asia Minor by the Turkish emirs is depicted in the works of medieval Turkish writers (Hodza Hussein, Asik Pacha Zadé, Nesri, Seadeddin, and others) as a blessing for the population, which, from then on, supposedly started to live in peace and tranquility under the protection of the conquerors. The authors especially praise the Osmanli sovereigns Osman and Orkhan, to whom the greater part of medieval Turkish historiography is dedicated. In it, the most noble and exalted virtues are attributed to these sovereigns: justice, loyalty, modesty, and so on. We find these panegyrics and this way of idealizing matters and men to the utmost also in one part of the contemporary bourgeois Turkish historiography, which endeavors by all means to attribute to the conquest by the Osmanlis the character of a *civilizing and progressive mission*. There the thesis is maintained (among others) that the conquests by the Osmanlis and the establishment of their state made it possible to create economic unity in fourteenth-century Asia Minor, and to overcome the economic crisis that is said to have existed there until that time. A similar opinion is expressed, for example, in an article by Moustapha Agdatch, published in the review *Belleten*, vol. XIII (1949) pp. 497–569. In this article, Agdatch formulates and develops the thesis of a supposed *economic unity* that, according to him, was accomplished following extensive Turkish conquests and the aggrandizement of the Osmanli State in place of the vanished Seljuk Sultanate. The author tells us about the economic prosperity that is supposed to have united the population behind their emirs, about the resumption of trade relations between cities of Asia Minor and the Byzantine cities on the coast of Thrace, and so on.

In reality, the historical facts tell us something quite different. The information furnished us by the Turkish historians of the Middle Ages, notwithstanding their tendentious interpretations, and the many facts reported to us by the writers of that period, Byzantine and otherwise, clearly show us that the conquest of Asia Minor by the Turks was a genuine calamity for the population. This conquest had as a result the massive destruction of material goods, the ruination of entire cities, the massacre, deportation, and enslavement of thousands of inhabitants—in a word, a general and lasting decline in the productivity of the country. The Turkish clans that invaded Asia Minor in no way represented a supposedly superior culture, nor did they possess a higher degree of civic organization, as some contemporary Turkish historians maintain. Quite to the contrary, with respect to their level of development, they were still in the semibarbarian state and had preserved many elements of primitive clan life. These tribes were headed by a leading group that was already rather strong due to the power that it held, and whose sole purpose was war and pillage. These leaders enriched themselves by accumulating booty in the form of estates, slaves, money, and jewels. It was precisely this leading group—united around their chiefs, the emirs, and rendered fanatical by the dogmas of Islam—that invaded the territories that Byzantium possessed in Asia Minor, only to pillage them, to carve out vast dominions for themselves, to capture slaves and to make their fortune. That was its essential purpose, which corresponded well to the level of economic and social development at which the Turkish tribes found themselves at that time.

Destruction and plundering were the distinctive feature of the Turkish conquests, and this feature was already manifest during the course of the first incursions of the Asiatic invaders, in the period between 1262 and 1282. According to a communication by the Byzantine historian Georgius Pachymeres, a contemporary of the events, the Turks who had invaded the lands situated north of the Meander ruined a large number of towns, great and small, as well as a certain number of monasteries, thus obliging the population to run for their lives.[4] The lands east of Sangarios (in the province of Paphlagonia) were transformed, in the words of the same author, into a "Scythian desert." Some rich, fertile regions that until recently had been cultivated by hard-working peasants were soon covered with forests and undergrowth and became inaccessible to human beings.[5] When Michael Paleologus traveled there to stop the advance of the Turks, he began (to use Pachymeres' expression) to tear out his hair and to lament bitterly the lot of his subjects. The fact that the Byzantine troops, sent into that region in 1281 to repel the invaders, were unable to obtain provisions anywhere and had to turn back, shows the extent to which Paphlagonia had been devastated by the Turkish invasions.[6]

In addition to the wholesale destruction and depopulation, there were indiscriminate massacres, along with routine, large-scale enslavement of the populace. The Turkish invaders mercilessly crushed any attempt at resistance and put to death the entire male population of those places that had refused to surrender.[7]

Thus they carried out a terrible massacre after seizing the fortress in Trales (on the Meander), which had persisted in defending itself. After the massacres came the subjugation of the populace. Previously, during the course of the first incursions of the Turks in Caria and Paphlagonia, between 1262 and 1264, a large part of the population had been led off into slavery.[8] According to Nicephorus Gregoras, after the fall of Trales the conquerors reduced to servitude approximately twenty thousand men who, with their feet shackled, groaned in envy of the lot of those whom death had already carried off.[9] After Osman took the fortified town of Karadja Hissar, the entire population was doomed to slavery. The invaders pitilessly divided the living booty among themselves, separating children from their mothers, brothers from sisters. "Who would have the talent," wrote Gregoras in his *History*, "to compose an account more voluminous than the *Iliad*, an account worthy of the calamities that the Turks inflicted upon the Byzantines? If we were to combine all these horrors and relate them succinctly in a single chapter, it would tell the mind and the imagination nothing. . . . If, on the other hand, we tried to relate everything in detail, it would be beyond our strength."[10]

The campaigns of the Turks took on an especially devastating character at the beginning of the fourteenth century, when the last attempts of the Byzantine government to stop their advance ended in a debacle and the front in Asia Minor was breached in many places. First of all there was the catastrophe in Lydia. With unheard-of ferocity the Turks overran defenseless villages. A large part of the population, as Pachymeres testifies, was massacred, and the rest fled, taking refuge in the nearby islands or in Thrace. The Turks immediately invaded the abandoned countryside and settled there, finding provisions and goods in abundance.[11]

After devastating Lydia, the hordes of plunderers headed north, toward Mysia. Their advance struck terror into the population and precipitated a new wave of emigration. On this subject Pachymeres writes: "Seeing the evils and calamities that the Turks were perpetrating in the South of Pergamus, with no one capable of stopping them, none of the inhabitants could hope to save himself by staying in his home. Faced with this threat of danger, everyone fled. Some reached Pergamus, others went still farther to Atramit, and still others fled to the coast near the town of *Lampsaque*. A great number of them crossed the Dardanelles and settled on the opposite coast, a few of them even going to the interior of the country [Thrace—editor's note], seized with fear and having lost all hope of ever being able to return to their homes."[12] Every day new waves of refugees arrived from Asia Minor, panic-stricken, having abandoned everything to fate. According to Pachymeres, almost the entire population of Asia Minor went over to Europe, which contributed to an increase in poverty and lack of provisions.[13]

The islands of the Aegean Sea and the Sea of Marmara, too, were filled with refugees. Pachymeres describes the tragic lot of a group of fugitives who had taken refuge on the Isle of Princes. There the refugees fell into the hands of Venetian pirates. Those unfortunate souls, who had just barely escaped from the

Turks, now were in danger once again of losing their lives, because the pirates were planning to massacre them unless a large ransom was paid. Andronicus considered himself obliged to pay that ransom, and thus the prisoners were spared.[14]

While the Turks were occupying and devastating Lydia and Mysia, Osman attempted, after the battle of Bapheon (July 1301), to take the great pass [or breach: *trouée*] leading to Bythinia.[15] Like a torrent, devastating everything in its path, the Osmanlis overran the population in the countryside, which, at that time of the year, was busy with heavy field work while gathering the harvest. Many peasants were massacred, others taken as slaves. A few managed to find refuge in the nearby fortified towns. The majority of the refugees took shelter in the port of Nicomedia. Since the city was surrounded by mighty walls, Osman decided not to attack it. Every day, Pachymeres tells us, a veritable anthill of panic-stricken, exhausted people arrived in Nicomedia. Not one of these fugitives had been spared the loss of his property or the sorrow of lamenting the death of a near relative. The women bewailed the death of their husbands, mothers—the death of their children, sisters—the death of their brothers. Along the roads leading to Nicomedia lay women, the elderly, and abandoned children.[16] In the city itself, filled with refugees and besieged by the enemy, famine and sicknesses soon made their appearance.

The tragedy that had been inflicted upon the population of Asia Minor at the beginning of the fourteenth century was repeated with redoubled violence in the course of the final campaigns of the Osmanli invaders, between 1326 and 1337, campaigns that resulted in the fall of the three last fortified towns that Byzantium still had in Bythinia: Brousse, Nicea, and Nicomedia. Nicea, which succumbed after a long siege, was almost entirely ruined and depopulated. The conquerors pillaged the churches and carried off their treasures and the relics of the saints that were venerated there.[17] Blinded by their religious fanaticism, they began to force the inhabitants who had escaped the massacres to renounce Christianity and to convert to Islam. We find proof of this in a message that the patriarch of Constantinople, John XIX (1333–1347) wrote shortly after the city was seized. It says there that the invaders endeavored to impose their *impure religion* on the populace, at all costs, intending to make the inhabitants followers of Muhammad. The Patriarch advises the Christians to be steadfast in their religion and not to forget that the *agarians* are masters of their bodies only, but not of their souls.[18]

The capture of localities situated near Nicea was also accompanied by cruel devastation and large-scale massacres. According to Nicephorus Gregoras, the Osmanlis were prepared to massacre all the inhabitants of the conquered lands, and if they refrained from doing so, it was because they needed that population so as to be able to levy their tributes.[19]

We should note that the works of the Byzantine historians Pachymeres and Gregoras are not the only ones that provide us with information about the devastation the Turkish invaders perpetrated in Asia Minor throughout the duration of their conquests. We find similar information in the works of Turkish authors, notably in Seadeddin, Nesri, Munedjim Basi, and others. Although these historians strive to present the conquests in a more favorable light, as a series of brilliant victories, they nevertheless do not succeed in concealing the whole truth or in remaining silent about the devastation, the throngs of captives, the depopulation of entire regions, and so on. The descriptions of Munedjim Basi and Hodja Hussein, which are referred to in the above-cited study by A. S. Tviritinova, contain quite a large number of facts about the destruction of the fortified towns of Karadja Hissar, Anghelokoma, Ak Hissar, Nicomedia, and so on.[20] Information of the same sort is found also in the works of Ašikpašašade, Seadeddin, and other writers.

One source that is still insufficiently utilized, and which presents a very clear picture of the devastation perpetrated by the Turks in Asia Minor and of the evils endured by the population at the time of the Turkish conquest, is the work of the Arab traveler Ibn Batouta.[21] As everyone knows, Batouta visited the territories in Asia Minor that had been conquered by the Turkish emirs. This journey took place during the summer of 1333, that is to say, a short time after the campaigns undertaken by Orkhan to seize Brousse and Nicea. Batouta visited the most important cities in that country (Nicea, Laodicea, Ephesus, Attalia, Magnesia, Pergamus, etc.), and, being an attentive and conscientious observer, he had the opportunity to see and to hear many things.

Batouta's descriptions show us that the ruination caused by the Turkish invasion was quite considerable and that a certain number of towns had been unable to return to normal or else were still completely destroyed. The once-populous city of Pergamus, he writes, was "in ruins."[22] Most of the port of Smyrna had been destroyed.[23] Nicea, the capital of the Osmanlis Turks, "was in ruins and was inhabited only by a very small number of the emir's subjects."[24] In many localities, the Greek population was greatly reduced or had completely disappeared, and the Turks had settled in its place. The Christian churches were destroyed or had been turned into mosques. Such was the case, for example, with the exceptionally beautiful church of Ephesus, where now the worship prescribed by Muhammad was celebrated.[25] What Batouta tells us about the transformation of Christian churches into mosques is confirmed, moreover, by Turkish sources (Seadeddin, Nesri, the anonymous chronicles, etc.).[26]

In describing his travels through Asia Minor, Batouta often speaks of slaves, both male and female, whom the Turks used as domestic servants or in order to satisfy their desires. There were, for example, a large number of slaves at Laodicea, in the harems of the leading citizens.[27] Some of the slaves had arrived in the marketplaces in large quantities, and Batouta himself acquired a slave woman at Balikseri,[28] near Pergamus. One of the most famous slave traders in that period, who continually financed expeditions with his ships for this purpose was, according to Batouta, the emir of Smyrna, Omour Beg, who personally presented him with the gift of a slave woman.[29] Subject to such a tragic fate, the slaves sought to escape at all costs. Batouta describes how his slave fled from Magnesia together with another slave and how the two fugitives were later captured.[30] This information that the Arab traveler gives us concerning the institution of slavery among the Turks during that period in Asia Minor and in the neighboring islands is confirmed by other sources, notably by a letter from Pope Clement VI from the year 1343.[31]

The information that Batouta gives us concerning the political fragmentation of the land and the existence of a great number of emirs, each governing a given region or even just one town, is of particular interest. Batouta tells us about emirs (to whom he accords the title of sultans) in Miletus, Ephesus, Brousse, Attalia, Magnesia, Nicea, Pergamus, Balikseri, Larendah, Acridour, Koul-Hissar, Smyrna, and so on.[32] They all had their own army, palace, and policy. The general fragmentation of the land, divided up among a large number of emirs, was further complicated by the presence of different nomadic tribes that prowled about these provinces, independent of any governor. Batouta notes the existence of a horde of Turkmenian nomads which was said to have settled not far from the city of Kevnik, to the east of Sangarios.[33]

If we consider as a whole the information that Batouta gives us in his description of Asia Minor, we will arrive at the indisputable conclusion that the productivity of the country was in decline, the economy was in jeopardy, and the population was ruined and sorely oppressed. The fact that most of the cities were in ruins, that the greater part of the populace had been massacred, had fled or were subjugated, and that power was now divided up among a great number of emirs, clearly shows that there could not have been any welfare, economic prosperity or unity, as certain contemporary Turkish historians maintain. The Arab voyager, who was a keen observer, has confirmed in his account the same impression of the devastation and ruin caused by the Turkish invaders that one gets from reading the Byzantine works of that period or the works of medieval Turkish historians and chroniclers.

The conquest of Asia Minor by the Turkish emirs meant not only the decline of the country's productivity and general, lasting ruination, but also the establishment of a new and cruel system of feudal exploitation by a new feudal class, which arose from the leading groups of the different tribes and which would occupy an important place and wield great influence in the newly constituted emirates. In order to consolidate its position in relation to the masses of the Turkish population, which was economically much weaker, and above all to strengthen its power over the subjugated Christians, this new class needed a strong administration, a mechanism of coercion and subjection that the ancient military structure of the clans was no longer capable of providing. Thus the conquest of Asia Minor and the appearance of feudal ties made possible the creation of the first Turkish states, the primary purpose of which was to keep in submission the masses of subjugated Christians and to exploit them thoroughly.

The stages of this feudalization and of the development of a single Turkish state can be best observed, relatively speaking, in the history of the Osmanli Turks, about whom we have the most sources and who, as everyone knows, ultimately succeeded in subjugating all the other emirates and incorporating them into their state by subjecting them to their power. The testimonies that have come down to us clearly show that among the Osmanlis the nucleus of the feudal class was composed of the military leaders of the clans, the members of the emir's family and his entourage. These feudal lords became great landowners after the conquest of Asia Minor, having acquired (either by military force or as gifts from the emir) vast tracts of land, a multitude of slaves, entire towns and numerous villages, together with their inhabitants. It was from among the landed class that the high-ranking civil and military dignitaries were recruited, who made up the leading class of the new state that was taking shape.[34]

As of the end of the thirteenth century, at the time of the first victories of Osman, we can find among the Osmanlis bits of evidence for the formation of this landed aristocracy. According to the testimony of Turkish historians and chroniclers, Osman granted domains and gifts first and foremost to his military chiefs and to the members of his family. Thus, after the capture of the fortified towns of Aghelokoma and Yar Hissar, Osman gave them as gifts to two of his top military chiefs: Hassan Alp and Tougroud Alp.[35] The latter received the surrounding villages as well, which henceforth began to bear his name, since they had become his fief. After the battle of Bapheon (1301) another military chief, Elp Koukiar, received from the emir as a gift the fortified town of Kara Tchepis.[36] To Alp Khundiz, another military chief, Osman granted the region of Soubachilik.[37]

The members of the emir's family were not neglected either. Osman gave the region of Kara Hissar to his son Orkhan and made a gift of the revenues of the city of Biledjik to his father-in-law, Edé Balou.[38]

This practice of rewarding the military chiefs and the members of the emir's family was continued by Orkhan (1326–1359). After the fall of Nicomedia in 1337, a military chief, Kara Mursel, received the region located on the coast of Bythinia, along with the obligation to defend it against pirates.[39] All the other villages of this region fell under the power of Kara Mursel and were named after him from then on (according to Seadeddin). During the reign of Orkhan other military chiefs, for example Aktché Hodja and Yanchi Lala, likewise received significant gifts and vast domains.[40] Orkhan granted whole regions to his sons, Mourad and Suleyman. Suleyman received the region around Ghyonuk and Modreni, whereas Mourad received the region of Brousse.[41]

Alongside this upper class of feudal lords at the time of the conquest of Asia Minor and the establishment of the Ottoman state, a class of intermediate and small landowners developed, who were recruited from among the soldiers that made up the troops that had helped the Osmanli emirs carry out their conquests. These soldiers received lands in the conquered territories of Asia Minor as a reward for their military service. But they were obliged to remain in the ranks of the army in the future as well. Thus arose the system of military fiefs, which soon became the very basis of the political and social regime of the Ottoman state, and contributed in considerable measure to the success of the rapid, incessant campaigns of the Turks in Asia Minor. This system made its appearance already during the reign of Osman. As the sources testify, Osman had lands distributed more than once to his soldiers as a reward for their victories. The first time, Osman distributed military fiefs (*timaris*) to his soldiers after the fall of the fortified town of Anghelokoma (Aynéghiol) and the surrounding localities. New distributions of *timaris* took place between 1301 and 1310 after the defeat of the Byzantines at Bapheon, which signified the conquest of the greater part of Bythinia.[42] Subsequently, new *timaris* were distributed to the soldiers when Osman undertook his second offensive for the final conquest of Bythinia.[43] The emir likewise presented his soldiers with gifts of houses in which to live.[44] As Seadeddin puts it, this usage helped to maintain the warlike spirit of the troops and incited the soldiers to start new campaigns of conquest.[45]

The system of military fiefs became even more firmly established during the reign of Orkhan. He confirmed all the *timaris* distributed by his father[46] and continued the practice himself. Thus, after the fall of Nicea, the entire surrounding region was divided up into military fiefs.[47] The same thing happened after the capture of Nicomedia.[48] *Timaris* were distributed also in the region of Yaliakova, according to the account in an anonymous Ottoman chronicle.[49]

As a consequence of the establishment of a feudal regime and the partitioning of lands among the soldiers and the members of the sultan's entourage (high-ranking military dignitaries or members of the emir's family), the population of Asia Minor that had not fled and had escaped the massacres fell under the heavy yoke of the new conquerors. They had to bear the burden of taxes and fines, and it was upon their hard labor that the well-being of the ruling class was built. The plight of the peasants became especially difficult. The Osmanli sovereigns were well aware of the fact that, were it not for the masses of peasants, the essential object of their exploitation, they would not be able to attain their goals nor to solidify a system of military fiefs capable of satisfying the needs of the great and petty feudal lords and at the same time of guaranteeing the success of their new attempts at conquest. They could not do without the peasantry, which furnished them with free labor and from which they extracted the last penny through taxes and tributes of every kind. Nor could they do without the artisans in the towns, because of their products, their knowledge, and their skills in their trades. That is the reason why, despite the routine massacres and banishment, the Osmanli conquerors endeavored to keep the rest of the population in the occupied regions by compelling them, with military force, to remain in their homes. Osman's policy in this regard was quite significant. After the capture of the fortified towns of Biledjik, Aynéghiol, Yar Hissar, and Yeni Hissar, Osman (as Nesri observes) ordered the peasants of that whole region not to leave their homes.[50] It was the same situation after the battle of Bapheon, when Osman officially forbade inciting the peasants of Bythinia to emigrate.[51] Orkhan followed Osman's example. One very convincing testimony is provided by Nicephorus Gregoras. Speaking about the fall of Nicea (1331) and the occupation of the coast of Bythinia, he says: "The barbarians occupied the localities along the coast of Bythinia without encountering resistance, and they imposed their taxes on the other smaller places. It was because of them [the taxes] that they did not massacre the entire population, although they could have done so very easily and very quickly."[52] These remarks of Gregoras show very clearly how the conquerors' intention to massacre the "infidels" *en masse* gave way to the more prudent idea of making sure that they had free labor and subjects to tax. Without manual laborers, that is, in the absence of peasants with feudal ties to the land, the feudal class of Turks could not have accomplished its goals, because it would not have been able to benefit from the "surplus value."

The creation of a new army bearing the name of *Yeni Tcheri* ("new troops"), or Janissaries, was one of the most dire calamities that the population of Asia Minor had to suffer after the conquest by the Osmanlis. This army corps that Orkhan created was recruited from among Christian children, who were converted to the Muslim religion and raised in special barracks. For this elite corps the Turks chose well-built boys, whom they took from their parents at a very young age. The payment of this "blood tax" amounted to a terrible and merciless tribute, which caused the ruin of hundreds of thousands of families. The Janissaries, brought up in a spirit of religious fanaticism and imbued with an unshakable loyalty to the sultan, became a pitiless horde that was the most compliant force in support of the regime and carried out the plans for conquest devised by the Osmanli feudal lords.[53]

The invasion of the Balkan Peninsula by the Osmanlis and the conquest of Bulgaria, Byzantium, and Serbia, of Bosnia and Albania, had the same consequences as the conquest of Asia Minor, indeed, on an even larger scale.

The events pertaining to the occupation of the Balkan Peninsula are well-known, and we will be content with recalling them very briefly.[54] As everyone knows, the conquest of the Balkans was preceded by a series of invasions carried out by the Turkish emirs who had settled in Asia Minor. The first invasions date from the beginning of the fourteenth century, at the time of the plundering campaign undertaken by the Catalan Company in Thrace and Macedonia. Some Turkish troops arrived then in Europe as allies of the Catalans and devastated the southern regions of Thrace (1308–1311). From 1326 on, the raids by the emirs of Asia Minor occurred repeatedly, almost every year. The inhabitants of southern Thrace, of southern Macedonia, and of the coastland of central Greece suffered especially from these invasions. In 1337 Turkish troops, who had come as allies of the emperor Andronicus III Paleologus, invaded Epirus and Albania. As of

1341, when the fight between the party of John Kantakuzenos and that of John V Paleologus Apokaukos had broken out in Byzantium, the Turkish troops began to appear regularly in Thrace. Officially they came as allies of John Kantakuzenos, but in reality their goal was to plunder the population and to carry off booty. An important role in this fratricidal struggle was played by the emir of Smyrna, Omour Beg, whom we mentioned earlier, who supported John Kantakuzenos with his armies and his ships. Later on Orkhan, whose state in Bythinia had already been appreciably consolidated, began to interfere deliberately in the affairs of Byzantium. In 1352, taking advantage of the weakness of Byzantium, his son, Suleyman, occupied the little fortress of Tzympé on the peninsula of Gallipoli.[55] Two years later, after a violent earthquake, the important fortified town of Gallipoli and the surrounding localities fell into the hands of the Osmanlis.[56] Thus, toward the middle of the fourteenth century, the Osmanlis had gained a firm footing on the European continent, and all the efforts of Byzantium to persuade them to retreat to Asia Minor were in vain.

Around the year 1360, after strengthening their positions, the Osmanlis this time launched genuine campaigns of conquest, under the orders of Suleyman at first, and later under the orders of the new sultan, Mourad I (1359–1389). Between 1351 and 1371, they occupied a series of places in Byzantine and Bulgarian Thrace: Demotika, Andrinopolis, Kypsala, Kechan, Plovdiv (Philippopolis), Stara-Zagora (Beroe), Aytos, Yambol, Karnobat, and so on. It is impossible to establish the chronology of the occupation of these towns, since the reports contained in the Turkish sources in this regard are confusing and contradictory,[57] whereas the Byzantine, Bulgarian, and Serbian sources provide only incomplete and insufficient information.

After the battle of Čirmen (September 26, 1371), the Turks advanced deep into the west, and within the space of about fifteen years occupied a large number of towns in western Bulgaria and in Macedonia: Samokov, Kustendil, Sofia, Bitolia, Prilep, Niš, and so on. This is the period during which their invasions in the Peloponnisos, central Greece, Epirus, Thessaly, Albania, and Montenegro took place. In 1388 the greater part of northeast Bulgaria fell into the hands of the Turks, and from 1389 on, after the battle of Kosovo, Serbi found itself obliged to acknowledge the sultan's sovereignty. Then came the devastating campaigns undertaken by Mourad's successor, Bajazet I (1389–1402) in Bosnia, Hungary, and Walachia, as well as toward the south, in central Greece and in the Peloponnesian Peninsula. Constantinople was besieged by the Turks. In 1393 the kingdom of Tirnovo fell definitively into the hands of the conquerors, and three years later the kingdom of Vidina succumbed.

Between 1402 and 1413, the Osmanli campaigns ceased, for a time, following the invasion of Asia Minor by the Mongols and the defeat suffered by armies of Bajazet near Ankara. This period of relative calm in the Balkan Peninsula coincided with the reign of the sultan Mahomet [Muhammad] I (1413–1421).

But the Osmanli offensive recommenced as of 1421. The invaders launched a series of campaigns against Peloponnisos, Albany, Serbia, and Hungary, where the population put up fierce resistance to the Turks. Nevertheless the conquerors won considerable victories. The pressure of the Turks intensified especially after the unsuccessful campaign of the king of Poland and Hungary, Vladislav IV (in 1444), and after the defeat suffered in 1448 by the armies of the Transylvanian *voyevod*, John Hunyadi, in the plain of Kosovo. After that battle, the path was clear for the Turks to conquer Serbia and the other Balkan States.

The definitive conquest of the Balkan Peninsula took place after Mahomet II rose to power in 1451. On May 29, 1453, Constantinople was taken by storm. The Byzantine Empire had ceased to exist. In 1459 the Turks became the masters of Serbia, and the following year the despot of Peloponnisos submitted. In 1463 Mahomet completed the conquest of Bosnia and of the Empire of Trebizond. In 1468 the heroic resistance of the Albanian people—who under the leadership of Skanderbeg had struggled for decades against the invaders—was broken. Finally in 1483, Herzegovina fell under Turkish domination, and toward the end of the fifteenth century, Zeta (Montenegro) was conquered.

Thus, after obstinate struggles that lasted for a century and a half, the Osmanli feudal lords became the masters of the entire Balkan Peninsula and founded there an enormous state. We find, in numerous historical sources, the stages of this conquest of the Balkan peoples. A considerable number of works and documents of diverse origin—Turkish, Byzantine, Bulgarian, Serbian, Arabic, Rumanian, Hungarian, Italian, French, Polish, and so on—have been preserved down to the present day. They throw a more or less full light on the different phases of the successive campaigns of the invader, as well as on the resistance put up by the populace of the peninsula.[58] Naturally, the sources contain quite a few discrepancies and contradictions, with regard both to what is reported and to the explanation and interpretation of the events that are described. We find, first, one manner of examining and interpreting the military exploits of the Osmanlis: that of the Turkish historians and chroniclers, who never cease praising the sultans and their victories over the "infidels." A different way of interpreting the phases of the Osmanli conquest is found in Byzantine, Bulgarian, Serbian, and Albanian authors; these reflect a hatred of the invader, and their works include lively descriptions of the native peoples' resistance to the conquerors. These interpretations vary, not only according to the author's ethnicity, but also according to the social class to which he belonged. The Byzantine aristocrat Kritobulus, who was in the service of Mahomet II, endeavored, as a renegade and traitor, to glorify his master's reign. That is why he interprets the events in question as he does.[59]

These same events are set forth in an entirely different way in the anonymous and popular chronicles, which express the patriotic aspirations of the Byzantines. The interpretations vary considerably also depending on whether the works in question are of Balkan origin (Byzantine, Serbian, Bulgarian) or the works of Western authors (French, Italian, etc.). The first category show the influence of the Orthodox Church and its ideological opposition to the "heresy" of the West, against "the Latins," who are accused of indifference, or even of hostile sentiments at the time when the peninsula was reeling under the blows of the Turkish invaders. The others maintain the opposite point of view, accusing the Balkan peoples and their governments of unwillingness to ask for the assistance of the West in repelling the Turkish threat.

Despite these differences in opinion and interpretation due to ethnic, social, and religious factors, it is nevertheless true that these sources contain a very large number of reports concerning indisputable facts, which can be neither contested nor omitted, no matter what interpretation one wishes to give or the perspective from which one writes. No one can deny the multitude of facts contained in the works of the historians and chroniclers, and in the historical documents that have come down to us and which refer to the military campaigns of the conquerors, the destruction they caused, the resistance the populace put up, and so on. When selected and grouped in a chronological, systematic order, these facts are impressive by their sheer quantity. They speak to us in the language of numbers, and this is what counts in historical science, when it is a question of making a succinct analysis of an historic event as momentous as the conquest of the Balkan Peninsula by the Turks.

The first conclusion to be drawn from the analysis and systematization of the numerous facts furnished by the historical sources is that the conquest of the Balkan Peninsula accomplished by the Turks over the course of about two centuries caused the incalculable ruin of material goods, countless massacres, the enslavement and exile of a great part of the population—in a word, a general and protracted decline of productivity, as was the case with Asia Minor after it was occupied by the same invaders. This decline in productivity is all the more striking when one recalls that in the mid-fourteenth century, as the Osmanlis were gaining a foothold on the peninsula, the states that existed there—Byzantium, Bulgaria, and Serbia—had already reached a rather high level of economic and cultural development. Despite the fragmentation inherent in the feudal system that existed there, despite the internal conflicts that characterize that period of their history, the economic and cultural life there was already quite advanced. The large cities on the coast and in the interior of these lands already played an important role as commercial centers and cultural centers.[60] It is not appropriate for us, within the framework of this study, which is very limited in its purpose, to dwell any longer on this question. It is enough for us to recall that the most recent studies conducted by Soviet, Bulgarian, and other historians, which are based both on written sources and on the findings of archaeological digs, establish beyond doubt the considerable progress that the Balkan peoples had made in the thirteenth and fourteenth centuries in the economic and cultural realm.

It was precisely during this period that the invasion of the Turks began. The Turkish feudal aristocracy, eager for booty, rushed toward the Balkan territories. The feudal leaders were seeking new wealth, lands, and slaves. That is why their campaigns were above all operations of plundering and devastation and had disastrous consequences for the lives of the inhabitants, resulting in a general and prolonged decline in the economic and cultural realm.

Even the first offensive of the Osmanli conquerors, which brought them into eastern Thrace after 1361, was accompanied by widespread destruction and ruination. As one anonymous Turkish chronicler puts it, they raged on "by blood and by fire,"[61] mercilessly crushing all resistance on the part of the populace. In a short time, a large number of cities were ruined and their inhabitants massacred or led off into captivity. "Cursed be our time," exclaimed the Byzantine writer and diplomat Demetrius Khodon in 1366 in one of his discourses on the occasion of the invasion of Thrace by Mourad. "The Turks have ruined our cities, pillaged our sanctuaries, and filled it all with blood and corpses."[62] In a letter written sometime between 1383 and 1387 the same author notes that the Byzantine cities had been entirely depopulated, a part of the inhabitants had been massacred by the invaders, and the others had fled into neighboring countries.[63] The plentiful data contained in the works of Turkish historians allows us to estimate the extent of the destruction perpetrated by the Turks in Thrace.[64]

When the Turks invaded eastern Bulgaria and Macedonia beginning in 1371, and Serbia later on, the number of localities that had been ruined or burned down increased rapidly. In every place where the inhabitants defended themselves and refused to surrender, the invaders pillaged and burned down their dwellings, while the city walls behind which the defenders fought were literally demolished. This is how the city of Niche was destroyed in 1386, the inhabitants of which, as Seadeddin notes, had put up strong resistance to the invaders who had laid siege to the city.[65] The city of Pirote suffered the same fate, judging from testimony by the Turkish historian Nešri.[66]

The campaign launched by Ali Pacha in 1388 in the northeastern part of Bulgaria, too, was accompanied by massive devastation. As Nešri remarks, the Turkish military chief had given his troops the explicit order to ruin and plunder along the way the regions and places that they passed through.[67] Consequently the Bulgarian lands of the northeast were devastated and the population was massacred or else carried off into slavery.[68]

After the battle of Nicopol, which was disastrous for the Christians (1396), the Turkish armies horribly ravaged places in Serbia and Hungary. As the philosopher Constantine relates in his biography of Stefan Lazarevich,[69] the town of Zemlin was completely destroyed. According to the testimony of Schiltberger, who participated in the campaign of Sigismond, the town of Petau was entirely leveled.[70] In 1397 Belgrade, too, was ravaged after an invasion launched by a horde of pillaging Turks in the region of Srem.[71] The same year saw large-scale destruction perpetrated by the Turks in the Peloponnisos. The wall surrounding the city of Argos was razed and the inhabitants were reduced to slavery.[72]

The fratricidal war that broke out among the sons of Bajazet [= Bayezid], which played itself out mainly in the Balkan Peninsula, was likewise accompanied by countless instances of plundering and destruction. Moussa above all distinguished himself by the pitiless measures that he took, which caused incalculable harm to the population. As the chronicle of Dečan relates, Moussa's armies defeated the Serbian despot Stefan in 1413 and destroyed Krouchevatz, Petrus, Stalatch, Koprian, and a number of other Serbian towns, while at the same time massacring "a multitude of Christians."[73] Moussa was likewise guilty of wreaking havoc at that time in Thrace. Among other incidents, he had an entire village in eastern Thrace torched, along with all its inhabitants.[74]

The campaigns of Mourad II (1421–1451) and especially those of his successor, Mahomet II (1451–1481) in Serbia, Bosnia, Albania, and in the Byzantine princedom of the Peloponnisos, were of a particularly devastating character. During the campaign that the Turks launched in Serbia in 1455 and 1456, Belgrade, Novo-Bardo, and other towns were to a great extent destroyed.[75] The invasion of the Turks in Albania during the summer of 1459 caused enormous havoc. According to the account of it written by Kritobulos, the invaders destroyed the entire harvest and leveled the fortified towns that they had captured.[76] The country was afflicted with further devastation in 1466 when the Albanians, after putting up heroic resistance, had to withdraw into the most inaccessible regions, from which they continued the struggle.[77] Many cities were likewise ruined during the course of the campaign led by Mahomet II in 1463 against Bosnia—among them Yaytzé, the capital of the kingdom of Bosnia.[78]

But it was the Peloponnisos that suffered most from the Turkish invasions. It was invaded in 1446 by the armies of Mourad II, which destroyed a great number of places and took thousands of prisoners.[79] Twelve years later, during the summer of 1458, the Balkan Peninsula was invaded by an enormous Turkish army under the command of Mahomet II and his first lieutenant Mahmoud Pacha. After a siege that lasted four months, Corinth fell into enemy hands. Its walls were razed, and many places that the sultan considered useless were destroyed.[80] The work by Kritobulos contains an account of the Osmanli campaigns, which clearly shows us the vast destruction caused by the invaders in these regions. Two years later another Turkish army burst into the Peloponnisos. This time Gardiki and several other places were ruined.[81] Finally, in 1464, for the third time, the destructive rage of the invaders was aimed at the Peloponnisos. That was when the Osmanlis battled the Venitians and leveled the city of Argos to its foundations.[82]

The countless ruins and the havoc that the Turks perpetrated over the course of their campaigns in the Balkan Peninsula left a profound impression on a large number of the contemporaries of these events, especially on travelers who passed through the Balkan territories in the fifteenth and sixteenth centuries and thus had the opportunity to observe and to hear many things. Among these travelers we must mention first of all the famous French diplomat Bertrandon de la Broquières, who made his way through the Balkans in 1433 while returning from Asia Minor. La Broquières stopped for a time in Constantinople, then went to Adrianopolis; from there he visited eastern and southern Thrace, and then returned to France, following the itinerary Andrinopolis—Plovdiv (Philippopolis)—Sofia. In many places in his account, he speaks about ruined towns and localities. He reports that the Turks had destroyed the town of Réghion, formerly a powerful fortification, as well as Athira, Zambie, Tchoriou, and Lulé-Bourgas, all of them in eastern Thrace.[83] Khypsala, a once-prosperous city, was in ruins.[84] This city, as Kritobulos notes in his *History*, had formerly been a remarkable place, but at the time when he was writing, it was nothing more than a simple village.[85] According to La Broquières, Makri, a port on the Aegean Sea, was completely destroyed, with the exception of one section of its ramparts.[86] The port of Misi (Kavala) was in a lamentable state. "Misi," La Broquières writes, "had formerly been a fortified place with strong defenses, but now a part of its surrounding wall was destroyed. Everything in it is devastated and the city has no inhabitants."[87] Ruins piled up likewise in Peritheorion, a port on the Aegean Sea and formerly capital of Momtchil, the *voyevod* [leader] of the Rhodopes.[88] The fortified town of Vyra (Féré), which had been a place of considerable importance in the thirteenth and fourteenth centuries, was destroyed as well.[89]

After leaving Andrinopolis and going to Serbia, the French traveler encountered along the way some new ruins caused by the Turkish invaders. When he arrived in Sofia, he observed that its ramparts had been demolished down to their foundations.[90] Izvor, near Pirote (a place that was probably located not far from the city which today bears the name of Bela-Palanka), was entirely destroyed.[91] Niš, previously an important city, was in ruins. La Broquières wrote, "The Turks forcibly occupied this city fifty years ago and have completely ravaged it."[92] According to the traveler Petančić, who traveled through the Balkans in 1502, Niš was at that time nothing more than a simple village. Petančić writes, "As one can see from its ruins, it was formerly a proud city, but now it is hardly more than a village, inhabited by Turks and Bulgarians."[93] According to the description given by La Broquières, the double surrounding wall of Krouchevatz, a city that the Turks had occupied in 1427, was completely razed.[94]

This information that Bertrandon de la Broquières gives us concerning the mass destruction of cities is confirmed in a report that one of the counselors of the Duke of Burgundy filed in 1439, on the subject of a crusade against the Turks planned by Jean Toricello.[95] In this memoir the author analyzes the possibilities of fighting against the invaders and notes that at that time, following the campaigns launched by the Turks, "the walls of all the great cities of Greece are destroyed, with the exception of those belonging to Demothika and Constantinople."[96]

The enormous devastation caused by the Turks did not escape the notice of Philip Buonacuore (Kalimach), a diplomatic envoy of the King of Hungary, who in 1487 traveled through Thrace, Macedonia, and Mesia [in the Danube basin]. "Everywhere," he writes, "one encounters nothing but ruins and deserted places, like after a long, hard war."[97] We also find a very revealing report in the work of the Polish historian Jan Długosz, who describes the campaign led by Vladislav IV Jagiellon in 1444. According to this author, when the crusaders departed from Nicopol for the southern bank of the Danube and arrived in northern Bulgaria, they saw a number of superb and remarkable edifices built by Roman emperors and military leaders, as well as marble monuments—arches and columns— bearing inscriptions in Latin and Greek. "All of these monuments," this author notes, "were to a great extent destroyed by the Turks."[98] It should be recognized that the information that Długosz provides us with has been neglected until now, and that it has not been used as important evidence of the devastating character of the campaigns conducted by the Turks in northern Bulgaria. It is true that a portion of these artworks from the Roman and Byzantine eras had already been partially destroyed before the occupation of that region by the Turks, as a result of the invasions by the Slavs, the Protobulgarians, the Pechenegy, the Coumans, and other tribes. It is nevertheless true that the invasion by the Turks at the end of the fourteenth century contributed in still greater measure to the destruction of these vestiges of Roman and Byzantine civilization in northern Bulgaria and resulted in the mass destruction of monuments of great architectural value.

As one might expect, the devastation and wholesale destruction caused by the Osmanli feudal lords as they conquered the Balkan Peninsula caused a rapid decline in the economic life of all countries in that region. The plundering, the arson, and the incessant havoc caused a profound disruption of agriculture and breeding, which were the main occupation of the inhabitants of Byzantium, Serbia, Bulgaria, Albania, and Bosnia. A heavy blow was dealt to the trades and to commerce within the region and with its neighbors—livelihoods which, as we have already noted, were already flourishing in the Balkan countries in the thirteenth and fourteenth centuries, within the framework of a developed feudal system. Many regions, once rich and fertile, were transformed into wilderness. In many places, famines and epidemics made their appearance, and the population was reduced to indescribable misery.

This economic decline became evident initially in Thrace and Macedonia, where the Osmanli invaders made their first appearance in the peninsula, first as allies of John Kantakuzenos and, as of 1354, on their own account. Very revealing in this regard are certain statements made by Nicephorus Gregoras, a contemporary of these events, when he speaks to us about the economic disruption caused by the Turkish invasions in Thrace in the fourteenth century. "The interests of Byzantium," he writes, "are at their worst, and Thrace has become for us an uncivilized and almost impassable land. Hardly any villages there have retained remnants of their Byzantine population. Having neither outlying districts nor city gates, they are located at great distances from one another in depopulated regions, resembling the isolated stalks of grain that stand in a vast, rich field after the harvest." Further on the author laments, "The unfortunate inhabitants of Thrace are left without beasts of burden, without any flocks, without a single ox that could enable them to work their fields and guarantee them a daily pittance. That is why the lands lie fallow, entirely depopulated and, in a word, rendered completely uncivilized."[99] One result was a terrible famine that afflicted Thrace in the mid-fourteenth century, and which soon gripped the capital itself. "At that time," writes Nicephorus Gregoras, "the inhabitants of Constaninople, as well as the population of most of the Byzantine towns of Thrace, suffered from a lack of victuals. While civil war was exhausting Byzantium, the Turks conducted frequent [naval] incursions from Asia with the help of monemes and triremes [galley ships having, respectively, one and three banks of oars], making their way with impunity into Thrace, especially during harvest season, seizing livestock, carrying off women and children into slavery, and causing such evils that these regions afterward remained depopulated and uncultivated. That was one of the reasons for the famine that the Byzantines had to endure."[100]

Disasters similar to the ones that Nicephorus Gregoras described in Thrace at the time of the civil war struck Macedonia and the eastern territories of Bulgaria after the invasions that the Turks conducted in these regions from 1371 on. A very suggestive picture of the disruption of economic life and of the hardships endured by the population of these countries is provided in a note made in 1371 by Issaye, a monk belonging to one of the monasteries of Mount Athos, in the margin of a translation of the works of Dionysius the Areopagite. "The Ishmaelites," he writes, "scattered and flew throughout the earth like birds in the air. They massacred one part of the Christians with the sword, and led off others into slavery; the rest were carried off by a premature death. Those who had been preserved from death were decimated by famine, because over all of those lands raged a famine such as there has never been since the creation of the world—and may the merciful Lord grant that there shall never again be one like it. And those whom the famine had spared were, by a divine warrant, attacked and devoured by wolves, both day and night. Alas, what a sorrowful picture to behold! The land is left devoid of all goods, men, livestock, and other produce. . . . And then the living truly envied the dead. And—believe me—not I, who am ignorant in everything, but even Livanius, the wisest of the Hellenic authors, could not describe the evils that overwhelmed the Christians of the western lands."[101]

The economic distress and general impoverishment struck also the territories located between the Stara Planina and the Danube basin ("Mesia") after their occupation by the Turks between 1393 and 1396, when the kingdoms of Tirnovo and Vidina perished. Agriculture and the trades suffered an extremely heavy blow, commerce began to be in jeopardy, and the population was prey to famine and misery.

The economic distress and general misery that struck Thrace, Macedonia, and the region situated between the Danube and Stara Planina (northern Bulgaria) was felt for decades, long after the Ottoman feudal lords had become masters of these territories. It suffices to read once more the above-cited work of Bertrandon de la Broquières in order to realize the lamentable economic situation of the inhabitants of the territories conquered by the Turks, through which this author had traveled. It was the wilderness appearance of eastern Thrace and the prevailing misery there which especially struck this illustrious traveler. Between Constantinople and Andrinopolis, as La Broquières states, one could find fertile regions, rich in water-courses, yet entirely deforested, depopulated, and completely abandoned.[102] In the provinces still subject to the government in Byzantium, he could see only a few villages, ruined, impoverished, and widely separated.[103] He notes further on that Adrinopolis was the only city that was slightly more wealthy and populated. That was, after all, the sultan's residence. This general state of misery that he observed in eastern Thrace he likewise discovers in the localities situated along the coast of the Aegean Sea, as far as Serrès. In that region, once so rich, the journey was made particularly difficult by the fact that the travelers did not manage to find lodging or to procure food. "Nowhere can one find a place to stay," La Broquières laments in his record of his travels, "nowhere can one find victuals, except in the large towns. Each man must carry along the way everything that he needs."[104] Although we do not wish to deny a certain element of exaggeration in these words of the French diplomat, who was accustomed to more conveniences, it nevertheless remains indisputable that, at that time, the situation in Thrace was particularly dif-ficult, and that the general economic ruination precipitated by the campaigns and the ravages of the Osmanli Turks continued to mark everything with its imprint.

*   *   *

The Polish diplomat Kalimah, too, whom we have already cited, provides us with testimony concerning the great misery and general impoverishment that wracked Thrace, Macedonia, and northern Bulgaria during the period in question. "Nowhere can one see fortified places," he writes in his work, "nowhere can one find a city or town which would prove, by its appearance, that its founder had thought about war and had put it in a position to defend itself. Everywhere one finds nothing but abandoned, ruined lands, as after a long, hard war."[105] The sight of the tired, worn-out Turkish peasants whom he encountered made a profound impression on him. "When I saw them, I was astonished by their small numbers and especially by the miserable, ragged appearance of that unfortunate populace. It seemed to me that they lived, not in houses, but in gloomy pits, so miserable and overwhelmed was the expression on their faces."[106] If even the Turkish pop-ulation, which nevertheless enjoyed certain advantages compared with the rest of the population in the Balkan territories, found itself in such a miserable situation, it is evident, a fortiori, that the Christian inhabitants, whose goods and dwellings had been pillaged more than once by the Ottoman invaders, were reduced to an even more tragic fate.

Thrace, Macedonia, and northern Bulgaria were not the only lands to suffer from this profound disruption of economic life and from the general impoverishment that resulted. The northwestern and southwestern regions of the peninsula— Bosnia, Serbia, Dalmatia, Albania—and central and southern Greece had to undergo a similar fate. The economic troubles began as early as 1370, when the hordes of Mourad launched their first invasions in these countries. It was commerce that suffered first; trade at that time was already well developed, and Bosnia, Serbia, the Republic of Venice, and the wealthy cities on the coast of Dalmatia (Ragusa, first and foremost) played an important part in the commerce. The Turkish invasions provoked general unrest and a vehement reaction in the countries in question. A certain number of documents, especially those preserved in the archives of Ragusa and Venice, provide convincing proof of the serious decline of economic life in the northwestern regions of the peninsula during the second half of the fourteenth century, and testify to the incessant lamentation due to the plundering perpetrated by the Turks, as well as to the attempts made to organize armed resistance against the invaders. Among these documents, the oldest is a letter that the senate of Venice addressed in 1385 to Balcha, the sovereign of Zeta.[107] It says that the advance of the Turks toward Zeta represented, as Balcha himself put it, a great danger for the commerce of Venice and for the Venetian merchants who were in the country. It had been decided, therefore, that the Republic of Venice would come to Balcha's aide by sending him four galleys. The merchants of Ragusa, who at that time maintained significant commercial ties with Serbia, Albania, and Bosnia, in their turn had to suffer the Turkish invasions. In a letter from the year 1387, two Albanian feudal lords from the region of Doukatchin (on the border of Herzegovina, Zeta, and Serbia), Léka Doukatchin and his brother, Paul, announced to the Ragusians that they could henceforth trade peacefully with their country, given that they had already *made a pact* with the Turks.[108] One sees clearly here what a threat the Turkish incursions presented to the development of commerce in these regions. The situation of the Ragusian merchants became particularly difficult as of 1396, when the Turks launched their systematic campaigns against Serbia, Bosnia, and the Adriatic coast and captured the entire region lying between the Lim, Moratcha, and Zeta, thus cutting off all communication between Ragusa and the lands of the Serbian despot Stefan Lazarević.[109] Although the Serbian despot had requested and obtained from Bayezid freedom to trade for the Ragusian merchants in his state,[110] the latter were constantly being attacked and their merchandise pillaged by Turkish detachments. We find proof of this in several documents. Thus, for example, in a letter from October 1397, the Ragusians complain to Stefan Lazarević that the Turks were arresting their merchants and obstructing their business.[111] We find a similar complaint in a letter dated August

1398.[112] In a letter from October of the same year, addressed to Princess Milica and to Lazar, it says that some Turkish detachments seized five thousand sheep and led them off toward the Lim River, and that in Valjevo they arrested some Ragusian merchants, whom they were holding prisoner.[113] On July 23, 1393, a new complaint arrived, addressed by the Republic of Venice to the Turkish military chief, Sarkhan, which says that some Ragusian merchants had been robbed on the Tara by some unknown Turks and Walachians, and that their merchandise had been carried off. There are still other letters written by the Ragusians at that time that reveal the major obstacles to commerce and the complete disruption of economic life caused by the incessant attacks of the Turks in these regions.

The decline of economic life, the degeneration of agriculture, of the trades, and of commerce resulted in the general impoverishment of the populace in the eastern regions of the Balkan Peninsula. We find numerous proofs of this especially in the archives of Venice, particularly in matters concerning the fourteenth and fifteenth centuries. Thus, for example, in a document dated 1398 preserved in the archives of Venice, it says that the inhabitants of Durazzo (Drač) had reached a state of extreme poverty following the invasions of the Turks and other neighboring peoples. That is the reason why the senate of Venice, which especially valued that important port city, decided to send provisions to its inhabitants.[114] In a document from 1402, likewise in the archives of Venice, we read that the Turks by their invasions had caused such havoc in the Albanian territories that the peasants there could not cultivate the lands unless they were in the immediate vicinity of the cities and fortresses (. . . *nisi apud civitates et castra*).[115] During that same year, as another communication testifies, the inhabitants of Antivari were in terrible distress. It says that the surprise attacks of the Turks had reduced them to that state of extreme destitution (. . . *ad nihilum devoluti*).[116] A similar fate awaited the inhabitants of Drivasto and Skutari, where in the years 1403 to 1406 the invaders had perpetrated countless crimes of plundering and arson.[117] According to a communication from the senate of Venice in 1428, the region of Skutari had been devastated by the Turks to such an extent that it was impossible to collect taxes from the population, either in currency or in kind.[118] That was a cruel blow for the Republic of Venice, which at that time depended primarily on its rich colonies along the Adriatic coast. During the first half of the fifteenth century, the fate of the inhabitants of Durazzo became increasingly tragic. In a letter from the senate of Venice in 1414 it says that the Turks closed off that city's access to the merchandise that had previously been imported there, thus obliging the merchants to unload it in the port of Aviona.[119] There was a great danger, as the letter emphasizes, that the population might abandon the city and scatter in all directions. Another letter from the senate of Venice, this one dated 1437, already speaks about the depopulation of the city as an accomplished fact.[120] According to a communication from the year 1439, the inhabitants of Durazzo were no longer capable of exploiting their salt pits as a result of a Turkish blockade.[121] This was a new and considerable difficulty for the city, since the exploitation of the salt pits was the main livelihood and the chief source of revenue for the populace. Many other documents are extant, especially in the archives of Venice and Ragusa from the late fourteenth and early fifteenth centuries that contain numerous testimonies to the general impoverishment and the great calamities that the populations of the northwestern regions of the peninsula, especially those on the Adriatic coast, had to suffer as a result of the attacks of the Osmanli invaders.

The despotic realm of the Peloponnisos was especially affected by the general economic decline and the impoverishment of the entire population. This realm had to suffer Turkish incursions over the course of almost a century, and it ultimately collapsed in 1460 under the blows of Mahomet II. We find very precise evidence for this in the works of the Byzantine historians, as well as in the archives of the Republic of Venice, since the latter at that time had a lively interest in the fate of its possessions on the peninsula—the cities of Modon and Coron, in particular. The first blows to strike the Peloponnisos went back to the year 1397, when the hordes of Yakoub Pasha invaded the country. Soon famine and misery made their appearance. In a letter from the year 1403 (preserved in the archives of Venice), we read that the senate of Venice granted to Nicolas Karandoulo, governor of the fortress of Modon, [financial] assistance, given the fact that, according to his report, life there had become impossible. The Turks perpetrated terrible destruction in the vicinity of Modon, and no one felt safe outside of its surrounding walls.[122] Similar complaints arrived from the inhabitants of Coron. In 1407 an envoy of the populace of Coron, Francis Ghéso, appeared before the senate of Venice. He told the senate that as a result of the acts of banditry committed by the Turks, the labor force had been greatly diminished, and it was impossible to recruit farm workers, even in return for payment in gold. Consequently the farms of all the inhabitants of the town had been abandoned, and most of these lands were covered again with undergrowth.[123] In response to that communication, the Venetian senate granted the inhabitants of Coron the right to hire "woodcutters" for field work, that is to say, peasants from the mountainous regions of the Peloponnisos, who assuredly had not suffered as much from the Turkish invasion.

The calamities that battered the populace of the Peloponnisos at the time of the campaigns launched by Mourad's lieutenants and by the sultan himself in 1446 aggravated the already precarious situation of its inhabitants and threw the economy into even greater disarray. But the real catastrophe occurred in 1458, during the first great invasion led by Mahomet II. The invaders torched and destroyed all the fields, vineyards, and gardens in the area surrounding Corinth and everywhere that the invader had set foot.[124] Scarcely had they recovered from those terrible trials when the inhabitants of the Peloponnisos were once more attacked by the Turks, first in 1460, then in 1463. This despotic realm, formerly wealthy and powerful, where agriculture and husbandry, the trades, and commerce had been prospering, was reduced to ruins, and its population fell into the most horrible destitution.

Numerous reports by Byzantine authors and others have come down to us that testify to the profound economic distress that took hold of Serbia, Bosnia, and Albania after these countries had become the victim of the Osmanli feudal lords, as a result of the campaigns conducted during the reign of Mahomet II. The invasions of the Turks in Albania had a particularly devastating character. The invaders set fire to and destroyed the fields and the dwellings of the entire population. Even Kritobulos, whose work is an apologia for the reign of Mahomet, cannot conceal the cruel devastation and the countless calamities perpetrated by the Turkish hordes over the course of their invasions in Albania between 1459 and 1468.[125]

The economic ruin and general impoverishment of the population caused by the devastation perpetrated by the Turkish invaders throughout the territory of the Balkan Peninsula were accompanied by a depopulation of the conquered regions. This was due in part to the many and bloody battles the Balkan peoples waged against the invaders, which claimed thousands of victims. On the other hand, the invaders drove from their homes a large number of inhabitants, whom they then led off into slavery.

This massive enslavement by the Turks at the time when they conquered the peninsula is confirmed by many particulars contained in the historical sources from the fourteenth and fifteenth centuries. This is one of the most sorrowful pages in the history of the Balkan peoples. This practice was closely bound up with the policy and the interests of the Ottoman feudal class and corresponded to the goals that it was pursuing. The Osmanli feudal lords, as we have already noted, had been significantly enriched during the conquest of Asia Minor, and they now possessed vast estates and numerous slaves. But this was not enough to satisfy their longing for wealth—quite the contrary. The feudal ruling class, headed by the emir and his favorites, endeavored to extend its power even further, to amass still more booty and slaves. The feudal Turks in Asia Minor needed slaves, first of all, to make up for the labor shortage, since the majority of the population had perished or fled following the Turkish conquest. Second, the feudal ruling class needed slaves for the domestic work in their homes, or to satisfy their desires in their harems. Finally, in exchange for slaves, the feudal lords managed to acquire precious objects and jewels from abroad. As is well known, in the fourteenth century the economy in the Ottoman state was still at a rudimentary level, commerce and the trades had scarcely developed, money was rare and dear. In these conditions, slave owners could sell their slaves in economically more advanced countries so as to procure in exchange the articles and products that they needed. Ownership of slaves meant a source of wealth not only for the feudal ruling class, but also in large measure for the ordinary soldier who, by selling the prisoners that he captured, could obtain what he required to increase his welfare.

This is why the Turkish soldiers did all that they could to seize prisoners in the course of their campaigns of conquest, and the ruling class exploited this greed so as to foster warlike and aggressive feelings among the soldiers.

Evidently, then, the large-scale slavery practiced by the Turks during their conquest of the Balkan Peninsula was a consequence of the very character of the economic and social regime of the Turkish state and corresponded first and foremost to the interests and the aims of the feudal ruling class. But there was still another reason that prompted the invaders to uproot from their homes the inhabitants of the conquered regions and to lead them off as slaves into Asia Minor. By driving a large number of inhabitants from the peninsula in this way, the Osmanli feudal lords endeavored to weaken the subject nations, to limit their chances of resisting, and to assure their own dominion over them. That was an important military and strategic objective that the Turks had set for themselves from the very first years of their appearance in the Balkan Peninsula, and which later on would acquire an even greater, even decisive importance.

The initial enslavement was carried out at the time when the Turks appeared in the peninsula and the detachments of Suleyman occupied the localities situated in the peninsula of Gallipoli. As Seadeddin relates, when the Turks seized the fortified town of Haghya (near Gallipoli), Suleyman ordered that the entire garrison and the leading men of the city be sent to Asia Minor.[126] This was, clearly, a measure taken for reasons that were mainly military and strategic. Later on, when the Turks invaded eastern and central Thrace beginning in 1360 and seized a large number of Byzantine and Bulgarian cities—Khypsala, Tchorlou, Kechan, Demotika, Andrinopolis, Plovdiv (Philippopolis), Stara Zagora, Yambol, Karnobat, and so on—they subjugated the population on a vast scale. Many references to this have been preserved, notably in the works of Turkish writers (Nešri, Seadeddin, etc.). We find there detailed accounts of the incursions launched by the Turks, which concern slaves seized by the Osmanli armies and the capture of "handsome youths and beautiful girls, slaves as splendid as the moon, and women as beautiful as the sun." If we are to believe Seadeddin, at first large numbers of slaves were taken after the capture of Khypsala and Malagra (near Andrinopolis).[127] Instances of mass enslavement were perpetrated later on in the region of Plovdiv and Stara-Zagora, where the Turkish hordes were under the command of Lala Shahin [French: *Chahin*]. These slaves were led off to Mourad's camp in Asia Minor and distributed to the soldiers, whereas one share was reserved as the property of the Muslim religious leaders.[128] Another of Mourad's lieutenants, Timourtash, who had captured Yambol and other Bulgarian localities in Thrace, also took a great number of prisoners.[129] Again, the Turks led off many slaves after capturing the fortified town of Kirk-Klissé, in eastern Thrace.[130] Mass enslavement was carried out by the Turks also after their incursions into the regions of Samokov and Ichtiman.[131]

The Bulgarian chronicle of the beginning of the fifteenth century tells us also about mass deportations carried out by the Turks at the time of their initial campaigns in Thrace, first during the reign of Suleyman, then under Mourad. It tells of a battle between the Turks and the Bulgarians, the latter commanded by Michael, son of Ivan-Alexander, a battle that ended with the defeat of the Bulgarian armies, as the anonymous chronicler notes. The latter specifies that after this encounter, the Turks "took a great number of prisoners, whom they led off to Gallipoli."[132] We do not know precisely when and where this battle took place, but it should probably be dated between 1340 and 1355.

The works of Byzantine authors, too, contain information about the pillaging committed by the Turks and about the capture of many slaves. We should mention here a communication from Chalcocondyles, which says that when he arrived in the peninsula after the death of Suleyman, Mourad ravaged "the interior of Macedonia (i.e., Thrace) and captured a great number of slaves." Chalcocondyles writes, "To the Turks who had followed him in the hopes of becoming rich, Mourad gave as a reward some of the slaves and livestock that he had seized from the Bulgarians and the Greeks."[133] We find information about the slavery practiced by the Turks in Thrace in the works of Demetrius Kydones as well. One of his letters, written between 1383 and 1387, is very revealing in this regard. In it he explains that the Byzantine towns were entirely depopulated as a result of the Turkish incursions into Thrace. One part of the population is said to have fled to other regions; the rest were assumed to have been captured and sold to the Turks.[134] It is clear that the author is alluding here to the slave sales conducted by the simple soldiers who had no use for their prisoners and preferred to receive money or other goods in exchange for them. According to Seadeddin, the price of a slave increased at that time by half to 125 aspres.[135]

As of 1371, when the Turks seized a part of Macedonia and southwestern Bulgaria and launched their incursions into central Greece, the Peloponnisos, Epirus, Albania, Serbia, Bosnia, and along the Adriatic coast, the practice of slavery took on still larger dimensions. Many, many slaves were led off by the Turks after the capture of Niš, judging from an account by Seadeddin.[136] Numerous slaves were taken after the capture of the Macedonian towns of Prilep, Melnik, Debar, Skopié, Bitolia, Kostour, Vereya, Radovish, Devol, Veles, Vodena, and so on. These slaves were led off to Asia Minor, where later some of them were sold to Venitian merchants. In the archives of the notary Brechano, from Cyprus, we find data concerning 122 Bulgarians, both men and women, who were sold at Candia as slaves between 1381 and 1383. As this source notes, the buyers and the vendors were inhabitants of Candia, whereas the slaves being sold came mainly from the above-mentioned Macedonian cities.[137]

Large numbers of slaves were captured during the plundering campaigns conducted by Mourad's lieutenant, Timurtash, between 1375 and 1385 in Bosnia, Albania, Herzegovina, and Epirus. As Seadeddin mentions, many "handsome youths and pretty girls" were captured in Albania, and each soldier received a slave as a gift, whereas Timurtash received one-fifth of the booty.[138] The campaigns in Bosnia, Herzegovina, and Epirus ended in the same fashion.

The routine pillaging by the Turks became even more widespread when the Osmanli feudal lords took over northeastern Bulgaria, starting in 1388, and began to invade Hungary, Bosnia, central Greece, and the Peloponnisos after the battle of Kosovo. According to the indications that we find in the works of Nešri and other authors, slaves were led off in droves after the campaign launched in 1388 by Ali Pasha.[139] After the battle of Kosovo (1389), a number of slaves were taken from Serbia. During that same year the Turks launched countless incursions, accompanied by devastation and plundering, in Walachia, Albania, and Bosnia. These campaigns ended with the capture and exile of a large number of the inhabitants of these countries.[140] In 1391 the Turks attacked the vicinity of Constantinople and carried off slaves from this part of eastern Thrace.[141] Slaves were led into exile again in 1393 when the kingdom of Tirnovo fell definitively into the hands of the Osmanlis. As Gregory Tzamblak mentions in his eulogy of the patriarch Evtymy, under orders from Bayezid the most reputed families in the Bulgarian capital were led off to slavery in Asia Minor.[142]

Many slaves were captured by the Turks after the ill-starred campaign of Sigismond, which ended in the battle of Nicopol (September 1396). We find information about it in the works of eyewitnesses to this battle, Bouciquaut, Froissart, and Schiltberger, as well as in Byzantine and Turkish sources.[143] According to Schiltberger, all the prisoners who were not yet twenty years old were taken to Gallipoli and from there sent into Asia Minor.[144] After his victory near Nicopol, Bayezid set out for Mitrovica and Petau, captured these villages, and took sixteen thousand slaves. Some of these captives were settled in the vast estates that he owned in the Balkans, whereas the rest were sent to Asia Minor.[145]

The campaign which Yakoub Pasha, Bayezid's lieutenant, launched in 1397 in the Peloponnisos at the head of a large army was the one that procured the greatest number of slaves for the Turks. If we are to believe Sphrantzès and Chalkokondyles, the capture of Argos alone delivered thirty thousand prisoners to the Turks, who sent them to Asia Minor under orders from the sultan.[146]

To whom did this enormous number of slaves accrue? We can conclude from the information furnished by Seadeddin that during the first period of the Turkish conquests (1354–1362) the booty that was captured, both goods and persons, was divided in its entirety among the soldiers. Thus the simple soldier was considerably enriched by acquiring many slaves, jewels, and money. This historian notes that the soldiers, gorged with booty, were unwilling to continue their incursions in Thrace and wanted to return to their homes in Asia Minor.[147] This practice of dividing up the booty—persons and goods—in equal parts did not last for long. The leading feudal class, which organized the incursions and the pillaging and which numbered among its members the military chiefs who led the Turkish troops, soon began to reserve for itself the lion's share of the booty. Seadeddin mentions that in 1363, in the middle of the campaigns launched by the Turks in Thrace, one of the sultan's high-ranking dignitaries, Kara Roustem, arrived in the camp under Mourad's orders and decreed that henceforth the fifth part of the booty taken should be designated for the benefit of the state (that is, for the sultan).[148] This ordinance yielded huge profits, not only for the sultan, but also for his entourage, the high-ranking civil and military dignitaries, whose hands were thus untied so that they could seize the greater part of the booty. Among the most favored, obviously, were the military chiefs who directed the military operations; as a sign of his favor or of recognition for their accomplishments, the sultan allowed them to seize enormous quantities of goods and slaves. As we noted earlier, Timurtash, Mourad's lieutenant, seized during the course of an invasion in Albania one-fifth of the prisoners who had fallen into the hands of the invaders.[149] Following the example of Timurtash, other military leaders, such as Evrenos Beg, Lala Shahin, and Hadji Ilbeki, then enriched themselves in the same manner. We can get some idea of the enormous wealth that Mourad's lieutenants had amassed in the form of "live booty" from the gifts that they presented to the sultan on the occasion of the wedding of his son, Bayezid. According to the historian Munedjim Baši, Timurtash gave the sultan a present consisting of one hundred boys and one hundred girls. Each of the first ten slaves carried a silver goblet filled with gold coins; the next ten, a golden goblet filled with silver coins; and the eighty remaining slaves, silver candlesticks.[150] This gift, the Turkish historian notes, stupefied the foreign envoys present at the ceremony. On that same occasion, another well-known military chief, Evrenos Beg, presented the sultan with a gift of many slaves.[151] Most of the captured slaves were sent to the sultan's palace; we have mentioned, indeed, that the sultan had the legal right to one-fifth of the booty that was taken. The number of slaves was already large during the reign of Mourad, but the number increased considerably under Bayezid, who conducted dozens of campaigns involving pillaging and devastation. The most handsome and the strongest of the boys who were taken prisoner were sent to special barracks to add to the corps of janissaries. The other slaves remained in the sultan's palace, where they were employed as domestics or served to satisfy the sultan's desires. We find an interesting description of the life of the sultan's slaves in Doucas's history. Describing the palace of Bayezid in Brousse, Doucas notes, among other things, that "there one could find carefully selected boys and girls, with beautiful faces, sweet young boys and girls who shone more brightly than the sun. To what nations did they belong? They were Byzantines, Serbs, Walachians, Albanians, Hungarians, Saxons, Bulgarians, and Latins. Each of them sang songs in his native language, although reluctantly. He himself (the sultan) unceasingly gave himself over to pleasure, to the point of exhaustion, by indulging in debauchery with these boys and girls."[152]

Subjected to hard labor, obliged to satisfy the carnal desires of their masters in the dwellings of the Turkish feudal lords or in the palaces of the sultan, sold on the marketplace like cattle, the slaves thought only of escaping their tragic lot and of saving themselves by fleeing. As Bertrandon de la Broquières notes, the slaves who succeeded in escaping often sought refuge in the Genoese colony of Galata, although the Genoese had to return them to their masters in keeping with an agreement made with the sultan.[153] We find in the archives of Genoa two documents relating to fugitive slaves. These two documents are dated 1391.[154] The first deals with two Bulgarian slaves who had escaped from the Turks and who were being guarded for a time in the prison of Galata, where they were fed at the expense of the community. The second of these documents refers to a sum of money that the Genoese are said to have paid for the deliverance of a slave who had escaped from the Turks and taken refuge in the colony.

Between 1402 and 1413, when the Osmanli campaigns were temporarily interrupted as a result of the anarchy that shook the Turkish state, instances of enslaving the population ceased as well. But this truce did not last long. After the accession of Mahomet I (1413–1421), and especially after the arrival of Mourad II (1421–1451), the seizure of slaves was resumed with a vengeance when the Osmanlis again started their incursions on the peninsula. We find much information on this subject, which has yet to be properly utilized and systematized, in the works of Doucas, Chalkokondyles, Sphrantzès, in the anonymous Byzantine chronicle, as well as in certain Turkish and Western authors. Slaves in great numbers were captured, for example, during the war conducted by Mahomet against Venice and in 1417 during the invasion of Negrepont (Euboea, Evvoia). These slaves were later sold in Sicily, Catalogna, and Syria.[155] Some years later (1424), huge numbers of slaves were carried off after a surprise attack on Coron and Modon (in the Peloponnisos).[156]

The capture of Salonika by Mourad's armies in 1430 was followed by the mass enslavement of the population. We find a dramatic description of the capture and plundering of the city in an account by a contemporary author, Ioan Anagnostas, an eyewitness himself, since he was among the prisoners. As he tells it, the Turks led seven thousand slaves out of the city—men, women, and children, who were later divided up among the soldiers.[157] Loaded down with chains, exhausted, and panic-stricken, they presented a lamentable sight. The history by Doucas provides us also with a very detailed description of the outrages committed by the Turks at Salonika and of the tragic fate awaiting its population.[158] These events are mentioned also in a letter by Pope Eugene IV from the year 1438.[159] Some of the prisoners, as Anagnostas remarks, found the money needed to purchase their freedom, but those who had no means had to depart with their new masters and follow them into their homes, to serve them until the day when they would find some way of redeeming themselves.[160]

When the Turks launched their new invasions, from 1430 on, the number of slaves they brought back increased more and more. A multitude of slaves was captured in 1438 by the armies of Mourad II during his campaign against Hungary.

Ašik Pasha Zadé, who took part in that campaign, writes that the soldiers took so many prisoners that their price fell considerably. According to his account, one could obtain a slave in exchange for a pair of boots.[161] Not long afterward the Turks led off new slaves during their invasion of Albania (1440).[162] The same thing happened after the disastrous campaign of Vladislav IV Varnencik in 1444. But the Osmanli feudal lords seized the largest number of slaves during the campaign conducted by Mahomet in the Peloponnisos against the despot Constantine (1446). If we are to believe the reports of the Byzantine historians on this subject, which moreover are confirmed by some Western authors, the Turks then carried off into captivity around sixty thousand prisoners.[163]

This increase in the number of slaves over the course of the first half of the fifteenth century prompted the growth of slave auctions and revived the slave markets that had been organized in the main cities of the Turkish state in Asia Minor and in the Balkan Peninsula. Many slaves were bought by the sultan of Babylon, as indicated in a communication from the traveler Lanoix, who visited that country between 1421 and 1423. According to Lanoix, the sultan of Babylon owned around ten thousand slaves from different countries: Bulgaria, Hungary, Slavonia, Walachia, and Russia.[164] We also find interesting information on this subject in the work of Bertrandon de la Broquières. While he was staying in Andrinopolis in 1434, he saw slaves who were shackled and about to be sold, begging outside the city walls.[165] While returning from Andrinopolis he met along the way forty men in chains and twenty women. These people had been taken prisoner during a surprise attack in Bosnia and were now being led to Andrinopolis, escorted by two Turks, in order to be sold.[166] We likewise have testimonies concerning the sale of slaves in Crete, on Cyprus, in Catalogna, and in Syria.[167] Documents preserved in the archives of Ancona prove that slaves were sold in that city also.[168] The Turks also sold slaves to the inhabitants of Albania who, in turn, sold them to others. A document dated 1439 deals with the slaves that a citizen of Venice is said to have bought for forty ducats from some Albanians near Himara.[169]

A message from Pope Eugene IV, dated 1442, contains very revealing information about the Turkish practice of mass enslavement in the mid-fifteenth century and about the tragic fate of the slaves that they captured. The message says that the Turks conquered enormous territories in Thrace, Macedonia, Illyria, Albania, Bulgaria and Slavonia, from which they took many slaves. The Turks led their slaves, the pope writes, bound in chains and then killed in the cities or along the roads those among them who, because of old age, sickness, or fatigue due to the long journey, were no longer capable of walking.[170]

In order to escape their tragic lot, the slaves tried to save themselves by fleeing. Two documents of the Republic of Ragusa (Dubrovnik) from the years 1414 and 1420 mention such cases.[171]

This wave of mass enslavement reached its high point during the devastating campaigns conducted by Mahomet II (1451–1453), the successor of Mourad II. This was the period when the Osmanli feudal class had discovered that it was possible to amass more and more *live booty* and thus to guarantee for themselves a life of luxury and leisure. Above all it was the capture of Constantinople (May 29, 1453), which delivered an enormous number of prisoners to the Turks. According to Kritobulos, fifty thousand inhabitants of the Byzantine capital were led off into captivity, whereas a recently published anonymous Byzantine chronicle estimates the number at sixty thousand.[172] Doucas, who was an eyewitness to the capture and sack of Constantinople, recounts in vivid language the martyrdom of the inhabitants of the capital who fell into the hands of the conquerors. According to his account, the Turks led off the most captives from the Cathedral of Santa Sofia, where the terrified inhabitants had sought refuge in vain.[173] Bound with chains and cords, men, women, adolescents, monks, and priests were led off to the Osmanli camp, where they had to await the determination of their fate. Each Turkish soldier seized a prisoner and hurried to bring him to a secure place so as to return to the city to look for new victims. The Janissaries carried off the greater part of the booty. They seized such a large number of women and children belonging to the leading families of the capital that, if we are to believe Chalkokondyles, they didn't know what to do with them all.[174] After three days of plundering came the time to divide up the booty. Mahomet received his legal share (one-fifth of the booty) and, in addition, a large number of boys and girls selected from among the most handsome, several of whom he had redeemed from the soldiers. He likewise redeemed several of the more reputable inhabitants of the capital, such as Lucas Notaras and others. On June 18—that is, twenty days after the capture of Constantinople—Mahomet departed for Andrinopolis, bringing all of his booty with him: jewels, valuables, and slaves. Scarcely three days after the capture of Constantinople, the rest of the slaves captured by the soldiers and the Janissaries were led outside the city. Piled into ships and boats with all the rest of the booty—luxurious garments; vessels made of gold, silver, copper, and lead; and a great number of books—these unfortunate souls went into exile, where new sufferings awaited them.[175]

Shortly after the capture of Constantinople, Mahomet launched new campaigns against Serbia, Bosnia, the Peloponnisos, Albania, Hungary, Walachia, the islands of the Aegean Sea, and Trebizond. These campaigns delivered up to the Osmanlis, and especially to the Janissaries, enormous numbers of slaves. Many captives were led off after the campaign conducted by Mahomet in Serbia in 1455, which ended in the capture of Novo Bardo and other localities. According to Mihail Constantinović, almost all the inhabitants of Novo Bardo were taken into captivity and the sultan received 320 youths and 700 women as a personal gift.[176] The capture of another fortified town near Smederevo left all eight thousand of its inhabitants in the hands of the Turks. The sultan received half of them and settled them in the vicinity of Constantinople, while the rest were divided among the military leaders and the soldiers who had performed the most meritorious service during that campaign.[177] Many prisoners fell into the hands of the Turks over the course of their plundering raids in the Peloponnisos. When the Turks put down the Albanian uprising, they carried off ten thousand prisoners, according to the anonymous Byzantine chronicle.[178] As Kritobulos notes in his history, at the time of the campaign conducted by Mahomet and by Mahmoud Pasha during the summer of 1458 in the Peloponnisos, more than four thousand prisoners were led off by the conquerors from the fortified towns that they had occupied.[179] During the military operations launched by the Turks against Thomas Paleologus and his brother Demetrius, the number of prisoners allegedly increased to thirty thousand, according to the anonymous Byzantine chronicle. The fortified town of Salvari alone yielded ten thousand prisoners.[180] In certain towns, the invaders led off the entire population; in others, they allowed some of the inhabitants to remain in their homes. Thus, according to Chalkokondyles, after the capture of Salmenik, the Turks led into captivity the entire population of that fortified town, or approximately six thousand persons. These captives were given to the soldiers who had distinguished themselves most valiantly during that campaign; nine hundred children were selected to supplement the corps of Janissaries, and the rest were sold.[181] After the capture of the fortress of Greven, only one-third of the population was led off into captivity, while the rest of the inhabitants remained in their homes.[182]

The Turks took many, many prisoners whom they led off into captivity during their campaigns against Albania. According to Kritobulos, around twenty thousand prisoners fell into the hands of the invaders at the time of the campaign conducted in 1466 by Mahomet II.[183] By way of imposing a tribute, the Turks took a great number of children out of the country.[184] Many slaves were taken by the Turks in Hungary as well. As the anonymous Byzantine chronicle notes, just one invasion in that country delivered up ten thousand Hungarian prisoners to the Turks.[185] Some slaves were captured during the campaigns against Bosnia (1463) and the islands in the Aegean Sea—Euboea [Evvoia], Lesbos, Samothrace, Imbros, and so on. In violation of the custom that gave him a right to one-fifth of the booty, the sultan started to reserve one-half of it for himself. After the capture of Bobovik in Bosnia, the sultan ordered that one-third of the inhabitants be given to him; the second third was distributed among the soldiers and the rest were permitted to remain in their homes.[186] After the capture of Mitylene, Mahomet kept half of the captured inhabitants for himself.[187] The sultan reserved for himself the most handsome and the most graceful of the captive boys and girls. As Kritobulos notes, during the spring of 1456 he brought from Enos 150 children who were selected from among the most beautiful of the city.[188]

In the writings of Jacob Promontorio de Campis, who was procurator for the court of the sultans from 1433 to 1458, we find interesting details about Mahomet's palace and about his untold wealth in *live booty*. He writes that in the sultan's palace in Constantinople there were special living quarters for the youths, his favorites, selected from among the captive Christians and his own subjects. There were as many as 400 of them. Put on a special diet, treated with much care and kept under strict watch, these adolescents were trained to become the future high-ranking dignitaries of the empire, the sultan's most loyal and most intimate collaborators.[189] Furthermore there were two harems in the palace, in which the most beautiful female slaves were kept. The first consisted of around 400 young women; the second, around 250.[190]

Besides the sultan, who, as we have said, awarded himself the lion's share of the booty, his lieutenants and the high-ranking dignitaries of his court grew rich with their many slaves. Chalkokondyles mentions the military leader Dzagan, who derived huge profits from his campaign in the Peloponnisos and led off a multitude of prisoners into Thessaly.[191] The same individual is mentioned in the anonymous Byzantine chronicle. It says there, notably, that Dzagan became very wealthy from the pillaging to which he subjected the Peloponnisos by sending many slaves and large quantities of good to his property in Thessaly without the sultan's knowledge.[192] Mahmoud Pasha, one of the high-ranking dignitaries of the empire and an intimate of the sultan, was himself Serbian on his mother's side and Greek on his father's side; he had been captured by the Turks as a child and raised in the sultan's court, and he, too, owned a large number of slaves. According to Chalkokondyles, he was so rich that he was capable of maintaining his own army and had in his pay several functionaries who ended up being quite influential in the affairs of state.[193]

The Osmanli feudal lords employed many of the slaves that they captured on construction work, rebuilding the fortified towns that were ruined or half destroyed, reconstructing buildings, bridges, and so on. Kritobulos explicitly notes that the surrounding walls of Constantinople were restored by Byzantine prisoners who had fallen into the hands of the Turks when the city was captured.[194] Other slaves were employed as domestics in the dwellings of the aristocratic Turks or had the task of amusing their masters or of satisfying their taste for carnal pleasures. Some of the captured children were sent to the barracks to fill up the ranks of the Janissaries. According to Jacobo Promontorio de Campis, whom we cited earlier, every year twenty-five hundred youths of fifteen years of age were sent from all regions of Turkey to these barracks. They consisted mainly of young prisoners captured during the campaigns conducted by the sultan, but included also in their number were children whose parents had to pay the blood tax in this manner. As De Campis notes, for six years these youths received an education under the supervision of harsh masters. Then the sultan selected from among them fifteen hundred adolescents whom he enlisted in his corps of Janissaries. The total contingent of Janissaries amounted to six thousand. De Campis describes in detail their clothing and their armaments, while devoting a few lines as well to the organization of this army corps.[195]

Let us consider now, what were the consequences of these instances of mass enslavement carried out for more than a century on the Balkan Peninsula by the

Turkish invaders, starting with Suleyman and continuing to Mahomet II. The answer to this question is given to us by the Byzantine historian Doucas, who had the opportunity to see and to experience personally the dire consequences of the invasion of the peninsula by the Turks, and to realize clearly the tragedy and the evils experienced by the subject population. In his writings, Doucas dwells especially on the countless incidents of pillaging that accompanied the military actions of the Turks in the Balkan territories, as well as the large-scale depopulation of the towns and the countrysides that resulted from the massacres and the mass enslavement. "The Turks, more than any other people," he writes, "love plundering and wars. They demonstrate this in their mutual relations, so what hope is there, then for the Christians . . . ? The Turks journey on foot as far as the Danube to conquer the Christians. They invade a province by the tens of thousands, arriving like robbers and fleeing once they have pillaged it. These incursions have transformed all of Thrace, as far as Dalmatia, into a wilderness. They have reduced the number of Albanians, who are nevertheless a numberless people. All told, the Turks have annihilated the Walachians and the Serbs and the Byzantines. When they subjugate these peoples, they give one-fifth of the booty to their sultan, in conformity with their law. Thus they hand over this fifth and best part to the government. Then, when the representatives of the government notice a prisoner who is young and strong, they buy him for a ludicrous price and declare him a slave of the state. The sultan calls these pupils his new army or, in his language, *Janissaries*."[196]

Doucas doubtless exaggerates when he tells us about a total annihilation of the Balkan peoples resulting from the pillaging and enslavement perpetrated by the Turks. Here, too, as elsewhere, Doucas expresses in rhetorical language the sentiments of profound sorrow and despair that the conquest of the Balkan Peninsula aroused in him. The numerous reports concerning the number of Christians who became slaves, furnished by certain Byzantine authors and others, whom we have cited earlier, no doubt also contain exaggerations and inaccuracies. It is nonetheless true that the conquest by the Turks and their ceaseless invasions for almost a century and a half dealt an extremely harsh blow to the population of the peninsula and caused the depopulation of many regions and localities, by obliging the inhabitants to go off into captivity. The period following the accession of Mahomet II was especially disastrous for the population of the Balkans. It was precisely during this period that the conquering fever of the Osmanlis reached its apogee and all the states on the peninsula fell definitively under the power of the conquerors.

Given these circumstances, it is still important to refute the thesis maintained nowadays by certain Turkish historians, which supposes that the Osmanli conquest was almost a blessing for the Balkan peoples. This thesis endeavors to attribute to the Osmanli feudal lords a civilizing mission in the Balkans, claiming that these rulers, by their conquests in Asia Minor and Europe, laid the groundwork for a more highly developed economic and social regime, for a wealthier and more advanced civilization. Such a thesis is belied by the historical facts. It is in flagrant contradiction with the plentiful information furnished by the historical sources, which clearly prove the destructive nature of the Turkish conquests.

By practicing large-scale subjugation of the population, the Osmanli feudal lords caused a vast movement of migration and population shifts throughout the peninsula. This dislocation of the population and these migratory movements, which deprived entire regions and localities of their inhabitants—peasants, craftsmen, or professionals—naturally contributed to a great extent (and for the same reasons that we have noted) to a cessation of economic and cultural life and a decrease in productivity. The lands belonging to the farmers who were led off into captivity lay fallow, the workshops where hard-working artisans once plied their trades were shut down. As is well known, people, because of their experience and their knowledge, are one of the essential factors in productivity. Without people there can be no economic activity whatsoever, even if one has the best means of production at one's disposal.

The depopulation of the countryside and the dying out of the trades were detrimental to the Turkish feudal ruling class and the Osmanli state that was being built up on the Balkan Peninsula. Insufficient manpower constituted an hindrance to the exploitation of the workers in the regions conquered by the feudal class. It was also an obstacle to the accomplishment of the political and military goals set by the invaders. Already during their initial incursions in the Balkan Peninsula, the invaders realized the dangers posed for them by the depopulation and ruination of the conquered territories, dangers that later on became even more serious and more evident. In order to cope with them, the sultans had recourse to two expedients from the very outset of their conquests: on the one hand, they had Turkish colonists from Asia Minor settle in certain regions of the peninsula; on the other hand, they transferred the population from designated [*rectaines*, from Latin *rego*, to mark off boundaries] regions to places where manpower was lacking, as a result of the destruction and ruination that they themselves had perpetrated.

This policy of colonization practiced by the Osmanlis in the Balkans (the main purpose of which was to assure normal economic life in the first place and the exploitation of the masses by the feudal lords) also pursued strategic and military ends. By settling Turks in the occupied regions, the Osmanli feudal lords sought to strengthen the Muhammadan [Islamic] element of the population and thus to consolidate the invaders' power. The Osmanli feudal lords sought to increase the number of Mohammedans especially in the large urban centers. To that end, they settled not only enlisted men, but also civilians. This policy became quite evident especially after the conquest of Thrace and Macedonia, that is, during the initial period of the invasion of Europe by the Turks, at a time when it was necessary for them to establish a solid base for their subsequent undertakings. The transfer of the Balkan populations from one region to another, also, served military and strategic purposes. By these populations shifts the Osmanli feudal lords sought to reduce the Christian population in the regions where their own power was not yet entirely consolidated, and where the [native] population posed a danger to the authorities by their attempts to revolt. This was the purpose, for example, of the transfers of population in the Peloponnisos during the second half of the fifteenth century. The uprooted population was directed toward regions where the lack of manpower made itself felt with particular severity. By having recourse to such measures, the Osmanli feudal lords pursued the simultaneous accomplishment of two precise purposes, one strategic and the other economic.

This policy of colonization, which was applied from the very first Osmanli invasions in the Balkans, was pursued throughout the duration of the conquest of the Balkan territories. We can mark off the stages of this policy in numerous sources of Turkish, Byzantine, and other origin, some of which have already been utilized [in historical scholarship], although in an inadequate and incomplete manner.[197] The first transfers of Turkish colonists took place during the reign of Suleyman, the conqueror of the region around Kherson. In 1352, after the fall of Tzympé, as Seadeddin notes, a Turkish garrison three hundred strong was set up there, and the number of troops was subsequently increased to three thousand.[198] Later, when the Osmanlis occupied the entire peninsula of Gallipoli, the number of colonists increased, and this time Turkish civilian colonists from Asia Minor came to settle there. According to Nešri, some Arab nomads from the region of Karassi settled in 1354 in the vicinity of Gallipoli.[199] We likewise find in the writings of Kantakuzenos reports concerning the immigration of the Turks in the peninsula of Gallipoli.[200] Chalkokondyles gives us an interesting report. He writes that, after they found out about the occupation of Gallipoli by Suleyman's armies, many Turks arrived from Asia Minor and devoted themselves there to farming.[201]

After the accession of Mourad, when the Osmanlis launched their incursions into Thrace and occupied a large number of the Byzantine and Bulgarian localities, immigration into the occupied regions by Turks coming from Asia Minor continued at an accelerated pace. According to Seadeddin, some Turks were settled by Evrenos Beg and Halil Beg along the Marica, in the region of Kipsala, which had been entirely cleansed of "infidels."[202] Some Turkish garrisons were stationed in Plovdiv, Andrinopolis, Stara-Zagora, and other towns.[203] The reports given by Seadeddin agree with indications by Chalkokondyles, who notes that during the reign of Mourad I the plain of Zagora and the region surrounding Plovdiv were populated by Turkish colonists.[204] According to a communication from the grand mufti Hairoulah Effendi, who made use of unknown sources, around ten thousand Muslims from the provinces of Bigha, Keressi, and Aïdin settled in Thrace.[205] The economic recovery of the ruined and depopulated areas of Thrace was made possible thanks to this immigration, as Ašik Pasha Zadé notes.[206]

Demetrius Kydones, too, mentions the colonization of Thrace by the Muslims during the reign of Mourad. In his discourse of 1366, he bitterly recalls that "the Turks now live in Thrace with greater security than the Byzantines," and that this area had already been transformed into a Turkish domain.[207]

The immigration of Turks in Thrace continued during the reign of Bajazet as well. At his command, as Nešri and Ašik Pasha Zadé mention, his son Ertoghroul brought in nomadic colonists from the region of Sarouhan. This immigration was dictated by political considerations, notably because of the frequent uprisings of these nomads against the authorities.[208] These nomads occupied the region around Plovdiv and settled especially in the vicinity of Sarambey and in Sarambey itself (today Septemvri). From a family belonging to these nomadic tribes was descended the Turkish military leader Ighit Pasha, one of the first lieutenants of Bayezid during his campaigns against Serbia and Bosnia.

The colonization of Thrace by the Turks changed to some extent the aspect of its inhabited places, especially those situated in the eastern part of the land along the Aegean coast. We find confirmation of this in the writings of Bertrandon de la Broquières, who traveled through that region in 1434. He reports that the fortified town of Tchorlou already had a mixed population composed of Greeks and Turks.[209] Pirghisi (Lulé Bourgas, Arcadiopolis) was already an entirely Turkish city, and the traveler did not meet a single Christian there.[210] In certain places La Broquières saw new localities built and inhabited by the Turks. This was the case, for example, with the village of Yeni Bazar (probably near Lake Tahina, today Neohori).[211] A Turkish locality is said to have been constructed near the older city of Vyra (Féré). It was surrounded with defending walls and was evidently, as La Broquières put it, "a large city," populated by Greeks and Turks.[212]

Some Tartars, who had fled from the Crimea after its occupation by Timourlenk, came likewise to settle in Thrace during the reign of Bayezid. They were settled in the region of Plovdiv, where they received grants of land. They were headed by a chief, a certain Aktabey. According to his own testimony, he was capable of organizing and sending an army of thirty thousand men to aid the sultan.[213] From this we can gather that the Tartars must have been very numerous. A second group of Tartars was brought from Asia Minor in 1418, under orders from Mahomet I. They, too, were settled in the region of Plovdiv, and they would later be the founders of the city of Tatar Pazardjik.[214] The Turks also colonized Sofia, Pirote, and Niš after the Osmanlis had occupied those provinces beginning in 1380. We find information on this topic in the writings of Chalkokondyles and of certain Turkish authors, as well as in the accounts of travelers who went through these countries. Bertrandon de la Broquières, who traversed these provinces in 1433, writes that Pirote was a city populated exclusively by Turks.[215] Petančić tells us that Niš, to which he went in 1502, had a mixed population made up of Bulgarians and Turks.[216] The city of Sofia became the mainstay of the Turks; the Osmanlis made it the center of their dominion in southwest Bulgaria and the point of departure for their new invasions.

The Turks proceeded to colonize another important region in Macedonia, which they had begun to invade as early as 1371. The Turkish colonists were settled principally in the great urban centers: Seres, Skopié, Bitolia, and so on, while other colonists were settled in the villages. The region of Salonika and the lands along the Vardar River were colonized by the Turks during the reign of Mourad, as Chalkokondyles tells it.[217] The existence of Turkish habitations in the region of Salonika is confirmed in a communication from Doucas concerning the capture of the city by Mourad II in 1430. Doucas indicates that the city, which had lost many of its inhabitants, was repopulated at the sultan's command by Turks who came from neighboring localities and villages.[218] During the reign of Mourad, the region of Seres was likewise colonized. Nomads from Sarouhan were settled there in 1385 on the abandoned lands. We find information about this colonization in the anonymous Turkish chronicles as well as in the writings of Nešri, Ašik Pasha Zadé, and Oroudjadil.[219] It is possible that this colonization did not take place in 1385 but a little later, given that Sarouhan at that time was not yet under the power of the Osmanlis. Be that as it may, the fact itself is nonetheless true, and we have no reason to doubt it. It is a well-known fact that the regions surrounding Seres, Verh, Zihna, Kerapheria, and other localities were at that time depopulated as a result of the battles that had waged there and the flight of the populace.[220] That is what made it necessary to colonize them.

This colonization was continued during the reign of Bayezid, when all of Macedonia, with the exception of Salonika, fell under the power of the Osmanlis. The information available to us mainly concerns the colonization of Skopje and the region surrounding it.[221] As Chalkokondyles writes, Bayezid brought to Skopje, which fell into the invaders' hands in 1392, "from Asia Minor and Europe many Turks with their wives and children."[222] No doubt it was the sultan's intention not only to repopulate the devastated territories, but also to establish a solid base for his future aggressive military actions against Serbia, Bosnia, Hungary, and Walachia. And in fact Skopje became the center of Turkish power in Macedonia. The sultan stationed there two of his most loyal lieutenants, Ighit Pasha and Isaak Pasha.

The colonization of Thessaly by the Turks likewise began during the reign of Bayezid. Chalkokondyles expressly mentions this in his history.[223] Some more recent sources deal with this Turkish population as well as with the rich Turkish landowners in Thessaly.

It was also during the reign of Bayezid that the Turks undertook the colonization of the provinces located between the Stara Planina and the Danube, in northern Bulgaria, which finally fell under the power of the conquerors in 1396. First this colonization was limited to the establishment of Turkish garrisons in the principal towns which served as bases for the Turkish [military] authority. The existence of such garrisons is confirmed by Schiltberger, Bouciquaut, Froissart, and other authors who describe the campaign conducted by Sigismond in 1396. We find similar reports in the works of Długosz, Kalimah, Beheim, and other authors who treat the campaign launched in 1444 by Vladislav IV. These sources demonstrate that all of northern Bulgaria was riddled with Turkish garrisons which were responsible for guarding the defending the principal cities and forti-fied towns of the country. There were garrisons in the towns on the banks of the Danube—Vidin, Oriahovo, Silistra, Nicopol—as well as in the localities in the interior of the region along the Danube—Tirnovo, Šumen, Petartch, Varna, Galata, Caliacra, and so on.[224]

Not counting the garrisons established in various regions of northeastern Bul-garia, a certain number of Turkish colonists were brought into the country toward the end of the fourteenth century, no doubt immediately after the campaign con-ducted by Ali Pasha in 1388. This civilian population was settled in various towns and villages, or else in localities that the new colonists built themselves. Leon-clavius, who made use of reliable Turkish sources, indicates that the region between Silistria and Šumen (Kolarovgrad) was inhabited at the beginning of the fifteenth century by Turkish *akindji*, that is, by peasants farmers who worked their own lands and at the same time served in the army.[225] The presence of Turks in that region, which was later known as Deliorman (now called Loudogorié), is confirmed in some sources concerning the 1415 revolt of Bedredin Simavi, as well as in the writings of Seadeddin and others. Seadeddin writes that Bedredin carried out his subversive activity in Deliorman and that from there he sent his agitators to the other parts of the country,[226] which proves that the size of the Turkish population must have been considerable in these provinces. We find also in the account that Beheim has left us of the campaign conducted by Vladislav in 1444, indications of the presence of Turks in these areas. One can conclude from this author's words that after the capture of Novi Pazar (Jengepasser), the cru-saders found in this city, besides the garrison, some Turkish civilians who were massacred at the same time as the soldiers.[227] These were Turkish peasants who no doubt had fled the nearby villages to seek refuge in this fortified town. There were also some Turkish refugees in the mighty fortified town of Šumen, which the crusaders managed to seize after fierce fighting.[228] The words of Beheim are quite significant when he says that "the real Turkey" (*in dy rehten Turkei*)[229] began at the place where the crusaders had joined battle toward the south of the Danube, in the direction of Novi Pazar, and from there toward Šumen and Varna. This proves that those very regions had a considerable number of Turks alongside the Bulgarian population around the mid-fifteenth century, whereas their number was insignificant in the rest of northern Bulgaria.

The immigration of Turks into northeastern Bulgaria continued later on as well. Two registers dating from the beginning of the sixteenth century indicate the immigration of the Turks in the vicinity of Silistra.[230] It was perhaps at that time that the Turks settled in the region called Touzlouk, located to the southwest of Šumen.[231]

*   *   *

Some Turkish colonists settled in Albania also. The Turks began to infiltrate the country especially during the time of the great campaigns conducted by Mourad II (1421–1452) and later by Mahomet II (1452–1481), when the country was finally conquered after a fierce resistance. As Leonclavius indicates, during one of his devastating campaigns in 1440, Mourad drove the Albanians from the lands that they had occupied and settled Turkish colonists there.[232] The colonization affected most of all the cities where garrisons of janissaries were stationed. A similar garrison was established in Arghirocastron, which was besieged by Albanian insurgents under the leadership of Depa.[233]

The Turks also colonized Serbia, Bosnia, the Peloponnisos, and the islands in the Aegean Sea after those places were occupied by the invaders. Here, too, the colonization consisted chiefly in the establishment of garrisons in the principal cities and fortified towns. We find in the writings of Doucas information about the presence of Turkish garrisons in Serbia,[234] whereas from the writings of Kritobulos we can learn primarily about the existence of Turkish garrisons in the Peloponnisos.[235] Elsewhere the anonymous Byzantine chronicle and Chalkokondyles provide us with information about the Turkish garrisons in Bosnia.[236] Chalkokondyles also provides us with data concerning the Turkish garrisons in the islands of the Aegean Sea.[237]

If we follow the stages of this policy of colonization implemented by the Osmanlis in the Balkan Peninsula, we will discover that the colonization was on a larger scale during the first fifty years after the arrival of the conquerors in Europe. This period was characterized by the relocation from Asia Minor of significant masses of the Turkish populace, who were settled mainly in eastern Thrace, along the Aegean coast, in Macedonia, and in Thessaly. This colonization extended in some measure to certain regions of northeastern Bulgaria. From 1402 on the immigration of Turks to Europe diminished considerably and consisted only in the establishment of garrisons in the occupied countries (Albania, Serbia, the Peloponnisos, Bosnia).

Under these circumstances, it is inaccurate to say that the Muslim element was predominant in the peninsula during the fourteenth and fifteenth centuries and that the Balkans had been transformed into "Turkish territory," as certain contemporary Turkish historians claim, notably O. Barkan in the article cited above. This thesis is not in keeping with historical truth. We have plenty of indications dating from the fourteenth and fifteenth centuries that prove that, despite the Turkish immigration, the Christians made up the bulk of the population in the Balkan Peninsula. This is confirmed by the travelers who made their way through the peninsula during that period and whose writings have been preserved. Among these travelers we should cite in the first place Bertrandon de la Broquières, about whom we spoke earlier; in 1434 he traveled through Thrace, southern Macedonia, and southwestern Bulgaria, that is to say, precisely the territories where the Turkish colonization had been the most significant. It is evident from the works of Broquières that, despite this colonization, the greater part of the population in these territories occupied by the Turks was composed of Christians—Bulgarians and Greeks. He indicates that the cities of Misterio (perhaps ancient Messina) and Peritor were inhabited exclusively by Greeks.[238] His reports on the Bulgarian population in Thrace and eastern Bulgaria are even more certain and more precise. In speaking of Plovdiv, La Broquières explicitly says that "[m]ost of Philippopolis is inhabited by Bulgarians who abide by the Greek law, that is, Orthodoxy."[239] In writing the account of his journey from Plovdiv to Sofia, La Broquières mentions "two villages populated by Bulgarians,"[240] in one of which he spent the night. Speaking about the plain of Sofia, La Broquières remarks that it was "populated largely by Bulgarians." About Sofia and the surrounding region he tells us: "The inhabitants of the city are for the most part Bulgarians, and it is the same with the village. The Turks there are a very small minority, which arouses in the others a great longing to free themselves from their domination, if only there were someone to help them."[241] With respect to the region situated between Sofia and Pirote, toward the Serbian border, he writes: "The country is well populated and its inhabitants and Bulgarian Orthodox."[242]

This information provided by La Broquières, which pertains to a comparatively limited subset of the Turkish possessions in the Balkan Peninsula, are confirmed by the work of Philip Buonacuore (Kalimah), an envoy of the king of Poland, who in 1487 traveled through Thrace, Mesia, and Macedonia (we spoke of him earlier). The descriptions that he has left us of the regions through which he traveled show that the Christian population there was predominant. "Besides the ease and the charm of the journey, we should note the fact that we were traveling among people who are Christian and consequently friendly."[243] According to him the number of Turks was very small. "Previously and now once again I was able to see how small the numbers of Turks in Europe are, since when I was sent by the King to the Turk [i.e., the sultan] to make peace and to settle the affairs of Walachia, I traveled along the coast through Lower Thrace and Mesia and on my return trip through the Middle [Mesia] as far as Macedonia and Upper Mesia." Kalimach adds, with reference to the Turkish population: "The people are so few that when they gather in groups to watch travelers depart, something which is most amusing and interesting to them. . . . I was astonished, in looking at them, by their small numbers, and even more by the poverty and lack of cleanliness among that populace."[244]

The sources that refer to the two campaigns of Vladislav IV in 1443 and 1444 provide us also with information concerning the insignificant number of Turks settled in the peninsula in the fifteenth century. We find some particularly interesting details in the reports about the second of these campaigns, during which the crusaders traveled through northern and northeastern Bulgaria. From the descriptions given by Kalimah, Długosz, and Beheim we can deduce that, as noted above, there were no Turks except in the garrisons of the fortified towns (Nicopol,

Novi-Pazar, Šumen, Galata, Varna, Caliacra, etc.). Some Turks had partially set-
tled certain villages in the vicinity of Novi-Pazar and Šumen, as Beheim notes.
The rest of the country was populated by Christian Bulgarians who, according to
Kalimah and Długosz, had their own churches and spoke a language similar to
Polish. This population put up no resistance at all to the armies of crusaders; quite
to the contrary, the locals came to their aid, which allowed Vladislav to reach
Varna (Stalin) in a very short time.

The most conclusive albeit unsystematic data on the population of the peninsula after it
was occupied by the Turks, and on its ethnic composition, are contained in the
works of several sixteenth-century travelers: Felix Petanäić (who journeyed
through the region in 1502), Benedict Kouripešić (1530), Benedetto Ramberti
(1534), A. Bousbeck (1553), Hans Dernschwam (1553–1555), and Stefan Gerlach
(1573–1578). The works of all these authors show us that the Turkish population
scattered throughout the Balkan territories (Bosnia, Herzegovina, Serbis, Bulgaria, Greece), although making up the ruling class, were quite inferior in number
to the Christian population and could by no means change the ethnic aspect of the
peninsula.

The most conclusive testimony of this preponderance of the Christian population, in spite of the colonization undertaken by the Turks in the peninsula, is furnished by the statistical data about the number of families subject to taxes in the
various administrative regions of the peninsula and on the islands in the Aegean
Sea. These data were preserved in Turkish government registers and were compiled over the period between 1520 and 1530 for fiscal reasons. The table that
appears in the above-cited article by Barkan was drawn up on the basis of these
data. It clearly shows the correlation between the different ethnic groups in the
Balkan Peninsula at the beginning of the sixteenth century.[245] In the final analysis,
this table indicates that there were, at that time, in the peninsula and on the islands
of the Aegean Sea (including a part of Asia Minor and the Crimea), 832,707 Christian families, as opposed to 194,958 Muhammadan families. To put it another way,
the number of Christians at the beginning of the sixteenth century was more than
four times as much as the number of Muhammadans. It is true, as even the author
of that article admits, that these data are not entirely exact, since several categories
of inhabitants are not included (the *spahis*, the slaves, and the officials of the
administration). It is nonetheless true that the totals themselves are very suggestive
and prove the inconsistency of the thesis that claims that the Turks had colonized
the Balkan Peninsula en masse and that the Turkish element there was predominant. Even in Bosnia, where their number at that time was the highest as a result
of the numerous conversions to Islam, the Muhammadans made up only the
minority of the population. Indeed, the table shows 16,935 Muhammadan families
in that country, as opposed to 19,935 Christian families. This proportion is ever
greater in the Bulgarian territories, in Thrace, and in northern Bulgaria. The Turks
were more numerous in eastern Thrace, as is evident from the table. That was the

province the Turks occupied in the first place after their arrival in the peninsula, which they colonized more intensively so as to be able to pursue thereafter more successfully their military conquests in the rest of the Balkan region.

As we have already said, the Osmanli feudal lords, in undertaking that colonization, intended to establish strong strategic bases in the occupied regions and at the same time to compensate for the inadequacy of the labor force due to the massacres and deportations. The transfers of the Christian population from one place to another had a similar purpose: to provide the depopulated regions with the labor supply that they lacked. This is what Bayezid did in 1396, for example, after the battle of Nicopol and the devastating campaign that he had conducted in the central Danube region. At his orders, some of the prisoners who had been taken after the capture of Mitrovica and Passau were sent as colonists to other regions of the Balkan Peninsula.[246] It is not recorded precisely where that colonization took place.

Mahomet II, whose reign was remarkable for a series of devastating campaigns against Serbs, Albania, Hungary, and Walachia and for the definitive occupation of all the Balkan States, pursued even more rigorously this policy of relocating the population. Some prisoners taken by the Turks after their incursions in Hungary were subsequently brought to Macedonia and settled in Skopje.[247] The prisoners taken after the capture of Sinope were sent to Rumelia[248] (i.e., to the frontiers of the former Byzantine Empire). Mahomet endeavored above all to repopulate his capital, Constantinople, and the surrounding area. As we have said, Constantinople was terribly ravaged after it was taken by the Turks in May of 1453, and a large part of its population was massacred or led off into captivity. The surrounding villages were likewise depopulated or deserted. This was a major drawback that interfered with the sultan's plans. In the absence of a populace consisting of farmers and artisans, the ruined capital could not be rebuilt. Furthermore, they had to make sure that the city was supplied with food. Only on these conditions could the city become the center of Turkish rule in the Balkans and assume the status of the true capital of the conquerors, as Mahomet II wished.

Shortly after the capture of the city, Mahomet ordered that some Christians and Jews be settled there so as to compensate for the depopulation of the capital. We find a brief allusion to this measure taken by Mahomet in the writings of Kritobulos.[249] We find more information on this question in the works of Doucas, where the sultan is said to have drawn up a list of five thousand families settled in the West (i.e., in the Balkan territories conquered by the Turks) and in the East (in Asia Minor), who received orders to leave their homes at the end of September in 1453 and to come settle in Constantinople. They were liable to capital punishment in the case of noncompliance.[250] Sphrantzès, too, mentions that some new inhabitants were transferred to Constantinople immediately after its capture. According to him, the sultan conferred upon the newly elected patriarch of Constantinople, Ghennadios Scholarios, certain rights in order to attract Christians to the capital, which was in fact the result.[251] Sphrantzès adds that at the sultan's orders the capital was colonized by Turks from Kaffa, Sinope, and Asprocastron.[252]

Considering that these [initial] measures taken to repopulate the capital and the surrounding area were inadequate, the sultan continued this policy of colonization during the following years as well. After the campaign against Serbia, some Serbian prisoners were brought to Constantinople in 1455. Doucas records an interesting fact concerning the capture of a fortress near Smederevo during that campaign. The Turks captured all the inhabitants, who numbered eight thousand. The sultan had half of the prisoners distributed among the soldiers who had distinguished themselves during that campaign, while the other prisoners were sent to Constantinople and settled in the vicinity of the capital.[253] The anonymous Byzantine chronicle also mentions the relocation of Serbian prisoners during the reign of Mourad and their settlement in the villages around the capital.[254]

A new colonization of Constantinople took place in 1456. According to Kritobulos, colonists were brought from Asia Minor and Europe, especially Christians.[255] The immigration continued in 1457 as well. That year, as Kritobulos indicates, a large number of Serbs, Hungarians and Mesians [Bulgarians—Author's note] were settled in Constantinople at the sultan's orders.[256] Kritobulos adds that Mahomet, was well aware that the region surrounding the capital was fertile and that it was in the interests of Constantinople that the land there be farmed intensively. Furthermore he had discovered that these regions were deserted and dangerous for travelers. Precisely for this reason he undertook this colonization, which affected the Serbs and Hungarians captured during military operations as well as Bulgarian peasants who were forcibly carried off from their homes.

The colonization of the capital continued during the following years as well. In 1458, four thousand prisoners captured in the Peloponnisos were brought to Constantinople.[257] Those of them who had formerly worked as artisans were settled, at the sultan's orders, in Constantinople. The others were assigned to the surrounding villages and received, if we are to believe Kritobulos, a yoke of oxen and everything that they needed to begin farming.

In 1460 the sultan promulgated a new ordinance, according to which all the inhabitants who had left the city before or after its fall and had settled in other places in Asia Minor or on the [European] continent were obliged to go home again. Many of them, Kritobulos reports, had taken up residence in Andrinopolis, Gallipoli, Brousse, and other localities.[258] Now they were all brought back to Constantinople. Some of them received houses from the sultan; others, plots of land upon which they could build new dwellings. The colonization of Constantinople did not stop there. In 1460 new colonists were brought from the two cities in Asia Minor called Phocis, as well as from the islands of Thasos and Samothrace, which had fallen into the hands of the Turks.[259] Some families were brought from Athens.[260] In 1463, after the devastating campaign against Bosnia, one-third of the inhabitants of Dobobik were sent to Constantinople and settled there.[261] One-third of the inhabitants of Mitylene (on the island of Lesbos) were settled in Constantinople after Mahomet had seized that island.[262] Certain prisoners received houses; others, plots of land. The capital was colonized once again in 1464 by large numbers of prisoners captured during the military operations against the uprising in the Peloponnisos. At that time, according to Kritobulos, Argos was destroyed and all its inhabitants—men, women, and children—were brought to the former capital of Byzantium.[263]

Kritobulos's account, which is our primary source of information about the colonizing policy of Mahomet II, could leave us with the impression that the measures taken by the sultan were actually beneficial to the populace, that they allowed many, many inhabitants of Asia Minor and Europe to receive domiciles and lands in Constantinople and the vicinity and to acquire all that they needed to make a living. In this department, as in others, Kritobulos, a renegade Turkophile, strives clumsily to embellish the reality and to idealize the policy of the Osmanlis. In fact this incessant relocation to Constantinople of Bulgarians, Serbs, Hungarians, and Greeks constituted a veritable calamity for the populace. The Osmanli feudal lords snatched hundred and thousands of families from their homes, from their next of kin, from everything that was dear to them. The Osmanlis made use of this policy of colonization to break up the Christian population in the regions where they deemed that their own power had not yet been firmly established. They endeavored to reduce the strength of the resistance among the people, to make the Christian populace an inert, obedient mass that would carry out all the sultan's orders with docility. Along with the instances of mass enslavement, forced colonization was one of the most cruel measures to which the Osmanlis resorted, in their hope of consolidating for ever their ascendancy over the Balkan peoples that they had subjugated.

The conquest of the Balkan Peninsula by the Turks meant not only the massive destruction of productivity, the depopulation of the occupied regions, mass enslavement, and forced colonization, but also the founding of a new feudal system. This feudal system was the continuation, in a subsequent phase of development, of the Osmanli military feudalism that had been created in Asia Minor during the first half of the fourteenth century. In essence, this system did not modify the feudal ties that existed in the Balkan states at the time when they were conquered by the Turks, but compared with them, the system was at an inferior, barbarous level, having as its foundation brutal coercion and terror, since the Muslims had the privilege of resorting with impunity to violence against the Christian population and of subjecting it to unlimited exploitation.

This establishment of Ottoman feudalism in the Balkan Peninsula, which occurred at the same time as the conquest, can be verified by a large number of documents of Turkish, Byzantine, Serbian, Bulgarian, and other origin. This is a new and subject for inquiry which does not fit within the framework of the present study.

NOTES

1. See З. В. Удальцова, "О внутренних причинах падения Византии в XV веке," *Вопросы истории* 7 (1953): 102–21; А. С. Твиритинова, "Фальсификация истории Турции в кемалистской историографии," *Виз. Врем.* 7 (1953): 9–31; И. С. Достян, "Борьба южнославянских народов против турецкой агресии в XIV–XV вв.," *Виз. Врем.* 7 (1953): 32–49; J. Macurek, "Турецкая опасность в Средней Европе," *Byzantino-slavica* 14 (1953): 130–57; Д. Ангелов, "Турското завоевание и борбата на балканските народи нашествениците," *Ист. преглед* 9 (1953): 374–99.

2. On the conquest of Asia Minor by the Turks, see the information given by J. von Hammer, *Geschichte des osmanischen Reiches I* (Pesth, 1840); J. W. Zinkeisen, *Geschichte des osmanischen Reiches in Europa I* (Hamburg, 1840); N. Jorga, *Geschichte des Osmanischen Reiches I* (Gotha, 1908). See also the specialist studies: P. Wittek, *Das Fürstentum Mentesche, Studie zur Geschichte Westkleinasiens im 13.-15. Jahrh.* (Istanbul, 1934); G. Georgiades-Arnakes, Οι πρωτοι Ὀθωμάνοι, Συμβολη εις το πρόβλημα της πτώσεως του Ἑλλήνισμου της Μικρας Ἀσίας (Athens, 1947).

3. Nicephori Gregorae, *Byzantina Historia*, ed. L. Schopeni, I. Bonnae (1829), p. 214; Wittek, *Das Fürstentum Mentesche*, pp. 18 ff.

4. Georgii Pachymeris, *De Michaele et Andronico Paleologis, libri XIII*, ed. J. Bekkeri (Bonnae, 1835), vol. 1, pp. 310 ff.

5. Pachymeres, vol. 1, p. 502n14.

6. Ibid., pp. 504–505.

7. Ibid., pp. 469–74.

8. Ibid., pp. 222–23, 310.

9. Gregoras, vol. 1, p. 142.

10. Ibid., p. 141.

11. Pachymeres, vol. 2, p. 314.

12. Ibid., vol. 2, p. 318:5–13. See also Gregoras, vol. 1, p. 207.

13. Pachymeres, vol. 2, p. 493.

14. Ibid., pp. 325–26.

15. Concerning this battle, see Seadeddin, *Chronica dell' origine et progressi della casa ottomana composta da Saidino Turco eccellentissimo historico in lingua turca, parte prima, tradotta da Vincenzo Brattuti* (Vienna, 1469), pp. 15 ff.; Pachymeres, vol. 2, pp. 327–35.

16. Pachymeres, vol. 2, p. 335.

17. About the conquest of Nicea, see Gregoras, vol. 2, p. 458; Seadeddin, *Chronica dell' origine et progressi della cassa ottomana*, p. 44; Giese, *Die altosmanischen anonymen Chroniken* (Leipzig, 1925), pp. 14–16.

18. Cited in Miklosich-Müller, *Acta et diplomata graeca medii aevi sacra et profana I* (Vienna, 1860), pp. 197–98, 183–84.

19. Gregoras, vol. 1, p. 458.

20. Твиритинова, "Фальсификация истории Турции в кемалистской историографии," pp. 22–23.

21. Translated into French by C. Defrémery and R. R. Sanquinetti, *Voyages d'Ibn Batotah* (Paris, 1873). See also G. Arnakes, Ἡ περιήγησις του ίμπν Μπαττούτα ανά την Μικραν Ἀσίαν και η κατάστασις των Ἑλληνικων και των Τουρκικων πληθυσμων κατα του Τουρκικων πληθυσμων κατα τον ιδ΄ αιωνα. Ἐπετηρις Ἑτ. Βυζ. Σπ. 22 (1952): 135–49.

22. Batouta, p. 315.

23. Ibid., p. 310.

24. Ibid., p. 323. On the large-scale destruction of towns perpetrated by the Turks in Asia Minor, see Arnakes, Οι πρωτοι 'Οθωμάνοι, Συμβολη εις το πρόβλημα της πτώσεως του 'Ελληνισμου της Μικρας 'Ασίας p. 149.

25. Batouta, p. 308.

26. Cited in Seadeddin, *Chronica dell' origine et progressi della casa ottomana composta da Saidino Turco eccellentissimo historico in lingua turca, parte prima, tradotta da Vincenzo Brattuti*, pp. 35, 40, 50; Giese, *Die altosmanischen anonymen Chroniken*, pp. 18, 21; Arnakes, Οι πρωτοι 'Οθωμάνοι, Συμβολη εις το πρόβλημα της πτώσεως του 'Ελληνισμου της Μικρας 'Ασίας, p. 149.

27. Batouta, p. 272.

28. Ibid., p. 317.

29. Ibid., pp. 310–11.

30. Ibid., p. 314.

31. Cited in Raynaldus, *Annales ecclesiastici*, vol. 6, pp. 308–10.

32. Batouta, pp. 279, 308, 321, 312, 315, 267, 269, 257, 310.

33. Ibid., pp. 315, 330.

34. Concerning the question of the formation of the Ottoman state, see Твиритинова, "Фальсификация истории Турции в кемалистской историографии," pp. 13–15.

35. Giese, *Die altosmanischen anonymen Chroniken*, p. 13. See also Nesri in Nöldeke, "Auszüge aus Nesris Geschichte des osmanischen Hauses," in *Zeitschrift der deutschen morgenländischen Gesellschaft* (Leipzig, 1859), vol. 13, p. 211.

36. Seadeddin, *Chronica dell' origine et progressi della casa ottomana composta da Saidino Turco eccellentissimo historico in lingua turca, parte prima, tradotta da Vincenzo Brattuti*, p. 22.

37. Giese, *Die altosmanischen anonymen Chroniken*, p. 13.

38. Nöldeke, "Auszüge aus Nesris Geschichte des osmanischen Hauses," p. 211.

39. Seadeddin, *Chronica dell' origine et progressi della casa ottomana composta da Saidino Turco eccellentissimo historico in lingua turca, parte prima, tradotta da Vincenzo Brattuti*, p. 37; Giese, *Die altosmanischen anonymen Chroniken*, p. 21. See also Твиритинова, "Фальсификация истории Турции в кемалистской историографии," p. 15.

40. Giese, *Die altosmanischen anonymen Chroniken*, p. 21.

41. Ibid., p. 23.

42. Seadeddin, *Chronica dell' origine et progressi della casa ottomana composta da Saidino Turco eccellentissimo historico in lingua turca, parte prima, tradotta da Vincenzo Brattuti*, pp. 13, 16. On the initial distributions of military fiefs, see the information in Г. И. Ибрагимов, "Крестьянские восстання в Турции в XXV–XVI вв.," *Виз. Врем.* 7 (1953): 123.

43. Seadeddin, *Chronica dell' origine et progressi della casa ottomana composta da Saidino Turco eccellentissimo historico in lingua turca, parte prima, tradotta da Vincenzo Brattuti*, p. 19; Nöldeke, "Auszüge aus Nesris Geschichte des osmanischen Hauses," pp. 211–12.

44. Nöldeke, "Auszüge aus Nesris Geschichte des osmanischen Hauses," p. 211.

45. Seadeddin, *Chronica dell' origine et progressi della casa ottomana composta da Saidino Turco eccellentissimo historico in lingua turca, parte prima, tradotta da Vincenzo Brattuti*, p. 16.

46. Ibid., p. 56.

47. M. Nešri, *Kitabi Cihan Nüma I Cilt*. Türk tarih Kurumu yayinlarindan, III seri, no. 2 (Ankara, 1949), p. 158.

48. Giese, *Die altosmanischen anonymen Chroniken*, p. 21; Seadeddin, *Chronica dell' origine et progressi della casa ottomana composta da Saidino Turco eccellentissimo historico in lingua turca, parte prima, tradotta da Vincenzo Brattuti*, p. 36.

49. Giese, *Die altosmanischen anonymen Chroniken*, p. 21.

50. Nöldeke, "Auszüge aus Nesris Geschichte des osmanischen Hauses," pp. 204, 212.

51. Seadeddin, *Chronica dell' origine et progressi della casa ottomana composta da Saidino Turco eccellentissimo historico in lingua turca, parte prima, tradotta da Vincenzo Brattuti*, p. 16.

52. Gregoras, vol. 1, p. 458.

53. On the creation of the army of Janissaries, consult Seadeddin, *Chronica dell' origine et progressi della casa ottomana composta da Saidino Turco eccellentissimo historico in lingua turca, parte prima, tradotta da Vincenzo Brattuti*, p. 21. See also Ибрагимов, "Крестьянские восстання в Турции в XXV–XVI вв.," pp. 130–31.

54. On the conquest of the Balkan Peninsula by the Turks, see Hammer, *Geschichte des osmanischen Reiches*, vol. 1, pp. 116 ff.; J. Zinkeisen, *Geschichte des osmanischen Reiches in Europa*, vol. 1, pp. 184 ff.; J. Dräseke, "Der Übergang der Osmanen nach Europa im XIV. Jahrhundert," *Neue Jahrb. für das klassische Altertum, Geschichte, und deutsche Literatur*, 31 (1913): 476–504; A. A. Vasiliev, *Histoire de l'Empire byzantin II* (Paris, 1932), pp. 305 ff.; G. Ostrogorsky, *Geschichte des byzantinischen Staates* (München 1952), p. 383; П. Ников, "Турското завладяване на България и съдбата на последните Шишмановци," *Известия на Ист. дружество* VII–VIII (1928): 41–112; Ст. Новакович, *Срби и турци XIV и XVI века: Ист. студије о првим борбама с најездом турском пре и после боја на Косову* (Belgrade, 1893). Concerning the Turkish conquest, see also the articles in *Виз. Врем* 7 (1953) and *Byzantinoslavica* 14 (1953).

55. On the conquest of Tzympé: Seadeddin, *Chronica dell' origine et progressi della casa ottomana composta da Saidino Turco eccellentissimo historico in lingua turca, parte prima, tradotta da Vincenzo Brattuti*, pp. 61–62; Giese, *Die altosmanischen anonymen Chroniken*, p. 23. See also Gregoras, vol. 3, pp. 119, 203; J. Cantacuzeni imperatoris *Historiarum libri* IV, t. III (Bonnae, 1832), p. 276.

56. Kantakuzenos, op. cit., vol. 3, p. 278; Gregoras, vol. 3, p. 224. See also Ostrogorsky, *Geschichte des byzantinischen Staates*, p. 383; Vasiliev, *Histoire de l'Empire byzantin*, p. 307.

57. On this question see Fr. Babinger, *Beiträge zur Frühgeschichte der Türkenherrschaft in Rumelien (14–15 Jahrh.)* (München, 1944), and Ал. Бурмов, "Кога е завладян Одрин от турците," *Известия на Бълг. ист. дружество* 19 (1945): 23–33.

58. About the struggle of the Balkan peoples against the Ottoman invaders, see Д. Ангелов, "Турското завоевание и борбата на балканските народи нашествениците," *Ист. преглед* 9 (1953): 374–99; И. С. Достян, "Борьба южнославянских народов против турецкой агресии в XIV-XV вв.," *Виз. Врем.* 7 (1953): 32–52; Н. Д. Смирнова and Г. И. Сенкевич, "Освободительная борьба албанского народа против турецких поробителей в XV в.," *Вопросы истории* 12 (1953): 80–97.

59. See the article on Kritobulos by З. В. Удальцова, "Предательская политика

феодальной знати Византии в период турецкого завоевания," *Виз. Врем.* 7 (1953): 93–121.

60. On the question of the economic development of the Byzantine Empire in the thirteenth and fourteenth centuries, see the article by З. В. Удальцова, "О внутренних причинах падения Византии в XV веке," *Вопросы истории* 7 (1953): 106–109; Д. Ангелов, *История на Византия*, vol. 2 (Sofia, 1952). On the economic development of Bulgarian lands during the 13th and 14th centuries, see И. Съкъзов, *Bulgarische Wirtschaftsgeschichte* (Berlin-Leipzig, 1929), pp. 103 ff. See also *История на България*, Издание на Българската акад. на науките (Sofia, 1954), vol. 1, pp. 190–93; Д. Ангелов, "Към въпроса за стопанския облик на българските земи през XII-XIV вв.," *Ист. преглед* 7 (1951): 4–5; Ст. Цонев, "Стоковото производство в феодална България," *Ист. преглед* 10, no. 5 (1954): 51–81. On the economy of Serbia in the 13th and 14th centuries, see К. Јиречек, *Историја срба II* (Belgrade, 1923), pp. 34 ff. Interesting information about the wealth and the economic progress of Serbian lands at the time of the conquest by the Turks are provided by Kritobulos, who is cited in З. В. Удальцова, "Византийский историк Критовул о южных славянах и других народах балканского полуострова в XV веке," *Виз. Врем.* 4 (1951): 97 ff.

61. V. J. Leunclavius, *Annales sultanorum osmanidorum* (Frankfurt, 1588), p. 10.

62. Demetrios Kydones, *De subsidio Latinorum*, Migne, *P.G.*, 154, 965 ff.

63. Demetrios Kydones, *Correspondance*, ed. G. Cammeli (Paris, 1930), pp. 31, 89.

64. See, for example, Leunclavius, *Annales sultanorum osmanidorum*, p. 10; Giese, *Die altosmanischen anonymen Chroniken*, p. 25; Seadeddin, *Chronica dell' origine et progressi della casa ottomana composta da Saidino Turco eccellentissimo historico in lingua turca, parte prima, tradotta da Vincenzo Brattuti*, pp. 63 ff.

65. Seadeddin, *Chronica dell' origine et progressi della casa ottomana composta da Saidino Turco eccellentissimo historico in lingua turca, parte prima, tradotta da Vincenzo Brattuti*, p. 112.

66. Nešri, *Kitabi Cihan Nüma I Cilt*, p. 263.

67. Ibid., p. 268.

68. Concerning this campaign there is interesting information based on Turkish sources that have come down to us in incomplete form, cited in J. Leunclavius, *Historiae musulmanae turcorum de monumentis ipsorum exscriptae, libri XIII* (Frankfurt, 1591), pp. 269 ff. See also D. Angelov, op. cit., pp. 383 ff.

69. К. Философ, "Живот Стефана Лазаревича от Константина Философа," ed. В. Јагић, *Гласник српског научног друштва* 42 (1875): 271.

70. V. Schiltbergers aus München, *Reise in den Orient und wunderbarere Begebenheiten*, hrsg. A. Penzel (München, 1814), p. 16. See also Јиречек, *Историја срба II*, pp. 103–104.

71. Философ, "Живот Стефана Лазаревича от Константина Философа," p. 272; Ст. Новаковић, *Срби и турци*, p. 312.

72. Cited in Sphrantzès, *Chronicon* (Bonnae, 1838), p. 83, and in Laonici Chalcocondyle, *Historiarum demonstraciones*, rec. E. Darko I. Budapestini, 1922, p. 92.

73. Ст. Новаковић, *Срби и турци*, p. 358; Достян, "Борьба южнославянских народов против турецкой агресии в XIV–XV вв.," p. 39.

74. See Ducae Michaelis Ducae nepotis *Historia Byzantina*, rec. J. Bekkerus (Bonnae, 1834), pp. 90–93.

75. See Kritobulos, *Βίος του Μωαμεθ β'*, éd. Ph. A. Dethier, *Monumenta Hungariae Historica* XXI, 1, 157, sec. 46, 172, sec. 93.

76. Ibid., p. 223, sec. 96.

77. Ibid., p. 331, sec. 68–69.

78. Ibid., pp. 290–94, sec. 95–105.

79. Chalkokondyles, op. cit., vol. 2, pp. 113–20.

80. Kritobulos, *Βίος του Μωαμεθ β'*, p. 201, sec. 32; pp. 197–98, sec. 21, p. 206, sec. 48.

81. Ibid., p. 238, sec. 130, p. 240, sec. 136.

82. Ibid., p. 306, sec. 9.

83. See Bertrandon de la Broquières, *Le voyage d'Outremer*, ed. Ch. Schefer (Paris, 1892), pp. 168, 169, 170. See also К. Иречек, "Стари пътешествия по България," *Периодическо списание на Бълг. книжовно дружество* 2, no. 3 (1882): 68–69.

84. Bertrandon, *Le voyage d'Outremer*, p. 173.

85. Kritobulos, *Βίος του Μωαμεθ β'*, p. 166, sec. 78.

86. Bertrandon, *Le voyage d'Outremer*, p. 174.

87. Ibid., p. 175.

88. Ibid., p. 176.

89. Ibid., p. 180.

90. Ibid., p. 201; Иречек, "Стари пътешествия," p. 76.

91. Bertrandon, *Le voyage d'Outremer*, p. 204.

92. Ibid.

93. Иречек, "Стари пътешествия," vol. 4, p. 69.

94. Bertrandon, *Le voyage d'Outremer*, p. 206.

95. See this report in ibid., pp. 267–74.

96. Ibid., p. 272.

97. See Хр. Кесяков, "Положението на България към края на 15 в.," *4. Сборник за народни умотворения, наука и книжнина* 6 (1891): 180.

98. J. Dlugosii, *Historiae Polonicae*, 1. XII (Frankfurt, 1711), p. 800.

99. Gregoras, vol. 2, pp. 747–48.

100. Ibid., p. 683.

101. See Л. Стојановић, *Стари српски записи и натписи*, т. III, 51–52, No. 4944; И. Иванов, *Старобългарски разкази* (Sofia, 1935), pp. 53–54.

102. Bertrandon, *Le voyage d'Outremer*, p. 170.

103. Ibid., p. 169.

104. Ibid., p. 180.

105. See Кесяков, "Положението на България към края на 15 в.," p. 180.

106. Ibid., p. 181.

107. S. Ljubić, ed., *Monumenta spectantia historiam slavorum meridionalium*, t. 6 (Zagreb, 1876), no. 313, pp. 219–20.

108. Cited in М. Пуциђ, *Српски споменици* (Belgrade, 1858), vol. 2, p. 29; Новаковић, *Срби и турци*, p. 244.

109. Новаковић, *Срби и турци*, p. 250.

110. Пуциђ, *Српски споменици*, vol. 1, p. 12; Новаковић, *Срби и турци*, p. 253.

111. Пуциђ, *Српски споменици*, vol. 1, p. 15; Новаковић, *Срби и турци*, p. 253.

112. Новаковић, *Срби и турци*, p. 253, par. 1; Пуциђ, *Српски споменици*, vol. 1, p. 28.

113. Пуциђ, *Српски споменици*, vol. 1, p. 30; Новаковић, *Срби и турци*, p. 252, par. 1.

114. *Acta et diplomata res Albaniae mediae aetatis illustrantia*, ed. L. D. Thalloczy, K. Jireĉek, and E. Sufflay II (1918), document # 610.

115. Cited in N. Jorga, *Notes et extraits pour servir à l'histoire des Croisades au XVe sièclei*, vol. 1, p. 120.

116. *Acta et diplomata res Albaniae mediae aetatis illustrantia*, doc. 688.

117. Ibid., doc. 729, 779, 795.

118. Jorga, *Notes et extraits pour servir à l'histoire des Croisades au XVe sièclei*, vol. 1, p. 500.

119. Ibid., vol. 1, p. 284.

120. Ibid., vol. 3, p. 15.

121. Ibid., vol. 3, p. 43.

122. Ibid., vol. 1, p. 137.

123. Ibid., vol. 1, p. 158.

124. Kritobulos, *Βίος του Μωαμεθ β',* p. 195, sec. 17 ff.

125. Ibid., pp. 221–23, 331–36.

126. Seadeddin, *Chronica dell' origine et progressi della casa ottomana composta da Saidino Turco eccellentissimo historico in lingua turca, parte prima, tradotta da Vincenzo Brattuti*, p. 63.

127. Ibid., p. 67.

128. Ibid., pp. 87–88. See also Leunclvius, *Annales sultanorum*, p. 10.

129. Seadeddin, *Chronica dell' origine et progressi della casa ottomana composta da Saidino Turco eccellentissimo historico in lingua turca, parte prima, tradotta da Vincenzo Brattuti*, p. 101.

130. Ibid., pp. 87–88.

131. Ibid., p. 101.

132. Cited in И. Иванов, *Старобългарски разкази* (Sofia, 1935), p. 224.

133. Chalkokondyles, vol. 1, p. 30.

134. Kydones, *Correspondance*, no. 31, 89.

135. Seadeddin, *Chronica dell' origine et progressi della casa ottomana composta da Saidino Turco eccellentissimo historico in lingua turca, parte prima, tradotta da Vincenzo Brattuti*, p. 89.

136. Ibid., p. 112.

137. See И. Съкъзов, "Новооткрити документи от края на XIV в. за българи от Македония продавани като роби," *Македонски преглед* 7 (1832): 2–3, 23–62.

138. Seadeddin, *Chronica dell' origine et progressi della casa ottomana composta da Saidino Turco eccellentissimo historico in lingua turca, parte prima, tradotta da Vincenzo Brattuti*, pp. 121–22.

139. Nešri, *Kitabi Cihan Nüma I Cilt*, p. 247; Seadeddin, *Chronica dell' origine et progressi della casa ottomana composta da Saidino Turco eccellentissimo historico in lingua turca, parte prima, tradotta da Vincenzo Brattuti*, p. 137; Leunclavius, *Historiae musulmanae*, pp. 269 ff.

140. See Seadeddin, *Chronica dell' origine et progressi della casa ottomana composta da Saidino Turco eccellentissimo historico in lingua turca, parte prima, tradotta da Vincenzo Brattuti*, pp. 158–60; Chalkokondyles, vol. 1, p. 55.

141. Doucas, p. 49.

142. See the translation of the text into modern Bulgarian in В. Сл. Киселков, *Митрополит Григорий Цамблак* (Sofia, 1943).

143. See A. C. Buchon, *Chronique de J. Frossart* (Paris: Panthéon Littéraire, 1852), vol. 3, pp. 268–71; and Schiltberger, *Reise in den Orient und wunderbarere Begebenheiten*, p. 15. See also *Livre des faits du bon messire Jean le Maingre, dit Bouciquaut*, ed. A. C. Buchon (Paris: Panthéon Littéraire), vol. 3, pp. 596–97.

144. Schiltberger, *Reise in den Orient und wunderbarere Begebenheiten*, p. 15.

145. Ibid., pp. 16–17.

146. Chalkokondyles, vol. 1, p. 92; Sphrantzès, *Chronicon*, p. 53.

147. Seadeddin, *Chronica dell' origine et progressi della casa ottomana composta da Saidino Turco eccellentissimo historico in lingua turca, parte prima, tradotta da Vincenzo Brattuti*, p. 90.

148. Ibid., p. 89; Leunclavius, *Annales sultanorum*, p. 12.

149. Seadeddin, *Chronica dell' origine et progressi della casa ottomana composta da Saidino Turco eccellentissimo historico in lingua turca, parte prima, tradotta da Vincenzo Brattuti*, pp. 121–22.

150. Cited in Твиритинова, "Фальсификация истории Турции в кемалистской историографии," p. 24.

151. Seadeddin, *Chronica dell' origine et progressi della casa ottomana composta da Saidino Turco eccellentissimo historico in lingua turca, parte prima, tradotta da Vincenzo Brattuti*, p. 116.

152. Doucas, p. 57.

153. Bertrandon, *Le voyage d'Outremer*, p. 141.

154. Jorga, *Notes et extraits pour servir à l'histoire des Croisades au XVe sièclei*, vol. 1, pp. 47, 52.

155. Ibid., vol. 1, 63.

156. Ibid., vol. 1, 391.

157. See *J. Anagnostae de Thessalonicensi excidio narratio*, ed. Bonnae, 510, p. 14–15.

158. Doucas, p. 200.

159. Jorga, *Notes et extraits pour servir à l'histoire des Croisades au XVe sièclei*, vol. 2, p. 352.

160. Anagnostas, op. cit., pp. 517–18.

161. Cited in Твиритинова, "Фальсификация истории Турции в кемалистской историографии," p. 24.

162. Leunclavius, *Annales sultanorum*, p. 41. See also Chalkokondyles, vol. 2, pp. 119 ff.

163. Doucas, p. 223; Jorga, *Notes et extraits pour servir à l'histoire des Croisades au XVe sièclei*, vol. 3, p. 221. See also the account in Zakitenos, *Le despotat grec de Morée I* (Paris, 1932), p. 235.

164. Cited in Б. Цветкова, "Робството в османската империя и по-специално в българските земи под турска власт," *Ист. преглед* 10, no. 2 (1954): 85.

165. Bertrandon, *Le voyage d'Outremer*, p. 199.

166. Ibid., p. 200.

167. Jorga, *Notes et extraits pour servir à l'histoire des Croisades au XVe sièclei*, vol. 1, p. 263.

168. Ibid., vol. 2, p. 304.

169. Ibid., p. 356.

170. Raynaldus, *Annales ecclesiastici*, vol. 9, p. 413.

171. Jorga, *Notes et extraits pour servir à l'histoire des Croisades au XVe sièclei*, vol. 2, pp. 145, 181.

172. Kritobulos, *Βίος του Μωαμεθ β'*, p. 116, sec. 225. See also G. Zoras, ed., "Η άλωσις της Κωνσταντινουπόλεως και η βασιλεία Μωαμεθ β' του κατακτητου," *Επετηρις 'Ετ. Βυζ. Σπ.* 22 (1952): 256.

173. Doucas, pp. 291 ff.

174. Chalkokondyles, vol. 3, pp. 162–63.

175. Doucas, p. 312.

176. See "Михала Константиновића србина на Островице историја или летописи турски," *Гласник српског ученог друштва* 18 (1865): 116–17. See also Chalkokondyles, vol. 3, pp. 171, 12.

177. Doucas, p. 317.

178. Zoras, "Η άλωσις της Κωνσταντινουπόλεως και η βασιλεία Μωαμεθ β'του κατακτητου," p. 259.

179. Kritobulos, *Βίος του Μωαμεθ β'*, p. 203, sec. 38.

180. Zoras, ""Η άλωσις της Κωνσταντινουπόλεως και η βασιλεία Μωαμεθ β'του κατακτητου," p. 271.

181. Chalkokondyles, vol. 3, p. 235.

182. Ibid., p. 233n.

183. Kritobulos, *Βίος του Μωαμεθ β'*, p. 333, sec. 73.

184. Ibid., p. 223, sec. 97.

185. Zoras, "Η άλωσις της Κωνσταντινουπόλεως και η βασιλεία Μωαμεθ β'του κατακτητου," p. 286.

186. Chalkokondyles, vol. 3, p. 282.

187. Ibid., vol. 3, p. 273.

188. Kritobulos, *Βίος του Μωαμεθ β'*, p. 168, sec. 82.

189. See Jacobo de Promontorio de Campis, Governo et Entrate del Gran Turco, *Stato del Gran turco*, ed. П. П. Иковски, *Известия на Бълг. Ист. дружество* 9 (1929): 9–11.

190. Jacobo de Promontorio, *Stato del Gran turco*, p. 14.

191. Chalkokondyles, vol. 3, pp. 238, 8–9.

192. Zoras, "Η άλωσις της Κωνσταντινουπόλεως και η βασιλεία Μωαμεθ β'του κατακτητου," p. 274.

193. Chalkokondyles, vol. 3, pp. 196–97.

194. Kritobulos, *Βίος του Μωαμεθ β'*, p. 142, sec. 3.

195. Jacobo de Promontorio, *Stato del Gran turco*, p. 9.

196. Doucas, pp. 135–38.

197. On the colonizing policy of the Osmanlis in the Balkan Peninsula, see the remarks in П. Ников, "Турското завладяване на България и съдбата на последните Шишмановци," *Известия на Ист. дружество* 7–8 (1928): 46 ff.; М. Дринов, *Историческо осветление върху статистиката на народностите в източната част на княжество България*, Съч., т. I (1909), pp. 523–48; К. Иречек, *Княжество България* (Plovdiv, 1899), vol. 2, p. 145; Hammer, *Geschichte des osmanischen Reiches*, vol. 1, p. 206; П. Мутафчиев, "Добруджа," *Сборник от студии* 4 (1947): 215 ff.; О.

L. Barkan, "Les déportations comme méthode de peuplement et de colonisation dans l'Empire ottoman," *Revue de la Faculté des Sciences Économiques de l'Université d'Istanbul* 1–4 (October 1949–July 1950): 67–131.

198. Seadeddin, *Chronica dell' origine et progressi della casa ottomana composta da Saidino Turco eccellentissimo historico in lingua turca, parte prima, tradotta da Vincenzo Brattuti,* p. 62.

199. Cited in Barkan, "Les déportations comme méthode de peuplement et de colonisation dans l'Empire ottoman," p. 105.

200. Kantakuzenos, vol. 3, pp. 276–78.

201. Chalkokondyles, vol. 1, pp. 22–23.

202. Seadeddin, *Chronica dell' origine et progressi della casa ottomana composta da Saidino Turco eccellentissimo historico in lingua turca, parte prima, tradotta da Vincenzo Brattuti,* p. 83.

203. Ibid., pp. 86, 90.

204. Chalkokondyles, vol. 1, p. 94.

205. Barkan, "Les déportations comme méthode de peuplement et de colonisation dans l'Empire ottoman," p. 105.

206. Ibid.

207. Kydones, *De subsidio Latinorum,* pp. 154, 965.

208. Barkan, "Les déportations comme méthode de peuplement et de colonisation dans l'Empire ottoman," pp. 111–12.

209. Bertrandon, *Le voyage d'Outremer,* p. 169.

210. Ibid., p. 170.

211. Ibid., p. 176.

212. Ibid., p. 180.

213. Barkan, "Les déportations comme méthode de peuplement et de colonisation dans l'Empire ottoman," p. 119.

214. Ibid., p. 188, citing Seadeddin, *Chronica dell' origine et progressi della casa ottomana composta da Saidino Turco eccellentissimo historico in lingua turca, parte prima, tradotta da Vincenzo Brattuti,* p. 349.

215. Bertrandon, *Le voyage d'Outremer,* p. 204.

216. See К. Иречек, "Стари пътешествия по България," p. 69.

217. Chalkokondyles, vol. 1, p. 94.

218. Doucas, 200 n19.

219. Giese, *Die altosmanischen anonymen Chroniken,* p. 36; Leunclavius, *Historiae musulmanae,* p. 244; Barkan, "Les déportations comme méthode de peuplement et de colonisation dans l'Empire ottoman," p. 110.

220. Leunclavius, *Historiae musulmanae,* p. 244.

221. Chalkokondyles, vol. 1, p. 94n15.

222. Ibid., vol. 1, p. 54 n19.

223. Ibid., p. 94.

224. Cf. Schiltberger, *Reise in den Orient und wunderbarere Begebenheiten, p. 8; Froissart,* pp. 239, 244; Bouciquaut, p. 590; Dlugosii, *Historiae Poloniae,* vol. 12, pp. 799, 800, 801, 802. See also Philippi Callimachi, *De rebus a Vladislao Polonorum atque Hungarum rege gestis libri tres,* in the series: *Scriptorum rerum hungaricarum veteres ac genuini* (Vienna 1746), pp. 512 ff., and M. Beheim, *Zehn Gedichte Michael Beheims zur*

Geschichte Oesterreichs und Ungarns, ed. Thomas G. von Karajan (*Quellen und Forschungen zur vaterländischen Geschichte, Literatur und Kunst*) (Vienna, 1849), pp. 35–46.

225. Leunclavius, *Historiae musulmanae*, p. 311; Мутафчиев, "Добруджа," p. 216.

226. Seadeddin, *Chronica dell' origine et progressi della casa ottomana composta da Saidino Turco eccellentissimo historico in lingua turca, parte prima, tradotta da Vincenzo Brattuti*, pp. 355 ff.; Ибрагимов, "Крестьянские восстання в Турции в XXV–XVI вв.," p. 138.

227. Beheim, *Zehn Gedichte Michael Beheims zur Geschichte Oesterreichs und Ungarns*, verses 401–10.

228. Ibid., verses 430 ff.

229. Ibid., verse 396.

230. Barkan, "Les déportations comme méthode de peuplement et de colonisation dans l'Empire ottoman," p. 112.

231. See К. Иречек, *Пътувания по България* (Plovdiv, 1899), p. 882.

232. Leunclavius, *Annales sultanorum*, p. 41n25.

233. Chalkokondyles, vol. 2, p. 29n17.

234. Doucas, p. 209.

235. Kritobulos, *Βίος του Μωαμεθ β΄,* p. 206, sec. 47, p. 240, sec.136; Chalkokondyles, vol. 3, p. 211n3.

236. Zoras, "Η άλωσις της Κωνσταντινουπόλεως και η βασιλεία Μωαμεθ β΄ του κατακτητου," pp. 280–81; Chalkokondyles, vol. 3, p. 282.

237. Chalkokondyles, vol. 3, p. 274.

238. Bertrandon, *Le voyage d'Outremer*, pp. 169, 176.

239. Ibid., p. 200.

240. Ibid., p. 201.

241. Ibid., p. 202.

242. Ibid., p. 203.

243. Кесяков, "Положението на България към края на 15 в.," p. 180.

244. Ibid., p. 181.

245. Barkan, "Les déportations comme méthode de peuplement et de colonisation dans l'Empire ottoman," p. 129.

246. Schiltberger, *Reise in den Orient und wunderbarere Begebenheiten*, p. 16.

247. Zoras, "Η άλωσις της Κωνσταντινουπόλεως και η βασιλεία Μωαμεθ β΄ του κατακτητου," p. 268.

248. Giese, *Die altosmanischen anonymen Chroniken*, p. 149.

249. Kritobulos, *Βίος του Μωαμεθ β΄,* p. 142, sec. 1.

250. Doucas, p. 313.

251. Sphrantzès, *Chronicon*, p. 308.

252. Ibid.

253. Doucas, p. 317.

254. Giese, *Die altosmanischen anonymen Chroniken*, p. 148.

255. Kritobulos, *Βίος του Μωαμεθ β΄,* p. 160, sec. 57.

256. Ibid., p. 181, sec. 21.

257. Ibid., p. 203, sec. 38, p. 206, sec. 49, p. 212, sec. 68. See also Chalkokondyles,

vol. 3, p. 205, and Zoras, "Η άλωσις της Κωνσταντινουπόλεως και η βασιλεία Μωαμεθ β' του κατακτητου," p. 271.

258. Kritobulos, *Βίος του Μωαμεθ β'*, p. 224, sec. 101, p. 225, sec. 102.
259. Ibid., p. 225, sec. 103.
260. Chalkokondyles, vol. 3, p. 237.
261. Ibid., p. 282.
262. Ibid., p. 273; Kritobulos, *Βίος του Μωαμεθ β'*, p. 287, sec. 90.
263. Kritobulos, *Βίος του Μωαμεθ β'*, p. 306, sec. 9.

43

A MODERN
JIHAD GENOCIDE

Andrew G. Bostom

The Greater Boston Armenian Genocide Commemoration Committee issued a press release, April 7, 2003, noting that April 24, 2003, marked the eighty-eighth "anniversary" of the Armenian genocide. On April 24, 1915, the Turkish Interior Ministry issued an order authorizing the arrest of all Armenian political and community leaders suspected of anti-Ittihad ("Young Turk" government), or Armenian nationalist sentiments. In Istanbul alone, 2,345 such leaders were seized and incarcerated, and most of them were subsequently executed. The majority were neither nationalists, nor were they involved in politics. None were charged with sabotage, espionage, or any other crime, and appropriately tried.[1] As the Turkish author Taner Akcam recently acknowledged,

> Under the pretext of searching for arms, of collecting war levies, or tracking down deserters, there had already been established a practice of systematically carried-out plunders, raids, and murders [against the Armenians] which had become daily occurrences.[2]

Within a month, the final, definitive stage of the process which reduced the Armenian population to utter helplessness, that is, mass deportation, would begin.[3]

A TRUE GENOCIDE

Was the horrific fate of the Ottoman Empire's Armenian minority at the end of the nineteenth and early twentieth centuries, in particular during World War I, due to "civil war" or genocide? A seminal analysis by Professor Vahakn Dadrian published last year validates the conclusion that the Ottoman Turks committed a cen-

Andrew G. Bostom, "A Modern Jihad Genocide," FrontPageMagazine.com, April 28, 2003, http://www.frontpagemag.com/Articles/ReadArticle.asp?ID=7519.

trally organized mass murder, that is, a genocide, against their Armenian population.[4] Relying upon a vast array of quintessential, primary source documents from
the World War I allies of the Ottoman Empire, Germany, and Austria-Hungary,
Dadrian obviated the intractable disputes surrounding the reliability and authenticity of both Ottoman Turkish and Armenian documents. He elucidated the truly
unique nature of this documentary German and Austro-Hungarian evidence:

> During the war, Germany and Austria-Hungary disposed over a vast network of
> ambassadorial, consular, military, and commercial representatives throughout the
> Ottoman Empire. Not only did they have access to high-ranking Ottoman offi-
> cials and power-wielding decision-makers who were in a position to report to
> their superiors as locus in quo observers on many aspects of the wartime treat-
> ment of Ottoman Armenians. They supplemented their reports with as much
> detail as they could garner from trusted informers and paid agents, many of
> whom were Muslims, both civilians and military.[5]

Moreover, the documents analyzed possessed another critical attribute: they
included confidential correspondence prepared and sent to Berlin and Vienna,
which were meant for wartime use only.[6] This confidentiality, Dadrian notes,
enabled German or Austro-Hungarian officials to openly question the contentions
of their wartime Ottoman allies, when ascertaining and conveying facts truthfully
to their superiors in Europe. Dadrian cites the compelling example of the
November 16, 1915, report to the German chancellor by Aleppo Consul Rossler.
Rossler states,

> I do not intend to frame my reports in such a way that I may be favoring one or
> the other party. Rather, I consider it my duty to present to you the description of
> things which have occurred in my district and which I consider to be the truth.[7]

Rossler was reacting specifically to the official Ottoman allegation that the
Armenians had begun to massacre the Turkish population in the Turkish sections
of Urfa, a city within his district, after reportedly capturing them. He dismissed
the charge, unequivocally, with a single word: "invented."[8]

Amassed painstakingly by Dadrian, the primary source evidence from these
German and Austro-Hungarian officials—reluctant witnesses—leads to this
inescapable conclusion: the anti-Armenian measures, despite a multitude of
attempts at coverup and outright denial, were meticulously planned by the
Ottoman authorities, and were designed to destroy wholesale, the victim population. Dadrian further validates this assessment with remarkable testimony before
the Mazhar Inquiry Commission, which conducted a preliminary investigation in
the postwar period to determine the criminal liability of the wartime Ottoman
authorities regarding the Armenian deportations and massacres. The December
15, 1918, deposition by General Mehmed Vehip, commander in chief of the

Ottoman Third Army and ardent CUP (Committee of Union and Progress, that is, the "Ittihadists" or "Young Turks") member, included this summary statement:

> The murder and annihilation of the Armenians and the plunder and expropriation of their possessions were the result of the decisions made by the CUP. . . . These atrocities occurred under a program that was determined upon and involved a definite case of willfulness. They occurred because they were ordered, approved, and pursued first by the CUP's [provincial] delegates and central boards, and second by governmental chiefs who had . . . pushed aside their conscience, and had become the tools of the wishes and desires of the Ittihadist society.[9]

Dadrian's own compelling assessment of this primary source evidence is summarized as follows:

> Through the episodic interventions of the European Powers, the historically evolving and intensifying Turko-Armenian conflict had become a source of anger and frustration for the Ottoman rulers and elites driven by a xenophobic nationalism. A monolithic political party that had managed to eliminate all opposition and had gained control of the Ottoman state apparatus efficiently took advantage of the opportunities provided by World War I. It purged by violent and lethal means the bulk of the Armenian population from the territories of the empire. By any standard definition, this was an act of genocide.[10]

JIHAD: A MAJOR DETERMINANT OF THE ARMENIAN GENOCIDE

The wartime reports from German and Austro-Hungarian officials also confirm independent evidence that the origins and evolution of the genocide had little to do with World War I "Armenian provocations." Emphasis is placed, instead, on the larger prewar context dating from the failure of the mid-nineteenth-century Ottoman Tanzimat reform efforts.[11] These reforms, initiated by the declining Ottoman Empire (i.e., in 1839 and 1856) under intense pressure from the European powers, were designed to abrogate the repressive laws of *dhimmitude*, to which non-Muslim (primarily Christian) minorities, including the Armenians, had been subjected for centuries following the Turkish jihad conquests of their indigenous homelands.[12]

Led by their patriarch, the Armenians felt encouraged by the Tanzimat reform scheme, and began to deluge the Porte (Ottoman seat of government) with pleas and requests, primarily seeking governmental protection against a host of mistreatments, particularly in the remote provinces. Between 1850 and 1870 alone, 537 notes were sent to the Porte by the Armenian patriarch characterizing numerous occurrences of theft, abduction, murder, confiscatory taxes, and fraud by government officials.[13] These entreaties were largely ignored and, ominously, were even considered as signs of rebelliousness. For example, British consul (to Erzurum) Clifford Lloyd reported in 1890,

> Discontent, or any description of protest is regarded by the local Turkish Local Government as seditious.[14]

He went on to note that this Turkish reaction occurred irrespective of the fact that "the idea of revolution" was not being entertained by the Armenian peasants involved in these protests.[15]

The renowned Ottomanist Roderick Davison has observed that under the Shari'a (Islamic Holy Law) the "infidel gavours ["*dhimmis*," "*rayas*"]" were permanently relegated to a status of "inferiority" and subjected to a "contemptuous half-toleration." Davison further maintained that this contempt emanated from "an innate attitude of superiority," and was driven by an "innate Muslim feeling," prone to paroxysms of "open fanaticism."[16] Sustained, vehement reactions to the 1839 and 1856 Tanzimat reform acts by large segments of the Muslim population, led by Muslim spiritual leaders and the military, illustrate Davison's point.[17] Perhaps the most candid and telling assessment of the doomed Tanzimat reforms, in particular the 1856 act, was provided by Mustafa Resid, Ottoman grand vizier, at six different times between 1846 and 1858. In his denunciation of the reforms, Resid argued the proposed "complete emancipation" of the non-Muslim subjects, appropriately destined to be subjugated and ruled, was "entirely contradictory" to "the 600-year traditions of the Ottoman Empire." He openly proclaimed the "complete emancipation" segment of the initiative as disingenuous, enacted deliberately to mislead the Europeans, who had insisted upon this provision. Sadly prescient, Resid then made the ominous prediction of a "great massacre" if equality was in fact granted to non-Muslims.[18]

Despite their "revolutionary" advent and accompanying comparisons to the ideals of the French Revolution, the CUP's "Young Turk" regime eventually adopted a discriminatory, antireform attitude toward non-Muslims within the Ottoman Empire. During an August 6, 1910, speech in Saloniki, Mehmed Talat, preeminent leader of the Young Turks, disdainfully rejected the notion of equality with "gavours," arguing that it "is an unrecognizable ideal since it is inimical with Sheriat [Shari'a] and the sentiments of hundreds of thousands of Muslims."[19] Roderick Davison notes that in fact "no genuine equality was ever attained," reenacting the failure of the prior Tanzimat reform period. As a consequence, he observes, the CUP leadership "soon turned from equality . . . to Turkification."[20]

During the reign of Sultan Abdul Hamid, the Ottoman Turks massacred over two hundred thousand Armenians between 1894 and 1896. This was followed, under the Young Turk regime, by the Adana massacres of twenty-five thousand Armenians in 1909, and the first formal genocide of the twentieth century, when in 1915 alone, an additional six hundred thousand to eight hundred thousand Armenians were slaughtered.[21] The massacres of the 1890s had an "organic" connection to the Adana massacres of 1909, and more important, the events of 1915. As Vahakn Dadrian argues, they facilitated the genocidal acts of 1915 by providing the Young Turks with "a predictable impunity." The absence of adverse consequences for the Abdul Hamid massacres in the 1890s allowed the Young Turks to move forward without constraint.[22]

Contemporary accounts from European diplomats make clear that these brutal massacres were perpetrated in the context of a formal jihad against the Armenians who had attempted to throw off the yoke of *dhimmitude* by seeking equal rights and autonomy. For example, the Chief Dragoman (Turkish-speaking interpreter) of the British embassy reported regarding the 1894–1896 massacres:

> [The perpetrators] are guided in their general action by the prescriptions of the Sheri [Sharia] Law. That law prescribes that if the "rayah" [*dhimmi*] Christian attempts, by having recourse to foreign powers, to overstep the limits of privileges allowed them by their Mussulman [Muslim] masters, and free themselves from their bondage, their lives and property are to be forfeited, and are at the mercy of the Mussulmans. To the Turkish mind the Armenians had tried to overstep those limits by appealing to foreign powers, especially England. They therefore considered it their religious duty and a righteous thing to destroy and seize the lives and properties of the Armenians.[23]

The scholar Bat Ye'or confirms this reasoning, noting that the Armenian quest for reforms invalidated their "legal status," which involved a "contract" (i.e., with their Muslim Turkish rulers). This

> breach . . . restored to the umma [the Muslim community] its initial right to kill the subjugated minority [the *dhimmis*], [and] seize their property.[24]

An intrepid Protestant historian and missionary Johannes Lepsius, who earlier had undertaken a two-month trip to examine the sites of the Abul Hamid era massacres, traveled again to Turkey during World War I. Regarding the period between 1914 and 1918, he wrote:

> Are we then simply forbidden to speak of the Armenians as persecuted on account of their religious belief? If so, there have never been any religious persecutions in the world. . . . We have lists before us of 559 villages whose surviving inhabitants were converted to Islam with fire and sword; of 568 churches thoroughly pillaged, destroyed and razed to the ground; of 282 Christian churches transformed into mosques; of 21 Protestant preachers and 170 Gregorian (Armenian) priests who were, after enduring unspeakable tortures, murdered on their refusal to accept Islam. We repeat, however, that those figures express only the extent of our information, and do not by a long way reach to the extent of the reality. Is this a religious persecution or is it not?[25]

Finally, Bat Ye'or places the continuum of massacres from the 1890s through World War I in an overall theological and juridical context, as follows:

> The genocide of the Armenians was the natural outcome of a policy inherent in the politico-religious structure of dhimmitude. This process of physically eliminating a rebel nation had already been used against the rebel Slav and Greek Christians, rescued from collective extermination by European intervention, although sometimes reluctantly.
>
> The genocide of the Armenians was a *jihad*. No rayas took part in it. Despite the disapproval of many Muslim Turks and Arabs, and their refusal to collaborate in the crime, these masssacres were perpetrated solely by Muslims and they alone profited from the booty: the victims' property, houses, and lands granted to the *muhajirun*, and the allocation to them of women and child slaves. The elimination of male children over the age of twelve was in accordance with the commandments of the *jihad* and conformed to the age fixed for the payment of the jizya. The four stages of the liquidation—deportation, enslavement, forced conversion, and massacre—reproduced the historic conditions of the *jihad* carried out in the *dar-al-harb* from the seventh century on. Chronicles from a variety of sources, by Muslim authors in particular, give detailed descriptions of the organized massacres or deportation of captives, whose sufferings in forced marches behind the armies paralleled the Armenian experience in the twentieth century.[26]

CONCLUSIONS

The Ottoman Turkish destruction of the Armenian people, beginning in the late nineteenth and intensifying in the early twentieth century, was a genocide, and jihad ideology contributed significantly to this decades long human liquidation process. These facts are now beyond dispute. Milan Kundera, the Czech author, has written that man's struggle against power is the struggle of memory against forgetting.[27] In his thoughtful analysis of the Armenian genocide, *The Banality of Indifference*, Professor Yair Auron reminds us of the importance of this struggle:

> Recognition of the Armenian genocide on the part of the entire international community, including Turkey (or perhaps first and foremost Turkey), is therefore a demand of the first order. Understanding and remembering the tragic past is an essential condition, even if not sufficient in and of itself, to preventing the repetition of such acts in the future."[28]

NOTES

1. E. Uras, *The Armenians and the Armenian Question in History*, 2nd ed. (Istanbul, 1976), p. 612.

2. T. Akcam, *Turkish National Identity and the Armenian Question* (Istanbul, 1992), p. 109.

3. R. Hovanissian, *Armenia on the Road to Independence* (Berkeley, CA, 1967), p. 51.

4. V. Dadrian, "The Armenian Question and the Wartime Fate of the Armenians as Documented by the Officials of the Ottoman Empire's World War I Allies: Germany and Austria-Hungary," *International Journal of Middle Eastern Studies* 32 (2002): 59–85.

5. Ibid., p. 60.

6. Ibid., p. 76.

7. Ibid., with specific primary source documentation, p. 84n109.

8. Ibid.

9. Ibid., p. 77, with specific primary source documentation, pp. 84–85n111.

10. Ibid., p. 77.

11. R. Davison, "Turkish Attitudes Concerning Christian-Muslim Equality in the Nineteenth Century," *American Historical Review* 59 (1954): 844–64.

12. Bat Ye'or, *The Decline of Eastern Christianity under Islam* (Cranbury, NJ: Fairleigh Dickinson University Press, 1996).

13. V. Dadrian, *Warrant for Genocide: Key Elements of Turko-Armenian Conflict* (New Brunswick, NJ: Transaction, 1999), p. 39.

14. Ibid., p. 61, with specific primary source documentation, p. 79n11.

15. Ibid.

16. Davison, "Turkish Attitudes Concerning Christian-Muslim Equality in the Nineteenth Century," p. 855.

17. Bat Ye'or, *Decline of Eastern Christianity under Islam*, pp. 395–433.

18. Dadrian, "The Armenian Question and the Wartime Fate of the Armenians," pp. 61–62, with specific primary source documentation, p. 79n14.

19. Ibid., pp. 61–62, with specific primary source documentation, p. 79n15.

20. R. Davison R, "The Armenian Crisis, 1912–1914," *American Historical Review* 53 (1948): 482–83.

21. V. Dadrian, *The History of the Armenian Genocide* (Providence, RI: Bergahn Books, 1997), pp. 155, 182, 225, 233n44; Y. Auron, *The Banality of Indifference* (New Brunswick, NJ: Transaction Publishers, 2000), p. 44.

22. Dadrian, *History of the Armenian Genocide*, pp. 113–84.

23. Ibid., p. 147, with primary source documentation, p. 168n199.

24. Bat Ye'or, *The Dhimmi: Jews and Christians under Islam* (Cranbury, NJ: Fairleigh Dickinson University Press, 1985), pp. 48, 67, 101.

25. M. C. Gabrielan, *Armenia: A Martyr Nation* (New York/Chicago: Fleming H. Revell, 1918), p. 269.

26. Bat Ye'or, *Decline of Eastern Christianity under Islam*, p. 197.

27. M. Kundera, *The Book of Laughter and Forgetting* (New York: Harper Collins, 1999).

28. Auron, *Banality of Indifference*, p. 56.

44

TEXTBOOK JIHAD IN EGYPT

Andrew G. Bostom

A "mock beheading" video located at radical Sheikh Abu Hamza's Web site (www.shareeah.org), which featured three young Muslim boys who pretended to behead a fourth,[1] has elicited the appropriate public revulsion. But little fanfare, let alone outrage, has accompanied the release of a detailed study of Egyptian children's textbooks, whose inculcation of anti-infidel hatred is potentially far more damaging.[2] For example, explicit sanctioning for jihad-related beheadings is provided in a seemingly pedestrian manner:

Studies in Theology: Tradition and Morals, **Grade 11 (2001), pp. 291–92:**

This noble [Qur'anic] Surah [Surat Muhammad] . . . deals with questions of which the most important are as follows: Encouraging the faithful to perform jihad in God's cause, to behead the infidels, take them prisoner, break their power, and make their souls humble—all that in a style which contains the highest examples of urging to fight. You see that in His words: "When you meet the unbelievers in the battlefield strike off their heads and, when you have laid them low, bind your captives firmly. Then grant them their freedom or take a ransom from them, until war shall lay down its burdens."

Commentary on the Surahs of Muhammad, Al-Fath, Al-Hujurat and Qaf, **Grade 11 (2002), p. 9:**

When you meet them in order to fight [them], do not be seized by compassion [towards them] but strike the[ir] necks powerfully. . . . Striking the neck means fighting, because killing a person is often done by striking off his head. Thus, it has become an expression for killing even if the fighter strikes him elsewhere. This expression contains a harshness and emphasis that are not found in the word

Andrew G. Bostom, "Textbook Jihad in Egypt," FrontPageMagazine.com, June 30, 2004, http://www .frontpagemag.com/Articles/ReadArticle.asp?ID=14017.

"kill," because it describes killing in the ugliest manner, i.e., cutting the neck and making the organ—the head of the body—fly off [the body].

Although chilling to our modern sensibilities, particularly when being taught to children, these are merely classical interpretations of the rules for jihad war, based on over a millennium of Muslim theology and jurisprudence.[3] And the context of these teachings is unambiguous, as the translator makes clear:

[the] concept of jihad is interpreted in the Egyptian school curriculum almost exclusively as a military endeavor . . . it is war against God's enemies, i.e., the infidels . . . it is war against the homeland's enemies and a means to strengthening the Muslim states in the world. In both cases, jihad is encouraged, and those who refrain from participating in it are denounced.

Teaching Egyptian school children anti-infidel jihad hatred is clearly a long, ongoing, and ignoble tradition even within the modern era. As the scholar E. W. Lane reported after several years of residence in both Cairo and Luxor (initially in 1825–1828, then in 1833–1835),

I am credibly informed that children in Egypt are often taught at school, a regular set of curses to denounce upon the persons and property of Christians, Jews, and all other unbelievers in the religion of Mohammad.[4]

Lane's nephew Edward Stanley Poole (who edited the 1860 reissue of his uncle's classic work), was provided such a prayer, which he translated from a contemporary nineteenth-century Arabic text, containing a typical curse on non-Muslims, recited daily by Muslim schoolchildren:

I seek refuge with God from Satan the accursed. In the name of God, the Compassionate, the Merciful. O God, aid El-Islam, and exalt the word of truth, and the faith, by the preservation of thy servant and the son of thy servant, the Sultan of the two continents (Europe and Asia), and the Khakan (Emperor or monarch) of the two seas [the Mediterranean and Black Seas], the Sultan, son of the Sultan (Mahmood) Khan (the reigning Sultan when this prayer was composed). O God, assist him, and assist his armies, and all the forces of the Muslims: O Lord of the beings of the whole world. O God, destroy the infidels and polytheists, thine enemies, the enemies of the religion. O God, make their children orphans, and defile their abodes, and cause their feet to slip, and give them and their families, and their households and their women and their children and their relations by marriage and their brothers and their friends and their possessions and their race and their wealth and their lands as booty to the Muslims: O Lord of the beings of the whole world.[5]

The modern scholar of Islamic civilization S. D. Goitein warned more than a century later, in 1949, speaking of the Arab world generally, in particular Egypt:

Islamic fanaticism . . . is now openly encouraged . . . writers whose altogether Western style (was mentioned earlier) have been vying with each other for some time in compiling books on the heroes and virtues of Islam. . . . What has now become possible in educated circles may be gathered from the following quotation from an issue of the New East, an Arab monthly periodical describing itself as the "organ of the academic youth of the East":

> "Let us fight fanatically for our religion; let us love a man—because he is a Moslem; let us honor a man—because he is a Moslem; let us prefer him to anyone else—because he is a Moslem; and never let us make friends with unbelievers, because they have nothing but evil for us."[6]

And a decade later, in 1958, Lebanese law professor Antoine Fattal, a noted scholar of the legal condition of non-Muslims living under the Sharia, lamented,

> No social relationship, no fellowship is possible between Muslims and dhimmis. . . . Even today, the study of the jihad is part of the curriculum of all the Islamic institutes. In the universities of Al-Azhar, Nagaf, and Zaitoune, students are still taught that the holy war is a binding prescriptive decree, pronounced against the Infidels, which will only be revoked with the end of the world.[7]

Sadly, almost fifty years after Fattal made his observations, the sacralized hatred of jihad is still being inculcated as part of the formal education of Muslim youth in Egypt, the most populous Arab country, and throughout the Arab Muslim and larger non-Arab Muslim world. We in the West must press our political and religious leaders to demand that such bellicose, hate-mongering "educational" practices be abolished in Islamic nations, under threat of severe, broad-ranging economic sanctions.

NOTES

1. "Muslim Kids Stage Mock Beheading," *WorldNet Daily*, June 26, 2004, http://www.wnd.com/news/article.asp?ARTICLE_ID=39145.

2. "Jews, Christians, War and Peace in Egyptian School Textbooks," Center for Monitoring the Impact of Peace, http://www.edume.org/reports/13/toc.htm.

3. Andrew Bostom, "Treatment of POWs," FrontPageMagazine.com, March 28, 2003, http://www.frontpagemag.com/Articles/ReadArticle.asp?ID=6929; "The Sacred Muslim Practice of Beheading," FrontPageMagazine.com, May 13, 2004, http://www.frontpagemag.com/Articles/ReadArticle.asp?ID=13371.

4. E. W. Lane, *An Account of the Manners and Customs of the Modern Egyptians* (New York: Dover, 1973), p. 276.

5. Lane, *An Acccount of the Manners and Customs of the Modern Egyptians*, p. 575. Edward Stanley Poole includes the following explanatory note, accompanying his (i.e., Poole's) English translation of the Arabic prayer:

My friend Mr. Burton (who, in the course of his long residence in Egypt, has acquired an ample fund of valuable information respecting its modern inhabitants, as well as other subjects), has kindly communicated to me an Arabic paper containing the forms of imprecation to which I have alluded in a note subjoined to p. 276 of this work. They are expressed in a "hezb" (or prayer) which the Muslim youths in many of the schools of Cairo recite, before they return to their homes, every day of their attendance, at the period of the " 'asr" except on Thursday, when they recite it at noon; being allowed to leave the school on this day, at the early hour of the "duhr," in consideration of the approach of Friday, their Sabbath and holiday.

6. S. D. Goitein, "Cross-Currents in Arab National Feeling," *Commentary* (January 1949): 161.

7. Antoine Fattal, *Le Statut Legal de Musulmans en Pays' d'Islam* (Beiru, 1958), pp. 369, 372.

PART 7
Jihad Slavery

45

THE ORIGINS OF MUSLIM SLAVE SYSTEM

K. S. Lal

From the day India became a target of Muslim invaders its people began to be enslaved in droves to be sold in foreign lands or employed in various capacities on menial and not-so-menial jobs within the country. To understand this phenomenon it is necessary to go into the origins and development of the Islamic system of slavery. For, wherever the Muslims went, mostly as conquerors but also as traders, there developed a system of slavery peculiar to the clime, terrain and populace of the place. For example, simultaneously with Muhammad bin Qasim's invasion of Sindh in early eighth century, the expansion of Arab Islam had gone apace as far as Egypt, North Africa, and the Iberian Peninsula in the West, as well as in Syria, Asia Minor, Palestine, Iraq, Iran, Khurasan, Sistan, and Transoxiana. In all these countries Muslim slave system grew and developed in its own way. There was constant contact between India and most of these countries in the medieval times. For example, as early as during the reigns of the slave sultans Iltutmish and Balban (1210–1286), there arrived at their courts in Delhi a large number of princes with their followers from Iraq, Khurasan, and Mawar-un-Nahr

---

K. S. Lal, "The Origins of Muslim Slave System," in *Muslim Slave System in India* (New Delhi: Aditya Prakashan, 1994), pp. 9–16.

because of the Mongol upheaval.[1] Many localities in Delhi and its environs were settled by these elites and their slaves, soldiers and scholars. In Balban's royal procession 500 Sistani, Ghauri, and Samarqandi slave-troops with drawn swords used to march by his side pointing to the fact that a large number of foreign slaves from these lands had come to India in thirteenth and fourteenth centuries.[2] When the Mughals launched their conquest of India, there was the establishment of the Ottoman Empire in Turkey, which at its height included present-day Albania, Greece, Bulgaria, Serbia, Romania, and several other contiguous countries. Then there was the Safavid Empire in Iran. The Ottoman Empire traded with Europe and imported "there indispensable stock of slaves. (Slav, as the word indicates), supplied by merchants, sometimes Jewish, from Verdun, Venice or elsewhere in Italy. Other slaves were brought from black Africa, eastern Europe and Turkish Central Asia."[3]

The Mughals of India had very close contacts with the Turkish Ottoman and Iranian Safavid empires. This contact certainly included exchange of slaves and ideas on slavery. But any attempt in this area of study, which is so vast and labyrinthine, is bound to deflect us from our main theme which is restricted to India. We shall therefore confine ourselves to the barest particulars of the beginnings of the institution outside India which will suffice for understanding the Muslim slave system in India in the medieval period.

Prophet Muhammad found slavery existing in Arabia, and recognised it in the Quran. The origins of Muslim slave system can thus be traced to Arabia, the original Muslim homeland, and the regions into which Islam spread. Quranic injunctions, Islamic conquests, and Muslim administrative institutions gave it a continuity and legitimacy. According to T. P. Hughes, "Slavery is in complete harmony with the spirit of Islam. . . . That Muhammad ameliorated the condition of the slave, as it existed under the heathen law of Arabia, we cannot doubt; but it is equally certain that the Arabian legislator intended it to be a permanent institution."[4] D. S. Margoliouth elaborates on the theme adding that "[o]n the whole . . . the Prophet did something to alleviate the existence of the captives . . . manumission was declared by him to be an act of piety . . . and murder or maiming of slaves was to be punished by retaliation."[5] In one of his last sermons, Muhammad exhorted his followers thus: "And your Slaves! See that ye feed them with such food as ye eat yourselves; and clothe them with the stuff ye wear. And if they commit a fault which ye are not inclined to forgive, then sell them, for they are the servants of the Lord, and are not to be tormented."[6] His first orthodox biographer, Ibn Ishaq, however, mentions a transaction which set a precedent for Islamic slave trade at a later, stage: "Then the apostle sent Sa'd b. Zayd Al-Ansari . . . with some of the captive women of Banu Qurayza to Najd and he sold them for horses and weapons."[7] The women had been made captive after their menfolk had been slaughtered en masse in the market place at Medina.

STATUS OF SLAVES IN ISLAM

The appeal of Muhammad contained some fundamental perceptions about the status of slaves in Islam. It recognised the slave as the property of the master. A slave could be sold but, being a Muslim or servant of the Lord, was not to be treated harshly. Here it needs to be observed that in the early days of Islam it was the scum of the society that flocked to the standard of Muhammad and became his fighting force. "Koran acknowledges so distinctly that the followers of the Prophet were the lowest of the people."[8] Arabian aristocracy "requested him to send away this scum before they would argue with him,"[9] (as did the Turkish ruling classes treat the early Muslim converts in India). But the mission of Muhammad was to spread his creed and any non-humane regulations would have presented a very unfavourable picture of Islam to the captives. This would have discouraged prose-lytization. On conversion also Muslim slaves could not be treated badly for that again would have been damaging to the reputation of the new creed and galling to the lives of the new converts. How these injunctions were later on followed or flouted by Muslim invaders and rulers in other countries is a different matter. In the original land of Islam, in Arabia, it was enjoined not to treat the slaves harshly; instead the masters were encouraged to utilize to the best the services of men slaves and enjoy the intimate company of women slaves.[10]

This tolerant treatment was not without conditions. A slave was the property of his master. His tenor of life was determined by the latter. For example, he could not marry without the master's permission. Although he was free to move from place to place, he could not hold pleasure parties nor pay visits to friends. A slave could not bestow aims or grant a loan or make a pilgrimage.[11] If he managed to accumulate any property, it was inherited not by his sons but by the master.[12] In theory a slave could purchase his freedom, but bond of freedom was granted to a slave in return for money paid, and until full money was paid there was no total redemption.[13] A slave should not seek his emancipation by running away, "The slave who fled from his master committed an act of infidelity," says Muhammad.[14]

The emancipation of slaves was not unknown in pre-Islamic Arabia. It was an old custom among the Arabs of more pious disposition to will that their slaves would be freed at their death. To Muhammad, the freeing of a slave was an act of charity on the part of the master, not a matter of justice, and only a believing slave deserved freedom.

In short, slavery in Islam is a permanent and perennial institution. As Margo-liouth points out, "the abolition of slavery was not a notion that ever entered the Prophet's mind."[15] "The fact remains," writes Ram Swarup, "that Muhammad, by introducing the concept of religious war and by denying human rights to non-Muslims, sanctioned slavery on an unprecedented scale . . . (and on) such massive proportions. Zubair, a close companion of the Prophet, owned one thousand slaves when he died. The Prophet himself possessed at least fifty-nine slaves at one stage or another, besides thirty-eight servants, both male and female. Mirk-hond, the Prophet's fifteenth century biographer, names them all in his Rauzat-us-Safa. The fact is that slavery, tribute, and booty became the main props of the new Arab aristocracy. . . ."[16] "The Slavery of Islam is interwoven with the Law of marriage, the Law of sale, and the Law of inheritance, of the system, and its abolition would strike at the very foundations of the code of Muhaminadanism."[17]

EXTENSION OF ISLAMIC SLAVERY

Islamic slave system spread and developed wherever Muslim rule was established. Ghulam or quallar ("slave") was the creation of the Safavid state. Mamluks were found in Egypt. In the Ottoman empire they were called *kapi-kulus*. "Kapi-kulu were recruited originally from the Sultan's share of prisoners of war, and subsequently from a periodical levy (devshirme) of Christian boys. Most of the youths entered the Janissary corps."[18] Christian slaves were drawn from the ranks of the Georgian, Armenian, and Circassian prisoners or their descendants."[19] Black slaves, natives of East Africa, were called *Zanj*.[20] Majority of slaves who penetrated and flourished in India were Turks.

Immediately after its birth, Muhammadanism entered upon a career of aggressive and expansionist conquest. Its Caliphs conquered extensively and set up autocratic governments based on the tenets of Islam rather than democratic governments based on the will of the people. Conquests required large armies; despotic governments could not be run without a train of bureaucrats. From the ninth to the thirteenth century in particular it was a period of feverish activity in Muslim Asia; empires were established and pulled down; cities were founded and destroyed. In other words, the whole of Central Asia, Transoxiana, and Turkistan was a very disturbed region in the medieval period. Armies and bureaucrats were needed in large numbers to administer the ever expanding dominions of Islam. The Turks came handy for such services.

TURKISH SLAVES

The Abbasids had built up a very large empire with capital at Baghdad,[21] and its provinces were administered by their Turkish slave officers and Turk mercenary troops. Caliph al-Mutasim (833–842 CE) introduced the Turkish element into the army, and he was the first Caliph to have Turkish slaves under his employment.[22] For it was soon discovered that the young slaves acquired from Turkistan and Mawar-un-Nahr formed an excellent material for such a corps.

Turks is a generic term comprehending peoples of sundry denominations and tribes. The Turkistan of the medieval historians was an extensive country. It was bounded on the east by China, on the west by Rum or Turkey, on the north by the walls of Yajuj and Majuj (Gog and Magog), and on the south by the mountains of Hindustan.[23] The Turks as a people were both civilised town-dwellers and the migratory tribes trekking across the desert or wilderness. With the extension of the Muslim frontier to the north and west of Persia one tribe after another, like Turks, Tartars, Turkomen, and even Mongols and Afghans came under subjection. They attracted the attention of their conquerors by their bravery and spirit of adventure. They were acquired in groups and droves as slaves. The Caliphs of Islam also purchased Turkish slaves to manage their far-flung empire. The Turkish slaves helped the cause of Islam through their fighting spirit.

But as their numbers grew, they became unmanageable. For example, Caliph al-Mutasim's own guard was of 4,000 Turks; the number later rose to 70,000 slave mercenaries.[24] With time the tyranny, lawlessness, and power of the Turks went on increasing.[25] The unscrupulous policy of religious persecution followed by the Caliph Mutawakkil was responsible for the alienation of the subject races. His own son entered into a conspiracy with the Turks, which ended in the Caliph's murder in 861. The Caliph Mutadid (892–902) was unable to suppress the power of the Turks. The final decline of the Caliphate set in just after the murder of Muqtadir in 932 CE. "The Turkish soldiers made and murdered Caliphs at their pleasure."[26] As the Caliphal empire disintegrated, in the third century of Islam, its provincial governors became independent.[27]

But technically these Turkish governors were only slaves and their tenure of power rested on military force and chance-victory and not on any moral foundations. On the other hand, the Caliphs were objects of respect. The first four Caliphs were directly related to Muhammad. Muawiyah, the founder of the Ummayad Caliphate, was a cousin of Abbas, an uncle of the Prophet. Abbas himself was founder of the Abbasid Caliphate. The Turkish slaves, therefore, considered it politic to keep a sort of special relationship with the Caliph: they went on paying him tribute and seeking from him recognition of their "sovereignty." That is how, in course of time, their political power was firmly established.

NOTES

For clarification of any citations, the reader is referred to the original, K. S. Lal, "The Origins of Muslim Slave System," in *Muslim Slave System in India* (New Delhi: Aditya Prakashan, 1994), pp. 178–88.

1. Minhaj, pp. 598–99; Farishtah, vol. 1, pp. 73, 75.
2. Barani, pp. 57–58.
3. *Cambridge History of Islam*, vol. 2, p. 524. The word *slave*, observes Ram Swarup, "is derived from Stavs, the Slavonic peoples of Central Europe. When they were captured and made bondsmen, they gave birth to die word 'slave.'" *The Word as Revelation: Names of Gods*, p. 23; also J. H. Kremers, *The Legacy of Islam*, p. 101.

4. *Dictionary of Islam*, pp. 596, 600.

5. Margoliouth, *Mohammed and the Rise of Islam*, pp. 461–62.

6. Cited in Muir, *The Life of Mahomet*, p. 473.

7. *The Life of Muhammad*: A translation of Ibn Ishaq's *Sirat Rasul Allah* by A. Gillaume (Karachi: CUP, 1955), p. 466.

8. Margoliouth, p. 98, quoting Qur'an 11.27.

9. Ibid., p. 97

10. Ibid., p. 406–407; Qur'an 4.3, 4.24, 4.25, 23.6; Muir, *Life of Mahomet*, pp. 334–35, 365, 421.

11. Hughes, *Dictionary of Islam*, p. 598.

12. *Sahib Muslim*, Hadis, 3584, 3585, 3595.

13. Qur'an 24.33.

14. Ram Swarup, *Understanding Islam through Hadis*, p. 76.

15. Margoliouth, *Mohammed and the Rise of Islam*, p. 461.

16. Ram Swarup, *Understanding Islam through Hadis*, p. 75.

17. Hughes, *Dictionary of Islam*, p. 600.

18. *Cambridge History of Islam*, vol. 1, p. 280 and n342.

19. Ibid., pp. 415, 407.

20. Ibid., pp. 129–30, 179.

21. Ruben Levy, *The Baghdad Chronicle* (Cambridge, 1929), p. 13.

22. Hamdullah Mustaufi, *Tarikh-i-Guzidah*, ed. E. G. Browne (London, 1910), p. 318.

23. Fakr-i-Mudabbir, *Tarikh-i-Fakhruddin Mubarak Shah*, p. 38.

24. *Cambridge History of Islam*, vol. 1, p. 125.

25. Ibn Asir, *Kamil-ut-Tawarikh*, Urdu trs. (Hyderabad, 1933), vol. 6, p. 319.

26. P. M. Sykes, *History of Persia* (London, 1915), vol. 2, p. 83.

27. Ruben Levy, *The Social Structure of Islam* (Cambridge, 1962), p. 282.

46

SLAVE-TAKING DURING MUSLIM RULE

K. S. Lal

Slavery forms an integral part of the history of Islam. The Turks practised it on a large scale before they entered India as invaders. Slaves were abducted or captured by marauders (Subuktigin, Balban), they were sold by jealous or needy relatives (Iltutmish), and they were purchased by slave-traders to be sold for profit (Aibak). These methods were known to Muslim rulers in India. All these and many other methods were employed by them and their nobles in making slaves in India. The phenomenon and its application was shocking to the Hindu mind; the Muslims, however, thought otherwise. According to Ibn Khaldun, the captives were "brought from the House of War to the House of Islam under the rule of slavery, which hides in itself a divine providence; cured by slavery, they enter the Muslim religion with the firm resolve of true believers. . . ."[1] Muslims took pride in enslaving people; the feelings of Hindu victims were just the opposite.

Qutbuddin Aibak entered upon a series of conquests. He dispatched Ikhti-yaruddin Bakhtiyar Khalji to the East and himself concentrated in Hindustan proper. He captured Kol (modern Aligarh) in 1194. There "those of the garrison who were wise and cute were converted to Islam, but those who stood by their ancient faith were slain with the sword."[2] Surely, those who embraced Islam during or immediately after the battle were "cute" and wise, because by this initiative on their part they were counted as free-born Muslims as against those who fought, were captured in battle, and then enslaved. T. P. Hughes gives the legal position: "If a captive embraced Islam on the field of battle he was a free man; but if he were made captive, and afterwards embraced Islam, the change of creed did

K. S. Lal, "Slave-Taking during Muslim Rule," in *Muslim Slave System in India* (New Delhi: Aditya Prakashan, 1994), pp. 41–59.

not emancipate him." Women captives were invariably taken prisoner. "Atiyat-ul-Qurazi relates that, after the battle with the Banu Quraizah, the Prophet ordered all those who were able to fight to be killed, and the women and children to be enslaved."[3]

Both these traditions were followed in India. In 1195 when Raja Bhim was attacked by Aibak twenty thousand slaves were captured, and fifty thousand at Kalinjar in 1202. "The temples were converted into mosques," writes Hasan Nizami, "and the voices of the summoners to prayer ascended to the highest heavens, and the very name of idolatry was annihilated."[4] Call to prayer five times a day with a loud voice carried an invitation and a message—join us, or else. People "could refuse this invitation or call at their own peril, spiritual and physical. As His followers became more powerful, the peril became increasingly more physical."[5] This process helped in the conversion of captives. Murry Titus pertinently remarks that "we may be sure that all those who were made slaves were compelled to embrace the religion of the masters to whom they were allotted."[6] Farishtah specifically mentions that during the capture of Kalinjar "fifty thousand kaniz va ghulam, having suffered slavery, were rewarded with the honour of Islam." Thus enslavement resulted in conversion and conversion accelerated the growth of the Muslim population.

Minhaj Siraj assigns twenty (lunar) years to Qutbuddin's career in Hindustan from "the first taking of Delhi" up to his death, both as a commander of Sultan Muizzuddin and as an independent ruler.[7] During this period Aibak captured Hansi, Meerut, Delhi, Ranthambhor, and Kol.[8] When Sultan Muizzuddin personally mounted another campaign against Hindustan, Aibak proceeded as far as Peshawar to meet him, and the two together attacked the Khokhar stronghold in the Koh-i-Jud or the Salt Range. The Hindus (Khokhars) fled to the highest in the mountains. They were pursued. Those that escaped the sword fled to the dense depth of the jungle; others were massacred or taken captive. Great plunder was obtained and many slaves.[9] According to Farishtah three to four hundred thousand Khokhars were converted to Islam by Muizzuddin;[10] but this figure is inflated. More than a hundred years later, Amir Khusrau refers to Khokhars as a non-Muslim tribe, and the way they were constantly attacked and killed by Sultans Iltutmish and Balban confirms Khusrau's contention.[11] Minhaj also says that "the Khokhars were not annihilated in this affair (Muizzuddin-Aibak attack) by any means, and gave great trouble in after years."[12]

Under Aibak most of Hindustan from Delhi to Gujarat, and Lakhnauti to Lahore, was brought under the sway of the Turks. In his time a large number of places were attacked and many more prisoners were captured than for which actual figures are available. Figures of slaves made during campaigns of Kanauj, Banaras (where the Muslims occupied "a thousand" temples),[13] Ajmer (attacked thrice), Gujarat, Bayana, and Gwalior are not available. Similar is the case with regard to Bihar and Bengal. About the end of the twelfth or the beginning of the thirteenth century, Ikhtiyaruddin Bakhtiyar Khalji marched into Bihar and attacked the University centres at Nalanda, Vikramshila, and Uddandpur.[14] The Buddhist monks and Brahmans mistaken for monks were massacred and the common people, deprived of their priests and teachers, became an easy prey to capture and enslavement. But no figures of such captives are known. Ibn Asir only says that Qutbuddin Aibak made "war against the provinces of Hind. . . . He killed many, and returned with prisoners and booty."[15] In Banaras, according to the same author, "the slaughter of the Hindus was immense, none was spared except women and children,"[16] who would have been enslaved as per practice. Habibullah writes that Muslim sway extended from Banaras through the strip of Shahabad, Patna, Monghyr, and Bhagalpur districts,[17] and repeated references to the presence of Muslims in this tract from the early times indicates that taking of slaves and conversion was common in the region. Fakhr-i-Mudabbir informs us that as a result of the Turkish achievements under Muizzuddin and Aibak, "even [a] poor (Muslim) householder became owner of numerous slaves."[18]

The narratives of contemporary and later chroniclers should not lead us to the conclusion that taking of Hindus as slaves was a child's play. There was stiff resistance to Muslim conquest and Muslim rule. Besides, the Sultans of Delhi had always to deal with a number of problems simultaneously. Most of the time of Sultan Iltutmish (1210–1236) was spent in suppressing his Turkish opponents, Qutbi and Muizzi Amirs in Delhi and rivals Yaldoz and Qubacha in Punjab and Sindh. He also faced the threat of invasion from the Mongol conqueror Chingiz Khan and the Khwarizmi Prince Jalaluddin Mangbarni fleeing before Chingiz. Therefore it was only sixteen years after his accession that he could march against Ranthambhor in 1226. During this period many Hindu kingdoms subdued by Aibak were becoming independent. Mandor near Jodhpur was attacked a little later. Here "much booty fell into the hands" of the victors, which obviously included slaves also.[19] The year 1231 witnessed his invasion of Gwalior where he "captured a large number of slaves." In 1234–35 he attacked Ujjain, broke its temple of Mahakal, and as usual made captives "women and children of the recalcitrants."[20] But most of his compatriot Muslims were not satisfied with the Sultan's achievements in the sphere of slave-taking and converting the land into Dar-ul-Islam all at once.

It is true that foreign Muslims—freemen and slaves—were flocking into Hindustan and this development was of great significance for the Sultanate. Adventurers and job seekers were flocking into Hindustan, the new heaven of Islam. More importantly, because of the Mongol upheaval, as many as twenty-five Muslim refugee princes with their retinues arrived at the court of Iltutmish from Khurasan and Mawaraun Nahr.[21] During the reign of Balban fifteen more refugee rulers and their nobles and slaves arrived from Turkistan, Khurasan, Iraq, Azarbaijan, Persia, Rum (Turkey), and Sham (Syria).[22] Their followers comprised masters of pen and of sword, scholars and Mashaikh, historians and poets. The pressure of these groups on the Sultan for Islamization of Hindustan would have been great. In 1228 CE Iltutmish received a patent of investiture from Al-Mustansir Billah, the Khalifa of Baghdad, in recognition of his enormously augmenting the prestige of the Muhammadan government in India. This was a booster as well as a further pressure. No wonder, the capital city of Delhi looked like Dar-ul-Islam and its ruler the leader of the eastern world of Islam.[23] But since the whole country was not conquered and converted, it did not amuse the Ulama and the Mashaikh.

SLAVE-TAKING A MATTER OF POLICY

Some Ulama therefore approached the "pious" Sultan Iltutmish to rule according to the Shariat and confront the Hindus with choice between Islam and death. Muslims had set up their rule and so the country had become Dar-ul-Islam. Any opposition to it was an act of rebellion. The Hindus who naturally resisted Muslim occupation were considered to be rebels. Besides they were idolaters (*mushrik*) and could not be accorded the status of Kafirs, of the People of the Book—Christians and Jews. For them the law provided only Islam or death. Islamic jurisprudence had crystallized over the last five centuries. Besides the evolvement of the four schools of Islamic jurisprudence, Shaikh Burhauddin Ali's Hidayah (530–596 H/1135–1199 CE), the Compendium of Sunni Law, based on the Quran and the Hadis, was also readily available in the time of Iltutmish. Muslim scriptures and treatises advocated jihad against idolaters for whom the law advocated only Islam or death.

In such a situation the answer of the Sultan to the Ulama was: "But at the moment in India . . . the Muslims are so few that they are like salt (in a large dish). . . . However, after a few years when in the capital and the regions and all the small towns, when the Muslims are well established and the troops are larger . . . it would be possible to give Hindus, the choice of death or Islam."[24] Such an apologetic plea was not necessary to put forward. The fact was that the Muslim regime was giving a choice between Islam and death only. Those who were killed in battle were dead and gone; but their dependents were made slaves. They ceased to be Hindus; they were made Musalmans in course of time if not immediately after captivity.

There was thus no let up in the policy of slave-taking. Minhaj Siraj writes that Ulugh Khan Balban's "taking of captives, and his capture of the dependents of the great Ranas cannot be recounted." Talking of his war in Avadh against Trailokyavarman of the Chandela Dynasty (Dalaki va Malaki of Minhaj), the chronicler says that "[a]ll the infidels' wives, sons and dependents . . . and children . . . fell into the hands of the victors." In 1253, in his campaign against Ranthambhor also, Balban enslaved many people. In 1259, in an attack on

Haryana, many women and children were enslaved.[25] Twice Balban led expeditions against Kampil, Patiali, and Bhojpur, and in the process enslaved a large number of women and children. In Katehar he ordered a general massacre of the male population of over eight years of age and carried away women and children. In 658 H (1260 CE) Ulugh Khan Balban marched with a large force on a campaign in the region of Ranthambhor, Mewat, and Siwalik. He made a proclamation that a soldier who brought a live captive would be rewarded with two silver tankahs and one who brought the head of a dead one would get one silver tankah. Soon three to four hundred living and dead were brought to his presence.[26] Like Balban other slave commanders of Iltutmish, or the "Shamsia Maliks of Hind" were marching up and down the Hindustan, raiding towns and villages and enslaving people. This was the situation prevailing from Lakhnauti to Lahore and from Ajmer to Ujjain. The Hindus used to reclaim their lands after the Muslim invaders had passed through them with fire and sword, and Turkish armies used to repeat their attacks to regain control of the cities so lost. But the captives once taken became slaves and then Musalmans for ever. The exact figures of such slaves have not been mentioned and therefore cannot be computed. All that is known is that they were captured in droves. Only one instance should suffice to convey an idea of their numbers. Even in the reign of a weak Sultan like Nasiruddin, son of Iltutmish, the ingress of captives was so large that once he presented forty beads of staves to our chronicler Minhaj Siraj to send to his "dear sister" in Khurasan.[27]

ENSLAVEMENT UNDER THE KHALJIS

The process of enslavement during war gained momentum under the Khaljis and the Tughlaqs. In two or three generations after Iltutmish the Muslims were digging their heels firmly into the country. Their territories were expanding and their armies were becoming larger. All the time, the desire to convert or liquidate the idolaters remained ever restless. Achievements in this regard of course depended on the strength, resources, and determination of individual Muslim rulers. For example, although Jalaluddin Khalji was an old and vacillating king, even he did not just remain content with expressing rage at the fact of not being able to deal with the Hindus according to the law.[28] During six years of his reign (June 1290–July 1296), he mounted expeditions and captured prisoners. While suppressing the revolt of Malik Chhajju, a scion of the dynasty he had ousted, he marched towards Bhojpur in Farrukhabad district and ruthlessly attacked Hindus in the region of Katehar (later Rohilkhand). During his campaign in Ranthambhor he broke temples, sacked the neighbouring Jhain and took booty and captives, making "a hell of paradise."[29] Later on Malwa was attacked and large quantity of loot, naturally including slaves, was brought to Delhi.[30] His last expedition was directed against Gwalior.[31]

Jalaluddin's nephew and successor Alauddin Khalji (1296–1316) turned out to be a very strong king. He marched against Devagiri in 1296. On his way through Gondwana and Khandesh he took prisoners a large number of Mahajans and cultivators, and ransomed them for wealth.[32] At Devagiri he enslaved a number of the Raja's relatives, and Brahmans and Mahajans. He put them in shackles and chains and paraded them in front of the fort to pressure the besieged king. After victory, he released many of the captives because of compulsions of the situation. He was only a prince who had marched to the Deccan without the Sultan's permission. But his taking of slaves in large numbers was in consonance with the policy of Muslim sultans and gave a foretaste of what was to follow during the course of his reign.

After ascending the throne, Alauddin Khalji embarked upon a series of conquests. He turned out to be the greatest king of the Sultanate period (c. 1200–1500), and his success as regards capture of slaves was stupendous. He started by seizing the families and slaves of his brothers and brother-in-law.[33] In 1299 he despatched a large army for the invasion of Gujarat. There all the major towns and cities like Naharwala, Asaval, Vanmanthali, Surat, Cambay, Somnath, et cetera were sacked. There the temples were broken, wealth looted and large numbers of captives of both sexes captured, including the famous Malik Kafur[34] and the Vaghela king's consort Kamala Devi.[35] In the words of Wassaf, the Muslim army in the sack of Somnath "took captive a great number of handsome and elegant maidens, amounting to 20,000, and children of both sexes . . . the Muhammadan army brought the country to utter ruin, and destroyed the lives of inhabitants, and plundered the cities and captured their offspring. . . ."[36] In 1301 Ranthambhor was attacked and in 1303 Chittor. In the invasion of Chittor, thirty thousand people were massacred in cold blood and obviously females and minors of their families were captured.[37] Slaves were also taken in large numbers in the expeditions to Malwa, Sevana, and Jalor (1305–1311); these will be referred to again in the course of this study. Maybe the number of captives obtained from Rajasthan was not that large knowing the bravery and chivalry of the Rajputs and their prevailing customs of Jauhar and Sati. But the highly successful Deccan campaigns of Malik Kafur must have supplied a large corps of captives. Besides, Alauddin did not confine to obtaining Hindu slaves. During the invasion of the Mongol Saldi (1299), the commanders of the Sultan captured seventeen hundred of his officers, men, and women and sent them as slaves to Delhi.[38] During the raid of Ali Beg, Tartaq and Targhi (1305), eight thousand Mongol prisoners were executed and their heads displayed in the towers of the Siri Fort which were then under construction.[39] The women and children accompanying the Mongol raiders Kubak and Iqbalmand were sold in Delhi and the rest of Hindustan. "The Mongol invaders were certainly infidels," says Mahdi Husain. This enslavement was as beneficial to Islam as that of the Hindus. Muslims were not enslaved because they were already Muslim.[40]

Sultan Alauddin's collection of slaves was a matter of successful routine. Under him the Sultanate had grown so strong that, according to Shams Siraj Afif, in his days "no one dared to make an outcry."[41] Similar is the testimony of the Alim and Sufi Amir Khusrau. In Nuh Sipehr he writes that "the Turks, whenever they please, can seize, buy or sell any Hindu."[42] No wonder, under him the process of enslavement went on with great vigour. As an example, he had fifty thousand slave boys in his personal service[43] and seventy thousand slaves worked continuously on his buildings.[44] We must feel obliged to Muslim chroniclers for providing such bits of information on the basis of which we can safely generalize. For instance, it is Barani alone who writes about the number of slaves working on buildings and Afif alone who speaks about the personal "boys" of Sultan Alauddin who looked after his pigeons. Ziyauddin Barani's detailed description of the Slave Markets in Delhi and elsewhere during the reign of Alauddin Khalji, shows that fresh batches of captives were constantly arriving there.[45]

ENSLAVEMENT UNDER THE TUGHLAQS

All sultans were keen on making slaves, but Muhammad Tughlaq became notorious for enslaving people. He appears to have outstripped even Alauddin Khalji and his reputation in this regard spread far and wide. Shihabuddin Ahmad Abbas writes about him thus: "The Sultan never ceases to show the greatest zeal in making war upon infidels. . . . Everyday thousands of slaves are sold at a very low price, so great is the number of prisoners."[46] Muhammad Tughlaq did not only enslave people during campaigns, he was also very fond of purchasing and collecting foreign and Indian slaves. According to Ibn Battuta one of the reasons of estrangement between Muhammad Tughlaq and his father Ghiyasuddin Tughlaq, when Muhammad was still a prince, was his extravagance in purchasing slaves.[47] Even as Sultan, he made extensive conquests. He subjugated the country as far as Dwarsamudra, Malabar, Kampil, Warangal, Lakhnauti, Satgaon, Sonargaon, Nagarkot, and Sambhal to give only few prominent place-names.[48] There were sixteen major rebellions in his reign which were ruthlessly suppressed.[49] In all these conquests and rebellions, slaves were taken with great gusto. For example, in the year 1342 Halajun rose in rebellion in Lahore. He was aided by the Khokhar chief Kulchand. They were defeated. "About three hundred women of the rebels were taken captive, and sent to the fort of Gwalior where they were seen by Ibn Battutah."[50] Such was their influx that Ibn Battutah writes: "At (one) time there arrived in Delhi some female infidel captives, ten of whom the Vazir sent to me. I gave one of them to the man who had brought them to me, but he was not satisfied. My companion took three young girls, and I do not know what happened to the rest."[51] Iltutmish, Muhammad Tughlaq, and Firoz Tughlaq sent gifts of slaves to Khalifas outside India. To the Chinese emperor Muhammad Tughlaq sent, besides other presents, "100 Hindu slaves, 100 slave girls, accomplished in song and dance . . . and another 15 young slaves."[52]

Ibn Battutah's eye-witness account of the Sultan's gifting captured slave girls to nobles or arranging their marriages with Muslims on a large scale on the occasion of the two Ids, corroborates the statement of Abbas. Ibn Battutah writes that during the celebrations in connection with the two Ids in the court of Muhammad bin Tughlaq, daughters of Hindu Rajas and those of commoners, captured during the course of the year were distributed among nobles, officers and important foreign slaves. "On the fourth day men slaves are married and on the fifth slave-girls. On the sixth day men and women slaves are married off."[53] This was all in accordance with the Islamic law. According to it, slaves cannot marry on their own without the consent of their proprietors.[54] The marriage of an infidel couple is not dissolved by their jointly embracing the faith.[55] In the present case the slaves were probably already converted and their marriages performed with the initiative and permission the Sultan himself were valid. Thousands of non-Muslim women[56] were captured by the Muslims in the yearly campaigns of Firoz Tughlaq, and under him the Id celebrations were held on lines similar to those of his predecessor.[57] In short, under the Tughlaqs the inflow of women captives never ceased.

Similar was the case with males, especially of tender and young age. Firoz Tughlaq acquired them by all kinds of methods and means, so that he collected 180,000 of them.[58] Shams Siraj Afif, the contemporary historian, writes that under Firoz, "slaves became too numerous" and adds that "the institution took root in every centre of the land." So that even after the Sultanate broke up into a number of kingdoms, slave-hunting continued in every "(Muslim) centre of the land."[59]

SUFFERINGS OF THE ENSLAVED

This is the version of the slave-capturing victors. The humiliation and suffering of the victims finds no mention in Muslim chronicles. Sustained experience of grief and pain and loss of dignity and self-respect used to turn them into dumb driven animals. The practice and pattern of breaking the spirit of the captives under Aibak, Iltutmish, and Balban, indeed throughout the medieval period, was the same as during the days of the Khaljis and the Tughlaqs. Only one case may be cited as an instance. Balban, when he was Ulugh Khan Khan-i-Azam, once brought to Delhi (in about 1260) 250 "Hindu leading men and men of position" from Mewar and Siwalik, bound and shackled and chained. During the expedition he had proclaimed that a royal soldier would be rewarded with two silver tankahs if he captured a person alive and one tankah if he brought the head of a dead one. They brought to his presence 300 to 400 living and dead everyday. The reigning Sultan Nasiruddin ordered the death of the leading men. The others accompanying them were shaken to the bones and completely tamed. Depiction of their suffering is found in an Indian work—Kanhadade Prabandha. Written in "old Rajasthani or old Gujarati," it was composed in the mid-fifteenth century and records the exploits of King Kanhardeva of Jalor against Alauddin's General Ulugh Khan who had attacked Gujarat in 1299 and taken a number of prisoners. In the Sorath (Saurashtra) region "they made people captive—Brahmanas and children, and women, in fact, people of all (description) . . . huddled them and tied them by straps of raw hide. The number of prisoners made by them was beyond counting. The prisoners' quarters (bandikhana) were entrusted to the care of the Turks." The prisoners suffered greatly and wept aloud. "During the day they bore the heat of the scorching sun, without shade or shelter as they were [in the sandy desert region of Rajasthan], and the shivering cold during the night under the open sky. Children, torn away from their mother's breasts and homes, were crying. Each one of the captives seemed as miserable as the other. Already writhing in agony due to thirst, the pangs of hunger . . . added to their distress. Some of the captives were sick, some unable to sit up. Some had no shoes to put on and no clothes to wear. . . . Some had iron shackles on their feet. Separated from each other, they were huddled together and tied with straps of hide. Children were separated from their parents, the wives from their husbands, thrown apart by this cruel raid. Young and old were seen writhing in agony, as loud wailings arose from that part of the camp where they were all huddled up. . . . Weeping and wailing, they were hoping that some miracle might save them even now."[60] The miracle did happen and Kanhardeva was successful in rescuing them after a tough fight.

But the description provides the scenario in which the brave and the strong, the elite and the plebeian, were made captives and their spirit broken. That is how Timur was enabled to massacre in one day about one hundred thousand of captives he had taken prisoner on his march to Delhi. They had been distributed among his officers and kept tied and shackled. That is how Maulana Nasiruddin Umar, a man of learning in Timur's camp, "slew with his own sword fifteen idolatrous Hindus, who were his captives." If the prisoners could "break their bonds," such a carnage could not have been possible. Prisoners were often brought to Timur's presence with hands bound to their necks.[61] Jahangir (1605–1627) also writes that "prisoners were conducted to my presence yoked together."[62] Most of them were kept yoked together even when they were sent out to be sold in foreign lands or markets in India.

The captives, on their part, clung together and did not separate from one another even in their darkest hour. Nor were they permitted an opportunity to do so under Islamic law, which the victors always observed with typical Muslim zeal. The Hidayah lays down that "if the Mussulmans subdue an infidel territory before any capitation tax be established, the inhabitants, together with their wives and children, are all plunder, and the property of the state, as it is lawful to reduce to slavery all infidels, whether they be Kitabees, Majoosees or idolters."[63] The Hidayah also lays down that "whoever slays an infidel is entitled to his private property,"[64] which invariably included his women and children. That is how a large number of people were involved, whether it was a matter of taking captives, making converts, or ordering massacres. About women and children of a single family of a slain infidel, or of droves of slaves captured in an attack on a region or territory Fakhre Mudabbir furnishes information on, both counts during the campaigns of Muhammad Ghauri and Qutbuddin Aibak. He informs us that during their expeditions ghulams of all descriptions (har jins) were captured in groups and droves (jauq jauq) so that even a poor householder (or soldier) who did not possess a single slave (earlier) became the owner of numerous slaves. . . ."[65]

In short, the captives swam or sank together so that if they were captured they were taken in large numbers. A manifest example of this phenomenon is that during a rebellion-suppressing expedition of Muhammad bin Tughlaq in the Deccan (1327), all the eleven sons of the Raja of Kampil (situated on the River Tungbhadra, Bellary District), were captured together, and made Muslims.[66] Generally, able-bodied men and soldiers were massacred, and their helpless women and children were made prisoners in large numbers or groups.[67] Even in peace times people of one or more villages or groups acted in unison. When Firoz Shah Tughlaq proclaimed that those who accepted Islam would be exempted from payment of Jizyah, "great number of Hindus presented themselves. . . . Thus they came forward day by day from every quarter. . . ."[68] Similarly, from the time of entering Hindustan, up to the time of reaching the environs of Delhi, Amir Timur had "taken more than 100,000 infidels and Hindus prisoners. . . ."[69] Timur massacred them all, but the fact that people could be made slaves in such unbelievably large numbers was due to their keeping together through thick and thin, howsoever desperate the situation. Nobody knew the reality better than Ibn Battuta who travelled in India extensively. During his sojourn he found villages after villages deserted.[70] Nature's ravages or man's atrocities might have made them flee, or more probably they would have been enslaved and converted, or just carried away. But the fact of habitations being completely deserted shows that large groups suffered together and did not forsake one another in times of trial and tribulation. This factor swelled the number of slaves.

SPECIAL SLAVES OF FIROZ SHAH TUGHLAQ

By the time of Firoz Shah Tughlaq, the institution of slavery had taken root in every region of Muslim domination. The Sultanate of Delhi was now two hundred years old and well entrenched. The need of slaves for all kinds of errands was great. So that slaves were ever needed in hundreds, and slave-taking did not remain confined to their capture during wars. Firoz Tughlaq resorted to some other methods of acquiring slaves. One of these was akin to the famous Dewshrime [devshirme] widely practised in the Ottoman Empire.

The practice of Devshirme (Greek for "collecting boys"), "is the name applied to the forcible pressing of Christian children to recruit the janissary regiments . . . of the Turkish Empire . . . mainly in the European parts with a Christian population (Greece, Macedonia, Albania, Serbia, Bosnia and Herzegovina, and Bulgaria)."[71] These Christians, Jews, and Gypsies turned Muslims were trained to fight against their own erstwhile brethren. "Instituted by Urkhan in 1330, it formed for centuries the mainstay of the despotic power of the Turkish sultans, and was kept alive by a regular contribution exacted every four years (or so), when the officers of the Sultan visited the districts over and made a selection from among the children about the age of seven. The Muhammadan legists attempted to apologise for this inhuman tribute by representing these children as the fifth of the spoil which the Quran assigns to the sovereign."[72]

Sultan Firoz commanded his great fief-holders and officers to capture slaves whenever they were at war, and to pick out and send the best for the service of the court. The fifth part of slaves captured in war in India were always despatched to the ruler (or Caliph) ever since the days of Muhammad bin Qasim. Firoz Tughlaq desired slaves to be collected in the Devshirme fashion. Great numbers of slaves were thus collected, and when they were found to be in excess, the Sultan sent them to Multan, Dipalpur, Hissar Firozah, Samana, Gujarat, and all the other feudal dependencies."[73]

The policy of Delhi Sultanate of leaving the bare minimum to the peasant helped in Firoz's "Devshirme." Under Muslim rule, a substantial portion of the agricultural produce was taken away by the government as taxes and the people were left with the bare minimum for subsistence in order to impoverish them because it was thought that "wealth" was the source of "rebellion and disaffection."[74] This policy was in practice throughout the medieval period, both under the Sultans and the Mughals. Conditions became intolerable by the time of Shahjahan as attested to by Manucci and Manrique. Peasants were compelled to sell their women and children to meet the revenue demand. Manrique writes that "the peasants were carried off . . . to various markets and fairs (to be sold), with their poor unhappy wives behind them carrying their small children all crying and lamenting, to meet the revenue demand." Bernier too affirms that "the unfortunate peasants who were incapable of discharging the demand of their rapacious lords, were bereft of their children who were carried away as slaves."[75] As in the Ottoman Empire, Christians and Jews turned Muslim were trained to fight their erstwhile brethren, so also in India in the medieval period Hindus captured and converted were made to fight their erstwhile brethren in Muslim wars of conquest. Trained or accustomed to fighting their own people, these converts to Islam are posing various kinds of problems in the present-day India and Eastern Europe.

NOTES

For clarification of any citations, the reader is referred to the original, K. S. Lal, "Slave-Taking during Muslim Rule," in *Muslim Slave System in India* (New Delhi: Aditya Prakashan, 1994), pp. 178–88.

1. Ibn Khaldun; Ibar, trans. Bernard Lewis in *Islam*, p. 98.
2. Hasan Nizami, *Taj-ul-Maasir*, E.D., vol. 2, p. 222.
3. *Dictionary of Islam*, p. 597.
4. Hasan Nizami, *Taj-u-Maasir*, p. 231; Farishtah, vol. 1, p. 62.
5. Ram Swarup, introduction to the reprint of William Muir's *The Life of Mahomet* (New Delhi, 1992), p. 9.
6. Titus, *Islam in India and Pakistan*, p. 31.
7. Minhaj, p. 523n; also Farishtah, vol. 1, p. 63.
8. Minhaj, p. 528.
9. Ibid., pp. 483–84.
10. Farishtah, vol. 1, pp. 59–60.
11. Amir Khusrau, *Tughlaq Nama*, Aurangabad text, p. 128.
12. Minhaj, p. 484n.
13. Farishtah, vol. 1, p. 58.
14. Opinions differ on the date of this raid. Ishwari Prasad, *Medieval India*, p. 138, places it probably in 1197; Wolseley Haig, C.H.1, vol. 3, pp. 45–46, a little earlier than this, and Habibullah, pp. 70, 84, in 1202–03.
15. Ibn Asir, *Kamil-ut-Tawarikh*, E.D., vol. 2, p. 250.
16. Ibid., p. 251.
17. Habibullah, op. cit., p. 147.
18. Tarikh-i-Fakhruddin Mubarak Shah, p. 20.
19. Minhaj, p. 611.
20. Farishtah, vol. 1, p. 66.
21. Ibid., p. 73; Minhaj, pp. 598–99.
22. Farishtah, vol. 1, p. 75. Also Habibullah, p. 272.
23. Barani, pp. 57–58; Farishtah, vol. 1, p. 75; Habibullah, pp. 294–95.
24. Ziyauddin Barani, *Sana-i-Muhammadi*, trans. in *Medieval India Quarterly*, (Aligarh), I, Part III, 100–105.
25. Minhaj, pp. 680, 683, 391, 828; E.D., vol. 2, pp. 348, 367, 371, 380–81, Farishtah, vol. 1, p. 73.
26. Farishtah, vol. 1, p. 73.
27. Minhaj, pp. 686, 675n5, 719–868.
28. Barani, pp. 216–17.
29. Khusrau, *Miftah-ul-Fatuh*, Aligarh text (1954): 35–36; Barani, p. 213.
30. Khusrau, *Miftah-ul-Fatuh*, pp. 38–39; Farishtah, vol. 1, p. 94.
31. Barani, pp. 222–23; Farishtah, vol. 1, pp. 95–97.
32. Farishtah, vol. 1, pp. 95–96.
33. Barani, p. 249; Farishtah, vol. 1, p. 102; Badaoni, *Ranking*, vol. 1, p. 248.
34. Isami, p. 243; Barani, pp. 251–52.
35. For detailed references see Lal, *Khaljis*, pp. 69–71.

36. Wassaf, bk. 4, p. 448. Also trans. in E.D., vol. 3, p. 43.

37. Khazain, Habib trans., p. 49; Lal, *Khaljis*, p. 101.

38. Barani, pp. 253–54; Farishtah, vol. 1, p. 103: Futuh, p. 241.

39. Farishtah, vol. 1, pp. 114–15; Barani, p. 320; Khazain, *Habib*, p. 28; Wassaf, vol. 4, pp. 526–27. The walls of the towers popularly known as Chor Minar in modern Hauz Khas Enclave are pierced with 225 holes. In medieval India apertures on the walls of towers were used by Muslims not only as windows but also to display heads of captured and executed prisoners. The custom was to cut off their heads and stick them into those holes, to be seen by everybody. During wars, only the heads of chiefs were displayed; those of common soldiers were simply piled into pyramids.

40. For references, Lal, *Khaljis*, pp. 146–48.

41. Afif, pp. 37–38.

42. Trans, in E.D., vol. 3, p. 561. Also in his Ashiqa, ibid., pp. 545–46.

43. Afif, p. 272.

44. Barani, p. 341.

45. Ibid., p. 318; Lal, *Khaljis*, pp. 214–15.

46. Masalik-ul-Absar, E.D., vol. 3, p. 580.

47. Ishwari Prasad, *Qaraunh Turks*, pp. 39–40, citing Battutah, *Def. and Sang.*, vol. 2, pp. 212–14.

48. Prasad, *Qaraunah Turks*, pp. 96, 126, 129–30, 173.

49. Mahdi Husain, *Tughlaq Dynasty*, pp. 195–257.

50. Prasad, *Qaraunah Turks*, p. 148, citing Battutah, *Def. and Sang.*, vol. 3, p. 332.

51. Battutah, p. 123.

52. Prasad, *Qaraunah Turks*, pp. 138–39.

53. Battutah, p. 63; Hindi trans. by S. A. A. Rizvi in Tughlaq Kalin Bharat, part 1 (Aligarh, 1956), p. 189.

54. Hamilton, *Hedaya*, vol. 1, p. 161.

55. Ibid., p. 174.

56. Afif, p. 265; also pp. 119–20.

57. Ibid., p. 180.

58. Ibid., pp. 267–73.

59. Ibid., pp. 270–71.

60. Padmanabh, *Kanhadade Prabandh*, trans. Bhatnagar, pp. 11, 16, 18.

61. Yazdi, *Zafar Nama*, vol. 2, pp. 92–95; Mulfuzat-i-Timuri, trans. E.D., vol. 3, pp. 436, 451.

62. Tarikh-i-Salim Shahi, p. 165. This was the fate of the captives throughout the medieval period and therefore there is no need to cite any more instances.

63. Hamilton, *Hedaya*, vol. 2, p. 213.

64. Ibid., p. 181.

65. Tarikh-i-Fakkruddin Mubarak Shah, ed. Denison Ross, p. 20.

66. Battutah, p. 95. For details see Prasad, *Qarunab Turks*, pp. 65–66; Mahdi Husain, *Tughlaq Dynasty*, pp. 207–208.

67. Barani, p. 56; Afif, pp. 119–20; Lal, *Growth of Muslim Population*, pp. 106, 113–16, 211–17 for copious references from Muslim chronicles.

68. Fatuhat-i-Firoz Shah, E.D., vol. 3, p. 386.

69. Mulfuzat-i-Timuri, E.D., vol. 3, pp. 435–36; Z. N. Yazdi II, p. 192, Rauzat-us-safa, vol. 6, p. 109.

70. Battuta, pp. 10, 20, 155–56.

71. *Encyclopaedia of Islam*, 1st ed. (1913–38), vol. 2, p. 952.

72. Arnold, *The Preaching of Islam*, p. 150; Qur'an 8.42. Bernard Lewis, *Islam*, pp. 226–27, also traces its origin to the fourteenth century.

73. Afif, pp. 267–73.

74. Barani, *Tarikh*, vol. 2, pp. 16–17, 287, 291, 430; and Fatawa-i-Jahandari, pp. 46–48; Afif, E.D., vol. 3, pp. 289–90.

75. Manucci, vol. 2, p. 451; Manrique, vol. 2, p. 272; Bernier, p. 205. For details, see Lal, *Legacy*, pp. 249–55.

47

ENSLAVEMENT OF HINDUS BY ARAB AND TURKISH INVADERS

K. S. Lal

Turks were not the first Muslims to invade India. Prior to the coming of Turks the Arab general Muhammad bin Qasim invaded Sindh in the early years of the eighth century. In conformity with the Muslim tradition, the Arabs captured and enslaved Indians in large numbers. Indeed from the days of Muhammad bin Qasim in the eighth century to those of Ahmad Shah Abdali in the eighteenth, enslavement, distribution, and sale of Hindu prisoners was systematically practised by Muslim invaders and rulers of India. It is but natural that the exertion of a thousand years of slave-taking can only be briefly recounted with a few salient features of the system highlighted.

ENSLAVEMENT BY THE ARABS

During the Arab invasion of Sindh (712 CE), Muhammad bin Qasim first attacked Debal, a word derived from *Deval* meaning temple. It was situated on the sea-coast not far from modern Karachi. It was garrisoned by four thousand Kshatriya soldiers and served by three thousand Brahmans. All males of the age of seventeen and upwards were put to the sword and their women and children were enslaved.[1] "[Seven hundred] beautiful females, who were under the protection of

K. S. Lal, "Enslavement of Hindus by Arab and Turkish Invaders," in *Muslim Slave System in India* (New Delhi: Aditya Prakashan, 1994), pp. 17–24.

Budh (that is, had taken shelter in the temple), were all captured with their valuable ornaments, and clothes adorned with jewels."[2] Muhammad dispatched one-fifth of the legal spoil to Hajjaj which included seventy-five damsels, the other four-fifths were distributed among the soldiers.[3] Thereafter whichever places he attacked like Rawar, Sehwan, Dhalila, Brahmanabad, and Multan, Hindu soldiers and men with arms were slain, the common people fled, or, if flight was not possible, accepted Islam, or paid the poll tax, or died with their religion. Many women of the higher class immolated themselves in Jauhar, most others became prize of the victors. These women and children were enslaved and converted, and batches of them were despatched to the Caliph in regular installments. For example, after Rawar was taken Muhammad Qasim "halted there for three days during which he massacred 6000 (men). Their followers and dependents, as well as their women and children were taken prisoner." Later on "the slaves were counted, and their number came to 60,000 (of both sexes?). Out of these, 30 were young ladies of the royal blood. . . . Muhammad Qasim sent all these to Hajjaj" who forwarded them to Walid the Khalifa. "He sold some of these female slaves of royal birth, and some he presented to others."[4] Selling of slaves was a common practice. "From the seventh century onwards and with a peak during Muhammad al-Qasim's campaigns in 712–13," writes Andre Wink, "a considerable number of Jats was captured as prisoners of war and deported to Iraq and elsewhere as slaves."[5] Jats here is obviously used as a general word for all Hindus. In Brahmanabad, "it is said that about six thousand fighting men were slain, but according to others sixteen thousand were killed," and their families enslaved.[6] The garrison in the fort-city of Multan was put to the sword, and families of the chiefs and warriors of Multan, numbering about six thousand, were enslaved.

In Sindh female slaves captured after every campaign of the marching army were converted and married to Arab soldiers who settled down in colonies established in places like Mansura, Kuzdar, Mahfuza, and Multan. The standing instructions of Hajjaj to Muhammad bin Qasim were to "give no quarter to infidels, but to cut their throats," and take the women and children as captives.[7] In the final stages of the conquest of Sindh, "when the plunder and the prisoners of war were brought before Qasim . . . one-fifth of all the prisoners were chosen and set aside; they were counted as amounting to twenty thousand in number . . . (they belonged to high families) and veils were put on their faces, and the rest were given to the soldiers."[8] Obviously a few *lakh* women were enslaved in the course of Arab invasion of Sindh.

GHAZNAVID CAPTURE OF HINDU SLAVES

If such were the gains of the "mild" Muhammad bin Qasim in enslaving *kaniz wa ghulam* [i.e., acquiring (wealth and slaves)] in Sindh, the slaves captured by

Mahmud of Ghazni, "that ferocious and insatiable conqueror," of the century beginning with the year 1000 CE have of course to be counted in hundreds of thousands. Henry Elliot and John Dowson have sifted the available evidence from contemporary and later sources—from Utbi's Tarikh-i-Yamini, Nizamuddin Ahmad's Tabqat-i-Akbari, the Tarikh-i-Alai, and the Khulasat-ut-Tawarikh to the researches of early European scholars. Mohammad Habib, Muhammad Nazim, Wolseley Haig, and I myself have also studied these invasions in detail.[9] All evidence points to the fact that during his seventeen invasions, Mahmud Ghaznavi enslaved a very large number of people in India. Although figures of captives for each and every campaign have not been provided by contemporary chroniclers, yet some known numbers and data about the slaves taken by Mahmud speak for themselves.

When Mahmud Ghaznavi attacked Waihind in 1001–1002, he took 500,000 persons of both sexes as captive. This figure of Abu Nasr Muhammad Utbi, the secretary and chronicler of Mahmud, is so mind-boggling that Elliot reduces it to 5,000.[10] The point to note is that taking of slaves was a matter of routine in every expedition. Only when the numbers were exceptionally large did they receive the notice of the chroniclers. So that in Mahmud's attack on Ninduna in the Punjab (1014), Utbi says that "slaves were so plentiful that they became very cheap; and men of respectability in their native land (India) were degraded by becoming slaves of common shop-keepers (in Ghazni)."[11] His statement finds confirmation in later chronicles including Nizamuddin Ahmad's Tabqat-i-Akbari, which states that Mahmud "obtained great spoils and a large number of slaves." Next year from Thanesar, according to Farishtah, "the Muhammadan army brought to Ghaznin 200,000 captives so that the capital appeared like an Indian city, for every soldier of the army had several slaves and slave girls."[12] Thereafter slaves were taken in Baran, Mahaban, Mathura, Kanauj, Asni, and so on. When Mahmud returned to Ghazni in 1019, the booty was found to consist of (besides huge wealth) 53,000 captives. Utbi says that "the number of prisoners may be conceived from the fact that, each was sold for from two to ten dirhams. These were afterwards taken to Ghazna, and the merchants came from different cities to purchase them, so that the countries of Mawarau-un-Nahr, Iraq and Khurasan were filled with them." The Tarikh-i-Alfi adds that the fifth share due to the Saiyyads was 150,000 slaves, therefore the total number of captives comes to 750,000.[13]

Before proceeding further, let us try to answer two questions which arise out of the above study. First, how was it that people could be enslaved in such large numbers? Was there no resistance on their part? And second, what did the victors do with these crowds of captives?

During war it was not easy for the Muslim army to capture enemy troops. They were able-bodied men, strong and sometimes "demon like." It appears that capturing such male captives was a very specialised job. Special efforts were made by "experts" to surround individuals or groups, hurl lasso or ropes around them, pin them down, and make them helpless by binding them with cords of hide, ropes of hessian, and chains and shackles of iron. Non-combatant males, women, and children of course could be taken comparatively easily after active soldiers had been killed in battle. The captives were made terror-stricken. It was a common practice to raise towers of skulls of the killed by piling up their heads in mounds. All captives were bound hand and foot and kept under strict surveillance of armed guards until their spirit was completely broken and they could be made slaves, converted, sold or made to serve on sundry duties.

In a letter Hajjaj instructed Muhammad bin Qasim on how to deal with the adversary. "The way of granting pardon prescribed by law is that when you encounter the unbelievers, strike off their heads . . . make a great slaughter among them. . . . (Those that survive) bind them in bonds . . . grant pardon to no one of the enemy and spare none of them," etc., etc.[14] The lives of some prisoners could be spared, but they could not be released. That is how the Arab invaders of Sindh could enslave thousands of men and women at Debal, Rawar, and Brahmanabad. At Brahmanabad, after many people were killed, "all prisoners of or under the age of 30 years were put in chains. . . . All the other people capable of bearing arms were beheaded and their followers and dependents were made prisoners."[15]

That is also how Mahmud of Ghazni could enslave five hundred thousand "beautiful men and women" in Waihind after he had killed fifteen thousand fighting men in a "splendid action" in November 1001 CE. Utbi informs us that Jaipal, the Hindu Shahiya king of Kabul, "his children and grandchildren, his nephews, and the chief men of his tribe, and his relatives, were taken prisoners, and being strongly bound with ropes, were carried before the Sultan (Mahmud) like common evil-doers. . . . Some had their arms forcibly tied behind their backs, some were seized by the cheek, some were driven by blows on their neck."[16] In every campaign of Mahmud large-scale massacres preceded enslavement.

The sight of horrendous killing completely unnerved the captives. Not only were the captives physically tortured, they were also morally shattered. They were systematically humiliated and exposed to public ridicule. When prisoners from Sindh were sent to the Khalifa, "the slaves, who were chiefly daughters of princes and Ranas, were made to stand in a line along with the menials (literally shoe-bearers)."[17] Hodivala gives details of the humiliation of Jaipal at the hands of Mahmud. He writes that Jaipal "was publicly exposed at one of the slave-auctions in some market in Khurasan, just like the thousands of other Hindu captives. . . . (He) was paraded about so that his sons and chieftains might see him in that condition of shame, bonds and disgrace . . . inflicting upon him the public indignity of 'commingling him in one common servitude.'"[18] No wonder that in the end Jaipal immolated himself, for such humiliation was inflicted deliberately to smash the morale of the captives. In short, once reduced to such straits, the prisoners, young or old, ugly or handsome, princes or commoners could be flogged, converted, sold for a tuppence or made to work as menials.

It may be argued that Mahmud of Ghazni could enslave people in hundreds of thousands because his raids were of a lightning nature when defence prepared-ness was not satisfactory. But even when the Muslim position was not that strong, say, during Mahmud's son Ibrahim's campaign in Hindustan when "a fierce struggle ensued, but Ibrahim at length gained victory, and slew many of them. Those who escaped fled into the jungles. Nearly 100,000 of their women and chil-dren were taken prisoners. . . ."[19] In this statement lies the answer to our first problem. There was resistance and determined resistance so that all the people of a family or village or town resisted the invaders in unison. If they succeeded, they drove away the attackers. If not, they tried to escape into nearby forests.[20] If they could not escape at all they were made captives but then all together. They did not separate from one another even in the darkest hour. Indeed adversity automati-cally bound them together. So they determined to swim or sink together.

Besides, right from the days of prophet Muhammad, and according to his instructions, writes Margoliouth, "parting of a captive mother from her child was forbidden. . . . The parting of brothers when sold was similarly forbidden. On the other hand captive wife might at once become the concubine of the conqueror."[21] This precept of not separating the captives but keeping them together was moti-vated by no humanitarian consideration but it surely swelled their numbers to the advantage of the victors. Hence large numbers of people were enslaved.

And now our second question—what did the victors do with slaves captured in large crowds? In the days of the early invaders like Muhammad bin Qasim and Mahmud Ghaznavi, they were mostly sold in the Slave Markets that had come up throughout the Muslim-dominated towns and cities. Lots of profit was made by selling slaves in foreign lands. Isami gives the correct position. Muhammad Nazim in an article has translated relevant lines of Isami's metrical composition.[22] "He (Mahmud) scattered the army of the Hindus in one attack and took Rai Jaipal prisoner. He carried him to the distant part of his kingdom of Ghazni and deliv-ered him to an agent of the Slave Market (dalal-i-bazar). I heard that at the com-mand of the king (Mahmud), the Brokers of the Market, (maqiman-i-bazar in the original) sold Jaipal as a slave for 80 Dinars and deposited the money realised by the sale in the Treasury."[23]

When Muslim rule was established in India, the sale of captives became restricted. Large numbers of them were drafted for manning the establishments of kings and nobles, working as labourers in the construction of buildings, cutting jungles and making roads, and on so many other jobs. Still they were there, enough and to spare. Those who could be spared were sold in and outside the country, where slave markets, slave merchants and slave brokers did a flourishing business, and the rulers made profit out of their sale.

Mahmud of Ghazni had marched into Hindustan again and again to wage jihad and spread the Muhammadan religion, to lay hold of its wealth, to destroy its tem-ples, to enslave its people, sell them abroad and thereby earn profit, and to add to Muslim numbers by converting the captives. He even desired to establish his rule in India.[24] His activities were so multi-faceted that it is difficult to determine his priorities. But the large number of captives carried away by him indicates that taking of slaves surely occupied an anteriority in his scheme of things. He could obtain wealth by their sale and increase the Muslim population by their conversion.

NOTES

For clarification of any citations, the reader is referred to the original, K. S. Lal, "Enslavement of Hindus by Arab and Turkish Invaders," in *Muslim Slave System in India* (New Delhi: Aditya Prakashan, 1994), pp. 178–88.

1. C.H.I., vol. 3, p. 3.

2. Al Kufi, Chachnama, Kalichbeg, p. 84.

3. C.H.I., vol. 3, p. 3.

4. Chachnama, Kalichbeg, p. 154. Raja Dahir's daughters also were counted among slave girls, 196. E.D., vol. 1, pp. 172–73 gives the number of captives as 30,000.

5. Andre Wink, *Al Hind*, p. 161.

6. Mohammad Habib, "The Arab Conquest of Sind," in *Politics and Society During the Early Medieval Period, being Collected Works, of Habib*, ed. K. A. Nizami, vol. 2, pp. 1–35. Al Biladuri, p. 122, has 8,000 to 26,000.

7. Chachnama, Kalichbeg, 155; E.D.I, 173, 211.

8. Ibid., 163; E.D., I, 181.

9. Appendix D, "Mahmud's invasions of India," in E.D., vol. 2, pp. 434–78; Habib, *Sultan Mahmud of Ghazni*, pp. 23–59; M. Nazim, *The Life and Times of Mahmud of Ghazni*, pp. 42–122; Lal, *Growth of Muslim Population*, pp. 102–104, 211–16.

10. Tarikh-i-Yamini, E.D., vol. 2, p. 26; Elliot, appendix, p. 438; Farishtah, vol. 1, p. 24.

11. Utbi, E.D., vol. 2, p. 39.

12. Farishtah, vol. 1, p. 28.

13. Lal, *Growth of Muslim Population in Medieval India*, pp. 211–13; also Utbi, E.D., vol. 2, p. 50 and n 1.

14. Chachnama, Kalichbeg, p. 155 and n.

15. Ibid., pp. 83–86, 154, 159, 161 ff.

16. Utbi, E.D., vol. 2, p. 26; Minhaj, p. 607 n5; Al Utbi and other chroniclers refer to Jaipal on many occasions. H. G. Raverty suggests that "Jaipal appears to be the title, not the actual name, of two or more persons," Minhaj, p. 81n.

17. Chachnama, Kalichbeg, p. 152.

18. Hodivala, pp. 192–93.

19. Maulana Ahmad and others, *Tarikh-i-Alfi*, E.D., vol. 5, p. 163; Farishtah, vol. 1, p. 49.

20. Lal, *Legacy*, pp. 263–68.

21. Margoliouth, *Muhammad*, p. 461; also Gibbon, vol. 2, p. 693.

22. In his article "Hindu Shahiya kingdom of Ohind," in *J.R.A.S.* (1927).

23. Cited in Hodivala, pp. 192–93.

24. C. E. Bosworth, *The Ghaznavids*, p. 235.

48

THE IMPACT OF DEVSHIRME ON GREEK SOCIETY

Vasiliki Papoulia

Although there has been some satisfactory research concerning the institution of the devşirme additional work dealing with this Ottoman practice is still needed. One very important difficulty encountered by the researcher is the dearth of statistical data, but he faces also a methodological and, indeed, a logical difficulty. Most of those who wrote about the influence of the devşirme on the Christian population really discussed only the negative aspect of this influence. Yet to determine the true extent of this influence it is important to find out what the situation of the Christian population would have been if such an institution had not existed. To state simply that it totally silenced the *reaya* is inconclusive. The great historian Leopold von Ranke had such a statement in mind when he wrote that the first heroic song of Christos Melionis rang out in the mountains only after the abolition of this heavy tithe of blood.[1] On the other hand, one could maintain that this oppressive measure rendered the Turkish rule so hateful that it led eventually to the uprisings of the Christians. It is quite possible that the devşirme was both stultifying and incendiary. In other words, this institution could have played a restraining role for as long as it lasted while creating conditions which were so traumatic that they brought about the uprising even after its disappearance.[2] One is forced, therefore, to hypothesize with regard to the impact of this institution. The ground is much firmer when some aspects related to the function of this institution are studied: for example, the number of the recruited children; the resist-

Vasiliki Papoulia, "The Impact of Devshirme on Greek Society," in *East Central European Society and War in the Prerevolutionary Eighteenth Century*, ed. Gunther E. Rothenberg, Béla K. Király, and Peter F. Sugar (Boulder: Social Science Monographs/New York: Columbia University Press, 1982), pp. 549–62.

ance of the population; the reasons for the abolition of he devşirme; the frequency of recruitment; the phenomenon of the alienation from the ethnic milieu of a segment of the population; the Islamization which is related to the alienation, in spite of the fact that the available data are restricted. We are, therefore, confronted with a peculiar situation. As far as the impact of the devşirme as a whole is concerned, we are, on the one hand, not bound so much by statistical data, but we must be very careful because of the resulting general methodological difficulty which is, after all, present in every aspect of scientific research and especially in history. On the other hand, as far as the particular aspects of the institution are concerned, we do not have such methodological reservations, but we deal with insufficient data. We are therefore obliged to consider both sides of the problem and thus arrive, both indirectly and directly, at the essence.

Before presenting my views on the devşirme, I would like to mention those of Arnold Toynbee. According to him, nomadic states collapse due to their unsatisfactory adaptation to life in partibus agricolarum. There is, however, the exception of the Ottoman Empire which was able to flourish for over 300 years. Toynbee tried to find an explanation for this exception in the successful substitution of an essential element of the nomadic life, the nonhuman actor, the secondary animals, by humans. These animals played a very important role in the nomadic life because, although they were not productive, they assisted the nomads in their work: for example, they protected the herds and kept them in obedience. The same function was performed by the *Kapi kullari*, the slaves of the Porte. The sultans recruited Christian children who fell into their hands either by capture, by purchase or by tithe of blood. In Ottoman Society the nomadic life is represented by three elements: the sultan and his military caste (the feudal cavalry); the enslaved population—the *rayah* (the herd); and the Kapikullars including the IçOğlan, the Acemi Oğlans, the janissaries, the spahis of the Porte, etc. Here in a rather figurative sense, we have an adaptation of the nomadic life to a settled environment. I cannot discuss here the explanatory value of Toynbee's theory. I have done this in an article, "Uber die Knabelese im osmanischen Reich: Bemerkungen zur Theorie Arnold Toynbees," Byzantina, III (1971), 389–407. I just want to point out that it lacks specific explanatory value because it is too general and therefore it applies to all repressive societies in which the ruling class kept a part of the population in obedience, in subjection, by means of specialized forces which play the role of watchdogs. Nevertheless, Toynbee's picture is valuable because it enables us to capture an essential dimension of the whole phenomenon. However, in order to grasp better this essence we must complete the picture presented by Toynbee with results of a different level of research.

In my view,[3] the creation of all the slave guards in the Islamic world constitute an attempt by the Islamic nomadic societies to adapt to the new conditions that they faced during the transitory stage between the collapse of the tribal society, the old foundation of the ruling order, and the establishment of permanent settlements. These guards constituted a sort of artificial tribal grouping affiliation (a fake adoption) by the sovereign who did not possess those social elements from which a sovereign could draw support. The Islamic factor is an important one because only in the Islamic world do we encounter the phenomenon of military slavery to a highly developed degree. The elevation of elements, of alien ethnic origin to a special imperial bodyguard, devoted to the sovereign and having special privileges as a result of its direct dependence on him, was possible only on the basis of Islamic law which declares: "Those who submit to the true faith become brothers through Islam." This principle permitted the overcoming of the narrow-minded solidarity of the asabiyyah. The result was the very peculiar phenomenon of the creation of new bonds of social solidarity on the basis of an artificial kinship between the sovereign and his slaves. This bodyguard had the task of protecting the sovereign from internal and external enemies. In order to fulfill this task it was subjected to very rigorous and special training, the janissary education famous in Ottoman society. This training made possible the spiritual transformation of Christian children into ardent fighters for the glory of the sultan and their newly acquired Islamic faith. Besides these two main factors, Islamic law and nomadic tradition, that made the devşirme possible, there is a third important one, the absolute character of the dynastic power. It functioned as a leveling instrument on the social status of all subjects and created the necessary institutional frame for the elevation of these slaves to the status of the ruling class for more than three centuries, discriminating to the detriment of the native Muslim element. It must be noted that no native Muslim rose above the rank of *sanjakbey* for a considerable time span.

Although Toynbee's and my interpretations are based on differing approaches, they converge on significant points. First, in both analyses an integrative process of new elements into Ottoman society appears and, second, this integration is seen as the result of a complete alienation of its new members from their origins.[4] Toynbee's concept differs from mine because he sees these children as substitutes for secondary animals, while I feel that they were degraded to the level of animals, as shown by their dog-like devotion to the sultan in time of peace and their wild behavior when in revolt, reminiscent both of the blind devotion of domestic animals and their occasional feral outbursts. Contemporary texts also allude to this behavior pattern. It is interesting to note that this type of alienation corresponds from the point of view of philosophical anthropology to the alienation of the Middle Ages when the alienated man was regarded not as a thing (res) as in the ancient Mediterranean societies (characteristic of commercial societies), but as a semi-animal, semi-human being, according to Friedrich Tomberg in his work, Polis and Nationalstaat. He was still considered semi-human because he still deserved respect as a Christian who can win the kingdom of God in the next world (he had a soul), and as a semi-animal because he was treated as one in the present world by the powers which required his services.[5] In the same manner a janissary was a human because he could attain the Muslim paradise, but in life he was at the disposal of his master who had the power to kill him without justification, load him own with all burdens of everyday life and with all the tasks necessary for the preservation of order in the reaya society as well as with the defense of the sovereign from every enemy. That this task raised the slaves to a ruling class does not change the essence of their situation, the alienation of the man. Tomberg does not mention it, or does Toynbee allude to this dimension of the devşirme system. This institution is a representative example of the alienation of the man's personality, of his inner transformation into an instrument in the hands of a militant political power.[6] This sort of alienation corresponds to the semi-nomadic, semi-agrarian Ottoman society.

To what extent was this inner transformation of the children and young boys complete? This question is hard to answer given the paucity of relevant sources. This dearth of information is, of course, another expression of the alienation of these children. Nevertheless we do learn from certain sources that it was not rare for these young men to attempt to preserve their faith and some recollection of their homeland and their families. For instance, Stephan Gerlach writes:

> They gather together and one tells another of his native land and of what he heard in church or learned in school there, and they agree among themselves that Muhammad is no prophet and that the Turkish religion is false. If there is one among them who has some little book or can teach them in some other manner something of God's world, they hear him as diligently as if he were their preacher.[7]

The Greek scholar Janus Kaskaris, who visited Constantinople in 1491, found among the janissaries many who not only remembered their former religion and their native land but also favored their former coreligionists. The renegade Hersek, the sultan's relative by marriage, told him that he regretted having left the religion of his fathers and that he prayed at night before the cross which he kept carefully concealed.[8]

It is possible that the characterization of Gerlach with regard to two renegades that they were "neither Christian nor Turk" also holds true for several others of these Christian children. We also know that the patron of the janissary corps was Hacci Bektas, the founder of the Bektasi Order, which, like all Islamic orders, had many syncretic elements as a result of the symbiosis of the Turks and Christians in Asia Minor and in the Balkans. The lack of family ties—the Greeks named them *apatores* and *amitores* (fatherless and motherless)—had as a result that the janissary corps took on the characteristics of a brotherhood, of a *Männerbund*, with strong solidarity bonds. The discrepancy between the external peaceful appearance of the janissaries giving the impression of monks (after the vivid description of Busbeck in his *De re militari*)[9] and their dreadful activities not only against enemies but also against the Christian and Turkish population in time of war or revolt is an expression of their peculiar situation. They are the *pessimum hominum genus*, the *diaboli aulici* of the Greeks.[10]

The consciousness that they had been born of Christian parents naturally bred in them feelings of guilt resulting in a strong aversion to their fellow countrymen. One might say that it was this guilt that drove them to such outbursts of fanaticism—the other side of alienation. For the essence of alienation is the individual's confusion between himself and his controlling environment.

The cultural *niveau* of a society is in direct correlation to its ability to understand and to feel events that affect its existence. The higher this *niveau*, the deeper the tragedy is felt. It is easy, therefore, to understand the dramatic tone of the relevant Greek texts that have survived. For the parents this complete transformation of the children with its familiar consequences meant the total loss, as fatal as death. In the Tübingen manuscript written by Andre Argyros and John Tholoites and given in 1585 to Martin Crusius, these feelings are vividly described:

> You understand, then, my lords and Christian gentlemen, what sorrow the Greeks bear, the fathers and the mothers who are separated from their children at the prime of life. Think ye of the heart-rending sorrow! How many mothers scratch out their cheeks! How many fathers beat their breast with stones! What grief these Christians experience on account of their children who are separated from them while alive, and how many mothers say, "It would have been better to see them dead and buried in our church, rather than to have them taken alive in order to become Turks and abjure our faith. Better that you had died."[11]

It seems that this sentiment was often expressed because Gerlach cites the case of a woman from Panormos in Asia Minor who had two handsome sons and daily begged God to take them away because she would soon have to give up one of them.[12] The distress expressed here was motivated not only by religious considerations, which are easy to understand during that particular period, but also by the low opinion which the Byzantines held about the barbarians.[13]

It is obvious that the population strongly resented the recruitment of their children and that this measure could be carried out only by force. Those who refused to surrender their sons—the healthiest, the handsomest, and the most intelligent—were on the spot put to death by hanging.[14] Nevertheless we have examples of armed resistance. In 1565 a revolt took place in Epirus and Albania. The inhabitants killed the recruiting officers and the revolt was put down only after the sultan sent five hundred janissaries in support of the local sanjakbey.[15] We are better informed, thanks to the historic archives of Yerroia, about the uprising in Naousa in 1705 where the inhabitants killed the Silandar Ahmed Celebi and his assistants and fled to the mountains as rebels. Some of them were later arrested and put to death.[16]

Since there was no possibility of escaping recruitment the population resorted to several subterfuges,[17] some left their villages and fled to certain cities which enjoyed exemption from the child levy or migrated to Venetian-held territories. The result was a depopulation of the countryside. Others had their children marry at an early age. Many exchanged their children with those of their Muslim neighbors who hoped that their son would thus attain a successful career, or purchased uncircumcised boys from poor Muslims. Often they sent their children to hide in the mountains or in the homes of Turkish officials who, according to Nicephorus Angelus, were friendly towards the Greeks.[18] The same writer states that at times the children ran away on their own initiative, but when they heard that the authorities had arrested their parents and were torturing them to death, returned and gave themselves up. La Guilletière cites the case of a young Athenian who returned from hiding in order to save his father's life and then chose to die himself rather than abjure his faith.[19] According to the evidence in Turkish sources, some parents even succeeded in abducting their children after they had been recruited. The most successful way of escaping recruitment was through bribery. That the latter was very widespread is evident from the large amounts of money confiscated by the sultan from corrupt recruiting officials. Finally, in their desperation the parents even appealed to the Pope and the Western powers for help.[20] Of course, the reactions of the population were not always the same. As it is shown from the writings of Trevisano, Crusius, and Gerlach, parents in times of great need wished that their children were among the chosen—since they usually took the best-looking, healthiest, and most intelligent—sometimes bringing themselves their children to those who came to collect them in order to get rid of the burden of supporting them. Hoping that their children would thus have a better opportunity.[21] These cases, however, must be the exceptions and not the rule, since it is contrary to human nature for parents to part happily with their children forever.

The methods that were used for the child recruitment as well as its results regarding the loss of a vital segment of the population constitute the elements which define it within the frame of political theory as a de facto state of war. The fact also that the Greek term *paidomazoma*[22] does not appear—to be exact—before the seventeenth century, and that the sources speak of *piasimo* (seizure), *aichmalotos paidon* (capture), and *arpage paidon* (grabbing of children)[23] indicates that the children lost through the devşirme were understood as casualties of war. [24] Of course, the question arises whether, according to Islamic law, it is possible to regard the devşirme as a form of the state of war, although the Ottoman historians during the empire's golden age attempted to interpret this measure as a consequence of conquest by force *be'anwa*. It is true that the Greeks and the other peoples of the Balkan peninsula did not as a rule surrender without resistance, and therefore the fate of the conquered had to be determined according to the principles of the Koran regarding the Ahl-al-Qitâb: i.e., either to be exterminated or be compelled to convert to Islam or to enter the status of protection, of aman, by paying the taxes and particularly the *cizye* (poll-tax). The fact that the Ottomans, in the case of voluntary surrender, conceded certain privileges, one of which was exemption from this heavy burden, indicates that its measure was understood as a penalization for the resistance of the population and the devşirme was an expression of the perpetuation of the state of war between the conqueror and the conquered. We cannot, unfortunately, discuss here in detail the subtleties of Islamic law regarding the state of war, but the sole existence of the institution of devşirme is sufficient to postulate the perpetuation of a state of war. I can only mention here that we cannot view devşirme as being in accordance with the holy law.[25]

In conclusion, in order to determine the number of Greek casualties in this peculiar case of a society at war, we need adequate statistics which we unfortunately lack.[26] Of course, a very important element in determining the number of losses is the exact date of the beginning of child-levy. It is evident that the earlier it started, the greater the losses. Another important point concerns the frequency of recruitment and the number of children recruited. Unfortunately the sources do not present a clear picture regarding these matters. Nevertheless we can arrive, directly or indirectly, at certain conclusions and determine certain stages in the process. As far as the beginning of the institution is concerned, there is no reason to doubt the testimony of the historians of the empire's golden age, Idris and Saadeddin, that devşirme was introduced during the reign of Orhan, about 1330. It is, however, certain that recruitment was not frequent until the time of Murad II who reorganized the janissary corps and established periodic recruitment every five years.[27] But this was not a regular procedure. Recruitment could take place every four, three, or two years, and at times even annually, according to the needs of the sultan. The biggest losses in children coincided with the peak of Ottoman expansion in the fifteenth and sixteenth centuries under Selim I and Süleyman the Magnificent. A decline in the numbers occurred during the reign of Selim II when the sons of janissaries were permitted to join the janissary corps. At a diminishing rate the recruitment of Christian children continued in later centuries to meet the needs of the Porte for slaves. From the seventeenth century the levy of children continued to lose its importance until it slowly disappeared. Occasional recruitments took place until the rebellion of 1705 and perhaps also later. Finally, though a final consideration of the total losses is impossible, there is no doubt that this, heavy burden was one of the hardest tribulations of the Christian population.

A general estimation of the influence of the institution within the framework of the Greek society results in the conclusion that this influence was mainly defined by the perpetuation of the state of war mentioned above and had its impact not only on the demographical level, but also on the psychological, because it sharpened, to a great degree, the hostile relations between the conqueror and the conquered. Certainly it cannot be coincidental that the evolution of the Ottoman society is characterized by a deep antithesis that led to the creation of fighting gangs in mountainous regions whose members eventually became the liberation armies of the Christian population. To what extent there existed a direct relation between the two phenomena, of the instutiton of devşirme and the revolutionary movements, is not easy to define nor the degree of this negative demographic influence be assessed because without doubt this institution was a bleeding for the Greek, and more generally, for the Christian community of the Ottoman Empire. In a text from the beginning of the seventeenth century, the threnos of Metropolitan Matthaios Myreon, we can find an allusion to a revolutionary attitude. On the one hand, he scorns the Greeks for expecting their liberation for pseudo-prophecies and the Great Powers, and on the other hand, he enumerates the evils of the Turkish domination, among them the devşirme.[28] Clearer is the relationship between revolutionary attitudes and the existence of this institution, which was felt as a calamity, in the petition of Janus Lascaris to Emperor Charles V.[29] It can be said that a connecting link in this evolution was the revolt of the inhabitants of Naousa in 1705, at which time they killed the Turks who were entrusted with the levy of the children.

The appearance of outlaw bands in the mountains was, in part, a result of the repressive character of the Turkish domination. These groups formed a kind of "subculture" that arose from the reaction to it. This subculture meant a regression from the social point of view, a regression to patriarchical [*sic*] patterns of social action, but it led through revolutionary activity to a new political organization. It seems as if a state of permanent war passed from the conquered to the conquerors. Nevertheless, we cannot postulate a direct causal relation between the two phenomena. devşirme and revolutionary gangs were parallel phenomena but on different levels. We understand this better if we remember that these slave guards were sort of artificial tribes, which the sovereign needed after the dissolution of the original social order as a result of his domain's growth. Robbery, as a way to solve the economic problem and as a way to escape from a humiliating reaya existence as a cultivator of the great domains of the Turkish landowners and timarh, belongs to the same level of social activity, to a patriarchical [*sic*] conception of life. Naturally it would be a simplification if we wanted to maintain that this characteristic concerns the whole social structure of the Ottoman Empire. It is a phenomenon that appears in some regions. It is an expression of the "segmentary" nature of the Turkish Empire in the sense that E. Durkheim gives to the term, as we pointed out in another context speaking about professional differentiation and the social mobility in the Ottoman society. It is perhaps owing to this segmentary nature of Ottoman society that one cannot strictly speak of a direct connection between these related phenomena.

NOTES

1. Leopold von Ranke, *Die Osmanen and die spanische Monarchie im sechzehnten and siebzehnten Jahrhundert, 4. Aufl.* (Berlin, 1877), pp. 69–70; G. F. Herzberg, *Geschichte der Byzantiner und des Osmanischen Reiches bis gegen Ende des sechzehnten Jahrhunderts* (Berlin, 1883), p. 121, agrees with Ranke: "Nun erst Konnte wieder von

einem Aufblühen der physischen wie der moralischen Volkskraft die Rede sein, seitdem nicht mehr die besten jügendlichen Kräfte der Nation ihr für immer entfremdet wurden. Wie aber die Dinge in Griechenland einmal lagen, wirkte die Abstellung des Knaben-Gins hier zuerst am fühlbarsten zurück auf den Aufschwung des Klephtenthums. Ein grosser Historiker macht mit gewohntem Scharfblicke darauf aufinerksam, dass der erste Klephte, den die Lieder der Neugriechen preisen, noch in dem siebzehnten Jahrhundert seine wilde Laufbahn eröffnet." Here it is clear that Herzberg finds, as Ranke does, a close relationship between the abolition of the devşirme and the revolutionary activity of the enslaved Greeks.

2. This is demonstrated by the various petitions that are mainly directed to the influential men of that time, begging them to free them from the Turkish yoke (see n20 below). *The "Digisis synoptiki" [Brief Accounts] of Ioannis Axagioles in Karolos o E'tis Germanias kai i pros apeleftherosin prospathia* [Charles V of Germany and Attempts toward Liberation], ed. G. Zoras, *Proceedings of the School of Philosophy, Athens University* 2 (1954): 420–72, describes the lamentation of parents who take refuge in monasteries and beg God with tears in their eyes to deliver them from the Turkish yoke. In a song of Epirus (P. Aravantinos, *Syllogi dimodon asmaton tis Epirou* [Society of the Popular Songs of Epirus] [Athens, 1880], p. 3) the sultan is anathematized for this evil deed. "Damn you king and damn you again for the evil you have done, the evil you are doing. You push aside the old men, the elders, and the clergy. You gather all the young ones and make them janissaries. Cry you mothers for the young, sisters for the brothers, and I cry and despair, last year they took my son, this year my brother."

3. Cf. B. Papoulia, *Ursprung and Wesen der "Knabenlese" im Osmanischen Reich* (München, 1963) (Südosteuropäische Arbeiten 59), where the older bibliography and all the known sources concerning the devşirme can be found.

4. The term *alienation* is used here in a broad sense to include the economic as well as the moral and spiritual dependency and exploitation of the people. Regarding the stages of this alienation cf. my work mentioned above regarding Toynbee (pp. 404–407).

5. Friedrich Tomberg, *Polis and Idationalstaat Eine vergleichende Überbau Analyse im Anschluss an Aristoteles* (Darmstadt and Neuwied; Sammlung Luchterhand, 93), p. 184.

6. Leopold von Ranke describes very characteristically this development as a result of complete seclusion and severe collective life, a principle that was once proposed by a German philosopher allowing a new will to appear in the place of the old: "Die hier erzogenen, ihrer ersten Jugend, ihrer Eltern, ihrer Heimat vergessend, kennen kein Vaterland als das Serai, keinen Herrn und Vater als den Grossherrn, keinen Willen als den seinen, keine Hoffnung als auf seine Gunst; sie kennen kein Leben als in strenger Zucht und in unbedingtem Gehorsam, keine Beschäftigung als den Krieg zu seinem Dienst, für sick keinen Zweck als etwa im Leben Beute, im Tode das Paradies, das der Kampf dür den Islam eröffnet." Was der Philosoph zur Bildung von Sittlichkeit, Religion und Gemeinschaft in der Idee vorgeschlagen hat, ist hier, Jahrhunderte vor ihm zur Entwicklung eines zugleich sklavischen und doch kriegerischen Sinnes in Ausführung gebracht. *Die Osmanen and die spanische Monarchie*, p. 12.

7. Stephan Gerlach, *Tage-Buch der von . . . Kaysern Maximiliano and Rudolpho an die ottomanische Pforte . . . abgefertigten Gesandtschaft herfür gegeben durch Samuel Gerlach* (Frankfurt am Main, 1674), p. 3. See also Denys A. Zakythinos, *The Making of Modern Greece. From Byzantium to Independence* (Oxford, 1976), pp. 26–30.

8. E. Legrand, *Bibliographie hellénique*, p. clvi; Sathas, *Tourkokratoumeni Elias* [Turkish-Occupied Greece] (Athens, 1868), p. 85. The same information is also given by Bartholomeo Georgewitz, *De Turcarum moribus epitome*, p. 100. See also A. E. Vakalopoulos, *Istoria tou Neou Ellenismou [History of Neo-Hellenism], B', Tourkokratia 1453–1669* II (Thessaloniki, 1964), p. 55n2.

9. Cf. Augerius Gislenius Busbequius, *De legationis Turcicae epistolae quatuor . . . eiusdem de re militari contra Turcam instituenda consilium* (Hanover, 1605), p. 15 (text of the English translation, p. 87): "These janissaries generally came to me in pairs. When they were admitted to my dining room they first made a bow and then came quickly up to me, all but running and touched my dress or hand, as if they intended to kiss it. After this they would thrust into my hand a nosegay of hyacinth or narcissus; then they would run back to the door almost as quickly as they came, taking care not to turn their backs, for this, according to their code, would be a serious breach of etiquette. After reaching the door, they would stand respectfully with their arms crossed, and their eyes bent on the ground, looking more like monks than warriors. On receiving a few small coins (which was what they wanted) they bowed again, thanked me in loud tones and went off blessing me for my kindness. To tell you the truth, if I had not been told beforehand that they were janissaries, I should, without hesitation, have taken them for members of some order of Turkish monks or brethren of some Moslem College. Yet there are the famous janissaries, whose approach inspires terror everywhere."

10. Martin Crusius, ed. *S. Cabasilas, Turcograeciae libri octo* (Basiliae, 1584), annotations, p. 193.

11. K. Dyobuniotes, *Anakoinosis . . .* [Communication . . .] (Athens: Proceedings of the Academy of Athens, 1936), p. 275.

12. Gerlach, *Tagebuch*, p. 257.

13. S. Vryonis, "Isidore Glabas and the Turkish Devshirme," *Speculum* 31 (1956): 433–44.

14. Cf. K. Vasdravelle, *Istorikon archion Verroias* [Historical, Archives of Verroia] (Thessaloniki, 1942), pp. 10–12, where orders to the Beylerbey of Rumeli, dated March 29, 1601, can be found that include the following: "You must also know that the bubasirides that will be sent will have by my permission the right to enforce, when necessary, the provisions of the holy fetva according to which parent of the infidel or anyone else, resists the surrender of his janissary son, is to be hanged at his front door, his blood regarded of no value."

15. Cf. J. W. Zinkeisen, *Geschichte des Osmanischen Reiches in Europa* (Hamburg, 1955), vol. 3, pp. 220–21; E. Charrière, *Négotiation de la France dans le Levant* (Paris, 1850), vol. 2, p. 802; also Papoulia, *Ursprung und Wesen den Kanben leve Istorikon Arhion Verrias* [Historical Archives of Verria], p. 109n3.

16. Ch J. K. Basdrabelles, p. 45 ff., *Armatoloi Kai Klephteseis tin Makedonian* [Armatoles and Klephts in Macedonia] (Thessaloniki: Makedonike Bibliothese, 1948), pp. 13 ff., 54 ff., 70 ff.

17. The case of Giovan Antonio Menavino, author of *Trattato de costumi et vita de Turchi* (Firenze, 1548), is an interesting one. He managed to escape after 10 years of service as iç Oğlan, and to return to this home in Vultri, Italy. He had been captured by Turkish pirates at the age of twelve. His escape and return had a meaning only because his family lived outside of the Ottoman realm. Such an escape was not possible for the Greek

and other Christian youths of the Balkans, as shown in the related documents. Cf. Ahmet Refik, *Devşirme usulü Acemi O lanlar* (Edebiyat-Fakultesi Meĝgmû asî, 5, 1927), p. 10.

18. Nichephoros Angelos, *Enchiridium de statu hodiernorum Graecorum . . . cum versione latine . . .* (Lipsiae, 1666), p. 62.

19. La Guilletière, *Athènes ancienne et nouvelle*, 3rd ed. (Paris, 1676). This incident is confirmed by J. B. Babin, *Relation de l'état présent de la ville d'Athènes* (Lyon, 1674), pp. 56 f.

20. For the petition of the Greeks of Asia Minor addressed to the Grand Master of the Knights Hospitalers of Rhodes, Jacques de Milly (1451–61), see F. Miklosich J. Miler, *Acta et diplomata medaevi sacra et profana* (Vienna, 1860–1890). The English translation from Speros Vryonis Jr., *The Decline of Medieval Hellenism in Asia Minor and the Process of Islamization from the Eleventh through the Fifteenth Century* (Berkeley and Los Angeles: University of California Press, 1971), p. 442. We have also another petition of the inhabitants of Himara from the year 1581, addressed to the Pope: "Holiest father, if you could convince him and save us and the children of Greece, that are taken every day and are turned into Turks, if you could only do this, God may bless you. Amen" A. Theiner F. Miklosich, *Monumenta spectantia ad unionem ecclesiarum* (Vienna, 1872), p. 59. Cf. the other sources concerning the reaction of the Greek population in Papoulia, *Ursprung and Wesen*, pp. 109–11.

21. Ibid., p. 112n11.

22. As "Paidomazoma," "jannitsaromazoma" (ibid., pp. 59n49, 80n12, 94n14, 109n3).

23. As "piasmos paidon," "arpaqi paidon," "dekatismos paidon," "syllogi paidon," "poniron ethos" (ibid., pp. 49n16, 80nn11–12).

24. H. A. R. Gibb and H. Bowen, *Islamic Society and the West* (London, 1957), vol. 1, part. 2, p. 223, sees the *paidomazoma* as "penalization on this score for the sins of their fathers."

25. Papoulia, *Ursprung and Wesen*, pp. 47–54.

26. There have been some efforts to calculate the population losses resulting from the devşirme. Joseph v. Hammer (*Geschichte des Osmanischen Reiches* [Pest, 1934], vol. 1, p. 98) expressed the opinion that the recruited children must have been 500,000 while K. Paparregopoulos (*Istoria tou hellenikou ethnous* [History of the Greek People], vol. 5, part. 1, p. 15) raised the number to one million. As A. Vakalopoulos (op. cit., p. 59) pointed out these numbers are not based on real evidence. The losses of the Greeks were heavy in the early period of occupation but with time they succeeded to restrict them. From Giovio (Jovius Paulus), *Turcicarum rerum commentarius* (Paris, 1538), p. 94, and Charles Richer, *Des Coustumes et manières de vivre des Turcs* (Paris, 1542), we learn that the janissaries of their time spoke mostly a Slavonic dialect.

27. A. E. Vakalopoulos, "Provlimata tis istorias tou paidmazomatos" [Problems Concerning the History of the Child-Levy], *Hellinika* 13 (1954): 274–93.

28. E. Legrand, *Bibliothèque grecque vulgaire* (Paris, 1881), vol. 2, pp. 313, 321, 322.

29. B. Knös, *Un ambassadeur de l'hellénisme -Janus Lascaris- et la tradition grécobyzantine dans l'humanisme français* (Uppsala-Paris, 1945), p. 191.

49

THE ROLE OF SLAVES IN FIFTEENTH-CENTURY TURKISH ROMANIA

M.-M. Alexandrescu-Dersca Bulgaru

In the fifteenth century the system of slavery (*kul, ghulam*) regulated by *kanuns* [from the same Greek word as "canons"] and *firmans* [sultan's orders] in accordance with the prescriptions of Muslim law (sharia) constituted one of the pillars supporting the centralized Ottoman Empire of Bayezid I (1389–1402) and Mehmed II (1444–1445, 1451–1481).

According to the Ottoman, Byzantine, and Latin sources, in Turkish Romania there were slaves born in a state of servitude, slaves introduced through commerce or recruited by *devshirme* (παιδωμάζωμα), and prisoners of war who were reduced to slavery.

Since Turkish Romania was a region, or rather a frontier (*uğ*) in constant contact with the Dar al-Harb, that is, with the theater of conflict which included all lands that had not yet fallen under the power of Islam, slavery was promoted there during the fifteenth century, above all by war, as well as by the incursions (*akin, haramlik*) into Christian territory. For the law of war provided that those prisoners unable to redeem themselves should be reduced to slavery.

It is well known that after the chaotic years (1402–1413) following the battle of Ankara (July 28, 1402), Mehmed I the Unifier (1413–1421) and Murad

---

M.-M. Alexandrescu-Dersca Bulgaru, "Le rôle des esclaves en Romanie turque au XVᵉ siecle," *Byzantinische Forschungen* 11 (1987): 15–22. English translation by Michael J. Miller.

[Mourad] II (1421–1444, 1449–1451) attempted the arduous task of reestablishing the unity of the Ottoman state and of extending its boundaries from the Danube—through the occupation by Giurgiu (Yerkökü) and Severin—to the Aegean Sea by the conquest of Thessalonika (1430). Through the capture of Constantinople (May 29, 1453), Mehmed II became the true restorer of the empire, based on Islamic, Turkish, and Byzantine traditions, with the sultan playing the part of the *basileus*.

The contemporary Turkish, Byzantine, and Latin chroniclers are unanimous in recognizing that during the campaigns conducted on behalf of the unification of Greek and Latin Romania and the Slavic Balkans under the banner of Islam, as well as during their *razzias* [raids] on Christian territory, the Ottomans reduced masses of inhabitants to slavery. The Ottoman chronicler Ašikpašazade relates that during the expedition of Ali pasha Evrenosoghlu in Hungary (1437), as well as on the return from the campaign of Murad II against Belgrade (1438), the number of captives surpassed that of the combatants.[1] The Byzantine chronicler Ducas [Doucas] states that the inhabitants of Smederevo, which was occupied by the Ottomans, were led off into bondage.[2] The same thing happened when the Turks of Menteše descended upon the islands of Rhodes and Cos[3] and also during the expedition of the Ottoman fleet to Enos[4] and Lesbos.[5] Ducas even cites numbers: seventy thousand inhabitants carried off into slavery during the campaign of Mehmed II in Morée (1460).[6] The Italian Franciscan Bartholomé de Yano (Giano dell'Umbria) speaks about sixty thousand to seventy thousand slaves captured over the course of two expeditions of the *akinğis* in Transylvania (1438)[7] and about three hundred thousand to six hundred thousand Hungarian captives.[8] If these figures seem exaggerated, others seem more accurate: forty inhabitants captured by the Turks of Menteše during a *razzia* in Rhodes,[9] seven thousand inhabitants reduced to slavery following the siege of Thessalonika (1430), according to John Anagnostes,[10] and ten thousand inhabitants led off into captivity during the siege of Mytilene (1462), according to the Metropolitan of Lesbos, Leonard of Chios.[11]

Given the present state of the documentation available to us, we cannot calculate the scale on which slaves were introduced into Turkish Romania by this method. According to Bartholomé de Yano, it would amount to four hundred thousand slaves captured in the four years from 1437 to 1443.[12] Even allowing for a certain degree of exaggeration, we must acknowledge that slaves played an important demographic part during the fifteenth-century Ottoman expansion. Recall, too, that the slave women who populated the harems also contributed mightily toward increasing the population in Turkish Romania. Ducas reports that the harem of Bayezid I was populated by Greek, Serbian, Rumanian, Albanian, Hungarian, Bulgarian, and Latin slave women.[13] The Turkish *pashas* and high-ranking dignitaries also had very populous harems. According to Muslim law, slave women who gave sons to their masters could no longer be sold, and upon the death of their masters, they became free.[14]

Beside the wars and the *razzias* (*akin*), which dumped considerable numbers of slaves onto the market, the slave trade played a role. The Tartars led the prisoners that they captured during their incursions in Russian and Polish territories to Azov, Kerch and Taman, and from there to Caffa so as to exchange them for materials supplied by the Turkish cloth merchants of Anatolia.[15]

In the first half of the fifteenth century most of the slaves that made up the merchandise of the slave trade were steered toward Adrianople (modern Edirne)—the capital of the Ottoman State until 1455. Bartholomé de Yano paints a gripping picture of their sufferings: "Priests, monks, the young and the aged who could scarcely walk, were shackled and drawn by horses," whereas the able-bodied men were led with the women and children like a flock being guarded by dogs. "Those who lingered along the way because of weariness, thirst, or rather their sufferings, were killed on the spot."[16] Others succumbed to their illnesses. Bartholomé de Yano saw in the streets of Adrianople heaps of corpses partially devoured by the dogs.[17]

After the conquest of Constantinople, which became again the capital of a great, full-blown empire, whole convoys of captives were sent on toward the banks of the Bosphorus. Others were led to Sinope and Inebolu.[18] Some black slaves were the object of commercial transactions conducted at the market of Antalya, where merchants from Brousse had set up shop to export white slaves.[19]

In keeping with a regulation issued by Mehmed II, after 1461 the sale of slaves was permitted only at the slave markets: *esir bazar* for the men, *avret bazar* for the women, as well as at the covered market (*bazzaristan*) in Istanbul.[20] There were other slave markets in Adrianople, Üsküb (Skopje), Haskovo, Akče Kazanlîk, and Nova Zagora,[21] as well as in Tulcea in Dobrudja.

The commercial transactions took place in the presence of slave brokers (*dellal*), who were placed under the orders of the *amil*[22] of the market (*kaban*). The latter official was obliged to record all the transactions concluded through these intermediaries, under penalty of being fined a thousand *aspres* (*akče*). This same regulation, along with the one concerning the market in Gallipoli, forbade the merchants and all those who engaged in the slave trade from doing so secretly, under pain of being punished by the magistrate in charge and being expelled from the market (*bazar*).[23]

All these transactions were subject to the payment of a sales tax (*bağ*) set by a regulation (*kanun*) of Mehmed II at two *akče* per slave,[24] as was customary for the sale of an ox. Another *kanun*, probably issued by Bayezid II (1481–1512), stipulates that upon the sale of a slave, a *bağ* should be collected consisting of two *aspres* from the vendor and an additional two *aspres* from the buyer.[25]

For the prisoners (*esir*) who made their way into Turkish Romania via the seaports—Gallipoli, Istanbul, Ineboli—or by the Danube River ports in Walachia (Giurgiu), Dobrudja (Isaccea), and Bulgaria, one paid a tax or a fee of twenty *aspres*[26] instead of the fifth (*pengyek*). The collectors of the fifth (*pengyekği*) or the customs officers were obliged to file with their masters a receipt (*tezkere*) bearing the description, the name, age, birthplace, and nationality of each of their slaves. According to Jacopo de Promontorio de Campis, the state also levied a customs tax of two *aspres* for the slaves who went on foot and five *aspres* for those who traveled horseback.[27]

The price of the slaves varied according to their age, sex, health, physical and intellectual qualities, and their occupations. Ašikpašazade paid 100 *akče* for a six- or seven-year-old boy and 150 *akče* for a stable-boy.[28] According to Jacopo de Promontorio, the price of slaves ranged from five ducats (240 *akče*) to seven ducats (336 *akče*).[29]

Prices varied especially according to the law of supply and demand. After the battle of Golubać (1428), the slave market in Adrianople was filled with so many Hungarian captives that the prices did not exceed 300 *akče*.[30] Ašikpašazade sold at Adrianople some slaves captured during the expedition of Murad II against Belgrade (1438) at a price of 200 or 300 *akče*.[31] After the expedition into Serbia, the price of little four-year-old boys fell to 20 *akče* on the market in Üsküb.[32] The Ottomans had led off so many prisoners into slavery that a very beautiful slave woman was exchanged for a pair of boots,[33] and four Serbian slaves were traded for a horse.[34]

Despite the fluctuation of prices and the fact that many slaves died en route and in the streets of Adrianople,[35] commerce in slaves proved to be very lucrative for the merchants who followed the Ottoman armies onto the battlefield, for the combatants as well as for the individuals [who acquired slaves]. Registers maintained by the *kadis* in the Ottoman cities show that the purchase of slaves represented one of the best investments [then available].[36] There was also a Turkish saying to the effect that someone who owned a slave was not a poor man.

Due to their market value, and also because of the ransoms paid to set them free, slaves were an important source of revenue for individual [citizens].

The State also profited from them by collecting the *beğet* and the custom duty (*gümrük*). According to Jacopo de Promontorio, the sultan received twelve thousand ducats per year for renting out (*iltizam*, *mukata'a*) [i.e., subcontracting the collection of] the custom duty imposed on slaves passing through Adrianople, and fifty thousand ducats per year for the slaves that went through Gallipoli and Istanbul.[37] It is clear from this that slaves played an important role, not only in the private economy of the Ottomans, but also in the fiscal organization of the Empire.

An equally important role was assigned to them in the Ottoman agricultural economy, which depended on their labor, especially when peasants (*reaya*) were lacking. For in Turkish Romania the problem that they faced was not that of [adequate] land, but that of [sufficient] cultivated land; the owners of *khass*, *ziamet*, and *timar* employed those who were born into slavery or those who were brought in through the slave trade, as well as the prisoners of war who did not manage to redeem themselves, or peasants who had been reduced to slavery.

According to a document that seems to have been issued by Bayezid II, the *khass* in the vicinity of Istanbul were cultivated by slaves (*kul*).[38] The same document also mentions laborers who sowed the fields of the *khass* in conjunction (*ortaklik*) with the state, which procured the seed for them. No doubt it is a question here of prisoners of war (*ortakği kullari*), employed as laborers in keeping with the system instituted by Orkhan Ghazi[39] in the fourteenth century. Kritobulos of Imbros reports that after the campaign of Morea (1460), Mehmed II had led off the prisoners that were reserved for him by title of the "fifth" (*pengyek*) and had settled them in villages that were founded in the vicinity of Istanbul so that they could cultivate the land. This was first and foremost a matter of guaranteeing the food supply for Istanbul, which had again become a great city. The Byzantine chronicler explains that the sultan had made available to them seed for sowing, teams of oxen, and plowing implements.[40] In exchange, the *ortakğis* were obligated to hand over to the state one-half of their harvest of wheat and rice. They were also employed on the estates (*čiftlik*) of the high-ranking Ottoman dignitaries[41] and on the lands of the religious establishments (*vakf*). The *ortakğ is* were subject to a special law, regulated by *kanun*, by virtue of which they were not allowed to marry outside their group. Some slaves recruited from the slave trade could also work the land as *ortakğis*. It was not until the sixteenth century that the *ortakğis* obtained the status of *reayas*.[42]

The slaves were also employed as laborers in the works of fortification and in the construction of mosques, palaces, and buildings for public use (minaret, caravansary, baths (*hamam*), schools (*mektub*), schools of theology (*medrese*), bridges, etc.). After the conquest of Constantinople (May 29, 1453), Mehmed II built the old Seraglio, the construction of which lasted for four years (1453–1457),[43] and then the new Seraglio (Yeni Saray, later called Topkapi Sarayi) in 1476, the mosque Mehemmediye (1462–1470) and four other mosques—the mosque of the Sheikh Ebul Wefa, the mosque of the Sheikh Bukhari, Orta Ğami, and the mosque of Eyub[44]—while employing slave labor. Kritobulos of Imbros has left us a few precise details on the working conditions. The chronicler reports that the famous fortress of the Seven Towers (Yedi Kule) was built by Byzantine slaves, who were enslaved as a result of the war. They received six *aspres* per day from the sultan and sometimes even more. Kritobulos implies that the laborers in question were prisoners of war who had been reduced to slavery and belonged to individuals. For he states that the sultan gave them this money not only to pay for their keep but more importantly, to provide them with the means of paying their ransoms to their masters so that they could settle down in Istanbul and repopulate the city.[45]

NOTES

1. Ašikpašazade, *Die altosmanische Chronik des Ašikpašazade auf Grund mehrerer neuentdeckter Handschriften*, ed. Fr. Giese (Leipzig, 1924), pp. 109, 112.

2. Ducas, *Historia turco-byzantine* (1341–1462), ed. B. Grecu (Bucarest, 1958), p. 399.

3. Ibid., p. 403.

4. Ibid., p. 419.

5. Ibid., p. 421.

6. Ibid., p. 279. The testimony of Ducas is confirmed by Tursun beg, "Tarikh-i Ebul Feth," in Gliša Elezović, *Turski izvori za istorija Jugoslaven* [Turkish Sources on the History of Yugoslavia] (Belgrade, 1932), p. 62, who relates that the slaves assembled before the tents of the Ottoman combatants were so numerous that those present had the impression that they were at genuine slave markets.

7. Bartholomé de Yano, *Epistola de crudelitate Turcorum*, in Migne, *Patrologia graeca*, t. 158, col. 1061. The figure of 70,000 slaves captured in Transylvania is found also in the *Annales Melicenos*, ed. W. Wattenberg, *Monumenta Germaniae Historica, Scriptores* (Hanover, 1851), vol. 9 p. 519.

8. De Yano, *Epistola de crudelitate Turcorum*, col. 1062.

9. Ducas, *Historia turco-byzantine*, p. 403.

10. J. Anagnostes, *De extremo Thessalonicensi exidio narratio*, ed. Leone Allatio (Bonn, 1838), pp. 510–11.

11. See the letter written by Leonard of Chios to Pope Pius II in Charles Hopf, *Chroniques gréco-romaines* (Berlin, 1873), pp. 359–66.

12. See the letter by Bartholomé de Yano (1443) in Odoricus Raynaldus, *Annales ecclesiastici* (Luca, 1752), vol. 9, p. 413. See also N. Iorga, "Aventures 'sarasines' des Français de Bourgogne au XVe siècle," in *Mélanges d'Histoire générale* (Cluj, 1927), vol. 1, p. 36.

13. Ducas, *Historia turco-byzantine*, p. 87.

14. A. Heidborn, *Droit public et administratif de l'Empire-Ottoman* (Vienne/Leipzig, 1908), vol. 1, pp. 78–79.

15. H. Inalcik, *The Ottoman Empire: The Classical Age 1300–1600*, trans. N. Itzkovitz and C. Imber (London, 1973), p. 131.

16. De Yano, *Epistola de crudelitate Turcorum*, col. 1059.

17. Ibid.

18. Inalcik, *Ottoman Empire*.

19. H. Inalcik, "Bursa and the Commerce of the Levant," *Journal of Economic and Social History of the Orient* 3, no. 2 (1960): 143.

20. N. Beldiceanu, *Les actes des premiers sultans conservés dans les manuscrits turcs de la Bibliothèque Nationale à Paris*, vol. 1: *Actes de Mehmed II et de Bayezid II du MS fonds turc ancien 39* (Paris: La Haye, 1960), p. 131, doc. 43.

21. Bistra Cvetkova, "Robstvoto v Osmanskata imperiia a po spetialno v bǎlgarskite zemi pod turska vlast" [Slavery in the Ottoman Empire and More Particularly in the Bulgarian Territories under Ottoman Rule], in *Istoriceski Pregled* 10, no. 2 (1955): 178–80.

22. *Amil*, someone who farmed lands belonging to the Ottoman state.

23. Beldiceanu, *Actes*, vol. 1, p. 134, doc. 46.

24. See the *kanun* issued by Mehmed II during the last decade of ğumada II 893 (June 2–10, 1488) in Fr. Kraelitz-Greifenhorst, "Kanunname Sultan Mehmeds des Eroberers: Die ältesten osmanischen Straf- und Finanzgesetze," in *Mitteilungen zur osmanischen Geschichte* (Vienna, 1921), vol. 1, p. 33.

25. Istanbul, Topkapi Sarayi R 1936, fol. 153 verso–155 recto. N. Beldiceanu, *Recherches sur la ville ottomane au XVe siècle: Études et actes* (Paris, 1973), p. 282, doc. 25. The rate for the *bağ* is the same in the *nahiye* of Haskovo, Akče Kazanlik, and Novo Zagora. Ö. L. Barkan, *XV ve XVI inci asirlarda osmanli Imparatorlu unda zirai ekonominin hukukî ve malî esaslari*, vol. 1: *Kanunlar* (Istanbul, 1943), pp. 257, 258.

26. See the report of the kadi of Akčekazanlik dated April 15, 1520, on the duties collected on the seaports of Walachia, Bulgaria, and Dobrudja in N. Beldiceanu, "Fiscalité et institutions de plusieurs échelles danubiennes," in *Le monde ottoman des Balkans (1402–1566): Institutions, société, économie* (London, 1976), pp. 99–100.

27. Fr. Babinger, "Die Aufzeichnungen des Genuesen Jacopo de Promontorio de Campis," in *Sitzungsberichte der Bayerischen Akademie, Philologische-Historische Klasse, 1956* (Munich, 1957), vol. 8, p. 62.

28. Ašikpašazade, *Die altosmanische Chronik*, p. 113.

29. Fr. Babinger, "Die Aufzeichnungen des Genuesen Jacopo de Promontorio de Campis," p. 62.

30. Ašikpašazade, *Die altosmanische Chronik*, p. 106.

31. Ibid., p. 112.

32. Ibid., p. 113.

33. Ibid., p. 112.

34. Gliša Elezović, *Turski spomeniki* (Belgrade, 1940, vol. 1, no. 1), pp. 169–70.

35. De Yano, *Epistola de crudelitate Turcorum*, col. 1059.

36. On the registers of the *kadis* in the 15th century, see H. Inalcik, "15. asir Turkiye iktisadi ve ictimai tarihi kaynaklari," *Iktisat Fakültesi Mecmuasi* 15 (1953–1954): 52–61.

37. Fr. Babinger, "Die Aufzeichnungen des Genuesen Jacopo de Promontorio de Campis," p. 62.

38. Beldiceanu, *Actes*, vol. 1, p. 166. See also the regulation issued by Bayezid II, May 12–21, 1499, in Barkan, *Kanunlar*, pp. 90–103.

39. Barkan, *Kanunlar*, pp. 86–109; "XV ve XVI asirlarda Osmanli imparatorluğunda toprak isciliğinin organizasyono sekilleri," *Iktisat Fakültesi Mecmuasi* 1 (1939): 29–74, 198–245, 397–447.

40. Kritobulos of Imbros, *De rebus per annos 1451–1467 a Mechemete II gestis*, ed. B. Grecu (Bucarest, 1963), p. 237.

41. Defter de Pašagaghi de 859/1455, Istanbul, Belediye Kütübhanesi, Cevdet Kit, no. 089.

42. Inalcik, *Ottoman Empire*, p. 113.

43. Johann von Hammer, *Constantinopolis und der Bosporos* (Pest, 1822), vol. 1, p. 322.

44. Ibid., pp. 397–99.

45. Kritobulos, *De rebus per annos 1451–1467*, pp. 171–73.

50

MY CAREER REDEEMING SLAVES

John Eibner

Nur Muhammad al-Hasan emerges from the Sudanese bush. His loose, once-bright white jalabiya flutters as he strides towards me. I in turn step through the long, dry grass towards him, stooping slightly as I walk under the weight of a US army kit bag full of grimy Sudanese bank notes. It is April 1999 and the midday sun is oppressive. Nur and I greet each other with a handshake and "Salam 'alaykum." We slip under the shade of an enormous mango tree where we have some important business to discuss: The liberation of slaves, mainly women and children.

Our enterprise is not to everyone's liking. Last spring, Sudan's government, the radical Islamist regime of the National Islamic Front (NIF) headed by Hasan at-Turabi and Gen. 'Umar al-Bashir, protested to the United Nations Commission on Human Rights about our work. The regime claims that my organization, Christian Solidarity International (CSI), is the main source of the abduction and kidnapping of children in southern Sudan.[1] In April, the Khartoum regime also initiated proceedings to deny CSI its consultative status at the United Nations (UN), alleging that we act contrary to the purposes and principles of the UN charter.[2]

About the same time, the world's richest and most influential child welfare organization, the United Nations International Children's Emergency Fund (UNICEF), ended its long silence on the enslavement of Sudanese woman and children. Instead of condemning the slavers, UNICEF—whose mandate requires it to work in partnership with the government of Sudan—echoed Khartoum by calling our liberation of slaves "absolutely intolerable," and by accusing us of vio-

John Eibner, "My Career Redeeming Slaves," *Middle East Quarterly* 4, no. 4 (December 1999), http://www.meforum.org/article/449.

lating the Slavery Convention.[3] Others, with agendas of their own, perhaps working with the Sudanese regime or trying to salvage their own tarnished reputations, have spread rumors of fraud about these activities.[4] Then in late October, the UN Economic and Social Council voted by a tally of 26 to 14 (with 12 abstentions) to withdraw our consultative status, thus effectively excluding CSI from the UN system. Yet if anything is "absolutely intolerable," it is that the international community has allowed slavery and other crimes against humanity to be institutionalized by a member state of the United Nations.

FREEING THE SLAVES

Nur heads one of four networks of Arab Muslim retrievers of slaves; CSI pays for the slaves he acquires and then frees them. Over the previous two months (mid-February to mid-April), he had trekked through the woods and scrubland of southern Darfur and Kordofan (provinces in the central region of Sudan), visiting the cattle camps and farms of the nomadic Baqqara Arabs in search of black African slaves. In most cases, he gains custody of the slaves by posing as a slave owner who wants to add to his stock of concubines, domestics, and agricultural laborers. Sometimes, he is able to arrange for the release of slaves through Arab chiefs. In rare cases, he is able to whisk an unattended slave away to freedom, without payment, or he finds a jealous wife only too happy secretly to hand over her husband's sex slave.

This time, Nur has brought back 316 slaves to their homeland in northern Bahr al-Ghazal Province; another 1,467 slaves returned via three other retrieval networks. Virtually all of these 1,783 individuals are women and children of the Dinkas, a Nilotic, black African tribe, with approximately three million members concentrated mainly in Bahr al-Ghazal. They sit fifty yards away from Nur and me under another huge shade tree. They sit there bewildered, not knowing what might happen next. Will mothers and children be separated? Will children be sold to work the fields? I greet them, talking through my Dinka translator, Joseph Garang, and introduce both my CSI colleague, Gunnar Wiebalck, and journalists who have accompanied us (from *Newsweek* and the *New York Times*).[5] We reassure them not to be afraid. Gunnar and I then count the slaves and do a random spot check of the names on the list of returnees. Everything is in good order. Nur then confirms our long-standing agreement: he will take 50,000 Sudanese pounds (currently the equivalent of two goats or $50) for every slave we buy from him.

Under the scrutiny of Nur and the journalists, I carefully count out 15,800,000 Sudanese pounds, then announce to the slaves that the money to redeem them has been paid. "You are all free to return to your homes," I tell them. A handful of newly liberated slaves are met right there by loved ones but most rise slowly and drift gradually away, knowing they may have to walk for several days before they reach their families. All the now ex-slaves share one thing in common, though: a deep relief at being far away from their former masters and happy to be back with their own people.

CSI began redeeming slaves in October 1995; as of October 1999, it has freed 15,447. An impressive number, perhaps, but it pales in comparison with the total number of slaves in Sudan. Our own estimate, based on the pattern of slave raiding over the past fifteen years and the observations of Western and Arab travelers in southern Darfur and Kordofan, conservatively puts the number of chattel slaves[6] close to or over 100,000. There are many more in state-owned concentration camps, euphemistically called "peace camps" by the government of Sudan, and in militant Qur'anic schools, where boys train to become mujahidun (warriors of jihad).[7]

Nur and his colleagues have established retrieval networks that are the Sudanese equivalent of the "underground railroad" in pre–Civil War America. They emerged and grew within the context of local peace agreements signed in the early 1990s when some Baqqara Arabs of southern Darfur and Kordofan came to the conclusion that the long-term interests of their people are irrevocably bound to peace with their neighbors, the black African Dinkas of northern Bahr al-Ghazal. These agreements benefit both sides: Arab signatories have the right to graze cattle during the dry season in the well-watered land south of the Bahr al-Arab River and trade unmolested in specified Dinka markets. In return, they agree both to resist Khartoum's jihad against the Dinka and to help retrieve Dinka slaves. Dinka community leaders invited CSI to support this initiative in 1995. In this way, CSI found itself in the slave-redeeming "business."

On his own, Nur cannot retrieve hundreds of slaves. To acquire such numbers, he depends on a broad array of friends and relatives who assist him, especially with logistics and security. His work is dangerous and must be executed covertly. He tells of having been arrested and tortured in 1995 on suspicion of retrieving slaves. A year later, he says, Khartoum's security agents ransacked and burned down his house. His family now lives in hiding. He can no longer travel to the towns in his region in daylight. In such places the government's brutal and ever-present security apparatus lies in wait for him.

SLAVE STORIES

I always interview at length some of the redeemed slaves. Here are four stories:

Adior Ajang Jongkor, a 35-year-old woman, was enslaved for two years by 'Ali in the village of Shetef. He changed her name to Huwa, Arabic for "Eve," had her perform domestic labor, repeatedly raped her, and slashed her with a knife when she resisted his advances. Her body now bears the many scars that resulted from her resistance.

Achol Tong Nyan, a Christian wife and mother in her mid-20s, was enslaved in March 1998. During a two-week forced march to the north she had to carry on her head a heavy load of tea and clothing—her captor's inanimate booty. At night, she was beaten and repeatedly gang-raped. Her master, Isma'il 'Ali Mahdi, gave her the name Howeva, forced her to perform Islamic rituals, and used her as a concubine. As a result of sexual relations with her master, she now has a baby girl, Paulina.

Wol Dut Deng, a boy in his mid-teens, was captured by the government of Sudan's Popular Defence Force (PDF) in the spring of 1996. On the forced march to Matarik, he witnessed the execution of his two brothers, Kak Deng Aguer and Deng Deng Aguer. His master, Hamdan, routinely beat and insulted him. After Deng tried to run away, Hamdan threatened to kill him and tied him up with a rope, leaving scars on his legs.

Nyanut Adwal Anei, a teenage girl, was enslaved by PDF troops in 1997. She was forced to live as the concubine of her master, Mahmud, who had her genitals excised.

Such dehumanizing abuse is not exceptional. Severe physical and psychological torture is the norm for the contemporary chattel slaves of Sudan, as are forced labor, forced conversion to Islam, death threats, beatings, and exemplary executions (usually by cutting the throat). Women endure rape and, in some cases, genital excision. Boys are sometimes trained as mujahidun and then sent to fight against their own people.

Note the absence of adult males: able-bodied men do not make passive, reliable slaves. Better able than women and children to resist cultural assimilation, more difficult to control physically, they are normally spared the humiliation of enslavement and are shot dead on sight during slave raids or are executed after carrying heavy booty to the north. Testimony from some redeemed slaves contain scores of grizzly eyewitness reports of many boy slaves unsuccessfully assimilated into servitude whose throats are cut just as they become physically strong.

HISTORICAL ROOTS

Slavery, an ancient institution, has been practiced in most parts of the world. In the territory that makes up the present Sudan, a deadly combination of intertribal warfare, despotic rulers, and commercial greed, meant slavery was an established institution in the pre-Islamic kingdoms of Nobatia, Makuria, and Alwa. With the coming of Islam in the mid-seventh century, a new political dynamic entered the region: jihad. It added a new dimension to the institution of slavery, for Islamic law gave religious legitimacy to the enslavement of non-Muslims captured in the course of jihad. As the scholar Majid Khadduri explains, the Shari'a (sacred law of Islam) had quite precise rules for non-Muslims captured in jihad:

[T]he Imam [ruler] may condemn the population of the conquered countries, in case they do not accept Islam and the Imam does not demand that they shall work and pay the tribute, to be slaves and be divided among the Jihadists as *ghanimah* (the spoils of war). The owner of a slave had the liberty to treat him any way he liked. If the slave were a woman, he was allowed to have sexual connection with her without marriage.[8]

Nor were slaves confined to war: the first truce between the Christian king of Makuria and the Muslim colonizers of Egypt, in 653 AD, required him to deliver annually 360 slaves as tribute to the "Treasury of the Muslims" and forty slaves to the governor of Egypt.[9] Soon, Sudanese slaves became a valuable commodity throughout the Middle East. According to Bernard Lewis:

From early Islamic times there are reports of gangs of black slaves employed in draining the salt flats of southern Iraq. Poor conditions led to a series of slave uprisings. Other black slaves were employed in the gold mines of upper Egypt and the Sudan, and in the salt mines of the Sahara.[10]

By the ninth century, Sudanese and Turkic slaves, known as the *jihadiya*, made up the bulk of the mighty army of the Arab Muslim empire.[11]

Throughout subsequent centuries, slave raiding and trading continued in Sudan, reaching its apogee in the nineteenth century. About 5,000 captives passed annually through the great slave market at Shendi in 1814, according to the Swiss scholar-explorer John Lewis Burckhardt[12]—a trickle compared to what was to come. The ruler of Egypt, Muhammad 'Ali (r. 1804–1849) seeking a huge slave-based army but unable to import from the usual sources, used the power of his modernizing state to expand the slave trade in Sudan, which now reached near-industrial proportions. The great slave traders established zaribas (primitive camps enclosed by thorn branches) throughout southern Sudan, devastated huge tracts of land, and transported slaves by the hundreds and thousands to the north by caravan and steamer. Slaves not absorbed into the army or domestic economy of Egypt were exported and sold to masters abroad, mainly in the Middle East. In 1833, the London-based Anti-Slavery Society estimated that his troops annually exported 20,000 slaves out of Sudan.[13]

The Mahdist jihad of 1881–1898 disrupted this lucrative export of Sudanese slaves but the slave trade lived on. Domestic servitude continued unabated in the Mahdist state, while the Mahdi and his successor, the Khalifa, required ever more slave soldiers to sustain their jihad. Military expeditions went south—using "fire and sword" in the words of eyewitness Rudolf Slatin Pasha, the ex-governor of Darfur—to subjugate southern tribes and capture fresh black African troops to fight for the Mahdi against the infidel (*kafir*)—meaning Egyptian Muslims and their European Christian allies.[14]

So devastating were the slave raids and plundering by Egyptian and Mahdist forces that the nineteenth century became known as "the time when the world was spoiled" in the collective consciousness of the Dinka of northern Bahr al-Ghazal.[15] More: the historical experience of slavery was so brutally powerful, it has left a deep scar on the communal psyche of the Sudanese. Echoes of the master-slave relationship continue to reverberate in Sudan and to stimulate contemporary racism.[16] Oliver Albino, a southern Sudanese intellectual, notes that it is a delusion to think, as is commonplace among northern Sudanese, that Western missionaries were responsible for instilling in the southerners a strong consciousness of slavery and the role of Arabs in the slave trade, for this awareness was passed on from generation to generation primarily within southern families.[17]

Serious efforts by the European abolitionist movement to end the Sudanese slave trade began in the mid-nineteenth century. In imperial Britain, the Anti-Slavery Society was a mighty influence and although Sudan was under Egyptian, not British control, after the death in 1849 of Muhammad 'Ali, the British role in Egypt increased to the point of occupying the country in 1882. The British pressured Egyptian authorities to combat vigorously the commercial slave trade; the famous general Charles Gordon (along with other Europeans) was enlisted by the Egyptian government to lead the campaign against slavery. Their success was limited, however. After Sir Herbert Kitchener defeated the Mahdists in 1898, the ensuing Anglo-Egyptian condominium, which governed Sudan until independence in 1955, resumed the abolitionist struggle. The condominium had great success in repressing the slave trade but failed to eliminate it. According to a former governor of Darfur, K. D. D. Henderson: "Up till the middle-twenties the Baqqara were still lifting slaves . . . and disposing of them to inaccessible markets far to the north."[18] As late as 1947, a memorandum prepared by British civil servants noted that

> [t]he educated northerner has dismissed the idea of slavery from his mind . . . but the Arab tribesman has not. In the late 'twenties an extensive trade in slaves from Ethiopia was unmasked and even today there are occasional kidnappings, and the victims are hurried into the hands of the desert nomads of the far north.[19]

Independence did nothing to change fundamentally this assessment. During the 1970s Sudanese sociologists noted the lingering existence of domestic slavery behind closed doors in some northern provincial towns; the same was undoubtedly true on remote farms.

The Baqqara nomadic cattlemen are among the poorest Arab tribes of northern Sudan; they have a long tradition of raiding the cows and goats of their sedentary neighbors. According to J. Spencer Trimingham, author of the classic *Islam in the Sudan*,

> They found still another livestock in the sedentary black population of these lands, which they also raided to perform the menial tasks of home and field and

plain, and whose women also served to keep their own diminishing social body restocked.[20]

Trimingham observed in 1949 that the Baqqara, whose economy and life style were cramped by the suppression of slavery, "still hanker after the practice."[21]

Looking over this long history, while there have been instances of Arabs being enslaved by blacks, the latter have been overwhelmingly the principal victims; for example, there has never been state-sponsored or commercial enslavement of Arabs by blacks. In all, 95 percent or more of Sudanese slaves have been non-Arab.[22]

THE REVIVAL OF SLAVERY AFTER 1983

Slavery is found today in many parts of the world, including Mauritania, Pakistan, India, Burma, and Saudi Arabia. But Sudan is the only place where chattel slavery is not just surviving but experiencing a great revival. This renascence of the slave trade began in the mid-1980s and resulted directly from an upsurge of Islamism in Sudan at that time, and especially from the Islamist emphasis on the renewal of jihad. After gaining the upper-hand in Khartoum by about 1983, the Islamists' immediate goal was to transform the multi-ethnic, multi-religious population of Sudan into an Arab-dominated Muslim state, and to do so through jihad. Under Turabi's powerful influence, the ruler of the time, Ja'far an-Numayri, declared himself to be (sounding like a caliph of old), the "rightly guided" leader of an Islamic state. Numayri then abrogated the autonomy agreement he had earlier reached with southern Sudan and imposed the Shari'a on the whole country. Armed resistance to these changes also began in 1983 with the formation of the Sudan People's Liberation Movement/Army (SPLM/A) under the leadership of Colonel John Garang.

Numayri responded militarily, initiating a process that has since assumed genocidal proportions. At least 1.9 million black Africans, out of an initial population of no more than 6 million people in the southern and central war zone, have died as a direct result of government policy. Over 4 million incidents of displacement have occurred, with some being temporary and some individuals experiencing multiple displacements.[23] In 1983–1984, Numayri initiated a policy of arming some Baqqara tribal militias (of the Riziqat and Misiriyiah tribes of southern Darfur and Kordofan) and unleashing them on the Dinkas of northern Bahr al-Ghazal.[24] Indeed, slave raids against the Dinka became an instrument in Khartoum's war effort. When the Baqqara won access to automatic weapons from the state at that time, the balance of power between them and the Dinka was fundamentally changed. Bands of Baqqara militiamen, known as *murahhilin* (resettlers) began to attack Dinka villages and cattle camps, stealing cows, goats, grain, women, and children, removing them as booty, killing adult males, and burning in their wake the huts and property they could not carry away.

The overthrow of Numayri in 1985 resulted in a suspension of this policy, only to find it resumed again after the election of Sadiq al-Mahdi as prime minister in 1986. The *murahhilin* raids were again accompanied by the "deliberate killing of tens of thousands of civilians; [and] the abduction of women and children, who were forced into slavery."[25] Atrocities of all sorts accompanied the slave raids. In one horrifying incident in 1987, over a thousand Dinka civilians were roasted alive in railway box cars by Riziqat *murahhilin* in the town of El Diein.[26] The great famine in northern Bahr al-Ghazal of 1987–89, during which more than 150,000 Dinkas starved to death, or died as a result of famine-related disease, saw no letup in the raiding. Dinkas fleeing the famine ran the risk of attack by the *murahhilin* as they trekked northwards in search of aid.

Murahhilin raiding became yet more widespread and institutionalized following the military coup of 1989 and the coming to power of a junta composed mainly of hard-line Islamist army officers headed by an NIF loyalist, General 'Umar al-Bashir. This seizure of power permitted the NIF, headed by Turabi, to gain complete control of the Sudanese state, something it had failed to do through electoral politics. The NIF's raison d'être is the Islamization and Arabization of Sudan (and the rest of Africa) by means of jihad. For the first time since the nineteenth century, slavery in Sudan has become an instrument of a state-sponsored jihad.

Bernard Levin, the British columnist, has described Sudan under the NIF regime as "a slave state of our time,"[27] and this is the case not only in practice but also in law. Although the government of Sudan is a signatory to the major international instruments prohibiting slavery, the creation of an Islamic state and the imposition of Shari'a law superimposed a new universal legal system on the country, one that the authorities view as paramount.[28] The conflict between Shari'a norms and international instruments regarding the legality of slavery was made explicit by former prime minister Sadiq al-Mahdi, imam of the Ansar movement:

> The traditional concept of JIHAD . . . is based upon a division of the world into two zones: one the zone of Peace, the other the zone of War. It requires initiating hostilities for religious purposes. . . . It is true that the [NIF] regime has not enacted a law to realize slavery in Sudan. But the traditional concept of JIHAD does allow slavery as a by-product [of jihad].[29]

During mass jihad rallies in towns (Muglad, Mieriam, El Diein, Babanusa) to mobilize Baqqara boys and men to join the jihad against the Dinka, senior NIF officials explicitly call for the killing and enslavement of "infidels."[30]

SLAVE RAIDING

Shortly after coming to power, the NIF regime promulgated the Popular Defence Act, which established the Popular Defence Force as a branch of the Sudanese armed forces. In contrast to the regular army, with its non-political career officers, the PDF leadership embraces the NIF's objectives and thinks of itself as a force of mujahadun. In southern Darfur and Kordofan, the PDF has largely incorporated the tribal murahhilin militias.[31] By 1991, the PDF had become an effective fighting force that the NIF used consistently to spearhead its declared jihad against the SPLA and those black African communities sympathetic to it.

The principal victims have been the Dinkas of northern Bahr al-Ghazal, together with the black African Nuba tribes of southern Kordofan. Some of the Nubas joined the SPLA's armed resistance in 1991. In response, the NIF unleashed the full fury of its jihad on them. So far, the jihad in the Nuba mountains has been, if anything, more ferocious than that in northern Bahr al-Ghazal, due to the mountains' political and strategic importance in northern Sudan. The fact that many Nubas, perhaps a majority, are Muslims, has not deterred the vigorous prosecution of jihad against them. In April 1992, imams loyal to the NIF issued a remarkable fatwa (edict) against the Nuba Muslims, reading them out of the religion:

> An insurgent who was previously a Muslim is now an apostate; and a non-Muslim is a nonbeliever standing as a bulwark against the spread of Islam, and Islam has granted the freedom of killing both of them.[32]

Some Nuba captives end up as chattel slaves but the overwhelming majority are deported to concentration camps elsewhere in Sudan, where they serve in slave-like conditions. The children are sent to militant Qur'anic schools, while the women are sent out to work without pay as day laborers on farms and in private homes. Sexual abuse is rife.

The most devastating recorded slave raids against the Dinka of Bahr al-Ghazal took place in the spring of 1998. The PDF, supported by the regular army, swept through Aweil West County, and penetrated deep inside Aweil West, Twic, and Abyei counties. Over 300,000 persons were displaced; the total number killed and enslaved is still not known. Slaves captured in this offensive and subsequently redeemed testified that thousands of women were placed in a pen, stripped of their clothing and video taped by 'Abd ar-Rahman Qidr, the government's commissioner in El Diein.

Following this onslaught, Santino Deng, a Dinka political advisor to the governor of northern Bahr al-Ghazal State, broke ranks with the government in defense of his own people when he stated that the Islamic militias were holding 50,000 Dinka children captive in Babanusa, Western Kordofan. "Some of our children," he declared with exceptionally rare candor for a government official, "are taken as slaves and sent to Qur'anic schools in Djibouti, Mauritania, Gabon, and Cameroon, the kingdom of Saudi Arabia, and Libya."[33]

Slave raids continue to the present time. The UNICEF rapid assessment team in northern Bahr al-Ghazal found that the PDF enslaved 2,064 people and killed 181 others in raids between December 1998 and February 1999 (during a UN-brokered "humanitarian" cease-fire, no less). The UN investigators reported that, after having been gang-raped by PDF members, a woman was forced to drink her own urine to survive; another woman had part of her breast bitten off by a sexual assailant.[34] In 1999, there have been markedly fewer slave raids and women and children taken into bondage than in the previous year, thanks largely to improved SPLA defenses in northern Bahr al-Ghazal.[35]

MODERN ABOLITIONISM

Last spring, the leader of the Sudan Peoples Liberation Movement/Army, John Garang, posed concisely the key theoretical question facing the international community regarding the revival of slavery in Sudan at the United Nations in Geneva: "Is the call for jihad against a particular people a religious right by those calling for it, or is it a human rights violation against the people on which jihad is declared and waged?"[36] This question touches the heart of relations between the Muslim and the non-Muslim world; it needs to be addressed forthrightly by academics and diplomats.

International law has a clear answer, for it defines slavery as a "crime against humanity." Slavery directly contravenes the Slavery Convention of 1926 and Article II (e) of the Genocide Convention of 1948.[37]

The first protests against the revival of slavery in Sudan came from the Sudanese themselves. In 1987, Bona Malwal, a Dinka leader and former government minister, then editor of the *Sudan Times* in Khartoum, published a series of articles exposing the resurgence of slavery and the El Diein massacre. For this, the prime minister of the day branded him "public enemy number one." Then two young Muslim academics, Ushar Mahmoud and Süleyman Ali Baldo, set out for western Sudan to investigate. They found that Malwal was right and published their findings as a report.[38] For revealing the truth, Mahmoud and Baldo served time in a Sudanese prison. Also in 1987, the Catholic bishop of Al-Obeid, Macram Max Gassis, who had personally redeemed members of his flock from bondage, testified about slavery before a congressional committee in Washington. Detained by the authorities in 1990, the bishop left the country after his release and was subsequently warned not to return to Sudan.

An important milestone towards abolition was reached in November 1995 when leaders of Sudan's banned northern opposition parties and movements joined together with the southern parties and movements to condemn "the sustained, systematic and grave violations of human rights committed or encouraged by the government of the Sudan, especially the kidnapping of children, the practice of slavery, and the forcible conscription of minors, as reported by the then-U.N. special rapporteur on Sudan, Gaspar Biro."[39] Hitherto, they had regarded slavery as a taboo subject, thereby keeping the issue off the national political agenda. A great debate on slavery among northern Sudanese was ignited in the spring of 1999 when Hamouda Fathelrahman and Abdon Agaw of the Sudan Human Rights Organization (based in Cairo) traveled on a fact-finding visit to Bahr al-Ghazal and issued a report which confirmed the irrefutable evidence on slavery published by the UN special rapporteurs and CSI.[40]

Some non-Sudanese human rights groups and activists have also responded energetically to the plight of the Sudanese slaves. An antislavery movement is growing in North America and Europe; prominent campaigners include Charles Jacobs of the American Anti-Slavery Group, Sam Cotton and Sebit Alley of the Coalition against Slavery in Mauritania and Sudan (CASMAS), Colorado school teacher Barbara Vogel, and the Reverend Charles Singleton. Their efforts, together with those of CSI, have resulted in a dynamic program combining the liberation of slaves with moral and material support for the victimized Dinka communities; the documentation of slave raids and cases of slavery; international media exposure; campaigning at the United Nations, in Washington, and other Western capitals; and support for local, national and international peace initiatives.

The rising tide of abolitionism is reflected in stirrings on Capitol Hill. Last July, Senators Sam Brownback (R–KS), Russell Feingold (D–WI), William Frist (R–TN), and Joseph Lieberman (D–CT) introduced the "Sudan Peace Act." It condemns

> the ongoing slave trade in Sudan and the role of the Government of Sudan in abetting and tolerating the practice; and the Government of Sudan's increasing use and organization of 'Murahalliin, Popular Defence Forces (PDF), and regular Sudanese Army units into organized and coordinated raiding and slaving parties in Bahr al-Ghazal, Nuba Mountains, Upper Nile and southern Blue Nile regions.[41]

Efforts against slavery in Sudan are slowly making progress, especially in the United States where the neo-abolitionist movement has been making steady headway. The momentum appears unstoppable. To give this movement an additional boost, a great international statesman or religious or business leader needs to devote his or her time and resources single-mindedly to this cause, much as William Wilberforce did two centuries ago. If anything, such a person needs to summon even more bravery than did Wilberforce, for the threat of terrorist attacks by the NIF and its doctrinal ally Usama bin Ladin cannot be dismissed.

UN AGENCIES AND WESTERN GOVERNMENTS

All of this campaigning has had some effect, making the "out of sight, out of mind" attitude less tenable. In February 1999, soon after Dan Rather of CBS News highlighted the plight of Sudanese slaves and CSI's role in freeing them, UNICEF broke its silence and admitted: "Slavery in Sudan exists."[42]

Even as it said this, however, UNICEF appeased the Khartoum regime by condemning the redemption of slaves as "absolutely intolerable." UNICEF had good reason to be concerned about the wrath of the government of Sudan. Shortly after UNICEF's admission of slavery, Sudan's deputy foreign minister, Hasan 'Abdin, threatened to disrupt UNICEF's work in Sudan unless it retracted its statement.[43] This kind of threat against the United Nations works. Although UNICEF has not denied and will not now deny that there is slavery in Sudan, it will (together with other UN agencies), for the sake of "operationality," cooperate with those who are waging a genocidal jihad and taking slaves in the process. With a view to assuaging the wrath of Khartoum, UNICEF's executive director Carol Bellamy made a series of widely publicized press statements attacking CSI's antislavery campaign, claiming that Dinka efforts to retrieve their enslaved women and children contravenes the Slavery Convention and is not in their own best interests.[44]

Bellamy also announced a four-point antislavery plan, which on paper looks very similar to the CSI program, minus slave redemption. It called for

> [a] firm commitment, from all those directly and indirectly responsible to end the slave trade in Sudan; freedom of movement for international verifiers; full support for retrieval tracing and reunification programs; and a specific plan and provision of free access to document all phases of a full-scale effort to bring the slave trade to an end, to free its victims and to restore them to their rightful communities and families.[45]

Stated in the abstract, Bellamy's four points seem merely to reiterate the CSI program. Operationally, however, UNICEF's proposal differs fundamentally from CSI's: UNICEF, as a state-oriented organization, depends upon partnership with the regime in Khartoum. CSI, on the other hand, as a manifestation of civil society, acts in partnership with the victimized community. Even so, the government of Sudan has yet to accept the UNICEF proposal, instead denying the very existence of slavery. In addition, according to UNICEF spokesman Peter Crowley, as of July 1999, the UNICEF plan had no budget. The UNICEF effort remains in limbo, while slaves who long to be freed remain in bondage.

The UN High Commissioner for Human Rights, Mary Robinson, has also kept mum on the issue, despite her own staff and independent UN special rapporteurs confirming the existence of slavery in Sudan and the government's key role in abetting the slave trade—in particular, the reports submitted by the former Special Rapporteur on Sudan Gaspar Biro and his successor Leonardo Franco. The 1999 Sudan Resolution of the UN Commission on Human Rights failed even to mention the word "slavery." The UN secretary-general, Kofi Annan, has also never publicly condemned the revival of slavery in Sudan.

And the US government? It too is reluctant. In 1999, for the first time in six years, Washington declined to serve as the main sponsor of the Commission on Human Rights' Sudan resolution, leaving this responsibility to the lukewarm European Union; and the Clinton administration assented to the commission's "slavery-free" resolution. Why the change? Because in return, the Sudanese were prepared not to press hard for a condemnation of the United States for the rocket attack on Khartoum's Ash-Shifa pharmaceutical factory in August 1998. However, with an eye on the abolitionist movement at home, the State Department tried to maintain the moral high ground by condemning the (US-supported) Sudan resolution as "deeply flawed" for failing to "confront fully the practice of slavery."[46] This did not convince; just four days later, the Clinton administration announced a weakening of sanctions on Sudan (by allowing the sale of agricultural goods and pharmaceuticals).[47]

Could it be that the wobble in America's Sudan policy is finally straightening out? The assistant secretary of state for African affairs, Susan Rice, and the US ambassador at large for war crimes, David Scheffer, publicly appealed in September 1999 for concerted international action to end slavery and other related war crimes in Sudan.[48] Time will tell whether this appeal is a signal for a serious policy initiative backed by the president, or if it reflects no more than posturing within a divided administration.

The sad truth must be acknowledged: Sudanese slaves and other victims of the NIF's genocidal jihad count for little in a world preoccupied with other matters. Millions of lives have been lost and disrupted while the world has largely turned a blind eye toward gross violations of human rights in Sudan.

Whatever may be the future of the international abolitionist movement, the Dinkas are right not to wait for help from the UN or any state but to find their own ways to liberate their people from bondage. Still, they can count on my colleagues and me, as well as a growing number of abolitionists for support until the last slave is free.

NOTES

1. Statement by Ali Mohamed Osman Yasin, minister of justice and attorney general, Republic of Sudan, to the fifty-fifth session of the United Nations Commission on Human Rights, Geneva, April 7, 1999.

2. A. M. Rosenthal, "When Is It News?" *New York Times*, September 3, 1999.

3. Agence France Presse, February 5, 1999; Carol Bellamy, "Buying Slaves Is Wrong," *International Herald Tribune*, May 13, 1999.

4. One reporter, Richard Miniter, used the pages of the *Atlantic Monthly* to do just this in its July 1999 issue ("The False Promise of Slave Redemption"). My investigation into his accusations, including an on-the-spot inquiry in July, has revealed several dismaying facts: (1) Jim Jacobson, Miniter's guide and one of his principal sources, was banned by Sudanese community leaders from further "slave redemption" activity after he had taken part in a bogus "redemption" in July 1998. After having been found out, Jacobson announced that he would no longer raise funds for "slave redemption," and began his campaign to discredit the integrity of the victims of slave raids and the community leaders who ended his unethical activity among their people. (2) According to local eyewitnesses, Miniter's field research in the area afflicted by slave raids amounted to no more than an hour at each of two locations. (3) Commissioner Aleu Akechak Jok, whom Miniter portrays as being opposed to slave redemption, is a long-standing supporter of this method of freeing his enslaved people. The commissioner rejected Jacobson's financial incentive to participate in a false redemption and ordered the two to leave the area forthwith. Commissioner Jok was also one of the community leaders who ordered the banning of Jacobson last February. (4) Miniter's article does not include interviews with slaves, ex-slaves, or slave retrievers, presumably because he did not encounter any. (5) Not only have three of Miniter's four cited local sources, Chief Longar Awie Ayuel, Commissioner Aleu Akechak Jok, and Adelino Rip Gee, claimed that Miniter grossly misrepresented their views, but the chief, supported by eye-witnesses, claims that the reporter did not even speak with him. (6) Miniter portrays Adelino Rip Gee as the "official spokesman" for the local administration, whereas he is in fact an unemployed intellectual who arrived in the area one and a half years ago from the government garrison town of Wau.

5. For reports on their experiences, see *Newsweek*, May 3, 1999; *New York Times*, April 25, 1999.

6. Chattel slaves are the private property of individual masters. They may be bought and sold. Other slaves belong to the state or to state-controlled institutions.

7. Bat Ye'or has noted the striking similarity between the enslavement of non-Muslim boys for service in the government of Sudan's jihad and the devshirme system in the Ottoman Empire. Bat Ye'or, *The Decline of Eastern Christianity under Islam: From Jihad to Dhimmitude* (Cranbury, NJ: Fairleigh Dickenson University Press, 1996), pp. 259–61. For the historical background of the training and use of child slave soldiers in Islamic societies, see Daniel Pipes, *Slave Soldiers and Islam* (New Haven, CT: Yale University Press, 1981).

8. Majid Khadduri, *The Law of War and Peace in Islam: A Study in Muslim International Law* (London: Luzac, 1940), p. 62.

9. According to the ninth-century historian Abu Khalif al-Bhuturi, quoted in Giovanni Vantini, *Christianity in the Sudan* (Bologna: EMI, 1981), pp. 65–67.

10. Bernard Lewis, *The Middle East: 2,000 Years of History from the Rise of Christianity to the Present Day* (London: Phoenix Giant, 1996), p. 209.

11. S. Abdullah Schleifer, "Jihad and the Traditional Islamic Consciousness, Part II," *Islamic Quarterly* 4 (1983): 187; Daniel Pipes, "Black Soldiers in Early Muslim Armies," *International Journal of African Historical Studies* 13 (1980): 87–94.

12. John Lewis Burckhardt, *Travels in Nubia*, 2nd ed. (London: John Murray, 1822), p. 290.

13. Carolyn Fleuhr-Lobban, "Islamization in Sudan: A Critical Assessment," *Middle East Journal* (Autumn 1990): 611.

14. Rudolf C. Slatin, *Fire and Sword in the Sudan: A Personal Narrative of Fighting*

and Serving the Dervishes, 2nd ed. (London: Edward Arnold, 1896), pp. 554–57; Robert O. Collins, *The Southern Sudan, 1883–1898: A Struggle for Control* (New Haven, CT: Yale University Press, 1962), pp. 57–58, 76–77, 139–40, 179.

15. Francis Mading Deng, *Africans of Two Worlds: The Dinka in Afro-Arab Sudan* (New Haven, CT: Yale University Press, 1978), p. 132.

16. In North America a dark-skinned person with some African ancestry is regarded as "black"; skin color is far more subtle in Sudan, where great importance is attached to the fact that true Arabs are lighter in skin color than the black Africans of the south. This said, cultural differences (language and religion) are even more important.

17. Oliver Albino, *The Sudan: A Southern Viewpoint* (London: Oxford University Press, 1970), p. 79.

18. K. D. D. Henderson, *Sudan Republic* (London: Ernest Benn, 1965), p. 162.

19. Ibid., p. 197.

20. J. Spencer Trimingham, *Islam in the Sudan* (London: Oxford University Press, 1949), p. 29.

21. Ibid.

22. Mohamed Omer Beshir, *The Southern Sudan: Background to Conflict* (London: C. Hurst, 1968), p. 11; Deng, *Africans of Two Worlds*, pp. 138–40.

23. Millard Burr, *Quantifying Genocide in Southern Sudan and the Nuba Mountains, 1983–1998* (Washington, DC: US Committee for Refugees, 1998).

24. Helen Chapin Metz, ed., *Sudan: A Country Study*, 4th ed. (Washington, DC: Library of Congress, 1992), p. 257.

25. Ibid.

26. Ushari Ahmad Mahmud and Süleyman Ali Baldo, *El Diein Massacre: Slavery in the Sudan* (London: Sudan Relief and Rehabilitation Association, 1987), abridged edition of *El Diein Massacre* (Khartoum: n.p., 1987).

27. The *Times* (London), May 31, 1996.

28. As symbolized by its adoption, together with the other members of the Organization of the Islamic Conference, of the Cairo Declaration on Human Rights in Islam, which conditions respect for human rights on Shari'a norms. The Cairo Declaration was reprinted in *Human Rights: A Compilation of International Instruments*, vol. 2: *Regional Instruments* (New York and Geneva: United Nations, 1997), pp. 474–84. See: Littman, "Islamism Grows Stronger at the United Nations," pp. 59–64.

29. As-Sadiq Al-Mahdi to Mary Robinson, UN High Commissioner for Human Rights (Section III: War Crimes), March 24, 1999.

30. According to the testimony of Arab traders and former slaves.

31. *Situation of Human Rights in the Sudan,* visit of the special rapporteur, Mr. Leonardo Franco, to the Republic of the Sudan, February 13–24, 1999, unedited version, UN Commission on Human Rights, fifty-fifth session, addendum to E/CN.4/1999/38, pp. 19–20, 56–57.

32. Quoted from the 1993 and 1994 reports of the UN special rapporteur, Gaspar Biro, in "The UN Finds Slavery in the Sudan," *Middle East Quarterly* (September 1996): 89–92.

33. Inter Press Service (Khartoum), July 24, 1998.

34. Rapid Assessment Report, *Rapid Assessment of Affected Locations in Twic, Aweil East, Aweil West and Wau Counties, March 13 and 25, 1999* (Lokichoggio: UNICEF/OLS Rapid Assessment Team, 1999).

35. SPLM press statement by Justin Yaac Arop, Nairobi, August 19, 1999.

36. SPLM press statement, United Nations, Geneva, March 22, 1999.

37. Alison Wiebalck, "Slavery in the Sudan: A Challenge to International Law," *Comparative and International Law Journal of Southern Africa* 31 (1998): 38–60; *Racism: Leading to Genocide and Slavery in the Sudan*, written statement by Christian Solidarity International, United Nations Economic and Social Council, Commission on Human Rights, fifty-fifth session, item 6, E/CN.4/1999/NGO/5, January 29, 1999.

38. Mahmud and Baldo, *El Diein Massacre.*

39. *Senior Representatives of the banned Political Parties and Social Movements of Sudan, Final Communiqué, Peace & Democracy in Sudan: The Development of the IGADD and Asmara (NDA) Processes* (London: Christian Solidarity International Conference, 1995).

40. Report by the Sudan Human Rights Organization (Cairo) on investigation of slavery by Hamouda Fathelrahman and Abdon Agaw, June 1999; Hamouda Fathelrahman, "A Personal Experience, A Sincere Appeal," Cairo, June 1999.

41. US Congress, Senate, 106th Cong., 1st sess., S. 145, "Sudan Peace Act," Section 4, paragraphs C & D, July 28, 1999.

42. Agence France Press, February 5, 1999.

43. British Broadcasting Corporation (BBC) News, March 18, 1999.

44. M2 Presswire (Geneva), March 16, 1999; Bellamy, "Buying Slaves Is Wrong."

45. M2 Presswire, March 16, 1999.

46. Harold Hongju Koh, assistant secretary of state for human rights, at the UN Commission on Human Rights, April 23, 1999.

47. Reuters, April 27, 1999.

48. Susan Rice and David Scheffer, "Sudan Must End Its Brutal War against Civilians," *International Herald Tribune*, September 1, 1999.

PART 8

Muslim and Non-Muslim Chronicles and Eyewitness Accounts of Jihad Campaigns

51

JIHAD CAMPAIGNS IN THE MIDDLE EAST, NORTH AFRICA, SPAIN, ASIA MINOR, GEORGIA, AND PERSIA—SEVENTH THROUGH SEVENTEENTH CENTURIES

A. EGYPT, PALESTINE, TRIPOLITANIA (640–646)[1]

The Capture of the Fayyum

Theodosius, the general, learning of the arrival of the Ishmaelites [Arabs], moved from place to place in order to observe the enemy. The Ishmaelites attacked, killed the commandant, massacred all his troops and immediately seized the town <of Behnesa? > Whoever approached them was massacred; they spared neither old men, nor women, nor children.

After the Flight of the Greek Army Near Nikiou

Then the Muslims arrived in Nikiou [on the Nile, near Damanhur]. There was not one single soldier to resist them. They seized the town and slaughtered everyone they met in the street and in the churches—men, women, and children, sparing nobody. Then they went to other places, pillaged and killed all the inhabitants they found. In the town of Sa they caught unawares Esqutaos and his men, of the tribe of Theodore the general, who were hidden in the vineyards, and they slew them. But let us now say no more, for it is impossible to describe the horrors the Muslims committed when they occupied the island of Nikiou, on Sunday, the eighteenth day of the month of Guenbot, in the fifteenth year of the lunar cycle, as well as the terrible scenes which took place in Cesarea in Palestine.

Amr [b. al-'As] oppressed Egypt. He sent its inhabitants to fight the inhabitants of the Pentapolis [Tripolitania] and, after gaining a victory, he did not allow them to stay there. He took considerable booty from this country and a large number of prisoners. Abulyanos . . . governor of the Pentapolis, with his troops and the leading citizens of the province withdrew to the town of Teycheira, which was heavily fortified, and shut themselves up there. The Muslims returned to their country with booty and captives.

The patriarch Cyrus felt deep grief at the calamities in Egypt, because Amr, who was of barbarian origin, showed no mercy in his treatment of the Egyptians and did not fulfil the covenants which had been agreed with him.

Amr's position became stronger from day to day. He levied the tax that had been stipulated; but he did not touch the property of the churches, preserved them from all pillage and protected them during the entire length of his government. After taking possession of Alexandria, he had the town's canal drained, following the example set by Theodore the evildoer. He raised the tax to as much as twenty-two batr of gold, with the result that the inhabitants, crushed down by the burden and is no position to pay it, went into hiding.

But it is impossible to describe the lamentable position of the inhabitants of this town, who came to the point of offering their children in exchange for the enormous sums that they had to pay each month, finding no one to help them because God had abandoned them and had delivered the Christians into the hands of their enemies.

Note

1. John of Nikiou, from *Chronique de Jean, Eveque de Nikiou,* trans. Hermann Zoten-berg (Paris, 1879), pp. 228–29, 243–44, 262–63. English trans. Bat Ye'or, *The Decline of Eastern Christianity under Islam* (Cranbury, NJ: Fairleigh Dickinson University Press, 1996), pp. 271–72.

B. IRAQ[1]

Letter from Umar b. al-Khattab (633–643) to Sa'd b. abi Wakkas after the Conquest of Sawad (Iraq)

I have received thy letter in which thou statest that thy men have asked thee to divide among them whatever spoils Allah has assigned them. At the receipt of my letter, find out what possessions and horses the troops on "horses and camels" [Koran 59.6] have acquired and divide that among them, after taking away one-fifth. As for the land and camels, leave them in the hands of those men who work them, so that they may be included in the stipends [pensions] of the Moslems. If thou dividest them among those present nothing will be left for those who come after them.

Al-Husain from Abdullah b. Hazim: The latter said, "I once asked Mujahid regarding the land of as-Sawad and he answered. "It can neither be bought nor sold. This is because it was taken by force and was not divided. It belongs to all the Moslems."

Al-Walid b. Salih from Sulaiman ibn-Yasar: "Umar b. al-Khatab left as-Sawad for those who were still in men?s loins and mothers? wombs [i.e., posterity], considering the inhabitants dhimmis from whom tax [jizya] should be taken on their person, and kharaj on their land. They are therefore dhimmis and cannot be sold as slaves."

Umar b. al-Khattab, desiring to divide as-Sawad among the Moslems, ordered that they [the inhabitants] be counted. Each Moslem had three peasants for his share. Umar took the advice of the Prophet's Companions, and Ali said, "leave them that they may become a source of revenue and aid for the Moslems."

Note

1. al-Baladhuri, *The Origins of the Islamic State* [*Kitab Futuh Al-Buldan*], trans. Philip K. Hitti (New York: Columbia University Press, 1916), pp. 422–23.

C. IRAQ, SYRIA, AND PALESTINE[1]

Umar Ibn al-Khattab Replies to the Muslim Soldiers Who Demand the Sharing-out of the Conquered Lands

But I thought that we had nothing more to conquer after the land of Kesra [Persia], whose riches, land, and people Allah has given us. I have divided the goods and chattels among those that conquered them after having subtracted a fifth, which under my supervision was used for the purpose for which it was intended. I thought it necessary to reserve the land and its inhabitants, and levy from the latter the kharaj by virtue of their land, and the capitation [jizya] as a personal tax on every head, this poll tax constituting a fay in favor of the Muslims who have fought there, of their children and of their heirs. Do you think that these borders could remain without warriors to defend them? Do you think that these vast countries, Syria, Mesopotamia, Kufa, Basra, Misr [Egypt] do not have to be covered with troops who must be well paid? Where can one obtain their pay if the land is divided up, as well as its inhabitants?

Umar's decision against the dividing up among the conquerors of the conquered territories, as soon as Allah had shown him the decisive passages of his Holy Book [the Koran] concerning this subject, constituted for him and his work a sign of divine protection and a blessing for all the Muslims. His resolution to levy the kharaj, so that the revenues could be shared among the Muslims was beneficial to all the Community [umma], for had it not been reserved to pay the wages and food of the warriors, the border provinces would never have been populated, the troops would have been deprived of the necessary means to carry on the holy war [jihad], and one would have been afraid that the infidels would return to their former possessions, since these would not have been protected by soldiers and mercenaries. Allah knows best where is the good!

Note

1. Abu Yusuf, *Le livre de l'impot foncier* [*Kitab al-Kharadj*], trans. Edmond Fagnan (Paris: Paul Geuthner, 1921), pp. 40–41, 43; English trans. in Bat Ye'or, *The Decline of Eastern Christianity under Islam* (Cranbury, NJ: Fairleigh Dickinson University Press, 1996), pp. 273–74.

D. ARMENIA (642)[1]

The ravaging army <of Arabs> left Assyria [upper Mesopotamia] and, by way of Dzor [southwest of Lake Van],[2] entered the Taron region, which it seized, as well as the districts of Bezhnunik and Agh'iovit [west of Lake Van]; then, turning toward the valley of Berkri via Ordoru and Kogovit [south of Mount Ararat], it spread out into Ararat.

There would have been no one among the Armenians able to sound the alarm in the [market] town of Dvin, [near modern Yerevan–Erevan], had it not been for three chiefs who had come running up at the time to gather the scattered troops, Theodosius Vahevonni, Katchian Araveghian and Shapuh Amatuni.

They fled in haste towards Dvin. When they reached the bridge of [the] Medzamor [tributary of the Araxes], they destroyed it behind them and managed to impart the sad news of the enemies' approach to the inhabitants: they made all the people of the land, who had come for the wine harvest, go into the fortress. But Theodore <Reshtuni> [Theodore Reshtuni, general-in-chief of Byzantine Armenia. Dismissed by Emperor Constans II (641–668), he went over to the Arab side and was recognized by Mu'awiya as head of Armenia and Georgia up to the region of the Karabagh in the east], for his part, had gone to the town of Nakhidijevan.

When the enemy arrived at the bridge of [the] Medzamor, they could not go across; but as they had Vartig, prince of Mogk [district of Greater Armenia], known as Aghdznik, as their guide, they crossed the bridge, and invaded the whole region. After taking a considerable quantity of booty and captives, they camped at the edge of the forest of Khosrovakert.

On the fifth day [Thursday], they launched an attack on the town of Dvin, and it fell to them; for they had shrouded it in clouds of smoke and, by this means and by arrow shots, they drove back the men who were defending the ramparts. Then, having set up their ladders, they climbed on to the walls, hurled themselves into the square, and opened the gates.

The enemy's army rushed in and butchered the inhabitants of the town by the sword. After gorging itself on booty, it returned to its encampments, outside the town.

After a few days' rest, the Ishmaelites [Arabs] went back whence they had come, dragging after them a host of captives, numbering thirty-five thousand.

Meanwhile, the prince of Armenia, Theodore, ruler of Reshtunik, had laid an ambush with a few men in the district of Kogovit, and pounced on them; but he was beaten and forced to flee. The infidels set off in pursuit of him and killed many of his men; after which they returned to Assyria.

Notes

1. Sepeos [Sebeos], *Histoire d'Heraclius*, trans. Frederic Macler (Paris: Imprimerie National, 1904), pp. 227–28; English trans. in Bat Ye'or, *The Decline of Eastern Christianity under Islam* (Cranbury, NJ: Fairleigh Dickinson University Press, 1996), pp. 274–75.

2. For these events, cf. Ghévond, *Histoire des guerres et des conquêtes des Arabes en Arménie* (Paris: C. Meyrueis, 1856), p. 5.

E. CYPRUS, THE GREEK ISLANDS, AND ANATOLIA (649–654)[1]

Mu'awiya and his suite turned towards constantia, the capital of the whole country. They found it entirely full of people. They established their rule over this town by a great massacre. . . . They collected gold from the whole island, riches and slaves, and they shared out the booty. The Egyptians took one part of it, they took another, and they went back [whence they had come].

But, as the Lord [Almighty] had set his eyes on the island, with a view to laying it to waste, he shortly after urged on Abu l-A'war and his army, which went to Cyprus for a second time, because they had learned that its inhabitants had joined forces. When they arrived, the inhabitants were seized with terror. When the Taiyaye entered, they made the inhabitants come out from the caves and pillaged the whole island. They laid siege to the town of Pathos and reduced it by battle. When the inhabitants asked to negotiate, Abu l-A'war informed them that he would take gold, silver and riches and that he would do no harm to the inhabitant. They opened the town: the Taiyaye collected its riches and returned to Syria.

Then, Mu'awiya laid siege to the town of Arwad which is an island, but he was not able to take it. He sent word to Bishop Thomas that the inhabitants should forsake the town and go in peace. They did not agree; and Mu'awiya returned to Damascus. When the spring came, Mu'awiya returned to the siege of Arwad. Then all the people forsook it and Mu'awiya destroyed it so that it could no longer be inhabited.

Abu l-A'war and his army came down by sea and arrived at the island of Cos. Through the treachery of its bishop, he captured [the island]. He laid waste and pillaged all its riches, slaughtered the population and led the remnant into captivity, and destroyed its citadel. He moved into Crete and pillaged it.

They went to Rhodes, and devastated it in the year 965 [654 CE] of the Greeks.

The seven-year truce that the Romans [Byzantines] had made with the Taiyaye expired in this period. The Taiyaye plundered all the lands of Asia, Bithynia and Pamphylia. There was a serious plague in the lands of Mesopotamia. The Taiyaye pillaged anew and laid waste [to lands] as far a field as Pontus and Galatia.

Note

1. Michael the Syrian, *Chronique*, ed. and trans. Jean-Baptiste Chabot, vol. 2 (Paris, 1899–1905), pp. 442, 450; English trans. in Bat Ye'or, *The Decline of Eastern Christianity under Islam* (Cranbury, NJ: Fairleigh Dickinson University Press, 1996), pp. 275–76.

F. CILICIA AND CESAREA OF CAPPADOCIA (650)[1]

They [the Taiyaye] moved into Cilicia and took prisoners; they came to Euchaita [a town on the river Halys in Armenia] without the population becoming aware of it; they took the ports by surprise, and when Mu'awiya arrived he ordered all the inhabitants to be put to the sword; he placed guards so that no one escaped. After gathering up all the wealth of the town, they set to torturing the leaders to make them show them things [treasures] that had been hidden. The Taiyaye led everyone into slavery—men and women, boys and girls—and they committed much debauchery in that unfortunate town: they wickedly committed immoralities inside churches.

They returned to their country rejoicing.

Mu'awiya, the Taiyaye general, divided his troops into two camps. At the head of one he put Habib [Habib b. Maslama conquered the Armenian regions of Lake Van, Vaspurakan, Siunia, and Georgia), a nasty Syrian, whom he sent to Armenia in the month of Tesrin <October> [the Arabs ravaged Armenia in the course of campaigns that were renewed annually]. When these troops arrived, they found the land filled with snow. Employing a ruse, they brought in oxen which they led before them to clear the road. In this way, they advanced without being impeded by the snow. The Armenians, who had not foreseen this, were attacked when they did not expect it. The Taiyaye embarked on devastation and pillage. They took captive the population, set fire to the villages and returned to their country joyfully.

The other army, which remained with Mu'awiya, advanced into the region of Cesarea of Cappadocia. Passing through Callisura, they found the villages full of men and animals and seized them. After collecting booty from the whole country, Mu'awiya attacked the town. He fought against it for ten days. Then, they totally devastated the whole province, left the town abandoned and withdrew. A few days later, they came back to Cesarea for a second time. They fought against it for many days. The inhabitants of Cesarea, seeing that a great wrath had fallen upon them and that they had no liberator, then agreed to negotiate for their lives. The leaders went out and consented to pay a tribute. When the sons of Hagar [Arabs] entered the town and saw the beauty of the buildings, churches and monasteries, and its great opulence, they regretted their promises to them. But as they could not go back on their pledges, they took everything they wanted and went away to the region of Amorium. When they saw the charms of the region, which was like paradise, they caused no damage, but turned towards the town. After surrounding it, realising that it was impregnable, they suggested to its inhabitants that they negotiate with them and open the town to them. As the latter did not agree, Mu'awiya sent his troops to ravage the countryside: they plundered gold, silver, riches like dust, and returned to their country.

Note

1. Michael the Syrian, *Chronique*, ed. and trans. Jean-Baptiste Chabot, vol. 2 (Paris, 1899–1905), pp. 431, 441; English trans. in Bat Ye'or, *The Decline of Eastern Christianity under Islam*, pp. 276–77.

G. CAPPADOCIA, UNDER THE CALIPHS SULAYMAN AND UMAR II (715–720)[1]

In the year 1028 <716–717 CE>, Maslama crossed into the Roman [Byzantine] Empire [Maslama, son of the caliph Abd al-Malik and half-brother of the ruling caliph, Sulayman. In 715, the Muslims launched raids on Amorium, Cappadocia, and Pergamum. In 717–718, Maslama laid siege to Constantinople]. Countless Arab troops assembled and began to invade the territory of the Romans. All [those from] the lands of Asia and Cappadocia took flight before them, as well as [those from] the whole coastal region.

They made their way to Mount Maurus [the Amanus, north of Antioch] and Lebanon, as far as Melitene, and on the river Arzanius,[2] and as far as the interior of Armenia. All this region was remarkable for the density of its population and the abundance of its vineyards, its cereals and its magnificent trees of every kind. Henceforth, it was laid waste and these lands are no longer inhabited.

In the year 1032 <720–721 CE>, which was the first year of Umar [Umar b. Abd al-Aziz, 717–720. There is a discordance in the dates], king of the Arabs, and the fourth of Leo [III, the Isaurian, 717–741], emperor of the Romans, Maslama left their territory, after having pillaged and devastated all that region which he transformed into an arid desert.

Notes

1. [Pseudo] Dionysius of Tell-Mahre, pp. 12, 14; English trans. in Bat Ye'or, *The Decline of Eastern Christianity under Islam* (Cranbury, NJ: Fairleigh Dickinson University Press, 1996), p. 281.

2. The author does not specify if this is the Arzan that flows into the Tigris or the eastern branch of the Euphrates, both in Armenia. For the topography of Christian Assyria, cf. J.-M. Fiey, *Assyrie Chrétienne* (Beirut, 1965), and Fiey, *Mossoul Chrétinne* (Beirut: Imprimerie Catholique, 1959).

H. SPAIN AND FRANCE (793–860)[1]

In 177 <17 April 793 CE>, Hisham, prince of Spain, sent a large army commanded by Abd al-Malik b. Abd al-Wahid b. Mugith into enemy territory, and which made forays as far as Narbonne and Jaranda <Gerona>. This general first attacked Jaranda where there was an elite Frank garrison; he killed the bravest, destroyed the walls and towers of the town, and almost managed to seize it. He then marched on to Narbonne, where he repeated the same actions, then pushing forward, he trampled underfoot the land of the Cerdagne [district of La Cerdana, region around Puigcerda, near Andorra]. For several months he traversed this land in every direction, raping women, killing warriors, destroying fortresses, burning and pillaging everything, driving back the enemy who fled in disorder. He returned safe and sound, dragging behind him God alone knows how much booty. This is one of the most famous expeditions of the Muslims of Spain.

In 210 <23 April 825>, Abd ar-Rahman b. al-Hakam sent a strong troop of cavalry commanded by Ubayd Allah—known by the name of Ibn al-Balansi—into Frank territory. This officer led razzias in all directions, embarked on murder and pillage, and took prisoners. In Rebi I <June–July 825>, an encounter which took place against the troops of the infidels ended in the rout of the latter, who lost many people; our men won an important victory there.

In 223 <2 December 837>, Abd ar-Rahman b. Al-Hakam, sovereign of Spain, sent an army against Alava; it camped near Hisn al-Gharat, which it besieged; it seized the booty that was found there, killed the inhabitants and withdrew, carrying off women and children as captives.

In 231 <6 September 845>, a Muslim army advanced into Galicia on the territory of the infidels, where it pillaged and massacred everyone. It advanced as far as the town of Leon, which it besieged with catapults. The terrified inhabitants fled, abandoning the town and what it contained, so that the Muslims plundered it as they pleased, then reduced what was left to ruins. But they withdrew without having been able to destroy the walls, because they were seventeen cubits wide, and they could do no more than open many breaches in them.

In 246 <27 March 860>, Muhammad b. Abd ar-Rahman advanced with many troops and a large military apparatus against the region of Pamplona. He reduced, ruined and ravaged this territory, where he pillaged and sowed death.

Note

1. Ibn al-Athir, *Annales du Maghreb et de l'Espagne* [*Al-Kamil fi al-tarikh/Grande Chronique*], trans. Edmond Fagnan (Algiers: Aldolphe Jourdon, 1898), pp. 144, 211, 222, 236; English trans. in Bat Ye'or, *The Decline of Eastern Christianity under Islam* (Cranbury, NJ: Fairleigh Dickinson University Press, 1996), pp. 281–82.

I. ANATOLIA—THE TAKING OF AMORIUM (838)[1]

Thousands of men on both sides died during the three days of battle. Then the king [the caliph al-Mu'tasim 833–842, brother of al Ma'mun 813–833] was shown a cleft in the wall. They concentrated all the ballistas and all the battering rams against that place; when they had assailed that place for two days, they suddenly made a breach in the walls, and a burst of lamentation came from within and a shout <of joy> from without. The many fighters who had been killed were piled up over this breach so that it was filled in with corpses, and the besiegers were not able to enter. Abu Ishaq grew angry; gathering together his Moorish and Turkish slaves, he positioned them in front and his troops behind them: whoever turned his back was killed.

Then the Romans [Byzantines] asked to come and see him, and he consented. The bishop and three notables came forward; they asked him if they could evacuate the town and leave. The king, in his pride, hardened his heart and did not agree. As they returned, one of them, called Bodin, went back to the king and promised to betray the town to him by a ruse. The king accepted with pleasure and gave him ten thousand darics. The traitor gave them this signal: "When you see me standing on the wall, raising my hand and removing my cap from my head, you will know that I have sent the fighters away from the breach, draw near and enter." The bishop, seeing Bodin going back to the king, realized that he intended to betray the town.

When the inhabitants realized that Bodin was letting the Taiyaye enter the town, they took flight, some to the church, crying Kyrie eleison, some into houses, others into cisterns, still others into ditches; the women covered their children, like chickens, so as not to be separated from them, either by the sword or by slavery. The sword of the Taiyaye began the slaughter and heaped them up by piles; when their sword was drunk with blood, the order came to massacre no more, but to take the population captive and to lead it away.

Then they pillaged the town. When the king entered to see the town, he admired the beautiful structure of the temples and palaces. As news came which worried him, he set the town on fire and burned it down. There were so many women's convents and monasteries that over a thousand virgins were led into captivity, not counting those that had been slaughtered. They were given to the Moorish and Turkish slaves, so as to assuage their lust: glory to the incomprehensible judgements <of God!>. They burned all those who were hidden in houses or who had climbed up to the church galleries.

When the booty from the town was collected in one place, the king, seeing that the population was very numerous, gave the order to kill four thousand men. He also gave the order to take away the fabrics and the gold, silver, and bronze objects and the rest of the yield from the pillage. They also began to take away the population: and there was a clamor of lamentation from the women, men, and children, when children were separated and removed from the arms of their parents; they shouted and howled. When the king heard their cries of lamentation and knew their cause, he was angry that they had begun to take the population away without his permission. In his anger, he got on his horse, and he struck and killed with his own hands three men whom he met leading slaves away. He immediately had the population assembled on the place where it was; on his orders, one part was given to the officers of the troop, and one part to the Turks, the king's slaves; and one part was sold to merchants. A family was sold as a whole; and parents were not separated from children.

At this period [841], Theophilus [829–842], emperor of the Romans, sent gifts to Abu Ishaq, king of the Taiyaye, and asked for an exchange of Roman prisoners against the Taiyaye. Abu Ishaq accepted the gifts, sent back even larger ones, and said: "We Arabs cannot agree to compare Muslims with Romans, because God values them more highly than the latter. However, if you return the Taiyaye to me and ask for nothing in exchange, we can return twice as many and outdo you in everything." The envoys returned with fifty camel-loads of princely gifts. And peace between the kings was restored.

Note

1. Michael the Syrian, *Chronique*, ed. and trans. Jean-Baptiste Chabot, vol. 3 (Paris, 1899–1905), pp. 98–100, 102; English trans. in Bat Ye'or, *The Decline of Eastern Christianity under Islam* (Cranbury, NJ: Fairleigh Dickinson University Press, 1996), pp. 282–84.

J. ARMENIA—UNDER THE CALIPH AL-MUTAWAKKIL (847–861)[1]

Provoked by the depredations of tax collectors and religious persecutions, the Armenian nobles rebelled and expelled the emirs of Taron and Vaspurakan. In order to subdue them, the caliph gathered an immense army under the orders of the emir Yusuf.

The following year [851] the monarch, with his counselors and all the grandees of Babylonia [Baghdad], decided and firmly resolved to strip all the Armenian princes of their domains in order, they said, to appropriate their heritage for themselves. It was first necessary to seize Ashot [Ardzruni] and his family, Bagarat [Bagratuni] and his family. They added, "For once these latter are removed, no one would be able to hold his position and stand up against them." At the same time, he assembled troops, formed battalions of horsemen, bold soldiers and captains; he entrusted them to a certain Yusuf, son of Abuseth, and charged him with the command of the country in place of his father, who had died on the road in the lands of Assyria [Iraq], when he was marching towards Armenia in order to punish it according to the agreed plan. "If you succeed," he told him, "in carrying out our plans against Armenia and its princes; if matters are brought to a successful conclusion just as I could wish; and if you are able to let me see the princes of Armenia in irons, particularly Ashot, prince of Vaspurakan, I will give you, you and your son, this land as an inheritance. Hasten, therefore, fly on his tracks, have no hesitation nor weakness nor delay nor tardiness in this matter which is yours."

The general left immediately, committed to the evil designs of his plan. He entered the canton of Aghbak, a province of Vaspurakan, via Atrpatakan, and camped at Adamakert [in the canton of Little Aghbak, on the Greater Zab river], the residence of the Ardzruni. From there he sent his messengers to pillage and gather up, with atrocious cruelty, the takings of his devastations.

He summoned the prince [Ashot] in amicable and peaceful terms, on the pretext of royal taxes; but the latter was advised not to present himself in person, by someone from the army of the Tadjics [Arabs], who disclosed to him the evil intentions formed against him.

Ashot Takes Flight and Sends a Letter to Yusuf

In addition, Ashot's mother, sister of Sahak and Bagarat, prince of Taron, an intelligent woman both in word and deed, as pious as she was prudent, went to Yusuf with many gifts and begged him to establish peaceful good relations with her sons and with the whole land of Vaspuakan. Her gifts were accepted and her request fulfilled; in addition, the emir obtained for himself illustrious and respected hostages. As for Ashot's mother, he sent her away with great honors, and he, himself, quietly crossed Vaspurakan, without causing it great damage, with the hostages in his suite. Crossing the district of Bznunik, he went to Khlath because he wanted to wait for a favorable occasion to attack his quarry by trickery and deceit.

Once he had arrived at Khlath [on Lake Van], the emir entered and camped his troops in the citadel of the town. He sent messengers to Bagarat and an invitation to present himself without fear or delay. His handwritten letter stated that he entrusted him with the affairs of Armenia, so that he himself could return to the court on the pretext of the approach of winter and the bitterness of the winds from the north and the frosts, to which he was not acclimatized.

Bagarat, who had no suspicion of the perfidy of the monarch and his men, with the confidence which unreserved devotion gives, made his arrangements and preparations in accordance with the will of God. To obey the monarch's order, he followed the messengers, without suspecting either a trap or deceit; in this, he was mistaken. He was equipped with the Holy Testaments, divine scriptures, and took with him a host of servants and various members of the clergy. The emir seized him and all his Bagratide relations, loaded them with chains, and, having sent them to Samara [near Baghdad], went in person to spend the winter in Mush, a town in the Taron, taking in his suite the hostages, either grandees of the house of Ardzruni or notables and their dependants. As for the inhabitants, he took them captive in order to sell them in Assyria and in all the places where the Tadjics ruled. Half of them were destined for service in the towns, as water-carriers, woodcutters, subjected to the roughest work during the harsh winter. Those who escaped fled in all directions, their homeland being completely devastated, except for the heights and fortresses of Khouth, occupied by mountain-dwellers.

In order to avenge their prince, the mountain-dwellers assassinated Yusuf (852). The caliph recruited an army of two hundred thousand men from all the provinces of the empire, and placed it under the orders of the Turk Bugha.

At this time Bugha, having divided his troops into two bodies and crossed the land of Apahunik, came and entered the town of Khlath [the Armenian text indicates that Bugha divided his troops after entering Khlath, not before. The translation into English has been made from Brosset's French translation of Ardzruni, with improvements when that text differed from the Armenian original]. He gave the order to enter Vaspurakan, to swamp the region, to carry off from there captives and booty, to empty the densely populated villages and market towns, to drag away all the rest [as] prisoners, women and children, and to load Ashot with irons and bring him to the monarch so that he could be punished for his past deeds and for his revolt against the Tadjics. Having entrusted one part of his troops to a commander called Jirak, he instructed him to move toward Reshtunik [south of Lake Van, in the province of Mogk], and he himself entered the borders of Apahunik with the strongest body, like hunters of lions or of other such species surrounding a shallow ditch, in order to seize in his clutches the powerful Ashot, prince of the bold—while still watching out that he did not slip through their hands and that he did not cause them some terrible disaster by nocturnal attacks. Meanwhile, as the stronghold of Hoghts [in the district Aghdznik—(Greater Armenia), north of Tigris] was massive, Jirak very quickly proceeded to the district of Reshtunik and poured his soldiers into the valley of Arhovank, on the borders of Mogk where was gathered the population of Reshtunik, which fell into the teeth of merciless dogs that tore the men apart, feeding on their corpses: he had them put to the sword and flooded the land with their blood. One part was led into slavery; the dwellings towns and fields were burned, depopulated of men and animals. Having taken the town of [Rhami] Noragiugh, in the district of Reshtunik, they led the people to the market place, cords around their necks, and put them to the sword.

Bugha succeeded in subduing Arab Armenia by a general massacre. The Armenian leaders, after having betrayed one another, were executed or sent with their families to the caliph who forced them to abjure their faith.

Thenceforth all the Armenian grandees began to separate to form different factions and to take refuge in the strongholds and citadels of Vaspurakan, each as fast as he could. The troops scattered, dispersed in the land, in order to fulfil the word [of God]. . . .

The general [Bugha], therefore, saw that everything had succeeded as he had wished; that, according to the intentions of the ungodly king, the wicked plans which they had envisaged for the principality of Vaspurakan had had a favorable outcome. All the valiant men having been eliminated, there was no longer any one in a position to stand up firmly and resist him. The bands of Tadjics and their clans, having followed the trail, began to disperse and spread out over the surface of the land, with unrestrained boldness. They set about dividing up the lands, drawing lots for them among themselves and measuring boundaries with ropes, and settling down peacefully in the strongholds, as they were now absolutely reassured regarding the sides from whence came their anxieties. It was a painful distress for the country such as had never been and would not be seen again. Villages, fields, and market towns turned into deserts, lost their charm and their attractiveness; likewise the various plants and trees covering the land lost their order and alignment. This is the evil, whose invasion the prophet Joel deplored [Joel 2:25]. It seems that the grasshopper, large and small, that the caterpillar and the worm have borne down upon us altogether, that they have swooped down upon the fruit trees, overladen with noxious plants. So it was that the works and possessions of man were lost and annihilated, precisely as it is said in the book of the prophet Joel's vision.

Then, having given the order to sell the captives to whomsoever one wished, Bugha went to the town of Dvin, where his winter quarters were prepared, while waiting for the days of spring. He was overburdened with prisoners, and our land was desolated by his passage and his departure.

When he [Bugha] entered the town with an innumerable quantity of prisoners and captives, he had them sold as slaves to foreign tribes, in order to remove them far from their fathers' houses and their inheritances.

Note

1. Thomas Ardzruni, "Historie des Ardazrouni (X^e siecle)," in *Collection d'Historiens Arméniens*, ed. Marie Felicite Brosset, vol. 1 (Paris: Geuthner, 1874–1876), pp. 102–104, 110, 127–28, 138; English trans. in Bat Ye'or, *The Decline of Eastern Christianity under Islam* (Cranbury, NJ: Fairleigh Dickinson University Press, 1996), pp. 286–89.

K. SICILY AND ITALY (835–851 AND 884)[1]

Another raid directed at Etna and the neighbouring strongholds resulted in the burning of harvests, the slaughter of many men and pillage. Another raid was again organised in the same direction by Abu al-Aghlab in 221 <25 December 835 CE>; the booty brought back was so extensive that slaves were sold for almost nothing. As for those who took part in this expedition, they returned safe and sound. In the same year, a fleet was sent against the <neighbouring> islands; after having taken rich booty and conquered several towns and fortresses there, they returned safe and sound.

In 234 <5 August 848>, the inhabitants of Ragusa made peace with the Muslims in exchange for surrendering the town and what it contained. The conquerors destroyed it after having taken away everything that could be transported.

In 235 <25 July 849>, a troop of Muslims marched against Castrogiovanni and returned safe and sound, after having subjected that town to pillage, murder and fire.

Redjeb 236 <January 851> saw the death of the Muslim emir of Sicily, Muhammad b. Abd Allah b. al-Aghlab, who had wielded power for nineteen years. He resided in Palermo, which he did not leave; he contented himself with sending out troops and columns for there, who served as his instruments of conquest and pillage.

Also, in 271 [884?] a strong Muslim column was directed against Rametta; it wrought great ravages and returned with much booty and many prisoners. As it chanced that the emir of Sicily, al-Husayn b. Ahmad, had died at that time, he was replaced by Sawada b. Muhammad b. Khafadja Temimi. When the latter arrived on the island, he led a strong army against Catania and destroyed everything which was to be found in <the neighbourhood>. He then went on to wage war against the inhabitants of Taormina, and ravaged the crops of the land. He was continuing his advance when a messenger from the Christian patrician came to beg for a truce and an exchange of prisoners. Sawada granted a three-month truce and redeemed three hundred Muslim prisoners, after which he returned to Palermo.

Note

1. Ibn al-Athir, *Annales du Maghreb et de l'Espagne* [*Al-Kamil fi al-tarikh/Grande Chronique*], trans. Edmond Fagnan (Algiers: Aldolphe Jourdon, 1898), pp. 192–93, 217–18, 261; English trans. in Bat Ye'or, *The Decline of Eastern Christianity under Islam* (Cranbury, NJ: Fairleigh Dickinson University Press, 1996), pp. 289–90.

L. JIHAD CAPTURE AND PILLAGE OF THESSALONIKI IN 904 CE[1]

[John Cameniates provided an eyewitness account of these events. Cameniates, his elderly father, and his brother, taken prisoner while they tried to escape by the ramparts, were spared their lives because they promised their captors a large amount of money. They were marched as prisoners through the city, and thus witnessed the terrible carnage of their fellow townspeople who had sough refuge in the church of Saint George. A summary, and excerpts from Cameniates narrative reveals that]:

The Thessalonians tried to escape through the streets, pursued by the Saracens, who were unleashed like wild beasts. In their panic, men, women, the elderly, and children, "fell into each other's arms to give each other one last kiss." The enemy hit with no mercy. Parents were killed while trying to defend their children. No one was spared: women, children, the elderly, all were immediately pierced by the sword. The poor wretches ran through the town, or tried to hide inside the caves; some of them, believing they could find refuge inside a church, would seek shelter inside, while others tried to scale the walls of the ramparts, from where they jumped into the void and crashed to the ground. Nuns, petrified with fear, with their hair disheveled, tried to escape, and ended up by the thousands in the hands of the barbarians, who killed the older ones, and sent the younger and more attractive ones into captivity and dishonor. . . . The Saracens also massacred the unfortunate people who had sought refuge inside churches.

The church [of Saint George] was full of wretches who had sought safety within it. There were about three hundred of them, as we learned later. A great number of murderous enemies came in. Immediately their leader bounced onto the holy altar, where the divine offices are held by the priests: there, crouching down with his legs crossed, in the manner of the barbarians, he sat, full of rage and arrogance, looking at the crowd of those people, full of the evil spirit of what he intended to commit. After grabbing my father and my brother with his hands, and after ordering that we be guarded in an area near the entrance by some of his men whom he had chosen, he gave a sign to his men to do away with the crowd. Like wild wolves when they meet their prey, they began to massacre the poor creatures quickly and mercilessly, and, overflowing with rage, they inquired with their eyes as to what the terrible judge wished to do with us: but he stopped them from doing anything against us, for the moment. . . . After the end of the massacre of those poor people, the entire floor was covered with bodies, with a lake of blood in the middle. Then, as the murderer could not get out, he ordered that they pile up the bodies one on top of the other, on the two sides of the church; then he quickly jumped down from the altar, came up to us, and grabbed my father and my brother with his hands.

Note

1. O. Tafrali, "The Capture and Pillage of Thessaloniki by the Saracens (in the Year 904)," *Thessalonique—Des Origines au XVI Siecle*, chap. 6, pp. 151–54. English translation by Ughetta Lubin.

M. MESOPOTAMIA—CAUSES OF THE INVASIONS BY THE TURKS (ELEVENTH CENTURY)[1]

As the Arabs, that is to say the Taiyaye, grew weaker and as the Greeks [Byzantines] seized many countries, the Taiyaye had to call on the Turks to assist them. They marched with the Arabs as subjects and not as masters.

However, as they acted bravely and gained victories wherever they went, they gradually became accustomed to triumphing. They loaded the riches of the region and carried them off to their land, and showed them to others, urging them to depart with them and go and live in an excellent region, filled with such goods.

Note

1. Michael the Syrian, *Chronique*, ed. and trans. Jean-Baptiste Chabot, vol. 3 (Paris, 1899–1905), pp. 154, 158–60; English trans. in Bat Ye'or, *The Decline of Eastern Christianity under Islam* (Cranbury, NJ: Fairleigh Dickinson University Press, 1996), pp. 290–92.

N. MESOPOTAMIA—PILLAGE OF MELITENE (MALATIA) (1057)[1]

At this same period, the dominion of the Turks began in some regions of Persia. Actually, a sultan called Tughril-Beg [Tughril Beg, 1038–1063, founder of the dynasty of the Seljuks] occupied the throne of the kingdom in the Khurasan, in the year 430 of the Arab empire. He sent troops who reached the regions of the Armenians, who were under the domination of the Romans [Byzantines]. They set about taking prisoners, pillaging, and burning in a barbarous manner. On several occasions they took prisoners and led them away without anyone coming out to meet them. [The Seljuk Turks ravaged Armenia from the beginning of the eleventh century. Here the author is referring to the campaigns of 1048–54.]

They reached the stronghold of Melitene, to the number of three thousand, during the winter of the year 1369 [1057]; and as it did not have a wall, because Cyriacus [the fortifications of Melitene had been destroyed in 934 by Joannes Kurkuas domestikos, and the Armenian leader Mleh] had destroyed it when he had seized it from the Taiyaye, the inhabitants began to flee to the mountain, where they died of cold and hunger. The first day, the Turks began by slaughtering mercilessly; so that many hid themselves under the corpses of those <persons> killed. The Turks set up their camp outside the town on the flank of a hill; none of ,them spent the night outside of the camp and the candles of the churches remained lit throughout the night.

The second day they set to torturing men so that they would show them hidden things [treasures]; and several died in torments; for example, the deacon Petrus, writer and schoolteacher. . . .

The Turks stayed at Melitene for ten days, laying waste and pillaging. Then they set fire to the wretched town, devastated the area within a day's march around and burned the whole land.

During this pillaging, the convent of Bar Gagai [in the area of Melitene] was seized and laid waste. After taking the population away, they departed; they strayed from the road and fell upon difficult mountains and rivers. While they were camping in a valley in the neighborhood of the mountain of the Sinisaya [the inhabitants of Sasun], heavy snow fell which hampered their progress. The Sinisaya having observed this, came down, occupied the roads and paths in front of them on all sides, and they died there of cold and hunger; those who survived were killed by the Sinisaya; none whatsoever escaping. The captive people from Melitene, all those who had escaped death, assisted in the massacre, and those who were hidden in the mountains likewise took part.

The emperor [Michael VI Stratioticus, 1056–1057], seeing that the Turks were moving up and had got as far as the sea of Pontus [the Black Sea], taking captives, pillaging and burning, took pity on the Christian people and sent horses and chariots, and after they had loaded their possessions, took them across the sea. <The Turks> pillaged towns and villages in the whole region of Pontus. As they were empty of inhabitants, this benefited the Turks who found there a place to live. And while everyone blamed the emperor, we for our part say that this came not from him but from above.

Note

1. Michael the Syrian, *Chronique*, ed. and trans. Jean-Baptiste Chabot, vol. 3 (Paris, 1899–1905), pp. 154, 158–60; English trans. in Bat Ye'or, *The Decline of Eastern Christianity under Islam* (Cranbury, NJ: Fairleigh Dickinson University Press, 1996), pp. 290–92.

O. ARMENIA, ANATOLIA, AND GEORGIA (ELEVENTH AND TWELFTH CENTURIES)

Matthew of Edessa

In the beginning of the year 465 [1015–16 CE] a calamity proclaiming the fulfill-ment of divine portents befell the Christian adorers of the Holy Cross. The death-breathing dragon appeared, accompanied by a destroying fire, and struck the believers in the Holy Trinity. The apostolic and prophetic books trembled, for there arrived winged serpents cone to vomit fire upon Christ's faithful. I wish to describe in this language, the first eruption of ferocious beasts covered with blood. At this period there gathered the savage nation of infidels called Turks. Setting out, they entered the province of Vaspuracan and put the Christians to the sword. . . . Facing the enemy, the Armenians saw these strange men, who were armed with bows and had flowing hair like women.[1]

During the year 551 [the date is wrong and could be 511, 1062] of the Armenian era, the Turks under the command of three of Sultan Tughril [Beg]'s generals, called Slar Khorasan, Mdjmdj [Medjmedj] and Isulv, [brought about a torrent of blood on the Christian nation and they] invaded the district of Baghin in the Fourth Armenia and sacked it. From there [like a venomous snake], they moved into the adjacent districts of Thelkhum and Arghni, where they took the Christians by surprise and exterminated them. The massacre began on the 4th of the month of Areg, a Saturday, at the eighth hour of the day [there follows a vivid description of massacre that is not translated by Dulaurier. The translation into English has been made from Dulaurier's French translation, with omissions rein-tegrated in square brackets].[2]

Everywhere throughout the Cilicia, up to Taurus, Marash, and Deluh and the environs, reigned agitation and trouble. For populations were precipitated into these regions en masse, coming by the thousands and crowding into them. They were like locusts, covering the surface of the land. They were more numerous, I might add seven times more numerous, than the people whom Moses led across the Red Sea; more numerous than the pebbles in the desert of Sinai. The land was inundated by these multitudes of people. Illustrious personages, nobles, chiefs, women of posi-tion, wandered in begging their bread. Our eyes witnessed this sad spectacle.[3]

Toward the beginning of the year 528 [1079–80] famine desolated . . . the lands of the worshippers of the Cross, already ravaged by the ferocious and san-guinary Turkish hordes. Not one province remained protected from their devasta-tions. Everywhere the Christians had been delivered to the sword or into bondage, interrupting thus the cultivation of the fields, so that bread was lacking. The farmers and workers has been massacred or lead off into slavery, and famine extended its rigors to all places. Many provinces were depopulated; the Oriental nation [Armenians] no longer existed, and the land of the Greeks was in ruins. Nowhere was one able to procure bread.[4]

Samuel of Ani—The Taking of Ani by Seljuk Sultan Alp Arslan (1064)

In 513 of the Armenian era [1064], at the time of the festival of the Virgin, on a Monday, the town of Ani was taken by the Sultan Alp Arslan [1063–73], who massacred its inhabitants, apart from the women and children whom he led into captivity. . . .[5]

Anna Comnena

And since the succession of Diogenes the barbarians tread upon the boundaries of the empire of the Rhomaioi . . . the barbarian hand was not restricted until the reign of my father. Swords and spears were whetted against the Christians, and also battles, wars, and massacres. Cities were obliterated, lands were plundered, and the whole land of the Rhomaioi was stained by blood of Christians. Some fell piteously [the victims] of arrows and spears, other being driven away from their homes were carried off captive to the cities of Persia. Terror reigned over all and they hastened to hide in the caves, forests, mountains, and hills. Among them some cried aloud in horror at those things which they suffered, being led off to Persia; and others who yet survived (if some did remain within the Rhomaic boundaries), lamenting, cried, the one for his son, the other for his daughter. One bewailed his brother, another his cousin who had died previously, and like women shed hot tears. And there was at that time not one relationship which was without tears and without sadness.[6]

Georgian Chronicler

The emirs spread out, like locusts, over the face of the land. . . . The countries of Asis-Phorni, Clardjeth, up to the shores of the sea, Chawcheth, Adchara, Samtzkhe, Karthli, Argoueth, Samokalako, and Dchqondid were filled with Turks, who pillaged and enslaved all the inhabitants.

In a single day they burned Kouthathis, Artanoudj, the hermitages of Clardjeth, and they remained in these lands until the first snows, devouring the land, massacring all those who had fled to the forests, to the rocks, to the caves. . . .

The calamities of Christianity did not come to and end soon thereafter, for the approach of spring, the Turks returned to carry out the same ravages and left [again] in the winter. The [inhabitants] however were unable to plant or to harvest. The land, [thus] delivered to slavery, had only animals of the forests and wild beasts for inhabitants. Karthli was in the grip of intolerable calamities such as one cannot compare to a single devastation or combination of evils of past times. The holy churches served as stables for their horses, the sanctuaries of the Lord served as repairs for the abominations [Islam]. Some of the priests were immolated during the Holy Communion itself, and others were carried off into harsh slavery without regard to their old age. The virgins were defiled, the youths circumcised, and the infants taken away. The conflagration, expending its ravages, consumed all the inhabited sites, the rivers, instead of water, flowed blood. I shall apply the sad words of Jeremiah, which he applied so well to such situations: "The honorable children of Zion, never put to the test by misfortunes, now voyaged as slaves on foreign roads. The streets of Zion now wept because there was no one [left] to celebrate the feasts. The tender mothers, in place of preparing with their hands the nourishment of the sons, were themselves nourished from the corpses of these dearly loved. Such and worse was the situation at that time . . ."

As Isaiah said: "Your land is devastated, your cities reduced to ashes, and foreigners have devoured your provinces, which are sacked and ruined by barbarian nations."[7]

Notes

1. Matthew of Edessa, from Edouard Dulaurier, *Recherches sur la Chronologie Arménienne, Technique et Historique. Ouvrage formant les Prolégomènes de la Collection Intitulée Bibliotheque Historique Arménienne*, vol. 1 (Paris: Imprimerie Imperiale, 1859), pp. 40–41; English trans. in Speros Vryonis Jr., *The Decline of Medieval Hellenism in Asia Minor and the Process of Islamization from the 11th through the 15th Century* (Berkeley and Los Angeles: University of California Press, 1971), pp. 80–81.

2. Matthew of Edessa, from Edouard Dulaurier, *Recherches sur la Chronologie Arménienne*, vol. 1, p. 296; English trans. in Bat Ye'or, *The Decline of Eastern Christianity under Islam* (Cranbury, NJ: Fairleigh Dickinson University Press, 1996), p. 292.

3. Matthew of Edessa, English trans. in Vryonis, *Decline of Medieval Hellenism in Asia Minor*, p. 170.

4. Ibid., pp. 181–82.

5. Samuel of Ani, "Tables Chronologiques," in *Collection d'Historiens Arméniens*, ed. Marie Felicite Brosset, vol. 2 (Paris: Geuthner, 1874–1876), p. 297; English trans. in Bat Ye'or, *Decline of Eastern Christianity under Islam*, p. 292.

6. Anna Comnèna, *Anne Comnène. Alexiade, text établi et traduit*, vol. 3 (Paris: B. Leib, 1937–1945), p. 229; English trans. in Vryonis, *Decline of Medieval Hellenism in Asia Minor*, p. 164.

7. Marie Brosset, *Histoire de la Géorgie*, vol. 1 (St. Petersburg: Impr. de l'Académie impériale des sciences, se vend chez W. Eggers et comp., 1849), pp. 346–50; English trans. in Speros Vryonis Jr., "Nomadization and Islamization in Asia Minor," *Dumbarton Oaks Papers* 29 (1975): 50–51. Vryonis comments further, regarding the pattern of depredations by the nomadic Turks,

In the spring they began to ascend the mountains of Somkheth and Ararat, where they again found the necessary pasturage and relief from the heat. But at no time did they cease to raid and devastate the adjoining territories of their Christian neighbors for booty and prisoners. (p. 51)

P. SYRIA AND PALESTINE (ELEVENTH CENTURY)[1]

As the Turks were ruling the lands of Syria and Palestine, they inflicted injuries on Christians who went to pray in Jerusalem, beat them, pillaged them, levied the poll tax at the gate of the town and also at Golgotha and the [Holy] Sepulchre; and in addition, every time they saw a caravan of Christians, particularly of those <who were coming> from Rome and the lands of Italy, they made every effort to cause their death in diverse ways. And when countless people had perished as a result, the kings and counts were seized with [religious] zeal and left Rome; troops from all these countries joined them, and they came by sea to Constantinople [First Crusade (1096–1099)].

Note

1. Michael the Syrian, *Chronique*, ed. and trans. Jean-Baptiste Chabot, vol. 3 (Paris, 1899–1905), p. 182; English trans. in Bat Ye'or, *The Decline of Eastern Christianity under Islam* (Cranbury, NJ: Fairleigh Dickinson University Press, 1996), pp. 292–93.

Q. JIHAD DESTRUCTION OF EDESSA IN 1144–1146 CE

[Professor J. B. Segal reviewed[1] the destruction of the Christian enclave of Edessa in 1144–1146 CE, during the Crusades, using primary source documentation, including a contemporary account by Michael the Syrian]:

Thirty thousand souls were killed. Women, youths, and children to the number of sixteen thousand were carried into slavery, stripped of their cloths, barefoot, their hands bound, forced to run beside their captors on horses. Those who could not endure were pierced by lances or arrows, or abandoned to wild animals and birds of prey. Priests were killed out of hand or captured; few escaped. The Archbishop of the Armenians was sold at Aleppo. . . . The whole city was given over to looting, "for a whole year," resulting in "complete ruin." From this disaster the Christian community of Edessa never recovered.

[Michael the Syrian (Patriarch of Antioch from 1166–1199) chronicled[2] the two devastating jihad attacks (1144 and 1146 CE) by the Seljuk Turks, which included the mass murder of noncombatants, as follows]:

The Turks entered with their swords and blades drawn, drinking the blood of the old and the young, the men and the women, the priests and the deacons, the hermits and the monks, the nuns, the virgins, the infants at the breast, the betrothed men and the women to whom they were betrothed! . . . Ah! what a bitter tale! The city of Abgar, the friend of Christ, was trampled underfoot because of our iniquity: the priests were massacred, the deacons immolated, the subdeacons crushed, the temples pillaged, the altars overturned! Alas! what a calamity! Fathers denied their children; the mother forgot her affection for her little ones! While the sword was devouring and everyone was fleeing to the mountaintop, some gathered their children, like a hen her chicks, and waited to die together by the sword or else to be led off together into captivity! Some aged priests, who were carrying the relics of the martyrs, seeing this raging destruction, recited the words of the prophet: "I will endure the Lord's wrath, because I have sinned against Him and angered Him." And they did not take flight, nor did they cease praying until the sword rendered them mute. Then they were found at the same spot, their blood spilled all around them. . . .

The Turks descended from the citadel upon those who had remained in the churches or in other places, whether because of old age, or as a result of some other infirmity, and they tortured them, showing no pity. Those who had escaped from being suffocated or trampled [in the crush] and had left the city with the Franks were surrounded by the Turks, who rained down upon them a hail of arrows which cruelly pierced them through. O cloud of wrath and day without mercy! In which the scourge of violent wrath once again struck the unfortunate Edessenians. O night of death, morning of hell, day of perdition! which arose against the citizens of that excellent city. Alas, my brethren! Who could recount or hear without tears how the mother and the infant that she carried in her arms were pierced through by the same arrow, without anyone to lift them up or to remove the arrow! And soon, [as they lay] in that state, the hooves of the horses of those who were pursuing them pounded them furiously! That whole night they had been pierced by arrows, and at daybreak, which was for them even darker, they were struck by the swords and the lances! . . . And then the earth shivered with horror at the massacre that took place: like the sickle on the stalks of grain, or like fire among wood chips, the sword carried off the Christians. The corpses of priests, deacons, monks, noblemen and the poor were abandoned pell-mell. Yet, although their death was cruel, they nevertheless did not have as much to suffer as those who remained alive; for when the latter fell in the midst of the fire and the wrath of the Turks, [those barbarians] stripped them of their clothing and of their footwear. Striking them with rods, they forced them—men and women, naked and with their hands tied behind their backs—to run with the horses; those perverts pierced the belly of anyone who grew faint and fell to the ground, and left him to die along the road. And so they became the prey of wild beasts, and then they expired, or else the food of birds of prey, in which case they were tortured. The air was poisoned with the stench of the corpses; Assyria was filled with captives.

Notes

1. J. B. Segal, *Edessa—The Blessed City* (Oxford: Clarendon Press, 1970), pp. 252–54.
2. Michael the Syrian, *Chronique*, ed. and trans. Jean-Baptiste Chabot, vol. 3 (Paris, 1899–1905), pp. 261–62, 270–71; English trans. Michael J. Miller.

R. JIHAD IN NORTH AFRICA AND SPAIN UNDER THE ALMOHADS (MID-TWELFTH CENTURY)

[Professor H. Z. Hirschberg[1] includes this summary of a contemporary Judeo-Arabic account by Solomon Cohen (which comports with Arab historian Ibn Baydhaq's sequence of events), from January 1148 CE, describing the Muslim Almohad conquests in North Africa, and Spain]:

Abd al-Mumin . . . the leader of the Almohads after the death of Muhammad Ibn Tumart[2] the Mahdi . . . captured Tlemcen [in the Maghreb] and killed all those who were in it, including the Jews, except those who embraced Islam. . . . [In Sijilmasa] One hundred and fifty persons were killed for clinging to their [Jewish] faith. . . . All the cities in the Almoravid [dynastic rulers of North Africa and Spain prior to the Almohads] state were conquered by the Almohads. One hundred thousand persons were killed in Fez on that occasion, and 120,000 in Marrakesh. The Jews in all [Maghreb] localities [conquered] . . . groaned under the heavy yoke of the Almohads; many had been killed, many others converted; none were able to appear in public as Jews. . . . Large areas between Seville and Tortosa [in Spain] had likewise fallen into Almohad hands.

Notes

1. H. Z. Hirschberg, *A History of the Jews of North Africa*, vol. 1 (Leiden: Brill, 1974), pp. 127–28.
2. Spiritual leader of the Muslim Almohads.

S. JIHAD CONQUEST OF THESSALONIKI (1430 CE)

Vryonis, in his discussion of the jihad conquest of Thessaloniki in 1430.[1] compiled extensive excerpts from the key primary sources—the (Greek Christian) *Diegesis*, and corroborating Ottoman chronicles by Orudj, Ashikpashazade, and Neshri. He highlights the major points of agreement between the sources, and then offers his own conclusions:

[T]he fact that the sultan gave the order to sack the city; that there was widespread enslavement and rich booty; that the city and its houses remained empty; that the sultan reconstituted it . . . that the Turks of Yenitse were settled there; that henceforth the newly settled city had an Islamic aspect. Thus the Turkish sources though not detailed, and though they are not sensitive to the nuances are nevertheless in overall agreement with the *Diegesis*.[2]

The conquest was brutal and left Thessaloniki completely depopulated, partially destroyed, and thoroughly looted. The estimates are that 7,000 were enslaved, possibly 6,000 were slain, and the looting was such that it went beyond moveable property to the dismantling of real property as well. All the city was claimed by the sultan as *khass*.[3]

Summary of the Ottoman Sources (by Vryonis)

Orudj states that the city was sacked and that the Turkish soldiers became very rich from the plundered wealth. Ashikpashazade has a somewhat longer account, mentioning the mustering of the army at Serez, the canons, and siege machines. He asserts that as the siege took many days, Ali Beg the son of Evrenos advised Murad that such a city could only be taken if the sultan allowed it to be plundered. Thus the sultan proclaimed that the army could plunder the city. At that point the ghazis brought ladder to the walls allowing the defenders no respite, and captured the city. They took much booty and many prisoners. As the houses of the city remained empty those who wished to stay there were allowed to have these houses without paying for them. The sultan then brought the inhabitants of Vardar Yenichesi into the city which now was transformed from a domain of idolaters to a domain of Islam. After the newly won city was put in order, Murad addressed the ghazis telling them what a fortunate thing the plundering of a city was and also the conversion of the idolaters to Islam by the sword.

The late sixteenth century *munsheatdji* of the sultan's court, Feridun, includes in his collection of documents one which purports to be a *fetihname* sent by Murad II to the sultan of Egypt announcing the conquest of the city of Thessaloniki. In it Murad is quoted as having informed the Mamluk ruler:

> The warriors returned with all the booty and they shattered their idols and crosses, laid waste their houses and palaces, and enslaved their women, girls, and makes. They made of their churches *djamiis* and *masdjids* and we proclaimed in them the ceremonies of Islam and we recited.

From the Diegesis, with Commentary by Vryonis

[In chapter four of the Diegesis *the Thessalonians receive the first report that the Turks are advancing, and the author takes chapters five and six to put the Turks in situ outside the city's walls before Murad unleashes his attack in chapter seven.*

This first report arrived at just that time when the Thessalonians, still shocked at having lost the metropolitan Symeon, were unhappy by reason of the fact that it was not possible for them to surrender the city to the Turks so as to avoid the sort of thing that actually did happen after the capture. That is to say they wished to avoid mass enslavement and destruction.—Vryonis⁴]

And the Turks advanced, like a swarm of bees, thirsting for our blood and striving wholly to devour all of us. Having approached the city and having set their tents as is the custom, they surrounded the city in the manner of a fortress, so that there was hardly visible a region empty of men. . . . At the beginning of the fourth day, before the sun had dawned clearly, we observe(d) according to the previous report, the entire multitude advancing toward the wall, some bearing ladders, others planks, still others "shields" woven from branches all armored simply, bearing siege machines, as is customary, frenzied by the desire for our destruction and urging one another on to our slaughter.⁵

[On the third hour of the fourth day, March 29, 1430, the Turks overcame the few defenders who by now had been largely killed and wounded, or were completely fatigued by the three days of exertion, and some of whom had previously abandoned the walls when the Venetians archers had been removed.—Vryonis⁶]

They raced into the city, swords in hands, one outracing another, as though competing who would first reach the inhabited portion of the city and particularly the section along the sea, for they thought most had fled there, especially the Latins because of their galleys. Accordingly all of us, as quickly as each one of us was able, rushed some to our houses, others fled to the holy churches, and others of us struggled fearfully to go underground in sewers and graves or in whatever might be convenient to our salvation, others in great fear reached other ships. . . . As the enemies entered the city, via the leaders and breaches as we have already said, some ran toward the houses and the people, others spread out to the gates of the city so that Murad could enter the city with the entire army. You saw them entering like bees or wild animals, howling and breathing out our murder, and they went through the city on foot or horseback. As the city and everything (else) were full of Turks, that is holy churches, divine monasteries, streets, and houses, then it was that there was perpetrated an affair worthy of many laments and tears. When they had entered the city, as we mentioned, and had attacked us like oppressive wolves, they hastened to plunder everything according to the promise of the ruler. For he had said during the fighting that if the city should be captured and his wish be brought to pass, every (soldier) should possess fully whatever he might take and that it would be inalienable from the side of anyone else. They were dragging off together, men, women, children of all age, fettered, like senseless animals, and they led them all off to the camp outside the city. I pass over in silence those who fell, who were not beyond numbers along the walls and streets, who had not been given burial, "lying about as prey for dogs and all birds," according to Homer, not only men but women as well and of these the oldest and the sickest. Each one of the enemy was hastening, by dint of the multitude of those whom he held, to lead them out hurriedly and to turn them over to his colleagues in the tents, lest this gain become the profit of someone stronger. Whence if he saw someone of the captives not able to keep up with the others because of old age or illness, he cut off his head reckoning this as but a small loss. Then for the first time were miserably separated children from parents, women from husbands, friends from friends, and blood relatives. We entertained the thought, incorrectly, that we would perish. The city was thrown into confusion, and a combined cry arose from all, and everything was filled with noises and moans. There were those who were leading off the unfortunate in chains, while others were pouring in, hastening to seize those who had previously escaped them. However the spoils did not fall equally to all of them. For so great was their number that a section of them (the Turks) *emptied the city of people* and their wealth and particularly that section (of the Turks) which had entered the city on foot by use of the ladders.[7]

[In chapter 21, the author of the Diegesis goes on to lament the final fate and shape of the city of Thessaloniki.—Vryonis[8]]

As affairs took this course, and as the Turks, to the number of 1,000 reached the city and they all took houses and churches as houses, and as they took up their dwelling in a mixed fashion throughout the city, the city garbed itself in disorder as though it were a garment of lamentation. It was deprived of its dignity which it would have had if the evil counsel had not taken place, and it removed its adornment in which it did not rejoice long, and it now moaned, as though in lamentation that an earthquake did not bury it or that fire did not consume it or that water . . . did not cover and flood it. It would have been better that it had never existed on the face of the earth than that it would be seen thus. Some of the hold houses were transformed, as we said, into common houses, and to speak in the manner of the prophet. "They destroyed the altars of God with axe and pick." Others retain only the traces of their former beauty and of their location. Some others, indeed most of them, have collapsed entirely so that it is not even possible to recognize where they once were. Their building materials were plundered and were incorporated into other newer buildings, and especially into the public bath house which is to be seen in the middle of the city. And one can hear only from the more aged people that such and such a church was here, another one was there, and what the beauty and charms of each of these churches had been. And this was the fate of the churches and monasteries throughout the city . . . (and are now) the cause of lamentation to those who contemplate them, not only because they are devoid of monks, who were evilly driven out and who have settled in other cities, but also because they have deprived them of all their beauty. They stripped them of their marbles, and all other materials which had been added originally for their building and beauty, were delivered up to the rapacity of whomsoever desired them.[9]

Notes

1. Speros Vryonis Jr., "The Ottoman Conquest of Thessaloniki in 1430," in *Continuity and Change in Late Byzantine and Early Ottoman Society—Papers Given at a Symposium in Dumbarton Oaks in May 1982*, ed. Anthony Bryer and Heath Lowry (Washington, DC: Dumbarton Oakes, Research Library and Collection, 1986), pp. 281–321.

2. Ibid., p. 312.

3. Ibid., p. 320; *khass* meaning "pertaining or belonging to the (Ottoman) state or ruler."

4. Ibid., p. 289.

5. Ibid., pp. 290, 292.

6. Ibid., p. 293.

7. Ibid., pp. 293–94.

8. Ibid., p. 298.

9. Ibid., p. 299.

T. JIHAD CONQUEST OF CONSTANTINOPLE (1453 CE)

[Both Turkish and Christian chroniclers provide graphic evidence of the wanton pillage and slaughter of noncombatants following the Ottoman jihad conquest of Constantinople in 1453. First from the Turkish sources]:

Sultan Mehmed (in order to) arouse greater zeal for the way of God issued an order (that the city was to be) plundered. And from all directions they (gazis) came forcefully and violently (to join) the army. They entered the city, they passed the infidels over the sword (i.e., slew them) and . . . they pillage and looted, they took captive the youths and maidens, and they took their goods and valuables whatever there was of them. . . ." [Urudj][1]

The gazis entered the city, cut off the head of the emperor, captured Kyr Loukas and his family . . . and they slew the miserable common people. They placed people and families in chains and placed metal rings on their necks." [Neshri][2]

[Speros Vryonis Jr. has summarized the key contents of letters sent by Sultan Mehmed himself to various Muslim potentates of the Near East]:

In his letter to the sultan of Egypt, Mehmed writes that his army killed many of the inhabitants, enslaved many others (those that remained), plundered the treasures of the city, "cleaned out" the priests and took over the churches. . . . To the Sherif of Mecca he writes that they killed the ruler of Constantinople, they killed the "pagan" inhabitants and destroyed their houses. The soldiers smashed the crosses, looted the wealth and properties and enslaved their children and youths. "They cleared these places of their monkish filth and Christian impurity." . . . In yet another letter he informs Cihan Shah Mirza of Iran that the inhabitants of the city have become food for the swords and arrows of the gazis; that they plundered their children, possessions and houses; that those men and women who survived the massacre were thrown into chains.[3]

[The Christian sources, include this narrative by Ducas, who gathered eyewitness accounts, and visited Constantinople shortly after its conquest]:

(Then) the Turks arrived at the church [the great church of St. Sophia], pillaging, slaughtering, and enslaving. They enslaved all those that survived. They smashed the icons in the church, took their adornments as well as all that was moveable in the church. . . . Those of (the Greeks) who went off to their houses were captured before arriving there. Others upon reaching their houses found them empty of children, wives, and possessions and before (they began) wailing and weeping were themselves bound with their hands behind them. Others coming to their houses and having found their wife and children being led off, were tied and bound with their most beloved. . . . They (the Turks) slew mercilessly all the elderly, both men and women, in (their) homes, who were not able to leave their homes because of illness or old age. The newborn infants were thrown into the streets. . . . And as many of the (Greek) aristocrats and nobles of the officials of the palace that he (Mehmed) ransomed, sending them all to the "speculatora" he executed them. He selected their wives and children, the beautiful daughters and shapely youths and turned them over to the head eunuch to guard them, and the remaining captives he turned over to others to guard over them. . . . And the entire city was to be seen in the tents of the army, and the city lay deserted, naked, mute, having neither form nor beauty.[4]

[From the contemporary fifteenth-century historian Critobulus of Imbros]:

Then a great slaughter occurred of those who happened to be there: some of them were on the streets, for they had already left the houses and were running toward the tumult when they fell unexpectedly on the swords of the soldiers; others were in their own homes and fell victims to the violence of the Janissaries and other soldiers, without any rhyme or reason; others were resisting relying on their own courage; still others were fleeing to the churches and making supplication—men, women, and children, everyone, for there was no quarter given. . . . The soldiers fell on them with anger and great wrath. . . . Now in general they killed so as to frighten all the City, and terrorize and enslave all by the slaughter.[5]

Notes

1. English trans. from Speros Vryonis Jr., "A Critical Analysis of Stanford J. Shaw's *History of the Ottoman Empire and Modern Turkey*, vol. 1: *Empire of the Gazis: The Rise and Decline of the Ottoman Empire, 1280–1808,*" *Balkan Studies* 24 (1983): 57–58.
2. Ibid., pp. 58–59.
3. Ibid., p. 59.
4. Ibid., pp. 60, 62.
5. Ibid., p. 68.

U. JIHAD CONQUEST OF METHONE (GREECE) (1499)[1]

And Bayezid [II, Ottoman Sultan], as I have mentioned, went to the city Methone, which belonged to the Venetians also, and besieged it day and night with cannons and mortars. Mortars are short cannons with wide mouths into which they place gunpowder and bullets; they are positioned upright so that their bullets shoot up high; on the way down, they destroy houses, human beings, and everything that they happen to encounter. He attacked the city with all sorts of weapons and bolts, while the janissaries employed fire arms. But the walls of Methone are high and strong; furthermore, there were many defenders inside and he proved unable to seize it; so he wished to depart and move on. But sin intervened and three Venetian galleys arrived in the harbor of the city with provisions, I mean biscuits, flour, wine, gunpowder, and other materials necessary for the defense of the city. When the inhabitants of Methone, men, women, and children, saw the galleys, they abandoned the walls that they were guarding and, with joy, they rushed to the shore in order to unload the provisions. It was early in the morning when the galleys came. The Turks, who were outside the walls, saw that the walls were deserted, with no people; within the hour they placed ladders and big wedges against the lowest, weakest spots of the walls and began to climb. The janissaries were the first; they held small standards which they erected all around the fortifications. The pitiable inhabitants of Methone, who had gathered at the harbor, did not know that the janissaries had scaled the walls and entered the city and that they had erected their standards. Suddenly they heard the war cry that they raised and the Methonians rushed back with their weapons. On their way they encountered the multitude of the Turks; they [the Turks] routed them and seized women and children. They [the Turks] slaughtered the pitiable inhabitants of Methone and also bound some of them; they were bound and dragged, as if they were sheep. In order to force the Turks out, the Methonians started fires in many parts of the city.

But they [the Turks] displayed fear neither for fire nor for other weapons. Thus houses, workshops, and churches burned down. The Turks took possession of this city and included it within their borders.[2] Then Sultan Bayezid came inside; he entered and prayed in the Frankish church which he converted into a mosque, as it remains to the present day. They butchered the pitiable Christians. They say that the slaughter was so great that blood ran to the sea and stained it red. From there, after Bayezid had prayed, he went to the lord's palace and established himself with great glory and in joyful shouting. He ordered all Methonians captured alive, young and old, to be brought before him. He ordered the execution of all those who were ten years or older; and so it happened. They gathered their heads and bodies, put them together, and built a big tower outside the city, which can still be seen nowadays. This happened in 1499.[3]

Notes

1. Marios Philippides, trans., *Byzantium, Europe, and the Early Ottoman Sultans, 1373–1513: An Anonymous Greek Chronicle of the Seventeenth Century (Codex Barberinus Graecus 111)* (New Rochelle, NY: A. D. Caratzas, 1990), pp. 101–102, 189–90 [i.e., text for notes 2–3, below].

2. After the surrender of Naupaktos, Rhion, and Antirrhion, the two forts guarding the entrance of the Gulf of Corinth fell to the Turks within three months. Thus by 1500 control of the Gulf had passed into the hands of Bayezid II; the invasion of the Morea then began. First he attacked Nauplion but he failed to scale its fortifications. Then he moved to the southern regions and invested Methone. The population of this city had been reinforced with waves of refugees from the previous Ottoman invasions of the Morea. Methone was surrounded by formidable fortifications and had been prepared for the siege. Most of the women had already been sent to Crete while five hundred artillery pieces had been deployed on the walls. After one month, four Corfiot vessels came to the harbor. While the inhabitants were at the port, Bayezid II launched his main assault. No mercy was shown to the survivors, after intense fighting in the streets. The Catholic bishop of Methone was slain and large numbers of inhabitants were sold into slavery throughout the Ottoman Empire. Methone fell on August 9, 1500; thus ended three centuries of Venetian rule.

3. The fall of Methone precipitated the surrender of Korone and of Navarino. As soon as Contarini, Navcarino's commander, discovered that Methone had fallen, he surrendered his city, despite the fact that he commanded a strong garrison. The authorities of Korone decided to resist but they were overruled by the inhabitants who had been terrified by the fate of Methone's citizens. At Korone the sultan prayed in the cathedral, which was thus turned into a mosque. The lives of the inhabitants were spared but they were sent to exile. Korone and Methone were then assigned to Mecca, which enjoyed their revenues.

V. JIHAD CAMPAIGNS IN GEORGIA OF SAFAVID RULER SHAH TAHMASP (D. 1576) (1540, 1546, 1551, AND 1553 CE)[1]

First Expedition of the Shah against Georgia (1540 CE)

This year [1540] the Shah went against the Georgians—hunting on the way to Bargshat and being joined by Chiefs and their forces from all parts. One night the Muslim army poured upon Tiflis, and plundered the city, and took captive women and children. Gulbad the Georgian, one of the chief nobles of Lawasan, took refuge in the Tiflis court, asking for quarter. And he surrendered the fort, and became a Muslim. The Ghazis raided the country. Hish, who was one of the greatest chiefs of Lawasan, threw himself into the fort of Birtis; but the Gabrs [infidels, in this case, Christians][2] surrendered it, and those who accepted Islam were spared, and the rest were slaughtered. Then the army marched against the mountains of Didku and Georgia, which they took, killing a number of the enemy in the passes of the hills; and the rest were scattered. Then the Shah went to the Kur river, and Lawasan, the Ruler of that land, fled to the hills and forests, and escaped. And the Shah returned to Tabriz.

Second Expedition of the Shah against Georgia (1546 CE)

[T]he Shah set out for Georgia with a large army, passed Shura-i-gil, and reached Aq Shahr. There, at a time of great cold, he made a night attack on the Gabrs, and covered the snow with their blood, and captured oxen and sheep, and burnt houses.

Third Expedition of the Shah against Georgia (1551 CE)

[T]he Shah marched with speed from Shaki, and the Ghazis surrounded the hills and dales of the infidels, and leveled every place of refuge, nor did any escape. And the families and possessions of those polytheists were transferred to their slayers, as their lawful heirs. And the young women were taken captive. Then some took refuge in the hills, and in caves, and others in the forts of Malinkot, Arqaru, Darzabad, and in a wondrous church. And the Muslims slew many, and took the fort of Tumuk, and the other forts . . . the Shah ordered Badr Khan Ustajlu and Ali Sultan Takalu to attack the fort (of Darzabad), which therefore they surrounded. Now it was on a height, near the gate of Tumuk and the source of the river Kur, and in strength it was like the wall of Alexander and the castle of Khaybar. In the middle of the fort they had hollowed out a place ten cubits high, and made a church of four rooms, and a long bench, and had painted its walls without and within with gold and lapis lazuli and pictures of idols, and arranged a throne in the second room, and an idol gilt and covered with precious stones, and with two rubies for the eyes of the lifeless form, and within the church was a narrow way one hundred fifty cubits long to go up, cut into the solid rock. And they had two hidden kiosks for use in times of trouble, and there were doors of iron and steel in the outer rooms, and a golden door in the inner ones. Then the Ghazis fell upon that place, and climbed above the fort, and slew the men, and took captive their wives and children. And the Shah and his nobles went to see the church, and they slew twenty evil priests, and broke the bell of seventeen maunds weight seven times cast, and destroyed the doors of iron and gold and sent them to the treasury. And Badr Khan Ustalju broke four candles, each being sixty maunds of wax. Thus the Shah got great booty; and in it were two rubies being the eyes of the idol, each worth fifty tumans. And they leveled the fort with the ground, so the Georgian Chiefs could go to no other place . . . and the Shah put to death Wakhush and Shir Mazan Ughali, who were Governors of that country.

Fourth Expedition of the Shah against Georgia (1553 CE)

At this time it was reported that the Gabrs were rebelling. So therefore the Shah set out to destroy the land of the infidels. And all that country was forest. So that the wind could not blow through the trees. And the infidels scattered, and Lawasan, the son of Daud, the Governor of the land, fled to a place of refuge. And the Georgians, being sore afraid, escaped to the hills and caves and forests, and were besieged in forts. And the Ghazis slew the men, and took capture their wives and children, and took booty, of cattle and sheep. Then the army marched on Gori, the capital of Lawasan, and plundered that land, and took prisoner fair young women and round-faced boys. Then they reached the fort of Mazrut, which never yet had been conquered by the Muslims. And the troops surrounded it, and the Kotwal Parsatan was dismayed, and left the fort, and yielded it up. Then the Shah set out for the fort of Aydin . . . and Lawasan had left his mother there. The Persians fell upon the defenders, and destroyed them with cannon and mines, and assaulted and entered the fort and captured the mother of Lawasan and most of the (defenders). Then the Shah was told that there was a fort hard by, where the Georgians had taken refuge. Shah Virdi Sultan Ziyad Ughali was appointed to take that fort. And he did so; and returned to camp. The army took many forts, and many prisoners, even more than thirty thousand, and much booty; and came to Barda. Then proclamations were sent around Persia with the glad tidings.

Notes

1. C. N. Seddon, trans., *A Chronicle of the Early Safawis—Being the Ahsanu't-Tawarikh of Hasan-I-Rumlu*, vol. 2 (Baroda: Oriental Institute, 1934), pp. 135, 143, 159, 168–69.

2. Seddon includes this note, stating (according to Gibbon): "'Gabour is no more than

Gheber, which was transferred from Persian to the Turkish language, from the worshippers of fire to those of the crucifix.' The Zafarnama commonly calls Hindus Gabrs." Ibid., p. 274.

W. DEPORTATION[1] OF THE POPULATION OF ARMENIA BY SHAH ABBAS I (1604)[2]

[Shah-Abbas] summoned his officers into his presence and chose the leaders and administrators of the population from among them, one commandant per district. Emir Guna-Khan was especially put in charge of the town of Erevan, of the land of Ararat, and of the small districts in the vicinity. They had for instructions, wherever their power could reach, to hunt down and take everything away everything—down to the last living dog—either Christians or subjected Muslims; for those who resisted and rebelled against the royal order—the sword, death, and captivity.

Having received this cruel and deadly order from the monarch, the generals departed, each with his division, and went to the districts of Armenia that had been assigned to them. It was like a flame spread by the wind among reeds. Immediately, in all haste and without drawing breath, the inhabitants of the provinces, forced to leave their dwellings and exiled from their homeland, were driven forward like herds of light and heavy cattle, violently dragged and forced back into the province of Ararat, where they filled the vast plain from one end to the other. . . . The Persian troops entrusted with the operation, gathered the population together no matter where, in villages or towns, and consigned houses and buildings to the flames; they burned and destroyed the stores of forage, piles of corn, barley, and other useful things; they pillaged, they cleared out everything, so that the Osmanli [Ottoman] troops should be destitute and die, and that the deportees, seeing this, would lose the hope and thought of return.

While the Persian soldiers charged with escorting these masses were dragging them towards the plain of Etchmiadzin, Shah Abbas was in Aghdja-Ghala [Yervandashat], and the Osmanli sardar [commander], Dshqal-Oghli, arrived with his troops at Kars. Knowing that he was not able to keep up the campaign against the Osmanlis, whose numerical superiority discouraged him, Shah Abbas turned towards Nakhidjevan and, with all his men, set out to follow in the tracks of the hordes going to Persia. The Osmanlis, for their part, set out hot on the heels of the Persians. There were therefore three great and endless assemblies: that of the populations; of the Persians; and of the Osmanlis. As a result, it came to pass that when the populations began to move off, Shah Abbas and the Persians swooped down on their former camp and, when they left the place, it was occupied by Dshqal-Oghli, with the Osmanli troops. They followed one after another, putting their feet in the same tracks, until the people and the Persians had reached the village of Julfa and the Osmanlis Nakh-ovan [Nakhidjevan]. From then on, the Persians did not allow the people to halt not even for an hour: they hustled them, hurried them, caused some of them to die from blows with sticks, cut the ears or noses off others, cut off heads and stuck them on posts. It was in this way that Iohandjan, brother of the Catholics Arakel, and another man had their heads cut off and stuck onto a pole by the side of the river Araxes. The purpose of these tortures and even worse inflicted on the population, was to force them by excessive terror to make haste and cross the river. The cunning Persian nation tormented the people in this way, out of fear of the Osmanlis advancing behind them: they saw the people's camp, crowded to overflowing—with their own men, also very numerous—and they understood that many days would be required to make the crossing. They were afraid that the Osmanlis would take advantage of this delay and hurl themselves upon them unawares and inflict a disaster upon them, or that they would take the population away form them and lead them back, which would later cause them considerable harm. That is why they harassed the people and hurried them to cross. But there were not enough boats and chests for such a throng. Many boats had been brought along from various places and a number of chests constructed on the spot, but the people and the Persians formed such a large body that nothing sufficed. The Persian warriors, charged with escorting the deportees surrounded them and watched that no one fled, dealt blows with sticks, broke everything, drove the people into the water, overflowing its [deep] banks, so that the sufferings and dangers for the people were appalling.

The wretched multitude saw the vast river, that sea that was going to swallow them; at their backs, the murderous sword of the Persians, leaving no hope of flight. A concert of heart-breaking lamentations, floods of tears, forming another Araxes, cries, groans, sobs, howls of grief, invectives, harrowing wailing; pleas and shrieks mingled: neither pity nor means of salvation appeared form any quarter.

Here, our people would have needed Moses of ancient times and his disciple Joshua to extricate Israel from the hands of another Pharaoh, to calm the waves and the swell of the great, wide river; but they did not have them, because the multitude of our crimes had closed the righteous God's gates of mercy.

The cruel Persian soldiers, escorting the crowd, filled the river with them, and themselves amid the waters, caused redoubled cries and lamentations, torn from their breasts by the danger. Some clung to the planks of the boats or even the chests, others seized the tails of horses, oxen, and buffalo; still others swarm across. Those who did not know how to swim, the weak, old men and women, children, young girls and boys covered the surface of the water which swept them along like autumnal current; some succeeded in crossing, many drowned there and met their death.

Some Persian Horsemen, who had sturdy mounts, or were endowed with strength themselves, went among the Christians, observed the girls and boys, and if one of them pleased them—woman, boy, or girl—deceived their master [their father or relative] by saying to him; "Give, I will take them across to the other side"; having crossed, instead of setting them down on the ground, they took them away to suit their fancy. Others carried them swimming, others took them away, killed the master, and led them off; others went off, throwing the children on the road and abandoning them; the masters escaped themselves, leaving the sick, because of the intolerable dangers and fatigues to which they were exposed. In a word, I say that our nation was prey to such misery and intolerable dismay and torment that I am incapable of recounting the details of the mortal hardship which broke the Armenian nation, crushed by such calamities. . . . At last it came about that the whole throng crossed the river, and pell-mell with them, the Persian army. Emir-Guna, their leader until then, was ordered by Shah Abbas to join his army, leaving Khalifalu Elias-Sultan, to guide the throng, with orders to lead these people on forced marches, to distance them from the Osmanlis and to deposit them on Persian soil. As for the shah, he marched straight to Tauriz [Tabriz] with his troops, following the royal route or *dshadeh*, but the throng did not follow the road going straight to the town, for fear that, marching behind the king, they would be separated from him and taken away by the Ottomans. He had therefore instructed Elias-Sultan to lead them by roundabout routes, through placed which were difficult to approach, where the Osmanlis could not follow them. Elias made the multitude march and guided them through valleys where the Araxes followed its course, through mountain gorges, rough both to enter and to descend, as well as through small valleys and narrow places. They did not cross mountain gorges or move from one rough spot to another without pain and suffering. . . .

The Hunt for Fugitives

When this matter was ended, the khan and his troops marched against other refuges from the same district of Garhni-Zur: those they succeeded in halting, they despoiled, slaughtered, and took with them. By coming and going, they reached the large valley called Kurhudara. Although there were several caves and fortified places in this valley where Christians were hiding, they neglected them in favor of the famous cave of Iakhsh-Khan where a thousand Christians, men and women, had gathered, attracted by its strong position, and who carefully watched over its approaches. The Persian soldiers had attacked them in vain for a long time, but they obtained no results from down below because it was a very high position. Their diabolical imagination presented them with another method. A detachment of two hundred men left the valley and scaled the rocks, where stones formed tiers up to the peak. Having fastened themselves together by long ropes, they went down, one after the other, from one level to the next, and in this way reached the level of the summits where the cave was. There, they clothed four of their men with iron breast-plates, covering them from head to toe, to which four or five swords were attached. Each man had a bared sword in his hand and four or five ropes around his body, so that if one were cut the other would hold him. They suspended these people from a dizzy height until they had reached the cave. When they arrived at the center of the hideout, they began to strike the men and women mercilessly with their swords, like wolves who had entered an enclosure tearing sheep to shreds. At the sight of the Persian swords, bent on slaughtering them, the wretched Christians set up a great cry of grief; there were sobs, lamentations, tears, and groans torn from them by mortal horror; they moved about, became restless, jostled each other in disarray, went to and fro from side to side like the waves of a stormy sea, seeking safety where there was no way out. Hearing the cries and understanding what had happened, the people who guarded the paths leading to the cave abandoned their posts out of concern for their comrades and went within to help them. When they saw the guards arrive outside, the Persians went altogether into the cave and fell on the Christians with their swords. From the entrance up to the furthermost corner of the hideout, it was like mown grass, all were slaughtered and hurled down below. Old men and women and those who did not please them were killed and the floor of the cave ran with Christian blood which reddened all the stones. The child was torn form its mother's breast and thrown below. A few women, young men, and young girls, who escaped the carnage, seeing themselves given into the hands of these fierce, inhuman beasts who would lead them into captivity, torture them and sully their purity, preferred death to a short and fleeting life full of crime and suffering. Many of them covered their heads with veils or with their gowns and threw themselves from the top of the cave into the abyss, and thus met their death. However, there was a dense forest in the valley. Some of those who threw themselves form the cave were caught in the branches went through their stomachs and came out of the backs of some of them; they reached the hearts and tore the shoulders of others, and their death was all the more cruel and painful. Lastly, those who remained were pillaged and robbed, and the rich booty shared out among the Persian soldiers, who seized them and took them to the main camp.

Thus the deportation to Persia did not extend to one or two districts but to a large number, from Nakhidjevan to Eghegadzor, on the frontier of Gegham, and to Lore on Hamzatshimar and Aparan; to Charap-Khan and Chiracavan; to Zarishat and to part of the villages of Kars [near Ani]; the whole Gaghzvan valley, to all the territory of Alashkert, to the village of Macon and to the land of Aghbak; to Salamast and Khoy, to Urmi, to all the foreigners and transitory people, who had remained in Tauriz and in its villages; to the entire plain of Ararat and the town of Yerevan; to the lands of Kerkh-Bulaqh and Dzaghcnots-Dzor, to Garni-Dzor and Urtza-Dzor, and earlier to the districts of Karin, Basen, Khnus and Manazkert, Artzke, Ardjesh, Berkri, and Van, where the inhabitants had been dragged to Yerevan in captivity and taken further afield.

All these districts of the beautiful land of Armenia, with their dependencies, where the population had been taken away forceably to Persia by order of the shah, were sacked and depopulated.

Many depopulated villages and sizable market towns can still be seen today on their rich and fertile soil, their fields and gardens.

After Having Ruined the Region of Ararat, the Jelalis Moved on to Ghegharkunik and Pillaged Its Villages (1605)

In addition, they seized women and children and took them away with them into captivity in order to force their masters to redeem them with gold and silver. After having done everything to their hearts' content, they made the captive women and children march, loaded the beasts of burden and the oxen, using the guards who had fallen into their hands, then they took the many flocks of sheep, the provisions, and the herds of horses on the road with them. As this expedition was taking place in winter—and the cold season that year was harsh, the snow heavy—they had not marched for two days when the exhausted animals fell by the way and hey divided the loads of those who failed and distributed them among the captive women and children. In this way, they crossed the mountain and arrived in the village of Karbi. How much suffering was endured by the wretched people employed in this task! Some of them lost hands, feet, and ears from the frost and it cut into their flesh; for others, the icy breezes took their breath away and they fell by the road and expired. These died as it were on the journey; the survivors were taken to Karbi, some sold for silver, others reserved as slaves to serve the Jelalis, who rested until the spring.

Notes

1. Large-scale deportations and population transfers accompanied the jihad campaigns waged by the Arabs, the Seljuk and Ottoman Turks, and the Safavides. For examples, see Michael Morony, *Iraq after the Muslim Conquest* (Princeton, NJ: Princeton University Press, 1984), pp. 195–96; S. D. Goitein, "Changes in the Middle East (950–1150) as Illustrated by the Documents of the Cairo Geniza," in *Islamic Civilisation 950–1150*, ed. D. S. Richards (Oxford: Cassirer, 1973), pp. 17–32; Speros Vryonis Jr., *The Decline of Medieval Hellenism in Asia Minor and the Process of Islamization from the 11th through the 15th Century* (Berkeley and Los Angeles: University of California Press, 1971), p. 169; Bar Hebraeus, *Chronography*, p. 264; Joseph Hacker, "The Sürgün System and Jewish Society in the Ottoman Empire during the 15th–17th Centuries," in *Ottoman and Turkish Jewry-Community and Leadership* (Bloomington: Indiana University Turkish Studies, 1992), pp. 1–65. Bat Ye'or in *The Decline of Eastern Christianity under Islam* (Cranbury, NJ: Fairleigh Dickinson University Press, 1996), p. 465n79, elucidates some of the salient features, and lasting impact, of these deportations:

These transfers, motivated by economic causes, affected dhimmi populations and were not reserved exclusively for newly subjugated or enslaved populations. Some chronicles provide information on these transfers. Departures had to take place on the same day or at very short notice, two or three days, making it impossible for the deportees to sell their possessions. In order to discourage flight, they were counted, closely supervised, and forbidden to move from their new places of residence, generally very far from their places of origin. When all the village inhabitants were deported, the houses were burnt down and the entire village destroyed. Thus the community archives, the libraries, and even the memory of the deportees were annihilated.

2. Arakel of Tauriz, "Livre d'Histoires," in Marie Brosset, *Histoire de la Géorgie*, vol. 1 (St. Petersburg: Impr. de l'Académie impériale des sciences, se vend chez W. Eggers et comp., 1849), pp. 287–95, 309–10; English trans. in Bat Ye'or, *Decline of Eastern Christianity under Islam*, pp. 362–69.

52

JIHAD ON THE INDIAN SUBCONTINENT— SEVENTH THROUGH TWENTIETH CENTURIES

A. CAMPAIGNS IN SIND (711–712 CE) LED BY MUHAMMAD BIN QASIM[1]

Muhammad took the fort [of Rawar] and stayed there for two or three days. He put six thousand fighting men, who were in the fort, to the sword, and shot some with arrows. The other dependents and servants were taken prisoners, with their wives and children. . . . When the number of the prisoners was calculated, it was found to amount to thirty thousand persons, amongst whom thirty were the daughters of chiefs, and one of them was Rai Dahir's sister's daughter, whose name was Jaisiya. They were sent to Hajjaj. The head of Dahir and the fifth part of the prisoners were forwarded in charge of Ka'ab, son of Mharak. When the head of Dahir, the women, and the property all reached Hajjaj, he prostrated himself before Allah, offered thanksgivings and praises. . . . Hajjaj then forwarded the head, the umbrellas, and wealth, and the prisoners to Walid the Khalifa. When the Khalifa of the time had read the letter, he praised Almighty Allah. He sold some of those daughters of the chiefs, and some he granted as rewards. . . . It is said that after the conquest was effected and the affairs of the country were settled and the report of the conquest had reached Hajjaj, he sent a reply to the following effect. "O my cousin! I received your life-inspiring letter. I was much pleased and overjoyed when it reached me. The events were recounted in an excellent and beautiful style, and I learnt that the ways and rules you follow are conformable to the Law. Except that you give protection to all, great and small alike, and make no difference between enemy and friend. Allah says,—Give no quarter to Infidels, but cut their throats. Then know that this is the command of the great Allah. . . ."

Muhammad bin Qasim marched from Dhalila, and encamped on the banks of the stream of the Jalwali to the east of Brahmanabad. He sent some confidential messengers to Brahmanabad to invite its people to submission and to the Muham-madan faith, to preach to them Islam, to demand the jizya, or poll tax, also to inform them that if they would not submit, they must prepare to fight. . . . [After the fort of Brahmanabad was taken, following a six-month siege]. . . . When the plunder and the prisoners of war were brought before Qasim, and enquiries were made about every captive, it was found that Ladi, the wife of Dahir, was in the fort with two daughters of his by his other wives. Veils were put on their faces, and they were delivered to a servant to keep them apart. One-fifth of all the prisoners were chosen and set aside; they were counted as amounting to twenty thousand in number, and the rest were given to the soldiers . . . (Qasim) sat on the seat of cruelty, and put all those who had fought to the sword. It is said that about six thousand fighting men were slain, but according to some, sixteen thousand were killed. . . .

[W]hen the Arabs reached the fort [of Multan], and the fight commenced [i.e., with the Hindu inhabitants who refused to submit to Islam], no place was found suitable for digging a mine until a person came out of the fort and sued for mercy. Muhammad Qasim gave him protection, and he pointed out a place towards the north on the banks of a river. A mine was dug, and in two or three days the walls fell down, and the fort was taken. Six thousand warriors were put to death, and all their relations and dependants taken as slaves. . . ."[1]

. . . There was at Debal a loft temple (budd) surmounted by a long pole, and on the pole was fixed a red flag, which when the high breeze blew was unfurled over the city. The budd is a high steeple, below which the idol or idols are deposited, as in this instance. The Indians give in general the name of budd to any-thing connected with their worship or which forms the object of their veneration. So an idol is called a budd. . . . (The Muslims) brought down the flagstaff (with one of their catapult war machines), and it was broken; at which the infidels were sore afflicted. The idolators advanced to the combat, but were put to flight; lad-ders were then brought and the Musulmans escaladed the wall. . . . The town was thus taken by assault, and the carnage endured for three days. The governor of the town, appointed by Dahir fled, and the priests of the temple were massacred. Muhammad bin Qasim marked out a place for the Musulmans to dwell in, built a mosque, and left four thousand Musulmans to garrison the place.[2]

Notes

1. H. M. Elliot and John Dowson, *The History of India as Told by Its Own Historians: The Muhammadan Period*, vol. 1 (1867–1877; repr., Delhi: Elibron, 2001), pp. 164, 172–73, 176, 181, 204–205, *Chachnama* of Al-Kufi.

2. Ibid., p. 120, *Al-Baladhuri*.

B. JIHAD BY YAQUB IBN LAYTH AGAINST THE HINDU KINGDOM OF KABUL (870 CE)[1]

Yaqub Ibn Layth now had recourse to stratagem and deception. He sent one of his confidential servants to Rusal [Hindu King] with a message to say that he wished to come and meet him and render homage. . . . When the ambassadors of Yaqub came to Rusal and delivered the message to him, it was very agreeable to him, because he was greatly harassed by Yaqub, who continually made incursions into his country, and attacked it in different directions. He made the ambassadors welcome, and sent messages to Yaqub, giving him many kind promises and holding out hopes for perferment. . . . A day was fixed for a parley between the parties. It was not the habit of Rusal to ride a horse, but he used to sit on a throne which a party of his servants carried on their shoulders. When both armies were drawn up in array, Rusal seated himself and ordered his troops to stand in line on each side of it. Yaqub with his three thousand brave horsemen advanced between these two lines, and his men carried their lances concealed behind their horses and wearing coats of mail under their garments. . . . When Yaqub drew near Rusal, he bowed his head as if to do homage, but he raised the lance and thrust it into the back of Rusal, so that he died on the spot. His people also fell like lightning upon the enemy, cutting them down with their swords, and staining the earth with the blood of the enemies of religion [Islam]. The infidels, when they saw the head of Rusal upon the point of a spear, took to flight, and great bloodshed ensued. The bride of victory drew aside her veil and Yaqub returned victorious. Next day six horsemen thousand of the infidels were sent prisoners to Sistan. He also placed sixty of their officers on assess, and having hung the ears of the slain upon the necks of these officers, he sent them in this manner to Bust. In this conquest he obtained such immense treasure and property that conjecture cannot make estimate of them. . . . The hostility which the people of Bust had shown to Yaqub, he now retaliated upon them. He fixed the same poll tax upon them as was levied from the Jews, and this was collected with severity. This victory which he achieved was the result of treachery and deception, such as no one had ever committed.

Note

1. H. M. Elliot and John Dowson, *The History of India as Told by Its Own Historians: The Muhammadan Period*, vol. 2 (1867–1877; repr., Delhi: Elibron, 2001), pp. 177–78, *Jam-Ul-Hikayat* of Muhammad Ufi. Yaqub Ibn Layth's successful treachery, according to A. L. Srivstava ("Indian Resistance to Medieval Invaders," *Journal of Indian History* 43 [1965]: 355), made the Brahman minister (and de facto Hindu ruler) Lallya's position,

> untenable after the . . . disaster [described above] and he abandoned Kabul. . . . This happened in 265 A.H. corresponding to 870 A.D., and ended Hindu rule in Afghanistan.

C. CAMPAIGNS OF SUBUKTIGIN OF GHAZNI (977–997 CE)[1]

The Sultan therefore sharpened the sword of intention in order to make an incursion upon his [Jayapal's] kingdom, and cleanse it from impurity and from his rejection of Islam. . . . The Amir marched out towards Lamghan, which is a city celebrated for its great strength and abounding in wealth. He conquered it and set fire to the places in its vicinity which were inhabited by infidels, and demolishing the idol-temples, he established Islam in them. He marched and captured other cities and killed the polluted wretches, destroying the idolatrous and gratifying the Musulmans. After wounding and killing beyond all measure, his hands and those of his friends became cold in counting the value of the plundered property. On the completion of his conquest he returned and promulgated accounts of the victories obtained for Islam, and every one, great and small, concurred in rejoicing over this result and thanking Allah.

Note

1. H. M. Elliot and John Dowson, *The History of India as Told by Its Own Historians: The Muhammadan Period*, vol. 2 (1867–1877; repr., Delhi: Elibron, 2001), p. 22, *Al-Utbi*.

D. MAHMUD OF GHAZNI'S CONQUEST[1] OF THANESAR,[2] KANAUJ, AND SIRSAWA, NEAR SAHARANPUR (1018–1019 CE)

The Sultan learned that in the country of Thanesar there were large elephants of Sailaman (Ceylon) breed, celebrated for military purposes. The chief of Thanesar was on this account obstinate in his infidelity and denial of God. *So the Sultan marched against him with his valiant warriors, for the purpose of planting the standards of Islam and extirpating idolatry* . . . after a vigorous attack on the part of the Musulmans, the enemy fled, leaving their elephants, which were all driven into the camp of the Sultan, except one, which ran off and could not be found. . . . The blood of the infidels flowed so copiously that the stream was discolored, notwithstanding its purity, and the people were unable to drink it. Had not night come on and concealed the traces of their flight, many more of the enemy would have been slain. The victory was gained by God's grace, who has established Islam forever as the best of religions, notwithstanding that idolators revolt against it. The Sultan returned with plunder which it is impossible to recount. Praise be to God, the protector of the world for the honor he bestows upon Islam and Musulmans!

The Sultan advanced to the fortifications of Kanauj, which consisted of seven distinct forts, washed by the Ganges, which flowed under them like the ocean. In

Kanauj there were nearly ten thousand temples, which the idolators falsely and absurdly represented to have been found by their ancestors two or three hundred thousand years ago. They worshipped and offered their vows and supplications to them, in consequence of their great antiquity. Many of the inhabitants of the place fled and were scattered abroad like so many wretched widows and orphans, from the fear which oppressed them, in consequence of witnessing the fate of their deaf and dumb idols. Many of them thus affected their escape, and those who did not fly were put to death. The Sultan took all seven forts in one day, and gave his soldiers leave to plunder them and take prisoners.

The Sultan summoned the most religiously disposed of his followers, and ordered them to attack the enemy immediately. Many infidels were consequently slain or taken prisoner in this sudden attack, and the Mussulmans paid no regard to the booty till they had satiated themselves with the slaughter of the infidels and worshippers of the sun and fire. The friends of God searched the bodies of the slain for three whole days, in order to obtain booty. . . . The booty amounted in gold and silver, rubies and pearls, nearly to three thousand thousand dirhams, and the number of prisoners may be conceived from the fact that each was sold for from two to ten dirhams. These were afterwards taken to Ghazna, and merchants came from distant cities to purchase them, so that the countries Mawarau-n nahr, Iraq, and Khurasan were filled with them, and the fair and the dark, the rich and the poor, were commingled in common slavery.

Notes

1. H. M. Elliot and John Dowson, *The History of India as Told by Its Own Historians: The Muhammadan Period*, vol. 2 (1867–1877; repr., Delhi: Elibron, 2001), pp. 40–41, 46, 49–50; *Al-Utbi*; introductory text from Elliot and Dowson (vol. 2, p. 14) indicates that the author of this text was Abu Nasr Muhammad ibn Muhammad al Jubbaru-l Utbi, or *Al-Utbi*. He was secretary to Sultan Mahmud, and as such "he enjoyed excellent opportunities of becoming fully acquainted with the conqueror." Al-Utbi's writings cover the entire reign of Mahmud's predecessor, Nasiru-d din Subuktigin, and part of that of Mahmud, until 1020 CE.

2. Thanesar (place of the god), an ancient town of British India, in Karnal district of the Punjab, on the river Saraswati, 100 miles by rail North of Delhi: population (1901) 5,066. As the center of the tract called Kurukshetra in the Mahabharata, it has always been a holy place, and was in the seventh century the capital of King Harshavardhana, who ruled over all northern India.

E. AN ALMOST CONTEMPORARY ACCOUNT OF MAHMUD'S INVASIONS OF INDIA

Mahmud's invasions of India have always attracted the attention of Indian historians. Unfortunately, however, not many contemporary accounts of it have come down to us. For a long time students of history were content to depend upon Firishta's history and Utbi's *Katab-ul-Yamini*. Utbi's account, however, is very meager and lacks details whereas Firishta's distance from his subject matter does not lend much authority to this work. The publication of the Persian text of a part of the *Zainul Akhbar* of Girdizi edited by Professor Muhammad Nazim in 1928 made available an account of Mahmud's invasions of India written, at the latest, in 1052 CE, that is, within twenty two years of Mahmud's death. Its account of Mahmud's invasions of India therefore deserves the foremost place among original authorities on Mahmud's reign and as such it is sure to interest students of Indian history. In the following pages an attempt has been made at providing readers of Indian history with a translation of Girdizi's Persian account, Sri Ram Sharma, "An Almost Contemporary Account of Mahmud's Invasions of India," *Studies in Medieval Indian History* (1956): 22–33.

When Mahmud became Amir of Khurasan, the Caliph of Baghdad gave him the title of Yamin-ul-Daulat wa Amin-ul-Millit.[1]

In 930 AH (1000 CE) Mahmud left for India from Ghazni and conquered many forts.[2]

On 5 Ramazan 391 AH (August 28, 1001 CE) Mahmud reached Heart and left for Ghazni. He left Ghazni for India and encamped at Peshawar. He has ten thousand soldiers with him. Jaipal, king of India, with twelve thousand horse, 30,000 foot and 300 elephants came out to oppose him. Both the armies were drawn up in battle array. Soon the battle began. God gave victory to the Muslims. Mahmud was victorious. Jaipal was defeated. Many infidels were killed. The Muslims killed 5,000 Hindus in that battle and Jaipal was made a prisoner. Fifteen of his sons and brothers also fell into their hands. A good deal of booty was taken. It is said that the necklace that Jaipal was wearing was valued at 180,000 Dinars. Similarly other Hindu chiefs who were taken prisoner were found wearing valuable ornaments round their necks. This victory was gained on Friday,[3] 8 Muharram, 392 AH (November 27, 1001 CE).

From here Mahmud marked on Waihind.[4] This country was also ravaged. When spring came, Mahmud returned to Ghazni.[5]

When Mahmud returned to Ghazni (from Sistan in 393 AH; 1003–1004 CE), he decided to attack Bhatia. He marched by way of Walihtan (Sibbi) and Hissar and reached Bhatia.[6] Here a battle raged for three days. Bajrao formed his troops in line of battle and sent them against Mahmud. He himself left for the bank of river Sasana. When Mahmud learned this, he sent some of his men in pursuit in order to capture Bajrao and his companions. When Bajrao learned of the pursuit, he left his main body and killed himself. Mahmud's soldiers took his head and captured all his companions and brought them before Mahmud who was overjoyed. By his orders all of them were killed. Two hundred eighty elephants fell into his hands.[7]

In 396 AH (1006 CE) Mahmud decided to make a surprise attack on Multan. He was afraid that if he marched by the direct route, Daud would get to know of it and make preparations to oppose him. He chose therefore a roundabout way to Multan. Anand Pal, son of Jaipal, contested his progress. Mahmud directed his army to attached Anand Pal's territories. Many men were taken prisoners and many were killed, the country was ravaged.[8]

Anand Pal ran away to the mountains of Kashmir. Mahmud reached Multan. He besieged it for a week till the garrison sued for peace. They agreed to pay 20,000 Dinars in two installments every year. Mahmud now returned to Ghazni.[9]

When Mahmud was free from his struggle against Ilak Khan (defeated in January 1008), he heard that Shokpal, grandson of Jaipal, who had fallen into the hands of Abuali at Nishapur and been converted to Islam, had abjured his religion. Mahmud turned towards him and captured him in the hills of Kashnod. He undertook to pay 400,000 Dinars. He was entrusted to Hakin Khazan and imprisoned. He died in prison.[10]

From here Mahmud left for India. In 399 AH (1008–1009 CE) he fought against Anand Pal and defeated him. Thirty elephants were taken and a large number of prisoners were made.[11] From here Mahmud marched on to Bhim Nagar and besieged it. For three days the siege continued. Mahmud then succeeded in entering the fort with some of his companions. Gold, silver, and diamonds that had been accumulating since the days of Bhim Pandom in this fort fell into his hands. Booty beyond counting fell into Mahmud's hands. Mahmud now returned to Ghazni. A throne of gold and silver was built. The booty was displayed at Ghazni for the people to stare at.[12]

From Ghazni in 400 AH (1010 CE) he left for Multan. The territory left unconquered last time was conquered now. Many Carmathians there in Multan were captured, some were slain, other mutilated, and made to suffer otherwise so that all of them died. Daud was also captured and taken to Ghazni and sent to Ghorak where he died.[13]

In 402 AH (1012 CE), Mahmud left Ghazni for Thanesar. When Trilochanpal, emperor of India, heard this, he sent messengers and offered 50 elephants if Mahmud would not march on Thanesar. Mahmud paid no heed to his words. When his armies reached the Camp of Ram, his men disputed his path. From their protected places, they attacked the Muslims, many of whom were killed.

When Mahmud reached Thanesar, he found the city deserted. Whatever fell into the hands of his men was destroyed. Many of the idols were broken. Jogar Om (which was the most famous idol in that Mecca of the Hindus)[14] was carried away to Ghazni and placed at the Durgah. People flocked to see it.[15]

In the year 404 AH (1014 CE), Mahmud decided to take Nanda.[16] When Trilochanpal, king of India, learnt about it, he sent tried veterans to the fort in order to guard the fort and himself left for the passes in Kashmir. When Mahmud reached the place, it was invested thoroughly. When the besieged felt helpless, they asked for peace and surrendered the fort. Mahmud, with some of his men, entered the fort and took away all the valuables and arms that were in the fort. Mahmud left Mir Saraggh in charge of the fort and himself left for the pass in Kashmir where Trilochanpal was hiding. When he heard of the enemy's approach, Trilochanpal ran away from there as well. Mahmud so arranged matters that the forts in the pass were taken and pillaged. His army captured a good deal of property and a large number of men. Many Hindus accepted Islam. The same year he issued orders that in the places conquered, mosques be raised and Hindus be converted to Islam by men appointed for the purpose. Mahmud himself returned to Ghazni. This victory was secured in the year 405 AH (1015 CE).[17]

When the year 407 AH (1016 CE) began, Mahmud decided to attack Kashmir. From Ghazni he set out for Kashmir. When he reached the pass, winter set in. Beyond the pass was the fort of Lohkot (Loharin) strong as of iron. It was invested. When the siege was turning to be successful, the severity of winter and the snow helped the garrison which was reinforced by the arrival of fresh troops, from Kashmir. Mahmud sought safety in retirement. He returned to Ghazni in the spring.[18]

In the beginning of the year 409 AH (1018 CE) Mahmud decided to attack Kanauj, a very populous and prosperous country. Crossing seven waters, Mahmud reached the frontiers of the kingdom, when Bakorah, the warden of the marches,[19] sent a messenger and submitted. From here he advance to Baranunder (Buland Shahr) Hardat himself fled and left his tribesmen to guard the fort. But Mahmud's armies broke their defenses and overpowered them. They bought themselves back to paying 1,000,000 dirhams and thirty elephants.

From here Mahmud advanced to Mahaban (near Muttra) on the Jumna then under Kala Chand. When he heard of Mahmud's advance, he selected his best elephant, mounted it, and tried to cross the river. Mahmud learned of his attempt at escape and ordered his men to watch the roads. In despair Kala Chand killed himself.[20] Mahaban was taken, 165 elephants and booty beyond imagination fell into Mahmud's hands. From here Mahmud advanced to Muttra, a very great city of the Hindus, sacred as the birth place of Krishna son of Vasudeva. Here is a great Hindu temple. When Mahmud reached Muttra no one opposed him. He ordered his men to spread over the whole kingdom, destroy all idols or burn them, and take possession of all property. From the temples, treasures and property beyond counting fell into Mahmud's hands. One sapphire weighed 450 mithgals. No one had ever seen such a stone. Gold and silver idols beyond estimate were taken. One gold idol was ordered to be broken and 98,300 mithgals of gold was founded therein. In this way much property and many of stones were captured.

From here Mahmud advanced to Kanauhj where the Rai was captured. Mahmud now set out of Ghazni. On the way a peerless elephant of Chand Rai of Kanauj, which Mahmud had heard of and sought for in vain, fell into his hands.

It has run away from Chand Rai's ranks and with the Mahaot was now captured. Mahmud named it Khudadad (God's gifts).

When Mahmud reached Ghazni, the booty was valued at 2,000,000 Dinars, 53,000 slaves, and 350 elephants.[21]

In the month of Tir in the year 410 AH (1019 CE) Mahmud decided to advance against Nanda. He had killed Rajpal.[22] He had decided to join Trilochanpal, make him victorious, and bring back his armies to his own kingdom. When he head the news of Mahmud's advance Trilochanpal crossed the Ganges towards Bari. Mahmud also crossed the river and defeated all the Hindu armies. Trilochanpal ran away with some Hindus and did not dispute Mahmud's path. Mahmud now decided to attack the city of Bari. They found it deserted. All the temples were burnt. They carried away every thing they could lay their hands on. From here, Mahmud decided to march towards Nanda's country. After crossing many rivers, Mahmud reached its frontiers. Nanda had heard of the advance of the army of Islam. He had gathered together a good many arms and a large army. It is said his army consisted of 36,000 calvary, 124,000 foot, 650 elephants. This should give some idea of his resources. When Mahmud approached his enemy's encampments, he disposed his troops in battle array and divided then into the usual sections for battle. He encamped taking cover to protect himself. He then sent a messenger to Nanda asking him to become a Muslim and save himself from all harm and distress. Nanda returned the reply that he had nothing to say to Mahmud except on the battlefield. It is said that Mahmud ascended a height in order to get a view of Nanda's army. He saw a world of tents and encampments, besides immovable horsemen, foot soldiers, and elephants. He felt distressed. He prayed to God to grant him victory. When the night fell, God struck fear into Nanda's heart. He left camp and ran away. When Mahmud sent a messenger next day, he found Nanda's camp deserted. They had left all their arms and taken away their horses and elephants. The messenger returned and informed Mahmud who left his place of refuge and went towards the enemy's camp and found it deserted. Mahmud thanked God and ordered the camp of Nanda to be looted. A good deal of property of all kinds was thus destroyed.

From here victorious Mahmud set out towards Ghazni. On their way back a forest fell in their way. The army entered it, 580 elephants of Nanda fell into their hands which they captured and brought to the Muslim camp.

Then they brought the news that there are two strongly fortified passes, Nur and Qirat. Here the inhabitants are Kafirs and idolatrous. Mahmud resolved to attack them. He ordered that a large number artisans such as blacksmiths, masons, and stone cutters should accompany the troops so that they might level up the roads, cut down the trees, and break stones. When the army reached there, it was resolved to attack Qirat first. Qirat is a pleasant place and its inhabitants worship the lion. Its climate is cold and fruits abound here. When the Shah of Qirat got the news, he advanced to meet them, submitted, and sought protection. Mahmud accepted his submission and spared its territories. The Shah of Qirat became Muslim and many of the inhabitants of Qirat as well accepted Islam. The inhabitants of Nur, however, refused to comply with Mahmud's demands. Mahmud ordered Hajib Ali to proceed to Nur and conquer it. A fort was built here. Mir Ali was appointed Kotwal of the fort. He was ordered to put Islam round their neck by sword. Islam now made its appearance in their country. This was in 411 AH (1020 CE).[23]

When the year 412 AH (1021 CE) began, Mahmud decided to attack Kashmir. The fort of Loharkot[24] was invested. A month was spent here. As the fort was very strong, it could not be taken. Thereupon Mahmud came out of the great pass and went towards Lahore and Takeshar[25] and spread his armies. When the spring came, Mahmud went back to Ghazni.[26]

When the year 413 AH (1022 CE) began, Mahmud decided to attack Nanda's territory. When the fort of Swalior was reached, it was invested. It was, however, a very strong fort and Mahmud failed to take it. He remained investing it for four days and nights. The commander of the fort then sent a messenger and sought for peace. He surrendered 35 elephants. The army of Mahmud now retreated from here and advanced towards Kalinjar, which was under Nanda. Nanda was himself in the fort with his officers and near relatives. Mahmud ordered that the fort be surrounded on all sides. Many plans were thought of. But the fort was so situated that no man could scale its heights. It was not even possible to attack the fort by cutting down stones at its base. No plan seemed possible. Some days were passed in this fashion. Nanda, however, felt uncomfortable in the fort as all roads had been closed to him. He sent messengers and offered to pay the jizya,[27] Hudya, and 300 elephants. This was agreed to. Nanda gladly sent 300 elephants and drove them out of the fort without Mahaots. Mahmud ordered him men who came up to the pack of elephants and mounted them. The garrison was very much surprised at this daring of Mahmud's soldiers. Nanda was a poet. He wrote a verse in Hindi and sent it to Mahmud. Mahmud had this recited to the Hindu,[28] Persian, and Turkish poets. Everyone liked the verse and declared that it was not possible to write more elegant or more high flown lines. Mahmud therefore had an order drawn up conferring on Nanda 15 forts in return for the verse that Nanda had composed in his honour. Besides this he sent many presents; women, jewels, and dresses. Nanda also sent a good deal in return. Mahmud returned to Ghazni from there.[29]

When winter came, as usual, Mahmud went towards India in order to gain religious merit. Someone said, "On the seashore there is a great city, Somnath by name. Hindus regard it with the same respect which the Muslims reserve for Mecca. There are gold and silver idols in the temple. The idol Manat, which the prophet had removed from Ka'aba, had reached this place via Aden. They had bought it. In the treasury of that temple they have placed precious stones and a good deal of property. But the way thereto is very dangerous."

When Mahmud heard this he planned to go to that city and destroy the idols. From Hindustran he now set his forces towards Somnath. When he approached the city and was seen by the Brahmanas and Sramanas, they all busied themselves in worshipping their idols. The chief officer of the city left it and taking his family and men with him, sailed down the river in a boat seeking refuge on an island where he remained surrounding the city. When the Muslim army approached the city, they besieged it and began to attack it. Before many days had passed a breach was effected, Mahmud's army entered the city and began to kill. Many Hindus were killed. Mahmud asked the Muazzan to go to the camp and announce the time of prayers. As he announced the call to prayers, all the idols were broken, burnt, or otherwise destroyed. The stone idol of Manat was dug from its foundation in the ground and broken into small pieces. Some of these, were taken to Ghazni on camels where they are still found under the steps of the mosque. There was some treasure under the idols. All that treasure was taken. A large amount of property was thus got—silver idols, jewels, and treasure of various kinds.

Mahmud now returned. For Parm Dev, Badshah of the Hindus, stood in his way disputing his path. Mahmud decided therefore to leave the right road back to Ghazni, for fear lest this great victory of his should turn into defeat (results of this great victory be thrown away). He left by way of Mansura towards Multan. His soldiers suffered many hardships partly on account of want of water and party on account of Jats of Sind and on other grounds. Many of the soldiers of Islam lost their lives on the way. At last Multan was sighted and from there Mahmud marched on to Ghazni.[30]

Mahmud had been greatly enraged at the conduct of the Jats of Multan and Bhatis of the Indus on account of their molesting his armies when he was returning from Somnath. He wanted to take vengeance on them for their conduct and punish them. Hence in the year 418 AH (1027 CE), he collected his armies for the twelfth time and set out towards Multan. When he reached the city, he ordered 1,400 strong boats to be built. They were fitted with three iron spikes each, strong and sharp, one at the bow and one each on the sides. They were so strong and sharp that they were capable of piercing, wrecking, and destroying whatever they struck against. Fourteen hundred boats were set afloat on the river. Every boat seated 20 well-equipped soldiers with bows, arrows, spears, and shields. When the Jats heard of Mahmud's approach, they carried their families to far off islands. They took up arms, equipped 4,000, and according to some accounts, 8,000 boats. Every boat contained many well-armed men. They set off to attack the enemy. When they came opposite the Muslim army, the Muslims shot arrows at them, the firemen threw rockets. When the Muslim boats came near the boats of the Jats, the spikes struck the Jat boats. In this way the Jat boats were either wrecked, drowned, or damaged. On the bands of the river, horsemen, foot soldiers and elephants had been placed. When any Jat appeared on the banks, he was again thrown in. The Muslim army marched on the banks of the river, till they sighted the camp of the refugee families. They were robbed. A good deal of booty was obtained. From there the Muslim army left with flying colors for Ghazni.

Notes

1. Girdizi, p. 62.
2. Girdizi is our only contemporary or semicontemporary authority for this invasion.
3. Utbi has Thursday (below, p. 39), which seems to be the correct day of the week.
4. Waihind was wrongly identified as Bhatinda in the later compilations. Mahmud could not easily have penetrated so far into India in so short a time. Both Utbi and Girdizi have Waihind. It seems to stand for Hund on the right tank of the Indus about fifteen miles from Attock.
5. Girdizi, pp. 65, 66. Dr. M. Nazim (*Life and Times of Sultan Mahmud of Ghazni* [Lahore: Khalil, 1931], p. 67) has stated on the authority of Girdizi that fifteen sons and grandsons of Jaipal were captured. The text has some sons and brothers.
6. Girdizi, pp. 66, 67; Bhatia is probably Bhera. It is situated some eighty miles from Waihind on the Jehlum.
7. Ibid.
8. Ibid., pp. 67, 68.
9. Ibid., p. 68.
10. Ibid., p. 69. He had been left at Waihind as Mahmud's governor. Dr. Nazim (*Life and Times of Sultan Mahmud of Ghazni*, p. 98) located the rebellion of Sukhpal in the Salt Range in the Punjab and converts Kashnod into the Salt Range. Kashmir would be a nearer guess. There is nothing improbable in Sukhpal being captured and kept prisoner.
11. Girdizi, p. 69.
12. Ibid., pp. 69, 70. Bhim Nagar is Nagar Kot, Kangra.
13. Ibid., p. 70.
14. Ibid.
15. Ibid., pp. 70, 71.
16. Nandana, see below.
17. Girdizi, p. 72.
18. Ibid., pp. 72, 73.
19. Ibid., pp. 74, 76, obviously Kashmir. Utbi calls him Sibli bin Shahi bin Bahmi. See below, p. 58.
20. Cf. Utbi below.
21. Girdizi, pp. 74–76.
22. Raja of Kanauj.
23. Girdizi, 76–79.
24. Loharin.
25. Takeshar seems to be the name given to the plains of the Punjab to the west of the Chenab.
26. Girdizi, p. 79.
27. Jizya, payable by a ruler, is used here for tribute rather than capitation tax payable by the non-Muslim subjects of a Muslim king.
28. Presence of Hindu poets in Mahmud's army may imply the presence of Hindus. But if Mahmud has in his army Persian and Turkish scholars who knew Hindi (or were the

verses in Sanskrit?), it would imply much greater interchange of cultures between the people on both sides of Hindukoh. Was an Alberuni on Mahmud's staff?

29. Girdizi, pp. 79, 80.

30. Ibid., 84, 85.

F. THE CONQUEST OF SOMNAT MAHMUD BIN SUBUKTIGIN (1025 CE)[1]

When the Sultan Yaminu-d Daula Mahmud bin Subuktigin went to wage religious war against India, he made great efforts to capture and destroy Somnat, in the hope that the Hindus would then become Muhammadans. He arrived there in the middle of Zi-l k'ada, 416 AH (December 1025 CE). The Indians made a desperate resistance. They would go weeping and crying for help into the temple, and then issue forth to battle and fight till all were killed. The number of the slain exceeded 50,000. The king looked upon the idols with wonder, and gave orders for the seizing of the spoil and the appropriation of the treasures. There were many idols of gold and silver and vessels set with jewels, all of which had been sent there by the greatest personages in India. The value of the things found in the temples of the idols exceeded twenty thousand, thousand dinars.

Note

1. H. M. Elliot and John Dowson, *The History of India as Told by Its Own Historians: The Muhammadan Period*, vol. 1 (1867–1877; repr., Delhi: Elibron, 2001), p. 98, *Al-Kazwini*.

G. THE CONQUEST OF AJMER BY MUHAMMAD GHAURI (1192 CE)[1]

The victorious army on the right and on the left departed towards Ajmer. . . . When the crow-faced Hindus began to sound their white shells on the backs of the elephants, you would have said that a river of pitch was flowing impetuously down the face of a mountain of blue. . . . The army of Islam was completely victorious, and a hundred thousand grovelling Hindus swiftly departed to the fire of hell. . . . He destroyed (at Ajmer) the pillars and foundations of the idol temples, and built on their stead mosques and colleges, and the precepts of Islam, and the customs of the law were divulged and established.

Note

1. H. M. Elliot and John Dowson, *The History of India as Told by Its Own Historians: The Muhammadan Period*, vol. 2 (1867–1877; repr., Delhi: Elibron, 2001), pp. 214–15, *Hasan Nizami*.

H. JIHAD CAMPAIGNS OF ALAUDDIN KHILJI (1296–1316 CE)[1]

When Sultan Alau-d din, the Sultan of Delhi, was well established in the centre of his dominion and had cut off the heads of his enemies and slain them, the vein of the zeal of religion beat high for the subjection of infidelity and destruction of idols, and in the month of Zi'l-hijja 698 H (1298 CE) his brother Malik Mu'izzu-d din and Nusrat Khan, the chief pillar of the state and the leader of his armies, a generous and intelligent warrior, were sent to Kambayat,the most celebrated of the cities of Hind in population and wealth. . . . With a view of holy war, and not for the lust of conquest, he enlisted under their banners about 14,000 cavalry and 20,000 infantry, which in their language are called dakk.

They went by daily marches through the hills, from stage to stage, and when they arrived at their destination at early dawn they surrounded Kambayat and the idolaters were awakened from their sleepy state of carelessness and were taken by surprise, not knowing where to go, and mothers forgot their children and dropped them from their embrace. The Muhammadan forces began to "kill and slaughter on the right and on the left unmercifully, throughout the impure land, for the sake of Islam," and blood flowed in torrents. They plundered gold and silver to an extent greater than can be conceived, and an immense number of brilliant precious stones, such as pearls, diamonds, rubies, and emeralds, etc. as well as a great variety of cloths, both silk and cotton, stamped, embroidered, and colored.

They took captive a great number of handsome and elegant maidens, amounting to 20,000, and children of both sexes, "more than the pen can enumerate." . . . In short, the Muhammadan army brought the country to utter ruin, and destroyed the lives of the inhabitants, and plundered the cities, and captured their off-spring, so that many temples were deserted and the idols were broken and trodden under foot, the largest of which was one called Somnat. . . . The fragments were conveyed to Delhi, and the entrance of the Jami Masjid was paved with them, that people might remember and talk of this brilliant Victory.

The tongue of the sword of the Khalifa of the time, which is the tongue of the flame of Islam, has imparted light to the entire darkness of Hindustan by the illumination of its guidance. . . . On the other side, so much dust arose from the battered temple of Somnat that even the sea was not able to lay it, and on the right hand and on the left hand the army has conquered from sea to sea, and several capitals of the gods of the Hindus, in which Satanism has prevailed since the time of the Jinns, have been demolished. All these impurities of infidelity have been cleansed by the Sultan's destruction of idol-temples, beginning with his first holy expedition against Deogir,[2] so that the flames of the light of the law illumine all these unholy countries, and places for the criers to prayer are exalted on high, and prayers are read in mosques. Allah be praised! . . .

On Sunday, the 23rd, after holding a council of chief officers, he [Malik Kafur, converted Hindu and commander of the Muslim army] took a select body of cavalry with him and pressed on against Billal Deo, and on the 5th of Shawwal reached the fort of Dhur Sammund[3] after a difficult march of twelve days over the hills and valleys, and through thorny forests. "The fire-worshipping" Rai, when he learnt that "his idol-temple was likely to be converted into a mosque," despatched Kisu Mal. . . . The commander replied that he was sent with the object of converting him to Muhammadanism, or of making him a zimmi, and subject to pay tax, or of slaying him if neither of these terms were assented to. When the Rai received this reply, he said he was ready to give up all he possessed, except his sacred thread.

Notes

1. H. M. Elliot and John Dowson, *The History of India as Told by Its Own Historians: The Muhammadan Period*, vol. 3 (1867–1877; repr., Delhi: Elibron, 2001), pp. 42–44, 85 (p. 85, Translation of Tarikh-i-'Alai of Amir Khusru, poet and sufi disciple of Nizamuddin Awliya, the famed Chishtiyya sufi of Delhi), 88–89. Translation of Tarikh-i-Wassaf of Abdullah Wassaf.

2. Devagiri in Maharashtra, renamed Daulatabad by Muhammad bin Tughlaq.

3. Dwarasamudra in Karnataka, capital of the Hoysala Kingdom at that time.

I. MUSLIM DEVASTATION OF BUDDHIST TEMPLES AND PLIGHT OF THE BUDDHIST COMMUNITY IN NORTHERN INDIA (BIHAR) (EARLY THIRTEENTH CENTURY CE)[1]

The Djarmasvamin said that "when they had reached the city of Vaisali, all the inhabitants had fled at dawn from fear of the Turushka [Muslim] soldiery."[2]

Vikramasili was still existing in the time of the Elder Dharmasvamin [1153–1261 CE] and the Kashmir [1145–1225 CE], but when the Dharmasvamin visited the country there were no traces left of it, the Turushka soldiery having raised it to the ground, and thrown the foundation stones into the Ganga [Ganges River]. At the time of Dharmasvamin's visit to Vajrsana, the place was deserted and only four monks were found staying (in the Vihara). One (of them) said, "It is not good! All have fled from fear of the Turushka soldiery." They blocked up the door in front of the Mahabodhi image with bricks and plastered it. Near it they placed another image as a substitute. They also plastered the outside door (of the temple). On its surface they drew the image of Mahesvara in order to protect it from non-Buddhists. The monks said, "We five do not dare to remain here and shall have to flee." As the day's stage was long and the heat great, said the Dharmasvamin, they felt tired, and as it became dark, they remained there and fell asleep. Had the Turushkas come, they would not have known it. At daybreak they fled towards the North following the rut of a cart, and for seventeen days the Dharmasvamin did not see the face of the image (i.e., the Mahabodhi image). At that time also a woman appeared, who brought the welcome news that the Turushka soldiery had gone far away.[3]

Notes

1. George Roerich, trans., *Biography of Dharmasvamin* (Patna: K. P. Jayaswal Research Institute, 1959). Dharmasvamin was a highly educated Tibetan monk who traveled in northern India from 1234–1236 CE. Independent evidence confirming the veracity of his chronicle demonstrates that King Ramasimha of Tirhut and Buddhasena of Bodha-Gaya, whom Dharmasvamin met during his short sojourn in India, were actually ruling at that time. Moreover, in the introduction to the text [on p. xii] by A. S. Altekar, it is noted that, "He [Dharmasvamin] resists the temptation of exaggerating the destruction wrought by the Muslim conquerors."
2. Ibid., p. 62.
3. Ibid., p. 64.

J. JIHAD CAMPAIGNS AT THE END OF THE THIRTEENTH CENTURY AND FIRST THREE DECADES OF THE FOURTEENTH CENTURY, FROM THE HINDU CHRONICLE *KANHADADE PRABANDHA*

[These campaigns vanquished extensive regions (Malwa, Gujarat, Ranthambhor, Siwana, Jalor, Devagiri, Warangal, Ma'bar, and Ramesvaram) and resulted in the death or enslavement of perhaps millions of Hindus.[1] The devastating nature of such attacks, which included deliberate targeting of non-combatants, is captured in the account, below]:

A farman (firman) was now given to Gori Malik (to sack Bhinmal). . . . The Turkish [Muslim] invaders entered the town making dreadful din and clamor. Orders were issued clear and terrible: 'The soldiers shall march into the town spreading terror everywhere! Cut down the Brahmanas [Brahman priests], wherever they may be—performing homa or milking cows! Kill the cows—even those which are pregnant or with newly born calves!" The Turks ransacked Bhinmal and captured everybody in the sleepy town. Thereafter, Gori Malik gleefully set fire to the town in a wanton display of force and meanness.[2]

Notes

1. V. S. Bhatnagar, trans., *Kanhadade Prabandha* (New Delhi: Aditya Prakashan, 1991), p. xii.
2. Ibid., p. 49.

K. BRUTALITY OF SULTAN OF MA'BAR (GHAYASUDDIN) WITNESSED BY IBN BATTUTA (C. 1345 CE)[1]

The country we had to traverse was an impenetrable jungle of trees and reeds. The Sultan ordered that every one in the army, great and small alike, should carry a hatchet to cut down these obstacles. When the camp was struck, he set out on horseback towards the forest together with his soldiers who felled the trees from morning to noon . . . they resumed cutting trees till the evening. All the infidels found in the jungle were taken prisoners; they had stakes sharpened at both ends and made the prisoners carry them on their shoulders. Each was accompanied by his wife and children, and they were thus led to the camp. It is the practice here to surround the camp with a palisade, called a katkar and having four gates. They make a second katkar around the king's habitation. Outside the principal enclosure, they raise the platforms about three feet high, and light fires on them at night. Slaves and sentinels spend the night here, each holding in his hand a bundle of very thin reeds. When the infidels approach for a night attack on the camp, all the sentries light their faggots, and thanks to the flames, the night becomes as bright as day, and the cavalry sets out in pursuit of the idolaters.

In the morning, the Hindus who had been made prisoners the day before, were divided into four groups, and each of these was led to one of the four gates of the main enclosure. There they were impaled on the posts they had themselves carried. Afterwards their wives were butchered and tied to the stakes by their hair. The children were massacred on the bosoms of their mothers, and their corpses left there. Then they struck camp and started cutting down trees in another forest, and all the Hindus who were made captive were treated in the same manner.[2]

Notes

1. Ibn Battuta 1304–1368/?1377, was one of the world's most famous travelers. Departing from Tangiers in 1325, he trekked extensively, across North Africa, through Egypt to Syria, Mecca (multiple pilgrimages), Iraq, the Red Sea, Yemen, Mogadishu, and the trading ports of East Africa, Oman, and the Persian Gulf; Asia Minor, including a visit

to Constantinople, Transoxiana, and Afghanistan; through northern and southern India, the Maldives, the Sumatra, and China (the Chinese port of Zaytun and Tsuan-chou), before returning to North Africa via Sumatra, Malabar, the Persian Gulf, Iraq, Syria, Egypt. Additional treks included visits to Sardinia, the kingdom of Granada, a journey across the Sahara, and to the country of Niger.

2. K. A. Nilakanta Sastri, ed., *Foreign Notices of South India* (Madras: University of Madras, 2001), pp. 278–79.

L. THE JIHAD CAMPAIGNS OF AMIR TIMUR (1397–1399 CE)[1]

About this time there arose in my heart the desire to lead an expedition against the infidels, and to become a ghazi; for it had reached my ears that the slayer of infidels is a ghazi, and if he is slain he becomes a martyr. It was on this account that I formed this resolution, but I was undetermined in my mind whether I should direct my expedition against the infidels of China or against the infidels and polytheists of India. In this matter I sought an omen from the Kuran, and the verse I opened upon was this, "O Prophet, make war upon infidels and unbelievers, and treat them with severity." (Qur'an 66.9). My great officers told me that the inhabitants of Hindustan were infidels and unbelievers. In obedience to the order of Almighty Allah I ordered an expedition against them. . . .

Then the Prince Muhammad Sultan said: "The whole country of India is full of gold and jewels, and in it there are seventeen mines of gold and silver, diamond and ruby and emerald and tin and steel and copper and quicksilver, etc., and of the plants which grow there are those fit for making wearing apparel, and aromatic plants, and the sugar-cane, and it is a country which is always green and verdant, and the whole aspect of the country is pleasant and delightful. Now, since the inhabitants are chiefly polytheists and infidels and idolators and worshippers of the sun, by the order of Allah and his prophet, it is right for us to conquer them." Some of the nobles said, "By the favor of Almighty Allah we may conquer India, but if we establish ourselves permanently therein, our race will degenerate and our children will become like the natives of those regions, and in a few generations their strength and valor will diminish." The amirs of regiments (kushunat) were disturbed at these words, but I said to them, "My object in the invasion of Hindustan is to lead an expedition against the infidels that, according to the law of Muhammad (upon whom and his family be the blessing and peace of Allah), we may convert to the true faith the people of that country, purify the land itself from the filth of infidelity and polytheism; and that we may overthrow their temples and idols and become ghazis and mujahids before Allah."

They gave an unwilling consent, but I placed no reliance upon them. At this time the wise men of Islam came before me, and a conversation began about the propriety of a war against infidels and polytheists; they gave it as their opinion that it is the duty of the Sultan of Islam, and all the people who profess that "there is no god but Allah, and Muhammad is the prophet of Allah," for the sake of preserving their religion and strengthening their law, to exert their utmost endeavor for the suppression of the enemies of their faith. And it is the duty of every Muslim and true believer to use his utmost exertions in obedience to his ruler. When the edifying words of the wise men reached the ears of the nobles, all their hearts were set upon a holy war in Hindustan, and throwing themselves on their knees, they repeated the Chapter of Victory.[2]

When I girded up my loins for the expedition, I wrote to Hazrat Shaikh Zainu-d-din[3] to the effect that I had determined on a religious expedition to Hindustan. He wrote in the margin of my letter: "Be it known to Abu–1-Ghazi Timur (whom may Allah assist) that great prosperity in this world and the next will result to you from this undertaking, and you will go and return in safety." He also sent me a large sword which I made my scepter. . . .

The ruler of Kator[4] had a fort, on one side of which was a river, and beyond the river a lofty mountain reaching down to the water. . . . When I advanced into the neighborhood of the fort I did not perceive a trace of the infidels, and when I came to the place itself I saw that they had abandoned it and fled. I obtained a booty of many sheep and some other things here, and ordered that they should set fire to the houses and buildings of the city, in the midst of which the fort was built, and that they should level it with the ground. Then crossing the river in haste and pursuing the track of the enemy, I reached the skirts of the mountain on the top of which the infidels had taken up their position in defiles and other strong places. I immediately gave orders to my valiant and experienced troops to ascend. Raising their war-cry and shouting the takbir, they rushed to the attack. . . . They all proved their zeal for Islam on the unbelieving foe, and having overpowered the infidels they put many of them to death and took possession of their fastnesses. Only a few of the enemy succeeded in sheltering themselves, wounded and worn out with fatigue, in their caverns. I sent Ak Sultan to them with the message that if they would consent to submit unconditionally and would all become Musulmans and repeat the creed, I grant them quarter, but otherwise I would exterminate them to a man. . . . They all proffered submission, and repeating the necessary formula, embraced the Muhammadan faith. . . .

I was informed that the blessed tomb of Hazrat Shaikh Farid Ganj-shakar (whom may Allah bless) was in this city [Ajodhan], upon which I immediately set out on pilgrimage to it. I repeated the Fatiha, and the other prayers, for assistance, etc., and prayed for victory from his blessed spirit, and distributed large sums in alms and charity among the attendants on the holy shrine.[5] I left Ajodhan on Wednesday, the 26th of the month on my march to Bhatnir.[6] The raja of that place was called Dul Chain. He had assembled a body of Rajputs, a class which supplies the most renowned soldiers of India, and with these he waited ready to do battle. . . .

So in all directions the brave warriors of Islam attacked the infidels with lion-like fury, until at length by the grace of Allah, victory beamed upon the efforts of my soldiers. In a short space of time all the people in the fort were put to the sword, and in the course of one hour the heads of ten thousand infidels were cut off. The sword of Islam was washed in the blood of the infidels, and all the goods and effects, the treasure and the grain which for many a long year had been stored in the fort, became the spoil of my soldiers. They set fire to the houses and reduced them to ashes, and they razed the buildings and the fort to the ground. When this victory had been accomplished I returned to my tent. All the princes and amirs waited upon me to congratulate me upon the conquest and upon the enormous booty which had fallen into my hands. It was all brought out and I distributed it among my brave amirs and soldiers.

When I made inquiries about the city of Sarsuti,[7] I was informed that the people of the place were strangers to the religion of Islam, and that they kept hogs in their houses and ate the flesh of those animals. When they heard of my arrival, they abandoned their city. I sent my cavalry in pursuit of them, and a great fight ensued. All these infidel Hindus were slain, their wives and children were made prisoners, and their property and goods became the spoil of the victors. The soldiers then returned, bringing with them several thousand Hindu women and children who became Muhammadans, and repeated the creed. . . .

It was again brought to my knowledge that these turbulent Jats were as numerous as ants or locusts. . . . They had now taken fright, and had gone into jungles and deserts hard to penetrate. My great object in invading Hindustan had been to wage a religious war against the infidel Hindus, and it now appeared to me that it was necessary for me to put down these Jats. On the 9th of the month I dispatched the baggage from Tohana,[8] and on the same day I marched into the jungles and wilds, and slew 2,000 demon-like Jats. I made their wives and children captives, and plundered their cattle and property. . . . On the same day a party of saiyids, who dwelt in the vicinity, came with courtesy and humility to wait upon me and were very graciously received. In my reverence for the race of the prophet, I treated their chiefs with great honor. . . .

On the 29th I again marched and reached the river Jumna. On the other side of the river I descried a fort, and upon making inquiry about it, I was informed that it consisted of a town and fort, called Loni.[9] . . . I determined to take that fort at once. . . . Many of the Rajputs placed their wives and children in their houses and burned them, then they rushed to the battle and were killed. Other men of the garrison fought and were slain, and a great many were taken prisoners. Next day I gave orders that the Musalman prisoners should be separated and saved, but that the infidels should all be despatched to hell with the proselyting sword. I also ordered that the houses of the saiyids, shaikhs, and learned Musalmans should be preserved but that all the other houses should be plundered and the fort destroyed. It was done as I directed and a great booty was obtained. . . .

Next day, Friday the 3rd of the month, I left the fort of Loni and marched to a

position opposite to Jahan-numa[10] where I encamped. . . . I now held a Court. . . .
At this Court Amir Jahan Shah and Amir Sulaiman Shah and other amirs of experience, brought to my notice that, from the time of entering Hindustan up to the present time, we had taken more than 100,000 infidels and Hindus prisoners, and that they were all in my camp. On the previous day, when the enemy's forces made the attack upon us, the prisoners made signs of rejoicing, uttered imprecations against us, and were ready, as soon as they heard of the enemy's success, to form themselves into a body, break their bonds, plunder our tents, and then to go and join the enemy, and so increase his numbers and strength. I asked their advice about the prisoners, and they said that on the great day of battle these 100,000 prisoners could not be left with the baggage, and that it would be entirely opposed to the [Islamic] rules of war to set these idolaters and foes of Islam at liberty. In fact, no other course remained but that of making them all food for the sword. When I heard these words I found them in accordance with the rules of war, and I directly gave my command for the tawachis[11] to proclaim throughout the camp that every man who had infidel prisoners was to put them to death and whoever neglected to do so should himself be executed and his property given to the informer. When this order became known to the ghazis of Islam, they drew their swords and put their prisoners to death. One hundred thousand infidels, impious idolaters, were on that day slain. Maulana Nasiru-d-din 'Umar, a counsellor and man of learning, who, in all his life, had never killed a sparrow, now, in execution of my order, slew with his sword fifteen idolatrous Hindus who were his captives. . . .

On the 16th of the month some incidents occurred which led to the sack of the city of Delhi, and to the slaughter of many of the infidel inhabitants. . . . The Hindus set fire to their houses with their own hands, burned their wives and children in them, and rushed into the fight and were killed. . . . On that day, Thursday, and all the night of Friday, nearly 15,000 Turks were engaged in slaying, plundering, and destroying. . . . The following day, Saturday, the 17th, all passed in the same way, and the spoil was so great that each man secured from fifty to a hundred prisoners—men, women, and children. There was no man who took less than twenty. The other booty was immense in rubies, diamonds, pearls, and other gems; jewels of gold and silver; ashrafis; tankas of gold and silver of the celebrated 'Alai coinage; vessels of gold and silver; and brocades and silks of great value. Gold and silver ornaments of the Hindu [12] women were obtained in such quantities as to exceed all account. Excepting the quarter of the saiyids, the 'ulama, and the other Musulmans, the whole city was sacked. . . .

I had been at Delhi fifteen days, which time I had passed in pleasure and enjoyment, holding royal Courts and giving great feasts. I then reflected that I had come to Hindustan to war against infidels, and my enterprise had been so blessed that wherever I had gone I had been victorious. I had triumphed over my adversaries. I had put to death some lakhs [1 lakh = 100,000] of infidels and idolaters, and I had stained my proselyting sword with the blood of the enemies of the faith.

Now this crowning victory had been won, and I felt that I ought not to indulge in ease but rather to exert myself in warring against the infidels of Hindustan. . . .

On the 1st Jumada-i-awwal I placed the left wing of the army under the command of Amir Jahan Shah, with orders to march up the Jumna, to take every fort and town and village he came to, and to put all the infidels of the country to the sword. The amir led off his army to execute my commands. . . . My brave fellows pursued and killed many of them, made their wives and children prisoners, plundered their property and goods, and secured a vast number of cows and buffaloes. When by the favor of Allah, I had secured this victory, I got off my horse and prostrated myself on the ground to pay my thanks. . . .

Pressing on with all haste I passed the jungles and thickets, and arrived in front of the infidels [at Kutila].[13] After a slight resistance the enemy took flight, but many of them fell under the swords of my soldiers. All the wives and children of the infidels were made prisoners, and their property and goods, gold, money and grain, horses, camels (shutur), cows, and buffaloes in countless numbers, fell as spoil into the hands of my soldiers. Satisfied with this rout of the enemy, I said the afternoon prayers in public in that desert, and I returned thanks to Allah. . . . My brave men displayed great courage and daring; they made their swords their banners, and exerted themselves in slaying the foe (during a bathing festival on the bank of the Ganges). They slaughtered many of the infidels, and pursued those who fled to the mountains. So many of them were killed that their blood ran down the mountains and plain, and thus (nearly) all were sent to hell. The few who escaped, wounded, weary, and half dead, sought refuge in the defiles of the hills. Their property and goods, which exceeded all computation, and their countless cows and buffaloes, fell as spoil into the hands of my victorious soldiers. . . .

When I was satisfied with the destruction I had dealt out to the infidels, and the land was cleansed from the pollution of their existence, I turned back victorious and triumphant, laden with spoil. On that same day I crossed the Ganges, and said my mid-day prayers in the congregation, on the banks of that river. I prostrated myself in humble thanks to Allah, and afterwards again mounting my horse, marched five miles down the river and then encamped. It now occurred to my mind that I had marched as a conqueror from the river Sind to Delhi, the capital of the kings of India. I had put the infidels to the edge of the sword on both sides of my route, and had scoured the land. . . . I had crossed the rivers Ganges and Jumna, and I had sent many of the abominable infidels to hell, and had purified the land from their foul existence. I rendered thanks to Almighty Allah that I had accomplished my undertaking, and had waged against the infidels that holy war I had resolved upon; then I determined to turn my course towards Samarkand, my capital and paradise. . . .

Amir Sulaiman Shah . . . and other amirs . . . said: "So long as we your servants, are able to move hand and foot, we will execute your orders . . . and (you) should now order us to march against the infidels of the Siwalik, [14] and to rout and destroy them." I replied: "My principal object in coming to Hindustan and in undergoing all this toil and hardship, has been to accomplish two things. The first was to war with the infidels, the enemies of the Muhammadan religion; and by this religious warfare to acquire some claim to reward in the life to come. The other was a worldly object; that the army of Islam might gain something by plundering the wealth and valuables of the infidels: plunder in war is as lawful as their mothers' milk to Musulmans who war for their faith, and the consuming of that which is lawful is a means of grace."

On the 10th Jumada-i-awwal I mounted my horse and drew my sword, determined on fighting the infidels of the Siwalik. . . . The infidel gabrs[15] were dismayed at the sight, and took to flight. The holy warriors pursued them, and made heaps of slain. A few Hindus, in a wretched plight, wounded and half dead, escaped, and hid themselves in holes and caves. An immense spoil beyond all compute, in money, goods and articles, cows and buffaloes, fell into the hands of my soldiers. All the Hindu women and children in the valley were made prisoners.

On the following day, the 14th Jumada-i-awwal, I crossed the river Jumna with the baggage, and encamped in another part of the Siwalik hills. Here I learned that in this part of the Siwalik there was a raja of great rank and power, by name Ratan Sen. . . . In the front of this valley Raja Ratan Sen had drawn out his forces. At the first onset, the Hindus broke and fled, and my victorious soldiers pursued, slashing their swords killing many of the fugitives, and sending them to hell. Only a few of them escaped, wounded and dispirited, and hiding themselves like foxes in the woods, thus saved their lives. When the soldiers gave up killing the infidels, they secured great plunder in goods and valuables, prisoners, and cattle. No one of them had less than one or two hundred cows, and ten or twenty slaves—the other plunder exceeded all calculation.

When I entered the valley on that side of the Siwalik, information was brought to me about the town (shahr) of Nagarkot,[16] which is a large and important town of Hindustan and situated in these mountains. . . . I instantly ordered Amir Jahan Shah, whom I had sent to the front with the forces of the left wing and the army of Khurasan, to attack the enemy. The amir, in obedience to my order, advanced and charged the enemy. At the very first charge the infidels were defeated and put to flight. The holy warriors, sword in hand, dashed among the fugitives, and made heaps of corpses. Great numbers were slain, and a vast booty in goods and valuables, and prisoners and cattle in countless numbers, fell into the hands of the victors who returned triumphant and loaded with spoil.

Notes

1. H. M. Elliot and John Dowson, *The History of India as Told by Its Own Historians: The Muhammadan Period* (1867–1877; repr., Delhi: Elibron, 2001), pp. 394–98, 403–405, 421–22, 427–29, 432–33, 435–36, 445–46, 448, 451–54, 457–58, 459–66. Translation of Malfuzat-i-Timuri of Timur.

2. Al-Fatiha, the opening chapter of the Quran.

3. A well-known sufi.

4. A town in North-West Frontier Province.

5. None of the devotees of Baba Farid, the famous Chishtiyya sufi, is known to have disapproved of the acts committed by Timur.

6. Modern Hanumangarh in the Ganganagar district of Rajasthan.

7. The ancient name of Sirsa, now headquarters of a district in Haryana.

8. A town in Jind district of Haryana.

9. A town opposite Delhi across the Jamuna.

10. Firoz Shah Tughlaq's palace on the Ridge, now Bara Hindu Rao Hospital.

11. Drum beaters.

12. The word *Hindu* in this citation was omitted in Mohammad Habib and K. A. Nizami, eds., *A Comprehensive History of India,* vol. 5: *The Sultanat* (New Delhi: People's Publishing House, 1970), p. 122.

13. A town on the east bank of the Jamuna.

14. Region round Dehradun and neighbouring districts of Himachal Pradesh.

15. A term used for Zoroastrians of Iran to start with, it became a term of contempt for Hindu warriors, meaning vagabonds.

16. Ancient name of Kangra, now a district headquarters in Himachal Pradesh.

M. JIHAD CAMPAIGNS OF BABUR (1519–1530 CE)[1]

[Attack on the small Hindu principality of Bajaur in the North-West Frontier Province at the start of his first invasion of India in 1519 CE.]

As the Bajauris were rebels and at enmity with the people of Islam, and as, by reason of the heathenish and hostile customs prevailing in their midst, the very name of Islam was rooted out from their tribe, they were put to general massacre and their wives and children were made captive. At a guess more than 3,000 men went to their death; as the fight did not reach to the eastern side of the fort, a few got away there. The fort taken, we entered and inspected it. On the walls, in houses, streets and alleys, the dead lay, in what numbers! Corners and goers to and from were passing over the bodies. . . . With mind easy about the important affairs of the Bajaur fort, we marched, on Tuesday the 9th of Muharram, one kuroh [two miles] down the dale of Bajaur and ordered that a tower of heads should be set up on the rising ground.[2]

[Babur's self-proclaimed jihad against the Rajput Confederacy led by Maharana Sangram Singh of Mewar, in 1527 CE. His account is punctuated with Qur'anic verses and references.]

On Monday the 9th of the first Jumada, we got out of the suburbs of Agra, on our journey (safar) for the Holy War, and dismounted in the open country, where we remained three or four days to collect our army and be its rallying-point. . . . On this occasion I received a secret inspiration and heard an infallible voice say: "Is not the time yet come unto those who believe, that their hearts should humbly submit to the admonition of Allah, and that truth which hath been revealed?" Thereupon we set ourselves to extirpate the things of wickedness. . . . Above all, adequate thanks cannot be rendered for a benefit than which none is greater in the world and nothing is more blessed, in the world to come, to wit, victory over most powerful infidels and dominion over wealthiest heretics, "these are the unbelievers, the wicked." In the eyes of the judicious, no blessing can be greater than this. . . .

Previous to the rising in Hindustan of the Sun of dominion and the emergence there of the light of the Shahansha's (i.e., Babur's) Khalifate the authority of that execrated pagan (Sanga)—at the Judgment Day he shall have no friend—was such that not one of all the exalted sovereigns of this wide realm, such as the Sultan of Delhi, the Sultan of Gujarat, and the Sultan of Mandu, could cope with this evil-dispositioned one, without the help of other pagans. . . . Ten powerful chiefs, each the leader of a pagan host, uprose in rebellion, as smoke rises, and linked themselves, as though enchained, to that perverse one (Sanga); and this infidel decade who, unlike the blessed ten, uplifted misery-freighted standards which denounce unto them excruciating punishment, had many dependents, and troops, and wide-extended lands. . . .

The protagonists of the royal forces fell, like divine destiny, on that one-eyed Dajjal who to understanding men, showed the truth of the saying, When Fate arrives, the eye becomes blind, and setting before their eyes the scripture which saith, Whosoever striveth to promote the true religion, striveth for the good of his own soul, they acted on the precept to which obedience is due, Fight against infidels and hypocrites. . . . The pagan right wing made repeated and desperate attack on the left wing of the army of Islam, falling furiously on the holy warriors, possessors of salvation, but each time was made to turn back or, smitten with the arrows of victory, was made to descend into Hell, the house of perdition: they shall be thrown to burn therein, and an unhappy dwelling shall it be. Then the trusty amongst the nobles, Mumin Ataka and Rustam Turkman, betook themselves to the rear of the host of darkened pagans. . . . At the moment when the holy warriors were heedlessly flinging away their lives, they heard a secret voice say, Be not dismayed, neither be grieved, for, if ye believe, ye shall be exalted above the unbelievers, and from the infallible Informer heard the joyful words, Assistance is from Allah, and a speedy victory! And do thou bear glad tiding to true believers. Then they fought with such delight that the plaudits of the saints of the Holy Assembly reached them and the angels from near the Throne, fluttered round their heads like moths. . . .

And victory the beautiful woman (shahid) whose world-adornment of waving tresses was embellished by Allah will aid you with a mighty aid, bestowed on us the good fortune that had been hidden behind a veil, and made it a reality. The absurd

Hindus, knowing their position perilous, dispersed like carded wool before the wind, and like moths scattered abroad. Many fell dead on the field of battle; others, desisting from fighting, fled to the desert exile and became the food of crows and kites. Mounds were made of the bodies of the slain, pillars of their heads.

After this success, Ghazi (jihad warrior) was written amongst the royal titles. Below the titles (tughra) entered on the Fath-nama, I wrote the following quatrain:

> For Islam's sake, I wandered in the wilds,
> Prepared for war with pagans and Hindus,
> Resolved myself to meet the martyr's death,
> Thanks be to Allah! a ghazi I became.[3]

Notes

1. Founder of the Mughal Empire.

2. A. S. Beveridge, trans., *Babur-Nama* (Lahore: Sange-Meel Publications, 1975), pp. 370–71.

3. Ibid., pp. 547, 554, 560–63, 569, 572–75.

N. JIHAD AGAINST VIJAYANAGARA BY SULTAN ADIL SHAHI OF BIJAPUR AND HIS ALLIES (1565 CE)

[The battle took place on Tuesday, 23 January 1565. The Vijayanagara army commenced attack in right earnest and the right and left wings of the confederate army were thrown into such disorder that their commanders were almost prepared to retreat when the position was saved by Hussain who opposed the enemy with great valour. The fighting was then continued and the loss of life on both sides was heavy. But it did not last long and its fate was determined by the desertion of two Muhammadan commanders under Ramaraja. Caesar Frederick, who visited Vijayanagara in 1567, said that each of these commanders had under him seventy to eighty thousand men and the defeat of Vijayanagara was due to their desertion. Ramaraja fell into enemy's hands and was beheaded on the order of Hussain.][1]

The Hindoos, according to custom, when they saw their chief destroyed, fled in the utmost disorder from the field, and were pursued by the allies with such success, that the river was dyed red with their blood. It is computed, by the best authorities, that above one hundred thousand infidels were slain during the action and in the pursuit. The plunder was so great that every private man in the allied army became rich in gold, jewels tents, horses, and slaves, the kings permitting every person to retain what he acquired, reserving the elephants only for their own use. Letters with accounts of this important victory were despatched to their several dominions, and to the neighbouring states, while the kings themselves, shortly after the battle, marched onwards into the country of Ramraj, as far as Anagoondy, and the advanced troops penetrated to Beejanuggur which they plundered, razed the chief buildings to the ground, and committed every species of excess.[2]

[The third day saw the beginning of the end. The victorious Mussulmans had halted on the field of battle for rest and refreshment, but now they had reached the capital, and from that time forward for a space of five months Vijayanagar knew no rest. The enemy had come to destroy, and they carried out their object relentlessly. They slaughtered the people without mercy; broke down the temples and palaces, and wreaked such savage vengeance on the abode of the Kings, that, with the exception of a few great stone-built temples and walls, nothing now remains but a heap of ruins to mark the spot where once stately buildings stood. They demolished the statues, and even succeeded in breaking the limbs of the huge Narasimha monolith. Nothing seemed to escape them. They broke up the pavilions standing on the huge platform from which the kings used to watch festivals, and overthrew all the carved work. They lit huge fires in the magnificently decorated buildings forming the temple of Vitthalaswami near the river, and smashed its exquisite stone sculptures. With fire and sword, with crowbars and axes, they carried on day after day their work of destruction. Never perhaps in the history of the world has such havoc been wrought, and wrought so suddenly, on so splendid a city; teeming with a wealthy and industrious population in the fun plenitude of prosperity one day, and on the next seized, pillaged, and reduced to ruins, amid scenes of savage massacre and horrors beggaring description. . . . The loot must have been enormous. Couto states that amongst other treasures was found a diamond as large as a hen's egg, which was kept by the Adil Shah.][3]

Notes

1. R. C. Majumdar, ed., *The History and Culture of the Indian People*, vol. 7: *The Mughal Empire* (Bombay, 1973), p. 425.

2. John Briggs, trans., *History of the Rise of the Mahomedan Power in India* (New Delhi, 1981), volume 3, p. 79.

3. Robert Sewell, *A Forgotten Empire* (New Delhi: National Book Trust, 1962), pp. 199–200.

O. JIHAD CAMPAIGNS OF AHMAD SHAH ABDALI [DURRANI] (1757, 1760, AND 1761 CE)[1]

Abdali's Attack on Gokul

Moving a fortnight behind his vanguard, the Abdali king himself came upon the scene. He had stormed Ballabhgarh on 3rd March and halted there for two days. On 15th March he arrived near Mathura, and wisely avoiding that reeking human shambles crossed over to the eastern bank of the Jamuna and encamped at Mahavan, six miles south-east of the city. Two miles to his west lay Gokul, the seat of the pontiff of the rich Vallabhacharya sect. The Abdali's policy of frightfulness had defeated his cupidity: dead men could not be held to ransom. The invader's unsatisfied need of money was pressing him; he sought the help of Imad's local knowledge as to the most promising sources of booty. A detachment from his camp was sent to plunder Gokul. But here the monks were martial Nagasannyasis of upper India and Rajputana. Four thousand of these naked, ash-smeared warriors stood outside Gokul and fought the Afghans, till half of their own number was killed after slaying an equal force of the enemy. Then at the entreaty of the Bengal subahdar's envoy (Jugalkishor) and his assurance that a hermitage of faqirs could not contain any money, the Abdali recalled the detachment. "All the vairagis perished but Gokulnath [the deity of the city] was saved," as a Marathi newsletter puts it.[2]

Describing Afghan atrocities at this time, Munshi Sadasukh Dehlawi wrote, "I have myself seen the depredations of the Afghans round Dehli and Mattra. God defend us from them! It makes the very hair of the body stand on end to think of them. Two hundred thousand men were destroyed in these massacres, and the hordes of the enemy were without number. Such atrocities, forsooth, were perpetrated in compliance with their religion and law! What cared they for the religion, the law, the honour and reputation of the innocent sufferers? It was enough for such bigots that splendour accrued by their deeds to the faith of Muhammad and 'Ali!"[3]

Eyewitness Account [of Mir Taqi] from Luni, near Delhi (January 1760)

In the evening Raja Nagar Mal (Mir's patron at the time) left the city, and in due course safely reached the forts of Suraj Mal (ruler of the Jat kingdom). I stayed behind to look after my family. After evening, proclamation was made that Shah Abdali had granted security to all, and that none of the citizens should be in any fear. But night had scarcely fallen when the outrages began. Fires were started in the city and houses were burnt down and looted. The following morning all was uproar and confusion. The Afghans and Rohillas (Najib's soldiers) started their work of slaughter and plunder, breaking down the doors, tying up those they found inside, and in many cases burning them alive or cutting off their head.

Everywhere was bloodshed and destruction, and for three days and three nights this savagery continued. The Afghans would leave no article of food or clothing untouched. They broke down the walls and roofs of the houses, and ill-treated and tormented in inhabitants. The city was swarming with them. Men who had been pillars of the state were brought to nothing, men of noble rank left destitute, family men bereft of all their loved ones. Most of them roved the streets amid insult and humiliation. Men's wives and children were made captive, and the killing and looting went on unchecked. The Afghans humiliated and abused their victims and practiced all kinds of atrocities upon them. Nothing which could be looted was spared, and some would strip their victims even of their underclothing. The new city (Shahjahanabad) was ransacked.

On the third day some sort of law and order was introduced, but the officer in charge himself completed the work of despoliation; and when at last the looters were driven out of the new city, they simply turned their attention to the old, where they put countless people to the sword. For seven or eight days the tumult raged. Nobody was left with clothes to wear or with enough food even for a single meal. Many died of the wounds they had received, while others suffered greatly from the cold. The looters would carry off men's stores of grain and then sell it at an extortionate price to those who needed it. The cry of the opposed rose to heaven, but the king (Abdali), who considered himself a pillar of true religion, was quite unmoved. Large numbers of people left the city and fled into the open country, where many of them died. Others were carried off by force to the invader's camp. I, who was already poor, became poorer. My house, which stood on the main road, was leveled with the ground.[4]

Jihad at Panipat (1761 CE)

Next morning the sun revealed a horrid spectacle on the vast plain south of Panipat. On the actual field of the combat thirty-one distinct heaps of the slain were counted, the number of bodies in each ranging from five hundred upwards to one thousand and in four up to fifteen hundred, a rough total of twenty-eight thousand. In addition to these, the ditch round the Maratha camp was full of dead bodies, partly the victims of disease and famine during the long siege and partly wounded men who had crawled out of the fighting to die there. West and south of Panipat city, the jungle and the road in the line of Maratha retreat were littered with the remains of those who had fallen unresisting in the relentless Durrani pursuit or from hunger and exhaustion. Their number—probably three-fourths noncombatants and one-fourth soldiers—could not have been far short of the vast total of those slain in the battlefield. The hundreds who lay down wounded, perished from the severity of the cold.

After the havoc of combat followed massacre in cold blood. Several hundreds of Marathas had hidden themselves in the hostile city of Panipat through folly or helplessness; and these were hunted out next day and put to the sword. According to one plausible account, the sons of Abdus Samad Khan and Mian Qutb received the Durrani king's permission to avenge their father's death by an indiscriminate massacre of the Marathas for one day, and in this way nearly nine thousand men perished; these were evidently non-combatants. The eyewitness Kashiraj Pandit thus describes the scene: "Every Durrani soldier brought away a hundred or two of prisoners and slew them in the outskirts of their camp, crying out, When I started from our country, my mother, father, sister, and wife told me to slay so many kafirs for their sake after we had gained the victory in this holy war, so that the religious merit of this act [of infidel slaying] might accrue to them. In this way, thousands of soldiers and other persons were massacred. In the Shah's camp, except the quarters of himself and his nobles, every tent had a heap of severed heads before it. One may say that it was verily doomsday for the Maratha people."

The booty captured within the entrenchment was beyond calculation and the regiments of Khans [i.e., eight thousand troopers of Abdali clansmen] did not, as far as possible, allow other troops like the Iranis and the Turanis to share in the plunder; they took possession of everything themselves, but sold to the Indian soldiers handsome Brahman women for one tuman and good horses for two tumans each. The Deccani prisoners, male and female reduced to slavery by the victorious army numbered twenty-two thousand, many of them being the sons and other relatives of the sardars or middle class men. Among them "rose-limbed slave girls" are mentioned. . . . Besides these twenty-two thousand unhappy captives, some four hundred officers and six thousand men fled for refuge to Shuja-ud-daulah's camp, and were sent back to the Deccan with monetary help by that nawab, at the request of his Hindu officers. The total loss of the Marathas after the battle is put at fifty thousand horses, captured either by the Afghan army or the villagers along the route of flight, two hundred thousand draught cattle, some thousands of camels, five hundred elephants, besides cash and jewelry. Every trooper of the Shah brought away ten, and sometimes twenty camels laden with money. The captured horses were beyond count but none of them was of value; they came like droves of sheep in their thousands.[5]

Notes

1. Abdali is the former name of the Afgan tribe now known as Durrani.

2. Jadunath Sarkar, *Fall of the Mughal Empire*, 4th ed., vol. 2 (New Delhi, 1991), pp. 70–71.

3. *Muntakhab-ut-Tawarikh*, in H. M. Elliot and John Dowson, *The History of India as Told by Its Own Historians: The Muhammadan Period*, vol. 8 (1867–1877; repr., Delhi: Elibron, 2001), pp. 405–406.

4. Saiyid Athar Abbas Rizvi, *Shah Wali-Allah and His Times* (Canberra, Australia: Ma'rifat Publishing House, 1980), pp. 304–305.

5. Sarkar, *Fall of the Mughal Empire*, pp. 210–11.

P. JIHAD IN SOUTHERN INDIA (THE MALABAR DISTRICT): THE MOPLAH "REBELLION" (1921)[1]

During the past one hundred years not fewer than 51 outbreaks of Moplah[2] fanaticism have been recorded. The *West Coast Spectator*[3] of July 6, 1922, prints part of a song which is sung by Moplah braves. It describes in detail the loveliness of the *houris* (virgins) that wait with caparisoned horses to take straight to heaven all those faithful that die in battle, and it is said that every Moplah on the warpath carried with him a copy of this song.

. . . The nature of these outbreaks has been well summed up in a decision of the three judges that sat on the Special Tribunal, Calicut, to try some of the principal offenders. They say in part,

> For the last hundred years at least, the Moplah community has been disgraced from time to time by murderous outrages. In the past these have been due to fanaticism. They generally blazed out in the Ernad Taluk (county), where the Moplahs were . . . their untutored minds were particularly susceptible to the inflammatory teachings that Paradise was to be gained by killing Kafirs. They would go out on the warpath, killing Hindus, no matter whom . . . no grievance seems to have been necessary to start them on their wild careers. . . . Their intention was, absurd as it may seem, to subvert the British Government, and substitute a Khalifate Government by force of arms.

. . . In the rebellion of 1921 it was certainly not agrarian troubles that started them on their mad career. The evidence now clearly shows that the Khalifate and Non-Cooperation agitation must be given credit for having inflamed the minds of the Moplahs with a vain hope of *swaraj* (self-rule) and eternal bliss. . . . There are no doubt agrarian difficulties in Malabar as there are serious tenancy difficulties, but from personal observation, I would say that the Hindu coolies of the Mohammedan tenants of the Brahmin and Nair landlords are worse off than their employers.

. . . [T]he Hindu population fell easy prey to their (i.e., the Molpah) rage and the atrocities committed defy description. . . . The tale of atrocities committed makes sad reading indeed. A memorial submitted by women of Malabar to Her Excellency the Countess of Reading mentions such crimes as wells filled with mutilated bodies, pregnant women cut to pieces, children torn from mother's arms and killed, husbands and fathers tortured, flayed, and burned alive before the eyes of their wives and daughters; women forcibly carried off and outraged; homes destroyed; temples desecrated . . . not less than 100 Hindu temples were destroyed or desecrated; cattle slaughtered in temples and their entrails placed around the necks of the idols in place of garlands of flowers; and wholesale looting. No fiendish act seems to have been too vile for them to perpetrate.

. . . There were, during the rebellion, many cases of forced conversion from Hinduism to Mohammedanism. There was a double difficulty about restoring these people to their old faith. In the first place there is a severe penalty resting on any Mohammedan that perverts . . . and in the second place there is really no door save birth into Hinduism.

Notes

1. J. J. Banninga, "The Moplah Rebellion of 1921," *Moslem World* 13 (1923): 379–87, excerpts from pp. 379–80, 382–84, 386. Banninga (1875–1963) graduated from the Western Theological Seminary and received an honorary Doctor of Divinity from Hope College, Michigan, in 1917. He left for India in 1901 and served there for forty-two years. In 1917, Banninga became the principal of the Union Theological Seminary at Pasumalai in South India, a position he would hold for twenty-five years. The school served as a training ground for Indian pastors and evangelists. Banninga opens his analysis with the following overview, to put these excerpts in context:

> Sufficient time has elapsed since the Moplah Rebellion of 1921 took place to estimate, more accurately than could have been done before, the causes, the course and consequences of that uprising. Within the past few months the report of the Commander-in-Chief has appeared together with other documents that make a study of the rebellion possible. Court decisions, magazine articles, reports of reconstruction officers, both public and private, and many other sources of information are now available.

2. Molpahs are Muslims of Arabic and Hindu descent from the Malabar district of South India. The names Moplah or Mapillai mean "bridegroom" or "son-in-law," respectively, referring to the intermarriage of Arab traders and indigenous Hindu women.

3. An English weekly which started publication in 1879 from Kozhikode. It was printed by Vakil Poovadan Raman from the Spectator Press, and edited by an Englishman, Dr. Keys. In later years the weekly was renamed the *Malabar Spectator*, and was quite popular locally.

53

JIHAD SLAVERY IN THE SUDAN— LATE NINETEENTH CENTURY[1]

[I]f trade in general is in a state of depression, there is one trade to which the advent of the Mahdi and Khalifa gas given a great impulse. I refer, of course, to the slave-trade. As, however, the export of slaves to Egypt is strictly prohibited, this trade is confined entirely to the provinces under the Khalifa's control. In prohibiting the export of slaves, the Khalifa acts on the wise principle that he should not increase the power of his adversaries at his own expense. It is, of course, quite impossible for him to absolutely prevent slaves being taken occasionally to Egypt or Arabia; but the slave-caravans which were formerly sent from the Sudan have now almost completely stopped. A few years ago quantities of slaves were sent from Abyssinia by Abu Darfur and the Nuba mountains by Osman Wad Adam, and were generally sold by public auction for the benefit of the Beit el Mal or the Khalifa's private treasury. The transport of slaves is carried on with the same execrable and heartless cruelty which characterizes their capture. Of the thousands of Abyssinian Christians seized by Abu Anga, the majority were women and children, and under the cruel lash of the whip they were forced to march on foot the whole distance from Abyssinia to Omdurman. Wrenched from their families, provided with scarcely enough food to keep body and soul together, barefooted, and almost naked, they were driven through the country like herds of cattle. The great number of them perished on the road, and those who arrived in Omdurman were in so pitiable a condition that purchasers could scarcely be found for them, whilst numbers were given away for nothing by the Khalifa. After the defeat of the

Shilluks, Zeki Tummal packed thousands of these wretched creatures into the small barges used for the transport of his troops, and dispatched them to Omdurman. Hundreds died from suffocation and overcrowding on the journey, and on the arrival of the remnant, the Khalifa appropriated most of the young men as recruits for his bodyguard, whilst the women and young girls were sold by public auction, which lasted several days. Hungry, and in many cases naked, these unfortunate creatures lay huddled together in front of the Beit el Mal. For food, they were given an utterly inadequate quantity of uncooked dhurra. Hundreds fell ill, and for these poor wretches it was also impossible to find purchasers. Wearily they dragged their emaciated bodies to the river bank, where they died, and as nobody would take the trouble to bury them, the corpses were pushed into the river and swept away.

But a worse fate than this befell the slaves who has the misfortune to be sent from Darfur along the broad stretches of the waterless desert which lie between that province and Omdurman. These miserable creatures were mercilessly drive forward day and night, and it would be impossible for me to describe here the execrable measures adopted by these brutal slave drivers to force on their pray to their destination. When the poor wretches could go no further their ears were cut off as a proof to the owner that his property had died on the road. Some of my friends told me that on one occasion they had found an unfortunate woman whose ears had been cut off, but who was still alive. Taking pity on her, they brought her to El Fasher, were she eventually recovered, whilst her ears had been duly exposed in Omdurman as proof of her death.

Latterly, no large caravans of slaves have arrived in Omdurman, because the majority of the slave producing districts, such as Darfur, have become depopulated, or, in some cases, the tribes, such as the Tama, Massalit, etc., have thrown off allegiance to the Khalifa. Consignments, however, still come from Reggaf, but, owing to the long and tedious journey, numbers of them perish on the way. As the supplies from Gallabat, Kordofan, and Darfur have considerably diminished, the Khalifa now allows the Emirs to sell slaves to the itinerant Gellabas, and the latter are obliged to sign a paper giving a descriptive return of their purchase, and the amount paid. They are permitted to resell on the same conditions.

There is, of course, a daily sale of slaves in Omdurman; but the purchase of male slaves is forbidden, as they are looked upon as the Khalifa's monopoly, and are generally turned into soldiers. Anyone wishing to dispose of a male slave must send him to the Beit el Mel, where a purely nominal price is paid for him, and he is then, if likely to make a good soldier, recruited for the mulazemin, but if unsuitable, he is sent off to work as a laborer in his master's fields. The sale of women and girls is permissible everywhere, with the proviso that a paper must be signed by two witnesses of the sale, one of whom, if possible, should be a Kadi, certifying that the slave sold is the actual property of the vendor. This system was brought into force because slaves frequently ran away from their masters, and were caught and sold by other persons as their own property, and thus theft of slaves was a very common practice in Omdurman. They were frequently enticed into other people's houses, or secretly induced to leave the fields, then thrown into chains and carried off to distant parts of the country, where they were sold at very low rates. In accordance with the Mohammedan law, slaves cannot be witnesses, and being well aware of their inferior position, these stolen creatures, as long as they are kindly treated, are not dissatisfied with their lot.

In Omdurman itself, in an open space a short distance to the south-east of the Beit el Ma, stands a house roughly built of mud bricks, which is known as the Suk er Rekik (slave market). Under the pretext that I wanted to buy or exchange slaves, I several times received the Khalifa's permission to visit it, and found ample opportunity for closely observing the conduct of the business. Here professional slave dealers assemble to offer their wares for sale. Round the walls of the house numbers of women and girls stand or sit. They vary from the decrepit and aged half-clad slaves of the working class to the gaily decked surya (concubine); and, as the trade is looked upon as a perfectly natural and lawful business, those put up for sale are carefully examined from head to foot, without the least restriction, just as if they were animals. The mouth is opened to see if the teeth are in good condition. The upper part of the body and the back are laid bare, and the arms carefully looked at. They are then told to take a few steps backward or forward in order that their movements and gait may be examined. A series of questions are put to them to test their knowledge of Arabic. In face, they have to submit to any examination the intending purchaser may wish to make. Suryas, of course, vary considerably in price; but the whole matter is treated by the slaves without the smallest concern. They consider it perfectly natural, and have no notion of being treated otherwise. Only occasionally one can see by the expression of a woman or girl that she feels this close scrutiny; possibly her position with her former master was rather that of a servant than a slave, or she may have been looked upon almost as a member of the family, and may have been brought to this unhappy position by force of circumstances, or through some hateful inhumanity on the part of her former master. When the intending purchaser has completed his scrutiny, he then refers to the dealer, asks him what he paid for her, or if he has any other better wares for sale. He will probably complain that her face is not pretty enough, that her body is not sufficiently developed, that she does not speak Arabic, and so on, with the object of reducing the price as much as possible; whilst on the other hand, the owner will do his utmost to show up her good qualities, charms, etc., into the detail of which it is not necessary to enter here. Amongst the various "secret defects" which oblige the dealer to reduce his price are snoring, bad qualities of character, such as thieving, and many others; but when at last the sale has been finally arranged, the paper is drawn out and signed, the money paid, and the slave becomes the property of her new master. Payment is always made in local currency (Omla Gedida dollars), and runs approximately as follows:

For an aged working slave, fifty to eighty dollars; for a middle-aged woman, eight to one hundred twenty dollars; for young girls between eight and eleven years of age, according to looks, one hundred ten to one hundred sixty dollars; and for suryas, according to looks, one hundred eighty to seven hundred dollars. These rates, of course, vary also according to market value, or special demand for a particular race.

Note

1. R. Slatin and F. R. Wingate, *Fire and Sword in the Sudan: A Personal Narrative of Fighting and Serving the Dervishes, 1879–1895* (London: Edward Arnold, 1903), pp. 337–41.

54

OTTOMAN MASSACRES OF THE BULGARIANS IN 1876

Three contemporary investigators who visited only a small number of the localities where the atrocities were reported to have been committed—Eugene Schuyler, James F. Clarke, and Walter Baring—agreed that there were between ten and fifteen thousand innocent people slain in the districts directly affected by the revolt. Modern Bulgarian historians estimate that as many as thirty thousand were murdered. Moreover, three thousand children were orphaned, thousands of Bulgarians were imprisoned and exiled, sixty to eighty villages and towns were destroyed, while an additional two hundred were plundered, and three hundred thousand livestock—cattle, sheep, and goats—and countless personal goods were confiscated as "booty" from a defenseless populace[1] long exploited during centuries of oppressive Ottoman rule.[2] Bulgarian revolutionaries did kill some Ottoman troops and officials engaged in the fighting, as well as few hundred Muslim irregulars who also fought against them. However, as the consensus reports of Baring, Schuyler, and Clarke substantiated, very few peaceful Muslims were killed by the Bulgarian insurgents.[3] Furthermore, the 1986 analysis by Shashko of American and British diplomatic reports from Bulgaria provides convincing evidence of

> some kind of pre-meditated scheme that entailed coordinated action of Ottoman officials, *bashi-bazouks*, Circassians, and the army against not just rebels, but unarmed Bulgarians as well. . . . The fact that Ottoman authorities were aware of the planned uprising and the swiftness with which they acted against the rebels, as well as the immediate dispatch of *bashi-bazouks* and Circassians against the unarmed people, strongly suggest the possibility of pre-meditated action.[4]

ACCOUNT OF AMERICAN CORRESPONDENT JANUARIUS A. MacGAHAN— OBSERVATIONS AT BATAK, JULY–AUGUST 1876[5]

At the point where we descended into the principal street of the place, the people who had gathered around us pointed to a heap of ashes by the roadside, among which could be distinguished a great number of calcined bones. Here a heap of dead bodies had been burnt, and it would seem that the Turks had been making some futile and misdirected attempts at cremation.

A little further on we came to an object that filled us with pity and horror. It was the skeleton of a young girl not more than fifteen, lying by the roadside, and partly covered with the debris of a fallen wall. It was still clothed in a chemise; the ankles were enclosed in footless stockings; but the little feet, from which the shoes had been taken, were naked and owing to the fact that the flesh had dried, instead of decomposing, were nearly perfect. There was a large gash in the skull, to which a mass of rich brown hair nearly a yard long still clung, trailing in the dust. It is to be remarked that all the skeletons of women were found here dressed in a chemise only, and this poor child evidently had been stripped to her chemise, partly in the search for money and jewels, partly out of mere brutality, then outraged, and afterwards killed. We have talked with many women who had passed through all parts of the ordeal but the last, and the procedure seems to have been as follows: They would seize a woman, strip her carefully to her chemise, laying aside articles of clothing that were valuable, with any ornaments and jewels she might have about her. Then as many of them as cared would violate her, and the last man would kill her or not as the humor took him.

At the next house a man stopped us to show where a blind little brother had been burnt alive, and the spot where he had found his calcined bones, and the rough, hard-visaged man sat down and cried like a child. . . .

On the other side of the way were the skeletons of two children lying side by side, partly covered with stones, and with frightful saber cuts in their little skulls. The number of children killed in these massacres is something enormous. They were often spitted on bayonets, and we have several stories from eye-witnesses who saw little babes carried about the streets, both here and at Otluk-kui, on the point of bayonets. The reason is simple. When a Mahometan has killed a certain number of infidels, he is sure of Paradise, no matter what his sins may be . . . the ordinary Mussulman takes the precept in broader acceptation, and counts women and children as well. Here in Batak the Bashi-Bazouks, in order to swell the count, ripped open pregnant women, and killed the unborn infants. As we approached the middle of the town, bones, skeletons, and skulls became more numerous. There was not a house beneath the ruins of which we did not perceive human remains, and the street besides were strewn with them.

And now we begin to approach the church and schoolhouse. The ground is covered here with skeletons, to which are clinging articles of clothing and bits putrid flesh; the air is heavy with a faint sickening odor, that grows stronger as we advance. It is beginning to be horrible. The school is one side of the road, the church on the other. The schoolhouse, to judge by the walls that are in part standing, was a fine large building, capable of accommodating two or three hundred children. Beneath the stones and rubbish that cover the floor to the height of several feet, are the bones and ashes of two hundred women and children burnt alive between those four walls. Just beside the schoolhouse is a broad shallow pit. Here were buried a hundred bodies two weeks after the massacre. But the dogs uncovered them in part. The water flowed in, and now it lies there a horrid cesspool, with human remains floating about or lying half exposed in the mud. Nearby, on the banks of the little stream that runs through the village, is a sawmill. The wheel-pit beneath is full of dead bodies floating in the water. The banks of this stream were at one time literally covered with corpses of men and women, young girls and children, that lay there festering in the sun, and eaten by dogs. But the pitiful sky rained down a torrent upon them, and the little stream swelled and rose up and carried the bodies away, and strewed them far down its grassy banks, through its narrow gorges and dark defiles beneath the thick underbrush, and the shady woods as far as Pestera, and even Tatar Bazardjik, forty miles distant. We entered the churchyard, but the odor here becomes so bad that it was almost impossible to proceed. We took a handful of tobacco, and held it to our noses while we continued our investigations.

Notes

1. Philip Shashko, "The Bulgarian Massacres of 1876 Reconsidered: Reaction to the April Uprising or Premeditated Attack?" *Études Balkaniques* 22 (1986): 18–25.

2. See, for example, Ivan Snegarov, *Turkish Rule as an Obstacle for the Cultural Development of the Bulgarian People and the Other Balkan Peoples* (Sofia: Bulgarian Academy of Science, 1958); Bistra Cvetkova, "Typical Features of the Ottoman Social and Economic Structure in Southeastern Europe during the 14th to the 16th Centuries," *Études Historique* 9 (1979): 129–49.

3. Shashko, "The Bulgarian Massacres of 1876 Reconsidered," p. 19.

4. Ibid., p. 25

5. Januarius A. MacGahan, *The Turkish Atrocities in Bulgaria* (Geneva, 1976), pp. 52–56.

55

JIHAD GENOCIDE OF THE ARMENIANS BY THE OTTOMAN TURKS

A. TWO ACCOUNTS OF THE MASSACRES OF 1894–1896

Massacres of the Armenians at Sasun, Istanbul, Trebizond, Erzurum, and Urfa[1]

In the region of Sasun, south of Mush, the exactions of the Kurdish chieftains had evolved into an organized system of tribute by blackmail, paid for their protection by the Armenian population. On top of this the Turkish authorities now chose to demand payment of arrears of government tax—which in the circumstances had for some years been tacitly remitted. When the Armenians refused to submit to this double exaction, Turkish troops were called into the area, in close concert with the Kurdish tribesmen. Soon they were indiscriminately slaughtering the helpless Armenians. The soldiers pursued them throughout the length and breadth of the region, hunting them "like wild beasts" up the valleys and into the mountains, respecting no surrender, bayoneting the men to death, raping the women, dashing their children against the rocks, burning to ashes the villages from which they had fled. For this operation the Turkish commander, Zeki Pasha, was awarded an appropriate gratuity by the Sultan.

Leakage of the news of these first Armenian massacres, which the Porte had hoped to brush aside as a trifling incident, aroused strong liberal protests throughout Europe, prompting demands by the three powers—Britain, France, and Russia—for a commission of enquiry. This was duly appointed by the Sultan, in 1895, "to enquire into the criminal conduct of Armenian brigands"—thus hoping to preempt further investigation and prove the Porte's version of events. Following this mockery of justice the powers, reinforced by mass meetings in London and Paris, put forward a scheme for Armenian reform, which the Sultan made a show of accepting in a watered-down version, with a profusion of unfulfilled paper promises.

Meanwhile, the Armenians themselves, led by the Hunchaks, staged a demonstration as they marched through the city of Istanbul to present a petition to the Porte, voicing their protests and demands for reform. Despite counsels of patience from their Patriarch, the demonstrators got out of hand when one of them (from Sasun) shouted "Liberty or Death!" The cry was taken up by the rest, breaking into a revolutionary song and provoking intervention by the police, who bludgeoned many of them to death on the spot. Meanwhile, the fanatical Moslem elements, without police intervention, ran wild through the streets, routing out Armenians and slaughtering them with clubs. There followed ten days of violence and terror, from which Armenians by the thousand took refuge in their churches, persuaded to emerge only by guarantees for their safety from the foreign embassies, on condition that they lay down their arms.

This coincided with the news, from the captain of a foreign vessel, of a great massacre in Trebizond. Powerless, he had watched as Armenian fugitives, swimming out to his ship, were knocked on the head by Moslem boatmen or forced underwater till they drowned. Nearly a thousand had been killed in the town, with indigenous Laz tribesmen from the mountains, broke into the Armenian quarter and for five hours kept up a murderous fusillade, despoiling and subsequently gutting by fire the Armenian shops in the market.

This heralded throughout eastern Turkey a series of organized massacres, coinciding with the Sultan's pretended acceptance of a new plan from the powers for Armenian reform. A telltale feature of them all was that they began and ended, as a matter of routine, with a bugle call, like any planned military operation. For such indeed they were. Here were no fortuitous police measures, forced on the authorities by outbreaks among the Sultan's Armenian subjects. Here on the contrary was an official campaign by force of arms against the Armenians as against any foreign enemy, calculated among his military forces in the Armenian centers of the six eastern provinces.

Their tactics were based on the Sultan's principle of kindling religious fanaticism among the Moslem population. Abdul Hamid briefed agents, whom he sent to Armenia with specific instructions as to how they should act. It became their normal routine first to assemble the Moslem population in the largest mosque in a town, then to declare, in the name of the Sultan, that the Armenians were in general revolt with the aim of striking at Islam. Their Sultan enjoined them as good Moslems to defend their faith against these infidel rebels. He propounded the precept that under the holy law the property of rebels might be looted by believers, encouraging Moslems to enrich themselves in the name of their faith at the expense of their Christian neighbours, and in the event of resistance, to kill them. Hence, throughout Armenia, "the attack of an ever increasing pack of wolves against sheep."

. . . The conduct of these operations was placed in the hands of Shakir Pasha, one of the Sultan's more sinister advisors, who had once served him as ambassador in St. Petersburg. His ostensible post was that of "inspector of certain localities in the provinces of Asiatic Turkey" in connection with the Sultan's own pretended reform plans. Under this cover his actual role was the planning and execution of massacres in each specified locality. Their objective, based on the convenient consideration that Armenians were now tentatively starting to question their inferior status, was the ruthless reduction, with a view to elimination, of the Armenian Christians, and the expropriation of their lands for the Moslem Turks.

Each operation, between the bugle calls, followed a similar pattern. First into a town there came the Turkish troops, for the purpose of massacre; then came the Kurdish irregulars and tribesmen for the purpose of plunder. Finally came the holocaust, by fire and destruction, which spread, with the pursuit of fugitives and mopping-up operations, throughout the lands and villages of the surrounding province. This murderous winter of 1895 thus saw the decimation of much of the Armenian population and the devastation of their property in some twenty districts of eastern Turkey. Often the massacres were timed for a Friday, when the Moslems were in their mosques and the myth was spread by the authorities that the Armenians conspired to slaughter them at prayer. Instead they were themselves slaughtered, when the Moslems emerged to forestall their design. The total number of victims was somewhere between fifty and a hundred thousand, allowing for those who died subsequently of wounds, disease, exposure, and starvation.

In each of thirteen large towns the numbers of those dead ran well into four figures. In Erzurum, the bazaar of a thousand shops was looted and wrecked by the Moslems, while some three hundred Christians were buried the next day in a single massed grave.

Cruelest and most ruinous of all were the massacres at Urfa, where the Armenian Christians numbered a third of the total population. Here in December 1895, after a two-months' siege of their quarter, the leading Armenians assembled in their cathedral, where they drew up a statement requesting Turkish official protection. Promising this, the Turkish officer in charge surrounded the cathedral with troops. Then a large body of them, with a mob in their wake, rushed through the Armenian quarter, where they plundered all houses and slaughtered all adult males above a certain age. When a large group of young Armenians were brought before a sheikh, he had them thrown down on their backs and held by their hands and feet. Then, in the words of an observer, he recited verses of the Koran and "cut their throats after the Mecca rite of sacrificing sheep."

When the bugle blast ended the day's operations some three thousand refugees poured into the cathedral, hoping for sanctuary. But the next morning—a Sunday—a fanatical mob swarmed into the church in an orgy of slaughter, rifling its shrines will cries of "Call upon Christ to prove Himself a greater prophet than Mohammed." Then they amassed a large pile of straw matting, which they spread over the litter of the corpses and set alight with thirty cans of petroleum. The woodwork of the gallery where a crowd of women and children crouched, wailing in terror, caught fire, and all perished in the flames. Punctiliously, at three-thirty in the afternoon the bugle blew once more, and the Moslem officials proceeded around the Armenian quarter to proclaim that the massacres were over. They had wiped out 126 complete families, without a woman or a baby surviving, and the total casualties in the town, including those slaughtered in the cathedral, amounted to eight thousand dead.

Note

1. Lord Kinross, *The Ottoman Centuries* (New York: Morrow Quill Paperbacks, 1977), pp. 457–60.

Massacres of the Armenians at Ayintab, Birecik, and Severek[1]

[The British Consul Barnham, whose district's consular jurisdiction included the cities of Ayintab and Birecik in Aleppo province, in his report to his government underscored the religious avowals of the gangs and mobs perpetrating the massacre in Ayintab.]

The butchers and the tanners, with sleeves tucked up to the shoulders, armed with clubs and cleavers, cut down the Christians, with cries of "Allahu Akbar!" broke down the doors of the houses with pickaxes and levers, or scaled the walls with ladders. Then when mid-day came they knelt down and said their prayers, and then jumped up and resumed the dreadful work, carrying it on far into the night. Whenever they were unable to break down the doors they fired the houses with petroleum, and the fact that at the end of November petroleum was almost unpurchasable in Aleppo suggests that enormous quantities were brought up and sent north for this purpose. . . . Much of this has been told before, but it is evidence which must be emphasized in order to refute the accusations so wantonly hurled against these poor Armenians of Aintab.

[Speaking of similar atrocities in nearby Birecik, the consul provided these details.]

On the 1st of January, about two hours after sunrise, the massacre began without apparent cause, and continued until night. The soldiers and Moslems of the city generally participated in the work. . . . Profession of Islamism or death was the alternative. . . . Many of the victims were dragged to the Euphrates, and with weights tied to their feet thrown in. . . .

[Here is a description by one of the survivors of an assault of this type, involving two Armenian churches in Severek (Diyarbekir province), a Gregorian, and subsequently, a Protestant one.]

The mob had plundered the Gregorian church, desecrated it, murdered all who had sought shelter there, and as a sacrifice, beheaded the sexton on the stone threshold. Now it filled out yard. The blows of an axe crashed in the church doors. The attacker rushed in, tore the Bibles and hymnbooks to pieces, broke and shattered whatever they could, blasphemed the cross and, as a sign of victory, chanted the Mohammedan prayer "La ilaha ill-Allah, Muhammedin Rasula-Ilah" (There is no other God but one God, and Mohammed is his Prophet). We could see and hear all these things from the room in which we huddled. . . . They were coming up the stairs . . . now butchers and victims were face to face. The leader of the mob cried: "Muhammede salavat" (Believe in Mohammed and deny your religion). [Disregarding our supplications to be spared] squinting horribly, he repeated his words in a terrifying voice. [When no one responded] the leader repeated again and gave orders to massacre. The first attack was on our pastor. The blow of an axe decapitated him. His blood, spurting in all directions, spattered the walls and ceilings with red. Then I was in the midst of the butchers. One of them drew his dagger and stabbed my left arm. . . . Another second, I lost consciousness. . . .

Note

1. Vahakn Dadrian, *The History of the Armenian Genocide* (Providence, RI: Bergahn Books, 1995), pp. 148, 150.

B. TWO EYEWITNESS ACCOUNTS OF THE PLIGHT OF THE ARMENIANS DURING WORLD WAR I

Palestine (1915)[1]

It has been more than proved (of their own admission!) that it was the Germans who "organized" the control and "correction" of the Armenians. Yet, these messengers from hell, who claim to be superior to others in many things, also describe themselves as "better Christians" than all the others (do relish William's[2] prose . . .). Now, the Turks have promised that only 500,000 of the 2,500,000

Armenians living in the empire will be left at the end of the war. As far as these promises are concerned, have faith in the Turks. They are on the way to keeping their word. On our road [in Palestine], one sees long files of young and old men engaged in forced labour: from time to time, someone sick enough is borne on the shoulders of a helpful comrade in misfortune; sometimes, someone lying on the road whose sufferings will soon have ceased.

Even better: these wretches are pursued along the [railway] line of the Hedjaz: old men, old women, children. Sometimes they are allowed to camp down. No bread, no clothing, not a [piece of] cloth on their heads [as protection] against sun or cold, not a tool with which to work. Yet these wretches sometimes have the courage to ask: Will we stop here at last? The reply is invariably: "It is not know!" and the worst torture is added to all the rest: the torture of uncertainty. In many places, it is forbidden to give alms to this hapless people.

Even better: do you know what was done with the young girls and young women?! Yes, as soon as you read my question, you, who know Islam, have guessed. However, this will not stop me telling you: THEY HAVE BEEN SOLD! Yes, yes: sold, every girl from the age of seven or eight upwards. They are not expensive. Although it is difficult to feed even the animals in this starving country, there were found among the "faithful," bidders ready to pay from five to a hundred francs for a piece of white flesh. Do not console yourself with the idea that I am reporting gossip! Vain consolation! Things seen, witnessed, proven, official! Very small girls torn from their mothers, young brides taken from their husbands, young girls "kaffirs" [infidels] become the slaves of the debauchery of the "faithful!" The children of a race of martyrs, a race which is claimed to be physically beautiful, and which is undeniably of an acute superiority of intelligence. . . .

As for me, I no longer have teeth to gnash, whose turn is it now? For I came into my country, on the holiest ground, on the road from Jerusalem, and I asked myself if we were in 1915 or in the days of Titus and Nebuchadnezzar. For I, a Jew, I forgot that I was Jewish—it is very difficult to forget this "privilege"!—and I asked myself if I had the right to week solely for the grief of my nation and if Jeremiah [8:21] did not shed his tears of blood for the Armenians too?!

And, lastly, since the Christians—some of whom sometimes claim a monopoly of works of Love, of Charity, and of Solidarity—are silent, there is need once again for a son of the Old Race who disregards the Pain, overcomes the Torture, or denies the Death which for twenty centuries is offered to us more often than is our share; it would need a drop of blood form the Patriarchs and of Moses, of the Maccabbees from arid Judea, of Jesus, the dreamer by the side of the blue lake of sweet Galilee, and of Bar Kochba; it would need to drop of the blood that had escaped from the slaughter, to rise up and say: Look! You who refuse to open your eyes.

Listen! You whose ears refuse to hear! What have you done with the secrets of Love and Charity entrusted to you?! To what purpose has served the spilled streams of our blood?! What are you doing in Life with your lofty words?!

And while a night's journey from here thousands and thousands of Englishmen, Canadians, and Australians—all volunteers who have come to fight—remain inactive, a few Arab dogs and Turkish hyenas are wallowing in a charnel-house which they create and maintain. And to know that whips would suffice to drive out all this cowardliness. Alas! The torture of being powerless and disarmed.

The valiant soldiers who would arose a Halleluya of liberation and joy do not come. . . . But tomorrow an official will come and teach us that the "Hasan" mosque of Jaffa is sacred and infinitely respectable because . . . a bandit built it with stones from stolen houses, and that some Muslim wearing an immaculately white "Lafeh" [gown] is worthy of respect and honor because he keeps well imprisoned in his harem two Armenians, bought "on the cheap," or, to use the words of the Holy Bible, "for a pair of shoes."

Forgive this tone, lieutenant! The roots of my past are in this country, my dreams for the future too; . . . I have my whole heart here and it is bleeding and wailing, forgive me.

And while the accursed German flood the world with their printed lies, their treachery built into professions of faith . . . , why are you silent?! Silent scorn and mistrust are fine, but bot Ecclesiastes say: "A time to keep silence, and a time to speak." . . . Especially, as honest people, should one not speak out, and is it a young, rebellious Jew who once again must do it?!

Extract from a report in French "PRO ARMENIA" (Athlit, 22 November 1915) by Absalom Feinberg[3] to Lt. C. Z.Wooley, British naval officer in Port Said, Egypt.

Notes

1. Reproduced from Bat Ye'or, *The Decline of Eastern Christianity*, pp. 439–41.
2. William II, German emperor.
3. Absalom Feinberg (1889–1917). Born at Gedera (Palestine). Agronomist and co-founder with Aharon Aaronsohn of Nili, the Palestinian Jewish intelligence service, which worked with British intelligence during World War I. He was assassinated by Bedouins near Gaza while traveling to Egypt in January 1917. A palm tree grew from the date seeds in his pocket. In 1967, after the Six Day War, his remains were discovered under the tree indicated by a Bedouin and buried in Israel on Mount Herzl.

IRAQ, 1915–1917[1]

Constantinople, April 3, 1919

. . . As I am reflecting in order to coordinate my ideas and describe to you with some precision the situation of Mosul during this war, I am overwhelmed by a feeling of sickness and embarrassment; for I find that the pen is too imperfect an instrument to convey truthfully all the horrors that I have seen, all the images which today fill my mind.

When I remember again, only a few months afterwards, the painful scenes which we have witnessed; when I think of that crowd of gaunt, fleshless specters, their faces white as corpses, filing through the streets and over countryside in search of a carcass or a few herbs to cheat their hunger; when I think of others, with limbs and cheeks bloated in the air, who came to ask for alms, collapsing from exhaustion on my doorstep, I come to the point of doubting myself. Was it a nightmare? What pen, what words could ever describe the distress, the agony of Mosul in 1918? What words could render the evil sight of those children's heads severed form their bodies and paraded in the streets to summon weeping mothers to recognize their stolen children, stolen in the street by ferocious starvelings, for whom this was the last resort? However improbable this may appear, it is—unless I am still dreaming—something I have see, a reality experiences.

D. Sasson, report No. 4 (extract) Archives, AIU, Iraq, I.C.2.

Constantinople, April 30, 1919

. . . 1915 saw the massacre of the Armenians; 1916 saw—O divine vengeance— the explosion of a dreadful epidemic. The fetid decomposition of Armenian corpses which were found abandoned in the open fields; those that were foolishly thrown into the nutritive waters of the Tigris emitted vengeful germs of inexorable diseases which, alas, mowed down entirely innocent population. There was typhoid fever, malaria, yellow fever, cholera. The uninterrupted exodus of depor- tees and emigrants brought with it exanthematic typhus, the most terrible of calamities, which decimated the population and which unfortunately claimed an immense and harsh tribute from our coreligionists. Oh! What a sad Passover it was that year! It found our quarter in mourning and almost every family weeping at the grave of a deceased or at the bedside of someone agonizing.

D. Sasson, report No. 5 (extract) Archives, AIU, Iraq, I.C.2.

Note

1. Translation reproduced from Bat Ye'or, *The Decline of Eastern Christianity*, pp. 441–42.

Appendix A

TOWNS AND VILLAGES RAVAGED DURING THE SELJUK-OTTOMAN JIHAD CONQUESTS OF ASIA MINOR, ELEVENTH THROUGH FIFTEENTH CENTURIES

Reconstructed from Speros Vryonis Jr.

Key: **P = pillaged, X= sacked or destroyed, E = enslaved, C = captured, M = massacred, B = besieged, F = flight]**

WESTERN ASIA MINOR

Towns and Villages	*Environs of Towns and Villages*	*Provinces*
Cyzicus (C, C, C, X)		West Anatolia (X)
Apollonius (C, X)	Apollonias (P)	Dorylaeum-Iconium (P, E, P, E)
Lopadium (X)	Lopadium (P)	Thynia-Bithynia (P, P, P, P)
Cius (C)	Poimamenum (P)	Propontis and Mysia (P, P, P)
Poimamenum (X)	Abydus (P, P)	Caius, Hermus, Cayster, and Maeander (P, P, P)
Adramyttium (X)	Adramyttium (P, P, F)	Phyrgia (P)
Calamus (X)	Chliara (F, P)	Paphlogonia (P)
Meleum (X)	Pergamum (F, P)	Pisidia (P)
Smyrna (C, X)	Smyrna (P)	Lycia (P)
Clazomenae (C, X)	Clazomenae (P)	
Phocaea (C, X)	Phocaea (P)	
Sardes (C)	Ephesus (P, P)	
Nymphaeum (C)	Philadelpheia (P)	
Ephesus (C, X)	Attaleia (P)	
Philadelpheia (C)	Dorylaeum (P)	
Tralles (X)	Cotyaeum (X)	
Louma (X)	Sozopolis (P)	
Pentacheir (X)	Lampe (P)	
Melanoudium (X)	Laodiceia (P)	
Latrus (X)	Chonae (P)	
Strobilus (X)		
Attaleia (X, B)		
Nicomedia (C, X)		
Nicaea (C, X, B)		
Prusa (C, X, B)		
Claudiopolis (B)		
Pithecas (X)		
Malagina (X)		
Dorylaeum (X, C)		
Cotyraeum (X, X)		
Amorium (X)		
Cedrea (C)		
Polybotus (C)		
Philomelium (C, X, X)		
Myriocephalum (X)		
Sozopolis (C, B, X)		
Chonae (X, C)		
Laodiceia (C, C, X)		
Hierapolis (X)		

Reconstructed from Speros Vryonis Jr., *The Decline of Medieval Hellenism in Asia Minor and the Process of Islamization from the Eleventh through Fifteenth Century* (Berkeley and Los Angeles: University of California Press, 1971), pp. 166–67.

Tripolis (X)
Tantalus (X, E)
Caria (X, E, X, E)
Antioch and Meandrum (X)
Choma-Soublaion (X)

EASTERN ASIA MINOR

Towns and Villages	Environs of Towns and Villages	Provinces
Caesareia (X)	Marash (P, C)	Cappodocia (P, P, P, F)
Arabissus (X)	Kaisum (S, M, E, P, X, X)	Pyramus River (E, P)
Albistan (E, X)	Tell Bashir (S, M, E, P, X, X)	Armenia (M, E, F, P)
Kaisum (F, X, E, X)	Edessa (P, X, P, P)	Lake Van (P, P)
Edessa		
(B, B, X, B, X, E, M, M)	Hisn Mansur (M, E)	
Nisibis (X)	Gargar (P)	
Gargar (X, E, X, E)	Seveverek (P)	
Melitene		
(X, M, E, X, C, X, B)	Melitene (P, P, P, X, E)	
Bar Mar Sauma (B, B, B, C)	Chliat (P)	
Sebasteia		
(X, N, E, C, X, X, C)	Perkri (P)	
Artze (X, F)		
Ani (X, C)		
Zorinak (X, M)		

NORTHERN ASIA MINOR

Towns and Villages	Environs of Towns and Villages	Provinces
Sinope (X, C)	Gangra (X, F)	
Trebizond (X, C)	Castamon (X, F)	
Amisus (C)	Amaseia (X, F)	
Paipert (B, C)		
Coloneia (B, C)		
Neocaesareia (X, C)		
Amaseia (B, C)		
Castamon (X, X)		
Doceia (C)		
Comana (C)		
Euchaita (C)		
Pimolissa (C)		
Gangra (C, X)		
Dadybra (C, F)		

SOUTHERN ASIA MINOR

Towns and Villages	Environs of Towns and Villages	Provinces
		Pyramus Valley (P)
Seleucia		
Mopsuestia (X)		
Corycus (X)		
Adana (X, E)		
Pracana (X)		

CENTRAL ASIA MINOR

Towns and Villages	Environs of Towns and Villages	Provinces
Iconium (X, M)	Ankara (P, P)	
Ankara (X, C, C)	Iconium (P, P, P)	
Coloneia Archelais (X)		
Laodiceia Combusta (X)		

The following relevant commentary is excerpted from Speros Vryonis's "The Conditions and Cultural Significance of the Ottoman Conquest in the Balkans," *Congres International des Etudes du Sud-Est Europeen* (Athens, 1970), pp. 7–9:

The [Turkish] conquests in Anatolia were prolonged, repeated (lasting from the 11th–15th centuries), quite destructive and disruptive of life and property.

The conquest of Asia Minor virtually destroyed the Anatolian Church. The ecclesiastical administrative documents reveal an almost complete confiscation of church property, income, buildings, and the imposition of heavy taxes by the Turks. In addition, they furnish evidence for further irregularity in ecclesiastical life due to the fact that the conquerors frequently prohibited the entrance of bishops and metropolitans, and often expelled them from their seats.

The conquests of Asia Minor were accompanied by large influxes of Turkmen nomads. Consequently, we are dealing not only with a conquest but with an ethnic migration. However, it was not only the numbers which contributed to the Turkification of Anatolia but also the very character of nomadism. Nomadism brought with it political decentralization, instability, and intermittent anarchy; it brought a nomadic economy based on pastoralism, banditry, and slave trading, all of which constituted a heavy burden for the sedentary Christians. These were instrumental in the devastation and disruption of Christian rural life throughout much of Anatolia. The Anatolian place names, so heavily Turkified, seem to reflect the disruption of much of the Christian rural society.

Appendix B

JIHAD SLAVE RAIDS (*RAZZIAS*) BY THE TATARS, MID-FIFTEENTH THROUGH LATE SEVENTEENTH CENTURIES

Fisher's caveat:

> The sources for these raids are incomplete and there is no doubt that there were many more slave raids that the author has not uncovered. (p. 579, n.17)

DATE	PLACE	NUMBER OF CAPTIVES
1463	Poland	18,000
1474	Galicia	7,000
1482	Kiev	Thousands
1498	Lvov	100,000

Constructed from Alan Fisher, "Muscovy and the Black Sea Slave Trade," *Canadian American Slavic Studies* (1972): 580–82.

1500	South Russia	50,000
1512	South Russia	25,000
1515	South Russia	60,000
1516	South Russia	5,000
1516	Galicia	40,000
1516	Galicia	50,000–100,000
1516	Galicia	Thousands
1521	Moscow	800,000
1527	South Russia	25,000
1533	South Russia	100,000
1533	Poland	Thousands
1534	Volynia	15,000
1537	Volynia	15,000
1555	South Russia	200,000
1571	Moscow	100,000
1575	South Russia	35,000
1585	Lvov	"immense"
1598	South Russia	Thousands
1612	Poland	50,000
1615	Ukraine	18,000
1616	Poland	Thousands
1618	Lvov	453
1621	Poland	36
1622	Galicia	229
1622	Lvov	150
1623	Poland	10,000
1624	Poland	900
1624	Poland	600
1626	Poland	60
1626	Poland	250
1632	Poland	2,260
1633	Poland	57
1633	South Russia	1,500
1636	South Russia	5,700
1637	Poland	2,280
1643	Chuguev	87
1644	Poland	10,000
1644	South Russia	6,000
1645	South Russia	5,700
1645	South Russia	6,200
1646	South Russia	60,000
1648	Poland	100,000

1648	Poland	40,000
1651	Poland	2,000
1654	Ukraine	300,000
1655	Poland	27,000
1656	Poland	34,000
1657	Kiev	50
1658	Ukraine	7,000
1659	Poland	11,060
1662	Ukraine	20,000
1676	Volynia	400,000
1678	Ukraine	30,000
1680	Ukraine	Whole town of Valki
1681	Ukraine	200
1693	Kharkov	Thousands
1694	Poland	Thousands

Excerpted commentary by Fisher regarding the plight of those enslaved:

[T]he first ordeal [of the captive] was the long march to the Crimea. Often in chains and always on foot, many of the captives died en route. Since on many occasions the Tatar raiding party feared reprisals or, in the seventeenth century, attempts by Cossack bands to free the captives, the marches were hurried. Ill or wounded captives were usually killed rather than be allowed to slow the procession. [Heberstein wrote] . . . "the old and infirm men who will not fetch much as a sale, are given up to the Tatar youths either to be stoned, or thrown into the sea, or to be killed by any sort of death they might please." An Ottoman traveler in the mid-sixteenth century who witnessed one such march of captives from Galicia marveled that any would reach their destination—the slave markets of Kefe. He complained that their treatment was so bad that the mortality rate would unnecessarily drive their price up beyond the reach of potential buyers such as himself. A Polish proverb stated: "Oh how much better to lie on one's bier, than to be a captive on the way to Tartary." (pp. 582–83)

Appendix C

MUSLIM JURISTS, THEOLOGIANS, AND HISTORIANS

ABU HANIFA (d. 767). An-Nu'man b. Thabit b. Zuta abu Hanifa. Theologian and jurisconsult, founder of the Hanafi school of jurisprudence. Died in Baghdad.

Abu Yusuf Ya'qub (731–798). A renowned jurist of the Hanafi school of law. Author of a basic treatise on public finance.

AL-AMILI (1547–1621). Born in Syria, he emigrated to Persia and eventually obtained an honored position at the court of Shah Abbas I. Al-Amili wrote an important exposition of Shi'ite jurisprudence, in Persian, the *Jami-i-Abbasi*.

AL-BALADHURI (d. 892). Eminent Persian historian who lived at the caliphs' court from 847 to 892. Author of Book of Conquests.

AL-BAYDAWI (1286–1316?). Shafiite jurist of the thirteenth/early fourteenth century, who attained the position of chief kadi of Shiraz. He had a reputation for wide learning, and wrote on a number of subjects most notably, Qur'anic exegesis, and jurisprudence. His most famous work is a Qur'anic commentary that is largely a condensed and amended edition of Al-Zamakshary's *al-Kashaf*.

ALBERUNI [AL-BIRUNI] (973–1048 CE). Born in Khwarazm (presently in Uzbekistan), was one of the greatest scholars of medieval Islam. A mathematician, astronomer, physicist, encyclopedist, philosopher, astrologer, traveller, historian, and pharmacist, Alberuni was also an impartial observer of customs and creeds. Retained at the Court of Ghazna, perhaps as official astrologer, Alberuni accompanied Sultan Mahmud on several of his military expeditions to northwest India. There he taught the Greek sciences while learning Sanskrit and various local dialects, and amassing the incalculable sum of information which he compiled in his monumental *Description of India*, completed in 1030, just prior to Mahmud's death.

AL-BUKHARI (d. 869). Born in Bukhara, he died in Samarkand. Author of the most important of the six compilations of traditions (hadith), being the acts and sayings attributed to the Prophet Muhammad.

AL-GHAZALI (1058–1111). Born at Tus in Khurasan, near modern Meshed, and became a renowned theologian, jurist, and mystic. Al-Ghazali's early training was as a jurist, and he continued to have an interest in jurisprudence throughout his career, writing a work the *Wadjiz*, dated 1101, in the last decade of his life. W. M. Watt wrote of Al-Ghazali, "acclaimed in both the East and West as the greatest Muslim after Muhammad, and he is by no means unworthy of that dignity. . . . He brought orthodoxy and mysticism into closer contact . . . the theologians became more ready to accept the mystics as respectable, while the mystics were more careful to remain within the bounds of orthodoxy."

AL-HILLI, AL-MUHAQQIQ (1206–1277 CE). He was a thirteenth-century Shi'a jurist and scholar noted for his interpretation of Islamic law according to the Shi'ite tradition, *Shara 'i'u 'l-Islam (Kitabu 'n-Nikah)*.

AL-MALIKI, ABU BAKR ABD ALLAH (eleventh century). Tunisian historian. Author of the famous chronicle *Riyad an-Nufus*.

AL-MAQRIZI [MAKRIZI] (1364–1442). Renowned historian, born in Cairo. Author of several works, particularly on the Mamluk sultans of Egypt.

AL-MARRAKUSHI [MERRAKECHI], ABD AL-WAHID (d. 1224). North African historian of the Almohads.

AL-MAWARDI [MAWERDI] (d. 1058). Famous Shafii jurist of Baghdad. Author of an important law treatise, *Al-ahkam as-Sultaniyya*, and a treatise on morality.

YUSUF AL-QARADAWI (b. 1926). A modern Muslim scholar and preacher best known for his popular al-Jazeera program, *ash-Shari'a wal-Hayat* (Sharia and Life), and his Web site IslamOnline. He has also published some fifty books, including *The Lawful and the Prohibited in Islam and Islam: The Future Civilization*. Al-Qaradawi was born in Egypt, and attended the Al-Azhar Theological Seminary. A follower of Muslim Brotherhood founder Hasan al-Banna during his youth, he was imprisoned first under the monarchy in 1949, then three times after the release of his *Tyrant and the Scholar*, poetic Islamic plays expressing political messages. He has also worked in the Egyptian Ministry of Religious Endowments, been the dean of the Islamic Department at the Faculties of Sharia and Education in Qatar, and been chairman of the Islamic Scientific Councils of Algerian Universities and Institutions. Qaradawi is a member of the Muslim Brotherhood, and the head of the European Council for Fatwa and Research.

AL-SHAFI'I (d. 820). Born in Gaza. Theologian and jurisconsult, disciple of Malik, founder of the Shafii school of jurisprudence.

AL-SHAYBANI (d. 805). Jurist of the Hanafi school of jurisprudence, disciple of Abu Yusuf. Author of several authoritative works, particularly an important work on jihad, *The Islamic Law of Nations.*

AL-SUYUTI (1445–1505). Born in Cairo, where his father taught Shaf'i law and acted as a substitute kadi. Al-Suyuti is presently recognized as the most prolific author in the realm of Islamic literature. A brilliant multidisciplinary scholar, Al-Suyuti was a learned jurist, historian, and biographer. Among his many scholarly contributions are about twenty works of Qur'anic studies, including seminal Qur'anic commentaries.

AL-TABARI (838–923). Born in Tabaristan, died in Baghdad. Historian, theologian, and jurisconsult. Author of a monumental commentary on the Koran and a universal history, *Annals*, and *Kitab al-Jihad* (Book of the Holy War).

AL-ZAMAKHSHARI (1070?–1143). Persian scholar who was born at Zamakhshar, a village of Khwarizm, studied at Bukhara and Samarkand, and enjoyed the fellowship of the jurists of Baghdad. He stayed at Mecca for many years, becoming known as Jar-idlah ("God's client"). Later he returned to Khwarizm, where he died at the capital Jurjaniyya. Zamakhshari's fame as a scholar rests upon his commentary on the Qur'an, called *al-Kashshaf* (The Revealer), which was the basis of the widely read commentary of Al-Baydawi.

ZIYAUDDIN BARANI (C. 1285–1357). A historian and writer on government under the Delhi sultanate. Well-connected with Delhi ruling circles, he became a companion of Sultan Muhammad b. Tughluq during the period between 1325–1351. Barani's major works (*Tarikh-i-Firoz Shahi* and *Fatawa-i-Jahandari*) attempt to educate the sultans in their duty toward Islam, that is, to curb unorthodoxy, abase the infidel, employ only pious servants, and remain inwardly humble toward God, despite governing with pomp and circumstance.

SHEIKH BURHANUDDIN ALI OF MARGHINAN (1135–1183). Born in Transoxiana, he composed the important Sunni text of Islamic law the *Hidayah*, which was translated into English in 1791 by Charles Hamilton.

MUHAMMAD B. AHMAD IBN ABDUN (d. 1134). Andalusian author of an authoritative legal treatise on Seville.

IBN ABI ZAYD AL-QAYRAWANI (922–996). Head of the North African Maliki school of Qairuan. Author of several legal works and of a compendium that ensured the triumph of the Maliki school of jurisprudence.

IBN AL-ATHIR (1160–1233). Born in Jazirat Ibn Umar on the Tigris (Iraq); lived in Mesopotamia and Palestine. Author of historical works on the Zangrid dynasty of Mosul (al-Bahir) and of a vast corpus of *Chronicles* (*al-Kamil fi't-tarikh*).

IBN BATTUTA (1304–c. 1368). Born and died in Tangiers. Author of accounts describing places visited in the course of several lengthy travels throughout the Islamic world, including India and China.

IBN AL-FUWATI (1244–1323). Born in Baghdad, historian and librarian in Maragha and Baghdad. Author of several historical works and bibliographies.

IBN HANBAL (d. 855). Theologian and jurisconsult, editor of a corpus of traditions, and founder of the Hanbali school of jurisprudence.

IBN HAZM (994–1064). Born in Cordoba, he was a poet, historian, jurist, and theologian, considered to be one of the seminal thinkers in Arabo-Muslim civilization. Ibn Hazm codified the literalist Zahiri doctrine, and according to Roger Arnaldez, "applied himself to reconstructing a legal system stripped of all that he considered to be additions made by the jurists who came after the Prophet and the Companions."

IBN HISHAM (d. 813). Born and died in Egypt. Grammarian and genealogist, famous for his recension of Ibn Ishaq's biography of Muhammad.

IBN HUDAYL (late fourteenth century). He was an Andalusian man of letters and writer from Granada. At the request of sultan Muhammad b. Yusuf b. Ismail (known as Al-Ghani), who reigned in the sixth and seventh decades of the fourteenth century, Ibn Hudayl wrote his masterpiece, a treatise on jihad "holy war," aimed at convincing the Andalusian Muslims to revive the cavalry and match the glory of their illustrious ancestors.

IBN ISHAQ (d. 761). Author of the most famous biography of Muhammad.

IBN KATHIR (1300–1373). One of the best-known historians and traditionalists of Syria during the reign of the Bahri Mamluks, compiling an important history of

Islam, as well as a Qur'anic commentary that foreshadows in its style the commentary of Al-Suyuti.

IBN KHALDUN (1332–1406). Born in Tunis, died in Cairo. Jurist, qadi (Maliki), renowned philosopher, historian, and sociologist. Author of a history of the Berbers and a universal history, preceded by an introduction to history (*al-Muqqddima*).

IBN AQYYIM AL-JAWZIYYA (d. 1351). Theologian, follower of Ibn Taymiya.

IBN RUSHD (1126–1198). Known as Averroes in the medieval West, Ibn Rushd was a scholar of the Qur'anic sciences and natural sciences (physics, medicine, biology, astronomy), theologian, and philosopher. Between 1153–1195, under the Almohad Caliphs 'Abd al-Mu'min, Abu Ya'kub Yusuf, and Ya'kub al-Mansur, he served as either a kadi or a physician in both North Africa (Marrakush) and Andalusia (Seville and Cordoba).

IBN TAGHRIBIRDI, ABU L-MAHASIN (d. 1469). Historian of the Mamluks.

IBN QUDAMA (1147–1223). An important jurisconsult and traditionalist theologian of the Hanbali school.

TAQI AL-DIN AHMAD IBN TAYMIYA (1263–1328). Syrian theologian and jurisconsult of the Hanbali school of jurisprudence under the Mamluks; active in Damascus, where he died. He left a considerable body of jurisprudence. His doctrine inspired the Wahhabi movement in eighteenth-century Arabia.

AYATOLLAH SEYYED RUHOLLAH KHOMEINI (1900–1989). An Iranian Shiite cleric and the political and spiritual leader of the 1979 revolution that overthrew Mohammad Reza Pahlavi, the then shah of Iran, restoring a Shiite theocracy. He was considered the supreme spiritual leader to many Shiite Muslims and ruled Iran from 1979 until his death in 1989. Khomeini wrote and lectured extensively on Islamic government and law (including the provision of formal legal rulings) for more than five decades.

KHUSRAU, AMIR (Khusro, or Khusraw) (1253–1325 CE). Poet, Sufi mystic, and spiritual disciple of Nizamuddin Auliya of Delhi. He wrote in both Persian and Hindustani. Associated with royal courts of more than seven rulers of the Delhi Sultanate (and a friend of the historian and writer Barani), Amir Khusrau's work *Khamsa* was considered to be one of the great classics of Persian poetry during the later Timurid period in Transoxiana.

MULLA MUHAMMAD BAKR MAJLISI (1627–1698). An authoritative jurist and prolific hadith collector, Majlisi was also well educated in Islamic philosophy and mysticism. During the late Safavid period, he became a dominant authority in politics, social and judicial matters. Majlisi's professed goal in his Persian writings was to disseminate the Shia ethos to "the masses of believers and common Shia" who had "no familiarity with the Arabic language." Majlisi had very close relationships with at least two of the Safavid monarchs, Shah Sulayman (d. 1694) and Shah Sultan Husayn (d. 1713). In 1686 he was appointed the Shaykh al-Islam by Shah Sulyaman. Upon Shah Husayn's accession to the throne in 1694, his title was changed to Mullabashi. Majlisi personally undertook legal matters and proceedings while holding these supreme institutionalized clerical offices. During the last four years in this official state office under Shah Sultan Husayn, Majlisi was the de facto ruler of Iran.

MALIK B. ANAS (710–795). Theologian and jurisconsult from Medina, founder of the Maliki school of jurisprudence. Author of *al-Muwatta*, the oldest extant treatise of Islamic law as practiced in the Hijaz.

MUSLIM (d. 874). Disciple of al-Bukhari and compiler of one of the most important corpus of traditions (hadith), being the acts and sayings (al-Shaih) attributed to the Prophet Muhammad.

SAYYID QUTB (1906–1966). One of the great Islamic scholars of the twentieth century. Qutb served a long sentence in prison for his Islamic and political opinions and was sentenced to death in Nasser's Egypt in 1966. Posthumously he has remained a popular Islamic spiritual guide. Qutb's conception of religion and its relation to secular modernity has had a pervasive influence throughout the Muslim world, particularly in Egypt and other Arab countries. He wrote the extensive Qur'anic commentaries *In the Shade of the Qur'an*, and is also remembered for his work on Islam's socioeconomic nature, *'Adalah fi al-ijtimaiyah fi al-Islam* (1949), and its translation, *Social Justice in Islam* (1953).

SHAYKH AHMAD SIRHINDI (1564–1624). Sirhindi was an eminent Sufi mystic, connected with several Sufi orders (including the Naqshbandi order), who contributed considerably toward the revival of orthodox Islam following the heterodox experiments of Akbar's reign (1556–1605). He published a number of tracts and letters promoting these views.

SHAH ALADIHLAWI WALI-ALLAH (1703–1762). Born in Delhi in 1703, Shah Wali-Allah was a theologian, pioneering Persian translator of the Qur'an, Sufi traditionalist, and political activist. Shah Wali-Allah's letters to Afghan ruler Ahmad Shah Abdali (Durrani), as well as prominent local Muslim leaders urging them to cooperate with Durrani in undertaking a jihad against the (Hindu) Marathas and Jats, reveal his persistent efforts to establish a (foreign, if necessary) and more militant Muslim dynasty within India. Shah Wali-Allah was thus not only an inspiration for Durrani's invasions of 1756–1757 and 1760–1761, he was also responsible for helping to organize a confederacy of Muslim powers against the Marathas in Northern India.

Appendix D

NON-MUSLIM HISTORIANS, AUTHORS, AND ISLAMIC SCHOLARS

ARAKEL OF TAURIZ (TABRIZ) (c. 1600–c. 1670). Armenian author who, at the request of the Catholicos Philippos, wrote a book of histories on the deportation of the Armenians in Persia. He continued to work in Isfahan from 1661 to 1662 at the request of the Catholicos Jacob of Julfa. His book is a valuable source of firsthand information on the condition of the Armenians and the patriarchs at that period.

BAR HEBRAEUS (ABUL-FARAJ) (1226–1286). Born in Melitene (Malatia in Upper Mesopotamia) of a Jewish father. Jacobite Bishop of Gubbos, Labakin, and Aleppo; Maphrian of the East, he died in Maraga. Author of *The Chronography* and other important historical and theological works.

REV. DR. RICHARD BELL (1876–1952). Bell was educated at Edinburgh University, where he studied Semitic languages and divinity. He became a minister of the Church of Scotland in 1904, and ordained to the parish of Wamphrey in 1907. After fourteen years in the parish ministry, Bell returned to Edinburgh as lecturer in Arabic, attaining the position of reader in Arabic in 1938, a position he held until his retirement in 1947. His major writings include *The origin of Islam in its Christian environment* (1925), The *Qur'an, translated, with a critical re-arrangement of the Surahs* (1937–1939), *Introduction to the Qur'an* (1953), and *A commentary on the Qur'an* (1991) [edited by C. E. Bosworth].

MARIE FELICITE BROSSET (1802–1880). Born in Paris, February 5, 1802, Brosset originally pursued ecclesiastic studies, and eventually studied Oriental languages. After working a few years as a printer, he found a position as a teacher of Caucasian languages in St. Petersburg in 1837. Later Brosset became a member of the Russian academy, and a librarian, before returning to Paris where he died September 3, 1880. Brosset is best known for his elegant translations from Georgian and Armenian, *Chronique géorgienne* (1829–1831), *Histoire de la Géorgie: depuis l'antiquité jusqu'au XIXe siècle* (1849–1858); *Histoire de la Siounie* (1864–1866), *Deux historiens arméniens Kiracos de Gantzac, XIIIe s., Histoire d'Arménie; Oukhtanes d'Ourha, Xe s., Histoire en trois parties* (1870–1871). He also wrote an original work, *Les ruines d'Ani, capitale de l'Arménie sous les rois Bagratides, aux xe et xie s; histoire et description* (1860–1861).

ANNA COMNENA (COMNENE) (1083–1153). A daughter of the Byzantine emperor Alexius I Comnenus, Anna Comnena became a chronicler/historian, trained in the study of poetry, science, and Greek philosophy. Following Anna's participation in a failed conspiracy in 1118 to depose her brother John after his accession, her life was spared, though she forfeited her property and fortune. Soon afterwards, Anna was dispatched to a convent where she wrote the *Alexiad*—a history in Greek of her father's life and reign. The *Alexiad* describes the political and military history during the reign of Alexius I Comnenus (1081–1118), making it one of the most important contemporary sources for the study of the Byzantine Empire.

DIONYSIUS OF TELL-MAHRE (d. 845). Patriarch of the Jacobites, his *Chronicle* has disappeared but extracts from it were preserved in Michael the Syrian's twelfth-century *Chronicle*. The *Chronicle* wrongly attributed to him was completed in c. 775, before his time. (*See* Pseudo-Dionysius of Tell Mahre.)

JEAN PAUL LOUIS FRANÇOIS EDOUARD DULAURIER (1807–1881). Born in Toulouse, he came to Paris as a young man, studied Arabic and Turkish under Silvestre de Sacy, and became interested in ancient Egyptian studies. He went to London in 1838 to study Hieroplyphic and Coptic texts. After he added Armenian to his expertise, he was appointed professor of Armenian at the Ecole des langues orientales vivantes, Paris. His *Recherches sur la Chronologie Armeninne, Technique et Historique*, 1859 includes important French translations of Armenian historians and chroniclers, such as Sebeos and Matthew of Edessa. He died in Meudon (auts-de-Seine).

GHEVOND. Armenian historian of the second half of the eighth century. Author of *History of the Wars* and *Conquests of the Arabs in Armenia*.

JOHN OF NIKIOU (seventh century). Coptic bishop. Author of an important account of the Arab conquest of Egypt, of which only an Ethiopian translation remains.

MATTHEW OF EDESSA (d. after 1136). Armenian chronicler and author of *Chronological Tables*.

MICHAEL THE SYRIAN. Jacobite patriarch of Antioch from 1166 to 1199. Author of a famous *Chronicle* that reproduces earlier sources, before describing contemporary events.

PSEUDO-DIONYSIUS OF TELL MAHRE (eighth century). Anonymous author of a *Chronicle* wrongly attributed to the ninth-century patriarch of the same name. It provides a valuable description of the peasant condition in Mesopotamia from personal experience.

SAMUEL OF ANI. Armenian author of a *Chronicle* from the second half of the twelfth century.

SAWIRUS (SEVERUS) B. AL-MAQAFFA. Coptic bishop of Ashmunein (Egypt) from 955 to 987. Author of a history of the patriarchs of Alexandria. After his death, it was continued from 886 to 1046 by Michael, bishop of Tinnis; then up to the thirteenth century by other ecclesiastics.

SEPEOS (SEBEOS). Armenian bishop active in the third quarter of the seventh century. Author of a history of Heraclius from the end of the fifth century to 661, he describes the events of his times.

THEOPHANES. Monastic chronicler of the Byzantine Empire, born sometime between 752–760. His *Chronographia*, which describes events from the end of the third through the beginning of the eighth centuries (from the accession of Emperor Diocletian to that of Leo V, 284–813), is considered to be of unique value because it utilizes a Greek translation of a late eighth-century chronicle originally written in Syriac. This particular source is believed to account for Theophanes accurate information on events in Muslim-held territory. Moreover Theophanes was a contemporary of the events he describes during the fratricidal war that erupted between the brothers al-Amin and al Ma'mun, following the death of Caliph Harun al-Rashid in 809 CE.

THOMAS ARDZRUNI (d. EARLY TENTH CENTURY). Armenian historian and author of *History of the Ardzrunis*, in which he describes contemporary events. It was continued by others from 907 to 1226.

MAJOR CONTRIBUTORS

NICOLAS P. AGHNIDES, fl. 1916, wrote a comprehensive analysis of Islamic law, *Mohammedan Theories of Finance with an Introduction to Mohammedan Law* (1916). Despite the title, this treatise was not limited to financial matters per se, covering a very broad range of issues, including important discussions of jihad and *dhimmi* regulations.

MARIA MATILDA ALEXANDRESCU-DERSCA's writings include numerous essays and *La campagne de Timur en Enatolie* (1942) and *Nicolae Iorga, a Roumanian Historian* (1972).

DIMITUR SIMEONOV ANGELOV graduated from Sofia University and subsequently became a professor of history. His writings in French and English include *Le Bogomilisme en Bulgarie* (1972), *Les Balkans au moyen age* (1978), *Formation of the Bulgarian Nation* (1978), and *Bulgaria's Contribution to the Development of Spiritual Culture in the Middle Ages* (1980).

ROGER ANTOINE ARNALDEZ was a professor of philosophy at universities in Egypt and France until his retirement in 1978. His writings include *Mahomet* (1970), *Le Coran* (1983), *Trois messengers pour un seul Dieu* (1983), *L'islam* (1985), *Aspects de la pensee musulmane* (1987), and *Jesus dens la pensee arabe* (1988).

DEMETRIOS JOHN (DIMITRIS STACHYS) CONSTANTELOS was educated at Holy Cross Greek Orthodox Theological School, Princeton Theological Seminary, and Rutgers University, where he received a PhD in 1965 for his thesis *Philanthropia and Philanthropic Institutions in the Byzantine Empire, 330–1204*. He was a pastor in Perth Amboy, NJ, and later served as a professor of history and religious studies at Stockton State College. His English writings include numerous essays, and *Orthodox Theology and Diakonia* (1981) and *Byzantine Society and Church Philanthropy from the Fourth Crusade through the Fall of Constantinople* (1985).

CHARLES EMMANUEL DUFOURCQ (1914–1982) was educated at Alger and completed his formal education with the *agregation d'histoire et geographie* at the Sorbonne. In 1937 he started his university career at the Lycee Carnot de Tunis.

After World War II and the Algerian war for independence, he became a professor of history in France, first at the Universite d'Amiens and later at Paris-Nanterre, where he remained until his death. His writings include numerous research articles and the major works *L'Espagne catalane et les Maghribaux* (1966), which was originally his doctoral thesis, and *La vie quotidienne dans l'Europe medievale sous domination arabe* (1978).

JOHN EIBNER is a historian and human rights specialist who received his MA from the University of London in 1978. Since 1990, he has served as assistant to the international president of Christian Solidarity International (CSI). He has led over twenty fact-finding visits to Sudan and neighboring countries and pioneered CSI's antislavery program.

JACQUES ELLUL (1912–1994) was for much of his professional life a professor of history of law at the Universite de Bordeaux. He wrote more than forty books that fused his sociological beliefs in Marxism and Christianity, including *Homme et l'argent* (1979) and its translation, *Money and Power* (1984), *Perspectives on Our Age: Jacques Ellul Speaks on His Life and Work* (1981), *FLN Propaganda in France during the Algerian War* (1982), and *Anarchie et christiansme* and its translation, *Anarchy and Christianity* (1991). During the last 25 years of his life, Ellul wrote important essays on Islam, including long prefaces to the original French versions of Bat Ye'or's *The Dhimmi* and *The Decline of Eastern Christianity Under Islam*.

EDMOND FAGNAN (1846–1931) earned a doctorate in law from the Université de Liege and later he obtained a diploma in Arabic, Persian, Turkish, and Hebrew from the Ecole des langues orientales vivantes, Paris. In 1873 he joined the Departement des manuscrits of the Bibliotheque nationale, where he collaborated in the production of Oriental historians in the Persian at l'Ecole des lettres d'Alger, a post he held until his retirement in 1919. From 1892 to 1904 he belonged to the Bordeau de la Societe historique algerienne. His writings include *Concordance du manuel de droit de Sidi Khalil* (1889) and *Additions aux dictionnaires arabes* (1923).

ALAN WASHBURN FISHER was a graduate of DePauw University and received his PhD in 1967 from Columbia University for the thesis *The Russian Annexation of the Crimea, 1774–1783*. In 1966 he began his lifelong teaching career at the Department of History of Michigan State University, specializing in Russian and Turkish history. His writings include *The Crimean Tatars* (1978).

W. R. GARDNER was affiliated with the Christian Literature Society for India. He wrote *Christianity and Muhammedanism* (1910), *The Doctrine of Man* (1913),

The Qur'anic Doctrine of Salvation (1914), *The Qur'anic Doctrine of Sin* (1914), and *Al-Ghazali* (1919).

HARRY W. HAZARD (1918–1989) received his PhD in Oriental studies from Princeton University in 1948. He subsequently taught at Princeton's program in Near Eastern Studies. In addition to writing numerous scholarly articles, Professor Hazard compiled the unique *Atlas of Islamic History* (1951). He also wrote *The Art and Architecture of the Crusader States* (1977) and was a collaborating author on both *The Impact of the Crusades on the Near East* (1985) and *The Impact of the Crusades on Europe* (1989).

CLEMENT HUART (1854–1926) was an eminent scholar of Arabic, Persian, and Turkish from the Ecole des Langues Orientales Vivantes, and was widely published in the late nineteenth and early twentieth centuries. Some of his major works include: *A History of Arabic Literature* (1901); *Histoire de Bagdad dans les temps modernes* (1901); *Histoire des Arabes* (1912–1913); and *La Perse antique et la civilisation iranienne* (1925). Earlier in his career, he was the chancellor at the French Consulate in Damascus, and subsequently also served as dragoman (interpreter), then consul, for the French Embassy in Constantinople.

MAJID KHADDURI, a professor Emeritus of Middle Eastern Studies, joined the Johns Hopkins School for Advanced International Studies in 1949, and directed the Middle East Studies Program until 1980. A prolific and acclaimed writer on the legal and political problems of the Middle East, he was the author of many published essays and a number of books, including, most notably, *War and Peace in the Law of Islam* (1955), *The Islamic Law of Nations: Shaybani's Siyar* [which he translated, introduced, and annotated] (1966), and *The Islamic Conception of Justice* (1984).

K. S. LAL (1920–2002) received his doctorate in medieval Indian history from the University of Allahabad in 1945. Starting as a lecturer in the same university, he served in the Madhya Pradesh Education Service from 1945 to 1963 and taught at Government Colleges in Nagpur, Jabalpur, and Bhopal. He was reader in the University of Delhi for ten years (1963–1973) and, for the next ten years, professor and head of the Department of History in the University of Jodhpur (1973–1979) and the University of Hyderabad (1979–1983). He published a number of articles and monographs on medieval Indian history, including *The History of the Khaljis* (1950), *Twilight of the Sultanate* (1963), *The Mughal Harem* (1988), *The Legacy of Muslim Rule in India* (1992), and *Theory and Practice of Muslim State in India* (1999).

VASILIKE D. PAPOULIA received a D.phil. in 1964 from the Universitat Munchen with a thesis entitled *Ursprung und Wesen der "Knabenlese" im Osmaniscen Reich.*

RUDD PETERS received a doctorate at Amsterdam in 1979 and in 1989 started his academic career at the Department of Arabic and Islamic Studies at the Universiteit van Amsterdam. His writings include *Jihad in Mediaeval and Modern Islam: The Chapter of Jihad from Averroes'* . . . *and Mahmud Shaltut* (1979) and its Persian translation in 1986. He was joint editor of *The Challenge of the Middle East: Middle Eastern Studies at the University of Amsterdam* (1982).

ARAM NAAPETOVICH TER-GHEVONDIAN graduated in 1954 from the Philological Faculty, State University, Erevan, and received his first degree in history in 1959. After his graduation he was affiliated with the Institute of History, Armenian Academy of Science. His major work translated into English (from Armenian) is *The Arab Emirates in Bagratid Armenia* (1976).

BASSAM TIBI received a traditional Islamic education in Damascus. In 1971 he earned a doctorate at the Universitat Frankfurt am Main with a thesis entitled *Zum Nationalismus in der "Dritten Welt" am arabischen Exempel.* Since 1973 he has been a professor of politics at Gottingen. His writings include *Die Krise des modernen Islams* (1981), *Die fundamentalistische Herausforderung* (1992), *Arab Nationalsm* (1981), *The Crisis of Modern Islam* (1988), *Conflict and War in the Middle East* (1993), *Im Schatten Allahs* (1994), and *Aufbruch am Bosporus* (1998).

SPEROS P. VRYONIS graduated in 1950 from Southwestern College and received his PhD in 1956 from Harvard. He was affiliated with UCLA as a professor of history. In addition to his major work, *The Decline of Medieval Hellenism in Asia Minor* (1971), his writings include *Byzantium and Europe* (1967), a collection of his articles, *Byzantium* (1971), *The Turkish State and History* (1991), and *The Mechanism of Catastrophe—The Turkish Pogrom of September 6–7, 1955* (2005). He also edited *Individualism and Conformity in Classical Islam* (1977).

JOHN RALPH WILLIS was a graduate of the University of Arizona and received a PhD in 1970 from School of Oriental and Asiatic Studies (London) for *al-Hajj 'Umar b. Sa'id al-Futi al-Turi and the Doctrinal Basis of His Islamic Reformist Movement.* In 1995, he was a professor in the Department of Near Eastern Languages and Literature at Princeton. He wrote *Studies in West African Islamic History* (1979), *Slaves and slavery in Muslim Africa* (1985), and *In the Path of Allah: The passion of Al-Hajj 'Umar* (1989).

BIBLIOGRAPHY

Major books, articles, and hyperlinks mentioned in text, documents, and notes are listed here. Inconsistences in the names or text are not necessarily reproduced in the bibliography and index.

Abbreviations used:
an.: annotations/annotated by
col.: collected by
ed.: editor/edited by/edition
Eng.: English
trans.: translation/translator
DOP: Dumbarton Oaks Papers
E & D: Elliot and Dawson, *The History of India as Told by Its Own Historians*
G & S: Goldziher and Schacht, *The Encyclopedia of Islam*
PG: Patrologiae cursus completes, Series Graeca, ed. J.-P. Migne, 161 volumes in 116 parts (Paris, 1857–1866)
*PPS*b: Pravoslavnij Palestinskij Sbornik

Abd al-Halim Mahmud. *Al-Jihad wa al-nasr.* Cairo, 1968.
Abd-Allah ibn Muftah. *Sharh al-Azhar*, vol. 5. Cairo, A.H. 1358.
Abd-ul-Hack. In *Le Mecherouttiete*, ed. Sherif Pasha. Paris, August 1912.
Abel, Armand. "Le Chapitre CI du Livre des Hérésies de Jean Damascene: Son inauthenticité." *Studia Islamica* 19 (1963).
———. "L'Etranger dans L'Islam Classique." *Recueils de la Société Jean Bodin* 9 (1958).
Abou El Fadl, Khaled. "The Rules of Killing at War: An Inquiry into Classical Sources." *Muslim World* 89 (1999).
———. *The Place of Tolerance in Islam.* Boston, MA, 2002.
Abu Da'ud. *Sunan*, vol. 3. Cairo, 1935.
Abu-I-Mahasin Ibn Taghre Birdi. *al-Nujum al-Zahira.* Cairo, 1929.
Abuquarca, Theodore. *PG*, 97.
Abu Talib Husaini, trans. (Persian). *Malfuzat-i-Timuri.* In E & D.
Abu Yusuf, Ya'qub. *Kitab al-Kharaj (Le livre de l'impôt foncier).* Trans. and an. Edmond Fagnan. Paris, 1921. Eng. trans. in Bat Ye'or, *The Dhimmi* and *The Decline.*
Adjarian, H. *Andsnanunneri Bararan* [Dictionary of Names]. Erevan, 1948.
Afif, Shams Siraj. *Tarikh-i-Firoz Shahi.* Calcutta, 1890.
Agdac, Moustapha. In *Belleten*, vol. 13, 1949.
Aghnides, Nicolas P. *Mohammedan Theories of Finance with an Introduction to Mohammedan Law.* New York, 1916.
Ahmad, Aziz. *Studies in Islamic Culture in the Indian Environment.* Oxford, 1964.
Ahmad, Maulana, et al. *Tarikhi-Alfi.* Trans. in E & D, vol. 5.

Ahmad, Rif'at Sayyid, and Al-Rafidun Al-Juz' Al-Awwal. *Dar Riyad Al-Rayyis Lil-Kutub Wal-Nashr.* London, 1991.

Ajayi, Jacob, and Michael Crowder. *A History of West Africa,* vol. 1. 1971.

Akcam, T. *Turkish National Identity and the Armenian Question.* Istanbul, 1992.

al-Amili, Baha' ad-din Muhammad ibn Husayn. *Jami'-i 'Abbasi: yakdawrah-i fiqh-i Farsi.* Eng. trans., Fatemeh Masjedi. Tehran, 1980s.

al-Armanazi, Najib. *Al-Shan' al-duwali fi al-Islam.* London, 1990.

al-Baghdadi, 'Abd al-Qahir. *Kitab Usul al-Din,* vol. 1. Istanbul, 1928.

Al-Baladhuri. *Liber expugnationis regionum.* Lugd. Bat., 1856.

al-Banna, Hasan. *Majmu'at rasail al-imam al-Shahid Hasan al-Banna.* Cairo, 1990.

al-Beidawi. *Anwar al-Tanzil. . . ,* vol. 1. Ed. H. O. Fleischer, 1846–48; Osnabrueck, 1968.

Al Biladuri. *Futuh-ul-Buldan.* Written 9th cent. CE. *See in* E & D, vol. 1.

Alberuni, Abu Raihan Muhammad. *Alberuni's India—An Account of the Religion, Philosophy, Literature, Geography, Chronology, Astronomy, Customs, Laws, and Astrology of India (about 1030 C.E.).* Trans. and ed. Edward C. Sachau, 1888, New Delhi, 1993; 2 vols. London, 1910.

Albino, Oliver. *The Sudan: A Southern Viewpoint.* London, 1970.

Alexandrescu-Dersca Bulgaru, M-M. *La campagne de Timur en Enatolie.* 1942.

———. *Nicolae Iorga, a Roumanian historian.* 1972.

———. "Le role des ecsalves en Romanie turque au XVe siecle." *Byzantinische Forschungen* 11 (1987).

al-Fattah, Nabil 'Abd. *Al-Mashaf wa al-saif.* Cairo, 1984.

Al-Ghazali. *Kitab al-Wagiz fi fiqh madhab al-imam al-Safi'i.* Eng. trans. Dr. Michael Schub. Beirut, 1979.

al-Hidayah. *The Hedaya, or Guide—A Commentary on the Mussulman Laws,* vol. 2. Trans. Charles Hamilton, 1791; New Delhi, 1982.

al-Hilli, Ibn al-Mutahhar. *Shara'i`u 'l-Islam.* See Querry, *Droit Musulman.*

———. *Tabsirat al-Muta'allimin fi Ahkam al-Din.* Damascus, A.H. 1342.

Alishan, Gh. *Ayrarat.* Venice, 1890.

Al-Kufi, *The Chachnāmah.* Trans. Mirza Kalichbeg Fredunbeg. Delhi, 1979. Trans. in E & D, vol. 1.

———. *Kitab al-Futuh.* 8 vols. Haydarabad, 1968, 1975.

al-Latif Husni, Abd. *Al-Islam wa al-'alaqat al-duwaliyya: Namudhaj Ahmad bin Khalid al-Nasiri.* Casablanca, 1991.

Al-Majlisi. "The Treatise Lightning Bolts against the Jews." Trans. V. B. Moreen. *Die Welt des Islams* 32 (1992).

Al-Makine. *Chronikon. See* N. A. Miednikow, *Palestine.*

Al Masudi. *Muruj-ul-Zuhab* (941 CE). Trans. in E & D.

al-Mawardi, Abu al-Hassan. *El-Ahkâm es-Soulthânîya* [A Treatise on Moslem Public Law]. Trans. into French and an. Count Léon Ostrorog, vol. 2, 1st part. Paris, 1906.

———. *The Laws of Islamic Governance.* London, 1996.

al-Mu'mini, (al-Mugaddam) Ahmad. *Al-Tabi'a al jihadiyya fi al-Islam.* Constantine, Algeria, 1991.

Al-Muntakha fii Tafsiir al-Qur'aan al-Kariim [The Culled Qur'aan Commentary]. 11th ed. Cairo, 1985.

al-Nasiri, Ahmad bin Khalid. *Al-Istigsa' fi akhbar al-Maghrib al-agsa.* 9 vols. Casablanca, 1955.

al-Qaradawi, Yusuf. *The Lawful and the Prohibited in Islam.* http://www.witness-pioneer.org/vil/Books/Q_LP/.

————. *Islam: The Future Civilization.* Cairo, 1419 AH/1998 AC.

————. *The Scholar and the Tyrant.* CA, Swansea, UK.

————. Discussion at *Al-Jazeera Television*, Qatar, June 19, 2001. *See in* "The Prophet Muhammad as a *Jihad* Model." *Middle East Media Research Institute* 246 (2001). http://memri.org/bin/articles.cgi?Page=archives&Area=sd&ID=SP24601.

————. Speech at the July 2003, European Council for Fatwa and Research, headed by Sheikh Al-Qaradawi, which convened in Stockholm. Reported in *Al-Sharq Al-Awsat*, London, July 19, 2003. See also "Al-Qaradhawi Speaks in Favor of Suicide Operations at an Islamic Conference in Sweden." *Middle East Media Research Institute* 542 (2003). http://memri.org/bin/articles.cgi?Page=archives&Area=sd&ID=SP54203.

al-Shaybani. *al-Siyar al-Kabir.* With Sarakhsi's commentary. Vol. 1. Hyderabad, A.H. 1335.

————. *The Islamic Law of Nations: Shaybani's Siyar.* Trans. and an. Majid Khadduri. Baltimore, 1966.

al-Suyuti. *al-Ashbah wa'l-Naza'ir.* Cairo, 1938.

————. *Durr al-Manthur*, vol. 3. Beirut, n.d.

————. *Tafsir al-Jalalayn.* Beirut, 1404/1984.

al-Tabari. *Annales*, vol. 2. 1354.

————. *The History of al-Tabari (Ta'rikh al rusul wa'l-muluk).* Albany, NY, 1989.

————. *Jami` al-Bayan*, vol. 10. Ed. M. Shakir. Beirut, 1421/2001.

————. *Kitab al-Jihad* (Book of the Holy War).

————. *Tarikh.* Cairo, 1964.

————. *Ta'rikh.* Ed. de Goeje. Series 1, vol. 4. Leiden, 1890.

al Umri, Shihabuddin. *Masalik-ul-Absar fi Mumalik-ul-Amsar.* Written mid-14th cent. CE. Trans. in E & D, vol. 3.

————/OLS Rapid Assessment Team. *Rapid Assessment Report, Rapid Assessment of Affected Locations in Twic, Aweil East, Aweil West and Wau Counties, March 13 and 25, 1999.* Lokichoggio, April 1999.

al-Zamakhshari. *Al-Kashshaaf . . .* [The Revealer], vol. 2. Ed. M. Ahmad. Cairo, 1365; 1946.

Amar, E., trans. and ed. "Consultations juridiques des fakihs du Maghreb." *Archives Marocaines*, Paris, 1908.

Amari, Michele. *Storia dei Musulmani di Sicilia*, vol. 1. Ed. G. Nallino. Catane, 1933–1939.

Anagnostas, J. *Anagnostae de Thessalonicensi excidio narratio.* Bonnae.

————. *De extremo Thessalonicensi exidio narratio.* Ed. Leone Allatio. Bonn, 1838.

Andric, Ivo. *The Development of Spiritual Life in Bosnia under the Influence of Turkish Rule.* 1924 doctoral dissertation. Eng. trans. Durham, NC, 1990.

Anetsi, Samuel. *Havakmunk i grots patmagrats* [Collection of the Writings of Historians]. Vagharshapat, 1893.

Angelos, Nichephoros. *Enchiridium de statu hodiernorum Graecorum . . . cum versione latine . . .* Lipsiae, 1666.

Angelov, Dimitar. *Les Balkans au moyen age. La Bulgarie des Bogomils aux Turcs.* London, 1978.

————. "Certain aspects de la conquête des peuples balkaniques par les Turcs." *Byzantinoslavica* (1956).

an-Na'im, Abdullahi Ahmed. *Toward an Islamic Reformation: Civil Liberties, Human Rights and International Law.* Syracuse, NY, 1990.

Arakelian, B. "Hayeri Apestambutiune Arabakan Ldsi Dem [The Insurrection of Armenians Against Arab Yoke]." *Teghekagir* 5–6 (1941).

Arakel of Tauriz. *Livre d'Histoires. See in* Brosset, *Collection.* Eng. trans. in Bat Ye'or, *The Decline.*

Aravantinos, P. *Syllogi dimodon asmaton tis Epirou* [Society of the Popular Songs of Epirus]. Athens, 1880.

Ardzruni, Thomas. *Histoire des Ardazrouni (Xᵉ siècle). See in* Brosset, *Collections.* Eng. trans. in Bat Ye'or, *The Decline.*

Arié, Rachel. *L'Espagne musulmane au temps des Nasrides.* Paris, 1973.

Arnaldez, Roger Antoine. "La guerre sainte selon Ibn Hazm de Courdoue." *Etudes d'Orientalisme Dediées à la Mémoire de Lévi-Provençal*, vol. 2, Paris, 1962.

Arnold, T. W. *The Preaching of Islam.* Westminister, 1896.

Arnold, T. W., and A. Guillaume, eds. *The Legacy of Islam.* Oxford, 1931.

Ašikpašazade. *Die altosmanische Chronik des Ašikpašazade auf Grund mehrerer neuentdeckter Handschriften.* Ed. Fr. Giese. Leipzig, 1924.

Assemani, Josepho Aloysio. *De Catholicis seu patriarehis Chaldaeorum et Nestorianorum Commentarius historicochronologicus.* Rome, 1775.

Atil, Esin. *Süleymanname: The Illustrated History of Süleyman the Magnificent.* New York, 1986.

Auron, Yair. *The Banality of Indifference.* New Brunswick, NJ, 2000.

Avgerian, M. *Liakatar vark ev vkayapanutiun hayots*, vol. 1.

Ayalon, David. "On the Eunuchs in Islam." *Jerusalem Studies in Arabic and Islam* 1 (1979).

Babin, J. B. *Relation de l'état présent de la ville d'Athènes.* Lyon, 1674.

Babinger, Fr. *Beiträge zur Frühgeschichte der Türkenherrschaft in Rumelien (14–15 Jahrh.).* Munich, 1944.

————. "Die Aufzeichnungen des Genuesen Jacopo de Promontorio de Campis." *Sitzungsberichte der Bayerischen Akademie, Philologische-Historische Klasse, 1956*, vol. 8. Munich, 1957.

Babur, Zahiruddin Muhammad. *Babur Nama or Tuzuk-i-Baburi.* Trans. A. S. Beveridge, 2 vols. London, 1922. Trans. from Persian by John Leyden and William Erskine as *Memoirs of Babur*, London, 1926.

Badalian, *Oratsuytsi Patmutiun* [History of the Calendar]. Erevan, 1970.

Badaoni, Abdul Qadir Ibn-i-Muluk Shah. *Muntakhab-ut-Tawarikh.* Ed. Ahmad All (Persian text), Calcutta, 1864–1867; Eng. trans. George S. A. Ranking, Calcutta, 1898.

Baghishetsi, David. *Manr Zhamanakagrutiunner* [Minor Chronicles], vol. 2. Erevan, 1956.

————. *The Origins of the Islamic State*, vol. 1. Trans. Philip K. Hitti. New York, 1916; Beirut, 1966.

————. *The Origins of the Islamic State (Kitab Futuh Al-Buldan).* Part 2. Trans. F. C. Murgotten. New York, 1924.

Ballis, William. *The Legal Position of War: Changes in Its Practice and Theory.* The Hague, 1937.

Banninga, J. J. "The Moplah Rebellion of 1921." *Moslem World* 13 (1923).

Barani, Ziyauddin. *Fatawa-i Jahandari*, circa 1358–1359 CE. *See in* Habib, *The Political Theory*.

———. "Sana-i-Muhammadi." Trans. in *Medieval India Quarterly* 1, part 3.

———. *Tarikh-i-Firoz Shahi*. Calcutta, 1864.

Bar Hebraeus. *Chronicon Ecclesiasticum*, vol. 3. Ed. J. B. Abbeloos and Th. J. Lamy. Paris and Rome, 1877.

———. *The Chronography*, vol. 1. Trans. E. A. Wallis Budge. London, 1932.

Barkan, Ö. L. *XV ve XVI inci asirlarda osmanli Imparatorluğunda zirai ekonominin hukukî ve malî esaslari*, vol. 1. Istanbul, 1943.

———. "XV ve XVI asirlarda Osmanli imparatorluğunda toprak isciliğinin organizasyono sekilleri." *Iktisat Fakültesi Mecmuasi*, vol. 1, 1939.

———. "Les déportations comme méthode de peuplement et de colonisation dans l'Empire ottoman." *Revue de la Faculté des Sciences Économiques de l'Université d'Istanbul*, nos. 1–4 (1949–1950).

Bartikian, H., trans. *The Chronical of Theophanes*. Unpublished MS.

Basdrabelles, Ch. J. K. *Armatoloi Kai Klephteseis tin Makedonian* [Armatoles and Klephts in Macedonia]. Thessaloniki, 1948.

Bat Ye'or. *The Decline of Eastern Christianity under Islam*. Cranbury, NJ, 1996.

———. *The Dhimmi. Jews and Christians under Islam*. Trans. David Maisel, Paul Fenton, and David Littman. Preface by Jacques Ellul. Cranbury, NJ, 1985.

———. *Eurabia—The Euro-Arab Axis*. Cranbury, NJ, 2005.

———. *Islam and Dhimmitude: Where Civilizations Collide*. Madison, NJ, 2002.

Becker, Carl H. *The Cambridge Medieval History*, vol. 2. Cambridge, 1913.

Beheim, M. *Zehn Gedichte Michael Beheims zur Geschichte Oesterreichs und Ungarns*. Ed. Th. G. von Karajan. Vienna, 1849.

Beldiceanu, N. *Les actes des premiers sultans conservés dans les manuscrits turcs de la Bibliothèque Nationale à Paris*. T. I. Paris, La Haye, 1960.

———. *Le monde ottoman des Balkans (1402–1566): Institutions, société, économie*. London, 1976.

———. *Recherches sur la ville ottomane au XVe siècle: Études et actes*. Paris, 1973.

Bell, Richard. *A Commentary on the Qur'an*, vol. 1 (Surahs I–XXIV). Manchester, 1991.

———. *The Origin of Islam in Its Christian Environment*. London, 1926.

———. *The Qur'an*, vol. 1. Edinburgh, 1937.

Bellamy, Carol. "Buying Slaves Is Wrong." *International Herald Tribune*, May 13, 1999.

Benjamin, Israel Joseph. *Eight Years in Asia and Africa—From 1846–1855*. Hanover, 1859.

Bernier, Francois. *Travels in the Mogul Empire (1656–1668)*. Revised by V. A. Smith. Oxford, 1934.

Beshir, Mohamed Omer. *The Southern Sudan: Background to Conflict*. London, 1968.

Bhatnagar, V. S., trans., ed., and an. *Kanhadade Prabandh*. New Delhi, 1991.

Bianchi, Th. X., and J. D. Kieffer. *Dictionnaire turc-français*. Paris, 1850.

Binyamin. *Eight Years in Asia and Africa from 1846 to 1855*. Hanover, 1859.

Biro, Gaspar. "The U.N. Finds Slavery in the Sudan." *MEQ* (September 1996).

Boland, B. J. *The Struggle of Islam in Modern Indonesia*. The Hague, 1971.

Bonwetsch, N., ed. "Doctrina Jacobi nuper baptizati." *Abhandlungen der Koniglicben Gesellschaft der Wusenscbaften zu Gottingen*, Philologisch-historiche Klasse, 12.03.1910.

Bostom, Andrew. "A Modern Jihad Genocide." FrontPageMagazine.com, April 28, 2003. http://www.frontpagemag.com/Articles/ReadArticle.asp?ID=7519.
———. "The Sacred Muslim Practice of Beheading." FrontPage Magazine.com, May 13, 2004. http://www.frontpagemag.com/Articles/ReadArticle.asp?ID=13371.
———. "Textbook Jihad in Egypt." FrontPageMagazine.com, June 30, 2004. http://www.frontpagemag.com/Articles/ReadArticle.asp?ID=14017.
———. "Treatment of POWs." FrontPageMagazine.com, March 28, 2003. http://www.frontpagemag.com/Articles/ReadArticle.asp?ID=6929.
Bosworth, C. E. *The Ghaznavids*. Edinburgh, 1963.
———. *See* Joseph Schacht, *The Legacy of Islam*.
Bouquet, Martin, et al., eds. *Recueil des Historiens des Gaules et de la France*. Paris, 1738–1833, 1869–1880.
Bousquet, G. H. *L'Ethique sexuelle de l'Islam*. Paris, 1966.
———. "Islamic Law and Customary Law in French North Africa." *Journal of Comparative Legislation and International Law* (1950).
Bowen, H. *See* H. A. R. Gibb, *Islamic Society*.
Boyce, Mary. *A Persian Stronghold of Zoroastrianism*. Based on the Ratanbai Katrak lectures, 1975. Lanham, MD, 1989.
———. *Zoroastrians: Their Religious Beliefs and Practices*. London, 1979, 2001.
Brockelmann, C. *Geshichte der Arabischen Litteratur*, vol. 1. Leiden, 1937.
———. *History of the Islamic Peoples*. Trans. J. Carmichael and M. Perlmann. New York, 1960.
———. *Kitab al-Mi'yar al-mughrib wa'l-jami `al-mu `rib amma tadammanahu Fatawi `Ulama' Ifrigiya wa'l-Andalus wa'l-Maghrib*. 12 vols. (Fas), A.H.1315. *See also* Amar, "Consultations."
Brosset, Marie Felicité. *Collection d'Historiens Arméniens*, vol. 1. Paris, 1874–1876.
———. *Histoire de la Géorgie*, vol. 1. St. Petersburg, 1849. Eng. trans. in Speros, "Nomadization."
Brown, Kenneth. "Profile of a Nineteenth-Century Moroccan Scholar." *See in* Keddie, *Scholars*.
Browne, E. G. *A Literary History of Persia in Four Volumes*, vol. 3. Cambridge, 1928.
Brownlow, Canon, trans. *The Hodoeporicon of Saint Willibald*. London, 1895.
b. Sa'id, 'Umar. *Fatwa*. f.3. *See* Willis, "The Writings."
Buchon, A. C. *Chronique de J. Frossart*. T. III. Paris, 1852.
———, ed. *Livre des faits du bon messire Jean le Maingre, dit Bouciquaut*. T. III.
Budge, Ernest A. Wallis, trans. *The Chronography of Bar Hebraeus*. London, 1932.
Buhuti, Kashshaf al-Qina'. *An Matn al-Igna*, vol. 3. Cairo, A.H. 1366.
Bukhari, Sahih. *Hadiths*. Trans. M. Muhsin Khan. http://www.usc.edu/dept/MSA/fundamentals/hadithsunnah/bukhari/.
———. *Kitab al-Jami' al-Sahih*, vol. 2. Leiden, 1864.
———. *Translation of Sahih Bukhari* by M. Muhsin Khan. http://www.usc.edu/dept/MSA/fundamentals/hadithsunnah/bukhari/.
Bull, Hedley, and Adam Watson, eds. *The Expansion of International Society*. Oxford, 1984.
Burckhardt, John Lewis. *Travels in Nubia*. 2nd ed. London, 1822.
Burr, Millard. *Quantifying Genocide in Southern Sudan and the Nuba Mountains, 1983–1998*. Washington, DC, 1998.

Busbequius, Augerius Gislenius. *De legationis Turcicae epistolae quatuor . . . eiusdem de re militari contra Turcam instituenda consilium.* Hanover, 1605.

Caetani, Prince. *Annali dell'Islam*, vol. 2. Milan, 1907.

Cahen, Claude. See in *Bulletin de la faculté des lettres de Strasbourg* 29 (1950).

———. *Past and Present* 6 (1954).

"Cairo Declaration on Human Rights in Islam." In vol. 2: *Regional Instruments of Human Rights: A Compilation of International Instruments.* New York and Geneva, 1997.

Callimachi, Philippi. *De rebus a Vladislao Polonorum atque Hungarum rege gestis libri tres. In the series: Scriptorum rerum hungaricarum veteres ac genuini.* Vindobonae [Vienna], 1746.

Canard, Marius. "Textes relatifs à l'emploi du feu grégeois par les Arabes." *Bulletin des Études arabes* 26. Algiers, 1946.

Chabot, Jean-Baptiste, trans. *Chronique de Denys de Tell-Mahre.* Paris, 1895; Eng. trans. in Bat Ye'or, *The Decline.*

———, ed. and trans. *Chronique de Michel Le Syrien*, vols. 2–3. Paris, 1899–1905; Brussels, 1963. Eng. trans. in Bat Ye'or, *The Decline.*

Chalcocondyle, Laonici. *Historiarum demonstraciones.* Rec. E. Darko I. Budapestini, 1922.

Charnay, Jean-Paul. *L'Islam et la guerre: De la guerre juste à la revolution sainte.* Paris, 1986.

Charrière, E. *Négotiation de la France dans le Levant*, vol. 2. Paris, 1850.

Chehata, Chafik. "Dhimma." *See in* G & S, vol. 2, 2nd ed.

Chozebites, Antonios. "Vita S. Georgii Chozebitae." *AB*, 7, 1888.

Christian Solidarity International. *Racism: Leading to Genocide and Slavery in the Sudan.* Written statement, United Nations Economic and Social Council, Commission on Human Rights, 55th session, item 6, E/CN.4/1999/NGO/5, January 29, 1999.

———. *Senior Representatives of the Banned Political Parties and Social Movements of Sudan, Final Communiqué, Peace and Democracy in Sudan: The Development of the IGADD and Asmara (NDA) Processes.* London, 1995.

Christides, V. "Arabs as 'Barbaroi' before the Rise of Islam." *Balkan Studies* 10 (1969).

Churchill, Winston. *The River War*, vol. 2. London, 1899.

Cicero. *Offices, Essays and Letters.* Bk. 1 (Everyman's ed.).

CMIP Reports. "Jews, Christians, War and Peace in Egyptian School Textbooks." http://www.edume.org/reports/13/toc.htm.

Codera, Francisco. "Narbona, Gerona y Barcelona bajo la dominación musulmana." *Anuari—Institut d'Estudìs Catalans*, Barcelona, 1909–1910.

Collins, Robert O. *The Southern Sudan, 1883–1898: A Struggle for Control.* New Haven, 1962.

Colom, Sevillano. "Mercaderes y navegantes." *See in* Mascaro, *Historia.*

Combefis, F. *Illustrium Christi martyrum lecti triumphi.* Paris, 1660.

Comnena, Anna. *Anne Comnene. Alexiade, texte établi et traduit*, vol. 3. Paris, 1937–1945. Eng. trans. in Speros Vryonis, *The Decline.*

Constantelos, Demetrios John (Dimitris Stachys). *Christian Hellenism: Essays and Studies in Continuity and Change.* New Rochelle, NY, 1998.

———. "The 'Neomartyrs' as Evidence for Methods and Motives Leading to Conversion and Martyrdom in the Ottoman Empire." *Greek Orthodox Theological Review* 23 (1978).

Cousins, Norman, ed. *The Words of Albert Schweitzer.* New York, 1996.

Crone, Patricia. *God's Rule. Government and Islam.* New York, 2004.

Crusius, Martin, and S. Cabasilas, eds. *Turcograeciae libri octo.* Basiliae, 1584.

Cunningham, A. *Coins of Medieval India.* London, 1894; Varanasi, 1967.

Cuoq, Joseph M. *Recueil des sources arabes concernant l'Afrique Occidentale du VIIIe au XVIe Siecle (Bilad al-Sudan).* Paris, 1975.

Curtin, Philip D., Roger Antsey, J. E. Inikori. *Journal of African History* 17 (1976).

Cvetkova, Bistra. "Robstvoto v Osmanskata imperiia a po spetialno v bälgarskite zemi pod turska vlast [Slavery in the Ottoman Empire and More Particularly in the Bulgarian Territories under Ottoman Rule]." *Istoriceski Pregled* 10, no. 2 (1955).

———. "Typical Features of the Ottoman Social and Economic Structure in Southeastern Europe During the 14th to the 16th Centuries." *Etudes Historique* 9 (1979).

Dadrian, Vahakn N. "The Armenian Question and the Wartime Fate of the Armenians as Documented by the Officials of the Ottoman Empire's World War I Allies: Germany and Austria-Hungary." *International Journal of Middle Eastern Studies* 32 (2002).

———. *The History of the Armenian Genocide. Ethnic Conflict from the Balkans to Anatolia to the Caucasus.* Providence, RI, 1995; 2003.

———. *Warrant for Genocide: Key Elements of Turko-Armenian Conflict.* New Brunswick, NJ, 1999.

Darbinian-Melikian, M. "Ditoghutiunner Hovhannes Draskhanakerttsu Patmutian Veraberial [Observations on the History of Hovhannes Draskhanakerttsi]." *Patma-Banasirakan-Handes* 3 (1981).

Darimi. *Sunan,* vol. 2. Damascus, A.H. 1349.

Davison, Roderick. "The Armenian Crisis, 1912–1914." *American Historical Review* 53 (1948).

———. "Turkish Attitudes Concerning Christian-Muslim Equality in the Nineteenth Century." *American Historical Review* 59 (1954).

Dawood, N. J., trans. *Koran.* 4th ed. London and New York, 1974.

de Bellefonds, Y. Linant. "Ihya." *See in* G & S, 2nd ed., vol. 3.

de Crémone, Liutprand. *Chronique.* Édition Petz, 1839.

Defrémery, C., and Dr. R. R. Sanquinetti, trans. *Voyages d'Ibn Batotah.* Paris, 1873.

de la Broquières, Bertrandon. *Le voyage d'Outremer.* Paris, 1892.

de la Martinière, Bruzon. *Dictionnaire géographique et historique,* vol. 1. Paris, 1768.

Deleyaye, H. "Passio sanctorum sexaginta martyrum." *AB,* 23, 1904.

Demetrios. *Correspondance.* Paris, 1930.

de Negri, Ossian. *Storia di Genova.* Milan, n.d.

Deng, Francis Mading. *Africans of Two Worlds: The Dinka in Afro-Arab Sudan.* New Haven, 1978.

Deng, Santino. Quoted in *Inter Press Service.* Khartoum, July 24, 1998.

Dennett, D. C. *Conversion and the Poll Tax in Early Islam.* Boston/Cambridge, MA, 1950.

D'Entreves, A. P. *Aquinas: Selected Political Writings.* Oxford, 1948. Devic (Dom) and Vessete (Dom). *Histoire générale du Languedoc,* vol. 1. Toulouse, 1882.

de Pašagaghi, Defter. *Istanbul, Belediye Kütübhanesi.* Cevdet Kit, no. 089.

de Promontorio de Campis, Jacobo. *Stato del Gran turco.* Ed. П. П. Иковски, *Известия на Бълг. Ист. дружесмво* 9 (1929).

Derdir. *Commentaire [sur] Khalil d'Abd el-Baki.* MS 1178. Algiers.

de Yano, Bartholomé. *Epistola de crudelitate Turcorum*, in Migne, *Patrologia graeca*, t. 158, col. 1061.

Dionisius of Tell Mahre, Pseudo-. *Chronique de Denys de Tell-Mahre*. Paris, 1895. Eng. trans. in Bat Ye'or, *The Decline*.

Dlugosii, Joannis. *Historiae Polonicae*. 1. 12. Frankfurt, 1711; Warsaw, 1985.

Donaldson, Dwight M. *The Shiite Religion*. London, 1933.

Donner, Fred M. *The Early Islamic Conquests*. Princeton, NJ, 1981.

Dozy, Reinhart. *Spanish Islam: A History of the Muslims in Spain*. London, 1915.

Dräseke, J. "Der Übergang der Osmanen nach Europa im XIV. Jahrhundert." *Neue Jahrb. für das klassische Altertum, Geschichte, und deutsche Literatur* 31 (1913).

Ducas. *Historia turco-byzantine (1341–1462)*. Ed. B. Grecu. Bucarest, 1958.

Ducellier, Alain. *Le Miroir de l'Islam*. Paris, 1971.

Dufourcq, Charles-Emmanuel, and J. Gautier-Dalché. *Histoire économique et sociale de l'Espagne chrétienne au Moyen Age*. Paris, 1976.

———. "Les Mozarabes du XIIe siècle et le prétendu 'Evêque' de Lisbonne." *Revue d'Histoire et de Civilisation du Maghreb* 5 (1968).

———. *La vie quotidienne dans l'Europe médiévale sous domination arabe*. Paris, 1978.

Dulaurier, Edouard. *Recherches sur la Chronologie Arménienne, Technique et Historique. Ouvrage formant les Prolégomènes de la Collection Intitulée Bibliothèque Historique Arménienne*, vol. 1. Paris, 1859. Eng. trans. in Vryonis, *The Decline*, and in Bat Ye'or, *The Decline*.

Dyobuniotes, K. "Anakoinosis . . . [Communication . . .]." *Proceedings of the Academy of Athens*, no. 11 (1936).

———. "Iakobos o Neobaptistos." *Hieros Syndermos*, 7.183. Athens, 1911.

Eibner, John. "My Career Redeeming Slaves." *Middle East Quarterly* 4, no. 4 (December 1999). http://www.meforum.org/article/449.

Eichner, W. "Die Nachrichten fiber den Islam bei den Byzantinern." *Der Islam* 23 (1936).

El-Boukhârî, Sahîh. *Livre LVI: Les Traditions islamiques*, vol. 2. Trans. Houdas and Marçais.

Elezović, Gliša. *Turski izvori za istorija Jugoslaven* [Turkish Sources on the History of Yugoslavia]. Belgrade, 1932.

———. *Turski spomeniki*, vol. 1, no. 1. Belgrade, 1940.

Eliade, M. *Histoire des croyances et des idées religieuses*. Paris, 1983.

Elliot, H. M., and John Dowson. *The History of India as Told by Its Own Historians*, vols. 1–8. 1867–1877; Delhi, 2001.

Ellul, Jacques. Foreword to Bat Ye'or, *The Decline*.

———. *The Subversion of Christianity*. Trans. Geoffrey Bromiley. Grand Rapids, MI, 1986.

el Masri, F. H., ed. and trans. *Uthman b. Fudi, Bayan Wujub al-Hi jra `ala'l-`Ibad*. Khartoum and Oxford, 1978.

Encyclopaedia of Islam, vol. 1. Leyden and London, 1960. 1st ed., 1913–1938.

Engelhardt, Edouard. *La Turquie et Le Tanzimat*. Paris, 1882. Eng. trans. in Bat Ye'or, *Islam*.

Epstein, John. *The Catholic Tradition of the Law of Nations*. London, 1935.

Eremites, Nilos. "Narrationes 2." *PG*, 79.

Esposito, John. *Islam: The Straight Path*. New York, 1994.

European Council for Fatwa and Research. *Al-Sharq Al-Awsat*. London, July 19, 2003. *Middle East Media Research Institute*, no. 542 (July 24, 2003). http://memri.org/bin /articles.cgi?Page=archives&Area=sd&ID=SP54203.

Eutychios of Alexandria. "Annales." *PG*, 3.

Fagnan, Edmond, trans. and notes. *Annales du Maghreb et de l'Espagne (Al-Kamil fi al-tarikh/Grande Chronique)*. Algiers, 1898. Eng. trans. in Bat Ye'or, *The Decline*.

————. *Le djihad ou guerre sainte selon l'école malikite*. Algiers, 1908.

————, trans. *Kitab al-Kharaj (Le livre de l'impôt foncier)*. Paris, 1921. Eng. trans. in Bat Ye'or, *The Dhimmi*.

Fakhr-i-Mudabbir. *Adabul Harb wa Shujaat*. Photocopy British Museum, Add. 1653. Hindi trans. in Rizvi, *Adi Turk*.

————. *Tarikh-i-Fakhruddin Mubarak Shah*. Ed. Sir Denison Ross. London, 1927.

Faraj, Abd al-Salam. *al-Farida al-Gha'ib* [The Absent Duty]. *See in* Ahmad, *Dar Riyad*.

Farishtah, Muhammad Qasim Hindu Shah. *Gulshan-i-Ibrahimi*. Also known as *Tarikh-i-Farishtah*. Persian text, Lucknow, 1865.

Fathelrahman, Hamouda. "A Personal Experience, a Sincere Appeal." Cairo, June 1999.

————, and Agaw, Abdon (Sudan Human Rights Organization). *Report*. Cairo, June 1999.

Fattal, Antoine. *Le Statut Légal des Non-Musulmans en Pays d'Islam*. Beirut, 1958.

Fayruzabadi. *Qamus al-Munit*, vol. 1. Cairo, 1933.

Feinberg, Absalom. *"PRO ARMENIA."* Report. Athlit, 22 November 1915. *See in* Bat Ye'or, *The Decline*.

Fetscher, Iring, and Herfried Miinkler, eds. *Pipers Handbuch der politischen Ideen*, vol. 5. Munich, 1987.

Février, Paul-Albert. *Le Développement urbain en Provence, de l'époque romaine à la find du XIVe siècle*. Paris, 1964.

Firoz Shah Tughlaq. *Futuhat-i-Firoz Shahi*. Aligarh, 1954.

Fisher, Alan Washburn. "Muscovy and the Black Sea Slave Trade." *Canadian American Slavic Studies* 6 (1972).

Fleuhr-Lobban, Carolyn. "Islamization in Sudan: A Critical Assessment." *Middle East Journal* (Autumn 1990).

Foi et Vie. "Islam et Christianisme." Special issue (1983).

Font Obrador. *Historia de Llucmayor*, vol. 1. Palma, 1972.

Friedmann, Yohanan. *Shaykh Ahmad Sirhindi: An Outline of His Thought and a Study of His Image in the Eyes of Posterity*. Montreal, 1971.

Gabrielan, M. C. *Armenia: A Martyr Nation*. New York, Chicago, 1918.

Gabrieli, Francesco. "Greeks and Arabs in the Central Mediterranean Area." *DOP* 18 (1964).

Gairdner, W. H. T. "Muhammad without Camouflage." *Moslem World* 9 (1919).

Gardner, W. R. W. "Jihad." *Moslem World* 2 (1912).

Georgewitz [Georgieuiz], Bartholomaeo Peregrino. *De Turcarum moribus epitome*. Lyon, 1554.

Gerlach, Stephan. *Tage-Buch der von . . . Kaysern Maximiliano and Rudolpho an die ottomanische Pforte . . . abgefertigten Gesandtschaft herfür gegeben durch Samuel Gerlach*. Frankfurt/M, 1674.

Ghevond. *History of the Wars and Conquests of the Arabs in Armenia*. Paris, 1856.

Gibb, H. A. R. "Arab-Byzantine Relations under the Umayyad Caliphate." *DOP* 12 (1958).

————, and Bowen, H. *Islamic Society and the West*, vol. 1, pt. 2. London, New York, Toronto, 1957.

Gibbon, Edward. *History of the Decline and Fall of the Roman Empire*, vol. 6. London, Bury, 1898.

Giese. *Die altosmanischen anonymen Chroniken*. Leipzig, 1925.

Gil, Moshe. "The Constitution of Medina: A Reconsideration." *Israel Oriental Studies* 4 (1974).

————. "Dhimmi Donations and Foundations for Jerusalem (638–1099)." *Journal of the Economic and Social History of the Orient* 37 (1984).

————. *A History of Palestine, 634–1099*. Cambridge, 1992.

Gillaume, A., trans. *The Life of Muhammad: A Translation of Ibn Ishaq's Sirat Rasul Allah*. Karachi, 1955, 1987.

Giovio (Jovius Paulus). *Turcicarum rerum commentarius*. Paris, 1538.

Glubb, J. B. *The Life and Times of Muhammad*. New York, 1970.

Goghtnatsi, Vahan, ed. *Soperk Haykakank*, vol. 2.

————. "Vkayapanutiun Vahana Goghtnatsvo [Martyrology of Vahan Goghtnatsi]." *Soperk Haykakan* 13.

Goitein, S. D. "Changes in the Middle East (950–1150) as Illustrated by the Documents of the Cairo Geniza." *See in* Richards, *Islamic Civilization*.

————. "Cross-Currents in Arab National Feeling." *Commentary* (February 1949).

————. "Evidence on the Muslim Poll Tax from Non-Muslim Sources." *Journal of the Economic and Social History of the Orient* 6 (1963).

Goldziher, Ignaz. *Introduction to Islamic Theology and Law*. Princeton, NJ, 1981.

————, and J. Schacht. *The Encyclopedia of Islam*. Leyden/London, 1960. 1st ed., 1913–38. CD-ROM ed., v.1.1.

Gordon, Murray. *Slavery in the Arab World*. New York, 1989.

Green, D. F., ed. *Arab Theologians on Jews and Israel*. Geneva, 1974.

Greenstone, Julius. "The Turcoman Defeat at Cairo." *American Journal of Semitic Languages and Literatures* 22 (1906).

Grégoire, H. "Mahomet et le Monophysisme." *Mélanges Diehl*, vol. 1, 1930.

Gregorae, Nicephori. *Byzantina Historia*. Ed. L. Schopeni. Bonnae, 1829.

Grotius, Hugo. *De Jure Belli ac Pacis*. 1625; Oxford, 1925.

Grousset, René. *L'Empire Des Steppes. Attila, Gengis-Khan, Tamerlan*. Paris, 1952.

————. *The Empire of the Steppes*. Trans. Naomi Walford. New Brunswick, NJ, 1970.

Grumel, V. *La chronologie*. Paris, 1958.

Habib, Mohammad. *Campaigns of Alauddin Khilji*. Trans. of Khusrau's *Khazain*. Bombay, 1933.

————. *The Political Theory of the Delhi Sultanate*. Allahabad, 1961.

————. *Politics and Society during the Early Medieval Period*. Ed. K. A. Nizami.

————. *Sultan Mahmud of Ghaznin*. Delhi, 1951.

Habib, Mohammad, and K. A. Nizami, eds. *A Comprehensive History of India*, vol. 5. New Delhi, 1970.

Habibullah, A. B. M. *The Foundation of Muslim Rule in India*. Lahore, 1945; revised, Allahabad, 1961.

Hacker, Joseph. "Ottoman Policy toward the Jews and Jewish Attitudes toward the Ottomans during the Fifteenth Century." In *Christians and Jews in the Ottoman Empire: The Functioning of a Plural Society*, ed. Benjamin Braude and Bernard Lewis. New York, 1982.

————. "The Sürgün System and Jewish Society in the Ottoman Empire during the 15th–17th Centuries." See in *Ottoman and Turkish Jewry-Community and Leadership*. Bloomington, IN, 1992.

Haig, Wolseley, ed. *The Cambridge History of India*. Delhi, 1958.

Hamidullah, Muhammad. *The Muslim Conduct of State*. Lahore, 1977.

Hamilton, Charles, trans. *Hidayah*, 4 vols. London, 1791. Repr., vols. 1–2, New Delhi, 1985.

————. *Geschichte des Osmanischen Reiches*, vol. 1. Pest, 1840, 1934.

Haneberg. "Das muslimische Kriegsrecht." *Bayerische Akten der Wissenschaft* 12 (1871).

Hattab. MS 1175, Algiers.

Hazard, Harry W. *Atlas of Islamic History*. Princeton, NJ, 1951/1954.

Heer, Nicholas, ed. *Islamic Law and Jurisprudence*. Seattle, 1990.

Heffening. "Wakf." *See in* G & S, 1st ed.

Heidborn, A. *Droit public et administratif de l'Empire-Ottoman*, vol. 1. Vienna, Leipzig, 1908.

Henderson, K. D. D. *Sudan Republic*. London, 1965.

Herzberg, G. F. *Geschichte der Byzantiner and des Osmanischen Reiches bis gegen Ende des sechzehnten Jahrhunderts*. Berlin, 1883.

Hirschberg, H. Z. *A History of the Jews of North Africa*, vol. 1. Leiden, 1974.

Hitti, P. K., ed. *'Abd al-Qahir al-Baghdadi, Mukhtasar Kitab al-Farq Bayn al-Firaq*. Summarized by al-Ras'ani. Cairo, 1924.

————. *The Arabs: A Short History*. London, 1948.

————. *History of the Arabs*. London, 1960.

————. *Origins of the Islamic State*. Beirut, 1966.

Hodgson, Marshall G. S. *The Venture of Islam*. 3 vols. Chicago, 1974.

Hodivala, S. H. *Studies in Indo-Muslim History*. Bombay, 1939.

Hogendorn, Jan. "The Hideous Trade. Economic Aspects of the 'Manufacture' and Sale of Eunuchs." *Paideuma* 45 (1999).

Hopf, Ch. *Chroniques gréco-romaines*. Berlin, 1873.

Hovanissian, Richard G. *Armenia on the Road to Independence*. Berkeley, CA, 1967.

————, ed. *Ethics in Islam*. Malibu, CA, 1985.

Huart, Clément. "Le droit de la guerre." *Revue du monde musulman* 2 (1907).

Hughes, Thomas P. *A Dictionary of Islam*. London, 1895, 1994.

Hugo, Victor. *Hernani*. 1830.

Huntington, Samuel P. "The Clash of Civilizations?" *Foreign Affairs* 72 (1993).

Hunwick, J. O. "Some Notes on the Term 'zanj' and Its Derivatives in a West African Chronicle." *Research Bulletin* 4, nos. 1–2. Ibadan, 1968.

Husain, Mahdi. *Shah Namah-i-Hind*. Trans. of Isami's *Futuh-us-Salatin*. 3 vols. Aligarh, 1976–77.

————. *Tughluq Dynasty*. Calcutta, 1963.

Ibn 'Abd-Allah, Al-Hasan. *Athar al-Uwal fi Tartib al-Duwal*. Cairo, A.H. 1295.

Ibn Abi Zayd al-Qayrawani. *La Risala ou Epitre sue les elements du dogme de la loi d'Islam*. Trans. from Arabic by Leon Bercher, Algiers, 1945, 1980. Eng. trans. in Bat Ye'or, *The Decline*.

Ibn al-Athir. *al-Ramil fi-t-tarikh*. Cairo, 1934–1935.

Ibn al-Fakih. *Kitab al-Buldan*. Lugd Bat, 1885.

Ibn al-Humam. *Sharh Fath al-Qadir*, vol. 4. Cairo, A.H. 1316.
Ibn Batouta [Ibn Battuta]. *Voyages d'Ibn Batotah*. French trans. C. Defrémery and Dr. R. R. Sanquinetti. Paris, 1873.
Ibn Battuta. *The Rehla of Ibn Battuta*. Eng. trans. Dr. Mahdi Husain, 1953; French trans. C. Defremery and B. R. Sanguinetti, *Ibn Batoutahs Voyages*. Paris, 1857.
Ibn Hauqal, *Ashkalal-ul-Bilad* (written 976 CE). Trans. in E & D.
Ibn Hazm. *Kitab al-Fasl fi al-Milal wa'l-Ahwa' wa'l-Nihal*, vol. 4. Cairo, A.H. 1321.
Ibn Hudhayl. *L'ornement des âmes*. French trans. Louis Mercier. Paris, 1939.
———. *Tuhfat al-Anfus wa Shi'ar Sukkan al-Andalus*. Ed. Louis Mercier. Paris, 1936.
Ibn Kathir. *Tafsir Ibn Kathir*. Riyadh, 2000.
Ibn Khaldun. *Al-Muqaddima*. Paris, 1858.
———. *The Muqudimmah. An Introduction to History*, trans. Franz Rosenthal. New York, 1958.
Ibn Majah Qazwini, Imam Hafiz Abu Abad. *Sunan ibn Majad*. Arabic text, Urdu trans. Abdul Hakim Khan Shahajahanpuri. 2 vols. Delhi, 1986.
Ibn Rushd. *Kitab al-Mugaddimat al-Mumahhidat*, vol. 1. Cairo, A.H. 1325.
Ibn Taymiyyah. *See in* Peters, *Jihad in Classical and Modern Islam.*
Ibn Warraq. *Why I Am Not a Muslim*. New York, 1995.
Idrisi. *Nuzhat-ul-Mushtaq* (12th cent. CE). *See in* E & D.
Inalcik, Halil. "15. asir Turkiye iktisadi ve ictimai tarihi kaynaklari." *Iktisat Fakültesi Mecmuasi* 15 (1953–1954).
———. "Bursa and the Commerce of the Levant." *Journal of Economic and Social History of the Orient* 3, no. 2 (1960).
———. *The Ottoman Empire: The Classical Age 1300–1600*. Trans. N. Itzkovitz and C. Imber. London, 1973.
———. "The Rise of the Turcoman Maritime Principalities in Anatolia: Byzantium and the Crusades." *Byzantinische Forschungen* (1986).
Injijian, Gh. *Hnakhosutiun Ashkharhagrakar; Hayastaneata Ashkharhi* [Geographic Archaeology of Armenia]. Venice, 1835.
Iorga, N. "Aventures 'sarasines' des Français de Bourgogne au XVe siècle." In *Mélanges d'Histoire générale*, vol. 1. Cluj, 1927.
———. *Geschichte des Osmanischen Reiches*, vol. 1. Gotha, 1908.
———. *Notes et extraits pour servir à l'histoire des Croisades au XVe siècle*, vol. 1.
Isamic, Khwaja Abdulla Malik. *Futuh-us-Salatin*. Persian text ed. Agha Mahdi Husain. Agra, 1938. Eng. trans., *see* Husain, *Shah.*
Istin, B. M., ed. "Otkrovenie Mefodiia Patarskago i Apokrificheskiia Videnia Daniela v Vizantiiski i Slaviano-Russkoi Literaturakh." *Chteniia v Imperatorskom Obschchestvie Istorii i Drevnostei Rossiskikh pri Moskovskom Universitetie*, 193. Moscow, 1897.
Ivars. *Dues creudades valenciano-mallorquines*. Valencia, 1921.
Jad al-Haqq `Ali Jad al-Haqq. *al-Azhar, Bayan ila al-nas*. 2 vols. Cairo, 1984–1988.
Janina, Na'mat-Allah. *Tanzim al jihad*. Cairo, 1988.
Jarry, Jacques. *Hérésies et factions dans l'empire byzantin du IVe au VIIe siècle*. Cairo, 1968.
Jeffery, Arthur. "Ghevond's Text of the Correspondence between Omar II and Leo III," *Harvard Theological Review* 37 (1944).
———. "The Political Importance of Islam." *Journal of Near Eastern Studies* 1 (1942).

————. "Present Day Movements in Islam." *Moslem World* 33 (1943).

John of Damascus. *De Haeresibus*. *PG*, 94.

John of Nikiu. *The Chronicle*. 111.540. Trans. R. H. Charles from *Zotenberg's Ethiopic Text*. Oxford, 1916.

————. *Chronique de Jean, Eveque de Nikiou*. An., French trans. Hermann Zotenberg. Paris, 1879. English trans. in Bat Ye'or, *The Decline*.

Jones, A. H. M. "Were Ancient Heresies National or Social Movements in Disguise?" *Journal of Theological Studies*, n.s., 10 (1959).

Jones, W. R. "The Image of the Barbarian in Medieval Europe." *Comparative Studies in Society and History* 13 (1971).

Jurjani, Minhaj Siraj. *Kitab al-Ta'rifat*, ed. Gustavus Fülgel. Leipzig, 1845.

————. *Tabqat-i-Nasiri*. Calcutta, 1864. Eng. trans. Major H. R. Raverty. London, 1881.

Juwaini. *Tarikh-i-Jahan Kusha*. Trans. in E & D, vol. 2.

Kaegi, Walter Emil. *Byzantium and the Early Islamic Conquests*. Cambridge, 1992.

————. "Initial Byzantine Reactions to the Arab Conquests." *Church History* 38 (1969).

Keddie, Nikki, ed. *Scholars, Saints, and Sufis: Muslim Religious Institutions in the Middle East since 1500*. Berkeley and Los Angeles, 1972.

Kelly, J. B. *Arabia, the Gulf, and the West*. New York, 1980.

————. *Britain and the Persian Gulf*. Oxford, 1968.

Kelsay, John. *Islam and War: A Study in Comparative Ethics*. Louisville, KY, 1993.

Kestenberg Amighi, Janet. *The Zoroastrians of Iran: Conversion, Assimilation, or Persistence*. New York, 1990.

Khadduri, Majid, trans. *al-Imam Muhammad ibn Idris al-Shaf'i's al-Risala fi us ul al-fiqh: Treatise on the Foundations of Islamic Jurisprudence*. Cambridge, UK, 1997.

————. Introduction to al-Shaybani, *The Islamic Law of Nations*.

————. *The Law of War and Peace in Islam: A Study in Muslim International Law*. London, 1940.

————. *War and Peace in the Law of Islam*. Baltimore, MD, 1955.

Khoury, Adel Th. *Les Théologiens Byzantins et l'Islam: Textes et auteurs (VIIIᵉ–XIIIᵉ siècles)*. Louvain and Paris, 1969.

————. *Der theologische Streit der Byzantiner mit dem Islam*. Paderborn, 1959.

————, trans. *Koran*. Giitersloh, 1987.

Khusrau, Abul Hasan Amir. *Asbiqa*. Aligarh, 1917.

————. *Khazain-ul-Futuh*. See Habib, *Campaigns*.

————. *Miftah-ul-Fatuh*. Aligarh Text, 1954.

————. *Tughlaq Nama*. Ed. Hashim Faridabadi. Aurangabad, 1933.

Kinross, Lord. *The Ottoman Centuries*. New York, 1977.

Kister, M. J. "The Massacre of the Banu Qurayzy.a: A Re-Examination of a Tradition." *Jerusalem Studies in Arabic and Islam* 8 (1986).

Knös, B. *Un ambassadeur de l'hellénisme—Janus Lascaris—et la tradition grécobyzantine dans l'humanisme français*. Uppsala-Paris, 1945.

Koefler, H. ed. "Badr al-Din Ibn Jama'a, Tahrir al-Ahkam fi Tadbir Ahl al-Islam." *Islamica* 6 (1934).

Koikylides. *Peri ton en Palaistine Archaion kai Neoteron Hellenikon Monasterion*. Jerusalem, 1906.

————. *Ta kata ten Lauran kai ton Cheimaron tou Houzinba*. Jerusalem, 1901.

Kraelitz-Greifenhorst, Fr. "Kanunname Sultan Mehmeds des Eroberers: Die ältesten osmanischen Straf- und Finanzgesetze." *Mitteilungen zur osmanischen Geschichte*, vol. 1. Vienna, 1921.

Kramer, Martin. "Hizbullah: The Calculus of Jihad." *See in*, Marty, *Fundamentalisms*.

Kritoboulos of Imbros. "Βίος του Μωαμεθ β΄." Ed. Ph. A. Dethier, in *Monumenta Hungariae Historica* 21.

———. *De rebus per annos 1451–1467 a Mechemete II gestis*. Ed. B. Grecu. Bucarest, 1963.

Kuckertz, Beate, ed. *Das Grune Schwert: Weltmacht Islam*. Munich, 1992.

Kundera, M. *The Book of Laughter and Forgetting*. New York, 1999.

Kurdi, Abdulrahman A. *The Islamic State*. London, 1984.

Kydones, Demetrios. *De subsidio Latinorum*. Migne, *PG*.

Lacam, J. *Les Sarrasins dans le haut Moyen Age français*. Paris, 1965.

La Guilletière. *Athènes ancienne et nouvelle*. 3rd ed. Paris, 1676.

Lal, K. S. *Early Muslims in India*. New Delhi, 1984.

———. *Growth of Muslim Population in Medieval India*. Delhi, 1973.

———. *History of the Khaljis*. 1950; Bombay, 1967; New Delhi, 1980.

———. *Indian Muslims: Who Are They?* New Delhi, 1990.

———. *The Legacy of Muslim Rule in India*. New Delhi, 1992.

———. *Muslim Slave System in India*. New Delhi, 1994.

———. *Theory and Practice of Muslim State in India*. New Delhi, 1999.

———. *Twilight of the Sultanate*. 1963; New Delhi, 1980.

Lambton, A. K. S. "Filaha," "agriculture." *See in* G & S.

Lammens, Henri. *Le Berceau de l'Islam*, vol. 1. Rome, 1914.

———. *Islam—Beliefs and Institutions*. Trans. E. Denison Ross. London, 1929; New Delhi, 1998.

Lane, E. W. *An Account of the Manners and Customs of the Modern Egyptians*. New York, 1973.

———. *An Arabic-English Lexicon*. London, 1865.

L'anonyme de Cordoue. Paris, 1885.

Laoust, Henri, trans. *Le précis de droit d'Ibn Qudama, jurisconsulte musulman d'école hanbalite né à Jérusalem en 541/1146, mort à Damas en 620/1223*. Livre 20. Beirut, 1950.

Last, Murray. *Sokoto Caliphate*. London, 1967.

Laurent, J. *L'Arménie entre Byzance et l'Islam*. Lisbon, 1980.

Legrand, E. *Bibliographie Hellenique ou Description Raisonnée des Ouvrages Publies en Grec par des Grecs aux XVe et XVIe Siècles*. Paris, 1885–1906.

———. *Bibliothèque grecque vulgaire*, vol. 2. Paris, 1881.

Lekkegaard, F. "Ghanima." *See in* G & S, 2nd ed.

Leo. *Hayots Patmutiun* [History of the Armenians]. Erevan, 1967.

Leunclavius, V. J. *Annales sultanorum osmanidorum*. Frankfurt, 1588.

———. *Historiae musulmanae turcorum de monumentis ipsorum exscriptae*. Libri 13. Frankfurt, 1591.

Lévi-Provençal, Evariste. *Histoire de l'Espagne musulmane*. 3 vols. Paris-Leyde, 1950–1953.

Levtzion, Nehmia. "A Seventeenth-Century Chronicle by Ibn al-Mukhtar: A Critical Study of Ta'rikh al-Fattash." *Bulletin of the School of Oriental and African Studies* 34 (1971).

———. *Ancient Ghana and Mali.* See Willis, Review.

Levy, Ruben. *The Baghdad Chronicle.* Cambridge, 1929.

———. *The Social Structure of Islam.* Cambridge, 1957, 1962.

Lewis, Bernard. *The Emergence of Modern Turkey.* Oxford University Press, 1968, 2002.

———. *Islam and the West.* New York, 1993.

———, ed. *Islam, from the Prophet Muhammad to the Capture of Constantinople.* 2 vols. New York, 1974.

———. *Islam in History: Ideas, People, and Events in the Middle East.* Chicago, 1993.

———. *The Middle East, 2,000 Years of History from the Rise of Christianity to the Present Day.* London, 1996.

———. *The Muslim Discovery of Europe.* New York, 1982; 2001.

———. "Politics and War." See Schacht, *The Legacy of Islam.*

———. *What Went Wrong? Western Impact and Middle Eastern Response.* London, 2002.

Lewis, Naphtali. "New Light on the Negev in Ancient Times." *Palestine Exploration Quarterly* 80 (1948).

Liakatar Vark ev Vkayabanutiun Srbots [Complete Hagiography and Martyrology of the Saints], vol. 6. Venice, 1813.

Littman, David G. Introduction to Gaspar Biro, "The U.N. Finds Slavery."

———. "Islamism Grows Stronger at the United Nations." *See in* Robert Spencer, *The Myth of Islamic Tolerance.* Amherst, NY, 2005.

———. "Jews under Muslim Rule: The Case of Persia." *Weiner Library Bulletin* 32 (1979).

———. "Jews under Muslim Rule in the Late Nineteenth Century." *Wiener Library Bulletin* 28 (1975).

Ljubi?, S., ed. *Monumenta spectantia historiam slavorum meridionalium* 6, no. 313. Zagreb, 1876.

Lloyd, Christopher. *The Navy and the Slave Trade.* London, 1949.

Loeb, Laurence. *Outcaste-Jewish Life in Southern Iran.* New York, 1977.

MacAlister, R. A. S. Article in *Encyclopaedia Britannica,* 11th ed., vol. 9. Cambridge, UK, 1910.

MacGahan, Januarius A. *The Turkish Atrocities in Bulgaria.* Repr., Geneva, 1976.

Mahmud, Ushari Ahmad, and Süleyman Ali Baldo. *El Diein Massacre: Slavery in the Sudan.* London, 1987. Abridged ed.: *El Diein Massacre.* Khartoum, 1987.

Maine, Sir Henry. *International Law.* London, 1888.

Majumdar, R.C., ed. *The History and Culture of the Indian People,* vols. 3, 6, 7. Bombay, 1954–1973.

———, ed. *The Mughul Empire.* Bombay, 1974.

Makdisi, George. "Ethics in Islamic and Rationalist Doctrine." *See in* Hovannisian, *Ethics.*

Malcolm, Napier. *Five Years in a Persian Town.* New York, 1905.

Malik b. Anas. *Muwatta.* Book 21, "Jihad." http://www.usc.edu/dept/MSA/fundamentals /hadithsunnah/muwatta.

Malkhasiants, S., ed. *Ghevondia Patmutiun Medal Vartapeti Hayots* [History of Armenians by Ghevond, the Great Vardapet]. St. Petersburg, 1887.

Manrique. *Travels of Frey Sebastian Manrique.* Trans. Eckford Luard. 2 vols. London, 1927.

Manucci, Niccolao. *Storia do Mogor.* Trans. W. Irvine, 4 vols. London, 1906.

Margoliouth, D. S. *Mohammed and the Rise of Islam.* London, 1905, reprinted in New Delhi, 1985.

Marty, Martin, and Scott Appleby, eds. *Fundamentalisms and the State.* Chicago, 1993.

Mascaro. *Historia de Mallorca.* Palma, 1971.

Mathur, Rakesh. "Hindu Origins of Romani Nomads." In *Hinduism Today*, Malaysia ed. (August/September 1990).

Matthew of Edessa. *See in* Dulaurier, *Recherches.*

Maximos the Confessor. "Ep. XIV ad Petrum Illustrem." *PG*, 91.

Mayer, Ann E. *Islam and Human Rights: Tradition and Politics.* Boulder, CO, 1991.

———. "The Shari'a: A Methodology or a Body of Substantive Rules?" *See in* Heer, *Islamic Law.*

———. "War and Peace in the Islamic Tradition: International Law." Mimeo, ref. no. 141, Philadelphia, n.d.

Meliaras, Kallistos. *Hoi Hagion Topoi en Palestine*, vol. 1. Jerusalem, 1928.

Melikoff, I. "Ghazi." Vol. 2. *See in* G & S, 2nd ed.

Menavino, Giovan Antonio. *Trattato de costumi et vita de Turchi.* Firenze, 1548.

Merrakechi, Abd El-Wâh'id [al-Marrukushi]. *Histoire des Almohades.* Trans. Edmond Fagnan. Algiers, 1893 (*Revue Africaine*, no. 202–7).

Metz, Helen Chapin, ed. *Sudan: A Country Study.* 4th ed. Washington, DC, 1992.

Meyendorff, J. "Byzantine Views of Islam." *DOP* 18 (1964).

Michaelis Ducae Nepotis, Ducae. *Historia Byzantina.* Rec. J. Bekkerus. Bonnae, 1834.

Miednikow, N. A., ed. *Palestine from the Arabic Conquest to the Crusades according to the Arabic Sources* (in Russian), vol. 2. Cited by Chr. Papadopoulos in *Historia.*

Miklosich, F., and J. Müller. *Acta et diplomata graeca medii aevi sacra et profana.* 6 vols. Vienna, 1860–1890. *See Eng. trans. in* Vryonis, *The Decline.*

———, and A. Theiner. *Monumenta spectantia ad unionem ecclesiarum graece et latinae.* Vienna, 1872.

Miles, George C. "Byzantium and the Arabs: Relations in Crete and the Aegean Area." *DOP* 18 (1964).

Millas Vallicrosa, José-Maria. "La Conquista musulmana de la región pirenaica." *Pirineos* 2 (1946).

Miniter, Richard. "The False Promise of Slave Redemption." *Atlantic Monthly* (July 1999).

Mirkhond. *Rauzat-us-Safa.* Trans. Rehatsek. London, 1892.

Mitchell, Richard. *The Society of Muslim Brothers.* Oxford, 1969.

Mitev, Yono. *The April Uprising and European Public Opinion.* Sofia Press, 1978.

Modern Cyclopaedia. 8 vols. London, 1901.

Monachos, John. "Narratio." *PG*, 109.

Moreen, V. B., trans. "Risala-yi Sawa'iq al-Yahud [The Treatise Lightning Bolts against the Jews]." *Die Welt des Islams* 32 (1992).

Morony, Michael. *Iraq after the Muslim Conquest.* Princeton, NJ, 1984.

Muir, William. *The Life of Mahomet.* New Delhi, 1992.

Muller, A. *Istoria Islama.* 1895.

Mustaufi, Hamdullah. *Tarikh-i-Guzidah.* Ed. E. G. Browne. London, 1910.

Nalbandian, H. "Arabatsi Vostikannere Hayastanum [Arab Governors in Armenia]." *Teghekagir* 8 (1956).

Nardin, Terry, ed. *The Ethics of War and Peace: Religious and Secular Perspectives.* Princeton, NJ, 1996.

Nau, F. "Abraham de Beit-Hale." *DHGE* 1, col. 165, no. 20. Paris, 1912.

Nazim, Muhammad. "Hindu Shahiya Kingdom of Ohind." *Journal of Royal Asiatic Society* (1927).

———. *The Life and Times of Sultan Mahmud of Ghazna.* Cambridge, 1931.

Nešri, M. "Kitabi Cihan Nüma I Cilt." *Türk tarih Kurumu yayinlarindan,* III seri, no. 2. Ankara, 1949.

Nikephoros. *Chronographikon Syntomon.* Ed. K. de Boor. Leipzig, 1880.

Nilakanta Sastri, K. A., col. and ed. *Foreign Notices of South India.* Madras, 2001.

Nisan, Mordechai. *Identity and Civilization.* Lanham, MD, 1999.

Nizami, Hasan. *Taj-ul-Maasir.* Trans. S. H. Askari in *Patna University Journal* (Arts) 18, no. 3 (1963). Also in E & D, vol. 2.

Noble Qur'an, The. http://www.usc.edu/dept/MSA/quran.

Nöldeke. "Auszüge aus Nesris Geschichte des osmanischen Hauses." *Zeitschrift der deutschen morgenländischen Gesellschaft.* Leipzig, 1859.

Obbink, Herman Theodorus. *De Heilige Oorlog Volgen den Koran.* Leiden, 1901.

Ormanian, M. *Azgapatum.* 1. Beirut, 1959.

Ostrogorsky, G. *Geschichte des byzantinischen Staates.* München, 1952.

Pachymeris, Georgii. *De Michaele et Andronico Paleologis,* libri 13, vol. 1. Bonnae, 1835.

Padmanabh. *Kanhadade Prabandh.* Trans. and an. V. S. Bhatnagar. New Delhi, 1991.

Panagiotakes, N. M. "Zetemata tes katakteseos tes Kretes hypo ton Arabon." *KretChron* 15–16 (1961–1962).

Papadopoulos, Chr. *Historia tes Ekklesias Alexandreias.* Alexandria, 1935, 1951.

———. *Historia tes Ekklesias Hierosolymon.* Jerusalem and Alexandria, 1910.

Papadopoulos-Kerameus, A., ed. *Analekta Ierosolymitikes Stachyologias,* vol. 5. St. Petersburg, 1888, repr., Brussels, 1963.

———, ed. "Hypomnema kath' historian tes athleseos tou hagiou . . . Ella tou Neou." *PPSb* 19 (1907).

———, A., ed. "Martyrion ton hagion endoxon Martyron tou Christou exekonta kai trion." *PPSb* 19 (1907).

———. "Martyrion ton hagion exekonta neon Martyron." *PPSb* 12 (1892).

Paparregopoulos K. *Istoria tou hellenikou ethnous* [History of the Greek People]. Athens, 1925.

Papoulia, Vasiliki [B]. "The Impact of Devshirme on Greek Society." *See in* Rothenberg, *East Central.*

———. *Ursprung and Wesen der "Knabenlese" im Osmanischen Reich.* Munich, 1963.

———. "Ursprung und Wesen den Kanben leve Istorikon Arhion Verrias." *Historical Archives of Verria* 3.

Paret, Rudi, trans. *Der Koran.* Stuttgart, 1979.

———. "Sure 9, 122 and der Gihad." *Welt des Islam,* n.s., 2 (1953).

Parfitt, Tudor. *The Jews of Palestine.* Suffolk, UK, 1987.

Patmutiun Hovhanu Katoghikosi [History of Hovhan Catholicos]. Jerusalem, 1867.

Patmutiun Movseq Kaghankatvatso [History of Movses Kaghankatvetsi]. Tiflis, 1912.

Pellat, Charles, ed. and trans. *Calendrier de Cordoue de l'an 961.* Leyde, 1961.

Perlmann, Moshe. "Eleventh Century Andalusian Authors on the Jews of Granada." *Proceedings of the American Academy for Jewish Research* 18 (1948–1949).

Peters, Rudolph. *Islam and Colonialism: The Doctrine of Jihad in Modern History.* The Hague, 1979.

———. *Jihad in Classical and Modern Islam.* Princeton, NJ, 1996.

———, trans., an. *Jihad in Mediaeval and Modern Islam: The Chapter on Jihad from Averroes' Legal Handbook 'Bidayat al-mudjtahid'.* Leyden, 1977.

Philippides, Marios, trans. *Byzantium, Europe, and the Early Ottomans 1373–1513. An Anonymous Greek Chronicle of the Seventeenth Century. (Codex Barberinius Graecus 111).* New York, 1990.

Phillipson, Coleman. *The International Law and Custom of Ancient Greece and Rome,* vol. 2. London, 1911.

Pidal, Ramon Menendez, ed. *Historia de España,* vols. 4–5. Madrid, 1950, 1957.

Pipes, Daniel. "Black Soldiers in Early Muslim Armies." *International Journal of African Historical Studies* 13 (1980).

———. *Slave Soldiers and Islam.* New Haven, 1981.

Pirenne, H. *Mahomet et Charlemagne.* Paris, 1937.

Piscatori, James. *Islam in a World of Nation-States.* Cambridge, 1986.

———, ed. *Islamic Fundamentalisms and the Gulf Crisis.* Chicago, 1991.

Pomjalovskij, I. *Zitie ize vo sv. otca nasege Theodora akrchiep. edeskago.* St. Petersburg, 1892.

Porphyrogennitos, Constantine. *De Administrando Imperio* 20. Ed. and trans. G. Moravcsik and R. J. H. Jenkins. Washington, DC, 1967.

Poussy, Claire. *La Conquête de la mer par les Arabes en Méditerranée occidentale.* Master's thesis, typewritten. Paris-Nanterre, 1975.

Prasad, Ishwari. *A History of the Qaraunah Turks in India.* Allahabad, 1936.

———. *Medieval India.* Allahabad, 1940.

Price, David, trans. *Memoirs of the Emperor Jahangueir, Written by Himself* [The Tuzuk-i-Jahangiri or Tarikk-i-Salim Shahi]. London, 1829.

Qadi Nu'man. *Da'a'im al-Islam,* vol. 1. Ed. Asif ibn 'Ali Faydi (Fyzee). Cairo, 1951.

Querry, A. *Droit Musulman, Recueil des lois concernant les Musulmans Schyites.* Paris, 1871/1981.

Qutb, Sayyid. *Al-Islam wa mushiklat al-hadarah.* 9th legal ed. Cairo, 1988.

———. *Al-Mustaqbal li hadha al-din.* Cairo, 1981.

———. *Al-Salam al- alami wa al-Islam.* 10th legal ed. Cairo, 1992.

———. *In the Shade of the Qur'an,* vol. 8. Leicester, UK, 2003.

———. "Jihaad in the Cause of God." *Milestones,* Cedar Rapids, IA, 1993.

———. *Ma alim fi al-tariq.* 13th legal ed. Cairo, 1989.

Rahman, Fazlur. *Islam and Modernity.* Chicago: University of Chicago Press, 1982.

Ralston, David B. *Importing the European Army: The Introduction of European Military Techniques and Institutions into the Extra-European World, 1600–1914.* Chicago, 1990.

Raverty, H. C. *Notes on Afghanistan.* London, 1886.

Raynaldus, Odoricus. *Annales ecclesiastici* 6, 9. Luca, 1752.

Refik, Ahmet. "Devşirme usulü Acemi Oğlanlar." *Edebiyat—Fakultesi Meğmû asî* 5 (1927).

Ricaut, Paul. *The Present State of the Greek and Armenian Churches, Anno Christi 1678.* London, 1679; New York, 1970.

Rice, Susan, and David Scheffer. "Sudan Must End Its Brutal War against Civilians." *International Herald Tribune*, September 1, 1999.

Richards, D. S., ed. *Islamic Civilization 950–1150*. Oxford, 1973.

Richer, Ch. *Des Coustumes et manières de vivre des Turcs*. Paris, 1542.

Ricks, Thomas. "Slaves and Slave Trading in Shi'i Iran, AD 1500–1900." *Journal of Asian and African Studies* 36 (2001).

Rida, Rashid, ed. *Ibn Qudama, al-Mughni*. Cairo, A.H. 1367.

Rieu, Charles. *Catalogue of the Persian Manuscripts in the British Musem*. London, 1966.

———. *Supplement to the Catalogue of the Persian Manuscripts in the British Museum (now in the British Library)*. London, 1977.

Rizvi, Saiyid Athar Abbas. *Adi Turk Kalin Bharat*. Aligarh, 1956.

———. *A History of Sufism in India*. 2 vols. 1978, 1983.

———. *Muslim Revivalist Movements in Northern India in the Sixteenth and Seventeenth Centuries*. Agra, Lucknow, 1965.

———. *Shah Wali-Allah and His Times*. Canberra, 1980.

———. *Tughlaq Kalin Bharat*. 2 parts, 1956, 1957.

Rodinson, Maxime. "The Western Image and Western Studies of Islam." *See in* Schacht, *The Legacy*.

Roerich, G., trans. *Biography of Dharmasvamin (Chag lotsava Chos-rje-dpal), a Tibetan Pilgrim*. Patna, 1959.

Rosenthal, A. M. "When Is It News?" *New York Times*, September 3, 1999.

Rosenthal, Franz. "Hurriyya," *E.I.*, vol. 3.

———. *The Muslim Concept of Freedom*. Leiden, 1960.

———. "On Suicide in Islam." *Journal of the American Oriental Society* 66 (1946).

Rothenberg, Gunther E., Béla K. Király, and Peter F. Sugar, eds. *East Central European Society and War in the Prerevolutionary Eighteenth Century*. New York, 1982.

Rouche, Michel. "Les Aquitains ont-ils trahi avant la bataille de Poitiers?" *Le Moyen Age* (1968).

Rubin, Barry, and Judith Colp Rubin. *Anti-American Terrorism and the Middle East*. Oxford: Oxford University Press, 2002.

Sahih Muslim. *Translation of Sahih Muslim*. Trans. Abdul Hamid Siddiqui. http://www.usc.edu/dept/MSA/fundamentals/hadithsunnah/muslim/.

Said, Edward. *Orientalism*. London and Henley, 1978.

Saint Martin, Antoine Jean. *Mémoires Historiques et Géographiques*. Paris, 1819.

Sale, George, trans. *The Koran: Commonly Called the Alkoran of Mohammed*. London, 1734; New York, 1880.

Samuel of Ani. See Brosset, *Tables Chronologiques*.

Santamaria, Alvaro. "Olfo de Procida." *Hispania*, vol. 25. Madrid, 1965.

Sarhindi, Yahiya. *Tarikh-i-Mubarak Shahi*. Ed. M. Hidayat Husain. Calcutta, 1931; Eng. trans. K. K. Basu. Baroda, 1932.

Sarkar, Jadunath. *Fall of the Mughal Empire*, vol. 2. New Delhi, 1991.

———. *History of Aurangzib*. London, 1929.

———. *Military History of India*. Calcutta, 1960.

Sasson, D. *Report No. 4* and *Report No. 5*. Archives, Alliance Israelite Universelle, I.C.2, Iraq. Trans. in Bat Ye'or, *The Decline*.

Sathas. *Tourkokratoumeni Elias* [Turkish-Occupied Greece]. Athens, 1868.

Schacht, Joseph. *An Introduction to Islamic Law*. Oxford, 1982.

————. "Umm al-Walad." *See in* G & S, 1st ed.

Schacht, Joseph, and C. E. Bosworth, eds. *The Legacy of Islam*. 2nd ed. Oxford, 1974.

Schiltbergers aus München. V. *Reise in den Orient und wunderbarere Begebenheiten*, hrsg. A. Penzel. München, 1814.

Schleifer, S. Abdullah. "Jihad and the Traditional Islamic Consciousness, Part II." *Islamic Quarterly* 4 (1983).

Schopen, L. *Ioannis Cantacuzeni eximperatoris Historiarum libri IV*. Bonn, 1832.

Seadeddin. *Chronica dell' origine et progressi della casa ottomana composta da Saidino Turco eccellentissimo historico in lingua turca, parte prima*. Trans. Vincenzo Brattuti. Vienna, 1469.

Seddon, C. N. *A Chronicle of the Early Safawis—Being the Ahsanu't-Tawarikh of Hasan-I-Rumlu*, vol. 2. Baroda, 1934.

Segal, J. B. *Edessa—The Blessed City*. London, 1970.

Sepeos [Sebeos]. *Histoire d'Heraclius*. Trans. Frederic Macler. Paris, 1904. Eng. trans. in Bat Ye'or, *The Decline*.

Servier, André. *Islam and the Psychology of the Musulman*. Trans. A. S. Moss-Blundell. London, 1924.

Setton, Kenneth M. "On the Raids of the Moslems in the Aegean in the Ninth and Tenth Centuries." *American Journal of Archaeology* 58 (1954).

Sewell, Robert. *A Forgotton Empire (Vijayanagar)*. Delhi, 1962.

Sezgin, F. *Gechichte der Arabischen Schrifttumss*, vol. 1. Leiden, 1967.

Shadid, Muhammad. *Al-Jihad fi al-Islam*. 7th ed. Cairo, 1989.

Shafi'i. *Kitab al-Umm*, vol. 4. Cairo, A.H. 1321.

Shahrastani. *Kitab al-Milal wa'l-Nihal*. Ed. Cureton. London, 1840.

Shaltut, Mahmud. *Al-Islam 'aqida wa shari a*. 10th ed. Cairo, 1980.

Sharma, Sri Ram. "An Almost Contemporary Account of Mahmud's Invasions of India." *Studies in Medieval Indian History* (1956).

Shashko, Philip. "The Bulgarian Massacres of 1876 Reconsidered: Reaction to the April Uprising or Premeditated Attack?" *Etudes Balkaniques* 22 (1986).

Shaw, Stanford. *History of the Ottoman Empire and Modern Turkey*. 2 vols. Cambridge, 1976.

Shawish, Sheikh (believed author). *Aljihad*. American Agency and Consulate, Cairo, Egypt, in US State Department document 867.4016/57, March 10, 1915.

Shedd, William A. *Islam and the Oriental Churches*. Philadelphia, 1904.

Sherburne, John H. *Life and Character of John Paul Jones—A Captain in the Navy of the United States*. 1825.

Sijistani, Imam Daud. *Sunan ibn Daud*. Arabic text, Urdu trans. Allama Wahid-uz-Zaman. 3 vols. Delhi, 1986.

Simonet, Francisco-Javier. *Historia de los Mozarabes de España*. Madrid, 1897–1903; Amsterdam, 1967.

Sinaites, Anastasios. "Sermon no. 3." *PG*, 89.

Singhal, D. P. *India and the World Civilization*. 2 vols. Delhi, 1972.

Slatin, Rudolf C., and F. R. Wingate. *Fire and Sword in the Sudan, a Personal Narrative of Fighting and Serving the Dervishes, 1879–1895*. London, 1896/1903.

Smith, Vincent A. *Akbar the Great Mogul*. Delhi repr., 1962.

————. *The Oxford History of India*. Oxford, 1928.

Snegarov, Ivan. *Turkish Rule as an Obstacle for the Cultural Development of the Bulgarian People and the Other Balkan Peoples*. Sofia, 1958.

Snouck Hurgronje, C. *The Acehnese*, vol. 1. Leyden, 1906.
———. *Mohammedanism*. New York, 1916.
Sophronios, Archbishop of Jerusalem. "Logos eis to hagion Baptisms." *See in* Papadopoulos-K., *Analekta*.
Soroudi, Sarah (Sorour). "The Concept of Jewish Impurity and Its Reflection in Persian and Judeo-Persian Traditions." *Irano-Judaica* 3 (1994).
Sourdel, D. *L'Islam médiéval*. Paris, 1979.
Sphrantzès. *Chronicon*. Bonnae, 1838.
Spyridakes, G. K. "To Thema tes Kretes pro tes katakteseos tes nesou Wct ton Arabon." *EBBS* 21 (1951).
Srivastava, A. L. *The History of India (1000 A.D.–1707 A.D.)*. Agra, 1964.
———. "Indian Resistance to Medieval Invaders." *Journal of Indian History* (1965).
———. *The Sultanate of Delhi (711–1526 A.D.)*. Agra, 1950.
———. "A Survey of India's Resistance to Medieval Invaders from the North-West: Causes of Eventual Hindu Defeat." *Journal of Indian History* (1965).
Stepanos Asoghik of Tarim. *Stepanosi Taronetsvo Asogilkan Patrautiun Tiezerakan* [The Universal History of Stepanos Asoghik of Tarim]. St. Petersburg, 1885.
Stowasser, Barbara F., ed. *The Islamic Impulse*. Washington, DC, 1987.
Stratus, Andrea. N. *To Byzantio ston 7on Aiona* [Seventh Century Byzantium]. Athens, 1969/1977.
Strauss, Leo. *The Political Philosophy of Hobbes*. Oxford, 1936.
Strothmann, R. *Das Staatrecht de Zaiditen*. Strassburg, 1912.
Swarup, Ram. See introduction to Muir, *The Life of Mahomet*.
———. *Understanding Islam through Hadis*. Indian repr., New Delhi, 1983.
Sykes, P. M. *History of Persia*. 2 vols. London, 1915.
Syros, Michael. See Chabot, *Chronique de Michel*.
Tafrali, O. *Thessalonique—Des Origines au XVI Siècle*. Paris, 1919.
Tahqiq al-isma li-Jami' Tabaqat hadihi 'l-umma. Arabic manuscript. C.A.D./20, 14ff. Ibadan, n.dd. See also Last, *Sokoto*.
Talbi, Mohammed. *L'Émirat aghlabide*. Paris, 1966.
Ter Ghevondian, Aram. *The Arab Emirates in Bagratid Armenia*. Trans. Nina G. Garsoian. Lisbon, 1976.
———. "The Armenian Rebellion of 703 against the Caliphate." Trans. M. A. Arakelian. *Armenian Review* 36 (1983).
———. *Armensk i arabskii khalifat*. Erevan, 1977.
———. "Arminiya Vostikanneri Zhamanakagrutiune [The Chronology of Governors of Arminiya]." *Patma-Banasirakan Handes* 1 (1977).
Thalloczy, L. D., Dr. K. Jireček, and E. Sufflay, eds. *Acta et diplomata res Albaniae mediae aetatis illustrantia*, 2, doc. #610 (1918).
Theophanes. *Chronographia*, vol. 1. Ed. K. de Boor. Leipzig, 1883–1885.
Thomas, Edward. *Chronicles of the Pathan Kings of Delhi*. London, 1871.
Tibi, Bassam. *Arab Nationalism: A Critical Inquiry*. 2nd ed. New York: St. Martin's Press, 1991. Enlarged 3rd ed. with new subtitle, *Between Islam and the Nation State*, 1997.
———. "Politische Ideen in der 'Drifter Welt' wahrend der Dekolonisation." *See in* Fetscher, *Pipers*.
———. "Universality of Human Rights and Authenticity of Non-Western Cultures: Islam

and the Western Concept of Human Rights" (review article). *Harvard Human Rights Journal* 5 (1992).

———. *Conflict and War in the Middle East.* New York, 1993.

———. *The Crisis of Modern Islam: A Preindustrial Culture in the Scientific-Technological Age.* Salt Lake City, 1988. Trans. of *Die Krize.*

———. "Culture and Knowledge." *Theory, Culture, and Society* 12 (1995).

———. *Die fundamentalistische Herausforderung: Der Islam and die Weltpolitik.* Munich, 1992.

———. "Islam and Arab Nationalism." *See in* Stowasser, *The Islamic Impulse.*

———. *Islam and the Cultural Accommodation of Social Change.* Boulder, CO, 1990.

———. *Islamischer Fundamentalismus, moderne Wissenschaft and Technologic.* Frankfurt am Main, 1992.

———. *Der Kreig der Zivilisationen.* Hamburg, 1995.

———. *Die Verschworung: Das Trauma arabischer Politik.* Hamburg, 1993.

———. "War and Peace in Islam." *See in* Nardin, *The Ethics.*

Timur, Amir. *Malfuzat-i-Timuri.* Trans. in E & D, vol. 3.

Titus, Murray. *Islam in India and Pakistan.* Calcutta, 1959.

Toledano, Ehud. "The Imperial Eunuchs of Istanbul: From Africa to the Heart of Islam." *Middle Eastern Studies* (1984).

———. *The Ottoman Slave Trade and Its Suppression.* Princeton, NJ, 1982.

———. *Slavery and Abolition in the Ottoman Middle East.* Seattle, 1998.

Tomadakes, N. "Problemata tes en Krete Arabokratias (826–961)." *EEBS* 30 (1960).

Tomberg, Friedrich. *Polis and Nationalstaat Eine vergleichende Überbau Analyse im Anschluss an Aristoteles.* Darmstadt and Neuwied.

Topkapi Sarayi. R 1936, fol. 153 verso–155 recto. Istanbul.

Toynbee, Arnold. See foreword to Albino, *The Sudan.*

Trimingham, J. Spencer. *Islam in the Sudan.* London, 1949.

Tripathi, R. P. *Some Aspects of Muslim Administration.* Allahabad, 1936.

Tritton, A. S. *The Caliphs and Their Non-Muslim Subjects.* London, 1930.

Tu'ayma, Sabir. *Al-Shari 'a al-Islamiyya fi 'asr al-Um.* Beirut, 1979.

Tuffrau, Paul. *La Légende de Guillaume d'Orange.* Adaptation. Paris, 1920.

Tursun Beg. "Tarikh-i Ebul Feth." *See in* Gliša Elezović, *Turski izvori.*

Tusi, Nizamul Mulk. *Kitab Masa'il al-Khilaf.* Tehran, A.H. 1370.

———. *Siyasat Nama.* Ed. Shefer. Tehran.

Ubicini, Abdolonyme. *Lettres Sur La Turquie*, vol. 2. Paris, 1854. Eng. trans. in Bat Ye'or, *The Decline.*

Ufi, Muhammad. *Jami-ul-Hikayat.* Trans. in E & D, vol. 2.

United Nations Commission on Human Rights. *Situation of Human Rights in the Sudan, Visit of the Special Rapporteur, Mr. Leonardo Franco, to the Republic of the Sudan, Feb. 13–24, 1999.* Unedited version, 55th session, addendum to E/CN.4/1999/38.

United States Congress, Senate, 106th Cong., 1st sess., S. 145, "Sudan Peace Act." Section 4, paragraphs C and D, July 28, 1999.

Uras, E. *The Armenians and the Armenian Question in History.* Istanbul, 1976.

Usener, H., ed. "Weihnachtspredigt des Sophronios." *Rheinisches Museum für Philologie* 4 (1886).

Usuman Dan Fodio, Shehu. *Bayan wujub al-hijra.* 1806.

————. *Tahqiq*, f.3 (b). See also *Tahqiq*.

Utbi, Abu Nasr Muhammad. *Kitab-i-Yamini*. Trans. James Reynolds. London, 1858. Also in E & D.

————. *Tarikh-i-Yamini*. See in E & D, vol. 2.

Vacalopoulos, Apostolos E. "Background and Causes of the Greek Revolution." *Neo-Hellenika* (1975).

————. *The Greek Nation, 1453–1669*. New Brunswick, NJ, 1976.

————. *Istoria tou Neou Ellenismou* [History of Neo-Hellenism], vol. 2. Thessaloniki, 1964.

————. *Origins of the Greek Nation—The Byzantine Period, 1204–1461*. New Brunswick, NJ, 1970.

————. "Provlimata tis istorias tou paidmazomatos [Problems concerning the History of the Child-Levy]." *Hellinika* 13 (1954).

Vajda, Georges. "À propos de la situation des Juifs et des Chrétiens à Séville au début du XIIe siècle." *Revue des Études Juives* 99 (1935).

Valldeavellano, Luis de Garcia. *Historia de España*, vol. 1, 2nd ed. Madrid, 1955.

van Berchem, Max. *La Propriété territoriale et l'Impôt foncier sous les premiers califes*. Geneva, 1886.

Vantini, Giovanni. *Christianity in the Sudan*. Bologna, 1981.

Vardan. *Tiezerakan Patmutiun* [Universal History]. Moscow, 1861.

Vasdravelle, K. *Istorikon archion Verroia*s [Historical, Archives of Verroia]. Thessaloniki, 1942.

Vasiliev, A. A. *Histoire de l'Empire byzantin*, vol. 2. Paris, 1932.

————, ed. "Kitab al-Unwan." *PO*, 8.3. Paris, 1912.

Vasilievskij, B. G. *PPSb* 2 (1886).

Vaux, Kenneth L. Ethics *and the Gulf War: Religion, Rhetoric, and Righteousness*. Boulder, CO, 1992.

Von Elbe, J. "The Evolution of the Concept of the Just War in International Law." *American Journal of International Law* 33 (1939).

von Hammer, J. *Constantinopolis und der Bosporos*, vol. 1. Pest, 1822.

von Kremer, A. *Culturgeschichte des Orients*. Vienna, 1877.

————. *Geschichte des herrschenden Ideen des Islam*. Leipzig, 1868.

von Ranke, Leopold. *Die Osmanen and die spanische Monarchie im sechzehnten and siebzehnten Jahrhundert*. Berlin, 1877.

Vryonis, Speros P. "Byzantium and Islam: Seventh–Seventeenth Century." *East European Quarterly* 2 (1968).

————. "The Conditions and Cultural Significance of the Ottoman Conquest in the Balkans." *Congres International des Etudes du Sud-Est Europeen*. Athens, 1970.

————. "A Critical Analysis of Stanford J. Shaw's 'History of the Ottoman Empire and Modern Turkey. Volume 1. Empire of the Gazis: The Rise and Decline of the Ottoman Empire, 1280–1808.'" Off-print, *Balkan Studies* 24 (1983).

————. *The Decline of Medieval Hellenism in Asia Minor and the Process of Islamization from the Eleventh through the Fifteenth Century*. Berkeley, CA, 1971. Paperback, 1986.

————. "The Experience of Christians under Seljuk and Ottoman Domination, Eleventh to Sixteenth Century." In *Conversion and Continuity: Indigenous Christian Communities in Islamic Lands, Eighth to Eighteenth Centuries*. Ed. Michael Gervers and Ramzi Jibran Bikhazi. Toronto, 1990.

———. "Isidore Glabas and the Turkish Devshirme." *Spéculum* 31 (1956).

———. "Nomadization and Islamization in Asia Minor." *DOP* 29 (1975).

———. "The Ottoman Conquest of Thessaloniki in 1430." *DOP* (1986).

———. "Seljuk Gulams and Ottoman Devshirmes." *Der Islam* 41 (1965).

Waliullah, Shah. *Qurrat al-aynain fi tafil al-shaykhayan.* Delhi, 1893.

Warner, Oliver. *William Wilberforce and His Times.* London, 1962.

Wassaf, Abdullah. *Tajziat-ul-Amsar wa Tajriyat-ul-Asar,* also called *Tarikh-i-Wassaf.* Written 1327 CE. Bombay, 1877.

Watson, Adam. *The Evolution of International Society.* London, 1992.

Watt, William Montgomery, trans. *The Faith and Practice of Al-Ghazali.* Oxford, UK, 1953.

———. "Badw," "Hidjra." *See in* G & S, 2nd ed.

———. "Economic and Social Aspects of the Origin of Islam." *Islamic Quarterly* 1 (1954).

———. *Islamic Fundamentalism and Modernity.* London, 1988.

———. *Muhammad Prophet and Statesman.* Oxford, 1961.

Wattenberg, W., ed. "Annales Melicenos." In *Monumenta Germaniae Historica, Scriptores* IX. Hanover, 1851.

Wellhausen, J. *The Arab Kingdom and Its Fall.* Trans. M. G. Weir. Calcutta, 1927; London, 1973.

Wiebalck, Alison. "Slavery in the Sudan: A Challenge to International Law." *Comparative and International Law Journal of Southern Africa* 31 (1998).

Willis, John Ralph. "Jihad and the Ideology of Enslavement." In *Slaves and Slavery in Muslim Africa,* vol. 1: *Islam and the Ideology of Enslavement,* Totowa, NJ, 1985.

———. "Jihad fi sabil Allah—Its Doctrinal Basis in Islam and Some Aspects of Its Evolution in Nineteenth-Century West Africa." *BAH* 3 (1967).

———. Review of: "N. Levtzion, Ancient Ghana and Mali." *International Journal of African Historical Studies* 8, no. 1.

———. "The Torodbe Clerisy: A Social View." *J.A.H.* 19, no. 2 (1978).

———. "The Western Sudan from the Moroccan Invasion (1591) to the Death of Mukhtar al-Kunti (1811)." *See in* Ajayi, *A History.*

———, ed. "The Writings of al-Hajj ʿUmar al-Futi and Shaykr Mukhtar b. Wadiʾat Allah: Literary Themes, Sources and Influences." *Studies* 1.

Wink, André. Al-Hind, *The Making of the Indo-Islamic World,* vol. 1. Delhi, 1990.

Wittek, Paul. *Das Fürstentum Mentesche, Studie zur Geschichte Westkleinasiens im 13.–15. Jahrh.* Istanbul, 1934.

———. *The Rise of the Ottoman Empire.* London: Royal Asiatic Society of Great Britain and Ireland, 1938; 1966.

WorldNetDaily. "Muslim Kids Stage Mock Beheading." http://www.wnd.com/news/article .asp?ARTICLE_ID=39145.

Wright, John. "The Mediterranean Middle Passage: The Nineteenth Century Slave Trade Between Triploi and the Levant." *Journal of North African Studies* 1 (1996).

Wright, Quincy. *A Study of War,* vol. 1. Chicago, 1942.

Yadgar, Ahmad. *Tarikh-i-Salatin-i-Afghana.* Calcutta, 1936. Trans. in E & D, vol. 5.

Yakubi. *Tarikh.* Beirut, 1960.

Yasin, Muhammad N. *Al-Jihad: Mayadinahu wa asalibahu.* Algiers, 1990.

Yazdi, Sharafuddin. *Zafar Nama*. 2 vols. Calcutta, 1885–1888.

Yule, Sir Henry, and Cordier, H. *The Book of Sir Marco Polo*. 2 vols. New York, 1903.

Zachariadou, Elizabeth. "The Holy War in the Aegean during the Fourteenth Century." See in *Latins and Greeks in the Eastern Mediterranean after 1204*. Totowa, NJ, 1989.

Zakitenos. *Le despotat grec de Morée*. Paris, 1932.

Zakythinos, Denys A. *The Making of Modern Greece. From Byzantium to Independence*. Oxford, 1976.

Zettersteen, K. V. "Abd-al-Malik." See in *Encyclopaedia of Islam*.

Zinkeisen, W. *Geschichte des Osmanischen Reiches in Europa*, vol. 3. Hamburg, 1955.

Zoras, G., ed. *Karolos o E'tis Germanias kai i pros apeleftherosin prospathia* [Charles V of Germany and Attempts toward Liberation]. Athens, 1954.

INDEX OF PERSONS, PEOPLES, TRIBES, AND INSTITUTIONS

Spelling irregularities in some source documents have been retained. Alternative names are mentioned in square brackets. Full names can be found in the text.

INDEX OF PLACES

Spelling irregularities in some source documents have been retained. Alternative names are mentioned in square brackets.

745